# CHALMERS AND GUEST ON BILLS OF EXCHANGE, CHEQUES AND PROMISSORY NOTES

AUSTRALIA
Law Book Co.
Sydney


CANADA AND USA
Carswell
Toronto


HONG KONG
Sweet & Maxwell Asia


NEW ZEALAND
Brookers
Wellington


SINGAPORE and MALAYSIA
Sweet & Maxwell Asia
Singapore and Kuala Lumpur

# CHALMERS AND GUEST ON BILLS OF EXCHANGE, CHEQUES AND PROMISSORY NOTES

## SIXTEENTH EDITION

By

## A.G. GUEST, CBE, Q.C., M.A., FBA

*Bencher of Gray's Inn; formerly Professor of
English Law, King's College,
University of London; Fellow of the Chartered
Institute of Arbitrators*

LONDON
SWEET & MAXWELL
2005

| First edition | (1878) by Sir M.D. Chalmers, KCB |
| Second edition | (1881) by Sir M.D. Chalmers, KCB |
| Third edition | (1883) by Sir M.D. Chalmers, KCB |
| Fourth edition | (1891) by Sir M.D. Chalmers, KCB |
| Fifth edition | (1896) by Sir M.D. Chalmers, KCB |
| Sixth edition | (1903) by Sir M.D. Chalmers, KCB |
| Seventh edition | (1909) by Sir M.D. Chalmers, KCB |
| Eighth edition | (1919) by Sir M.D. Chalmers, KCB |
| Ninth edition | (1927) by Sir M.D. Chalmers, KCB |
| Tenth edition | (1932) by A.D. Gibb |
| Eleventh edition | (1947) by F.R. Batt |
| Twelfth edition | (1952) by Barry Chedlow |
| Thirteenth edition | (1964) by David A.L. Smout |
| Fourteenth edition | (1991) by A.G. Guest |
| Fifteenth edition | (1998) by A.G. Guest |
| Sixteenth edition | (2005) by A.G. Guest |

Published in 2005 by
Sweet & Maxwell Limited of 100 Avenue Road, London, NW3 3PF
*http://www.sweetandmaxwell.co.uk*

Typeset by Interactive Sciences Limited, Gloucester
Printed and bound in Great Britain by
William Clowes Ltd

No natural forests were destroyed to make this product;
only farmed timber was used and re-planted.

**British Library Cataloguing in Publication Data**

A CIP catalogue record for this book
is available from the British Library

ISBN 0421 877 10 3

*The information contained in this book is not intended to be a substitute for
specific legal advice, and readers should obtain advice from a
qualified adviser in relation to individual transactions.*

Coventry University

# PREFACE

The last edition of this book was published in 1998. Since that time there have been a number of significant decisions of direct relevance to the law of negotiable instruments. Most of these concern cheques, for example *Dextra Bank & Trust Co. v Bank of Jamaica* (on what constitutes delivery of a cheque), *Smith v Lloyds TSB Group plc* ( on the effect of alteration of a cheque), *Honourable Society of the Middle Temple v Lloyds Bank plc* and *Linklaters v HSBC Bank plc* (on the standard of care required of a banker when collecting a cheque crossed "account payee") and *Fiorentino Comm Giuseppe Srl v Farnesi* (on dispensation from the need to present a cheque for payment). But some cases have concerned bills of exchange, including *Hong Kong and Shanghai Banking Corporation Ltd v G D Trade Co Ltd* and *Novaknit Hellas SA v Kumar Brothers International Ltd*, where the Court of Appeal leaned heavily in favour of upholding bills despite defects in their wording and suggested that defects in the wording of bills as originally drawn might be cured by the language of the acceptance.

On a more general level there have been other decisions of some importance to banks, such as *Hollicourt (Contracts) Ltd v Bank of Ireland* (on the effect of presentation of a winding-up petition on a customer's account) and *Saudi Arabian Monetary Agency v Dresdner Bank AG* (on the right of a banker to set-off its customer's accounts). And the House of Lords has, in a somewhat controversial decision, in *Twinsectra Ltd v Yardley* defined what constitutes "dishonesty" in cases of alleged dishonest assistance, and the Court of Appeal has likewise attempted to define what constitutes "knowing" (or now "unconscientious") receipt of trust moneys in *Bank of Credit & Commerce International (Overseas) Ltd v Akindele*.

Perhaps the area in which there has been most movement is that of the recovery of money paid under a mistake and the defences available to the recipient (such as estoppel and change of position) as exemplified in such cases as *Kleinwort Benson Ltd v Lincoln City Council, Bank of America v Arnell, Philip Collins Ltd v Davis, Scottish Equitable plc v Derby, Niru Battery Manufacturing Co v Milestone Trading Ltd, Papamichael v National Westminster Bank plc* and *Barros Mattos Junior v MacDaniels Ltd.*

Revisions of the Banking Code and of the Business Banking Code have brought the two codes up to date to March 2005. There have also been a number of statutory changes since the last edition, of which perhaps the most significant relates to money laundering in the Proceeds of Crime Act 2002. The difficulties that the "tipping off" provisions in this legislation pose to banks have been considered in *Bank of Scotland v A Ltd.*

v

As in previous editions the opportunity has been taken to include a number of decisions from Commonwealth and other jurisdictions where the Bills of Exchange Act 1882 has been enacted with or without modification.

It has unfortunately not been possible to take account of the Gambling Act 2005 which was enacted too late for inclusion in this edition. It will, when it enters into force, render largely obsolete the discussion relating to gaming and wagering contracts contained in paragraphs 4–016 to 4–020.

*London, July 22, 2005*                                                    A.G.G.

# CONTENTS

## BILLS OF EXCHANGE ACT 1882

### PART I
### PRELIMINARY

### PART II
### BILLS OF EXCHANGE

### Capacity and Authority of Parties

### The Consideration for a Bill

### Negotiation of Bills

### General Duties of the Holder

## Liabilities of Parties

## Discharge of Bill

## Acceptance and Payment for Honour

## Lost Instruments

## Bill in a Set

## Conflict of Laws

# PART II
# CHEQUES ON A BANKER

## Crossed Cheques

# PART IV
# PROMISSORY NOTES

# PART V
# SUPPLEMENTARY

## Schedules to Act

# CHEQUES ACT 1957

# APPENDICES

# TABLE OF CASES

# TABLE OF STATUTES

*(References in bold indicate where legislation is cited in full)*

# TABLE OF STATUTORY INSTRUMENTS

# TABLE OF INTERNATIONAL LEGISLATION

# TABLE OF EU LEGISLATION

# TABLE OF INTERNATIONAL CONVENTIONS

**United States**

# BILLS OF EXCHANGE ACT 1882

## (45 & 46 Vict., c.61)

*An Act to codify the law relating to Bills of Exchange, Cheques, and Promissory*    1–001
*Notes.*                                                      [18th August 1882.]

**Be it enacted by the Queen's most Excellent Majesty, by and with the advice and consent of the Lords Spiritual and Temporal, and Commons, in this present Parliament assembled, and by the authority of the same, as follows:**

## PART I

## PRELIMINARY

### Short title

**1. This Act may be cited as the Bills of Exchange Act 1882.**    1–002

#### COMMENT

**Codification.** The expressed purpose of the Act was to codify the law    1–003
relating to bills of exchange, cheques and promissory notes. It was, as
Chalmers pointed out,[1] the first enactment codifying any branch of the
common law which found its way into the Statute Book. The Act does
not, in general, extend to other forms of negotiable instrument.[2]

**Territorial application.** The Bill as originally drafted applied only to    1–004
England and Ireland. The clause excluding Scotland was struck out in
committee.[3] The Act therefore applies to the whole of the United Kingdom. Specific provision is made in section 72 for certain situations where
laws conflict.

---

[1] Preface to the Third Edition. See also Chalmers (1886) 2 L.Q.R. 125; (1903) 19 L.Q.R. 10.
[2] But see s.95 of this Act and s.5 of the Cheques Act 1957; below, para.17–075.
[3] Chalmers (9th ed.), p.1.

1–005     **Construction of the Act.** Section 7(3) of the Act provides that, where the payee is a fictitious or non-existing person, the bill may be treated as payable to bearer. In *Vagliano Brothers v Bank of England*[4] the Court of Appeal qualified the wording of this subsection by introducing a limitation, to be found in the common law, that the principle applied only against the parties who at the time they became liable on the bill were cognisant of the fictitious character or non-existence of the payee. This reference to the common law at the time of the passing of the Act was rejected by the House of Lords.[5] Lord Herschell said[6]:

> "My Lords, with sincere respect to the learned Judges who have taken this view, I cannot bring myself to think that this is the proper way to deal with such a statute as the Bills of Exchange Act, which was intended to be a code of the law relating to negotiable instruments. I think the proper course is in the first instance to examine the language of the statute and to ask what is its natural meaning, uninfluenced by any considerations derived from the previous state of the law, and not to start with inquiring how the law previously stood, and then, assuming that it was probably intended to leave it unaltered, to see if the words of the enactment will bear an interpretation in conformity with this view.
>
> If a statute, intended to embody in a code a particular branch of the law, is to be treated in this fashion, it appears to me that its utility will be almost entirely destroyed, and the very object with which it was enacted will be frustrated. The purpose of such a statute surely was that on any point specifically dealt with by it, the law should be ascertained by interpreting the language used instead of, as before, by roaming over a vast number of authorities in order to discover what the law was, extracting it by a minute critical examination of the prior decisions, dependent upon a knowledge of the exact effect even of an obsolete proceeding such as a demurrer to evidence. I am of course far from asserting that resort may never be had to the previous state of the law for the purpose of aiding in the construction of the provisions of the code. If, for example, a provision be of doubtful import, such resort would be perfectly legitimate. Or, again, if in a code of the law of negotiable instruments words be found which have previously acquired a technical meaning, or been used in a sense other than their ordinary one, in relation to such instruments, the same interpretation might well be put upon them in the code. I give these as examples merely; they, of course, do not exhaust the category. What, however, I am venturing to insist upon is, that the

---

[4] (1889) 23 Q.B.D. 243, 260.
[5] *Bank of England v Vagliano Brothers* [1891] A.C. 107 (s.7, Illustration 4).
[6] At 144–145. See also Lord Halsbury at 120, Lord Selborne at 127, Lord Morris at 162.

first step taken should be to interpret the language of the statute, and that an appeal to earlier decisions can only be justified on some special ground.

One further remark I have to make before I proceed to consider the language of the statute. The Bills of Exchange Act was certainly not intended to be merely a code of the existing law. It is not open to question that it was intended to alter, and did alter it in certain respects. And I do not think it is to be presumed that any particular provision was intended to be a statement of the existing law, rather than a substituted enactment."

In view of these observations it may be thought surprising that in this work so many pre-Act cases are referred to. But there are reasons for this. First, there are relatively few reported cases on bills and notes since the passing of the Act. The reader may nevertheless wish to see how the provisions of the statute operate in practice, and cases decided under the common law often provide useful illustrations, even though they may not be referred to as authorities. Secondly, there are some (admittedly very few) instances where the provisions of the code are, in the words of Lord Herschell, "of doubtful import", and rather more instances where the precise application of those provisions is uncertain. Common law cases may here be of some guidance. Thirdly, there are situations where the statutory provision is not exhaustive. An example is section 29(2) of the Act, which gives certain examples of defects of title, but does not purport to set out a definitive list. The sub-section may be supplemented by examples derived from the common law. Fourthly, common law cases may be used to interpret the technical meaning of expressions used in the Act. Fifthly, section 97(2) of the Act provides that: "The rules of common law, including the law merchant, save in so far as they are inconsistent with the express provisions of this Act, shall continue to apply to bills of exchange, promissory notes, and cheques." The law relating to negotiable instruments is not an isolated phenomenon; the transactions which give rise to the instrument, and certain aspects of the instrument itself, are subject to the common law.[7] Sixthly, it may be of some interest to trace the common law origins of the rule now codified in the Act. For these reasons, pre-Act cases are often cited, though not with the object of inciting the practitioner to disregard Lord Herschell's admonition.

**Changes in the law.** According to Chalmers[8]:                        **1–006**

"The Bill as originally drafted was intended to reproduce the then existing law as exactly as possible, but certain amendments of the

---

[7] See below, para.16–025.
[8] (9th ed.), p.2.

law were introduced in committee. Provisions which alter the law are s.4(2), s.7(2) and (3), s.12, s.14(1), s.15, s.18(3), s.33, s.36(3), s.39(4), s.41(2), s.44(2), s.49(6), s.51(2), s.61, s.62, s.64, s.73, s.74, ss.91–95, s.100."

1–007      **Cheques Act 1957.** This Act is to be construed as one with the 1882 Act.[9]

1–008      **Review Committee on Banking Services.** In January 1987 the Government, jointly with the Bank of England, commissioned a Review of Banking Services Law and Practice. The Review Committee was chaired by Professor Robert Jack CBE. The chief objective of the Review was to:

> "examine the law and its practical implications from the points of view of banker, customer and the general public interest in the availability, reliability, security and effective operation of payment, remittance and other banking services".

The report of the Committee was published in 1989.[10] Much of the report concerns aspects of banking law and practice which fall outside the scope of the present work. However, the Review Committee recommended a number of changes in the law which, if adopted, would affect the then current legislation contained in the 1882 Act and in the Cheques Act 1957. In particular, the Review Committee recommended that the law relating to cheques should be re-enacted in a new Act, to be called the "Cheques and Bank Payment Orders Act".[11] The new Act would make a number of amendments to the law relating to cheques[12] and would include provisions permitting the introduction of a new non-transferable instrument (the "bank payment order") the proceeds of which could be collected only by a bank and solely for the account of the named payee.[13]

So far as the law relating to negotiable instruments (other than cheques and payment orders) is concerned, the Review Committee recommended that there should be a new Negotiable Instruments Act covering not only bills of exchange and promissory notes, but also, in so far as their negotiability is concerned, all other negotiable instruments.[14] However, the language and style of the 1882 Act should be retained since it was clear, concise and well understood.[15] In view of the technical nature of

---

[9] Cheques Act 1957, s.6(1). See below, para.17–077.
[10] (1989) Cm.622.
[11] (1989) Cm.622, Rec.7(1).
[12] (1989) Cm.622, Rec.7(2)–7(13).
[13] (1989) Cm.622, Rec.7(7).
[14] (1989) Cm.622, Rec.8(1).
[15] (1989) Cm.622, Rec.8(2).

this branch of the law, the Review Committee commissioned a report from an expert (Dr A.M. Shea), which itself set out recommendations for the enlargement of the scope of the 1882 Act and for the amendment of certain of its provisions.[16] Included in this sub-report was "draft legislation" prepared by Dr Shea to illustrate his proposals. After consultation, the Review Committee adopted a considerable number of Dr Shea's recommendations.

In 1990 the Government presented a White Paper setting out its **1–009** response to the report of the Review Committee.[17] It did not accept that there was a need for a new Cheques and Bank Payment Orders Act or for the introduction of a new instrument, the bank payment order.[18] It preferred instead an alternative course mentioned by the Review Committee which was to clarify the effect of the existing markings and crossings on cheques.[19] Legislation would be introduced whereby cheques crossed generally would be "not negotiable"[20]; the need for a clear method of making cheques non-transferable, where this was required, would be met by giving statutory status to the words "account payee" written on the face of a crossed cheque, so ensuring that the cheque could only be paid into the bank account of the named payee.[21] Recommendations of the Review Committee accepted in the White Paper, and dealt with later in this book, included the repeal and re-enactment in substance of the differing statutory provisions which at present protect the paying banker,[22] an amendment to the 1882 Act to facilitate the truncation of cheques,[23] a reconsideration of the principle of attachment of funds in Scotland,[24] the equation of Government-payable orders to cheques[25] and a clarification of the legal effect of bank giro credits.[26]

The Government agreed with the Review Committee that the structure and language of the 1882 Act should be retained, but did not accept the need to extend the 1882 Act to other instruments.[27] Certain limited changes to the Act were nevertheless necessary to bring the law up to date with modern circumstances, as mentioned in the Review Committee's recommendations. Amendments would be introduced to facilitate the denomination of instruments in units of account,[28] to abolish the

---

[16] Report, App.A.
[17] (1990) Cm.1026.
[18] (1990) Cm.1026, Annex 5, para.5.4.
[19] (1989) Cm.622, para.7.18.
[20] Annex 5, para.5.5.
[21] Annex 5, paras 5.6–5.8.
[22] Rec.7(5); Annex 5, para.5.9; below, paras 8–043, 14–024 and 17–005.
[23] Rec.7(8); Annex 5, paras 5.11–5.13; below, para.13–023.
[24] Rec.7(10); Annex 5, paras 5.15–5.18; below, para.7–008.
[25] Rec.7(11), 7(12); Annex 5, paras 5.19–5.20; below, para.13–014.
[26] Rec.7(13); Annex 5, paras 5.21–5.22; below, para.7–011.
[27] (1990) Cm.1026, Annex 6, paras 6.2, 6.3.
[28] Rec.8(5); Annex 6, para.6.4; below, para.2–014.

mandatory requirement of noting and protest of foreign bills and to introduce a simpler form of protest on a voluntary basis,[29] to afford legal recognition to the "aval",[30] to give transactions in dematerialised instruments the same status as transactions in negotiable instruments generally,[31] and to allow notice of dishonour to be given by electronic communication or by telecommunication.[32]

**1–010**     **Statutory implementation.** The Government's proposals have so far only been implemented by statute in the Cheques Act 1992 and the Deregulation (Bills of Exchange) Order 1996.[33] The 1992 Act gave statutory recognition to the words "account payee" or "a/c payee" on a crossed cheque by introducing into the 1882 Act a new section 81A, subsection (1) of which provides that a crossed cheque bearing these words across its face is not transferable, but is only valid as between the parties thereto.[34] Consequential amendments were made to the 1882 Act and to the Cheques Act 1957. The 1996 Order, made under the Deregulation and Contracting Out Act 1994, introduced into the 1882 Act a new section 74B in order to facilitate the truncation of cheques,[35] with consequential amendments to the 1882 Act and to the Cheques Act 1957. The remainder of the proposals have not yet been implemented.

**1–011**     **Banking Codes.** Of particular importance in the wider scope of the banker–customer relationship was the Government's acceptance of much of the Review Committee's recommendation relating to the introduction of a code of banking practice.[36] A Code of Banking Practice (now called "The Banking Code") was, in consequence, drawn up by the British Bankers' Association, the Building Societies Association and the Association for Payment Clearing Services. It was published in 1992, and revised in 1994, 1997, 2001, 2003 and 2005. The Code is voluntary and binds only those institutions which subscribe to it. Its aim is to set out standards of good banking practice to be followed by banks and building societies in their relations with *personal* customers, that is to say any person who is acting for purposes which are not linked to their trade, business or profession. Most of the provisions of the Code concern the banker–customer relationship and payment cards, and are not concerned directly with the payment or collection of bills, cheques and promissory notes. But some provisions are relevant incidentally to cheques and these are noted

---

[29] Rec.8(8); Annex 6, para.6.7; below, para.6–144.
[30] Para.8.16; Annex 6, para.6.8; below, para.7–039.
[31] Rec.8(9); Annex 6, paras 6.9, 6.10; below, paras 2–011 and 5–004.
[32] Technical Recommendation 36; Annex 6, para.6.11; below, para.6–100.
[33] SI 1996/2993.
[34] See below, para.14–037.
[35] See below, para.13–023.
[36] Annex 1.

at the appropriate places in this book. A second banking code, the "Business Banking Code", for business customers (including associations, charities and clubs) with an annual turnover (or income) of less than £1 million, was also published in 2003 and 2005. Both banking codes can be obtained online.[37]

**Other codifications.** International conferences were held in The Hague 1–012 in 1910 and 1912 with a view to unifying the various systems of bills of exchange law prevailing in the main commercial countries of the world. The United Kingdom was represented at these conferences. The resulting Convention on the Unification of the Law relating to Bills of Exchange and Promissory Notes, and Uniform Regulation,[38] was not adhered to by the United Kingdom and never entered into force. In 1930 and 1931, under the auspices of the League of Nations at Geneva, six further conventions were formulated. Two of these dealt with substantive law: a Convention providing a Uniform Law for Bills of Exchange and Promissory Notes ("ULB")[39] and a Convention providing a Uniform Law for Cheques ("ULC").[40] These two conventions have been ratified or acceded to by a large number of civil law countries, but not by the United Kingdom or the United States or other countries of a common law tradition. Two conventions dealt with the conflict of laws: a Convention for the Settlement of Certain Conflicts of Laws in connection with Bills of Exchange and Promissory Notes[41] and a Convention for Settlement of Certain Conflicts of Laws in connection with Cheques.[42] The United Kingdom is not a party to these two conventions. The last two conventions dealt with stamp laws: a Convention on the Stamp Laws in connection with Bills of Exchange and Promissory Notes[43] and a Convention on the Stamp Laws in connection with Cheques.[44] The United Kingdom became a party to these two conventions in 1934 and 1932 respectively.

In the United States, a Negotiable Instruments Law was promulgated by the National Conference of Commissioners on Uniform State Laws in 1896, and was subsequently enacted in every American jurisdiction. It largely followed the 1882 Act in its wording, although the arrangement was different.[45] The law relating to negotiable instruments in the United

---

[37] From *www.bba.org.uk* or *www.bankingcode.org.uk*.
[38] League of Nations, document C. 234. M. 83. 1929. II, pp.33–49.
[39] League of Nations, *Treaty Series*, vol.CXLIII, p.259, No.3313 (1933–1934).
[40] League of Nations, *Treaty Series*, vol.CXLIII, p.357, No.3316 (1933–1934).
[41] League of Nations, *Treaty Series*, vol.CXLIII, p.319, No.3314 (1933–1934).
[42] League of Nations *Treaty Series*, vol.CXLIII, p.409, No.3317 (1933–1934).
[43] League of Nations *Treaty Series*, vol.CXLIII, p.339, No.3315 (1933–1934).
[44] League of Nations *Treaty Series*, vol.CXLIII, p.9, No.3301 (1933–1934).
[45] See Brannan, *The Negotiable Instruments Law Annotated* (9th ed., 1926).

States has since been substantially revised and modernised in the Uniform Commercial Code ("UCC"), Article 3—Commercial Paper.

There are thus three major extant codifications: first, the Geneva Uniform Laws on Bills of Exchange and Promissory Notes ("ULB") and on Cheques ("ULC"); secondly, the Bills of Exchange Act 1882; and thirdly, Article 3 of the Uniform Commercial Code ("UCC"). To these there must now be added the United Nations Convention on International Bills of Exchange and International Promissory Notes ("UNB").[46] This convention, formulated by the United Nations Commission on International Trade Law, attempted to bridge the differences between the civil law systems on the one hand and the common law systems on the other. It envisaged a new form of International Bill of Exchange and International Promissory Note, governed by the regime of the convention and expressly so denoted, for *optional* use. The convention does not apply to cheques. Despite its worthy objective, the convention seems unlikely to achieve a sufficient degree of support among nations for it to enter into force.[47]

### Interpretation of terms

1–013     2. In this Act, unless the context otherwise requires—
"Acceptance" means an acceptance completed by delivery or notification.
"Action" includes counterclaim and set off.
"Banker" includes a body of persons, whether incorporated or not, who carry on the business of banking.
"Bankrupt" includes any person whose estate is vested in a trustee or assignee under the law for the time being in force relating to bankruptcy.
"Bearer" means the person in possession of a bill or note which is payable to bearer.
"Bill" means bill of exchange, and "note" means promissory note.
"Delivery" means transfer of possession, actual or constructive, from one person to another.
"Holder" means the payee or indorsee of a bill or note who is in possession of it, or the bearer thereof.
"Indorsement" means an indorsement completed by delivery.

---

[46] See the 15th edition of this book, App.C.
[47] The convention enters into force on the first day of the month following the expiration of 12 months after the date of deposit of the tenth instrument of ratification, acceptance, approval or accession (art.89(1)).

"Issue" means the first delivery of a bill or note, complete in form to a person who takes it as a holder.
"Person" includes a body of persons whether incorporated or not.
"Postal operator" has the meaning given by section 125(1) of the Postal Services Act 2000.
"Value" means valuable consideration.
"Written" includes printed, and "writing" includes print.

Amendment
The definition of "postal operator" was inserted by the Postal Services Act 2000 (Consequential Modifications No.1) Order 2001 (SI 2001/1149), art.3(1) and Sch.1, para.4.

COMMENT

"Acceptance". By section 17(1) of the Act, the acceptance of a bill is the signification by the drawee of his assent to the order of the drawer. It must be written on the bill and signed by the drawee.[48] The requirements of a valid acceptance are set out in sections 17 to 19. The reference to delivery or notification to complete an acceptance reflects the provisions of section 21(1) of the Act and the proviso thereto. As to acceptance for honour, see section 65. **1–014**

"Action". See section 30(2) (presumption as to holder in due course) and section 70 (lost bill), which require this definition. Contrast the definitions in section 151(1) of the Supreme Court Act 1981 and section 147(1) of the County Courts Act 1984. The definition is, of course, inclusive. **1–015**

"Banker". This definition could be criticised as unhelpful, since it does not go on to define what is "the business of banking". It may, however, be impossible to arrive at any satisfactory definition of "bank" or "banker" or to identify what are the essential characteristics of "the business of banking".[49] **1–016**
The main regulatory statute, the Financial Services and Markets Act 2000, avoids any definition as such of the term "bank". It refers instead to an "authorised person", that is to say, a person authorised for the purposes of the Act (*e.g.* granted permission to accept deposits by the Financial Services Authority),[50] or an "EEA firm" qualifying for authorisation

---

[48] s.17(2)(a).
[49] See the Report of the (Jenkins) Company Law Committee (1962) Cmnd.1749, § 405.
[50] ss.31(1)(a), (2).

under Schedule 3 of the Act (exercising EEA passport rights in the UK).[51] The Bankers' Books Evidence Act 1879 (as amended) also, in effect, employs the same terminology when defining the expressions "bank" and "banker" for the purposes of the Act (but in addition includes the National Savings Bank and the Post Office in the exercise of its powers to provide banking services).[52] Other statutes tend to follow the same pattern[53] or simply refer to "a bank within the meaning of the Bankers' Books Evidence Act 1879."[54] It does not, however, follow that, because an institution is a bank for the purposes of some other Act, it is necessarily a "banker" for the purposes of the present Act.

The words "the business of banking" are likewise incapable of precise definition for a number of reasons. First, those institutions which are entitled to call themselves banks do not all conduct their business in a uniform manner. The range of activities engaged in by the clearing banks differs from that, for example, of the merchant banks. Secondly, in the last 25 years, institutions such as savings banks, building societies,[55] finance houses and the Post Office[56] have moved into areas which were previously the preserve of the clearing banks. They now offer current account—as well as deposit account—facilities, overdrafts and loans, and some foreign exchange services, though not as a general rule finance through the medium of bills of exchange and promissory notes. It has therefore become more difficult to define the business of banking by reference to business carried on by the clearing banks alone. Thirdly, the nature of banking business changes from time to time. The merger of smaller banks into larger entities, and the expansion in the numbers of those maintaining accounts with financial institutions, has altered the way in which banking business is carried on. In particular, the electronic revolution has had a marked effect on banking practices. Accounts have been computerised, and electronic processes are used to clear cheques. More cash withdrawals are now made from personal accounts through automated teller machines (ATMs) than by cheque[57]; EFTPOS systems (Electronic Funds Transfer at Point of Sale) have been set up, by which payments for retail sales can be made by transferring funds from the customer's account to the retailer's account without the use of cash,

---

[51] ss.31(1)(b), (2). See also the Financial Services and Markets Act 2000 (EEA Passport Rights) Regulations 2001 (SI 2001/2511).

[52] s.9(1).

[53] *e.g.* Agricultural Credits Act 1928, s.5(7) (as amended); Solicitors Act 1974, s.87(1) (as amended); Postal Services Act 2000, s.7(5) (as amended).

[54] See, *e.g.* Consumer Credit Act 1974, s.74(3A).

[55] Building Societies Act 1997, s.12(3).

[56] Post Office Act 1969, s.7(1)(b)(2) (as amended by s.58(1) of the British Telecommunications Act 1981 and s.115(1) the Postal Services Act 2000).

[57] See below, para.13–002.

cheques or paper vouchers[58]; and the legal framework is at least in place for the introduction of "cheque truncation", whereby cheques would be cleared electronically, only the data on them being transmitted to the paying banker without any need to move the paper instrument.[59] Banking may even be conducted by telephone only. These developments suggest that it would be unwise to determine the nature and scope of the business of banking by reference to banking practices as at a particular time.[60]

In 1914, in *Commissioners of the State Savings Bank of Victoria v Permewan,* **1–017** *Wright & Co. Ltd,*[61] Isaacs J. considered that the fundamental meaning of the term was not different in Australia from that obtaining in England, and said:

> "The essential characteristics of the business of banking ... may be described as the collection of money by receiving deposits upon loan, repayable when and as expressly or impliedly agreed upon, and the utilization of the money so collected by lending it again in such sums as are required."

In 1948 the Judicial Committee of the Privy Council, in *Bank of Chettinad Ltd of Colombo v Commissioners of Income Tax, Colombo,*[62] accepted as in no way conflicting with the meaning attached to the word "bank" in England in 1932 the definition of a "banking company" in the Ceylon Companies Ordinance 1938 as: "a company which carries on as its principal business[63] the accepting of deposits of money on current account or otherwise, subject to withdrawal by cheque, draft or order". And in 1966, in *United Dominions Trust Ltd v Kirkwood,*[64] the Court of Appeal unanimously held that the payment and collection of customers' cheques was, in modern times, an essential constituent of the business of banking.[65] In that case, the point at issue was whether a finance house was "bona fide carrying on the business of banking" within the meaning of section 6(d) of the Moneylenders Act 1900 so as to exempt it from the provisions of the Moneylenders Acts 1900 to 1927. All the members of the Court considered

---

[58] See below, para.13–002.
[59] See below, para.13–023. But full cheque truncation is still "some way off", see Paget (12th ed.), 17.121.
[60] *Bank of New South Wales v The Commonwealth* (1948) 76 C.L.R. 1, 334; *Woods v Martins Bank Ltd* [1959] 1 Q.B. 55, 70; *United Dominions Trust Ltd v Kirkwood* [1966] 2 Q.B. 431, 446.
[61] (1915) 19 C.L.R. 457, 470–471. This was approved by the High Court of Australia in *Australian Independent Distributors Ltd v Winter* (1965) 112 C.L.R. 443, 454.
[62] [1948] A.C. 378, 383.
[63] But see *Re Roe's Legal Charge* [1982] 2 Lloyd's Rep. 370.
[64] [1966] 2 Q.B. 431. See also *Re Birkbeck Permanent Benefit Building Socy.* [1912] 2 Ch. 183; *London & Harrogate Securities Ltd v Pitts* [1976] 1 W.L.R. 1063; *Re Roe's Legal Charge,* above, at 381.
[65] At 446, 458, 465.

that the definition of Isaacs J. in the Australian case was too wide.[66] Lord Denning M.R. stated[67] that: "no person can be considered a banker unless he handles cheques as freely as cash". He said[68]:

> "There are . . . two characteristics usually found in bankers today: (i) They accept money from, and collect cheques for, their customers and place them to their credit; (ii) They honour cheques or orders drawn on them by their customers when presented for payment and debit their customers accordingly. These two characteristics carry with them also a third, namely: (iii) They keep current accounts, or something of that nature, in their books in which the credits and debits are entered."

The Court of Appeal, by a majority,[69] held that the finance house fell within the exemption. But they did so also on the ground that it had acquired so widespread and unqualified a reputation among bankers and commercial men as to discharge the burden of proof that it was bona fide carrying on the business of banking.[70]

Since the definition of "banker" is used in the present Act and in the Cheques Act 1957 principally in relation to cheques,[71] it may be that the characteristics referred to by Lord Denning M.R. would similarly still be regarded as essential to carrying on the business of banking for the purposes of the Act. But the "march of time"[72] could takes us to the position where banking business might quite feasibly be carried on without any need for cheques or other paper-based orders to pay[73] and it does not therefore appear sensible that the definition should be interpreted by reference to one only of a number of ways in which money may be withdrawn from or paid into customers' accounts.

1–018     **"Bankrupt".** This definition appears to be inclusive. For the vesting (in England) of the bankrupt's estate in the trustee in bankruptcy or official receiver, see section 306 of the Insolvency Act 1986. For the vesting (in Scotland) of the estate of the debtor in the permanent trustee, see section 31 of the Bankruptcy (Scotland) Act 1985. See sections 41(d), 49(10) and 51(5) of the Act, which require this definition.

---

[66] At 446, 457–458, 464.
[67] At 446.
[68] At 447.
[69] Lord Denning M.R. and Diplock L.J. (Harman L.J. dissenting).
[70] At 453–456, 474–475.
[71] *cf.* s.60.
[72] An expression used by Lord Denning M.R. in *United Dominions Trust Ltd v Kirkwood*, above, at 446.
[73] See also below, para.13–023 (truncation of cheques).

**"Bearer".** By section 8(3) of the Act, a bill is payable to bearer which is 1–119
expressed to be so payable, or on which the only or last indorsement is an
indorsement in blank. By section 34(1), an indorsement in blank specifies
no indorsee, and a bill so indorsed becomes payable to bearer. As a
general rule, the possessor of a bill or note payable to order is not its
"bearer" unless and until it has been indorsed in blank and negotiated by
delivery.[74] However, by section 7(3), where the payee is a fictitious or
non-existing person the bill may be treated as payable to bearer. Further,
by section 2 of the Cheques Act 1957, a banker who gives value for, or has
a lien on, a cheque payable to order which the holder delivers to him for
collection without indorsing it, has such (if any) rights as he would have
had if, upon delivery, the holder had indorsed it in blank. A banker to
whom a cheque is so delivered becomes a bearer of the instrument.[75]

For the negotiation of a bill payable to bearer, see section 31(2); and for
the liability of a holder who negotiates a bill payable to bearer, see section
58.

**"Bill" and "note".** For the operative definition of these terms, see 1–020
sections 3 and 83 of the Act. For the definition of a cheque, see section
73.

**"Delivery".** Section 61(1) of the Sale of Goods Act 1979 defines deliv- 1–021
ery to mean *"voluntary* transfer of possession from one person to
another". Chalmers observed that a wider definition was required by the
1882 Act "because of instruments payable to bearer"[76]: even an involun-
tary transfer of possession, *e.g.* by theft, constitutes delivery of a bill or
note payable to bearer, at least in favour of a holder in due course.[77]

Possession is nowhere defined in the Act; the draftsman no doubt
wisely refrained from the attempt. It is a concept notoriously resistant to
definition.[78] As used in the Act, possession may be either rightful or
wrongful, actual or constructive.

"A person is said to have constructive possession of a thing when it
is in the actual possession of his servant or agent on his behalf[79];

---

[74] It appears that the payee in possession of a bill or note payable to order could not become
the bearer of it by indorsing it in blank, since he could not complete the indorsement by
delivering it to himself.
[75] *Midland Bank Ltd v R.V. Harris Ltd* [1963] 1 W.L.R. 1021; below, para.17–022. But this does
not apply to cheques crossed "account payee": below, para.17–017.
[76] Chalmers (9th ed.), p.6.
[77] s.21(2) (conclusive presumption of delivery). *cf. McKenty v Vanhorenback* (1911) 21
Man.L.R. 360.
[78] See Pollock and Wright, *An Essay on Possession in the Common Law* (1888); Harris, *Oxford
Essays in Jurisprudence* (1961), p.69.
[79] *Silk Bros Interstate Traders Pty Ltd v Security Pacific National Bank* (1989) 16 N.S.W.L.R. 446.
See below, para.5–057 (s.38). See also para.5–057 joint possession.

therefore delivery may be effected without change of actual possession in three cases namely:

(1) a bill is held by C on his own account; he subsequently holds it as agent for D;
(2) a bill is held by C's agent, who subsequently attorns to D, and holds it as his agent;
(3) a bill is held by D as agent for C; he subsequently holds it on his own account."[80]

For the necessity for delivery to complete the contracts of the drawer, acceptor or an indorser of a bill, see section 21; for the necessity for delivery of a promissory note to the payee or bearer, see section 84. See also the definitions of "acceptance", "indorsement" and "issue".

Delivery may be relevant to the question whether property in the instrument has passed to the intended transferee,[81] who is the "true owner" of the instrument,[82] whether payment has been made if the instrument is lost in transit,[83] and what is the place where the contract is made for the purpose of the rules relating to the conflict of laws.[84] For delivery by post, see the Comment on section 21, below, para.2–151.[85]

1–022     **"Holder".** The concept of the holder is central to the Act and to the law of negotiable instruments. "Holder" includes alike the payee, the indorsee,[86] and the bearer of a bill or note. It signifies the mercantile owner of the instrument, who may or may not be the legal owner of it. Even a thief may be the holder of a bill payable to bearer. But if a bill payable to order is stolen, and the indorsement of the payee or of an indorsee is forged, neither the thief nor any person who subsequently comes into possession of the instrument will be a holder, as the forged signature is wholly inoperative.[87]

It is to be noted that possession is an essential part of the definition.[88]

---

[80] Chalmers (9th ed.), p.6, citing *Field v Carr* (1828) 5 Bing. 13; *Bosanquet v Forster* (1841) 9 C. & P. 659; *Belcher v Campbell* (1845) 8 Q.B. 1. See also *Lysaght v Bryant* (1850) 9 C.B. 46 (s.21, Illustration 7); *Ancona v Marks* (1862) 7 H. & N. 686. *cf. Brind v Hampshire* (1836) 1 M. & W. 365 (s.21, Illustration 4).

[81] See below, para.2–151 (s.21).

[82] See below, para.3–051 (s.24).

[83] See below, para.2–151 (s.21).

[84] s.72(1)(2).

[85] See below, para.2–151.

[86] See "Indorsement", below, para.1–024.

[87] s.24; see below, para.3–066.

[88] See the Comment on "Delivery", above, para.1–021.

A holder may be a mere holder[89] holder for value[90] or a holder in due course.[91] The original payee of a bill or note, in whose possession the instrument remains, is a holder, but cannot be a holder in due course.[92] An agent, *e.g.* a banker, to whom an order or bearer instrument is delivered for collection is a holder of it.[93] But a banker upon whom a cheque is drawn and to whom it is presented for payment is not a holder of the cheque.[94]

The holder may sue on the bill in his own name.[95] He may (unless the    **1–023** bill is in its origin or by indorsement made non-transferable)[96] negotiate the bill.[97] If he obtains payment of the bill the person who pays him in due course gets a valid discharge for the bill.[98]

A person to whom an order bill is transferred without indorsement is not a holder until the indorsement of the transferor is obtained.[99]

**"Indorsement".** This definition reiterates the requirement, derived    **1–024** from the common law[1] and also to be found in sections 21(1) and 31(3) of the Act, that an indorsement must be completed by delivery. For delivery, see the definition of that term, above at para.1–021, and section 21.

The indorsement of the holder is required in order to negotiate a bill or note which is payable to order.[2] For the requisites of a valid indorsement, see section 32. As a general rule, it must be written on the instrument,[3] and, as the word "indorsement" indicates, is usually (but not necessarily) placed on the back of the instrument. An indorsement may be a special indorsement[4] or an indorsement in blank,[5] and it may be qualified[6] conditional[7] or restrictive.[8]

---

[89] See below, para.4–028.
[90] ss.27(2)(3); see below, para.4–024.
[91] s.29(1); see below, para.4–049.
[92] *Jones (R.E.) Ltd v Waring and Gillow Ltd* [1926] A.C. 670 (s.29, Illustration 6); below, para.4–059.
[93] *Akrokerri (Atlantic) Mines Ltd v Economic Bank* [1904] 2 K.B. 465, 472; *Sutters v Briggs* [1922] 1 A.C. 1; *Baker v Barclays Bank Ltd* [1955] 1 W.L.R. 822. But not an instrument which is non-transferable: see below, para.14–043.
[94] *Coats v Union Bank of Scotland* 1929 S.C., H.L., 114. But see below, para.4–060 (s.29).
[95] s.38(1). For the other rights of the holder, see the Comment on s.38; below, para.4–028.
[96] ss.8(1), 35, 81A. Contrast s.81 (cheques crossed "not negotiable").
[97] s.31.
[98] ss.38(3)(b), 59.
[99] s.31(4). But exceptions exist by virtue of s.7(3) of the 1882 Act and s.2 of the Cheques Act 1957.
[1] *Marston v Allen* (1841) 8 M. & W. 494, 504. See also *Adams v Jones* (1840) 12 A. & E. 455; *Lloyd v Howard* (1850) 15 Q.B. 995, 999; *Denton v Peters* (1870) L.R. 5 Q.B. 475.
[2] s.31(3). But see s.7(3) of the 1882 Act and s.2 of the Cheques Act 1957.
[3] s.32(1). The exceptions are there mentioned.
[4] ss.32(6), 34(2).
[5] ss.32(6), 34(1).
[6] s.16(1).
[7] s.33.
[8] s.35.

An indorsement which operates as a negotiation must be distinguished from the so-called "anomalous indorsement" under section 56 of the Act whereby a person backs a bill with his signature, and thereby incurs the liability of an indorser to a holder in due course.[9] It must also be distinguished from an "indorsement" which is merely a signature by way of receipt.[10]

**1–025**    The term "indorser" denotes the former holder of a bill or note who has indorsed it. For the liability of an indorser, see section 55(2). The first indorser of a note is deemed to correspond with the drawer of an accepted bill payable to drawer's order.[11] The term is, however, often used to denote an anomalous indorser under section 56. The term "indorsee" is primarily used to denote a person to whom an instrument payable to order has been specially indorsed. But it is probable that the bearer of an order instrument indorsed in blank—that is, any person who makes title to it through an indorsement—is also an indorsee.[12] In *Midland Bank Ltd v R.V. Harris Ltd*,[13] Megaw J. stated that an indorsee meant: "a person who has the rights which are given by statute in respect of a bill or cheque by virtue of an indorsement".

**1–026**    **"Issue".** See sections 9(3), 12 and 72(1), which require this definition. For delivery, see the definition of that term, above, and section 21.

Some difficulty is caused by the words "complete in form". It follows from this requirement that a bill or note will not be issued if it is delivered to a holder when it is incomplete, *i.e.* when one or more of the requisites of a valid bill or note are not present on the instrument. However, in *Gerald McDonald & Co. v Nash & Co.*,[14] the House of Lords held that, once a bill is duly and timeously completed in accordance with section 20 of the Act, then it is to be treated as if it had not been defective at all; it is retrospectively validated. But a mental element is in that case involved. The proviso to section 20(2), which protects a holder in due course to whom an incomplete instrument is negotiated after completion notwithstanding that it was not duly and timeously completed, applies only if the person signing it intended it to become a bill. If an incomplete bill is stolen from the signatory and filled up as a bill, he will not be liable even to a holder in due course.[15] And if he hands an incomplete note to his

---

[9] See below, para.7–030.
[10] See below, para.5–006.
[11] s.89(2).
[12] *Barber v Richards* (1851) 6 Exch. 63, 65.
[13] [1963] 1 W.L.R. 1021, 1024 (a case on s.2 of the Cheques Act 1957).
[14] [1924] A.C. 625, 647 (s.20, Illustration 15).
[15] *Baxendale v Bennett* (1878) 3 Q.B.D. 525 (s.20, Illustration 20).

agent as bailee only, and without the intention the agent should issue it as a promissory note, he will not be liable if the note is completed by the agent and negotiated to a holder in due course.[16] The necessary *animus emittendi* will not be present.

A bill or note will not be issued unless and until it is delivered to a person who takes it as a holder. In most cases that person will be the payee of the instrument. But the lodging of a bill with the drawee for acceptance does not constitute issue of the bill, since the drawee does not take it as a holder. Nor does the mere drawing of a bill or cheque by the drawer payable to his own order constitute issue, since the drawer cannot deliver it to himself.

See also sections 1(2)(a) and 4(2)(b) of the Cheques Act 1957 (documents issued by customer of banker).

**"Person".** See in particular sections 3, 4, 5, 8, 15, 20, 23, 24, 26, 28, 29, **1–027** 31, 34, 36, 38, 41, 45, 46, 49, 50, 51, 52, 54, 56, 65, 68, 69, 70, 71, 72, 74, 78, 81, 83, 85, 91, which require this definition. The definition is inclusive and similar to that contained in section 5 and Schedule 1 of the Interpretation Act 1978.

**"Postal operator".** See sections 41(1)(e), 45(8), 49(15) and 51(6) which **1–028** require this definition. Section 125(1) of the Postal Services Act 2000 defines "postal operator" to mean "a person who provides the service of conveying postal packets from one place to another by post or any of the incidental services of receiving, collecting, sorting and delivering such packets."[17]

**"Value".** What constitutes valuable consideration for a bill is set out in **1–029** section 27(1) of the Act. For "holder for value" see section 27(2) and (3). See also section 2 of the Cheques Act 1957 (banker who has given value for an order cheque delivered to him unindorsed for collection).

**"Written" and "writing".** This definition is inclusive.[18] For a wider **1–030** definition, see section 5 and Schedule 1 of the Interpretation Act 1978: " 'Writing' includes typing, printing, lithography, photography and other modes of representing or reproducing words in a visible form, and expressions referring to writing are construed accordingly."

---

[16] *Smith v Prosser* [1907] 2 K.B. 735 (s.20, Illustration 22).
[17] For "postal packet", see also s.125(1) of the Act.
[18] A bill or note may be written in pencil: *Geary v Physic* (1826) 5 B. & C. 234. See also the Comment on s.3; below, para.2–011.

The definition is required, in particular, by sections 3, 17, 21, 26, 32, 34, 49, 51, 62, 65, 71, 83, 91. For "signature" see sections 23 and 91.

Where the instrument is partly in handwriting and partly printed, it would seem that the general rule of construction[19] would apply, and that, if there be any inconsistency in the two forms, the handwritten words should prevail over the printed.

---

[19] See *Chitty on Contracts* (29th ed., Sweet & Maxwell), Vol.I, para.12–070.

# PART II

# BILLS OF EXCHANGE

## Form and Interpretation

### Bill of exchange defined

3. (1) A bill of exchange is an unconditional order in writing, 2–001
    addressed by one person to another, signed by the person
    giving it, requiring the person to whom it is addressed to pay
    on demand or at a fixed or determinable future time a sum
    certain in money to or to the order of a specified person, or to
    bearer.

   (2) An instrument which does not comply with these conditions,
    or which orders any act to be done in addition to the payment
    of money, is not a bill of exchange.

   (3) An order to pay out of a particular fund is not unconditional
    within the meaning of this section; but an unqualified order
    to pay, coupled with (a) an indication of a particular fund out
    of which the drawee is to re-imburse himself or a particular
    account to be debited with the amount, or (b) a statement of
    the transaction which gives rise to the bill, is uncondi-
    tional.

   (4) A bill is not invalid by reason—
    (a) That it is not dated;
    (b) That it does not specify the value given, or that any value
        has been given therefor;
    (c) That it does not specify the place where it is drawn or the
        place where it is payable.

| Definitions | Comparison | 2–002 |
|---|---|---|
| "bearer": s.2. | UCC: §§ 3–103 to 3–113. | |
| "bill": s.2. | ULB: arts 1–4. | |
| "determinable future time": s.11. | UNB: arts 2, 3, 11. | |
| "person": s.2. | | |
| "value": s.2. | | |
| "writing": s.2. | | |

COMMENT

**2–003**    **Bills of exchange.** A bill of exchange is sometimes called a "draft"[1] and, when accepted, an "acceptance". A bill drawn by one trader on another against a trade transaction, but not bearing a bank indorsement, is known as a "trade bill" or "trade draft"; when accepted it is known as a "trade acceptance". A bill bearing the indorsement of a bank is referred to as a "bank bill" and a bill accepted by a bank as a "bankers' acceptance". A draft drawn by a bank on itself is a "bankers' draft". It is, in fact, not a bill of exchange.[2]

**2–004**    **Parties.** The person who draws the bill and gives the order to pay is called the "drawer".[3] The person upon whom the bill is drawn and who is thereby ordered to pay is called the "drawee". When the drawee signifies his assent to the order of the drawer in due form ("acceptance"),[4] he is then called the "acceptor".[5] An acceptance must be written on the bill and be accompanied by or consist of the signature of the drawee.[6] The person specified in the bill as the person to or to whose order the money is to be paid is called the "payee",[7] or, if the bill is drawn payable to bearer and he is in possession of the bill, the "bearer".[8]

Unless the bill is so drawn,[9] or indorsed[10] as to prohibit transfer, the bill may be "negotiated", *i.e.* transferred, to a third party.[11] A bill payable to order is negotiated by the indorsement of the payee (or of a subsequent transferee) completed by delivery.[12] The person indorsing the bill is called the "indorser"[13] and the person to whom it is indorsed, the "indorsee". To operate as a negotiation, the indorsement must be written on the bill and be accompanied by or consist of the signature of the indorser.[14] A bill payable to bearer is negotiated by mere delivery.[15]

---

[1] UCC, § 3–104(e). In commercial usage, the term "draft" is ordinarily used to denote an unaccepted bill.
[2] See below, para.2–012.
[3] For the liability of the drawer, see s.55(1).
[4] s.17(1).
[5] For the liability of the acceptor, see s.54.
[6] s.17(2).
[7] s.7.
[8] s.2.
[9] s.8(1). See also s.81A (cheques crossed "account payee").
[10] s.35.
[11] s.31(1).
[12] s.31(3).
[13] For the liability of the indorser, see s.55(2).
[14] s.32.
[15] s.31(2).

The payee or an indorsee of a bill who is in possession of it, or the bearer, is called the "holder".[16]

Other persons who may be encountered with respect to bills of exchange are the "referee in case of need",[17] the "acceptor for honour",[18] the "accommodation party",[19] the "anomalous" or "quasi-" indorser[20] and the giver of an *"aval"*.[21]

**Cheques and promissory notes.** A cheque is a bill of exchange drawn on a banker payable on demand.[22] Except as otherwise provided in Part III of the Act, the provisions of the Act applicable to a bill of exchange payable on demand apply to a cheque.[23] But a cheque which is crossed "account payee" is not transferable[24]: it is a mere payment order and not a negotiable instrument.

**2–005**

A promissory note is not a bill of exchange.[25] Promissory notes are dealt with in Part IV of the Act, but subject to the provisions of Part IV, and except as provided by section 89, the provisions of the Act relating to bills of exchange apply, with the necessary modifications, to promissory notes.[26] The person who promises to pay is known as the "maker" of the note. In applying the provisions of the Act he is deemed to correspond with the acceptor of a bill.[27]

**Form of a bill.** The detailed content of bills of exchange will vary, but the following example of an export bill will illustrate the way in which a bill of exchange is drawn, and the requirements of section 3(1) of the Act:

**2–006**

*£68,376*                                        *LONDON 29th October 2004*

At *sixty days* after *sight* pay to the Order of *Exporters Ltd*            the sum of *sixty eight thousand three hundred and seventy six pounds* Value received

*Drawn under Bank of Ruritania Credit No. 5498/86 covering shipment of 30 cases of machine tools from U.K. to Ruritania*

[16] s.2. For "holder for value", see s.27(2). For "holder in due course", see s.29.
[17] s.15.
[18] ss.65–68.
[19] s.28.
[20] s.56.
[21] See below, para.7–039 (s.56).
[22] s.73.
[23] s.73.
[24] s.81A(1).
[25] s.83(1).
[26] s.89(1).
[27] s.89(2).

| To Bank of Ruritania (U.K.) Ltd | for and on behalf of |
|---|---|
| 67 Chatterton Street | EXPORTERS LIMITED |
| London EC2 | (signed) P.F. Smith |
| | Director |

This bill of exchange was drawn in London on October 29, 2004. It contains an unconditional order ("pay") in writing addressed by Exporters Limited, the drawer, to Bank of Ruritania (U.K.) Ltd, the drawee, signed on behalf of Exporters Limited by P.F. Smith, a director, requiring the drawee to pay at a fixed or determinable future time ("sixty days after sight") a sum certain in money (£28,376) to the order of a specified person ("Exporters Ltd"), the payee of the bill.

Neither the words "Value received" nor the clause in the centre of the bill recording the fact that the bill is drawn under a letter of credit are essential to or prejudice the validity of the bill, but it is usual to insert such a statement of value and the clause serves to identify the transaction which gives rise to the bill.

**2–007**      **Subsection (1): definition of bill.** This subsection sets out the requirements with which an instrument must comply if it is to be a bill of exchange. Apart from these requirements, no special form of words is essential to the validity of a bill.[28] It need not contain the words "Bill of Exchange"[29] nor need it be expressly payable to bearer or "to order".[30] It may be drawn in any language.[31]

Bills are normally written on paper, but presumably may be on any material that will receive writing.[32] It would seem that a bill must be a single instrument, though it could comprise more than one page.[33]

---

[28] *Morris v Lee* (1725) 2 Ld.Raym. 1396 (note); *Ellison v Collingridge* (1850) 9 C.B. 570 ("Credit Messrs P. & Co., or order . . . " instead of "Pay"). See also (notes), below, para.15–003 (s.83). Story, *Bills of Exchange*, § 33.

[29] Contrast ULB, art.1; UNB, art.1.

[30] s.8(4). Contrast UCC, §§ 3–104(a), 3–109 (unless payable to bearer).

[31] *Re Marseilles Extension Railway and Land Co.* (1885) 30 Ch.D. 598; *Credit Lyonnais v P. T. Barnard & Associates Ltd* [1976] 1 Lloyds Rep. 557; *Maxform Spa. v Mariani and Goodville Ltd* [1979] 2 Lloyds Rep. 385, affirmed [1981] 2 Lloyd's Rep. 54; *Banco Atlantico S.A. v British Bank of the Middle East* [1990] 2 Lloyd's Rep. 504.

[32] Sir Alan Herbert MP—creator of Albert Haddock and author of *Uncommon Law*—was no stranger to eccentric cheques. He wrote them on napkins, a brandy bottle and even on an egg. The egg had to be boiled by the bank to send it through the central clearing house. In August 1970 he was presented with a cheque for £5 written on a golden Guernsey cow called Elba. This recalled the case of *Board of Inland Revenue v Haddock* in which Mr Haddock had paid the Collector of Taxes a cheque for £57 written on "a large white cow of malevolent aspect". The cow exhibited some reluctance to be indorsed.

[33] *K.H.R. Financings Ltd v Jackson* 1977 S.L.T. (Sh.Ct) 6 (note). See also s.71 (bills in a set).

**"Order."** A bill is an order.[34] It must require, and not merely request, **2–008**
the drawee to pay. It must, therefore, in its terms be imperative and not
precative.[35] But the insertion of mere terms of courtesy will not make it
precative.[36] An authority to pay, for example "we hereby authorise you to
pay to our account to the order of G", is not an order to pay,[37] nor is a
building society withdrawal form.[38]

Where an instrument is so ambiguously worded that it is doubtful
whether it was intended for a bill or for a note, the holder may treat it at
his option as either.[39]

An instrument which orders the drawee to pay without acceptance is
nevertheless a bill of exchange.[40]

**"Unconditional."** It is of the essence of a bill that it should be payable **2–009**
at all events.[41] Although an acceptance,[42] indorsement[43] or delivery[44] of a
bill may be conditional, the order given by the drawer to the drawee must
be unconditional. Likewise the promise to pay contained in a promissory
note must be unconditional[45]:

> "The reason is (and it is equally applicable to all negotiable instru-
> ments) that it would greatly perplex the commercial transactions of
> mankind, and diminish and narrow their credit, circulation, and
> negotiability, if paper securities of this kind were issued out into the
> world encumbered with conditions and contingencies, and if the
> persons, to whom they were offered in negotiation, were obliged to
> enquire, when those uncertain events would probably be reduced to
> a certainty. And hence, the general rule is, that a Bill of Exchange
> always implies a personal general credit, not limited or applicable to
> particular circumstances and events, which cannot be known to the
> Holder of the Bill, in the general course of its negotiation."[46]

---

[34] See also UCC, § 3–104(e); ULB, art.1(2); UNB, art.3(1)(a).

[35] *Little v Slackford* (1828) M. & M. 171 (Illustration 1).

[36] *Ruff v Webb* (1794) 1 Esp. 129 (Illustration 2); *Brookler v Security National Insurance Co. of Canada* (1915) 23 D.L.R. 595. *cf. R. v Ellor* (1784) 1 Leach C.C. 323.

[37] *Hamilton v Spottiswoode* (1849) 4 Exch. 200, 210.

[38] *Weir v National Westminster Bank* 1994 S.L.T. 1251.

[39] *Edis v Bury* (1827) 6 B. & C. 433 (Illustration 3); *Lloyd v Oliver* (1852) 18 Q.B. 471; *Fielder v Marshall* (1861) 9 C.B.N.S. 606. See also *Shuttleworth v Stevens* (1808) 1 Camp. 407; *Allan v Mawson* (1814) 4 Camp. 115; *Armfield v Allport* (1857) 27 L.J.Ex. 42; *Mason v Lack* (1929) 45 T.L.R. 363; UCC, § 3–104(e).

[40] *R. v Kinnear* (1838) 2 Moo. & R. 117; *National Park Bank of New York v Berggren & Co.* (1914) 30 T.L.R. 387.

[41] See also; UCC, §§ 3–104, 3–106, ULB, art.1(2); UNB, art.3(1)(a).

[42] s.19.

[43] s.33.

[44] s.21(2).

[45] s.83(1).

[46] Story, *Bills of Exchange*, § 46, *Carlos v Fancourt* (1794) 5 T.R. 482, 485, 487.

If the order to pay is subject to any condition or qualification, the instrument will not be a bill of exchange. In particular, section 11 of the Act provides: "An instrument expressed to be payable on a contingency is not a bill, and the happening of the event does not cure the defect."[47]

An order addressed to the drawee requiring him to pay, provided that he first verifies the identity of the payee[48] or provided that a receipt form on the instrument is duly signed,[49] is conditional. But a direction in a bill that a receipt form must be duly signed, if addressed to the payee and not to the drawee, does not render the bill conditional.[50] In the case of a note, it is a question of construction whether a direction to the payee to do some act, *e.g.* to surrender a document, renders the promise of the maker to pay conditional upon such act being performed, or whether the act is to be performed merely in consequence of payment.[51] A direction on a dividend warrant that the warrant "will not be honoured after 3 months from the date of issue unless specially indorsed by the Secretary" has been held not to render the order to pay conditonal.[52]

References to other agreements or transactions are sometimes placed upon bills of exchange and promissory notes.[53] The question then arises whether the terms of the reference are such as to qualify the drawer's order or the maker's promise to pay. A bill drawn in the form "as per advice" is not conditional.[54] Nor is a bill or note conditional if it states that it is drawn or made in accordance with or pursuant to or "as per" another agreement or transaction,[55] unless the order or promise to pay is subject to or governed by that other agreement or transaction. References of this nature will ordinarily be understood to be a statement of the transaction which gave rise to the instrument[56] or to have been included for information only,[57] and not to qualify the order or promise to pay. An express statement on a note that it is to be held as collateral security would

---

[47] But see s.11(2).

[48] *Ong Kim Lian v Kwek Beng Choo* (1914) 14 S.S.L.R. 10 (Straits Settlements).

[49] *Bavins Jnr & Sims v London and South Western Bank Ltd.* [1900] 1 Q.B. 270 (Illustration 4); *Capital and Counties Bank Ltd v Gordon* [1903] A.C. 240, 252. But see Cheques Act 1957, ss.1(2)(a), 4(2)(b), 5; below, paras 17–013, 17–064 and 17–075.

[50] *Nathan v Ogdens Ltd* (1905) 93 L.T. 553, affirmed (1905) 94 L.T. 126 (Illustration 5). See also *Thairlwall v G.N.Ry* [1910] 2 K.B. 509, 519 (dividend warrant); *Roberts & Co. v Marsh* [1915] 1 K.B. 42 (s.73, Illustration 1); *London and Montrose Shipbuilding and Repairing Co. Ltd v Barclay's Bank Ltd* (1925) 31 Com.Cas. 67, reversed on its facts (1926) 31 Com.Cas. 182.

[51] *O'Grady v Lecomte* (1918) 40 D.L.R. 378.

[52] *Thairlwall v G.N. Ry*, above, at 518, 520.

[53] See, in particular, references in notes to the fact that the note is secured, below, para.15–028 (s.83).

[54] Story, *Bills of Exchange*, § 65, Contrast Chitty, *Bills* (11th ed., 1878), p.118.

[55] *Jury v Barker* (1858) E. B. & E. 459 (note).

[56] s.3(3)(b).

[57] *Brill v Crick* (1836) 1 M. & W. 232. See also *Williams & Glyns Bank Ltd v Belkin Packaging Ltd (No.2)* (1979) 17 B.C.L.R. 153; 123 D.L.R. (3d) 612; 147 D.L.R. (3d) 577.

probably make its payment contingent,[58] but not simply a statement that collateral security has been deposited with the payee.[59]

A statement on an instrument that the consideration is executory does **2–010** not render it conditional[60] unless payment is made conditional upon performance of the consideration.[61]

An instrument containing an arbitration clause would not be a bill of exchange.[62]

See also subsections (2) and (3), below.

**"Writing."** The order must be in writing. "Writing" includes print.[63] **2–011** Further, by section 5 of and Schedule 1 to the Interpretation Act 1978, in any Act, unless the contrary intention appears, "writing" includes typing, printing, lithography, photography and other modes of reproducing words in visible form.[64]

It is at least arguable that a bill could be issued by electronic means, provided that it could be reproduced in visible form, *e.g.* printed out or seen on a video-display unit. But difficulty would also arise from the fact that the order to pay would not be "signed" by the drawer.[65] Following the Report of the Review Committee on Banking Services Law and Practice in 1989,[66] the Government concluded that there would be considerable gains in efficiency if negotiable instruments could be "dematerialised", that is to say, issued and traded in purely electronic form, in a depositary system.[67] It therefore proposed to introduce legislation to give transactions in dematerialised instruments the same status as transactions in negotiable instruments generally.[68] Section 8 of the Electronic Communications Act 2000 empowers the appropriate Minister to modify, by order made by statutory instrument, the provisions of any enactment for the purpose of authorising or facilitating the use of electronic communications or electronic storage for certain purposes. But there is as yet no indication that the Government intends to implement its proposal by an order made under this section modifying the 1882 Act.

Nevertheless a limited step towards dematerialisation has already been made in regulations made by the Treasury under section 207 of the

---

[58] *Leeds v Lancashire* (1809) 2 Camp. 205; *Hall v Merrick* (1877) 40 U.C.Q.B. 566; *Shaw v Agnew* [1941] 2 D.L.R. 587.
[59] s.83(3); *Wise v Charlton* (1836) 4 A. & E. 786; *Fancourt v Thorne* (1846) 9 Q.B. 312; *Chesney v St John* (1879) 4 O.A.R. 150, 156; *O'Grady v Lecomte* (1918) 40 D.L.R. 378.
[60] *Merchants Bank of Canada v Bury* (1915) 21 D.L.R. 495.
[61] *Drury v Macaulay* (1846) 16 M. & W. 146 (note).
[62] *Nova (Jersey) Knit Ltd v Kammgarn Spinnerei GmbH.* [1977] 1 W.L.R. 713, 716.
[63] s.2.
[64] *cf.* UCC, § 201(46).
[65] See below, para.3–021 (s.23).
[66] (1989) Cm. 622, rec. 8(9); above, para.1–008.
[67] See below, para.5–004 (s.31).
[68] (1990) Cm. 1026, Annex 6, paras 6.9, 6.10.

Companies Act 1989.[69] These allow for the evidencing and transfer of title to "eligible debt securities" (including bankers' acceptances) in accordance with a computer based system and procedures.[70]

2–012     **"Addressed by one person to another."** The order must be addressed by one person (the drawer) to another (the drawee). If, therefore, the drawer draws a bill on himself, the instrument is not a bill of exchange.[71] Thus a bankers' draft, drawn by a banker upon himself, whether payable at the head office or some other office of his bank, is not a bill (or a cheque).[72] However, by section 5(2) of the Act, where in a bill drawer and drawee are the same person, the holder may treat the instrument, at his option, either as a bill of exchange or as a promissory note.[73]

      The drawee must be named or otherwise indicated in a bill with reasonable certainty.[74] A bill may be addressed to two or more drawees whether they are partners or not, but an order addressed to two drawees in the alternative or to two or more drawees in succession is not a bill of exchange.[75] Where the drawee is a fictitious person or a person not having capacity to contract, the holder may again treat the instrument, at his option, either as a bill of exchange or as a promissory note.[76]

      The Act recognises[77] that a bill may be drawn by one person for the account of another.[78] The person for whose account the bill is drawn is sometimes known as "the third account".

2–013     **"Signed by the person giving it."** The order must be signed by the drawer.[79] The signature may be added at any time,[80] and a bill may be

---

[69] Uncertificated Securities Regulations 2001 (SI 2001/3755); Uncertified Securities (Amendment) (Eligible Debt Securities) Regulations 2003 (SI 2003/1633).
[70] See below, para.5–004.
[71] *cf.* ULB, art.3; UNB, art.11.
[72] *Capital and Counties Bank v Gordon* [1903] A.C. 240, 250; *McClintock v Union Bank of Australia Ltd* (1920) 20 S.R.(N.S.W.) 494; [1922] 1 A.C. 240, 248. The decision to the contrary in *Ross v London County Westminster and Parr's Bank Ltd* [1919] 1 K.B. 678 cannot be supported: *Slingsby v Westminster Bank Ltd* [1931] 1 K.B. 173, 187. The instrument is in effect a promissory note made and issued by the bank: *Commercial Banking Co. of Sydney Ltd v Mann* [1961] A.C. 1, 7. However, protection is afforded to a banker in the case of such instruments by ss.1 and 4 of the Cheques Act 1957 (see ss.1(2)(b), 4(2)(d)). See also s.5 of the 1957 Act (crossed cheques).
[73] See below, para.2–040.
[74] s.6(1).
[75] s.6(2).
[76] s.5(2).
[77] ss.65(1), 68(1).
[78] ULB, art.3.
[79] See also UCC, § 3–103(a); ULB, art.1(8); UNB, art.3(1)(d).
[80] s.20.

accepted before it has been signed by the drawer.[81] But until it is so signed the instrument is inchoate[82] and not a bill. Thus B draws a bill on A, but does not sign it. A accepts, and the instrument is transferred for value to C. Without B's signature, A is not liable as acceptor on the bill,[83] but may possibly be liable as the maker of a promissory note.[84]

If the signature of the drawer is forged or placed on the bill without his authority, the signature is wholly inoperative,[85] although certain estoppels may arise as against the drawer[86] and, under the Act, against the acceptor[87] and any indorser[88] of the bill.

For the meaning of "signature", see section 23, below. The seal of a corporation is equivalent to a signature.[89] See also section 23(1)(2) (signature in assumed or firm name), section 25 (procuration signature) and sections 26 and 91(1) (signature by agent or representative).

**"A sum certain in money."** The order must require the drawee to pay   2–014
a sum in money.[90] "Money" is not defined in the Act, but clearly includes legal tender[91]; and a bill may be drawn payable in a foreign currency.[92] But an instrument payable in "good East India bonds"[93] or in gold dust,[94] and an order to deliver to bearer on demand a certain quantity of iron,[95] is not a bill of exchange. See also subsection (2), below.

---

[81] s.18(1).
[82] s.20.
[83] *Stoessiger v S.E. Ry Co.* (1854) 3 E. & B. 549; *Goldsmid v Hampton* (1858) 5 C.B., N.S. 94; *M'Call v Taylor* (1865) 19 C.B., N.S. 301; *South Wales & Cannock Chase Coal Co. Ltd v Underwood* (1899) 15 T.L.R. 157. See also *Ex p. Hayward* (1871) 6 Ch.App. 546 (no issue); *Ayres v Moore* [1940] 1 K.B. 278, 286 (irregularity).
[84] *cf.* the cases cited above, note 83. But these are not consistent with *Mason v Lack* (1929) 140 L.T. 696 (although in that case the name of the drawer was subsequently added). See also *Haseldine v Winstanley* [1936] 2 K.B. 101 (s.64, Illustration 3).
[85] s.24. *cf.* s.23(1) (assumed name). It may be argued that if the drawer's signature is forged, then the instrument is not a bill at all (*Arrow Transfer Co. Ltd v Royal Bank of Canada* (1972) 27 D.L.R. (3d) 81, 104: forged signature of the drawer of a cheque). See below, para.3–062 (s.24).
[86] See below, para.3–079 (s.24).
[87] s.54(2)(a).
[88] s.55(2)(b).
[89] s.91(2). See also s.36A of the Companies Act 1985 (inserted by s.130(2) of the Companies Act 1989).
[90] See also s.17(2)(b) (acceptance); UCC, §§ 3–104(a), 3–107; ULB, art.1(2); UNB, art.3(1)(a).
[91] For legal tender, see the Currency and Bank Notes Act 1954, s.1; Coinage Act 1971, s.2; Currency Act 1983, s.1. See also s.2 of the Decimal Currency Act 1969 (if the sum payable is an amount of money wholly or partly in shillings or pence).
[92] *John v Boulken* (1920) 36 T.L.R. 767, but other instances abound. See also ss.9(1)(d), 57 and UCC, §§ 1–201(24), 3–107.
[93] Buller N.P. (7th ed., 1817), p.272b.
[94] *McDonald v Belcher* [1904] A.C. 429 (note).
[95] *Dixon v Bovill* (1856) 3 Macq.H.L. 1.

It is doubtful whether an instrument denominated in units of account such as Special Drawing Rights (SDRs) would be a bill of exchange or promissory note. However, following a recommendation made by the Review Committee on Banking Services Law and Practice,[96] the Government proposed that such instruments should be brought clearly within the Act,[97] and that the Act should be modified so that the expression "a sum certain in money" is defined to include a monetary unit of account established by an intergovernmental institution or by agreement between two or more states.[98] The euro is, of course, a currency.

The sum required to be paid must be certain.[99] A sum is not certain if it is susceptible of contingent or uncertain additions or deductions.[1] Thus an order to pay a specified sum "and also all other sums which may be due"[2] or with the addition of bank charges,[3] or with the costs of collection or an attorney's fee or both on default,[4] is not a bill of exchange; nor would an order to pay a specified sum, first deducting therefrom any money which may be owed, be a bill. The sum must be capable of being ascertained from the instrument itself without reference to external facts which may be put in evidence in the case.[5]

2–015     It seems that the principle lying behind this requirement is that, at the time of payment,[6] it should be possible to determine from the instrument what sum is payable with any necessary computation. Thus it has been held[7] that, if an instrument is payable at a fixed time, the sum must be certain at that time, so that an instrument payable 60 days after sight which provided for payment of a specified sum, together with interest at a specified rate "until arrival of payment in London", did not satisfy the requirements of certainty.

It seems probable that the sum payable is certain even though it is to be

---

[96] (1989) Cm. 622, rec. 8(3).
[97] (1990) Cm. 1026, Annex 6, para.6.4.
[98] See UCC, § 1–201(24)
[99] *Jones v Simpson* (1823) 2 B. & C. 318 (Illustration 6); *Davies v Wilkinson* (1839) 10 A. & E. 98 (Illustration 7). See also *Standard Bank v Marais* (1895) 12 Cape S.C. 342; *MacMillan v Macmillan* (1977) 76 D.L.R. (3d) 760.
[1] Byles, *Bills of Exchange* (27th ed.), Sweet & Maxwell, pp.24–25; *Standard Trusts Co. v La Valley* [1931] 1 D.L.R. 149, affd [1931] 4 D.L.R. 634.
[2] *Smith v Nightingale* (1818) 2 Stark 375 (note). See also *Bolton v Dugdale* (1833) 4 B. & Ad. 619 (note); *Ayrey v Fearnsides* (1838) 4 M. & W. 168.
[3] *Standard Bank of Canada v Wildey* (1919) 19 S.R.(N.S.W.) 384; *Hamman v Van der Merwe* 1947 (1) S.A. 631, 632; *Dalgety Ltd v John J. Hilton Pty Ltd* [1981] 2 N.S.W.L.R. 169.
[4] *Temple Terrace Assets Co. Inc. v Whynot* [1934] 1 D.L.R. 124. *cf.*, UCC, § 3–104(a).
[5] *Standard Bank of Canada v Wildey*, above, at 389; *Macleod Savings & Credit Union Ltd v Perrett* (1981) 118 D.L.R. (3d) 193. But see s.9(1)(c)(d).
[6] As opposed to the time of issue.
[7] *Rosenhain v Commonwealth Bank of Australia* (1922) 31 C.L.R. 46, 51–52.

paid with a stated discount or addition if paid before or after the date fixed for payment.[8]

The requirement of certainty is supplemented by section 9 of the Act (interest and exchange). It also applies to promissory notes.[9]

**"On demand or at a fixed or determinable future time."**[10] The order                2–016
must require the drawee to pay the sum specified in the bill either on demand or at a fixed or determinable future time.[11]

By section 10(1) of the Act, a bill is payable on demand: (a) which is expressed to be payable on demand, or at sight, or on presentation; or (b) in which no time for payment is expressed. See also section 11.

A bill may be drawn payable at a fixed time, for example "on 28th August, 2004"; or it may be drawn payable at a determinable future time, as defined in section 11 of the Act.

There is no limit as to the length of time at which a bill may be payable.[12]

**"To or to the order of a specified person, or to bearer."** The order must          2–017
require the drawee to pay the sum specified in the bill to or to the order of a specified person, or to bearer.[13]

As to when a bill is payable to order, see section 8(4) of the Act. The effect of a bill drawn payable "to the order of C" is no different from that of a bill drawn payable "to C or order", and it is payable to the payee or his order at his option.[14]

Where a bill is not payable to bearer, the payee must be named or otherwise indicated therein with reasonable certainty.[15] A bill may be drawn payable to, or to the order of, the drawer or the drawee.[16] It may also be drawn payable to two or more payees jointly or to one or more of several payees in the alternative, or to the holder of an office for the time being.[17] Where the payee is a fictitious or non-existing person the bill may be treated as payable to bearer.[18]

---

[8] But if certainty must exist at the time of issue, as opposed to the time of payment (see above, para.2–015, n.6), the sum would not be certain.
[9] s.83(1).
[10] See also UCC, §§ 3–104(a), 3–108, ULB, arts 1, 2; UNB, art.3(1)(b).
[11] But not both: *Toronto-Dominion Bank v Parkway Holdings Ltd* (1969) 1 D.L.R. (3d) 716.
[12] *Colehan v Cooke* (1742) Wills 393 (s.11, Illustration 4).
[13] See also UCC, §§ 3–104(a), 3–109. *cf.* ULB, arts 1, 3; UNB, art.3(1)(a).
[14] s.8(5). But see para.2–068, n.26.
[15] s.7(1).
[16] s.5(1).
[17] s.7(2).
[18] s.7(3).

**2–018**    Considerable difficulty may arise if the name of the payee is left blank. But the omission of the name of the payee will not necessarily invalidate the instrument as a bill of exchange or as a promissory note. This question is discussed in the comment to section 7(1) of the Act, below.

As to when a bill is payable to bearer, see section 8(3) of the Act.

An instrument drawn payable to "cash or order" is not a bill of exchange, nor (if addressed to a banker) is it a cheque, since it is not payable to a specified person or to bearer.[19] Similarly, an instrument payable to or to the order of something other than a person, *e.g.* to "wages", to "office", "housekeeping" or a ship,[20] or to "the pump at Aldgate,"[21] is not a bill of exchange. But if a bill is drawn payable to "cash or bearer" or to something other than a person "or bearer", it would appear to be a valid bill, payable to bearer.[22]

**2–019**    **Subsection (2): non-compliance.** This subsection reinforces subsection (1) by providing that, to be valid, a bill of exchange must be limited to the payment of money. No other act beyond the payment of money can be required.[23] Thus an order to pay a specified sum and in addition to deliver up horses and a wharf[24] or to give real security[25] is not a bill of exchange. Nor, it seems, can a bill stipulate for some other act as an alternative to payment.[26]

An instrument which does not comply with the requirements of subsection (1), or which orders any act to be done in addition to the payment of money, is not a bill of exchange. If an instrument is defective as a bill

---

[19] *North and South Insurance Corp. Ltd v National Provincial Bank Ltd* [1936] 1 K.B. 328; *Cole v Milsome* [1951] 1 All E.R. 311; *Orbit Mining and Trading Co. Ltd v Westminster Bank Ltd* [1963] 1 Q.B. 794 (Illustration 8); *Gader v Flower* (1979) 129 N.L.J. 1266; *Hills v Venter* 1983 (4) S.A. 22; *Christeller v Brahberg Boerdery (Edms) Bpk* 1983 (4) S.A. 87; *H. & F. Spares Centre (Pty) Ltd v Grand Prix Spares* 1986 (4) S.A. 974. But if the instrument is issued by a customer of a banker, the banker may claim the protection afforded by ss.1, 4 of the Cheques Act 1957 (see ss.1(2)(a); 4(2)(a)). See also s.5 of the 1957 Act (crossed instruments). Moreover, in *North and South Insurance Corp. Ltd v National Provincial Bank Ltd*, above, at 336, Branson J. said that the direction to a bank to pay cash was by necessary implication to pay it to the bearer of the document, and in *Orbit Mining and Trading Co. Ltd v Westminster Bank Ltd*, above, at 811, Sellars L.J. said that the effect was that the direction was equivalent to payment to bearer. In *Judmaier v Standard Bank of Canada* [1927] 1 W.W.R. 270, such a document was held to be a bearer instrument. See also UCC, § 3–109(a)(3) (instrument payable to "cash" or to the order of "cash" is payable to bearer).
[20] *cf. Grant v Vaughan* (1764) 3 Burr. 1516.
[21] *Tatlock v Harris* (1789) 3 Terin Rep. 174.
[22] *Grant v Vaughan*, above.
[23] *Dickie v Singh* 1974 S.L.T. (Notes) 3. *cf.* UCC, § 3–104(a)(3).
[24] *Martin v Chauntry* (1747) 2 Stra. 1271 (note).
[25] *Follett v Moore* (1849) 4 Exch. 410 (note). *cf.* s.87(3) and *Fancourt v Thorne* (1846) 9 Q.B. 312.
[26] *Smith v Boheme* (1724), cited 2 Ld.Raym. 1362, 1396. See also *Savage v Uwechia* [1961] 1 W.L.R. 455 (note), although in this case the question at issue was the enforceability of a promise to convey land on default in payment.

or note, it may still be valid as some other transaction, for instance, as a receipt or as evidence of a contract,[27] or as a mandate to pay.[28]

**Subsection (3): particular fund.** This subsection amplifies and eluci- **2–020** dates the meaning of "unconditional" in subsection (1). An order to pay out of a particular fund is not unconditional. The order is qualified to the extent that the fund may not be in or come into existence or that it may not be available for payment or that it may be insufficient to enable payment to be made. Thus an order addressed to the drawee requiring him to pay a specified sum out of the proceeds of sale of a certain property, or from moneys held by him and belonging to the drawer or to a third party, or out of moneys to be received or becoming payable by him is not a bill of exchange.[29]

On the other hand, an unqualified order to pay, coupled with an indication of a particular fund out of which the drawee is to reimburse himself or a particular account to be debited with the amount is unconditional.[30]

Bills of exchange are frequently "claused" with words that refer to the transaction underlying the bill, *e.g.* "Drawn under credit no. 80276 against shipment of seventeen cases of machine parts from U.K. to Hong Kong *per* m.v. 'Orient' ". In most cases, such words appear in the bill after the words "Value received". A reference of this nature does not normally render the order to pay conditional: "such an expression is used . . . simply to denote the fact that the draft is drawn as part of a mercantile transaction, and not to indicate that the fund produced by the goods referred to is the only fund from which the amount of the draft is to be paid".[31] Section 3(3)(b) also provides that an unqualified order to pay, coupled with a statement of the transaction which gives rise to the bill, is unconditional. But an order to the drawee to pay, or to accept the bill,

---

[27] *Smith v Nightingale* (1818) 2 Stark. 375; *Canada Permanent Trust Co. v Kowal* (1981) 120 D.L.R. (3d) 691, 698. But see *Savage v Uwechia*, above, where the words "value received", if referring to past consideration, were held insufficient to support a contract for the sale of land.

[28] *North & South Insurance Corp. Ltd v National Provincial Bank Ltd* [1936] 1 K.B. 328.

[29] *Josselyn v Lacier* (1715) 10 Mod. 294; *Jenney v Herle* (1723) 2 Ld. Raym. 1361 (Illustration 9); *Banbury v Lisset* (1744) 2 Stra. 1211; *Dawkes v Lord DeLorane* (1771) 3 Wils. K.B. 207 (Illustration 10), *Carlos v Fancourt* (1794) 5 T.R. 482 (Illustration 11); *Hill v Halford* (1801) 2 B. & P. 413 (Illustration 12); *Fisher v Calvert* (1879) 27 W.R. 301. Contrast UCC, § 3–106(b).

[30] *Macleod v Snee* (1728) 2 Stra. 762 (Illustration 13); *Haussoullier v Hartsinck* (1798) 7 T.R. 733; *Griffin v Weatherby* (1868) L.R. 3 Q.B. 753 (Illustration 14); *Banner v Johnston* (1871) L.R. 5 H.L. 157; *Re Boyse (No.3)* (1886) 33 Ch.D. 612 (Illustration 15); *Guaranty Trust Co. of New York v Hannay* [1918] 2 K.B. 623 (Illustration 16); *Peacocke & Co. v Williams* (1909) 28 N.Z.L.R. 354.

[31] *Guaranty Trust Co. of New York v Hannay*, above, at 656, see also at 630, 666; *The Elmville* [1904] P. 319. *cf. Brown Shipley & Co. v Kough* (1885) 29 Ch.D. 848.

only against the tender of certain documents other than the bill would appear to be conditional.[32]

**2–021**    Although an instrument directing payment to be made out of a particular fund is not a bill of exchange, it may yet be a valid equitable assignment of part of the fund[33] or an effective mandate for payment[34] which, when carried out by the addressee, gives him rights or an effective discharge against the author of the instrument; and although an instrument promising that payment will be made out of a particular fund is not a promissory note, it may yet be a contract or evidence of a contract by the promisor to pay the sum mentioned therein.[35]

**2–022**    **Subsection (4): date, value and place.** A bill is not invalid by reason that it is not dated.[36] Nevertheless it is irregular to issue it undated and a banker is not bound to honour an undated cheque.[37] In the case of the omission of a date in a bill payable after date, any holder may insert the true date of issue.[38] Otherwise, *e.g.* in the case of a cheque, the person in possession of it has prima facie authority to fill up the omitted date,[39] but in order to bind prior parties it must be filled up within a reasonable period of time, and strictly in accordance with the authority given.[40] See also section 13 of the Act. The alteration of the date is a material alteration.[41]

**2–023**    A bill is not invalid by reason that it does not specify the value given, or that any value has been given therefor. In England it is usual to insert in the bill either a statement of the value or the words "value received";

---

[32] *Lister v Schulte* [1915] V.L.R. 374, 379. Contrast *Rosenhain v Commonwealth Bank of Australia* (1922) 31 C.L.R. 46 ("documents against acceptance" left open whether unconditional); *Korea Exchange Bank v Debenhams (Central Buying) Ltd* [1979] 1 Lloyds Rep. 100, 548 ("D/A" in commercial usage not part of the order to pay directed to the drawee and so bill not conditional); *Novaknit Hellas SA v Kumar Brothers International Ltd* [1998] Lloyd's Rep. Bank. 287 (documents include the bill).

[33] *Brice v Bannister* (1878) 3 Q.B.D. 569; *Buck v Robson* (1878) 3 Q.B.D. 686; *Fisher v Culvert* (1879) W.R. 301; *Re Kent and Sussex Sawmills Ltd* [1947] Ch. 177. But the direction must be *irrevocable*: see *Percival v Dunn* (1885) 29 Ch.D. 128; *Re Williams* [1917] 1 Ch. 1; *Rekstin v Severo, etc., and Bank for Russian Trade Ltd* [1933] 1 K.B. 47; *James Talcott Ltd v John Lewis & Co. Ltd* [1940] 3 All E.R. 592; *Re Danish Bacon Co. Ltd Staff Pension Fund Trusts* [1971] 1 W.L.R. 248.

[34] *Bell v London and North Western Ry* (1852) 15 Beav. 548; *ex p. Hall* (1878) 10 Ch.D. 615. See also *North & South Insurance Corp. Ltd v National Provincial Bank Ltd* [1936] 1 K.B. 328.

[35] Provided that the other requirements of a contract are satisfied, *i.e.* consideration moving from the promisee. See *White v North* (1849) 3 Exch. 689; *Drury v Macaulay* (1846) 16 M. & W. 146; *Kirkwood v Smith* [1896] W.N. 46; *Black v Pilcher* (1909) 25 T.L.R. 497; *Abacus Cities Ltd v Cornwall* (1982) 43 C.B.R.(N.S.) 56 (Alberta).

[36] See also UCC, art.3–113(b). *cf.* ULB, art.1(7); UNB, arts 2, 3.

[37] *Griffiths v Dalton* [1940] 2 K.B. 264.

[38] s.12.

[39] s.20(1).

[40] s.20(2). See also *Griffiths v Dalton*, above, (reasonable time for filling in date of cheque).

[41] s.64(2).

but this has long been held not to be essential.[42] Every party whose signature appears on a bill is prima facie deemed to have become a party thereto for value,[43] and where value has at any time been given for a bill the holder is deemed to be a holder for value as regards the acceptor and all parties to the bill who became parties prior to such time.[44]

In the case of an accepted bill payable to drawer's order, the words "value received" mean value received by the acceptor[45]; while in a bill payable to a third party, they mean prima facie value received by the drawer from the payee.[46]

A bill is not invalid by reason that it does not specify the place where    2–024
it is drawn.[47] Nevertheless, it is usual and convenient to state in a bill the place where it is drawn and such place may be relevant to the status of the bill as an inland or foreign bill[48] and to the application of section 72 of the Act (conflict of laws).

A bill is not invalid by reason that it does not specify the place where it is payable.[49] As to presentment for payment where no place of payment is specified, see section 45(4) of the Act. The acceptor may fix the place of payment by a local acceptance.[50] It seems that a bill may state an alternative place of payment.[51] Where a bill is made payable elsewhere than at the residence or place of business of the drawee, the bill is said to be "domiciled" where payable.[52]

ILLUSTRATIONS

1. An instrument reading: "Mr Little, please to let the bearer have    2–025
seven pounds, and place it to my account and you will oblige. Your humble servant, R. Slackford" is not a bill of exchange, since it does not purport to be a demand (order) made by a party having a right to call on the other to pay.[53]

---

[42] *Hatch v Trayes* (1840) 11 A. & E. 702.
[43] s.30(1).
[44] s.27(2).
[45] *Highmore v Primrose* (1816) 5 M. & S. 65.
[46] *Grant v Da Costa* (1815) 3 M. & S. 351. In a note, they mean value received by the maker from the payee: *Clayton v Gosling* (1826) B. & C. 360.
[47] *cf.* ULB, arts 1, 2; UNB, art.2.
[48] s.4. See also *Koch v Dicks* [1933] 1 K.B. 307 (material alteration).
[49] See also UCC, § 3–111. *cf.* ULB, arts 1, 2; UNB, art.2.
[50] s.19(2)(c).
[51] *Beeching v Gower* (1816) Holt N.P. 313 (note); *Pollard v Herries* (1803) 3 B. & P. 335 (note).
[52] *cf.* ULB, art.4.
[53] *Little v Slackford* (1828) M. & M. 171.

2. An instrument reading: "Mr Nelson will much oblige Mr Webb by paying to J. Ruff or order, twenty guineas on his account" is a bill of exchange, in that it is an order by one person to another to pay money to the payee or his order.[54]

3. Bury gives to Edis, for goods sold and delivered, an instrument addressed to Grutherot reading: "Three months after date I promise to pay Mr John Bury, or order, forty-four pounds eleven shillings and five pence, value received (Signed) John Bury." Grutherot's name is written on the instrument as an acceptance and Bury's name on the back as an indorsement. Edis is entitled to treat Bury either as the drawer of a bill or maker of a note, and is therefore not obliged to give him notice of dishonour.[55]

**2–026**      4. The Great Northern Railway Company draws an instrument in the form of a cheque addressed to the Union Bank of London ordering that bank to pay to the claimants the sum of £69 7s., "provided the receipt form at foot hereof is duly signed, stamped and dated". The instrument is stolen from the claimants, the receipt being then unsigned. The claimants' indorsement and receipt on the document are forged and it is collected by the defendant bank for a customer. The instrument is not a cheque within section 73 of the Act because it is not an unconditional order for the payment of money within section 3, subsection (1), of the Act. The defendant bank is liable to the claimants in an action for money had and received and (*per* A.L. Smith and Vaughan Williams L.JJ.) in conversion for the amount of the instrument.[56]

5. An instrument is drawn in the form of a cheque with a note at the foot of the instrument which reads: "The receipt at the back hereof must be signed, which signature will be taken as an indorsement." This is a cheque, for the direction is to the payee and not to the drawee banker.[57]

6. Blackburn writes and sends to Simpson the following order: "Mr R. Simpson, please to pay to Nelson, on account of the assignees of Oakley, Overend and Oakley, the proceeds of a shipment of twelve bales of goods, value about £2,000, consigned by me to you." The order is not a bill of exchange, the sum not being certain.[58]

---

[54] *Ruff v Webb* (1794) 1 Esp. 129.
[55] *Edis v Bury* (1827) 6 B. & C. 433.
[56] *Bavins Jnr & Sims v London and South Western Bank Ltd* [1900] 1 Q.B. 270. But see now s.4(2)(b) of the Cheques Act 1957.
[57] *Nathan v Ogdens Ltd* (1905) 93 L.T. 553, affirmed (1905) 94 L.T. 126.
[58] *Jones v Simpson* (1823) 2 B. & C. 318.

7.  An instrument is made in the following form: "I agree to pay to Mr    **2–027**
Charles Davies, or his order, the sum of £695, at four instalments [total-
ling £600] . . . .; the remainder, £95, to go as a set-off for an order of Mr
Reynolds to Mr Thompson, and the remainder of his debt owing from C.
Davies to him. (Signed) James Wilkinson." The instrument is not a promissory note.[59] If made in the form of a bill, the fact that part of the sum
was, by agreement, not to be paid but treated as a set-off would similarly
prevent the instrument from being a bill of exchange.

8.  A cheque form addressed to a bank reading "Pay cash or order" is
not a cheque because it is not a bill of exchange; it is not payable to or to
the order of a specified person and it is not payable to bearer.[60]

9.  An instrument ordering the drawee to pay £1,945 upon demand out
of money in the drawee's hands belonging to the proprietors of certain
mines and quarries is no more a bill of exchange than an order directing
payment "out of my rents in your hands".[61]

10.  An instrument ordering the drawee to pay to Miss R: "£32 17s. out    **2–028**
of W. Steward's money, as soon as you receive it", is not a bill of exchange
since it is made payable out of a particular fund.[62]

11.  A promise to pay £10 "out of the money arising from my reversion
of £43 when sold" is not a promissory note because the money is payable
upon a contingency.[63]

12.  A promise to pay £190 "on the sale of the produce immediately
when sold of the White Hart, St. Alban's, Herts., and the goods, etc., value
received" is not a promissory note.[64]

13.  An instrument requiring the drawee to pay to M or order £9 10s.    **2–029**
"as my quarterly half-pay, to be due from 24th June to 27th September
next, by advance" is a valid bill of exchange, the mention of half-pay
being only by way of direction how the drawee shall reimburse himself.[65]

14.  An instrument reading "Please pay to Messrs Griffin & Co. or order
£600, on account of moneys advanced by me for the Isle of Man Slate and

[59] *Davies v Wilkinson* (1839) 10 A. & E. 98.
[60] *Orbit Mining and Trading Co. Ltd v National Westminster Bank Ltd* [1963] 1 Q.B. 794. See also
below, para.17–072 (Cheques Act 1957, s.4, Illustration 17).
[61] *Jenney v Herle* (1723) 2 Ld.Raym. 1361.
[62] *Dawkes v Lord De Lorane* (1771) 3 Wils. K.B. 207.
[63] *Carlos v Fancourt* (1794) 5 T.R. 482.
[64] *Hill v Halford* (1801) 2 B. & P. 413.
[65] *Macleod v Snee* (1728) 2 Stra. 762.

Flag Company Ltd" is a valid bill of exchange: it is not an order to pay out of a particular fund.[66]

15. An instrument addressed to the Bank of England reading "Pay to my order £7,000 sterling, which sum is on account on the dividends and interests due on the capital and dividends registered in the books of the Bank of England in the name of C and [the drawer], which you will please charge to my account and credit according to a registered letter I have addressed to you" is a valid bill of exchange: it states merely what the fund is out of which the drawee is to reimburse himself and what is the account to be debited with the amount.[67]

2–030    16. An instrument reading: "Pay to the order of ourselves £1,464 9s. value received and charge the same to account of 100 RSML bales of cotton" is a bill of exchange and negotiable.[68]

### Inland and foreign bills

2–031    **4. (1) An inland bill is a bill which is or on the face of it purports to be (a) both drawn and payable within the British Islands, or (b) drawn within the British Islands upon some person resident therein. Any other bill is a foreign bill.**

**For the purposes of this Act "British Islands" mean any part of the United Kingdom of Great Britain and Ireland, the islands of Man, Guernsey, Jersey, Alderney, and Sark, and the islands adjacent to any of them being part of the dominions of Her Majesty.**

**(2) Unless the contrary appear on the face of the bill the holder may treat it as an inland bill.**

Definitions
"bill": s.2.
"holder": s.2.
"person": s.2.

### COMMENT

2–032    **Inland and foreign bills.** The importance of the distinction between an inland and a foreign bill is this: a foreign bill, *appearing on the face of it*

---

[66] *Griffin v Weatherby* (1868) L.R. 3 Q.B. 753.
[67] *Re Boyse (No.3)* (1886) 33 Ch.D. 612.
[68] *Guaranty Trust Co. of New York v Hannay* [1918] 2 K.B. 623.

*to be such*, must be duly protested for non-acceptance and for non-payment[69]; and, where a foreign bill has been accepted as to part, it must be protested as to the balance.[70] An inland bill *may* be noted for non-acceptance or for non-payment, but it is not necessary to note or protest any such bill in order to preserve the recourse against the drawer or indorsers.[71] However, if any party is resident abroad, it should, as a matter of prudence, be protested for the purpose of recourse against him in his own country.[72]

The distinction between inland and foreign bills is also relevant in the conflict of laws, where an inland bill is indorsed in a foreign country.[73]

Before the abolition of stamp duty on bills and notes by the Finance Act 1970,[74] a distinction also existed between inland and foreign bills for the purposes of stamp duty under the Stamp Act 1891, but the definition of a foreign bill or note differed from that in the 1882 Act.

The corresponding provision in relation to promissory notes is section 83(4); but protest of a foreign note is unnecessary.[75]

**Subsection (1): inland bill.** A bill of exchange will be an inland bill if    **2–033** in fact it satisfies the requirements of paragraph (a) or (b),[76] or if on its face it purports to satisfy those requirements whether in fact it does so or not. Subject to subsection (2), any other bill is a foreign bill.

As to a bill where no place of payment is specified, see section 45(4) of the Act.

The British Islands no longer include the Republic of Ireland.[77]

**Subsection (2): face of bill.** It has been stated[78] that the result of this    **2–034** subsection: "appears to be that, though a bill purports to be a foreign bill, the holder may nevertheless show that it is in fact an inland bill for the purpose of excusing protest; while if it purports to be an inland bill, though really a foreign bill, he may treat it, at his option, as either". This statement seems to be incorrect. In either case, the bill would be an inland

---

[69] s.51(2). Contrast (foreign notes), s.89(4).

[70] s.44(2).

[71] s.51(1).

[72] See ULB, art.44, and below, para.12–031.

[73] s.72(2), proviso.

[74] s.32 and Sch.7.

[75] s.89(4).

[76] *Amner v Clark* (1835) 2 G.M. & R. 468; *Lebel v Tucker* (1867) L.R. 3 Q.B. 77. A bill may not be an inland bill under s.4(1)(b) if it is drawn upon a foreign agency of a United Kingdom bank, as the foreign agency is not a person "resident" in the British Islands: *Canada Life Assurance Co. v Canadian Imperial Bank of Commerce* (1980) 98 D.L.R. (3d) 670.

[77] Irish Free State (Consequential Adaptation of Enactments) Order, S.R. & O. 1923 No.405, para.2, made under s.6 of the Irish Free State (Consequential Provisions) Act 1922.

[78] Chalmers, *Bills of Exchange* (9th ed.) p.19. It is further stated that subs.(2) altered the law.

bill under subsection (1). Subsection (2) in its terms does no more (and no less) than provide that the holder may treat a bill as an inland bill unless, on its face, it appears to be a foreign bill. The intention appears to be that, if it is uncertain from the face of the bill whether it is an inland or foreign bill, but the bill is in fact a foreign bill, the holder may treat it as an inland bill.[79]

ILLUSTRATIONS

2–035   1. A bill is drawn in Liverpool on a merchant in London. It is payable in London, but is indorsed in Paris. This is an inland bill.[80]

2. A bill is drawn in Liverpool on B, who resides in London. It is payable in Paris. This is an inland bill.[81]

3. A bill is drawn in London on a merchant in Paris, payable in London, and is accepted. This is an inland bill.[82]

2–036   4. A bill is drawn in London on C who resides in Paris. No place of payment is specified and C accepts the bill as drawn. The bill may be treated by the holder as an inland bill.[83]

5. A bill is, and is stated on its face to be, drawn in London on D, who resides in Paris. It is payable in Paris. This is a foreign bill.[84]

6. A bill is, and is stated on its face to be, drawn in Paris on a merchant in London. It is payable in London. This is a foreign bill.[85]

7. A bill is drawn on a merchant in London. It is in fact drawn in Paris but purports on its face to be drawn in London. It is payable in London. This is an inland bill.[86]

---

[79] Illustrations 4 and 9. But such a bill would not require to be protested under s.51(2) as a foreign bill, since it does not appear on its face to be such.
[80] s.4(1)(a). See also s.72(2), and *Lebel v Tucker* (1867) L.R. 3 Q.B. 77 (Section 72, Illustration 2).
[81] s.4(1)(b).
[82] s.4(1)(a); *Amner v Clark* (1835) 2 C.M. & R. 468.
[83] s.4(2).
[84] s.4(1).
[85] s.4(1); *Koch v Dicks* [1933] 1 K.B. 307 (after alteration).
[86] s.4(1)(a); *Koch v Dicks*, above (before alteration).

8. A bill is drawn on E, who resides in London. It is in fact drawn in    2–037
London but purports on its face to be drawn in Paris. It is payable in
Paris. This is an inland bill.[87]

9. A bill is drawn in Paris on a merchant in London. The place where
the bill is drawn does not appear on the face of the bill. It is payable in
London. The holder may treat it as an inland bill.[88]

## Effect where different parties to bill are the same person

5. (1) A bill may be drawn payable to, or to the order of, the drawer;    2–038
or it may be drawn payable to, or to the order of, the
drawee.
(2) Where in a bill drawer and drawee are the same person, or
where the drawee is a fictitious person or a person not having
capacity to contract, the holder may treat the instrument, at
his option, either as a bill of exchange or as a promissory
note.

| Definitions | Comparison |
|---|---|
| "bill": s.2. | UCC: §§3–103(a)(6), 3–104(e). |
| "holder": s.2. | ULB: arts 1, 3. |
| "person": s.2. | ULC: arts 1, 6. |
| "promissory note": s.83(1). | UNB: arts 3, 11. |

### COMMENT

**Subsection (1): bill payable to drawer or drawee.** Bills of exchange are    2–039
frequently drawn payable to, or to the order of, the drawer, either by
name or in the form "Pay to my/our order" or "Pay to the order of
ourselves".[89] Cheques may be drawn payable to, or to the order of, the
drawer where a customer of a bank wishes to obtain cash over the
counter, *e.g.* "Pay self". By section 8(5) of the Act, where a bill is expressed
to be payable to the order of a specified person, and not to him or his
order, it is nevertheless payable to him or his order at his option. However, in *McDonald (Gerald) & Co. v Nash & Co.*[90] differing views were

---

[87] s.4(1)(b).
[88] s.4(2).
[89] See also *Chamberlain v Young and Tower* [1893] 2 Q.B. 206 (bill payable "to       order", the
blank not being filled in, held to be a bill payable to drawer's order).
[90] [1924] A.C. 625 (Section 20, Illustration 15); see also below, paras 2–135 and 7–032.

expressed in the House of Lords as to whether a bill expressed to be payable to the order of the drawer was a complete bill before its indorsement by the drawer.[91] But their Lordships agreed that, under section 20 of the Act, the drawer was entitled to indorse the bill as payee and enforce the bill as so indorsed against a party who had previously indorsed the bill with the intention of making himself liable as guarantor.

Very occasionally bills are drawn payable to, or to the order of, the drawee, *e.g.* "Pay yourselves" or "Pay to your own order". A bill may be drawn in this form where the drawee acts in two different capacities, for example, if he is in business on his own account, and also as agent for some other person interested in the bill.[92] But cheques are sometimes drawn payable to the drawee bank where a customer wishes to obtain cash over the counter, travellers' cheques or a bankers' draft,[93] or wishes the bank to make payment from his account under a credit transfer to the account of another. A cheque drawn payable to the drawee bank or order, if not by way of payment, is a direction to the bank to hold the amount for which it is drawn and to apply it in accordance with the mandate given by the customer.[94]

2–040     **Subsection (2): drawer and drawee same person.** An instrument drawn by the drawer on himself is not a bill of exchange, since it is not an order addressed by one person to another.[95] But where in a bill drawer and drawee are the same person, the holder may treat the instrument, at his option, either as a bill of exchange or as a promissory note.[96] This option is only available to a holder.[97]

If he treats it as a bill of exchange, he has the rights of a holder against a drawer of a bill.[98] But by section 50(2)(c), notice of dishonour is dispensed with as regards the drawer where the drawer and the drawee are the same person.

---

[91] [1924] A.C. 625 at 633–634, 652.

[92] *Holdsworth v Hunter* (1830) 10 B. & C. 449. But, in such a case, it is clear that the bill is not an instrument that can be enforced until the drawee has indorsed it away. *cf.*, *R. v Bartlett* (1841) 2 Moo. & R. 362.

[93] *Australian Bank of Commerce Ltd v Perel* [1926] A.C. 737.

[94] *Australian Bank of Commerce Ltd v Perel* [1926] A.C. 737. See also *Bank of Montreal v Dominion Gresham Guarantee & Casualty Co. Ltd* [1930] 4 D.L.R. 689, 692, [1930] A.C. 659, PC.

[95] s.3(1).

[96] *Miller v Thomson* (1841) 3 M. & G. 576 (Illustration 2); *Davis v Clarke* (1844) 6 Q.B. 16 (Illustration 1); *Allen v Sea, Fire and Life Assurance Co.* (1850) 9 C.B. 574 (Illustration 4); *Willans v Ayers* (1877) 3 App. Cas. 133; *Re Commercial Bank of South Australia* (1887) 36 Ch.D. 522, 525; *Capital and Counties Bank Ltd v Gordon* [1903] A.C. 240, 250; *Re British Trade Corp. Ltd* [1932] 2 Ch. 1 (Illustration 3); *Commercial Banking Co. of Sydney Ltd v Mann* [1961] A.C. 1, 7; *Yan v Post Office Bank Ltd* [1994] 1 N.Z.L.R. 154.

[97] *Capital and Counties Bank Ltd v Gordon* [1903] A.C. 240, 250; *Orlando Fine Foods (Pty) Ltd v Sun International (Bophutswana) Ltd* 1994 (2) S.A. 249.

[98] ss.38, 55(1).

If he treats it as a promissory note, he has against the drawer the rights of a holder against a maker of a promissory note.[99] The provisions of the Act relating to presentment for acceptance and acceptance do not apply.[1] Presentment for payment is not normally necessary to render the drawer liable[2] and notice of dishonour is dispensed with as regards the drawer.[3]

It has, however, been stated that this right of election can be availed of    **2–041** by the holder only when he puts the instrument in suit against any of the other parties to it, and not for any other purpose; thus he will not be allowed to elect when he is sued for converting the instrument.[4]

Subsection (2) also provides that the holder may, at his option, treat the instrument either as a bill of exchange or as a promissory note where the drawee is a fictitious person[5] or a person not having capacity to contract.[6] In each of these situations the Act further states that:

(a) presentment for acceptance is excused,[7]
(b) notice of dishonour is dispensed with as regards the drawer,[8] and
(c) notice of dishonour is dispensed with as regards the indorser where the indorser was aware of the fact at the time he indorsed the bill.[9]

By section 46(2)(b) presentment for payment is dispensed with where the drawee is a fictitious person.

ILLUSTRATIONS

1. J.H. draws a bill addressed to J.H., payable to himself or order, and    **2–042** indorses it to the claimant. If J.H. (the drawer) and J.H. (the drawee) are

---

[99] *cf.* ss.88, 89(2).
[1] s.89(3).
[2] s.87(1).
[3] ss.48, 50(2)(c).
[4] *McClintock v Union Bank of Australia Ltd* (1920) 20 S.R. (N.S.W.) 494, 503–504 (reversed [1922] 1 A.C. 240). See also *Capital and Counties Bank Ltd v Gordon,* above, at 250 (cheque).
[5] This presumably includes a non-existing person: *cf.* s.7(3). See *Smith v Bellamy* (1817) 2 Stark. 223 (Illustration 5).
[6] See s.22, below, paras 3–001, *et seq.*
[7] s.41(2)(a).
[8] s.50(2)(c).
[9] s.50(2)(d).

in fact the same person, the instrument is not a bill of exchange but a promissory note.[10]

2. A banking partnership carries on business in London with a branch office at Dorking. The manager of the Dorking branch, acting on behalf of the partners, draws an instrument on the head office in London, reading "Six months after date, pay, without acceptance to the order of F £100 value received". The instrument is indorsed by the payee to the claimant. The claimant may treat it as a promissory note, and the omission of any allegation of presentment or of matter of excuse for presentment is immaterial.[11]

3. In 1920 the Batoum branch of a company draws on the London office of the company an instrument, reading: "At sight pay this sole exchange to the order of M the sum of one thousand pounds sterling value received which place to account No. 2." The instrument is successively indorsed over to the order of I, J and the claimant. In 1931, the claimant seeks to prove in the liquidation of the company. He may elect to treat the instrument as a promissory note and it need not be presented for payment to render the maker (the company) liable. The fact that it is addressed to the London office is not for the purpose of section 87(1) of the Act a requirement set out in the body of the document making it payable at a particular place. But since time runs from the date of the instrument, the claimant's claim is barred by limitation.[12]

2–043     4. The directors of a company draw an instrument addressed to "the cashier" [*i.e.* of the company], reading "Ninety days after date, credit Mrs. A, or order, with the sum of £311 9s. 6d., claims *per* Susan King, in cash on account of this corporation." The instrument contains all that is essential as a promissory note.[13]

5. The defendant draws a bill upon Stevenson payable in London to the defendant's own order. The bill is subsequently indorsed to the claimant as second indorsee. It has writing on it purporting to be the acceptance of Stevenson, who cannot be found. The claimant must either allege the acceptance to be genuine (in which case he must prove a presentment for payment or an excuse for non-presentment) or must

---

[10] *Davis v Clarke* (1844) 6 Q.B. 16. But since the Act it may only be *treated* as a promissory note. See also s.17, Illustration 3.
[11] *Miller v Thomson* (1841) 3 M. & G. 576.
[12] *Re British Trade Corp. Ltd* [1932] 2 Ch. 1.
[13] *Allen v Sea, Fire and Life Assurance Co.* (1850) 9 C.B. 574.

charge the defendant with his drawing a bill on a non-existent person whereby the drawer himself is liable.[14]

### Address to drawee

6. (1) **The drawee must be named or otherwise indicated in a bill**  2–044
   **with reasonable certainty.**
   (2) **A bill may be addressed to two or more drawees whether they**
   **are partners or not, but an order addressed to two drawees in**
   **the alternative or to two or more drawees in succession is not**
   **a bill of exchange.**

Definitions                    Comparison
"bill": s.2.                   UCC: § 3–103.
                            ULB: art.1.

### COMMENT

**Subsection (1): the drawee.** A bill of exchange is an order addressed  2–045
by one person to another (the drawee).[15] Speaking of the indication of the
drawee, Story[16] says:

> "This seems indispensable to the rights, duties, and obligations of all
> the parties; for the Payee cannot otherwise know, upon whom he is
> to call, to accept and pay the Bill; nor can any other person know,
> whether it is addressed to him, or not, and whether he would be
> justified in accepting and paying the Bill, on account of the
> Drawer."

Only the drawee can accept a bill.[17]

Where the drawee is named in the bill, it is immaterial that the word
"at", instead of "to", is inserted before his name,[18] and a mere error of
description, the drawee and acceptor being admittedly the same person,

---

[14] *Smith v Bellamy* (1817) 2 Stark. 223.
[15] s.3(1).
[16] *Bills of Exchange*, § 58.
[17] s.17 (except in the case of acceptance for honour (s.65)); *Jackson v Hudson* (1810) 2 Camp.
447; *Davis v Clarke* (1844) 6 Q.B. 16 (s.17, Illustration 3).
[18] *Shuttleworth v Stevens* (1808) 1 Camp. 407.

will not invalidate the acceptance.[19] Where no drawee was named, but the bill was addressed to be payable at a stated address, an acceptance by the person who lived at that address was held to impose liability on him as acceptor.[20] But this decision "goes to the verge of the law."[21]

An instrument in which the drawee is neither named nor indicated with reasonable certainty is not a bill of exchange.[22] If a person writes an "acceptance" on such an instrument, he is not liable as an acceptor, but may be liable as the maker of a promissory note.[23] The instrument may, however, be completed in accordance with the conditions of section 20 of the Act. Thus, after acceptance, his name may be inserted as drawee,[24] and he is then liable as acceptor.[25]

For cases where the drawee is a fictitious person or a person not having capacity to contract, see section 5(3) of the Act.

2–046    **Subsection (2): two or more drawees.** There may be two or more drawees of a bill. The acceptors of a bill can only be liable jointly,[26] whereas the makers of a note may be liable jointly, or jointly and severally, according to its tenor.[27] The acceptance of one or more of the drawees, but not of all, is a qualified acceptance.[28]

Though a bill may not be addressed to two drawees in the alternative,[29] or to two or more drawees in succession,[30] it may name a referee in case of need[31]; but his status is wholly different from that of an ordinary drawee. Alternative or successive drawees would give rise to difficulty as to the recourse if the bill were dishonoured.

---

[19] *Dermatine Co. Ltd v Ashworth* (1905) 21 T.L.R. 510.
[20] *Gray v Milner* (1819) 8 Taunt. 739 (Illustration 1).
[21] *Byles on Bills of Exchange* (27th ed.), para.10–02; *Davis v Clarke*, above; *Peto v Reynolds* (1854) 9 Exch. 410, 416.
[22] *Mason v Lack* (1929) 45 T.L.R. 363 (Illustration 2); *Haseldine v Winstanley* [1936] 2 K.B. 101, 105 (s.64, Illustration 3).
[23] *Peto v Reynolds*, above, affirmed *sub. nom. Reynolds v Peto* (1855) 11 Exch. 418; *Fielden v Marshall* (1861) 9 C.B., N.S. 606; *Mason v Lack*, above; *Haseldine v Winstanley*, above. *cf. Britannia Electric Lamp Works Ltd v D. Mandler & Co. Ltd* [1939] 2 K.B. 129 (s.87, Illustration 3).
[24] s.20(1)(2).
[25] *cf. Haseldine v Winstanley*, above, where, after acceptance, the name of the defendant who accepted was put on the bill as drawee in place of the drawer's name which had been inserted as drawee by mistake. Horridge J. held that the defendant was liable, either as acceptor if the alteration made the instrument a good bill of exchange, or as the maker of a promissory note if it did not.
[26] *Re Barnard* (1886) 32 Ch.D. 447. *cf. Other v Iveson* (1855) 3 Drew. 177 (cheque).
[27] s.85(1).
[28] s.19(2)(e). See also s.44(1).
[29] *cf.* UCC, § 3–103(a)(6).
[30] *Jackson v Hudson* (1810) 2 Camp. 447, 448.
[31] s.15.

ILLUSTRATIONS

1. An instrument is drawn by S, payable to himself or order. The name 2–047
of the drawee is not stated, but the instrument is addressed "Payable at
No. 1 Wilmot Street, opposite the Lamb, Bethnal Green, London". It is
accepted by the defendant, M, who resides at that address. A verdict is
obtained against the defendant at the suit of the claimant, an indorsee of
the instrument. The instrument is a bill of exchange, it being directed to
a particular place, which could only mean to the person who resides
there.[32]

2. An instrument purporting to be a bill of exchange is drawn by the
claimant and accepted by the defendant. When accepted, it bears no other
names at all (*i.e.* neither the name of the drawer nor that of the drawee),
except that it states that the bill is payable at Lloyd's Bank, High Street,
Shoreditch. Subsequently the claimant puts his name on the bill as
drawer, but no drawee is ever named. The defendant is liable as the
maker of a promissory note, since the instrument fulfils the requirements
of section 83(1) of the Act.[33]

## Certainty required as to payee

7. (1) Where a bill is not payable to bearer, the payee must be 2–048
     named or otherwise indicated therein with reasonable cer-
     tainty.
   (2) A bill may be made payable to two or more payees jointly, or
     it may be made payable in the alternative to one of two, or
     one or some of several payees. A bill may also be made
     payable to the holder of an office for the time being.
   (3) Where the payee is a fictitious or non-existing person the bill
     may be treated as payable to bearer.

| Definitions | Comparison |
|---|---|
| "bearer": s.2. | UCC; §§ 3–109, 3–110, 3–404. |
| "bill": s.2. | ULB: arts 1, 3. |
| "person": s.2. | ULC: art.5. |
| | UNB: arts 3, 10. |

[32] *Gray v Milner* (1819) 8 Taunt. 739.
[33] *Mason v Lack* (1929) 45 T.L.R. 363.

COMMENT

2–049    **Subsection (1): the payee.** "Every Bill of Exchange", says Story,[34] "ought to specify, to whom the same is payable; for in no other way can the Drawee, if he accepts it, know to whom he may properly pay it, so as to discharge himself from all further liability." For this reason, and because it may be necessary to establish whether it was in fact the payee who indorsed the bill,[35] unless the bill is payable to bearer, the payee must be named or otherwise indicated in it with reasonable certainty.[36]

The payee, though not named, may be indicated by description, *e.g.* "The Treasurer General of the Royal Treasury of Portugal"[37] or "the trustees of the Wesleyan Chapel, Harrogate".[38] Extrinsic evidence is then admissible to determine who was at the time the person so described and intended to be the payee. Extrinsic evidence is also admissible to resolve an ambiguity, for example where there are two persons (father and son) of the same name, to show which of the two was intended to be the payee,[39] or to identify the payee when misnamed.[40] Where such evidence is admitted, the criterion is the intention of the drawer of the bill or, in the case of a note, the maker of the note.[41] Further, by section 32(4) of the Act, where, in a bill payable to order, the payee is wrongly designated, or his name is misspelt, he may indorse the bill as therein described, adding, if he thinks fit, his proper signature.

Where the name of the payee is left blank, the instrument is incomplete and the person in possession of it may insert the name of the payee in accordance with and subject to the conditions set out in section 20 of the Act. But until this be done, the authorities are divided as to whether the instrument can be a valid bill or note.[42] In a number of older cases it was

[34] *Bills of Exchange,* § 54.
[35] s.32; *Mead v Young* (1790) 4 T.R. 28.
[36] *Chadwick v Allen* (1726) 2 Stra. 706 (note); *Green v Davies* (1825) 4 B. & C. 235 (note).
[37] *Soares v Glyn* (1845) 8 Q.B. 24 (indorsement).
[38] *Holmes v Jaques* (1866) L.R. 1 Q.B. 376. See also *Megginson v Harper* (1834) 2 C. & M. 322 (trustees under the will of W).
[39] *Sweeting v Fowler* (1815) 1 Stark. 106; *Stebbing v Spicer* (1849) 8 C.B. 827. But these cases could be explained on the ground that either person so named may indorse the bill: *cf. Mead v Young* (1790) 4 T.R. 28.
[40] *Willis v Barrett* (1816) 2 Stark. 29; *Seref Bros (S.A.) (Pty) Ltd v Khan Brothers Wholesale* 1976 (3) S.A. 339, 340; *Standard Mineral Water Works v Grobler* 1977 (4) S.A. 66; *Adam Associates (Strathclyde) Ltd v CGU Insurance plc* [2001] SLT (Sh.Ct.) 18. See also *Bird & Co. v Thos Cook and Son* [1937] 2 All E.R. 227, 230–231 (indorsement).
[41] *Mead v Young* (1790) 4 T.R. 28. See also *Bird & Co. v Thos Cook and Son,* [1937] 2 All E.R. 227 (intention of indorser).
[42] Extrinsic evidence is not admissible to explain away an uncertainty patent on the bill. In *Polish Combatants' Association Credit Union Ltd v Moge* (1984) 9 D.L.R. (4th) 60 rectification was allowed to insert the name of the payee even though this was not in time within s.20. *Sed quaere?*

held that an instrument payable "to        or order" was not a bill of exchange.[43] But in *Chamberlain v Young*,[44] where a bill was drawn "Pay to        order" (and not "to        or order") and was indorsed by the drawer, it was construed as being payable "to my order", *i.e.* to the drawer's order, and held to be a valid bill. It may be that, in similar circumstances, a bill payable "to        or order" would now be construed as payable "to myself or order"; but the matter is still in doubt.[45]

Where an instrument was made by the defendant in the form of a     **2–050** promissory note, but containing no payee's name or any statement that it was payable to bearer, and it was handed by the defendant to the claimant's agent with the intention that it should operate as a note, it was held to have the effect of a note payable to bearer "because that is the natural legal effect".[46] But it would be difficult to contend,[47] that a bill or note payable "to        or order" would have that effect, since the words "or order" would negate any inference that it was payable to bearer.

A bill or cheque drawn payable "to cash or order", or to or to the order of anything other than a person, is not a bill of exchange.[48]

See also subsection (3), below (fictitious or non-existing payee). Section 34(3) of the Act applies the provisions of the Act relating to the payee (with necessary modifications) to an indorsee under a special indorsement.

**Subsection (2): two or more payees.** A bill may be made payable to     **2–051** two or more payees jointly, *e.g.* "Pay C and D" or "Pay to the order of C and D". Where a bill is payable to the order of two or more payees who are not partners all must indorse, unless the one indorsing has authority to indorse for the others.[49]

Before the Act, a bill was void if payable to two payees in the alternative unless there was apparent community of interest.[50] But the subsection permits a bill to be made payable in the alternative to one of two, or one of some of several, payees, *e.g.* "Pay C or D" or "Pay to the order of

[43] *R. v Richards* (1811) Russ. & Ry. 193; *R. v Ryan* (1811) Russ. & Ry. 195 (Illustration 1).
[44] [1893] 2 Q.B. 206 (Illustration 2).
[45] [1893] 2 Q.B. 206 at 209, 210; *North and South Insurance Corp. Ltd v National Provincial Bank Ltd* [1936] 1 K.B. 328, 335. Contrast *Henderson, Sons & Co. Ltd v Wallace and Pennell* 1902 5 F. 166(where Lord Traynor said the signatories of a cheque were rather in the position of the makers of a note).
[46] *Daun & Vallentin v Sherwood* (1895) 11 T.L.R. 211. See also *J.I. Case Threshing Machine Co. v Desmond* (1914) 22 D.L.R. 455 (payee inferred). Contrast; *Amerongen (Liquidator) v Hamilton* (1957) 22 W.W.R. 377.
[47] *cf. Wookey v Pole* (1820) 4 B. & Ald. 1 (treasury bill in this form payable to bearer). The UCC, §3–109(a)(2), would make such an instrument payable to bearer.
[48] See the Comment to s.3(1), above.
[49] s.32(3).
[50] *Blanckenhagen v Blundell* (1819) 2 B. & Ald. 417. *cf. Watson v Evans* (1863) 1 H. & C. 662.

C or D". Presumably any such payee may indorse the bill.[51] Where it cannot be determined from the face of the instrument whether the instrument is payable to two or more payees jointly or in the alternative, extrinsic evidence is presumably admissible to prove the intention of the drawer or maker in this regard.

A bill may also be made payable to the holder of an office for the time being. A common law, a bill payable to the holder of an office for the time being was invalid.[52]

**2–052**     **Subsection (3): fictitious or non-existing payee.** Where the payee is a fictitious or non-existing person the bill may be treated as payable to bearer. The importance of this provision lies in the fact that, if the payee's indorsement is forged on the bill, the right of the holder will not be defeated by the operation of section 24 of the Act. The forged indorsement may be disregarded and the bill treated as a bearer instrument. Not only the holder, but any person to whose interest it is so to treat the bill may do so, *e.g.* a banker who has paid such a bill, domiciled with him on a forged indorsement,[53] or a person who is sued for conversion of the bill.[54] The effect therefore is that loss falls on the acceptor, maker or drawer of the instrument.[55]

It is immaterial for the purposes of the sub-section whether or not the acceptor or other party liable on the bill knew that the payee was a fictitious or non-existing person.[56]

The payee will be a non-existing person if, though once in existence, he has ceased to exist, as, for example, where the payee is deceased[57] or is firm or company which no longer exists.[58] The payee will also be such a person where he is not yet in existence[59] or has never existed,[60] or where he is an imaginary person. Thus if the drawer is fraudulently induced by

---

[51] *Watson v Evans* (1863) 1 H.&C. 662.

[52] *Cowie v Sterling* (1856) 6 E. & B. 333; *Yates v Nash* (1860) 8 C.B.N.S. 581. *cf. Holmes v Jacques* (1866) L.R. 1 Q.B. 376; *Watson v Evans,* above.

[53] *Bank of England v Vagliano Bros.* [1891] A.C. 107 (Illustration 4).

[54] *cf. North and South Wales Bank Ltd v Macbeth* [1908] A.C. 137 (Illustration 6).

[55] The UCC has eliminated the artificiality of treating a bill payable to order as one payable to bearer. UCC, § 3–404, contains a more extensive provision, which includes cases where the payee is non-existent or is intended to have no interest in the instrument, whereby (although a regular chain of indorsements is required) a person can effectively indorse in the name of the payee. See also UCC, § 3–405.

[56] *Bank of England v Vagliano Brothers* [1891] A.C. 107 at 120, 129–130, 134, 146–147, 160–161. Before the Act, it was held that the holder was entitled to treat the bill as payable to bearer only if the acceptor, at the time of acceptance, knew the payee to be fictitious.

[57] *Canada Trust Co. v R.* [1982] 2 F.C. 722 (Canada); *Ashpitel v Bryan* (1863) 3 B. & S. 474, affd (1864) 5 B. & S. 723 (but this was a case of estoppel under the previous law). Contrast *Murray v East India Co.* (1821) 5 B. & Ald. 204.

[58] *cf. City Bank v Rowan* (1893) 14 N.S.W.L.R. 127 (fictitious person).

[59] *Rutherford Copper Mining Co. v Ogier* (1905) 1 Tas.L.R. 156 (note).

[60] *Canadian Bank of Commerce v Rogers* (1911) 23 O.L.R. 109.

a rogue to draw a cheque payable to "B. Crawford or order", and B. Crawford is an imaginary person invented by the rogue who forges B. Crawford's indorsement and obtains payment of the cheque, then B. Crawford is a non-existing person, and the cheque may be treated as payable to bearer.[61]

The meaning of "a fictitious person" was considered by the House of 2–053 Lords in *Bank of England v Vagliano Brothers,*[62] the facts of which are set out in Illustration 4. In that case, the bills in question were drawn payable to a named payee *who was in existence.* But the signature of the drawer on the bills was forged by the person drawing them. The drawee accepted the bills in ignorance of the forgery, intending by his acceptance to incur liability to the named payee. The forger thus obtained a genuine acceptance of forged bills. However, the forger did not intend the named payee to receive payment. He intended to and did forge the indorsement of the payee, and himself obtained payment of the bills. The question at issue in the case was whether the defendant bank, with whom the bills were domiciled for payment and who had paid out on the bills, was entitled to debit the account of its customer, the acceptor, in respect of the amounts paid out. The House of Lords by a majority (Lords Bramwell and Field dissenting) held that it was entitled to do so. Four of their Lordships (Lord Halsbury L.C. and Lords Selborne, Watson and Macnaghten)[63] based their decision mainly on the ground that, in the circumstances of the case, the acceptor had, albeit innocently, misled the bank and induced it to make the payments which it made, and could not therefore hold the bank responsible for such payments. But five of their Lordships (Lord Halsbury L.C. and Lords Watson, Herschell, Macnaghten and Morris)[64] held that, assuming the documents were in fact bills of exchange,[65] the fact that the name of an existing person had been selected by the forger as the payee of the bill did not prevent the payee from being "a fictitious person" within the meaning of section 7(3) of the Act. "Fictitious" did not mean "imaginary". The proper meaning of the word was "feigned" or "counterfeit".[66] Lord Macnaghten said[67]:

---

[61] *Clutton & Co. v Attenborough & Son* [1897] A.C. 90 (Illustration 3) (fictitious or non-existing person); *Royal Bank of Canada v Concrete Column Clamps (1961) Ltd* (1977) 74 D.L.R. (3d) 26 (Illustration 7).

[62] [1891] A.C. 107. See Chalmers (1891) 7 L.Q.R. 216; Adams (1891) 7 L.Q.R. 295; Butterworth (1894) 10 L.Q.R. 40.

[63] Lord Herschell also stated (at 156) that he did not dissent from this ground.

[64] Lord Selborne (at 129) doubted the majority view on this point.

[65] Lords Watson and Macnaghten stated that the documents were not bills of exchange to which s.7(3) was intended to apply (at 134, 160). Lord Halsbury L.C. considered that they were not bills at all, but, applying the doctrine of estoppel against the acceptor, "one may consider whether as against him they may not possess qualities which, in their inception, they did not possess" (at 120).

[66] At 122, 153, 161.

[67] At 161.

"It seems to me that the [persons] named as payees on these pre-tended bills were, strictly speaking, fictitious persons. When the bills came before [the drawee] for acceptance they were fictitious from beginning to end. The drawer was fictitious; the payee was fictitious; the person indicated as agent for presentation was fictitious. One and all they were feigned and counterfeit persons put forward as real persons, each in a several and distinct capacity; whereas, in truth, they were mere make-believes for the persons whose names appeared on the instrument. They were not, I think, the less fictitious because there were in existence real persons for whom these names were intended to pass muster."

And Lord Herschell concluded[68]:

" . . . whenever the name inserted as that of the payee is so inserted by way of pretence merely, without any intention that payment shall only be made in conformity therewith, the payee is a fictitious person within the meaning of the statute, whether the name be that of an existing person, or of one who has no existence, and that the bill may, in each case, be treated by a lawful holder as payable to bearer".

Lord Herschell also considered[69] that, even if the drawer's name had not been forged, but the drawer had himself inserted the name of the payee as a pretence without intending any such person to receive payment, the bills would still have been bills whose payee was a fictitious person.

2–054    *Vagliano*'s case was, however, distinguished in a number of subsequent cases where cheques were drawn payable to existing persons. In these cases[70] the drawer drew the cheque intending the named payee to receive payment, although such intention was induced by the fraud of another who subsequently forged the payee's indorsement and obtained payment for himself. It was held that the payee was not a fictitious person within the meaning of section 7(3): "Where there is a real drawer who has

---

[68] At 153. See also Lord Halsbury (at 121, 122) and Lord Watson (at 134); *Edinburgh Ballarat Gold Quartz Mine Co. Ltd v Sydney* (1891) 7 T.L.R. 656; *Fok Cheong Shing Investments Ltd v Bank of Nova Scotia* (1983) 146 D.L.R. (3d) 617; *Kelly Funeral Homes Ltd v Canadian Imperial Bank of Commerce* (1990) 72 D.L.R. (4th) 276; *Bank of Nova Scotia v Toronto—Dominion Bank* (2001) 200 D.L.R. (4th) 549, leave to appeal refused 208 D.L.R. (4th) vi.

[69] At 153–154.

[70] *Vinden v Hughes* [1905] 1 K.B. 795 (Illustration 5); *Macbeth v North and South Wales Bank Ltd* [1908] A.C. 137 (Illustration 6); *Town and Country Advance Co. v Provincial Bank of Ireland* [1917] 2 I.R. 421; *Goldman v Cox* (1924) 40 T.L.R. 744. See also *Harley v Bank of Toronto* [1938] 2 D.L.R. 135; *Bank of Toronto v Smith* [1950] 3 D.L.R. 169; *Zurich Life Insurance Co. of Canada v Royal Bank of Canada* (1973) 36 D.L.R. (3d) 750; *Royal Bank of Canada v Concrete Column Clamps (1961) Ltd* (1977) 74 D.L.R. (3d) 26 (Illustration 7); *Boma Manufacturing Ltd v Canadian Imperial Bank of Commerce* (1997) 140 D.L.R. (4th) 463.

designated an existing person as the payee, and intends that the person should be the payee, it is impossible that the payee can be fictitious".[71]

It therefore appears that whether or not the payee is a fictitious person depends on the intent of the drawer.[72] If the person drawing the bill —whether he is the genuine drawer or a person who forges the drawer's signature—inserts the name of the payee by way of pretence only without the intention that he should receive payment, the payee is a fictitious person notwithstanding that he in fact exists. But if the drawer inserts the name of an existing person, intending that payment shall be made to that person, then, even though that intention is induced by the fraud of a third party who intends to misappropriate the bill, the payee is neither a fictitious nor a non-existing person, and the bill cannot be treated as payable to bearer.

The above principles can lead to certain anomalies in situations of "payroll padding",[73] where an employee prepares cheques for signature by his employer payable to persons whom he has fraudulently added to the payroll of his employer's business. He then negotiates or himself obtains payment of the cheques. If the persons so added are non-existing persons, names invented by the employee, then the loss falls on the employer, for the cheques may be treated as payable to bearer.[74] But if the payees are existing persons, for example, former employees who are no longer employed by the employer, then the loss falls on the subsequent indorsee, or the drawee[75] of the cheque, since it was the intention of the employer when drawing the cheque (though induced by the fraud of the employee) that the payees named should receive the proceeds, and they are not fictitious or non-existing persons.[76] It might be thought that, in

---

[71] *Macbeth v North and South Wales Bank Ltd*, [1908] A.C. 137 at 139.

[72] But the intention of the drawer is immaterial if the payee is a *non-existing* person: *Clutton & Co. v Attenborough & Son* [1897] A.C. 90 (Illustration 3). In *Kelly Funeral Homes Ltd v Canadian Imperial Bank of Commerce* (1990) 72 D.L.R. (4th) 276, where two persons signed a cheque as drawers, it was held that the intention of the dominant signatory was relevant. In *Boma Manufacturing Ltd v Canadian Imperial Bank of Commerce* (1997) 140 D.L.R. (4th) 463, an employee of a company with authority to sign cheques signed on behalf of the company a number of cheques payable to existing persons but without the intention that they should receive payment. A majority of the Supreme Court of Canada held that the relevant intention was that of the drawer (the company) and not of the signatory, and that s.7(3) did not therefore apply. La Forest and McLachlin JJ. dissented on the ground that the intention of the signatory should be attributed to the company, see also *Rhostar (Pvt.) Ltd v Netherlands Bank of Rhodesia Ltd* 1972 (2) S.A.703. cf. *Bank of Nova Scotia v Toronto—Dominion Bank* (2001) 200 D.L.R. (4th) 549.

[73] See *Royal Bank of Canada v Concrete Column Clamps (1961) Ltd* (1977) 74 D.L.R. (3d) 26; (Illustration 7).

[74] *Clutton & Co. v Attenborough & Son* [1897] A.C. 90 (Illustration 3).

[75] Unless protected by ss.60, 80 of the Act or s.1 of the Cheques Act 1957.

[76] *Vinden v Hughes* [1905] 1 K.B. 795 (Illustration 5); *Macbeth v North and South Wales Bank Ltd* [1908] A.C. 137 (Illustration 6).

either case, the loss should fall upon the employer as a risk of his business rather than upon the subsequent indorsee or drawee.[77]

If the name of a real and existing payee is inserted by the drawer of a bill, the subsequent alteration of that name by another does not mean that the payee is a fictitious or non-existing person or convert a bill payable to order into a bill payable to bearer.[78]

2–055    **Cheques crossed "account payee."** By section 81A(1) of the Act, a crossed cheque which bears on its face the words "account payee" or "a/c payee", either with or without the word "only", is not transferable and is only valid as between the parties thereto. The majority of cheques currently issued in the United Kingdom are so crossed. Where such a cheque is drawn payable to a fictitious or non-existing person, it is submitted that a collecting banker, for example, cannot rely on subsection (3) to establish that he is the holder of a bearer instrument as the cheque is incapable of transfer.[79] The same reasoning would also apply to a bill, note or cheque drawn "Pay X only" or which contains words prohibiting transfer or indicating that it should not be transferable.[80]

ILLUSTRATIONS

2–056    1. R is tried and convicted for forging and uttering a navy pay bill purporting to be drawn by S and payable "to        or order", and also for forging and uttering an indorsement upon it in the name of J. The conviction is wrong. The instrument is not a bill of exchange because there is no payee.[81]

2. T draws a bill on Y, reading "Five months after date pay to        or-der the sum of one hundred and fifty pounds for value received". The bill is accepted by Y, indorsed by T and handed to the claimant for value. T and Y, as drawer and acceptor, are liable to the claimant on the bill. The bill must be construed as meaning that it is payable to "my order", that

---

[77] See the dissent in *Royal Bank of Canada v Concrete Column Clamps (1961) Ltd* (1977) 74 D.L.R. (3d) 26; and the dissent in *Boma Manufacturing Ltd v Canadian Imperial Bank of Commerce* (1997) 140 D.L.R. (4th) 463; UCC, § 3–405. Contributory negligence on the part of the employer is irrelevant. *Boma*, at 476.

[78] *Goldman v Cox* (1924) 40 T.L.R. 744.

[79] Illustration 8.

[80] s.8(1). See *Rhostar (Pvt) Ltd v Netherlands Bank of Rhodesia Ltd* 1972 (2) S.A. 703, 709–711. *cf. Bank of Credit and Commerce Zimbabwe Ltd v UDC Ltd* 1991 (4) S.A. 660.

[81] *R. v Ryan* (1811) Russ & Ry. 195.

is, to the order of the drawer, and having been indorsed by him is a valid bill of exchange.[82]

3. P is employed by the claimants, a firm of land agents, as a clerk in their accounts department. He induces the claimants to draw cheques payable to the order of "George Brett", whom he represents to be entitled to payment for work and materials supplied to the firm. There is no such person as George Brett, and no such consideration as represented. P obtains possession of the cheques, indorses them in the name of George Brett and negotiates them to the defendants, who give value for them in good faith. The cheques are collected by the defendants' bankers and the proceeds credited to the defendants' account. The claimants claim against the defendants the amounts so received as money paid under a mistake of fact. The claim fails. Although the claimants believed and intended the cheques to be payable to a real person, "George Brett" is a fictitious or non-existing person within the meaning of section 7(3) of the Act. The cheques may therefore be treated as payable to bearer. As against the defendants, who are holders in due course, the claimants cannot assert that the cheques were never "issued", as defined in section 2 of the Act.[83]

4. The claimant, trading as Vagliano Brothers, has a foreign correspondent, Vucina, in Odessa. The claimant is in the habit of accepting bills drawn on him by Vucina and payable to the order of P & Co., a firm carrying on business in Constantinople. One Glyka, a clerk employed by the claimant, forges Vucina's signature as drawer on a number of such bills. The claimant, in ignorance of the forgery, accepts these bills payable (as usual) at the defendant bank. Glyka then forges the indorsement of P & Co. to non-existent indorsees, presents the bills for payment to the bank and obtains cash for them. The claimant claims against the bank a declaration that he is entitled to be credited by the bank with the amount so paid, which he alleges to have been wrongfully and without authority debited to his account. His action fails. Assuming the documents in question to be bills of exchange, the bank is protected by section 7(3) of the Act. The named payee (P & Co.) is "a fictitious person" within the meaning of that subsection, and the documents may be treated by the bank as payable to bearer.[84]

2–057

5. C is employed as a confidential clerk by the claimants, a partnership firm of salesmen in Covent Garden market. Part of his duties consists of

---

[82] *Chamberlain v Young and Tower* [1893] 2 Q.B. 206.
[83] *Clutton & Co. v Attenborough & Son* [1897] A.C. 90.
[84] *Bank of England v Vagliano Brothers* [1891] A.C. 107. The facts are set out in the judgment of Charles J. (1888) 22 Q.B.D. 103.

filling up cheques payable to the order of customers of the claimants for whom fruit and vegetables have been sold. C fills out 7 cheques payable to such customers and gets one of the partners to sign them as drawer. Instead of posting these cheques to the payees, C forges the payees' indorsement on them and cashes them from time to time with the defendant, a shopkeeper with whom he deals. The cheques are collected by the defendant's bank and the proceeds credited to the defendant's account. The claimants claim from the defendant the amount so received. The payees are not "fictitious persons" within the meaning of section 7(3) of the Act and the claimants are entitled to judgment for the amount claimed.[85]

6. W, by falsely representing to the claimant that he has agreed to buy from one T.A. Kerr certain shares and arranged to re-sell them at a profit, induces the claimant to finance the transaction. The claimant draws a cheque in payment for the shares payable to "T.A. Kerr or order". Kerr is a real person, but the share transaction is fictitious. W forges Kerr's indorsement to the cheques and pays it into his own bank, the defendant bank, which collects the cheque from the claimant's bank. The claimant is entitled to damages for conversion of the cheque by the defendant bank.[86] T.A. Kerr is not a fictitious, but a real, person, and intended by the drawer of the cheque to receive the proceeds.[87]

2–058     7. The claimant company employs a payroll clerk, G, whose normal duty it is to prepare cheques for wages due to employees of the company. G perpetrates a fraud by including among the cheques presented to the authorised signatory of the company for signature a number of cheques payable to persons to whom no wages are owing by the company. Some of the payees are chosen at random by G from some unknown source, perhaps the telephone directory or invented by G. But others are persons who have been employed by the company in the past but to whom no payment is due. The company's signing officer signs the cheques without investigation. G abstracts these cheques, forges the indorsements and obtains payment from the defendant bank on whom the cheques are drawn. An action is brought by the company against the bank claiming that its account has been wrongly debited with the amounts so paid out. The bank is not liable with respect to the cheques drawn payable to payees whose names are chosen at random, for these may be treated as

---

[85] *Vinden v Hughes* [1905] 1 K.B. 795.

[86] It being conceded that the protection of s.82 of the Act is not available: *Macbeth v North & South Wales Bank* [1906] 2 K.B. 718, 723. See now s.4 of the Cheques Act 1957, below, para.17–028.

[87] *Macbeth v North & South Wales Bank Ltd* [1908] A.C. 137.

payable to bearer. But the bank is liable[88] in respect of the cheques payable to former employees, since the payees are not fictitious or non-existing persons.[89]

8. Over a period of time D, who is employed by E Ltd, induces the finance director of the company to draw a number of cheques on the company's account with the X Bank payable to "Charles Robinson" by falsely representing that payments are due to Robinson for services provided. "Charles Robinson" is an imaginary person and no services have in fact been provided. Each of the cheques is crossed "Account payee only". D opens an account with the Y Bank in the name of "Charles Robinson". Before opening the account the Y Bank takes no steps to verify the identity of its customer. D deposits the cheques with the Y Bank for collection. They are collected by the Y Bank and the proceeds credited to the account. D absconds with the proceeds. (*Semble*) the Y Bank is liable to the company for conversion[90] of the cheques, subject to any defence that it may successfully raise under section 4 of the Cheques Act 1957 that it has acted bona fide and without negligence.[91] The "Account payee" crossing renders the cheques non-transferable under section 81A of the 1882 Act. Even if, under section 7(3), the Y Bank may treat the cheques as payable to bearer, it acquires no title to the cheques as they are incapable of transfer.

**What bills are negotiable**

8. **(1) When a bill contains words prohibiting transfer, or indicating**   2–059
**an intention that it should not be transferable, it is valid as**
**between the parties thereto, but is not negotiable.**
**(2) A negotiable bill may be payable either to order or to**
**bearer.**
**(3) A bill is payable to bearer which is expressed to be so paya-**
**ble, or on which the only or last indorsement is an indorse-**
**ment in blank.**
**(4) A bill is payable to order which is expressed to be so payable,**
**or which is expressed to be payable to a particular person,**
**and does not contain words prohibiting transfer or indicating**
**an intention that it should not be transferable.**
**(5) Where a bill, either originally or by indorsement, is expressed**
**to be payable to the order of a specified person, and not to**

---

[88] There being no equivalent to s.60 of the Act in the Canadian statute.
[89] *Royal Bank of Canada v Concrete Column Clamps (1961) Ltd* (1977) 74 D.L.R. (3d) 26 (Supreme Ct of Canada).
[90] But see below, para.3–050.
[91] See below, para.17–028.

him or his order, it is nevertheless payable to him or his order
at his option.

Definitions                          Comparison
"bearer": s.2                        UCC: §§3–104(d), 3–109,
"bill": s.2                          3–205(b).
"indorsement": s.2                   ULB: arts 1, 11—14, 75, 77.
"person": s.2                        ULC: art.5.
                                     UNB: arts 3, 13.

COMMENT

2–060   **Negotiable bills.** Section 3(1) of the Act states that a bill of exchange
may be payable (i) to a specified person, or (ii) to the order of a specified
person, or (iii) to bearer. The present section, however, distinguishes
between bills that are negotiable and those that are not negotiable. In this
section, the word "negotiable" is used to mean "transferable". An instrument may not be transferable but still be a valid bill of exchange.

2–061   **Subsection (1): words prohibiting transfer.** A drawer may wish to
create a bill of exchange but not allow for its transfer or negotiation. An
indorsee of a bill may likewise wish by his indorsement (a "restrictive
indorsement") to prohibit the further transfer of the bill by the indorsee.[92]
A bill will be negotiable, when drawn, unless it contains words prohibiting transfer, or indicating an intention that it should not be transferable.
It will remain negotiable until it is restrictively indorsed, or discharged by
payment or otherwise.[93]

The usual way in which a drawer creates a non-negotiable bill is by
drawing the bill payable to a specified person only, e.g. "Pay X only".[94]
But the same effect may be achieved by writing the words: "Not Transferable" on the face of the bill or, it seems, in the case of a bill (but not of a
cheque)[95] the words "Not Negotiable",[96] A crossed cheque which bears
on it the words "Not Negotiable" remains transferable, but the holder
acquires no better title than that of his transferor.[97]

---

[92] s.35(1).
[93] s.36(1).
[94] *Hibernian Bank Ltd v Gysin and Hanson* [1939] 1 K.B. 483 (Illustration 1). See also *T.S.
Aroonasalam Chitty v Seah Eng Koon* [1934] M.L.J. 164 ("I promise to pay S. personally" on
note).
[95] As to the special statutory meaning attaching to: "not negotiable" on a crossed cheque, see
s.81; and for the effect the words "a/c payee" on a cheque, see below, para.2–063.
[96] *Hibernian Bank Ltd v Gysin and Hanson* [1939] 1 K.B. 483. But see below, para.14–033
(s.81).
[97] s.81; below, para.14–030.

At one time there was authority for the view that a bill expressed to be payable to order must always be negotiable and could not be made not transferable.[98] But in *Hibernian Bank Ltd v Gysin and Hanson*,[99] where a bill (not a cheque) was drawn: "Pay... to the order of X Ltd only" and crossed "Not Negotiable", it was held that, notwithstanding that the bill was expressed to be payable to order, the words on the bill were such as to make the bill not transferable. There is little doubt that, at the present day, if a printed form of order cheque is employed and the cheque is drawn "Pay X only or order", the cheque would not be transferable, if only because the written word: "only" would be held to prevail over the printed words "or order".

**Assignment.** An instrument containing words prohibiting transfer or indicating an intention that it should not be transferable, is nevertheless effective to create a debt or obligation owed to the original payee. It is therefore arguable that, although the instrument itself cannot be transferred by negotiation, the payee's contractual rights on the instrument could be validly transferred by him to a third party by assignment.[1] So if the payee indorses and delivers the instrument to a third party, his rights on the instrument would pass to the third party by assignment. However, certain forms of wording on the instrument, *e.g.* "Pay X only", would probably be construed as words prohibiting assignment and so render ineffective, as against the debtor or obligor, the transfer of any of the payee's rights as such to the assignee.[2] The prohibition would, on the other hand, not necessarily invalidate the contract of assignment between the payee and the assignee[3] nor would it prevent the transfer of ownership of the paper to the third party so as to preclude any action in conversion against a paying or collecting banker by the payee.[4]                    2–062

**Cheques crossed "account payee".** Previously it was held that the words "account payee" or "a/c payee" on a cheque did not indicate that the cheque should not be transferable.[5] But, since the passing of the Cheques Act 1992, a crossed cheque which bears these words across its                    2–063

[98] *National Bank Ltd v Silke* [1891] 1 Q.B. 435, *per* Lindley and Fry L.JJ. at 439.
[99] [1938] 2 K.B. 384, affd [1939] 1 K.B. 483 (Illustration 1).
[1] *Chandler v Portland Edmond Cement Co. Ltd* (1917) 33 D.L.R. 302; see below, para.5–067.
[2] *Linden Gardens Trust Ltd v Lenesta Sludge Disposals Ltd* [1944] A.C. 85. See also below, para.14–044, *cf. Brice v Bannister* (1878) 3 Q.B.D. 569, 581.
[3] *Linden Gardens Trust Ltd v Lenesta Sludge Disposals Ltd* [1944] A.C. 85 at 108. The assignment, though prohibited, might also be capable of operating as a declaration of trust of his contractual rights by the payee in favour of the assignee: *Re Turcan* (1888) 49 Ch.D. 5; *Spellman v Spellman* [1961] 1 W.L.R. 921, 925; *Don King Productions Ltd v Warren (No.1)* [2000] Ch.291.
[4] *Absa Bank Ltd v Greyvenstein* 2003 (4) SA 537; see below, paras 3–050, 3–051 and 14–044.
[5] *National Bank Ltd v Silke* [1891] 1 Q.B. 435.

face is not transferable and is only valid as between the parties thereto.[6] Since most cheque forms pre-printed by banks in the United Kingdom are now crossed and bear these words across their face, it follows that the vast majority of cheques are no longer negotiable instruments but are merely payment orders issued by the customer to his bank instructing the bank to pay the sum mentioned in the cheque to the named payee.

2–064      **Subsection (2): order and bearer bills.** Cheques are commonly drawn payable to bearer, bills but rarely so.[7]

2–065      **Subsection (3): bearer bills.** A bill is payable to bearer which is expressed to be so payable, *e.g.* "Pay Bearer". A bill payable "to C or bearer" is payable to bearer,[8] and a bill payable "to bearer or order" is also presumably so payable.[9] A bill (or cheque) drawn payable to "cash or order" is not a bill payable to bearer, since it is not expressed to be so payable, and is not a bill of exchange at all[10]; but a cheque so drawn may be a valid mandate to the bank on which it is drawn to pay cash to the bearer of the instrument.[11]

The second part of this subsection altered the law.[12] It was intended to bring the law into accordance with the mercantile understanding by making a special indorsement control a previous indorsement in blank. Before the Act it was held that once a bearer bill always a bearer bill, and so where a bill was indorsed in blank, its negotiability was unaffected by a subsequent special indorsement. Now a bill is a bearer bill if the only or last indorsement is an indorsement in blank, or if it is expressed to be payable to bearer. See section 34 of the Act as to blank indorsements, and converting blank indorsements into special indorsements.

It is questionable whether a bill which was originally drawn payable to bearer can be converted into one payable to order by a special indorsement, *i.e.* by an indorsement which specifies the person to whom, or to

---

[6] s.81A(1), inserted by s.1 of the Cheques Act 1992; see below, para.14–037.

[7] ULB, arts 1, 75, does not permit bills or notes to be drawn payable to bearer, but does permit (arts 12, 13, 14, 77) indorsements to bearer or indorsements in blank. But ULC, art.5, permits cheques to be made payable to the bearer.

[8] *MK International Development Co. Ltd v Housing Bank* [1991] 1 Bank.L.R. 74; *Hunter BNZ Finance Ltd v Australian and New Zealand Banking Group Ltd* [1990] V.R. 41; *Ramsukh v Diesel Electric (Natal) Pty Ltd* 1994 (1) S.A. 876. *cf. House Property Co. of London Ltd v London County and Westminster Bank* (1915) 31 T.L.R. 479 (cheque payable to X or bearer crossed "a/c payee").

[9] UCC, § 3–109(a)(1).

[10] See the Comment on s.3(1), above, para.2–018.

[11] *North and South Insurance Corp. Ltd v National Provincial Bank Ltd* [1936] 1 K.B. 328, 336; *Orbit Mining and Trading Co. Ltd v Westminster Bank Ltd* [1963] 1 Q.B. 794, 811. *cf.* UCC, § 3–109(a)(3).

[12] *Walker v Macdonald* (1848) 2 Exch. 527. See also *Smith v Clarke* (1794) Peake 295.

whose order, the bill is to be payable. According to an Australian authority,[13] such a bill remains payable to bearer notwithstanding such an indorsement, since it can be negotiated by mere delivery.

If the drawer strikes through the words "or bearer" on a standard form, **2–066** so that the instrument reads simply "Pay C", the instrument is now payable to a particular person, and is in consequence payable to or to that person's order.[14]

By section 2 of the Cheques Act 1957, a banker who gives value for, or has a lien on, a cheque payable to order which the holder delivers to him for collection[15] without indorsing it, has such (if any) rights as he would have had if, upon delivery, the holder had indorsed it in blank. Thus, in the circumstances envisaged by that section,[16] a cheque, though payable to order, is in the hands of the banker deemed to be payable to bearer.[17]

For the warranty given by the holder of a bill payable to bearer who negotiates it by delivery without indorsing it, see section 58 of the 1882 Act.

**Subsection (4): order bills.** This subsection altered the law.[18] Before **2–067** the Act it was held in England that a bill or note drawn payable to a specified person, *e.g.* "Pay C", without the addition of the words authorising transfer was not negotiable.[19] The Act adopted the Scottish rule that a bill or note was negotiable unless it contained words prohibiting transfer or indicating an intention that it should not be transferable, as, for instance, "Pay C only".

A bill is payable to order which is expressed to be so payable, for example, "Pay my order", "Pay C or order", "Pay to the order of C"[20] or "Pay to C",[21] subject to subsection (1).

---

[13] *Miller Associates (Australia) Pty Ltd v Bennington Pty Ltd* [1975] 7 A.L.R. 144. See also *Pienaar v Moritz* 1985 (1) S.A. 547. *cf.* UCC, § 3–205(a).

[14] s.8(4).

[15] The section applies whether the holder pays the cheque into his own account or into the account of another: *Westminster Bank Ltd v Zang* [1966] A.C. 182. (Cheques Act 1957, s.2, Illustration 2).

[16] See below, para.17–015.

[17] *Midland Bank Ltd v R.V. Harris Ltd* [1963] 1 W.L.R. 1021 (Cheques Act 1957, s.2, Illustration 1); *Westminster Bank Ltd v Zang* [1966] A.C. 182. But this does not apply to cheques crossed "account payee": see below, para.17–017.

[18] *Edwards v Walters* [1896] 2 Ch. 157 (Illustration 2) (note).

[19] *Plimley v Westley* (1835) 2 Bing. N.C. 249; *Edwards v Walters* [1896] 2 Ch.157. But the indorser of such a note, though he could not thereby render the maker liable, was liable on his indorsement to the indorsee: *Plimley v Westley* (1835) 2 Bing. N.C. 249 at 251, 252; *Gwinnell v Herbert* (1836) 5 A. & E. 436, 441. Contrast (indorsements to a named payee only) *Edie v East India Co.* (1761) 2 Burr. 1216, and see s.34(2) below, para.5–027.

[20] See s.8(5) below para.2–068.

[21] *Edwards v Walters* [1896] 2 Ch.157.

If the word or words "order" or "or order" on a printed form of bill or cheque are struck through, so that the instrument reads simply "Pay C", it might be thought that the drawer thereby indicated an intention that the instrument should not be transferable. But since the instrument is then expressed to be payable to a particular person, the effect of subsection (4) appears to be that the bill remains payable to order.[22] Upon the deletion of the word "order", "the effect of the 4th subsection of the 8th section of the Bills of Exchange Act is immediately to put the word in again".[23]

A cheque crossed "account payee" is not payable to order since it is not transferable.[24]

2–068 **Subsection (5): to or to order.** This subsection was declaratory of the common law.[25] It provides that a bill payable "to the order of C" is in legal effect payable "to C or order", *i.e.* that C can make an effective demand for payment without giving a responsible indorsement. It rests with the payee whether he will himself present, or negotiate, the bill.[26]

ILLUSTRATIONS

2–069 1. The Irish Casing Co. Ltd draws upon the defendants a bill of exchange as follows: "Three months after date pay against this first of exchange to the order of the Irish Casing Co. Ltd *only* the sum of £500 effective value received." The bill is further crossed "Not negotiable". It is accepted by the defendants, indorsed by the drawers and transferred to the claimant for value. An action by the claimant (as holder and indorsee) fails. The crossing "not negotiable" and the word "only" in the body of the bill sufficiently prohibited transfer so as to render the bill non-negotiable.[27]

2. A promissory note, dated August 1, 1865, reads: "I, W.W., of &c., promise to pay to the Rev. A. Edwards on demand the sum of £200, with

---

[22] *H. Meyer & Co. Ltd v Jules Decroix, Verley et Cie.* (1890) 25 Q.B.D. 343, affirmed [1891] A.C. 520 (s.19, Illustration 1).
[23] (1890 25 Q.B.D. 343 at 347; see also at 350.
[24] See s.81A(1) (inserted by s.1 of the Cheques Act 1992); above, para.2–063 and below, para.14–037.
[25] *Smith v M'Clure* (1804) 5 East. 476.
[26] But see the differing views expressed in *McDonald (Gerald) & Co. v Nash & Co.* [1924] A.C. 625, 633, 634, 652, as to whether an instrument drawn payable to the drawer is a complete bill before it has been indorsed by the drawer.
[27] *Hibernian Bank Ltd v Gysin and Hanson* [1939] 1 K.B. 483.

interest for the same at the rate of 4 per cent per annum." Before the 1882 Act, the note was not negotiable, being payable to a person designated without the addition of "or order" or "bearer". But section 8(4) of the Act applies to it and makes it negotiable after the Act comes into force.[28]

3. A draws a cheque "Pay B £100". The cheque is drawn on a pre-printed cheque form which is crossed and bears the words "Account payee" across its face. B has no bank account and persuades C, a shop-keeper, to give him cash for the cheque. He indorses the cheque and delivers it to C. The cheque is dishonoured. By section 81A(1) of the 1882 Act (inserted by section 1 of the Cheques Act 1992) the cheque is not transferable.[29] C cannot sue A on the cheque.

## Sum payable

9.—(1) The sum payable by a bill is a sum certain within the mean-    2–070
ing of this Act, although it is required to be paid—
   (a) With interest.
   (b) By stated instalments.
   (c) By stated instalments, with a provision that upon default in payment of any instalment the whole shall become due.
   (d) According to an indicated rate of exchange or according to a rate of exchange to be ascertained as directed by the bill.

(2) Where the sum payable is expressed in words and also in figures, and there is a discrepancy between the two, the sum denoted by the words is the amount payable.

(3) Where a bill is expressed to be payable with interest, unless the instrument otherwise provides, interest runs from the date of the bill, and if the bill is undated from the issue thereof.

---

[28] *Edwards v Walters* [1896] 2 Ch. 157.
[29] See below, para.14–037. Contrast (before the 1992 Act) *National Bank Ltd v Silke* [1891] 1 Q.B. 435.

| Definitions | Comparison |
|---|---|
| "bill": s.2. | UCC: §§3–104(a), 3–108(b), 3–112, |
| "issue": s.2 | 3–114. |
| | ULB: arts 5, 6. |
| | ULC: art.7. |
| | UNB: arts 7, 8 |

COMMENT

2–071     **Subsection (1)(a): interest on bill.** The sum payable by a bill is a sum certain although it is required to be paid with interest. "Interest proper",[30] that is to say, interest reserved by the instrument must be distinguished from interest by way of damages for dishonour, as to which see section 57. Interest reserved by the instrument is recoverable as part of the amount of the instrument.[31]

Bills of exchange seldom carry stipulations as to interest, but promissory notes often do. The rate of interest is usually specified, *e.g.* "12 per cent per annum". It may be that, in England, a stipulation for payment of a specified sum "with interest" (but not stating a rate) would be a valid bill or note[32] on the ground that 5 per cent is the understood rate.[33] But in a Scottish case[34] a note to pay a specified sum: "together with any interest that may accrue thereon" was held not to be promissory note within the Act as the sum was uncertain.

An instrument which permits a party to vary the specified rate would not, it is submitted, be a valid bill or note.[35] It is also doubtful whether an instrument which provides for interest to vary with a base rate, *e.g.* "2 per cent above the base lending rate of     Bank plc", or with an inter-bank

---

[30] See s.57(3). It may be presumed that the instrument can expressly provide for the same rate of interest to be paid after default as is stipulated to be paid as "interest proper" before default, but such a stipulation would not be part of the bill or note.

[31] See below, para.7–047 (s.57); *Watkins v Morgan* (1834) 6 C. & P 661; *Hudson v Fossett* (1844) 13 L.J.C.P 141. See also ICC Uniform Rules for Collections (1995), Brochure No.522, art.20.

[32] *Clayton v Gosling* (1826) 5 B. & C. 360 ("with lawful interest"); *Warrington v Early* (1853) 2 E. & B. 763 (with lawful interest); *Roffey v Greenwell* (1839) 10 A. & E. 222 ("with legal interest").

[33] *Re Commercial Bank of South Australia* (1887) 36 Ch.D. 522, 529. See also UCC, § 3–112(b) (judgment rate).

[34] *Lamberton v Aiken* (1899) 1 Ct. of Sess.Cas. 189. See also *Macleod Savings & Credit Union Ltd v Perrett* (1981) 118 D.L.R. (3d) 193.

[35] *Bank of Montreal v Dezcam Industries Ltd* (1983) 147 D.L.R. (3d) 359 (interest at a rate from time to time applied to advances to "most credit-worthy" customers invalidates instrument).

rate, would be valid.[36] The sum to be paid would not be ascertainable from the instrument itself, but only by reference to external facts which would have to be adduced in evidence.[37] The Review Committee on Banking Law and Practice questioned whether floating rate instruments should be brought within the Act,[38] but the Government has concluded that there is no need at present to make provision for floating rate instruments.[39]

The period for which interest is payable must be certain. The date from which interest is to run may be specified in the instrument or determined in accordance with subsection (3). But an instrument which provides for interest to commence on "the date of delivery of the goods"[40] or to run from "the date of the advance"[41] (that date not appearing on the instrument) will be invalid as a bill or note. It has also been held in Australia[42] that a bill drawn payable at a fixed date which provided for interest at a specified rate "until arrival of payment in London" was not a bill.     **2–072**

Interest may be specified at a yearly rate, or at a rate for a period of less than a year, *e.g.* "2 per cent per month". Unless compounding is expressly provided for, a rate of interest will probably be construed as simple interest.[43] Trade custom might be admissible that interest is to be calculated on a 360-day basis.

An unauthorised insertion of a rate of interest, or the alteration of the specified rate, is a material alteration.[44]

**Subsection 1(b) and (c): instalments.** The sum will also be a sum certain if it is payable by stated instalments.[45] Both the amounts and times for the payment of the instalments must be stated,[46] but presumably a stipulation for payment of a total specified sum by (say) "12 equal instalments" on specified dates would suffice. A provision that upon     **2–073**

[36] See *Bank of Montreal v A. & M. Investments Ltd* (1982) 136 D.L.R. (3d) 181 (interest at $1\frac{3}{4}$ per cent above bank's base rate invalidates instrument). But see *Royal Bank of Canada v Reed and Wakefield Construction Ltd* [1983] 2 W.W.R. 419; *Royal Bank of Canada v Stonehocker* (1985) 61 B.C.L.R. 265. See also UCC, § 3–112(b) and UNB, art.8(6).

[37] See above, para.2–015 (s.3). But this principle is already breached in s.9(1)(d).

[38] (1989) Cm. 622, rec. 8(5).

[39] (1990) Cm. 1026, Annex 6, para.6.5.

[40] *Del Confectionery Ltd v Winnipeg Cabinet Factory Ltd* [1941] 4 D.L.R. 795, See also *Bank of British Columbia v Coopers & Lybrand Ltd* (1985) 15 D.L.R. (4th) 714 (date of construction of building).

[41] *Macleod Savings & Credit Union Ltd v Perrett* (1981) 118 D.L.R. (3d) 193.

[42] *Rosenhain v Commonwealth Bank of Australia* (1922) 31 C.L.R. 46.

[43] *Daniell v Sinclair* (1881) 6 App. Cas. 181.

[44] *Warrington v Early* (1853) 2 E.&B. 763; *Bellamy v Porter* (1913) 28 O.L.R. 572; *Allen v Gray* (1917) 38 D.L.R. 41. See s.64. But, in Canada, there is a division of authority as to whether a rate of interest may be supplied under s.20 where the instrument as signed provides for interest at a rate left blank: see *Crawford and Falconbridge* (8th ed.), p.1317.

[45] *Oridge v Sherborne* (1843) Car. & M. 16.

[46] *Moffat v Edwards* (1841) Car. & M. 16; *MacMillan v MacMillan* (1977) 76 D.L.R. (3d) 760.

default in payment the whole shall become due is also permitted.[47] An instrument is not invalid as a bill or note because it contains a provision that giving time shall not prejudice the rights of the holder.[48] But a provision in a note that instalments are to cease upon the death of the payee makes it invalid.[49]

2–074   **Subsection 1(d): rate of exchange.** The sum payable will further be certain if it is payable according to an indicated rate of exchange, or according to a rate of exchange to be ascertained as directed by the bill. Thus a bill may be drawn in United States dollars payable in London "at the current rate of exchange for sight drafts in New York".[50] The order to pay may also contain words such as "exchange per indorsement".[51] The unauthorised addition, either on the face of the bill or to the indorsements, of the rate of exchange according to which the bill is to be paid is a material alteration.[52]

Where a bill is denominated in a foreign currency, judgment may be given in that foreign currency.[53]

2–075   **Subsection (2): discrepancy in words and in figures.** The Act does not require, as a condition for the validity of a bill of exchange or promissory note, that the sum payable be stated in a particular way or that it be stated both in words and in figures.[54] But where the sum payable is expressed in words and also in figures, and there is a discrepancy between the two, the sum denoted by the words is the amount payable.[55] The discrepancy must be clear.[56]

Bills of exchange are usually drawn with the sum to be paid expressed in words in the body of the bill and with the same sum in figures superscribed (in the older cases referred to as "the marginal figures" or

---

[47] *Blake v Lawrence* (1802) 4 Esp. 147; *Carlon v Kenealy* (1843) 12 M. & W. 139; *Monetary Advance Co. v Cater* (1888) 20 Q.B.D. 785; *Kirkwood v Carroll* [1903] 1 K.B. 531 (s.83, Illustration 1). In *Canada Permanent Trust Co. v Kowal* (1981) 120 D.L.R. (3d) 691, such a provision for acceleration "at the option of the holder" was also permitted.

[48] *Yates v Evans* (1892) 61 L.J.Q.B. 446; *Kirkwood v Carroll* [1903] 1 K.B. 531.

[49] *Worley v Harrison* (1835) 3 A. & E. 669.

[50] See *Pollard v Herries* (1803) 3 B. & P. 335 (note).

[51] *Suse v Pompe* (1860) 8 C.B.N.S. 538; *Rouquette v Overmann* (1875) L.R.10 Q.B. 525. But not "plus all bank charges": *Standard Bank of Canada v Wildey* (1919) 19 S.R. (N.S.W.) 384, 388. cf. *Tropic Plastic and Packaging Industry v Standard Bank of South Africa Ltd* 1969 (4) S.A. 108.

[52] *Hirschfield v Smith* (1866) L.R. 1 C.P. 340 (Section 72, Illustration 16). See s.64.

[53] See below, para.7–046 (s.57). s.72(4) of the Act was repealed by s.4 of the Administration of Justice Act 1977.

[54] s.3(1).

[55] See also UCC, §3–114; UCP, art.6; ULC, art.9; UNB, art.8(1). For approval of this rule as applied to cheques, see (1989) Com. 622, rec. 7(9); (1990) Com. 1026, Annex 5, para.5.14.

[56] *Dependable Aluminium Windows and Doors C.C. v Antoniades* 1993 (2) S.A. 49.

"the marginal figure") at the head of the bill. If there is a discrepancy, subsection (2) establishes the primacy of the sum expressed in words. But it has been stated[57] that:

> "the marginal figure at the head of a bill, which has since become a matter of common usage, was probably added at a very early date, in order that the amount of the bill might strike the eye immediately, and was in fact a note, index, or summary of the bill which followed".

The marginal figure may be looked at to resolve an ambiguity in the amount expressed in words.[58] But, where the sum expressed in words is smaller than that of the marginal figure, evidence to show that the larger figure was intended to be the amount of the bill is inadmissible.[59] Further, it has been held[60] that, if a bill is accepted at a time when the marginal figure only is present on the bill and the amount to be expressed in words in the body of the bill has yet to be filled in, the bill is incomplete.[61] The person in possession of the bill has prima facie authority from the acceptor to fill in, in words, the amount of the marginal figure.[62] But if that person fills in, in words, a larger amount than that of the marginal figure and alters the marginal figure accordingly, or even if he does not alter the marginal figure,[63] and the bill is then negotiated to a holder in due course,[64] the bill is valid and effectual in the hands of such a holder for the larger amount.

Pre-printed cheque forms issued by banks contemplate that the order     **2–076**
to pay will be expressed both in words and in figures. If there is a discrepancy between the two, the practice is to return the cheque unpaid,[65] with the remark "words and figures differ". Unlike a bill of exchange, the amount expressed in figures is placed in the body of the cheque. It might therefore be supposed that, if the amount payable is expressed in figures only, the cheque is nevertheless a complete instrument, since the Act does not require the amount to be expressed both in

---

[57] *Garrard v Lewis* (1882) 10 Q.B.D. 30, 33.

[58] *R. v Elliott* (1777) 1 Leach C.C. 175 (Illustration 1); *Hutley v Marshall* (1882) 46 L.T. 186.

[59] *Saunderson v Piper* (1839) 5 Bing. N.C. 425, 561, (Illustration 2). *Sed quaere? cf. Irvani v G. & H. Montage GmbH* [1990] 1 W.L.R. 667 (foreign law).

[60] *Garrard v Lewis* (1882) 10 Q.B.D. 30 (Illustration 3). Contrast *Scholfield v Earl of Londesburgh* [1896] A.C. 514, where both words and figures were on the bill when accepted, but they were subsequently altered.

[61] See s.20. But this is surprising in view of the fact that the Act does not require the amount to be expressed in words.

[62] s.20(1) (2).

[63] *Garrard v Lewis* (1882) 10 Q.B.D. 30 at 34. But it is submitted that such a bill would be irregular; see below, paras 4–052—4–053.

[64] See s.20(2).

[65] *London Joint Stock Bank Ltd v Macmillan* [1918] A.C. 777, 832. But the banker might pay, or offer to pay, the smaller amount: *London Joint Stock Bank Ltd v Macmillan* [1918] AC 777, [1917] 2 K.B. 439, 448, CA.

words and in figures.[66] In *London Joint Stock Bank Ltd v Macmillan*,[67] Viscount Haldane[68] and Lord Parmoor[69] were agreed that, if the sum payable is stated in figures only, the statement in words being omitted from the space provided for it, the banker on whom the cheque is drawn would probably be justified in refusing to pay it, since he has a right to insist that the customer's mandate be given in proper form. But Viscount Haldane stated[70] that such an instrument would be a complete order for payment within the definition in section 3 of the Act, whereas Lord Parmoor considered[71] that it was "wanting in a material particular" and would not be a complete cheque. This difference of opinion may be of relevance in circumstances where the amount of a cheque, at the time when it is drawn, is expressed in figures only and the drawer delivers the cheque to another who inserts a larger amount in words and alters the figures accordingly. The question will arise, if the cheque is negotiated to a holder in due course,[72] whether the holder can rely on section 20 of the Act (inchoate instruments) to claim from the drawer the larger amount. However, it is clear that, in those circumstances, the drawee banker who pays the cheque can debit the drawer's account with the larger amount, since the relationship between the bank and its customer, the drawer, is such as to impose upon the drawer a duty to the bank to take reasonable care to ensure that, when the document leaves his possession, it is fully and properly filled up.[73]

Promissory notes are often made in the same form as bills of exchange, that is to say, with the sum payable expressed in words in the body of the instrument and the same sum expressed in marginal figures at the head of the note. But notes are also frequently made with the sum payable expressed both in words and in figures in the body of the note.

It is sufficient if the sum payable is expressed in an instrument in words which, though inaccurate, are intelligible, for example, "Pay X twenty five-50" with the word "pounds" omitted.[74]

An instrument where there is a discrepancy between the currency of the words and figures may be irregular.[75]

---

[66] The practice of banks is to return cheques where the amount is expressed in figures only.

[67] [1918] A.C. 777 (s.64, Illustration 5).

[68] [1918] A.C. 777 at 816.

[69] [1918] A.C. 777 at 831.

[70] [1918] A.C. 777 at 816.

[71] [1918] A.C. 777 at 831–832. See also Lord Finlay L.C. at 812.

[72] s.20(2).

[73] *London Joint Stock Bank Ltd v Macmillan* [1918] A.C. 77.

[74] *Phipps v Tanner* (1833) 5 C. & P. 488.

[75] *Banco di Roma SpA v Orru* [1973] 2 Lloyd's Rep. 505 (s.29, Illustration 4).

**Subsection (3): calculation of interest.** This subsection is declaratory    2–077
of the common law.[76] "Issue" is defined in section 2.

1. E is charged with and convicted of forging a bank note purporting to    2–078
have been made by T, on behalf of the Bank of England, for the payment
of the sum of £50 to C or bearer on demand. The note reads "I promise to
pay to C, or bearer, on demand, the sum of fifty". In the margin the sum
"£.Fifty" appears. E is rightly convicted. The sum in the margin of the
note removes every doubt and shows that the "fifty" in the body of the
note was intended for £50.[77]

2. M & Co. draw a bill on the defendants payable to their own order.
The sum expressed in words in the body of the bill is £200 but the sum
expressed as a marginal figure at the head of the bill is £245. The defendants accept the bill as so drawn. The claimants discount the bill for M &
Co., paying them £245, less the discount for the same. The claimants as
indorsees of the bill can recover from the defendants £200 only. The
words, and not the figures, determine the sum to be paid, and extrinsic
evidence is not admissible to show that it was intended as a bill for
£245.[78]

3. B draws a bill on the defendant payable to himself. The sum to be
mentioned in words in the body of the bill is left blank but the sum of £14
0s. 6d. is expressed as a marginal figure at the head of the bill. The
defendant accepts the bill in that condition, intending to accept for the
sum so stated. B subsequently fills in words in the body the sum of £164
0s. 6d. and fraudulently alters the marginal figure to that sum. He indorses the bill to the claimant, who takes it as a bona fide holder for value for
the larger amount. The defendant is liable to the claimant for the larger
amount. The marginal figure is not an essential part of the bill. An
acceptor in blank holds out the person to whom he entrusts the bill to
have authority to fill in the bill for any amount the stamp will cover, and
no alteration (even if fraudulent or unauthorised) of the marginal figure
can vitiate the bill as a bill for the full amount inserted in the body when

---

[76] *Kennerley v Nash* (1816) 1 Stark. 452; *Hopper v Richmond* (1816) 1 Stark. 507, 508; *Clayton v Gosling* (1826) 5 B. & C. 360; *Richards v Richards* (1831) 2 B. & Ad. 447; *Roffey v Greenwell* (1839) 10 A. & E. 222. cf. *Doman v Dibben* (1826) Ry. & M. 381.
[77] *R. v Elliott* (1777) 1 Leach C.C. 175.
[78] *Saunderson v Piper* (1839) 5 Bing. N.C. 425, 561.

it reaches the hands of a bona fide holder for value without notice of the alteration.[79]

### Bill payable on demand

2–079    10. (1) A bill is payable on demand—
        (a) Which is expressed to be payable on demand, or at sight, or on presentation; or
        (b) In which no time for payment is expressed.
    (2) Where a bill is accepted or indorsed when it is overdue, it shall, as regards the acceptor who so accepts, or any indorser who so indorses it, be deemed a bill payable on demand.

| Definitions | Comparison |
|---|---|
| "acceptance": s.2. | UCC: §3–108. |
| "bill": s.2. | ULB: arts 2, 33, 34. |
| "indorsement": s.2. | ULC: art.28. |
| | UNB: art.9. |

### COMMENT

2–080    **Demand instruments.** This section explains the meaning of the words "on demand" in section 3(1) of the Act (definition of a bill of exchange). A promissory note may also be made payable on demand.[80]

A cheque is a bill of exchange drawn on a banker payable on demand.[81]

2–081    **Subsection (1): demand bills.** An instrument will not be a bill payable on demand by virtue of paragraph (b) of this subsection ("in which no time for payment is expressed") if a time for payment *is* expressed but that time is not a fixed or determinable future time within sections 3(1) and 11 of the Act, nor (*semble*) will it be such a bill if the wording intended to express a time for payment is defective or unintelligible.[82]

As to presentment for payment of bills payable on demand, see section 45(2) of the Act[83]; as to when a bill payable on demand is overdue, see section 36(3).

---

[79] *Garrard v Lewis* (1882) 10 Q.B.D. 30.
[80] s.83(1).
[81] s.73.
[82] This question was left open in *Korea Exchange Bank v Debenhams (Central Buying) Ltd* [1979] 1 Lloyd's Rep. 548, 550.
[83] See also s.86(1) (note payable on demand).

**Subsection (2): overdue bills.** As to the acceptance of an overdue bill,     2–082
see section 18(2) of the Act. As to the indorsement of an overdue bill, see
section 36.[84]

### Bill payable at a future time

**11. A bill is payable at a determinable future time within the mean-     2–083
ing of this Act which is expressed to be payable—**
    **(1) At a fixed period after date or sight.**
    **(2) On or at a fixed period after the occurrence of a specified event
       which is certain to happen, though the time of happening may
       be uncertain.**
**An instrument expressed to be payable on a contingency is not a
bill, and the happening of the event does not cure the defect.**

| Definition | Comparison |
|------------|------------|
| "bill": s.2. | UCC: § 3–108. |
| | ULB: art.33. |
| | ULC: art.28. |
| | UNB: art.9. |

### COMMENT

**Future time.** Section 3(1) of the Act stipulates that the order contained     2–084
in a bill of exchange must require the drawee to pay a sum of money on
demand or at a fixed or determinable future time, and that the order must
be unconditional. The present section amplifies the meaning of "at a
determinable future time" and also deals with the effect of an instrument
expressed to be payable on a contingency. Section 83(1) of the Act likewise
requires that the promise contained in a promissory note must engage the
maker to pay a sum of money on demand or at a fixed or determinable
future time, and that the promise must be unconditional. In cases both
ancient and modern the principles set out in these provisions have sometimes been applied very strictly but at other times more loosely. The
current tendency of the courts is to uphold, where possible, the negotiability of the instrument as a bill or note even though, on one construction,

---

[84] See also s.86(3) (negotiation of a note payable on demand).

it is open to question. In *Hong Kong and Shanghai Banking Corporation Ltd. v G.D. Trade Co. Ltd.*[85] the Court of Appeal observed "[a bill] is a document in use in hundreds of commercial transactions and, in the case of an instrument which has been drawn as a bill with the plain intention that it should take effect as such, the court should lean in favour of a construction which upholds its validity as a bill where that is reasonably possible".

**2–085**　　　**Date.** A bill may be payable at a fixed future time, that is to say, on a specified date.[86] But in *Williamson v Rider*[87] the Court of Appeal held, by a majority,[88] that an instrument payable "on or before" a specified date was invalid as a note since it was not payable at a fixed future time. The option reserved to the maker to pay at an earlier date than the specified date created an uncertainty and contingency in the time of payment. This decision was followed by the same Court in the later case of *Claydon v Bradley*,[89] where an instrument payable "by July 1, 1983" was held not to be a note. It is, however, submitted that the dissenting judgment of Ormerod L.J. in *Williamson v Rider* is to be preferred[90]: he considered that the terms of the note created no uncertainty, as the maker would not be under any obligation to pay the note until the specified date arrived. But these decisions can only be overruled by the House of Lords. It must follow, too, that an instrument which provides alternative dates of payment, for example, a promissory note in which payment is promised on a specified date, but with an option given to the maker to pay at a later date (usually on more onerous terms), is similarly invalid.[91]

A bill may be payable at a fixed period after date, for example "30 days after date" or "three months after date".[92] But an instrument payable "after date" or "on or after" a particular date or "*after* 12 months after date" would not be a valid bill.[93]

---

[85] [1998] C.L.C. 238. See also *Novaknit Hellas SA v Kumar Brothers International Ltd* [1998] Lloyd's Rep. Bank. 287.

[86] See also ss.13, 14.

[87] [1963] 1 Q.B. 89 (Illustration 1). See also *Salot v Naidoo* 1981 (3) S.A. 959; *Standard Credit Corp. v Kleyn* 1988 (4) S.A. 441.

[88] Willmer and Danckwerts L.JJ., relying in part on *Alexander v Thomas* (1851) 16 Q.B. 333 (Illustration 3) and on *Crouch v Credit Foncier of England Ltd* (1873) L.R. 8 Q.B. 374.

[89] [1987] 1 W.L.R. 521 (s.83, Illustration 5).

[90] At 101. See also *John Burrows Ltd v Subsurface Surveys Ltd* (1968) 68 D.L.R. (2d) 354; *Creative Press Ltd v Harman* [1973] I.R. 313; *Kiat v Ng* (1992) 128 N.B.R. (2d) 374; UCC § 3–108(b)(c); Hudson (1962) 25 M.L.R. 593.

[91] Contrast (in Canada) *Hogg v Marsh* (1849) 5 U.C.Q.B. 319, approved in *John Burrows Ltd v Subsurface Surveys Ltd* (1968) 68 D.L.R. (2d) 354.

[92] Where such a bill is issued undated, see ss.12, 20. See also s.14(2) as to fixing the due date of such bills in ordinary cases.

[93] *Gaudet v Comeau* [1936] 1 D.L.R. 754.

**Sight.** A bill may be payable at a fixed period after sight, for example,    **2–086**
"60 days after sight".[94] "Sight" means presentment for acceptance,
whether the bill is actually accepted or not.[95] Where a bill is payable after
sight, presentment for acceptance is necessary in order to fix the maturity
of the instrument.[96] Again, however, a bill payable simply "after sight" or
"*after* 60 days after sight" would be invalid. But a bill payable "at sight"
is a valid bill as it is payable on demand.[97] It would appear that a bill
cannot be drawn payable at a fixed period after *acceptance*, since it is not
payable at a fixed period after sight and it is uncertain whether the
drawee will accept or refuse to accept the bill.[98] Yet instruments which
were construed to read "90 days after acceptance/sight" were upheld as
valid, being payable 90 days after their presentment for acceptance
regardless of whether or not the drawee accepted them.[99] An instrument
payable "90 days after sight or when realised" (the words "or when
realised" meaning when the drawee had the money to pay) has been held
not to be a bill of exchange.[1]

**Event.** A bill may be payable on or at a fixed period after the occur-     **2–087**
rence of a specified event which is certain to happen, though the time of
happening may be uncertain. Bills which are payable on the death of a
person or (say) 12 months after the death of a person, are obvious
examples where the bill will be valid.[2] In some older cases, decided before
the Act, the requirement that the event must be certain to happen was
only loosely applied. Thus a note payable "On 12th June, 1750, when G
should come of age"[3] and a note payable two months after a Royal Navy
ship was paid off[4] were held to be valid (even though G might die before
attaining majority or the ship never be paid off). Such decisions would
not be followed at the present day. It was also held that a note payable
"on having 12 months' notice" was not payable on a contingency and was

---

[94] Where the acceptance of such a bill is undated, see s.12. See also s.14(2) and (3) as to fixing
the due date of such bills in ordinary cases, s.18(3) as to acceptance after a prior refusal
to accept, and s.65(5) on the maturity of such a bill accepted for honour.

[95] *Korea Exchange Bank v Debenhams (Central Buying) Ltd* [1979] 1 Lloyd's Rep. 548, 553. *cf.*
*Campbell v French* (1795) 6 T.R. 200, 212.

[96] s.39(1).

[97] s.10(1)(a).

[98] *Korea Exchange Bank v Debenhams (Central Buying) Ltd* [1979] 1 Lloyd's Rep. 548 (Illustration 2). *Cooperative Exportvereniging "Vecofa" U.A. v Maha Syndicate* [1970] 1 M.L.J. 187
(Singapore) ("at 60 days sight D/A on arrival of steamer").

[99] *Hong Kong and Shanghai Banking Corpn. Ltd v G.D. Trade Co. Ltd* [1998] C.L.C. 238 (Illustration 3).

[1] *Alexander v Thomas* (1851) 16 Q.B. 333.

[2] *Colehan v Cooke* (1742) Willes 393 (Illustration 5). See also *Roffey v Greenwell* (1839) 10 A. &
E. 222.

[3] *Goss v Nelson* (1757) 1 Burr. 226.

[4] *Andrews v Franklyn* (1717) 1 Str. 24.

payable at a time which the court had to suppose would arrive[5] and a note payable "two months after demand in writing" was assumed to be valid.[6] But it is doubtful whether such instruments satisfy the requirements of section 11.

2–088    **Contingency.** A bill or note cannot be expressed[7] to be payable on a contingency,[8] and the happening of the event does not cure the defect. "Certainty", said Ashurst J.,[9] "is a great object in negotiable instruments; and unless they carry their own validity on the face of them, they are not negotiable: on that ground bills of exchange, which are only payable on a contingency, are not negotiable, because it does not appear on the face of them whether or not they will ever be paid." Thus it has been held that a note payable "within two months after I should be lawfully married to X" was invalid[10] and that an instrument payable "at such period of time that my circumstances will admit without detriment to myself or family" was not a promissory note.[11] Likewise, an instrument drawn payable at 30 days after the arrival of a ship at Calcutta was not a bill of exchange but "mere waste paper".[12] On the other hand, it has been more recently held that an instrument drawn payable "60 days after first presentation of documents" was valid as a bill since the phrase "presentation of documents" was no less certain than "sight" (it being common ground that "documents" included the bill).[13] More contentiously in the same case it was held that an instrument expressed to be payable "on 60 days from shipment" was similarly valid on the ground that "shipment is certain to have taken place prior to presentation of documents including the bill and, in that event, there would ... be a date certain for the purpose of calculating maturity of the bill".[14]

The fact that a place of payment is specified in a bill does not make it contingent.[15]

---

[5] *Clayton v Gosling* (1826) 5 B. & C. 360 (Illustration 6).

[6] *Prince v Taylor* (1860) 5 H. & N. 540 (the point was not argued) (s.26, Illustration 4).

[7] cf. *Eastern Elevator Services Ltd v Wolfe* (1981) 119 D.L.R. (3d) 643 (agreement that cheque to be cashed only upon a contingency rendered it not a bill of exchange): but this case is clearly wrong on this point.

[8] Nor can liability be defeasible upon a contingency: *Worley v Harrison* (1835) 3 A. & E. 669.

[9] *Carlos v Fancourt* (1794) 5 T.R. 482, 486.

[10] cf. *Pearson v Garrett* (1689) 4 Mod. 242.

[11] *Ex p. Tootell* (1798) 4 Ves. Jun. 372.

[12] *Palmer v Pratt* (1824) 2 Bing. 185. See also *MacMillan v MacMillan* (1977) 76 D.L.R. (3d) 760 ("starting with payment from 1969 crop").

[13] *Novaknit Hellas SA v Kumar Brothers International Ltd* [1998] Lloyd's Rep. Bank. 287 (Illustration 4).

[14] [1998] Lloyd's Rep. Bank. 287 at 291.

[15] s.45(4). See also s.87(1) (note).

**Cure by acceptance.** It has not yet been decided whether an instrument which is defective as a bill when originally drawn in respect of the time of payment can be "cured" on acceptance, where the form of acceptance is certain and unconditional. In *Hong Kong & Shanghai Banking Corporation Ltd. v G.D. Trade Co. Ltd.*[16] and in *Novaknit Hellas SA v Kumar Brothers International Ltd.*[17] the view was expressed that a defect which affected the bill as originally drawn could thus be cured by acceptance, although in neither case was the Court of Appeal prepared to decide the issue. It is, however, submitted that an acceptance which is certain and unconditional in its terms cannot retrospectively convert an instrument which is invalid as a bill under section 11 into a valid bill of exchange.[18] But the acceptor may be liable as the maker of a promissory note, since the instrument then fulfils the requirements of section 83(1) of the Act.[19]

2–089

ILLUSTRATIONS

1. R makes an instrument which reads "In consideration of the loan of £100 from G of 26 Ashley Drive, Leighton-on-Sea, Essex, I, R, of 48, Battledean Road, Highbury, London, N5, agree to repay to G the sum of £100 on or before December 31, 1956". The instrument is not a promissory note. The option reserved by the instrument to pay at an earlier date than the fixed date creates an uncertainty and a contingency in the time for payment.[20]

2–089A

2. An instrument on a bill of exchange form reads "BILL OF EXCHANGE Date SEPT. 28, 1974 Seoul Korea FOR U.S. $298,048.00 At 90 days D/A SIGHT OF THIS FIRST BILL OF EXCHANGE ... PAY TO Korea Exchange Bank OR ORDER. ... ". The word "SIGHT", which is part of the original printed form of the instrument coming between the typed letters "D/A" and the printed word "OF" is deleted by overtyping. The instrument is not a bill of exchange, since it is not expressed to be payable at a fixed or determinable future time. For a bill to be expressed to be payable at a fixed period after sight, the word "sight" must be used. Even if the instrument can be construed as meaning "at 90 days after acceptance" it is invalid, because it is neither expressed to be payable at a fixed period after sight (though sight may include acceptance) nor is it

---

[16] [1998] C.L.C. 238 (Illustration 3).
[17] [1998] Lloyd's Rep. Bank. 287 (Illustration 4).
[18] As is the case under ss.12 and 20 of the Act.
[19] See below, para.15–001.
[20] *Williamson v Rider* [1963] 1 Q.B. 89.

expressed to be payable at a fixed period after the occurrence of a specified event which is certain to happen, as the drawee may accept or refuse to accept the bill.[21]

3. Drawees, using blank forms of bills of exchange supplied by a bank, insert the words "90 days after acceptance" in the blank space left between the printed words "At" and "sight". An unsuitably large type face is employed with the result that the letters sometimes overlap. The bills are not payable on a contingency. They are construed as expressed to be payable "90 days after acceptance/sight". As "sight" refers to present-ment for acceptance, the bills are payable 90 days after presentment for acceptance, regardless of whether or not the drawee accepts them. *Quaere* whether acceptance of a bill in terms requiring payment on a particular date cures any defect in the bill as originally drawn.[22]

4. A number of bills are drawn on the defendant company. Some of these are expressed to be payable "on 60 days from first presentation of documents" and a further bill is expressed to be payable "on 60 days from shipment". They are accepted by two officers of the company on its behalf in the form "Accepted payable at United Bank Limited Manchester at/after sight 60 days from today" and the acceptances are signed and dated. The required certainty as to the date of maturity in the event of non-acceptance is present by use of the phrase "presentation of docu-ments" which it is common ground includes the bill. As to the phrase "on 60 days from shipment", shipment is certain to have taken place prior to presentation of the documents including the bill, and in that event there would be a date certain for calculating maturity of the bill, *i.e.* 60 days from the date of shipment. Further any defect in the form of the bills is arguably cured by the terms of their acceptance and, in any event, even if defective, the instruments could take effect as promissory notes.[23]

**2–090**      5. The defendant makes a note whereby he promises to pay to D or order 150 guineas 10 days after the death of his father for value received. The note is duly indorsed by D to the claimant. The claimant, as indorsee, is entitled, after the death of the defendant's father, to recover from the defendant the amount of the note. The note does not depend on a contingency, but there is a certain promise to pay at the time of the giving of the note, and the money will certainly become payable one time or other, though it is uncertain when that time will come. It is a valid promissory note.[24]

---

[21] *Korea Exchange Bank v Debenhams (Central Buying) Ltd* [1979] 1 Lloyd's Rep. 548.
[22] *Hong Kong & Shanghai Banking Corp. Ltd v G.D. Trade Co. Ltd* [1998] C.L.C. 238.
[23] *Novaknit Hellas SA v Kumar Brothers International Ltd.* [1998] Lloyd's Rep. Bank. 287.
[24] *Colehan v Cooke* (1742) Willes 393.

6. Before the Act, the defendant and B jointly make a note, reading "On having 12 months' notice we jointly and severally promise to pay [the claimant] or order, £200 for value received, with lawful interest". The defendant subsequently becomes bankrupt and a commission is issued against him. The next day following the issue of the commission the claimant gives notice to the defendant to pay in 12 months the £200 and interest secured by the note. The debt is proveable in the bankruptcy. Interest runs from the date of the note. There is no contingency as to the debt, for the words "value received" acknowledge the debt to be due. Nor is the time of payment contingent, as the note is payable at a time which it must be supposed will arrive.[25]

## Omission of date in bill payable after date

**12. Where a bill expressed to be payable at a fixed period after date is issued undated, or where the acceptance of a bill payable at a fixed period after sight is undated, any holder may insert therein the true date of issue or acceptance, and the bill shall be payable accordingly.**

**Provided that (1) where the holder in good faith and by mistake inserts a wrong date, and (2) in every case where a wrong date is inserted, if the bill subsequently comes into the hands of a holder in due course the bill shall not be avoided thereby, but shall operate and be payable as if the date so inserted had been the true date.**

2–091

| Definitions | Comparison |
|---|---|
| "bill": s.2. | UCC: §§ 3–113, 3–115, 3–407, 3–409(c). |
| "good faith": s.2. | ULB: arts 1, 10. |
| "holder": s.2. | ULC: arts 1, 13. |
| "holder in due course": s.29. | UNB: art.12. |
| "issue": s.2. | |

### Comment

**Insertion of date by holder.** A bill is not invalid by reason that it is not dated.[26] But where a bill is expressed to be payable at a fixed period after date, a date will be required to determine the maturity of the bill.[27] If such

2–092

[25] *Clayton v Gosling* (1826) 5 B. & C. 360. *Sed quaere?*
[26] s.3(3).
[27] s.14(2).

a bill is issued undated, this section permits any holder to insert in the bill the true date of issue, and the bill is then payable accordingly.

The acceptance of a bill need not be dated.[28] But where a bill is payable at a fixed period after sight and is accepted, then, for the purpose of determining the day on which it falls due, time begins to run from the date of the acceptance.[29] If the acceptance of such a bill is undated, this section permits any holder to insert in the bill the true date of acceptance, and the bill is then payable accordingly.

The section is, however, of relatively narrow application. First, it only applies where the bill is payable at a fixed period after date or sight. It does not apply if the bill is payable at a fixed date or on demand. Thus a holder cannot, for example, by virtue of this section insert the date of acceptance in a bill payable on a fixed date, or the date of issue in a cheque or in a bill payable on demand. Secondly, the only dates which the section allows to be inserted are the true dates of issue or acceptance, as the case may be.[30] Thirdly, the section permits only the holder (as defined by section 2), and no other person, to insert the relevant date. Fourthly, the section only applies if the relevant date is omitted. It does not apply if the relevant date is on the bill, and that date is altered.[31] But see section 20 of the Act for the more general rule as to the filling up of material omissions in a bill.

**2–093** The proviso[32] to the section is inelegantly phrased. Since the proviso derogates from the main provision of the section, the words "a wrong date" must be taken to refer to a wrong date for the issue or acceptance of the bill (as the case may be). Where the conditions referred to in the proviso are satisfied, the bill is not avoided by the insertion of the wrong date, but operates and is payable as if the date so inserted had been the true date.

The first part of the proviso covers the situation where the holder in good faith and by mistake inserts a wrong date. Its scope is more limited than might at first sight appear. In *Foster v Driscoll*[33] a bill of exchange, accepted but undated, was delivered to the drawer for completion. The bill was expressed to be payable to the drawer 90 days after date. It had previously been agreed between the drawer and two of the three acceptors of the bill that the bill should be payable 90 days after November 26. Contrary to that agreement, the drawer inserted December 3 as the date of the bill. The Court of Appeal held that section 12 did not apply as

---

[28] s.17(1).
[29] s.14(3).
[30] *Foster v Driscoll* [1929] 1 K.B. 470, 495 (Illustration).
[31] s.64.
[32] Chalmers commented that, before its enactment, the English law on the subject dealt with was very obscure (9th ed., p.38).
[33] [1929] 1 K.B. 470 (Illustration).

between the immediate parties to a bill where the date which had to be inserted was that fixed by some agreement, and the holder inserted an incorrect date (although in good faith and by mistake). The bill was avoided as against the acceptors,[34] even though the incorrect date was in their favour.

The second part of the proviso covers every case where a wrong date is inserted, *e.g.* if it is not inserted in good faith or by mistake or (*semble*) not by a holder, where the bill subsequently comes into the hands of a holder in due course (as defined by section 29 of the Act).


Illustration


On October 26, 1927, an agreement is entered into between (*inter alios*) L,    **2–094**
D and M for the sale of a quantity of whisky by L to D and M. The agreement provides for payment by a bill of exchange for £4,812 at 90 days' sight from November 26, 1927, accepted by A, D and M, the bill to be drawn and accepted on signing of the agreement and handed to L to hold as security. Pursuant to this provision, on the day of the agreement, a document, undated and on unstamped paper, is handed to L's agent. It purports to be a bill of exchange, payable to L 90 days after date, accepted by A, D and M, but having no name as drawer. L subsequently completes the bill by signing his name as drawer and at the same time alters the printed place of drawing (London) to the place where the bill is in fact drawn (Lausanne) so that it becomes a good foreign bill.[35] He also inserts as the date of the bill December 3, 1927, believing this to be the date required by the prior agreement. The bill is dishonoured by non-payment. The bill is avoided as against the acceptors because an incorrect and unauthorised date has been inserted.[36] The correct date should have been November 26, 1927. L cannot rely on section 12: that the wrong date was inserted by him in good faith and by mistake. The section refers only to a case where a bill is issued undated or where the acceptance is undated. The date which the section allows to be inserted is the date of issue or acceptance. L did not insert either of these dates or intend to insert them. He intended to insert what he thought was the date in the agreement under which the bill was given and did not insert the correct date. As between immediate parties, the section does not apply to a case where the date which has to be inserted in the bill is fixed by some other agreement.[37]

[34] s.64.
[35] s.20.
[36] s.64.
[37] *Foster v Driscoll* [1929] 1 K.B. 495, 524.

### Ante-dating and post-dating

2–095      13. (1) Where a bill or an acceptance or any indorsement on a bill is dated, the date shall, unless the contrary be proved, be deemed to be the true date of the drawing, acceptance, or indorsement, as the case may be.

            (2) A bill is not invalid by reason only that it is ante-dated or post-dated, or that it bears date on a Sunday.

| Definitions | Comparison |
|---|---|
| "acceptance": s.2. | UCC: § 3–113. |
| "bill": s.2. | ULC: art.28. |
| "indorsement": s.2. | |

2–096      **Subsection (1): presumption as to date being true date.** This subsection is declaratory of the common law.[38] The prima facie presumption arising from the date may be rebutted by proof that the date in question is not the true date.[39] It is arguable, however, that evidence to correct an incorrect date should be admissible only between immediate parties[40] or at least not so as to prejudice a holder in due course of the instrument.

2–097      **Subsection (2): ante-dating and post-dating.** The validity of a bill is not affected by reason only that it is ante-dated or post-dated. This subsection also resolves any doubt that previously existed at common law as to the validity of a bill issued on a Sunday.[41]

2–098      **Post-dated cheques.** Cheques are often issued post-dated, that is to say, bearing a date later than that on which they are in fact issued. The purpose of issuing a post-dated cheque is to prevent the drawee banker from paying the cheque to the payee or a holder before the date written on the cheque.[42] It is clear that the instrument is a cheque once the date written on it arrives.[43] But its status is unclear prior to that date. It is

---

[38] *Roberts v Bethell* (1852) 12 C.B. 778, 788.

[39] *Pasmore v North* (1811) 13 East 517; *Armfield v Allport* (1857) 27 L.J. Ex. 42. See also the cases cited in para.2–098, n.52, where evidence to prove that cheques were post-dated was adduced to support the argument that they were insufficiently stamped.

[40] For the distinction between immediate and remote parties, see below, para.4–005.

[41] *Begbie v Levi* (1830) 1 Cr. & J. 180.

[42] For the position of the banker who pays a post-dated cheque in advance of its due date, see below, para.13–009. For the position of a banker who collects such a cheque, see below, para.17–065. For the marking of post-dated cheques, see below, para.7–009.

[43] *Robinson v Benkel* (1913) 29 T.L.R. 475, 476. See also *Royal Bank of Scotland v Tottenham* [1894] 2 Q.B. 715 (Illustration).

arguable that, between the date of its issue and the date written on the cheque, it is not payable on demand[44] and so cannot be a cheque but an instrument of a different kind.[45] The view has been expressed[46] that: "so far as regards its practical effect, a post-dated cheque is the same thing as a bill of exchange at so many days' date as intervene between the day of delivering the cheque and the date marked upon the cheque". It has also been stated[47] that the effect of issuing a post-dated cheque is equivalent to giving a promissory note not payable until the date written on the cheque.

On the other hand, in *Hodgson & Lee Pty Ltd v Mardonius Pty Ltd*,[48] the Court of Appeal of New South Wales concluded that, since a post-dated cheque is not payable at a fixed or determinable future time,[49] it was payable on demand,[50] and was therefore a cheque.[51] It is submitted that this opinion is to be preferred.[52] In any event, there is no doubt that, first, in view of sub-section (2) of the present section, a post-dated cheque is not invalid.[53] Secondly, if payable to order or to bearer, it can be negotiated between the date of its issue and the date written upon it.[54] The mere fact that it is post-dated does not mean that it is delivered in escrow, subject to a condition suspending the operation of the instrument until the date written upon it arrives.[55] Thirdly, a person who takes a post-dated order or bearer cheque in good faith and for value may become a holder in due course: the instrument is not incomplete or irregular on the face of it because it is post-dated.[56]

---

[44] *cf.* s.73.
[45] *Brien v Dwyer* (1978) 141 C.L.R. 378, 394.
[46] *Foster v Mackreth* (1867) L.R. 2 Exch. 163, *per* Kelly C.B. at 167. See also Martin B., *ibid.* at 166; *Keyes v Royal Bank of Canada* [1947] 3 D.L.R. 161, 169; *Brien v Dwyer* (1978) 141 C.L.R. 378 at 408. *cf. Pollock v Bank of New Zealand* (1901) 20 N.Z.L.R. 174.
[47] *Ex p. Richdale* (1882) 19 Ch.D. 409, 417.
[48] (1986) 5 N.S.W.L.R. 496.
[49] ss.3, 11.
[50] ss.3, 10.
[51] See also *Shapiro v Greenstein* (1970) 10 D.L.R. (3d) 746.
[52] Contrast Brindle and Cox, *Law of Bank Payments* (3rd ed.), 7–036.
[53] *Royal Bank of Scotland v Tottenham* [1894] 2 Q.B. 715. The validity of a post-dated cheque was also challenged (unsuccessfully) on the grounds of non-compliance with the former requirements relating to stamping the instrument: *Gatty v Fry* (1877) 2 Ex.D. 265; *Hitchcock v Edwards* (1889) 60 L.T. 636; *Robinson v Benkel* (1913) 29 T.L.R. 475.
[54] *Hitchcock v Edwards* (1889) 60 L.T. 636; *Carpenter v Street* (1896) 6 T.L.R. 410; *Royal Bank of Scotland v Tottenham* [1894] 2 Q.B. 715; *Robinson v Benkel* (1913) 29 T.L.R. 475; *Guildford Trust Ltd v Goss* (1927) 43 T.L.R. 167 (s.20, Illustration 13).
[55] *Guildford Trust Ltd v Goss* (1927) 43 T.L.R. 167. See s.21(2)(b).
[56] *Hitchcock v Edwards* (1889) 60 L.T. 636; *Carpenter v Street* (1896) 6 T.L.R. 410; *Royal Bank of Scotland v Tottenham* [1894] 2 Q.B. 715; *Robinson v Benkel* (1913) 29 T.L.R. 475; *Guildford Trust Ltd v Goss* (1927) 43 T.L.R. 167; *Chartered Bank v Yeoh Bok Han* [1965] 2 M.L.J. 125; *Shapiro v Greenstein* (1969) 10 D.L.R. (3d) 746, 752; *Liang Tai Trading Co. Ltd v Toh Thye Guan* [1970] 2 M.L.J. 269. See s.29(1).

ILLUSTRATION

2–099   On August 3 the defendant draws a cheque for £250, dated August 10, payable to the order of H. H indorses the cheque and hands it to M. M, on August 8, pays the cheque into her account with the claimant bank, which undertakes to give her credit to the amount of the cheque. On August 10, the defendant orders the drawee bank to stop payment of the cheque. The claimant bank, as holder for value, can recover against the defendant on the cheque. The cheque is not invalid by reason only that it is post-dated.[57]

## Computation of time of payment

2–100   **14. Where a bill is not payable on demand the day on which it falls due is determined as follows:**

   **(1) The bill is due and payable in all cases on the last day of the time of payment as fixed by the bill or, if that is a non-business day, on the succeeding business day.**

   **(2) Where a bill is payable at a fixed period after date, after sight, or after the happening of a specified event, the time of payment is determined by excluding the day from which the time is to begin to run and by including the day of payment.**

   **(3) Where a bill is payable at a fixed period after sight, the time begins to run from the date of the acceptance if the bill be accepted, and from the date of noting or protest if the bill be noted or protested for non-acceptance, or for non-delivery.**

   **(4) The term "month" in a bill means calendar month.**

Amendment
S.14(1) was substituted by s.3(2) of the Banking and Financial Dealings Act 1971.

| Definitions | Comparison |
|---|---|
| "acceptance": s.2. | UCC: §§ 3–108, 3–502. |
| "bill": s.2. | ULB: arts 35–37. |
| "business day": s.92. | UNB: art.9. |
| "delivery": s.2. | |
| "non-business day": s.92. | |

---

[57] *Royal Bank of Scotland v Tottenham* [1894] 2 Q.B. 715.

COMMENT

**Date of maturity.** Subsection (1), as originally enacted, provided that three days, called days of grace, were, in every case where the bill itself did not otherwise provide, added to the time of payment as fixed by the bill, and the bill was due and payable on the last day of grace.[58] Days of grace likewise applied to promissory notes. But, by an amendment of the subsection effected by section 3(2) of the Banking and Financial Dealings Act 1971, days of grace were abolished.

**2–101**

"Business day" and "non-business day" are defined by section 92 of the Act.[59]

For the maturity of a bill payable after sight which is accepted for honour, see section 65(5) of the Act.

**Conflict of laws.** Where a bill is drawn in one country and is payable in another, the due date thereof is determined according to the law of the place where it is payable.[60] The law of that place may provide for days of grace.[61] Or a moratory law of that place may postpone the due date of payment.[62]

**2–102**

**Noting or protest.** Noting or protest (as referred to in subsection (3)) is dealt with in section 51 of the Act.[63]

**2–103**

ILLUSTRATIONS

1. A bill is drawn payable on January 1 (New Year's day). New Year's day is a non-business day.[64] The bill is due and payable on January 2, if that day is a business day.[65]

**2–104**

2. A note dated January 1 is made payable one month after date. It is due on February 1. A similar note, dated January 31, would be due on February 28 (or February 29, if a leap year).[66]

---

[58] The date of maturity was advanced (s.14(1)(a) or postponed (s.14(1)(b)) if the last day of grace fell on a non-business day.

[59] s.1(1) and Sch.1 of the Banking and Financial Dealings Act 1971 determined what are "Bank Holidays" in England and Wales, Scotland and Northern Ireland.

[60] s.72(5).

[61] See below, para.12–031 (s.72).

[62] *Rouquette v Overmann* (1875) L.R. 10 Q.B. 525; *Re Francke and Rasch* [1918] 1 Ch. 470 (s.72, Illustrations 18 and 19).

[63] See below, para.6–143. For protest for non-delivery, see s.51(8).

[64] By royal proclamation in England, and by Sch.1, para.2, of the Banking and Financial Dealings Act 1971 in Scotland.

[65] s.14(1).

[66] s.14(2)(4).

3. A bill is payable three months after sight. The acceptance bears date January 1. The bill is due on April 1.[67]

4. The holder of a foreign bill, payable 60 days after sight, makes an agreement that if it be dishonoured by non-acceptance, he will represent it for payment at maturity. Acceptance is refused. The time of payment must be calculated from the day the bill was protested, and not from the day of presentment to the drawee for acceptance.[68]

**Case of need**

2–105      **15. The drawer of a bill and any indorser may insert therein the name of a person to whom the holder may resort in case of need, that is to say, in case the bill is dishonoured by non-acceptance or non-payment. Such person is called the referee in case of need. It is in the option of the holder to resort to the referee in case of need or not as he may think fit.**

| Definitions | Comparison |
|---|---|
| "bill": s.2. | UCC: § 4–503 |
| "holder": s.2. | ULB: art.60. |
| "person": s.2. | |

COMMENT

2–106      **Referee in case of need.** An order addressed to two drawees in the alternative or to two or more drawees in succession is not a bill of exchange.[69] But the drawer of a bill and any indorser may insert in it the name of a person to whom the holder may resort in case the bill is dishonoured by non-acceptance or by non-payment. Such person is called "the referee in case of need", or sometimes "the drawee in case of need", or simply the "case of need". Although he is named in the bill, the referee in case of need must be distinguished from an accommodation party who has signed the bill as acceptor.[70] His position is also distinct from that of the drawee. Under section 67(1), before a bill is presented for payment to a referee in case of need, it must be protested[71] for non-payment. The Act

---

[67] ss.14(2)(3)(4).
[68] s.14(3). See *Campbell v French* (1795) 6 T.R. 200.
[69] s.6(2).
[70] s.28(1).
[71] Or noted: s.93.

does not specifically provide that the bill must be protested for non-acceptance, but presumably this would be required by section 65.

Resort to the referee in case of need is optional and not obligatory.[72] Reference in case of need is, in practice, obsolete.[73]

### Optional stipulations by drawer or indorser

**16. The drawer of a bill, and any indorser, may insert therein an express stipulation—**  2–107
**(1) Negativing or limiting his own liability to the holder:**
**(2) Waiving as regards himself some or all of the holder's duties.**

| Definitions | Comparison |
|---|---|
| "bill": s.2. | UCC:§§ 3–414(e), 3–415(b), |
| "holder": s.2. | 3–504. |
| | ULB: arts 9, 15. |
| | ULC: art.18. |
| | UNB: arts 38, 44, 56, 67. |

### COMMENT

**Subsection (1): special stipulations negativing or limiting liability.** This subsection permits the drawer of a bill and any indorser to negative or limit his own liability to the holder. It accords this privilege only to a drawer or an indorser, but it has been held that the privilege also extends to an anomalous indorser under section 56 of the Act.[74] An acceptor may accept conditionally,[75] but he could not "accept" a bill in terms which negatived[76] completely his liability as acceptor. The stipulation by the drawer or indorser must be express and it must be inserted in the instrument itself, otherwise it will be ineffective against a holder in due course.[77]   2–108

---

[72] This settled a moot point at common law; *Chalmers* (9th ed.), p.45.
[73] But see ICC Uniform Rules for Collections (1995), Brochure No.522, art.25 (Case of need (principal's representative)); see below, para.6–044 (s.45).
[74] *Wakefield v Alexander & Co.* (1901) 17 T.L.R. 217 (cheque).
[75] s.19.
[76] *cf. Decroix Verley et Cie v Meyer & Co. Ltd* (1890) 25 Q.B.D. 343, 347 (affirmed [1891] A.C. 520). See also below, para.2–126 (qualified acceptance).
[77] An agreement, off the instrument, to the same effect between an indorser and his immediate indorsee may, however, be a good defence to that indorser who is sued by that indorsee: *Pike v Street* (1828) M. & M. 226; *Castrique v Buttigieg* (1855) 10 Moore P.C. 94 (s.21, Illustration 35); see below, para.2–167.

The drawer may negative his own liability to the holder.[78] But, if he does so, it is questionable whether the instrument is in fact a bill of exchange until some other signature (*e.g.* an acceptance) is placed on the instrument, as there will be no party liable until that time. He may also limit his own liability to the holder, for example, by making that liability conditional. But the order to pay addressed to the drawee must be unconditional for the bill to be valid.[79]

More frequently it is the indorser who, in his indorsement, negatives or limits his liability to the holder. Such an indorsement is sometimes called a qualified indorsement. It must be distinguished from a conditional indorsement (section 33) and a restrictive indorsement (section 35). Examples of such an indorsement would be an indorsement with the words "without recourse" or "without recourse to me" or "*sans recours*" or "without recourse, unless presented within 30 days". The indorser thereby passes his interest to the indorsee, but negatives or limits his own liability as an indorser.[80] Any ambiguity in the indorsement would presumably be construed against the indorser (*contra proferentem*).

**2–109**    **Forfaiting.**[81] Forfaiting is a means by which an exporter may obtain medium-term finance for the export of his goods without recourse to himself in the event of default in payment by the importer. The exporter draws a time bill, or a series of time bills maturing at successive dates, upon the importer, the bills being drawn "without recourse" to himself. The bills are presented for acceptance to the importer and his acceptance obtained. As a normal rule, the arrangements between the exporter and the importer will require that the importer's liability on the bills be guaranteed by a bank in the importer's country, either by means of an "aval"[82] written on the bill or by a guarantee on a separate document executed by the bank. The bills are then indorsed "without recourse" by the exporter and discounted or sold by him in the *à forfait* market.

Alternatively, and perhaps more frequently,[83] the instruments employed will be promissory notes made by the importer, which are likewise guaranteed by a bank, indorsed "without recourse" by the exporter and discounted or sold by him. At maturity, the then holder of the instrument will present it for payment to the importer. If the instrument is dishonoured by non-payment, the holder will look to the guarantor bank for payment (which, in turn, will seek reimbursement from the

---

[78] Release by the drawer from his guarantee of payment is not permitted by ULB, art.9. Contrast UNB, art.38(2) and UCC, § 3–414(e) (but these provisions do not apply to cheques).

[79] s.3(1).

[80] *cf. Castrique v Buttigieg* (1855) 10 Moore P.C. 94 at 110–112.

[81] See Guild and Harris, *Forfaiting* (Universe Books, New York).

[82] See below, para.7–039 (s.56).

[83] Possibly as a result of ULB, art.9; above, para.2–108, n.78.

importer, if possible). The exporter thus obtains immediately the cash value of the instrument, less a fee for the facility and a discount charge at a fixed rate for the period of the credit, but without any recourse to himself in the event of default. The credit risk, and the foreign exchange, economic and political risks, are borne by the forfaiter, who also carries the responsibility of presenting the instrument for payment and obtaining payment from the obligors.

**Warranties on transfer.** In a forfaiting transaction, the exporter will **2–110** normally sell or discount the instrument to a bank ("the introducing bank"), which in turn will sell it on into the *à forfait* market. Since each transfer of the instrument is effected "without recourse", the ultimate holder will have no right of recourse against the drawer and prior indorsers if payment cannot be obtained. The question, however, arises whether, on transfer, warranties might be held to be impliedly given by each transferor to his immediate transferee similar to those given by a transferor by delivery under section 58(3) of the Act,[84] namely: "that the bill is what it purports to be, that he has a right to transfer it, and that at the time of the transfer he is not aware of any fact which renders it valueless".

It may, therefore, be that, notwithstanding that the transfer is "without recourse", a transferor warrants to his immediate transferee that the instrument is formally valid,[85] that the signatures of the acceptor or maker and that of the avalising bank are genuine and authorised, that each prior indorsement is valid and that he is not aware that instrument relates other than to a bona fide transaction.[86] Moreover, the *à forfait* market deals almost exclusively in trade-backed instruments, that is to say, bills or notes where the underlying contract is a contract of sale of goods or similar contract, as opposed to a financial transaction, *i.e.* where the "importer" is borrowing funds for use in his business. It has been suggested[87] that there may be a duty on the introducing bank to check the nature of the transaction giving rise to the instrument which is offered to it, and that, unless the contrary is expressly stated, each transferor in the market might be held to represent or warrant that the instrument sold is a trade-backed instrument.

---

[84] See below, para.7–069.

[85] In an expert market, however, it may be that each purchaser is expected to satisfy himself that the instrument is valid under the governing law. *cf.* s.72(1); below, para.12–001.

[86] I am indebted to the suggestions made by Mr M.C. Johns, in an unpublished paper on (*inter alia*) this point. See also the American case of *Dumont v Williamson* (1867) 17 L.T. 71, 72 and the further American cases cited in Britton, *Cases on the Law of Bills and Notes* (5th ed.), pp.707–708; UCC, § 3–416.

[87] By Mr M.C. Johns, above, n.86.

**2–111**    **Subsection (2): waiving holder's duties.** This subsection permits the drawer of a bill and any indorser to waive as regards himself some or all of the holder's duties.[88] It is again limited to the drawer or an indorser and again the waiver must be express and inserted in the instrument.[89] Such a waiver does not affect the negotiation of the bill. Thus, for example, C, the holder of a bill, may indorse it to D, adding the words: "notice of dishonour waived". No subsequent party is then obliged to give notice of dishonour to C. The waiver is, however, personal to the person making it. In the above example, such an indorsement by C would not dispense with notice to the drawer or any other indorser.[90] Even if the waiver is inserted by the drawer when drawing the bill, it would not dispense with notice being given to other parties.[91]

In South Africa it has been held that the signature on the back of a promissory note under the imprint of a rubber stamp which bore the words: "I waive my right to notice of dishonour and presentation", operated both as an indorsement and as a waiver.[92]

### Definition and requisites of acceptance

**2–112**    **17. (1) The acceptance of a bill is the signification by the drawee of his assent to the order of the drawer.**

   **(2) An acceptance is invalid unless it complies with the following conditions, namely:**

   **(a) It must be written on the bill and be signed by the drawee. The mere signature of the drawee without additional words is sufficient.**

   **(b) It must not express that the drawee will perform his promise by any other means than the payment of money.**

| Definitions | Comparison |
|---|---|
| "acceptance": s.2. | UCC: 3–409 |
| "bill": s.2. | ULB: art.25. |
| "written": s.2 | UNB: art.43. |

---

[88] *e.g.* presentment for acceptance (s.39), presentment for payment (s.45), notice of dishonour (s.48) and protest (s.51).

[89] But see s.46(2)(e), 50(1)(b), 51(9).

[90] Unless, possibly, there was a general statement on the bill to the effect that (for example) the waiver extended to all indorsers.

[91] But see below, para.6–128 (s.50) as to the persons to whom the benefit of such a waiver enures.

[92] *Blou v Georgiades* 1959 (1) S.A. 219.

## COMMENT

**Acceptance.** This section defines the nature of an acceptance and the    2–113
requirements which must be satisfied for it to be valid. Section 18 of the
Act deals with the time for acceptance and section 19 with the kinds of
acceptance that may be signified on the bill.

An acceptance is, in effect, a promise in writing on the bill by the
drawee[93] to pay, when the bill is due, a sum of money to the holder of the
bill in accordance with the terms of the acceptance. Elsewhere in the Act,
an acceptance is referred to variously as a "contract"[94] or an "engagement".[95] If the drawee does not accept as required by the Act, he is not
liable on the instrument.[96] After the drawee has accepted, he is thence-
forth termed the "acceptor". By section 2, "acceptance" means an acceptance completed by delivery or notification, and such delivery or
notification is dealt with in section 21. Until delivery or notification, the
contract constituted by the acceptance is incomplete and revocable.[97]

The provisions of the Act relating to acceptance do not apply to promissory notes.[98] Although a cheque is a bill of exchange, it is a bill of
exchange of a special type.[99] The holder of a cheque, as between himself
and the drawer, has no right to require acceptance,[1] and in the ordinary
course a cheque is not accepted.[2] While it cannot be said that a cheque can
never be accepted,[3] it is only done in very unusual and special circumstances, and would require strong and unmistakable words.[4] The marking or certification of a cheque is not an acceptance.[5]

As to the liability of an acceptor and estoppels binding on him, see    2–114
section 54 of the Act.

A bill of exchange signed by the drawer, though unaccepted by the
drawee, is *vis-à-vis* a holder in due course "complete and regular on the
face of it" for the purposes of section 29(1).[6]

---

[93] But see s.65 (acceptance for honour).
[94] s.21(1).
[95] s.54(1).
[96] s.53(1).
[97] s.21(1).
[98] s.89(3).
[99] See below, para.13–003.
[1] *Bank of Baroda Ltd v Punjab National Bank Ltd* [1944] A.C. 176, 184 (s.53, Illustration 5).
[2] *Ramchurn Mullick v Luchmeechund Radakissen* (1854) 9 Moo. P.C. 46, 69; *Bank of Baroda Ltd v Punjab National Bank Ltd* [1944] A.C. 176 at 184. See also below, para.13–003.
[3] *Keene v Beard* (1860) 8 C.B., N.S. 372, 380. See *Broadhead v Royal Bank of Canada* (1968) 70 D.L.R. (2d) 445, where a cheque was held to have been accepted.
[4] *Bank of Baroda Ltd v Punjab National Bank Ltd* [1944] A.C. 176.
[5] [1944] A.C. 176. Contrast UCC, § 3–409(d). See below, para.7–009 (s.53).
[6] *National Park Bank of New York v Berggren & Co.* (1914) 30 T.L.R. 387.

**2–115**      **Subsection (1): acceptance by drawee.** A person who is not a party already liable on a bill may in certain circumstances intervene and accept the bill *suprà protest* for honour[7]; and an officer of a company or a person on its behalf who signs or authorises to be signed on behalf of the company an acceptance of a bill of exchange will, under section 349(4) of the Companies Act 1985,[8] be personally liable to the holder (unless the bill is duly paid by the company) if in the bill the company's name is not mentioned in accordance with the statutory requirements of subsection (1) of that section.[9] Subject to these qualifications, it is clear law, both in England and Scotland, that no person other than the drawee can be liable as the acceptor of a bill.[10] If a person other than the drawee purports to accept a bill, intending to incur liability on it, it is possible that he could incur liability as an anomalous indorser under section 56 of the Act, but not as acceptor.[11]

The drawee and the acceptor of the bill must therefore be the same person. If the drawee is not named in the bill, but is otherwise indicated in it with reasonable certainty,[12] an acceptance by him will be valid.[13] Also, if the name of the drawee is misdescribed in the bill, and it is accepted by him in his true name, this will not invalidate the acceptance, provided it is clear that drawee and acceptor are in fact the same person.[14] Likewise a mere error of description in the acceptance will not render the acceptance invalid if drawee and acceptor are admittedly the same.[15] But if an acceptance is written on a bill in which no person is named as drawee or otherwise indicated with reasonable certainty, the signatory of the acceptance will not be liable as acceptor (unless and until his name as drawee is inserted in accordance with section 20 of the Act), but may be liable as the maker of a promissory note.[16]

---

[7] s.65.

[8] Replacing s.108(4) of the Companies Act 1948.

[9] See below, para.3–026.

[10] *Jackson v Hudson* (1810) 2 Camp. 447 (Illustration 1); *Polhill v Walter* (1832) 3 B. & Ad. 114, 122; *Bult v Morrell* (1840) 12 A. & E. 745 (Illustration 2); *Davis v Clarke* (1844) 6 Q.B. 16 (Illustration 3); *Nicholls v Diamond* (1853) 9 Exch. 154, 157; *Steele v M'Kinlay* (1880) 5 App. Cas. 754 (Section 56, Illustration); *Stacey & Co. v T.H. Wallis Ltd* (1912) 28 T.L.R. 209, 211; *Maxform Spa v Mariani and Goodville Ltd* [1979] 2 Lloyd's Rep. 385, 387, affirmed [1981] 2 Lloyd's Rep. 54 (s.23, Illustration 15).

[11] *cf. Steele v M'Kinlay* (1880) 5 App. Cas. 754.

[12] s.6(1).

[13] *Shuttleworth v Stephens* (1808) 1 Camp. 407; *Gray v Milner* (1819) 8 Taunt. 739. See above, para.2–045.

[14] *Lloyd v Ashby* (1831) 2 B. & Ad. 23. See also *Odell v Cormack Bros* (1887) 19 Q.B.D. 223, 226; *Maxform Spa v Mariani and Goodville Ltd* [1979] 2 Lloyd's Rep. 385 (bill drawn on person in his trade name may be accepted in his true name).

[15] *Dermatine Co. Ltd v Ashworth* (1905) 21 T.L.R. 510: acceptance omits "Limited" (s.23, Illustration 9).

[16] *Peto v Reynolds* (1854) 9 Exch. 410, affirmed (1855) 11 Exch. 418; *Fielder v Marshall* (1861) 9 C.B., N.S. 606; *Mason v Lack* (1929) 45 T.L.R. 363 (s.6, Illustration 2); *Haseldine v Winstanley* [1936] 2 K.B. 101 (s.64, Illustration 3); see below, para.8–090.

The acceptance is distinct from the bill.[17] But, in construing the acceptance, the address, or order, to the drawee should be read together with the acceptance so as to give validity (if possible) to the instrument.[18]

A bill may be addressed to two or more drawees whether they are **2–116** partners or not.[19] The acceptance of some one or more of the drawees, but not all, is a qualified acceptance[20]: the holder of the bill may refuse to take such a qualified acceptance and treat the bill as dishonoured by non-acceptance.[21] But any one of two or more drawees may accept so as to bind himself.[22]

A partnership firm name or signature is merely a compendious form of expressing the names or signatures of all the partners in that firm.[23] If a bill is addressed to a firm, an acceptance by the signature of the name of the firm is equivalent to the signature by the person so signing of the names of all persons liable as partners in that firm.[24] An acceptance by a partner in the name of the firm is an acceptance by the firm and does not make that partner separately liable, even though he adds his own name to the acceptance.[25] But if a bill is addressed to a firm, and one of the partners accepts it in his own name on behalf of the firm but without the authority of his co-partners, then he is liable as acceptor.[26] Conversely, where a bill is addressed to a member of a firm in his personal character, though describing him as an officer of the firm, an acceptance by him on behalf of the firm will impose liability on him as acceptor.[27]

An agent who accepts without authority a bill addressed to his principal will not be liable as acceptor, but may be liable to the holder in an action for falsely representing that he had authority, or for breach of his

---

[17] *H. Meyer & Co. Ltd v Jules Decroix, Verley et Cie* (1890) 25 Q.B.D. 343, 348 (affirmed [1891] A.C. 520).

[18] s.26(2). See *Mare v Charles* (1856) 5 E. & B. 978, 981; *Penrose v Martyr* (1858) E. B. & E. 499 (s.23, Illustration 7); *Okell v Charles* (1876) 34 L.T. (N.S.) 822 (Illustration 4); *Herald v Connah* (1876) 34 L.T. (N.S.) 885 (Illustration 5); *Stacey & Co. v T.H. Wallis Ltd* (1912) 28 T.L.R. 209 (s.23, Illustration 10); *Elliott v Bax-Ironside* [1925] 2 K.B. 301 (Illustration 6). cf. *Maxform Spa v Mariani and Goodville Ltd* [1981] 2 Lloyd's Rep. 54 (s.23, Illustration 15); *Novaknit Hellas SA v Kumar Brothers International Ltd* [1998] Lloyd's Rep. Bank. 287 (s.11, Illustration 4).

[19] s.6(2).

[20] s.19(2)(e).

[21] s.44(1).

[22] *Bult v Morrell* (1840) 12 A. & E. 745 (Illustration 2); *Owen v Van Uster* (1850) 10 C.B. 318 (Illustration 8). See also s.19(2)(e).

[23] But this is not so in the case of a limited liability partnership formed by being incorporated under the Limited Liability Partnerships Act 2000 where the signature of a partner will (as in the case of a company) be construed as being made on behalf of the body corporate: see below, para.3–035.

[24] s.23(2). See also Partnership Act 1890, s.6.

[25] *Re Barnard, Edwards v Barnard* (1886) 32 Ch.D. 447 (Illustration 7).

[26] *Owen v Van Uster* (1850) 10 C.B. 318 (Illustration 8). If he accepts in his own name, and with the authority of the firm, but not on behalf of the firm, the acceptance will be binding on him: *Geo. Thompson (Aust.) Pty Ltd v Vittadello* [1978] V.R. 199 (co-partner not bound).

[27] *Nicholls v Diamond* (1853) 9 Exch. 154 (Illustration 9).

implied warranty of authority.[28] But if the bill is addressed to both principal and agent, or to the agent alone, and he accepts for himself and, without authority, for his principal, the agent will be liable as acceptor, but his principal will not be liable on the acceptance.[29] Where an agent accepts (even with authority) a bill addressed to his principal, but does so in his own name only and without any addition of the name of his principal, it would appear that neither the principal nor the agent will be liable as acceptor,[30] since the principal's signature as acceptor has not been written on the bill[31] and the agent cannot accept the bill as it is not addressed to him.

**2–117**     **Subsection (2): requirements of form.** An acceptance must be written[32] on the bill. An acceptance will therefore be invalid if it is made orally, or in writing but separately from the bill,[33] or if it is sought to be inferred from the retention of the bill by the drawee without objection for a long period of time,[34] or from the terms of a collection letter.[35] As to the acceptance of a bill in a set, see section 71(4).

An acceptance must be signed by the drawee.[36] The drawee may sign by the hand of his agent.[37] The usual mode of accepting is for the drawee to write "accepted" across or on the face of the bill, and then to sign his name underneath. But the drawee may use any form of words from which the intention to pay may be gathered[38]; and the mere signature of the drawee without additional words is sufficient.[39] The signature of the drawee on the back of the bill probably suffices. As between immediate parties, a signature placed on the face of the bill will not be an acceptance if it is placed there by or on behalf of the drawee merely in order to

---

[28] *Polhill v Walter* (1832) 3 B. & Ad. 114; *Collen v Wright* (1857) 7 E. & B. 301; *West London Commercial Bank v Kitson* (1884) 13 Q.B.D. 360 (see s.22, Illustration 2).

[29] *Nicholls v Diamond* (1853) 9 Exch. 154.

[30] In *Lindus v Bradwell* (1848) 5 C.B. 583, a bill addressed to William B. was accepted by his wife, signing "Mary B.", and it was held that if he had authorised her so to accept, or afterwards ratified her acceptance, he would be liable as acceptor. The reasoning was (at 591) that the drawee could accept in any name he chose to adopt, and William B. chose to adopt *pro hac vice* the name of his wife to accept it. It is doubtful whether this is consonant with s.17. But see *Eccles v Merchant Bank of Canada* [1923] 3 D.L.R. 1103; *Maxform Spa v Mariani and Goodville Ltd* [1981] 2 Lloyd's Rep. 54 (s.23, Illustration 15).

[31] ss.17(2), 23, 91(1).

[32] Defined in s.2. See also Interpretation Act 1978, s.5 and Sch.1.

[33] *Bank of Ireland v Archer* (1843) 11 M. & W. 383 (promise to accept bill not yet drawn).

[34] Contrast *Harvey v Martin* (1803), cited 1 Camp. at 425 (common law). *cf. Jeune v Ward* (1818) 1 B. & Ald. 653.

[35] *Man (E.D. & F.) (Coffee) Ltd v Miyazaki S.A. Commercial Agricola* [1991] 1 Lloyd's Rep. 154, 159–160.

[36] For "signature", see below, para.3–023.

[37] s.91(1).

[38] *Smith v Vertue* (1860) 9 C.B. (N.S.) 214; *Humphreys v Taylor* [1921] N.Z.L.R. 343.

[39] Contrast *Hindhaugh v Blakey* (1878) L.R. 3 C.P. 136 (common law).

authorise payment, and not as an acceptance,[40] unless the bill is subsequently delivered to a holder in circumstances where the signatory is unable to show that the delivery was conditional.[41]

An acceptance by the drawee to perform his promise by, for example, the provision of bills or goods to the value of the bill drawn upon him is not a valid acceptance,[42] since an acceptance must not express that the drawee will perform his promise by any other means than the payment of money. But an acceptance to pay at a bank "from external account" of another company is valid.[43] If it is construed to mean that the acceptor will pay with someone else's money and out of that other person's account, it may well be a qualified acceptance[44]; but it is not a promise to pay by other means than the payment of money. Although a bill is invalid unless the order is to pay a sum certain in money,[45] there is no requirement that an acceptance must be for a sum certain. Thus an acceptance to pay the amount of the bill "plus all bank charges, commission and stamps" is a valid (but qualified) acceptance.[46] An acceptance will also be valid (though qualified) even if it is conditional or if it provides for payment to be made otherwise than on demand or at a fixed or determinable future time.[47] It does not have to meet the requirements stipulated for the order to pay in a bill of exchange.

## ILLUSTRATIONS

1. The claimant draws a bill payable to himself or order. It is addressed   **2–118**
to I, but is accepted both by I and by the defendant. The defendant is not
liable as acceptor. A bill drawn upon one person may not be accepted by
a second person.[48]

2. P draws a bill payable to J or order. It is addressed to the: "Directors
of the Imperial Salt and Alkali Co.". The acceptance reads: "Accepted for
the Imperial Salt and Alkali Co." and it is signed by three of the four
directors of the company as directors, and also by P as manager. P is not

[40] *Smith v Commercial Banking Co. of Sydney Ltd* (1910) 11 C.L.R. 667.
[41] (1910) 11 C.L.R. 667 at 674. See s.21.
[42] *Russell v Phillips* (1850) 14 Q.B. 891, 901.
[43] *Banca Popolare di Novara v John Livanos & Sons Ltd* [1965] 2 Lloyd's Rep. 149 (overruled on other grounds in *Oesterreichische Länderbank v S'Elite Ltd* [1981] Q.B. 565).
[44] s.19.
[45] See above, para.2–014 (s.3).
[46] *Bank of Lisbon v Optichen Kunsmis* 1970 (1) S.A. 447 (Illustration 10). Contrast *Perry & Co. v Nelco Floors* 1956 (2) S.A. 711, 713.
[47] s.19(2).
[48] *Jackson v Hudson* (1810) 2 Camp. 447.

a director of the company. The three directors are liable as acceptors, but P is not so liable as the bill is not addressed to him.[49]

3. J.H. draws a bill on J.H. payable to himself or order. It is accepted by the defendant, and indorsed by J.H. to the claimant. Even if the instrument is or may be treated as a bill of exchange,[50] the defendant is not liable as acceptor. He is not the drawee and his acceptance is not in fact an acceptance.[51]

**2–119**  4. A bill addressed to: "The Great Snowdon Mountain Copper Mining Company (Limited) Lombard Street" is accepted as follows: "Accepted payable at Messrs B & Co., J.M. and R.C. Directors of the Great Snowdon Mountain Copper Mining Company (Limited) D.B.C., Secretary." Since the company is the drawee of the bill and the acceptance complies with section 47 of the Companies Act 1862, the acceptance is on behalf of the company, and the directors are not personally liable.[52]

5. A bill is addressed to: "H.C, General Agent of L'Unione Compagna D'Assicurazione General (Firenze), 8 York Street, Manchester". It is accepted as follows: "Accepted, payable at 8 York Street, Manchester, on behalf of the company. H.C." The bill is directed to H.C. personally, and he must therefore be taken to have accepted it, so as to render himself personally liable upon it.[53]

6. A bill is addressed to F.F.E. Ltd. It is accepted by B and M, directors of the company, as follows: "Accepted payable at the Westminster Bank Ltd, Piccadilly Branch. B, M, directors. F.F.E. Ltd." As required by the drawer, the bill is also indorsed by them as follows "F.F.E. Ltd, B, M, directors". In signing the acceptance, the directors are signing on behalf of the company and not in their individual capacity, for the reason that the bill is addressed to the company and the company alone is intended to accept it. But the directors are personally liable as indorsers.[54]

**2–120**  7. A draws a bill upon Messrs B & Co., a partnership firm consisting of two partners. One of the partners, B, accepts the bill in the following form: "Accepted; payable at the Imperial Bank, Lothbury. B & Co." with the name of B written underneath. The bill is indorsed to the claimant.

---

[49] *Bult v Morrell* (1840) 12 A. & E. 745.
[50] s.5(2).
[51] *Davis v Clarke* (1844) 6 Q.B. 16. See also s.5, Illustration 1.
[52] *Okell v Charles* (1876) 34 L.T. (N.S.) 822.
[53] *Herald v Connah* (1876) 34 L.T. (N.S.) 885.
[54] *Elliott v Bax-Ironside* [1925] 2 K.B. 301. See also s.26 (Illustration 11).

The acceptance is that of B & Co., and only binds the firm of B & Co. It does not make B separately liable on the acceptance.[55]

8. The claimant draws a bill directed to: "Allty-Crib Mining Company, near Talybout, Aberystwyth." The company is unincorporated and consists of four persons, of whom U, the defendant, is one. The defendant writes an acceptance on the bill, as follows: "Per proc. The Allty-Crib Mining Company... U, London Manager". The acceptance is made without the authority of his co-partners. The defendant is liable as acceptor. He is one of those to whom the bill is addressed and is in consequence liable upon his acceptance.[56]

9. The claimants draw two bills of exchange directed "To D, Purser, West Downs Mining Company" and these are accepted by D, the defendant, in the following form: "D, accepted, per proc. West Downs Mining Company". The company so named is not a corporate body and D is a member of the company, but has no authority to accept bills on the company's behalf. D is liable as acceptor. The bills are drawn on him in his personal character, and the acceptance is not the less a good acceptance by him, because he happens also to accept them for others, which he had no right to do.[57]

10. A bill is drawn in Lisbon addressed to a drawee in Johannesburg   2–121
requiring the drawee to pay a sum in US dollars on April 7, 1968. The bill is accepted as follows: "Accepted payable on 7.4.1968 at the sight selling rate of exchange on the date of payment plus all bank charges, commission and stamps for US$41,446.93. Documents received." This is a valid (though qualified) acceptance. It is not stated in the statute that the acceptance must constitute an engagement consistent with all the requirements, *e.g.* a "sum certain", laid down for the order in the definition of a bill of exchange.[58]

## Time for acceptance

18. A bill may be accepted.                                          2–122
  (1) Before it has been signed by the drawer, or while otherwise
      incomplete:
  (2) When it is overdue, or after it has been dishonoured by a
      previous refusal to accept, or by non-payment:

---

[55] *Re Barnard. Edwards v Barnard* (1886) 32 Ch.D. 447.
[56] *Owen v Van Uster* (1850) 10 C.B. 318.
[57] *Nicholls v Diamond* (1853) Exch. 154.
[58] *Bank of Lisbon v Optichen Kunsmis* 1970 (1) S.A. 447.

(3) When a bill payable after sight is dishonoured by non-acceptance, and the drawee subsequently accepts it, the holder, in the absence of any different agreement, is entitled to have the bill accepted as of the date of first presentment to the drawee for acceptance.

| Definitions | Comparison |
|---|---|
| "acceptance": s.2,17(1). | UCC: § 3–409. |
| "bill": s.2. | ULB, arts 10, 21–23. |
| "holder": s.2. | UNB: art.42. |

## COMMENT

2–123   **Subsection (1): acceptance while incomplete.** A bill may be accepted before it has been signed by the drawer, or while otherwise incomplete.[59] Provision is made in section 20 of the Act for the insertion of the name of the drawer or for the completion of an otherwise incomplete bill. Until the drawer's signature is inserted, the instrument is not a bill of exchange.[60]

**Subsection (2): acceptance of overdue or dishonoured bill.** A bill may be accepted when it is overdue.[61] Thus if B draws a bill on A, payable three months after date, it may be accepted in the fourth month notwithstanding that it is then overdue; and, as regards the acceptor who so accepts, it is deemed to be a bill payable on demand.[62] However, if there is nothing on the face of a bill to show when it was accepted, it is presumed, unless the contrary is proved, that the bill was accepted before maturity and within a reasonable time after its issue.[63]

A bill may be accepted when it has been dishonoured by non-acceptance or non-payment. So, for example, if the holder of a bill payable one month after sight presents it to the drawee for acceptance, and acceptance is refused, he may subsequently present it again for acceptance. If it is then accepted, the acceptance is valid.

---

[59] See the cases cited in the Comment and Illustrations to s.20.

[60] s.3(1). As to whether the acceptor may be liable as the maker of a promissory note, see above, para.2–013.

[61] *cf.* ULB, art.21.

[62] s.10(2). See *Mutford v Walcot* (1698) I Ld.Raym. 574; *Wynne v Raikes* (1804) 5 East 514, 521; *Christie v Peart* (1841) 7 M. & W. 491.

[63] *Roberts v Bethell* (1852) 12 C.B. 778.

**Subsection (3): subsequent acceptance of dishonoured after sight** 2–124
**bill.** This subsection applies only to a bill payable after sight.[64] It is
intended to secure that, apart from special agreement, the holder should
be put, as far as possible, in the same position as if the bill had not been
dishonoured before its ultimate acceptance.[65]

## General and qualified acceptances

19. (1) An acceptance is either (a) general or (b) qualified. 2–125

    (2) A general acceptance assents without qualification to the
order of the drawer. A qualified acceptance in express terms
varies the effect of the bill as drawn.

    In particular an acceptance is qualified which is—

    (a) conditional, that is to say, which makes payment by the
acceptor dependent on the fulfilment of a condition
therein stated:

    (b) partial, that is to say, an acceptance to pay part only of the
amount for which the bill is drawn:

    (c) local, that is to say, an acceptance to pay only at a partic-
ular specified place:

    An acceptance to pay at a particular place is a general accep-
tance, unless it expressly states that the bill is to be paid there
only and not elsewhere:

    (d) qualified as to time:

    (e) the acceptance of some one or more of the drawees, but
not of all.

| Definitions | Comparison |
|---|---|
| "acceptance": ss. 2, 17(1) | UCC: §§ 3–409, 3–410. |
| "bill": s.2 | ULB: arts 26, 27. |
| | UNB: art.43. |

### COMMENT

**Types of acceptance.** This section permits the drawee to give a qual- 2–126
ified acceptance to the order of the drawer contained in a bill[66] and

---

[64] See s.11. It is, perhaps, somewhat strange that subs.(3) does not also apply to a bill payable
at sight.

[65] The subs. was added in committee: *Chalmers* (9th ed.), p.52.

[66] Contrast ULB, art.26, which only allows a partial acceptance. But the acceptor is nevertheless bound according to the terms of his qualified acceptance.

distinguishes an unqualified or "general" acceptance from one that is qualified. A general acceptance assents without qualification to the order of the drawer. If the acceptance is qualified in one of the ways listed in subsection (2) or otherwise, then it is a qualified acceptance. It is necessary, however, to consider whether the acceptance is merely qualified or no acceptance at all. For example, the drawee could not validly accept a bill with a stipulation to the effect that he was not to be liable on the bill,[67] *e.g.* "without recourse to me", and probably could not accept in terms such as to make himself secondarily, and not primarily, liable on the bill.[68]

The holder of a bill may refuse to take a qualified acceptance, and if he does not obtain an unqualified acceptance may treat the bill as dishonoured by non-acceptance.[69] If a qualified acceptance is taken, then, unless the drawer or an indorser has expressly or impliedly authorised the holder to take such an acceptance, the holder must give notice to the drawer and any indorser, who (except in the case of a partial acceptance)[70] may decline to be bound by it and be discharged from his liability on the bill.[71]

When a bill is accepted generally, presentment for payment is not necessary in order to render the acceptor liable.[72] But the terms of a qualified acceptance may require presentment for payment.[73]

**2–127**    **Qualified acceptance.** A qualified acceptance in express terms varies the effect of the bill as drawn. In order to produce that effect, it has been said[74] that: "the words of qualification must ... be incorporated in the acceptance, or at least so connected with the acceptance as obviously to form part of it; and must also be such as to indicate clearly and unequivocally the nature of the restriction which they are meant to introduce". Thus when drawees accepted a bill and wrote above their acceptance "In favour of Mr. F only", the House of Lords held[75] that the words so placed could not be regarded as part of the acceptance or to have the effect of

---

[67] See also *Canadian Bank of Commerce v B.C. Interior Sales Ltd* (1957) 11 D.L.R. (2d) 609 (acceptance "subject to our adjustments" not to be construed as subject to a general right of set-off rendering the acceptance nugatory).

[68] But in *H. Meyer & Co. Ltd v Jules Decroix, Verley et Cie* [1891] A.C. 520, it appears to be assumed (especially by Bowen L.J. in the Court of Appeal (1890) 25 Q.B.D. 343, 350) that an acceptor could qualify his acceptance by clear words to the effect that his undertaking to pay was to the payee only, thus prohibiting the transfer of the bill (*cf.* Bowen L.J. (1890) 25 Q.B.D. at 347): see s.8(1). *cf.* ss.16(1), 35.

[69] s.44(1).

[70] s.44(2).

[71] ss.44(2)(3); App.A, Notice 5.

[72] s.52(1).

[73] s.52(2). See s.19(2)(a), (c), below, para.2–127.

[74] *H. Meyer & Co. Ltd v Jules, Decroix, Verley et Cie* [1891] A.C. 520, *per* Lord Watson at p.525.

[75] [1891] A.C. 520, Lords Bramwell and Morris dissenting.

qualifying its terms.[76] An acceptance is, whenever possible, to be construed as general, not qualified; and a mere memorandum, such as a wrong due date, inconsistent with such construction, has been rejected as being no part of the acceptance.[77] Whether acceptance is general or qualified is a question of law.[78]

The particular cases of qualified acceptance in subsection (2) do not profess to be exhaustive.[79] If, for example, a bill were drawn in United States dollars, but accepted payable in London only in naira (Nigerian currency)[80] or "at the sight selling rate of exchange on the date of payment",[81] the acceptance would be qualified. But those listed are qualified acceptances.

(a) *Conditional acceptance.* This makes a payment by the acceptor dependent upon the fulfilment of a condition therein stated, for example: "Accepted, payable on giving up bills of lading",[82] "to pay the bill when goods sent to me [the drawee] are sold",[83] or payable "when in cash for the said vessel's cargo"[84] "when in funds".[85] An acceptance to pay out of a particular fund would presumably be conditional.[86] An acceptance is conditional if it requires presentment for payment, either with or without an added express stipulation that presentment must be made on the date of maturity.[87]

(b) *Partial acceptance.* This is an acceptance to pay part only of the amount for which the bill is drawn, *e.g.* acceptance as to £100 of a bill drawn for £127.[88]

(c) *Local acceptance.* This is an acceptance to pay *only* at a particular specified place. An acceptance to pay at a particular place, *e.g.* at a

---

[76] *H. Meyer & Co. Ltd v Jules, Decroix, Verley et Cie* [1891] A.C. 520 (Illustration 1). See also *Canadian Bank of Commerce v B.C. Interior Sales* (1957) 11 D.L.R. (2d) 609 ("subject to our adjustments").

[77] *Fanshawe v Peet* (1857) 2 H. & N. 1.

[78] *Sproat v Matthews* (1786) 1 T.R. 182.

[79] *Decroix, Verley et Cie v Meyer & Co. Ltd* (1890) 25 Q.B.D. 343, 348.

[80] *Boehm v Garcias* (1808) 1 Camp. 425n.

[81] *Bank of Lisbon v Optichen Kunsmis* 1970 (1) S.A. 447 (s.17, Illustration 10).

[82] *Smith v Vertue* (1860) 9 C.B.N.S. 214 (Illustration 2) See also *Sproat v Matthews* [1786] 1 T.R. 182; *Ex p. Brett* (1871) 6 Ch.App. 838; *Humphreys v Taylor* [1921] N.Z.L.R. 343. *cf. Benjamin's Sale of Goods* (6th ed.), § 22–104.

[83] *Smith v Scarffe* (1741) 7 Mod. 426.

[84] *Julian v Shobrooke* (1753) 2 Wils. K.B. 9.

[85] *Smith v Vertue* (1860) 9 C.B.N.S. 214, at 225; *Potters v Taylor* (1888) 20 N.S.R. 362.

[86] *Banca Popolare di Novara v John Livanos & Sons Ltd* [1965] 2 Lloyd's Rep. 149 (overruled on other grounds in *Oesterreichische Länderbank v S'Elite Ltd* [1981] Q.B. 565). See also s.3(3) (order to pay).

[87] s.52(2).

[88] *Wegersloffe v Keene* (1719) 1 Stra. 214. See also s.44(2), and App.A, Notice 4.

particular branch of a named bank,[89] is a general acceptance unless it expressly states that the bill is to be paid there only and not elsewhere. Notwithstanding the wording of sub-section (2)(c), it would appear that, to constitute a qualified acceptance, it is unnecessary that both the word "only" and the phrase "and not elsewhere" be expressly stated,[90] but one or other of those expressions can (and must) appear. See also sections 45(4)(a), 52(2).

(d) *Qualified as to time.* An acceptance will be qualified as to time if, for example, a bill is drawn payable two months after date and is accepted by the drawee payable six months after date[91] or on condition of its being renewed until a later date.[92] It is a moot point whether an acceptance which is certain and unconditional as to the time of payment can "cure" and so render valid a bill which, as originally drawn, is defective and invalid as a bill of exchange under section 11 of the Act.[93]

(e) *Acceptance by some one or more of the drawees, but not of all.* An acceptance will be qualified if, for example, it is addressed to two drawees, A and B, and A only accepts, or if it is addressed to a partnership firm in the firm's name but is accepted by one of the partners in his own name.[94] See also sections 6(2) and 17(1).

This section does not apply to promissory notes.[95]

ILLUSTRATIONS

2–128     1. A bill of exchange is drawn by F on the defendants, reading "On October 31st after date pay to order Mr F £778 4s. 2d. Value received". The defendants accept the bill, and above their acceptance write "In favour of Mr F only." The word "order" in the bill is also struck out. F sends the bill to the claimants, bankers, who discount it for him. The striking through of the word "order" probably has no effect.[96] In any event, the words above the acceptance are not sufficiently plain and unequivocal to qualify

[89] *Ex p. Hayward* (1887) 3 T.L.R. 687 (Illustration 3); *Bank Polski v K.J. Mulder & Co.* [1942] 1 K.B. 497 (Illustration 4). Contrast (before the Act) *Rowe v Young* (1820) 2 Bligh 391.

[90] *Bank Polski v K.J. Mulder & Co.* [1942] 1 K.B. 497, at 501. *cf. Higgins v Nicholls* (1839) 7 Dowl. 551; *Halstead v Skelton* (1843) 5 Q.B. 86.

[91] *cf. Fanshawe v Peet* (1857) 2 H. & N. 1.

[92] *Russell v Phillips,* (1850) 14 Q.B. 891.

[93] *Hong Kong & Shanghai Banking Corpn. Ltd v G.D. Trade Co. Ltd* [1998] C.L.C. 238 (s.11, Illustration 4). See above para.2–089.

[94] See the Comment to s.17(1), above, para.2–116.

[95] s.89(3).

[96] (1890) 25 Q.B.D. 343. See s.8(4).

its operation. The acceptance is a general acceptance of a negotiable bill.[97]

2. A bill is accepted by the defendants as follows: "Accepted, payable on giving up bill of lading for 76 bags of clover-seed per 'Amazon' at the London and Westminster Bank, Borough Branch." The claimants are indorsees of the bills so accepted. The acceptance is clearly conditional. The claimants are only entitled to receive the amount of the bill on delivery to the defendants of the bill of lading. But they are not bound to hand over the bill of lading on the day the bill falls due, for it is not necessary to present the bill for payment on the precise day on which it is due.[98]

3. Bills of exchange are drawn abroad addressed to the defendants and expressed to be payable in Ceylon. They are accepted in London by the defendants payable at the Chartered Mercantile Bank, Kandy, Ceylon. This is a general acceptance, and the defendants can be sued in England on the bills.[99]

4. L draws a bill of exchange on the defendants for Dutch florins 22,140 **2–129** payable to L's order at the Twentsche Bank, Amsterdam. The bill is accepted by the defendants, and indorsed by L to the R Bank, which indorses it to the claimants. The insertion by the drawer of terms regarding the place of payment has the same effect as if such terms had been inserted by the defendants as part of their acceptance. The acceptance is a general acceptance, and the fact that the bill is payable in Dutch currency does not displace the application of section 19(2)(c). Presentment for payment is not necessary to render the acceptors liable.[1]

**Inchoate instruments**

20. (1) Where a simple signature on a blank paper is delivered by the **2–130** signer in order that it may be converted into a bill, it operates as a prima facie authority to fill it up as a complete bill for any amount, using the signature for that of the drawer, or the acceptor, or an indorser; and, in like manner, when a bill is wanting in any material particular, the person in possession

---

[97] *H. Meyer & Co. Ltd v Jules Decroix, Verley et Cie* [1891] A.C. 520.
[98] *Smith v Vertue* (1860) 9 C.B.N.S. 214.
[99] *Ex p. Hayward* (1887) 3 T.L.R. 687.
[1] *Bank Polski v K.J. Mulder & Co.* [1941] 2 K.B. 266; [1942] 1 K.B. 497. See also s.72, Illustration 9.

of it has a prima facie authority to fill up the omission in any
way he thinks fit.

(2) In order that any such instrument when completed may be
enforceable against any person who became a party thereto
prior to its completion, it must be filled up within a reasonable time, and strictly in accordance with the authority given.
Reasonable time for this purpose is a question of fact.

Provided that if any such instrument after completion is negotiated to a holder in due course it shall be valid and effectual for
all purposes in his hands, and he may enforce it as if it had been
filled up within a reasonable time and strictly in accordance with
the authority given.

Amendment
Subs.(1) was repealed in part by s.36(8), and Sch.8, Pt V, of the Finance Act
1970.

| Definitions | Comparison |
|---|---|
| "bill": s.2. | UCC: §§ 3–115, 3–407, 4–401(d). |
| "delivery": s.2. | ULB: art.10. |
| "holder in due course": s.29. | ULC: art.13. |
| "person": s.2. | UNB: art.12. |

COMMENT

2–131    **Completion of an incomplete instrument.** An instrument wanting in
some one or more requisites prescribed by section 3(1) of the Act is not a
bill of exchange. But a person may sign a document and deliver it to
another in order that it may be subsequently filled up and issued as a bill.
Such a document is an "inchoate" instrument, for it is not yet a complete
bill of exchange. The purpose of this section is to confer prima facie
authority on the holder or the person in possession of the instrument to
supply the omission and convert the document into a valid bill. In *Glenie
v Bruce Smith*,[2] Fletcher Moulton L.J. said[3]:

> "The logical order of operations with regard to a bill is, no doubt,
> that the bill should be first filled up, then that it should be signed by
> the drawer, then that it should be accepted, then that it should be
> negotiated, and then that it should be indorsed by the persons who
> become successively holders; but it is common knowledge that par-
> ties very often vary, in a most substantial manner, the logical order of

[2] [1904] 1 K.B. 263.
[3] At 267–268.

those proceedings, and s.20 of the Bills of Exchange Act is intended to deal with those cases. . . . If you choose to anticipate the logical order of events and give [the] uncompleted document to a person in order that it may be made a complete bill, then he has a prima facie authority to fill up the omission."

There will also be cases where the instrument, though valid as a bill, lacks some element which is necessary to implement the agreement of the parties in relation to the intended effect of the bill. The section again confers prima facie authority to supply the omission.[4]

The authority conferred is in effect a transferable authority to complete the bill. In order that the instrument, when completed, may be enforceable against a person who became a party to it prior to its completion, it must be filled up within a reasonable time and strictly in accordance with the authority given.[5] Once, however, it has been duly and timeously completed, the result of completion is the same as if the bill had never been defective at all; the efficacy of the section is not limited to rights which only come into existence after the omission is supplied.[6] But the liabilities of the parties accrue only from the time when the bill is issued in a complete form.[7]

A bill of exchange is nevertheless a negotiable instrument, and it is **2–132** necessary to protect a person to whom the completed instrument is transferred and who takes it innocently and for valuable consideration.[8] Accordingly, even though the instrument is not filled up within a reasonable time or not filled up in accordance with the authority given, if it is negotiated after completion to a holder in due course, that holder can enforce the instrument against a person who became a party to it prior to its completion as if it had been properly completed, and in accordance with its terms.[9]

The section re-enacts, in substance, the previous common law. It leaves open, however, for determination by the law outside the Act the question how the authority given is to be proved.[10]

The section also applies to promissory notes which are incomplete.[11]

**Subsection (1): completion.** The first part of this subsection deals with **2–133** the case of "a simple signature on a blank paper". The paper so signed

---

[4] See, *e.g. Gerald McDonald & Co. v Nash & Co.* [1924] A.C. 625 (Illustration 15) and the cases cited in para.2–133, nn.18 to 27, below.
[5] s.20(2).
[6] *Gerald McDonald & Co. v Nash & Co.* [1924] A.C. 625, at 647.
[7] *Goldsmid v Hampton* (1858) 5 C.B., N.S. 94; *Ex p. Hayward* (1871) 6 Ch.App. 546.
[8] *Foster v Mackinnon* (1869) L.R. & C.P. 704, 712.
[9] s.20(2), proviso.
[10] *London Joint Stock Bank Ltd v Macmillan* [1918] A.C. 777, 816–817.
[11] See also s.84.

must be delivered by the signer in order that it may be converted into a bill. This requirement (which may be taken to apply to the whole of subsection (1)) is of particular relevance where the completed bill is negotiated to a holder in due course. It is therefore dealt with in the Comment on the proviso to subsection (2). If such a paper is so delivered, then it operates as a prima facie authority to fill it up for any amount, using the signature for that of the drawer, or the acceptor, or an indorser. As originally enacted, this provision referred to "a blank *stamped* paper" and to "any amount *the stamp will cover*". But with the abolition of stamp duty on bills and notes by the Finance Act 1970, it was amended[12] to its present form, and the amount is therefore now unlimited.

Where the signature is used for that of the drawer,[13] the prima facie authority conferred extends to the insertion of an order to pay, the amount of the bill, the date, the maturity, and the names of the drawee and payee. Where the signature is used for that of the acceptor,[14] the bill may likewise be completed, together with the signature of the drawer. Where the signature is used for that of an indorser,[15] the bill may be completed in its entirety, leaving the signature as an indorsement on the back of the bill. In the case of a promissory note, the signature may be used as that of the maker of the note[16] or of an indorser.[17]

The second part of the subsection deals with a bill which is "wanting in any material particular". In like manner, the person in possession of the bill has a prima facie authority to fill up the omission in any way he thinks fit. For example, there may be inserted: the signature of the drawer of the bill,[18] the place where it is drawn,[19] the name of the drawee[20] or of

---

[12] Finance Act 1970, s.36(8) and Sch.8, Pt V.

[13] See, for example, *Collis v Emett* (1790) 1 H.B. 313; *Usher v Dauncey* (1814) 4 Camp. 97 (Illustration 3); *Barker v Sterne* (1854) 9 Exch. 684 (Illustration 9); *Guildford Trust Ltd v Goss* (1927) 43 T.L.R. 167 (Illustration 13).

[14] See, for example, *Molloy v Delves* (1831) 7 Bing. 428; *Schultz v Astley* (1836) 2 Bing. N.C. 544 (Illustration 6); *Montague v Perkins* (1853) 22 L.J.C.P. 187 (Illustration 8); *Hatch v Searles* (1859) 2 Sm. & G. 147 (Illustration 4); *Goldsmid v Hampton* (1858) 5 C.B., N.S. 94; *Foster v Mackinnon* (1869) L.R. 4 C.P. 704, 712; *London and South Western Bank Ltd v Wentworth* (1880) 5 Ex.D. 96 (Illustration 7); *Glenie v Bruce Smith* [1904] 1 K.B. 263 (Illustration 14). See also *G. & H. Montage GmbH v Irvani* [1988] 1 W.L.R. 1285 affirmed [1990] 1 W.L.R. 667).

[15] *Russel v Langstaffe* (1780) 2 Dougl. 514, 516; *Foster v Mackinnon* (1869) L.R. 4 C.P. 704, at 712; *Glenie v Bruce Smith*, [1904] 1 K.B. 263.

[16] *Temple v Pullen* (1853) 8 Exch. 389; *Herdman v Wheeler* [1902] 1 K.B. 361 (Illustration 10); *Lloyd's Bank Ltd v Cooke* [1907] 1 K.B. 794 (Illustration 21).

[17] *Bank of Nova Scotia v Hogg* (1979) 99 D.L.R. (3d) 729.

[18] *Scard v Jackson* (1875) 34 L.T. (N.S.) 65 (Illustration 5); *Harvey v Cane* (1876) 34 L.T. (N.S.) 64; *Hogarth v Latham* (1878) 3 Q.B.D. 643 (Illustration 12); *Carter v White* (1883) 25 Ch.D. 666 (Illustration 2); *Faulks v Atkins* (1893) 10 T.L.R. 178; *Foster v Driscoll* [1929] 1 K.B. 470 (s.12, Illustration). See also *Snaith v Mingay* (1818) 1 M. & S. 87, 92; *Bank of Nova Scotia v Hogg* (1979) 99 D.L.R. (3d) 729 (maker of note).

[19] *Foster v Driscoll* [1929] 1 K.B. 470.

[20] *Haseldine v Winstanley* [1936] 2 K.B. 101 (s.64, Illustration 3).

the payee,[21] the amount of the bill in words,[22] the date of payment,[23] the drawer's indorsement to himself as payee on a bill drawn payable to his order,[24] the payee's indorsement of a note already indorsed by a stranger,[25] or the place of payment of a promissory note.[26] Particular provison is made by section 12 of the Act, where a bill expressed to be payable at a fixed period after date is issued undated, or where the acceptance of a bill payable at a fixed period after sight is undated, for the insertion by a holder in the bill of the true date of issue or acceptance. But even where section 12 does not in its terms apply, the subsection authorises the insertion of an omitted date, *e.g.* of a cheque.[27]

The prima facie authority conferred by subsection (1) is not limited to the person to whom the incomplete document is delivered: any bona fide holder may fill it up.[28] If given for valuable consideration, the authority is irrevocable, *e.g.* by the death of the person giving it[29]; but if, as in the case of an accommodation acceptance, the authority is given without receiving value, then it will terminate upon the death of the person giving it, since the authority is not coupled with an interest.[30] The death of the person to whom the bill is delivered for completion does not terminate the authority, and the bill may be completed by his personal representatives after his death.[31]    **2–134**

**Guarantee indorsements.** Subsection (1) may also be invoked where a bill or note is drawn or made payable to order and a third party "backs" the instrument by adding his name as indorser with the intention of guaranteeing payment of the instrument. Suppose that B is willing to sell goods to A, but only on condition that C guarantees the payment by A for the goods, which C agrees to do. B draws a bill on A payable to B's order. The bill is accepted by A and indorsed by C with the intention of making    **2–135**

[21] *Crutchley v Mann* (1814) 5 Taunt. 529 (Illustration 1); *Awde v Dixon* (1851) 6 Exch. 869 (Illustration 11); *Re Gooch* [1921] 2 K.B. 593.

[22] *Garrard v Lewis* (1882) 10 Q.B.D. 30 (s.9, Illustration 3). *cf. London Joint Stock Bank v Macmillan* [1918] A.C. 777 (s.64, Illustration 5). Contrast *Burns v Forman* 1953 (2) S.A. 226 (amount in pencil).

[23] See note to s.12, above, para.2–092.

[24] See the cases cited in nn.34–36, below.

[25] *Erikssen v Bunting* (1901) 20 N.Z.L.R. 388; *Ferrier v Stewart* (1912) 15 C.L.R. 32, 38–39; *Durack v West Australian Trustee Executor & Agency Co. Ltd* (1944) 72 C.L.R. 189.

[26] *Automobile Finance Co. of Australia Ltd v Law* (1933) 49 C.L.R. 1, 10–11.

[27] *Tan Chong Keng v Vincent Lim Bak Keng* [1986] 2 M.L.J. 327, 331 (Singapore). *cf. Griffiths v Dalton* [1940] 2 K.B. 264.

[28] *Crutchley v Mann* (1814) 5 Taunt. 529 (Illustration 1); *Harvey v Cane* (1876) 34 L.T., N.S. 64; *Faulks v Atkins* (1893) 10 T.L.R. 178; *Bank of Nova Scotia v Manchur* [1978] 5 W.W.R. 323. *cf.* "the person in possession of it" in the case of material omissions.

[29] *Usher v Dauncey* (1814) 4 Camp. 97 (Illustration 3); *Carter v White* (1882) 20 Ch.D. 225, affd (1883) 25 Ch.D. 666 (Illustration 2).

[30] *Hatch v Searles* (1854) 2 Sm. & G. 147 (Illustration 4).

[31] *Scard v Jackson* (1875) 34 L.T. (N.S.) 65 (Illustration 5). *cf. Lawson's Executors v Watson* (1907) 9 F. 1353, 1357, 1359.

himself liable to B in the event of A's default in payment of the bill when it falls due. As the bill now stands, C is not liable to B on the bill.[32] But if B is permitted to and does add his indorsement as payee above that of C, then the bill may be read to mean that B, as payee, has indorsed the bill (gratuitously) to C and that C has reindorsed the bill (for value) to B.[33] B can recover against C, as a prior indorser. In *McDonald (Gerald) & Co. v Nash & Co.,*[34] the House of Lords held that subsection (1) entitled the drawer of a bill payable to his order to insert his indorsement in blank as payee above that of the guarantee indorser and so render the bill retro-spectively valid against such indorser.[35] The bill, as drawn, was "wanting in a material particular", namely the indorsement by the drawer of his name as payee, which the guarantee indorser authorised the drawer to insert in order to render him liable to the drawer on the bill. In sub-sequent cases[36] it has been further held that the order of the indorsements is not conclusive, so that the subsection may be invoked by the payee even though he has added his indorsement beneath that of the guarantee indorser. And in *Yeoman Credit Ltd v Gregory,*[37] where the payee's indorse-ment was a restrictive indorsement, and not an indorsement in blank, the subsection was likewise applied.

**2–136**    **Subsection (2): conditions for completion.** This subsection expresses a condition of general application to all the cases covered by subsection (1).[38] It first provides that, for the completed instrument to be enforceable against any person who became a party to it prior to its completion it must be filled up within a reasonable time,[39] and strictly in accordance

---

[32] C, as indorser, is not liable to B as drawer or payee; nor is s.56 of the Act applicable, as B is not a holder in due course.

[33] *Glenie v Bruce Smith* [1907] 2 K.B. 507, 512 (affirmed [1908] 1 K.B. 263).

[34] [1924] A.C. 625 (Illustration 15), applying *Glenie v Bruce Smith* [1908] 1 K.B. 263 (Illustration 14) and *Re Gooch* [1921] 2 K.B. 593, and distinguishing *Steele v M'Kinlay* (1880) 5 App. Cas. 754 (s.56, Illustration). See also *Erikssen v Bunting* (1901) 20 N.Z.L.R. 388 (note).

[35] At 647, 648. See also below, para.2–136, n.47.

[36] *National Sales Corp. Ltd v Bernardi* [1931] 2 K.B. 188 (Illustration 16); *McCall Bros Ltd v Hargreaves* [1932] 2 K.B. 423 (Illustration 18); *Lombard Banking Ltd v Central Garage and Engineering Co. Ltd* [1963] 1 Q.B. 220 (Illustration 17); *Yeoman Credit Ltd v Gregory,* [1963] 1 W.L.R. 343 (Illustration 19). See also *Penny v Innes* (1834) Cr. M. & R. 439; *Glenie v Bruce Smith* [1907] 2 K.B. 507 (affirmed [1908] 1 K.B. 263); *Durack v West Australian Trustee & Agency Co. Ltd* (1944) 72 C.L.R. 189 (note); *H. Rowe & Co. Pty Ltd v Pitts* [1973] 2 N.S.W.L.R. 159. *cf. Jenkins & Sons v Coomber* [1898] 2 Q.B. 168; *Shaw (M.T.) & Co. Ltd v Holland* [1913] 2 K.B. 15.

[37] [1963] 1 W.L.R. 343 (Illustration 19).

[38] *Gerald McDonald & Co. v Nash & Co.* [1924] A.C. 625, 648.

[39] See *e.g. Temple v Pullen* (1853) 8 Exch. 389; *Montague v Perkins* (1853) 22 L.J.C.P. 187 (Illustration 8); *Hatch v Searles* (1854) 2 Sm. & G. 147 (Illustration 4); *Griffiths v Dalton* [1940] 2 K.B. 264, (18 months too long in case of a cheque). It may be completed when it is overdue: *Scard v Jackson* (1875) 34 L.T. (N.S.) 65 (Illustration 5); *Maclean v McEwan & Son* (1899) 1 F. 381. *Quaere* whether completion may take place after action brought: see *Trimble v Thorne* [1914] v L.R. 41; *Amerongen (Liquidator) and Others v Hamilton* (1957) 22 W.W.R. 337; *Polish Combatants Association Credit Union Ltd v Moge* (1984) 9 D.L.R. (4th) 60.

with the authority given.[40] Reasonable time for this purpose is a question of fact. If it is not filled up within a reasonable time or not in accordance with the authority given, then it is not enforceable against such a prior party by a holder[41] (other than a holder in due course).[42] The extent of the authority given to complete the instrument must be determined by reference to matters outside the bill.[43] Since the person in possession of the bill has prima facie authority to complete the bill in any way he thinks fit, the burden of proving want of authority rests upon the person alleging authority to be absent.[44]

It follows from the subsection that filling in an omission in a bill under proper authority to do so makes a bill complete and thereupon enforceable, without which it could not have been enforced.[45] "The plain meaning of [this] enactment" said Fletcher Moulton L.J.,[46] "is that in the case of a bill so filled up persons have just the same rights as persons in the same position with regard to an ordinary bill, provided that there has not been a *de facto* exceeding of the authority, and provided the bill is filled up in a reasonable time. . . . and therefore a party, even though he knew all the circumstances of the case, and even though he became a party to it while it was still incomplete, is entitled to all the rights of a holder in due course." Thus a holder who takes a bill not complete and regular on its face can, when the bill is duly completed, turn himself retrospectively into a holder in due course.[47] And a person who signed the instrument in its incomplete state will not be permitted to raise the defence that the usual order of operations for completion of the bill were not done in the proper order.[48]

---

[40] "Strict compliance" may be achieved more easily if the authority is broad in scope, *e.g.* an implied authority to complete the bill in any way necessary to achieve the desired result: *Mazur v Imperial Investment Corp. Ltd* (1963) 39 D.L.R. (2d) 631; *Bank of Nova Scotia v Manchur* [1978] 5 W.W.R. 323. But it seems that completion of a bill by a person acting within his usual or ostensible authority, but outside or in excess of his actual authority, would not be "strictly" in accordance with the authority given: *cf. Bank of Montreal v Casa* (1975) 63 D.L.R. (3d) 78.

[41] *Awde v Dixon* (1851) 6 Exch. 869 (Illustration 11); *Hatch v Searles* (1854) 2 Sm. & G. 147 (Illustration 4); *Hogarth v Latham* (1878) 3 Q.B.D. 643 (Illustration 12); *Oakley v Boulton, Maynard & Co.* (1888) 5 T.L.R. 60; *Watkins v Lamb* (1901) 85 L.T. 483; *Herdman v Wheeler* [1902] 1 K.B. 361 (Illustration 10).

[42] Under the proviso.

[43] *Gerald McDonald & Co. v Nash & Co.* [1924] A.C. 625, at 648; *McCall Bros Ltd v Hargreaves* [1932] 2 K.B. 423, 427; and see the cases cited in n.39, above.

[44] *Anderson v Somerville, Murray Co.* (1898) 1 F (Ct.Sess.) 90; *George v Allen* [1953] 3 D.L.R. 551; *S. Cohen & Sons Ltd v Hoddinott* (1961) 29 D.L.R. (2d) 69.

[45] *Gerald McDonald & Co. v Nash & Co.* [1924] A.C. 625, at 647.

[46] *Glenie v Bruce Smith* [1908] 1 K.B. 263, 268–269.

[47] *National Sales Corp. Ltd v Bernardi* [1931] 2 K.B. 188, 192. See also *Gerald McDonald & Co. v Nash & Co.* [1924] A.C. 625, at 636, 647, 648; *Lombard Banking Ltd v Central Garage and Engineering Ltd* [1963] 1 Q.B. 220, 230; *Yeoman Credit Ltd v Gregory* [1963] 1 W.L.R. 343, 352.

[48] *Glenie v Bruce Smith* [1908] 1 K.B. 263, at 269 (Illustration 14).

2–137       **The proviso.** The proviso to subsection (2) is intended to protect a
holder in due course to whom the instrument is negotiated after completion. Even if the instrument has not been filled up within a reasonable
time or not been filled up in accordance with the authority given, it is
valid and effectual for all purposes in his hands as if it had been duly and
properly completed.[49] To entitle such a holder to the benefit of the
proviso, certain conditions must be satisfied.

First, the document must have been delivered by the signer in order
that it may be converted into a bill.[50] This requirement is imported into
the proviso from subsection (1) by the words "any such instrument", *i.e.*
an instrument such as is referred to in subsection (1). Delivery is defined
by section 2 of the Act to mean "transfer of possession, actual or constructive, from one person to another". Delivery by the signer is essential,
as is also the intention that the document shall be converted into a bill.[51]
Thus, if an acceptance is written on a blank paper and the paper is
subsequently stolen from the signatory and filled up as a bill, the signatory will not be liable even if it is negotiated to a holder in due course.[52]
More difficulty may arise, however, as to the intention of the signer where
he has handed the document to another. In *Smith v Prosser*,[53] Fletcher
Moulton L.J. expressed the view that section 20 was based upon the
doctrine of common law estoppel as it existed at the date of the Act, and
said[54]:

> " . . . both the common law and the statute realized the possibility of
> two rival dangers—on the one hand, a person who did nothing more
> than sign a blank stamped paper might find himself in the position
> of being the maker of a bill or note; on the other hand, a man might
> issue an incomplete bill or note and place it in the hands of an agent
> with a limited authority to fill it up, and the agent might fill it up
> without due regard to the limitations of his authority and put it into
> circulation and thereby injure innocent persons. They therefore drew
> the line as regards the protection of third parties in the following
> very reasonable and intelligible way: if the signer intended it to

---

[49] *Collis v Emett* (1790) 1 H.Bl. 313; *Usher v Dauncey* (1814) 4 Camp. 97 (Illustration 3); *Schultz
v Astley* (1836) 2 Bing. N.C. 544 (Illustration 6); *Montague v Perkins* (1853) 22 L.J.C.P. 187
(Illustration 8); *Barker v Sterne* (1854) 9 Exch. 684 (Illustration 9); *Garrard v Lewis* (1882) 10
Q.B.D. 30 (s.9, Illustration 3); *Dunn v Jefferson* (1925) 69 S.J. 725; *Guildford Trust Ltd v Goss*
(1927) 43 T.L.R. 167 (Illustration 13); *Golden-Prism v But-Shop Investments & Distributors
(Pty) Ltd* 1978 (1) S.A. 512; *Ramsukh v Diesel Electric (Natal) Pty Ltd* 1994 (1) S.A. 876. See
also UCC, §§ 3–115, 3–407.
[50] *cf.* UCC, § 3–115(a).
[51] *Smith v Prosser* [1907] 2 K.B. 735, 744, 753; *Baxendale v Bennett* (1878) 3 Q.B.D. 525
(Illustration 20).
[52] *Herbert v Steele* 1953 (3) S.A. 271 (cheque).
[53] [1907] 2 K.B. 735 (Illustration 22).
[54] At 753–754.

become a bill, it was for him to see that it was issued in accordance with his intentions, and if he did not do this, third parties would not be affected; on the other hand, if he did not intend it to become a bill, there would be no such duty incumbent upon him, and he would be in the same position as if he had merely signed it as an autograph. There would in that case be no *animus emittendi*, and he would therefore not be liable for the act of a bailee who turned the document into a negotiable instrument."

The line of demarcation is not, however, always an easy one to draw. In the case in which these words were spoken[55] promissory notes were signed in blank and delivered to an agent as custodian only, though pending instructions in the future from the signer for their issue as promissory notes and as to the amount to be filled in. The agent fraudulently completed the notes and gave them to the payee, who received them in good faith and for value. Since the signer did not have the intention that the agent should issue them as promissory notes, he was not estopped[56] from saying that he was not the maker of the notes. On the other hand, where post-dated cheques were signed in blank and delivered to the signer's copartner to be used for the purpose of the partnership business, and the cheques were fraudulently completed and negotiated (while still post-dated) to a holder in due course, the signer was held liable as drawer of the cheques.[57]

Secondly, the person seeking to enforce the instrument must not himself have completed the instrument, and the instrument must have been completed before it was negotiated to him. In *Hatch v Searles*,[58] Stuart V.-C. said[59]:                                                                      **2–138**

"As to a bona fide holder, the question as to the effect of the acceptance or indorsement having been written on a blank piece of paper can be of no importance, unless he is fastened with notice of that imperfection. If the holder has notice of the imperfection, he can be in no better situation than the person who took it in blank, as to any right of the acceptor or indorsee who gave it in blank."

---

[55] *Smith v Prosser* [1907] 2 K.B. 735, which has been followed in Canada in *Hubbert v Home Bank of Canada* (1910) 20 O.L.R. 651; *Ray v Willson* (1911) 45 Can. S.C.R. 401; *Campbell v Bourque* (1914) 17 D.L.R. 262; *Frontier Finance Ltd v Hynes and Niagara Sewing Machine Co.* (1957) 10 D.L.R. (2d) 206; *Commercial Acceptance Corp. v Paris* (1964) 45 D.L.R. (2d) 493; *Nordic Acceptance Ltd v Switzer* (1965) 50 D.L.R. (2d) 600; affirmed 55 D.L.R. (2d) 385n. But see the criticism in *Crawford and Falconbridge* (8th ed.), § 5001.6 (pp.1321–1323).

[56] The proviso to s.20(2) did not apply, as the notes were not negotiated after completion to a holder in due course: see n.62, below. But presumably the result would have been the same had the notes so been negotiated. For estoppel, see below, para.2–139.

[57] *Guildford Trust Ltd v Goss* (1927) 43 T.L.R. 167 (Illustration 13). See also the cases cited in para.2–136, n.49, above.

[58] (1854) 2 Sm. & G. 147 (Illustration 4).

[59] At 153. See also *Awde v Dixon* (1851) 6 Exch. 869 (Illustration 11).

And in *France v Clark*,[60] where this observation was approved by the Court of Appeal, Lord Selborne L.C. said[61]: "The defence of purchaser for valuable consideration without notice, by any one who takes from another without inquiry an instrument signed in blank by a third party, and then himself fills up the blanks, appears to us to be altogether untenable."

Thirdly, the instrument must, after completion, have been negotiated to him. If an instrument is filled up in a manner contrary to the authority given and is then delivered to the named payee of the instrument who gives value for it in good faith, there will be no "negotiation" of the instrument to him (as the word is understood in the proviso) as a holder in due course.[62]

Fourthly, he must be a holder in due course, as defined by section 29 of the Act. In particular, there must be nothing in the transaction to lead him to suspect that it was not bona fide.[63]

**2–139**     **Estoppel.** The subject of signature on blank paper is not exhaustively covered by section 20 of the Act and there is still room for the operation of an estoppel at common law.[64]

First, a person who signs a negotiable instrument in blank or while it is otherwise incomplete may be estopped from denying the validity of the completed instrument as against a holder who has acted to his detriment in reliance upon it, even in circumstances where the holder would not be protected by the proviso to subsection (2). In *Lloyds Bank Ltd v Cooke*,[65] the defendant signed a blank paper which he intended to become a promissory note and to be made use of as security for an advance. He handed it to C, authorising him to fill it up and raise money on it. C exceeded the authority so given to him, because, instead of confining himself to the authorised amount, he fraudulently filled up the note for a greater amount payable to the claimant bank, and delivered it to the bank as security for a loan which the bank advanced to him in reliance upon it. As the bank was the original payee of the note, the proviso to subsection (2) was of no assistance: the note had not been negotiated after completion to a holder in due course.[66] But the defendant was held to be estopped as

---

[60] (1884) 26 Ch.D. 257.

[61] At 262.

[62] *Herdman v Wheeler* [1902] 1 K.B. 361 (Illustration 10); *Smith v Prosser* [1907] 2 KB. 735, 742, 752 (Illustration 22). See also *Jones (R.E.) Ltd v Waring & Gillow Ltd* [1926] A.C. 670. But *cf. Lloyds Bank Ltd v Cooke* [1907] 1 K.B. 794, below, para.2–147 (Illustration 21).

[63] *Hogarth v Latham* (1878) 3 Q.B.D. 643 (Illustration 12); *Ben Baron and Partners v Henderson* 1959 (3) S.A. 188.

[64] *Wilson and Meeson v Pickering* [1946] K.B. 422, 426.

[65] [1907] 1 K.B. 794 (Illustration 21).

[66] The contrary view expressed in the case by Fletcher Moulton L.J. was disapproved in *R.E. Jones Ltd v Waring and Gillow Ltd* [1926] A.C. 670. See above, para.2–138; below, para.4–059.

against the bank from denying the validity of the note.[67] On the other hand, where a document on which there was an acceptance signed in blank was stolen from the signer and converted into a bill of exchange,[68] and where a document in the form of a promissory note was signed in blank and entrusted to the signer's agent as custodian for safe keeping, but not with the intention that it be issued as a promissory note,[69] the signer was held not to be estopped from denying the validity of the instrument as against one who took it in good faith and for value. Further, in *Wilson and Meeson v Pickering*,[70] the claimants delivered to one of their employees a crossed cheque form signed on their behalf in blank and bearing the words "Not negotiable". The employee was instructed to fill up the form as a cheque for a specified amount payable to the Inland Revenue, but she fraudulently filled it up for a larger amount payable to the defendant and handed it to the defendant in satisfaction of an existing debt. Although the defendant received the cheque in good faith and without notice of the fraud, she could not, as original payee of the cheque, rely on the proviso to subsection (2); but she sought to contend that the claimants were estopped from denying the validity of the instrument. The Court of Appeal held that the claimants were not so estopped,[71] because the defendant had not acted to her detriment in reliance on the cheque and because she had taken a crossed cheque which bore on it the words "not negotiable", so that under section 81 of the Act[72] she had no better title to the cheque than that which the person from whom she took it had.

Secondly, if a customer of a bank signs a cheque in blank or while it is otherwise incomplete, and leaves it to an employee or other person to fill it up, he is bound, as against the bank, by the instrument as filled up by his agent.[73] By virtue of the relationship of banker and customer, the drawer is under a duty to the bank to take reasonable care to ensure that, when the document leaves his possession, it is fully and properly filled up.[74] The bank can therefore debit its customer's account with the amount paid out. The same principle might be applied where a bill of

---

[67] Relying, in particular, or *Brocklesby v Temperance Permanent Building Society* [1895] A.C. 173.

[68] *Baxendale v Bennett* (1878) 3 Q.B.D. 525 (Illustration 20).

[69] *Smith v Prosser* [1907] 2 K.B. 735 (Illustration 22).

[70] [1946] K.B. 422 (Illustration 23).

[71] The Court of Appeal also stated that the common law estoppel only applied to negotiable instruments. But, on this point, it has subsequently been held that the signature of a document in blank may preclude the person signing it from contesting its validity as against an innocent third party, even though the document signed is not a negotiable instrument: see *Mercantile Credit Co. Ltd v Hamblin* [1965] 2 Q.B. 242, 274–275, 278–279; *United Dominions Trust Ltd v Western* [1976] Q.B. 513 (overruling on this point *Campbell Discount Ltd v Gall* [1961] 1 Q.B. 431).

[72] See below, para.14–031 (s.81).

[73] *London Joint Stock Bank Ltd v Macmillan* [1918] A.C. 777, 811 (s.64, Illustration 5); *Verjee v CIBC Bank & Trust Co. (Channel Islands) Ltd* [2001] Lloyd's Rep. Bank. 279.

[74] [1918] A.C. 777.

exchange is domiciled for payment at a specified bank and is accepted in blank or while otherwise incomplete by a customer of that bank.[75] It is much more doubtful, however, whether a bank would similarly succeed against its customer if a cheque signed in blank by the customer were stolen from him[76] or if he entrusted such a cheque to another as custodian, but with no present intention that it should be completed and used.[77] But it is arguable that the bank should not be held responsible for paying a cheque signed by its customer in an incomplete state if, due to the negligence of the customer, another is enabled to complete the cheque and present it for payment to the bank, which pays it in good faith.[78]

2–140      **Non est factum.**[79] Section 20 will not apply where a person signs an incomplete instrument in the belief that he is signing a document which is essentially different in substance or in kind,[80] since he does not then deliver the document in order that it may be converted into a bill or note.

Illustrations

2–141      1. A bill for £200 is drawn by C on the defendant payable at 60 days sight, but the name of the payee is left blank. The defendant accepts the bill in that condition. Any bona fide holder may complete the bill by the insertion of his name as payee, and sue on the bill.[81]

2. R owes £500 to the defendant. He accepts two bills drawn on him, each for £250, and duly filled up, except that the name of the drawer is omitted. These bills are handed to the defendant. N also deposits with the defendant certain stock as security for the debt. R dies. An action is brought by the claimant, trustee in bankruptcy of N, claiming to be relieved from his suretyship. The action fails. R's acceptance is given for valuable consideration, and the authority to complete the bills is not revoked by his death. The failure by the defendant to fill in the drawer's name and to give notice of non-payment of the bills to the claimant does not discharge the claimant from his suretyship.[82]

---

[75] *Bank of England v Vagliano Brothers* [1891] A.C. 107 (s.7, Illustration 4: but this was not a case of an incomplete bill).

[76] *cf. Baxendale v Bennett* (1878) 3 Q.B.D. 525 (Illustration 20); *Herbert v Steele* 1953 (3) S.A. 271.

[77] *cf. Smith v Prosser* [1907] 2 K.B. 735 (Illustration 22).

[78] See UCC, §§ 3–115, 4–401.

[79] See below, para.3–022 (s.23).

[80] See, *e.g. Lewis v Clay* (1898) 67 L.J.Q.B. 224 (Section 23, Illustration 5) (note signed in belief that signature was merely that of a witness).

[81] *Crutchley v Mann* (1814) 5 Taunt. 529.

[82] *Carter v White* (1882) 20 Ch.D. 225, affirmed (1883) 25 Ch.D. 666.

3. The defendants carry on business as a partnership firm in which D is a partner. In February, D draws and indorses in blank a bill of exchange and hands the bill to a clerk to be completed as the exigencies of the business may require. In March D dies. In April the clerk inserts the names of the other parties in the firm and the amount of the bill. The bill is accepted by the firm. It is discounted by the claimant in good faith and for value. The surviving partners are liable on the bill.[83]

4. S gives C a blank acceptance on stamped paper to accommodate him, **2–142** and without receiving value. After S's death the signed paper is filled up as a bill and discounted to X, who sees it filled up. The death of S terminates the authority to complete and negotiate the bill, as the authority is not coupled with an interest. X cannot recover on the bill because he had notice of the acceptance in blank.[84]

5. The defendant accepts a bill of exchange drawn on him with a blank space left for the drawer's name. The bill comes into possession of the claimant, as administratrix of the estate of W, after it is overdue. The claimant may insert her own name as drawer and sue on the bill as administratrix.[85]

6. The defendant signs his acceptance on a blank stamped paper. The paper so signed is subsequently filled up as a bill payable to the order of the drawer, a fictitious signature being inserted as that of the drawer and indorser. The completed bill is then negotiated to the claimant, who takes it in good faith and for value. The claimant can recover against the defendant on the bill.[86]

7. The defendant writes his acceptance upon a blank stamped paper, **2–143** and hands the paper so signed to a moneylender to secure repayment with interest of a promised loan of £500. A receipt given by the moneylender indicates the intention that the document is to be negotiated, but nothing is said as to who should draw or indorse the bill. The bill, when completed, bears the signature of one "S.H.H." as drawer and the bill is drawn payable to himself. It purports to be indorsed by "S.H.H." to the claimant bank, which takes it as a bona fide holder for value. The defendant has been cheated out of his acceptance and receives no money. But since he delivered the document for the purpose of having the name of the drawer and indorser inserted, and of its being negotiated, the bill

---

[83] *Usher v Dauncey* (1814) 4 Camp. 97.
[84] *Hatch v Searles* (1854) 2 Sm. & G. 147.
[85] *Scard v Jackson* (1875) 34 L.T. (N.S.) 65.
[86] *Schultz v Astley* (1836) 2 Bing. N.C. 544.

is enforceable against him by the claimant. Even if "S.H.H." is a fictitious name, the defendant is liable.[87]

8. The defendant writes his acceptance on a blank stamped paper and delivers it to S for completion as a bill. 12 years later S fills it up as a bill drawn by himself on the defendant requiring the defendant to pay to S or order £200 five months after date. S indorses the bill so completed to H, who indorses it to the claimant, a bona fide holder for value. The jury find that the bill has not been completed within a reasonable time. This finding is immaterial, as delay in completion does not affect the rights of a bona fide holder for value. The defendant is liable to the claimant on the bill.[88]

9. M, in Bavaria, signs as drawer a blank form of a bill of exchange and sends it with a consignment of goods to his correspondents, Messrs S in London, for acceptance by the purchaser of the goods. Messrs S fill up the blanks by inserting the date, amount, etc., and procure its acceptance by the defendant. Then, in fraud of the drawer, they indorse it away for a private debt to the claimant, who takes it in good faith and for value. The claimant can recover against the defendant on the bill, and it is immaterial that the paper was not stamped, as it was not an inland bill.[89]

2–144      10. The defendant borrows £15 from A. He signs his name on a blank stamped paper and hands it to A with authority to complete it as a promissory note payable to A for £15. A fraudulently fills up the paper as a promissory note for £30 payable to the claimant. He hands it to the claimant, who takes it in good faith and for value. The claimant cannot recover against the defendant on the note. The delivery of the note by A to the claimant is not a negotiation of it within the proviso to section 20(2) of the Act.[90]

11. The defendant and his brother, X, sign as makers an instrument in the form of a promissory note, the name of the payee being left blank. The defendant signs on condition that the note shall only be issued if R will also join as a maker. R refuses to join. X, who is in possession of the note, represents that he has authority to deal with it. He fills in the name of the claimant as payee and delivers the note to the claimant for value. The claimant cannot recover against the defendant on the note. X's authority

[87] *London and South Western Bank Ltd v Wentworth* (1880) 5 Ex.D. 96.
[88] *Montague v Perkins* (1853) 22 L.J.C.P. 187.
[89] *Barker v Sterne* (1854) 9 Exch. 684.
[90] *Herdman v Wheeler* [1902] 1 K.B. 361.

to complete the note was limited and the claimant knew that the note was incomplete.[91]

12. The defendants, L and F, are partners in the firm of L & Co., F accepts in his firm's name bills of exchange payable to "our order" (*i.e.* to the order of the drawers) but with the drawers' name left blank. F has no authority from his co-partner to accept the bills. F hands the bills to C, who is a partner with the claimant in the firm of H & C. C gives the bills in their incomplete state to the claimant for a private debt. The claimant fills in the firm name of H & C as drawers. The claimant is not a bona fide holder as he suspected that something was wrong and cannot recover on the bill from L (as L & Co.).[92]

13. The defendant is in partnership with H and others. He draws a **2–145** post-dated cheque and signs it in blank, believing that, as usual, the rubber stamp of the partnership will be added and that the cheque will be used for the partnership business. H fills up the cheque payable to himself, but does not add the partnership stamp, so that the cheque appears to be the personal cheque of the defendant. H indorses the cheque while still post-dated to the claimants, moneylenders, who take it in good faith in return for a loan to H. Despite the fact that the cheque is post-dated, the claimants are holders in due course and can recover against the defendant on the cheque.[93]

14. The defendant enters into an agreement with the claimant to guarantee the payment by T for goods sold to T by the claimant, and for that purpose to indorse bills accepted by T. T writes his acceptance on a blank bill form, and the defendant adds his signature as indorser. The document is handed to the claimant, who fills it up as a bill payable to drawer's order, signs the bill as drawer and indorses the bill (in blank). The claimant can recover against the defendant on the bill. The bill has been completed in accordance with section 20(1) of the Act and the defendant is estopped from saying that the operations leading to completion of the bill were not done in the proper order.[94]

15. The claimants sell goods to A & Co. and the defendants undertake to guarantee payment for them. The claimants draw bills on A & Co expressed to be payable to the claimants' order. These bills are accepted by A & Co., indorsed by the defendants (in blank) and handed by the defendants to the claimants in exchange for delivery orders. Shortly

[91] *Awde v Dixon* (1851) 6 Exch. 869.
[92] *Hogarth v Latham* (1878) 3 Q.B.D. 643.
[93] *Guildford Trust Ltd v Goss* (1927) 43 T.L.R. 167.
[94] *Glenie v Bruce Smith* [1908] 1 K.B. 263.

before the bills become due the claimants indorse their name as payees on the bills above the defendants' signature. The bills are duly presented to A & Co. for payment, but are dishonoured. The claimants give notice of dishonour and claim payment from the defendants. The defendants are liable to the claimants on the bills. The bills, when handed to the claimants, were wanting in a material particular within the meaning of section 20(1) of the Act by reason of the absence of any indorsement by the claimants above the signature of the defendants, and the claimants have implied authority to fill in their name as payees over the name of the defendants. When so filled up, the bills became retrospectively enforceable.[95]

2–146      16. A Ltd are indebted to the claimants. It is agreed that A Ltd will accept bills of exchange drawn upon them by the claimants for the amount of the debt, and that the defendant will indorse the bills, in consideration of time being given, so as to render himself liable to pay if A Ltd do not do so. The claimants draw a series of bills addressed to A Ltd and payable to the claimants' order. These are accepted by A Ltd and indorsed by the defendant, who puts his signature on the back of the bills close to the top. The bills are subsequently indorsed by the claimants (in blank), their signature being written on the back of the bills below that of the defendant. The bills are dishonoured by non-payment at maturity. Subject to proper notice of dishonour, the defendant is liable to the claimants on the bills. Section 20(1) of the Act is satisfied. The order of signatures on the back of the bills is not conclusive and should not be held to nullify the intentions of the parties, but to be a mere inadvertence, not changing the rights of the parties.[96]

17. The claimants agree to advance to C Ltd £8,000 upon the basis of three bills to be accepted by C Ltd and indorsed "as guarantees" by the defendants, directors of C Ltd. Three bills drawn by the claimants upon C Ltd payable to the claimants' order are accepted by C Ltd and indorsed by the defendants by signing the bills on their backs. Before the bills are presented for payment, the claimants' indorsement is put upon them, but in each case, below the signatures of the defendants. It is the claimants' policy so to indorse bills taken by way of security. The defendants are (subject to proper notice of dishonour) liable to the claimants on the bills. The parties intended that the claimants should be at liberty to complete the bills by indorsement, and the claimants intended to do what was

---

[95] *Gerald McDonald & Co. v Nash & Co.* [1924] A.C. 625.
[96] *National Sales Corp. Ltd v Bernardi* [1931] 2 K.B. 188.

necessary to complete them by adding their indorsement. The position of the claimants' indorsement does not nullify that intention.[97]

18. The claimants are unwilling to supply further goods to W Ltd unless the bills of W Ltd are backed by the defendant, who is a director of the company. Nine bills are drawn by the claimants on W Ltd payable to their own order. These are accepted by W Ltd and indorsed by the defendant. The claimants themselves then indorse the bills by writing their name underneath, not above, that of the defendant. W Ltd fail to pay the bills. The defendant is liable to the claimants by reason of his indorsement. Under section 20 of the Act, the claimants had authority to complete the bills by adding their own indorsement. The fact that the signatures are out of order is no answer to the claimants' claim. Although the oral contract between the defendant and the claimants was a contract of guarantee, the Statute of Frauds cannot be set up as a defence to a claim on the bills.[98]

19. The claimants provide finance for hire-purchase transactions car-    **2–147** ried out by E Ltd by drawing bills of exchange payable to the claimants' order for the sums advanced, the bills being accepted by E Ltd and indorsed by the defendant, the managing director of E Ltd, as surety. One of the bills so accepted and indorsed is subsequently indorsed by the claimants beneath the signature of the defendant as follows: "Pay to Barclays Bank Ltd value on collection, per pro [the claimants]". The bill is dishonoured by non-payment. Subject to proper notice of dishonour, the defendant is liable to the claimants on the bill. Having regard to the intention of the parties, the claimants' indorsement may be treated, under section 20 of the Act, as though it had been made first as an indorsement in blank, which would validate the defendant's signature as an indorser, and, secondly, as a restrictive indorsement for collection. It does not therefore prevent the bill from being complete and regular on the face of it within section 29(1) of the Act nor the claimants from being a holder in due course within section 56.[99]

20. The defendant writes his acceptance on a blank stamped paper to accommodate H, but H, being no longer in need of accommodation returns the paper to the defendant in its incomplete state. The defendant places the paper in an unlocked drawer from which it is stolen. The paper reappears as a bill of exchange which purports to have been drawn by C

---

[97] *Lombard Banking Ltd v Central Garage and Engineering Co. Ltd* [1963] 1 Q.B. 220. See also below, para.6–118 (s.49, Illustration 20).
[98] *McCall v Hargreaves* [1932] 2 K.B. 423.
[99] *Yeoman Credit Ltd v Gregory* [1963] 1 W.L.R. 343. See also below, para.6–065 (s.45, Illustration 2) and para.6–118 (s.49, Illustration 21).

payable to himself, and indorsed by C to D and by D to the claimant. The claimant receives the bill in good faith and for value. The defendant is not liable to the claimant on the bill. After the return of the blank acceptance the defendant never authorised anyone to fill in the drawer's name and never issued the acceptance intending it to be used. There is no estoppel to prevent the defendant from setting up the true facts and, even if the defendant was negligent, the negligence was not the proximate of effective cause of the fraud.[1]

21. C informs the defendant that he is applying for a loan of £500 from the claimant bank and asks him to join in giving promissory notes by way of security for the loan. The defendant signs two blank stamped pieces of paper and it is agreed that C will fill each of them up as a promissory note for £250 payable to the claimants. C fraudulently fills up one of the pieces of paper as a promissory note for £1,000 payable to the claimants. He delivers it to the claimants, who, in reliance on it, make an advance to C of £1,000. The defendant is estopped from denying the validity of the note as between himself and the claimants. He is not allowed to assert that C exceeded the authority given to him.[2]

**2–148**  22. The defendant, in South Africa, being about to leave for England, signs his name on two blank unstamped pieces of paper, which are lithographed forms of promissory notes. He entrusts these to T his agent, to be retained by T until the defendant shall by letter or telegram from England give instructions for their issue as promissory notes and as to the amount to be filled in. T, without any instructions from and in fraud of the defendant, asks the claimant to buy the notes, which the claimant knows are made in blank, telling the claimant that he is acting under a power of attorney from the defendant. The claimant declines to purchase the notes unless they have two other signatures appended, so T himself and another, R, also sign the notes. The notes are completed for a large sum and the name of the claimant, as payee, inserted. They are purchased by the claimant for almost their full value and without knowledge of the fraud. The proviso to section 20(2) does not apply because the notes have not been negotiated after completion to a holder in due course. The defendant is not estopped from denying the validity of the notes as between himself and the claimant, since he delivered the notes to T as custodian, and not with the intention that they should be issued as negotiable instrument. No action can be maintained by the claimant against the defendant on the notes.[3]

---

[1] *Baxendale v Bennett* (1878) 3 Q.B.D. 525.
[2] *Lloyds Bank Ltd v Cooke* [1907] 1 K.B. 794.
[3] *Smith v Prosser* [1907] 2 K.B. 735.

23. A partner in the claimant firm signs on behalf of the claimants a blank crossed cheque form with the words "Not negotiable" printed on it. He hands the form to P, a secretary employed by the firm, with instructions to fill it up for £2 payable to the Inland Revenue. P fraudulently fills it up as a cheque for £54 4s. 0d. and inserts the name of the defendant as payee. P then hands the cheque to the defendant in payment of an existing debt for that amount owed by P to the defendant. The defendant receives the cheque in good faith and without notice of the fraud, and obtains payment of the cheque through her bankers. In an action by the claimants against the defendant to recover the sum so paid, the claimants rely on section 81 of the Act whereby the defendant, as payee, acquires no better title to the cheque than P from whom she took it. The claimants are not estopped as against the defendant from denying that the cheque was filled up in excess of their agent's authority because the defendant did not act to her prejudice in reliance on the cheque and because, in any event, the words "not negotiable" amounted to an express statement, to any person taking the cheque, that she would get no better title than that possessed by the person from whom she took it.[4]

## Delivery

21. (1) Every contract on a bill, whether it be the drawer's, the accep-    2–149
tor's, or an indorser's, is incomplete and revocable, until
delivery of the instrument in order to give effect thereto.

      Provided that where an acceptance is written on a bill, and
the drawee gives notice to or according to the directions of the
person entitled to the bill that he has accepted it, the acceptance then becomes complete and irrevocable.

  (2) As between immediate parties, and as regards a remote party
other than a holder in due course, the delivery—

    (a) in order to be effectual must be made either by or under
the authority of the party drawing, accepting, or indorsing, as the case may be:

    (b) may be shown to have been conditional or for a special
purpose only, and not for the purpose of transferring the
property in the bill.

    But if the bill be in the hands of a holder in due course a
valid delivery of the bill by all parties prior to him so as to
make them liable to him is conclusively presumed.

---

[4] *Wilson and Meeson v Pickering* [1946] K.B. 422

(3) **Where a bill is no longer in the possession of a party who has signed it as drawer, acceptor, or indorser, a valid and unconditional delivery by him is presumed until the contrary is proved.**

Definitions
"acceptance": s.2
"bill": s.2.
"delivery": s.2.
"holder in due course": s.29.
"person": s.2.

Comparison
UCC: §§ 3–105, 3–201, 3–203,
3–305, 3–409.

COMMENT

2–150    **Subsection (1): delivery to complete contract.** The contract constituted by the signature of the drawer[5] or of an indorser[6] on the bill is not complete until delivery of the instrument in order to give effect to it, and until that time the contract can be revoked.[7] "To constitute a contract", said Bovill C.J.,[8] "there must be a delivery over of the instrument by the drawer or indorser for a good consideration: and as soon as these circumstances take place the contract is complete, and it becomes a contract in writing." By section 2 of the Act, "delivery" means transfer of possession, actual or constructive,[9] from one person to another.

In the case of an acceptance, the contract of the acceptor[10] will likewise become complete and irrevocable upon delivery.[11] But an acceptance will also become complete and irrevocable if the drawee gives notice to or according to the directions of the person entitled to the bill that he has

---

[5] s.55(1).
[6] s.55(2).
[7] See (no delivery): *Cox v Troy* (1822) 5 B. & Ald. 474; *Brind v Hampshire* (1836) 1 M. & W. 365 (Illustration 4); *Bromage v Lloyd* (1847) 1 Exch. 32 (Illustration 2: note); *Re Devize* (1873) L.R. 9 Ch. App. 27; *Arnold v Cheque Bank* (1876) 1 C.P.D. 578, 584 (Illustration 1); (delivery): *Lysaght v Bryant* (1850) 9 C.B. 46 (Illustration 7); *Re Richards* (1887) 36 Ch.D. 541 (Illustration 3). Partial delivery is ineffectual: *Smith v Mundy* (1860) 3 E. & E. 22.
[8] *Abrey v Crux* (1869) L.R. 5 C.P. 37, 42. See also *Denton v Peters* (1870) L.R. 5 Q.B. 475, 477.
[9] See above, para.1–021 (s.2).
[10] s.54(1).
[11] It appears that the acceptor's signature must be on the bill at the time of the delivery of the instrument in order to give effect thereto: *Smith v Commercial Banking Co. of Sydney Ltd* (1910) 11 C.L.R. 667, 674, 676.

accepted it.[12] An acceptance must be completed either by delivery or by notification.[13]

Delivery is also necessary to pass the property in the bill, *i.e.* from the drawer to the payee or bearer, or from an indorser to an indorsee.[14] "In order to make the property in the bills pass" said Mellish L.J.,[15] "it is not sufficient to indorse them; they must be delivered to the indorsee or to the agent of the indorsee. If the indorser delivers them to his own agent, he can recover them; if to the agent of the indorsee, he cannot recover them".

A promissory note is inchoate and incomplete until delivery thereof to the payee or bearer.[16]

**Delivery by post.** There is considerable uncertainty whether an instru-   2–151
ment which is sent by post is delivered when it is posted or only when it is received. Where a cheque is sent by post by a debtor to his creditor in payment of a debt, this does not normally amount to payment if the cheque is lost in the post.[17] But there is authority for the view that, if the creditor expressly or impliedly[18] requests or authorises payment through the post, the debtor will be discharged if he complies with the request or authority by posting the cheque in a properly addressed letter to the creditor even though it does not reach him,[19] provided that the creditor's directions are complied with[20] and the cheque is in a form appropriate to be sent by post.[21] These cases lie somewhat uncomfortably side by side with others which establish that payment made by cheque is effected when the cheque is received and accepted in conditional payment of the

---

[12] *Cox v Troy* (1822) 5 B. & Ald. 474 at 478; *Chapman v Cottrell* (1865) 3 H. & C. 865, 867. *cf. Nova (Jersey) Knit Ltd v Kammgarn Spinnerei* [1977] 1 W.L.R. 713. As the drawee has no property in the bill, less is required to make him attorn to the holder.

[13] s.2 "Acceptance". See *Bank of Van Diemen's Land v Bank of Victoria* (1871) L.R. 3 P.C. 526 (Illustration 5).

[14] *Brind v Hampshire* (1836) 1 M. & W. 365; *Latter v White* (1872) L.R. 5 H.L. 578 (Illustration 6); *Arnold v Cheque Bank* (1876) 1 C.P.D. 578. See also below, para.3–051 (s.24).

[15] *Re Devize* (1873) L.R. 9 Ch. App. 27, 31–32.

[16] s.84. See also *Latter v White* (1872) L.R. 5 H.L. 578.

[17] *Luttges v Sherwood* (1895) 11 T.L.R. 233; *Pennington v Crossley & Sons Ltd* (1897) 77 L.T. 43; *Baker v Lipton Ltd* (1899) 15 T.L.R. 435; *Acraman v South Australian Gas Co.* [1910] S.A.L.R. 59.

[18] In *Mitchell-Henry v Norwich Union Life Insurance Socy Ltd* (1917) 34 T.L.R. 77, 78, it was stated that very little was needed to raise such an implication. But contrast *Pennington v Crossley & Sons Ltd* (1897) 77 L.T. 43 (course of dealing not sufficient).

[19] *Norman v Ricketts* (1886) 3 T.L.R. 182 (cheque stolen and cashed); *Thairlwall v Great Northern Ry* [1910] 2 K.B. 509 (dividend warrant); *Channon v English Scottish and Australian Bank* (1918) 18 S.R. (N.S.W.) 30; *ABSA Bank Ltd v Mutual and Federal Insurance Co. Ltd* 2003 (1) S.A. 635. See also *Tankexpress A/S v Compagnie Financière des Petroles* [1949] A.C. 76 (delay).

[20] *London Bank of Australia Ltd v Kendall* (1920) 28 C.L.R. 401.

[21] *Robb v Gow* 1905 8 F. 90 (uncrossed bearer cheque sent by post). *cf. Ose Gesellschaft v Jewish Colonial Trust* (1937) 43 T.L.R. 398.

debt[22] or sometimes only when the cheque is cleared and the proceeds credited to the payee's account.[23] They appear to determine upon whom the risk falls if a cheque sent by post is misappropriated and cashed.

The same principles might also be applied to determine whether delivery is complete and the property passes in an instrument despatched by post,[24] both when it does and when it does not reach the recipient. The former may be important, for example, in deciding in which country the contract of a party on the bill is made[25]; the latter as to who is the "true owner"[26] of an instrument which is stolen before it is received. There is, on the other hand, some force in the contention that, since United Kingdom postal regulations do not permit the sender to reclaim letters once posted, delivery should in any event be considered complete and the property should pass immediately the instrument is posted.[27] However, other cases indicate that an instrument sent by post is only delivered when received[28] and it is submitted that this is the better view.

2–152    **Subsection (2): defences.** This subsection permits certain defences to be raised with respect to the delivery of a bill. These defences cannot, however, be raised against a holder in due course. For the definition of a holder in due course, see section 29 of the Act.

By paragraph (a) it may be shown that the delivery referred to in subsection (1) was ineffectual because it was not made either by or under the authority of the party drawing, accepting or indorsing as the case may be.[29] The ordinary law of principal and agent will determine whether delivery has been made under the authority of that party.[30] However, in *Dextra Bank & Trust Co. Ltd v Bank of Jamaica*[31] the drawer of a cheque argued that, although he had authorised one P to deliver the cheque to

---

[22] *Pearce v Davis* (1834) 1 M. & R. 365; *Felix Hadley & Co. v Hadley* [1898] 2 Ch. 680; *Marreco v Richardson* [1908] 2 K.B. 584; *The Brimnes* [1975] Q.B. 929, 948, 969; *Homes v Smith* [2000] Lloyd's Rep. Bank. 139.

[23] *Re Owen decd* [1949] 1 All E.R. 901; *Re Hone* [1951] Ch. 85. See (1951) 72 J.I.B. 89.

[24] *London Bank of Australia Ltd v Kendall* (1920) 28 C.L.R. 401.

[25] See below, para.12–007 (s.72).

[26] See below, para.3–051 (s.24).

[27] *Re Devize* (1873) L.R. 9 Ch.App. 27 at 32. See also *ABSA Bank Ltd v Mutual and Federal Insurance Co. Ltd* 2003 (1) S.A. 635, 638. Contrast *London Bank of Australia Ltd v Kendall* (1920) 28 C.L.R. 304.

[28] *Chapman v Cottrell* (1865) 3 H. & C. 865; *London Bank of Australia Ltd v Kendall* (1920) 28 C.L.R. 304; *Nova (Jersey) Knit Ltd v Kammgarn Spinnerei* [1977] 1 W.L.R. 713, 718, 724, 733. See also *Davidovich and Mandel v Hill* [1948] 2 D.L.R. 613; *Re Northern Ontario Power Co.* [1954] 1 D.L.R. 627, 637; *Bordo v 403512 Ontario Inc.* (1983) 145 D.L.R. (3d) 235, 242.

[29] *Marston v Allen* (1841) 8 M. & W. 494.

[30] Compare *Bromage v Lloyd* (1847) 1 Exch. 32 (Illustration 2) with *Re Richards* (1887) 36 Ch.D. 541 (Illustration 3). See also *Cox v Canadian Bank of Commerce* (1911) 21 Man. R. 1, affirmed (1912) 5 D.L.R. 372.

[31] [2002] 1 All E.R. (Comm.) 193 (s.59, Illustration 21).

the payee, he had not authorised delivery of the cheque by B, an intermediary employed by P to hand over the cheque. The delivery of the cheque
to the payee was therefore ineffectual as it was not made by or under his
authority. This argument was rejected by the Judicial Committee of the
Privy Council. Lord Bingham and Lord Goff said[32]:

> " . . . s.21(2)(a) is concerned with authority to deliver and not with
> the precise mode of delivery which is authorised. The distinction
> makes good sense. If a cheque is drawn in favour of a named payee
> and is placed, for example, in a file, from which it is abstracted by a
> thief or mischief-maker by whom it is handed to the payee, it seems
> just that the drawer should not be liable since he has never author-
> ised delivery at all. But if the drawer prescribes delivery by one
> method and physical transfer is effected by another, in circumstances
> where the payee gives value and does not (and ordinarily could not)
> know of the method of transfer prescribed by the drawer, it would
> seem neither just nor consistent with the objective of achieving
> maximum certainty in mercantile transactions to deny the transferee
> a right to recover. It was accepted that the [payee] gave value for the
> cheque".

By paragraph (b) it may be shown that the delivery was conditional or
for a special purpose only, and not for the purpose of transferring the
property in the bill. Thus it may be shown that the delivery was in escrow,
i.e. that the instrument was to be delivered so as not to take effect as a bill
until a certain condition should have been fulfilled.[33] Or it may be shown,
for example, that the bill was indorsed and delivered so that it might be
discounted or realised, the property not to pass until that time,[34] or so that
the indorsee might collect payment of the bill, but not with the intention
of transferring to him the property in the bill.[35] The condition or special
purpose must, however, be communicated by the transferor to the transferee.[36] A bill may also be delivered conditionally as collateral security, it
being agreed that it will become operative only in the event of default.[37]

---

[32] [2002] 1 All E.R. (Comm.) 193 at [23].

[33] *Jefferies v Austin* (1725) 1 Stra. 674 (Illustration 8); *Bell v Lord Ingestre* (1848) 12 Q.B. 317
(Illustration 9); *Druiff v Parker* (1868) L.R. 5 Eq. 131, 137; *Insurance Corpn. of Ireland plc v
Dunluce Meats Ltd* [1991] N.I. 286.

[34] *Goggerley v Cuthbert* (1806) 2 B. & P. N.R. 170; *Cranch v White* (1835) 1 Bing. N.C. 414; *Adams
v Jones* (1840) 12 A. & E. 455; *Lloyd v Howard* (1850) 15 Q.B. 995 (Illustration 11); *Muttyloll
Seal v Dent* (1853) 8 Moore P.C. 319; *Dawson v Isle* [1906] 1 Ch. 633, 639.

[35] *Ex p. Twogood* (1812) 19 Ves. Jun. 229, 231–232; *Castrique v Buttigieg* (1855) 10 Moore P.C.
94, 108–109; *Denton v Peters* (1870) L.R. 5 Q.B. 475 (Illustration 10). See also *Novaknit Hellas
SA v Kumar Brothers International Ltd* [1998] Lloyd's Rep. Bank. 287.

[36] *Dextra Bank & Trust Co. Ltd v Bank of Jamaica* [2002] 1 All E.R. (Comm.) 193 at [19] (s.59,
Illustration 21).

[37] *Alsager v Close* (1842) 10 M. & W. 576.

Upon fulfilment of the condition, a conditional delivery becomes complete and takes effect at that time.[38]

**2–153**     The fact that the delivery was invalid or not unconditional may be raised as between immediate parties and in principle as regards a remote party other than a holder in due course.[39] A party sued on a bill may therefore plead the defect in delivery against a person with whom he has no direct relationship. For example, if an acceptor is sued by an indorsee of a bill, he may show that the indorsement was not completed by a valid and unconditional delivery to the indorsee, and that the indorsee has in consequence no title to sue.[40] On the other hand, if the drawer of a cheque hands the cheque to his agent with instructions (though subject to certain conditions) to deliver the cheque to the payee and the agent so delivers the cheque without observing or notifying to the payee the conditions to which his authority to deliver is subject, the payee will acquire a good title to the cheque, provided he gives value and has no notice of the agent's limited authority.[41]

The defect in delivery may be established by oral evidence.[42] The parol evidence rule (see below) does not apply. This is in conformity with the common law which admits oral evidence to show that what purports to be a written contract is no contract at all[43] or to prove an agreement that a written contract is not to come into operation until a certain condition is fulfilled.[44] In practice, however, it may be difficult to distinguish[45] between situations where it is orally agreed that the bill is not to become operative pending the fulfilment of a condition (in which case oral evidence of the conditional delivery will be admitted) and situations where the bill is delivered operatively but subject to an oral agreement in defeasance of a party's liability on the bill (in which case oral evidence to qualify the terms of the written instrument will normally not be admitted).[46]

Where a person to whom a bill is delivered conditionally or for a special purpose misappropriates it, the true owner may sue that person, and any person other than a holder in due course who deals with the bill

---

[38] *Clifford Chance v Silver* [1992] 2 Bank L.R. 11 (s.29, Illustration 8).

[39] For the distinction between immediate and remote parties, see below, para.4–005.

[40] *Bell v Lord Ingestre* (1848) 12 Q.B. 317; *Lloyd v Howard* (1850) 15 Q.B. 995.

[41] *Watson v Russell* (1862) 3 B. & S. 34, (1864), 5 B. & S. 968 (s.38, Illustration 2); *Dextra Bank & Trust Co. Ltd v Bank of Jamaica* [2002] 1 All E.R. Comm. 193 at [22]. This is so even though the payee of a cheque cannot be a holder in due course: see below, para.4–059.

[42] See the cases cited in nn.33 and 34, above.

[43] *Chitty on Contracts* (29th ed.), Vol.I, § 12–106.

[44] *Chitty on Contracts*, Vol.I, § 12–109.

[45] See *Young v Austen* (1869) L.R. 4 C.P. 553, 556; *Hitchings and Coulthurst Co. v Northern Leather Co. of America and Doushkess* [1914] 3 K.B. 907 (Illustration 25); *Guildford Trust Ltd v Goss* (1927) 43 T.L.R. 167 (s.20, Illustration 13).

[46] See below, para.2–155.

in a manner inconsistent with his rights, for conversion of the bill[47]; or if the bill has been collected, the true owner may claim the proceeds by an action in restitution.[48]

The provisions of the subsection apply, with the necessary modifications, to promissory notes.[49]

**Subsections (2) and (3): presumptions as to delivery.** If a bill is in the hands of a holder in due course[50] a valid delivery of the bill by all parties prior to him so as to make them liable to him is conclusively presumed. So, for example, if a completed cheque drawn payable to bearer is stolen from the drawer and delivered by the thief to a holder in due course,[51] or if the drawer is induced by the fraud of an employee to draw a cheque payable to the order of a fictitious or non-existing person (which cheque may be treated as payable to bearer)[52] and to hand the cheque to the employee who negotiates it to a holder in due course,[53] the drawer cannot assert, as against such a holder, that the cheque was never "issued" by delivery. So also if the holder of a bill indorses the instrument to an indorsee in escrow or for a special purpose only, and the indorsee in breach of trust transfers the instrument to a holder in due course, the indorser will be liable to that holder on the instrument.[54]

Where a bill is in the hands of a person, *e.g.* the payee or a holder for value or a collecting banker,[55] who is not a holder in due course, the conclusive presumption as to prior deliveries does not apply. But he may be assisted by the rebuttable presumption in subsection (3) which effectively places the burden of proof[56] upon the person against whom the bill is sought to be enforced, to show that there was no delivery by the

2–154

---

[47] *Goggerley v Cuthbert* (1806) 2 B. & P.N.R. 170; *Cranch v White* (1835) 1 Bing.N.C. 414; *Alsager v Close* (1842) 10 M. & W. 576. But see, in relation to cheques, Cheques Act 1957, s.4; below, para.17–028.

[48] *Muttyloll Seal v Dent* (1853) 8 Moore P.C. 319. See also *Arnold v Cheque Bank* (1876) 1 C.P.D. 517 (no delivery).

[49] s.89.

[50] Defined in s.29. The conclusive presumption also applies where the holder is a "sheltered holder" within s.29(3): *Insurance Corp. of Ireland plc v Dunluce Meats Ltd* [1991] N.I. 286. But the original payee of a bill in whose possession it remains cannot be a holder in due course. See below, para.2–155.

[51] *Ingham v Primrose* (1859) 7 C.B.N.S. 82, 85. Contrast *Baxendale v Bennett* (1878) 3 Q.B.D. 524 (*incomplete* and undelivered instrument: s.20, Illustration 20).

[52] s.7(3).

[53] *Clutton & Co. v Attenborough & Sons* [1897] A.C. 90, 95 (s.7, Illustration 3).

[54] *Marston v Allen* (1841) 8 M. & W. 494, 504; *Lloyd v Howard* (1850) 15 Q.B. 995, 998; *Barber v Richards* (1851) 6 Exch. 63.

[55] Whether or not the banker is a holder: *Surrey Asset Finance Ltd v National Westminster Bank* [2001] E.W.C.A. Civ. 60.

[56] See *Colin v Gibson* (1927) 27 S.R. (N.S.W.) 328, 331; *Equitable Securities Ltd v Neal* [1987] 1 N.Z.L.R. 233, 240; *Midland Bank plc v Brown Shipley & Co. Ltd* [1991] 1 Lloyd's Rep. 576, 583; *National Bank of Canada v Tardival Associates* (1994) 109 D.L.R. (4th) 126; *Surrey Asset Finance Ltd v National Westminster Bank*, above, n.55.

drawer, acceptor[57] or indorser (as the case may be) or that the delivery was defective.

**2–155**    **Admissibility of extrinsic evidence.** The contracts of the various parties to a bill of exchange or promissory note are contracts which are required by law to be in writing.[58] They are, therefore, like any other contract which has been reduced to writing, subject (in England)[59] to what is commonly known as the "parol evidence rule".[60] The rule has been summarised as follows: "Parol testimony cannot be received to contradict, vary, add to or subtract from the terms of a written contract, or the terms in which the parties have deliberately agreed to record any part of their contract."[61] The effect is to bind a party to his contract as written on the instrument: extrinsic evidence[62] is, in general, inadmissible to prove that the terms of the contract differed from those expressed in writing on the bill or note.[63]

The merits of the rule are a matter of dispute.[64] Moreover, the rule is in no sense an absolute one. The courts are prepared to admit extrinsic evidence of terms additional to those contained in a written document if it is shown that the document was not intended to express the entire agreement between the parties.[65] However, since the contracts of the parties to a bill or note must be in writing, *oral* evidence is in principle excluded by the operation of the rule, even as between immediate parties[66] to the instrument.[67] There is, perhaps, less injustice in this than at first sight appears. In view of the formal nature of negotiable instruments, it is arguable that to admit such evidence would undermine the certainty and finality which ought to attach to each party's promise on the instrument. "What is to become of bills of exchange and promissory notes",

---

[57] Or the maker of a note, see s.89(2); *Yan v Post Office Bank Ltd* [1994] 1 N.Z.L.R. 154.

[58] See s.3(1) (drawer), s.17(2) (acceptor), s.32(1) (indorser), s.83(1) (maker).

[59] *cf.* s.100 (Scotland).

[60] See *Chitty on Contracts* (29th ed.), Vol.I, §§ 12–095 *et seq.*

[61] *Bank of Australasia v Palmer* [1897] A.C. 540, *per* Lord Morris at 545. See also *Goss v Lord Nugent* (1833) 5 B. & Ad. 58, 64; *Young v Austen* (1869) L.R. 4 C.P. 553, 556; *Abrey v Crux* (1869) L.R. 5 C.P. 37; *Maillard v Page* (1870) L.R. 5 Exch. 312, 319; *Hill v Wilson* (1873) L.R. 8 Ch. App. 888, 898; *New London Credit Syndicate v Neale* [1898] 2 Q.B. 487; *Hitchings & Coulthurst Co. v Northern Leather Co. of America and Doushkess* [1914] 3 K.B. 907.

[62] Whether oral or written; but see below, para.2–156.

[63] See the cases cited in n.60 (above) and n.69 (below).

[64] See The Law Commission Report (Law Com. 154) (1986). The Commission recommended no legislative action to reform or clarify the rule.

[65] *Harris v Rickett* (1859) 4 H. & N. 1; *Malpas v L. & S.W. Ry* (1866) L.R. 1 C.P. 336; *Mercantile Bank of Sydney v Taylor* [1893] A.C. 317, 321; *Gillespie Bros & Co. v Cheney, Eggar & Co.* [1896] 2 Q.B. 59, 62; *J. Evans & Son (Portsmouth) Ltd v Andrea Merzario Ltd* [1976] 1 W.L.R. 1078; *Haryanto (Yani) v E.D. & F. Man (Sugar) Ltd* [1986] 2 Lloyd's Rep. 44, 46–47.

[66] See below, para.4–005 (s.27).

[67] See the cases cited in n.60 (above) and n.69 (below).

said Lord Ellenborough,[68] "if they may be cut down by a secret agreement that they shall not be put in suit?"

Most cases where the parol evidence rule has been applied are cases where a party to a bill or note has sought to qualify his absolute undertaking on the instrument by adducing evidence of a contemporaneous oral agreement in defeasance of that undertaking, that is to say, that his liability is to be enforceable against him only in certain contingencies or that it is to be postponed to a time later than that expressed on the face of the instrument.[69] Since the effect of such evidence would be to contradict the terms of the written instrument, it is inadmissible.

On the other hand, "a written agreement on a distinct paper, to renew, **2–156** or in other respects to qualify, the liability of the maker or acceptor, is good as between the original parties".[70] Indeed, it would seem that, as between immediate parties,[71] evidence may always be given of a *written* agreement to vary the effect of the instrument and regulate their rights as between themselves.[72] Yet in order to afford a defence to liability it must be shown that the written agreement was supported by valuable consideration[73] and that it was not collateral to the instrument, *e.g.* because persons other than the parties to the instrument are parties to the agreement,[74] but that the writing and the instrument form only one contract.[75] Such a situation may arise where a bill or note is given contemporaneously with a credit agreement—for example, a mortgage[76] or hire-

---

[68] *Hoare v Graham* (1811) 3 Camp. 57.

[69] *Hoare v Graham* (1811) 3 Camp. 57 (Illustration 12); *Free v Hawkins* (1817) 8 Taunt. 92 (Illustration 13); *Rawson v Walker* (1816) 1 Stark. 361 (Illustration 14); *Woodbridge v Spooner* (1819) 3 B. & Ald. 233 (Illustration 15); *Campbell v Hodgson* (1819) Gow 74 (Illustration 16); *Moseley v Hanford* (1830) 10 B. & C. 729 (Illustration 18); *Foster v Jolly* (1835) 1 C.M. & R. 703 (Illustration 19); *Adams v Wordley* (1836) 1 M. & W. 374 (Illustration 20); *Besant v Cross* (1851) 10 C.B. 895 (Illustration 21); *Drain v Harvey* (1855) 17 C.B. 257 (Illustration 22); *Abrey v Crux* (1869) L.R. 5 C.P. 37 (Illustration 23); *Young v Austen* (1869) L.R. 4 C.P. 553, 556; *Maillard v Page* (1870) L.R. 5 Exch. 312, 319; *Stott v Fairlamb* (1883) 52 L.J.Q.B. 420; *New London Credit Syndicate v Neale* [1898] 2 Q.B. 487 (Illustration 24); *Union Bank v MacCullough* (1912) 7 D.L.R. 694; *Hitchings and Coulthurst Co. v Northern Leather Co. of America and Doushkess* [1914] 3 K.B. 907 (Illustration 25).

[70] *Byles* (26th ed.), p.401.

[71] See below, para.4–005 (s.27).

[72] *Bowerbank v Monteiro* (1813) 4 Taunt. 844, 846; *Young v Austen* (1869) L.R. 4 C.P. 553 (Illustration 26); *Maillard v Page* (1870) L.R. 5 Exch. 312, 319 (Illustration 27).

[73] *Bowerbank v Monteiro* (1813) 4 Taunt. 844. See also *McManus v Bark* (1870) L.R. 5 Exch. 65.

[74] *Webb v Simpson* (1849) 13 Q.B. 894; *Salmon v Webb* (1852) 3 H.L.C. 310 (Illustration 28).

[75] *Young v Austen* (1869) L.R. 4 C.P. 553 at 556, 557; *Maillard v Page* (1870) L.R. 5 Exch. 312 at 319. See also the cases cited, above, n.65. If the agreement is merely collateral, it only affords ground for a cross-action, and not for a defence to liability on the instrument: *Maillard v Page* (1870) L.R. 5 Exch. 312, at 319. See also *Salmon v Webb* (1852) 3 H.L.C. 310.

[76] *Walker v Jones* (1865) L.R. 1 P.C. 50.

purchase agreement[77]—and as collateral security for the liability of the debtor under that agreement: the terms of the instrument may be subject to and controlled by the terms of the credit agreement.

**2–157**     **Exceptions to the parol evidence rule.** There are a number of exceptions to the parol evidence rule, or, more accurately, situations where the parol evidence rule will not be applied.[78] The dividing line between the rule and the "exceptions" is often subtle, and it is not particularly useful to try to reconcile apparently conflicting decisions. In the result, the scope of application of the rule is an area of difficulty and uncertainty for the practitioner. That difficulty and uncertainty is exacerbated by the fact that, in relation to bills and notes, the majority of the decisions on the application or non-application of the rule date from the nineteenth century and do not necessarily reflect the somewhat more relaxed approach which is adopted by the courts in respect of contracts generally.

Where the exceptions apply, even oral evidence may be admitted to qualify the ostensible contract of a party on the instrument. However, a person to whom a bill or note is negotiated or delivered is entitled to assume that each party's promise is absolute and unqualified unless it is otherwise indicated on the instrument itself. In most cases,[79] therefore, extrinsic evidence will be admissible only as between immediate parties, or as regards a remote party[80] who took the instrument with knowledge of the qualification.

**2–158**     **Evidence of the validity or effectiveness of the contract on the bill.** Parol evidence is admissible to prove the presence of a vitiating factor that deprives the ostensible contract written on the bill of its binding character. For example:

**2–159**     (i) *No contract*: Parol evidence will be admitted to show that what appears to be a valid and binding contract is in fact no contract at all.[81] Thus a party who has signed a bill or note may adduce such evidence to establish the defence of *non est factum, i.e.* to show that he believed that he was signing a fundamentally different document,[82] or to prove that his contract was incomplete because there was no effective delivery of the instrument in order to give effect thereto.[83]

---

[77] *United Dominions Trust Ltd v Bycroft* [1954] 1 W.L.R. 1345. But see now, in relation to agreements regulated by the Consumer Credit Act 1974, s.123(3) of that Act.

[78] See *Chitty on Contracts* (29th ed.), Vol.I, §§ 12–105—12–116.

[79] *cf.* the defence of *non est factum*, below, para.3–022.

[80] For the distinction between immediate and remote parties, see below, para.4–005 (s.27).

[81] See *Chitty on Contracts* (29th ed.), Vol.I, § 12–106.

[82] See below, para.3–022. This defence is available against a holder in due course: *Foster v Mackinnon* (1869) L.R. 4 C.P. 704.

[83] ss.21(1)(2)(a), above, para.2–154.

(ii) *Consideration*: Parol evidence is admissible to impeach the con- **2–160**
sideration for the contract.[84] A bill is not invalid by reason that it does not
specify the value given, or that any value has been given therefor.[85] But,
whether or not a bill expresses that value has been given, parol evidence
is admissible[86] to show want of or failure of consideration for the contract.[87] The words "value received" do not therefore preclude a party
from showing that no consideration has in fact been given[88] or that an
executory consideration has wholly or partly failed.[89] It seems, however,
that parol evidence may not be admissible to prove a real consideration
inconsistent with that expressed in the instrument.[90]

(iii) *Conditional contract*: Parol evidence is admissible to prove a con- **2–161**
temporaneous oral agreement that the contract was not to become operative except upon the fulfilment of a condition.[91]

(iv) *Fraud, illegality etc.*: Parol evidence will always be admitted to **2–162**
show that the contract was vitiated by fraud, illegality, misrepresentation,
mistake, duress, undue influence or any other ground which would
render a contract voidable or unenforceable at law or in equity.[92]

(v) *Agency*: Parol evidence is admissible to show that an agent signing **2–163**
per pro. was, in so signing, acting outside the actual limits of his authority[93] and generally to show that a person purporting to act on behalf of
another had no authority so to act.[94] It may possibly also be admitted, in

---

[84] See *Chitty on Contracts* (29th ed.), Vol.I, § 12–108.

[85] s.3(4)(b).

[86] But only between immediate parties, or as between remote parties if the holder is not a
holder for value: see ss.27(2), 30(1); below, paras 4–024 and 4–080.

[87] *Abbott v Hendrix* (1840) 1 M. & G. 791, 794, 796 (Illustration 30); *Young v Austen* (1869) L.R.
4 C.P. 553, 556; *Abrey v Crux* (1869) L.R. 5 C.P. 37, 45. See also *Thompson v Clubley* (1836)
1 M. & W. 212; *Glesby v Mitchell* [1932] 1 D.L.R. 641.

[88] *Abbott v Hendrix* (1840) 1 M. & G. 791 at 795.

[89] *Solly v Hinde* (1834) 2 Cr. & M. 516 (Illustration 29). See also below, paras 4–008 and
4–009.

[90] *Ridout v Bristow* (1830) 9 Exch. 48 (Illustration 17). But see *Abbott v Hendrix* (1840) 1 M. &
G. 791 at 796; *Clifford v Turrell* (1845) 14 L.J.Ch. 390; *Turner v Forwood* [1951] 1 All E.R. 746.
cf. *Peffer v Rigg* [1977] 1 W.L.R. 285, 293.

[91] s.21(2)(b), above, para.2–152. See also *Chitty on Contracts* (29th ed.), Vol.I, § 12–109; *Pym
v Campbell* (1856) 6 E. & B. 370; *Ontario Ladies' College v Kendry* (1905) 10 O.L.R. 324;
*Williams & Glyn's Bank Ltd v Belkin Packaging Ltd (No.2)* (1981) 123 D.L.R. (3d) 612, affirmed
(1983) 147 D.L.R. (3d) 577; *Eastern Elevator Services Ltd v Wolfe* (1981) 119 D.L.R. (3d) 643;
*Equitable Securities Ltd v Neil* [1987] N.Z.L.R. 233, 239–240. Such evidence is, however, only
admissible as between immediate parties and in any event is to be contrasted with
evidence in defeasance of a party's liability on the bill: see above, para.2–155.

[92] See *Chitty on Contracts* (29th ed.), Vol.I, § 12–112. Although these defences cannot be set
up against a holder in due course, parol evidence is admissible to show that a holder is
not a holder in due course. See also s.30(2).

[93] s.25.

[94] But the defence of want of authority may not be available against a holder in due course
or by reason of estoppel: see, *e.g.* the Comment to ss.20, 21, above, paras 2–137 and
2–139.

cases of ambiguity, to show that a signatory did or did not sign as agent.[95]

**2–164**      **Evidence of the true nature of the agreement or relationship between the parties.** Parol evidence is admissible to prove the true nature of the contract, or the legal relationship of the parties, even though this may vary or add to the ostensible contract written on the bill.[96] In *Macdonald v Whitfield*[97] Lord Watson said[98]:

> "... it is a well established rule of law that the whole facts and circumstances attendant upon the making, issue, and transference of a bill or note may be legitimately referred to for the purpose of ascertaining the true relation to each other of the parties who put their signatures upon it, either as makers or as indorsers; and that reasonable inferences, derived from these facts and circumstances, are admitted to the effect of qualifying, altering, or even inverting the relative liabilities which the law-merchant would otherwise assign to them."

The following provide illustrations:

**2–165**      (i) *Accommodation acceptance*: Parol evidence will be admitted to show that a bill has been accepted for the accommodation of, say the drawer.[99] In that case, as between the acceptor and the drawer, the acceptor is in substance a mere surety for the drawer: the drawer is ultimately liable and the acceptor, if forced to pay the holder, has a right of recourse against the drawer.[1] Parol evidence is therefore admissible to prove that the acceptor is to have the rights of a drawer and that the drawer is subject to the liabilities of an acceptor.[2]

**2–166**      (ii) *Suretyship*: Parol evidence may be adduced to prove that a party signed a bill or note in the capacity of surety.[3] So, for example, such evidence is admissible to show that it was the common intention, both of the original payee of a bill and of an indorser, that the latter should be

---

[95] *Albert Pearl (Management) Ltd v J.D.F. Builders Ltd* (1971) 22 D.L.R (3d) 532, revd 31 D.L.R. (3d) 690, varied 49 D.L.R. (3d) 422; *Rolfe Lubell & Co. v Keith* [1979] 1 All E.R. 860. But contrast *Chapman v Smethurst* [1909] 1 K.B. 927, 930; *Kettle v Dunster and Wakefield* (1927) 43 T.L.R. 770.

[96] See *Chitty on Contracts* (29th ed.), Vol.I, § 12–113.

[97] (1883) 8 App. Cas. 733.

[98] At 745. See also his earlier statement in similar terms in *Steele v M'Kinlay* (1880) 5 App. Cas. 754, 778–779.

[99] See s.28.

[1] *Thompson v Clubley* (1836) 1 M. & W. 212; *Lazarus v Cowie* (1842) 3 Q.B. 459; *Ewin v Lancaster* (1865) 6 B. & S. 571 (Illustration 31); *Overend Gurney & Co. v Oriental Finance Co.* (1874) L.R. 7 H.L. 348 (s.28, Illustration 3); *Solomon v Davis* (1883) 1 Cab. & E. 83 (Illustration 32).

[2] *Steele v M'Kinlay* (1880) 5 App. Cas. 754 at 779.

[3] *Chitty on Contracts* (29th ed.), Vol.I, § 12–116.

directly liable to the former on the bill as surety for the liability of the acceptor,[4] or to show that successive indorsers were in fact cosureties,[5] or to show that a maker of a note signed it as surety for the comaker of the note.[6]

(iii) *Indorsements without liability*: Parol evidence is admissible of an **2–167** agreement between an indorser and his immediate indorsee that the instrument is to be indorsed to the indorsee for a special purpose only, but not with the intention of enabling him to claim against the indorser.[7] In *Castrique v Buttigieg*[8] it was said[9]:

"The liability of an indorser to his immediate indorsee arises out of a contract between them, and this contract in no case consists exclusively in the writing popularly called an indorsement, and which is indeed necessary to the existence of the contract in question, but that contract arises out of the written indorsement itself, the delivery of the Bill to the indorsee, and the intention with which that delivery was made and accepted, as evinced by the words, either spoken or written, of the parties, and the circumstances (such as the usage at the place, the course of dealing between the parties and their respective situations) under which the delivery takes place: thus a Bill, with an unqualified written indorsement, may be delivered and received for the purpose of enabling the indorsee to receive the money for account of the indorser, or to enable the indorsee to raise money for his own use on the credit of the signature of the indorser, or with an express stipulation that the indorsee, though for value, is to claim against the drawer and acceptor only, and not against the indorser, who agrees to sell his claim against the prior parties, but stipulates not to warrant their solvency. In all these cases the indorser is not liable to the indorsee, and they are all in conformity with the general law of contract, which enables parties to them to limit and modify

---

[4] *Gerald McDonald & Co. v Nash & Co.* [1924] A.C. 625 (see s.20, Illustration 15), distinguishing *Steele v M'Kinlay* (1880) 5 App. Cas. 754, which was not followed in *McCall Bros Ltd v Hargreaves* [1932] 2 K.B. 423; *Rolfe Lubell & Co. v Keith* [1979] 1 All E.R. 860.

[5] *Macdonald v Whitfield* (1883) 8 App. Cas. 733 (Illustration 33).

[6] *Hill v Wilcox* (1831) 1 M. & Rob. 58 (Illustration 34). See also *McIntosh v McNaughton* [1935] 2 D.L.R. 237; *Glatt v Ritt* (1973) 34 D.L.R. (3d) 295.

[7] *Ex p. Twogood* (1812) 19 Ves. Jun. 229, 231; *Castrique v Buttigieg* (1855) 10 Moore P.C. 94; *Novaknit Hellas SA v Kumar Brothers International Ltd* [1998] Lloyd's Rep. Bank. 287. Where the indorsement is for a special purpose only, and not for the purpose of transferring the property in the bill, this will fall within s.21(2)(b). But the indorsement may be made for a special purpose only, and for the purpose of transferring the property in the bill: *Castrique v Buttigieg* (1855) 10 Moore P.C. 94. Where the indorser is also the drawer, the agreement may also relieve him of liability as drawer: see *Pike v Street* (1828) M. & M. 226.

[8] (1855) 10 Moore P.C. 94 (Illustration 35).

[9] At 108–109.

their liabilities as they think fit, provided they do not infringe any prohibitory law."

But, as against a holder in due course, any stipulation which negatives or limits the liability of an indorser must be expressed and inserted in the instrument itself.[10]

**2–168**  (iv) *Order of indorsements*: Parol evidence is admissible to displace the order of the indorsements as they appear on the instrument[11] and in general to show the purpose with which an indorsement was made.[12]

It would seem clear, however, that parol evidence of the true nature of the agreement or relationship between the parties ought not to be admitted so as to prejudice the position of a holder in due course[13] or the position of a payee or another party to the instrument who was not privy to the agreement relied on.[14] Each of these should be entitled to enforce the instrument as written.

**2–169**  **Evidence of discharge or variation.** Parol evidence is admissible to show that the written contract has been discharged by payment, release or otherwise.[15] However, the absolute and unconditional renunciation by the holder, at or after maturity of a bill, of his rights against the acceptor must be in writing unless the bill is delivered up to the acceptor.[16] The written contract may also be varied by a subsequent agreement for valuable consideration[17]; but since the contract is one which, by law, is required to be in writing it can in principle only be varied by writing,[18] it is questionable whether, in the case of a bill or note, a mere assurance given by one person to another that he will forbear to enforce his strict legal rights would have effect between them as a waiver or equitable

---

[10] s.16.

[11] *National Sales Corp. Ltd v Bernardi* [1931] 2 K.B. 188 (s.20, Illustration 16); *Lombard Banking Ltd v Central Garage and Engineering Co. Ltd* [1963] 1 Q.B. 220 (s.20, Illustration 17). See also ss.32(5), 55(2)(a), (c).

[12] *ibid.*; see also *Gerald McDonald & Co. v Nash & Co.* [1924] A.C. 625 (s.20, Illustration 15); *McCall Bros Ltd v Hargreaves* [1932] 2 K.B. 423 (s.20, Illustration 18); *McIntosh v McNaughton* [1935] 2 D.L.R. 237; *Yeoman Credit Ltd v Gregory* [1963] 1 W.L.R. 343 (s.20, Illustration 19); *Rolfe Lubell & Co. v Keith* [1979] 1 All E.R. 860.

[13] *Fox v Toronto General Trust Corp.* [1934] 4 D.L.R. 759.

[14] *Wadgery v Fall* [1926] 4 D.L.R. 333; *Traders Group Ltd v Carroll* (1970) 2 N.S.R. (2d) 321.

[15] *Morris v Baron & Co.* [1918] A.C. 1; *National Manufacturing Co. v Stepa* (1922) 65 D.L.R. 284. See also ss.59(1), 63.

[16] s.62(1). See also s.89 (notes). *cf.* s.62(2).

[17] *McManus v Bark* (1870) L.R. 5 Exch. 65. But waiver or equitable forbearance (below) does not require consideration to support it: *Chitty on Contracts* (29th ed.), Vol.I, §§ 3–081, 22–044.

[18] *Goss v Lord Nugent* (1833) 5 B. & Ad. 58; *Noble v Ward* (1867) L.R. 2 Ex. 135; *British and Beningtons Ltd v N.W. Cachar Tea Co. Ltd* [1923] A.C. 48; *United Dominions Trust (Jamaica) Ltd v Shoucair* [1969] 1 A.C. 340.

forbearance so as to preclude the party giving the assurance from going back on it if in all the circumstances it would be inequitable for him to do so.[19]

**Evidence to interpret or explain the written contract.** As in the case of   **2–170** any other written contract,[20] the parol evidence rule does not preclude the court from considering the "factual matrix" of the transaction to interpret or explain the words used.[21] But such evidence will seldom be relevant, having regard to the plain undertaking of each party to a bill or note. In any event, direct evidence of a party's subjective intentions with respect to the wording of an instrument is normally inadmissible.[22] Such evidence may nevertheless sometimes be admitted, for example, where there are two payees of the same name, to identify the intended payee,[23] or to identify a payee who is referred to by description only,[24] or to identify (and correct) the name of a drawee, payee or indorsee who is misnamed.[25] But extrinsic evidence is not admissible to supply a patent omission, as where the name of the payee of a bill is left blank,[26] or to render certain that which is uncertain on the face of the instrument.[27]

**Evidence for rectification of the written contract.** Parol evidence is   **2–171** admissible where it is sought, on the basis of that evidence, to rectify the written contract on the ground that it does not give effect to the real agreement between the parties.[28] Thus, in equity, parol evidence has been admitted to show that the claimant's name had by accident been inserted as that of the drawer, although such evidence would not have been admissible at common law.[29] Even at common law, however, parol evidence is admissible to prove the true date of the drawing, acceptance or

---

[19] *Chitty on Contracts* (29th ed.), Vol.I, §§ 3–085, 22–042; *W.J. Alan & Co. Ltd v El Nasr Export and Import Co.* [1972] 2 Q.B. 189, 212–214, 218, 221. See also ss.50(1)(b), 51(9).

[20] *Chitty on Contracts* (29th ed.), Vol.I, §§ 12–117 *et seq.*

[21] *ibid.*, § 12–118. See *Macdonald v Whitfield* (1883) 8 App. Cas. 733, 745. But contrast *Macleod Savings & Credit Union Ltd v Perrett* (1981) 118 D.L.R. (3d) 193.

[22] *Grant v Grant* (1870) L.R. 5 C.P. 727, 728; *LCC v Henry Boot & Sons Ltd* [1959] 1 W.L.R. 1069, 1065; *Prenn v Simmonds* [1971] 1 W.L.R. 1381, 1385; *Reardon Smith Line Ltd v Yngvar Hansen-Tangen* [1976] 1 W.L.R. 989, 996; *Harmony Shipping Co. S.A. v Saudi-Europe Line Ltd* [1981] 1 Lloyd's Rep. 377, 416.

[23] *Sweeting v Fowler* (1815) 1 Stark. 106; *Stebbing v Spicer* (1849) 8 C.B. 827.

[24] See above, para.2–049.

[25] *Willis v Barrett* (1816) 2 Stark. 29; *Dermatine Co. Ltd v Ashworth* (1905) 21 T.L.R. 510; *Bird & Co. (London) Ltd v Thomas Cook & Son Ltd* [1937] 2 All E.R. 227, 230–231.

[26] s.7. See above, para.2–049.

[27] *Macleod Savings & Credit Union Ltd v Perrett* (1981) 118 D.L.R. (3d) 193 (interest expressed to run "from the date of the advance": evidence not admissible to prove date of advance).

[28] *Murray v Parker* (1854) 19 Beav. 305, 308; *Henderson v Arthur* [1907] 1 K.B. 10, 13; *Lovell and Christmas Ltd v Wall* (1911) 104 L.T. 85. See *Chitty on Contracts* (29th ed.), Vol.I, § 5–092.

[29] *Druiff v Parker* (1868) L.R. 5 Eq. 131 (Illustration 36); *cf. Steele v M'Kinlay* (1880) 5 App. Cas. 754, 773, 774. See also *Royal Bank of Canada v Mendel* [1977] 6 W.W.R. 10.

an indorsement of a bill in contradiction of the date stated therein,[30] or, where a relevant date has been omitted, that date.[31]

ILLUSTRATIONS

**2–172**     1. The claimants are the holders for value of a bill of exchange drawn payable to their order. They indorse it specially to W & Co. and place it, together with a letter, in an envelope addressed to W & Co. The envelope with the letter and the bill enclosed, which is put in the claimants' office posting box, is stolen by H, the claimants' clerk. H forges the indorsement of W & Co. and procures the defendant bank to present the bill for payment and obtain payment of it on his behalf. The property in the bill remains in the claimants. The claimants, unless estopped (which they are not), may maintain an action against the defendant bank for money had and received.[32]

2. The defendants make a promissory note whereby they promise to pay H or order £300 on demand, and deliver it to H. H indorses the note, but does not deliver it. H dies. His executrix delivers the note after his death to the claimants, but without indorsing it. The claimants cannot sue the defendants on the note. There is a writing of his name by the deceased, and a delivery by his executrix. These acts do not constitute an indorsement of the note to the claimants.[33]

3. R hands to C, her solicitor, a promissory note for £200 signed by herself and payable on demand to her servant, H. R tells C not to mention the note to anyone, to retain it until her death, and then to hand it to H if still in her service. R dies, not having revoked her direction to C. C hands the note to H. H may prove for the £200 in R's estate.[34]

**2–173**     4. U is the holder of a bill of exchange for £300, at 90 days after sight, payable to himself or order. U specially indorses it to the claimant in payment for his children's board and education, and transmits the bill to his agent, the defendant, with instructions to deliver it to the claimant.

---

[30] s.13(1); *Pasmore v North* (1811) 13 East 517; *Armfield v Allport* (1857) 27 L.J. Ex. 42. See also (post-dated cheques) above, para.2–098.

[31] *Davis v Jones* (1856) 17 C.B. 625; *Spiers & Knox v Semple* 1901 9 S.L.T. 153. See also ss.12, 20 (insertion of date). Contrast *Macleod Savings & Credit Union Ltd v Perrett* (1981) 118 D.L.R. (3d) 193.

[32] *Arnold v Cheque Bank* (1876) 1 C.P.D. 578. But see now Cheques Act 1957, s.4 (cheques).

[33] *Bromage v Lloyd* (1847) 1 Exch. 32.

[34] *Re Richards* (1887) 36 Ch.D. 541; but see the criticism of this case in *Re Whitaker* (1889) 42 Ch.D. 119, 125.

The defendant obtains the acceptance of the drawees. He informs the claimant that he has received the bill, but does not contract to hold it as agent for the claimant. U then countermands and revokes his instructions to the defendant. The claimant cannot maintain trover against the defendant, as the property in the bill is still in U.[35]

5. G. draws a bill for £3,000 at 15 days after sight on G & Co. payable to the order of the claimants. The claimants indorse the bill to the defendants, their agents, and send it to them with instructions to obtain G & Co.'s acceptance of the bill. The bill is presented to G & Co. for acceptance and left with them. G & Co. write their acceptance on the bill. When the defendants call for the bill, they are merely informed that it has been mislaid, and are requested to call on the next working day. On that day, the defendants call again for the bill, but are told that the relevant clerk is not available. They are requested to call the next day. When they do call the next day, they obtain the bill; but the acceptance of G & Co. on it has been cancelled. In the interval, G & Co. have heard that a remittance is not likely to be forwarded by G to meet the bill, and so have cancelled their acceptance, which they are entitled to do. G becomes insolvent. The defendants are not liable to the claimants in negligence, since, in the circumstances, they have not been negligent in failing to obtain G & Co.'s acceptance of the bill.[36]

6. A deed of composition is entered into with creditors and promissory notes are handed to the trustees under the deed. The trustees are in the position of stakeholders. If a person who makes a note instructs trustees not to hand them over to a particular creditor, the creditor cannot maintain detinue, as the notes are not in his possession actually or constructively.[37]

7. L and S carry on business together as a partnership firm. The firm is 2–174 indebted to the claimant in the sum of £6,000. L (who acts throughout as the claimant's agent) with the concurrence of S, and in his presence, indorses a bill of exchange for £800 in the name of the firm to the claimant. He places the bill among some securities which he holds for the claimant, but the fact of the indorsement is not communicated by him to the claimant. This constitutes a valid delivery of the bill. Upon dishonour of the bill by the drawee, the claimant is entitled as indorsee to recover against the defendant who drew the bill.[38]

---

[35] *Brind v Hampshire* (1836) 1 M. & W. 365.
[36] *Bank of Van Diemen's Land v Bank of Victoria* (1871) L.R. 3 P.C. 526.
[37] *Latter v White* (1872) L.R. 5 H.L. 578.
[38] *Lysaght v Bryant* (1850) 9 C.B. 46.

8. The defendant makes a promissory note payable to the claimant, who sues him on it. The defendant may show that the note was delivered in the nature of an escrow, namely as a reward, in case the claimant procured the defendant to be restored to an office, which the claimant did not in fact effect.[39]

9. Two bills of exchange, one for £2,000 and the other for £2,118, are drawn by E upon, and accepted by, the defendant payable to E. E indorses the bills to the claimant and transmits them by letter to the claimant for the express purpose of retiring certain overdue bills (to the amount of about £4,000) given by E to the claimant, and on the express condition that the overdue bills should be returned to him by the next post. The condition is not complied with. The defendant is not liable to the claimant on the two bills. Until the condition was performed, no interest was to pass to the claimant as indorsee.[40]

2–175    10. The claimant and the defendant are partners in a speculation in currants. J gives the defendant a bill in payment for some currants. The defendant indorses his name on the bill and hands it to the claimant, requesting him to try to obtain payment from J. The bill is dishonoured by J. The defendant is not liable as indorser to the claimant on the bill. The intention of the parties was not that the claimant should become the sole owner of the bill as against the defendant, but that he should hold it for the joint benefit of himself and the defendant, in whom the property in half the bill remained.[41]

11. C draws a bill of exchange upon the defendant payable to himself. The bill is accepted by the defendant. C indorses the bill to the order of M, and hands it to M so that he may get it discounted for him. M does not get it discounted, but indorses it and hands it to the claimant without value and after it is overdue. The defendant is not liable to the claimant on the bill. C gave M possession of the bill merely for a collateral purpose and without the intention to make him transferee of the property in the bill.[42]

*Admissibility of parol evidence*

2–176    12. A promissory note for £4,500 is made by G and B payable to the defendants two months after date. It is indorsed by the defendants to G

---

[39] *Jefferies v Austin* (1725) 1 Stra. 674.
[40] *Bell v Lord Ingestre* (1848) 12 Q.B. 317.
[41] *Denton v Peters* (1870) L.R. 5 Q.B. 475.
[42] *Lloyd v Howard* (1850) 15 Q.B. 995.

& Son, who indorse it to the claimant. Evidence is not admissible to prove a contemporaneous oral agreement between the claimant and the defendants at the time the defendants indorsed the note that it would be renewed when it fell due.[43]

13. A promissory note for £1,000 is made by S payable 12 months after date to the defendant or order and indorsed by the defendant to the claimant. The note is dishonoured by non-payment by S but no notice of dishonour is given to the defendant. Evidence is not admissible to prove a contemporaneous oral agreement at the time of making and indorsing the note that payment should not be demanded until after the sale of the estates of S, so as to waive notice of dishonour.[44]

14. A promissory note for £66 is made by the defendants payable to the claimant on demand. Evidence is not admissible to prove that payment was to be made out of a particular fund and that the defendants were to be liable only if the fund was insufficient to discharge the debt.[45]

15. B makes a promissory note for £100 payable to the claimant on    **2–177**
demand. B dies, and an action is brought by the claimant against the defendant, the executrix of B's estate. Evidence is not admissible to prove an oral agreement that the note should not be payable until after the death of B (in which case it would be void as a testamentary gift).[46]

16. The defendant accepts a bill of exchange for £250 drawn upon him and payable to the claimant in six months. The bill is given under an oral understanding that payment is not to be demanded in the event of the claimant being able to reimburse himself out of the effects of a third party. This bill is renewed for another bill at three months. Evidence of the oral understanding is inadmissible and it is no defence to an action on the bill that the claimant has received £1,700 from the effects of the third party.[47]

17. A widow makes a promissory note for £100 payable 12 months after date to the claimant or order "Value received by my late husband." The note is valid on the face of it, and evidence is not admissible to show a consideration different from that expressed in the note, namely, that the

[43] *Hoare v Graham* (1811) 3 Camp. 57.
[44] *Free v Hawkins* (1817) 8 Taunt. 92.
[45] *Rawson v Walker* (1816) 1 Stark. 361.
[46] *Woodbridge v Spooner* (1819) 3 B. & Ald. 233.
[47] *Campbell v Hodgson* (1819) Gow. 74.

note was given as a mere indemnity on behalf of liabilities incurred by the widow's late husband.[48]

**2–178**    18. The defendant makes a promissory note for £233 payable to R or his order on demand. The claimant is the trustee in bankruptcy of R. Evidence is not admissible to prove an oral agreement between the defendant and R that the note was to be paid upon R giving up possession of certain premises and accounting for the rent, as this would be to contradict by parol the note itself.[49]

19. A promissory note for £12 is made by the defendant payable to the claimant 14 days after date. Evidence is not admissible to prove that the note was given under an oral agreement that it should not be enforced if the claimant obtains a verdict in an action against third parties, since this would contradict the express contract to pay at a specified time.[50]

20. The claimant draws two bills of exchange on the defendant for £45 each, one payable six months, and the other, 12 months, after date. The bills are accepted by the defendant. Evidence is not admissible to prove a contemporaneous oral agreement that the claimant would not call for payment on the bills until he should recover, or if he should not recover, payment on a promissory note. The defendant is estopped from saying that he made any other contract than the absolute one on the bills.[51]

**2–179**    21. The defendant accepts a bill of exchange for £98 19s. 6d. drawn upon him by T and payable to T's order four months after date. The bill is indorsed by T to the claimant. Evidence is not admissible to prove that, before the making and accepting of the bill, it was orally agreed between the defendant and T that £65 only should be paid, by four instalments, even though the indorsement to the claimant was without value or consideration. Such an agreement would vary the terms of the contract on the face of the bill by parol, which cannot be done.[52]

22. A bill of exchange for £20 is drawn by the claimant upon, and accepted by, the defendant payable to the claimant three months after date. The bill is dated 12 July. In answer to a claim by the claimant on the bill, the defendant pleads "a defence on equitable grounds" that the bill ought to have been, and was represented by the claimant to be, drawn on the 25 July, and that the action was commenced before the bill would have

---

[48] *Ridout v Bristow* (1830) 9 Exch. 48.
[49] *Moseley v Hanford* (1830) 10 B. & C. 729.
[50] *Foster v Jolly* (1835) 1 C.M. & R. 703.
[51] *Adams v Wordley* (1836) 1 M. & W. 374.
[52] *Besant v Cross* (1851) 10 C.B. 895.

been due if properly dated. The plea discloses no equitable defence and is not to be allowed.[53]

23. The defendant draws a bill of exchange payable to the claimant 12 months after date. It is dishonoured by non-payment by the acceptor. In an action by the claimant against the defendant as drawer of the bill, it is sought to introduce evidence of an oral agreement between the claimant, the defendant and the acceptor that the acceptor would deposit certain securities with the claimant as security for payment of the bill and in case the bill should not be duly paid, the claimant should sell the securities and apply the proceeds in liquidation of the bill, and that until the claimant should have sold the securities the defendant should not be liable to be sued on the bill. Such evidence is inadmissible, since it contradicts and is contrary to the contract on the face of the bill.[54]

24. A bill of exchange for £110 is drawn upon the defendant payable to **2–180** the order of the drawers three months after date. It is accepted by the defendant and indorsed by the drawers to the claimants. In an action by the claimants against the defendant on the bill, the defendant raises the defence that, at the time the bill was accepted by him, it was orally agreed between the drawers and the defendant that the drawers would renew the bill if the defendant could not meet it at maturity. Evidence of that oral agreement is inadmissible, even though the claimants acquired the bill with notice of the circumstances in which it was accepted, and so could not stand in any better position than the drawers.[55]

25. The N Company makes and delivers to the claimants a promissory note in respect of goods supplied to it by the claimants. The note is expressed to be payable to the claimants 60 days after date, and is indorsed by the defendant as surety. Evidence is not admissible to prove an oral agreement between the defendant and the claimants, contemporaneous with the note, that the defendant should not be called upon to pay if the goods supplied should be unequal to sample. The agreement is not one suspending the coming into force of the contract of the defendant on the note, but an agreement in defeasance of that contract and which contradicts the terms of the instrument.[56]

26. The claimants draw a bill of exchange upon the defendant for £21 14s. 4d. payable to themselves two months after date and the defendant accepts the bill. In answer to a claim against him on the bill the

---

[53] *Drain v Harvey* (1855) 17 C.B. 257.
[54] *Abrey v Crux* (1869) L.R. 5 C.P. 37.
[55] *New London Credit Syndicate v Neale* [1898] 2 Q.B. 487.
[56] *Hitchings and Coulthurst Co. v Northern Leather Co. of America and Doushkess* [1914] 3 K.B. 907.

defendant pleads that he accepted the bill upon a certain condition agreed between himself and the claimants as part of the consideration for the bill that the claimants would renew the bill for a further term of two months if, when the bill became due, the defendant should not have received a sum of money from a third party. The omission of a plea that the agreement was in writing does not make the plea bad. Although the defendant could not have set up a contemporaneous oral agreement to contradict the contract on the face of the bill, he can set up a written agreement entered into at the time the bill was accepted.[57]

**2–181**   27. The defendant accepts a bill of exchange drawn upon him by the claimant for £5,000 payable at six months. When the defendant accepts the bill, the claimant agrees in writing that he will renew the bill should any circumstances prevent the defendant from meeting it at maturity. The defendant makes no application for renewal during the currency of the bill; but on the claimant's presenting it for payment shortly after it becomes due, he claims to have it renewed according to the agreement, circumstances having in fact prevented him from meeting it. The agreement is admissible in evidence. It is contemporaneous, in writing, and is not collateral, the bill and the writing forming only one contract; and the bill is sued upon by the drawer himself. The defendant is not bound to apply for a renewal during the currency of the bill, but may do so within a reasonable time after it becomes due.[58]

28. The defendant makes a promissory note for £106 15s. 8d., with interest at the rate of 4 per cent, payable on demand to the claimants, the executors of D. A written agreement is entered into between the defendant and the legatees of D's estate which provides that the note in question shall not be sued on until the youngest legatee reaches the age mentioned in D's will. The claimants do not sign this agreement, but, when it has been signed by the other parties, then take it into their possession. When sued on the note, the defendant pleads the terms of the written agreement (the youngest legatee still being under age). The plea is bad, since the agreement is collateral and is not between the same parties as the note.[59]

29. U, being very ill, tells C that C is to have £100 for acting as his (U's) executor. U makes a promissory note for £100 "for value received" payable to C on demand, and gives this note to C. U recovers. C dies before U. C's executor sues U's executor on the note. U's executor may resist the

---

[57] *Young v Austen* (1869) L.R. 4 C.P. 553.
[58] *Maillard v Page* (1870) L.R. 5 Ex. 312.
[59] *Salmon v Webb* (1852) 3 H.L.C. 510.

claim by showing that the consideration for the note has totally failed.[60]

30. The defendant makes a promissory note for £500 payable to the order of the claimant two years after date. The consideration expressed on the face of the note is for commission due to the claimant for business transacted for the defendant. In answer to a claim by the claimant against the defendant on the note, the defendant pleads that the true consideration was for services to be thereafter rendered by the claimant to the defendant, and that the claimant has not rendered those services. Parol evidence is admissible to show no consideration or that the consideration has failed.[61]   **2–182**

31. B draws three bills of exchange on the defendant payable to B's order three months after date. These bills are accepted by the defendant and indorsed by B to the claimant. After the bills become due, the claimant enters into an agreement with B that, in consideration of B giving him a mortgage for these bills and other debts, he will deliver up the bills to be cancelled, and give up his claim on all parties. The mortgage security is given accordingly. Parol evidence is admissible to show that the defendant accepted the bills for the accommodation of B (the drawer) and that the claimant knew of this fact when he entered into the agreement with B. The defendant is in the position of surety in relation to B, the principal debtor, and is discharged by reason of the agreement between the claimant and B.[62]

32. The claimant is the holder of a bill of exchange for £100 drawn by I upon and accepted by the defendant. Before the bill becomes due, I makes a composition with his creditors. The claimant, as one of those creditors, accepts a composition of £7 10s. He then sues the defendant as acceptor for £100. Parol evidence is admissible to show that the defendant accepted the bill for the accommodation of I, the drawer. Where a bill is accepted for the accommodation of the drawer, it is the drawer who is ultimately liable, and the acceptor, if he is forced to pay the holder, has recourse against the drawer. In the case of such a bill, payment by the drawer is *pro tanto* a discharge to the acceptor.[63]

33. A bank in Canada agrees to extend further credit to a company, but on condition that the loan is guaranteed by the personal guarantee of the directors of the company. Promissory notes to cover the amount of the   **2–183**

---

[60] *Solly v Hinde* (1834) 2 Cr. & M. 516.
[61] *Abbott v Hendrix* (1840) 1 M. & G. 791.
[62] *Ewin v Lancaster* (1865) 6 B. & S. 571.
[63] *Solomon v Davis* (1883) 1 Cab. & E. 83.

loan are therefore made by the secretary of the company and signed by him on behalf of the company. The name of the defendant, a director of the company, is inserted as payee and the notes are then successively indorsed by the defendant and by three other directors of the company, namely the claimant, C and M, in that order. The notes are dishonoured by non-payment by the company. In an action by the claimant against the defendant as prior indorser for a complete indemnity in respect of the claimant's liability on the notes, parol evidence is admissible to show that the claimant and the defendant made their indorsements on the notes, together with the other directors of the company, as cosureties for the company, and are, in that capacity, entitled and liable only to equal contribution *inter se*.[64]

34. H and the defendant jointly make a promissory note for £50 payable to the claimant. The claimant accepts a composition of his debt from H. Parol evidence is admissible to show that the defendant joined in making the note merely as surety for H and that the claimant knew of this fact. The composition with H, the principal debtor, being without the consent of the defendant, discharges the defendant as surety.[65]

35. The defendant habitually acts as agent for the claimant in procuring and remitting for him bills on England, on account of money received by him for the claimant in Malta. In the course of that agency, the defendant purchases bills in Malta drawn payable to his order, indorses them specially to the claimant, and transmits them to the claimant in London. The indorsement is not made "without recourse" nor is there any other reservation in the indorsement as to the defendant's liability. The bills are dishonoured. The defendant is not liable as indorser to the claimant, since the circumstances are such as to show that no liability was intended.[66]

**2–184** 36. The claimant's husband makes an advance to G and the defendant upon two bills of exchange each for £500. After the husband's death, the bills are not paid at maturity and it is agreed that they will be renewed by the issue of fresh bills. One of these renewed bills is drawn out by the claimant's daughter with a blank for the drawer's name, but she, by mistake or inadvertence, puts the claimant's name in the place where the name of the drawer should be. The bill is then sent to G and the defendant for signature. The defendant signs his name as drawer beneath the name of the claimant and G writes his acceptance on the bill. The bill is payable to the order of the defendant and indorsed by the defendant to

---

[64] *Macdonald v Whitfield* (1883) 8 App. Cas. 733.
[65] *Hill v Wilcox* (1831) 1 M. & Rob. 58.
[66] *Castrique v Buttigieg* (1855) 10 Moore P.C. 94.

the claimant. The bill is not paid by G and the claimant sues the defendant as drawer at law. Upon the defendant pleading that the claimant's name appears as drawer of the bill, the claimant files a suit in equity that the bill be rectified by striking out her name as drawer. Parol evidence is admissible to prove the real contract.[67]

## Capacity and Authority of Parties

### Capacity of parties

22. (1) **Capacity to incur liability as a party to a bill is co-extensive**   3–001
**with capacity to contract.**
    **Provided that nothing in this section shall enable a corporation to make itself liable as drawer, acceptor, or indorser of a bill unless it is competent to it so to do under the law for the time being in force relating to corporations.**

  (2) **Where a bill is drawn or indorsed by an infant, minor, or corporation having no capacity or power to incur liability on a bill, the drawing or indorsement entitles the holder to receive payment of the bill, and to enforce it against any other party thereto.**

| Definitions | Comparison |
|---|---|
| "bill": s.2. | UCC: §§ 3–202, 3–305. |
| "holder": s.2. | ULB: art.7. |
| "indorsement": s.2. | ULC: art.10. |
| | UNB: arts 28, 30. |

### COMMENT

**Capacity to incur liability.** This section, which deals with capacity to   3–002
incur liability as party to a bill, is the first of a group of sections (sections 22 to 26) headed "Capacity and Authority of Parties".

Capacity must be distinguished from authority. Capacity means power to contract so as to bind oneself. Authority means power to contract on behalf of another so as to bind him. Capacity to contract is the creation of law. Authority is derived from the act of the parties themselves. Want of

[67] *Druiff v Parker* (1868) L.R. 5 Eq. 131.

capacity may, in certain circumstances,[1] be incurable. Want of authority may be cured by ratification. Capacity or no capacity is a question of law. Authority or no authority is usually a question of fact.

Capacity must also be distinguished from immunity from suit or inability to sue. A foreign state, sovereign or ambassador has capacity to incur liability, but is, in certain circumstances, immune from the jurisdiction of the English courts[2]; and an alien enemy can incur liability (and be sued) but cannot sue in the Queen's courts, except under royal licence.[3]

Capacity must further be distinguished from illegality. A person of full capacity may enter into a contract the enforcement of which is prohibited either by statute or at common law, or the making or performance of which may involve the commission of an unlawful act. The question whether the liability incurred under such a contract can be enforced will depend upon the purpose and intent of the statute or rule of public policy concerned and, in many cases, upon whether the person seeking to enforce the liability knew of or participated in the unlawful act.[4]

3–003     **Subsection (1): capacity.** This subsection is declaratory of the common law. The first sentence states that capacity to incur liability as a party to a bill (or note)[5] is to be determined by reference to the general law relating to capacity to contract.

3–004     **Corporations and companies.** The proviso to this subsection makes it clear that the section does not enlarge the capacity of a corporation to incur liability as a party to a bill, which is to be determined by the law for the time being in force relating to corporations.

At common law, a corporation incurred no liability by drawing, accepting or indorsing a bill of exchange,[6] unless expressly or impliedly authorised by its act of incorporation so to do. In the case of a trading corporation, the fact of incorporation for the purpose of a trade normally conferred upon it, among other incidental powers, the capacity to draw, accept, or indorse bills of exchange.[7] In the case of a non-trading corporation, however, the power had to be expressly given, or there had to be

---

[1] *e.g.* previously in the case of the *ultra vires* contracts of companies: *Ashbury Railway Carriage & Iron Co. v Riche* (1875) L.R. 7 H.L. 653. But contrast mental incapacity, where the contract may be ratified: *Matthews v Baxter* (1873) L.R. 8 Ex. 132.

[2] See *Chitty on Contracts* (29th ed.), Vol.I., §§ 11–001 *et seq. cf., Central Bank of Yemen v Cardinal Investments Corpn. (No.1)* [2001] 1 Lloyd's Rep. Bank 1.

[3] *Chitty on Contracts* (29th ed.), Vol.I, §§ 11–024 *et seq.*

[4] *Chitty on Contracts* (29th ed.), Vol.I, §§ 16–001 *et seq.*

[5] See s.89.

[6] The same rule applied to promissory notes.

[7] *Re Peruvian Rys Co.* (1867) L.R. 2 Ch. App. 617.

terms in the act of incorporation wide enough to include it.[8] If a company entered into a contract which was in excess of its capacity, the transaction was *ultra vires* and absolutely void,[9] and it was irrelevant whether or not the person contracting with the company had notice of the want of capacity.

So far as third parties are concerned, the *ultra vires* rule has now been effectively abolished for most companies by section 35(1) of the Companies Act 1985,[10] which provides: "The validity of an act done by a company shall not be called into question on the ground of lack of capacity by reason of anything in the company's memorandum." It still remains the duty of the directors to observe any limitations on their powers flowing from the company's memorandum,[11] for breach of which duty they will be liable. But this internal limitation will not affect the capacity of the company to incur liability on the bill.

Two restrictions are, however, imposed on this principle. First, the *ultra vires* rule continues to apply to the acts of a company which is a charity, except in favour of a person who—(a) gives full consideration in money or money's worth in relation to the act in question, and (b) does not know that the act is not permitted by the company's memorandum, or who does not know at the time the act is done that the company is a charity.[12] Secondly, when the board of directors of a company has exceeded any limitation of their powers under the company's constitution in a transaction where the third party is a director of the company or of its holding company, or is a person connected with such director or a company with whom such a director is associated, then the transaction is voidable at the company's option.[13] But the transaction ceases to be voidable if (*inter alia*) rights acquired bona fide for value and without actual notice of the directors' exceeding their powers by a person who is not party to the transaction would be affected by the avoidance.[14] These two restrictions are unlikely to affect a holder in due course of any bill cheque or note to which a company is a party.

3–005

---

[8] *Bateman v Mid Wales Ry* (1866) L.R. 1 C.P. 499 (Illustration 1); *Re Peruvian Rys Co.* (1867) L.R. 2 Ch. App. 617 at 622. See also *Bramah v Roberts* (1837) 3 Bing. N.C. 963; *Dickinson v Valpy* (1829) 10 B. & C. 128; *Steele v Harmer* (1845) 14 M. & W. 831; *West London Commercial Bank v Kitson* (1884) 13 Q.B.D. 360 (Illustration 2). But it is doubtful whether this rule applied to cheques, as even a non-trading corporation could not operate without maintaining a bank account and drawing cheques on it. See also now s.3A of the Companies Act 1985 (inserted by s.110 of the Companies Act 1989).

[9] *Ashbury Railway Carriage & Iron Co. v Riche* (1875) L.R. 7 H.L. 653; *Wenlock (Baroness) v River Dee Co. (No.1)* (1885) 10 App. Cas. 354.

[10] Section 35 was substituted by s.108 of the Companies Act 1989.

[11] s.35(3) of the 1985 Act (subject to ratification).

[12] Charities Act 1993, ss.65–68.

[13] Companies Act 1985, s.322A, inserted by s.109 of the Companies Act 1989.

[14] Companies Act 1985, s.322A(5)(c).

Directors who sign a bill or note on behalf of a company which has no capacity to incur liability thereon may be personally liable to the holder for falsely representing that the company has the power to incur liability or for breach of an implied warranty of authority.[15]

**3–006**     **Authority of directors.** The authority of directors to bind the company is also affected by the *ultra vires* rule, since they have no authority to exceed any limitation on their powers flowing from the company's memorandum[16] or to exercise those powers for an *ultra vires* purpose. However, section 35A(1) of the 1985 Act[17] provides that, in favour of a person dealing with[18] a company in good faith, the power of the board of directors to bind the company, or authorise others to do so, shall be deemed to be free of any limitation under the company's constitution. There is a presumption of good faith[19] and section 35A(2)(b) provides that a person shall not be regarded as acting in bad faith by reason only of his knowing that an act is beyond the powers of the directors under the company's constitution.[20]

Section 35A(1) covers only want of authority which derives from a limitation under the company's constitution.[21] But acts of a director or other officer of a company which are outside his authority may be validated under the rule in *Royal British Bank v Turquand*[22] or by more general principles of the law of agency.[23]

**3–007**     **Instruments signed on behalf of a company before its incorporation.** Where a bill or note is signed by a promoter or other person on behalf of a company before it has been formed, the company can incur no liability on the instrument as drawer, acceptor, maker or indorser, since it cannot be bound by a contract made when it is non-existent.[24] Further it cannot, after incorporation, ratify or adopt the signature of its agent.[25]

---

[15] *West London Commercial Bank v Kitson* (1884) 13 Q.B.D. 360 (Illustration 2). But see *Chitty on Contracts* (29th ed.), Vol.I, § 9–041.

[16] Companies Act 1985, s.35(3), inserted by s.108 of the Companies Act 1989.

[17] s.35A was likewise inserted by s.108 of the 1989 Act.

[18] Defined in s.35(2)(a). It is submitted that the holder of a bill or note "deals with" a company if he takes an instrument on which the company's name appears as drawer, acceptor, maker or indorser by virtue of the privity created by the instrument.

[19] s.35A(2)(c).

[20] See also s.35B.

[21] But see s.35A(3).

[22] (1856) 6 E. & B. 327. See *Chitty on Contracts* (29th ed.), Vol.I, § 9–042.

[23] See below, para.16–005.

[24] See *Chitty on Contracts* (29th ed.), Vol.I, §§ 9–012—9–018.

[25] *Kelner v Baxter* (1866) L.R. 2 C.P 174; *Scott v Lord Ebury* (1867) L.R. 2 C.P. 255, 267; *North Sydney Investment & Tramway Co. v Higgins* [1899] A.C. 263.

However, by section 36C(1) of the Companies Act 1985,[26] a contract which purports to be made by or on behalf of a company[27] at a time when the company has not been formed,[28] has effect, subject to any agreement to the contrary,[29] as one made with the person purporting to act for the company or as agent for it, and he is personally liable on the contract accordingly. It would appear that, notwithstanding section 26(1) of the 1882 Act,[30] even though the person signing adds words to his signature, indicating that he signs for or on behalf of a principal, or in a representative capacity, he will be personally liable on the bill or note if he purports to draw, accept, make or indorse the instrument on behalf of a company which has not been formed.[31]

**Liquidators, etc.** A liquidator, (whether in a winding up by the court or in a voluntary winding up)[32] an administrator,[33] an administrative receiver[34] and a Scottish receiver[35] have each the power to draw, accept, make and indorse any bill of exchange or promissory note in the name and on behalf of the company. 3–008

**Bankrupts.** A bankrupt has capacity to incur contractual liability on an instrument after he is adjudicated bankrupt.[36] 3–009

**Public authorities.**[37] By section 2 of the Local Government Act 2000, a local authority[38] has power to do anything (including the power to incur expenditure, give financial assistance to any person and enter into arrangements with any person) which it considers likely to achieve promotion or improvement of the economic, social or environmental well- 3–010

---

[26] Inserted by s.130(4) of the Companies Act 1989, and replacing the previous s.36(4) of the 1985 Act. See the First Directive of the Council of the EC on Harmonisation of Company Law (68/151) originally implemented by s.9(2) of the European Communities Act 1972. See also Griffiths (1993) 13 *Legal Studies* 241.

[27] *cf. Rover International Ltd v Cannon Film Sales Ltd (No.2)* [1987] B.C.L.C. 540 (foreign company excluded).

[28] *cf. Oshkosh B'Gosh Inc. v Dan Marbel Ltd* [1989] B.C.L.C. 507 (change of name); *Cotronic (UK) Ltd v Dezonie* [1991] B.C.C. 200 (no intention to form company at time of contract); *Badgerhill Properties Ltd v Cottrell* [1991] B.C.L.C. 805 (agency).

[29] *cf. Phonogram Ltd v Lane* [1982] Q.B. 938.

[30] See below, para.3–105.

[31] *Phonogram Ltd v Lane* [1982] Q.B. 938.

[32] Insolvency Act 1986, ss.165, 167; Sch.4, para.9.

[33] Insolvency Act 1986, s.14; Sch.1, para.10.

[34] Insolvency Act 1986, s.42; Sch.1, para.10. But see Enterprise Act 2002, s.250 (prohibition of appointment).

[35] Insolvency Act 1986, s.55; Sch.2, para.10.

[36] See *Chitty on Contracts* (29th ed.), Vol.I, § 20–053.

[37] See Mitchell, *The Contracts of Public Authorities* (1954); Aronson and Whitmore, *Public Torts and Contracts* (1982); Arrowsmith, *Civil Liability and Public Authorities* (1992); *Chitty on Contracts* (29th ed.), Vol.I, §§ 10–013 *et seq.*

[38] A local authority (even a parish council) is a body corporate.

being of its area. It is submitted that this power is wide enough, in principle,[39] to confer upon a local authority the capacity to draw, accept, make or indorse a bill of exchange or promissory note. Local authorities are, however, subject to the *ultra vires* rule, so that the contract constituted by the signature by a local authority of a bill or note will be unenforceable against the authority[40] if it is *ultra vires*.

With respect to any other public authority whose powers are defined by statute, its capacity to incur liability upon a bill or note must be determined by reference to the powers, express or implied, conferred upon it by the statute.

Sections 35 to 35C of the Companies Act 1985 do not apply to public authorities.

3–011    **Unincorporated associations.** An unincorporated association is not a legal person and cannot incur liability upon a bill or note. As a general rule, if one or more persons contract on behalf of an unincorporated association, then, by the rules of agency, the members of the association may individually become parties to the contract and be sued in a representative action.[41] But, in the case of a bill or note, it seems unlikely that so large a number of persons would be held to have incurred liability on the instrument[42] and it is more probable that those members alone who sign the instrument will incur liability,[43] even if they add words to their signature indicating that they sign for or on behalf of the association, or in a representative character.[44]

3–012    **Trade unions.** In consequence of the Trade Union and Labour Relations Act 1974, a trade union, though technically not a body corporate,[45] is capable of making contracts[46] and in consequence has capacity to incur liability on a bill or note.

---

[39] See also Local Government Act 1972, s.111, and in particular Sch.13, Pt I, paras 2(1)(e), 5 (power to raise money by the issue of bills); Local Government Act 2003, ss.1–8 (power to borrow etc.).

[40] *LCC v Att.-Gen.* [1902] A.C. 165; *Att.-Gen. v Manchester Corp.* [1906] 1 Ch. 643; *Att.-Gen. v Fulham Corp.* [1921] 1 Ch. 440; *Rhyl UDC v Rhyl Amusements Ltd* [1959] 1 W.L.R. 465; *Hazell v Hammersmith and Fulham London B.C.* [1992] 2 A.C. 1; *Credit Suisse v Allerdale B.C.* [1997] Q.B. 306. But see Local Government (Contracts) Act 1997 (as amended); Local Government Act 2003, s.6. *cf. Westdeutsche Girocentrale Landesbank v Islington B.C.* [1996] A.C. 669 (restitution).

[41] See *Chitty on Contracts* (29th ed.), Vol.I, §§ 9–068 *et seq.*

[42] *M'Meekin v Easton* (1889) 16 R. 363 (Scotland). Contrast s.23(2) (firm).

[43] *M'Meekin v Easton* (1889) 16 R. 363; *Rew v Pettet* (1834) 1 A. & E. 196; *Austin v Hober* [1917] W.W.R. 994.

[44] *cf.* s.26(1) of the Act. But see s.26(2).

[45] s.2 of the 1974 Act.

[46] s.2(1)(a) of the 1974 Act. See *Chitty on Contracts* (29th ed.), Vol.I, §§ 9–085 *et seq.*

**Limited liability partnerships.** A limited liability partnership incorpo- **3–013** rated under the Limited Liability Partnerships Act 2000 has unlimited capacity.[47]

**Minors.** The age of majority is 18 years.[48] All persons under that age **3–014** are known technically as minors (or infants).[49] Although, by sub-section (1), the capacity of a minor to incur liability as a party to a bill is stated to be coextensive with capacity to contract, it has long been the law that a minor incurs no liability by drawing, indorsing, accepting or making[50] a bill or note, even at the suit of a holder in due course.[51] Indeed, in *Re Soltykoff*[52] Lord Esher M.R. said[53]: "[An infant] is not liable upon a bill of exchange or a promissory note under any circumstances". If this statement is correct, then a minor may be in a more favourable position in respect of bills and notes than under the general law of contract. Since the repeal of section 1 of the Infants Relief Act 1874,[54] no other contract by a minor is absolutely void. At most, a minor's contract is "voidable", being either not binding on him unless ratified after attaining majority[55] or binding on him unless repudiated within a reasonable time of attaining majority.[56] Further, under the general law of contract, contracts for necessaries and certain other beneficial contracts are binding on a minor.[57] It might be supposed that, if a minor entered into such a contract, a bill or note issued in performance of his obligations under the contract would likewise be enforceable against him. But it has been held[58] that, if a bill is accepted by a minor in payment for necessaries supplied to him, any liability of the minor will be upon the underlying contract and not upon the instrument. Thus, no claim can be brought, *e.g.* by an indorsee of the bill, who did not himself supply the necessaries to the minor.

Previously, by virtue of section 2 of the Infants Relief Act 1874 and section 5 of the Betting and Loans (Infants) Act 1892, if a minor incurred a debt and, after attaining majority, drew or accepted a bill or made a promissory note to pay that debt, he would not be liable to a holder of the

[47] Limited Liability Partnerships Act 2000, s.1(3).
[48] Family Law Reform Act 1969, s.1. See also Age of Majority (Scotland) Act 1969, s.1.
[49] Family Law Reform Act 1969, s.12.
[50] *Levene v Brougham* (1909) 25 T.L.R. 265 (note).
[51] See the cases cited in *Re Soltykoff* [1891] 1 Q.B. 413, 414. It is immaterial that the minor has misrepresented his age: *Bartlett v Wells* (1862) 1 B. & S. 836.
[52] [1891] 1 Q.B. 413 (Illustration 3).
[53] At 415.
[54] Minors' Contracts Act 1987, ss.1, 4(2).
[55] *Chitty on Contracts* (29th ed.), Vol.I, §§ 8–005, 8–042. In *Hunt v Massey* (1834) 5 B. & Ad. 902 it was held that an acceptance during minority could be ratified, and so validated, after attaining majority.
[56] *Chitty on Contracts* (29th ed.), Vol.I, §§ 8–005, 8–030.
[57] *Chitty*, §§ 8–007 *et seq.*
[58] *Re Soltykoff* [1891] 1 Q.B. 413 (Illustration 3).

instrument with notice of the circumstances in which it was given[59] and probably not even to a holder in due course.[60] These two statutory provisions have, however, now been repealed.[61] In consequence, a bill, cheque or note which has been drawn, indorsed, accepted or made by a person of full age in respect of a debt contracted during minority will be binding on him, and this will be so whether his signature of the instrument constitutes merely a ratification by him of the debt or a fresh promise, based on new consideration, to pay the debt.[62]

If a minor draws a post-dated cheque, dating it as of a date after attaining his majority, he is not liable on the cheque, even after he is of full age.[63] But if a person of full age accepts a bill drawn on him while still a minor, he will be liable on it.[64]

A bank is entitled to pay a cheque drawn on it by a minor[65] and will not be liable to repay money received by it upon the collection of a minor's cheque.

**3–015**      **Mental disorder and drunkenness.** It is uncertain whether a patient[66] whom a judge of the Court of Protection has found (under Part VII of the Mental Health Act 1983) to be incapable, by reason of mental disorder, of managing and administering his property and affairs[67] or one in respect of whose property a receiver has been appointed[68] can in any circumstances enter into a valid contract.[69] It may well be that any such contract would be absolutely void,[70] so that such a patient would not be liable for drawing, accepting, making or indorsing a bill or note even to a holder in due course.[71]

Otherwise a person who signs a bill or note while suffering from mental disorder must, in order to escape liability, prove, not merely that he was so insane at the time that he did not know what he was doing, but

---

[59] *Smith v King* [1892] 2 Q.B. 543. See also *Ex p. Kibble* (1875) L.R. 10 Ch. 373.

[60] See, in particular, s.5 of the 1892 Act.

[61] Minors' Contracts Act 1987, ss.1, 4(2).

[62] Any distinction drawn by s.2 of the 1874 Act between ratification and a fresh promise to pay is now obsolete. See also s.27(1)(b) of the 1882 Act; below, para.4–021.

[63] *Hutley v Peacock* (1913) 30 T.L.R. 42 (Illustration 4). But it is possible that the signature might now be ratified after majority: see *Hunt v Massey* (1834) 5 B. & Ad. 902.

[64] *Stevens v Jackson* (1815) 4 Camp. 164.

[65] *Freeman v Bank of Montreal* (1912) 5 D.L.R. 418.

[66] Defined in s.96 of the Mental Health Act 1983.

[67] Mental Health Act 1983, s.96.

[68] Mental Health Act 1983, s.99.

[69] See *Re Walker* [1905] 1 Ch. 160; *Re Marshall* [1920] 1 Ch. 284. Contrast *Baldwyn v Smith* [1900] 1 Ch. 588; *In the Estate of Walker* (1912) 28 T.L.R. 466. But these decisions related to the Lunacy and Mental Treatment Acts 1890 to 1930 (now repealed).

[70] See *Chitty on Contracts* (29th ed.), Vol.I, § 8–078; Treitel, *Law of Contract* (9th ed.), p.514; Fridman (1963) 79 L.Q.R. 502; (1964) 80 L.Q.R. 84. *cf.*, s.96(1)(b) of the 1983 Act.

[71] *Stevenson Estate v Siewart* (2000) 191 D.L.R. (4th) 151, (2001) 202 D.L.R. (4th) 295. (Alberta).

also that the person with whom he contracted knew him to be so insane as not to be capable of understanding what he was about.[72] The same rule would appear to apply to drunken persons[73] or those under the influence of drugs.[74] Once, however, the cause of the incapacity ceases, it is open to the incompetent to ratify the contract constituted by his signature of the instrument.[75]

It is clear that mental disorder and drunkenness may be raised as a defence against an immediate party with knowledge of the incapacity,[76] and the defence would also probably be available against a remote party who took the instrument with such knowledge.[77] It is less clear, however, whether the defence is a real defence, that is to say, like *non est factum*,[78] is available against all the world, including a holder in due course, or whether a remote party, taking the instrument without knowledge of the incapacity, could enforce it against the incompetent. There is no case which decides this issue, although the fact that the contract on the instrument is not void but voidable and the leading case of *Imperial Loan Co. v Stone*[79] (which concerned immediate parties) both suggest that lack of knowledge on the part of the person seeking to enforce the instrument would cause the defence to fail.[80]

**Subsection (2): liability of other parties.** This subsection deals with, and is limited to, the situation where a bill is drawn or a bill (or note) is indorsed by a minor or corporation having no capacity or power to incur liability on the instrument. It provides, first, that the drawing or indorsement entitles the holder to enforce it against any other party to the instrument, *i.e.* any party other than the minor or incapable corporation.[81] Thus if a minor makes a promissory note payable to order which is subsequently indorsed by the payee, the indorsee may enforce the note

3–016

---

[72] *Molton v Camroux* (1849) 4 Exch. 17; *Imperial Loan Co. v Stone* [1892] 1 Q.B. 599, 601, 602, 603; *McLaughlin v Daily Telegraph Newspaper Co. Ltd* (No.2) (1904) 1 C.L.R. 243; *Hart v O'Connor* [1985] A.C. 1000. On the degree of incapacity with respect to a cheque, see *Manches v Trimborn* (1946) 115 L.J.K.B. 305 (senile degeneration).

[73] *Gore v Gibson* (1845) 13 M. & W. 623; *Matthews v Baxter* (1873) L.R. 8 Ex. 132; *Irvani v Irvani* [2000] 1 Lloyd's Rep. 412, 425. There does not appear to be any wider doctrine of "unconscionability": *Irvani v Irvani* at 425.

[74] *Irvani v Irvani* [2000] 1 Lloyd's Rep 412 at 425.

[75] *Matthews v Baxter* (1873) L.R. 8 Ex. 132.

[76] *Imperial Loan Co. v Stone* [1892] 1 Q.B. 599.

[77] *Grant v Imperial Trust* [1935] 3 D.L.R. 660; *McNab v Imperial Trust Co.* [1935] 4 D.L.R. 570.

[78] See below, para.3–022; *Falconbridge* (7th ed.), p.549.

[79] [1892] 1 Q.B. 599 (Illustration 5).

[80] But this would not appear to be a case where the burden of proof is shifted under s.30(2).

[81] *Grey v Cooper* (1782) 3 Doug. 65; *Taylor v Croker* (1802) 4 Esp. 187; *Smith v Johnson* (1858) 3 H. & N. 222.

against the payee, though not against the minor. In this respect, the subsection merely restates in part a general rule of the common law that the incapacity of one or more of the parties to a bill or note in no way diminishes the liability of the other parties to the instrument.[82]

Secondly, it provides that the drawing or indorsement by the minor or corporation entitles the holder to claim payment of the bill. Thus, if a bill is drawn payable to the order of the drawer and indorsed by him to a statutory corporation having no capacity or power to incur liability on the instrument, a subsequent indorsement by the corporation passes the property in the bill to the indorsee, even though the corporation itself may not be liable as indorser.[83] At common law, however, in situations which fall outside the subsection, as in the case of mental disorder or drunkenness, an indorsement which is void because of the incapacity of the indorser may not transfer title to the instrument so as to constitute the indorsee the holder.[84]

It has been pointed out[85] that the subsection does not cover the case of the acceptance of a bill by a person having no capacity to incur liability. But section 5(2) of the Act provides that, where the drawee is a person not having the capacity to contract, the holder may treat the instrument, at his option, either as a bill of exchange or as a promissory note.[86] Neither the drawer nor any indorser could therefore raise lack of capacity on the part of the drawee as a defence to liability on the bill.

3–017    **Estoppels.** Subsection (2) is buttressed by certain estoppels which are raised in favour of a holder in due course. The acceptor of a bill is precluded from denying to a holder in due course: (i) the capacity of the drawer to draw the bill,[87] (ii) in the case of a bill payable to drawer's order, the then capacity of the drawer to indorse,[88] and (iii) in the case of a bill payable to the order of a third person, the then capacity of the payee to indorse.[89] The drawer of a bill and the maker of a note are likewise precluded from denying to a holder in due course the then capacity of the payee to indorse.[90]

---

[82] *Burgess v Merrill* (1812) 4 Taunt. 468; *Wauthier v Wilson* (1912) 28 T.L.R. 239 (Illustration 6).

[83] *Smith v Johnson* (1858) 3 H. & N. 222. See also *Grey v Cooper* (1782) 3 Doug. 65; *Drayton v Dale* (1823) 2 B. & C. 293.

[84] *Alcock v Alcock* (1841) 3 M. & G. 268; *Stevenson Estate v Siewert* (2000) 191 D.L.R. (4th) 151, (2001) 202 D.L.R. (4th) 295. But see the estoppels referred to below, para.3–017.

[85] *Byles* (27th ed.), para.6–01.

[86] See above, para.2–041. See also ss.41(2)(a), 50(2)(c), 50(2)(d).

[87] s.54(2)(a). See below, para.7–017.

[88] s.54(2)(b). See below, para.7–017.

[89] s.54(2)(c). See below, para.7–018.

[90] ss.55(1)(b), 88(2).

Further estoppels against the indorser of a bill or note are contained in section 55(2)(b) and (c),[91] although it is to be noted that these provisions do not refer to the *capacity* of the other parties referred to.

ILLUSTRATIONS

1. A railway company is incorporated under a private Act which limits **3–018** the borrowing powers of the company and contains no provision in terms empowering the company to draw, accept, make or indorse bills of exchange and promissory notes. By order of the board of directors the company accepts several bills of exchange to which the seal of the company is attached. An action is brought on the acceptances by indorsees of the bills. The acceptances are not binding on the company. The legislature has not expressed an intention to entrust to the company the power to accept bills.[92]

2. A bill of exchange payable to order and addressed to the B. & I. Company, which is incorporated under local Acts and has no power to accept bills, is accepted by the defendants, who are two of the directors of the company, and also by the secretary, as follows: "Accepted for and on behalf of the B. & I. Company, G.K., F.S.P., directors; B.W., secretary." The bill so accepted is given to the drawer, the engineer of the company, on account of the company's debt to him for professional services. He is told by the defendants that they are giving the bill on the understanding that he will not negotiate it, and only as a recognition of the company's debt to him, since the company has no power to accept bills. But the defendants know that he will discount, and so negotiate, it. The bill is negotiated to the claimants for value and without notice of the understanding. The defendants are personally liable for the amount of the bill.[93]

3. S, during his minority, accepts certain bills of exchange drawn on him in payment for necessary goods supplied to him by the drawer. M petitions for S's bankruptcy, founding his claim upon the debt due to him as indorsee of the bills. The petition must be dismissed. S is not liable upon his acceptance of the bills.[94]

4. The defendant, before July 29, gives to B a cheque payable to order **3–019** for £250 post-dated August 14. On August 11, B transfers the cheque for

[91] See below, para.7–028.
[92] *Bateman v Mid Wales Ry* (1866) L.R. 1 C.P. 499.
[93] *West London Commercial Bank v Kitson* (1884) 13 Q.B.D. 360.
[94] *Re Soltykoff* [1891] 1 Q.B. 413.

value to the claimant. On August 14, the cheque is presented for payment, but is returned marked "account closed". The defendant attained his majority on July 29. The claimant cannot recover from the defendant on the cheque.[95]

5. The defendant signs as surety a promissory note. The agent of the claimants is present when the note is signed. Subsequent to the making of the note, the defendant is found by inquisition to be a lunatic. The jury agree that the defendant, when he signed the note, was so insane as not to be capable of understanding what he did, but they cannot agree whether this fact was known to the claimants' agent. A new trial is ordered. The jury have disagreed on a material question in the cause, since the allegation as to the knowledge of the claimants' agent is a necessary averment and it must be proved by the defendant in order to succeed.[96]

6. A father and son make a joint and several promissory note payable to the claimant in respect of a loan advanced by the claimant to the son, who at the time is still a minor. The loan is void under the Infants Relief Act 1874. The father is liable on the note. The intention was that he should act as principal borrower together with his son, and not as guarantor of his son's (void) debt.[97]

### Signature essential to liability

3–020       **23. No person is liable as drawer, indorser, or acceptor of a bill who has not signed it as such: Provided that**

        **(1) Where a person signs a bill in a trade or assumed name, he is liable thereon as if he had signed it in his own name:**

        **(2) The signature of the name of a firm is equivalent to the signature by the person so signing of the names of all persons liable as partners in that firm.**

| Definitions | Comparison |
|---|---|
| "bill": s.2. | UCC: §§ 1–201, 3–401. |
| "person": s.2. | ULB: arts 7, 8. |
| | ULC: arts 10, 11. |
| | UNB: arts 33, 34. |

---

[95] *Hutley v Peacock* (1913) 30 T.L.R. 42.
[96] *Imperial Loan Co. Ltd v Stone* [1892] 1 Q.B. 599.
[97] *Wauthier v Wilson* (1912) 28 T.L.R. 239.

COMMENT

**Signature of a bill.** Signature of a bill is essential to liability on it.[98] As **3–021** a general rule, a person is liable as drawer, acceptor or indorser of a bill only if he has signed it as such.[99] The same rule applies with respect to the maker or indorser of a promissory note.[1] However, by section 91(1) of the Act, where any instrument or writing is required to be signed by any person, it is not necessary that he should sign it with his own hand, but it is sufficient if his signature is written thereon by some other person by or under his authority. The signature may therefore be written by an agent, although the signature must be that of the principal and not of the agent. If an agent signs a bill or note in his own name, the principal will not be liable on it, even if the payee is aware that the signer is an agent.[2] Bills and notes constitute an exception to the ordinary rule[3] that, where an agent is authorised by his principal to enter into a contract and does so in his own name, evidence is admissible to charge the undisclosed principal, though not to discharge the agent. A person who signs only the name of another, whether with or without authority, will not ordinarily be liable on the bill or note, as he has not signed it in his own name.[4]

**Non est factum.** The drawer, acceptor, maker or indorser must sign the **3–022** bill or note *as such*. If he signs the instrument in the belief that he is signing a document which is essentially different in substance or in kind from that which he believed it to be—for example, where he signs his indorsement of a bill in the belief that he is signing a personal guarantee[5] or where he signs as maker of a promissory note in the belief that he is signing a document merely as a witness[6]—he may raise the defence of

---

[98] See also s.3(1) (bill must be signed by drawer), s.83(1) (note must be signed by maker), s.17(2)(a) (signature by drawee necessary for acceptance), s.32(1) (indorsement must be signed by the indorser), s.56 (signature of anomalous indorser).

[99] *Fenn v Harrison* (1790) 3 T.R. 757, 761; *Vincent v Horlock* (1808) 1 Camp. 442 (Illustration 1); *Siffkin v Walker* (1809) 2 Camp. 307 (Illustration 3); *Leadbitter v Farrow* (1816) 5 M. & S. 345, 349, 350 (Illustration 2); *Re Adansonia Fibre Co.* (1874) L.R. 9 Ch. App. 635, 643.

[1] ss.83(1), 89(1); *Central Bank of Yemen v Cardinal Financial Corpn.* [2001] Lloyd's Rep. Bank. 1 at [8] [14].

[2] *Ducarrey v Gill* (1830) M. & M. 450; *Leadbitter v Farrow* (1816) 5 M. & S. 345 at 349, 350 (Illustration 2); *Ex p. Rayner* (1868) 17 W.R. 64; *Churchill & Sim v Goddard* [1937] 1 K.B. 92, 111; *Central Bank of Yemen v Cardinal Financial Investment Corpn.* [2001] Lloyd's Rep. Bank 1 at [8] [14].

[3] *Bowstead and Reynolds on Agency* (17th ed.), §§ 8–070, 8–091, 9–047.

[4] *Wilson v Barthrop* (1837) 2 M. & W. 863. But, if without authority, he may be liable for misrepresentation or for breach of warranty of authority: *Starkey v Bank of England* [1903] A.C. 114.

[5] *Foster v Mackinnon* (1869) L.R. 4 C.P. 704 (Illustration 4). See also *R. v Davies* [1982] 1 All E.R. 513.

[6] *Lewis v Clay* (1898) 67 L.J.Q.B. 224 (Illustration 5).

*non est factum*, even against a holder in due course.[7] But, for this defence to succeed, the document must be radically or essentially or fundamentally different from the document as it was believed to be,[8] and the signer must prove that he acted carefully.[9]

3–023      **Meaning of signature.** The Act contains no definition of "signed" or "signature". But "signature" may perhaps be defined as the writing of a person's name on a bill or note in order to authenticate and give effect to some contract thereon.[10] A handwritten signature will clearly suffice, even if in pencil[11]; and a signature made by another person, but attested by a mark, is sufficient.[12] There is some doubt whether a lithograph or stamped facsimile of a signature would be sufficient, but it appears that it will be so.[13] However, it has not yet been held that a firm or company can "sign" as drawer by its name affixed by a rubber stamp, unaccompanied by any signature in verification,[14] and it seems unlikely that a signature by a mere mark,[15] symbol[16] or printed name[17] would suffice. Nevertheless, a note which ran, "I, John Stiles, promise to pay" (in the hand of the maker), instead of the usual "I promise to pay" with the signature subscribed, was held sufficiently signed[18]; but such a signature, or a signature by initials only,[19] is inconvenient and irregular.

---

[7] *Foster v Mackinnon* (1869) L.R. 4 C.P. 704.

[8] *Saunders v Anglia Building Society* [1971] A.C. 1004, 1017, 1019, 1021, 1026, 1039.

[9] [1971] A.C. 1004 at 1016, 1019, 1027, 1038; *Crédit Lyonnais v P.T. Barnard & Associates Ltd* [1976] 1 Lloyd's Rep. 557 (Illustration 6); *Marvo Color Research Ltd v Harris* (1982) 141 D.L.R. (3d) 577. This does not depend upon the principle of estoppel but on the principle that no man can take advantage of his own wrong: *Saunders v Anglia Building Society* [1971] A.C. 1004 at 1019, 1038. In *Petelin v Cullen* (1975) 132 C.L.R. 355, the Australian High Court held that the question of negligence is irrelevant where no innocent third party is involved; but see *Crédit Lyonnais v P.T. Barnard & Associates Ltd* [1976] 1 Lloyd's Rep. 557. See also *Puffer v Mastorkis* (1966) 59 D.L.R. (2d) 427.

[10] See *Grondin v Tisi and Turner* (1912) 4 D.L.R. 819, 825.

[11] *Geary v Physic* (1826) 5 B. & C. 234; *Importers Co. Ltd v Westminster Bank Ltd* [1927] 1 K.B. 869, 874.

[12] *George v Surrey* (1830) M. & M. 516.

[13] *Bennett v Brumfitt* (1867) L.R. 3 C.P. 28; *Re London and Mediterranean Bank* (1868) L.R. 3 Ch. App. 651, 654; *Goodman v J. Eban Ltd* [1954] 1 Q.B. 550; *Lazarus Estates Ltd v Beasley* [1956] 1 Q.B. 702, 710. cf. *Meyappen v Manchanayake* (1961) 62 N.L.R. (Ceylon) 529; *Silk Bros v Security Pacific National Bank* (1987) 16 N.S.W.L.R. 434, 441 (affd (1989) 16 N.S.W.L.R. 446).

[14] *Lazarus Estates Ltd v Beasley* [1956] 1 Q.B. 702 at 710; *Meyappen v Manchanayake* (1961) 62 N.L.R. (Ceylon) 529. cf. *Bird & Co. v Thomas Cook & Son Ltd* [1937] 2 All E.R. 227 (indorsement).

[15] *Morton v French* 1908 S.C. 171. cf. *George v Surrey* (1830) M. & M. 516; UCC, § 3–401.

[16] cf. UCC, § 1–201 (39).

[17] *Sniderman v McGarry* (1966) 60 D.L.R. (2d) 404, 408 (name of drawer printed on cheque form). As to typewritten signatures, see *McBeath's Trustees v McBeath* 1935 S.C. 471; *Goodman v J. Eban Ltd* [1954] 1 Q.B. 550 at 559; *Firstpost Homes Ltd v Johnson* [1995] 1 W.L.R. 1567, 1575. cf. UCC, § 3–401.

[18] *Taylor v Dobbins* (1719) 1 Stra. 399. See also *Ruff v Webb* (1794) 1 Esp. 129; *Evans v Hoare* [1892] 1 Q.B. 593; *Wood v Smith* [1993] Ch. 90.

[19] *Dansereau et Fils v Aubert Construction* [1967] C.S. 41 (Quebec).

Section 7 of the Electronic Communications Act 2000 provides that an electronic signature incorporated into or logically associated with a particular electronic communication or electronic data is to be admissible in evidence (though not conclusive) in any legal proceedings in relation to any question as to the authenticity or integrity of the communication or data. It is, however, submitted that this does not validate an electronic signature of a bill or note, if only because a bill or note is not yet such a communication or data.[20] Nevertheless, at common law, if an instrument in the form of a bill or note is signed by its maker and transmitted by fax to a recipient with the intention that the recipient should utilise the received copy as a bill or note, it could be argued that the copy has been "signed" by the maker. In *Re a Debtor (No.2021 of 1995)*[21] the question arose whether a faxed proxy form had been signed by the creditor as required by the Insolvency Rules 1986. Laddie J. said that "the receiving fax [machine] was instructed by the transmitting creditor to reproduce his signature on the proxy form which was itself being created at the receiving station".[22] Moreover, it could be argued that, provided the necessary *animus emittendi* is present,[23] there is a sufficient transfer of possession of the instrument to the recipient to amount to a "delivery" to him of the instrument. However, in a New Zealand case, *Cahayag v Removal Review Authority*,[24] a facsimile of a cheque was held not to be payment to the recipient of a fee payable for an immigration appeal: it was a "copy of proposed payment, not payment itself". It is submitted that, in most cases, the transmission to a recipient of a facsimile of a signed bill or note will similarly be intended merely to provide the recipient with a copy of the instrument (perhaps to show that the original instrument exists or what are its terms) and not to create an instrument to be utilised by the recipient.

**Liability outside the instrument.** A person who has not signed, **3–024** though not liable on the instrument, may nevertheless be liable on the original obligation for which the instrument was given, either unconditionally or conditionally upon the dishonour of the instrument, or for breach of an agreement to sign, or for breach of an oral guarantee of payment where the Statute of Frauds is satisfied.

---

[20] *cf.* s.8 of the Act of 2000 (which requires to be applied by statutory instrument: see above, para.2–011). The Electronic Signatures Regulations 2002, SI 2002/318, do not affect this issue. Contrast Gamertsfelder [1998] U.N.S.W.L.J. 54.
[21] [1996] 2 All E.R. 245.
[22] At p.351. See also *The Anemone* [1987] 1 Lloyd's Rep. 546; *Good Challenger Navegante SA v Metalexportimport SA* [2003] 1 Lloyd's Rep. 471 at [61], [2003] EWCA Civ 1668, [2004] 1 Lloyd's Rep. 67 at [20–28].
[23] See above, paras 1–026, 2–137, 2–150.
[24] [1998] 2 N.Z.L.R. 72.

**3–025** **Corporations and companies.** The seal of a corporation is equivalent to a signature.[25] But a bill or note of a corporation is not required by the Act to be under seal,[26] and by section 37 of the Companies Act 1985 a bill of exchange or promissory note is deemed to have been made, accepted or indorsed on behalf of a company if made, accepted or indorsed in the name of, or by or on behalf or on account of, the company by a person acting under its authority. It should be noted that a bill or note will be validly made, accepted or indorsed even if the name of the company alone is placed, with authority, on the instrument.[27] The word "made" presumably includes "drawn" and the expression "bill of exchange" will include a cheque.

**3–026** **Personal liability of officers, etc., of company.** By section 349(1) of the Companies Act 1985, every company is required to have its name mentioned in legible characters in all bills of exchange, promissory notes, endorsements, cheques and orders for money or goods purporting to be signed on behalf of the company. If a company fails to comply with this subsection it is liable to a fine.[28] Subsection (4) of section 349 also provides:

> "If an officer of a company or a person on its behalf signs or authorises to be signed on behalf of the company any bill of exchange, promissory note, endorsement, cheque or order for money or goods in which the company's name is not mentioned as required by subsection (1), he is liable to a fine; and he is further personally liable to the holder of the bill of exchange, promissory note, cheque or order for money or goods for the amount of it (unless it is duly paid by the company)."

This section replaces a similar provision in previous Companies Acts,[29] and it has been very strictly applied. The signatory will be personally liable if the correct name of the company is not mentioned in the instrument, even though he is innocent of moral blame[30] and even though the holder has in no way been misled.[31] Thus, if the name of the company is incorrect, for example, because the wording of the company's name is

---

[25] s.91(2). See also s.36A of the Companies Act 1985 (inserted by s.130(2) of the Companies Act 1989).

[26] s.91(2).

[27] But in the case of cheques, banks require the name of the company to be accompanied by the signature of the person signing, and either a "per pro." or other representative indication, and/or a designation of the position held by the signatory.

[28] Companies Act 1985, s.349(2).

[29] *e.g.* Companies Act 1948, s.108(4).

[30] *Rafsanjan Pistachio Producers Co-operative v S. Reiss* [1990] B.C.L.C. 352.

[31] *Atkins v Wardle* (1889) 58 L.J.Q.B. 377 (affirmed 5 T.L.R. 734) (Illustration 8); *Scottish & Newcastle Breweries Ltd v Blair* 1967 S.L.T. 72 (Illustration 11). Contrast *Penrose v Martyr* (1858) E.B. & E. 499, 503; *Jenice Ltd v Dan* [1993] B.C.L.C. 1349.

confused[32] or added to[33] or a word is omitted[34] such as the word "Limited"[35] or even an ampersand,[36] personal liability will be incurred. Certain abbreviations are, nevertheless, permitted, *e.g.* "Ltd" for "Limited"[37] and "Co." for "Company,"[38] but not "M" for "Michael" in the company's true name.[39]

However, subsection (1) of the section is complied with if the name of the company is mentioned somewhere in the instrument, so that a bill which is addressed to the company in its correct name will not give rise to personal liability on the part of a person signing an acceptance on behalf of the company if the company's name is wrongly stated in the acceptance[40] or not stated in the acceptance at all.[41] If a bill is addressed to a company by an incorrect name and is accepted by a director of the company in his own name, he can incur no liability as acceptor, since the bill is not addressed to him.[42] But he will incur liability under section 349(4) if, looking at the bill as a whole, it is apparent that it "purports to be signed on behalf of the company".[43] The name that is required to be stated in the instrument is the name of the company as registered under the Companies Acts, and a trading or business name[44] will not suffice.[45]

In *Durham Fancy Goods Ltd v Michael Jackson (Fancy Goods) Ltd*,[46] however, the holders of a bill of exchange were held to be precluded from enforcing the personal liability of a director who had accepted a bill on behalf of a company when they had addressed the bill to the company by an incorrect name and also inscribed on the bill a form of acceptance

---

[32] *Penrose v Martyr* (1858) E.B. & E. 499 (Illustration 7); *Atkins v Wardle* (1889) 58 L.J.Q.B. 377.

[33] *Nassau Steam Press v Tyler* (1894) 70 L.T. 376.

[34] *Scottish & Newcastle Breweries Ltd v Blair* 1967 S.L.T. 72; *Durham Fancy Goods Ltd v Michael Jackson (Fancy Goods) Ltd* [1968] 2 Q.B. 839 (Illustration 13).

[35] *Penrose v Martyr* (1858) E.B. & E. 499; *Atkins v Wardle* (1889) 58 L.J.Q.B. 377; *British Airways Board v Parish* [1979] 2 Lloyd's Rep. 361 (Illustration 14); *Blum v O.C.P. Repartition S.A.* [1988] B.C.L.C. 170; *Lindholst & Co. A/S v Fowler* [1988] B.C.L.C. 166; *Novaknit Hellas SA v Kumar Brothers International Ltd* [1998] Lloyd's Rep. Bank. 287; *Fiorentino Comm. Giuseppe Srl v Farnesi* [2005] 2 All E.R. 737.

[36] *Hendon v Adelman* (1973) 117 S.J. 631 (Illustration 12).

[37] *F. Stacey and Co. Ltd v Wallis* (1912) 106 L.T. 544 (Illustration 10).

[38] *Banque de L'Indochine et de Suez S.A. v Euroseas Group Finance Co. Ltd* [1981] 3 All E.R. 198 (Illustration 16).

[39] *Durham Fancy Goods Ltd v Michael Jackson (Fancy Goods) Ltd* [1968] 2 Q.B. 839.

[40] *Dermatine Co. Ltd v Ashworth* (1905) 21 T.L.R. 510 (Illustration 9).

[41] *F. Stacey and Co. Ltd v Wallis* (1912) 106 L.T. 544.

[42] See s.17 above, para.2–115.

[43] *Maxform SpA v Mariani and Goodville Ltd* [1979] 2 Lloyd's Rep. 385, affirmed [1981] 2 Lloyd's Rep. 54 (Illustration 15); *Novaknit Hellas SA v Kumar Brothers International Ltd* [1998] Lloyd's Rep. Bank. 287.

[44] See now Business Names Act 1985.

[45] *Maxform SpA v Mariani and Goodville Ltd* [1979] 2 Lloyd's Rep. 385.

[46] [1968] 2 Q.B. 839 (Illustration 13). In *Blum v O.C.P. Repartition S.A.* [1988] B.C.L.C. 170, May L.J. (at 175) expressly reserved his position as to whether this case was rightly decided.

describing the company by the same incorrect name, which the director had accordingly signed. But such an estoppel will not be raised if the holder has merely addressed the bill to the company by an incorrect name, since it is open to the person signing the acceptance to correct the name of the company in the acceptance.[47] The fact that the error is due to the fault of a third party, *e.g.* of the drawee bank, which has printed the incorrect name of the company on the company's cheques, will not take away the personal liability of the signatory.[48]

3–027     The personal liability imposed by the subsection will only arise if the instrument is not duly paid by the company.[48a] But it is not to be equated with that of a guarantor or surety, so that, for example, giving time to the company to discharge the debt constituted by the instrument will not discharge the signatory.[49] Nevertheless, the signatory could probably recover from the company in restitution the amount he has been compelled to pay as money paid to its use, on the grounds that, as between himself and the company, the company was primarily liable to pay the instrument, and the company has obtained the benefit of the payment by the discharge of its liability.[50]

Rectification of the instrument will not be ordered so as to enable the signatory to avoid his statutory liability.[51]

3–028     **Subsection (1): trade or assumed name.** Where a person signs a bill in a trade or assumed name, he is liable thereon as if he had signed it in his own name.[52]

3–029     **Subsection (2): partnership firms.** This subsection makes special provision for partnerships.[53] The signature of the name of a firm[54] is deemed to be the signature of all persons who are partners in the firm, whether working, dormant,[55] or secret,[56] or who, by holding themselves out as

---

[47] *Scottish & Newcastle Breweries Ltd v Blair* 1967 S.L.T. 72; *Maxform SpA v Mariani and Goodville Ltd* [1979] 2 Lloyd's Rep. 385; *Lindholst & Co. A/S v Fowler* [1988] B.C.L.C. 166.

[48] *Hendon v Adelman* (1973) 117 S.J. 631; *British Airways Board v Parish* [1979] 2 Lloyd's Rep. 361.

[48a] *Fiorentino Comm. Giuseppe Srl v Farnesi* [2005] 2 All E.R. 737 (present liability must have arisen).

[49] *British Airways Board v Parish* [1979] 2 Lloyd's Rep. 361.

[50] *Moule v Garrett* (1872) L.R. 7 Ex. 101, 104; *Brook's Wharf and Bull Wharf Ltd v Goodman Brothers* [1937] 1 K.B. 534, 543–544. See *Chitty on Contracts* (29th ed.), Vol.I, § 29–099.

[51] *Blum v O.C.P. Repartition S.A.* [1988] B.C.L.C. 170; *Rafsanjan Pistachio Producers Co-operative v S. Reiss* [1990] B.C.L.C. 352.

[52] *Forman v Jacob* (1815) 1 Stark. 46, 47; *Wilde v Keep* (1834) 6 C. & P. 235 (Illustration 17); *Lindus v Bradwell* (1848) 5 C.B. 583, 591.

[53] See *Lindley and Banks on Partnership* (17th ed.), § 12–175.

[54] *cf. Ringham v Hackett, The Times,* February 9, 1980, CA (Illustration 18); *Central Motors (Birmingham) v P.A. & S.N.P. Wadsworth* [1983] C.L.Y. 6. See also *Raman Chitty v Ng Siang Ee* (1904) 9 S.S.L.R. 90 (Straits Settlements).

[55] *Swan v Steele* (1806) 7 East 210; *Wintle v Crowther* (1831) 1 Cr. & J. 316.

[56] *Pooley v Driver* (1876) 5 Ch.D. 458.

partners, are liable as such to third parties.[57] However, in the absence of evidence to the contrary, a partner has no authority to use for partnership purposes any other name than the name of the firm. If, without authority,[58] he varies the firm style, then, unless the variation is insubstantial,[59] no action can be maintained against the firm on the instrument,[60] although the individual partner who signs will be personally liable.[61]

A firm is not liable on a bill or note signed in the name of one of the partners only, even if the proceeds are applied for partnership purposes,[62] unless his name is that of the firm.[63] Thus, if A, B and C are in partnership and arrange that C shall draw bills in his own name on A and B, C's signature to such bills does not bind the others, even though the bills are drawn in the course of the partnership transactions.[64] It follows that, where there is no distinct firm name, the firm has no name by which it can draw, make, accept or indorse bills or notes; and it is not to be assumed that the name of a partner upon the instrument is to be considered as being *pro hac vice* the name of the firm.[65] However, in such a case a partner could for firm purposes sign the individual names of his copartners.[66]

Where the name of a firm and the name of one of the partners in it are the same, and that partner draws, accepts or indorses a bill in the common name, the signature is prima facie deemed to be that of the firm, at least where he carries on no business separate from the business of the firm.[67] But this presumption may be rebutted by showing that the bill was not given for partnership purposes or under the authority of the firm, and it is then immaterial that a bona fide holder took the bill as a bill of the persons who constitute the partnership, whoever they may be, and not merely as the bill of the individual partner.[68]

---

[57] *Gurney v Evans* (1858) 3 H. & N. 122; *Yorkshire Banking Co. v Beatson (No.1)* (1880) 5 C.P.D. 109, 124. See Partnership Act 1890, ss.6, 14.

[58] *cf. Williamson v Johnson* (1823) 1 B. & C. 146 (managing partner in habit of indorsing bills in former name of firm).

[59] *Leonard v Wilson* (1834) 2 Cr. & M. 589; *Kirk v Blurton* (1841) 9 M. & W. 284, 289; *Forbes v Marshall* (1855) 11 Ex. 166, 180.

[60] *Faith v Richmond* (1840) 11 A. & E. 339 (Illustration 19); *Kirk v Blurton* (1841) 9 M. & W. 284 (Illustration 20); *Re Adansonia Fibre Co.* (1874) L.R. 9 Ch. App. 635; *Odell v Cormack & Co.* (1887) 19 Q.B.D. 223, 226.

[61] *Faith v Richmond* (1840) 11 A. & E. 339; *Kirk v Blurton* (1841) 9 M. & W. 284: see also *Wilde v Keep* (1834) 6 C. & P. 235.

[62] *Siffkin v Walker* (1809) 2 Camp. 307 (Illustration 3); *Emly v Lye* (1812) 15 East 7; *Nicholson v Ricketts* (1860) 2 E. & E. 497; *Re Adansonia Fibre Co.* (1874) L.R. 9 Ch. App. 635; *Geo. Thompson (Aust.) Pty. Ltd v Vitadello* [1978] V.R. 199.

[63] See below.

[64] *Nicholson v Ricketts* (1860) 2 E. & E. 497 at 526; *Re Adansonia Fibre Co.* (1874) L.R. 9 Ch. App. 635 at 644.

[65] *Re Adansonia Fibre Co.* (1874) L.R. 9 Ch. App. 635 at 643, 644.

[66] *Ex p. Buckley* (1845) 14 M. & W. 469; *Norton v Seymour* (1847) 3 C.B. 792.

[67] *Yorkshire Banking Co. v Beatson* (1880) 5 C.P.D. 109, 123–124.

[68] *Yorkshire Banking Co. v Beatson* (1880) 5 C.P.D. 109 (Illustration 21).

**3–030**   Where two firms carry on business in the same firm name, a person who is a partner in both firms is liable to be sued on any bills signed in that name, and binding on either firm. If the defendant is a partner in only one of the firms, and a bill is indorsed by his copartners in that firm for a debt due to the other firm, in fraud of the defendant, it has been held[69] that he will be liable to a bona fide holder of the bill without notice of the fraud. Further, in *Baker v Charlton*,[70] in a like situation, where a bill was drawn by his copartners, who were members of both firms, the defendant was not permitted to raise the defence that the bill was not drawn by the firm to which he belonged; but it has been contended that this case can no longer be relied on.[71]

See also the Comment on section 17 of the Act (Acceptance of Bill).[72]

**3–031**   **Authority of partner to bind firm.**[73]  By section 5 of the Partnership Act 1890:

> "every partner is an agent of the firm and his other partners for the purposes of the business of the partnership; and the acts of every partner who does any act for carrying on in the usual way business of the kind carried on by the firm of which he is a member bind the firm and his partners, unless the partner so acting has in fact no authority to act for the firm in the particular matter, and the person with whom he is dealing knows that he has no authority or does not know or believe him to be a partner."

If a partner, for the purposes of the business of the partnership, signs a bill or note in the firm's name when expressly authorised so to do by his co-partners, the signature will bind the firm and his partners. Further, even though he has no express authority, he will have implied authority to bind the firm and his partners if, by signing the bill or note, he does an act for carrying on in the usual way business of the kind carried on by the firm. However, it is open to partners to agree among themselves that one or more of them shall have no authority to sign bills or notes in the name of the firm, either generally or in respect of a particular transaction or transactions.[74] And a partner may, for example, in fraud of his co-partners, accept a bill or make a note in the name of the firm, and give the bill or note in payment of a private debt of his own.[75] In such a case, as

---

[69] *Swan v Steele* (1806) 7 East 210.

[70] (1791) 1 Peake 111.

[71] *Lindley and Banks on Partnership* (18th ed.), § 12–189. See also *Fleming v M'Nair* (1812) 3 Dow at 229, and note (b) at 1 Peake 112.

[72] See above, para.2–116.

[73] *Lindley and Banks on Partnership* (18th ed.), Ch.12.

[74] Partnership Act 1890, ss.8, 19, 46.

[75] Partnership Act 1890, s.7.

between the partnership and third parties, the firm may still be bound. If the holder of the instrument took it with knowledge of the partner's want of authority, he will not be able to enforce it against the firm. But if the instrument was signed in the name of the firm with the apparent, though not with the real, authority of his co-partners, the firm will be bound to a holder who took it for value without knowledge of the partner's want of authority.

A partner in a trading partnership has implied authority to bind the firm by drawing, making, accepting and indorsing bills and notes in the firm name for the purposes of the partnership.[76] There is no authoritative definition of a trading partnership, but it has been stated that "trade" is not co-extensive with "business"[77] and that "trading" implies the buying and selling of goods.[78] His authority is to bind his co-partners jointly with himself, and not to bind himself and them jointly and severally.[79] If, in fact, he has no authority to sign the bill or note in the name of the firm, then the firm and his partners will not be liable to one who takes the instrument with notice of his want of authority[80]; but they will be bound to one who takes the instrument for value without such notice.[81]

A partner in a non-trading partnership has prima facie no authority to render the firm and his partners liable by signing a bill or note in the firm name. Professional partnerships (*e.g.* solicitors),[82] mining partnerships,[83]

---

[76] *Lane v Williams* (1692) 2 Vern. 277; *Pinkney v Hall* (1696) 1 Salk. 126; *Sutton v Gregory* (1797) Peake Add. Cas. 150; *Gallway v Mathew and Smithson* (1808) 10 East 264, 266; *Davidson v Robertson* (1815) 3 Dow 218; *Dickinson v Valpy* (1829) 10 B. & C. 128, 138; *Thicknesse v Bromilow* (1832) 2 C. & J. 425, 435; *Hedley v Bainbridge* (1842) 3 Q.B. 316, 320; *Bank of Australasia v Breillat* (1847) 6 Moo.P.C. 152, 194; *Stephens v Reynolds* (1860) 5 H. & N. 513; *Ex p. Darlington Joint Stock Banking Co.* (1865) 4 De G.J. & S. 581, 585; *Wheatley v Smithers* [1906] 2 K.B. 321, 322 (revd on other grounds [1907] 2 K.B 664). cf. *Levieson v Lane* (1862) 13 C.B., N.S. 278; *Re Cunningham & Co. Ltd* (1887) 36 Ch.D. 532. But a bill accepted in blank is not binding on the firm except in favour of a bona fide holder without notice of the way the bill was accepted: *Hogarth v Latham* (1878) 3 Q.B.D. 643.
[77] *Harris v Amery* (1865) L.R. 1 C.P. 148, 154.
[78] *Wheatley v Smithers* [1906] 2 K.B. 321, 322 (reversed on other grounds [1907] 2 K.B. 664); *Higgins v Beauchamp* [1914] 3 K.B. 1192, 1195; *Finny v Bergum* [1926] 3 D.L.R. 798.
[79] *Maclae v Sutherland* (1854) 3 E. & B. 1, 33. But it is otherwise if several partners sign a note personally. See s.85, and *Healey v Story* (1848) 3 Exch. 3; *Penkivil v Connell* (1850) 5 Exch. 381; *Bottomley v Fisher* (1862) 1 H. & C. 211.
[80] *Arden v Sharpe* (1792) 2 Esp. 524; *Gallway v Mathew and Smithson* (1808) 10 East 264; *Ex p. Darlington Joint Stock Banking Co.* (1865) 4 De G.J. & S. 581; *Heilbut v Nevill* (1870) L.R. 5 C.P. 478.
[81] *Sutton v Gregory* (1797) Peake Add. Cas. 150; *Swan v Steele* (1806) 7 East 210; *Ridley v Taylor* (1810) 13 East 175; *Thicknesse v Bromilow* (1832) 2 C. & J. 425; *Lewis v Reilly* (1841) 1 Q.B. 349; *Wiseman v Easton* (1863) 8 L.T., N.S. 837. See also (burden of proof) s.30(2) and *Hogg v Skeen* (1865) 18 C.B., N.S. 426.
[82] *Hedley v Bainbridge* (1842) 3 Q.B. 316; *Forster v Mackreth* (1867) L.R. 2 Ex. 163; *Garland v Jacomb* (1873) L.R. 8 Ex. 216, 219.
[83] *Dickinson v Valpy* (1829) 10 B. & C. 128; *Ricketts v Bennett* (1847) 4 C.B. 686, 689; *Brown v Byers* (1847) 16 M. & W. 252.

and partnerships of commission agents,[84] cinema proprietors,[85] and auctioneers,[86] have been held to be non-trading partnerships.[87] The holder of the instrument, even if he is a holder in due course,[88] must therefore prove actual authority or that such authority is to be implied, *i.e.* that it is customary or usual in a business of that nature or is necessary for the purposes of carrying on the business of the partnership.[89]

3–032　With respect to cheques, a partner has implied authority to bind the firm by drawing cheques in the firm's name on the bankers of the firm,[90] but not to post-date them.[91]

An unauthorised signature may be ratified by the firm.[92]

3–033　**Authority of partner to transfer.** A partner who has no authority to bind the firm by his indorsement may yet transfer the property in the instrument by negotiating it in the firm name.[93] But where a bill belonging to a firm is indorsed away by one partner in the firm name, in fraud of his co-partners, the property in it does not pass to an indorsee who takes with notice of the fraud.[94]

3–034　**Ex-partners.** After the dissolution of a partnership the authority of each partner to bind the firm terminates, except so far as may be necessary to wind up the affairs of the partnership, and to complete transactions begun but unfinished at the time of the dissolution.[95] Nevertheless, as between the partnership and third parties, such authority can only effectively be determined by due notice of the dissolution.[96] Notice in the *London Gazette* is sufficient notice as to persons who had no dealings with

---

[84] *Yates v Dalton* (1858) 28 L.J. Ex. 69.

[85] *Higgins v Beauchamp* [1914] 3 K.B. 1192.

[86] *Wheatley v Smithers* [1906] 2 K.B. 321.

[87] See also *Greenslade v Dower* (1828) 7 B. & C. 635 (no authority with respect to bills in respect of foundation of agricultural partnership). *cf. Bank of Australasia v Breillat* (1847) 6 Moo.P.C. 152 (banking partnership).

[88] *Dickinson v Valpy* (1829) 10 B. & C. 128.

[89] *Dickinson v Valpy* (1829) 10 B. & C. 128 at 137, 139; *Hedley v Bainbridge* (1842) 3 Q.B. 316, 321. See also *Bank of Australasia v Breillat* (1847) 6 Moo.P.C. 152.

[90] *Laws v Rand* (1857) 3 C.B., N.S. 442, 447; *Backhouse v Charlton* (1878) 8 Ch.D. 444.

[91] *Forster v Mackreth* (1867) L.R. 2 Ex. 163 (solicitors' firm). But see *Guildford Trust Ltd v Goss* (1927) 136 L.T. 725 (where there was nothing to put the transferee of the cheque on inquiry).

[92] s.24.

[93] *Smith v Johnson* (1858) 3 H. & N. 222 (company); see above, para.3–016.

[94] *Heilbut v Nevill* (1870) L.R. 5 C.P. 478; *Creighton v Halifax Banking Co.* (1890) 18 S.C.R. 140. *cf. Ross v Chandler* (1911) 45 S.C.R. 127.

[95] Partnership Act 1890, s.38. *cf. Kilgour v Finlyson* (1789) 1 H.Bl. 155; *Abel v Sutton* (1800) 3 Esp. 108; *Anderson v Weston* (1840) 6 Bing.N.C. 296.

[96] Partnership Act 1890, s.36(1). Contrast *Lewis v Reilly* (1841) 1 Q.B. 349, which is said in *Lindley and Banks on Partnership* (18th ed.), § 13–63, to be "perplexing". See also the Limited Liability Partnerships Act 2000, s.6(3)

the firm before the date of the dissolution[97]; but otherwise it must be shown that the third party was aware of the dissolution.[98] Likewise, where a partner retires from his firm, but the business is carried on, he may still be liable on the firm's bills and notes if he has not given due notice of his retirement.[99]

**Limited liability partnerships.** A limited liability partnership incorpo- **3–035** rated under the Limited Liability Partnerships Act 2000 is a legal entity distinct from its members.[1] Accordingly the law relating to partnerships does not apply in principle to a limited liability partnership.[2] Every member of such a partnership is the agent of the partnership.[3] But the partnership is not bound by anything done by a member in dealing with a person if (a) the member in fact has no authority to act for that partnership by doing that thing, and (b) the person knows that he has no authority or does not know or believe him to be a member of the partnership.[4] Liability for the wrongful acts or omissions of a member of a partnership in the course of the business of the partnership or with its authority is imposed on the wrongdoing member and the partnership, but not on other members individually.[5]

ILLUSTRATIONS

1. J, the drawer and payee of a bill, indorses it in blank to H & Co. One **3–036** of the partners in that firm writes above J's signature "Pay the contents to V & Co.", without signing his own name or that of his firm. Neither the partner nor his firm are liable as indorsers, since their name does not appear written on the bill with intent to indorse.[6] The partner has only converted the blank indorsement of J into a special indorsement (as now permitted by section 34(4)).

2. The defendant, who is agent for the D Bank, draws in his own name a bill for £50 payable to the claimant. The claimant knows that the

---

[97] Partnership Act 1890, s.36(2).
[98] *Re Fraser* [1892] 2 Q.B. 633, 637.
[99] *Parkins v Carruthers* (1800) 3 Esp. 248. He may also be liable if he continues to hold himself out as partner: *Williams v Keats* (1817) 2 Stark. 290; *Dolman v Orchard* (1825) 2 C. & P. 104. cf. *Re Fraser* [1892] 2 Q.B. 633, see s.14 of the 1890 Act.
[1] Limited Liability Partnerships Act 2000, s.1(1).
[2] Limited Liability Partnerships Act 2000, s.1(5).
[3] Limited Liability Partnerships Act 2000, s.6(1).
[4] Limited Liability Partnerships Act 2000, s.6(2).
[5] Limited Liability Partnerships Act 2000, s.6(4). See *Lindley and Banks on Partnership* (18th ed.), para.28–11.
[6] *Vincent v Horlock* (1808) 1 Camp. 442.

defendant is only an agent. The defendant is liable as the drawer of the bill.[7] The D Bank is not liable.[8]

3. The defendants, W and R, are jointly indebted to the claimant in the sum of £300. W alone makes a promissory note payable to the claimant for the amount of the debt. W alone is liable on the note, even though it is given for a joint debt.[9]

3–037
4. The defendant, a gentleman advanced in life, is induced by C to indorse a bill of exchange for £3,000 in the belief that it is a guarantee of a similar nature to one which he has previously signed. By subsequent indorsements the bill comes into the hands of the claimant, who takes it in good faith and for value. The defendant is not liable on the bill, as he never intended to make such a contract and was not negligent.[10]

5. Lord N comes to the defendant and asks him to witness some deeds for him. He produces a roll of papers covered by blotting paper, in which there are cut four openings, explaining that the matter is a private one. Believing that he is witnessing Lord N's signature, the defendant signs in the spaces indicated. The papers are two promissory notes for £11,000 payable to the claimant, and two letters authorising the claimant to pay the proceeds of the notes to Lord N. The claimant receives the notes in good faith and for value. The defendant is not liable, as he acted without negligence and his mind never went with the transaction.[11]

6. Two bills of exchange, in French, are drawn by a French company on the defendants, an English company, in relation to watches supplied to the defendants by the French company. The claimants, a French bank, discount the bills and credit the French company's account. They present the bills to the defendants for acceptance, and the bills are accepted by the defendants' managing director, B, on behalf of the defendants. In an action by the claimants against the defendants on the bills, the defendants plead *non est factum*, alleging that B is ignorant of the French language and had believed that the documents were merely receipts acknowledging the arrival in England of consignments of the watches. The defence fails, as the defendants have not discharged the burden of proving that B acted carefully.[12]

---

[7] *Leadbitter v Farrow* (1816) 5 M. & S. 345.
[8] (1816) 5 M. & S. 345 at 349, 350.
[9] *Siffkin v Walker* (1809) 2 Camp. 307.
[10] *Foster v Mackinnon* (1869) L.R. 4 C.P. 704.
[11] *Lewis v Clay* (1898) 67 L.J.Q.B. 224.
[12] *Crédit Lyonnais v P. T. Barnard & Associates Ltd* [1976] 1 Lloyd's Rep. 557.

7. The defendant is the secretary of a company whose true name is "The **3–038** Saltash Watermen's Steam Packet Company Limited". The plaintiff draws a bill addressed to "The Saltash Watermen's Steam Packet Company, Saltash", omitting the word "Limited". The bill is accepted by the defendant "J.M., Secretary to the said company". The bill is dishonoured by non-payment. The defendant is personally liable under section 31 of the Joint Stock Companies Act 1856 as he has signed a bill on behalf of the company without the company's name on it.[13]

8. The defendants are directors of a company named "South Shields Salt Water Baths Company (Limited)". The claimant, a shareholder in the company, draws a bill addressed to "Salt Water Baths Company (Limited) South Shields" and the bill is accepted by the defendants on behalf of "South Shields Salt Water Baths Company", omitting the word "Limited". The defendants are personally liable, upon dishonour of the bill, under section 42 of the Companies Act 1862. They have accepted a bill without the name of the company on it.[14]

9. The claimant draws a bill of exchange addressed to "The Motor and General Tyre Company (Limited)". It is accepted by the defendants, directors of the company, "For the Motor and General Tyre Company. A, T, Directors". The word "Limited" is omitted from the acceptance because the rubber stamp impressed on the bill is longer than that part of the bill on which the acceptance is stamped. The company does not pay the bill. The defendants are not personally liable under section 42 of the Companies Act 1862. There is only one company on whose behalf it was intended to accept the bill and that company's name has been mentioned, *i.e.* in the address, on the bill.[15]

10. The defendants are the directors and secretary of a company named **3–039** "J and T H Wallis Limited". The claimants draw a bill of exchange addressed to "Messrs J and T H Wallis Ltd, Beddington, Surrey". The bill is accepted by the defendants as follows "Accepted payable at the London and County Bank, Croydon Branch—Jas. Wallis, Thomas H. Wallis; Henry Bowles, Secretary." The company goes into liquidation and the bill is unpaid. The defendants are not personally liable under section 63 of the Companies (Consolidation) Act 1908. The abbreviation "Ltd" for "Limited" is permissible, and it is sufficient if the name of the company appears correctly in the address of the bill without also being mentioned in the acceptance.[16]

[13] *Penrose v Martyr* (1858) E.B. & E. 499.
[14] *Atkins v Wardle* (1889) 58 L.J.Q.B. 377 (affirmed 5 T.L.R. 734).
[15] *Dermatine Co. Ltd v Ashworth* (1905) 21 T.L.R. 510.
[16] *Stacey (F.) and Co. Ltd v Wallis* (1912) 106 L.T. 544.

11. The defenders are the directors and secretary of a company named "Anderson & Blair (Property Development) Limited". The pursuers draw a bill addressed to "Messrs Anderson & Blair, Windmill Hotel, Arbroath", and the bill is signed by the defenders on behalf of the company as accepted. The bill is unpaid. The defenders are personally liable under section 108(4) of the Companies Act 1948, even though the pursuers have not been deceived or misled. The pursuers are under no personal bar, for they have done nothing to mislead the defenders.[17]

12. The defendants are directors of a company named "L & R Agencies Limited". They draw a cheque on behalf of the company payable to the claimant. The cheque bears the printed words "L R Agencies Limited". (omitting the ampersand) which have been placed there by the drawee bank. The cheque is unpaid. The defendants are personally liable under section 108 of the Companies Act 1948.[18]

3–040     13. The claimants draw a 90-day bill by typing the text of the bill on the right-hand side of their own printed letter paper. The bill is addressed to "M. Jackson (Fancy Goods) Ltd, 263 Bury New Road, Manchester". On the left-hand side of the paper the following words are also typed by the claimants: "Accepted payable; Westminster Bank Ltd, 110 Regent Road, Salford 5. For and on behalf of: M. Jackson (Fancy Goods) Ltd, Manchester". The defendant, a director of the company, accepts the bill by adding his signature beneath the typed words of acceptance. The true name of the company is "Michael Jackson (Fancy Goods) Limited". The bill is unpaid and the company goes into liquidation. The defendant is personally liable on the bill under section 108 of the Companies Act 1948 since "M" is not an abbreviation of "Michael". But the claimants have implied that acceptance of the bill in this form would be accepted by them as a regular acceptance and it is inequitable that the claimants should be allowed to enforce the defendant's liability without giving him the opportunity to regularise the acceptance by inscribing the correct name of the company on the bill, which it is now too late to do. The claimants' action therefore fails.[19]

14. The defendant is the managing director of a company named "Watchstream Limited", which is indebted to the claimants for considerable sums. The defendant draws a cheque on the company's account for £50,000 payable to the order of the claimants. The cheque has printed on it the name "Watchstream", the word "Limited" being omitted. The cheque is dishonoured. An offer by the company to discharge its debts to

---

[17] *Scottish & Newcastle Breweries Ltd v Blair* 1967 S.L.T. 72.
[18] *Hendon v Adelman* (1973) 117 S.J. 631.
[19] *Durham Fancy Goods Ltd v Michael Jackson (Fancy Goods) Ltd* [1968] 2 Q.B. 839.

the claimants, including its debt on the cheque, by instalments is accepted by the claimants. The defendant is personally liable under section 108(4) of the Companies Act 1948. The liability under that subsection is not one which is identical in legal consequences with the liability of a guarantor or surety under a contract of guarantee. Further, once the cheque was not duly paid, the liability of the defendant came into existence and could not, in any event, be affected thereafter in the way in which the liability of a guarantor would or might be affected under the ordinary law of principal and surety.[20]

15. The defendant is the sole director of and a majority shareholder in a company named "Mariani and Goodville Limited", which carries on business in London under the registered business name "Italdesign". The claimants draw bills of exchange addressed to "Italdesign". These are accepted by the defendant in his own name and without any addition to his signature. The bills are dishonoured by non-payment. The defendant is not liable as acceptor as he is not the drawee. But, although the drawee and the acceptor are different persons, if the bills are looked at as a whole, there is no doubt that the defendant purported to sign the bills on behalf of the drawee company. Since the true name of the company is not mentioned in the bills, section 108(4) of the Companies Act 1948 applies and the defendant is personally liable. The claimants are not estopped from enforcing that liability since, although the bills were addressed to "Italdesign", they did not suggest how the bills should be accepted, and there was nothing to prevent the defendant from accepting by signing "Mariani and Goodville Limited trading as Italdesign".[21]

16. The defendants are officers of a company whose registered name is **3–041** "Euroseas Group Finance Company Limited". Two cheques are drawn by the company in favour of the claimants and these bear the printed words "Per pro. Euroseas Group Finance Co. Ltd". The cheques are signed by the defendants, but are dishonoured. The defendants are not personally liable under section 108(4) of the Companies Act 1948, since "Co." is so generally accepted as an abbreviation of as to be treated as equivalent to "Company".[22]

17. The claimant draws a bill on the defendant, Joseph Keep, who accepts it in the name "John Keep & Co.". The defendant is a sole trader. He is liable on the bill.[23]

---

[20] *British Airways Board v Parish* [1979] 2 Lloyd's Rep. 361.
[21] *Maxform SpA v Mariani and Goodville Ltd* [1979] 2 Lloyd's Rep. 385, affirmed [1981] 2 Lloyd's Rep. 54.
[22] *Banque de l'Indochine et de Suez S.A. v Euroseas Group Finance Co. Ltd* [1981] 3 All E.R. 198.
[23] *Wilde v Keep* (1834) 6 C. & P. 235.

18. H and W set up business in partnership. A partnership account is established at a branch of Lloyds Bank and the bank issues two cheque books with "H/W Promotions" (the style of the partnership) printed on the cheques. H draws such a cheque for £500 payable to R, but without telling W. He signs his own name beneath the printed name of the partnership. W is liable to R on the cheque.[24]

3–042      19. R, B and H carry on business in partnership under the name of "The Newcastle and Sunderland Wall's End Coal Company". R makes a promissory note for £350, signing it "For The Newcastle Coal Company, R, Manager". B and H are not liable on the note, as they did not empower R to use any name but that of the firm.[25]

20. Blurton and Habershon carry on a partnership business as printers under the name of "John Blurton". Habershon draws and indorses a bill of exchange in the name of "John Blurton & Co.". Blurton is not liable to the claimant, a subsequent indorsee of the bill, since Habershon had no authority to bind Blurton, except in the partnership name.[26]

21. The defendants, B and M, carry on business in partnership. B is the only ostensible partner, the business being carried on in his name. M is a dormant partner. B enters into accommodation transactions and, without the authority of M, accepts and indorses bills of exchange in his own name. The accommodation transactions are entered into by B for his private purposes and are not entered in the books of the firm. One of the bills so accepted and another of the bills so indorsed by B are discounted in good faith and for value by the claimant bank. The bank takes the bills as the bills of the partnership business, whoever the proprietors might be, and not as the bills of B only. M is not liable on the bills as it has been proved that the bill was signed by B, not in the name of the partnership, but in an individual capacity for his own private purposes.[27]

### Forged or unauthorised signature

3–043      **24. Subject to the provisions of this Act, where a signature on a bill is forged or placed thereon without the authority of the person whose signature it purports to be, the forged or unauthorised signature is wholly inoperative, and no right to retain the bill or to give a discharge therefor or to enforce payment thereof against any party**

[24] *Ringham v Hackett, The Times,* February 9, 1980, CA.
[25] *Faith v Richmond* (1840) 11 A. & E. 339.
[26] *Kirk v Blurton* (1841) 9 M. & W. 284.
[27] *Yorkshire Banking Co. v Beatson* (1880) 5 C.P.D. 109.

**thereto can be acquired through or under that signature, unless the party against whom it is sought to retain or enforce payment of the bill is precluded from setting up the forgery or want of authority.**

**Provided that nothing in this section shall affect the ratification of an unauthorised signature not amounting to a forgery.**

| | |
|---|---|
| Definitions | Comparison |
| "bill": s.2. | UCC: §§ 1–201(43), 3–403, 3–405, |
| "person": s.2. | 3–406, 4–401, 4–406. |
| | ULB: arts 7, 16, 40. |
| | ULC: arts 10, 19, 35. |
| | UNB: arts 25, 26, 34. |

COMMENT

**Forged or unauthorised signature.** This section lays down the general rule that a forged signature, or a signature which is placed on a bill without the authority of the person whose signature it purports to be, is "wholly inoperative", and that no right to retain the bill[28] or to give a discharge therefor[29] or to enforce payment thereof[30] against any party thereto can be acquired through or under that signature. To this general rule, however, the section itself indicates three exceptions. These exceptions are: (i) those contained in other provisions of the Act; (ii) estoppel; and (iii) the ratification of an unauthorised signature not amounting to forgery.[31]

The section applies to any forged or unauthorised signature on a bill, whether it purports to be that of the drawee, the drawer or an indorser. It also applies to the signature of the maker or indorser of a promissory note[32] and to that of the drawer or indorser of a cheque.[33] But it does not relate to any fraudulent alteration in the body of the instrument (though this may constitute forgery),[34] which is dealt with by section 64.

**"Subject to the provisions of this Act".** The provisions referred to are: section 7(3) (fictitious or non-existing payee)[35]; section 25 (procuration

3–044

3–045

---

[28] See below, para.3–050.
[29] See s.59.
[30] See ss.38, 54(1), 55(1), (2).
[31] See also below, para.3–088 (adoption).
[32] s.89.
[33] s.73. But see below, paras 3–073, 8–043, 14–024 and 17–005 (forged indorsements).
[34] Forgery and Conterfeiting Act 1981, ss.9(1)(2).
[35] See above, para.2–052; below, para.3–078.

signatures)[36]; section 54(2)(a) (estoppel of acceptor)[37]; section 55(2)(b) (estoppel of indorser)[38]; section 60 (protection of banker paying a cheque on which there is a forged or unauthorised indorsement)[39]; and section 80 (protection of paying banker and drawer where cheque is crossed).[40]

Since the Cheques Act 1957 is to be read as one with the 1882 Act,[41] the section is also subject, in particular, to sections 1 and 4 of the 1957 Act.[42]

3–046    **Forgery.** This section, and section 60 of the Act, refer to "forged" and "unauthorised" signatures. The same consequences of invalidity apply in both cases, but the proviso to the section distinguishes, for the purposes of ratification, "an unauthorised signature not amounting to a forgery". It has been pointed out[43] that the forgery legislation in force at the time of the Act, namely, the Forgery Act 1861, established two relevant offences: first, under section 22(d), it was an offence to *forge* a bill or note, or any acceptance, indorsement or assignment thereof, with intent to defraud; secondly, section 24 of that Act created a separate and distinct offence[44] if a person:

> "should, with intent to defraud, draw, make, sign, accept or indorse any bill of exchange or promissory note or any order or request for the payment of money by procuration or otherwise, for, or in the name of, or on account of any other person, without lawful authority or excuse".

"Forged" and "forgery" are not defined by the 1882 Act. The words "where a signature on a bill is forged" in the present section may therefore have been intended to cover only the situation where the signature in question is counterfeited or falsely purports to be a genuine signature. In contrast, a signature would not be "forged" if it was merely placed on a bill without the authority of the person whose signature it purported to be. Nevertheless, in *Morison v London County and Westminster Bank Ltd*,[45] an attempt was made to extend the concept of forgery to the situation where an agent, having authority to draw and sign cheques per pro. for the purposes of his principal's business, for his own purposes and in

---

[36] See below, para.3–095.
[37] See below, paras 3–057 and 7–017.
[38] See below, paras 3–071 and 7–028.
[39] See below, para.8–043.
[40] See below, para.14–024. This section is extended to certain instruments other than cheques by s.95 and s.5 of the Cheques Act 1957: see below, paras 16–018 and 17–075.
[41] Cheques Act 1957, s.6(1).
[42] See below, paras 17–005 and 17–028.
[43] *Paget* (7th ed.), pp.407 *et seq.* (deleted from subsequent editions).
[44] *cf. R. v White* (1847) 2 Car. & K. 404.
[45] [1914] 3 K.B. 356 (Illustration 1); (the events in this case occurred before the Forgery Act 1913 came into force).

fraud of his principal, drew and so signed a number of cheques on his principal's bank account and applied the proceeds to his own use. The Court of Appeal held that the cheques were not forgeries.[46] The bank was bound to honour cheques so signed, and "[a] document cannot be a forged instrument as between certain persons and not as between others".[47] Phillimore L.J. said[48]:

> "Where there is a power to sign per pro., a document so signed is not a forgery to the party to whom it is addressed, and who can, or a fortiori must, act upon it, and therefore it is not a forgery at all. The misuse by an agent of his power of writing his principal's name either as a simple signature, or by signing per pro., may, however, be indictable as some form of fraud."

The Forgery Act 1913 altered and extended the definition of forgery in the criminal law. Subsequent to that Act, in *Kreditbank Cassel GmbH v Schenkers Ltd*,[49] the articles of a company contained very wide powers to delegate the drawing and indorsing of bills. A branch manager of the company, having no authority to draw or indorse bills of exchange, in fraud of the company drew and indorsed on behalf of the company a number of bills, signing them with the name of the company, his own name and a description of his position as branch manager. The Court of Appeal held that the bills were forgeries and the company was not liable on them. The rule that an outsider is not bound to inquire as to the "indoor management" of a company did not apply where the document in question was a forgery.[50] Scrutton L.J. reasoned[51]: "the bills are clearly forgeries within the Forgery Act, 1913, as they contain a false statement—namely, that [the branch manager] was acting for the company, and they purport to bind the company in fraud of the company". The inference might, therefore, appear to be that the words "where a signature is forged" in the present section must be interpreted in accordance with the current statutory definition of "forgery" for the purposes of the criminal law.

The current definition of forgery is contained in section 1 of the Forgery **3–047** and Counterfeiting Act 1981,[52] which provides: "a person is guilty of forgery if he makes a false instrument, with the intention that he or another shall use it to induce somebody to accept it as genuine, and by reason of so accepting it to do or not to do some act to his own or any

---

[46] It was also stated that the case did not fall within s.24 of the 1861 Act.
[47] [1914] 3 K.B. 356 at 374.
[48] [1914] 3 K.B. 356 at 381.
[49] [1927] 1 K.B. 826 (Illustration 2).
[50] *Ruben v Great Fingall Consolidated* [1906] A.C. 439.
[51] [1906] A.C. 439 at 840.
[52] s.13 of the Act abolishes the offence of forgery at common law.

other person's prejudice". By section 9(1), an instrument is false (*inter alia*):

> "(a) if it purports to have been made in the form in which it is made by a person who did not in fact make it in that form; or
>
> (b) if it purports to have been made in the form in which it is made on the authority of a person who did not in fact authorise its making in that form; or
>
> (c) if it purports to have been made in the terms in which it is made by a person who did not in fact make it in those terms; or
>
> (d) if it purports to have been made in the terms in which it is made on the authority of a person who did not in fact authorise its making in those terms; or
>
> . . . . . . .
>
> (h) if it purports to have been made . . . by an existing person but did not in fact exist."

Assuming the necessary *mens rea* to be present, it seems reasonably clear that, at least as regards the signature of the drawer of a bill or the maker of a note,[53] a signature placed on the instrument without the authority of the person whose signature it purports to be will be a forgery under the 1981 Act; and it is even possible that the per pro. signature in *Morison's Case* would also now be held to be a forgery.

It is, however, submitted that the definition of forgery in the 1981 Act should not be applied to the 1882 Act, and that the reference to forgery in section 24 should be construed more narrowly and in accordance with the intention of the section at the time the 1882 Act was passed.

3–048      **Unauthorised signatures.** Whether or not a signature is unauthorised is to be determined by applying ordinary principles of the law of agency,[54] although special rules may be applicable in the case of partnerships[55] and in the case of signatures on behalf of a company.[56] In particular, where the protection afforded by section 35A(1) of the Companies Act 1985[57] is not available, the holder of a bill or note signed on behalf of a company may be protected by the "indoor management" rule in *Royal British Bank v Turquand*.[58]

---

[53] The Act refers to the "making" of a false instrument, or ss.9(1)(e), (f), (g), (2), its alteration.

[54] See the Comment on s.91(1); below, para.16–004.

[55] See above, para.3–031 (s.23).

[56] *Bowstead and Reynolds on Agency* (17th ed.), § 8–032 *et seq*.

[57] Inserted by s.108(1) of the Companies Act 1989. See above, para.3–006.

[58] (1856) 6 E. & B. 327. See *Re Land Credit Co.* (1869) L.R.4. Ch. App. 460 (s.25, Illustration 5); *Biggerstaff v Rowatts Wharf Ltd* [1896] 2 Ch. 93; *Dey v Pullinger Engineering Co.* [1921] 1 K.B. 77. Contrast *Underwood A.L. Ltd v Bank of Liverpool Ltd* [1924] 1 K.B. 775 (Cheques Act 1957, s.4, Illustration 9); *Kreditbank Cassel GmbH v Schenkers Ltd* [1927] 1 K.B. 826 (Illustration 2); *Liggett B. (Liverpool) Ltd v Barclays Bank Ltd* [1928] 1 K.B. 48.

Authority to sign may be actual, express or implied, or an apparent (or ostensible) authority.[59] Difficulties may arise with respect to signatures authorised for one purpose but fraudulently used for another. As a general rule, however, an act of an agent within the scope of his actual or apparent authority does not cease to bind his principal merely because the agent was acting fraudulently and in furtherance of his own interests,[60] subject to section 25 of the 1882 Act[61] which provides that a signature by procuration operates as notice that the agent has but a limited authority to sign, and the principal is only bound by such signature if the agent in so signing was acting within the actual limits of his authority.

**Effects of forged or unauthorised signature.** The effects of a forged or 3–049
unauthorised signature on a bill, cheque or note will vary according to whether the signature purports to be that of the drawee or maker, the drawer, or an indorser. Before considering these effects, it is necessary to refer to two actions which may be available to the true owner of the instrument in certain circumstances against one who pays, receives payment, retains or deals with it contrary to his rights. These are the actions in conversion and in restitution (for money had and received). While they are dealt with here in the context of forged or unauthorised signatures, their availability extends, for example, to cases where a genuine signature has been obtained by a fraud which renders void the contract of the signatory on the instrument[62] or where authority to sign has been fraudulently misused.[63]

**Conversion.** Conversion may be defined as an act of wilful inter- 3–050
ference, without lawful justification, with any chattel in a manner inconsistent with the right of the person entitled to it. Although the interference must be wilful, it is unnecessary to show that the defendant knew of or intended to interfere with the proprietary or possessory right of the

---

[59] See s.91(1); below, para.16–004.
[60] *Bowstead and Reynolds on Agency* (17th ed.), § 8–064.
[61] See below, para.3–095.
[62] See, *e.g. Great Western Ry Co. v London and County Banking Co. Ltd* [1901] A.C. 414, 418, 419, 422, 424 (Cheques Act 1957, s.4, Illustration 3); *Tate v Wilts and Dorset Bank* (1899) 1 L.D.B. 286, 376. Contrast *Midland Bank plc v Brown Shipley & Co. Ltd* [1991] 1 Lloyd's Rep. 576; *Paget* (12th ed.), 23.5 (contract voidable but not void). *cf. Hunter BNZ Finance Ltd v C.G. Maloney Pty Ltd* (1988) 18 N.S.W.L.R. 420; *Australian Guarantee Corp. Ltd v Commissioners of the State Bank of Victoria* [1989] V.R. 617.
[63] See, *e.g. Morison v London County & Westminster Bank Ltd* [1914] 3 K.B. 356, 378 (Illustration 1); *Underwood A.L. Ltd v Bank of Liverpool* [1924] 1 K.B. 775 (Cheques Act 1957, s.4, Illustration 9); *Lloyds Bank v Chartered Bank of India, Australia and China* [1929] 1 K.B. 40 (Cheques Act 1957, s.4, Illustration 10); *Midland Bank Ltd v Reckitt* [1933] A.C. 1 (s.25, Illustration 9); *Nu-stilo Footwear Ltd v Lloyds Bank Ltd* (1956) 7 L.D.B. 121 (Cheques Act 1957, s.4, Illustration 16); *Orbit Mining and Trading Co. Ltd v Westminster Bank Ltd* [1963] 1 Q.B. 794 (Cheques Act 1957, s.4, Illustration 17).

claimant to the chattel. Conversion is a tort of strict liability and any inconsistent dealing with the chattel, however innocent, will amount to a conversion.

For the purposes of an action in conversion, a bill, cheque or note is treated as a chattel. It has repeatedly been held that a person converts an instrument if he or his principal has no title or a defective title to it and he deals with it in a manner inconsistent with the right of its true owner, as by obtaining payment of the instrument[64] or by paying it,[65] and in either case retaining the proceeds unlawfully or making them available to a person not entitled to them. The value of the instrument is deemed to be its face value and the true owner can recover against the tortfeasor damages of that amount.[66] The measure of the damages recoverable is not affected by the fact that the instrument (being a cheque) is crossed "not

[64] *Bobbett v Pinkett* (1876) 1 Ex.D. 368 (Illustration 9); *Arnold v Cheque Bank* (1876) 1 C.P.D. 578 (s.21, Illustration 1); *Bissell & Co. v Fox Bros & Co.* (1885) 53 L.T. 193; *Fine Art Society v Union Bank of London* (1886) 17 Q.B.D. 705; *Kleinwort Sons & Co. v Comptoir National Escompte de Paris* [1894] 2 Q.B. 157; *Lacave & Co. v Crédit Lyonnais* [1897] 1 Q.B. 148 (Cheques Act 1957, s.4, Illustration 2); *Great Western Ry Co. v London and County Banking Co. Ltd* [1901] A.C. 414 (Cheques Act 1957, s.4, Illustration 3); *Capital and Counties Bank Ltd v Gordon* [1903] A.C. 240 (Cheques Act 1957, s.4, Illustration 1); *Vinden v Hughes* [1905] 1 K.B. 795 (s.7, Illustration 5); *Bevan v National Bank Ltd* (1906) 23 T.L.R. 65; *Macbeth v North and South Wales Bank* [1908] A.C. 137 (s.7, Illustration 6); *Morison v London County and Westminster Bank Ltd* [1914] 3 K.B. 356 (Illustration 1); *Ladbroke & Co. v Todd* (1914) 30 T.L.R. 433 (Cheques Act 1957, s.4, Illustration 7); *Ross v London County Westminster and Parr's Bank Ltd* [1919] 1 K.B. 678 (Cheques Act 1957, s.4, Illustration 8); *Underwood (A.L.) Ltd v Bank of Liverpool Ltd* [1924] 1 K.B. 775 (Cheques Act 1957, s.4, Illustration 9); *Lloyds Bank Ltd v Chartered Bank of India Australia and China* [1929] 1 K.B. 40 (Cheques Act 1957, s.4, Illustration 10); *Midland Bank Ltd v Reckitt* [1933] A.C. 1 (s.25, Illustration 9); *Lloyds Bank Ltd v Savory (E.B.) & Co.* [1933] A.C. 20 (Cheques Act 1957, s.4, Illustration 11); *Motor Traders Guarantee Corp. v Midland Bank Ltd* [1937] 4 All E.R. 90 (Cheques Act 1957, s.4, Illustration 12); *Carpenters' Co. v British Mutual Banking Co. Ltd* [1938] 1 K.B. 511 (s.60, Illustration 1); *Bute (Marquess of) v Barclays Bank Ltd* [1955] 1 Q.B. 202 (Cheques Act 1957, s.4, Illustration 14); *Baker v Barclays Bank Ltd* [1955] 1 W.L.R. 822 (Cheques Act 1957, s.4, Illustration 15); *Nu-Stilo Footwear Ltd v Lloyds Bank Ltd* (1956) 7 L.D.B. 121 (Cheques Act 1957, s.4, Illustration 16); *Lumsden & Co. v London Trustee Savings Bank* [1971] 1 Lloyd's Rep. 114 (Cheques Act 1957, s.4, Illustration 20); *Lipkin Gorman v Karpnale Ltd* [1991] 2 A.C. 548 (s.29, Illustration 7); *Boma Manufacturing Ltd v Canadian Imperial Bank of Commerce* (1997) 140 D.L.R. (4th) 463; *Honourable Society of the Middle Temple v Lloyds Bank plc* [1999] 1 All E.R. (Comm.) 193 (Cheques Act 1957, s.4, Illustration 5).

[65] There is no clear decision on this point, but see *Smith v Union Bank of London* (1875) L.R. 10 Q.B. 291 (affirmed (1875) 1 Q.B.D. 31) (s.79, Illustration 1); *Bavins Jnr and Sims v London and South Western Bank Ltd* [1900] 1 Q.B. 270, 278. *El Awadi v Bank of Credit and Commerce International S.A.* [1990] Q.B. 606, 627; *Smith v Lloyds TSB Bank plc* [2000] 2 All E.R. (Comm.) 693, 697; *Stevenson Estate v Siewart* (2000) 191 D.L.R. (4th) 151, (2001) 202 D.L.R. (4th) 295. See also *Lacave & Co. v Crédit Lyonnais* [1897] 1 Q.B. 148 (Cheques Act 1957, s.4, Illustration 2), and below, paras 3–072 and 17–006. Contrast *Charles v Blackwell* (1877) 2 C.P.D. 151, 162–163. The matter is discussed in Ellinger, Lomnicka and Hooley, *Modern Banking Law* (3rd ed., 2002), 387–389.

[66] *Morison v London County and Westminster Bank Ltd* [1914] 3 K.B. 356, 365, 379; *Lloyds Bank v Chartered Bank of India, Australia and China* [1929] 1 K.B. 40, 55; *Smith v Lloyds TSB Bank plc* [2000] 2 All E.R. (Comm.) 693, 697; *Stevenson Estate v Siewart* (2000) 191 D.L.R. (4th) 151, (2001) 202 D.L.R. (4th) 295.

negotiable"[67] or that the true owner has an alternative remedy to recoup his loss against another person on or outside the instrument,[68] nor (possibly) by the fact that the instrument is a nullity because it lacks any operative signature.[69] It is, perhaps, questionable whether this same measure of damages applies to an instrument which is not transferable, for example a cheque drawn "Pay X only"[70] or crossed "account payee",[71] since such an instrument is in effect a mere payment order. But it is submitted that the "face value" rule would be applied even in this case.[72]

**True owner.** The person entitled to bring an action in conversion is referred to as the "true owner". This expression is used in the 1882 Act[73] and in the Cheques Act 1957,[74] but is not defined in either enactment. In fact, it is not necessary for the claimant to prove that he is the "owner", in the sense that the property in the instrument is in him.[75] It is sufficient for him to prove that he had actual possession or an immediate right to possession of it at the time of the conversion.[76] An equitable title is not in itself sufficient.[77] In deciding whether or not a person has title to sue in conversion, regard must be had to the provisions of the 1882 Act and (where applicable) of the 1957 Act, and in particular to the fact that the chattel which is the subject-matter of the action is a negotiable instrument. Normal proprietary or possessory rights in the instrument as a chattel may be overridden by its issue or negotiation or by its payment in

3–051

---

[67] s.81; *Great Western Ry Co. v London and County Banking Co. Ltd* [1901] A.C. 414; *Motor Traders Guarantee Ltd v Midland Bank Ltd* [1937] 4 All E.R. 90; *Bute (Marquess of) v Barclays Bank Ltd* [1955] 1 Q.B. 202.

[68] *Bobbett v Pinkett* (1876) 1 Ex.D. 368 (Illustration 9); *International Factors Ltd v Rodriguez* [1979] Q.B. 351.

[69] See below, para.3–062. But contrast (altered instrument) s.64, below, para.8–088.

[70] See above, para.2–059 (s.8).

[71] s.81A; below, para.14–037.

[72] See *Bavins Jnr and Sims v London and South Western Bank Ltd* [1900] 1 Q.B. 270 (s.3, Illustration 3); *Honourable Society of the Middle Temple v Lloyds Bank plc* [1999] 1 All E.R. (Comm.) 193 (Cheques Act 1957, s.4, Illustration 5). The amendment made to s.4(2)(a) of the Cheques Act 1957 by s.3 of the Cheques Act 1992 (below, para.17–063) assumes that the collecting banker requires protection against claims in respect of the conversion of such an instrument.

[73] ss.79(2), 80.

[74] s.4.

[75] For the passing of property, see above, para.2–150 (s.21).

[76] *Bute (Marquess of) v Barclays Bank Ltd* [1955] 1 Q.B. 202 (Cheques Act 1957, s.4, Illustration 14); *Lipkin Gorman v Karpnale Ltd* [1991] 2 A.C. 548 (s.29, Illustration 7). See also *Official Assignee v Oversea Bank Ltd* [1934] M.L.J. 76. But it would appear that the defendant could plead that another person has a better right than the claimant (the *jus tertii*): Torts (Interference with Goods) Act 1977, s.8(1).

[77] *MCC Proceeds Inc. v Lehman Brothers International (Europe)* [1998] 4 All E.R. 675; *Hounslow London BC v Jenkins* [2004] All E.R. (D) 160.

due course. So, for example, if an instrument payable to bearer is delivered to a holder in due course, he will become the owner of the instrument, as there is no one with a better title to it.[78]

The question whether a person was the "true owner" of a bill, note or cheque may be a matter of some nicety. Some examples (which are not exhaustive) may be given in the case of cheques. A person will be the true owner of a cheque form stolen from his cheque book on which his signature as drawer is forged.[79] The drawer of a cheque will be its true owner if he is induced by the fraud of a rogue to draw a cheque payable by mistake to the rogue[80] or if a rogue misuses the authority conferred upon him by the drawer to draw cheques in the name and on behalf of the drawer by drawing a cheque payable to himself.[81] The drawer of a cheque will also be its true owner if he is induced by the fraud of a rogue to draw a cheque payable to a third party which is then misappropriated by the rogue[82] or if a cheque drawn by him payable to a third party is stolen from him before despatch.[83] He will likewise be the true owner if such a cheque is sent to and misappropriated by his agent.[84]

More difficulty, however, arises where a cheque, drawn by a debtor and payable to his creditor, is stolen after despatch but before it reaches the

---

[78] *Smith v Union Bank of London* (1875) 1 Q.B.D. 31 (s.79, Illustration 1).

[79] But see the discussion, below, para.3–062.

[80] See *e.g. Great Western Ry Co. v London and County Banking Co. Ltd* [1901] A.C. 414, 418, 419, 422, 424 (Cheques Act 1957, s.4, Illustration 3). But contrast *Midland Bank plc v Brown Shipley & Co. Ltd* [1991] 1 Lloyd's Rep. 576 (voidable title), and above, para.3–049, n.62. *cf. Australian Guarantee Corp. Ltd v Commissioners of the State Bank of Victoria* [1989] V.R. 617.

[81] See, *e.g. Morison v London County and Westminster Bank Ltd* [1914] 3 K.B. 356 (Illustration 1); *Lloyds Bank Ltd v Chartered Bank of India, Australia and China* [1929] 1 K.B. 40 (Cheques Act 1957, s.4, Illustration 10); *Midland Bank Ltd v Reckitt* [1933] A.C. 1 (s.25, Illustration 9); *Nu-Stilo Footwear Ltd v Lloyds Bank Ltd* (1956) 7 L.D.B. 121 (Cheques Act 1957, s.4, Illustration 16); *Orbit Mining and Trading Co. Ltd v Westminster Bank Ltd* [1963] 1 Q.B. 794 (Cheques Act 1957, s.4, Illustration 17).

[82] See, *e.g. Macbeth v North and South Wales Bank* [1908] A.C. 137 (s.7, Illustration 6); *Crumplin v London Joint Stock Bank Ltd* (1913) 30 T.L.R. 99 (Cheques Act 1957, s.4, Illustration 6); *Motor Traders Guarantee Corp. Ltd v Midland Bank Ltd* [1937] 4 All E.R. 90 (Cheques Act 1957, s.4, Illustration 12); *Commercial Securities & Finance Ltd v ANZ Banking Group (NZ) Ltd* [1985] 1 N.Z.L.R. 728. *New Zealand Law Society v ANZ Banking Group Ltd* [1985] 1 N.Z.L.R. 280.; *Hunter BNZ Finance Ltd v C.G. Maloney Pty Ltd* (1988) 18 N.S.W.L.R. 420. See also *Basil Read Sun Homes (Pty.) Ltd v Nedperm Bank Ltd* 1999 (1) S.A. 831 (SCA) (drawer induced to part with possession of cheque by false representation by recipient that he was authorised by payee to receive cheque).

[83] *Akrokerri (Atlantic) Mines Ltd v Economic Bank* [1904] 2 K.B. 465; *Commissioners of Taxation v English, Scottish and Australian Bank Ltd* [1920] A.C. 683 (Cheques Act 1957, s.4, Illustration 4); *Carpenters' Co. v British Mutual Banking Co. Ltd* [1938] 1 K.B. 511 (s.60, Illlustration 1); *Lloyd's Bank Ltd v E.B. Savory & Co.* [1933] A.C. 221 (Cheques Act 1957, s.4, Illustration 11); *Marfani & Co. Ltd v Midland Bank Ltd* [1968] 1 W.L.R. 956 (Cheques Act 1957, s.4, Illustration 19); *Lumsden & Co. v London Trustee Savings Bank* [1971] 1 Lloyd's Rep. 114 (Cheques Act 1957, s.4, Illustration 20).

[84] *Importers Co. Ltd v Westminster Bank Ltd* [1927] 2 K.B. 297.

payee[85]; the question whether the drawer or payee is the true owner may possibly depend on whether the drawer was authorised to effect payment in that manner, *e.g.* by post.[86] But even if the drawer retains ownership of the instrument, it might still be the case that the payee is entitled to immediate possession of it and so has a sufficient title to sue in conversion.[87] In any event, under section 21(3) of the Act, the payee is presumed to have received a valid and unconditional delivery of the cheque from the drawer until the contrary is proved.[88]

Where a cheque drawn payable to a third party is stolen after it has been received by or on behalf of the payee, the payee is the true owner of the instrument.[89] If he indorses it specially, but the cheque is stolen or misappropriated before its despatch to the indorsee, he remains its true owner.[90] Likewise if he indorses it in blank; but in such a case he will lose his title to a holder in due course.[91] The rights of the true owner may also be extinguished by payment of the cheque in due course.[92]

---

[85] See *Kleinwort Sons & Co. v Comptoir Escompte de Paris* [1894] 2 Q.B. 157; *Lacave & Co. v Crédit Lyonnais* [1897] 1 Q.B. 148 (indorsements); *Ladbroke & Co. v Todd* (1914) 30 T.L.R. 433 (Cheques Act 1957, s.4, Illustration 7).; *Robinson v Midland Bank* (1925) T.L.R. 402; *Hunter BNZ Finance Ltd v Australian and New Zealand Banking Group Ltd* [1990] V.R. 41; *Honourable Society of the Middle Temple v Lloyds Bank plc* [1999] 1 All E.R. (Comm.) 193. See also, in Malaysia, *The Rubber Industry (Replanting) Board v Hongkong & Shanghai Banking Corp.* [1957] M.L.J. 103; *Oriental Bank of Malaya v Rubber Industry (Replanting) Board* [1957] M.L.J. 153; and, in South Africa, *Fedgen Insurance Ltd v Bankorp Ltd* 1994 (2) S.A. 399; *The Godfather v Commrs for Inland Revenue* 1993 (2) S.A. 426. *First National Bank of SA Ltd v Quality Tyres (1970) Pty. Ltd* 1995 (3) S.A. 556; *Absa Bank Ltd v Mutual & Federal Insurance Co. Ltd* 2003 (1) S.A. 635, 638.

[86] *London Bank of Australia Ltd v Kendall* (1920) 28 C.L.R. 40; *Absa Bank Ltd v Mutual & Federal Insurance Co. Ltd* 2003 (1) S.A. 635. See above, para.2–151 (s.21).

[87] Contrast *Barclays National Bank Ltd v Wall* 1983 (1) S.A. 149.

[88] See above, para.2–154.

[89] See, *e.g. Fine Art Society v Union Bank of London* (1886) 17 Q.B.D. 705; *Bavins Jnr and Sims v London and South Western Bank* [1900] 1 Q.B. 270 (s.3, Illustration 4); *Capital and Counties Bank Ltd v Gordon* [1903] A.C. 240 (Cheques Act 1957, s.4, Illustration 1); *Underwood (A.L.) Ltd v Bank of Liverpool* [1924] 1 K.B. 775 (Cheques Act 1957, s.4, Illustration 9); *United Australia Ltd v Barclays Bank Ltd* [1941] A.C. 1; *Baker v Barclays Bank Ltd* [1955] 1 W.L.R. 826 (Cheques Act 1957, s.4, Illustration 15); *Yorkshire Bank plc v Lloyds Bank plc* [1999] 2 All E.R. (Comm.) 154; *Surrey Asset Finance Ltd v National Westminster Bank* [2001] E.W.C.A. Civ 60; *Linklaters v HSBC Bank plc* [2003] EWHC 1113 (Comm.), [2003] 2 Lloyd's Rep. 545. See also *Bute (Marquess of) v Barclays Bank Ltd* [1955] 1 Q.B. 202 (Cheques Act 1957, s.4, Illustration 14); *Grantham Homes Pty Ltd v ANZ Banking Group Ltd* (1980) 26 A.C.T.R. 1; *United Malayan Banking Corp. Bhd v Kek Tek Huat* [1990] S.C.R. 31; *Lipkin Gorman v Karpnale Ltd* [1991] 2 A.C. 548; *Bond Equipment (Pretoria) Pty. Ltd v Absa Bank Ltd* 1999 (2) S.A. 63, affirmed 2000 (1) S.A. 372; *Energy Measurements (Pty) Ltd v First National Bank of South Africa Ltd* 2001 (3) S.A. 132; *Bank of Montreal v Ernst & Young* [2002] S.C. 81 (Canada). Contrast *Bobbett v Pinkett* (1876) 1 Ex.D. 368 (Illustration 9); *Commercial Banking Co. of Sydney Ltd v Mann* [1961] A.C. 1.

[90] *Arnold v Cheque Bank* (1876) 1 C.P.D. 578 (s.21, Illustration 1); *Ross v London County, Westminster and Parr's Bank Ltd* [1919] 1 K.B. 678 (Cheques Act 1957, s.4, Illustration 8). See also *Lacave & Co. v Crédit Lyonnais* [1897] 1 Q.B. 148 (Interception after despatch).

[91] *Smith v Union Bank of London* (1875) 1 Q.B.D. 31 (s.79, Illustration 1). See also Cheques Act 1957, s.2.

[92] See below, para.8–002 (s.59), ss.60 and 80 of the 1882 Act and s.1 of the Cheques Act 1957.

If an agent, in fraud of his principal, draws cheques on his principal's account and thereby obtains a banker's draft drawn by the bank payable to a third party or to bearer, the principal does not acquire any title to the draft.[93] But if the draft is drawn by the bank payable to the principal and delivered to the agent, the principal becomes its true owner since he has the immediate right to possession of the draft.[94]

3–052    **Restitution.** A claimant who has a remedy in conversion is entitled to "waive the tort" and sue in restitution for the same amount as money had and received to his use.[95] By converting the instrument the defendant becomes accountable to the claimant for the proceeds of his wrongful dealing with it. Claims for conversion and in restitution are usually made in the same action in the alternative, and in many cases there will be no substantial difference between them.[96] However, a restitutionary claim is subject to certain limitations[97] and is subject to certain defences[98] which do not apply to an action in conversion. In particular, a banker, who collects a bill, cheque or note for a customer with no title or a defective title to the instrument, receives the proceeds and pays them over to the customer before learning of the claim, will not be liable to an action in restitution, since, as agent, he has changed his position by payment to his principal.[99] But he nevertheless remains liable to an action in conversion based on his wrongful dealing with the instrument.

3–053    **Forged or unauthorised signature of the drawee.** Section 17(2)(a) of the Act requires that an acceptance must be written in the bill and signed by the drawee. If the signature of the drawee as acceptor is forged or unauthorised, it will be completely inoperative and will not bind the drawee[1] unless he is precluded from setting up the forgery or want of

---

[93] *Union Bank of Australia Ltd v McClintock* [1922] 1 A.C. 240; *Commercial Banking Co. of Sydney v Mann* [1961] A.C.1.

[94] *Lipkin Gorman v Karpnale Ltd* [1991] 2 A.C. 548 (s.29, Illustration 7).

[95] See *Marfani & Co. Ltd v Midland Bank Ltd* [1968] 1 W.L.R. 956, 971. By bringing an action for money had and received a claimant does not "waive", in the sense of abandon, his alternative claim for damages for conversion: *United Australia Ltd v Barclays Bank Ltd* [1941] A.C. 1.

[96] *cf. Bavins Jnr and Sims v London and South Western Bank* [1900] 1 Q.B. 270, 275, 276, 278 (s.3, Illustration 4). See also below, para.3–056 (forged or unauthorised signature of drawer) and para.12–030 (conflict of laws).

[97] See below, para.8–021.

[98] See below, paras 8–026 and 8–029 (s.59).

[99] See below, para.8–028.

[1] *Credit Lyonnais Bank Nederland N.V. v E.C.G.D.* [1998] 1 Lloyd's Rep. 19, 26, 39 (affirmed without consideration of this point [2000] 1 A.C. 486). *cf. Strathmore Group v Alexanders Discount* 1992 S.L.T. 846 (mere allegation of forgery: caution or consignment required in Scotland).

authority[2] or unless he adopts the forged,[3] or ratifies the unauthorised[4] signature. Should the drawee pay the bill in ignorance of the forgery, he will prima facie be entitled to recover the money from the recipient as money paid under a mistake.[5]

The fact that the drawee's signature is forged or unauthorised normally affords no defence to the drawer or an indorser of the bill.[6] Except in the cases specified in subsections (1) and (2) of section 39 of the Act,[7] presentment for acceptance is not necessary to render liable any party to the bill.[8] In consequence, a forged or unauthorised signature of the drawee will not affect the liability of other parties to the instrument. When the bill is presented to the drawee for payment, and payment is refused, the bill will be dishonoured by non-payment[9] and (provided that the requisite proceedings on dishonour are duly taken)[10] an immediate right of recourse against the drawer and indorsers accrues to the holder.[11] A guarantor outside the bill of the forged acceptance will not, however, be liable.[12]

Where a banker agrees to pay bills domiciled with him for payment which have been accepted by his customer, the drawee, he has no mandate to pay such a bill if the drawee's signature thereon is forged or unauthorised. If he pays the bill, he will not be entitled to debit the drawee's account with the amount paid, unless the drawee is estopped from denying the banker's authority to make the payment.[13] He will, however, prima facie be entitled to recover the money from the person to whom it was paid.[14]

If a bill is drawn upon two or more drawees and is accepted by one or more of them, their liability as acceptors will not be affected by the fact that the signature as acceptor of any co-drawee is forged or unauthorised.[15] However, if they accepted the bill as co-sureties, for example, to **3–054**

---

[2] See below, para.3–079; *Leach v Buchanan* (1802) 4 Esp. 226 (Illustration 10); *Mather v Maidstone* (1856) 18 C.B. 273 (s.59, Illustration 15).

[3] See below, para.3–088.

[4] See below, para.3–087. *cf. Brook v Hook* (1871) L.R. 6 Ex. 89 (Illustration 15).

[5] See below, para.8–021. *cf. Mather v Maidstone* (1856) 18 C.B. 273.

[6] At least against a holder in due course.

[7] See also s.40(1). The drawer and indorsers may, in consequence, in some cases be discharged by virtue of the fact that the bill has not been presented for acceptance: ss.39(2), 40(2); see below, para.6–008 (s.40).

[8] s.39(3).

[9] s.47(1).

[10] *i.e.* notice of dishonour and any necessary protest: see below, paras 6–096, 6–143.

[11] s.47(2).

[12] *Credit Lyonnais Bank Nederland N.V. v E.C.G.D.* [1998] 1 Lloyd's Rep. 19.

[13] See below, para.3–079.

[14] See below, para.8–021. *cf. Smith v Mercer* (1815) 6 Taunt. 76 (s.59, Illustration 11); *Cocks v Masterman* (1829) 9 B. & C. 902 (Section 59, Illustration 14).

[15] See above, para.2–116 (s.17(1)); *Owen v Van Uster* (1850) 10 C.B. 318 (s.17, Illustration 8).

accommodate the drawer, and on condition that that co-drawee would also accept the bill, then it seems that they could raise the absence of any signature by the co-drawee as a defence to an action against them by a holder who took the bill with knowledge that their acceptances were so conditioned,[16] though not against a holder in due course.

3–055 **Forged or unauthorised signature of the maker of a note.** A person will incur no liability on a promissory note if his signature as maker is forged or placed on the note without his authority, unless he is estopped[17] or adopts the forgery[18] or ratifies the unauthorised signature.[19] If he mistakenly pays the note, believing his signature to be genuine, he will prima facie be entitled to recover the money paid.[20]

Where the sole signature on the note is that of the maker, and that signature is forged or unauthorised, the instrument is a nullity, unless saved by adoption or ratification. If, however, a note payable to order is indorsed by the payee, then it would seem[21] that (subject to the requisite proceedings on dishonour being duly taken)[22] the payee and any subsequent indorser will be liable, since the first indorser of a note is deemed to correspond with the drawer of an accepted bill payable to drawer's order[23] and any indorser is precluded from denying to his immediate or a subsequent indorsee that the note was at the time of his indorsement valid and subsisting.[24] If the note is payable to bearer and is negotiated by the holder without indorsement, the transferor will be liable to his immediate transferee, being a holder for value, upon his warranty that the note is what it purports to be.[25]

The position of a banker with whom a note is made payable is the same as that of a banker with whom a bill is domiciled for payment.[26]

As in the case of joint acceptances, the forgery of one of two or more co-makers' names—the other signature or signatures being genuine—will not impair the enforceability of the note against any maker who signed

---

[16] *Evans v Bremridge* (1856) 8 De G.M & G. 100; *Greer v Kettle* [1938] A.C. 156, 165; *James Graham and Co. (Timber) Ltd v Southgate-Sands* [1986] Q.B. 80. Contrast *Capital Bank Cashflow Finance Ltd v Southall* [2004] EWCA Civ 817, [2004] 2 All E.R. (Comm.) 675 (mere expectation).

[17] See below, para.3–079.

[18] See below, para.3–088.

[19] See below, para.3–087.

[20] See below, para.8–021 (s.59).

[21] But it could be argued that there is no promissory note, as there is no signature of the maker.

[22] *i.e.* notice of dishonour see below, para.6–096.

[23] s.89(2).

[24] s.55(2)(c).

[25] s.58(3).

[26] See above, para.3–053.

it,[27] unless he signed as co-surety and on condition that the note would be signed by the person whose signature is forged.[28]

**Forged or unauthorised signature of the drawer.** Where the signature    **3–056**
of the drawer of a bill or cheque is forged or placed thereon without authority, then, unless the ostensible drawer is precluded from setting up the forgery or want of authority[29] or adopts[30] the forged or ratifies[31] the unauthorised signature, he cannot be held liable on the instrument.[32] Since the forged or unauthorised signature is stated to be "wholly inoperative", it might be thought that the instrument is a nullity, since the absence of any operative signature by a drawer would destroy the character of the document as a bill or cheque.[33] However, a party who signs such an instrument as acceptor or indorser may incur liability on it[34]; and even if the forged or unauthorised signature is the sole signature on the instrument, the true owner of the document may possibly be entitled to claim damages in conversion[35] or to claim money obtained by it as money had and received to his use.[36] Moreover, where such an instrument has been paid, other persons may acquire rights or incur liabilities by reason of its payment:

(i) *Acceptor*: Section 54(2)(a) of the Act provides that the acceptor of a    **3–057**
bill, by accepting it, is precluded from denying to a holder in due course the existence of the drawer, the genuineness of his signature, and his capacity and authority to draw the bill. The acceptor therefore engages that he will pay the bill to a holder in due course notwithstanding that the signature of the drawer is forged or unauthorised. This statutory estoppel operates, however, only in favour of a holder in due course,[37] and not in favour of any other holder, *e.g.* a holder for value[38] or the original payee of the bill (who cannot be a holder in due course).[39] It might be argued that, since the bill lacks any operative signature of a drawer, the acceptor is not liable to such a holder.[40] But there is some authority that, at

---

[27] *Banque Nationale v Payette* [1924] 1 D.L.R. 483. See also below, para.15–034.
[28] See above, para.3–054.
[29] See below, para.3–079.
[30] See below, para.3–088.
[31] See below, para.3–087.
[32] *Kreditbank Cassel GmbH v Schenkers Ltd* [1927] 1 K.B. 826 (Illustration 2).
[33] See *Arrow Transfer Co. Ltd v Royal Bank of Canada* (1972) 27 D.L.R. (3d) 81, 87, 104 (cheque). See also *Bank of England v Vagliano Bros* [1891] A.C. 108, 116, 162. *cf.* para.2–053 (bill).
[34] See below, paras 3–057, 3–058.
[35] See below, para.3–062. Contrast *Arrow Transfer Ltd v Royal Bank of Canada* (1972) 27 D.L.R. (3d) 81.
[36] See below, para.3–062.
[37] Defined in s.29(1).
[38] See below, para.4–024 (s.27).
[39] See below, para.5–072 (s.38).
[40] See above, para.2–013 (s.3).

common law, the acceptor of a bill is estopped from asserting against any bona fide holder for value that the drawer's signature was forged. In *Bank of England v Vagliano Brothers*,[41] where both the signatures of the drawer and of the payee were forged, Lord Halsbury L.C. said[42]:

> "I have designedly avoided calling these documents bills of exchange. They were nothing of the sort. But if they had got into the hands of an innocent owner for value without notice, Vagliano [the acceptor] would undoubtedly have been responsible upon them; for he had given them a genuineness as against himself by accepting them."

Alternatively the acceptor might be liable on the instrument as the maker of a promissory note.[43] However, the acceptance will very often have been obtained by fraud, giving rise to a defect of title,[44] or the payee's indorsement may also be forged or unauthorised,[45] in which case the acceptor may have a defence to liability on other grounds.

The acceptor will be discharged from liability on the bill if he pays it in due course, *i.e.* at or after maturity to the holder of the bill in good faith and without notice that the holder's title to the bill is defective.[46] The question then arises whether the acceptor, having paid the bill in ignorance of the fact that the drawer's signature thereon is forged or unauthorised, can recover the money so paid from the recipient as money paid under a mistake. It would seem that, where payment is made to a holder in due course, the money paid would be irrecoverable in view of the statutory preclusion in section 54(2)(a). But in cases where the recipient is not such a holder, some doubt exists due to the modern tendency of the courts to expand the remedy of recovery of money paid under a mistake, and, in particular, to reject as a ground for non-recovery that the drawee of a bill is required to know the signature of the drawer[47] or that, by paying, he impliedly represents that that signature is genuine.[48] The reader is referred to the discussion of this matter in the Comment on section 59.[49]

---

[41] [1891] A.C. 108 (Section 7, Illustration 4). See also *London and South Western Bank Ltd v Wentworth* (1880) 5 Ex D. 96 (Section 20, Illustration 7) (incomplete bill).

[42] [1891] A.C. 108 at 116. See also at 154 (Lord Herschell).

[43] *Mason v Lack* (1929) 140 L.T. 696; *Haseldine v Winstanley* [1936] 2 K.B. 101. See above, para.2–013 (s.3).

[44] s.29(2). See also *Ayres v Moore* [1940] 1 K.B. 278 (s.38, Illustration 4) and below, paras 4–063 and 5–072 (ss.29, 38).

[45] See below, para.3–066 (forgery of signature of indorser)

[46] s.59.

[47] See below, para.8–024 (s.59).

[48] See below, para.8–024 (s.59).

[49] See below, para.8–021. The rule in *Cocks v Masterman* (1829) 9 B. & C. 902 will not apply where there is no person to whom notice of dishonour need be given: see below, para.8–025 (s.59).

Where a banker accepts a bill drawn upon him for the accommodation of his customer, the drawer,[50] then, subject to the terms of any contract between them, he will not be entitled to be indemnified[51] by the drawer against his liability to the holder if the drawer's signature on the bill is forged or unauthorised, unless the drawer is estopped or ratifies or adopts the signature.

(ii) *Indorser*: The indorser of a bill or cheque, by indorsing it, is pre-   **3–058**
cluded from denying to a holder in due course the genuineness and regularity in all respects of the drawer's signature.[52] Provided that the requisite proceedings on dishonour are duly taken,[53] if the instrument is dishonoured, he will be liable to such a holder even though the drawer's signature is forged or unauthorised.[54] This estoppel does not, however, extend to a holder for value who is not a holder in due course[55] or to a mere holder[56] of the instrument. Where a bearer instrument is transferred by a holder without indorsement, the fact that the drawer's signature is forged or unauthorised may render the transferor liable to his transferee, being a holder for value, upon his warranty that the instrument is what it purports to be.[57]

(iii) *Drawee bank*: Where a banker pays a cheque drawn on him and on   **3–059**
which the signature of the drawer, his customer, is forged or unau-
thorised, he will not be entitled to debit the customer's account with the amount paid out. His duty is to pay in accordance with the customer's mandate, and, if the customer has not authorised the payment, he cannot charge the customer with it,[58] unless the customer is estopped by representation[59] or by negligence[60] from denying his authority to make the payment or adopts[61] or ratifies[62] the signature. No statutory protection is conferred on the banker in these circumstances. It has, however, been suggested that a banker can maintain the debit to his customer's account to the extent that he can show that the payment made by him discharged

---

[50] See s.28.
[51] See para.4–045 (s.28).
[52] s.55(2)(b).
[53] *i.e.* notice of dishonour and any necessary protest: ss.48, 51.
[54] See para.7–028.
[55] See para.4–024 (s.27) "Holder in due course" is defined in s.29(1).
[56] See para.4–028.
[57] s.58(3).
[58] This is the true ground for the banker's liability, not that the banker "is bound to know his customer's signature" and is negligent if he does not do so: see *London and River Plate Bank Ltd v Bank of Liverpool Ltd* [1896] 1 Q.B. 7, 10; *Liggett (B.) (Liverpool) Ltd v Barclays Bank Ltd* [1928] 1 K.B. 48; *National Westminster Bank Ltd v Barclays Bank International Ltd* [1975] Q.B. 654.
[59] See para.3–080.
[60] See para.3–085.
[61] See para.3–088.
[62] See para.3–087.

a debt of the customer[63] or otherwise conferred a benefit on the customer.[64] Even though the payment was made without authority, the banker is, so it is contended, subrogated to the rights of the creditor-payee and is entitled in equity to rely upon those rights when faced with a claim by the customer that his account be reinstated. In *Crantrave Ltd v Lloyds Bank plc*,[65] however, the Court of Appeal held that only a payment which was authorised by the customer or ratified by him would discharge a debt of the customer to his creditor. In the absence of such authorisation or ratification, payment to a third party could not of itself afford a defence to a banker against a claim by his customer for reinstatement of the customer's account. The Court of Appeal nevertheless left the door slightly ajar by saying that "there will be circumstances in which a court may intervene to prevent unjust enrichment either by the customer in having his money from the bank as well as having the claim of his creditor met, or by the creditor who has double payment of his debt"[66] or "in which it could nevertheless be unconscionable to allow the customer to recover from the bank the balance of his account without the deduction of a payment which the bank has made gratuitously".[67]

Where a joint account is opened, the banker may be instructed to pay cheques drawn on the account only when signed by all the account holders jointly. Particular problems arise where one joint account holder forges the signature of another and obtains payment of the cheque. These problems are discussed separately.[68]

The drawee banker who pays a cheque in ignorance of the fact that the drawer's signature thereon is forged or unauthorised is prima facie entitled to recover from the recipient the amount paid as money paid under a mistake.[69] He cannot, however, recover the money from a collecting banker who has paid over the proceeds of the cheque to his principal, before learning of the claim, but only from the principal.[70]

3–060      Since the unauthorised debit is ineffective to alter the true state of the account between the drawee banker and his customer, the cause of action against the drawee banker will accrue only when the customer demands

---

[63] *Liggett (B.) (Liverpool) Ltd v Barclays Bank Ltd* [1928] 1 K.B. 48 at 60, 63–64. See also *Lloyds Bank Ltd v Chartered Bank of India, Australia and China* [1929] 1 K.B. 40, 61; *Jackson v White and Midland Bank Ltd* [1967] 2 Lloyd's Rep. 68, 80; *Associated Midland Corp. v Bank of New South Wales* [1983] 1 N.S.W.L.R. 533; *H.J. Symons & Co. v Barclays Bank* [2003] EWHC 1249 (Comm) at [20] [65]. Ellinger and Lee [1984] L.M.C.L.Q. 459.

[64] *Liggett (B.) (Liverpool) Ltd v Barclays Bank Ltd* [1928] 1 K.B. 48 at 61. cf. *Re Cleadon Trust Ltd* [1939] Ch. 286, 302–305, 316, 321, 323, 327.

[65] [2000] Q.B. 917.

[66] [2000] Q.B. 917, 924 (Pill L.J.).

[67] [2000] Q.B. 917, 925 (May L.J.).

[68] para.3–064.

[69] *National Westminster Bank Ltd v Barclays Bank International Ltd* [1975] Q.B. 654 (s.59, Illustration 18); *Bank of America v Arnell* [1999] Lloyd's Rep. Bank 399; para.8–021.

[70] See para.8–028 (s.59).

repayment of the amount wrongly debited to the account and such repayment is refused. The limitation period, both in respect of the principal sum and interest (if the account is interest bearing), will commence to run from that time.[71] Also, interest on the amount paid away by the drawee banker is recoverable by the customer from the date on which he requires the banker to eliminate the unauthorised debit and to repay what is due, even though the sum wrongly debited is in a non-interest bearing account.[72]

(iv) *Bank where bill domiciled for payment*: When a customer accepts a **3–061** bill payable at his banker's, it is an authority to the banker to pay it. If the banker agrees to and does pay the bill, the customer cannot claim that the banker is not entitled to charge him with the amount so paid merely on the ground that the signature of the drawer on the bill is forged or unauthorised. In *Bank of England v Vagliano Brothers*,[73] Lord Macnaghten said: "The drawee of a bill is bound to know the drawer's signature. It is his fault if he writes his acceptance on a forged instrument. And it is his act of acceptance which sends the bill forward for payment to the banker." By writing his acceptance upon it, the customer accredits the instrument to the banker[74]: the acceptance is in itself a distinct assurance, upon which the banker is entitled to rely, that the bill bearing the customer's signature is a real draft upon him by the purported drawer.[75]

(v) *Collecting bank*: Where a banker collects a bill or cheque for a **3–062** customer, he runs the risk of being sued by the true owner of the instrument in conversion[76] or in restitution for money had and received[77] if his customer has no title to it. The measure of his liability is the face value of the instrument.[78] Suppose, therefore, that a thief steals a cheque book and draws a cheque payable to himself by forging the owner's signature thereon. The thief then delivers the cheque so drawn (without indorsement) to his own bank which presents it for payment, collects the proceeds and credits them to the thief's account. The question arises whether the owner of the cheque book, as true owner of the document which purports to be his cheque, has any claim in conversion for substantial damages,[79] or for money had and received, against the collecting

---

[71] *National Bank of Commerce v National Westminster Bank plc* [1990] 2 Lloyd's Rep. 514 (payment order).
[72] *Tai Hing Cotton Mill Ltd v Liu Chong Hing Bank Ltd* [1986] A.C. 80.
[73] [1891] A.C. 107, 158 (s.7, Illustration 4).
[74] [1891] A.C. 107 at 114–115 (Lord Halsbury L.C.).
[75] [1891] A.C. 107 at 133–134 (Lord Watson).
[76] See above, para.3–050; below, para.17–030.
[77] See above, para.3–052.
[78] See above, para.3–050. This also applies to non-transferable instruments, *e.g.* cheques crossed "account payee": *ibid.*
[79] As opposed to an action to enforce his right to possession of the instrument: *Bird v Discount Banking of England and Wales* (1894) 11 T.L.R. 103.

bank for collecting an instrument to which its customer had no title. At first sight, any such claim would appear to lack merit, since the owner is asserting that the forged signature is wholly inoperative. In consequence, he is the true owner, not of a cheque, but merely of a "piece of paper" which carries no rights or liabilities.[80] He should not therefore be permitted to claim damages in conversion based on the face value of the instrument.[81] However, although the document is in one sense worthless, money has been obtained by its use and his account has been depreciated by the amount paid out.[82] In English law, there is some authority for the view that the collecting bank may be liable in conversion at the suit of the true owner of a document purporting to be a cheque on which his signature as drawer has been forged or placed without authority.[83] Moreover, in that event it is arguable that the collecting bank would not be entitled to the protection afforded by section 4 of the Cheques Act 1957, since the instrument is not a cheque (not having been "drawn" on a banker) nor is it a document issued by a customer of a banker within section 4(2)(b) of the 1957 Act.[84] If the instrument collected is a bill of exchange, no statutory protection would in any event be available.[85] The purported drawer of a cheque is, however, sufficiently protected by his right to require the reinstatement of his account by the drawee bank[86] and it is submitted that there are no strong policy grounds for giving him an alternative remedy for substantial damages in conversion against the collecting bank.[87]

The same difficulty confronts the purported drawer of the cheque if he resorts to the alternative remedy of an action in restitution for money had and received based on a "waiver" of the tort of conversion.[88] But such an action could succeed if it was formulated as an action to recover money

---

[80] *National Westminster Bank Ltd v Barclays Bank International Ltd* [1975] Q.B. 654, 656. See also below, para.8–088 (altered cheque).

[81] See (in Canada) *Arrow Transfer Co. Ltd v Royal Bank of Canada* (1972) 27 D.L.R. (3d) 81, 87, 104; *Number 10 Management Ltd v Royal Bank of Canada* (1976) 69 D.L.R. (3d) 99, 105; and (in Australia) *Koster's Premier Pottery Pty Ltd v Bank of Adelaide* (1982) 28 S.A.S.R. 355. Contrast *Boma Manufacturing Ltd v Canadian Imperial Bank of Commerce* (1997) 140 D.L.R. (4th) 463 (unauthorised signature).

[82] *Morison v London County and Westminster Bank Ltd* [1914] 3 K.B. 356, 365.

[83] *Midland Bank Ltd v Reckitt* [1933] A.C. 1 (s.25, Illustration 9) (unauthorised signature). See also *Boma Manufacturing Ltd v Canadian Imperial Bank of Commerce* (1997) 140 D.L.R. (4th) 463.

[84] See below, para.17–063.

[85] But the purported drawer would, in many cases, experience difficulty in establishing that he was the true owner of the instrument.

[86] See above, para.3–059. However, it will be no defence for the collecting bank to plead that the owner has suffered no loss because he is entitled to such reinstatement: *Bobbett v Pinkett* (1876) 1 Ex. D. 368 (Illustration 9).

[87] This is also the view expressed in Brindle and Cox, *Lair of Bank Payments* (3rd ed.), 7–144.

[88] *United Australia Ltd v Barclays Bank Ltd* [1941] A.C. 1; see above, para.3–052.

paid under a mistake by his agent, the paying bank.[89] However, a restitutionary claim would not succeed against the collecting bank if, before learning of the claim, it had changed its position by paying over the amount of the collected cheque to its customer.[90]

(vi) *Person receiving payment*: By the same token, if an action for conversion or in restitution lies at the suit of the purported drawer, such an action would lie against the person who received payment of the instrument.[91] But, more usually in the case of a cheque, the claim will be made against the person receiving the payment (if he can be found) by the drawee bank to recover the amount paid as money paid under a mistake.[92]     3–063

**Joint accounts.** Where a joint account is opened in the name of two or more customers, the banker may be instructed to honour cheques only when signed by all the account holders jointly.[93] The question then arises as to his liability if he honours a cheque on which the signature of one of the joint account holders is forged or unauthorised, or is missing. In *Brewer v Westminster Bank Ltd*[94] one of two joint account holders, forging the signature of the other, drew cheques on the account and applied the proceeds to his own use. An action against the bank brought by the innocent account holder for a declaration that the joint account had been wrongly debited with the amount of the forged cheques was dismissed by McNair J. He held that the obligation undertaken by the bank to honour cheques if signed by both account holders jointly was a single obligation owed to them jointly. But both account holders, suing jointly, could not have obtained the declaration sought, since a party could not found an action on his own wrongdoing.     3–064

The decision in this case was, however, criticised,[95] and it has either been distinguished[96] or not followed[97] in a number of subsequent cases.

---

[89] See below, para.8–021. *cf. Agip (Africa) Ltd v Jackson* [1991] Ch. 547 (s.59, Illustration 20); *Bank of America v Arnell* [1999] Lloyd's Rep. Bank 399.

[90] See below, para.8–028.

[91] *Morison v Kemp* (1912) 20 T.L.R. 70 (s.25, Illustration 4); *Bank of America v Arnell* [1999] Lloyd's Rep. Bank 399. *cf. Agip (Africa) Ltd v Jackson* [1991] Ch. 547.

[92] See above, para.3–059; below, para.8–021.

[93] *cf. Hirschorn v Evans* [1938] 2 K.B. 801; *Re Bishop, National Provincial Bank v Bishop* [1965] Ch. 450; *Feaver v Feaver* [1977] 5 W.W.R. 271 (Canada).

[94] [1952] 2 All E.R. 650.

[95] Goodhart (1952) 68 L.Q.R. 446; Glanville Williams (1953) 16 M.L.R. 232. See also (1953) 69 L.Q.R. 157.

[96] *Welch v Bank of England* [1955] Ch. 508, 532; *Baker v Barclays Bank Ltd* [1955] 1 W.L.R. 822, 831.

[97] *Ardern v Bank of New South Wales* [1956] V.L.R. 569 (Australia); *Jackson v White and Midland Bank Ltd* [1967] 2 Lloyd's Rep. 68; *Catlin v Cyprus Finance Corp. (London) Ltd* [1983] Q.B. 759.

In particular, in *Jackson v White and Midland Bank Ltd*,[98] Park J. held that, by mandate, the bank not only made an agreement with the account holders jointly that it would honour any cheque signed by them jointly, but it also made an agreement with each account holder severally that it would not honour any cheques unless that account holder had signed them. For a breach of this latter agreement, the bank was liable. He therefore granted an injunction ordering the bank to credit the account with the amount paid on cheques signed by one of two joint account holders but on which that account holder had forged the signature of the other, appropriating the proceeds to his own use. Similar reasoning was adopted by Bingham J. in *Catlin v Cyprus Finance Corporation (London) Ltd*,[99] where a bank, in breach of its mandate to pay only against cheques or other payment orders signed by both husband and wife, made payments on instructions signed by the husband alone. In the light of these cases it is submitted that *Brewer's* case is no longer good law and that "it is highly undesirable that this question should continue to be litigated".[1]

The measure of the damages recoverable from the banker for breach of his mandate is the loss suffered by the account holder as a result of the wrongful payment. In *Jackson v White and Midland Bank Ltd*[2] the funds paid into the account, against which the forged cheques were drawn, represented funds paid in by the innocent account holder, and the full amount of the cheques was ordered to be credited. But more often the loss suffered will be only a half-share or other "moiety" of the amount paid out.[3]

Where the banker has made such a payment in breach of his mandate, he may be entitled to be indemnified by the recipient of the moneys on the ground that the payment was obtained by deceit[4] or to recover from the recipient the sum wrongfully paid as money paid under a mistake.[5]

3–065     **Authorised signatories.** A banker may be authorised by his customer to honour cheques drawn on him on behalf of the customer only when signed by two or more designated signatories. If he then honours a cheque on which the signature of one of the designated signatories is forged or unauthorised, or which is not signed by a sufficient number of

---

[98] [1967] 2 Lloyd's Rep. 68 (Illustration 3).
[99] [1983] Q.B. 759 (Illustration 4). See also *Simos v National Bank of Australasia Ltd* (1976) 10 A.C.T.R. 4 (Australia).
[1] [1983] Q.B. 759 at 770.
[2] [1967] 2 Lloyd's Rep. 68.
[3] *Twibell v London Suburban Bank* [1869] W.N. 127; *Ardern v Bank of New South Wales* [1956] V.L.R. 569 (Australia); *Catlin v Cyprus Finance Corp. (London) Ltd* [1983] Q.B. 759.
[4] *Catlin v Cyprus Finance Corp. (London) Ltd* [1983] Q.B. 759; *Simos v National Bank of Australasia Ltd* (1976) 10 A.C.T.R. 4 (Australia).
[5] See below, para.8–021 (s.59).

signatories, or which is signed by persons other than those specified in his mandate, he will be in breach of his contract with the customer and will prima facie not be entitled to debit the customer's account.[6] However, in *London Intercontinental Trust Ltd v Barclays Bank Ltd*,[7] where the defendant bank paid cheques drawn on behalf of the customer by only one signature when its mandate required two signatures, Slynn J. held that the bank could maintain the debit to the account since the transactions represented by the cheques were transactions which the sole signatory was authorised by the customer to effect. The bank was therefore entitled to act on the cheques drawn on his single signature, and the cheques were not invalidated by the fact that the bank held a mandate requiring two signatures.

**Forged or unauthorised indorsement.** An indorsement which is   3–066
forged or placed on a bill without the authority of the person whose signature it purports to be is "wholly inoperative". The purported signatory cannot be held liable on the bill unless he is precluded from setting up the forgery or want of authority[8] or adopts[9] the forged or ratifies[10] the unauthorised indorsement. Section 24 further provides that "no right to retain the bill or to give a discharge therefor or to enforce payment thereof against any party thereto can be acquired through or under that signature". So, for example, if B draws a bill payable to the order of C and the bill is stolen by a thief who forges C's indorsement and delivers the bill to D, then (i) D cannot enforce payment of the bill against B or C or (if the bill has been accepted) against the acceptor, (ii) D acquires no title to the bill, and (iii) the bill is not discharged by payment to D by or on behalf of the drawee or acceptor, even if payment is made in good faith and without notice that D has no title to the bill.

In the above example, it is immaterial that D takes the bill in good faith and for value and without notice that the indorsement is a forgery. D is not even a holder of the bill (as defined in section 2 of the Act), and cannot therefore be a holder in due course. He is not the payee of the bill; he is not an indorsee of the bill, the indorsement to him being wholly inoperative; and he is not the bearer of the bill, since the bill was neither drawn payable to bearer nor (if the purported indorsement is in blank) has it become payable to bearer by reason of the inoperative indorsement. This

---

[6] See above, para.3–059.
[7] [1980] 1 Lloyd's Rep. 241 (Illustration 14). See also *West v Commercial Bank of Australia Ltd* (1936) 55 C.L.R. 315 (estoppel); *H.J. Symons & Co. v Barclays Bank* [2003] EWHC 1249 (Comm.); *Harding v Standard Bank of South Africa Ltd* 2004 (6) S.A. 464.
[8] See below, para.3–079.
[9] See below, para.3–088.
[10] See below, para.3–087.

was the law before the Act[11] and section 24 is declaratory of the pre-existing law.[12]

If, however, after the forged or unauthorised indorsement, the bill is subsequently indorsed, then, under section 55(2)(b) of the Act,[13] the subsequent indorser or indorsers will be precluded from denying to a holder in due course the genuineness and regularity in all respects of the previous indorsements. Thus, in the above example, if D indorses the bill to E, being a holder in due course, E will have a right of recourse, supported by estoppel, against D. In this context, the expression "holder in due course" must be taken to include a person who would, but for the forged or unauthorised indorsement, have been a holder of the bill. The estoppel thus raised against D is nevertheless a limited one. It will not enable E to enforce payment against B (the drawer) or C (the payee whose indorsement was forged) nor, if the bill has been accepted, against the acceptor of the bill. Moreover, E will acquire no title to the bill and payment to him by the acceptor or drawee will not constitute a valid discharge. If, therefore, the drawee or acceptor pays the bill, the money so paid will prima facie be recoverable as money paid under a mistake and, in any event, E will be accountable for the proceeds to the true owner of the bill (C) in an action for conversion or for money had and received. E may, however, recoup his loss against D. In the absence of the forger, the risk arising from the forged indorsement will therefore ultimately fall on D, the person who took the bill from the forger.

3–067    The effects outlined above also ensue, in substance, in the case of a forged or unauthorised indorsement upon a promissory note or cheque; but, in the case of a cheque, statutory protection is afforded in certain circumstances to a banker who pays or collects a cheque bearing a forged or unauthorised indorsement.[14]

More particularly the effects of a forged or unauthorised indorsement upon the parties to a bill, cheque or note are as follows:

3–068    (i) *Acceptor.* There is no statutory estoppel which precludes the acceptor of a bill payable to order from denying the genuineness or validity of an indorsement. In any action against him on the bill, he may raise the defence that the ostensible holder is not the lawful holder of the instrument but derived his supposed title to it through or under a forged

---

[11] *Mead v Young* (1790) 4 T.R. 28 (Illustration 5); *Esdaile v La Nauze* (1835) 1 Y. & C. 394 (Illustration 6); *Johnson v Windle* (1836) 3 Bing. N.C. 225 (Illustration 7); *Robarts v Tucker* (1851) 16 Q.B. 560 (Illustration 8); *Bobbett v Pinkett* (1876) 1 Ex.D. 368 (Illustration 9). See also *Arnold v Cheque Bank* (1876) 1 C.P.D. 578 (s.21, Illustration 1).

[12] *Lacave & Co. v Crédit Lyonnais* [1897] 1 Q.B. 148, 152. See *Vinden v Hughes* [1905] 1 K.B. 795 (s.7, Illustration 5); *Macbeth v North & South Wales Bank* [1908] A.C. 137 (s.7, Illustration 6).

[13] See above, para.3–045 and below, para.7–028. See also s.55(2)(c).

[14] See below, paras 8–043, 14–024, 17–005 and 17–028.

indorsement.[15] If he pays the bill to such a person, he is not discharged, since payment has not been made to the holder.[16] He remains liable to the lawful holder of the bill, that is to say, to the person in possession[17] whose indorsement was forged or placed thereon without authority. This is so notwithstanding that he pays the bill in good faith and without knowledge that the indorsement is forged or unauthorised.[18] But he is prima facie entitled to recover the payment from the recipient as money paid under a mistake.[19]

An exception, however, exists where the payee is a fictitious or non-existing person. In such a case, under section 7(3) of the Act,[20] the bill may be treated as payable to bearer, and the presence of the forged or unauthorised indorsement is then immaterial. The acceptor will be liable to the person in possession of the bill and payment to that person in due course will operate as a discharge.

(ii) *Maker of a note.* The position of the maker of a promissory note payable to order is the same as that of the acceptor of an order bill.    **3–069**

(iii) *Drawer.* The drawer of a bill or cheque engages that, if it be dishonoured, he will compensate the holder or any indorser who is compelled to pay it, provided that the requisite proceedings on dishonour are duly taken.[21] But he is under no obligation to compensate a person in possession of a bill or cheque payable to order (unless the payee is a fictitious or non-existing person)[22] if that person derives his title to the instrument through or under a forged or unauthorised indorsement. Nor is he obliged to compensate any indorser to whom the instrument is transferred after such an indorsement. However, in the case of a cheque, the banker on whom the cheque is drawn is protected in certain circumstances if he pays it bearing a forged or unauthorised indorsement[23] and will in consequence be entitled to debit the drawer's account with the amount paid.[24] The loss will therefore fall on the drawer, unless he can recoup that loss by an action in conversion or for money had and received against the collecting banker (who will also normally be protected)[25] or against the person receiving payment of the cheque.[26]    **3–070**

---

[15] *i.e.* he may raise the defence of *jus tertii*. See *Mead v Young* (1796) 4 T.R. 28 (Illustration 5); *Esdaile v La Nauze* (1835) 1 Y. & C. 394 (Illustration 6).

[16] See below, para.8–011 (s.59).

[17] See s.2. He would have to obtain the bill, or (*semble*) proceed under ss.69, 70.

[18] See below, para.8–011 (s.59).

[19] See below, para.8–021 (s.59).

[20] See above, para.2–052 (s.7).

[21] s.55(1)(a).

[22] s.7(3).

[23] See ss.60, 80 of the Act and s.1 of the Cheques Act 1957.

[24] See below, para.3–073 (drawee bank).

[25] Cheques Act 1957, s.4, below, para.17–028.

[26] See below, para.3–076 (person receiving payment) and below, para.8–021 (s.59).

**3–071**     (iv) *Indorser.* The indorser of a bill, by indorsing it, is precluded from denying to a holder in due course the genuineness and regularity in all respects of all previous indorsements.[27] He will therefore be liable to a holder in due course if the bill is dishonoured, notwithstanding that an indorsement prior to his own on the bill was forged or unauthorised. He is also precluded from denying to his immediate or a subsequent indorsee that, at the time of his indorsement, he had then a good title to the bill.[28] As mentioned above, the effect of these provisions is that, in practice, where one or more indorsements are placed on an order bill subsequent to a forged or unauthorised indorsement, the loss will fall on the first such indorser after the invalid indorsement. Any indorser prior to such an indorsement will, of course, not be liable either to the ostensible holder or to any indorser subsequent to that indorsement. The same principles apply in the case of an indorser of a cheque or promissory note which is payable to order.

**3–072**     (v) *Drawee bank.* "A cheque drawn by the customer is in point of law a mandate to a banker to pay the amount according to the tenor of the cheque".[29] If a banker upon whom a cheque is drawn pays it in due course[30] and in accordance with the mandate of his customer, the drawer, he will be entitled to debit his customer's account. He has, however, no mandate to pay otherwise than to a holder. If, therefore, he pays a cheque payable to order on which any necessary[31] indorsement of the payee or a subsequent indorser is forged or unauthorised, he will not have paid in accordance with his mandate. Unless the payee is a fictitious or non-existing person[32] or the customer is estopped from relying on the forged or unauthorised signature,[33] he will not be entitled, in principle, to debit his customer's account with the amount paid.[34] Moreover, he is exposed to liability in conversion to the true owner of the cheque which he has paid.[35] His remedy—which may well be worthless—is to seek to recover

---

[27] s.55(2)(b) See above, para.3–045.
[28] s.55(2)(c).
[29] *London Joint Stock Bank Ltd v Macmillan* [1918] A.C. 777, 789 *per* Lord Finlay L.C.
[30] s.59(1).
[31] *i.e.* to establish the chain of title. *cf.* s.56 (anomalous indorsement).
[32] s.7(3).
[33] See below, para.3–079.
[34] *Slingsby v District Bank Ltd* [1932] 1 K.B. 544 (s.60, Illustration 2).
[35] *Smith v Union Bank of London* (1875) L.R. 10 Q.B. 291 (affirmed (1875) 1 Q.B.D. 31); *Bavins Jnr and Sims v London and South Western Bank Ltd* [1900] 1 Q.B. 270, 278; *El Awadi v Bank of Credit and Commerce International S.A.* [1990] Q.B. 606, 627; *Smith v Lloyds TSB Bank plc* [2000] 2 All E.R. (Comm.) 693, 697 and above, para.3–050, n.65. Contrast *Charles v Blackwell* (1877) 2 C.P.D. 151, 162–163. See also *Lacave & Co. v Crédit Lyonnais* [1897] 1 Q.B. 148. This matter is discussed in Ellinger, Lomnicka and Hooley, *Modern Banking Law* (3rd ed., 2002), pp.387–389.

the payment from the recipient as money paid under a mistake.[36] The payee of a cheque owes no duty to the drawee banker to prevent misappropriation of the cheque.[37]

Since, however, the drawee banker has no effective means of knowing whether or not a person presenting an order cheque for payment is the lawful holder of the instrument, a number of statutory provisions operate to protect him if he pays a cheque which bears a forged or unauthorised indorsement. First, under section 60 of the Act,[38] if he pays an order cheque in good faith and in the ordinary course of business, he is deemed to have paid it in due course although the indorsement of the payee or any subsequent indorsement has been forged or made without authority. Secondly, section 80 of the Act[39] protects him if he pays in good faith and without negligence a crossed cheque to a banker, and section 5 of the Cheques Act 1957[40] extends this protection to the payment of certain other crossed instruments. Thirdly, section 1 of the 1957 Act[41] provides that, if in good faith and in the ordinary course of business he pays a cheque[42] drawn on him which is irregularly indorsed,[43] he does not in doing so incur any liability by reason only of the irregularity in indorsement, and he is deemed to have paid in due course. But the protection afforded by these provisions need only be relied on by the drawee banker where an indorsement is required. By section 1 of the 1957 Act there are circumstances in which he need not concern himself with the absence of an indorsement.

3–073

(vi) *Bank where bill or note domiciled for payment:* If a customer accepts a bill or makes a note payable at his banker's, the banker is under no duty to pay it.[44] But if he undertakes such a duty to the customer, then the authority given to him by the customer is to pay the instrument to a person who is capable of giving a good discharge for it.[45] In consequence, where a bill or note is payable to order, payment to a person who has acquired it through or under a forged indorsement will not constitute a discharge and the banker will not be entitled to debit the customer's account with the amount paid. This was so decided in the case of *Robarts v Tucker*[46] in 1851. No

3–074

---

[36] See below, para.8–021 (s.59). *cf. London & River Plate Bank Ltd v Bank of Liverpool Ltd* [1896] 1 Q.B. 7 (s.59, Illustration 16).

[37] *Yorkshire Bank plc v Lloyds Bank plc* [1999] 2 All E.R. (Comm.) 153.

[38] See below, para.8–043 (s.60). See also Stamp Act 1853, s.19; below, para.8–045.

[39] See below, para.14–024.

[40] See below, para.17–075. See also s.95 of the 1882 Act.

[41] See below, para.17–005.

[42] Or certain other instruments referred to in s.1(2).

[43] *cf. Slingsby v District Bank Ltd* [1932] 1 K.B. 544.

[44] *Robarts v Tucker* (1851) 16 Q.B. 560, 579; *Bank of England v Vagliano Brothers* [1891] A.C. 107, 157.

[45] *Robarts v Tucker* (1851) 16 Q.B. 560. See also *Kymer v Laurie* (1849) 18 L.J.Q.B. 218.

[46] (1851) 16 Q.B. 560 (Illustration 8). This case was approved in *Bank of England v Vagliano Brothers* [1891] A.C. 107 at 117, 125, 131, 141, 155, 158–159, 166.

statutory protection[47] extends to the banker in such a case since the instrument is not drawn on him. Nevertheless, if the payee is a fictitious or non-existing person, he may treat the instrument as payable to bearer and pay it accordingly.[48] Moreover, in paying the instrument, he acts as the customer's agent, and the customer may be estopped from denying that the payment was properly made by his agent.

In *Bank of England v Vagliano Brothers*[49] a majority of the House of Lords held that the acceptor had, albeit innocently, misled his bankers into paying a number of order bills on which both the signature of the drawer and the indorsement of the payee had been forged, which payments had been made by them in good faith and in the ordinary and usual way of bankers, and that they could therefore debit the acceptor's account with the amounts paid. Lord Selborne said[50]:

> "I think that a representation made directly to the banker by the customer upon a material point, untrue in fact (though believed by the person who made it to be true), and on which the banker acted by paying money which he would not otherwise have paid, ought . . . to be an answer to that prima facie case [*i.e.* that the authority was only to pay to the order of the person named as payee upon the bill]. If the bank acted upon such a representation in good faith, and according to the ordinary course of business, and a loss has in consequence occurred which would not have happened if the representation had been true, I think that is a loss which the customer, and not the bank, ought to bear".

Negligence on the part of the customer, provided it led directly to the loss, would also suffice.[51]

A banker who pays a bill or note accepted or made payable at his bank to a person who claims through or under a forged indorsement will be liable to an action for conversion at the suit of the true owner of the instrument.[52]

3–075    (vii) *Collecting bank.* A banker who collects for a customer a bill, cheque or note payable to order on which any necessary indorsement is forged or unauthorised will prima facie be liable in conversion, or in

---

[47] Under ss.60, 80 of the Act, s.19 of the Stamp Act 1853 or s.1 of the Cheques Act 1957.
[48] s.7(3); *Bank of England v Vagliano Brothers* [1891] A.C. 107.
[49] [1891] A.C. 107 (s.7, Illustration 4).
[50] [1891] A.C. 107, 123, 124. See also 115, 134, 159, 162.
[51] [1891] A.C. 107, 115, 123.
[52] See above, para.3–072 (drawee). For recovery of the payment by the bank from the recipient, see below, para.8–021 (s.59).

restitution for money had and received, to the true owner of the instrument.[53] The measure of damages in conversion is the face value of the instrument.[54] However, in the case of cheques and certain analogous instruments, the banker is protected from liability to the true owner by section 4 of the Cheques Act 1957 where he collects for a customer such an instrument in good faith and without negligence.[55] But no statutory protection exists in the case of bills of exchange and promissory notes. The collecting banker might, however, escape liability if he could prove that the proceeds have discharged a debt owed by the true owner or been appropriated for his benefit.[56]

Since conversion is a tort of strict liability,[57] it is no defence, except under section 4 of the 1957 Act, for the collecting banker to plead that he acted without negligence. Nevertheless, the true owner may by his neglect or carelessness have facilitated the forgery of his indorsement. In *Morison v London County and Westminster Bank*[58] it was suggested that a lack of vigilance on the part of the true owner in detecting the fraud of his employee had "lulled to sleep" the collecting bank and so excused the bank's negligence. But this principle was not approved in later cases[59] and it appears that any "lulling to sleep" must now be such as to show an estoppel or ratification.[60] The extent to which contributory negligence can be raised as a defence to an action in conversion against the collecting bank is discussed later in the Comment on this section.[61]

Where the collecting banker is liable to the true owner for innocent conversion of a cheque, he may be entitled to be indemnified by his customer (who delivered the cheque to him as agent for collection) in

---

[53] *Arnold v Cheque Bank* (1876) 1 C.P.D. 578; *Kleinwort Sons & Co. v Comptoir National Escompte de Paris* [1894] 2 Q.B. 157; *Lacave & Co. v Credit Lyonnais* [1897] 1 Q.B. 148; *Bavins Jnr and Sims v London and South Western Bank* [1900] 1 Q.B. 270; *Capital and Counties Bank Ltd v Gordon* [1903] A.C. 240; *Akrokerri (Atlantic) Mines Ltd v Economic Bank* [1904] 2 K.B. 465; *Macbeth v North and South Wales Bank Ltd* [1908] A.C. 137; *Ladbroke v Todd* (1914) 30 T.L.R. 433; *Motor Traders Guarantee Corp. Ltd v Midland Bank Ltd* [1937] 4 All E.R. 90; *Carpenters' Co. v British Mutual Banking Co. Ltd* [1938] 1 K.B. 511; *Baker v Barclays Bank Ltd* [1955] 1 W.L.R. 822; *Marfani & Co. Ltd v Midland Bank Ltd* [1968] 1 W.L.R. 956, 971. In Scotland liability will only be in restitution: see Cusine (1978) 23 Jur. Rev. 223.

[54] See above, para.3–050.

[55] See below, para.17–028.

[56] *Reid v Rigby & Co.* [1894] 2 Q.B. 40; *Jacobs v Morris* [1902] 1 Ch. 816; *Underwood A.L. Ltd v Bank of Liverpool* [1924] 1 K.B. 775, 794; *B. Liggett (Liverpool) Ltd v Barclays Bank Ltd* [1928] 1 K.B. 48; *Lloyd's Bank Ltd v Chartered Bank of India, Australia and China* [1929] 1 K.B. 40, 61. But see *Crantrave Ltd v Lloyds Bank plc* [2000] Q.B. 917; above, para.3–059 (payment must be authorised to discharge debt).

[57] See above, para.3–050.

[58] [1914] 3 K.B. 356 (Illustration 1).

[59] *Lloyd's Bank Ltd v Chartered Bank of India, Australia and China* [1929] 1 K.B. 40 at 60, 79; *Lloyd's Bank Ltd v E.B. Savory & Co. Ltd* [1933] A.C. 201, 236; *Carpenters' Co. v British Mutual Banking Co. Ltd* [1938] 1 K.B. 511, 530, 535.

[60] *Bank of Montreal v Dominion Gresham Guarantee & Casualty Co. Ltd* [1930] A.C. 659, 666.

[61] See below, para.3–089.

respect of the amount paid in settlement of that liability[62] or to claim that amount from the customer for breach of an implied warranty that the customer was entitled to have the proceeds of the cheque paid to him.[63] Alternatively a claim for contribution may be made under section 2(1) of the Civil Liability (Contribution) Act 1978.[64]

3–076     (viii) *Person receiving payment*. A person who acquires a bill, cheque or note payable to order through or under a forged or unauthorised indorsement is not the holder of the instrument and obtains no title to it[65] even if he takes it in good faith and for value and without notice that the indorsement is forged or unauthorised.[66] He cannot, therefore, recover against the acceptor,[67] drawer[68] or maker[69] on the instrument, his only remedy being to seek reimbursement on dishonour against a prior indorser who indorsed it after the invalid indorsement.[70] If he obtains payment of the instrument, he will prima facie be liable to repay the amount paid to the person by whom it was paid.[71] He will also be liable to the true owner in an action for conversion or in restitution for money had and received.[72] Thus, if a cheque drawn payable to the order of C is stolen from C, C's indorsement is forged and the cheque is then "negotiated" to D, who gives value for it in ignorance of the forgery, the drawee bank which pays the cheque and the bank which collects it on D's behalf will normally be protected,[73] but D will be accountable to C, its true owner.

3–077     **Instruments indorsed abroad.** The section may not apply where an instrument is indorsed abroad. Under the English rules of private international law, the transfer of a chattel is governed by the law of the place of

---

[62] *Redmond v Allied Irish Bank plc* [1987] F.L.R. 307 (concessions made). But in this case Saville J. expressed doubt whether the concessions had been properly made. See also *Sheffield Corpn. v Barclay* [1905] A.C. 392; *Kai Yung v Hong Kong and Shanghai Banking Corp.* [1981] A.C. 787; *National Commercial Banking Corp. of Australia Ltd v Batty* (1985–1986) 160 C.L.R. 251, 273; *Honourable Society of the Middle Temple v Lloyds Bank plc* [1999] 1 All E.R. (Comm) 193 (Cheques Act 1957, s.4, Illustration 5); *Linklaters v HSBC Bank plc* [2003] EWHC 1113 (Comm), [2003] 2 Lloyd's Rep. 545.

[63] *Sheffield Corpn. v Barclay* [1905] A.C. 392, 402, 404; *Kai Yung v Hong Kong and Shanghai Banking Corp.* [1981] A.C. 787, 796, 798; *Honourable Society of the Middle Temple v Lloyds Bank plc* [1999] 1 All E.R. (Comm) 193; *Linklaters v HSBC plc* [2003] EWHC 113, [2003] 2 Lloyd's Rep. 545.

[64] cf. *Honourable Society of the Middle Temple v Lloyds Bank plc* [1999] 1 All E.R. (Comm) 193; *Linklaters v HSBC plc* [2003] EWHC 113, [2003] 2 Lloyd's Rep. 545.

[65] Except where the payee is a fictitious or non-existing person: s.7(3): *Clutton & Co. v Attenborough & Son* [1897] A.C. 90 (s.7, Illustration 3).

[66] See above, para.3–066.

[67] See above, para.3–068.

[68] See above, para.3–070.

[69] See above, para.3–069.

[70] See above, para.3–071.

[71] s.59(1); see below, para.8–021.

[72] *Johnson v Windle* (1836) 3 Bing. N.C. 225 (Illustration 7); *Bobbett v Pinkett* (1876) 1 Ex.D. 368 (Illustration 9); *Vinden v Hughes* [1905] 1 K.B. 795 (s.7, Illustration 5).

[73] See above, paras 3–073 and 3–075; below, paras 8–043, 14–024, 17–005 and 17–028.

transfer and "[t]he rule that the transfer of chattels must be governed by the law of the country where the transfer takes place applies to a bill or cheque".[74] Under the Geneva Uniform Law (ULB),[75] although the person whose indorsement is forged is not liable,[76] title to a bill may be acquired through or under a forged indorsement. By article 16 of that Law, the possessor of a bill of exchange is deemed to be the lawful holder (*porteur légitime*) if he establishes his title to the bill through an uninterrupted series of indorsements, even if the last indorsement is in blank. He will have title to the bill and will thus be entitled to exercise all rights derived therefrom, notwithstanding that he claims through or under an indorsement which is forged. The person who has been dispossessed of the bill will be able to claim it from him only if it is proved that he acquired the bill in bad faith or in acquiring it was guilty of gross negligence. Further, under article 40 of the Law, a person who pays the bill at maturity to a lawful holder is validly discharged, unless he has been guilty of fraud or gross negligence: he is bound to verify the regularity of the series of indorsements, but not the signature of the indorsers.[77] If, therefore, a bill drawn payable to order is stolen from the payee by a thief who forges the payee's indorsement and delivers the bill to X, who is paid by the drawee, the loss will normally fall on the payee and not, as under the 1882 Act, upon X who took the bill from the forger.

**Instruments payable or which may be treated as payable to bearer.** A    3–078
bill, cheque or note payable to bearer is negotiated by mere delivery.[78]
The person in possession of an instrument payable to bearer is a "holder" of it,[79] and, if he is a holder in due course,[80] he will obtain a good title to it and may enforce payment against all parties liable on the instrument despite any defect in title of prior parties[81] and despite the fact that it was lost or stolen or otherwise improperly obtained.[82] Payment to the bearer by or on behalf of the drawee or acceptor at or after maturity will constitute payment in due course and will discharge the instrument, provided the payment is made in good faith and without notice of the

---

[74] *Embiricos v Anglo-Austrian Bank* [1905] 1 K.B. 677, 683 (s.72, Illustration 6).
[75] See also the Geneva Uniform Law for Cheques (ULC), arts 19, 35, and Vis (1979) 27 *American Journal of Comparative Law* 547.
[76] ULB, art.7; ULC, art.10.
[77] In *Linklaters v HSBC Bank plc* [2003] EWHC 1113 (Comm), [2003] 2 Lloyd's Rep. 545 the words "Prior Endorsements Guaranteed" placed on a cheque by a Spanish bank collecting a cheque for a customer did not constitute any more than a guarantee that, in respect of the final indorsement, the bank had verified the *identity* of the signatory but not the authenticity of the signature.
[78] s.31(2).
[79] s.2.
[80] Defined in s.29(1).
[81] s.38(2).
[82] See below, para.4–066 (s.29(2)); para.5–074 (s.38(3)).

defect in or absence of title of the recipient.[83] Under section 7(3) of the Act,[84] where the payee is a fictitious or non-existing person, the instrument may be treated as payable to bearer and, in such a case, the presence of a forged or unauthorised indorsement is immaterial.

3–079 **Estoppel.** The section provides specifically for an exception to the effects of a forged or unauthorised signature where the party against whom it is sought to retain or enforce payment of the bill is precluded[85] from setting up the forgery or want of authority.

A party to a bill may be estopped from asserting that the signature of another party to the bill is forged or unauthorised. In addition to the statutory estoppels raised against the acceptor and the indorser of the bill by sections 54(2)[86] and 55(2)(b)[87] of the Act in favour of a holder in due course and against an indorser under section 55(2)(c)[88] in favour of his immediate or a subsequent indorsee, the acceptor of a bill may, for example, be estopped from denying the authenticity of the signature of the drawer to any innocent holder for value[89] or to the banker with whom he has domiciled the bill for payment[90] or, in certain circumstances, from raising against such a banker the fact that the payee's indorsement is forged.[91] One party to a bill may be estopped while another is not.

The party whose signature has been forged or placed on a bill without his authority may also be precluded from setting up the forgery or want of authority. The drawee of a bill may, for example, be estopped where he has represented to the holder that his signature as acceptor is genuine.[92] In particular, the drawer of a cheque may be estopped as against the drawee bank from asserting that his signature on the cheque is forged or unauthorised, with the result that the drawee bank is then entitled to debit his account with the amount which it has paid.[93]

Estoppel may arise by representation or by negligence.

---

[83] s.59(1); below, para.8–011.
[84] See above, para.2–052.
[85] The word "precluded" was inserted in the Act in committee in lieu of the word "estoppel," an English technical term unknown to Scots law.
[86] See above, para.3–057; below, para.7–017 (s.54).
[87] See above, para.3–058; below, para.7–028 (s.55).
[88] See above, para.3–071; below, para.7–028 (s.55).
[89] See above, para.3–057.
[90] See above, para.3–061.
[91] See above, para.3–074.
[92] *Leach v Buchanan* (1802) 4 Esp. 226 (Illustration 10). *cf. Brook v Hook* (1871) L.R. 6 Ex. 89 (Illustration 15).
[93] See, *e.g. Greenwood v Martins Bank Ltd* [1933] A.C. 51 (Illustration 11); *Brown v Westminster Bank Ltd* [1964] 2 Lloyd's Rep. 187. See also *West v Commercial Bank of Australia Ltd* (1936) 55 C.L.R. 315; *London Intercontinental Trust Ltd v Barclays Bank Ltd* [1980] 1 Lloyd's Rep. 241; *H.J. Symons & Co. v Barclays Bank* [2003] EWHC 1249 (Comm) (insufficient number of signatures).

**Estoppel by representation.** The essential features giving rise to an 3–080
estoppel by representation were stated by Lord Tomlin, delivering the
opinion of the House of Lords in *Greenwood v Martins Bank Ltd*,[94] to be as
follows:

"(1) A representation or conduct amounting to a representation
intended to induce a course of conduct on the part of the person to
whom the representation is made. (2) An act or omission resulting
from the representation, whether actual or by conduct, by the person
to whom the representation is made. (3) Detriment to such person as
a consequence of the act or omission".

In that case a husband discovered that his wife had forged his signature
as drawer to several cheques but refrained from informing the bank of the
forgeries as he did not wish to give his wife away. Later he decided to tell
the bank, and his wife committed suicide. An action brought by him
against the bank for wrongfully debiting his account was dismissed. The
House of Lords held that he was under a duty to inform the bank of the
forgeries, that his deliberate failure to do so amounted to a representation
by him that the cheques were genuine and that, by reason of the representation, the bank had been deprived of the opportunity of suing him
and his wife in respect of the tort of his wife committed before her
death.[95]

(i) *Representation*: There must be a representation by words or conduct, 3–081
or by silence amounting to a representation. The representation must be
clear and unequivocal.[96] In fact, there are very few cases of estoppel by an
express representation[97] other than cases where the drawee of a bill has
acknowledged a forged acceptance as his own.[98] Either the representation
is implied[99] or is constituted by silence.[1]

---

[94] [1933] A.C. 51, 57 (Illustration 11).
[95] The cause of action dropped with death, and the husband was at that time liable for his
wife's torts.
[96] *Bute (Marquess of) v Barclays Bank Ltd* [1955] 1 Q.B. 202, 213. See also *Woodhouse A.C. Israel
Cocoa Ltd S.A. v Nigerian Produce Marketing Co. Ltd* [1972] A.C. 741, 757, 758, 761, 762, 768,
771.
[97] But see *Tina Motors Pty. Ltd v Australian & New Zealand Banking Group Ltd* [1977] V.R.
205.
[98] *Leach v Buchanan* (1802) 4 Esp. 226 (Illustration 10); *Robarts v Tucker* (1851) 16 Q.B. 560, 577;
*Brook v Hook* (1871) L.R. 6 Ex. 89, 100; *Greenwood v Martins Bank Ltd* [1932] 1 K.B. 371, 375
CA. Contrast *Morris v Bethell (No.2)* (1869) L.R. 5 C.P. 47. See also below, para.3–088
(adoption).
[99] *Brown v Westminster Bank Ltd* [1964] 2 Lloyd's Rep. 187.
[1] *McKenzie v British Linen Co.* (1881) 6 App. Cas. 82, 109; *Greenwood v Martins Bank Ltd* [1932]
1 K.B. 371; *Ontario Woodsworth Memorial Foundation v Grozbord* (1966) 58 D.L.R. (2d) 21,
affirmed (1969) 4 D.L.R. (3d) 194; *Limpgrange Ltd v Bank of Credit and Commerce International S.A.* [1986] F.L.R. 36.

In *Greenwood v Martins Bank Ltd*, Lord Tomlin continued[2]: "Mere silence cannot amount to a representation, but when there is a duty to disclose deliberate silence may become significant and amount to a representation." It is clear from the use of the word "deliberate" that the person against whom the estoppel is raised must either have had actual knowledge that the signature was forged or unauthorised and failed to speak out or deliberately refrained from making inquiries which would have revealed the forgery or want of authority.[3] Silence due to ignorance will not be sufficient[4] nor will "constructive knowledge" suffice.[5] There must also be a duty to disclose. Assuming the requisite knowledge is present, a customer of a bank owes it a duty to disclose that his signature as the drawer of a cheque drawn on his account is forged or unauthorised.[6]

The duty of disclosure is nevertheless not confined to the banker and customer relationship: any person who becomes aware that his signature on a document has been forged is bound to repudiate the signature if the forgery is brought to his attention by one whom he knows will act upon it.[7] It would also appear that a person who becomes aware that his signature as drawer or indorser has been forged on a bill and who knows that the payee will advance money in reliance on the instrument is bound with reasonable diligence to warn the payee of the fact. If he does not do so, and the payee's position is thereby prejudiced, he will be estopped from setting up the forgery as against the payee.[8] But there is no duty to inform a person who knows of the forgery or whose agent is aware of the forgery and chooses not to inform his principal (unless the conduct of the agent is calculated to create, in the mind of a reasonable person of ordinary intelligence, a suspicion or belief that the agent means to betray his principal's interests).[9]

**3–082**     (ii) *Act or omission by representee.* The person to whom the representation is made must act or omit to act as a result of the representation. It is, however, unnecessary that the representor should actually have intended

---

[2] [1933] A.C. 51, 57.

[3] *Patel v Standard Chartered Bank* [2001] Lloyd's Rep. Bank 229.

[4] *Tai Hing Cotton Mill Ltd v Liu Chong Hing Bank Ltd (No.1)* [1986] A.C. 317.

[5] *Price Meats Ltd v Barclays Bank plc* [2000] 2 All E.R. (Comm) 346 (Illustration 13); *Patel v Standard Chartered Bank* [2001] Lloyd's Rep. Bank 229.

[6] *Ogilvie v West Australian Mortgage and Agency Corp. Ltd* [1896] A.C. 257, 270; *Greenwood v Martins Bank Ltd* [1932] 1 K.B. 371; *Brown v Westminster Bank Ltd* [1964] 2 Lloyd's Rep. 187. See also *Limpgrange Ltd v Bank of Credit and Commerce International S.A.* [1986] Fin.L.R. 36 (unauthorised transactions on account).

[7] *McKenzie v British Linen Co.* (1881) 6 App. Cas. 82, 109; *Ewing v Dominion Bank* (1904) 35 S.C.R. 133 (leave to appeal refused [1904] A.C. 806); *Fung Kai Sun v Chan Fui Hing* [1951] A.C. 489, 502; *Ontario Woodsworth Memorial Foundation v Grozbord* (1966) 58 D.L.R. (2d) 21.

[8] *McKenzie v British Linen Co.* (1881) 6 App. Cas. 82 at 109; *Ontario Woodsworth Memorial Foundation v Grozbord* (1966) 58 D.L.R. (2d) 21.

[9] *Ogilvie v West Australian Mortgage and Agency Corp. Ltd* [1896] A.C. 257.

to induce the representee to act (or refrain from acting) on the representation; it is sufficient if a reasonable man would take the representation to be true, and believe that he was meant to act upon it, and the person to whom it was made did in fact act upon it as true.[10]

(iii) *Detriment to representee.* The person to whom the representation is **3–083** made must suffer detriment as a result of the representation. In the case of a forgery, where there is a failure to disclose or delay in disclosing the forgery, there must be material loss or prejudice to the person who should have been informed and which prompt and reasonable information would have prevented.[11] Such loss or prejudice may be constituted, for example, by loss of the opportunity to sue the forger because of his death[12] or disappearance,[13] or (in the case of a bank) by the bank continuing to pay cheques drawn on the customer's account[14] or paying out money to the forger.[15] But if timely disclosure would not have prevented such loss or prejudice, no estoppel will arise.[16]

It appears to be immaterial that the person to whom the representation is made was himself negligent in failing to detect the forgery unless such negligence was the proximate cause of the detriment sustained.[17] Negligence in failing to detect the forgery may well be the proximate cause of loss sustained by paying on a forged instrument but yet not be the proximate cause of detriment suffered as a result of the representation in the loss of the opportunity to sue the forger.[18]

(iv) *Extent of the estoppel.* In *Brown v Westminster Bank Ltd*,[19] a customer **3–084** impliedly represented to her bank that certain cheques apparently drawn by her were genuine. It was held that she was estopped from setting up

---

[10] *Freeman v Cooke* (1848) 2 Exch. 654, 663; *Carr v London & N.W. Ry* (1875) L.R. 10 C.P. 307, 317; *Brown v Westminster Bank Ltd* [1964] 2 Lloyd's Rep. 187, 202.

[11] *McKenzie v British Linen Co.* (1881) 6 App. Cas. 82; *Ewing v Dominion Bank* [1896] A.C. 257 at 138; *Fung Kai Sun v Chan Fui Hing* [1951] A.C. 489.

[12] *Greenwood v Martins Bank Ltd* [1933] A.C. 51 (Illustration 11).

[13] *Ontario Woodsworth Memorial Foundation v Grozbord* (1966) 58 D.L.R. (2d) 21, affirmed (1969) 4 D.L.R. (3d) 194. *cf. Ogilvie v West Australian Mortgage and Agency Corp. Ltd* [1896] A.C. 257.

[14] *Brown v Westminster Bank Ltd* [1964] 2 Lloyd's Rep. 187.

[15] *Ewing v Dominion Bank* (1904) 35 S.C.R. 133.

[16] *McKenzie v British Linen Co.* (1881) 6 App. Cas. 82; *Fung Kai Sun v Chan Fui Hing* [1951] A.C. 489.

[17] *Greenwood v Martin's Bank Ltd* [1932] 1 K.B. 371 at 58. *cf. Barclays Bank DCO v Straw* 1965 (2) S.A. 93; *Varker v Commercial Banking Co. of Sydney Ltd* [1972] 2 N.S.W.L.R. 967. *Quaere* whether, in the case of a bank, the customer could now raise the defence of contributory negligence on the part of the bank: *contra, Tina Motors Pty Ltd v Australian and New Zealand Banking Group Ltd* [1977] V.R. 205, 208.

[18] *Greenwood v Martin's Bank Ltd* [1932] 1 K.B. 371, 382, 383, CA. See also *Ogilvie v West Australian Mortgage and Agency Corp. Ltd* [1896] A.C. 257 at 268; *Brown v Westminster Bank Ltd* [1964] 2 Lloyd's Rep. 187.

[19] [1964] 2 Lloyd's Rep. 187. See also *Tina Motors Pty Ltd v Australian & New Zealand Banking Group Ltd* [1977] V.R. 205.

the true facts, both in respect of the cheques which had already been forged and also in respect of further forged cheques presented to and paid by the bank after the representation.

3–085     **Estoppel by negligence.** In *London Joint Stock Bank Ltd v Macmillan*,[20] the House of Lords held that a duty of care is owed by the customer to his bank in the operation of a current account to refrain from drawing a cheque on the account in such a manner as may facilitate fraud or forgery. If, in breach of that duty, he so negligently draws a cheque as to enable a third party fraudulently to alter the cheque,[21] or if he draws a cheque in blank or while it is otherwise incomplete, leaving it to another to fill it up, and that other fraudulently completes it in an unauthorised manner,[22] the drawee bank will be entitled to debit the customer's account with the amount paid out on the cheque. In *Macmillan's* case, however, Lord Finlay L.C. said[23]:

> ".... the negligence must be in the transaction itself, that is, in the manner in which the cheque is drawn. It would be no defence to the banker, if the forgery had been that of a clerk of a customer, that the latter had taken the clerk into his service without sufficient inquiry as to his character."

The question whether a customer owes to his bank a wider duty to take reasonable precautions in the conduct of his business to prevent forged cheques being presented to the bank for payment was considered in *Tai Hing Cotton Mill Ltd v Liu Chong Hing Bank Ltd*.[24] In that case, due to the customer's failure to operate any adequate system for the prevention or detection of fraud, an accounts clerk employed by the customer was enabled over a long period of time to forge the customer's signature as drawer to a large number of cheques, which cheques were presented to and paid by the drawee bank. The Judicial Committee of the Privy Council held[25] that the customer owed no such wider duty to his bank,

---

[20] [1918] A.C. 777 (Section 64, Illustration 5). Contrast *Scholfield v Londesborough* [1896] A.C. 514; *Slingsby v District Bank Ltd* [1932] 1 K.B. 544; *Heskell v Continental Express Ltd* [1950] 1 All E.R. 1033.

[21] See below, para.8–085.

[22] See above, para.2–139.

[23] [1918] A.C. 777, 795. The illustration given by Lord Finlay reflects the facts in *Kepitigalla Rubber Estates Ltd v National Bank of India Ltd* [1909] 2 K.B. 1010.

[24] [1986] A.C. 80 (Illustration 12).

[25] See also *Lewes Sanitary Steam Laundry Co. Ltd v Barclay, Beavan & Co. Ltd* (1906) 11 Com.Cas. 255; *Kepitigalla Rubber Estates Ltd v National Bank of India Ltd* [1909] 2 K.B. 1010; *Columbia Graphophone Co. v Union Bank of Canada* (1916) 34 D.L.R. 743n.; *National Bank of New Zealand Ltd v Walpole and Patterson Ltd* [1975] 2 N.Z.L.R. 7; *Commonwealth Trading Bank of Australia v Sydney Wide Stores Pty Ltd* (1981) 148 C.L.R. 304; *Holzman v Standard Bank Ltd* 1985 (1) S.A. 360; *Canadian Pacific Hotels Ltd v Bank of Montreal* (1987) 40 D.L.R. (4th) 385; *National Australia Bank Ltd v Hokit Pty Ltd* [1997] 6 Bank.L.R. 177.

either in contract or in tort. Nor was the customer, in the absence of any knowledge of the forgeries, estopped from asserting that his account had been wrongly debited with the amounts paid out. Likewise, if a customer negligently loses his cheque book, or negligently fails to keep it in safe custody, with the result that it is taken by a stranger or employee who forges the customer's signature as drawer, the drawee bank which pays the forged cheque will nevertheless not be entitled to debit the customer's account with the amount of the cheque.[26]

**Failure to check bank statements.**[27] In *Tai Hing Cotton Mill Ltd v Liu*    3–086
*Chong Hing Bank Ltd*[28] it was expressly provided in the bank's rules or standard terms, incorporated into the contract between the customer and the bank, that the customer should notify the bank of any error in the monthly statements sent to him and, in the absence of any such notification within a specified period of time, the account should be deemed to be correct. The Privy Council held that this provision, though contractual in effect, did not sufficiently bring home to the customer the fact that it was intended to have conclusive effect against him if he raised no query. Lord Scarman said[29]:

> "If banks wish to impose upon their customers an express obligation to examine their monthly statements and to make those statements, in the absence of query, unchallengeable by the customer after expiry of a time limit, the burden of the objection and of the sanction imposed must be brought home to the customer. . . . Clear and unambiguous provision is needed if the banks are to introduce into the contract a binding obligation upon the customer who does not query his bank statement to accept the statement as accurately setting out the debit items in the accounts."

The customer in that case was not precluded, either by contract or by estoppel, from asserting that his current account was incorrectly debited. In the absence of any clear and unambiguous contractual provision, the importance of which is brought home to the customer, there is therefore no duty on the customer to examine with reasonable care periodic statements of account received from his bank.[30]

---

[26] *Bank of Ireland v Evan's Trustees* (1855) 5 H.L.C. 389, 410–411.
[27] See Pollock (1910) 26 L.Q.R. 4; Holden (1954) 17 M.L.R. 41.
[28] [1986] A.C. 80 (Illustration 12).
[29] [1986] A.C. 80 at 110.
[30] See also *Kepitigalla Rubber Estates Ltd v National Bank of India Ltd* [1909] 2 K.B. 1010; *Walker v Manchester & Liverpool District Banking Co. Ltd* (1913) 29 T.L.R. 492; *Wealden Woodlands (Kent) Ltd v National Westminster Bank Ltd* (1983) 133 N.L.J. 719; *Canadian Pacific Hotels Ltd v Bank of Montreal* (1987) 40 D.L.R. (4th) 385. Contrast UCC, § 4–406.

Canadian cases have, however, relieved banks from liability as the result of "verification agreements" by which the customer undertakes to examine such periodic statements and to notify the bank of any unauthorised debits within a certain time.[31] But in the United Kingdom, it is questionable whether such an undertaking in a bank's standard terms and conditions would be binding on a non-business customer, on the ground that it is "unfair" within the meaning of the Unfair Terms in Consumer Contracts Regulations 1999.[32]

3–087      **The proviso: ratification.** An unauthorised signature may be ratified.[33] Ratification can, however, occur only where the person whose act is in question professes or purports at the time of acting to do so as agent.[34] It may therefore be that the person whose signature is placed on a bill or note without his authority can be held to have ratified the signature only if the signature is by procuration or is accompanied by words indicating that it is signed by the purported agent, and not if his name alone is placed on the instrument.[35] Only the person whose signature is placed on the instrument without his authority can ratify the signature,[36] and he must at the time of the signature have been in existence[37] and have had capacity to incur liability as a party to the instrument.[38] Ratification may be by words or conduct,[39] but requires full knowledge on his part that the signature was unauthorised[40] and must be such as unequivocally to show that he treats the signature as authorised and becomes a party to the instrument.[41]

Ratification may also occur where a banker pays a cheque drawn on him in breach of his mandate from his customer, but the customer

---

[31] *Rutherford v Royal Bank of Canada* [1932] 2 D.L.R. 332; *B. & G. Construction Co. v Bank of Montreal* [1954] 2 D.L.R. 753; *Arrow Transfer Co. Ltd v Royal Bank of Canada* (1972) 27 D.L.R. (3d) 81; *Kelly Funeral Homes Ltd v Royal Bank of Canada* (1990) 72 D.L.R. (4th) 276; *Don Bodkin Leasing Ltd v Toronto-Dominion Bank* (1998) 40 O.R. (3d) 262. See also Bills of Exchange Act 1985, s.48 (Canada) and Bills of Exchange Act No.34 of 1964, s.72B (South Africa).

[32] SI 1999/2083, as amended by SI 2000/1186.

[33] *McKenzie v British Linen Co.* (1881) 6 App. Cas. 82, 99.

[34] *Bowstead and Reynolds on Agency* (17th ed.), § 2–061, citing *Keighley, Maxsted & Co. v Durant* [1901] A.C. 240, 247. cf. *Imperial Bank of Canada v Begley* [1936] 2 All E.R. 367, 374.

[35] *Newell v Royal Bank of Canada* (1997) 147 D.L.R. (4th) 268, 272.

[36] *Saunderson v Griffiths* (1826) 5 B. & C. 909, 913, 915; *Jones v Hope* (1880) 3 T.L.R. 247n., 251.

[37] *Kelner v Baxter* (1866) L.R. 2 C.P. 174.

[38] See *Bowstead and Reynolds on Agency* (17th ed.), § 2–060.

[39] *Bowstead and Reynolds on Agency* (17th ed.), § 2–070.

[40] *Bowstead and Reynolds on Agency* (17th ed.), § 2–067; *Aotearoa International Ltd v Westpac Banking Corp.* [1984] 2 N.Z.L.R. 34. cf. *Morison v London County and Westminster Bank Ltd* [1914] 3 K.B. 356 (Illustration 1); *London Intercontinental Trust Ltd v Barclays Bank Ltd* [1980] 1 Lloyd's Rep. 241, 249.

[41] *Bowstead and Reynolds on Agency* (17th ed.), § 2–070.

nevertheless approves the transaction or the breach of mandate, or elects to treat the transaction as valid.[42]

**Adoption of forged signature.** A forgery cannot be ratified.[43] A forger  **3–088** does not act, and does not purport to act, on behalf of the person whose name he forges and there is, therefore, nothing on which ratification can be grounded. This rule has, however, been criticised as being based on "arid logic"[44] and it has further been asserted[45] that the leading case, *Brook v Hook*,[46] was in fact decided on the ground that the acceptance of responsibility for the forged signature was, in the circumstances of the case, illegal. The justification for the rule does, nevertheless, appear to be correct. In *Greenwood v Martins Bank Ltd*,[47] Scrutton L.J. in the Court of Appeal accepted the proposition that a forgery could not be ratified, but went on to state[48]:

> "A forgery can however be adopted. The supposed signer may say, 'I will recognize this signature as my own; you may debit my account with these cheques', and in that case the Bank which has acted on this statement could successfully object to the customer's endeavouring to withdraw his adoption."

It is, however, uncertain whether the adoption of a forged signature is to be treated as a promise requiring consideration,[49] or as an example of estoppel by express representation,[50] or as an independent principle akin to ratification.

**Contributory negligence.** By section 11(1) of the Torts (Interference  **3–089** with Goods) Act 1977 "contributory negligence is no defence in proceedings founded on conversion, or on intentional trespass to goods". It is to be noted that the subsection does not refer to "wrongful interference" or

---

[42] *London Intercontinental Trust Ltd v Barclays Bank Ltd* [1980] 1 Lloyd's Rep. 241 (Illustration 13). *cf. Limpgrange Ltd v BCCI, S.A.* [1986] Fin.L.R. 36.

[43] *Brook v Hook* (1871) L.R. 6 Ex. 89; *Greenwood v Martin's Bank Ltd* [1932] 1 K.B. 371, 378–379 (affirmed [1933] A.C. 51); *Imperial Bank of Canada v Begley* [1936] 2 All E.R. 367, 374–375; *Rowe v B. & R. Nominees Pty Ltd* [1964] V.R. 477. Contrast *McKenzie v British Linen Co.* (1881) 6 App. Cas. 82, 99.

[44] Chalmers (11th ed.), p.75. See also Atiyah, *Vicarious Liability in the Law of Torts* (1967), p.315.

[45] See *Scott v Bank of New Brunswick* (1894) 23 S.C.R. 227.

[46] (1871) L.R. 6 Ex. 89 (Illustration 15).

[47] [1932] 1 K.B. 371 (affirmed [1933] A.C. 51) (Illustration 1).

[48] At 379. Contrast *Brook v Hook* (1871) L.R. 6 Ex. 89.

[49] *Greenwood v Martin's Bank Ltd* [1933] A.C. 51, 57. A forged signature cannot be adopted if the consideration for accepting responsibility for the forgery is an agreement not to prosecute the forger; such consideration is unlawful as being contrary to public policy: *Brook v Hook* (1871) L.R. 6 Ex. 89; *Newell v Royal Bank of Canada* (1997) 147 D.L.R. (4th) 268. But see *Chitty on Contracts* (29th ed.), Vol.I, § 16–035.

[50] See above, para.3–081, and *Leach v Buchanan* (1802) 4 Esp. 226 (Illustration 10).

"wrongful interference with goods" as defined in section 1 of the 1977 Act, and that "conversion" is broadly expressed without the reference to "goods", so that the restrictive interpretation of "goods" in section 14 does not appear to be applicable.[51] In consequence, contributory negligence cannot be raised as a defence to an action by the true owner in conversion[52] or in restitution.[53] However, section 47 of the Banking Act 1979 provides:

> "In any circumstances in which proof of absence of negligence on the part of a banker would be a defence in proceedings by reason of section 4 of the Cheques Act 1957, a defence of contributory negligence shall also be available to the banker notwithstanding the provisions of section 11(1) of the Torts (Interference with Goods) Act 1977."[54]

Section 4 of the Cheques Act 1957 is limited to the collection by a banker for a customer of cheques and certain other analogous instruments.[55]

On the other hand, where a customer seeks to charge his banker with breach of a duty of care in paying without inquiry a cheque drawn on the customer's account when the banker knew or ought reasonably to have concluded that the account was being operated in fraud of the customer,[56] there is some authority for the view that contributory negligence can be raised as a partial or total defence to the customer's claim. In *Lipkin Gorman v Karpnale Ltd*,[57] a partner in a firm of solicitors, with authority to draw cheques by his sole signature on the firm's client account, withdrew from the account and misappropriated over a period of time large sums in order to fund his gambling activities. In an action by the firm against the drawee bank based on breach by the bank of its contractual duty of care and as constructive trustee, Alliott J. (at first instance)[58] found the

---

[51] *Current Law Statutes Annotated*, 32/10–11 (1977), cited by Alliott J. in *Lipkin Gorman v Karpnale Ltd* [1987] 1 W.L.R. 987, 995. In any event, the definition of "goods" in s.14(1) would appear wide enough to cover a negotiable instrument.

[52] *Lipkin Gorman v Karpnale Ltd* [1987] 1 W.L.R. 987, 995, 996, [1989] 1 W.L.R. 1340, 1386 (s.29, Illustration 7). (This point did not arise on appeal in that case: [1991] 2 A.C. 548). See also *Wilton v Commonwealth Trading Bank of Australia* [1973] 2 N.Z.W.L.R. 644; *Day v Bank of New South Wales* (1978) 19 A.L.R. 32, 42; *Australian Guarantee Corp. v Commissioners of the State Bank of Victoria* [1989] V.R. 617; *Boma Manufacturing Ltd v Canadian Imperial Bank of Commerce* (1997) 140 D.L.R. (4th) 463, 477. Contrast *Lumsden & Co. v London Trustee Savings Bank* [1971] 1 Lloyd's Rep. 114. (Cheques Act 1957, s.4, Illustration 20); *Dairy Containers Ltd v NZI Bank Ltd* [1995] 2 N.Z.L.R. 30, 109–114.

[53] *Kelly v Solari* (1841) 9 M. & W. 54; *Dextra Bank & Trust Co. Ltd v Bank of Jamaica* [2002] 1 All E.R. (Comm) 193 at [40–46].

[54] See below, para.17–057.

[55] See below, para.17–063.

[56] See below, para.13–062 (s.75).

[57] [1987] 1 W.L.R. 987; [1989] 1 W.L.R. 1340; [1991] 2 A.C. 548 (s.75, Illustration 13). Contrast *Lewes Sanitary Laundry Co. Ltd v Barclay, Beavan & Co. Ltd* (1906) 11 Com.Cas. 255.

[58] [1987] 1 W.L.R. 987.

bank liable, but held that the defence of contributory negligence was available to the bank.[59] He acquitted the firm of any negligence in respect of its accounting system.[60] Nevertheless, it had come to the notice of another partner in the firm that the partner in question had fraudulently claimed a disproportionate amount by way of travelling expenses. Yet no steps were taken by the firm to cancel or curtail his signing powers. On this ground, Alliott J. held that, from the time of this discovery, the firm had "no one to blame but themselves for their loss, and it would be inequitable to grant them any relief".[61] On appeal to the Court of Appeal,[62] it was held that the bank was not in breach of any duty of care to its customer (the firm), nor had it acted in such a way as to render itself liable as constructive trustee. The question of contributory negligence did not, therefore, arise. But May L.J. was of the opinion[63] that the judge's decision on this point was correct, because:

> "authorities such as *Greenwood v Martin's Bank Ltd*[64] and *Tai Hing Cotton Mill Ltd v Liu Chong Hing Bank Ltd*[65] make it clear that it is an implied term of the relationship between a banker and his customer at least in relation to the operation of a current account that the latter will notify the former as soon as he learns that the account is being operated by a dishonest person".

However, it has subsequently been held that contributory negligence is at most a partial defence, and not a total defence.[66] The loss by the firm of any right to complain of the negligence of the bank is therefore better explained as an instance of estoppel[67] or as a case where, from the time the partner was discovered to be fraudulent, the firm's own conduct was the effective cause of its loss.[68]

## ILLUSTRATIONS

1. One Abbott, who is the manager of an insurance broker's business, **3–090** is authorised by the broker to draw cheques "per pro." for the purposes

---

[59] [1987] 1 W.L.R. 987, 997.
[60] [1987] 1 W.L.R. 987, 1014–1018.
[61] [1987] 1 W.L.R. 987, 1019.
[62] [1989] 1 W.L.R. 1340. The claim against the bank was not pursued in the House of Lords: [1991] 2 A.C. 548.
[63] [1989] 1 W.L.R. 1340, 1360.
[64] [1933] A.C. 51; above, para.3–081.
[65] [1986] A.C. 80; above, para.3–086.
[66] *Pitts v Hunt* [1991] 1 Q.B. 24.
[67] See above, para.3–079.
[68] [1987] 1 W.L.R. 987, 1019.

of that business; and the broker gives directions to his bank to honour cheques so drawn. Abbott opens a private banking account for his own purposes with the defendant bank and over a period of four years pays into that account 50 cheques which he has drawn and, when necessary, indorsed by means of the "per pro." signature in fraud of the broker. The cheques are collected in good faith and in the ordinary way by the defendant bank, which places the proceeds to the credit of Abbott's account. The broker sues the defendant bank for the amount of the cheques as damages for conversion or, alternatively, as money had and received. The action fails. The cheques signed by Abbott "per pro." as he was authorised to do, were not rendered forgeries by the fact that they were drawn for purposes outside and in fraud of that authority. With respect to cheques collected after the first year or two, the defendant bank could rely on the protection of section 82 of the 1882 Act[69]: the bank was not negligent in assuming that, having collected cheques for Abbott during the first year or two without protest from the broker, Abbott was acting within his authority.[70] The signature "per pro." did not operate, by virtue of section 25 of the Act, as notice that Abbott had but a limited authority to sign, since section 25 applied only to rights and liabilities while an instrument was current and not (as in the case of section 82) to rights to the proceeds arising when an instrument was discharged by payment.[71] With respect to cheques collected during the first year or two, even if the defendant bank had been negligent, the broker had ratified the acts of Abbott. At the end of this period, he had either himself or through his accountants become aware of the fraud and arranged to treat the cheques for the purposes of the firm's accounts as drawn upon the broker's current account with his bank and as items to be debited to Abbott in the accounts of the firm.[72]

2. The defendant company has by its memorandum of association power to draw and indorse bills of exchange, and by its articles of association the directors are empowered to determine who shall be entitled to draw and indorse bills on the company's behalf. The company employs, as manager of its Manchester branch, one Clarke, who has no authority on behalf of the company to draw or indorse bills of exchange. In fraud of the company, Clarke draws seven bills on behalf of the company "S. Clarke, Manchester Manager" to drawer's order. These bills are accepted by C.W. Ltd, a company in which Clarke has an interest, and are indorsed by him on behalf of the defendant company in like manner.

---

[69] See now s.4 of the Cheques Act 1957.
[70] cf. *Lloyd's Bank Ltd v E.B. Savory & Co.* [1933] A.C. 201, 230.
[71] This view was subsequently disapproved in *Midland Bank Ltd v Reckitt* [1933] A.C. 1, 16.
[72] *Morison v London County & Westminster Bank Ltd* [1914] 3 K.B. 356.

Clarke sends the bills to T in Germany in payment for goods supplied by T to C.W. Ltd and they are discounted by the claimants, who take them without notice of the fraud and want of authority. Upon dishonour of the bills by C.W. Ltd, the claimants sue the defendant company on them as drawers. The defendant company is not liable. The claimants did not know of the powers of delegation in the company's articles and so were not entitled to rely on the exercise of those powers; and, the bills being forgeries, they were not entitled to invoke the principle that they were not bound to enquire into the internal management of the company. Even if they had known of the power of delegation, they could not assume that a branch manager had ostensible authority to draw and indorse bills of exchange. There was further, nothing in the conduct of the defendant company to preclude it from setting up the forgery or want of authority.[73]

3. The claimant and the first defendant open a joint account with the second defendant bank on the terms of the bank's standard form of mandate which authorises the bank to debit to the account cheques signed by both of them and which further provides that their liability to the bank is joint and several. The claimant pays into the account £2,000 which is intended to be used for such purposes as the claimant and the first defendant shall mutually agree. The first defendant forges the claimant's signature to five cheques (totalling £763 5s. 1d.) which are honoured by the bank, and the first defendant misappropriates the proceeds. No partnership exists between the claimant and the first defendant. An injunction is granted ordering the bank to credit the joint account with the amount paid out on the forged cheques. The bank, by mandate, has agreed with the account holders jointly that it will honour any cheques signed by them jointly. But it has also separately agreed with each of the account holders severally that it will not honour any cheques unless he has signed them. The bank is liable to the claimant for breach of that separate agreement. An injunction is also granted ordering the first defendant to authorise the bank to honour any cheque drawn on the joint account by the claimant alone.[74-79]

4. The claimant and her husband deposit funds in a joint account with the defendant bank on terms of a written mandate that payments out of the account against cheques or other payment orders are to be made only if signed by both account holders. In breach of this mandate the bank transfers funds from the joint account to the use of the husband on instructions signed by him alone. The claimant, suing alone, is entitled to

**3–091**

---

[73] *Kreditbank Cassel GmbH v Schenkers Ltd* [1927] 1 K.B. 826.
[74-79] *Jackson v White and Midland Bank Ltd* [1967] 2 Lloyd's Rep. 68.

damages equal to her half-share in the funds so transferred. Her claim is not defeated by her failure to join her husband as a party to the action. In third party proceedings against the husband, the bank is entitled to be indemnified by him on the ground that he had deliberately misled the bank into believing that he had the claimant's authority to give instructions on her behalf.[80]

5. The defendant accepts a bill drawn on him by C payable to "Henry Davis, or order". The bill gets into the hands of a Henry Davis other than the one in whose favour it is drawn. That person indorses the bill and delivers it to the claimant, who takes it for value and without knowledge of the forgery. Evidence is admissible to prove that the bill was not indorsed by the payee and in consequence that no title has been derived by the claimant through the medium of the forged indorsement.[81]

6. G & Co. draw a bill of exchange for £500 on the claimants payable to Heyland or order. The bill gets into the hands of Heyland's agent, one Hitchcock, who forges Heyland's indorsement and transfers the bill for value to the defendant, the defendant being ignorant of the forgery. The defendant obtains the claimants' acceptance of the bill. After the bill arrives at maturity, the defendant becomes aware of the forgery and obtains a genuine indorsement from Heyland in consideration that Heyland be paid one-half of the amount received on the bill. The defendant brings an action against the claimants to recover the amount of the bill. The original (forged) indorsement confers no title on the defendant, even though he took the bill in good faith and for value. Nor does the subsequent (genuine) indorsement alter the case, since it was made after the bill was overdue. The claimants are therefore entitled in equity to an order to have the bill delivered up to be cancelled, and to an injunction to restrain the defendant's action on the bill.[82]

3–092    7. The defendant makes a promissory note payable to the claimant or order, and delivers it to the claimant. The note is stolen by W, a clerk employed by the claimant, who forges the claimant's indorsement. The note is transferred to a person who takes it in good faith and for value, and that person presents it for payment to the defendant's bankers. The bankers pay the note, debit the account of the defendant with the sum paid and hand over the note to the defendant. The claimant demands the note from the defendant, who refuses to give it up. The claimant can maintain an action in conversion against the defendant for the value of

[80] *Catlin v Cyprus Finance Corp. (London) Ltd* [1983] Q.B. 759.
[81] *Mead v Young* (1790) 4 T.R. 28.
[82] *Esdaile v La Nauze* (1835) 1 Y. & C. 394.

the note. No title to the note can be derived through the forged indorsement. It is no defence that six weeks elapsed before the claimant discovered and gave the defendant notice of the loss of the note.[83]

8. T, an agent of the claimant insurance company, draws on the claimant company a bill for £5,000 payable to the order of certain named payees, and hands the bill to the payees' solicitor. The solicitor forges the payees' indorsements on the bill, sends the bill to a bank in Stockport and receives value for it. The Stockport bank indorses the bill to J & L (London Bankers) and receives the money on account of the Stockport bank. J & L present the bill so indorsed to the claimant company for acceptance, and the claimant company accept the bill payable at their bankers, the defendants. On maturity, the defendants pay the bill to J & L and debit the claimant company's account. The defendants cannot maintain the debit to the account. In the absence of estoppel, a banker cannot debit his customer with a payment made to one who claims through a forged indorsement and so cannot give a valid discharge for the bill.[84]

9. The claimant draws a cheque on his bankers, M & Co., payable to the order of P and crosses it "L & C Bank". The cheque is sent to P, from whom it is stolen. The thief forges P's indorsement. The cheque ultimately passes to the defendant, who takes it in good faith, for value and without notice of the forgery. The defendant delivers it to his country bankers for presentation, and they in turn send it to their London agents. The London agents present the cheque to and receive payment from M & Co., who either do not observe or disregard the crossing "L & C Bank". The claimant brings an action against the defendant for the amount of the cheque as money had and received. Although the claimant could have disavowed the payment of the cheque and thrown the loss on his bankers, M & Co., who had paid the wrong bankers, he can nevertheless recover the amount of the cheque from the defendant, who acquired no title to the cheque through the forged indorsement.[85]

10. The defendant's acceptance to a bill of exchange is forged by the   **3–093** drawer. The bill is indorsed and transferred to the claimant who takes it in good faith. Before taking the bill, the claimant, not having perfect knowledge of the defendant's handwriting, sends a person with the bill to enquire whether the acceptance is in the defendant's handwriting, and is assured by the defendant that it is and that the bill will be duly paid.

---

[83] *Johnson v Windle* (1836) 3 Bing. N.C. 225.
[84] *Robarts v Tucker* (1851) 16 Q.B. 560.
[85] *Bobbett v Pinkett* (1876) 1 Ex.D. 368.

Having so accredited the bill, and induced the claimant to take it, the defendant is liable for the payment of it.[86]

11. G's wife forges his signature as drawer to a number of cheques, obtains payment from the drawee bank and uses the proceeds for her own purposes. G becomes aware of the forgeries but is persuaded to say nothing by his wife. He keeps silence for eight months. When eventually he decides to disclose the forgeries, his wife commits suicide. G brings an action against the drawee bank to recover the sums paid out of his account on the forged cheques. His action fails. G was under a duty to disclose the forgeries to the bank when he became aware of them so as to enable the bank to take steps to recover the money paid out. Through his failure to fulfil that duty, the bank lost its right to sue G and his wife for the tort committed by the wife, since (as the law then was) the bank's right of action abated on her death. G is therefore estopped from claiming the amounts paid out.[87]

12. A company is a customer of three banks and maintains with each of them a current account. The banks' rules or standard terms, incorporated in the company's contracts with the banks, include a requirement that the company shall notify the banks within a specified time of any errors in its monthly bank statements which will otherwise be deemed to be correct. Over a period of four years the banks honour by payment on presentation some 300 cheques totalling approximately HK $5.5 million which on their face appear to have been drawn by the company and to bear the signature of one Chen, the company's managing director, who is one of the company's authorised signatories to its cheques. In each instance the company's bank account is debited with the amount of the cheque. The signature of Chen on the cheques has been forged by an accounts clerk employed by the company, Leung Wing Ling. The forgeries are not known to the company because the company's system of internal financial control is unsound and, from the point of view of preventing or detecting fraud, inadequate. Upon discovering the forgeries, the company immediately institutes proceedings against the banks to recover the amounts paid out on the forged cheques. The banks are liable. The company owes no duty to the banks, whether in contract or in tort, to exercise such precautions as a reasonable customer in its position would take to prevent forged cheques being presented to the banks. And the express terms of the company's contracts with the banks are not sufficiently clear and unambiguous to impose upon the company a contractual obligation to examine its bank statements and to accept them as

[86] *Leach v Buchanan* (1802) 4 Esp. 226.
[87] *Greenwood v Martins Bank Ltd* [1933] A.C. 51.

accurately stating the debits if not challenged within the stipulated time or to estop the company from claiming that the accounts have been wrongly debited.[88]

13. The claimant company is a customer of the defendant bank. **3–094** Between 1993 and 1996 cheques totalling £172,229 drawn on the company's account are paid by the bank, the signatures on which are alleged to be forgeries. The company sues the bank for money had and received. The bank pleads in its defence that the company had constructive knowledge of the forgeries in that: (i) the company was alerted to need for inquiries into the reason why its overdraft was so large, (ii) there could not have been any vouchers to support the forged cheques, and (iii) the company failed to carry out investigations which would have revealed the forgeries. This part of the bank's defence is struck out. Constructive knowledge, that is, means of knowledge, is insufficient to amount to a defence to the claim.[89]

14. The defendant bank is authorised to honour cheques drawn on behalf of the claimant company provided that such cheques are signed by one director and the company secretary or by any two directors. A director of the company is authorised to transfer certain moneys for investment from the company to a firm of stockbrokers associated with the company. He does so by two cheques drawn on the company's account by his sole signature, which cheques are honoured by the bank notwithstanding the mandate requiring two signatures. The firm of stockbrokers gets into financial difficulties and goes into liquidation, and the company claims against the bank that its account has been wrongfully debited with the amounts paid on the cheques. The company's claim fails. Since the director was authorised to transfer the money by giving an instruction to the bank (whether by cheque or otherwise) the cheques were not invalidated by the fact that they bore his signature alone. The evidence further showed that the board of the company had subsequently approved the transaction as a whole, that the secretary of the company had authorised and ratified the payments by cheques bearing only one signature, and that the company had pursued its claim against the Stock Exchange and in the liquidation on the basis that the transactions were valid. The company had therefore ratified the payments. The company was also estopped from claiming the amounts of the two debits since it failed to notify the bank that the cheques had been drawn contrary to the mandate and this amounted to a representation that the cheques had been

---

[88] *Tai Hing Cotton Mill Ltd v Liu Chong Hing Bank Ltd* [1986] A.C. 80.
[89] *Price Meats Ltd v Barclays Bank plc* [2000] 2 All E.R. (Comm) 346.

validly drawn, which representation had been acted upon by the bank.[90]

15. The defendant's name is forged by J to a joint and several promissory note for £20 which purports to be made in favour of the claimant by the defendant and J. While the note is still current, the claimant encounters the defendant, who denies his signature to the note. Upon the claimant threatening to prosecute J for forgery, in order to prevent this, the defendant (while still protesting that the alleged signature is forged) gives the claimant a memorandum which states: "I hold myself responsible for a bill for £20, bearing my signature and J's, in favour of [the claimant]." The memorandum cannot be construed as a ratification, as a forgery cannot be ratified. It is an agreement by the defendant to treat the note as his own in consideration that the claimant will not prosecute J, and as such is void as founded on an illegal consideration.[91]

## Procuration signatures

3–095
**25. A signature by procuration operates as notice that the agent has but a limited authority to sign, and the principal is only bound by such signature if the agent in so signing was acting within the actual limits of his authority.**

Comparison
UCC: § 3–402.

### COMMENT

3–096
**Notice of limited authority to sign.** No act done by an agent in excess of his actual authority is binding on the principal with respect to persons having notice that in doing the act the agent is exceeding his authority.[92] The effect of section 25 "is to give notice of limited authority on the face of the document, and this operates as and when the document is negotiated or delivered".[93] The principal is only bound by a signature by procuration if the agent in so signing was acting within the actual limits

---

[90] *London Intercontinental Trust Ltd v Barclays Bank Ltd* [1980] 1 Lloyd's Rep. 241.
[91] *Brook v Hook* (1871) L.R. 6 Ex. 89.
[92] *Bowstead and Reynolds on Agency* (17th ed.), § 8–051.
[93] *Midland Bank Ltd v Reckitt* [1933] A.C. 1, 16, *per* Lord Atkin.

of his authority.[94] The section appears to be declaratory of the common law.[95] In *Attwood v Munnings*,[96] Bayley J. said[97]:

"This was an action on an acceptance importing to be by procuration, and, therefore, any person taking the bill would know that he had not the security of the acceptor's signature, but of the party professing to act for him in pursuance of an authority from him. A person taking such a bill, ought to exercise due caution, for he must take it upon the credit of the party who assumes the authority to accept, and it would be only reasonable prudence to require the production of that authority."

It follows that even a holder in due course of a bill so signed cannot enforce it against the principal if the agent has exceeded his authority.[98]

It is not, however, clear whether all forms of representative signature fall within the section. In an Irish case,[99] decided before the Act, Pigott C.B. stated that an acceptance "for Richardson & Son, Thomas Popple" was not equivalent in the law merchant to the form "per pro. Richardson & Son, Thomas Popple". The former expression did not, like the latter, import a special and limited authority, or put the drawer of the bill on discovery whether the agent had exceeded his authority. Dicta in subsequent English cases[1] also support the view that the section is confined to cases where the form of signature shows a special and limited authority as "per procuration" or "under power of attorney," and excludes cases of general authority as "A for B" (and, presumably, signatures "on behalf of" or "pro" the principal or "per" or "by" the agent).

*Byles*[2] further argues that section 25 falls between section 24, which speaks of unauthorised signatures, and section 26, which concerns signatures for or on behalf of a principal or in a representative character: "If

---

[94] *Attwood v Munnings* (1827) 7 B. & C. 727 (Illustration 1); *Alexander v Makenzie* (1848) 6 C.B. 76; *Balfour v Ernest* (1859) 5 C.B.N.S. 601, 627; *Stagg v Elliott* (1862) 12 C.B., N.S. 373; *Jonmenjoy Condo v Watson* (1884) 9 App. Cas. 561 (Illustration 2); *Employers' Liability Assurance Corp. v Skipper* (1887) 4 T.L.R. 55, 56; *Re Cunningham & Co. Ltd* (1887) 36 Ch.D. 532 (Illustration 3); *Reid v Rigby & Co.* [1894] 2 Q.B. 40, 42 (Illustration 7); *Gompertz v Cook* (1903) 20 T.L.R. 106; *Morison v Kemp* (1912) 29 T.L.R. 70 (Illustration 4); *Morison v London County & Westminster Bank Ltd* [1914] 3 K.B. 356, 367; *Alexander Stewart of Dundee Ltd v Westminster Bank Ltd* [1926] W.N. 271; *Midland Bank Ltd v Reckitt* [1933] A.C. 1 (Illustration 9); *Aotearoa International Ltd v Westpac Banking Corp.* [1984] 2 N.Z.L.R. 34.

[95] *Morison v London County & Westminster Bank Ltd* [1914] 3 K.B. 356 at 367.

[96] (1827) 7 B. & C. 278 (Illustration 1).

[97] (1827) 7 B. & C. 278 at 283.

[98] *Morison v London County & Westminster Bank Ltd* [1914] 3 K.B. 356 at 367; *Midland Bank Ltd v Reckitt* [1933] A.C. 1.

[99] *O'Reilly v Richardson* (1865) 17 I.C.L.R. 74.

[1] *McDonald (Gerald) & Co. v Nash & Co.* [1922] W.N. 272 (Scrutton L.J.), reversed [1924] A.C. 625; *Alexander Stewart of Dundee Ltd v Westminster Bank Ltd* [1926] W.N. 126 (Rowlatt J.) and [1926] W.N. 271 (Atkin L.J.).

[2] 27th ed., p.64.

section 25 had been intended to apply to all representative signatures, there would have been no need to refer to signatures by procuration and, accordingly, it is permissible to assume that some special authority was intended."[3] On the other hand, Chalmers considered that "the distinction does not seem founded on any clear principle",[4] and there is no recent case where it has clearly been held that signatures "for" or "on behalf of" the principal lie outside the section. A narrow interpretation may, perhaps, be defended on the ground of practicality: that a holder without knowledge that the agent is exceeding his authority should be entitled to rely on the apparent authority of the agent and should not, save in the exceptional case of a signature "per pro." or "under power of attorney", be bound to enquire into the authority of the self-described agent.

3–097   Particular difficulties arise in the case of the signature of companies, since the company will normally only be bound if the instrument is signed in the name of or by or on behalf or on account of the company by a person acting under its authority.[5] In the case of cheques, for example, the agent usually signs "per pro.", the company, or signs "for" or "on behalf of" the company or "per" the agent, adding his official position to his name.[6] It seems clear that section 25 will apply to signatures "per pro." a company as in the case of a private individual,[7] but it is doubtful whether the other forms of representative signature would attract the application of the section.

The effect of the section may possibly be less extensive than would appear from a literal reading of its provisions. Certain cases[8] suggest that, if the person signing as agent has apparent authority to sign under the terms of the document or other mandate conferring authority, the production of which should have been required by the person relying on the signature, the principal will be bound. In *Bryant, Powis and Bryant Ltd v Banque de Peuple*,[9] Lord Macnaghten cited with approval a dictum in an American case[10] as follows:

> "Whenever the very act of the agent is authorized by the terms of the power, that is, whenever by comparing the act done by the agent with the words of the power, the act is in itself warranted by the terms used, such act is binding on the constituent, as to all persons dealing in good faith with the agent; such persons are not bound to

[3] *Byles* (27th ed.), p.64.
[4] *Chalmers* (9th ed.), p.91.
[5] Companies Act 1985, s.37; above, para.3–025. But see Companies Act 1985, s.36A, and s.91(2) of the 1882 Act.
[6] See above, para.3–025.
[7] cf. *Alexander Stewart of Dundee Ltd v Westminster Bank Ltd* [1926] W.N. 126, 271.
[8] See the cases cited in n.11, below.
[9] [1893] A.C. 170, 180.
[10] *President, etc., of the Westfield Bank v Cornen* (1867) 47 N.Y.R. 320, 322.

inquire into facts aliunde. The apparent authority is the real authority."

Thus, if the agent had authority to sign, but abused that authority for his own purposes, or failed to observe the conditions attached to its exercise, this would not affect the rights of a holder without knowledge.[11] However, in *Midland Bank Ltd v Reckitt*,[12] a solicitor fraudulently and in abuse of a power of attorney given to him by his client drew cheques on his client's account with a signature by procuration ("by his attorney"). He then paid these cheques into his own bank account with the defendant bank. Lord Atkin said[13]:

> "The bank never in fact asked for or saw the terms of the document [the power of attorney]; and, for my part, I venture to doubt whether in such circumstances they could ever rely on any other than an actual authority. Ostensible authority appears to be excluded when the party averring it cannot show that any appearance of authority other than the actual authority was ever displayed to him by the principal. He neither shows a representation nor that he relied on it."

In any event, if the person relying on the signature knows that the agent, though acting within his apparent authority, has abused that authority or failed to observe the conditions attached to its exercise, then he is not protected, since the agent has not even apparent authority so far as that person is concerned.[14]

If money is obtained from a third party by the unauthorised act of an agent and is applied for the benefit of the principal, the money so applied may be recovered by the third party, whether in equity or in restitution as money had and received to his use.[15]

**Criticism of section.** There appears to be no compelling reason why    3–098
signatures by procuration should be treated any differently from other representative signatures, or why they should uniquely exclude the rule

---

[11] *Re Land Credit Co.* (1869) 4 Ch.App. 460 (Illustration 5); *Bryant, Powis and Bryant Ltd v Banque de Peuple* [1893] A.C. 170 (Illustration 6). See also *Bank of Bengal v Macleod* (1849) 7 Moore P.C. 35; *Bank of Bengal v Fagan* (1849) 7 Moore P.C. 61; *Hambro v Burnand* (1904) 2 K.B. 10; *Morison v London County & Westminster Bank Ltd* [1914] 3 K.B. 356 (s.24, Illustration 1). Contrast *Morison v Kemp* [1912] 29 T.L.R. 70 (Illustration 4); *Kreditbank Cassel GmbH v Schenkers Ltd* [1927] 1 K.B. 826 (s.24, Illustration 2); *Midland Bank Ltd v Reckitt* [1933] A.C. 1 (Illustration 9).

[12] [1933] A.C. 1 (Illustration 9).

[13] [1933] A.C. 1 at 17.

[14] *Balfour v Ernest* (1859) 5 C.B., N.S. 601; *Jacobs v Morris* [1902] 1 Ch. 816; *John v Dodwell & Co. Ltd* [1918] A.C. 563; *Reckitt v Barnett, Pembroke & Slater Ltd* [1929] A.C. 176 (s.91, Illustration 3); *Reckitt v Nunburnholme* (1929) 45 T.L.R. 629.

[15] *Reid v Rigby & Co.* [1894] 2 Q.B. 40 (Illustration 7); *Reversion Fund & Insurance Co. v Maison Cosway Ltd* [1913] 1 K.B. 364; *Bowstead and Reynolds on Agency* (17th ed.), § 8–201.

that a person is bound by the acts of another done within his apparent (or ostensible) authority. There is much to be said for the view that the section should be repealed.[16]

3–099 **Protection of paying or collecting banker.** The fact that an indorsement is signed by procuration does not deprive a paying banker of the protection afforded by sections 60[17] and 80[18] of the 1882 Act or by section 1 of the Cheques Act 1957.[19] With respect to a collecting banker, it was at one time thought[20] that section 25 was independent of section 82 (now re-enacted and extended by section 4 of the Cheques Act 1957,[21] which provides protection for a collecting banker who acts without negligence) and that this section related only to liabilities on the instrument and did not apply to the proceeds of a cheque which had been paid and discharged. That view, however, was rejected in *Midland Bank Ltd v Reckitt*.[22] It is now clear that a signature by procuration is a matter which must be taken into account in determining whether or not a collecting banker has acted without negligence. However, the fact that the signature of the drawer or of an indorser is by procuration, will not of itself deprive the banker of protection on the ground that he has been negligent unless other suspicious circumstances are present,[23] *e.g.* payment of a cheque by an agent into his private account. As regards negligence on the part of a collecting banker, the distinction between signatures strictly "per pro." and other forms of representative signature is probably irrelevant.

3–100 **Liability of agent signing without authority.** A person who, without authority, signs the name of another person to a bill, either simply or by procuration signature, is not liable on the instrument, except (i) in the special case provided for by section 349 of the Companies Act 1985,[24] (ii) where the alleged principal is a company which has not been formed,[25] and (iii) possibly, where he signs on behalf of an alleged principal who is fictitious or non-existent.[26] The self-described agent will, however, be

---

[16] Report by the Review Committee on Banking Services Law and Practice (1989) Cm. 622, App.A, pp.228–229.
[17] *Charles v Blackwell* (1877) 2 C.P.D. 151 (Illustration 8); See below, para.8–043.
[18] See below, para.14–024. But s.80 refers to "negligence".
[19] See below, para.17–005.
[20] *Morison v London County & Westminster Bank Ltd* [1914] 3 K.B. 356, 367–368, 375, 382. (s.24, Illustration 1).
[21] See below, para.17–028.
[22] [1933] A.C. 1, 16 (Illustration 9).
[23] See below, para.17–043 (Cheques Act 1957, s.4).
[24] See above, para.3–026.
[25] See above, para.3–007.
[26] *Bowstead and Reynolds on Agency* (17th ed.), § 9–081. *cf.*, *Deloitte & Touche v Meramveliotakis* (2000) 50 O.R. (3d) 577.

liable in tort for deceit if fraud and damage can be proved,[27] or strictly liable for breach of warranty of authority.[28]

ILLUSTRATIONS

1. M, who carries on business on his own account and is also in **3–101** partnership with others, goes abroad. He gives his wife a power of attorney to accept bills in his name in respect of his private business. His wife accepts a bill in M's name in respect of the partnership business, signing it "per pro.". The bill is negotiated. M is not liable on the acceptance.[29]

2. The claimant brings an action in detinue to recover a Government of India Note made payable to his order. The note was indorsed to the defendant by the claimant's agent in the form "J.W.M., by his attorney A.D.M." in pledge for a private debt of the agent's, though this fact was not known to the defendant. On its true construction, the power of attorney does not include a power to pledge. The defendant acquires no title to the note.[30]

3. The manager in South Africa of an English company, in order to obtain a guarantee for the company's business, gives a note signed "for myself and in representation of the company". This not being necessary, or in the ordinary course of the company's business, the note is not binding on the company.[31]

4. A manager is authorised to draw cheques "per pro." for the purposes **3–102** of his employers' business as insurance brokers. He draws a cheque "per pro." his employers, making it payable to a bookmaker for his private

---

[27] *Polhill v Walter* (1832) 3 B & Ad. 114.
[28] *West London Commercial Bank Ltd v Kitson* (1883) 12 Q.B.D. 157, 161–162 (affirmed (1884) 13 Q.D. 360). See also *Collen v Wright* (1857) 7 E. & B. 301 (affirmed (1857) 8 E. & B. 647); *Starkey v Bank of England* [1903] A.C. 140; *Bowstead and Reynolds, op. cit.*, § 9–060. *cf. Beattie v Ebury* (1872) L.R. 7 H.L. 102: *Gowers v Lloyds and National Provincial Foreign Bank Ltd* [1938] 1 All E.R. 766.
[29] *Attwood v Munnings* (1827) 7 B. & C. 278.
[30] *Jonmenjoy Condo v Watson* (1884) 9 App. Cas. 561.
[31] *Re Cunningham & Co Ltd* (1887) 36 Ch.D. 532. *cf.* s.35A of the Companies Act 1985; above, para.3–006 (s.22).

betting losses. The bookmaker gets the cheque cashed. The employers can recover the money from the bookmaker.[32]

5. By a resolution of the directors, the chairman of a company is authorised to accept bills drawn on the company by L against the deposit of securities to a certain amount. He accepts a bill drawn by L, signing it "on behalf of" the company, and L in return deposits some securities, but not nearly to the specified amount. The bill is negotiated to a bona fide holder. The company is liable on the acceptance.[33]

6. Two promissory notes are made by S.W. & Co. payable to the order of the appellant company. The company gives D a power of attorney which, on its true construction, authorises D to indorse bills and notes on behalf of the company. D indorses the notes "per pro." in the name of the company and dishonestly for his own purposes pledges them to the respondent bank as security for a personal loan. The company is liable on the notes.[34]

3–103     7. A, a manager employed by the defendants, is authorised to draw cheques on the defendants' bank account for the purposes of their business, but is not authorised by them to borrow money. He borrows £20 from the claimant, giving as security a cheque drawn "per pro." the defendants. He uses the £20 to pay the defendants' workmen. The claimant cannot recover on the cheque. But since the money lent has found its way into the defendants' possession, and been employed for their benefit, he is entitled to recover it.[35]

8. S.K. is the agent of the claimant firm. He has authority to sell goods for the firm and to receive payment therefor by cash or cheque, but has no authority to indorse cheques on behalf of the firm. He receives from the defendants, in payment for goods supplied, two cheques drawn on the defendants' bankers payable to the firm or order. He indorses the cheques "S & Co. [the firm] per S.K., agent," receives payment from the defendants' bankers and misappropriates part of the proceeds of the cheques. Payment by the bankers is within the protection of 16 & 17 Vict. c.59,[36]

---

[32] *Morison v Kemp* (1912) 29 T.L.R. 70.
[33] *Re Land Credit Co.* (1869) L.R. 4 Ch.App. 460.
[34] *Bryant, Powis and Bryant Ltd v Banque de Peuple* [1893] A.C. 170. But see above, para.3–097.
[35] *Reid v Rigby & Co.* [1894] Q.B. 40.
[36] Stamp Act 1853; below, para.8–045.

section 19, and the firm cannot maintain an action against the defendants either for the price of the goods or in respect of the cheques.[37]

9. Reckitt authorises T, his solicitor, by a power of attorney to draw cheques on his bank account with Barclays Bank and to apply the moneys for his purposes. T fraudulently and for his own purposes draws a number of cheques on the account, signing them "Harold G. Reckitt by T his attorney". T pays these cheques into his own account with the defendant bank, with whom he has an overdraft. In an action against the defendant bank for conversion of the cheques, the bank claims to be a holder in due course. It also seeks to rely on the protection afforded by section 82 of the 1882 Act, namely that it has in good faith and without negligence received payment for a customer of a crossed cheque.[38] The bank is a holder for value of the cheques, but section 25 defeats the bank's right to be considered a holder in due course. The protection of section 82 is denied, because the form of the cheques gave the bank notice that the money might not be the money of T and the bank was negligent in making no inquiry as to T's authority to make the payments into his own account.[39]

**Person signing as agent or in representative capacity**

26. **(1) Where a person signs a bill as drawer, indorser, or acceptor, and adds words to his signature, indicating that he signs for or on behalf of a principal, or in a representative character, he is not personally liable thereon; but the mere addition to his signature of words describing him as an agent, or as filling a representative character, does not exempt him from personal liability.**    3–104

    **(2) In determining whether a signature on a bill is that of the principal or that of the agent by whose hand it is written, the construction most favourable to the validity of the instrument shall be adopted.**

| Definitions | Comparison |
|---|---|
| "bill": s.2. | UCC: § 3–402. |
| "person": s.2. | ULB: arts 7, 8. |
| "written": s.2. | ULC: arts 10, 11. |
| | UNB: arts 26, 36. |

---

[37] *Charles v Blackwell* (1877) 2 C.P.D. 151.
[38] See now s.4 of the Cheques Act 1957; below, para.17–043.
[39] *Midland Bank Ltd v Reckitt* [1933] A.C. 1.

Comment

**3–105**      **Subsection (1): signature as agent.** Chalmers stated: "This section was re-drafted in committee, and perhaps somewhat modifies the rigour of the common law rule. At any rate, the older cases must be examined carefully with the words of the section."[40] Subsection (1) may, however, accurately have embodied the common law.[41] It has always been the case that, if an agent signs a bill or note, and adds words to his signature, indicating that he signs for or on behalf of a principal, or in a representative character, such as "per pro.", "for" or "on behalf of" the principal or "per" or "by" the agent, he is not personally liable on the instrument.[42] On the other hand, an agent who signs a bill in his own name only, without naming his principal, will incur personal liability even though he is known to be signing as agent[43] and even though he adds words to his signature indicating that he is signing as agent.[44] Further, even if he names his principal, words added to his signature such as "agent", "director", "secretary", "chairman", "manager", "trustee", "executor" or "receiver" have been treated merely as descriptive—a *designatio personae*—and so do not exempt him from personal liability.[45] In the words of Lord Ellenborough[46]:

> "Is it not a universal rule that a man who puts his name to a bill of exchange thereby makes himself personally liable, unless he states upon the face of the bill that he subscribes it for another, or by procuration of another, which are words of exclusion? Unless he says plainly, 'I am the mere scribe,' he becomes liable."

Nevertheless, the imposition of personal liability on the agent is applied less rigorously today than in the earlier cases. The main problem

---

[40] 9th ed., p.94.

[41] *Falconbridge* (7th ed.), p.599n. See *Dutton v Marsh* (1871) L.R. 6 Q.B. 361, 364.

[42] *Lindus v Melrose* (1857) 2 H & N. 293; (1858) 3 H. & N. 177 (Illustration 7); *Alexander v Sizer* (1869) L.R. 4 Ex. 102 (Illustration 8).

[43] *Leadbitter v Farrow* (1816) 5 M. & S. 345 (s.23, Illustration 2).

[44] *Thomas v Bishop* (1734) 2 Stra. 955 ("per").

[45] *Eaton v Bell* (1821) 5 B. & Ald. 34; *Rew v Pettet* (1834) 1 A. & E. 196 *(Illustration 2)*; *Penkivil v Connell* (1850) 5 Exch. 381; *Liverpool Borough Bank v Walker* (1859) 4 De G. & J. 24 (Illustration 3); *Price v Taylor* (1860) 5 H. & N. 540 (Illustration 4); *Bottomley v Fisher* (1862) 1 H. & C. 211; *Gray v Raper* (1866) L.R. 1 C.P. 694; *Courtauld v Saunders* (1867) 16 L.T. 562 (Illustration 5); *Dutton v Marsh* (1871) L.R. 6 Q.B. 361 (Illustration 1); *Imperial Land Building and Deposit Co. Ltd v Melvey* (1889) 6 W.N. 14; *Forwood v Mathews* (1893) 10 T.L.R 138 ("first minister of the Zanzibar Government"); *The Elmville (No.1)* [1904] P. 319; *Landes v Marcus* (1909) 25 T.L.R. 478; *Brebner v Henderson* 1925 S.C. 643; *Elliott v Bax-Ironside* [1925] 2 K.B. 301, 306, 307 (Illustration 11); *Kettle v Dunster and Wakefield* (1927) 43 T.L.R 770 (Illustration 6).

[46] *Leadbitter v Farrow* (1816) 5 M. & S. 345, 349.

which arises is where the name of the principal appears on the instrument, followed by the signature of his duly authorised agent, but omitting words indicating that he signs for or on behalf of a principal, or in a representative character. Typically the handwritten signature of the agent appears immediately below the printed or typewritten name of a company, whether or not accompanied by a description of the position held by the signatory, *e.g.* "director" or "secretary".[47] A strict application of the rule set out in subsection (1) would lead to the conclusion that the agent is personally liable.[48] But there are a number of cases to the contrary,[49] and in *Chapman v Smethurst*[50] Vaughan Williams L.J. remarked[51] that "[T]he decisions are bound to run rather near each other when the Court has to determine whether the company or the directors who sign a promissory note are liable upon it."

If an agent draws a bill or makes a promissory note in this form, it might be argued that the instrument is to be construed so as to create a joint liability on the part of the company and of the agent[52]: the company is liable as drawer or maker because its name has been placed on the instrument by an agent acting within his authority[53] and the agent is liable because he has signed the instrument as co-drawer or comaker. But it is difficult to believe that the parties truly intended to create a joint, or joint and several, liability, and the issue is normally whether the company or the agent is liable.[54] The modern tendency is to hold that the signature

[47] *i.e.* "as *filling* a representative character".
[48] *Dutton v Marsh* (1871) L.R. 6 Q.B. 361 (Illustration 1); *Landes v Marcus* (1909) 25 T.L.R. 478; *Elliot v Bax-Ironside* [1925] 2 K.B. 301, 306, 307 (Illustration 11); *Kettle v Dunster and Wakefield* (1927) 43 T.L.R. 770 (Illustration 6). See also *Locza v Ruthenian Farmers Co-operative Co.* (1922) 68 D.L.R. 535; *De Beer v Diesel and Electrical Engineering Co.* 1960 (3) S.A. 89; *Tsuida and Halkett Bay Logging Co. Ltd v Logan Mayhew Ltd* (1961) 28 D.L.R. (2d) 156; *Alliston Creamery v Grosdanoff* (1962) 34 D.L.R. (2d) 189; *Beaver Lumber Co. Ltd v Denis and Denis Sawmills Ltd* (1963) 41 W.W.R. 570; *Glatt v Ritt* (1973) 34 D.L.R. (3d) 295; *Bank of Nova Scotia v Radocsay* (1981) 125 D.L.R. (3d) 651; *Scania South Africa (Pty) Ltd v Smit* 2003 (1) S.A. 457.
[49] *Owen (D.) & Co. v Cronk* [1895] 1 Q.B. 265, 273 (Illustration 6, note); *Chapman v Smethurst* [1909] 1 K.B. 927 (Illustration 9); *Elliott v Bax-Ironside* [1925] 2 K.B. 30 (s.17, Illustration 7); *Britannia Electric Lamp Works Ltd v Mandler (D.) & Co.* [1939] 2 K.B. 129 (s.87, Illustration 3); *Bondina Ltd v Rollaway Shower Blinds Ltd* [1986] 1 W.L.R. 517 (Illustration 10). See also *Amalgamated Handwork Manufacturers Co. v Cole* [1935] V.L.R. 103; *Electrical Equipment of Australia Ltd v Peters* [1957] S.R. (N.S.W.) 361; *H.B. Etlin & Co. Ltd v Asselstyne* (1962) 34 D.L.R. (2d) 191; *Albert Pearl Management Ltd v J.D.F. Builders Ltd* (1972) 31 D.L.R. (3d) 690, varied (1975) 49 D.L.R. (3d) 422; *Medic v Taylor* (1976) 59 D.L.R. (3d) 321; *Allprint Co. Ltd v Irwin* (1982) 136 D.L.R. (3d) 587; *Schmidt v Jack Brillard Printing Services CC* 2000 (3) S.A. 824.
[50] [1909] 1 K.B. 927.
[51] [1909] 1 K.B. 927 at 929.
[52] *Mauch v Birt* (1964) 45 D.L.R. (2d) 187. *cf. Sniderman v McGarry* (1966) 60 D.L.R. (2d) 401.
[53] s.91(1); See above para.3–025.
[54] *Chapman v Smethurst* [1909] 1 K.B. 927, 930; *Bondina Ltd v Rollaway Shower Blinds Ltd* [1986] 1 W.L.R. 517, 520. See also *Albert Pearl Management Ltd v J.D.F. Builders Ltd* (1972) 31 D.L.R. (3d) 690, varied (1975) 49 D.L.R (3d) 422.

is that of the company by the hand of the agent, and it is the company, and not the agent, who is liable thereon.[55]

3–106     In *Chapman v Smethurst*,[56] Vaughan Williams L.J. said[57]:

> "To my mind, when you have once got a promissory note so drawn as to bind the company [the company's authority being admitted], and when the form of the note is such that no question of joint liability can possibly arise, it almost conclusively shews that the note is in such a form that the company alone is liable . . .".

In that case, a note was signed "J.H.S.'s Laundry and Dye Works Limited. J.H.S., Managing Director". It was held by the Court of Appeal that the note was the note of the company and that the managing director was not personally liable. And in *Bondina Ltd v Rollaway Shower Blinds Ltd*[58] a cheque was drawn on which the defendant company's name was pre-printed as drawer. Below the printed name of the company appeared the personal signatures of two directors of the company without any other addition. At the bottom of the cheque there was a printed line of figures, designating (*inter alia*) the number of the account which was the company's account. Dillon L.J. said[59]: "It shows plainly, as I construe it, looking no further than the form of the cheque itself, that the drawer of the cheque was the company and not the [directors]."

The reasoning in these cases appears to be that: (i) the question is one of construction of the instrument,[60] and (ii) the form of the instrument was such as to show, clearly and unambiguously, that the note or cheque was that of the company. In other (Canadian) cases,[61] however, it has been suggested that the printed name of a company, followed by the signature of the agent without any words indicating that he signs for or on behalf of the company or in a representative character, creates an ambiguity, which may be resolved by admitting parol evidence of the intention of the

---

[55] But, in Canada, the authorities are more divided: see *Crawford and Falconbridge* (8th ed.), pp.1406–1407.

[56] [1909] 1 K.B. 927.

[57] [1909] 1 K.B. 927 at 928.

[58] [1986] 1 W.L.R. 517. See also *Electrical Equipment of Australia Ltd v Peters* [1957] S.R. (N.S.W.) 361; *H.B. Etlin & Co. Ltd v Asselstyne* (1962) 34 D.L.R. (2d) 191; *Allprint Co. Ltd v Erwin* (1982) 136 D.L.R. (3d) 587; *Plascon Evans Paints (Tvl) Ltd v Ming* 1980 (3) S.A. 378; *Schmidt v Jack Brillard Printing Services CC* 2000 (3) S.A. 824; *Muirhead v Commonwealth Bank of Australia* [1996] Q.C.A. 241. Contrast *Akasia Finance v Da Souza* 1993 (2) S.A. 337.

[59] [1986] 1 W.L.R. 517, 520.

[60] *Chapman v Smethurst* [1909] 1 K.B. 927 at 930.

[61] *Tsuida and Halkett Bay Logging Co. Ltd v Logan Mayhew Ltd* (1961) 28 D.L.R. (2d) 156; *H.B. Etlin & Co. Ltd v Asselstyne* (1962) 34 D.L.R. (2d) 191; *Mauch v Birt* (1964) 45 D.L.R. (2d) 187; *Albert Pearl Management Ltd v J.D.F. Builders Ltd* (1972) 31 D.L.R. (3d) 690, varied 49 D.L.R. (3d) 422; *Medic v Taylor* (1976) 59 D.L.R. (3d) 321. Contrast *Glatt v Ritt* (1973) 34 D.L.R. (3d) 295. See also *Royal Bank of Canada v Mendel* [1977] 6 W.W.R. 10; *Dickinson v S.A. General Electric Co.* 1973 (2) S.A. 620; *Marshall v Bull Quip (Pty) Ltd* 1983 (1) S.A. 23; *Prince Albert Credit Union v Diehl* [1987] 4 W.W.R. 419 (rectification).

parties[62] or evidence that the person taking the instrument knew the instrument to be that of the company and was not therefore, as against the agent, a holder in good faith.[63]

**Subsection (2): construction.** Acceptances of a bill provide an illustra- 3–107 tion of this rule: that the construction most favourable to the validity of the instrument is to be adopted.[64] Since a bill cannot be accepted (except for honour) by a person other than the drawee,[65] an acceptance will (if possible) be construed as having been made by the person to whom the bill is addressed. Thus if a bill is addressed to the agent, and he accepts by words which indicate that he is accepting in a representative capacity on behalf of a principal, he may nevertheless be personally liable as acceptor.[66] Conversely, if a bill is addressed to the principal, and the agent accepts on behalf of the principal, but without adding words to his own signature indicating that he signs for or on behalf of the principal, or in a representative character, the acceptance will be construed as that of the principal and the agent will not be personally liable.[67]

Where a bill addressed to and accepted by a company is indorsed by a director on behalf of the company, the indorsement may be treated, not as the indorsement of the company,[68] but as the personal indorsement of the director, whether or not he adds to his signature words indicating that he signs for or on behalf of the company or in a representative character.[69] An indorsement by the company would add no greater validity to the bill than is already conferred by its acceptance. Therefore, under subsection (2), the construction that it is the personal indorsement of the director is to be adopted.[70] Alternatively, since such an indorsement is commercially

---

[62] See above, para.2–163 (but such evidence is only admissible as between immediate parties). Contrast *Chapman v Smethurst* [1909] 1 K.B. 927 at 930; *Kettle v Dunster and Wakefield* (1923) 47 T.L.R. 770 (Illustration 6) (parol evidence admissible).

[63] *Tsuida and Halkett Bay Logging Co. Ltd v Logan Mayhew Ltd* (1961) 28 D.L.R. (2d) 156 at 160. See also *Gordon v Roebuck* (1992) 92 D.L.R. (4th) 670.

[64] See above, paras 2–115 and 2–116.

[65] See above, para.2–115.

[66] *Mare v Charles* (1865) 5 E. & B. 978; *Herald v Connah* (1876) 34 L.T.(N.S.) 885 (s.17, Illustration 5). See also *Nicholls v Diamond* (1853) 9 Exch. 154 (s.17, Illustration 9). But s.26(1) may be said to negate such liability.

[67] *Penrose v Martyr* (1858) E.B. &. E. 499 (s.23, Illustration 7); *Okell v Charles* (1876) 34 L.T.(N.S.) 822 (s.17, Illustration 4); *Stacey & Co. Ltd v Wallis* (1912) 106 L.T. 544 (s.23, Illustration 10); *Elliott v Bax-Ironside* [1925] 2 K.B. 301 (s.17, Illustration 6); See also *Maxform SpA v Mariani and Goodville Ltd* [1979] 2 Lloyds Rep. 385, affirmed [1981] 2 Lloyds Rep. 54 (s.23, Illustration 15); *Novaknit Hellas SA v Kumar Brothers International Ltd* [1998] Lloyd's Rep. Bank. 287.

[68] *Britannia Electric Lamp Works Ltd v D. Mandler & Co. Ltd* [1939] 2 K.B. 129 (s.87, Illustration 3) (where s.26(2) was said to be inapplicable).

[69] *Elliott v Bax-Ironside* [1925] 2 K.B. 301 (Illustration 11); *Rolfe Lubell & Co. v Keith* [1979] 1 All E.R. 860 (Illustration 12).

[70] *Elliott v Bax-Ironside* [1925] 2 K.B. 301.

meaningless, it creates an ambiguity, so that parol evidence[71] is admissible as to the intentions of the parties with respect to the indorsement.[72]

ILLUSTRATIONS

3–108     1. A note is made in the form "We, the directors of the Isle of Man Slate and Flag Company, Limited, do promise to pay . . . " and is signed "R.M., Chairman, J.H., S.B., H.J.". The seal of the company is affixed and attested by a witness. The directors are personally liable.[73]

2. Money is lent to a parish. The defendants give a note for the amount, signing it "J.P. and Q.W., churchwardens for the Parish of Chingford. J.F., overseer". They are personally liable on the note as makers.[74]

3. X, by will, directs his executors to carry on his business and the executors do so. One of the executors, in the course of the business, accepts bills of exchange, signing them "P.pro. The executors of X. W.W.". The executors are liable on these acceptances.[75]

3–109     4. A note is made in the form "Two months after demand in writing we promise to pay etc." and is signed "W.H. and J.T. trustees. W.F. secretary". The signatories are personally liable.[76]

5. Money is lent to the F Company. A note for the amount is given in the form "Three months after date, we promise to pay etc." and is signed "H.W.S., W.W., R.J.B., W.W.P., Directors. The F Company. J.T. Manager". The persons who sign are personally liable as makers.[77]

6. The claimant, receiver of a company, draws a number of bills of exchange signing them "R.K., Receiver, Ford Paper Works (1923), Limited" as drawer. The bills are accepted by the defendants in respect of goods supplied to the company (liability for which had been expressly disclaimed by the claimant). The claimant personally is entitled to recover

---

[71] See above, paras 2–163 and 3–106. Contrast *Chapman v Smethurst* [1909] 1 K.B. 927, 930; *Kettle v Dunster and Wakefield* (1927) 43 T.L.R. 770 (Illustration 6).
[72] *Rolfe Lubell & Co. v Keith* [1979] 1 All E.R. 860. See also *Elliott v Bax-Ironside* [1925] 2 K.B. 301 at 306, 309.
[73] *Dutton v Marsh* (1871) L.R. 6 Q.B. 361.
[74] *Rew v Pettet* (1834) 1 A. & E. 196.
[75] *Liverpool Borough Bank v Walker* (1859) 4 De G. & J. 24.
[76] *Price v Taylor* (1860) 5 H. & N. 540; *cf.* s.11 of the Act.
[77] *Courtauld v Sanders* (1867) 16 L.T., N.S. 562.

against the defendants on the bills. The intention of the parties must be gathered from the terms of the document alone and the words added to the claimant's signature are words of description only.[78]

7. A note is made in the form "Three months after date we jointly promise to pay F.S. or order, six hundred pounds, for value received in stock on account of the London and Birmingham Iron and Hardware Company, Limited" and is signed "J.M., G.N.W., J.H., Directors". The note is binding on the company and the directors are not personally liable.[79]     **3–110**

8. A note is made in the form "On demand I promise to pay Messrs. A & Co., or order, etc." and is signed "For Mistley, Thorpe, and Walton Railway Company, J.S., Secretary". The secretary is not personally liable.[80]

9. A note is made in the form "Six months after demand I promise to pay Mrs M.C. the sum of £300 for value received together with six per cent. interest per annum" and is signed "J.H. Smethurst's Laundry and Dye Works, Limited, J.H. Smethurst, Managing Director". The note is the note of the company and the managing director is not personally liable.[81]

10. A post-dated cheque is drawn in favour of the claimant on a printed bank cheque form. The name of a company "Rollaway Shower Blinds Ltd" is pre-printed on the cheque as drawer and below this W and McM, directors of the company, place their personal signatures without any additional words. At the bottom of the cheque is a pre-printed line of figures designating the number of the cheque, the branch of the bank, and the number of the account which is the company's account. In an action by the claimant against the directors for summary judgment on the cheque, unconditional leave to defend is given, as it is plainly arguable that the directors are not personally liable.[82]     **3–111**

11. A bill addressed to F.F.E. Ltd is accepted by two directors on behalf of the company.[83] As required by the drawer, the bill is also indorsed by them as follows: "F.F.E. Ltd, B, M, directors". If the indorsement were

---

[78] *Kettle v Dunster and Wakefield* (1927) 43 T.L.R. 770. Contrast *Owen (D) & Co. v Cronk* [1895] 1 Q.B. 265, 273 ("Judd & Co. (Limited), S.C., receiver").
[79] *Lindus v Melrose* (1857) 2 H. & N. 293, (1858) 3 H. & N. 177.
[80] *Alexander v Sizer* (1869) L.R. 4 Ex. 102.
[81] *Chapman v Smethurst* [1909] 1 K.B. 927.
[82] *Bondina Ltd v Rollaway Shower Blinds Ltd* [1986] 1 W.L.R. 517.
[83] s.17, Illustration 6.

treated as that of the company, it would give no greater validity to the bill than is already contained in the acceptance. Therefore the construction that it is the personal indorsement of the directors is to be adopted and the directors are personally liable.[84]

12. A bill addressed to G.F. Ltd is accepted by the company. It is indorsed by a director who places his signature within a rubber-stamped box, so that it reads "For and on behalf of G.F. Ltd X (*signature*) director". The director is personally liable on this indorsement. The only way that validity can be given to the indorsement is by construing it to bind someone other than the acceptor. As soon as it becomes obvious that the indorsement as worded is meaningless there is a patent ambiguity which allows evidence to be admitted that the director agreed personally to indorse the bill.[85]

## The Consideration for a Bill

### Value and holder for value

4–001     27. (1) Valuable consideration for a bill may be constituted by—
         (a) Any consideration sufficient to support a simple contract;
         (b) An antecedent debt or liability. Such a debt or liability is deemed valuable consideration whether the bill is payable on demand or at a future time.
      (2) Where value has at any time been given for a bill the holder is deemed to be a holder for value as regards the acceptor and all parties to the bill who became parties prior to such time.
      (3) Where the holder of a bill has a lien on it, arising either from contract or by implication of law, he is deemed to be a holder for value to the extent of the sum for which he has a lien.

Definitions                     Comparison
"bill": s.2.                   UCC: §§ 3–303, 3–305, 4–211.
"holder": s.2.
"value": s.2.

COMMENT

4–002     **Consideration for a bill.** In English law, consideration is required for the enforcement of any contract which is not made by deed.[1] The Act,

---

[84] *Elliott v Bax-Ironside* [1925] 2 K.B. 301.
[85] *Rolfe Lubell & Co. v Keith* [1979] 1 All E.R. 860.
[1] *Rann v Hughes* (1778) 7 T.R. 350n. *cf. Oliver v Davis* [1949] 2 K.B. 727, 742.

however, nowhere expressly states that consideration is required to render enforceable the obligations of parties to a bill or note. But, for obligations governed by English law,[2] such a requirement may be deduced from the fact that the liabilities of the drawer,[3] acceptor,[4] indorser[5] and maker[6] are referred to in the Act as an "engagement", and section 21(1) specifically refers to the "contract on the bill" of the drawer, acceptor or indorser.[7] Further, there are many cases in which enforcement of such an obligation has been refused on the ground or absence of consideration or of the total failure of consideration.

The general law of consideration therefore applies to bills, cheques and notes.[8] However, the principles applied differ to some extent from those applicable in the case of ordinary contracts.

First, in contract law, past consideration is no consideration, and a promise will be unenforceable for want of consideration if the only consideration for it is an antecedent debt owed by the promisor to the promisee.[9] But valuable consideration for a bill may be constituted by an antecedent debt or liability.[10]

Secondly, section 2 of the Act defines "value" to mean valuable consideration. As a general rule in the law of contract, valuable consideration must move from, *e.g.* be given by, the promisee.[11] In the case of bills, as between immediate parties,[12] value must have been given by the holder who seeks to enforce the obligation.[13] But, as between remote parties,[14] value need not have been given by the holder as long as value has been given for the instrument after the defendant became a party to it.[15]    4–003

Thirdly, the burden of proving that consideration has been given normally lies upon the claimant who seeks to enforce the contract. But, in the case of bills, consideration is presumed until the contrary is proved.[16]

**Impeachment of value.** The question whether absence of consideration or its failure, total or partial, affords a good defence to a party sued    4–004

---

[2] See below, para.12–011 (conflict of laws).
[3] s.55(1)(a).
[4] s.54(1).
[5] s.55(2)(a).
[6] s.88(1).
[7] See also s.89(2) (notes).
[8] See *Chitty on Contracts* (29th ed.), Vol.I. Ch.3. The Review Committee on Banking Services Law and Practice (above, para.1–008) recommended that the need for consideration as a test of negotiability should be abolished: (1989) Cm. 622, rec. 8.4. But this recommendation was not accepted: (1990) Cm. 1026.
[9] See *Chitty on Contracts* (29th ed.), Vol.I, § 3–026.
[10] s.27(1)(b).
[11] See *Chitty on Contracts* (29th ed.), Vol.I, § 3–036.
[12] See below, para.4–005.
[13] See below, para.4–024.
[14] See below, para.4–005.
[15] s.27(2).
[16] s.30(1), (2).

on a bill depends upon the status of the holder, that is, whether he is a "mere holder",[17] a "holder for value"[18] or a "holder in due course",[19] and also upon the relationship of the party claiming payment and the party from whom payment is claimed, *e.g.* whether they are "immediate parties" or "remote parties".

4–005      **Immediate and remote parties.** "Immediate parties" are parties in direct relation with each other. All other parties are "remote".

Persons are immediate parties, relatively to each other, if their legal relations as parties to an instrument arise out of their direct dealings with each other.[20] Normally the following are immediate parties: the drawer and acceptor and the drawer and payee of a bill, the drawer and payee of a cheque, the maker and payee of a note, an indorser and his indorsee of a bill, cheque or note. They will usually be found to have dealt directly with each other, for example, by an agreement to sell goods or supply services, to extend credit or to purchase or discount the instrument.

Persons are remote parties, as regards each other, if their legal relations as parties to an instrument arise, not out of their direct dealings with each other, but out of their respective dealings with another party, or parties, to the instrument.[21] Normally the following are remote parties: the acceptor and payee of a bill (except where it is drawn payable to the order of the drawer), and an indorsee and the acceptor of a bill[22] or the maker of a note.

In all cases, however, it is their actual relationship which determines whether they are immediate or remote parties, and parol evidence is admissible to prove that relationship.[23]

4–006      **Rules as to impeachment of value.** The rules as to impeachment of value may be summarised as follows. They apply also to cheques and promissory notes.

4–007      (i) *Absence of consideration.* Absence of consideration, total or partial,[24] is a matter of defence against an immediate party.[25] Thus if A draws a

---

[17] See below, para.4–028.

[18] s.27(2); below, para.4–024.

[19] s.29(1); below, para.4–050.

[20] *Crawford and Falconbridge* (8th ed.), p.1519.

[21] *Crawford and Falconbridge* (8th ed.), p.1519.

[22] And an indorsee and the drawer of a bill, unless drawn payable to the drawer's order.

[23] See above, para.2–164.

[24] *Darnell v Williams* (1817) 2 Stark 166; *Forman v Wright* (1851) 11 C.B. 481; *Thoni GmbH & Co. K.G. v R.T.P Equipment Ltd* [1979] 2 Lloyd's Rep. 282 (Illustration 7); *MK International Development Co. Ltd v Housing Bank* [1991] 1 Bank. L.R. 74 (Illustration 25).

[25] *Holliday v Atkinson* (1826) 5 B. & C. 501; *Easton v Pratchett* (1835) 1 C.M. & R. 798, 808–809; *Milnes v Dawson* (1850) 5 Exch. 948, 950; *Churchill and Sim v Goddard* [1937] 1 K.B. 92, 110; *Oliver v Davis* [1949] 2 K.B. 727 (Illustration 18); *Hasan v Willson* [1977] 1 Lloyd's Rep. 431 (Illustration 19); *AEG (UK) Ltd v Lewis, The Times*, Dec. 29, 1992, CA.

cheque in favour of B and delivers it to B as a gift, B cannot recover from A.[26] And if C, the holder of a bill for value, indorses it to D by way of gift, the property in the bill passes to D, but he cannot recover from C.[27] Absence of consideration is likewise a good defence against a remote party who is not a holder for value,[28] *i.e.* where value has not at any time been given for the bill.[29] Thus if A accepts a bill drawn on him by B in order to accommodate B,[30] and B indorses the bill to C without value, C cannot recover from A (although the burden lies upon A to show that neither C nor any intervening holder was a holder for value).[31]

On the other hand, absence of consideration is no defence against a remote party who is a holder for value.[32] Thus if A accepts a bill drawn on him by B to accommodate B[33] and B indorses the bill to C for value, C can recover from A,[34] and it is immaterial that when C took the bill he knew that A was an accommodation party.[35] *A fortiori* absence of consideration is no defence against a remote party who is a holder in due course.[36]

(ii) *Total failure of consideration.*[37] A total failure of consideration will **4–008** occur when the party against whom liability is sought to be enforced received no part of the benefit for which he bargained in the transaction which led to him becoming a party to the bill, for example, where an advance or payment promised to him was never made, where goods agreed to be sold to him are never delivered[38] or, if delivered, are lawfully rejected by him before his obligation to pay matures,[39] or where his

---

[26] *Holliday v Atkinson* (1826) 5 B. & C. 501 *cf. Re Whitaker* (1889) 42 Ch.D. 119.
[27] *Easton v Pratchett,* (1835) 1 C.M. & R. 798 at 808–809; *Milnes v Dawson* (1850) 5 Exch. 948 at 950.
[28] *Mills v Barber* (1836) 1 M. & W. 425.
[29] s.27(2).
[30] s.28, below, para.4–041.
[31] *Mills v Barber* (1836) 1 M. & W. 425. See also s.30(1).
[32] *Charles v Marsden* (1808) 1 Taunt. 224; *Scott v Lifford* (1808) 1 Camp. 246 (Illustration 20); *Stein v Yglesias* (1834) 1 C.M. & R. 565; *Mills v Barber* (1836) 1 M. & W. 425; *Sturtevant v Ford* (1842) 4 M. & G. 101; (s.36; Illustration 6); *Petty v Cooke* (1871) L.R. 6 Q.B. 790. Contrast Geva [1980] C.L.J. 360.
[33] s.28.
[34] *Sturtevant v Ford,* (1842) 4 M. & G. 101. But it may be that if C paid less than the full amount of the bill, he can only recover the amount which he paid: below, para.4–010. *cf. Re Bunyard, Ex p. Newton* (1880) 16 Ch.D. 330 (Illustration 30).
[35] s.28(2) (unless there is an express or implied agreement not to negotiate the bill: *Parr v Jewell* (1855) 16 C.B. 684).
[36] s.38(2).
[37] See *Chitty on Contracts* (29th ed.), Vol.I, § 29–054.
[38] *Patrick v Harrison* (1792) 3 Bro.C.C. 476; *Behrend & Co. Ltd v Produce Brokers Co. Ltd* [1920] 3 K.B. 530; *Finch Motors Ltd v Quin* [1980] 2 N.Z.L.R. 573. But contrast *Mills v Buono* [1986] B.T.L.C. 399.
[39] *Kwei Tek Chao v British Traders & Shippers Ltd* [1954] 2 Q.B. 459, 475; *All Trades Distributors v Agencies Kaufman* (1969) 113 S.J. 995. *cf. Montebianco Industrie Tesselli SpA v Carlyle Mills (London) Ltd* [1981] 1 Lloyds Rep. 509 (Illustration 8).

acceptance is given against the receipt of a bill of lading which turns out to be a forgery.[40] Total failure of consideration is a defence against an immediate party,[41] and against a remote party who is not a holder for value.[42] It is not a defence against a remote party who is a holder in due course.[43] Nor, is seems, is it a defence against a remote holder for value without notice of the failure.[44] However, total failure of consideration may possibly be a defence against a remote holder for value with notice.[45] The reason may in some cases be that it is in the nature of a fraud, or breach of faith, to negotiate a bill when the holder knows that the consideration on which he received it has failed.[46]

When the consideration for a bill totally fails, the court may restrain its negotiation by injunction.[47]

**4–009**    (iii) *Partial failure of consideration.* Partial failure of consideration is a defence *pro tanto* against an immediate party, and against a remote party who is not a holder for value,[48] provided that the partial failure is an ascertained and liquid amount.[49] Thus if A accepts a bill drawn on him by B as the price of a specified quantity of goods at a certain price per tonne to be supplied by B to A, and B delivers part only of the contract quantity, A will have a good defence to an action against him by B on the bill to the extent of the excess in the price beyond the amount due (at the contractual rate) for the goods which are delivered. Likewise, if, before the

---

[40] *Robinson v Reynolds* (1841) 2 Q.B. 196, 203.
[41] *Solly v Hinde* (1834) 2 Cr. & M. 516 (s.21, Illustration 29); *Mills v Oddy* (1835) 2 Cr. M. & R. 103; *Abbott v Hendrix* (1840) 1 M. & G. 791 (s.21, Illustration 30); *Churchill and Sim v Goddard* [1937] 1 K.B. 92, 109; *Fielding & Platt Ltd v Najjar* [1969] 1 W.L.R. 357 (Illustration 4); *All Trades Distributors v Agencies Kaufman* (1969) 113 S.J. 995; *Nova (Jersey) Knit Ltd v Kammgarn Spinnerei GmbH* [1977] 1 W.L.R. 713, 722, 726, 732.
[42] *Astley and Williams v Johnson* (1860) 5 H. & N. 137.
[43] s.38(2). See also *Robinson v Reynolds* (1841) 2 Q.B. 196; *Guaranty Trust Co. of New York v Hannay* [1918] 2 K.B. 623, 652. This also applies to a holder claiming under a holder in due course: s.29 (3).
[44] *Watson v Russell* (1864) 5 B. & S. 968. See also *Misa v Currie* (1876) 1 App. Cas. 554, 556. Contrast *Byles* (27th ed.), p.212n.
[45] *Lloyd v Davis* (1824) 3 L.J. (O.S.) K.B. 38; *Traders Finance Corp. Ltd v Casselman* (1960) 22 D.L.R. (2d) 177. But contrast *Fairclough v Pavia* (1854) 9 Exch. 690, 695; *Ashley Colter Ltd v Scott* [1942] 3 D.L.R. 538.
[46] See *Parr v Jewell* (1855) 16 C.B. 684 (s.36, Illustration 2) and *Crawford and Falconbridge* (8th ed.), p.1461. *cf. Oulds v Harrison* (1854) 10 Exch. 572.
[47] *Patrick v Harrison* (1792) 3 Bro.C.C. 476; *Bainbrigge v Hemminway* (1865) 12 L.T. 74. Contrast *Glennie v Imri* (1839) 3 Y. & C. Ex. 436 (set-off).
[48] *Agra and Masterman's Bank v Leighton* (1866) L.R. 2 Ex. 56.
[49] *Forman v Wright* (1851) 11 C.B. 481, 492; *Agra and Masterman's Bank v Leighton* (1866) L.R. 2 Ex 56; *Saga of Bond Street Ltd v Avalon Promotions Ltd* [1972] 2 Q.B. 325 (Illustration 5); *Nova (Jersey) Knit Ltd v Kammgarn Spinnerei GmbH* [1977] 1 W.L.R. 713, 720, 732; *Thoni GmbH v R.T.P. Equipment Ltd* [1979] 2 Lloyds Rep. 282 (Illustration 7); *MK International Development Co. Ltd v Housing Bank* [1991] 1 Bank. L.R. 74 (Illustration 25); *Safa Ltd v Banque du Caire* [2000] 2 Lloyd's Rep. 600, 605.

bill is presented for payment, A justifiably rejects part of the goods because they do not correspond with the contract description, A will have *pro tanto* a defence against B.

However, even against an immediate party, an unliquidated cross-claim, *e.g.* for breach of warranty, cannot be set up as a defence to an action on the bill, whether the cross-claim arises out of the same or a different transaction.[50] Thus, in the above example, if the whole of the goods are delivered to A and are accepted by him, but they turn out to be of inferior quality, A will have no defence to an action against him by B on the bill. This is so even though, were B to sue A on the contract of sale for the price, A could set up against B the breach of warranty in diminution or extinction of the price.[51]

Partial failure of consideration, even if the loss is liquidated, is not a defence against a remote party who is a holder for value[52] or who is a holder in due course.[53]

**Part 24 proceedings.** Where an application is made by a claimant for summary judgment against a defendant in respect of a claim on a bill of exchange, cheque or promissory note, the general rule is that the court will give summary judgment for the claimant save in exceptional circumstances. "We have repeatedly said in this court that a bill of exchange or a promissory note is to be treated as cash. It is to be honoured unless there is some good reason to the contrary."[54] In most of the cases where this    **4–010**

---

[50] *Glennie v Imri* (1839) 3 Y. & C. Ex. 436, 442–443; *Trickey v Larne* (1840) 6 M. & W. 278; *Warwick v Nairn* (1855) 10 Ex. 762; *James Lamont & Co. Ltd v Hyland Ltd (No.1)* [1950] 1 K.B. 585 (Illustration 1); *Brown Shipley & Co. Ltd v Alicia Hosiery Ltd* [1966] 1 Lloyds Rep. 668 (Illustration 2); *Cebora S.N.C. v S.I.P. (Industrial Products) Ltd* [1976] 1 Lloyds Rep. 271 (Illustration 6); *Nova (Jersey) Knit Ltd v Kammgarn Spinnerei GmbH* [1977] 1 W.L.R. 713 at 720, 722, 726, 732; *Montecchi v Shimco U.K. Ltd* [1979] 1 W.L.R. 1180, 1183; *Montebianco Industrie Tessilli SpA v Carlyle Mills (London) Ltd* [1981] 1 Lloyds Rep. 509 (Illustration 8); *Handley Page Ltd v Rockwell Machine Tool Co. Ltd* [1970] 2 Lloyds Rep. 459, 465, [1971] 2 Lloyds Rep. 298. See also Summary Procedure on Bills of Exchange Act 1855, s.2 (now repealed).

[51] Sale of Goods Act 1979, s.53(1)(a). See also Sale of Goods Act 1979, s.48C.

[52] *Archer v Bamford* (1822) 3 Stark. 175; *Ashley Colter Ltd v Scott* [1942] 3 D.L.R. 538, 541. But see *Harris Oscar Son & Co. v Vallarman & Co.* [1940] 1 All E.R. 185.

[53] s.38.(2). This also applies to a holder claiming under a holder in due course: s.29(3).

[54] *Fielding & Platt Ltd v Najjar* [1969] 1 W.L.R. 357, 361, *per* Lord Denning M.R. See also *Brown Shipley & Co. Ltd v Alicia Hosiery Ltd* [1966] 1 Lloyds Rep. 668, 669; *Cebora S.N.C. v S.I.P. (Industrial) Products Ltd* [1976] 1 Lloyds Rep. 271, 274, 278, 279; *Montecchi v Simco (U.K.) Ltd* [1979] 1 W.L.R. 1180, 1183; *Montebianco Industrie Tessili SpA v Carlyle Mills (London) Ltd* [1981] 1 Lloyds Rep. 509, 511. Contrast *Aquaflite Ltd v Jaymar International Freight Consultants Ltd* [1980] 1 Lloyds Rep. 36 (bills surrendered in return for promise of cheque: no estoppel to allow claim as if on a cheque) and *Willment Brothers Ltd v N.W. Thames RHA* (1984) 26 B.L.R. 51 (mutual set-off in insolvency even though claim on bill of exchange).

point has arisen,[55] the claimant has been the original payee of the instrument and the defendant the party primarily liable on it, *i.e.* the acceptor of the bill, the drawer of the cheque or the maker of the note. The instrument has been given in respect of a contract between the claimant and the defendant under which the claimant has supplied or agreed to supply goods, services or work and materials to the defendant. The action has, therefore, been between immediate parties to the instrument. The cases clearly establish that the fact that the defendant may have a counterclaim for unliquidated damages arising out of the same or a closely related transaction is no defence to an action on the instrument,[56] even though the defendant would have been entitled to set up the counterclaim by way of set-off had the claimant's claim been on the underlying contract.[57] In *Nova (Jersey) Knit Ltd v Kammgarn Spinnerei GmbH*,[58] Lord Russell said[59]:

> "It is in my opinion well established that a claim for unliquidated damages under a contract for sale is no defence to a claim under a bill of exchange accepted by the purchaser: nor is it available as set-off or counterclaim. This is a deep rooted concept of English commercial law. A vendor and purchaser who agree upon payment by acceptance of bills of exchange do so not simply upon the basis that credit is given to the purchaser so that the vendor must in due course sue for the price under the contract of sale. The bill is itself a contract separate from the contract of sale. Its purpose is not merely to serve as a negotiable instrument, it is also to avoid postponement of the purchaser's liability to the vendor himself, a postponement grounded upon some allegation of failure in some respect by the

---

[55] *cf. Brown Shipley & Co. Ltd v Alicia Hosiery Ltd* [1966] 1 Lloyds Rep. 668 (Illustration 2); *Barclays Bank Ltd v Aschaffenburger Zellstoffwerke A.G.* [1967] 1 Lloyds Rep. 387 (Illustration 3).

[56] *James Lamont & Co. Ltd v Hyland Ltd* [1950] 1 K.B. 585 (Illustration 1); *Far East Corp. Ltd v Shun Cheong Steam Navigation Co. Ltd* [1962] M.L.J. 344; *Brown Shipley & Co. Ltd v Alicia Hosiery Ltd* [1966] 1 Lloyds Rep. 668 (Illustration 2); *Fielding & Platt Ltd v Najjar* [1969] 1 W.L.R. 357 (Illustration 4); *Cebora S.N.C. v S.I.P. Industrial Products Ltd* [1976] 1 Lloyds Rep. 271 (Illustration 6); *Nova (Jersey) Knit Ltd v Kammgarn Spinnerei GmbH* [1977] 1 W.L.R. 713, 720, 722, 726, 732; *Montecchi v Shimco (U.K.) Ltd* [1979] 1 W.L.R. 1180, 1183; *Montebianco Industrie Tessili SpA v Carlyle Mills (London) Ltd* [1981] 1 Lloyds Rep. 509 (Illustration 8); *International Ore & Fertilizer Corp. v East Coast Fertiliser Co. Ltd* [1987] I N.Z.L.R. 9; *Mobil Oil Australia Ltd v Caulfield Tyre Service Pty Ltd* [1984] V.R. 444; *International Ore and Fertilizer Corp. v East Coast Fertilizer Co. Ltd* [1987] 1 N.Z.L.R. 9; *Safa Ltd v Banque du Caire* [2000] 2 Lloyd's Rep. 600, 605. See also *Eldan Services v Chandag Motors* [1990] 3 All E.R. 459 (no injunction to restrain presentation of post-dated cheque).

[57] *Mondel v Steel* (1841) 8 M. & W. 858, 871; *Hanak v Green* [1958] 2 Q.B. 9; Sale of Goods Act 1979, ss.48C, 53(1)(a).

[58] [1977] 1 W.L.R. 713.

[59] [1977] 1 W.L.R. 713 at 732–733. See also *Central Bank of Yemen v Cardinal Financial Investments Corpn.* [2001] Lloyd's Rep. Bank 1.

vendor under the underlying contract, unless it be total or quantified partial failure of consideration."

The courts will not ordinarily grant a stay of execution of the judgment on the claim pending trial of such a counterclaim[60] (which of course the defendant remains at liberty to pursue in the action). But they might grant a freezing injunction to restrain the claimant from removing from the jurisdiction or otherwise dealing with the proceeds of an instrument pending trial of such a counterclaim.[61]

Nevertheless the orders the court may make on an application by a claimant under Part 24 remain a matter for the discretion of the court.[62] It would appear that, as between immediate parties, it is "beyond argument" that the application should be dismissed if there has been a total failure of consideration.[63] Moreover, in the exercise of its discretion, the court may dismiss the application in respect of part of the claimant's claim on the instrument if there has been a partial failure of consideration in a liquidated amount[64] or even if there is a liquidated counterclaim arising out of the same transaction which can be raised by way of legal set-off.[65] The dismissal may, however, be conditional upon payment into court of a sum of money, *e.g.* the amount in dispute.[66] But apart from cases of total or partial failure of consideration there could be exceptional circumstances where the court would exercise its discretion to dismiss the

---

[60] *Brown Shipley & Co. Ltd v Alicia Hosiery Ltd* [1966] 1 Lloyds Rep. 668, 669; *Cebora S.N.C. v S.I.P (Industrial Products) Ltd* [1976] 1 Lloyds Rep. 271; *Montecchi v Shimco (U.K) Ltd* [1979] 1 W.L.R. 1180; *Safa Ltd v Banque du Caire* [2000] 2 Lloyd's Rep. 600, 605. See also *Nova (Jersey) Knit Ltd v Kammgarn Spinnerei GmbH* [1977] 1 W.L.R. 713, 721–722, 726, 733 (arbitration); *Thoni GmbH v R.T.P. Equipment Ltd* [1979] 2 Lloyds Rep. 282, 285; *Montebianco Industrie Tessili SpA v Carlyle Mills (London) Ltd* [1981] 1 Lloyds Rep. 509. *cf. Cobury v Wolverhampton Metal* [1989] C.L.Y. 3065, CA.

[61] *Z Ltd v A–Z and AA–LL* [1982] Q.B. 558, 574, 591; *Bolivinter Oil S.A. v Chase Manhattan Bank N.A.* [1984] 1 W.L.R. 392, 393 (letters of credit). Contrast *Montecchi v Shimco (U.K.) Ltd* [1979] 1 W.L.R. 1180 *Intraco Ltd v Notis Shipping Corp.* [1981] 2 Lloyds Rep. 256; *Eldan Services v Chandag Motors* [1990] 3 All E.R. 459.

[62] *Cebora S.N.C. v S.I.P. (Industrial Products) Ltd* [1976] 1 Lloyd's Rep. 271 at 275, 278; *Montebianco Industrie Tessili SpA v Carlyle Mills (London) Ltd* [1981] 1 Lloyd's Rep. 509 at 511; *Safa Ltd v Banque du Caire* [2000] 2 Lloyd's Rep. 600, 605. Contrast *Isovel Contracts Ltd v ABB Building Technologies Ltd* [2002] 1 B.C.L.C. 390 at [15].

[63] *Montebianco Industrie Tessili SpA v Carlyle Mills (London) Ltd* [1981] 1 Lloyd's Rep. 509 at 511. See also *Fielding & Platt Ltd v Najjar* [1969] 1 W.L.R. 357 (Illustration 4); *All Trades Distributors v Agencies Kaufman* (1969) 113 S.J. 995; *Nova (Jersey) Knit Ltd v Kammgarn Spinnerei GmbH* [1977] 1 W.L.R. 713, 726, 732; *Finch Motors Ltd v Quin* [1980] 2 N.Z.L.R. 573.

[64] *Saga of Bond Street Ltd v Avalon Promotions Ltd* [1972] 2 Q.B. 325; *Thoni GmbH v R.T.P. Equipment Ltd* [1979] 2 Lloyds Rep. 282 (Illustration 7).

[65] *Barclays Bank Ltd v Aschaffenberger Zellstoffwerke A.G.* [1967] 1 Lloyds Rep. 387 (Illustration 3); *Hong Kong and Shanghai Banking Corpn. v Kloeckner & Co. AG* [1990] 2 Q.B. 514, 526.

[66] *All Trades Distributors v Agencies Kaufman* (1969) 113 S.J. 995; *Saga of Bond Street Ltd v Avalon Promotions Ltd* [1972] 2 Q.B. 325; *Thoni GmbH v R.T.P. Equipment Ltd* [1979] 2 Lloyd's Rep. 280. See also *Cobury v Wolverhampton Metal* [1989] C.L.Y. 3065, CA.

application,[67] although "the Courts should not . . . erode that rule [*i.e.,* that bills of exchange are treated as cash] by treating circumstances as exceptional wherever its application might cause injustice".[68]

Where a holder sues on behalf of or as trustee for another person, any defence or set-off available against that person may be raised against the holder[69] and in Part 24 proceedings judgment may be given for the whole amount of the bill but with a stay of execution in respect of the amount in dispute.[70]

4–011      **Subsection (1)(a): present consideration.** What is consideration sufficient to support a simple contract is to be determined by reference to the normal principles of contract law governing consideration.[71] As in the case of simple contracts, present consideration for a bill or note must move from the promisee but need not necessarily move to the promisor.[72] In particular the following have been held to constitute valuable consideration for a bill or note: a cross acceptance,[73] a fluctuating balance,[74] a promise to forbear to enforce an existing claim against a third party or an actual forbearance at the request (express or implied) of the promisor,[75] the compromise of a suit or claim even if the claim is invalid, provided it is not known to be invalid,[76] the restoration by a thief of stolen property,[77] a warranty by an auctioneer of his authority to accept a

---

[67] See the cases cited in n.62, above, and (misrepresentation) *Clovertogs v Jean Scenes* [1982] Com.L.R. 88, although this case may be of dubious authority on its facts: *Safa Ltd v Banque du Caire* [2000] 2 Lloyd's Rep. 600, 608; *Solo Industries UK Ltd v Canara Bank* [2001] 1 W.L.R. 1800 at [25–26]. See also (fraud) *Cobury v Wolverhampton Metal* [1989] C.L.Y. 3065, CA; *Marina Sports Ltd v Alliance Richfield Pte Ltd* [1990] 3 M.L.J. 5; *Solo Industries U.K. v Canara Bank* [2001] EWCA Civ 1041, [2001] 1 W.L.R. 1800 at [25]–[26]. *Cf. First Discount Ltd v Cranston* [2002] EWCA Civ 71.

[68] *Cebora S.N.C. v S.I.P (International Products) Ltd* [1976] 1 Lloyd's Rep. 271, *per* Stephenson L.J.

[69] *De la Chaumettc v Bank of England* (1829) 9 B. & C. 208 (as explained in *Currie v Misa* (1875) L.R. 10 Ex. 153, 169; (1876) 1 App. Cas. 554, 570); *Reid v Furnival* (1833) 1 C. & M. 538 (Illustration 29); *Thornton v Maynard* (1875) L.R. 10 C.P. 695 (s.38, Illustration 1); *Re Bunyard, Ex p. Newton* (1880) 16 Ch.D. 330 (Illustration 30); see below, para.4–030.

[70] *Barclays Bank Ltd v Aschaffenberger Zellstoffwerke A.G.,* [1967] 1 Lloyd's Rep. 387.

[71] See *Chitty on Contracts* (29th ed.), Vol.I, Ch.3.

[72] *Yan v Post Office Bank Ltd* [1994] 1 N.Z.L.R. 154.

[73] *Buckler v Buttivant* (1802) 3 East 72; *Hornblower v Proud* (1819) 2 B. & Ald. 327; *Rose v Sims* (1830) 1 B & Ad. 521, 526; *Burdon v Benton* (1847) 9 Q.B. 843; *Re London, Bombay and Mediterranean Bank* (1874) L.R. 9 Ch.App. 686.

[74] *Bosanquet v Dudman* (1814) 1 Stark 1; *Collenridge v Farquharson* (1816) 1 Stark 259; *Atwood v Crowdle* (1816) 1 Stark 483; *Pease v Hirst* (1829) 10 B. & C. 122; *Richards v Macey* (1845) 14 M. & W. 484. *cf. Re Boys* (1870) L.R. 10 Eq. 467.

[75] *Balfour v Sea Life Assurance Co.* (1857) 3 C.B. (N.S.) 300; *Crears v Hunter* (1887) 19 Q.B.D. 341 (Illustration 9); *Elkington v Cooke Hill* (1914) 30 T.L.R. 670; *MK International Development Co. Ltd v Housing Bank* [1991] 1 Bank. L.R. 74 (Illustration 25).

[76] *Cook v Wright* (1861) 1 B. & S. 559; *Kingsford v Oxenden* (1891) 7 T.L.R. 565. See also *Callisher v Bischoffsheim* (1870) L.R. 5 Q.B. 449; *Miles v New Zealand Alford Estate Co.* (1885) 32 Ch.D. 266.

[77] *London and County Banking Co. v London and River Plate Bank* (1888) 21 Q.B.D. 235.

cheque in payment of a deposit on a sale of land[78] and the acceptance of a cheque in lieu of immediate payment in cash.[79] But an instrument which is delivered as a gift[80] or in pursuance of a moral obligation owed to the recipient[81] is not given for valuable consideration.

Where a banker collects for a customer a cheque payable to order or bearer, he may do so merely as collecting agent. But he may also give present consideration for such a cheque and become a holder for value of it in his own right.[82] An obvious example is where he discounts or purchases the cheque for cash. The banker does not provide consideration merely by crediting the cheque to a customer's account before it is cleared.[83] But if he lends further against the cheque, or if he agrees to or does in fact allow the customer to draw against the cheque before clearance,[84] or if he honours cheques drawn by the customer which he would not have done if the cheque had not been delivered for collection,[85] then there is present consideration moving from him for the cheque.

As in the case of other simple contracts,[86] the courts do not normally concern themselves with the adequacy of consideration.[87] But inadequacy of consideration may be evidence of bad faith or unconscionable conduct.[88]

**Void consideration.** There is no consideration sufficient to support a **4–012** simple contract within subsection (1)(a) if the alleged consideration is in fact void. Where a loan is made and the circumstances are such that the loan is null and void by statute, a bill or note given by the borrower in respect of the loan will be unenforceable by the lender for want of consideration.[89] For the same reason a bill or note given in respect of a

---

[78] *Pollway v Abdullah* [1974] 1 W.L.R. 493 (Illustration 10).

[79] [1974] 1 W.L.R. 493.

[80] *Holliday v Atkinson* (1826) 5 B. & C. 501.

[81] *Eastwood v Kenyon* (1840) 11 A. & E. 435; *Re Whitaker* (1889) 42 Ch.D. 119.

[82] See below, paras 17–019 and 17–029.

[83] *Akrokerri (Atlantic) Mines Ltd v Economic Bank* [1904] 2 K.B. 465; *Re Farrow's Bank Ltd* [1923] 1 Ch. 41 (Illustration 26); *A.L. Underwood Ltd v Barclays Bank Ltd* [1924] 1 K.B. 775 (Cheques Act 1957, s.4, Illustration 9); *Westminster Bank Ltd v Zang* [1966] A.C. 182 (Cheques Act 1957, s.2, Illustration 1); *National Australia Bank Ltd v KDS Construction Services Pty Ltd* (1988) 76 A.L.R. 27.

[84] *Royal Bank of Scotland v Tottenham* [1894] 2 Q.B. 75 (s.13, Illustration); *Westminster Bank Ltd v Zang* [1966] A.C. 182 at 206, 207, 213; *Barclays Bank Ltd v Astley Industrial Trust Ltd* [1970] 2 Q.B. 527, 539–540 (Illustration 28). See below, para.17–020.

[85] *Barclays Bank Ltd v Astley Industrial Trust Ltd* [1970] 2 Q.B. 527. See below, para.17–020.

[86] See *Chitty on Contracts* (29th ed.), Vol.I, § 3–014.

[87] *Jones v Gordon* (1877) 2 App. Cas. 616, 631–632; *Adib el Hinnawi v Yacoub Fahmi* [1936] 1 All E.R. 638. But see *MK International Development Co. Ltd v Housing Bank* [1991] Bank.L.R. 74 (Illustration 25) (partial absence of consideration).

[88] *Allen v Davis* (1850) 4 De G. & S. 133; *Simmons v Cridland* (1862) 5 L.T. (N.S.) 524; *Jones v Gordon* (1872) 2 App.Cas. 616 at 632. See also *Chitty on Contracts* (29th ed.), Vol.I, §§ 3–021, 7–047, 27–032.

[89] *Sharp v Ellis* (1971) 20 F.L.R. 199.

contract or transaction which is null and void by statute or at common law will be unenforceable as between immediate parties[90] to the instrument.[91] As between remote parties,[92] however, it may be enforceable. A statute may, exceptionally, render the instrument void in whosesoever hands it may come.[93] But otherwise, if a bill or note given for a void consideration is negotiated to a third party, the holder will be entitled to enforce it against the defendant unless value has not at any time been given for the instrument after the defendant became a party to it.[94] The onus of proving absence of value rests upon the defendant.[95]

An instrument given in respect of a contract which is not void, but is merely unenforceable for failure to comply with certain requirements of form,[96] does not lack consideration. Thus an action could be brought on a cheque given in payment of a deposit under an oral contract for the sale of land even though the contract itself was unenforceable for want of any note or memorandum in writing as required by section 40 of the Law of Property Act 1925.[97] However, by section 2 of the Law of Property (Miscellaneous Provisions) Act 1989, a contract for the sale or other disposition of an interest in land can now only be made in writing and the document must be signed by or on behalf of each party to the contract. In the absence of any signed writing there is no contract. It would therefore seem that there would be no consideration for an instrument given in respect of such a transaction.

An instrument given in furtherance of an exchange contract which is unenforceable (though not illegal) under the Bretton Woods Agreement Order 1946 may itself be unenforceable, in whole or in part, in an English court.[98]

4–013     **Consumer Credit Act 1974.**[99] Section 123 of the Consumer Credit Act 1974 imposes restrictions upon the use of negotiable instruments in connection with a regulated consumer credit agreement or a regulated consumer hire agreement, other than in the case of non-commercial agreements,[1] *i.e.* agreements not made by the creditor or owner in the

---

[90] See above, para.4–005.
[91] *Richardson v Moncrieffe* (1926) 43 T.L.R. 32.
[92] See above, para.4–005.
[93] *e.g.* Gaming Act 1710, s.1 (as originally enacted); Betting and Loans (Infants) Act 1892, s.5 (now repealed).
[94] s.27(2). See *Fitch v Jones* (1855) 5 E. & B. 238 (Illustration 14); *Ong Guam Hua v Chong* [1963] M.L.J. 6.
[95] ss.30(1), (2).
[96] *e.g.* under s.4 of the Statute of Frauds 1677.
[97] *Low v Fry* (1935) 152 L.T. 585.
[98] *Mansouri v Singh* [1986] 1 W.L.R. 1393 (s.72, Illustration 13). See below, para.12–020 (s.72).
[99] See Guest and Lloyd, *Encyclopedia of Consumer Credit* (1975).
[1] Defined in s.189(1).

course of a business carried on by him. A consumer credit agreement[2] is an agreement between an individual[3] (including a sole trader, partnership or unincorporated association) ("the debtor")[4] and any other person ("the creditor")[5] by which the creditor provides[6] the debtor with credit not exceeding £25,000.[7] A consumer hire agreement[8] is an agreement made by a person with an individual[9] (the "hirer") for the bailment or (in Scotland) the hiring of goods to the hirer, being an agreement which (a) is not a hire-purchase agreement,[10] and (b) is capable of subsisting for more than three months, and (c) does not require the hirer to make payments exceeding £25,000.[11] A consumer credit or consumer hire agreement is a regulated agreement if it is not an exempt agreement by virtue of section 16 of the Act or of regulations made under that section.[12]

Section 123(1) of the Act provides that a creditor or owner shall not take a negotiable instrument,[13] other than a bank note or cheque,[14] in discharge of any sum payable by the debtor or hirer under a regulated agreement, or by any person as surety[15] under a regulated agreement. Subsection (3) of the same section prohibits the creditor or owner from taking a negotiable instrument as security[16] for the discharge of any sum payable as mentioned in subsection (1). A person who takes a negotiable instrument in contravention of section 123 (1) or (3) is not a holder in due course, and is not entitled to enforce the instrument.[17] Bills of exchange and promissory notes cannot, therefore, be taken in payment of any sum payable by the debtor or hirer, or by a surety, under a regulated agreement; nor can they be taken as security for any sum so payable. Cheques can be taken in payment, but not as security.[18] However, subsection (2)

---

[2] Defined in ss.8(2), 189(1).
[3] Defined in s.189(1).
[4] Defined in s.189(1).
[5] Defined in s.189(1).
[6] *i.e.* agrees to provide.
[7] The limit was raised from £5,000 from May 20, 1985 by SI 1983/1878 and to £25,000 from May 1, 1998, by SI 1998/996. Proposed legislation will abolish the limit.
[8] Defined in ss.15(1), 189(1).
[9] Defined in s.189(1).
[10] Hire-purchase agreements are deemed fixed-sum credit agreements; see s.9(3).
[11] The limit was raised from £5,000 from May 20, 1985 by SI 1983/1878 and to £25,000 from May 1, 1998, by SI 1998/996. A Bill has been introduced to remove the financial limit entirely.
[12] ss.8(3), 14(2). See the Consumer Credit (Exempt Agreements) Order 1989 (SI 1989/869) as amended.
[13] "Negotiable instrument" is not defined in the Act. It is questionable whether this expression includes an instrument which is not transferable and therefore not negotiable (see ss.8(1), 81A).
[14] "Cheque" is not defined in the Act, but presumably has the same meaning as in s.73.
[15] Defined in s.189(1).
[16] s.123(4).
[17] s.125(1).
[18] s.123(4).

provides that the creditor or owner shall not negotiate a cheque taken by him in payment except to a banker (within the meaning of the Bills of Exchange Act 1882).[19]

Any contravention of section 123 also renders the credit or hire agreement, and any security provided in relation to it, enforceable on an order of the court only.[20]

For the effect of the section on the rights of a transferee where an instrument has been taken or transferred in breach of its provisions, see the Comment on section 29, below, para.4–070.[21]

4–014    **Exemptions.** Certain important exemptions exist, either directly or indirectly, to the operation of section 123 of the 1974 Act. First, the Consumer Credit (Exempt Agreements) Order 1989[22] provides (*inter alia*) that the following are exempt, and not regulated, agreements: (i) a debtor–creditor–supplier agreement[23] for fixed-sum credit[24] under which the total number of payments[25] to be made by the debtor does not exceed four, and those payments are required to be made within a period of 12 months beginning with the date of the agreement[26]; (ii) a debtor–creditor–supplier agreement[27] for running-account credit[28] which provides for the making of payments[29] by the debtor in relation to specified periods and requires that the number of payments to be made by the debtor in repayment of the whole amount of the credit provided in each period shall not exceed one[30]; and (iii) a consumer credit agreement made in connection with trade in goods or services between the United Kingdom and a country outside the United Kingdom or within a country or between countries outside the United Kingdom, being an agreement under which credit is provided to the debtor in the course of a business carried on by him.[31] The first and second of these exemptions will usually exempt from being regulated agreements (and consequentially from the operation of section 123) those agreements where normal trade credit is provided, *e.g.* a sale of goods with an extension of the time of payment by the buyer. The third exemption will exempt from being a regulated

---

[19] s.2 of the 1882 Act; above, para.1–016.
[20] s.124. See also ss.106, 113.
[21] See below, paras 4–070—4–071.
[22] SI 1989/869, as amended.
[23] Defined in ss.12, 189(1) of the 1974 Act.
[24] Defined in ss.10(1)(b), 189(1) of the 1974 Act.
[25] "Payment" means a payment comprising an amount in respect of credit with or without any other amount. See also s.9(4) of the 1974 Act.
[26] Art.3(1)(a)(i) (subject to art.3(2)).
[27] Defined in ss.12, 189(1) of the 1974 Act.
[28] Defined in ss.10, 189(1) of the 1974 Act.
[29] See above, n.25.
[30] Art.3(1)(a)(ii) (subject to art.3(2)).
[31] Art.5(a).

agreement foreign trade transactions where, for example, payment is to be made by instalments. Bills and notes can therefore still be employed in relation to such foreign transactions. It does not matter whether the credit is extended under the transaction to or by a person in a foreign country. Moreover the extension of credit by a United Kingdom bank or financial institution to a sole trader or partnership in the United Kingdom to finance the import of goods from overseas would appear to fall within that exemption.

Secondly, the Consumer Credit (Negotiable Instruments) Order 1984[32] provides that section 123 shall not apply in the case of a consumer hire agreement where it is made in connection with trade in goods between the United Kingdom and a country outside the United Kingdom or within a country or between countries outside the United Kingdom, being an agreement under which goods are bailed or (in Scotland) hired to the hirer in the course of a business carried on by him.

The extent to which the 1974 Act otherwise applies to credit and hire agreements having a foreign connection or involving some foreign element is a matter of some difficulty and lies outside the scope of the present work.[33]

**Illegal consideration.** As in the case of any other contract,[34] the contract constituted by a person's signature of a bill or note may be unenforceable against him by reason of illegality. He may raise against an immediate party[35] the defence that his engagement was given for an illegal consideration.[36] Such a defence will also be available against a remote party who takes the instrument with knowledge of the illegality,[37] or when it is overdue,[38] but not against a holder in due course.[39] Normally a person to whom a bill or note is negotiated is prima facie deemed to be a holder in due course.[40] But section 30(2) of the Act provides that, if in an action on a bill it is admitted or proved that the acceptance, issue or subsequent negotiation of the bill is affected with illegality, the burden of proof is shifted, unless and until the holder proves that, subsequent to **4–015**

---

[32] SI 1984/435.
[33] See Guest and Lloyd, *Encyclopedia of Consumer Credit* (1975) §§ 2–194, *et seq.*
[34] See *Chitty on Contracts* (29th ed.) Vol.I, Ch.16.
[35] See above, para.4–005.
[36] *Howden v Haigh* (1840) 11 A. & E. 1033; *Jones v Merionethshire Permanent Benefit Building Soc.* [1892] 1 Ch. 173 (Illustration 11).
[37] *Hay v Ayling* (1851) 16 Q.B. 423, 431; *Shaw v Benson* (1883) 11 Q.B.D. 563 (Illustration 12); *Woolf v Hamilton* [1898] 2 Q.B. 337 (Illustration 13); *Robinson v Benkel* (1913) 29 T.L.R. 495; *Ladup Ltd v Shaikh* [1983] Q.B. 225 (Illustration 16).
[38] *Amory v Merryweather* (1824) 2 B. & C. 573 (s.36, Illustration 1); but contrast *Chalmers v Lanion* (1808) 1 Camp. 383 (s.36, Illustration 8).
[39] s.29.
[40] s.30(2).

the illegality, value has in good faith been given for the bill. If, therefore, the consideration is illegal, as opposed to being merely void, the onus under section 30(2) rests upon the holder to satisfy the court that value has been given for the instrument in good faith and without notice of the illegality.[41] However, a holder (whether a holder for value or not), who derives his title to a bill or note through a holder in due course, and who is not a party to any illegality affecting it, has all the rights of that holder in due course as regards the acceptor and all parties to the bill prior to that holder.[42] In such a case, mere knowledge of the illegality does not deprive him of those rights.

If a bill is accepted for lawful consideration, but is subsequently indorsed by the payee to a third party for an illegal consideration, it is submitted that the indorsee could not maintain an action on the bill either against the payee or against the acceptor.[43] It is further submitted that, if a bill is given for an illegal consideration, but is subsequently indorsed by the payee to a third party for value, the estoppel otherwise raised against the payee in favour of the indorsee by section 55(2)(c) of the Act would not be available if the indorsee knew, at the time he took the bill, that it had been given for an illegal consideration.[44]

**4–016**     **Gaming and wagering.**[45] The difference between void and illegal consideration may be illustrated by reference to the statutes which regulate gaming and wagering, namely, the Gaming Acts 1710, 1835, 1845, 1892 and 1968.

**4–017**     (i) *Instruments given in respect of gaming or wagering contracts.* Section 18 of the Gaming Act 1845 provides:

> "All contracts or agreements, whether by parole or in writing, by way of gaming or wagering,[46] shall be null and void; and . . . no suit shall be brought or maintained in any Court of Law or Equity for recovering any money or valuable thing alleged to be won upon any wager, or which shall have been deposited in the hands of any

---

[41] *Robinson v Benkel* (1913) 29 T.L.R. 475; *Tan Chow Soo v Ratna Ammal* [1969] 2 M.L.J. 49, PC.

[42] s.29(3). See also s.36(2) and *Chalmers v Lanion* (1808) 1 Camp. 383.

[43] The opinion to the contrary, expressed by Brett and Cotton L.JJ. in *Flower v Sadler* (1882) 10 Q.B.D., 572, 575, 576, cannot, it is submitted, be reconciled with s.30 (2).

[44] *Ladup Ltd v Shaikh* [1983] Q.B. 225 (Illustration 16). But in that case the cheque was crossed and bore the words "not negotiable", so that s.81 of the Act applied.

[45] The statutes referred to in paras 4–016 to 4–020 will be entirely repealed upon the entry into force of the Gambling Act 2005.

[46] It makes no difference that gaming is carried on, not with cash, but with gaming chips: *Lipkin Gorman v Karpnale Ltd* [1991] 2 A.C. 548.

person to abide the event on which any wager shall have been made."

Amounts won by gaming or wagering are therefore irrecoverable by action. Further, it has been held that, even though there is a fresh promise supported by fresh consideration by the loser to the winner to pay the amount of a lost bet, no action can be maintained, since it is a suit brought to recover a sum of money "alleged to be won upon any wager".[47] Although the section does not specifically refer to negotiable instruments given for the payment of money lost under a gaming or wagering contract, it is clear that, if such an instrument, *e.g.* a cheque, is given to the winner by the loser in payment, the winner can no more maintain an action against the loser on the cheque than on the original contract.[48] However, an instrument given in respect of a wagering contract rendered void by the 1845 Act is not given for an illegal consideration, but for no consideration.[49] If such an instrument is negotiated by the winner to a third party, the third party may enforce it if he is a holder for value of the instrument.[50] The burden of proving absence of value rests upon the defendant[51] and it is immaterial that the holder knew that the instrument was originally given in connection with a wager.[52]

Different considerations, however, apply where a negotiable instrument is given in respect of gaming (which includes horse racing).[53] Section 1 of the Gaming Act 1710 provided that securities of every kind given wholly or in part for any money or valuable thing won by gaming, or by playing at any game or by betting on any game,[54] or for repaying any money lent for such gaming or betting, or lent at the time and place of play to any person so gaming or betting, should be "'utterly void, frustrate, and of none effect". As a result, an instrument so given was unenforceable against the loser, not only by the winner, but also by a holder of the instrument who acquired it for value and in ignorance of its origin.[55] Section 1 of the Gaming Act 1835 therefore enacted that any security, including a bill or note, which would under the 1710 Act have been absolutely void, should be deemed and taken to have been made, drawn, accepted, given, or executed for an illegal consideration. So, for

---

[47] *Hill v William Hill (Park Lane) Ltd* [1949] A.C. 530, overruling *Hyams v Stuart-King* [1908] 2 K.B. 696.
[48] *Richardson v Moncrieffe* (1926) 43 T.L.R. 32; *Hill v William Hill (Park Lane) Ltd* [1949] A.C. 548.
[49] *Fitch v Jones* (1855) 5 E. & B. 238 (Illustration 14).
[50] s.27(2). See *Fitch v Jones* (1855) 5 E. & B. 238.
[51] ss.30(1), (2).
[52] *Lilley v Rankin* (1886) 56 L.J.Q.B. 248.
[53] *Applegarth v Colley* (1842) 10 M. & W. 723.
[54] cf. *Ladup Ltd v Shaikh* [1983] Q.B. 225 (Illustration 16).
[55] *Bowyer v Bampton* (1741) 2 Stra. 1155; *Shillito v Theed* (1831) 7 Bing. 405.

example, if the loser gives to the winner a cheque in settlement of a lost gaming bet, neither the winner nor any person to whom the cheque is negotiated by the winner and who has knowledge of its origin can enforce the cheque.[56] But a holder in due course can enforce it.[57] The holder must discharge the onus of proof placed upon him by section 30(2).[58]

**4–018**    (ii) *Instruments given in respect of loans to pay lost bets.* The 1710 and 1835 Acts do not appear to apply to instruments given in respect of loans to pay bets already lost, as the money is not lent "for gaming".[59] But, by section 1 of the Gaming Act 1892:

> "Any promise, express or implied, to pay any person any sum of money paid by him under or in respect of any contract or agreement rendered null and void by the Gaming Act, 1845 . . . shall be null and void, and no action shall be brought or maintained to recover any such sum of money."

Thus if A lends money to B to settle B's gaming or wagering losses, the loan will be irrecoverable if it has been paid direct to the winner, for the money lent has been paid by A "under or in respect of" a contract avoided by the Act of 1845.[60] Similarly, where such a loan is paid to the loser, it will be irrecoverable if it is made subject to a stipulation that it is to be used to settle gaming or wagering losses,[61] though not if it is advanced to the loser to use as he thinks fit.[62] If the circumstances are such that a loan is null and void by virtue of the 1892 Act, then it would appear that a negotiable instrument given by the borrower in respect of the loan will be unenforceable by the lender as the consideration will be void. But if the instrument were negotiated by the lender to a third party for value, the third party could enforce it notwithstanding that he knew the circumstances in which it had been given.[63] The burden of proving absence of value would rest upon the defendant.[64]

---

[56] *Hay v Ayling* (1851) 16 Q.B. 423, 431; *Woolf v Hamilton* [1898] 2 Q.B. 337 (Illustration 13); *Ladup Ltd v Shaikh* [1983] Q.B. 225 *cf. Robinson v Benkel* (1913) 29 T.L.R. 475.
[57] s.29.
[58] See above, para.4–015; below, para.4–082. But see also s.29(3).
[59] *Ex p. Pyke* (1878) 8 Ch.D. 754 (but the actual decision would not now be followed by reason of the Gaming Act 1892: *Macdonald v Green* [1951] 1 K.B. 594). Contrast *Parker v Alcock* (1831) You. 361; *Humphrey v Wilson* (1929) 141 L.T. 469.
[60] *Tatam v Reeve* [1893] 1 Q.B. 44; *Woolf v Freeman* [1937] 1 All E.R. 178. *C.H.T. Ltd v Ward* [1965] 2 Q.B. 63.
[61] *Macdonald v Green* [1951] 1 K.B. 594.
[62] *Re O'Shea* [1911] 2 K.B. 981.
[63] s.27(2).
[64] ss.30(1), (2).

(iii) *Instruments given in respect of loans for betting.* An instrument, *e.g.* a **4–019** cheque, given to repay money[65] lent for gaming will be caught by the Gaming Acts 1710 and 1835. It will be deemed by 1835 Act to have been given for an illegal consideration. As between lender and borrower it will be unenforceable.[66] Although the 1710 and 1835 Acts in their terms apply only to securities, it has been held that the lender can sue neither on the instrument nor on the underlying contract of loan.[67] If the lender nego- tiates the instrument for value to a third party, the third party cannot enforce it if he took it with knowledge of the circumstances in which it was given. In order to enforce it, a holder would have to discharge the onus of proof under section 30(2).[68]

A loan to enable a borrower to make a non-gaming wager will probably be void under the Gaming Act 1892 if made subject to a stipulation that it is to be used for betting.[69] In such a case, an instrument given in respect of such a loan would probably be held to have been given for a void, but not for an illegal, consideration.

(iv) *Gaming on licensed premises.* Validity is accorded in certain circum- **4–020** stances to cheques given in connection with gaming by section 16 of the Gaming Act 1968.[70] Part II of that Act establishes a system for the licens- ing and registration of premises for gaming. Subsection (1) of section 16 provides that, where gaming takes place on licensed premises, the licen- see "shall not make any loan or provide or allow to any person any credit,[71] or release,[72] or discharge on another person's behalf, the whole or part of any debt (a) for enabling any person to take part in the gaming, or (b) in respect of any losses incurred in the gaming". Subsection (2) provides that the licensee shall not accept a cheque and give in exchange for it cash or tokens for enabling any person to take part in the gaming

---

[65] Including gaming chips provided for gaming: *Stuart v Stephen* (1940) 56 T.L.R. 571; *Carlton Hall Club Ltd v Laurence* [1929] 2 K.B. 153. *cf. Cumming v Mackie* 1973 S.L.T. 242, but dicta in this case were disapproved in *R. v Knightsbridge Crown Court, Ex p. Marcrest Ltd* [1983] 1 W.L.R. 300, 310. Contrast s.16(4) of the Gaming Act 1968; below, para.4–020.
[66] *Moulis v Owen* [1907] 1 K.B. 746; *Stuart v Stephen* (1940) 56 T.L.R. 571.
[67] *Applegarth v Colley* (1842) 10 M. & W. 723; *Carlton Hall Club Ltd v Lawrence* [1929] 2 K.B. 153 discussed in *Chitty on Contracts* (29th ed.), Vol.II, §§ 40–066, 40–072, and see *C.H.T. Ltd v Ward* [1965] 2 Q.B. 63, 85, 86). But where a loan is made in, and governed by the laws of a foreign country to bet on a game that is legal there, then, even though the lender cannot sue on an instrument governed by English law, *e.g.* a cheque drawn on an English bank (*Moulis v Owen* [1907] 1 K.B. 746), he may nevertheless sue and recover on the contract of loan: *Quarrier v Colston* (1842) 1 Ph. 147; *Saxby v Fulton* [1909] 2 K.B. 208; *Société Anonyme des grands Etablissements du Touquet-Paris-Plage v Baumgart* (1927) 43 T.L.R. 278.
[68] But see s.29(3).
[69] See *Chitty on Contracts* (29th ed.), Vol.II, § 40–065.
[70] As amended by s.1 of the Gaming (Amendment) Act 1986.
[71] See *R. v Knightsbridge Crown Court, Ex p. Marcrest Properties Ltd* [1983] 1 W.L.R. 300, 306, 309, 310; *Crockfords Club Ltd v Mehta* [1992] 1 W.L.R. 355.
[72] See *Ladup Ltd v Shaikh* [1983] Q.B. 225; *R. v Knightsbridge Crown Court, Ex p. Marcrest Properties Ltd* [1983] 1 W.L.R. 300.

unless certain conditions are satisfied. These conditions are that the cheque must not be post-dated, and it must be exchanged for cash or tokens to the amount or value for which it is drawn.[73] By subsection (3), the holder of the licence must also cause the cheque to be delivered to a bank for payment or collection not more than two days after he has accepted it.[74] Subsection (4) of the section further provides that nothing in the Gaming Acts of 1710, 1835, 1845 or 1892 "shall affect the validity of, or any remedy in respect of, any cheque which is accepted in exchange for cash or tokens to be used by a player in gaming" to which Part II of the Act applies.

The effect of these complex provisions would appear to be as follows: first, if a licensee accepts a cheque[75] and gives in exchange for it cash or tokens for enabling a person to take part in gaming on the licensed premises, then, if the conditions specified in section 16(2) are satisfied, the cheque is enforceable[76] and its validity is not affected by the Gaming Acts 1710, 1835, 1845 or 1892.[77] Secondly, if a licensee accepts a cheque and gives in exchange for it cash or tokens for enabling a person to take part in gaming on the licensed premises, but the conditions specified in section 16(2) are not satisfied, then an offence is committed,[78] and the cheque would be considered to have been given for an illegal considera-tion.[79] Thirdly, if a licensee makes a loan or provides or allows credit in contravention[80] of section 16(1),[81] then any negotiable instrument (includ-ing a cheque) given to or by the licensee in connection therewith would be considered to have been given for an illegal consideration. Fourthly, neither section 16(2) nor 16(4) validates a cheque given by a licensee in exchange for tokens, *e.g.* when a player cashes in his chips.[82]

**4–021**  **Subsection (1)(b): antecedent debt or liability.** By way of introduction it should be recalled that, as a general rule in the law of contract, the mere

---

[73] Where these conditions are fulfilled, the giving of cash or tokens in exchange for a cheque is not to be taken to contravene subs. (1): see subs. (2). For redeemed cheques and substitute cheques given in exchange for a redeemed cheque, see s.1(2A)(3A) (inserted by s.1(3) of the Gaming (Amendment) Act 1968), and s.1(4).

[74] The effect of an infringement of subs. (3) on the enforceability of the cheque is uncertain. But if there is a common intention that there is to be no legal right to have the cheque honoured when presented, what is provided is a "sham": *R. v Knightsbridge Crown Court, Ex p. Marcrest Properties Ltd* [1983] 1 W.L.R. 300 at 308.

[75] Even a third-party cheque: *Crockfords Club Ltd v Mehta* [1992] 1 W.L.R. 355. Contrast *Lipkin Gorman v Karpnale Ltd* [1991] 2 A.C. 548 (banker's draft).

[76] As is also the contract of loan: *Crockfords Club Ltd v Mehta* [1992] 1 W.L.R. 355.

[77] *Lipkin Gorman v Karpnale Ltd* [1989] 1 W.L.R. 1340, 1363–1364. But these observations must be read in the light of the appeal to the House of Lords: [1991] 2 A.C. 548.

[78] s.23. See *Ladup Ltd v Shaikh* [1983] Q.B. 225; *R. v Knightsbridge Crown Court, Ex p. Marcrest Properties Ltd* [1983] 1 W.L.R. 300 at 308.

[79] *Ladup Ltd v Shaikh* [1983] Q.B. 225.

[80] s.23 (offence).

[81] *R. v Knightsbridge Crown Court, Ex p. Marcrest Properties Ltd* [1983] 1 W.L.R. 300 at 306.

[82] *Ladup Ltd v Shaikh* [1983] Q.B. 225.

existence of an antecedent debt due from the promisor to the promisee is no consideration for a promise since it amounts only to past consideration.[83] However, if the creditor (the promisee) in return for the promise[84] agrees to forbear to enforce his claim to the debt, even temporarily,[85] then there is consideration and the promise is binding.[86] Further, although the creditor does not agree to forbear, an actual forbearance at the request (express or implied) of the promisor is consideration for the promise.[87] But an actual forbearance which is not induced by the express or implied request of the promisor is no consideration.[88]

Before the Act it had long been held that, if a creditor took a bill or note payable at a future time in payment of an antecedent debt owed to him by the person giving the instrument, he became a holder for value.[89] The reason put forward was that the taking of such an instrument implied an agreement on the part of the creditor to suspend his remedies for the debt during the interval before the instrument became payable. In 1875, however, in *Currie v Misa*[90] a cheque payable on demand was taken by a creditor in respect of an antecedent debt due to him from his immediate transferor. The Court of Exchequer Chamber nevertheless held that the creditor was a holder of the cheque for value. Lush J., delivering the judgment of the majority of the court,[91] pointed out that, in view of the then practice of not presenting cheques for payment until the following day, consideration might be found in the benefit to the debtor by the holding over. But he preferred to rest his judgment on a different ground:

" . . . in truth, the title of a creditor to a bill given on account of a pre-existing debt, and payable at a future day, does not rest upon the implied agreement to suspend his remedies. The true reason is . . . that a negotiable security given for such a purpose is a conditional payment of the debt, the condition being that the debt revives if the

---

[83] *Chitty on Contracts* (29th ed.), Vol.I, § 3–026.
[84] *Wigan v English & Scottish Law Life Assurance Soc.* [1909] 1 Ch. 291.
[85] *Willatts v Kennedy* (1831) 8 Bing. 5; *Morton v Burn* (1837) 7 A. & E. 19; *Oldershaw v King* (1857) 2 H. & N. 517; *Fullerton v Provincial Bank of Ireland* [1903] A.C. 309, 313; *Board v Hoey* (1949) 65 T.L.R. 43.
[86] *Chitty on Contracts* (29th ed.), Vol.I, § 3–046.
[87] *Alliance Bank v Broom* (1864) 2 Dr. & Sm. 289, as explained in *Fullerton v Provincial Bank of Ireland* [1903] A.C. 309 at 313; *Crears v Hunter* (1887) 19 Q.B.D. 341, 342, 344, 346 (Illustration 9).
[88] *Combe v Combe* [1951] 2 K.B. 215. See also *Crears v Hunter* (1887) 19 Q.B.D. 341 at 344.
[89] See, *e.g. Poplewell v Wilson* (1720) 1 Stra. 264; *Baker v Walker* (1814) 14 M. & W. 465; *Balfour v Sea Fire Life Assurance Co.* (1857) 3 C.B. N.S. 300.
[90] (1875) L.R. 10 Exch. 153, affirmed *sub. nom. Misa v Currie* (1876) 1 App. Cas. 554 (Illustration 17).
[91] Lord Coleridge C.J. dissenting.

security is not realized. This is precisely the effect which both parties intended the security to have, and the doctrine is as applicable to one species of negotiable security as to another; to a cheque payable on demand, as to a running bill or a promissory note payable to order or bearer, whether it be the note of a country bank which circulates as money, or the note of the debtor, or of any other person. The security is offered to the creditor, and taken by him as money's worth, and justice requires that it should be as truly his property as the money which it represents would have been his had the payment been made in gold or a Bank of England note."[92]

There was therefore no distinction between an instrument payable at a future time and one payable on demand: consideration could be found in either case in the conditional payment of the debt.

It is against this background that section 27(1)(b) should be construed. It has been stated[93] that the first sentence was "intended to get over what would otherwise have been prima facie the result at common law that the giving of a cheque for an amount for which you are already indebted imports no consideration, since the obligation is past and has been already incurred". The second sentence was intended to resolve any doubt as to the correctness of the decision of the majority of the court in *Currie v Misa*.[94] The words "or liability" were added in committee. They perhaps extended the previous law.

4–022    It follows that, if the holder of an instrument negotiates it to his creditor in payment of a pre-existing debt owed by him, the creditor will give value for the instrument, and, if the other requirements of section 29(1) of the Act are satisfied,[95] will be a holder in due course.[96]

Where a customer delivers an order or bearer cheque to his banker for collection at a time when his account is overdrawn, the banker will become a holder for value of the cheque by virtue of section 27(1)(b) (irrespective of any lien on the cheque under section 27(3)[97] if the cheque is paid in for the express purpose of reducing the overdraft or if the banker expressly or impliedly agrees to accept it in conditional reduction of the overdraft.[98] But the mere fact that the banker credits the amount of

---

[92] (1875) L.R. 10 Exch. 153 at 163–164. But see *D. & C. Builders v Rees* [1966] 2 Q.B. 617.
[93] *Oliver v Davis* [1949] 2 K.B. 727, 735 *per* Evershed M.R.
[94] [1949] 2 K.B. 727 at 736.
[95] See below, para.4–050.
[96] *Golden Prism v But-Shor Investments and Distributors (Pty) Ltd* 1978 (1) S.A. 512.
[97] See below, paras 4–029 and 17–021.
[98] *Currie v Misa* (1879) L.R. 10 Exch. 153; *McLean v Clydesdale Banking Co.* (1883) 9 App. Cas. 95; *Midland Bank v Reckitt* [1933] A.C. 1, 18 (s.25, Illustration 9); *Re Keever* [1967] Ch. 182 (Illustration 27); *Barclays Bank Ltd v Astley Industrial Trust Ltd* [1970] 2 Q.B. 527, 539 (Illustration 28). See below, para.17–020.

such a cheque to the overdrawn account does not necessarily mean that he has given value for the cheque.[99]

**Antecedent debt or liability of third party:** The question has arisen as to whether the words "an antecedent debt or liability" in subsection (1)(b) extend to a debt or liability of a third party, *i.e.* of a person other than the promisor or drawer, maker or negotiator of the instrument. In *Oliver v Davis*,[1] A drew a cheque payable to B and forwarded it to B in respect of a debt owed by C to B. The Court of Appeal held, on the facts,[2] that B had provided no consideration for A's promise, as drawer, to pay the cheque. Somervell and Denning L.JJ. were of the opinion[3] that section 27(1)(b) did not apply to a promise to pay an antecedent debt or liability of a third party and that, in such a case, in order that the promise might be enforced, there had to be consideration sufficient to support a simple contract. But Evershed M.R., while concurring in this view, also stated:

4–023

> "This at any rate is plain—that if the antecedent debt or liability of a third party is to be relied upon as supplying 'valuable consideration for a bill' there must at least be some relationship between the receipt of the bill and the antecedent debt or liability".[4]

and that in such a case "you must find something in the transaction sufficient at the very least to connect the receipt of the bill with the antecedent debt or liability".[5]

It is clear that the Court of Appeal did not intend to cast any doubt on the rule that consideration could consist of a promise to forbear by the holder of the instrument, or by an actual forbearance on his part at the express or implied request of a party to the instrument, in regard to a third party's debt or liability.[6] But the consideration is then the forbearance, and not the antecedent debt or liability of the third party. *Oliver v Davis* therefore appears to establish the proposition that the antecedent debt or liability referred to in section 27(1)(b) must be an antecedent debt

---

[99] *Westminster Bank Ltd v Zang* [1966] A.C. 182 (where the banker continued to charge interest on the whole amount of the overdraft); *National Australia Bank Ltd v KDS Construction Services Pty Ltd* (1988) 76 A.L.R. 27. cf. *Barclays Bank Ltd v Astley Industrial Trust Ltd* [1970] 2 Q.B. 527. See below, para.17–019.

[1] [1949] 2 K.B. 727. See also *AEG (UK) Ltd v Lewis, The Times*, December 29, 1992, CA.

[2] Illustration 18.

[3] [1949] 2 K.B. 727 at 741, 742.

[4] [1949] 2 K.B. 727 at 735.

[5] [1949] 2 K.B. 727 at 736.

[6] *Oliver v Davis* [1949] 2 K.B. 727 at 743. See also *Balfour v Sea Life Assurance Co.* (1857) 3 C.B. N.S. 300; *Hasan v Willson* [1977] 1 Lloyd's Rep. 431, 441, *J.D.F. Builders Ltd v Albert Pearl (Management) Ltd* (1974) 49 D.L.R. (3d) 422.

or liability of the promisor or drawer, maker or negotiator of the instrument, and not of a stranger to the instrument, and this was the interpretation put upon the case by Goff J. in *Hasan v Willson*.[7] Moreover, in *MK International Development Co. Ltd v Housing Bank*[8] this proposition was adopted and applied by Mustill L.J. in the Court of Appeal. Nevertheless, certain problems remain. First, it is difficult to see why the principle in *Currie v Misa*, that consideration may be found in conditional payment of a debt, should not equally apply where the debt is that of a third party.[9] Secondly, the wider dicta of Evershed M.R. in *Oliver v Davis* have been relied on in New Zealand,[10] for example, in *Bonior v Siery Ltd*[11] where a cheque drawn by a company was taken by the payee in payment of an antecedent debt due to the payee from a director of the company, with the result that the company was entitled to reduce its indebtedness to the director by debiting his account with the company. It was held that "there was such a close relationship between payment on behalf of the third party and the affairs of [the company] as constitutes consideration". In England, however, it must now be taken to be settled law that the antecedent debt or liability referred to in section 27(1)(b) cannot be that of a stranger. This may be justified on the ground that, as between immediate parties,[12] consideration—whether present or past—must move from the promisee.

There may nevertheless be one situation where an antecedent debt or liability of one person could be relied on to enforce the instrument against another person who signed it without receiving value.[13] This is where the person whose liability it is sought to enforce signed the instrument as an accommodation party[14] and the antecedent debt or liability is that of the party accommodated.[15] So, for example, a debt of £1,000 is due and owing

---

[7] [1977] 1 Lloyd's Rep. 431 (Illustration 19).

[8] [1991] 1 Bank.L.R. 74 (Illustration 25) see also *AEG (UK) Ltd v Lewis, The Times*, December 29, 1992, CA.

[9] *Currie v Misa* (1875) L.R. 10 Exch. 153; *Ayres v Moore* [1940] 1 K.B. 279, 282. See also *Wragge v Sims Cooper & Co. (Australia) Pty Ltd* (1933) 50 C.L.R. 483, at 491–492; *Walsh v Hoag & Bosch Pty Ltd* [1977] V.R. 178. In *Oliver v Davis*, there was no acceptance by the creditor (B) of the cheque by way of conditional payment before payment was stopped.

[10] *Bonior v Siery Ltd* [1968] N.Z.L.R. 254. cf. *Electrical Technologies Ltd v Auckland Electrical Services Ltd* [1995] 3 N.Z.L.R. 726. See also *Finch Motors Ltd v Quin* [1980] 2 N.Z.L.R. 513; *International Ore and Fertiliser Corpn. v East Coast Fertiliser Co. Ltd* [1987] 1 N.Z.L.R. 9, and *Canadian Bank of Commerce v Pioneer Farm Co. Ltd* [1927] 4 D.L.R. 772; *J.D.F. Builders Ltd v Albert Pearl (Management) Ltd* (1974) 49 D.L.R. (3d) 422, 433; *Independent Wholesale Ltd v Steinke* (1996) 180 Alberta R. 58 (Canada); *Walsh v Hoag & Bosch Pty Ltd* [1977] V.R. 178 (Australia).

[11] [1968] N.Z.L.R. 254. But the court in this case also found a degree of forbearance by the payee.

[12] See above, para.4–005.

[13] *Crawford and Falconbridge* (8th ed.), pp.1426, 1427.

[14] s.28.

[15] *Gallagher v Murphy* [1929] 2 D.L.R. 124; *Mollot v Monette* (1982) 128 D.L.R. (3d) 577. Contrast *Stack v Dowd* (1907) 15 O.L.R. 331.

from C to B. A, to accommodate C, and at his request, joins with C in making a promissory note for £1,000 payable to B. The antecedent debt of C will be sufficient consideration to enable B to enforce the note against A.[16]

**Subsection (2): holder for value.** The holder of a bill or note is the payee or indorsee who is in possession of it, or the bearer of the instrument.[17] The holder may or may not be a holder for value.[18] By subsection (2) of this section, where value has at any time been given for a bill, the holder is deemed to be a holder for value as regards the acceptor and all parties to the bill who became parties prior to such time. If the holder has himself given value, the consequence is that he is a holder for value as regards all prior parties, even those who received no value.[19] Thus, for example, A draws an order cheque payable to B and delivers it to B as a gift. B deposits the cheque with his bank, which gives value for it.[20] The bank is a holder for value as regards A, even though A received no value for the cheque. Further, even though the holder does not himself give value, if value has *at any time* been given for the instrument, he will be a holder for value as regards the acceptor and all parties who became parties prior to such time.[21] For example, B draws a bill on A payable to C. A accepts gratuitously. C gives value for the bill and indorses it to D as a gift. Although D has not himself given value, he is a holder for value as regards A and B. The words "prior to such time" should not be construed too literally: a person may become a party to the bill and give value simultaneously.[22]

4–024

The subsection makes it clear that a holder may be a holder as regards some parties to a bill or note, but not as regards others. It is also clear that a holder can rely on the subsection to make him a holder for value as against a remote party even though he himself has not provided consideration for the instrument. But it is less clear whether the subsection is confined to cases where the holder and the party whose liability it is sought to enforce are remote parties, or whether its effect extends to cases where they are immediate parties.[23] In *Churchill and Sim v Goddard*,[24] Scott

---

[16] *Mollot v Monette* (1982) 12 8 D.L.R. (3d) 577. See also *Scott v Lifford* (1808) 1 Camp. 246 (Illustration 20).

[17] s.2; above, para.1–022.

[18] s.2; above, para.1–022.

[19] *Scott v Lifford* (1808) 1 Camp. 246 (Illustration 20); *Barber v Richards* (1851) 6 Exch. 63 (Illustration 23). See also *Munroe v Bordier* (1849) 8 C.B. 862; *Poirier v Morris* (1853) 2 E. & B. 89; Thorneley [1968] C.L.J. 196. Contrast Geva [1980] C.L.J. 360.

[20] See below, para.17–019 (Cheques Act 1957, s.2).

[21] *MK International Development Co. Ltd v Housing Bank* [1991] 1 Bank.L.R. 74 (Illustration 25).

[22] [1991] 1 Bank.L.R. 74.

[23] For the distinction between remote and immediate parties, see above, para.4–005.

[24] [1937] 1 K.B. 92, 110.

L.J. said: "As between immediate parties, the defendant is entitled to prove absence of consideration moving from the claimant as a defence to an action on the bill . . . " If this is correct, then, notwithstanding the terms of the subsection, between immediate parties, consideration must move from the claimant,[25] and the absence or failure of this is a good defence to the action. In *Hasan v Willson*,[26] Robert Goff J. expressed his support for the view[27] that, as between immediate parties, consideration must move from the promisee.

A second, but cognate, question is whether the words "where value has . . . been given" in section 27(2) extend to a case where the value referred to is given by a stranger, *i.e.* by a person who never becomes a party to the instrument. In *Diamond v Graham*,[28] the claimant agreed to lend a sum of money to H if H would obtain and deliver a cheque drawn by the defendant payable to the claimant. H obtained such a cheque from the defendant by giving the defendant his own cheque in return. Upon receipt of the defendant's cheque, the claimant released payment of his cheque for the loan. Both H's cheque in favour of the defendant and the defendant's cheque in favour of the claimant were dishonoured. The Court of Appeal held that the claimant had furnished consideration for the defendant's cheque by releasing payment of his cheque to H. But Danckwerts L.J. also considered, as an alternative, that value was given for the defendant's cheque when H (who was not, of course, a party to the defendant's cheque) gave the defendant his own cheque in return. "There is nothing in the subsection [subs. (2)]", he said,[29] which appears to require value to have been given by the holder as long as value has been given for the cheque." This has been interpreted[30] to mean that, in the view of Danckwerts L.J., the subsection permits value to be provided by a stranger to the instrument.

**4–025**      If this interpretation is correct,[31] then it must be pointed out that the view of Danckwerts L.J. was unnecessary to the decision, as it was held that consideration for the defendant's promise did in fact move from the claimant. Moreover, in *Pollway v Abdullah*[32] where a purchaser of property by auction gave to the auctioneers a cheque payable to their order for the amount of the deposit due under the terms of sale, Roskill L.J.[33] expressed

---

[25] But it need not move to the defendant.
[26] [1977] 1 Lloyd's Rep. 431, 442.
[27] Set out in *Byles* (2nd ed., 1972), p.190. *cf. Byles* (27th ed.), § 18–16.
[28] [1968] 1 W.L.R. 1061 (Illustration 24).
[29] [1968] 1 W.L.R. 1061 at 1064 (with whose judgment Diplock and Sachs L.JJ. agreed). See also *Wragge v Sims Cooper & Co. (Australia) Pty Ltd* (1933) 50 C.L.R. 483.
[30] By Robert Goff J. in *Hasan v Willson* [1977] 1 Lloyd's Rep. 431 at 441.
[31] In *MK International Development Co. Ltd v Housing Bank* [1991] 1 Bank.L.R. 74, Mustill L.J. stated that he did not read the judgment of Danckwerts L.J. in this sense.
[32] [1974] 1 W.L.R. 493 (Illustration 10).
[33] [1974] 1 W.L.R. 493 at 497.

considerable doubt as to whether the vendor's undertaking to sell the property could be the consideration for the cheque, as this consideration did not move from the promisee—the payees of the cheque, and stated that, notwithstanding *Diamond v Graham*, he would have required further argument as to the questions which might arise under section 27(2) of the Act. In *Hasan v Willson*[34] Robert Goff J. rejected the view that, for the purposes of subsections (1) or (2) of section 27, consideration could be provided by a stranger. The same stance was adopted by Mustill L.J. in the Court of Appeal in *MK International Development Co. Ltd v Housing Bank*[35] where, in an action by the payee against the drawer of a cheque, it was sought to rely on consideration provided by a third party as value given for the cheque under section 27(2). Mustill L.J. stated that the subsection was intended to apply where an instrument had been negotiated and in any event it was " not be read as envisaging value being provided by strangers to the instrument". This is, it is submitted, sufficient authority for the proposition that the words "where value has . . . been given" in the subsection mean "where any party to the bill has given value" and do not extend to value given by a stranger.

**Rights of holder for value.**[36] The rights of a holder for value, other than a holder in due course, are not set out in the Act. A holder for value will not qualify as a holder in due course[37] if he takes a bill which is not complete and regular on the face of it[38] or which is overdue,[39] or if at the time he becomes a holder he has notice that it has been previously dishonoured,[40] or if he does not take the bill in good faith,[41] or if at the time the bill is negotiated to him he has notice of a defect in the title[42] of the person who negotiated it,[43] or if he is the original payee of the bill.[44] The position of a holder to whom an overdue bill is negotiated and that of a holder who takes the bill with notice of previous dishonour are specifically dealt with in subsections (2) and (5) of section 36 of the Act.[45] The position of the payee-holder calls for special treatment and is accordingly dealt with later in this work.[46]

**4–026**

---

[34] [1977] 1 Lloyd's Rep. 431, 441–442.
[35] [1991] 1 Bank.L.R. 74 (Illustration 25).
[36] See Geva (1980–1981) 5 C.B.L.J. 53.
[37] s.29(1); below, para.4–050.
[38] s.29(1); below, para.4–052.
[39] ss.29(1)(a), 36(2); below, paras 4–054 and 5–039.
[40] ss.29(1)(a), 36(5); below, paras 4–055 and 5–045.
[41] ss.29(1)(b), 90; below, paras 4–056 and 16–001.
[42] s.29(2); below, para.4–062.
[43] s.29(1)(b); below, para.4–058.
[44] *Jones (R.E.) Ltd v Waring & Gillow Ltd* [1926] A.C. 670; below, para.4–059.
[45] See below, paras 5–039 and 5–045.
[46] See below, para.5–072.

A holder for value has the right, in common with any other holder, to sue on the bill in his own name.[47] But there is some uncertainty as to the defences which may be raised against him. It is clear that a defendant may raise against a holder for value any "real" or "absolute" defences.[48] But, in addition, since section 38(2) of the Act provides that a holder in due course holds the bill free from any defect of title of prior parties as well as from mere personal defences available to prior parties among themselves, it could be argued that it follows that the claim of a mere holder for value may be defeated both by defects of title of prior parties and by personal defences available to prior parties among themselves.[49]

With respect to "any defect of title of prior parties", a holder for value takes the bill subject to any defect of title[50] attaching to the bill at the time it is negotiated to him,[51] and it is immaterial whether his claim is against an immediate party or a remote party and whether or not he has notice of the defect.[52] "The difference between the rights of a 'holder in due course' and those of a 'holder' is that a holder in due course may get a better title than the person from whom he took, whereas a holder gets no better title."[53]

4–027   With respect to "mere personal defences available to prior parties among themselves", the Act expressly recognises that there may be personal defences and it neither defines or limits the number of such defences.[54] Prior to the Act, the defences now referred to as defects in title were known as "equities attaching to the bill"[55] in contrast with "equities between the parties", which is presumably what is meant by "mere personal defences". Such defences will include matters of set-off or counterclaim,[56] general contractual defences[57] and defences under statute.[58]

---

[47] s.38(1); below, para.5–055.

[48] See below, para.5–070.

[49] *Arab Bank Ltd v Ross* [1952] 2 Q.B. 216, 224.

[50] See below, para.4–062.

[51] *cf.* ss.36(2), (5).

[52] *Crossley v Ham* (1811) 13 East 498; *Amory v Merryweather* (1824) 2 B. & C. 573; *Lloyd v Howard* (1850) 15 Q.B. 995; *Parr v Jewell* (1855) 16 C.B. 684 (s.36, Illustration 2); *Holmes v Kidd* (1858) 3 H. & N. 891 (s.36, Illustration 3); *Shaw v Benson* (1883) 11 Q.B.D. 563 (Illustration 12); *Woolf v Hamilton* [1898] 2 Q.B. 337 (Illustration 13); *Arab Bank Ltd v Ross* [1952] 2 Q.B. 216, 229.

[53] *Arab Bank Ltd v Ross* [1992] 2 Q.B. 216 at 229 *per* Denning L.J.

[54] *Stock Motor Ploughs Ltd v Forsyth* (1932) 48 C.L.R. 125, 155.

[55] below, para.4–062.

[56] *Stein v Yglesias* (1834) 1 C.M. & R. 565; *Whitehead v Walker* (1842) 10 M. & W. 696; *Oulds v Harrison* (1854) 10 Exch. 572 (s.36, Illustration 7); *Re Overend Gurney & Co., Ex p. Swan* (1868) L.R. 6. Eq. 344.

[57] *e.g.* that the contract is conditional (see above, para.2–152) or that the signature was to be without liability (see above, para.2–167) or that the contract was procured by misrepresentation.

[58] *Stock Motor Ploughs Ltd v Forsyth* (1932) 48 C.L.R. 125.

Absence or failure of consideration is not an equity attaching to the bill[59] and may accordingly be classified as a personal defence. A personal defence will ordinarily be available between immediate parties.[60] But in principle it should *not* be available against a remote holder for value.[61] However, the question arises whether a defendant who has such a defence against a prior party can assert it against a remote holder for value who took the bill in good faith but with notice of the defence. It would appear that he cannot do so.[62] Yet there may be special circumstances, *e.g.* a known total failure of consideration,[63] where such a defence could be raised.

A holder for value will nevertheless be entitled to the benefit of the "shelter" rule in section 29(3) of the Act[64] where he derives his title to the bill through a holder in due course.

A holder for value does not enjoy the protection and privileges extended by the Act only to a holder in due course.[65]

**Rights of mere holder.** A holder (a "mere holder") who is not a holder    4–028
for value may sue on the bill in his own name,[66] but the Act does not indicate what defences may be raised against him. Where a holder has not himself given value, but value has at some time been given for the bill, then, under subsection (2), he is deemed to be a holder for value as regards the acceptor and all parties to the bill who became parties prior to such time. However, if value has not at any time been given for the bill, or, if value has been given, as regards those who became parties gratuitously after the giving of value,[67] it would seem that he could always be met by the defence of absence or failure of consideration, whether his claim is against an immediate or remote party.[68]

---

[59] *Stein v Yglesias* (1834) 1 C.M. & R. 565; *Sturtevant v Ford* (1842) 4 M. & G. 101 (s.36, Illustration 6); *Re Overend Gurney & Co., Ex p. Swan* (1868) L.R. 6 Eq. 344; *Ashley Colter Ltd v Scott* [1942] 3 D.L.R. 538. Contrast Geva [1980] C.L.J. 360.

[60] See above, paras 2–160, 4–006, 4–009. But see (unliquidated cross-claims), above, paras 4–009, 4–010.

[61] *Charles v Marsden* (1808) 1 Taunt. 224; *Archer v Bamford* (1822) 3 Stark. 175; *Burrough v Moss* (1830) 10 B. & C. 558; *Stein v Yglesias* (1834) 1 C.M. & R. 565; *Robinson v Reynolds* (1841) 2 Q.B. 196; *Sturtevant v Ford* (1842) 4 M. & G. 201; *Whitehead v Walker* (1842) 10 M. & W. 696; *Fitch v Jones* (1855) 5 E. & B. 238 (Illustration 14); *Re Overend Gurney & Co., Ex p. Swan* (1868) L.R. 6 Eq. 344. But see *Re European Bank, Ex p. Oriental Commercial Bank* (1870) 5 Ch.App. 358 (s.36, Illustration 4). Contrast Goode, *Commercial Law* (3rd ed.), p.515; Geva (1980) 5 Can. Bus L.J. 53 and [1980] C.L.J. 360.

[62] *Scott v Lifford* (1808) 1 Camp. 246 (Illustration 20) (see also s.28(2)); *Oulds v Harrison* (1854) 10 Exch. 572; *Lilley v Rankin* (1887) 56 L.J.Q.B. 248 (Illustration 15).

[63] See above, para.4–008.

[64] See below, para.4–072.

[65] See below, para.5–071 (s.38(2)).

[66] s.38(1).

[67] Other than the acceptor.

[68] See above, paras 4–006—4–009 (impeachment of value).

**4–029**     **Subsection (3): holder having a lien.** "A lien is a right in one man to retain that which is in his possession belonging to another, till certain demands of him the person in possession are satisfied."[69] A lien may arise from contract (express or implied) or by implication of law. Where the holder of a bill has a lien on it, he is deemed to be a holder for value to the extent of the sum for which he has a lien. The lien most frequently encountered in this connection is the banker's lien.[70]

"Bankers most undoubtedly have a general lien on all securities deposited with them, as bankers, by a customer, unless there be an express contract, or circumstances that show an implied contract inconsistent with lien."[71] The lien extends (*inter alia*) to bills of exchange, cheques and promissory notes,[72] but is not limited to fully negotiable securities.[73] The securities must come into the banker's hands in his capacity as banker and in the ordinary course of banking business.[74] Usually the lien attaches to secure the customer's total indebtedness to the bank at any one time.[75] Unlike other common law liens, a banker's lien confers upon the banker as holder the right to realise the instrument by claiming payment from those liable on it.[76]

A banker's lien attaches to a cheque deposited with him by a customer for collection.[77] Since a banker may at one and the same time be an agent for collection and the holder of a cheque payable to order or to bearer,[78] he may be deemed to be a holder for value under subsection (3) if he collects such a cheque for a customer whose account is

---

[69] *Hammonds v Barclay* (1802) 2 East 227, 235.

[70] See Ellinger, Lomnicka and Hooley, *Modern Banking Law* (3rd ed., 2002), p.779; *Paget* (12th ed.), 29.2.

[71] *Brandao v Barnett* (1846) 12 Cl. & Fin. 787, 806. See also *Jones v Peppercorne* (1858) John 430; *London Chartered Bank of Australia v White* (1879) 4 App. Cas. 413; *Re London and Globe Finance Corp.* [1902] 2 Ch. 416. cf. *General Produce Co. v United Bank Ltd* [1979] 2 Lloyd's Rep. 255.

[72] *Wylde v Radford* (1863) 33 L.J. Ch. 51, 53.

[73] See Ellinger, Lomnicka and Hooley, *Modern Banking Law* (3rd ed., 2002), p.780, *Paget* (12th ed.), 29.2. But under subs.(3), the bank must be a "holder".

[74] *Brandao v Barnett* (1846) 12 Cl. & Fin. 787 at 806.

[75] *Atwood v Crowdie* (1816) 1 Stark. 483; *Re European Bank* (1872) L.R. 8 Ch.App. 41; *Re London and Globe Finance Corp.* (1846) 12 Cl. & Fin. 787 at 420; *Re Keever* [1967] Ch. 182 (Illustration 27); *Bank of New South Wales v Ross, Stuckey and Morawa* [1974] 2 Lloyd's Rep. 110, 112. But see *Wilkinson v London and County Banking Co.* (1884) 1 T.L.R. 63; *Re Bowes* (1886) 33 Ch.D. 586.

[76] nn.94 and 95, below.

[77] *Johnson v Robarts* (1875) 10 Ch.App. 505; *Misa v Currie* (1876) 1 App. Cas. 554, 565, 569, 573; *Re Keever* [1967] Ch. 182; *Barclays Bank Ltd v Astley Industrial Trust Ltd* [1970] 2 Q.B. 527 (Illustration 28); *Bank of New South Wales v Ross, Stuckey and Morawa* [1974] 2 Lloyd's Rep. 110. cf. *Akrokerri (Atlantic) Mines Ltd v Economic Bank* [1904] 2 K.B. 465.

[78] *Sutters v Briggs* [1922] 1 A.C. 1; *Baker v Barclays Bank Ltd* [1955] 1 W.L.R. 822. See also Cheques Act 1957, s.2. But see below, paras 14–037 and 17–017 (cheques crossed "account payee").

overdrawn.[79] Alternatively he may sometimes rely upon the overdraft as an "antecedent debt or liability" and thus good consideration within section 27(1)(b).[80] When the cheque is paid by the drawee, the banker may apply the proceeds in reduction or extinction of the customer's indebtedness, unless they have been earmarked for a different purpose.[81]

It has been stated that bankers cannot claim a general banker's lien **4–030** except upon the customer's own property[82]; but this must be doubted so far as negotiable instruments are concerned.[83] With respect to subsection (3), the person seeking to rely on the subsection must be the "holder" of the bill.[84] So, for example, where an indorsement on an order bill is forged, the purported indorsee will not be a holder.[85] Nor will a person (other than the original payee) be the holder of an instrument which is not transferable, for example, one which is drawn "Pay X only"[86] or a cheque which is crossed "account payee".[87] But since it has been said that no distinction is to be drawn between the expressions "holder for value", "holder who has taken for value" and "holder who has given value" where they occur in the Act,[88] a holder who is deemed by subsection (3) to be a holder for value will be a holder in due course if the conditions set out in section 29(1) are satisfied.[89] If those conditions are not satisfied, then the holder will be subject to such defences as are available against a mere holder for value.[90] And in the case of a cheque crossed "not negotiable", the holder will hold it subject to any defects in title of his transferor.[91]

The deposit of a negotiable instrument by way of pledge to secure an advance or other indebtedness is technically different from the exercise of

---

[79] *Sutters v Briggs* [1922] 1 A.C. 1 at 18; *Midland Bank Ltd v Reckitt* [1933] A.C. 1, 18; *Re Keever* [1967] Ch. 182; *Barclays Bank Ltd v Astley Industrial Trust Ltd* [1970] 2 Q.B. 527; *Bank of New South Wales v Ross, Stuckey and Morawa* [1974] 2 Lloyd's Rep. 110; *National Australia Bank Ltd v KDS Construction Services Pty Ltd* (1988) 76 A.L.R. 27.

[80] See above, para.4–021; below, para.17–020.

[81] *Re Keever* [1967] Ch. 182. *cf. Halesowen Presswork and Assemblies Ltd v Westminster Bank Ltd* [1971] 1 Q.B. 1, 46; [1972] A.C. 785.

[82] *Cuthbert v Robarts, Lubbock & Co.* [1909] 2 Ch. 226, 233.

[83] *Brandao v Barnett* (1846) 12 Cl. & F. 787, 805–806; *Johnson v Robarts* (1875) 10 Ch.App. 505. See also *London Joint Stock Bank v Simmons* [1892] A.C. 201 (pledge).

[84] As defined in s.2, above, para.1–022.

[85] See above, para.3–066.

[86] s.8(1).

[87] s.81A.

[88] *Barclays Bank Ltd v Astley Industrial Trust Ltd* [1970] 2 Q.B. 927 at 539.

[89] [1970] 2 Q.B. 927. See also *Re Keever* [1967] Ch. 182.

[90] See above, para.4–024. See also *Ex p. Kingston* (1871) L.R. 6 Ch.App. 632; *Sheffield (Earl of) v London Joint Stock Bank Ltd* (1888) 13 App. Cas. 333; *Redfern & Son v Rosenthal* (1902) 86 L.T. 855 (no lien if securities known not to be property of pledgor); *Bank of Credit and Commerce International S.A. v Dawson and Wright* (1987) Fin.L.R. 342 (bank claiming lien privy to fraud).

[91] s.81; below, para.14–030.

a lien, but it probably falls within the subsection.[92] Indeed a banker's lien on negotiable securities has been judicially described as "an implied pledge".[93] A holder who has a lien or is a pledgee may recover from any party to the bill to the extent of the sum for which he has the lien or pledge.[94] If the person from whom he received the bill could have sued on the bill, he may recover the whole amount of the bill, and on recovery becomes a trustee for the person entitled to the remainder of the money, after deducting the sum for which he has the lien or pledge.[95] As regards the difference between that sum and the amount of the bill, the defendant can raise against him any defence or set-off available against the person for whom he is trustee.[96] It is the duty of the holder to present the instrument at maturity and to give proper notice of dishonour if it is not paid.[97]

The lien is lost if the holder parts with possession of the bill.[98] Where a banker discharges a bill by payment on behalf of his customer, the acceptor, the bill ceases to be negotiable under section 36 of the Act and he does not become a holder for value of the bill under subsection (3).[99]

The discounting of bills is not within the subsection; a discounter is a holder for full value.[1]

ILLUSTRATIONS

**4–031**      1. The defendants accept a bill of exchange for £20,000 drawn on them by the claimants in respect of repairs and alterations to be carried out by

---

[92] In any event, the pledgee has the same rights at common law: *Collins v Martin* (1797) 1 B. & P. 648; *Atwood v Crowdie* (1816) 1 Stark. 483; *Re Bunyard, Ex p. Newton* (1880) 16 Ch.D. 330 (Illustration 30).

[93] *Brandao v Barnett* (1846) 12 Cl. & Fin. 787, 806.

[94] *Collins v Martin* (1797) 1 B. & P. 648; *London Joint Stock Bank v Simmons* [1892] A.C. 201.

[95] *Reid v Furnival* (1833) 1 Cr. & M. 538 (Illustration 29); *Re Bunyard, Ex p. Newton* (1880) 16 Ch. D. 330.

[96] *Thornton v Maynard* (1875) L.R. 10 C.P. 695 (s.38, Illustration 1). See also *Barclays Bank Ltd v Aschaffenberger Zellstoffwerke A.G.* [1967] 1 Lloyd's Rep. 387 (Illustration 3) and above, para.4–010; below, para.5–060.

[97] *Peacock v Pursell* (1863) 14 C.B.N.S. 728; *Hamilton Finance Co. Ltd v Coverley, Westray, Walbaum and Tosetti Ltd* [1969] 1 Lloyd's Rep. 53, 72.

[98] *Lloyd's Bank v Swiss Bankverein* (1913) 18 Com. Cas. 79; *Westminster Bank Ltd v Zang* [1966] A.C. 182 (Cheques Act 1957, s.2, Illustration 2).

[99] *Auchteroni & Co. v Midland Bank Ltd* [1928] 2 K.B. 294, 300–301.

[1] *Ex p. Towgood* (1812) 19 Ves. Jun. 229; *Re Gomersall* (1875) 1 Ch.D. 137, 142. *cf. Re Firth, Ex p. Schofield (No.2)* (1879) 12 Ch. D. 337. Prima facie, where a bill is negotiated from one person to another, it is deemed to have been wholly transferred to the latter, and not to have been pledged or deposited as collateral security: *Ex p. Towgood* (1812) 19 Ves. Jun. 229; *Hills v Parker* (1866) 14 L.T. (N.S.) 107; *Re Boys* (1870) L.R. 10 Eq. 467.

the claimants to a ship. Upon an application by the claimants for summary judgment on the bill, the defendants allege that the claimants did not complete the repairs in time, whereby they lost profits of £100,000. This is no defence to the action on the bill and leave to defend is refused.[2]

2. Three bills of exchange totalling £9,000 are accepted by the defendants and indorsed to the claimant bankers. In proceedings under R.S.C. Order 14 brought by the claimants for summary judgment on the bills, the defendants counterclaim set-off in respect of amounts allegedly due under another transaction between the claimants and the defendants. Judgment is given for the claimants and a stay of execution pending trial of the counterclaim is refused.[3]

3. BCI Ltd agree to supply and erect certain machinery for the defendants. Pursuant to the agreement 18 bills of exchange are drawn by BCI Ltd and accepted by the defendants. These are indorsed by BCI Ltd and delivered to the claimant bankers. The claimants pay BCI Ltd only 73 per cent of the value of the bills, it being agreed that the balance of 27 per cent will be credited on receipt to the account of BCI Ltd. The eleventh and twelfth bills (totalling £96.812) are dishonoured. In proceedings for summary judgment brought by the claimants, the defendants claim to set-off liquidated damages for delay in the sum of £46,000, and in addition counterclaim damages of £2,000,000, in respect of the construction contract. Judgment is given for the claimants for the amount of bills but with a stay of execution as to 27 per cent of the claim. As to the 27 per cent, the claimants are trustees for BCI Ltd, and any defence or set-off in respect of the liquidated damages claim which the defendants have against BCI Ltd is available against the claimants so far as that proportion is concerned.[4]

4. The claimants contract to manufacture and deliver to the defendants certain machinery for a total sum of £235,000. Six promissory notes are made by the defendants, payable to the claimants at intervals during the progress of the work. The first note is not met and the claimants suspend work. The second note is presented and is unpaid. On an application for summary judgment in respect of these two notes, judgment is given for the claimants on the first note. This covered work in progress and was equivalent to cash. But leave to defend is given in respect of the second note. Since the claimants had suspended work before it became due, a defence is available on the ground of failure of consideration.[5]          4–032

[2] *James Lamont & Co. Ltd v Hyland Ltd* [1950] 1 K.B. 585.
[3] *Brown Shipley & Co. Ltd v Alicia Hosiery Ltd* [1966] 1 Lloyd's Rep. 668.
[4] *Barclays Bank Ltd v Aschaffenberger Zellstoffwerke A.G.* [1967] 1 Lloyd's Rep. 387.
[5] *Fielding & Platt Ltd v Najjar* [1969] 1 W.L.R. 357.

5. The defendants accept a bill of exchange for £7,208 drawn on them by the claimants as the price of 10,000 bottles of scent to be delivered by the claimants by a certain date. On the stipulated date only 5,144 bottles have been delivered. An application is made by the claimants for summary judgment on the bill. Judgment is given for the claimants for £314 admittedly due, with leave to defend as to the balance, which by agreement is to be brought into court.[6]

6. An application is made by the claimants for summary judgment on five bills of exchange, totalling £56,469, accepted by the defendants and payable to the claimants in respect of goods sold and delivered by the claimants to the defendants. The defendants counterclaim £42,461 as damages in respect of defects in the goods supplied, defects in goods supplied under other contracts and for failure to supply other goods ordered. Judgment is given for the claimants on the bills and a stay of execution refused.[7]

4–033      7. To settle an account relating to the supply of goods, the defendants accept a bill of exchange drawn on them by the claimants in the sum of Austrian schillings 1,000,000. In proceedings brought by the claimants for summary judgment on the bill, the defendants allege that their indebtedness to the claimants was only 400,897 schillings and in consequence that there was a failure of consideration in a liquidated amount of 599,103 schillings. Judgment is given for the claimants for 400,897 schillings with leave to defend as to the balance of 599,103 schillings on condition that that amount is brought into court.[8]

8. The defendants accept a number of bills of exchange drawn on them by the claimants in respect of 26,000 kilos of cloth delivered by the claimants to the defendants by instalments. In answer to an application by the claimants for summary judgment on the bills, the defendants claim that 17,200 kilos were unsatisfactory and not in accordance with the contract, and were of less value, and that they rejected the goods delivered. Judgment is given for the claimants for the amount of the bills. Having accepted the goods, the defendants were not entitled to reject them, and their claim in consequence was a counterclaim for unliquidated damages for defective goods.[9]

9. A debt is owed by the defendant's father to the claimant. A promissory note for the debt is drawn up and signed by the defendant's father

---

[6] *Saga of Bond Street Ltd v Avalon Promotions Ltd* [1972] 2 Q.B. 325n.
[7] *Cebora SNC v S.I.P. (Industrial Products) Ltd* [1976] 1 Lloyd's Rep. 271.
[8] *Thoni GmbH K.C. v R.T.P. Equipment Ltd* [1979] 2 Lloyd's Rep. 282.
[9] *Montebianco Industrie Tessilli SpA v Carlyle Mills (London) Ltd* [1981] 1 Lloyd's Rep. 509.

and the defendant by which they jointly and severally promise to pay the claimant the amount of the debt and in the meantime interest thereon at the rate of 5 per cent per annum half yearly. Interest is paid on the note. The claimant subsequently sues the defendant on the note for the principal sum. The jury is instructed that, if the note was signed by the defendant in order that the claimant might give time to his father, and the claimant did give time, there would be consideration for the making of the note by the defendant. The jury find for the claimant and their verdict is upheld by the Court of Appeal. Not only a promise by the creditor to forbear is good consideration, but also actual forbearance by him at the request, express or implied, of the debtor.[10]

10. The defendant purchases a property at auction. The conditions of sale provide for payment of a 10 per cent deposit of the purchase price to the auctioneers as agents for the vendors. The auctioneers accept for the deposit the defendant's cheque drawn payable to themselves. The defendant stops payment of the cheque and refuses to proceed with the sale. The auctioneers, as payees of the cheque, are entitled to judgment against the defendant, the drawer. The consideration provided by them for the cheque was either their warranty to the defendant of their authority to receive the cheque payable to themselves as named payees in diminution of the defendant's obligation to pay the full amount of the purchase price to the vendors or their acceptance of the cheque in place of legal tender, *i.e.* cash, due from the defendant.[11]    **4–034**

11. C embezzles the money of a building society. His wife and brother give promissory notes to the society for the amount, on the implied condition that he shall not be prosecuted. The notes are given upon an illegal consideration, and cannot be enforced.[12]

12. A note is made payable to an officer of an unregistered loan society, formed after the Companies Act 1862, the consideration being a loan by the society. The loan was made pursuant to the rules of the society, but the society consists of more than 20 members and is therefore illegal. The officer indorses the note to his successor. The indorsee cannot sue the maker.[13]

13. A cheque is given by the defendant in payment of bets upon horse races lost by him, and indorsed by the payee to the claimant for value with notice of the consideration for which it is given. The claimant cannot    **4–035**

---

[10] *Crears v Hunter* (1887) 19 Q.B.D. 341.
[11] *Pollway Ltd v Abdullah* (1974) 1 W.L.R. 493.
[12] *Jones v Merionethshire Permanent Benefit Building Society* [1892] 1 Ch. 173.
[13] *Shaw v Benson* (1883) 11 Q.B.D. 563.

enforce the cheque against the defendant, as it is deemed by the Gaming Act 1835 to have been given for an illegal consideration.[14]

14. The defendant makes a promissory note and delivers it to N in payment of a lost wager concerning the amount of hop duty in 1854. The note is indorsed by N to T and by T to the claimant. Since the note has been given in respect of a wagering contract rendered void by the Gaming Act 1845, it has been given, not for an illegal consideration, but for no consideration. The claimant is not required to prove that he gave consideration. It is for the defendant to prove that no consideration has been given for the note.[15]

15. The defendant makes two promissory notes for £1,000 and £8,000 payable to B in respect of gambling transactions on the stock exchange. The notes are indorsed by B to the claimant for value. Since the transactions were void, but not illegal, under the Gaming Act 1845, it is irrelevant whether the claimant was aware of the circumstances under which the notes were given and the claimant's claim on the notes succeeds.[16]

**4–036**  16. S, the first defendant, visits a casino run by the second defendants and obtains there a large amount of gaming chips in return for certain bank drafts. At the end of play, having lost a considerable amount, he exchanges his remaining chips for a crossed cheque for £45,000 drawn by the second defendants and stamped "account payee only not negotiable". S then goes to the claimants' casino, where he and his brother have incurred large gaming debts, and requests the claimants' manager to change the second defendants' cheque for him. The manager telephones the second defendants and is informed that the second defendants will pay on their cheque only if the drafts given to them by S are honoured. Nevertheless the claimants provide S with £37,500 worth of chips in exchange for the indorsement and delivery to them of the cheque, having first deducted £7,500 on account of the existing debts of S and his brother. Since the drafts given by S are not honoured, the second defendants countermand payment of their cheque. The claimants' action to enforce payment of the cheque against S and the second defendants fails. By virtue of the Gaming Acts 1710 and 1835, the cheque is deemed to have been given for an illegal consideration, and the claimants were aware of the illegality at the time they took the cheque. They cannot rely on the provisions of section 16 of the Gaming Act 1968 because (*inter alia*) the cheque was not drawn payable to the holder of a licence under the Act.

[14] *Woolf v Hamilton* [1898] 2 Q.B. 339.
[15] *Fitch v Jones* (1855) 5 E. & B. 238.
[16] *Lilley v Rankin* (1886) 56 L.J.Q.B. 248.

Further, as between themselves and S, the claimants contravened section 16 of the 1968 Act in that they supplied tokens of a value less than that for which the cheque was drawn.[17]

17. A cheque (or bill payable on demand) for £1,993 is drawn by the defendant on his bank payable to L or bearer. L is indebted to the claimants, who are his bankers, in substantial sums and is being pressed by them for payment. On the 13th, L hands the cheque to the claimants. On the 14th, the claimants present the cheque for payment and the amount of the cheque is credited to L's account. The defendant instructs the drawee bank to stop payment of the cheque. The claimants are holders for value of the cheque and can enforce it against the defendant. A creditor to whom a negotiable security is given on account of a pre-existing debt holds it by an indefeasible title, whether it be one payable at a future time or on demand.[18]

18. The claimant lends £350 to D who, in return, draws in favour of the claimant a post-dated cheque for £400. Before the cheque is presented D, who would be unable to meet it, persuades his fiancée, W, to draw in the claimant's favour a cheque for £400. D gives W's cheque to the claimant's wife in the absence of the claimant. Three days later the claimant returns and receives W's cheque. On the same day, W countermands payment of her cheque and informs the claimant that she has done so. The next day the claimant presents D's cheque for payment and it is dishonoured. Subsequently he presents W's cheque for payment and (payment having been stopped) it is dishonoured. W's promise, as drawer, to pay her cheque is unenforceable by the claimant. No consideration for the promises has moved from the claimant. Section 27(1)(b) of the Act does not apply where the antecedent debt or liability is not that of the person giving the cheque, but that of a third person.[19]

19. S, a director of P Ltd, is indebted to the claimant in the sum of £50,000. Arrangements are made whereby (i) S's wife draws on behalf of P Ltd a cheque for £55,000 payable to the defendant, (ii) the defendant draws a cheque for £50,000 payable to the claimant, and (iii) the defendant draws a cheque for £5,000 payable to P Ltd. When the claimant presents the defendant's cheque for £50,000 for special clearance, it is dishonoured, since the defendant has in the meantime discovered that P Ltd's cheque is worthless and so has stopped payment of both his cheques. The claimant claims damages from the defendant in respect of

**4–037**

[17] *Ladup Ltd v Shaikh* [1983] Q.B. 225.
[18] *Currie v Misa* (1875) L.R. 10 Exch. 727, affirmed *sub. nom. Misa v Currie* (1876) 1 App. Cas. 554.
[19] *Oliver v Davis* [1949] 2 K.B. 727.

the dishonour of the £50,000 cheque. The defendant raises the defence that this cheque was obtained from him by fraud on the part of S, and that there is no consideration for it. The defence of fraud fails, because the defendant fails to discharge the onus of proving that the claimant had notice of the fraud. The defence of absence of consideration succeeds. No consideration has been furnished by the claimant for the cheque. The "antecedent debt or liability" referred to in section 27(1)(b) of the Act must be a debt or liability of the drawer of the cheque and not that of a stranger.[20]

20. A is indebted to the claimant for £1,500. The claimant agrees to extend time for payment if A will accept a bill drawn on him by his uncle, the defendant, payable to the claimant. Since the claimant gave value for the bill to A, he is entitled to sue the defendant even though the defendant received no value.[21]

21. The claimant draws a bill on the defendant payable to his own order. The defendant, in order to accommodate the claimant, accepts it. Subsequently the claimant gives value for the bill. The claimant is a holder for value.[22]

4–038      22. The claimant is the treasurer and the trustee of a copartnership of which both he and the defendant, together with others are members. The defendant makes a promissory note for £45 payable to the claimant as security for a loan made to him by the copartnership. There is consideration for the note as between the claimant and the defendant, notwithstanding that both are jointly interested in the funds of the copartnership.[23]

23. E draws a bill on the defendant who accepts it. E indorses the bill in blank and delivers it to B, receiving no value. B pledges the bill with a pawnbroker, T, who gives value. T delivers the bill to the claimant. The claimant is a holder for value as regards the defendant.[24]

24. H requests the claimant to lend him £1,650. The claimant agrees to do so and gives H his cheque for £1,650 on condition that H undertakes to procure a cheque for £1,665 from the defendant by a certain date so that the claimant should have the defendant's cheque in his possession before

---

[20] *Hasan v Willson* [1977] 1 Lloyd's Rep. 431.
[21] *Scott v Lifford* (1808) 1 Camp. 246. (It was stated that this was not an accommodation bill as there was consideration between the payee and the acceptor).
[22] *Burdon v Benton* (1847) 9 Q.B. 843.
[23] *Lomas v Bradshaw* (1850) 19 L.J.C.P. 273.
[24] *Barber v Richards* (1851) 6 Exch. 63.

his own cheque is presented. The cheque from the defendant is not forthcoming in time, so the claimant stops payment of his cheque payable to H. A day later H obtains from the defendant a cheque for £1,665 drawn payable to the claimant by giving to the defendant a cheque drawn by H payable to the defendant for the same amount. H hands the defendant's cheque to the claimant, who pays it into his bank and authorises the bank to pay the cheque which he has drawn in H's favour. Both H's cheque in favour of the defendant and the defendant's cheque in favour of the claimant are dishonoured. Value has been given for the defendant's cheque, because the claimant himself gave value by releasing payment of his cheque to H after having stopped it and (*semble*) because value was given by H when he gave to the defendant the cheque drawn by H in favour of the defendant.[25]

25. N, a relative of the King of Jordan, requires office space and some **4–039** financial accommodation during a stay of a few months in London. K makes the necessary arrangements through two companies controlled by him. These are (i) the claimant, MKI Ltd, and (ii) Y Ltd. MKI Ltd provide the office space against N's undertaking to reimburse a share of the office expenses of £1,000 per month. Y Ltd make to N substantial loans. N defaults. K writes to the King, using MKI Ltd's letterhead, asking that pressure be put on N to repay his debts. K receives from the Royal Court a letter enclosing a cheque for £50,965 drawn by the defendant bank in Amman on the Arab Bank in London payable to "MKI Ltd or Bearer". Before the cheque is cleared N contacts the King's staff and denies the existence of any indebtedness. Payment of the cheque is countermanded and the cheque is accordingly dishonoured by the Arab Bank on presentation. MKI Ltd issue a writ claiming the amount of the cheque from the defendant bank and apply to serve the writ outside the jurisdiction. The application is resisted on the ground that there was no consideration for the cheque. Leave to serve the writ is given. Subject to determination of the truth of the above allegations at trial: (1) the antecedent debt of N, a stranger to the cheque, to MKI Ltd or Y Ltd would not be a valid consideration under section 27(1)(b); (2) an implied agreement by MKI Ltd to forbear to enforce its claim against N would be a valid consideration under section 27(1)(a), but MKI Ltd's claim on the cheque would be limited to the small amount owed to it; (3) value given by the King for the cheque would not cause MKI Ltd to be deemed a holder for value under section 27(2) since that subsection is intended to apply where the instrument has been negotiated and not in favour of the original payee and it requires value to have been given by a party to the cheque and not by a stranger; but (4) the cheque having being drawn payable to "MKI Ltd or

---

[25] *Diamond v Graham* [1968] 1 W.L.R. 1061.

Bearer" it is payable to bearer and in consequence the King might be considered the first holder, so that value given by the King for the cheque would then support the claim of MKI Ltd, a subsequent holder, to be a holder for value under section 27(2).[26]

26. V receives a crossed order cheque for £1,493 payable to him which he indorses and pays into his account with the F Bank. The F Bank forthwith credit him with the amount in their ledger and remit the cheque to the B Bank as their clearing agents, who credit it to the F Bank's account subject to recourse. The cheque is duly presented and paid. Before the B Bank advises the F Bank that the cheque has been cleared, and before the moneys are made available to the B Bank as the F Bank's agent, the F Bank suspends payment. The paying-in slip which accompanied V's payment in of the cheque stated that the F Bank reserved to itself the right, at its discretion, to defer payment of cheques against uncleared effects which might have been credited to the account. The liquidator of the F Bank must pay out of the assets of the bank the full amount of the cheque in question. The F Bank did not take the cheque as holders for value, but as agents for collection. The mere crediting by a bank of a cheque paid into the customer's account, without any knowledge of the customer or arrangement between him and the bank, does not convert the bank into a holder for value. This being so, the F Bank having received the money after they ceased to act as a going concern, the relationship between F Bank and V had not become that of debtor and creditor before the stoppage, but continued as that of agent and principal.[27]

27. On November 15 the M Bank receives from a customer for collection a cheque for £3,000 payable to order and credits it to the customer's account which is £352 overdrawn. There is also a debit balance of £1,000 on the customer's loan account. On November 16, the bank receives the proceeds of the cheque, unaware that a receiving order has that day been made against the customer. The bank is entitled to a lien on the cheque in the sum of £1,352 under section 27(3) and is also a holder in due course of the cheque.[28]

4–040 28. M Ltd are customers of the claimant bank and are overdrawn in excess of their authorised credit limit, their current overdraft being in excess of £4,600. They pay into their account five unindorsed[29] cheques drawn by the defendants payable to the order of M Ltd to the total value

---

[26] *MK International Development Co. Ltd v Housing Bank* [1991] 1 Bank.L.R. 74.
[27] *Re Farrow's Bank Ltd* [1923] 1 Ch. 41.
[28] *Re Keever* [1967] Ch. 182.
[29] Cheques Act 1957, s.2.

of £2,850. On receipt of these cheques and before they are cleared, the bank decides to honour certain cheques drawn on the account by M Ltd which the bank would otherwise have dishonoured. In the meantime the defendants discover that the transactions in respect of the five cheques are fraudulent and countermand payment. The bank has a lien on the five cheques and, under section 27(3), is deemed to be a holder for value to the extent of M Ltd's overdraft. Alternatively the bank is a holder for value because (i) it allowed M Ltd to draw against the uncleared cheques, and (ii) it accepted the cheques in conditional reduction of the overdraft. Having proved affirmatively absence of any knowledge of the fraud, the bank is a holder in due course.[30]

29. A bill is drawn by R on and accepted by the defendant for £300, payable three months after date to the drawer's order. The bill is indorsed by the drawer and passed to the claimant with a request that he get it discounted. The claimant hands the bill to the B Bank who agree to discount it against the claimant's guarantee but, since the whole amount of £300 is not immediately required, advance only £100 on it. The claimant is entitled to recover from the defendant the whole amount of the bill and not merely to the amount of his guarantee. As soon as the claimant recovers the whole amount, he becomes a trustee for the person entitled to the remainder of the money, after deducting the amount which he has advanced.[31]

30. B draws a bill for £300, which is accepted by B & Co. for his accommodation, and indorses it to N as security for performance of a contract. B becomes bankrupt. N can tender a proof for £300, but cannot recover dividends in excess of the debt due to him from B.[32]

### Accommodation bill or party

28. (1) An accommodation party to a bill is a person who has signed a bill as drawer, acceptor, or indorser, without receiving value therefor, and for the purpose of lending his name to some other person.   4–041

(2) An accommodation party is liable on the bill to a holder for value; and it is immaterial whether, when such holder took the bill, he knew such party to be an accommodation party or not.

---

[30] *Barclays Bank Ltd v Astley Industrial Trust Ltd* [1970] 2 Q.B. 527.
[31] *Reid v Furnival* (1833) 1 C. & M. 538.
[32] *Re Bunyard, Ex p. Newton* (1880) 16 Ch.D. 330.

| Definitions | Comparison |
|---|---|
| "bill": s.2. | UCC: § 3–419. |
| "holder": s.2. | |
| "person": s.2. | |
| "value".2. | |

COMMENT

4–042　**Accommodation bill.** Although the marginal note to this section refers to "Accommodation bill or party", the section only defines and deals with the liability of an accommodation party. The Act does not define the expression "Accommodation bill". Chalmers was of the view that the statement frequently made that a bill signed by one or more accommodation parties is an accommodation bill is incorrect[33]: "An accommodation bill is a bill whereof the acceptor (*i.e.* the principal debtor according to the terms of the instrument)[34] is in substance a mere surety for some other person who may or may not be a party thereto".[35] The distinction is of importance in relation to the discharge of the bill. Section 59(3) of the Act provides that, where an accommodation bill is paid in due course by the party accommodated the bill is discharged.[36] An accommodation bill is therefore discharged if it is discharged by the person who is in substance, though not in form, the principal debtor.[37]

The main commercial use of accommodation bills at the present day is the "acceptance credit".[38] which is a finance facility extended by a bank to its customer. The bank accepts bills drawn by the customer payable to himself at a future date. The signature of the bank as acceptor for the accommodation of the customer as drawer, enables the customer to discount the bill for cash in the commercial bills market. At maturity, the discounter presents the bill to the bank for payment. The customer is required on or before the due date to put the bank in funds to meet the bill.[39] But as against the discounter, the bank assumes the primary liability as acceptor to pay the bill.[40] The customer is thus enabled to obtain

---

[33] Citing *Scott v Lifford* (1808) 1 Camp. 246 (s.27, Illustration 20).
[34] Or the maker in the case of a promissory note: *Bechervaise v Lewis* (1872) L.R. 7 C.P. 372 (Illustration 2) or the drawer in the case of a cheque (*Sundelson v Knuttel*, 2000 (3) S.A. 513).
[35] Contrast *Byles* (27th ed.), § 19–37.
[36] Otherwise (s.59(2)) payment by the drawer or an indorser does not discharge the bill.
[37] See below, para.8–020.
[38] See Ellinger, Lomnicka and Hooley, *Modern Banking Law* (3rd ed., 2002), pp.690, 715.
[39] Or the bill is "rolled-over".
[40] s.54.

finance on the basis of the standing of the bank and its acceptance of the bill.[41]

The acceptance credit is essentially a short-term credit facility. But most acceptance credits are revolving credit facilities subject to a credit limit stipulated by the bank. When a bill is duly paid off by the customer, the amount becomes available to finance further bills unless the period of credit has expired and not been extended.

**Subsection (1): accommodation party.** The characteristics of an accom-  4–043
modation party can be elicited from the definition contained in this subsection. First, he is a person who has signed a bill as a drawer,[42] acceptor or indorser "without receiving value therefor".[43] Since every party whose signature appears on a bill is prima facie deemed to have become a party thereto for value,[44] the onus is on the person seeking to establish that the signatory is an accommodation party to prove that he signed the bill without receiving value. "Value" is defined by section 2 of the Act to mean valuable consideration.[45] In the case of an acceptance credit, the bank invariably receives a fee or commission. The question therefore arises whether the bank is an accommodation party and the bills drawn under the credit are accommodation bills. The authorities are divided,[46] but it is submitted that the bank is an accommodation party notwithstanding the charging of a fee or commission.[47] The provision of funds by the party accommodated in order to meet the bill when due does not appear to constitute the receipt of value by the accommodation party for the purposes of the present section.[48]

Secondly, an accommodation party must sign the bill "for the purpose of lending his name to some other person". *Byles*[49] interprets this to mean that the bill must be signed by the accommodation party in order that the person to whom he lends his name ("the person accommodated") may

---

[41] See Gillett, *The Bill on London*.

[42] *Sundelson v Knuttel*, 2000 (3) S.A. 513, 516 (cheque).

[43] The word "therefor" may mean "for the bill" or "for the signature".

[44] s.30(1).

[45] See also s.27(1).

[46] *Re Oriental Finance Corp. v Overend Gurney & Co.* (1871) L.R. 7 Ch.App. 142, 151 (affirmed (1874) L.R. 7 H.L. 348); *Re Yglesias, Ex p. Gomez* (1875) L.R. 10 Ch.App. 639, 643; *Re Securitibank Ltd* [1978] 1 N.Z.L.R. 97, 154; *K.D. Morris & Sons Pty Ltd v Bank of Queensland Ltd* (1980) 146 C.L.R. 165, 178, 201; *Coles Myer Finance Ltd v Commissioner of Taxation of the Commonwealth of Australia* (1993) 176 C.L.R. 640, 657, 683. See also *Bagnall v Andrews* (1830) 7 Bing. 217 222; *Re Overend Gurney & Co., Ex p. Swan* (1868) L.R. 6 Eq. 344, 356 (bill drawn against open account not an accommodation bill); Ellinger, Lomnicka and Hooley, *Modern Banking Law* (3rd ed., 2002), p.715.

[47] Accordingly the drawer cannot complain of want of due presentment, notice of dishonour or protest: see below, para.4–046.

[48] *National Office Supplies v Thazbhay* 1975 (3) S.A. 977; *Sundelson v Knuttel*, 2000 (3) S.A. 513, 518.

[49] 27th ed., § 19–37.

raise money upon it, or otherwise make use of it. However, it would appear also to be of the essence of accommodation that the accommodation party signs the bill as surety for the person accommodated. Although he is in form the drawer, acceptor or indorser of the bill, *vis-à-vis* the person accommodated he is a surety,[50] the implied agreement between them being that the person accommodated will provide the funds for the payment of the bill at maturity, or, if he fails to do so, will indemnify the accommodation party who is compelled to pay the bill.[51] It may therefore possibly be a requirement of accommodation that the person accommodated is or will be obliged to the principal creditor in respect of the debt in question.[52]

Parol evidence is admissible to show that a party to a bill is an accommodation party and the true relationship to each other of the signatories of the instrument.[53] Nevertheless, difficulties may arise in deciding whether a signatory is an ordinary party or an accommodation party.[54] In particular, a lender may agree to make an advance, allow credit or grant an extension of time to the person accommodated on condition that an accommodation signature is obtained. In such a case, valuable consideration will have been provided for the accommodation signature of the bill, but, since the accommodation party has not received value, he is not thereby deprived of his accommodation status.[55] In practice most anomalous indorsers under section 56 of the Act[56] will be found to be accommodation parties.

**4–044**     **Subsection (2): liability of accommodation party.** An accommodation party is liable on a bill to a holder for value.[57] The rule set out in this

---

[50] There may be contract of suretyship between the principal debtor and surety, but no contract of suretyship between the surety and the creditor: see *Chitty on Contracts* (29th ed.), Vol.II, § 44–003.

[51] *Reynolds v Doyle* (1840) 1 M. & G. 753; *Hawley v Beverley* (1843) 6 M. & G. 221, 227; *Asprey v Levy* (1847) 16 M. & W. 851; *Sleigh v Sleigh* (1850) 5 Exch. 514, 517; *Yates v Hoppe* (1850) 9 C.B. 541; *K.D. Morris & Sons Pty Ltd v Bank of Queensland Ltd* (1980) 146 C.L.R. 165, 202. See also *Batson v King* (1859) 4 H. & N. 739. cf. *Sleigh v Sleigh* (1850) 5 Exch. 514 (voluntary payment), but see *Ex p. Bishop* (1880) 15 Ch.D. 400, 410, 417. In *Coles Myer Finance Ltd v Commissioner of Taxation of the Commonwealth of Australia* (1993) 176 C.L.R. 640, 659, 689, the High Court of Australia rejected the proposition that the drawer of an accommodation bill only comes under an obligation to the acceptor when the acceptor pays the bill.

[52] *Smith v Bank of Montreal* (1976) 72 D.L.R. (3d) 154, 157. But see *Sundelson v Knuttel* 2000 (3) S.A. 513 and above, n.50.

[53] See above, para.2–164.

[54] See *Bagnall v Andrews* (1830) 7 Bing. 217, 222. cf. *Ex p. Swan* (1868) L.R. 6 Eq. 344, 357.

[55] cf. *Scott v Lifford* (1808) 1 Camp. 246 (s.27, Illustration 20).

[56] See below, para.7–031.

[57] See s.27(2), above, para.4–024. Contrast *Stack v Dowd* (1907) 15 O.L.R. 331 (no liability to payee who was not holder for value); *Sundelson v Knuttel* 2000 (3) S.A. 513, 518 (no liability to subsequent holder who had not given value).

subsection is consistent with the principle that the absence of consideration between prior parties, whether known to the holder or not, is no defence against a holder for value.[58] Thus, if a bill is accepted for the accommodation of the drawer, it is no defence to an action against the acceptor by an indorsee for value that the acceptor received no value for the bill.[59] However, there is some authority[60] for the view that, if the indorsee has not discounted the bill, but merely advanced money on it, he can recover no more than the amount of his advance. This may, perhaps, be justified on the ground that, with respect to the excess over the amount advanced, the holder sues on behalf of or as trustee for the person from whom he received the bill, *i.e.* the drawer, who as the person accommodated has no claim against the acceptor.[61]

Since an accommodation party is a party to the bill, he nevertheless has whatever defences are available to him in the capacity in which he signed the bill. Moreover, the position of an accommodation party is a privileged one in two respects. First, an accommodation party, known to be a surety, can avail himself of any defence against the holder, arising out of the bill transaction, which the person accommodated could have set up.[62] Secondly, although the holder is entitled to treat the accommodation party as the person primarily liable on the bill, as soon as he is affected with notice that the apparent principal is only a surety, the ordinary consequences which flow from that relationship ensue, and the holder disregards them at his peril. Any such dealing with the real principal or other sureties as would ordinarily discharge a surety discharges the accommodation party.[63] It is to be noted that, in this case, even though the holder took the bill without knowledge of the surety status of the accommodation party, he is bound to have regard to the suretyship of the accommodation party once this comes to his notice.[64]

In particular, if the holder of a bill with knowledge of the suretyship enters into a binding agreement with the person accommodated,[65] at any

---

[58] See above, para.4–007. *Mollot v Monette* (1982) 128 D.L.R. (3d) 577.
[59] *Collins v Martin* (1797) 1 B. & P. 648, 651; *Smith v Knox* (1799) 3 Esp. 46 (Illustration 1); *Sturtevant v Ford* (1842) 4 M. & G. 101 (s.36, Illustration 6).
[60] *Wiffen v Roberts* (1795) 1 Esp. 261; *Simpson v Clarke* (1835) 2 C.M. & R. 342. *cf.* above, para.4–030.
[61] But contrast *Re Bunyard, Ex p. Newton* (1880) 16 Ch.D. 330, 336 (s.27, Illustration 30).
[62] *Bechervaise v Lewis* (1872) L.R. 7 C.P. 372, 377 (Illustration 2).
[63] *Greenough v McClelland* (1860) 2 E. & E. 424, 429; *Overend, Gurney & Co. v Oriental Financial Corp.* (1874) L.R. 7 H.L. 348, 360. See *Chitty on Contracts* (29th ed.), Vol.II, Ch.44.
[64] *Overend, Gurney & Co. v Oriental Financial Corp.* (1874) L.R. 7 H.L. (Illustration 3). See also *Ewin v Lancaster* (1865) 6 B. & S. 571 (s.21, Illustration 31); *Rouse v Bradford Banking Co.* [1894] A.C. 586; *Royal Bank of Canada v Wagstaffe* (1919) 50 D.L.R. 717, 723–4; *Goldfarb v Barnett* [1920] 1 K.B. 639.
[65] *Lyon v Holt* (1839) 5 M. & W. 250; *Frazer v Jordan* (1858) 8 E. & B. 303; *Clarke v Birley* (1889) 41 Ch.D. 422.

time prior to judgment, to give time for payment,[66] this will discharge the accommodation party from liability,[67] unless either the accommodation party consents to the giving of time[68] or the holder expressly reserves his rights against the accommodation party when time is given.[69] But there must be a binding agreement to give time: mere delay or forbearance is insufficient.[70] An agreement by a bank to allow a customer to increase his overdraft is not a binding agreement not to sue for the original debt forthwith.[71] Likewise, if the holder by binding agreement releases the person accommodated from liability, this will discharge the accommodation party.[72] The release of a cosurety[73] or the surrender or impairment of securities deposited with the holder[74] may also, in certain circumstances, discharge the accommodation party.

It is no defence to an accommodation party that, at the time the bill was negotiated to a holder for value, it was overdue.[75]

4–045    **Rights of accommodation party.** It is the implied duty of the person accommodated to provide the funds to meet the bill at maturity. If he fails to do so, he must indemnify the accommodation party who is compelled

---

[66] See *Rowlatt on Principal and Surety* (5th ed.), Ch.8; O'Donovan and Phillips, *The Modern Contract of Guarantee* (English ed., 2003), 7–59.

[67] *Greenough v McClelland* (1860) 2 E. & E. 424, 429; *Bailey v Edwards* (1864) 4 B. & S. 761; *Overend, Gurney & Co. v Oriental Financial Corp.* (1874) L.R. 7 H.L. (Illustration 3); *Polak v Everett* (1876) Q.B.D. 669, 673–674. cf. *Torrance v Bank of British North America* (1873) L.R. 5 P.C. 246, 252; *Re a Debtor* [1913] 3 K.B. 11.

[68] *Clark v Devlin* (1803) 3 B. & P. 363; *Atkins v Revell* (1860) De G.F. & J. 360; *Polak v Everett* (1876) Q.B.D. 669 at 673–674.

[69] *Owen v Homan* (1853) 4 H.L.C. 997, 1037; *Oriental Financial Corp. v Overend, Gurney & Co.* (1871) 7 Ch.App. 142, 150 (affirmed (1874) L.R. 7 H.L. 348, 358); *Jones v Whitaker* (1887) 57 L.T. 216; *Mahant Singh v U Ba Yi* [1939] A.C. 610.

[70] *Goring v Edmonds* (1829) 6 Bing. 94; *Bell v Banks* (1841) 3 M. & G. 258; *Overend, Gurney & Co. v Oriental Financial Corp.* (1874) L.R. 7 H.L.; *Carter v White* (1883) 25 Ch.D. 666, 672; *Rowlatt on Principal and Surety* (5th ed.), pp.176–177; O'Donovan and Phillips, *The Modern Contract of Guarantee* (English ed., 2003), 7–65.

[71] *Rouse v Bradford Banking Co.* [1894] A.C. 586.

[72] *Ewin v Lancaster* (1865) 6 B. & S. 571 (s.21, Illustration 31).

[73] *Ward v National Bank of New Zealand* (1883) 8 App. Cas. 755, 764; *Mercantile Bank of Sydney v Taylor* [1893] A.C. 317. But see *Rowlatt on Principal and Surety* (5th ed.), Ch.12; O'Donovan and Phillips, *The Modern Law of Guarantee* (English ed., 2003), 8.21; *Chitty on Contracts* (29th ed.), Vol.II, § 44–101.

[74] *Pearl v Deacon* (1857) 1 De. G. & J. 461; *Re Darwen and Pearce* [1927] 1 Ch. 176; *Smith v Wood* [1929] 1 Ch. 14; *Guaranty Trust Co. of Canada v Seller's Oil Field Service Ltd* (1984) 12 D.L.R. (4th) 55. But see *Rowlatt on Principal and Surety* (5th ed.), Ch.12; O'Donovan and Phillips, *The Modern Law of Guarantee* (English ed., 2003), 8.46; *Chitty on Contracts* (29th ed.), Vol.II, § 44–102; and *Duncan Fox & Co. v N. & S. Wales Bank* (1880) 6 App. Cas. 1, 15; *Taylor v Bank of N.S.W.* (1886) 11 App. Cas. 596 (dealing with securities before dishonour of bill).

[75] *Charles v Marsden* (1808) 1 Taunt. 224; *Stein v Yglesias* (1834) 1 C.M. & R. 565; *Sturtevant v Ford* (1842) 4 M. & G. 101 (s.36, Illustration 6); *Re Overend, Gurney & Co., Ex p. Swan* (1868) L.R. 6 Eq. 344, 359. See s.36(2); below, para.5–041.

to pay the holder.[76] In addition to his rights against the person accommodated, the accommodation party has a right of contribution against cosureties.[77] Thus if two or more persons agree to become parties to a bill to accommodate a third, they will be entitled to contribution *inter se*, subject to any agreement between them.[78] This right of contribution is not affected by the order in which their indorsements appear on the instrument[79] or, for example, by the fact that one cosurety has signed a note as maker and the other as indorser,[80] and parol evidence is admissible to displace the ordinary priority attaching to their signatures.[81] As against the holder an accommodation party known to be a surety will have the right to securities belonging to the person accommodated which have been deposited with the holder as security for the debt which the accommodation party has paid.[82]

**Position of person accommodated.** As a general rule, the drawer or an    4–046
indorser, for whose accommodation a bill is accepted, cannot avail himself of want of due presentment for payment,[83] or of notice of dishonour[84] or of protest,[85] because it is his own duty to provide the funds to meet the bill at maturity. It must also follow from the nature of accommodation that the accommodation party cannot be liable to him on the bill.[86]

**Insolvency.** The bankruptcy of the person accommodated does not    4–047
discharge the accommodation party from liability on the bill.[87] If the person accommodated puts the accommodation party in funds to meet the bill, but becomes bankrupt before the bill matures, the accommodation party can retain those funds for the purpose of paying the bill.[88]

---

[76] See above, para.4–043. This indemnity may include costs which the accommodation party has been called upon to pay: *Jones v Brooke* (1812) 4 Taunt. 464; *Stratton v Matthews* (1848) 3 Exch. 48, 49; *Garrard v Cottrell* (1847) 10 Q.B. 679. *cf. Roach v Thompson* (1830) M. & M. 487; *Beech v Jones* (1848) 5 C.B. 696.

[77] *Reynolds v Wheeler* (1861) 10 C.B.N.S. 561 (approved in *Macdonald v Whitfield* (1883) 8 App. Cas. 753); *Godsell v Lloyd* (1911) 27 T.L.R. 383. See *Rowlatt on Principal and Surety* (5th ed.), p.163; O'Donovan and Phillips, *The Modern Law of Guarantee* (English ed., 2003), 11–175, 12–116.

[78] *Macdonald v Whitfield* (1883) 8 App. Cas. 753 (s.21, Illustration 33).

[79] *Macdonald v Whitfield* (1883) 8 App. Cas. 753.

[80] *Rutherford v Taylor* (1915) 24 D.L.R. 882.

[81] See above, para.2–168.

[82] *Bechervaise v Lewis* (1872) L.R. 7 C.P. 372, 377; *Gray v Seckham* (1872) L.R. 7 Ch.App. 680. See *Rowlatt on Principal and Surety* (5th ed.), p.156; O'Donovan and Phillips, *The Modern Law of Guarantee* (English ed., 2003), 12–254, 12–312. *cf. Scholefield Goodman & Sons Ltd v Zyngier* [1986] A.C. 562.

[83] s.46(2)(c)(d).

[84] s.50(2)(c)(4), (d)(3); *Collott v Haugh* (1812) 3 Camp. 281.

[85] s.51(9).

[86] *Raner v Benjamin Bros* [1910] T.P.D. 1324; *Sundelson v Knuttel* 2000 (3) S.A. 513, 518.

[87] *General Printers Employees' (Oshawa) Credit Union Ltd v Kemp* (1975) 57 D.L.R. (3d) 321 (note).

[88] *Yates v Hoppe* (1850) 9 C.B. 541.

Where a bill is accepted for the accommodation of the drawer, but the acceptor dishonours the bill by non-payment at maturity, this will not discharge the drawer from liability to the holder, and he may be sued by the holder on the bill[89] or on the underlying transaction between them. In consequence, should the drawer already have put the acceptor in funds before the acceptor becomes insolvent and fails to pay the bill, the drawer will be compelled to pay the amount of the bill over again. His only remedy will be to prove for the debt as a creditor of the insolvent acceptor.[90] However, if the acceptor evinces an intention not to honour the bill when it falls due, and the drawer has not yet provided the funds necessary to meet the bill, he will be released from his obligation to do so.[91]

ILLUSTRATIONS

4–048     1. A bill is drawn by V, payable to himself, upon the defendant, who accepts it. V indorses the bill to the claimant for value. The defendant's acceptance is given to accommodate V and without any consideration, which fact is known to the claimant. The claimant is entitled to recover the amount of the bill from the defendant, even though he had full knowledge of the transaction.[92]

2. The defendant and R jointly make a promissory note for £230 payable to the claimant. R dies. In an action by the claimant against the defendant on the note, the defendant pleads that, as the claimant well knew, he made the note merely as surety for R, that the note was given by R to the claimant in respect of certain partnership debts and that the claimant has in his hands partnership moneys of R more than sufficient to satisfy the note. In substance this is a plea by a surety of a set-off by the principal debtor, R, arising out of the same transaction out of which the liability of the surety arose, and it is a defence in equity against the claimant.[93]

3. Four bills are drawn by D upon and accepted by the F Corporation for the accommodation of McH and his principals, on payment of a commission for such acceptances. They are discounted with O & G, a

---

[89] s.55(1)(a).
[90] Except where, by agreement, security held by the acceptor has been specifically appropriated to meet the bill: see below, para.7–016 (s.54).
[91] *Sale Continuation Ltd v Austin Taylor & Co. Ltd* [1968] 2 Q.B. 849.
[92] *Smith v Knox* (1799) 3 Esp. 46. See now s.28(2).
[93] *Bechervaise v Lewis* (1872) L.R. 7 C.P. 372.

discount house. The bills are not paid but renewed. McH gives O & G his written guarantee that the renewed bills will be paid at maturity. They are not paid at maturity. O & G then become aware for the first time that the bills are accommodation bills and that the F Corporation is surety for McH and his principals. With this knowledge O & G enter into a binding agreement with McH for valuable consideration to suspend their right to sue on the bills. Subsequently an action is brought by O & G against the F Corporation to recover the amount of the bills. The F Corporation file a bill to restrain the action. The action is restrained, since, with knowledge of the suretyship, O & G have agreed after their right of action accrued to give time to McH, the principal debtor, and so discharged the F Corporation from liability on the bills.[94]

### Holder in due course

29. (1) **A holder in due course is a holder who has taken a bill,**    4–049
   **complete and regular on the face of it, under the following**
   **conditions; namely,**
   (a) **That he became the holder of it before it was overdue,**
      **and without notice that it had been previously dishon-**
      **oured, if such was the fact:**
   (b) **That he took the bill in good faith and for value, and that**
      **at the time the bill was negotiated to him he had no notice**
      **of any defect in the title of the person who negotiated**
      **it.**
   (2) **In particular the title of a person who negotiates a bill is**
      **defective within the meaning of this Act when he obtained**
      **the bill, or the acceptance thereof, by fraud, duress, or force**
      **and fear, or other unlawful means, or for an illegal considera-**
      **tion, or when he negotiates it in breach of faith, or under such**
      **circumstances as amount to a fraud.**
   (3) **A holder (whether for value or not), who derives his title to a**
      **bill through a holder in due course, and who is not himself a**
      **party to any fraud or illegality affecting it, has all the rights of**
      **that holder in due course as regards the acceptor and all**
      **parties to the bill prior to that holder.**

| Definitions | Comparison |
|---|---|
| "acceptance": ss.2,17(1). | UCC: 3–302, 3–304, 3–305. |
| "bill": s.2. | ULB: art.16. |
| "good faith": s.90. | ULC: art.19. |

---

[94] *Overend Gurney & Co. v Oriental Financial Corp.* (1874) L.R. 7 H.L. 348.

"holder": s.2.                              UNB: arts 29, 31.
"negotiate": s.31.
"person": s.2.
"value": s.2.


COMMENT


4–050    **Subsection (1): definition of holder in due course.** The Act substituted the term "holder in due course" for the more cumbrous "bona fide holder for value without notice", and its synonyms "bona fide holder", "innocent indorsee", etc.[95] This subsection sets out the requirements which must be satisfied for a person to be a holder in due course of a bill, cheque or note.

4–051    **"Holder who has taken a bill."** To qualify as a holder in due course, a person must first qualify as a holder. By section 2, "holder" means the payee or indorsee of a bill or note who is in possession of it, or the bearer thereof; and "bearer" means the person in possession of a bill or note which is payable to bearer. A person to whom an unindorsed order bill is delivered, but not negotiated,[96] is not a holder[97] and therefore cannot be a holder in due course. However, an exception exists under section 2 of the Cheques Act 1957,[98] which confers upon a banker who gives value for, or has a lien on, a cheque payable to order, which the holder delivers to him for collection without indorsing it, such rights as he would have had if, upon delivery, it had been indorsed in blank. As a general rule, a person cannot be the holder of an order bill if he takes the bill through or under a forged or unauthorised indorsement,[99] and in consequence cannot be a holder in due course.[1]

The holder must have "taken" the bill, that is to say, received it by negotiation.[2] Notwithstanding the definition of "holder" in section 2, the original payee of a bill in whose possession it remains cannot be a holder in due course.[3] No person can therefore be or become a holder in due

---

[95] *Lloyd's Bank Ltd v Cooke* (1907) 1 K.B. 794, 806.
[96] s.31(3).
[97] *Whistler v Forster* (1863) 14. C.B. N.S. 248 (Illustration 1).
[98] Below, para.17–015.
[99] s.24, above, para.3–066.
[1] But see s.55(2)(b) (estoppel); above, para.3–058; below, para.7–028. See also ss.1, 4 of the Cheques Act 1957; below, paras 17–005 and 17–028.
[2] *Jones (R.E.) Ltd v Waring and Gillow Ltd* [1926] A.C. 670 (Illustration 6). But see *Barclays Bank Ltd v Astley Industrial Trust Ltd* [1970] 2 Q.B. 527 (s.27, Illustration 28) (holder with a lien under s.27(3) may be a holder in due course).
[3] *Jones (R.E.) Ltd v Waring and Gillow Ltd*, [1926] A.C. 670 and below, para.4–059.

course of an instrument which is not transferable, *i.e.* one which contains words prohibiting transfer, or indicating that it should not be transferable,[4] or, in the case of a cheque, which is crossed "account payee".[5] Such an instrument is not negotiable and only the original payee can be a holder of it.

**Complete and regular on its face.** The rights of a holder in due course    **4–052**
can only be acquired by a holder who takes a bill "complete and regular on the face of it". If the bill itself conveys a warning, *caveat emptor.* Its holder, however honest, can acquire no better title than that of his transferor.[6] The words "on the face of it" are not, however, to be taken literally, and incompleteness or irregularity on the face or on the back of the bill (*e.g.* in an indorsement) will suffice.[7] But whether a bill is complete and regular on its face is to be determined by looking only at the bill.

An instrument will be incomplete if, at the time of its negotiation to the holder, it lacks one of the requirements[8] of a valid bill, cheque or note, or if it is wanting in any material particular.[9] Nevertheless, it has been held that a holder who takes an incomplete bill, may under section 20(2) of the Act, himself fill it up within a reasonable time and strictly in accordance with the authority given, and so convert himself retrospectively into a holder in due course,[10] although he cannot become a holder in due course for the purpose of the proviso to that subsection if he does not observe those conditions.[11] A bill is complete though not yet accepted by the drawee.[12] An undated bill would appear to be incomplete or at least irregular.[13]

The bill must be regular on its face. Presumably any alteration which would be a material alteration,[14] *e.g.* of the date, would, if apparent from the bill,[15] render it irregular, as would an obvious erasure.[16] In *Banco di*

---

[4] s.8(1).

[5] s.81A(1).

[6] See *Awde v Dixon* (1851) 6 Exch. 869 (s.20, Illustration 11).

[7] *Arab Bank Ltd v Ross* [1952] 2 Q.B. 216, 226; *Yeoman Credit Ltd v Gregory* [1963] 1 W.L.R. 343, 352.

[8] See above, paras 2–007—2–018; below, paras 13–001 and 15–001.

[9] s.20; above, paras 2–133—2–135.

[10] *Glenie v Bruce Smith* [1908] 1 K.B. 263, 268-269; *Gerald McDonald & Co. v Nash & Co.* [1924] A.C. 625, 647, 648; *National Sales Corp. v Bernardi* [1931] 2 K.B. 188, 192; *Lombard Banking Ltd v Central Garage and Engineering Ltd* [1963] 1 Q.B. 220, 230; *Yeoman Credit Ltd v Gregory* [1963] 1 W.L.R. 343 at 352; above, para.2–136.

[11] See above, para.2–138.

[12] *National Park Bank of New York v Berggren & Co.* (1914) 30 T.L.R. 387; above, para.2–114 (s.17).

[13] See above, paras 2–092 (s.12), 2–131 and 2–133, (s.20).

[14] s.64(2).

[15] *cf.* s.64(1)(proviso); below, para.8–079.

[16] *Mobeni Supersave v Suleman* 1992 (3) S.A. 660 (deletion of crossing).

*Roma SpA v Orru*,[17] it was held that a discrepancy between the currency of the words and figures on a bill,[18] though it constituted something that could not have misled anybody, was a sufficiently arguable point for refusing an application for summary judgment brought by a holder who claimed as holder in due course. It would seem that any feature of the bill which would reasonably put the holder on inquiry will make it irregular. However, for example, a statement in the body of the bill of the transaction which gives rise to the bill[19] is not an irregularity, nor is the fact that a cheque is post-dated[20] or that it has been completed in handwriting that obviously differs from the signature.[21] In the days when it was customary to divide bills in half, for security reasons, sending each half separately to the recipient, a bill which had been torn and the pieces pasted together might not necessarily be irregular,[22] but that would not be the position today.

4–053　　A bill will not be regular on its face if an indorsement is irregular. Speaking of irregular indorsements, Denning L.J. said[23]: "Regularity is a different thing from validity". An indorsement may be invalid, for example, because it is forged or unauthorised, but still be regular. Conversely, an indorsement may be irregular even though it is valid as an indorsement and transfers rights on the bill to the indorsee.[24] In *Arab Bank Ltd v Ross*,[25] the Court of Appeal held that the omission from an indorsement of the word "Company" on a note made payable to a Palestinian firm "Fathi and Faysal Nabulsy Company" did not invalidate the indorsement but rendered it irregular. The omission of the word "Company" from the indorsement would reasonably give rise to a doubt whether in point of personality the payees and the indorsers were necessarily the same.[26]

If a bill payable to "John Williams" is indorsed "J. Williams", the indorsement is not irregular,[27] and titles and descriptions, *e.g.* "Mr." or "the Hon." can often be omitted without impairing the regularity of the

---

[17] [1973] 2 Lloyd's Rep. 505 (Illustration 4).

[18] s.9(2).

[19] s.3(3)(b).

[20] *Hitchock v Edwards* (1889) 60 L.T. 636; *Guildford Trust Ltd v Goss* (1927) 136 L.T. 725 (s.20, Illustration 13). See above, para.2–098 (s.13).

[21] *Ierullo v Rovan* (2000) 46 O.R. (3d) 692.

[22] *Ingham v Primrose* (1859) 7 C.B.N.S. 82 (criticised in *Baxendale v Bennett* (1878) 3 Q.B.D. 525, 532; *Smith v Prosser* [1907] 2 K.B. 735, 146) *cf. Scholey v Ramsbottom* (1810) 2 Camp. 485; *Redmayne v Burton* (1860) 2 L.T. 324; *Nash v de Freville* [1900] 2 Q.B. 72, 89.

[23] *Arab Bank Ltd v Ross* [1952] 2 Q.B. 216, 226.

[24] *Leonard v Wilson* (1834) 2 Cr. & M. 589; *Hadley & Co. v Henry* (1896) 22 V.L.R. 230; *Bird & Co. (London) Ltd v Thomas Cook & Son Ltd* [1937] 2 All E.R. 227; *Arab Bank Ltd v Ross*, [1952] 2 Q.B. 216 below, para.5–015; *Navidos (Pty) Ltd v Essop* 1994 (4) S.A. 141. *cf. Slingsby v District Bank Ltd* [1932] 1 K.B. 544 (s.60, Illustration 2), below, para.5–015.

[25] [1952] 2 Q.B. 216 (Illustration 3). See also *Slingsby v District Bank Ltd* [1932] 1 K.B. 544.

[26] [1952] 2 Q.B. at 234.

[27] [1952] 2 Q.B. 216 at 222.

indorsement.[28] But if the payee is described in the instrument by the wrong name, for example. "James Williams", but then indorses it in his true name "John Williams", the indorsement is irregular.[29] Nice questions may arise as to the degree of correspondence required.[30] In *Arab Bank Ltd v Ross*[31] Denning L.J. said[32]:

> " . . . when is an indorsement irregular? The answer is, I think, that it is irregular whenever it is such as to give rise to doubt whether it is the indorsement of the named payee. A bill of exchange is like currency. It should be above suspicion. But if it is asked: When does an indorsement give rise to doubt? I would say it is a practical question which is, as a rule, better answered by a banker than a lawyer."

The fact that indorsements are out of sequence does not render a bill irregular.[33]

**Before it was overdue.** The holder must become the holder of the     4–054
instrument before it was overdue. Except where an indorsement bears date after the maturity of the bill, every negotiation is prima facie deemed to have been effected before the bill was overdue.[34] Where a bill or note is not payable on demand, the day on which it falls due is to be determined in accordance with section 14 of the Act.[35] A bill payable on demand, or a cheque, is deemed to be overdue when it appears on the face of it to have been in circulation for an unreasonable length of time.[36] But, where a note payable on demand is negotiated, it is not deemed to be overdue, for the purpose of affecting the holder with defects in title of which he had no notice, by reason that it appears that a reasonable time for presenting it for payment has elapsed since its issue.[37]

The position of a person to whom an overdue bill has been negotiated is specifically dealt with in section 36(2) of the Act.[38]

---

[28] [1952] 2 Q.B. 216 at 228.
[29] *Toronto Doninion Bank v Canadian Acceptance Corpn.* (1969) 7 D.L.R. (3d) 728. See s.32(4) for the correct course to be adopted in such a case.
[30] See the examples cited to the court in *Slingsby v District Bank Ltd* [1932] 1 K.B. 544.
[31] [1952] 2 Q.B. 216. See also *Mourgelas v Maidanos* 1973 (4) S.A. 297, 298; *Standard Bank of South Africa Ltd v Sappi* 1995 (4) S.A. 392, 401–402; *Cutfin (Pty.) Ltd v Sangio Pipe CC* 2002 (5) S.A. 156.
[32] [1952] 2 Q.B. 216 at 227.
[33] *Lombard Banking Ltd v Central Garage and Engineering Ltd* [1963] 1 Q.B. 220 (s.20, Illustration 17); *Yeoman Credit Ltd v Gregory* [1963] 1 W.L.R. 343 (s.20, Illustration 19).
[34] s.36(4).
[35] See above, para.2–100.
[36] s.36(3). What is an unreasonable length of time for this purpose is a question of fact. For overdue cheques, see below, para.5–043.
[37] s.86(3).
[38] See below, para.5–039.

**4–055**     **Without notice of dishonour.** The holder must become the holder of the bill without notice that it had been previously dishonoured, if such was the fact.[39] The dishonour may be by non-acceptance[40] or by non-payment.[41] It is clear that the "notice" here referred to means knowledge of dishonour, or suspicion coupled with the means of knowledge wilfully disregarded.[42] It does not refer to the formal notice of dishonour mentioned in section 48 of the Act.

The position of a person who takes a bill which is not overdue, but with notice of dishonour, is specifically dealt with in section 36(5) of the Act.[43]

**4–056**     **Good faith.** The holder must take the bill in good faith. The expression "good faith" is defined in section 90 of the Act and is discussed in the Comment on that section.[44]

**4–057**     **Value.** The holder must take the bill for value.[45] "Value" is defined in section 2 to mean valuable consideration, and this is dealt with in section 27.[46] Commentators have generally assumed that the words "took ...." for value "mean that a holder in due course must himself give value for the bill, and that it is insufficient for him to be, under section 27(2),[47] deemed to be a holder for value by virtue of the fact that value has been given by a previous holder of the bill.[48] In *Clifford Chance v Silver*,[49] however, the Court of Appeal held that solicitors to whom a cheque had been indorsed as stakeholders, and who were therefore alleged not to have given value, were nevertheless holders in due course because they were deemed to be holders for value pursuant to section 27(2). But it is not clear from the facts of the case[50] by whom and to whom value had been given for the cheque. Also in *MK International Development Co. Ltd v*

---

[39] *Hornby v McLaren* (1908) 24 T.L.R. 494 (cheque known to have been dishonoured) (s.36, Illustration 11).

[40] s.43.

[41] s.47.

[42] See below, para.4–058.

[43] See below, para.5–045.

[44] See below, para.16–001.

[45] *De la Chaumette v Bank of England* (1829) 9 B. & C. 208 (Illustration 2). It is not sufficient that value is given after the bill is negotiated to the holder: *Nalliah v Pure Beverages Co. Ltd* (1965) 68 N.L.R. (Ceylon) 311.

[46] See above, para.4–002.

[47] See above, para.4–024.

[48] See the 14th edition of this book, at p.274; Crawford and Falconbridge (8th ed.), p.1419; Cowen, *Law of Negotiable Instruments in South Africa* (5th ed.), p.58; Riley, *The Law relating to Bills of Exchange in Australia* (3rd ed.), p.91; Bradgate and Savage, *Commercial Law* (1991), p.412; Goode, *Commercial Law* (1st ed.), p.448; Geva [1980] C.L.J. 360, 364.

[49] [1992] 2 Bank L.R. 11.

[50] Illustration 8.

*Housing Bank*,[51] Mustill L.J. expressed the view (*obiter*) that section 27(2) must be read as "a special provision, directed to the position of a holder who wishes to establish that he is a holder for value in good faith without notice and must as a first step show that he is a holder for value; and it relieves him of the necessity to show that he himself gave value".[52] These cases therefore suggest that it is unnecessary for a holder in due course himself to have given value. But this view may require reconsideration.[53]

**No notice of defect in title.** At the time the bill was negotiated to him,    **4–058** the holder must have had no notice of any defect in the title of the person who negotiated it. The meaning of "defect in title" is dealt with in subsection (2) of this section. This requirement is distinct from that of good faith, but there is a tendency, particularly in the older cases, for them to merge into one another.

Notice in section 29(1)(b) means actual notice.[54] The concept of constructive notice does not apply to commercial transactions, including bills of exchange.[55] Notice consists either of actual knowledge of a fact (sometimes referred to as express notice) or of a suspicion of something wrong, coupled with a wilful disregard of the means of knowledge, *i.e.* "wilfully shutting one's eyes" (sometimes referred to as implied notice).[56] But mere negligence, that is to say, where the holder is "honestly blundering and careless",[57] is insufficient.[58] The notice must be of a defect in the title of the person who negotiated the bill. Although dicta suggest that the holder is affected with notice if he merely knows that there is "something wrong

---

[51] [1991] 1 Bank. L.R. 74 (s.27, Illustration 25). See also *Mills v Buono* [1986] B.T.L.C. 399 (concession made). This view may, perhaps, derive some further support from *Barclays Bank Ltd v Astley Industrial Trust Ltd* [1970] 2 Q.B. 527, 539 (s.27, Illustration 28) and *Re Keever* [1967] Ch. 182, 193 (s.27, Illustration 26).

[52] [1991] 1 Bank.L.R. 74 at 80.

[53] Hitchens [1993] J.B.L. 371; Goode, *Commercial Law* (3rd ed.), p.498; Sealy and Hooley, *Commercial Law, Text, Cases and Materials* (3rd ed.), p.527.

[54] *Baker v Barclays Bank Ltd* [1955] 1 W.L.R. 822, 834.

[55] *London Joint Stock Bank v Simmons* [1892] A.C. 201, 221; *Manchester Trust Co. v Furness* [1895] 2 Q.B. 539, 545; *Lloyds Bank v Swiss Bankverein* (1913) 108 L.T. 143.

[56] *May v Chapman* (1847) 16 M. & W. 351, 361; *Raphael v Bank of England* (1855) 17 C.B. 161, 174; *Jones v Gordon* (1877) 2 App. Cas. 616, 625, 628, 629, 633, 635 (Illustration 5); *London Joint Stock Bank v Simmons* [1892] A.C. 201 at 221; *Benjamin v Weinberg* [1956] S.C.R. 553; *Beneficial Finance Co. of Canada v Kulig* (1970) 13 D.L.R. (3d) 134; *Ng Kim Lek v Wee Hock Chye* [1971] 1 M.L.J. 148, 149; *Hasan v Willson* [1971] 1 Lloyd's Rep. 431, 444. See also *Lipkin Gorman v Karpnale Ltd* [1987] 1 W.L.R. 987, 994–995; [1989] 1 W.L.R. 1340, 1360; [1991] 2 A.C. 548.

[57] *Jones v Gordon* (1877) 2 App.Cas. 616 at 628, 629.

[58] *Goodman v Harvey* (1836) 4 A. & E. 870, 876; *Bank of Bengal v Fagan* (1849) 7 Moore P.C. 61, 72; *Raphael v Bank of England* (1855) 17 C.B. 161 at 175; *Jones v Gordon* (1877) 2 App.Cas. 616 at 628, 629, 632; *London Joint Stock Bank v Simmons* [1892] A.C. 201 at 219, 220; *Bank of Cyprus (London) Ltd v Jones* (1984) 134 N.L.J. 522.

in the transaction",[59] it seems clear that, in the present context, the thing that is wrong must be such as either to give rise to a defect in title or to give rise to a suspicion that further enquiry would reveal such a defect.[60] It is also evident from the wording of the provision that the relevant time is when the bill is negotiated to the holder[61]; after acquired knowledge by him is not to be taken into account.[62]

The question whether notice to an agent is equivalent to notice to his principal, and vice versa, is governed by the ordinary law of principal and agent[63] but the answer to the question may be one of considerable difficulty.[64] It should, however, be borne in mind that, where an agent is party or privy to the commission of a fraud upon his principal, his knowledge of such fraud, and of the facts and circumstances connected therewith, will not ordinarily be imputed to the principal,[65] and a reasonable time should be allowed for the principal to communicate notice received by him to his agents.[66]

**4–059**    **Payee not holder in due course.** The original payee of a bill, cheque or note who remains in possession of the instrument cannot be a holder in due course.[67] It was so decided by the House of Lords in *Jones (R.E.) Ltd v Waring & Gillow Ltd.*[68] This decision has been criticised,[69] but the

---

[59] *Jones v Gordon* (1877) 2 App.Cas. 616 at 628, 629, 633; *London Joint Stock Bank Ltd v Simmons* [1892] A.C. 201 at 221; *Beneficial Finance Co. of Canada v Kulig* (1970) 13 D.L.R. (3d) 134. But this may indeed be relevant to "good faith".

[60] But the holder need not know the exact defect, *e.g.* where the holder suspects that his transferor stole the bill, whereas in fact he obtained it by deception: *Jones v Gordon* (1877) 2 App.Cas. 616 at 628.

[61] See *Whistler v Forster* (1863) 14 C.B., N.S. 248 (Illustration 1).

[62] *Williams & Glyns Bank Ltd v Belkin Packaging Ltd* (1983) 147 D.L.R. (3d) 577; *Clifford Chance v Silver* [1992] 2 Bank L.R. 11 (Illustration 8). But *cf. Lipkin Gorman v Karpnale Ltd* [1987] 1 W.L.R. 987, 995; [1989] 1 W.L.R. 1340; [1991] 2 A.C. 548.

[63] See *Bowstead and Reynolds on Agency* (17th ed.), §§ 8–204–8–216. *cf. Bank of Credit and Commerce International S.A. v Dawson and Wright* [1987] Fin.L.R. 342 (notice to executive employee).

[64] *El Ajou v Dollar Land Holdings Ltd (No.1)* [1994] 2 All E.R. 685, 702; *Deutsche Ruckversicherung Aktiengesellschaft v Walbrook Insurance Co. Ltd* [1995] 1 Lloyd's Rep. 153, 164; *Ispahani v Bank Melli Iran* [1998] Lloyd's Rep. Bank. 133.

[65] *Re European Bank, Ex p. Oriental Bank* (1870) L.R. 5 Ch.App. 358; *Re Hampshire Land* [1896] 2 Ch. 743; *Houghton & Co. v Nothard, Lowe & Wills* [1928] A.C. 1; *Belmont Finance Corp. v Williams Furniture Ltd* [1979] Ch. 250. See *Bowstead and Reynolds on Agency* (16th ed.), § 8–207.

[66] *Willis v Bank of England* (1835) 4 A. & E. 21, 39.

[67] For the rights of the payee, see below, para.5–072.

[68] [1926] A.C. 670, 680, 687, 699 (Illustration 6) and re-affirmed in *Dextra Bank & Trust Co. Ltd v Bank of Jamaica* [2002] 1 All E.R. (Comm) 193 at [19], PC. Conflicting views had previously been expressed in *Lewis v Clay* (1897) L.J.Q.B. 224; *Herdman v Wheeler* [1902] 1 K.B. 361, 371; *Lloyd's Bank v Cooke* [1907] 1 K.B. 794, 805–808; *Glenie v Bruce-Smith* [1908] 1 K.B. 263.

[69] See *Crawford and Falconbridge* (8th ed.), pp.1474–1478. See also UCC, §3–302. But see the Report of the Review Committee on Banking Services Law and Practice (1989) Cm. 1026, Appendix A, Report, para. 20. 6.

reasoning seems to be virtually inescapable in view of the fact that the Act contemplates that a holder in due course must be a holder to whom the instrument is negotiated.[70] An instrument is not negotiated to the original payee.[71]

**Whether drawee a holder in due course.** The drawee or acceptor of a    4–060
bill or cheque, and the maker of a promissory note, to whom the instrument is presented for payment will ordinarily not be a holder in due course as the instrument will not be negotiated to him.[72] But the question arises whether the drawee of the cheque payable to order can in any circumstances become a holder in due course. Suppose that A by fraud induces B to draw a cheque payable to his order. The cheque is drawn on the X Bank. A is also a customer of the X Bank, but at a branch different from that on which the cheque is drawn. A deposits the cheque at his branch for credit to his account. The branch receives it in good faith and without notice of the fraud, and gives value for the cheque, *e.g.* by lending money against it. B countermands payment of the cheque. Can the X Bank claim payment from B as holder of the cheque in due course? It has been argued[73] that it cannot do so, because it received the cheque solely in the capacity of agent of A for collection and because it should not be entitled to claim as a holder in due course against its own customer, the drawer. But in *London Provincial & South Western Bank Ltd v Buszard*,[74] where no fraud was involved, judgment was given for the drawee bank as holder for value against its customer, the drawer, who had stopped payment of a cheque deposited by the payee for collection at another branch of the same bank. Following this case, there seems to be no reason why a drawee bank which collects payment of an order cheque both as agent for collection and in its own right[75] could not claim the status of a holder in due course. Even where a cheque is paid in for collection at the

---

[70] ss.20(2), 21(2), 29(1)(b).

[71] s.31.

[72] *Coats v Union Bank of Scotland* 1929 S.C. (H.L.) 114 (drawee banker not holder of paid cheque). But in certain pre-Act cases, where the drawee or acceptor of a bill paid it in part before maturity (*cf.* s.59(1)), it was held that this operated as a purchase of the instrument and, subject to s.61, he might reissue and further negotiate it: *Morley v Culverwell* (1840) 7 M. & W. 174 (s.59, Illustration 2); *Attenborough v Mackenzie* (1856) 25 L.J. Exch. 244 (s.37, Illustration 2). He was regarded as having discounted the bill. But this would not apply to an instrument payable on demand, *e.g.* a cheque. See also *Slingsby v District Bank Ltd* [1931] 2 K.B. 588, 600 (affirmed [1932] 1 K.B. 544).

[73] *Crawford and Falconbridge* (8th ed.), pp.1478–1480. The Canadian authorities are divided: see *Keyes v Royal Bank of Canada* [1947] 3 D.L.R. 161, 172; *Canadian Bank of Commerce v Brash* (1957) 10 D.L.R. (2d) 555; *Royal Bank of Canada v Boyce* (1966) 57 D.L.R. (2d) 683, 689; *William Ciurluini Ltd v Royal Bank of Canada* (1972) 26 D.L.R. (3d) 552; *Capital Associates Ltd v Royal Bank of Canada* (1973) 36 D.L.R. (3d) 579, affirmed 65 D.L.R. (3d) 384n.; *Bank of Nova Scotia v Gould* (1977) 79 D.L.R. (3d) 473.

[74] (1918) 35 T.L.R. 142 (Illustration 9).

[75] See below, para.17–019 (Cheques Act 1957, s.2).

same branch on which it was drawn, so that the drawee bank is both paying banker and collecting banker,[76] such a claim might still be available. It would be a question of fact whether the cheque was presented for payment to the drawee bank or whether the bank gave value for a cheque delivered to it for collection. If, however, a cheque is crossed "account payee" it is not transferable[77] and the drawee bank cannot become a holder of it, let alone a holder in due course.

4–061     **Rights of holder in due course.** The rights, powers and privileges of a holder in due course are dealt with in the Comment on section 38(2) of the Act.[78]

4–062     **Subsection (2): defects of title.** This subsection lists those circumstances in which a person's title to a bill will be defective for the purposes of the Act. The list may not be exhaustive.[79] Prior to the Act, defects of title were known as "equities attaching to the bill".[80] A person whose title is defective must be distinguished from a person with no title at all, and who can give none, such as a person purporting to make title to an order bill through or under a forged or unauthorised indorsement.[81]

4–063     **"Fraud."** Fraud is the ground most frequently alleged as a defect of title. If, for example, B by fraud obtains from A a cheque drawn payable to himself, or by fraud obtains A's acceptance of a bill drawn payable to himself, which he then negotiates to C, B's title to the instrument will be defective.[82]

However, subsection (2) refers only to the case where the negotiator obtains the bill, or the acceptance thereof, by fraud. If B by fraud induces A to give him a cheque, or accept a bill, drawn payable to C, which he then delivers to C, there is no negotiation of the instrument by B to C, the original payee.[83] The question therefore arises whether, for the purposes of the Act, C's title is defective if he negotiates the instrument to D. The answer is not entirely certain. But it would appear that C's title to the instrument will not be defective if he received it in good faith and for

---

[76] *Carpenters' Co. v British Mutual Banking Co. Ltd* [1938] 1 K.B. 511 (s.60, Illustration 1).

[77] s.81A (inserted by s.1 of the Cheques Act 1992).

[78] See below, para.5–069.

[79] *Central Bank of Yemen v Cardinal Investments Corpn.* [2001] Lloyd's Rep. Bank, 1 at [21].

[80] See above, para.4–027.

[81] s.24. But a thief who steals a bill payable to bearer, though he has no title to the bill, may yet pass a good title to holder in due course by delivery: see below, para.5–074 (s.38(3)).

[82] *Whistler v Forster* (1863) 14 C.B. N.S. 248 (Illustration 1). See also other instances of fraud cited above, para.3–051 (s.24) and *Lipkin Gorman v Karpnale Ltd* [1991] 2 A.C. 548 (Illustration 7).

[83] s.31. See *Jones (R.E.) Ltd v Waring & Gillow Ltd* [1926] A.C. 670.

value without notice of the fraud.[84] On the other hand, if C received it with notice of the fraud, it would seem that his title is defective, even though he obtained the instrument, not by his own fraud, but as the result of the fraud of a third party, B. Under section 30 (2) of the Act,[85] once the fraud is admitted or proved, the burden of proof is shifted to the holder, D, to prove that, subsequent to the alleged fraud, value has in good faith been given for the instrument either by himself or by C.

It has been stated that "fraud" in the relevant sections of the Act means common law fraud.[86] If this is correct, then equitable fraud, *e.g.* breach of trust or of fiduciary duty, is not "fraud" for the purposes of this subsection.[87] In *Osterreichische Länderbank v S'Elite Ltd*[88] it was held that fraud did not include a fraudulent and voidable preference under section 44 of the Bankruptcy Act 1914 unless actual fraud was present. Subject to this limitation, it would appear that the fraud could be practised on persons outside the bill, for example, where it is issued or accepted pursuant to an agreement to defraud third party creditors.[89]

A contract obtained by fraud is voidable and not void,[90] unless the **4–064** fraud is of such a nature as to give rise to an operative mistake[91] or to the defence of *non est factum*.[92] A person from whom an instrument or its acceptance has been obtained by fraud must therefore repudiate the transaction as soon as he acquires knowledge of the fraud. If, with knowledge of the fraud, he affirms the transaction, he will not be entitled to raise the fraud as a defence to an action against him.[93]

**"Duress, or force and fear."** The specific defects listed include **4–065** duress.[94] The words "force and fear" were inserted in committee as the equivalent of the English technical term "duress" which is unknown in Scots law.[95] In English law, a contract which has been obtained by illegitimate forms of pressure or intimidation is voidable on the ground of

---

[84] See below, para.5–072 (rights of the payee).

[85] See below, para.4–082.

[86] *Osterreichische Länderbank v S'Elite Ltd* [1981] 1 Q.B. 565. (Illustration 10).

[87] But since the list in this subs. may not be exhaustive, it is submitted that equitable fraud could still give rise to a defect of title.

[88] [1981] 1 Q.B. 565 (Illustration 10).

[89] *Jones v Gordon* (1877) 2 App. Cas. 616 (Illustration 5). See also *Cockshutt v Bennett* (1788) 2 T.R. 763; *Bryant v Christie* (1816) 1 Stark. 329; *Knight v Hunt* (1829) 5 Bing. 432.

[90] See *Chitty on Contracts* (29th ed.), Vol I, §§ 6–042, 6–100.

[91] *Chitty on Contracts* (29th ed.) Vol.I, Ch.5.

[92] *Chitty on Contracts* (29th ed.) Vol.I, § 5–086. See also above, para.3–022.

[93] *Archer v Bamford* (1822) 3 Stark. 175; *Dawes v Harness* (1875) L.R. 10 C.P. 166; *Kenton v Barclays Bank* [1977] C.L.Y. 189. *cf. Mills v Oddy* (1835) 2 Cr. & M. 103.

[94] *Duncan v Scott* (1807) 1 Camp. 100.

[95] Stair I, 9, 8; Ersk. III, 1, 16; IV, 1, 26; Bell, *Principles*, § 12. In Scots law, a contract is *void* and reducible if one party's consent was given under the influence of force and fear imposed by the other party (see Walker, *Principles of Scottish Law* (3rd ed., 1983), p.88) and accordingly might constitute a "real" or "absolute" defence (see below, para.5–070) but for the express wording of subs. (2).

duress.[96] At common law, duress consisted only of actual or threatened violence to the person or unlawful imprisonment. Equity, on the other hand, would treat contracts as voidable which had been induced by forms of pressure or coercion which did not amount to duress at common law,[97] and today the wider equitable rule prevails.[98] It is submitted that "duress" in subsection (2) comprehends duress both at common law and in equity, and that it also extends to economic duress.[99] Where it is sought to avoid a contract on the ground of duress exerted by a third party, it must be shown that the party seeking to enforce the contract was aware of the duress.[1] So it would appear that, if B by duress procures A to draw a cheque payable to C, which C then negotiates to D, C's title to the cheque will not be defective within the meaning of the Act if he receives the cheque in good faith and for value without notice of the duress.[2]

Undue influence[3] is not specifically referred to in the subsection as a defect of title. But there is little doubt that it is "an equity attaching to the bill",[4] and not a mere personal defence.[5] It could be brought within the subsection, preferably by enlarging the meaning of "duress", or as falling within the phrase "or other unlawful means". But in any event the subsection is not exhaustive. The title of a person who negotiates a bill will therefore be defective when he obtains the bill, or its acceptance, by undue influence.

A contract obtained by duress[6] or undue influence is voidable, but not void.[7] The party seeking to raise such a defence may be precluded from doing so by affirmation or acquiescence.[8]

---

[96] See *Chitty on Contracts* (29th ed.), Vol.I, § 7–001.

[97] *Williams v Bayley* (1886) L.R. 1 H.L. 200.

[98] *Mutual Finance Co. Ltd v John Wetton & Sons Ltd* [1937] 2 K.B. 389. See also *Société des Hotels Réunis v Hawker* (1913) 29 T.L.R. 578.

[99] For economic duress, see *Chitty on Contracts* (29th ed.) § 7–011. *cf Gordon v Roebuck* (1992) 92 D.L.R. (4th) 670.

[1] *Kesarmal s/o Letchman Das v Valliappa Chettiar (N.K.V.) s/o Nagappa Chettiar* [1954] 1 W.L.R. 380. *cf. Lancashire Loans Ltd v Black* [1934] 1 K.B. 380. But duress exerted by an agent may affect his principal: *Avon Finance Co. Ltd v Bridger* [1985] 2 All E.R. 281 (undue influence).

[2] *Talbot v Von Boris* [1911] 1 K.B. 854 (s.30, Illustration 6). But the position is not free from doubt: see para.5–072. See also s.30(2) (burden of proof).

[3] See *Royal Bank of Scotland v Etridge (No.2)* [2001] UKHL 44, [2002] 2 A.C. 773; *Chitty on Contracts* (29th ed.) § 7–047.

[4] *Archer v Hudson* (1846) 7 Beav. 551; *Maitland v Irving* (1846) 15 Sim. 437; *Espey v Lake* (1853) 10 Hare 260. *cf. Aylesford (Earl of) v Morris* (1873) L.R. 8 Ch.App. 484.

[5] See above, para.4–027.

[6] *cf.* Lanham (1966) 29 M.L.R. 615.

[7] *Pao On v Lau Yiu Long* [1980] A.C. 614, 635; *Universe Tankships Inc. of Monrovia v International Transport Workers Federation* [1983] 1 A.C. 366. *cf. Barton v Armstrong* [1976] A.C. 104, 120.

[8] See *Chitty on Contract* (29th ed.), § 7–083.

**"Other unlawful means."** The words "unlawful means" will include    4–066
theft, as where a thief steals an instrument payable to bearer and negotiates it by delivery to another.[9]

**"Illegal consideration."** The effect of illegal consideration has been    4–067
discussed in the Comment on section 27 of the Act.[10]

**"Negotiation in breach of faith, or under such circumstances as**    4–068
**amount to fraud."** A bill or its acceptance may be lawfully and properly
obtained, but yet the title of the negotiator will be defective if he negotiates it in breach of faith or under such circumstances as amount to a
fraud. So, for example, the acceptor of a bill who is sued by the holder
may raise the defence that the payee delivered the bill to another for the
purpose of getting it discounted, but that the person to whom the bill was
so delivered fraudulently or in breach of faith negotiated it by way of sale
or pledge instead of getting it discounted.[11] And the drawee of a bill
accepted by him for the accommodation of the drawer may show that the
drawer negotiated the bill in breach of an agreement between them that
the bill would not be negotiated.[12]

Under this heading we may also, perhaps, place *Holmes v Kidd*,[13] where
the defendant accepted a bill in consideration of a loan made to him by
the drawer-payee and at the same time deposited certain goods with the
drawer-payee as security for the loan, it being agreed between them that
the payee could sell the goods and apply the proceeds in payment of the
bill if not paid by the defendant when due. After the bill became due, the
payee sold the goods, but nevertheless indorsed the bill when overdue to
the claimant. It was held that the agreement was an equity attaching to
the bill, and not merely a personal right of set-off, so that the claimant
(who was not a holder in due course) took it subject to that agreement.

**Other instances.** It would appear that payment, in whole or in part,    4–069
before maturity, or in other circumstances which do not discharge the bill,
could give rise to a defect of title.[14] It was also held, before the Act, that,

---

[9] *De la Chaumette v Bank of England* (1829) 9 B. & C. 208 (Illustration 2). See also *Raphael v Bank of England* (1855) 17 C.B. 161.
[10] See above, para.4–015.
[11] *Barber v Richards* (1851) 6 Exch. 63; *Tatam v Haslar* (1889) 23 Q.B.D. 345. cf. *Lloyd v Howard* (1850) 15 Q.B. 995 (s.21, Illustration 11).
[12] *Parr v Jewell* (1855) 16 C.B. 684 (s.36, Illustration 2). See also *Hornby v McLaren* (1908) 24 T.L.R. 494 (cheque) (s.36, Illustration 11); *Nash v De Freville* [1900] 2 Q.B. 72 (note); *Banque Provinciale de Canada v Beauchemin* (1959) 18 D.L.R. (2d) 584 (cheque); *Barclays National Bank Ltd v Serfontein* 1981 (3) S.A. 244 (cheque); *Williams & Glyns Bank Ltd v Belkin Packaging Ltd* (1983) 147 D.L.R. (3d) 577 (restrictive indorsement).
[13] (1858) 3 H. & N. 891 (s.36, Illustration 3).
[14] *Brown v Davis* (1789) 3 T.R. 80 (s.36, Illustration 5); *Graves v Key* (1832) 3 B. & Ad. 313, 319.

where a bill was purchased with money stolen from a third party, the claim of the third party to the bill so purchased was an equity attaching to the bill.[15] The question has been left open[16] whether state immunity attaching to the maker of a promissory note gives rise to a defect of title on the part of the payee of the note, but it is submitted that it does not do so.

4–070    **Consumer Credit Act 1974.** It has already been explained[17] that section 123(1) of the Consumer Credit Act 1974 prohibits a creditor or owner from taking a negotiable instrument (other than a bank note or cheque) in discharge of any sum payable by the debtor or hirer under a regulated consumer credit or consumer hire agreement, or by any person as surety under a regulated agreement, and that section 123(3) prohibits the creditor or owner from taking a negotiable instrument (including a bank note or cheque) as security for the discharge of any sum payable as mentioned in subsection (1). Section 123(2) further provides that the creditor or owner shall not negotiate a cheque taken by him in payment except to a banker.

A person who takes a negotiable instrument in contravention of section 123(1) or (3) is not a holder in due course, and is not entitled to enforce the instrument.[18] That person may, however, negotiate the instrument to a third party, who takes it for value and without notice of the contravention. This possibility has been appreciated and dealt with in section 125(4), which provides that nothing in the Act affects the rights of a holder in due course of a negotiable instrument. In compensation, if the debtor, hirer or surety ("the protected person") becomes liable to a holder in due course of an instrument taken from the protected person in contravention of section 123(1) or (3), or taken from the protected person and negotiated in contravention of section 123(2), the creditor or owner must indemnify the protected person in respect of that liability.[19]

However, section 125(2) states that, where a person negotiates a cheque in contravention of section 123(2), *i.e.* other than to a banker, his so doing constitutes a defect in his title within the meaning of the Bills of Exchange Act 1882. If therefore, at the time when he takes the cheque, a holder has notice that it has been so negotiated, he will not be a holder in due course. Nevertheless he is still prima facie deemed to be a holder in due course,[20] and there is nothing in the 1974 Act to suggest that, under section 30(2) of

---

[15] *Re European Bank, Ex p. Oriental Bank* (1870) L.R. 5 Ch.App. 358 (s.36, Illustration 4). See also *Lipkin Gorman v Karpnale Ltd* [1991] 2 A.C. 548 (Illustration 7).

[16] *Central Bank of Yemen v Cardinal Financial Investments Corpn.* [2001] Lloyd's Rep. Bank 1 at [19].

[17] See above, para.4–013.

[18] s.125(1).

[19] s.125(3).

[20] s.30(2) of the 1882 Act.

the 1882 Act, the burden of proof shifts to him to re-establish his status as such a holder.

Somewhat surprisingly there is no express comparable provision to deal with the situation where an instrument is negotiated which has been taken in contravention of section 123(1) or (3). The 1974 Act does not state that so to take an instrument, or to negotiate it when it has been so taken, constitutes a defect in the title of the creditor or owner. The question therefore arises whether a holder, other than a holder in due course, could enforce the instrument against the debtor, hirer or surety from whom the instrument was taken, and in particular whether knowledge by the holder that it has been taken in contravention of section 123(1) or (3) precludes recovery. It might be argued that the title of the creditor or owner is defective because he has obtained the instrument "by unlawful means" or "for an illegal consideration". But the effect of a contravention of section 123(1) or (3) is merely to render the instrument unenforceable by the person who takes it,[21] and section 170(1) of the Act further provides that a breach of any requirement made (otherwise than by any court) by or under the Act is to incur no civil or criminal sanction as being such a breach, except to the extent (if any) expressly provided by or under the Act.

4–071

It might also be argued that, since the list of defects of title in section 29(2) of the 1882 Act is not exhaustive, it is open to the courts to hold that to obtain an instrument in contravention of section 123(1) or (3) is, though not expressly referred to in the 1974 Act, such a defect. But the express reference in section 125(2) to a defect in the title of a person who negotiates a cheque in breach of section 123(2) would appear to show an intention to exclude any other contravention of section 123 from giving rise to a similar defect: *expressio unius est exclusio alterius*. In conclusion it is submitted that contravention of section 123(1) or (3) by the creditor or owner does not constitute a defect in his title within the meaning of section 29(2).

**Subsection (3): holder claiming under a holder in due course.** Where a holder derives his title to a bill through a holder in due course and is not himself a party to any fraud or illegality affecting it, it is immaterial that he knew of such fraud or illegality[22] when he took the bill, since he has all the rights of that holder in due course as regards the acceptor and all parties to the bill prior to that holder.[23] This rule is sometimes referred to as the "shelter" rule, and it applies whether the holder is a holder for

4–072

---

[21] s.125(1).

[22] Or any other defect of title.

[23] *May v Chapman* (1847) 16 M. & W. 355, 360, 361 (Illustration 11). See also *Chalmers v Lanion* (1808) 1 Camp. 383 (s.36, Illustration 80); *Insurance Corp. of Ireland plc v Dunluce Meats Ltd* [1991] N.I. 286.

value or not. It has been justified on the ground that it is necessary for the protection of the holder in due course, for otherwise it might be impossible for him to negotiate a bill further by reason of irregularities becoming known after he acquired the bill for value without notice.[24]

Only a holder[25] can claim the benefit of the shelter rule and he must derive his title to it by negotiation[26] through a holder in due course. If an indorsement on a bill payable to order is forged or unauthorised, the rule will not apply, since the person in possession of the bill will not be a holder.[27] However, a banker to whom a cheque payable to order is validly indorsed and delivered for collection by a holder in due course could rely on the rule, and likewise a banker who gives value for, or has a lien on, a cheque payable to order which a holder in due course delivers to him for collection without indorsing it, since, under section 2 of the Cheques Act 1957, he has such rights as he would have had if, upon delivery, the holder had indorsed it in blank.[28] But, since the original payee of a bill, cheque or note cannot be a holder in due course,[29] a holder who receives an instrument by negotiation from the original payee does not qualify as a sheltered holder under the subsection.[30]

The subsection will apply notwithstanding that the holder took the bill when it was overdue. Although, under section 36(2) of the Act, when an overdue bill is negotiated, it can only be negotiated subject to any defect in title affecting it at its maturity, and thenceforward no person who takes it can acquire or give a better title than that which the person from whom he took it had, nevertheless if the holder derives his title through a holder in due course who acquired the bill (by definition)[31] before maturity and held it at maturity, the bill will not have been subject to any defect in title at that time.[32]

4–073     **Effect of rule.** The effect of the rule is to confer upon the sheltered holder all the rights of the holder in due course as regards the acceptor and all parties to the bill prior to that holder. But if, for example, a bill is negotiated to him by a holder in due course as a gift, although he could sue the acceptor and prior parties, he could not sue the holder in due course, since *vis-à-vis* that holder he has not provided any consideration for the bill.[33] Moreover, he has only the same rights as the holder in due

---

[24] *Crawford and Falconbridge* (8th ed.), p.1466.
[25] Defined in s.2.
[26] s.31(1).
[27] See above, para.3–066 (s.24).
[28] See below, para.17–015.
[29] *Jones (R.E.) Ltd v Waring & Gillow Ltd* [1926] A.C. 670 (Illustration 6).
[30] But see (before the Act) *Masters v Ibberson* (1849) 8 C.B. 100, 112.
[31] See above, para.4–054 (s.29(1)).
[32] *Insurance Corp. of Ireland plc v Dunluce Meats Ltd*, [1991] N.I. 286. See below, para.5–039.
[33] See above, para.4–007.

course through whom he derived his title to the bill. He can therefore be met by such "real" or "absolute" defences as are available even against a holder in due course.[34]

**Reacquisition of the instrument.** It is clear that if a bill is indorsed    4–074
back by a holder in due course to one who was himself a party to any fraud or illegality affecting it, that person cannot qualify as a sheltered holder under subsection (3). But the Court of Appeal has held, in an action by the payee of a bill against the acceptor, that the reacquisition of the instrument by the payee by negotiation from a holder in due course conferred upon him the rights of that holder under the subsection. In *Jade International Steel Stahl und Eisen GmbH & Co. KG v Robert Nicholas (Steels) Ltd*[35] a bill was drawn by a seller payable to himself or order and accepted by the buyer in respect of goods to be delivered. The seller indorsed and discounted the bill to his bank, and it was thereafter discounted through a chain of banks, but the bill was dishonoured by the buyer on presentation for payment owing to a dispute as to the quality of the goods. Following an indorsement in blank, the bill was then passed back down the chain of banks to the seller's bank which charged it back to his account and delivered the bill to him. In an action by the seller-payee against the buyer-acceptor on the bill, the buyer sought to raise as a defence the defects in the goods. But the Court of Appeal held that the action was not between immediate parties to the bill. The seller was not suing in his original capacity as payee, but as a holder who derived his title to the bill from the banks (who were holders in due course) and accordingly, by virtue of section 29(3), was entitled to the rights of the banks. This decision has, however, been criticised,[36] and in particular because the bill was in effect paid by the drawer-indorser (the seller) and section 59(2)(b) of the Act provides in such a case that such party "is remitted to his former rights against the acceptor".[37]

ILLUSTRATIONS

1. G, by fraud, induces the defendant to draw a cheque payable to    4–075
himself or order, which he then hands to the claimant, without indorsing it, in part satisfaction of an existing debt owed by him to the claimant. The claimant has no notice of the fraud. Subsequently the claimant obtains G's

---

[34] See below, para.5–070.
[35] [1978] Q.B. 917 (Illustration 12). See also *Hon Chee Enterprise v British Markitex Ltd* [1982] 1 M.L.J. 149.
[36] *Crawford and Falconbridge* (8th ed.), p.1467.
[37] But see s.37; below, para.5–050.

indorsement, by which time he has notice that the cheque has been fraudulently obtained. The claimant has "no title to sue".[38]

2. The defendants make a promissory note for £500 payable to bearer. The note is stolen from a holder and comes into the hands of O & Co. in France, who remit it to the claimant, their agent in England, to be presented for payment. At the time the claimant receives the note, O & Co. are indebted to him on the balance of account. The claimant is not a holder in due course, although the position might be otherwise had the claimant made a further advance or given further credit on the strength of the note. The claimant must be considered as representing O & Co. and, if he can recover at all, it must be upon their right. O & Co. must prove that they gave value in good faith for the note.[39]

3. Two promissory notes, each payable on demand, are made by the defendant payable to "Fathi and Faysal Nabulsy Company", a firm registered in Palestine of which Fathi and Faysal Nabulsy are the two partners. The notes are indorsed "Fathi and Faysal Nabulsy" (the word "Company" being omitted), this being the known and recognised signature of the partnership. They are discounted to the claimant bank. Although the indorsement is valid to pass title to the notes to the bank, the form of the indorsement renders the notes irregular on their face and the bank is not a holder in due course of the notes.[40]

4–076    4. Three bills of exchange are drawn by an Italian company on and accepted by the defendant as the price of goods to be sold and delivered by the company to the defendant. The bills are indorsed by the company to the claimants and presented for payment by them, but are dishonoured by non-payment on the ground that the goods delivered are defective. The bills are drawn in pounds sterling and the sterling amount is correctly expressed in figures in the top-right hand corner with the preface "Lgs", which is the Italian abbreviation for "pounds sterling". The same amount is expressed in Italian in words in the body of the bill, but prefaced by the printed word "Lire", which is neither altered or struck out. Upon an application for summary judgment by the claimants, claiming as holders in due course, leave to defend is given on terms, there being a sufficiently arguable point relating to the discrepancy between "Lgs" and "Lire" although it could not have misled anybody.[41]

---

[38] *Whistler v Forster* (1863) 14 C.B., N.S. 248.
[39] *De la Chaumette v Bank of England* (1829) 9 B. & C. 208, as explained in *Misa v Currie* (1876) 1 App. Cas. 554, 570; *McLean v Clydesdale Bank* (1883) 9 App. Cas. 95, 114.
[40] *Arab Bank Ltd v Ross* [1952] 2 Q.B. 216.
[41] *Banco di Roma SpA v Orru* (1973) 2 Lloyd's Rep. 505.

5. G and S, both being insolvent and contemplating bankruptcy, draw bills on each other and accept them. J knows that G is in embarrassed circumstances but believes that G possesses assets. He also knows that certain persons can give full information as to G's affairs, but makes no inquiry of them. J declines to discount the bills, but purchases four bills totalling £1,757 for £200. J's proof against G's estate in the bankruptcy is limited to £200. He must be taken to have known that the bills were fraudulent.[12]

6. B persuades the claimants to draw two cheques, one for £2,000 and the other for £3,000, payable to the order of the defendants, by falsely representing that the defendants are financing a new line of cars. The cheques are drawn in the mistaken belief that they are the required deposit for 500 cars. They are handed to B who gives them to the defendants in payment of a deposit of £5,000 payable by B to the defendants in respect of certain hire-purchase agreements for furniture. Objection being raised by the defendants as to the regularity of the claimant's signature on the cheques, it is agreed between the claimants and the defendants (no mention being made of the purpose of payment) that the two cheques will be returned and a fresh cheque for £5,000 will be signed and posted to the defendants. The defendants cash this cheque and release to B the furniture let under the hire-purchase agreements. Upon discovery of the fraud, they retake possession of the furniture. The claimants are entitled to recover the £5,000 from the defendants as money paid under a mistake, and they are not estopped. The original payee of a cheque in whose possession it remains cannot be a holder in due course.[43]

7. C is a partner in the claimant firm of solicitors and has authority to draw cheques on the firm's client account with the L. Bank. Cheques so drawn by him are used to obtain three drafts drawn by the bank on itself payable to the claimants. C takes one of these drafts to the defendants, a gaming club, indorses it and proffers it to the club in exchange for chips. After some hesitation, the club's employers accept the draft for that purpose. The club is liable to the claimants for conversion of the draft. The claimants had an immediate right to possession of the draft. The club is not a holder in due course of the draft as section 29(1)(b) of the Act has not been satisfied: the provision of chips for gaming does not constitute giving value for the draft.[44]     4–077

---

[42] *Jones v Gordon* (1877) 2 App. Cas. 616.
[43] *Jones (R.E.) Ltd v Waring & Gillow Ltd* [1926] A.C. 670.
[44] *Lipkin Gorman v Karpnale Ltd* [1991] 2 A.C. 548; see also below, para.13–071 (s.75, Illustration 13).

8. As part of a property transaction, the defendant draws a cheque for £100,000 payable to the order of F H & S, a firm of solicitors, who indorse it *"sans recours"* and deliver it to the claimants, solicitors acting for the vendor in the transaction. The cheque is in respect of a deposit and delivery of it is conditional on exchange of contracts. Contracts are duly exchanged but the cheque is dishonoured on presentation. The claimants apply for summary judgment on the cheque. Upon fulfilment of the condition delivery became complete and the claimants became holders in due course of the cheque. The claimants, though acting as stakeholders, took the cheque for value as required by section 29(1) because they were deemed to be holders for value under section 27(2), value having been given for the cheque by the exchange of contracts immediately prior to delivery. Judgment is given for the claimants for the amount of the cheque.[45]

9. The defendant draws a cheque for £100 on the Oxford Street branch of the claimant bank payable to the order of T. T indorses the cheque and pays it into her account at the Victoria Street branch of the same bank, and she is provided with £80 cash in respect of it. Unknown to the Victoria Street branch, payment of the cheque has already been countermanded by the defendant by notice to the Oxford Street branch, and the cheque is dishonoured when presented there. The bank is entitled to judgment against the defendant on the cheque. It is a holder for value of the cheque in good faith and without notice of the countermand. Notice of countermand to one branch of a bank is not notice to other branches of the same bank.[46]

**4–078**   10. An Austrian company draws a bill on the defendants, an English company, which the defendants accept. The bill is negotiated by the Austrian company to the claimant bank. The bank seeks summary judgment against the defendants on the bill, claiming as holder in due course. The defendants assert that they have an arguable defence to the claim, in that the bank is not a holder in due course since, when it took the bill, it knew that the Austrian company was insolvent and that the bill had been negotiated with the intention of preferring the bank to other creditors of the Austrian company in circumstances amounting to a fraudulent preference. This is no defence. Fraud in the relevant sections of the Act means common law fraud. A "fraudulent", *i.e.* voidable, preference under section 44 of the Bankruptcy Act 1914 is not without more fraudulent, and no charge of fraud has been made out.[47]

---

[45] *Clifford Chance v Silver* [1992] 2 Bank L.R. 11.
[46] *London Provincial & South Western Bank Ltd v Buszard* (1918) 35 T.L.R. 142.
[47] *Osterreichische Länderbank v S'Elite Ltd* [1981] 1 Q.B. 565.

11. The defendants, C and G, are in partnership trading as J.G. & Co. In fraud of his fellow partner, G draws a bill in the firm name upon W.C. payable to the order of the defendants. The bill is indorsed and discounted to B, who has no knowledge of the fraud. The claimant takes it by indorsement from B, he, the claimant, knowing of the circumstances under which it was originally drawn. No defence is made out. An innocent person may transfer title to a bill to a person who is not party to the original fraud, though he have knowledge of it.[48]

12. A bill of exchange, payable to the claimants or order at 120 days, is drawn by the claimants on the defendants in respect of the price of two consignments of steel to be supplied by the claimants to the defendants. The bill is indorsed and discounted by the claimants to the S Bank, by the S Bank to the D Bank, and by the D Bank to the M Bank, which opens the indorsement. The defendants accept the bill, but it is dishonoured on presentment for payment because of a dispute about the quality of the first consignment of steel. After dishonour, the bill is passed by the M Bank to the D Bank and by the D Bank to the S Bank, which debits the claimants' account with the amount of the bill and hands the bill back to the claimants. The claimants have lost the capacity which they had as drawers and immediate parties to the bill. They are holders for value of the bill and derive their title to it from the D Bank and the M Bank, who were holders in due course. They can rely, as against the defendants, on section 29(3) of the Act and are entitled to summary judgment on the bill.[49]

## Presumption of value and good faith

30. (1) Every party whose signature appears on a bill is prima facie deemed to have become a party thereto for value.    4–079

    (2) Every holder of a bill is prima facie deemed to be a holder in due course; but if in an action on a bill it is admitted or proved that the acceptance, issue, or subsequent negotiation of the bill is affected with fraud, duress, or force and fear, or illegality, the burden of proof is shifted, unless and until the holder proves that, subsequent to the alleged fraud or illegality, value has in good faith been given for the bill.

[48] *May v Chapman* (1847) 16 M. & W. 355, 360, 361.
[49] *Jade International Steel Stahl und Eisen GmbH & Co. KG. v Robert Nicholas (Steels) Ltd* [1978] Q.B. 917.

Definitions
"acceptance": ss.2, 17(1).
"action": s.2
"bill": s.2.
"good faith": s.90.
"holder": s.2.
"holder in due course": s.29.
"issue": s.2.
"value": s.2.

Comparison
UCC: § 3–308.
ULB: arts 16, 17, 18, 19.
ULC: arts 19, 21, 22, 23.
UNB: arts 15, 27, 28, 29, 32.

## COMMENT

4–080    **Subsection (1): presumption of signature for value.** Under the general law of contract, the party seeking to establish a contract must prove the consideration for it. But this is not so in the case of bills, cheques and notes. It is unnecessary for a person who seeks to enforce an instrument against a party liable to him thereon to plead or prove that the engagement of that party constituted by his signature of the instrument was given for consideration, since every party whose signature appears on the instrument is prima facie deemed to have become a party thereto for value. Conversely, if a person accepts a bill gratuitously for the accommodation of the drawer,[50] the burden of proof lies on him to show that he signed the bill as acceptor without receiving value therefor.[51]

4–081    **Subsection (2): presumption of holding in due course.** Every holder of a bill is prima facie deemed to be a holder in due course.[52] It would appear that, in order to rely on this presumption, a claimant must first prove that the instrument in question fulfils the requirements of a valid bill or note[53] and that it has been validly negotiated to him so as to constitute him a holder of the instrument.[54] The burden then ordinarily lies on the defendant to rebut the presumption by proving, for example,

---

[50] See above, para.4–042 (s.28).
[51] See above, para.4–043.
[52] *King v Milsom* (1809) 2 Camp. 6; *Fitch v Jones* (1855) 5 E. & B. 238 (s.27, Illustration 14). The holder is not compelled to rely on the presumption, but may establish his status by affirmative proof: *Barclays Bank Ltd v Astley Industrial Trust Ltd* [1970] 2 Q.B. 527 (s.27, Illustration 27).
[53] See above, para.2–001; below, para.15–003.
[54] *Thambirajah v Mahesvari* (1961) 62 N.L.R. (Ceylon) 519 (claimant required to show that notes payable to order had been validly indorsed to him).

that, at the time the claimant took the instrument, it was incomplete[55] or irregular,[56] or overdue,[57] or that the claimant did not take the instrument as holder for value.[58]

**Fraud, duress or illegality.** Subsection (2), however, goes on to provide  **4–082** that, if in an action[59] on a bill it is admitted or proved that the acceptance, issue or subsequent negotiation of the bill is affected with fraud, duress, or force and fear, or illegality, the burden of proof is shifted, unless and until the holder proves that, subsequent to the alleged fraud or illegality, value has in good faith been given for the bill.[60] If the holder succeeds in discharging that burden of proof, he will re-establish his status as a holder in due course,[61] although, presumably, it would then still be open to the defendant to prove that the claimant was not in fact a holder in due course, *e.g.* because he took the bill when it was overdue.

The words "if it is admitted or proved" mean no more than that some evidence of circumstances in the nature of fraud, etc., must be given sufficient to be left to a jury.[62] In Part 24 proceedings, it is sufficient that the defendant, in his affidavit in reply to an application for summary judgment, gives prima facie proof that the acceptance, issue or subsequent negotiation of the bill was affected by one of the vices mentioned in the subsection.[63]

In this subsection, as in section 29(2), "fraud" means common law fraud,[64] but can extend to fraud practised on third parties.[65] Fraud etc.

---

[55] See above, para.4–052.
[56] See above, para.4–053.
[57] See above, para.4–054.
[58] See above, para.4–057.
[59] This includes counterclaim and set-off: s.2. But the subs. does not apply to proceedings for an injunction to restrain the holder from negotiating a bill on the ground that it was obtained by fraud: *Hawkins v Troup* (1890) 7 T.L.R. 104.
[60] *Bailey v Bidwell* (1844) 13 M. & W. 73 (Illustration 1); *Smith v Braine* (1851) 16 Q.B. 244 (Illustration 2); *Berry v Alderman* (1853) 14 C.B. 95; *Hogg v Skeen* (1865) 18 C.B. (N.S.) 426 (Illustration 3); *Tatam v Haslar* (1889) 23 Q.B.D. 345 (Illustration 4); *Baker v Barclays Bank Ltd* [1955] 1 Q.B. 822 (Cheques Act 1957, s.4, Illustration 15); *Tan Chow Soo v Ratna Ammal* [1969] 2 M.L.J. 49; *Jebsen & Jessen (S) Pte Ltd v Yeung Hoi Kwang* [1978] M.L.J. 96.
[61] *Robinson v Benkel* (1913) 29 T.L.R. 475; *Bank für Gemeinwirtschaft A.G. v City of London Garages Ltd* [1971] 1 W.L.R. 149 (Illustration 5).
[62] *Hall v Featherstone* (1858) 3 H. & N. 284, 286–287; *Tatam v Haslar* (1889) 23 Q.B.D. 345, 348, 349; *Hawkins v Troup* (1890) 7 T.L.R. 104 at 105; *Bank of Cyprus (London) v Jones* (1984) 134 New L.J. 522. But see *Wallingford v Mutual Society* (1880) 5 App. Cas. 685, 697, 709 (general allegation of fraud insufficient).
[63] *Powszechny Bank Zwiazkowy W Polsce v Paros* [1932] 2 K.B. 353, 360. But see below, para.4–084.
[64] *Osterreichische Länderbank v S'Elite Ltd* [1981] 1 Q.B. 565 (s.29, Illustration 10). See above, para.4–063. *cf. Lloyd's Bank Ltd v Cooke* [1907] 1 K.B. 794, 807–808.
[65] See above, para.4–063.

affecting the acceptance[66] or issue[67] of the bill, or its subsequent negotiation,[68] will shift the burden of proof to the claimant. The meaning of duress, or force and fear, has already been discussed,[69] and it is submitted that this includes also undue influence.[70] The distinction in this regard between illegal transactions[71] and those which are merely void has been considered in the Comment on section 27 of the Act.[72]

4–083    No reference is made in the subsection to lost or stolen instruments. At common law, if it was proved that a bearer instrument had been stolen, the onus of proof shifted to the claimant,[73] and it is submitted that the common law rule continues to apply.[74] The position with respect to lost instruments was less certain at common law,[75] but it is submitted that the onus is again shifted if a lost instrument is appropriated in circumstances amounting to theft.[76]

Proof by a defendant that he is an accommodation party,[77] or that he received no value for his signature of the bill, does not require the holder to prove that he, or a previous holder, gave value for the bill: the 'burden of proof' rests on the defendant.[78]

4–084    **Re-establishing holder in due course status.** The holder can re-establish his status as a holder in due course by proving that, subsequent to the alleged fraud or illegality (or, presumably, duress) value has in good faith been given for the bill.[79] At the time of the passing of the Act, it was uncertain how much the claimant had to prove in cases where evidence of fraud had been given—whether the onus was shifted only to the extent of making the claimant prove that value was in fact given, or

---

[66] *Hogg v Skeen* (1865) 18 C.B. (N.S.) 426 (Illustration 3); *Banque du Rhône S.A. v Fuerst Day Lawson Ltd* [1968] 2 Lloyd's Rep. 153.

[67] *Bailey v Bidwell* (1844) 13 M. & W. 73 (Illustration 1).

[68] *Smith v Braine* (1851) 16 Q.B. 244 (Illustration 2); *Berry v Alderman* (1853) 14 C.B. 95; *Fuller v Alexander Bros* (1882) 47 L.T. 443; *Powszechny Bank Zwiazkowy W Polsce v Paros* [1932] 2 K.B. 353; *Baker v Barclays Bank Ltd* [1955] 1 W.L.R. 822 (Cheques Act 1957, s.4, Illustration 15). See also *Ben Baron and Partners v Henderson* 1959 (3) S.A. 188.

[69] See above, para.4–065.

[70] See above, para.4–065.

[71] See *Bailey v Bidwell* (1844) 13 M. & W. 73 (Illustration 1).

[72] See above, para.4–015.

[73] *De la Chaumette v Bank of England* (1829) 9 B. & C. 208 (s.29, Illustration 2). See also *Raphael v Bank of England* (1855) 17 C.B. 161.

[74] s.97(2).

[75] See *King v Milsom* (1809) 2 Camp. 5; *Paterson v Hardacre* (1811) 4 Taunt. 114; *Mills v Barber* (1836) 1 M. & W. 425, 432.

[76] Theft Act 1968, s.3(1).

[77] See above, para.4–041.

[78] *Mills v Barber* (1836) 1 M. & W. 425.

[79] *Robinson v Benkel* (1913) 29 T.L.R. 475; *Bank für Gemeinwirtschaft A.G. v City of London Garages Ltd* [1971] 1 W.L.R. 149 (Illustration 5); *Bank of Cyprus (London) Ltd v Jones* (1984) 134 New L.J. 522.

that it was also given bona fide.[80] The sub-section is, however, clear that both requirements must be satisfied.[81] "Value" is defined in section 2[82] and "good faith" in section 90 of the Act.[83] A person will not be in good faith if he received the bill with notice[84] of the fraud, etc., affecting it.

The subsection does not require that value be given in good faith by a person to whom the bill is negotiated. Thus if A by fraud obtains a cheque from B payable to C, which C negotiates to D, D may, in order to re-establish his status as a holder in due course, prove that C (the original payee) gave value in good faith for the cheque.[85]

In *Powszechny Bank Zwiazkowy W Polsce v Paros*[86] the Court of Appeal held that, on an application for summary judgment, where evidence of fraud is adduced by the defendant, the mere statement in the claimant's affidavit that he took the instrument in good faith and for value is not sufficient to decide the issue in favour of the claimant. But in the later case of *Bank für Gemeinwirtschaft Aktiengesellschaft v City of London Garages Ltd*,[87] the same court upheld an order for summary judgment against the defendant, notwithstanding evidence of fraud, where the claimant's affidavit and evidence were found to establish good faith and the giving of value with such a degree of probability that, if the case had gone for trial, the defendant's defence of fraud would have had no real chance of success.

Where a claimant brings an action against the acceptor of a bill, and the acceptor alleges that his acceptance was obtained by fraud, then if there is a triable issue as to the fraud and as to whether, subsequent to the fraud, value has in good faith been given for the bill, the court may in its discretion order the claimant to give security for the defendant's costs in the action.[88]

**Application to payee.** In *Talbot v Von Boris*[89] the Court of Appeal held   **4–085** that section 30(2) of the Act has no application to the original payee of an instrument in whose hands the instrument remains, and this was also the view expressed by Robert Goff J. in *Hasan v Willson*.[90] Where, therefore,

---

[80] *Tatam v Haslar* (1889) 23 Q.B.D. 345, 349, commenting on the views expressed by Parke B. in *Bailey v Bidwell* (1844) 13 M. & W. 73, 76 and Lord Blackburn in *Jones v Gordon* (1877) 2 App. Cas. 616, 628. See also *Smith v Braine* (1851) 16 Q.B. 244 and *Hogg v Skeen* (1865) 18 C.B. (N.S.) 426 (Illustrations 2 and 3).

[81] *Tatam v Haslar* (1889) 23 Q.B.D. 345 (Illustration 4).

[82] See above, para.1–029.

[83] See below, para.16–001.

[84] For the meaning of notice, see above, para.4–058.

[85] But in such a case, C's title may not in fact be defective: see above, para.4–063 (s.29).

[86] [1932] 2 K.B. 353. See also *Fuller v Alexander Bros* (1882) 47 L.T. 443.

[87] [1971] 1 W.L.R. 149 (Illustration 5).

[88] *Banque du Rhône S.A. v Fuerst Day Lawson Ltd* [1968] 2 Lloyd's Rep. 153. See CPR, Pt 25.

[89] *Talbot v Von Boris* [1911] 1 K.B. 854 (Illustration 6).

[90] [1977] 1 Lloyd's Rep. 431 (s.27, Illustration 19). See also *United Commercial Bank Ltd v New Era Corp.* [1976] M.L.J. 101.

the claimant is the original payee of the instrument, the defendant must prove that the claimant received the instrument with notice of the fraud, etc., with the curious result that in the matter of proof the original payee is in a more favoured position than a person to whom the instrument has been negotiated, since the burden does not shift to him to prove that, subsequent to the fraud, etc., value has in good faith been given for the instrument. Although the decision has been criticised,[91] it is in this respect[92] consistent with the later decision of the House of Lords in *Jones (R.E.) Ltd v Waring & Gillow Ltd*[93] in which it was held that the original payee of an instrument who remains in possession of it cannot be a holder in due course. If the original payee is not a holder in due course, he can scarcely be deemed to be such a holder under subsection (2).

4–086     **Sheltered holder.** Section 30(2) also does not apply to the "sheltered holder" referred to in section 29(3) of the Act,[94] that is to say, a holder (whether for value or not) who derives his title to a bill through a holder in due course, and who is not himself a party to any fraud or illegality affecting it.[95]

ILLUSTRATIONS

4–087     1. A promissory note is made by the defendant payable to B and indorsed by B to the claimant. When sued on the note, the defendant alleges that it was given for an illegal consideration, namely that B would not oppose a bankruptcy petition presented by the defendant. If a note is proved to have been obtained by fraud, or affected by illegality, such proof casts upon the claimant the burden of showing that he is a bona fide indorsee for value, which burden the claimant failed to discharge.[96]

2. The defendant accepts a bill drawn on him by B for the defendant's accommodation. The bill is indorsed in blank by B and delivered to the defendant in order that the defendant may get it discounted. The defendant delivers the bill to M to get it discounted, and M delivers the bill to C for the same purpose. C, in violation of that purpose and against good

---

[91] *Crawford and Falconbridge* (8th ed.), p.1470.
[92] But see below, para.5–072 (s.38).
[93] [1926] A.C. 670 (s.29, Illustration 6).
[94] See above, para.4–072.
[95] But if fraud or illegality is admitted or proved, the sheltered holder bears the burden of re-establishing the status of the "holder in due course" through whom he derives his title: *De la Chaumette v Bank of England* (1829) 9 B. & C. 208 (s.29, Illustration 2).
[96] *Bailey v Bidwell* (1844) 13 M. & W. 73.

faith, indorses the bill to the claimant. The onus lies on the claimant to prove that he gave value for the bill.[97]

3. V and S carry on business in partnership. V, for his own private purposes, accepts a bill in the name of the partnership without the authority of his fellow partner and in fraud of the partnership articles. The claimant, as indorsee of the bill, is required to prove that he gave value for the bill.[98]

4. A bill of exchange for £500 is drawn by J on, and accepted by, the **4–088** defendant payable to the order of J, and is indorsed by J to the claimant. In an action by the claimant against the defendant as acceptor, the defendant alleges that he accepted the bill and handed it to L to get it discounted for him, but that L fraudulently handed over the bill to J and that J fraudulently indorsed it to the claimant, who took it for no consideration and with notice of the fraud. Evidence of fraud having been given, the burden lies on the claimant to prove that, subsequent to the alleged fraud, value has in good faith been given for the bill.[99]

5. Ten bills of exchange, totalling £250,000, are drawn in London by N Ltd upon, and accepted by, CLG Ltd payable to B & S, Hamburg. Each bill is generally indorsed by the four defendants: N Ltd, CLG Ltd, W (a director of N Ltd and CLG Ltd) and the Central Bank of India. The bills are negotiated to a German company, which delivers them to the claimants who become holders for collection. The bills are dishonoured by non-payment. Notice of dishonour is duly given, and the bills are duly noted and protested. The claimants apply for summary judgment against all four defendants. The Central Bank of India obtains leave to defend the action on the ground that its London manager, who indorsed the bills on behalf of the Bank, was not authorised to bind the Bank by his sole signature. It is alleged that the issue, acceptance and indorsement of the bills was procured by the fraud of that London manager to conceal his defalcations. Notwithstanding this allegation of fraud, leave to sign judgment against the other three defendants is given. The claimants' affidavit is supported by unchallenged and unchallengeable contemporary documents so as to establish good faith and the giving of value with such a degree of probability that if the case went for trial the defendants' defence of fraud would have no real chance of success.[1]

---

[97] *Smith v Braine* (1851) 16 Q.B. 244.
[98] *Hogg v Skeen* (1865) 18 C.B. (N.S.) 426.
[99] *Tatam v Haslar* (1889) 23 Q.B.D. 345.
[1] *Bank für Gemeinwirtschaft A.G. v City of London Garages Ltd* [1971] 1 W.L.R. 149.

6. The defendants, husband and wife, make two joint and several promissory notes payable to the claimant in respect of sums of money to be advanced on the security of the notes by the claimant to the husband. In answer to the claimant's claim on the notes, the wife pleads that she was induced to sign the notes by duress on the part of her husband and that the claimant had notice of that duress. The burden of proof rests upon the wife to establish that the claimant knew of the duress. Section 30(2) of the 1882 Act does not apply to a case where the instrument, whether a bill or note or cheque, remains in the hands of the person to whom it was originally delivered and in whose possession it remains. The wife has failed to discharge that burden of proof, since in evidence she has stated that she did not think the claimant knew of the duress.[2]

## Negotiation of Bills

### Negotiation of bill

5–001    31. (1) A bill is negotiated when it is transferred from one person to another in such a manner as to constitute the transferee the holder of the bill.

(2) A bill payable to bearer is negotiated by delivery.

(3) A bill payable to order is negotiated by the indorsement of the holder completed by delivery.

(4) Where the holder of a bill payable to his order transfers it for value without indorsing it, the transfer gives the transferee such title as the transferor had in the bill, and the transferee in addition acquires the right to have the indorsement of the transferor.

(5) Where any person is under obligation to indorse a bill in a representative capacity, he may indorse the bill in such terms as to negative personal liability.

| Definitions | Comparison |
|---|---|
| "bearer": s.2. | UCC: §§ 3–104, 3–201, 3–203, |
| "bill": s.2. | 3–204. |
| "delivery": s.2. | ULB: arts 11–15. |
| "holder": s.2. | ULC: arts 14–17, 20. |
| "indorsement": s.2. | UNB: arts 13–16, 24, 45. |
| "person": s.2. | |

[2] *Talbot v Von Boris* [1911] 1 K.B. 854.

COMMENT

**Negotiation of a bill.** The primary characteristics of a negotiable    5–002
instrument are, first, that it is "transferable" in the sense that the rights
arising under it can be transferred by delivery of the instrument (together
with any necessary indorsement) so that it can be sued upon by the
person who is for the time being in possession of it, and, secondly, that it
is "negotiable" in the sense that such a transfer may, in addition, confer
upon the transferee a good title to the instrument notwithstanding a
defect in the title of the transferor.[1] The Act may have intended to
distinguish between "transferable" and "negotiable" in, for example,
section 8(1), which provides: "When a bill contains words prohibiting
transfer, or indicating an intention that it should not be transferable, it is
valid as between the parties thereto, but is not negotiable",[2] although it
has subsequently been stated that a bill (though not a cheque)[3] crossed
"not negotiable" is thereby rendered not even transferable.[4]

For the rest, however, the Act uses the words "negotiate", "negotiation" and "negotiable" sometimes to indicate transfer and transferability[5]
and sometimes to mean negotiability in the full sense.[6] As Byles remarks[7]:
"The terms 'transferable' and 'negotiable' are hopelessly mixed up in the
Act." But it is true to say that, neither in that work nor indeed in this one,
is the word "negotiable" used in a single consistent sense.

**Subsection (1): negotiation defined.** This subsection provides that a    5–003
bill is negotiated when it is transferred in such a manner as to constitute
the transferee the holder. "Transfer" is not defined in the Act; but
"holder" is defined in section 2 to mean "the payee or indorsee of a bill
or note who is in possession of it, or the bearer thereof". However, where
a bill or note is issued by first delivery to the payee, although the payee
is a holder of the instrument, there is no negotiation of it to him.[8]

By negotiation the holder does not necessarily become the owner of the
instrument and a person may be a holder without necessarily being its
owner.

The negotiation of a bill or note has been distinguished from the sale of
goods, by Holroyd J.[9]; from the transfer of shares in a company, by Byles

[1] *Crouch v Credit Foncier of England Ltd* (1873) L.R. 8 Q.B. 374, 381–382.
[2] See above, para.2–061.
[3] See below, para.14–030.
[4] *Hibernian Bank Ltd v Gysin and Hanson* [1939] 1 K.B. 483 (s.8, Illustration 1).
[5] *e.g.* s.36.
[6] *e.g.* ss.29(1)(2).
[7] 27th ed., 8–02.
[8] *Jones (R.E.) Ltd v Waring & Gillow Ltd* [1926] A.C. 670 (s.29, Illustration 6).
[9] *Wookey v Pole* (1820) 4 B. & Ald. 1, 10.

J.[10]; and from the transfer of an assignable Scottish bond, by Blackburn J.[11]

5–004     **Dematerialised instruments.** The section clearly contemplates the transfer of a paper instrument by delivery. But the Review Committee on Banking Services Law and Practice[12] was asked to examine, in the context of the existing law, proposals for negotiable instruments to be placed with a central depositary and thereafter transferred by means of a screen-based or book entry system. In its report,[13] the Committee rejected a purely contractual regime between members to overcome the legal difficulties involved:

> "What is required . . . is to make good the shortcomings of the con-tractual approach by replicating for screen-based transfers the law . . . in regard to bills of exchange. The objective will be to procure that the legal effect of an instrument and of transactions within the system, on the obligations of a party thereto, is precisely the same as it would have been had the same transaction occurred in the conventional way."[14]

The Committee also foresaw a system in which instruments were no longer created in paper form, but the obligations they would have repre-sented were recorded in electronic or "dematerialised" form only.[15] In such a system, "it would not simply be a question of trading an existing negotiable instrument without indorsement and delivery, but of trading an obligation which is not contained in any written instrument".[16] Again, the Committee considered that obligations equivalent to those attaching to negotiable instruments should be capable of being created and that parties to transactions in those obligations could be put in the same position as equivalent parties to transactions in negotiable instru-ments.[17]

Accordingly the Committee recommended that new legislation should "contain provisions giving to transactions taking place in a screen based or book entry depositary (or dematerialised) system operated by an Approved Depositary and satisfying certain basic statutory requirements the same status as equivalent transactions in negotiable instruments generally".[18]

---

[10] *Swan v North British Australasian Co.* (1863) 2 H. & C. 175, 184, 185.
[11] *Crouch v Credit Foncier of England Ltd* (1873) L.R. 8 Q.B. 374, 381.
[12] See above, para.1–008.
[13] (1989) Cm. 622.
[14] (1989) Cm. 622, para.8.35.
[15] (1989) Cm. 622, para.8.33; see above, para.2–011.
[16] (1989) Cm. 622, para.8.38.
[17] (1989) Cm. 622, para.8.40.
[18] (1989) Cm. 622, rec.8(9).

In 1990 the Bank of England commenced the provision of a service for screen-based settlement of money market instruments through its Central Moneymarkets Office (CMO). The service enabled its members to make screen-based transfers of money market instruments held in paper form in a central depository, which operated within existing legislation. In 2003 non-material equivalents of money market instruments (known as "eligible debt securities")[19] began to be issued into CREST[20] and in October 2003 the CMO system was shut down. Eligible debt securities include (*inter alia*) dematerialised bankers' acceptances.[21] The Bank of England purchases or holds as collateral eligible bankers' acceptances as part of its open market operations.[22]

**Subsection (2): bill to bearer.** A bill payable to bearer is negotiated by mere delivery, and no indorsement is required. A bill is payable to bearer which is expressed to be so payable, or on which the only or last indorsement is in blank.[23] "Bearer" and "delivery" are defined in section 2 of the Act.

5–005

Where the holder of a bill payable to bearer negotiates it by delivery without indorsing it, he is called a "transferor by delivery".[24] He is not liable on the instrument,[25] but by negotiating the bill gives certain warranties to his immediate transferee.[26]

**Subsection (3): bill to order.** A bill payable to order is negotiated by the indorsement of the holder completed by delivery. A bill is payable to order which is expressed to be so payable, or which is expressed to be payable to a particular person, and does not contain words prohibiting transfer or indicating an intention that it should not be transferable.[27] "Delivery", "holder" and "indorsement" are defined in section 2, and the requisites for a valid indorsement are set out in section 32. The indorsement may be a "full" indorsement, or it may be a qualified indorsement (*i.e.* one which negatives or limits the liability of the indorser to the

5–006

---

[19] For the legislative background see the Uncertificated Securities Regulations 2001 (SI 2001/3755) and the Uncertificated Securities (Amendment) (Eligible Debt Securities) Regulations 2003 (SI 2003/1633), made by the Treasury under s.207 of the Companies Act 1989. These allow for the evidencing and transfer of title to eligible debt securities in accordance with a computer-based system and procedures.

[20] For a description of this company, see *www.crestco.co.uk*.

[21] The Bank of England and Crest Co. have produced guides specifically for "acceptors" and "drawers" of bankers' acceptances.

[22] For a bankers' acceptance to be eligible it must meet certain requirements (detailed in notices issued by the Bank on August 27, 2003). The Bank also maintains a list of institutions whose acceptances are eligible for discount at the Bank.

[23] s.8(3). See also s.34(1).

[24] s.58(1).

[25] s.58(2).

[26] s.58(3).

[27] s.8(4). See also ss.8(5), 81A.

holder),[28] or a conditional[29] or restrictive[30] indorsement. The indorsement may be special[31] or in blank.[32] A bill cannot be negotiated through or under a forged or unauthorised indorsement.[33]

The indorsement of the holder is required in all cases for the negotiation of a bill of exchange or promissory note payable to order unless the instrument has become payable to bearer by reason of an indorsement in blank. But section 2 of the Cheques Act 1957 confers on a banker who gives value for, or has a lien on, a cheque payable to order, which the holder delivers to him for collection without indorsing it, such rights as he would have had if it had been indorsed in blank,[34] and it has been held that a cheque so delivered without an indorsement is negotiated to the banker, so that he may become a holder in due course.[35]

No indorsement of the holder is required unless it is sought to negotiate an instrument payable to order. The presentment of an instrument for payment is not a negotiation of it[36] and no indorsement is required. Nevertheless, before the passing of the Cheques Act 1957, it was the practice of bankers to require the "indorsement" of the payee when a cheque was presented to the drawee bank for payment. This is still required in the case of bills and may be required where, for example, a cheque is cashed over the counter.[37] Such an "indorsement" is, however, not strictly an indorsement, but operates as a receipt.[38]

5–007     **Subsection (4): transfer of a bill to order without indorsement.** If the holder of a bill payable to his order transfers it for value without indorsing it, the transferee does not become a holder of the instrument, since he is not the payee or indorsee of the instrument or the bearer thereof.[39] The transfer nevertheless gives the transferee such title as the transferor had in the bill. The position was thus explained by Willes J. in *Whistler v Forster*[40]:

[28] s.16(1).
[29] s.33.
[30] s.35.
[31] s.34(2).
[32] s.34(1).
[33] s.24. But see s.55(2).
[34] See below, para.17–015.
[35] *Midland Bank Ltd v R.V. Harris Ltd* [1963] 1 W.L.R. 1021 (Cheques Act 1957, s.2, Illustration 1). This does not apply to cheques crossed "account payee" which are not transferable: see below, para.14–037 (s.81A), para.17–017 (Cheques Act 1957, s.2).
[36] *Sharples v Rickhard* (1857) 2 H. & N. 57 (unless the drawee acceptor of a bill pays it in part before maturity: see above, para.4–060 (s.29), n. 72).
[37] See below, para.17–003.
[38] *Keene v Beard* (1860) 8 C.B. (N.S.) 372, 382; *McDonald (Gerald) & Co. v Nash & Co.* [1924] A.C. 625, 633–634.
[39] See s.2 (definition of "holder").
[40] (1863) 14 C.B. (N.S.) 248, 257–258, followed in *Volkskas v Darrenwood Electrical* 1973 (2) S.A. 386.

" ... the general rule of law is undoubted, that no one can transfer a better title than he himself possesses: *Nemo dat quod non habet*. To this there are some exceptions; one of which arises out of the rule of the law-merchant as to negotiable instruments. These, being part of the currency, are subject to the same rule as money: and if such an instrument be transferred in good faith, for value, before it is over-due, it becomes available in the hands of the holder, notwithstanding fraud which would have rendered it unavailable in the hands of a previous holder. This rule, however, is only intended to favour transfers in the ordinary and usual manner whereby a title is acquired according to the law-merchant, and not to a transfer which is valid in equity according to the doctrine respecting the assignment of choses in action, ... and it is therefore clear that, in order to acquire the benefit of this rule, the holder of the bill must, if it be payable to order, obtain an indorsement, and that he is affected by notice of a fraud received before he does so. Until he does so, he is merely in the position of an assignee of an ordinary chose in action, and has no better right than his assignor."

As assignee of a chose in action,[41] the transferee takes "subject to equities".[42] It would appear that these will include rights of set-off availa-ble to the party primarily liable on the instrument against the transferor in respect of debts which have accrued due before he receives notice of the assignment (whether or not these are payable before that date), and also debts arising out of the same contract as that which gave rise to the liability, or which are closely connected with that contract.[43]

Since the transferee is not a holder of the bill, he cannot claim the right conferred by section 38(1) of the Act to sue on the bill in his own name,[44] and, as equitable assignee, must probably join the transferor as a party to the action.[45] He cannot indorse the bill in the transferor's name[46] and cannot negotiate the bill by himself indorsing it.

---

[41] *Harrop v Fisher* (1861) 10 C.B. (N.S.) 196, 203 (Illustration 1); *Factory Investments (Pty) Ltd v Ismails* 1960 (2) S.A. 10; *Aldercrest Developments Ltd v Hamilton Co-Axial (1958) Ltd* (1973) 37 D.L.R. (3d) 254. *cf. Geo. Thompson (Australia) Pty Ltd v Vittadello* [1978] V.R. 199, 208–212.

[42] See *Chitty on Contracts* (29th ed.), Vol.I, § 19–069.

[43] *Newfoundland v Newfoundland Ry* (1888) 13 App. Cas. 199, 213; *Biggerstaff v Rowatts Wharf Ltd* [1896] 2 Ch. 93; *William Pickersgill & Sons Ltd v London & Provincial etc. Insurance Co. Ltd* [1912] 3 K.B. 614; *Rother Iron Works Ltd v Canterbury Precision Engineers Ltd* [1974] Q.B. 1; *Business Computers Ltd v Anglo-African Leasing Ltd* [1977] 1 W.L.R. 578, 585; *The Raven* [1980] 2 Lloyd's Rep. 266. See *Aldercrest Developments Ltd v Hamilton Co-Axial (1958) Ltd* (1973) 37 D.L.R. (32) 254.

[44] *Cunliffe v Whitehead* (1837) 3 Bing. N.C. 828, 830; *Harrop v Fisher* (1861) 10 C.B. (N.S.) 196; *Good v Walker* (1892) 61 L.J. Q.B. 736; *Bank of British Columbia v Coopers & Lybrand Ltd* (1985) 15 D.L.R. (4th) 714.

[45] See *Chitty on Contracts* (29th ed.), Vol.I, § 19–038.

[46] *Harrop v Fisher* (1861) 10 C.B. (N.S.) 196 (Illustration 1).

**5–008** However, if the holder transfers the bill for value, the transferee acquires the right to have the indorsement of the transferor,[47] and, by section 39 of the Supreme Court Act 1981, if the High Court has made an order directing the transferor to indorse the instrument, but the transferor neglects or refuses to comply with the order or cannot after reasonable inquiry be found, the High Court may order that the instrument be indorsed by such person as the court may nominate for that purpose. But the right to have such an indorsement is available only to the first transferee, since a subsequent transferee will not have had the bill transferred to him by a holder.

If the transferor does indorse the bill, the indorsement takes effect from that time,[48] so that the transferee will take the instrument subject to any defect of title of which he has become aware between the date of the transfer and the date of the indorsement.[49] If the bill is delivered to the transferor for indorsement, but he destroys it, the transferee cannot sue the acceptor on the bill.[50]

**5–009** **Subsection (5): indorsement by representative.** A person under an obligation to indorse a bill in a representative capacity, *e.g.* as executor or administrator, may indorse it in such terms as to negative personal liability. Indorsements limiting or negativing liability are dealt with in section 16(1) of the Act and indorsements in a representative capacity in section 26.

ILLUSTRATIONS

**5–010** 1. A bill is drawn by J, and accepted by the appellant payable to J's order, in respect of goods supplied and to be supplied by J to the appellant. J fails to supply the promised goods. He discounts the bill to R, but through ignorance or inadvertence R does not obtain J's indorsement. R then purports to indorse the bill as agent "per pro. J" and delivers the bill to the respondent in discharge of a debt due from him to the respondent. The respondent cannot maintain an action against the appellant on

---

[47] *Walters v Neary* (1904) 21 T.L.R. 146 (Illustration 2). If the transferor has died or is bankrupt, his personal representatives or trustee in bankruptcy can be compelled to indorse: *Ex p. Mowbray* (1820) 1 Jac. & W. 428; *Watkins v Maule* (1820) 2 Jac. & W. 237. Only a transferee in possession can call for an indorsement: *Bank of British Columbia v Coopers & Lybrand Ltd* (1985) 15 D.L.R. (4th) 714.

[48] *Day v Longhurst* (1893) 62 L.J. Ch. 334.

[49] *Whistler v Forster* (1863) 14 C.B. (N.S.) 248 (s.29, Illustration 1); *Imperial Bank of Canada v Dennis* [1925] 3 D.L.R. 488, [1926] 3 D.L.R. 168.

[50] *Edge v Bumford* (1862) 31 Beav. 247. But he will have an action against the transferor in conversion.

the bill. An order bill is properly transferable only by indorsement. Transfer without indorsement does not confer authority on the transferee to indorse the bill in the name of the transferor.[51]

2. The claimant agrees to advance money to C if C will accept a bill drawn on him by a responsible person. C persuades the defendant to draw a bill on him, which C accepts. The bill is drawn payable to order of the defendant, but the defendant fails to indorse it before it is handed to the claimant. The claimant does not notice the absence of an indorsement and advances the money to C. The bill is dishonoured by non-payment. The claimant has the right to compel the defendant to indorse the bill, with the result that the claimant can recover from the defendant as drawer.[52]

### Requisites of a valid indorsement

32. An indorsement in order to operate as a negotiation must comply with the following conditions, namely—　　　　5–011

    (1) It must be written on the bill itself and be signed by the indorser. The simple signature of the indorser on the bill, without additional words, is sufficient.

        An indorsement written on an allonge, or a "copy" of a bill issued or negotiated in a country where "copies" are recognised, is deemed to be written on the bill itself.

    (2) It must be an indorsement of the entire bill. A partial indorsement, that is to say, an indorsement which purports to transfer to the indorsee a part only of the amount payable, or which purports to transfer the bill to two or more indorsees severally, does not operate as a negotiation of the bill.

    (3) Where a bill is payable to the order of two or more payees or indorsees who are not partners all must indorse, unless the one indorsing has authority to indorse for the others.

    (4) Where, in a bill payable to order, the payee or indorsee is wrongly designated, or his name is mis-spelt, he may indorse the bill as therein described, adding, if he think fit, his proper signature.

    (5) Where there are two or more indorsements on a bill, each indorsement is deemed to have been made in the order in which it appears on the bill, until the contrary is proved.

---

[51] *Harrop v Fisher* (1861) 10 C.B. (N.S.) 196.
[52] *Walters v Neary* (1904) 21 T.L.R. 146.

**(6) An indorsement may be made in blank or special. It may also contain terms making it restrictive.**

| Definitions | Comparison |
|---|---|
| "bill": s.2. | UCC: §§ 3–201, 3–204, 3–415. |
| "indorsement": s.2. | ULB: arts 11–15. |
| "written": s.2 | ULC: arts 14–18, 20 |
|  | UNB: arts 13–20, 24. |

COMMENT

5–012    **Indorsement for negotiation.** This section deals with the requirements which must be satisfied for an indorsement to operate as a negotiation of a bill. By section 2 "indorsement" means an indorsement completed by delivery and "delivery" means transfer of possession, actual or constructive, from one person to another.[53] "Negotiation" is defined in section 31(1).

For the nature and effect of a so-called "anomalous" or quasi-indorsement by a person other than the holder, which does not in itself operate as a negotiation of the instrument, but by which the person signing guarantees payment, see section 56 of the Act.[54]

An indorsement is a contract by the indorser in the terms set out in section 55(2) of the Act; but the indorsement may be qualified,[55] conditional[56] or restrictive.[57]

5–013    **Subsection (1): formal requirements.** An indorsement must be written on the bill itself. The assignment of an instrument by a separate writing is not an indorsement,[58] nor is an express promise in writing to pay a bill.[59] In *K.H.R. Financings Ltd v Jackson*[60] it was said that "the purpose of the provision is to enable a bill to operate as a negotiable instrument by

---

[53] See also (delivery): s.21.
[54] See below, para.7–030.
[55] s.16(1).
[56] s.33.
[57] s.35.
[58] *Harrop v Fisher* (1861) 10 C.B. (N.S.) 196, 203–204. See also *Rose v Sims* (1830) 1 B. & Ad. 521.
[59] *Re Barrington* (1804) 2 Sch. & Lef. 112.
[60] 1977 S.L.T. (Sh. Ct.) 6.

ensuring that one piece of paper contains all the writing constituting the obligations of the bill and the names of the parties to it". Accordingly, the Sheriff Principal held that, where a promissory note was part of a larger document, a signature on the back of the document, though not on the back of the note itself, was an indorsement.

Two exceptions are, however, provided for in the subsection. The first is the case of an indorsement written on an "allonge". When there is no room on a bill for further indorsements, a slip of paper, called an "allonge", may be attached thereto. It becomes part of the bill, and indorsements may be written on it. "Allonges" are rarely found in the United Kingdom, but less rarely in civil law countries and in particular those which have adopted the Geneva Uniform Law on Bills of Exchange and Promissory Notes.[61] The second is an indorsement written on a "copy" of a bill issued or negotiated in a country where "copies" are recognised. "Copies" of a bill are specifically dealt with in Articles 67 and 68 of the Geneva Uniform Law[62] and must be distinguished from parts (*exemplaires*) of a bill drawn in a set.[63] A "copy" may be indorsed and guaranteed in the same manner and with the same effects as the original.[64]

Although indorsements are usually written on the back of the instrument, an indorsement on its face is valid.[65] But a person who, for example, signs a promissory note on its face intending thereby to indorse it runs the risk that his signature may be construed and held to be that of comaker of the note.[66]

**Signature.** The indorsement must be signed by the indorser; for the meaning of "signature", see the Comment on section 23, above. It is not necessary that the indorser should sign the instrument in his own hand. It is sufficient if his signature is written on it by some other person by or under his authority.[67] In the case of a corporation, the seal of the corporation is equivalent to a signature,[68] and a bill or note is deemed to have been indorsed on behalf of a company if it is indorsed in the name of, or

**5–014**

---

[61] ULB, art.13. Some civil law codes contain detailed provision with respect to "allonges".
[62] A "copy" must specify the person in possession of the original instrument (art.68).
[63] ULB, arts 64–66. See also s.71 of the Act (indorsement of parts of bills in a set).
[64] ULB, art.67.
[65] *R. v Bigg* (1716) 1 Stra. 18; *Young v Glover* (1857) 3 Jur. (N.S.) Q.B. 637; *Ex p. Yates* (1858) 2 De G. & J. 191; *Simonin v Philion* (1922) 66 D.L.R. 673; *Trimper v Frahn* [1925] S.A.S.R. 347; *Kupferschmidt v Ammoneit* [1931] 4 D.L.R. 550 (affd [1932] 4 D.L.R. 720).
[66] *Gorrie (A.D.) Co. Ltd v Whitfield* (1920) 58 D.L.R. 326; *Triggs v English* [1924] 4 D.L.R. 937.
[67] s.91(1).
[68] s.91(2). See also Companies Act 1985, s.36(A).

by or on behalf of or on account of, the company by a person acting under its authority.[69]

**5–015**    **Indorsement of holder.** In order to operate as a negotiation, the indorsement must be that of the holder. A cheque drawn "Pay X per Y or order" should be indorsed "X per Y" and not merely "X".[70] However, the name signed by the indorser need not necessarily correspond exactly with the name of the payee or indorsee on the instrument, although it is difficult to state precisely to what extent a discrepancy is permitted. In *Arab Bank Ltd v Ross*,[71] Denning L.J. said[72]:

> " . . . by a misnomer, a payee may be described on the face of the bill by the wrong name, nevertheless, if it is quite plain that the drawer intended him as payee, then an indorsement on the back by the payee in his own true name is valid and sufficient to pass the property in the bill".

Thus if a bill is drawn payable to "J.R. Smith or order", whereas the true name of the payee is "J.R. Smythe", an indorsement signed "J.R. Smythe" is a valid indorsement.[73] Conversely, in the same case, notes were made payable to "Fathi and Faysal Nabulsy Co. or order", the name being that of a firm in which Fathi and Faysal Nabulsy were the partners. The notes were indorsed "Fathi and Faysal Nabulsy", the word "company" being omitted. The Court of Appeal held that this indorsement was valid to pass title to the notes to the indorsee. However, there was evidence that the signature of the names of the two partners "Fathi and Faysal Nabulsy" was the known and recognised signature of the partnership. It does not follow that an instrument payable to the order of a partnership firm, *e.g.* "Hattons", could be validly indorsed by signing the name of one or more partners in the firm.[74] It would seem that an instrument payable to a sole trader in his trade name, *e.g.* "Pay Smith's Television or order" might be validly indorsed by signing his true name alone, *e.g.* "J.R. Smith".[75] But in all of the above cases, even if the indorsement is valid, it

---

[69] Companies Act 1985, s.37; see above, para.3–025 (s.23).

[70] *Slingsby v District Bank Ltd* [1932] 1 K.B. 544 (s.60, Illustration 2).

[71] [1952] 2 Q.B. 216 (s.29, Illustration 3).

[72] [1952] 2 Q.B. 216 at 226.

[73] *Leonard v Wilson* (1834) 2 Cr. & M. 589; *Hadley & Co. v Henry* (1896) 22 V.L.R. 230. See also *Bird & Co. (London) Ltd v Thomas Cook & Son Ltd* [1937] 2 All E.R. 227. Contrast *Bank of Montreal v Exhibit & Trading Co. Ltd* (1906) 22 T.L.R. 722.

[74] See above, para.3–029 (s.23): but the principles there set out relate to the *liability* of the partners, and not to the negotiation of the instrument. See also *Toronto-Dominion Bank v Canada Acceptance Corp. Ltd* (1969) 7 D.L.R. (3d) 728, 735. *cf. Forbes v Marshall* (1855) 11 Exch. 166 (immaterial discrepancy).

[75] This point was raised, but not determined, in *Walker v Macdonald* (1848) 2 Exch. 527. The instrument could be indorsed in the trade name: s.23(1).

is nevertheless irregular,[76] and the indorsee will in consequence not qualify as a holder in due course.[77]

**Intention to indorse.** Section 23 of the Act provides that no person is **5–016** liable as indorser of a bill who has not signed it *as such*, and it is sometimes said[78] that to constitute a valid indorsement the signature of the indorser must be placed on the bill *animo indorsandi* (with the intention to indorse), that is to say, with the intention of negotiating the instrument[79] and of incurring the liabilities of an indorser.[80] But this statement must be treated with some caution. There will undoubtedly be cases where the signature of the holder will not be considered as an indorsement because the necessary intent is absent, for example, where the signature is intended merely as a receipt[81] or where the stamp of a bank is placed on a cheque merely to identify it as the item of the bank in clearing. However, at least against a holder in due course, a holder will not be permitted to repudiate his signature as an ostensible indorser on the ground that he had no intention to indorse[82] unless he can establish one of the recognised "real" or "absolute" defences[83] such as *non est factum*.[84] As between an indorser and his immediate indorsee, parol evidence is admissible to show an agreement that, by his indorsement, the indorser is not to incur liability to the indorsee on the bill.[85] But, as against a holder in due course, any intention to qualify[86] or restrict[87] the liability of the indorser, or to render it conditional,[88] must be set out in writing on the bill itself.

**Additional words.** In addition to the signature, the words most usu- **5–017** ally found are those constituting a special indorsement,[89] *e.g.* "Pay D" or "Pay D or order". It would appear that words of absolute assignment, for example "I hereby assign this draft and all benefit of the money secured

---

[76] But see s.32(4).
[77] See above, para.4–053 (s.29).
[78] *Miller Associates (Australia) Pty Ltd v Bennington Pty Ltd* (1975) 7 A.L.R. 144; *Paget* (8th ed.), p.229. See also s.21(2) (delivery).
[79] s.31.
[80] s.55(2)(a).
[81] See above, para.5–006 (s.31).
[82] *Nedbank Ltd v Aldick* 1981 (3) S.A. 1007. See also 21(2) (conclusive presumption as to delivery).
[83] See below, para.5–070 (s.38).
[84] See above, para.3–022 (s.23).
[85] *Castrique v Buttigieg* (1855) 10 Moore P.C. 94 (s.21, Illustration 35). See also above, para.2–167 (s.21).
[86] s.16(1).
[87] s.35.
[88] s.33.
[89] s.34(2).

thereby to D",[90] without an order to pay, would be a valid indorsement: words of transfer or assignment in addition to a signature would probably be treated as mere surplusage.[91] Words of guarantee in addition to the signature of the holder, *e.g.* "Payment guaranteed", might be held to be a mere restatement of the indorser's liability under section 55(2)(a) of the Act[92] or to superimpose an added liability as surety, but would not invalidate the indorsement for the purposes of negotiation.

5–018     **Subsection (2): partial indorsement.** Two examples may be given. First, C, the holder of a bill for £100, indorses it "Pay £30 to D or order".[93] Secondly, C indorses it "Pay £50 to D or order, and £50 to E or order".[94] Both purported indorsements are invalid as a negotiation. Neither D nor E has any right of action on the bill and they cannot further indorse it.[95] Such an "indorsement" might, however, operate as an authority to receive payment of the amount thereby specified.[96]

An acceptance of a bill may be partial, that is to say, an acceptance to pay part only of the amount for which the bill is drawn.[97] An indorsement of a bill so accepted would doubtless be good.[98]

5–019     **Subsection (3): several payees or indorsees.** Except in the case of a bill payable to a partnership,[99] a bill payable to the order of two or more payees or indorsees must be indorsed by all of them, unless the one indorsing has authority to indorse for the others.[1] Thus, if a bill is payable "to the order of C and D" and D alone indorses it to E, the indorsement is invalid: E cannot sue on the bill.[2] But if D with C's authority were to

---

[90] *Richards v Frankum* (1840) 9 C. & P. 221, 225.

[91] *Edgar v Bahrs and Chapman* (1918) 43 D.L.R. 372; *Bank of Nova Scotia v Philpott* [1930] 4 D.L.R. 148; *Dodd v McGrath* [1952] 3 D.L.R. 566 (unless they also contained language which rendered the indorsement qualified, conditional or restrictive: *e.g. Moody v Scott and Klein* (1921) 68 D.L.R. 707, 710).

[92] See below, para.7–026 (s.55) or below, para.7–031 (s.56).

[93] *Hawkins v Cardy* (1699) 1 Ld. Raym. 360. Chalmers was of the opinion that such an indorsement would be valid if the holder (C) also acknowledges receipt of £70. But it is doubtful whether this is permitted by the subs.

[94] *Heilbut v Nevill* (1869) L.R. 4 C.P. 354, 358.

[95] Except with the authority of and in the name of the indorser.

[96] *Heilbut v Nevill* (1869) L.R. 4 C.P. 354, at 356, 358. *Byles* (27th ed.), 9–06 suggests that the indorsee is given a lien on the bill. But, for a lien to have the effect mentioned in s.27(3), the person claiming the lien must be a holder (as defined in s.2).

[97] s.19(2)(b).

[98] *Byles* (27th ed.), 9–06.

[99] See above, para.3–029 (s.23(2)).

[1] By s.97(3)(d), the usages with respect to dividend warrants or the indorsement thereof (where the practice was to pay on the indorsement of any one of two or more joint payees) is expressly preserved.

[2] *Carvick v Vickery* (1781) 2 Dougl. 653n; *Gough Electric Ltd v CIBC* (1986) 31 D.L.R. (4th) 307. But the "indorsement" may operate as an authority for the indorsee to receive the amount due to him: *Heilbut v Nevill* (1869) L.R. 4 C.P. 354, 356.

indorse it for himself and C, this is sufficient. A bill may, however, be made payable in the alternative to one of two, or one of some of several payees,[3] and it may be likewise indorsed to alternative indorsees.[4] Presumably any one of them may then indorse.[5]

Where an instrument is payable to an unincorporated association, it would seem that one or more officers, duly authorised for that purpose, could indorse the instrument in the name and on behalf of the association.[6]

**Subsection (4): misdescription of payee or indorsee.** It should be noticed that this subsection is not obligatory in its terms. It permits the payee or indorsee, if he is wrongly designated or his name is misspelt, to indorse the bill as therein described. Thus if a bill is drawn payable to "J.R. Smith or order", whereas the true name of the payee is "J.R. Smythe", he can validly negotiate the bill by signing it as "J.R. Smith".[7] But it is usual and proper for the holder to write first the name as described or spelt in the instrument, and adding underneath his proper signature. The indorsement is then regular. If he were to indorse the instrument in his true name only, the indorsement would in most cases be valid,[8] but irregular.

An instrument payable to "Mrs John Smith or order" should be indorsed "Ellen Smith, the wife of John Smith" or "Mrs John Smith —Ellen Smith". Cheques drawn payable to the order of a company may misdescribe or mis-spell the name of the company, and the practice was to indorse the cheque with a rubber stamp bearing a number of common variants of the company's name above the signature of the person signing on the company's behalf.[9] Since the Cheques Act 1957, the need for such niceties in the indorsement of cheques has largely disappeared.

**Subsection (5): order of indorsements.** By section 55(2)(a) of the Act, the indorser of a bill by indorsing it engages that if the bill be dishonoured he will compensate the holder or a *subsequent* indorser who is compelled to pay it, provided that the requisite proceedings on dishonour be duly taken. The presumption that each indorsement was made in time, in the order in which it appears on the bill may be displaced by proof to

5–020

5–021

---

[3] s.7(2).
[4] s.34(3).
[5] *cf. Watson v Evans* (1863) 1 H. & C. 662, 663.
[6] But see above, para.3–011 (s.22), as to the difficulties relating to liability on the indorsement.
[7] *Willis v Barrett* (1816) 2 Stark. 29 (not indorsement).
[8] *Leonard v Wilson* (1834) 2 Cr. & M. 589. See above, para.5–015.
[9] *Bird & Co. (London) Ltd v Thomas Cook & Son Ltd* [1937] 2 All E.R. 227.

the contrary.[10] Parol evidence is also admissible, for example, to show that successive indorsers were in fact co-sureties[11] or otherwise to show the relationship between them.[12]

**5–022** **Subsection (6): kinds of indorsement.** Indorsements in blank and special indorsements are described in section 34 of the Act, and restrictive indorsements in section 35. An indorsement may also be qualified[13] or conditional.[14]

### Conditional Indorsement

**5–023** **33. Where a bill purports to be indorsed conditionally the condition may be disregarded by the payer, and payment to the indorsee is valid whether the condition has been fulfilled or not.**

| Definition | Comparison |
|---|---|
| "bill": s.2. | UCC: § 3–206. |
| | ULB: art.12. |
| | ULC: art.15. |
| | UNB: art.18. |

### COMMENT

**5–024** **Conditional indorsement.**[15] Presumably an indorsement is conditional whether or not the condition is certain to be fulfilled.[16]

---

[10] *National Sales Corp. Ltd v Bernardi* [1931] 2 K.B. 188 (s.20, Illustration 16); *McCall v Hargreaves* [1932] 2 K.B. 423 (s.20, Illustration 18); *Lombard Banking Ltd v Central Garage and Engineering Co. Ltd* [1963] 1 Q.B. 220 (s.20, Illustration 17). See also above, para.2–168 (s.21); *Durack v West Australian Trustee Executor & Agency Co. Ltd* (1946) 72 C.L.R. 189; *cf. Ferrier v Stewart* (1912) 15 C.L.R. 32.

[11] *Macdonald v Whitfield* (1833) 8 App. Cas. 733 (s.21, Illustration 33).

[12] See the cases cited in n.10, above, and *Gerald McDonald & Co. v Nash & Co.* [1924] A.C. 625 (s.20, Illustration 15); *Yeoman Credit Ltd v Gregory* [1963] 1 W.L.R. 343 (s.20, Illustration 19); *Glatt v Ritt* (1973) 34 D.L.R. (3d) 295; *Rolfe Lubell & Co. v Keith* [1979] 1 All E.R. 860; and above, para.2–164 (s.21).

[13] s.16(1).

[14] s.33.

[15] The ULB does not recognise conditional indorsements (art.12). The UCC renders the condition ineffective (s.3–206(b)). The UNB Convention also states that an indorsement must be unconditional (art.18(1)); but *cf.* art.18(2). It seems that an instrument cannot be indorsed with a condition that, in a certain event, the indorsee shall not have the power to indorse: see *Byles* (27th ed.), 9–11, citing *Soares v Glyn* (1845) 8 Q.B. 24, 30.

[16] Contrast s.11(1).

This section altered the common law.[17] It was formerly held that if a bill was indorsed conditionally, the acceptor paid it at his peril if the condition was not fulfilled.[18] This was hard on him. If he dishonoured the bill, he might be liable in damages, and yet it might be impossible for him to find out if the condition had been fulfilled.

As between indorser and indorsee the condition will probably be operative.[19] If the indorsee receives payment without the condition being fulfilled, it is probable that he will be liable in restitution to account for the proceeds to the indorser.

## Indorsement in blank and special indorsement

34. (1) An indorsement in blank specifies no indorsee, and a bill so    5–025
    indorsed becomes payable to bearer.
   (2) A special indorsement specifies the person to whom, or to whose order, the bill is to be payable.
   (3) The provisions of this Act relating to a payee apply with the necessary modifications to an indorsee under a special indorsement.
   (4) When a bill has been indorsed in blank, any holder may convert the blank indorsement into a special indorsement by writing above the indorser's signature a direction to pay the bill to or to the order of himself or some other person.

Definitions:                  Comparison
"bearer": s.2.                UCC: § 3–205.
"bill": s.2.                  ULB: arts 12–14, 16, 20.
"holder": s.2.               ULC: arts 14–17, 20.
"indorsement": s.2.          UNB: arts 14–16.
"person": s.2.
"writing": s.2.

COMMMENT

**Subsection (1): indorsement in blank.** An indorsement in blank con-    5–026
sists of the signature of the indorser on the bill,[20] but does not specify any

---

[17] Chalmers (9th ed.), pp.2, 133.
[18] *Robertson v Kensington* (1811) 4 Taunt. 30.
[19] *Commercial Bank of Windsor v Morrison* (1902) 32 S.C.R. 98.
[20] s.32(1).

indorsee. A bill so indorsed becomes payable to bearer[21] and is negotiated by delivery.[22]

The effect of such an indorsement is as follows: A bill is payable to the order of John Smith. He signs on the back "John Smith". This act is interpreted as an indorsement in blank by John Smith, and operates as if he had written—(1) I hereby assign this bill to bearer. (2) I hereby undertake that if the bearer duly presents this bill and it is dishonoured I will indemnify him on receiving due notice thereof.

5–027      **Subsection (2): special indorsement.** A special indorsement specifies the person to whom, or to whose order, the bill is to be payable. It must be written on the bill itself and signed by the indorser.[23] "Pay D or order," "Pay to the order of D" and "Pay D" are all special indorsements and are of like effect: the bill is payable to D or his order at his option.[24] As a general rule,[25] an instrument so indorsed can only be negotiated by the indorsement of the holder completed by delivery.[26]

A special indorsement following an indorsement in blank displaces the previous indorsement in blank.[27] But it is probable that a bill originally drawn payable to bearer cannot be converted into an order bill by a special indorsement.[28]

5–028      **Subsection (3): provisions as to payee apply to indorsee.** A special indorsement is to this extent equated to the drawing or making of an instrument, the indorsee being treated as a new payee. For the provisions relating to the payee, see sections 7 and 8 of the Act, above, paras 2–048, 2–059.

5–029      **Subsection (4): conversion of blank into special indorsement.**[29] The holder of a bill may convert a blank into a special indorsement in accordance with this sub-section.[30] Thus the holder of a bill, indorsed by C in blank, may write above C's signature the words "Pay D" or "Pay to the order of D." The holder who does this is not liable as an indorser,[31] but

---

[21] Defined in s.2.

[22] s.31(2). "Delivery" is defined in s.2. See also s.21.

[23] s.32(1).

[24] ss.8(4), (5) (see above, para.2–067) and s.34(3).

[25] But see s.7(3), and s.2 of the Cheques Act 1957; below, para.17–015.

[26] s.31(3).

[27] s.8(3). But see below, para.5–029, n.31.

[28] *Miller Associates (Australia) Pty Ltd v Bennington Pty Ltd* [1975] 7 A.L.R. 144; see above, para.2–065 (s.8).

[29] This subs. may have altered the common law: see *Smith v Clarke* (1794) 1 Peake 295; *Walker v Macdonald* (1848) 2 Exch. 527. cf. *Clerk v Pigot* (1698) 12 Mod. 192.

[30] By itself, this is not a material alteration under s.64: *Hirschfield v Smith* (1866) L.R. 1 C.P. 340, 352–353.

[31] *Vincent v Horlock* (1808) 1 Camp. 442 (s.23, Illustration 1). See also s.23 (no person liable as indorser who has not signed it as such).

the indorsement operates as a special indorsement from C to D. Alternatively, he may convert a blank indorsement into a special indorsement by writing above C's signature a direction to pay the bill to or to the order of himself, in which case he elects to take as indorsee[32] and he can only further negotiate the bill by himself indorsing it.[33]

**Striking out indorsements.** The holder may at any time[34] strike out     5–030
any indorsement which is not necessary to his title.[35] The indorser, whose indorsement is intentionally[36] struck out, and all indorsers subsequent to him, are discharged from their liabilities.[37] Provision is also made in section 59(2)(b) of the Act[38] for striking out indorsements where a bill is paid by an indorser, or where a bill payable to drawer's order is paid by the drawer. The practice of striking out indorsements is now virtually obsolete in the United Kingdom.

### Restrictive indorsement

35. (1) An indorsement is restrictive which prohibits the further     5–031
negotiation of the bill or which expresses that it is a mere authority to deal with the bill as thereby directed and not a transfer of the ownership thereof, as, for example, if a bill be indorsed "Pay D only", or "Pay D for the account of X", or "Pay D or order for collection".

     (2) A restrictive indorsement gives the indorsee the right to receive payment of the bill and to sue any party thereto that his indorser could have sued, but gives him no power to transfer his rights as indorsee unless it expressly authorise him to do so.

     (3) Where a restrictive indorsement authorises further transfer, all subsequent indorsees take the bill with the same rights and subject to the same liabilities as the first indorsee under the restrictive indorsement.

---

[32] *Clerk v Pigot* (1698) 12 Mod. 192.

[33] If he wishes to do so without liability, he should indorse it "without recourse" (see s.16(1)).

[34] Even after the claimant has finished his case and the objection has been taken: *Mayer v Jadis* (1833) 1 M. & Rob. 247.

[35] *Mayer v Jadis*, (1833) 1 M. &. Rob. 247. *cf. Bartlett v Benson* (1845) 14 M. & W. 733; *Fairclough v Pavia* (1854) 9 Exch. 690, 695. See also s.37. It seems that indorsements for collection could also be struck out by the owner of the bill.

[36] *Aliter* if by mistake: *Wilkinson v Johnson* (1834) 3 B. & C. 428; s.63(3), below, para.8–073.

[37] s.63(2).

[38] See below, para.8–017.

| Definitions | Comparison |
|---|---|
| "bill": s.2. | UCC: § 3–206. |
| "indorsement": s.2. | ULB: arts 11, 15, 18, 19. |
| | ULC: arts 14, 18, 23. |
| | UNB: arts 17, 21, 22. |

## COMMENT

5–032    **Subsection (1): restrictive indorsement.**[39] This subsection provides for two distinct types of restrictive indorsement.

The first type is an indorsement "which prohibits further negotiation of the bill".[40] The example given is a bill indorsed "Pay D only".[41] By such an indorsement the indorser transfers his rights on the bill to the indorsee, but prevents the bill from being further negotiated.

The second type is an indorsement "which expresses that it is a mere authority to deal with the bill as directed and not a transfer of the ownership thereof", as exemplified by the other two indorsements referred to: "Pay D for the account of X" and "Pay D or order for collection". The object of this second type of indorsement is to procure that the proceeds of the bill, when received by the indorsee, shall be applied in the manner indicated in the indorsement. The direction may be that the proceeds be applied for the benefit or use of the indorser, *e.g.* "Pray pay the money to my use",[42] "Pay the money to my servant for my use,"[43] "Pay the contents to my use." "Pay to D, or his order, for my use",[44] "Pay to the order of D for the credit of [the indorser]".[45] Or the direction may be that the proceeds be applied for the benefit or use of another, *e.g.* "Pay D for the account of X",[46] "Pay to D or order for the account of X",[47] "Pay D or order for the use of X",[48] "Pay to the order of D under provision of my note in favour of X",[49] "Pay D for X".[50] Where a bill is thus restrictively indorsed, the relations between indorser and

[39] See Basse (1942) 52 Yale L.J. 890.
[40] *cf.* s.8(1).
[41] See also *Archer v Bank of England* (1781) 2 Dougl. 637 ("the within must be credited to D, value in account").
[42] *Snee v Prescot* (1743) 1 Atk. 245, 249.
[43] *Edie v East India Co.* (1761) 2 Burr. 1216, 1227.
[44] *Lloyd v Sigourney* (1829) 5 Bing. 525 (Illustration 1).
[45] *Merchants Bank of Canada v Brett* [1923] 2 D.L.R. 264.
[46] s.35(1).
[47] *Treuttel v Barandon* (1817) 8 Taunt. 100 (Illustration 2).
[48] *Evans v Cramlington* (1687) Carth. 5.
[49] *Wedlake v Hurley* (1830) 1 C. & J. 83 (Illustration 3).
[50] *Bute (Marquess of) v Barclays Bank* [1955] 1 Q.B. 202 (not indorsement).

indorsee are substantially those of principal and agent,[51] the indorsee holding the proceeds as fiduciary (or on trust)[52] for the indorser. Alternatively, the restrictive indorsement may be an indorsement for collection, e.g. "Pay D or order for collection",[53] "Pay D for collection", "Pay to D Bank, value on collection",[54] "Pay D Bank or order for collection for the account of Bank C [the indorser]",[55] and (presumably) "Pay any bank".[56] An indorsement for collection, or at least the indorsement of a cheque by a customer to his bank for collection, constitutes the bank the agent of the customer for that purpose.[57]

On the other hand, indorsements in the form "Pay D", "Pay D or **5–033** order" and "Pay to the order of D" are not restrictive. They are simply special indorsements.[58] A statement in an indorsement that the value for it has been furnished by some person other than the indorsee, e.g. "Value in account with the X Bank", does not make it restrictive.[59]

In *Yeoman Credit Ltd v Gregory*[60] bills of exchange drawn by the claimants on, and accepted by, E Ltd payable to the claimants' order were indorsed by the defendant, the managing director of E Ltd, as surety. They were then indorsed by the claimants, beneath the signature of the defendant "Pay to B. Bank, value on collection". The bill was dishonoured by non-payment. It was held that the defendant was liable to the claimants on the bill. Extrinsic evidence was admissible to explain the two indorsements and the intention of the parties that the defendant should be liable to the claimants if E Ltd defaulted on the bill.[61] The order of indorsements was not conclusive,[62] and the claimants' indorsement could be taken to be prior to that of the defendant.[63] But Megaw J. further stated[64] that the claimants' indorsement fulfilled a *dual* function: it was permissible

---

[51] *Williams, Deacon & Co. v Shadbolt* (1885) 1 T.L.R. 417, 1 Cab. & E. 529; *Merchants Bank of Canada v Brett* [1923] 2 D.L.R. 264.
[52] Although the indorsee is frequently referred to as a trustee, he is normally accountable for the proceeds only to his principal, and not to the person for whose benefit or use the indorser directs the proceeds to be applied: *Wedlake v Hurley* (1830) 1 C. &. J. 83 (Illustration 3). *cf. Treuttel v Barandon* (1817) 8 Taunt. 100 (Illustration 2).
[53] s.35(1).
[54] *Yeoman Credit Ltd v Gregory* [1963] 1 W.L.R. 343.
[55] *Williams, Deacon & Co. v Shadbolt* (1885) 1 T.L.R. 417.
[56] *cf.* UCC, s.3–206(c).
[57] *Capital and Counties Bank Ltd v Gordon* [1903] A.C. 240.
[58] s.34(2) (see also ss.8(4)(5), 34(3)). Extrinsic evidence is, however, admissible to show that such an indorsement is in fact restrictive, *e.g.* an indorsement for collection: *Novaknit Hellas SA v Kumar Brothers International Ltd* [1998] Lloyd's Rep. Bank. 287.
[59] *Potts v Reed* (1806) 6 Esp. 57; *Murrow v Stuart* (1853) 8 Moo. P.C. 267; *Buckley v Jackson* (1868) L.R. 3 Ex. 135.
[60] [1963] 1 W.L.R. 343 (s.20, Illustration 19).
[61] See above, para.2–168 (s.21).
[62] s.32(5).
[63] See above, para.2–135 (s.20).
[64] [1963] 1 W.L.R. 343 at 352.

"to treat this indorsement as though it had been made first as an indorsement in blank, which would validate the indorser's signature as an indorser, and, secondly, as a restricted indorsement for collection just as though the indorsement had been written on in blank at one moment of time, and at a subsequent moment of time there had been written above, as the holder was plainly entitled to do, a restriction".

**5–034**    **Subsection (2): effect of restrictive indorsement.** A restrictive indorsement gives the indorsee the right to receive payment of the bill and to sue any party thereto that the indorser could have sued.[65] So, for example, if an accepted bill is indorsed by the payee "Pay D Bank for collection", then the D bank is entitled to receive payment from the acceptor, which payment will discharge the bill if made in due course.[66] The D Bank can also sue the acceptor on the bill. A party who pays a bill to a restrictive indorsee is not responsible for the due application of the proceeds by the indorsee.

However, in certain circumstances, payment or settlement by the party liable of his indebtedness to the indorser will preclude the indorsee from suing on the bill, even though the indorsee has credited the indorser with the amount of the bill. In the two relevant cases the indorsements were respectively "Pay D Bank or order for collection for the account of C [the indorser]"[67] and "Pay to the order of D for the credit of C [the indorser]".[68] It was held that payment or settlement by the acceptor or maker of the instrument of his debt to the indorser was a good defence to an action against him by the indorsee: the relationship between the indorser and indorsee being one of principal and agent, the debtor was not prevented from paying his debt to the principal, *i.e.* to the real creditor.[69]

A restrictive indorsement gives the indorsee no power to transfer his rights as indorsee unless it expressly authorises him to do so. Such an express authority may be given, for example, by an indorsement "Pay to D or his order for my use", "Pay D or order for the use of X" or "Pay D or order for collection", the words "or order" conferring the required authority to transfer.

---

[65] *Evans v Cramlington* (1687) Carth. 5. But the indorsee cannot, by a restrictive indorsement, become a holder in due course: *Imperial Bank of Canada v Hays & Earl Ltd* (1962) 35 D.L.R. (2d) 136 (reversed by legislation in Canada). *cf.* UCC § 3–206(e).

[66] See below, para.8–011.

[67] *Williams, Deacon & Co. v Shadbolt* (1885) 1 T.L.R. 417, 1 Cab. & E. 529 (but the facts of this case are unclear).

[68] *Merchants Bank of Canada v Brett* [1923] 2 D.L.R. 264 (payment in good faith and without notice of transfer).

[69] [1923] 2 D.L.R. 264.

**Subsection (3): further transfer by indorsee.** Since all subsequent   5–035
indorsees take the bill with the same rights and subject to the same
liabilities as the first indorsee under the restrictive indorsement, they can
become holders of the bill, but not holders in due course.[70] Any defence
available to the party liable on the bill against the first indorsee is likewise
available against subsequent indorsees. A direction in the indorsement
that the indorsee is to apply the proceeds of the instrument for the benefit
or use of the indorser,[71] or of another[72] will be binding on a subsequent
indorsee.

ILLUSTRATIONS

1. The claimant indorses a bill "Pay to S.W., of London, or his order for   5–036
my use". S.W. applies to the defendants, his bankers, to discount the bill,
and they do so without further enquiry, placing the proceeds to the credit
of S.W. S.W. becomes bankrupt. The property in the bill remained in the
claimant and he is entitled to recover the amount from the defendants.[73]

2. The payee of a bill indorses it: "Pay to D, or order, for account of T
& Co. [the claimants]". D, as agent of the claimants, but without their
authority, pledges the bill to the defendants as security for cash advances
made by the defendants to D. The defendants have sufficient notice that
the bill is not the property of D and they are liable in trover to the
claimants.[74]

3. The claimant is the payee and holder of a promissory note made by
G. G indorses a Bank of England bill: "Pay to the order of H & Co. [the
defendants] under provision for my note in favour of W [the claimant]".
The defendants present the bank bill for payment and are duly paid. But

---

[70] But see *Yeoman Credit Ltd v Gregory* [1963] 1 W.L.R. 343 (s.20, Illustration 19) where Magaw
J. held that the plaintiffs were holders in due course for the purposes of s.56 of Act.
Assuming that this is correct, it depends on the finding of the dual function of the
particular indorsement: see above, para.5–033.
[71] *Lloyd v Sigourney* (1829) 5 Bing. 525 (Illustration 1).
[72] But in this case, unless the recipient is the agent of the person for whose use or benefit the
proceeds are held (*Treuttel v Barandon* (1817) 8 Taunt. 100 (Illustration 2)) only the owner
of the bill can sue, but not the "beneficiary" (*Wedlake v Hurley* (1830) 1 C. & J. 83
(Illustration 3)).
[73] *Lloyd v Sigourney* (1829) 5 Bing. 525.
[74] *Treuttel v Barandon* (1817) 8 Taunt. 100.

they refuse to pay over the proceeds to the claimant, claiming to set off the amount received against a debt due to them from G. G might have maintained an action against the defendants; but, since the defendants never assented or agreed to hold the bill or the proceeds for the claimant, the claimant's action to recover the proceeds fails.[75]

### Negotiation of overdue or dishonoured bill

5–037    36. (1) Where a bill is negotiable in its origin it continues to be negotiable until it has been (a) restrictively indorsed or (b) discharged by payment or otherwise.

(2) Where an overdue bill is negotiated, it can only be negotiated subject to any defect of title affecting it at its maturity, and thenceforward no person who takes it can acquire or give a better title than that which the person from whom he took it had.

(3) A bill payable on demand is deemed to be overdue within the meaning and for the purposes, of this section, when it appears on the face of it to have been in circulation for an unreasonable length of time. What is an unreasonable length of time for this purposes is a question of fact.

(4) Except where an indorsement bears date after the maturity of the bill, every negotiation is prima facie deemed to have been effected before the bill was overdue.

(5) Where a bill which is not overdue has been dishonoured any person who takes it with notice of the dishonour takes it subject to any defect of title attaching thereto at the time of dishonour, but nothing in this sub-section shall affect the rights of a holder in due course.

| Definitions | Comparison |
|---|---|
| "bill": s.2. | UCC: § 3–302, 3–304. |
| "holder": s.2. | ULB: art.20. |
| "holder in due course": s.29. | ULC: art.24. |
| "indorsement": s.2. | UNB: arts 24, 28, 29. |
| "negotiate": s.31. | |
| "person": s.2. | |

---

[75] *Wedlake v Hurley* (1830) 1 C. & J. 83.

COMMENT

**Subsection (1): how long a bill continues negotiable.** "A bill of    5–038
exchange" said Lord Ellenborough,[76] "is negotiable *ad infinitum* until it
has been paid by or discharged on behalf of the acceptor". A bill ceases
to be negotiable once it has been discharged.[77] A bill may, however, not be
negotiable in its origin, *i.e.* when it contains words prohibiting transfer, or
indicating an intention that it should not be transferable[78] or, in the case
of a cheque, where it is crossed "account payee",[79] or it may be rendered
non-negotiable by a restrictive indorsement which prohibits its further
negotiation.[80]

The fact that an action has been brought on a dishonoured bill does not
determine its negotiability,[81] so that the transferee may also sue on it,[82]
unless he has notice of the action.[83]

Provision is made in the Act for further negotiation of a bill by section
37 where the bill is negotiated back to a prior party and by section 59(2)(b)
where it is paid by an indorser or (in certain circumstances) by the
drawer.

**Subsection (2): negotiation of overdue bill.**[84] A person to whom an    5–039
overdue bill is negotiated cannot be a holder in due course[85] and so does
not hold the bill free from any defect of title of prior parties.[86] In *London
and County Banking Co. v Groome*,[87] Field J., speaking of an overdue bill or
note payable at a fixed date, said[88]:

> " . . . the reason of the rule is, that, inasmuch as these instruments are
> usually current only during the period before they become payable,
> and their negotiation after that period is out of the usual and ordi-
> nary course of dealing, that circumstance is sufficient of itself to
> excite so much suspicion that, as a rule of law, the indorsee must take

---

[76] *Callow v Lawrence* (1814) 3 M. & S. 95, 97.
[77] See below, para.8–003 (s.59).
[78] s.8(1).
[79] s.81A(1).
[80] s.35(1).
[81] But only until judgment, when the bill will be extinguished by merger as between the
defendant and the claimant or any subsequent party. *cf. Woodward v Pell* (1868) L.R. 4 Q.B.
55.
[82] *Deuters v Townsend* (1864) 5 B. & S. 613. *cf. Woodward v Pell* (1868) L.R. 4 Q.B. 55.
[83] *Marsh v Newell* (1808) 1 Taunt. 109 (stay of action); *Jones v Lane* (1838) 3 Y. & C. 281. But
see to the contrary *Deuters v Townsend* (1864) 5 B. & S. 613.
[84] See Donald (1970) 8 Alberta L.R. 75.
[85] s.29(1)(a).
[86] s.38(2). But see s.29(3).
[87] (1881) 8 Q.B.D. 288.
[88] (1881) 8 Q.B.D. 288 at 292.

it on the credit of and can stand in no better position than the indorser: *Brown v Davies.*"[89]

Or, in the more colourful words of Lord Ellenborough[90]: "After a bill or note is due, it comes disgraced to the indorsee, and it is his duty to make enquiries concerning it." The position of a holder who takes a bill when overdue is this: he is a holder with notice. He may or may not be a holder for value, and his rights will be regulated accordingly.[91] He is a holder with notice for this reason: he takes a bill which, on the face of it, ought to have got home and been paid. He is therefore bound to make two inquiries: (1) Has what ought to have been done really been done, *i.e.* has the bill in fact been discharged? (2) If not why not? Is there any equity attaching thereto, *i.e.* was the *title* of the person who held it at maturity defective?

5–040     **Overdue.** A bill or note not payable on demand will be overdue after the expiration of its due date determined in accordance with section 14 of the Act.[92] A bill payable on demand, or a cheque, will be deemed to be overdue in the circumstances set out in subsection (3) below.[93]

5–041     **Defect of title.**[94] The meaning of the words "defect of title" (which, prior to the Act, was referred to as "an equity attaching to the bill")[95] has been explained and discussed in the Comment on section 29(2) of the Act.[96] In particular, a holder to whom an instrument was negotiated when overdue has been held to take it subject to a defect of title arising from fraud,[97] illegality,[98] breach of an agreement between the acceptor and the payee that the bill was not to be negotiated[99] or as to how it was to be paid,[1] negotiation under such circumstances as amounted to fraud,[2] and

---

[89] (1789) 3 T.R. 80 (Illustration 5).
[90] *Tinson v Francis* (1807) 1 Camp. 19.
[91] See above, para.4–024 and 4–028 (s.27).
[92] See above, para.2–100. It is doubtful, where an instrument is required to be paid by stated instalments (see s.9(1)), whether it is "overdue" once the date for payment of the first instalment has expired. See *Union Investment Co. v Wells* (1908) 39 S.C.R. 625, 632 (interest). Contrast *Moothoo Raman Chetty v Aik Kah Pay* (1905) 9 S.S.L.R. 115 (Straits Settlements) (acceleration clause on default).
[93] That subs. does not apply to promissory notes payable on demand: see s.86(3).
[94] See *Central Bank of Yemen v Cardinal Financial Investments Corpn* [2001] Lloyd's Rep. Bank 1 at [20], [25–26], where this paragraph was cited with approval by the Court of Appeal.
[95] See above, para.4–027.
[96] See above, para.4–062.
[97] *Nash v De Freville* [1900] 2 Q.B. 72 (s.61, Illustration 1).
[98] *Amory v Merryweather* (1824) 2 B. & C. 573 (Illustration 1).
[99] *Parr v Jewell* (1855) 16 C.B. 684, 712 (Illustration 2).
[1] *Holmes v Kidd* (1858) 3 H. & N. 891 (Illustration 3).
[2] *Lloyd v Howard* (1850) 15 Q.B. 995 (s.21, Illustration 11).

the fact that the bill was purchased with money stolen from a third party.[3]

On the other hand, absence[4] or failure[5] of consideration is not an equity attaching to the bill.[6] It will not affect a holder who takes an overdue bill[7] if he himself has given value for the bill[8] or if value has at any time been given for the bill as respects the acceptor and parties who became parties to the bill prior to such time.[9] Likewise a holder for value of an overdue bill will not be affected by mere personal defences available to prior parties between themselves, for example, rights of set-off.[10]

**Affecting it at its maturity.** The holder of an overdue bill takes it 5–042 subject only to defects of title affecting it at its maturity. So, for example, it is no defence for the acceptor of a bill to plead that it was accepted for an illegal consideration if, before maturity, it was negotiated to a holder in due course, even though it was subsequently negotiated to the claimant when it was overdue.[11]

**Subsection (3): bill on demand, when overdue.** This subsection 5–043 applies to bills payable on demand,[12] but, by section 86(3), it does not apply to notes payable on demand, which are regarded as continuing securities.[13] By virtue of section 73, the subsection applies to cheques.

What is an unreasonable length of time is a question of fact. In a case in 1881,[14] where the previous decisions were reviewed, Field J. indicated that a cheque negotiated eight days after date was not to be considered to

---

[3] *Re European Bank, ex p. Oriental Bank* (1870) L.R. 5 Ch.App. 358 (Illustration 4).

[4] See above, para.4–007.

[5] See above, para.4–008. But see the doubts surrounding total failure of consideration in respect of a holder with knowledge: above, para.4–008.

[6] *Charles v Marsden* (1808) 1 Taunt. 224; *Scott v Lifford* (1808) 1 Camp. 246 (s.27, Illustration 20); *Stein v Yglesias* (1834) 1 C.M. & R. 565; *Sturtevant v Ford* (1842) 4 M. & G. 101 (Illustration 6); *Re Overend, Gurney & Co., Ex p. Swan* (1868) L.R. 6 Eq. 344. See also *Petty v Cook* (1871) L.R. 6 Q.B. 790. Contrast Geva [1980] C.L.J. 360.

[7] *Stein v Yglesias* (1834) 1 C.M. & R. 565; *Sturtevant v Ford* (1842) 4 M. & G. 101.

[8] See above, paras 4–011 and 4–021 (s.27).

[9] See s.27(2); above, para.4–024.

[10] *Stein v Yglesias* (1834) 1 C.M. & R. 565; *Whitehead v Walker* (1842) 10 M. & W. 696 (Illustration 10). *Oulds v Harrison* (1854) 10 Exch. 572 (Illustration 7); *Re Overend, Gurney & Co., Ex p. Swan* (1868) L.R. 6 Eq. 344. But *cf. Collenridge v Farquharson* (1816) 1 Stark. 259.

[11] *Chalmers v Lanion* (1808) 1 Camp. 383 (Illustration 8). See also *Fairclough v Pavia* (1854) 9 Exch. 690; *Insurance Corp. of Ireland Plc v Dunluce Meats Ltd* [1991] N.I. 286; and s.29(3) (sheltered holder); above, para.4–072.

[12] See s.10.

[13] But see the Comment on s.86(3); below, para.15–043.

[14] *London and County Bank v Groome* (1881) 8 Q.B.D. 288. *cf. Rothschild v Corney* (1829) 9 B. & C. 388 (six days); *Down v Halling* (1825) 4 B. & C. 330 (five days). But the subsection altered the common law: *Chalmers* (9th ed.) p.2. See also the Comment on s.74(2), below, para.13–019.

be on the footing of an overdue bill, but in an earlier case in 1850[15] a cheque presented two months after date was said to be stale. Bankers ordinarily refuse to pay a cheque (an "out-of-date" cheque) which is presented for payment after six months from the date written on the cheque. But such refusal takes place in the context of the banker-customer relationship.[16] It does not necessarily indicate what is an unreasonable length of time for the purpose of the subsection, although it probably provides some guidance.

5–044      **Subsection (4): presumption as to date of negotiation.** Where an indorsement is dated, the date is, unless the contrary be proved, deemed to be the true date.[17]

This subsection contains no presumption as to the exact time of negotiation.[18] The presumption that the negotiation was effected before the bill was overdue may be rebutted by proof[19] to the contrary.

5–045      **Subsection (5): bill known to be dishonoured.** Dishonour of a bill may be by non-acceptance[20] or non-payment.[21] A bill payable at a fixed date may be dishonoured by non-acceptance,[22] and a cheque or bill payable on demand may be dishonoured by non-payment,[23] before it is overdue. This subsection puts a bill known to be dishonoured on the same footing as an overdue bill, except that it refers to a defect of title[24] attaching to the bill at the time of dishonour and not at maturity. By section 29(1)(a) of the Act, a holder who becomes a holder with notice that the bill has been previously dishonoured, if such was the fact, cannot be a holder in due course.[25] Presumably in this subsection, as in the case of section 29, notice means actual knowledge of dishonour, or a suspicion thereof coupled with the means of knowledge wilfully disregarded.[26] It does not refer to the formal notice of dishonour provided for in section 48 of the Act.

---

[15] *Serrel v Derbyshire Ry* (1850) 9 C.B. 811 (date of negotiation uncertain). See also *Ballem v Fried* [1923] 4 D.L.R. 1203 (six months).
[16] See also ss.74(2), 75.
[17] s.13(1).
[18] *Anderson v Weston* (1840) 6 Bing. N.C. 296.
[19] *Lewis v Parker* (1836) 4 A. & E. 838. Contrast *Bounsall v Harrison* (1836) 1 M. & W. 611 (inference).
[20] s.43.
[21] s.47.
[22] *Crossley v Ham* (1811) 13 East 498 (Illustration 9).
[23] *Hornby v McLaren* (1808) 24 T.L.R. 494 (Illustration 11).
[24] See above, para.4–062 (s.29(2)). *cf. Whitehead v Walker* (1842) 10 M. & W. 696 (Illustration 10).
[25] See above, para.4–055.
[26] See above, para.4–058.

ILLUSTRATIONS

5–046

1. The defendant, by W as his agent, enters into unlawful contracts for buying and selling shares, and, for the purpose of securing the repayment of money paid by W in respect of those contracts, makes a promissory note payable to the order of W three months after date. Long after the note becomes due, W indorses the note to the claimants. The claimants cannot recover from the defendant on the note.[27]

2. Two bills of exchange are drawn by A on the defendant payable to A or order three months after date, and are accepted by the defendant. They are negotiated by A to the claimant when overdue. It is a good defence for the defendant to prove that he accepted the bills without consideration, and for the accommodation of A, and that they were indorsed by A in breach of an agreement not to indorse them away.[28]

3. The defendants apply to W to advance them the sum of £300, which W agrees to do upon terms that the defendants accept a bill of exchange drawn on them for the amount of the advance and deposit with W certain canvas (valued at £400) as security for payment of the bill. It is further agreed that, if the bill is not paid, W can sell the canvas and apply the proceeds in payment of the bill. W accordingly draws a bill on the defendants payable to himself or order, which the defendants accept. After the bill becomes due, W sells the canvas for £272, but nevertheless indorses the bill to the claimant. The claimant takes the bill subject to the equity of the proceeds of the sale of the canvas being applied to payment of the bill.[29]

5–047

4. P, the manager of the O Bank, steals monies from the bank, and purchases therewith certain overdue bills, which he negotiates to the E Company, a company promoted by himself and of which he is the sole director. The claim of the O Bank is an equity attaching to the bills, and the E Company took the bills subject to that equity as they were overdue. The O Bank, and not the E Company, is entitled to the bills and can prove in the insolvency of the acceptor.[30]

5. The defendant makes a note payable to S or order at a future date. S indorses it in blank and delivers it to T, by whom it is noted for non-

---

[27] *Amory v Merryweather* (1824) 2 B. & C. 573 (but the claimants also knew of the illegality).
[28] *Parr v Jewell* (1915) 16 C.B. 684, 712.
[29] *Holmes v Kidd* (1858) 3 H. & N. 891.
[30] *Re European Bank, Ex p. Oriental Bank* (1870) L.R. 5 Ch.App. 358.

payment. S is paid by the defendant, takes the note up from T and re-negotiates it to the claimant. The defendant may show that the note has been satisfied as between himself and S, the payee, and that it was indorsed to the claimant when it was overdue, and after satisfaction to S.[31]

6. A draws a bill on the defendant payable to A's order, which the defendant accepts for A's accommodation and without consideration. The bill is indorsed by A to the claimant for value when overdue. Absence of consideration is no defence. It is not an equity attaching to the bill.[32]

**5–048**    7. B draws a bill on the defendant, which the defendant accepts, payable to the order of B. B indorses the bill to the claimant. In reply to an action on the bill, the defendant pleads that the bill was indorsed to the claimant when overdue and that B was indebted to the claimant in a sum exceeding the amount of the bill and interest. This is no defence. Although the claimant took the bill subject to all equities attaching to it, the right of set-off is not an equity attaching to the bill.[33]

8. The defendant, the acceptor of a bill, alleges that he accepted it for a debt contracted in a smuggling transaction. It is shown that, before maturity, the bill was indorsed to a bona fide holder for value without notice of the illegality and was then, after it was overdue, indorsed to the claimant. The claimant can sue the defendant on the bill; at maturity, the bona fide holder had a good title to the bill.[34]

9. Two bills are drawn upon D & Co. payable at 60 days' sight to the defendant or order and are indorsed by the defendant to P. It is agreed between P and the defendant that, upon payment of one of the bills, the defendant shall be exonerated from both. The bills are presented to D & Co. for acceptance but are dishonoured by non-acceptance. One of the bills is indorsed after dishonour by P's agent to the claimant, who knows of the dishonour. The defendant takes up and pays the other bill. The claimant is bound by the agreement by which the defendant is discharged from liability on both bills, as this was an equity attaching to the bills against P. Whoever takes a bill after its dishonour takes it with all the infirmities belonging to it.[35]

**5–049**    10. The claimants are the assignees of the estate of B, a bankrupt. The defendant, payee of a bill, indorses it to S, who indorses it to W & S Co.,

[31] *Brown v Davies* (1789) 3 T.R. 80.
[32] *Sturtevant v Ford* (1842) 4 M. & G. 101.
[33] *Oulds v Harrison* (1854) 10 Exch. 572.
[34] *Chalmers v Lanion* (1808) 1 Camp. 383.
[35] *Crossley v Ham* (1811) 13 East 498.

who indorse it to B. When sued on the bill, the defendant pleads that B took the bill after dishonour by non-acceptance and subject to a set-off between B and W & S Co. This is no defence. The set-off is not an equity attaching to the bill.[36]

11. C owes £115 to the claimant in respect of dealings in shares. In order to provide funds to meet this debt, the defendant, at the request of C, draws a cheque for £115 payable to C or order. It is agreed that C will pay this cheque into his bank to meet his own cheque for the same amount drawn in favour of the claimant. The defendant changes his mind and stops payment of his cheque, whereupon C hands that cheque to the claimant, who takes it with notice that it has been dishonoured. The defendant is not liable to the claimant on the cheque. The claimant, having notice of dishonour, was not a holder in due course, and took the cheque with any defect in title attaching to it at the time of dishonour. As C negotiated it to the claimant in breach of faith, instead of paying it into his own bank, this was a defect in title within section 29 of the Act.[37]

### Negotiation of bill to party already liable thereon

**37. Where a bill is negotiated back to the drawer, or to a prior indorser or to the acceptor, such party may, subject to the provisions of this Act, re-issue and further negotiate the bill, but he is not entitled to enforce payment of the bill against any intervening party to whom he was previously liable.** 5–050

| Definitions | Comparison |
|---|---|
| "bill": s.2. | UCC: § 3–207. |
| "negotiate": s.31. | ULB: art.11. |
| | ULC: art.14. |
| | UNB: art.23. |

### COMMENT

**Reacquisition and reissue of bill.** A bill may be negotiated back to a prior party, *i.e.* to the drawer, or to a prior indorser, or to the acceptor. Such party may then, subject to the provisions of the Act, reissue and further negotiate the bill. Where the bill is negotiated back to the drawer 5–051

---

[36] *Whitehead v Walker* (1842) 10 M. & W. 696.
[37] *Hornby v McLaren* (1908) 24 T.L.R. 494.

or to a prior indorser, he may negotiate the bill away at any time, whether before or after maturity.[38] But where the reacquiring party is the acceptor, he can as a general rule only negotiate it away before maturity[39]: if he is or becomes the holder of it at or after its maturity, in his own right, the bill is discharged.[40] The words "subject to the provisions of this Act"[41] refer (*inter alia*)[41] to the fact that a bill may not be further negotiated[42] if it is restrictively indorsed[43] or discharged.[44]

Provision is also made in section 59(2)(b) of the Act[45] for the further negotiation of a bill by an indorser or (in certain circumstances) by the drawer who has paid the bill.

5–052    **Rights of reacquiring party.** There is little doubt that a party who thus reacquires an instrument does so, not in his original capacity,[46] but as a new holder of the instrument.[47] He can therefore claim the status of a holder in due course[48] or that of a "sheltered holder" under section 29(3) of the Act.[49] But the present section provides that he is not entitled to enforce payment of the bill against any intervening party to whom he was previously liable. This rule is designed to avoid circuity of action.[50] For example, C, the drawer of a bill drawn to drawer's order, indorses it for value to D, who indorses it to E, who indorses it back to C. C cannot recover from D or E, for they in turn could recover from him as drawer.[51]

However, the rule does not preclude the reacquiring party from enforcing payment against an intervening party to whom he was not previously liable. Two examples may be given. First, C, the payee of a note, indorses it "without recourse" to D, who indorses it to E, who indorses it back to C. C, in his character of third indorsee, can sue D and E. There is no circuity of action, for they have no claim against him as prior indorser.[52] Secondly, C draws a bill on A payable to C's order in respect of a debt due

---

[38] *Hubbard v Jackson* (1827) 4 Bing. 390 (Illustration 1). But this is probably a case now falling within s.59(2).

[39] *Attenborough v Mackenzie* (1856) 25 L.J. Exch. 266 (Illustration 2).

[40] s.61.

[41] See also s.59(2).

[42] s.36(1).

[43] s.35.

[44] ss.59(1), (3), 60–64, 68.

[45] See below, para.8–017.

[46] But see s.59(2).

[47] Chafee (1921) 21 Col.L.R. 538.

[48] s.29(1).

[49] *Jade International Steel Stahl und Eisen GmbH & Co. KG v Robert Nicholas (Steels) Ltd* [1978] Q.B. 917 (s.29, Illustration 12).

[50] *Holmes v Durkee* (1883) 1 Cab. & E. 23.

[51] *Bishop v Hayward* (1791) 4 T.R. 470; *Britten v Webb* (1824) 2 B. & C. 483, 486 (Illustration 3); *Wilkinson & Co. v Unwin* (1881) 7 Q.B.D. 636, 637.

[52] *Morris v Walker* (1850) 15 Q.B. 589, 594.

or to become due from A to C. It has been previously agreed that D will indorse the bill as surety for A's debt and in pursuance of this agreement C indorses the bill to D and D indorses it back to C. C can sue D. There is no circuity of action, for D has no right of action against C because the intention is that D shall be responsible for A's debt.[53]

ILLUSTRATIONS

1. M draws a bill on the defendant, which the defendant accepts, payable three months after date to the order of M. Before the bill is due, M indorses it to W. The bill is dishonoured by the defendant and W recovers from M the amount of the bill. About a year and a half afterwards, M indorses the bill to the claimant. The claimant can sue the defendant on the bill.[54]   **5–053**

2. T accepts a bill for £400 drawn by and payable to the defendant. The defendant indorses it and hands it to S to get it discounted. S offers it to B for this purpose, who takes it to T and gets from him £375, which is offered to and accepted by the defendant, who believes himself to be thereby discharged. Before maturity, T transfers the bill to A at a discount, and after the bill is due A transfers it to the claimant. The defendant is liable on the bill. It was discounted and not paid, and before maturity. T could reissue the bill.[55]

3. The claimants draw a bill for £500 upon W, which W accepts, payable six months after date to their order. The bill is indorsed by the claimants to the defendant and reindorsed by him to the claimants. The claimants cannot recover from the defendant as he in turn could recover against them.[56]

4. The claimants draw a bill on H payable to their order, which H accepts. The claimants indorse the bill to the defendants and the defendants indorse it back to the claimants. Upon dishonour of the bill by H, the claimants claim payment from the defendants. They are entitled so to do. Evidence is adduced by the claimants to show that the bill was   **5–054**

---

[53] *Wilders v Stevens* (1846) 15 M. & W. 208 (Illustration 4); *Morris v Walker* (1860) 15 Q.B. 589; *Wilkinson & Co. v Unwin* (1881) 7 Q.B.D. 636 (Illustration 5); *Glenie v Bruce Smith* [1907] 2 K.B. 507 (affirmed [1908] 1 K.B. 263) (s.20, Illustration 14); *Re Gooch* [1921] 2 K.B. 593, 600, 602, 605. See also *McDonald & Co. v Nash & Co.* [1924] A.C. 625 (s.20, Illustration 15).
[54] *Hubbard v Jackson* (1827) 4 Bing. 390.
[55] *Attenborough v Mackenzie* (1856) 25 L.J. Ex. 244.
[56] *Britten v Webb* (1824) 2 B. & C. 483, 486.

indorsed by the defendants as surety for a debt due from H to the claimants which the claimants had allowed H time to pay. There is no circuity of action because the claimants were not liable to the defendants on the bill.[57]

5. U accepts two bills drawn upon him by the claimants as the price of goods sold and delivered to him by the claimants, it being agreed that U will procure his mother, the defendant, to indorse the bills as surety for the price of the goods. The claimants indorse the bills and the defendant indorses them to the claimants. They are dishonoured at maturity and due notice of dishonour is given to the defendant. The defendant is liable to the claimants on the bills. No circuity of action is involved as the bills were indorsed by the defendant with the intention of becoming a surety and as intermediate indorser she had no right of action against the claimants.[58]

### Rights of the holder

5–055      **38. The rights and powers of the holder of a bill are as follows:**
        **(1)**   **He may sue on the bill in his own name:**
        **(2)**   **Where he is a holder in due course, he holds the bill free from any defect of title of prior parties, as well as from mere personal defences available to prior parties among themselves, and may enforce payment against all parties liable on the bill:**
        **(3)**   **Where his title is defective (a) if he negotiates the bill to a holder in due course, that holder obtains a good and complete title to the bill, and (b) if he obtains payment of the bill the person who pays him in due course gets a valid discharge for the bill.**

| Definitions | Comparison |
|---|---|
| "bill": s.2. | UCC: §§ 3–301, 3–302. |
| "holder": s.2. | ULB: arts 16–19, 40. |
| "holder in due course": s.29. | ULC: arts 19, 21–23. |
| "negotiates": s.31. | UNB: arts 27–30, 70, 72, 77. |
| "person": s.2. | |

---

[57] *Wilders v Stevens* (1846) 15 M. & W. 208.
[58] *Wilkinson & Co. v Unwin* (1881) 7 Q.B.D. 636.

## COMMENT

**Rights and powers of holder.** This section sets out, in part, the rights  5–056
and powers of the holder of a bill. It applies also to cheques and promissory notes. In addition to the rights and powers referred to, the holder is
entitled, for example, to negotiate the instrument,[59] to obtain a duplicate
of a lost instrument,[60] to insert (in certain circumstances) the true date of
issue or acceptance of the instrument,[61] to convert a blank indorsement
into a special indorsement,[62] to discharge the instrument or a party
thereto by renunciation,[63] and to cancel the instrument or a signature
thereon.[64]

**Subsection (1): holder may sue in his own name.** This subsection  5–057
does no more than provide that the holder of a bill may maintain an
action on it in his own name.[65] Whether or not he is entitled to recover in
such an action must be determined in accordance with other provisions of
the Act, and in particular this will depend on whether the action is
between immediate or remote parties[66] and upon the status of the holder,
*i.e.* whether he is a mere holder,[67] a holder for value[68] or a holder in due
course.[69]

"Holder" is defined in section 2 to mean the payee or indorsee of a bill
or note who is in possession of it, or the bearer thereof, and "bearer"
means the person in possession of a bill or note which is payable to
bearer. The claimant must, therefore, at the commencement of the
action,[70] be in possession of the instrument. Possession may, however, be
actual or constructive. A holder may have constructive possession where
the instrument is in the hands of his agent,[71] or where it has been
indorsed and delivered to another for collection,[72] or where he has possession jointly with others.[73] The holder is usually, but not necessarily, the

---

[59] s.31.
[60] s.69.
[61] s.12. Contrast s.20 (completion of incomplete instrument by "the person in possession of
it").
[62] s.33(4).
[63] s.62.
[64] s.63.
[65] *Stock Motor Ploughs Ltd v Forsyth* (1933) 48 C.L.R. 125, 143, 156.
[66] See above, para.4–005.
[67] See above, para.4–028.
[68] See above, para.4–024.
[69] See above, para.4–050; below, para.5–069.
[70] *Emmett v Tottenham* (1853) 8 Exch. 884.
[71] *Jenkins v Tongue* (1860) 29 L.J. Ex. 147; *Ancona v Marks* (1862) 7 H. & N. 686; *Silk Bros
Interstate Traders Pty Ltd v Security Pacific National Bank* (1989) 16 N.S.W.L.R. 446.
[72] *Clerk v Pigot* (1699) 12 Mod. 192.
[73] *Rordasnz v Leach* (1816) 1 Stark. 446; *Ord v Portal* (1812) 3 Camp. 239; *Low v Copestake* (1828)
3 C. & P. 300; *Wood v Connop* (1843) 5 Q.B. 292 (bearer instruments).

owner of the bill. He is entitled to maintain an action on it in his own name against all or any of the parties liable thereon, unless it is shown that the defendant is the true owner of the instrument or that he holds it adversely to the true owner.[74] It is always competent for the holder of a bill indorsed to him in blank to hand it over to another for the purpose of suing on it, because it is immaterial that the holder never had any interest in the bill[75] or that he has parted with his interest therein.[76]

5–058     **Action on bill payable specially.** A bill is payable specially where it is payable to or to the order of the payee or payees in whose possession it remains, or where it has been specially indorsed to or to the order of a specified indorsee or indorsees. Subject to the rules as to transmission,[77] when a bill is payable specially, the action must be brought in the name of the particular person or persons to whom the bill is payable.[78] So, for example, if a bill is specially indorsed to the partnership firm of "D & Co.", an action must be brought in the name of the firm, and the managing partner cannot sue in his own name.[79]

5–059     **Action on bill payable to bearer.** When a bill is payable to bearer, an action thereon may be brought in the name of any person who has either the actual or the constructive possession of the bill.[80] Thus if a bill is indorsed in blank to a partnership firm, any one of the partners may bring an action on it in his own name.[81]

5–060     **Holder suing as agent or trustee.** When the holder of a bill sues as agent for another person, for example, as agent for collection, he can sue on the bill in his own name. Even if he himself gave no value for the bill, he can rely on section 27(2) of the Act and claim as a holder for value if either his principal or a prior holder gave value for the instrument. But, if he sues as agent, without personal interest, any defence or set-off available against his principal is available against him.[82]

---

[74] *Jones v Broadhurst* (1850) 9 C.B. 173; *Agra and Masterman's Bank v Leighton* (1866) L.R. 2 Ex. 56, 63–65.
[75] *Law v Parnell* (1859) 7 C.B. (N.S.) 282.
[76] *Williams v James* (1850) 15 Q.B. 498; *Poirier v Morris* (1853) 2 E. & B. 89.
[77] See below, para.5–062.
[78] *Pease v Hirst* (1829) 10 B. & C. 122, 127.
[79] *Bawden v Howell* (1841) 3 M. & G. 638, 641.
[80] *Clerk v Pigot* (1699) 12 Mod. 192; *Ord v Portal* (1812) 3 Camp. 239; *Rordasnz v Leach* (1816) 1 Stark. 446; *Low v Copestake* (1828) 3 C. & P. 300; *Wood v Connop* (1843) 5 Q.B. 292; *Law v Parnell* (1859) 7 C.B. N.S. 282; *Jenkins v Tongue* (1860) 29 L.J. Ex. 147; *Ancona v Marks* (1862) 7 H. & N. 686. *cf. Emmett v Tottenham* (1853) 8 Exch. 884.
[81] *Wood v Connop* (1843) 5 Q.B. 292.
[82] *De la Chaumette v Bank of England* (1829) 9 B. & C. 208, as explained in *Currie v Misa* (1875) L.R. 10 Ex. 153, 164 (s.29, Illustration 2); *Re Anglo Greek Steam Navigation & Trading Co.* (1869) L.R. 4 Ch.App. 174.

The same principle applies where the holder sues wholly or in part for the benefit of and as trustee for another person. Any defence or set-off available against that person is available *pro tanto* against the holder.[83] There are three situations in particular where the holder will be considered to be trustee for another. First, where payment is made either partially or in full by the drawer to the indorsee of a bill, this does not preclude the indorsee as holder from suing the acceptor for the full amount of the bill; but the indorsee will hold on trust for the drawer, to the extent of the sum so paid, the amount recovered from the acceptor.[84] Secondly, where the payee of a bill indorses and discounts it to the holder, but on terms that the holder will pay to the payee immediately only a certain percentage of the value of the bill, the balance being credited to the payee's account if and when received from the acceptor, the holder can sue the acceptor for the full amount of the bill; but as to that balance the holder will sue as trustee for the payee.[85] Thirdly, where the holder has a lien on or is a pledgee of the bill, if the person from whom he received it could have sued on the bill, he may sue for the full amount of the bill; but he is a trustee of the amount recovered after deducting the sum for which he has the lien or pledge.[86]

However, the fact that the holder has acted in the transaction underlying the bill as agent for another does not necessarily mean that he will be subject to defences available against his principal. In *Churchill and Sim v Goddard*[87] the claimants were the *del credere* agents of Finnish timber importers to whom they were responsible for payment of the price of timber supplied. They drew bills on the defendant payable to their own order and forwarded these to the defendant for acceptance together with shipping documents representing timber sold by their principals to the defendant. They paid their principals the invoice price of the timber, less their commission. The defendant accepted the bills, but on presentment for payment the bills were dishonoured, the defendant having justifiably rejected the timber supplied. The Court of Appeal held that the claimants were not suing as agents or trustees for their principals. As payees, they were holders of the bills[88] and were, or were deemed to be, holders for value.[89] As between themselves and the defendant, there was no absence

---

[83] *Agra and Masterman's Bank v Leighton* (1866) L.R. 2 Ex. 56, 65; *Thornton v Maynard* (1875) L.R. 10 Ex. 695 (Illustration 1); *Barclays Bank Ltd v Aschaffenberger Zellstoffwerke A.G.* [1967] 1 Lloyd's Rep. 387 (s.27, Illustration 3).

[84] *Jones v Broadhurst* (1850) 9 C.B. 173; *Thornton v Maynard* (1875) L.R. 10 Ex. 695.

[85] *Reid v Furnival* (1833) 1 C. & P. 538 (s.27, Illustration 29); *Barclays Bank Ltd v Aschaffenberger Zellstoffwerke A.G.* [1967] 1 Lloyd's Rep. 387.

[86] *Re Bunyard, Ex p. Newton* (1880) 16 Ch.D. 330 (s.27, Illustration 30); see above, para.4–030.

[87] [1937] 1 K.B. 92.

[88] s.2.

[89] ss.27(1), 30(1).

or failure of consideration giving rise to a defence to liability on the bills.

**5–061**    **Holder's right of proof.** When a party to a bill becomes bankrupt, the holder, who could have maintained an action against such party if he had remained solvent, can prove against his estate in the bankruptcy. Any defence, set-off or counterclaim available in an action is available against a proof. In one respect the right of proof is more extensive than the right of action. An action can only be brought to recover a debt which is due. But, by virtue of the definition of "bankruptcy debt" in section 382 of the Insolvency Act 1986, that definition includes any debt or liability to which the bankrupt may become subject after the commencement of the bankruptcy (including after his discharge from bankruptcy) by reason of any obligation incurred before the commencement of the bankruptcy.[90] Further, it is immaterial whether the debt or liability is present or future, whether it is certain or contingent or whether its amount is fixed or liquidated, or is capable of being ascertained by fixed rules or as a matter of opinion.[91] Thus, if the acceptor of a bill not yet due becomes bankrupt, the holder may prove, and so might the drawer or indorser. So, too, the holder of an accepted bill may prove if the drawer or an indorser becomes bankrupt. Proof of debts takes place in accordance with the provisions of the Insolvency Act 1986 and the Insolvency Rules 1986.

Similar principles apply in the case of the winding-up of a company.[92]

**5–062**    **Transmission by operation of law.** The Act leaves untouched the rules of general law[93] which regulate the transmission of negotiable instruments by operation of law. Those rules apply to cheques and promissory notes as well as to bills of exchange.

**5–063**    (i) *Death.* On the death of a holder of a bill the title to the instrument passes to his personal representatives. Where the holder of a bill payable to order dies, his executor or administrator can enforce payment of it or indorse it away, using his own name.[94] In indorsing the bill, the executor or administrator may exclude personal liability.[95] As he is not the agent of the deceased, he cannot by his delivery complete an indorsement written

---

[90] s.382(1)(b).
[91] s.382(3).
[92] Insolvency Rules 1986, rule 13.12.
[93] See s.97(2).
[94] *Rawlinson v Stone* (1746) 3 Wils. K.B. 1; *Watkins v Maule* (1820) 2 Jac. & W. 237, 243. See also *Murray v East India Company* (1821) 5 B. & Ald. 204, 216. He should specify the capacity in which he indorses to make the title clear.
[95] s.31(5).

by the latter.[96] He must indorse it afresh. If the holder of a bill dies, having specifically bequeathed it to another, that legatee cannot sue on it or indorse it away, unless he first obtains the indorsement of the executor.[97]

(ii) *Bankruptcy.* If the holder of a bill becomes bankrupt, and at the **5–064** commencement of the bankruptcy[98] he is the beneficial owner[99] of it, title to the bill vests automatically in the trustee in bankruptcy.[1] Where a bill is given to a bankrupt after the commencement of the bankruptcy, the trustee may by notice in writing claim it for the bankrupt's estate.[2]

Title to the bill vests in the trustee immediately on his appointment taking effect or, in the case of the official receiver, on his becoming trustee.[3] With the consent of the creditors' committee or of the court he can bring an action to enforce payment of the bill[4] and will sue in his own name as trustee. Since he has power to sell any part of the property for the time being comprised in the bankrupt's estate,[5] it would seem that, for that purpose, he could indorse a bill payable to the order of the bankrupt, using his own name. He has power to give receipts for any money received by him and thereby discharge the person making the payment.[6]

By section 284(1) of the Insolvency Act 1986, where a person is adjudged bankrupt, any disposition of property made by that person between the day of the presentation of the petition for the bankruptcy order and the vesting of the estate in the trustee is void except to the extent that it is or was made with the consent of the court, or is or was subsequently ratified by the court. An indorsement by the bankrupt during that period would be subject to that provision. However, an indorsee who deals with the bankrupt in good faith who gives value and who has no notice of the presentation of the petition, is protected.[7] Payment of a bill to a holder who is adjudged bankrupt will, it seems, be

---

[96] *Bromage v Lloyd* (1847) 1 Ex. 32 (s.21, Illustration 2).
[97] *Bishop v Curtis* (1852) 18 Q.B. 878.
[98] Defined in s.278(a) of the Insolvency Act 1986.
[99] Contrast (in particular) bills held as agent: *Re Julians, Ex p. Oursell* (1756) Ambl. 297; *Ex p. Sayers* (1800) 5 Ves.Jun. 169; *Parke v Eliason* (1801) 1 East 544; *Jombart v Woollett* (1837) 2 My. & Cr. 389; *Edwards v Glyn* (1859) 2 E. & E. 29; bills entered "short" by banker: *Giles v Perkins* (1807) 9 East 12; *Thompson v Giles* (1824) 2 B. & C. 422; Byles 27th ed. 34–33; *cf.* bills given for the accommodation of the bankrupt: *Arden v Watkins* (1803) 3 East 317; *Wallace v Hardacre* (1807) 1 Camp. 45; *Willis v Freeman* (1810) 12 East 656; *Ramsbotham v Cator* (1816) 1 Stark. 228.
[1] Insolvency Act 1986, ss.283, 306, 311, 312.
[2] Insolvency Act 1986, ss.307, 309. But see s.307(4) (acquisition of bill in good faith, for value and without notice of bankruptcy).
[3] Insolvency Act 1986, s.306.
[4] Insolvency Act 1986, Sch.5, para.2.
[5] Insolvency Act 1986, Sch.5, para.9.
[6] Insolvency Act 1986, Sch.5, para.10.
[7] s.284(4). See also Insolvency Act 1986, s.284(5), below, para.13–048 (s.75).

valid and a good discharge if made before the estate vests in the trustee.[8]

**5–065**    (iii) *Liquidation.* Unlike bankruptcy, there is no automatic vesting of the property of the company in the liquidator. But the liquidator will take control of all the property and things in action to which the company is or appears to be entitled,[9] and, in a winding-up by the court, the court may by order direct that the property belonging to the company shall vest in the liquidator.[10] He may bring an action to enforce payment of a bill in the name and on behalf of the company[11]; he may sell a bill[12]; and he has power to execute a receipt,[13] and to indorse a bill,[14] in the name and on behalf of the company.

**5–066**    (iv) *Execution.* By virtue of section 12 of the Judgments Act 1838,[15] a bill, cheque or note may be seized in execution by the sheriff under a writ of *fieri facias.* The sheriff holds the instrument as security and can sue in his own name for recovery, although he is not bound to do so except against an indemnity by the judgment creditor against the costs and expenses of the action. Payment to the sheriff of an instrument so seized is a good discharge. He is responsible to the judgment debtor for any surplus over the amount of the judgment and costs. It is doubtful whether the sheriff has any power to indorse an instrument payable to order,[16] or to hand over to the judgment creditor, or sell, an instrument payable to bearer. Under section 89(1) of the County Courts Act 1984, a bailiff or officer executing a warrant of execution issued from a county court may seize a bill, cheque or note. Under section 91 of the 1984 Act the registrar holds instruments so seized as security for the benefit of the claimant, and the claimant may sue in the name of the defendant, or in the name of any person in whose name the defendant might have sued, for the recovery of the sum secured or made payable thereby, when the time for payment arrives.

**5–067**    **Assignment or sale.** A bill, cheque or note may be transferred by assignment or sale on the same conditions required for an ordinary chose

---

[8] There is no provision in the Insolvency Act 1986 equivalent to s.46 of the Bankruptcy Act 1914.

[9] Insolvency Act 1986, s.144.

[10] Insolvency Act 1986, s.145.

[11] Insolvency Act 1986, Sch.4, para.4 (in the case of a winding-up by the court, only with the sanction of the court or the liquidation committee).

[12] Insolvency Act 1986, Sch.4, para.6.

[13] Insolvency Act 1986, Sch.4, para.7.

[14] Insolvency Act 1986, Sch.4, para.9.

[15] As amended by the Courts Act 2003, s.109(1) and Sch.8, para.9.

[16] *cf. Mutton v Young* (1847) 4 C.B. 371, 373.

in action.[17] So, for example, if C is the holder of a note payable to his order, he may transfer his title to D by a separate writing assigning the note to D, or by a voluntary deed constituting a declaration of trust in favour of D,[18] or by a written contract of sale.

A bill is a chattel; therefore it may be transferred as a chattel.[19] A bill is a chose in action; therefore it may be assigned as a chose in action.[20] It is clear, however, that a subsequent title by negotiation will override a prior title under a sale or assignment under the general law, *e.g.* C, the holder of a bill payable to bearer, assigns by deed certain property, including the bill, to D. C no longer has any property in the bill, but he is still the holder of it, and if he negotiates the bill by delivery to E, who takes it as holder in due course, E's title overrides that of D.[21] Notice to a debtor, who has given a cheque or other negotiable instrument for his debt, that the debt has been assigned by the creditor can be disregarded by the debtor, even if the creditor who has assigned the debt is still the holder of the instrument.[22]

The transfer of a bill payable to order without indorsement is dealt with in section 31(4) of the Act.[23]

*Donatio mortis causa.* If the holder of a bill or promissory note deliv- **5–068** ers it to another by way of gift in contemplation of death, and dies, this is a valid *donatio mortis causa*. The title to the instrument will pass to the donee, whether it is payable to bearer[24] or to order,[25] but in the latter case the indorsement of the personal representative of the deceased will be required in order to enable the donee to sue on the bill.[26] However, the gift of a bill or note does not enable the donee to sue the deceased's estate on the instrument, for the donee will have provided no consideration for it.[27]

---

[17] But a non-transferable instrument probably cannot be assigned as against the debtor or obligor: see above, para.2–062; below, para.14–044.

[18] *Richardson v Richardson* (1867) L.R. 3 Eq. 686. *cf. Warriner v Rogers* (1873) L.R. 16 Eq. 340.

[19] *Embiricos v Anglo-Austrian Bank* [1905] 1 K.B. 677.

[20] *e.g.* as a book debt: *Dawson v Isle* [1906] 1 Ch. 633.

[21] *Aulton v Atkins* (1856) 18 C.B. 249. See also the Comment on s.31(4), above, para.5–007.

[22] *Bence v Shearman* [1898] 2 Ch. 582. See also *Davis v Reilly* [1898] 1 Q.B. 1; *Re a Debtor* [1908] 1 K.B. 344, 349.

[23] See above, para.5–007.

[24] *Miller v Miller* (1735) 3 P. Wms. 356.

[25] *Veal v Veal* (1859) 27 Beav. 303; *Austin v Mead* (1880) 15 Ch.D. 651; *Clement v Cheesman* (1884) 27 Ch.D. 631.

[26] *Bishop v Curtis* (1852) 18 Q.B. 878. *Quaere* whether the donee can compel the personal representative to indorse it to him. s.31(4) of the Act gives this right only in the case of a transfer for value.

[27] *Tate v Hilbert* (1793) 4 Bro. C.C. 286, 294; *Holliday v Atkinson* (1826) 5 B. & C. 501, 503. See also *Re Whitaker* (1889) 42 Ch.D. 119, 124, and above, para.4–007.

Different considerations apply to the gift, in contemplation of death, of a cheque drawn by the donor on his own bank[28]: the duty and authority of a banker to pay a cheque drawn on him by his customer are determined by notice of the customer's death.[29]

5–069      **Subsection (2): rights and powers of holder in due course.** "Holder in due course" is defined in section 29(1) of the Act.[30] By section 30(2) every holder of a bill is prima facie deemed to be a holder in due course.[31] A holder in due course holds the bill free from any defect of title of prior parties, as well as from mere personal defences available to prior parties among themselves. The meaning of the expression "defect of title" (formerly referred to as "an equity attaching to the bill") is explained in the Comment on section 29(2) of the Act[32] and that of "mere personal defences" (formerly referred to as "equities between the parties") in the Comment on section 27(2).[33]

A holder in due course is endowed with paramount rights over the bill. He may enforce payment against all parties liable on the bill. Whether or not a party is so liable must be determined by reference to the provisions of the Act as a whole. In particular, a defendant may be entitled to raise what are sometimes termed "real" or "absolute" defences so as to negate his liability on the bill. Such defences are available against any holder, including (unless otherwise provided in the Act) a holder in due course.

5–070      **Real or absolute defences.** "Real" or "absolute" defences arise from the invalidity or nullification of the instrument, or of the defendant's ostensible contract on the instrument. They are to be distinguished from the "defects of title" and "mere personal defences" referred to in subsection (2). Examples of such defences are:

(a) complete incapacity to incur liability as a party to a bill[34]: the incapable party may raise this as a defence even against a holder in due course;

(b) forged or unauthorised signature[35]: the person whose signature is forged or placed on a bill without his authority cannot, in the

---

[28] See below, para.13–046 (s.75).
[29] s.75(2).
[30] See above, para.4–050.
[31] See above, para.4–081.
[32] See above, para.4–062.
[33] See above, para.4–027.
[34] s.22. See above, para.3–010 (public authorities), para.3–014 (minors) *cf.* para.3–015 (mental disorder).
[35] s.24.

absence of estoppel, be held liable thereon even to a holder in due course[36];

(c) *non est factum*: the signatory is not bound by his signature of the instrument even to a holder in due course[37];

(d) absence of delivery of a complete bill: the contract of a party is incomplete and revocable until delivery,[38] although, in the hands of a holder in due course, a valid delivery by all parties prior to him so as to make them liable to him is conclusively presumed[39];

(e) absence of delivery of an incomplete bill: this is a defence even against a holder in due course[40];

(f) unauthorised or tardy completion of an incomplete bill: a person who became a party to the instrument prior to its completion may raise this as a defence, but not against a holder in due course[41];

(g) discharge of a bill by payment in due course[42]: by the acceptor becoming the holder of the bill at or after maturity in his own right,[43] by renunciation at or after maturity (although this is no defence against a holder in due course without notice of the renunciation)[44] or by intentional and apparent cancellation of the instrument[45];

(h) the intentional and apparent cancellation of the signature of a party by the holder or his agent: this is a defence available to the party whose signature is cancelled and to any indorser who would have had a right of recourse against that party[46];

(i) material alteration of a bill or acceptance: this is a defence except to a party who has himself made, authorised or assented to the alteration and subsequent indorsers, although in the hands of a holder in due course the bill may be enforceable according to its original tenor.[47]

The effect on the instrument itself of circumstances giving rise to a real or absolute defence will vary. For example, where the signature of the drawer is forged or unauthorised, and that signature is the sole signature

---

[36] See above, paras 3–044, 3–053, 3–055, 3–056 and 3–066.
[37] See above, para.3–022.
[38] s.21(1); above, para.2–150.
[39] s.21(2).
[40] See above, para.2–136 (s.20(2)).
[41] s.20(2); above, para.2–136.
[42] s.59(1) (2); below, para.8–003.
[43] s.61; below, para.8–056.
[44] s.62; below, para.8–064.
[45] s.63(1); below, para.8–071.
[46] s.63(2); below, para.8–072.
[47] s.64(1); below, para.8–079.

on the bill, then the bill is a nullity; but if such a bill is accepted or indorsed, then, by estoppel, the acceptor[48] and any indorser[49] will incur liability on it. Where a bill is discharged by payment in due course, it ceases to exist as a bill and becomes mere waste paper.[50] Where a bill is materially altered, the effect is that it is "avoided"; but, if the alteration is not apparent and the bill is in the hands of a holder in due course, he may nevertheless avail himself of it as if it had not been altered.[51] In each case, therefore, regard must be had to the particular provisions of the Act.

5–071    **Protection and privileges of holder in due course.** In addition to his right to enforce payment against all parties liable on the bill, a holder in due course is protected by the Act in a number of ways, and enjoys certain privileges which are not accorded to holders of a lesser status, *i.e.* to a holder for value[52] or a mere holder[53] of a bill. The relevant provisions of the Act are: section 12 (wrong date inserted deemed to be the true date),[54] section 20(2), proviso (completion of incomplete bill),[55] section 21(2) (conclusive presumption of valid delivery),[56] section 36(5) (dishonoured bill),[57] section 48(1) (failure to give notice of dishonour),[58] section 54(2)(a), (b) and (c) (estoppels of acceptor),[59] section 55(1)(b) (estoppel of drawer),[60] section 55(2)(b) (estoppel of indorser),[61] section 56 (liability of anomalous indorser),[62] section 62(2) (renunciation),[63] section 64(1) (enforcement of bill which has been materially altered),[64] section 71(4) and (5) (bills in a set),[65] section 88(2) (estoppel of maker of note).[66]

5–072    **Rights of the payee.** The original payee of a bill, cheque or note in whose possession the instrument remains cannot be a holder in due

[48] s.54(2)(a).
[49] s.55(2)(b).
[50] See below, para.8–003.
[51] s.64(1), proviso.
[52] See above, para.4–024.
[53] See above, para.4–028.
[54] See above, para.2–093.
[55] See above, para.2–137.
[56] See above, para.2–154.
[57] See above, para.5–065.
[58] See below, para.6–093.
[59] See below, paras 7–017—7–018.
[60] See below, para.7–025.
[61] See below, para.7–028.
[62] See below, para.7–031.
[63] See below, para.8–064.
[64] See below, para.8–079.
[65] See below, paras 11–006—11–007.
[66] See below, para.15–054.

course, as the instrument has not been negotiated to him.[67] He cannot therefore claim the protection and rights conferred by sub-section (2) upon a holder in due course. As a holder, he may sue on the instrument in his own name.[68] He may or may not be a holder for value.[69] But the Act nowhere states what defences may be raised against him by the original parties to the instrument, *i.e.* by the drawer and acceptor of a bill, the drawer of a cheque or the maker of a note. It is clear, however, that if he himself procures the issue of the instrument or its acceptance by fraud, duress or other unlawful means, or if as between himself and the person sought to be held liable on the instrument the consideration is illegal, then his title to the bill will be defective and such defect in title may be raised as a defence against him. Moreover, as between immediate parties,[70] subject to the rule that negotiable instruments are to be treated as cash in the hands of the recipient,[71] mere personal defences arising out of the underlying transaction, *e.g.* absence or failure of consideration, may also be raised.[72]

The position is less clear, however, where the fraud, duress, etc., is that of a third party, for example, where A by fraud procures B to draw a cheque payable to C. On one view, unless B proves that C received the cheque with notice of the fraud, or did not receive it for value or in good faith, then B will be liable to C on the cheque. In *Watson v Russell*,[73] Crompton J., in delivering the judgment of the majority of the court,[74] said:

> "If A, by means of a false pretence or a promise or condition which he does not fulfil, procures B to give him a note or cheque or acceptance in favour of C, to whom he pays it, and who receives it bona fide for value, B remains liable on his acceptance. His acceptance imports value and liability prima facie, and he can only relieve himself from his promise to pay C by shewing that C is not holder for value, or that he received the instrument with notice or not bona fide."

This statement was relied upon by Vaughan Williams L.J. in *Talbot v Von Boris*,[75] where the Court of Appeal held, in an action by the payee against

---

[67] *Jones (R.E.) Ltd v Waring & Gillow Ltd* [1926] A.C. 670 (s.29, Illustration 6); *Dextra Bank & Trust Co. Ltd v Bank of Jamaica* [2002] 1 All E.R. (Comm) 193 at [19]; see above, para.4–059.

[68] s.38(1).

[69] See above, para.4–024.

[70] See above, para.4–005.

[71] See above, para.4–010.

[72] See above, paras 4–007—4–009.

[73] (1862) 3 B. & S. 34, affirmed (1864) 5 B. & S. 968 (Illustration 2).

[74] (1862) 3 B. & S. 34 at 38.

[75] [1911] 1 K.B. 854 (s.30, Illustration 6).

the defendant and her husband as joint makers of a promissory note, that duress by her husband which induced her to make the note afforded no defence in the absence of proof that the duress was known to the claimant when he received the note. It was also relied upon by Robert Goff J. in *Hasan v Willson*.[76] In that case, S by fraud induced the defendant to draw a cheque payable to the claimant, which S then delivered to the claimant. Judgment was given for the defendant on the ground that the consideration for the cheque had wholly failed. But Robert Goff J. stated that, had value been given, the defendant would have been liable on the cheque since the defendant had not proved that the claimant received the cheque with notice of the fraud. In *Nelson v Larholt*[77] the executor of a deceased's estate fraudulently drew cheques on the executor's account payable to the defendant, a turf accountant. Denning J. held that the proceeds of the cheques were recoverable by the estate from the defendant, but on the specific ground that the defendant had implied notice of the executor's fraud and want of authority. In *Hindle v Brown*,[78] where the defendant was induced to purchase certain pictures at auction by a fraud on the part of their owner, and gave a cheque for the price to the auctioneer, the Court of Appeal held that the auctioneer, who in the meantime had settled with the owner,[79] was entitled to recover against the defendant on the cheque. Also, in the more recent case of *Dextra Bank & Trust Co. Ltd v Bank of Jamaica*[80] Lord Bingham and Lord Goff stated that if (as happened in the case) a third party obtains a cheque from the drawer in fraud of the drawer, the payee of the cheque will acquire a good title to it, provided he gives value and has no notice of the fraud.

5–073      All of these cases therefore suggest that the Act has not impaired the position of an innocent payee-holder for value of an instrument[81] who takes it free of any defence based upon fraud or duress by a third party. On the other hand, since section 38(2) confers a right to enforce the instrument despite defects in title of prior parties only on a holder in due course, it might be argued that the original payee receives the instrument subject to any defects of title affecting its issue or acceptance whether he knows of them or not. In *Jones (R.E.) Ltd v Waring & Gillow Ltd*,[82] the claimants were induced by an elaborate fraud on the part of B to draw a cheque payable to the claimants in the mistaken belief that it related to an entirely different transaction. The cheque was delivered by B to the

---

[76] [1977] 1 Lloyd's Rep. 431 (s.27, Illustration 19). See also *Karabus Motors (1959) Ltd v Van Eck* 1962 (1) S.A. 451; *Universal Import Export v Bank of Scotland*, 1994 S.C.L.R. 944, OH.

[77] [1948] 1 K.B. 339 (Illustration 5).

[78] (1908) 98 L.T. 791 (Illustration 3).

[79] It is to be noted that the auctioneer is not stated to have given value when he received the cheque, but see *Pollway v Abdullah* [1974] 1 W.L.R. 493 (s.27, Illustration 10).

[80] [2002] 1 All E.R. (Comm) 193 at [22] (s.59, Illustration 22).

[81] *Lloyds Bank Ltd v Cooke* [1907] 1 K.B. 794, 805–806.

[82] [1926] A.C. 670 (s.29, Illustration 6). See also *T. Place & Sons v Turner* (1951) 101 L.J. 93.

defendants in settlement of an existing debt owed by him to the defendants. Although the defendants received the cheque in good faith and for value, and without notice of the fraud of B, the House of Lords held that the claimants were entitled to recover from them the amount of the cheque as money paid under a mistake. The defendants relied (*inter alia*) on the dictum of Crompton J. in *Watson v Russell*,[83] but that case was distinguished on its facts[84] and the dictum was said to be inapplicable to the recovery of money paid under a mistake.[85] Lord Carson also said[86] that it went "further than the facts of the particular case and does not seem to me to have been necessary for the decision on the facts before the court". In *Ayres v Moore*,[87] the defendant was induced by the fraud of a rogue to accept two bills of exchange payable to the claimant. The rogue delivered the bills to the claimant, who received them in good faith and for value and without notice of the fraud, but at the time of their receipt the name of the drawer had not yet been inserted. Hallett J. held that the claimant could not recover against the defendant as acceptor of the bills. He could not claim as holder in due course because the bills were incomplete when received, and, in any event, as original payee, he could not be a holder in due course. In the course of his judgment, however, Hallett J. suggested[88] that fraud by a third party would constitute a good defence to an acceptor of a bill as against the original payee, irrespective of whether the payee had notice of the fraud.

Commenting on this issue, *Byles*[89] states that *Jones (R.E.) Ltd v Waring & Gillow Ltd*[90] "did not, specifically, at any rate, reduce the rights of a payee-holder for value below those of a holder in due course. And it is submitted that the decision did not affect the rights of a payee-holder for value whatever they may be." It does, indeed, appear that, as the authorities now stand, if the issue of a bill, cheque, or note, or its acceptance, is affected by fraud or duress on the part of a third party, this cannot be raised as a defence against the original payee of the instrument who has received it as holder in good faith and for value without notice of the defect.[91] Moreover, in one respect, the position of the payee-holder is more favourable than that of a holder to whom the instrument has been negotiated, since section 30(2) of the Act (which shifts the burden of proof

---

[83] (1862) 3 B. & S. 34.
[84] [1926] A.C. 670 at 682, 685, 687, 694, 709 as a case of an agent disregarding a limitation placed on his ostensible authority. (For the facts, see Illustration 2.)
[85] [1926] A.C. 670 at 682, 685, 687, 695, 700.
[86] [1926] A.C. 670 at 701. See also Lord Sumner at 694.
[87] [1940] 1 K.B. 278 (Illustration 4).
[88] [1940] 1 K.B. 278 at 288. *Talbot v Von Boris* [1911] 1 K.B. 854, and *Hindle v Brown* (1908) 98 L.T. 791, were not cited to him in the case.
[89] 27th ed., 18–36.
[90] [1926] A.C. 670.
[91] Whether the action is between immediate or remote parties. (For the distinction, see above, para.4–005) *cf. Universal Import Export v Bank of Scotland*, 1994 S.C.L.R. 944, OH.

to the holder in certain circumstances) does not apply to the case of the original payee of the instrument.[92] The party sued on the instrument bears the burden of proving that the payee took it with notice of the fraud or duress.[93] Nevertheless, the rights of the innocent payee-holder for value are, by implication, affected by the fact that, at least in certain situations,[94] the party liable to him on the instrument could apparently claim (or counterclaim) the sum due as money paid or payable under a mistake.[95]

In certain other respects,[96] it is, however, clear that the position of the original payee is not to be equated with that of a holder in due course. For example, in respect of the completion of an incomplete bill, the payee cannot take advantage of the proviso to section 20(2) of the Act, since the protection afforded by that proviso is available only to a holder in due course.[97] For a bill to be enforceable by a payee-holder against a person who became a party to it prior to its completion, the bill must have been filled up within a reasonable time and strictly in accordance with the authority given.[98] Secondly, the conclusive presumption as to the valid delivery of a bill by prior parties which is raised by section 21(2) of the Act does not apply to the original payee, but only to a holder in due course.[99] The rights of the payee-holder may therefore be defeated by proof[1] that the delivery was not made either by or under the authority of the drawer, acceptor or maker of the instrument or was conditional or for a special purpose only, and not for the purpose of transferring the property in the instrument.[2] Thirdly, where a bill or acceptance is materially altered without the assent of all parties liable on the bill, then the bill will be void in the hands of the payee.[3] He cannot take advantage of the privilege accorded by section 64(1) of the Act to a holder in due course to avail himself of the bill as if it had not been altered, and to enforce payment of it according to its original tenor. In these situations it is immaterial that the unauthorised completion, delivery or alteration was due to the fraud of a third party and that the payee had no knowledge of

---

[92] *Talbot v Von Boris* [1911] 1 K.B. 854 (s.30, Illustration 6). See above, para.5–072.

[93] *Talbot v Von Boris* [1911] 1 K.B. 854; *Hasan v Willson* [1977] 1 Lloyd's Rep. 431.

[94] See below, para.8–021 (s.59) for the principles governing claims for repayment.

[95] Contrast *Byles* (27th ed.), 32–36.

[96] In addition to the examples given here, see also the protection and privileges accorded by the Act solely to a holder in due course (above, para.5–071).

[97] See above, para.2–137 (s.20).

[98] *Herdman v Wheeler* [1902] 1 K.B. 361 (s.20, Illustration 10); *Smith v Prosser* [1907] 2 K.B. 735, 742, 751 (s.20, Illustration 22); *Wilson and Meeson v Pickering* [1946] K.B. 422 (s.20, Illustration 23). *cf. Lloyds Bank Ltd v Cooke* [1907] 1 K.B. 794 (s.20, Illustration 21) (estoppel).

[99] See above, para.2–154.

[1] For the burden of proof, see s.21(3).

[2] s.21(2).

[3] s.64(1) (except against a party who has himself made, authorised or assented to the alteration); see below, para.8–078.

it when he received the instrument.[4] Further, the estoppels raised by the Act in favour of a holder in due course, and, in particular, the estoppels raised against the acceptor by section 54(2)(a) and (b) of the Act,[5] do not in their terms extend to the original payee of a bill.

**Subsection (3): defective title.** The power to negotiate a bill must be distinguished from the right to negotiate it. The right to negotiate is an incident of ownership; the power to negotiate it is an incident of apparent ownership. Thus if a thief steals a bill payable to bearer, he acquires no title to the bill; but if he negotiates it by delivery to a holder in due course, that holder obtains a good and complete title to the bill. Likewise if a person obtains a bill payable to his order, or the acceptance thereof, by fraud or for an illegal consideration, his title to the bill is defective; but if he negotiates the bill by indorsing and delivering it to a holder in due course, the latter obtains a good and complete title to the instrument.

Again, a holder whose title to a bill is defective has no right to receive payment. But, if he obtains payment of the bill, a drawee or acceptor who pays him in due course, that is to say, at or after maturity in good faith and without notice that his title to the bill is defective, gets a valid discharge for the bill.[6]

5–074

ILLUSTRATIONS

1. The claimants sue as indorsees of nine bills of exchange drawn by R & Co. upon, and accepted by, the defendant, and indorsed by R & Co. to the claimants. The defendant pleads in defence that R & Co. became bankrupt and that the claimants received a dividend of £425 from the estate of R & Co. in respect of the amount of the bills; that, as to that sum, the claimants are suing only as trustee for the drawers (R & Co.); and that the defendant is entitled to set-off against that sum a debt due from R & Co. to the defendant. This is a good defence.[7]

5–075

2. A ship is chartered by the defendant to K for a period of six months on terms that the vessel may be withdrawn in case of non-payment of hire. K sub-charters the ship, through the claimant, to a third party. The hire money being in arrear, the defendant threatens to withdraw the ship

---

[4] *Herdman v Wheeler* [1902] 1 K.B. 361; *Lloyds Bank Ltd v Cooke* [1907] 1 K.B. 794; *Smith v Prosser* [1907] 2 K.B. 735.

[5] See below, para.7–017 (s.54). But see above, para.3–057 (s.24) for a possible estoppel at common law.

[6] s.59(1).

[7] *Thornton v Maynard* (1875) L.R. 10 Ex. 695.

unless the arrears are fully paid. K, being unable to remit this amount, applies to the claimant for assistance. The claimant draws a cheque payable to the defendant for one-half of the amount due and hands this to K, as his agent, with instructions to deliver it to the defendant on terms that K is to inform the defendant that it is given in consideration that the ship is to perform the charter. K sends the cheque to the defendant but omits to inform him of the condition on which it has been given. The defendant cashes the cheque, but, the balance of hire being unpaid, stops the ship. The claimant is not entitled to recover from the defendant the amount of the cheque.[8]

3. At a sale by auction, the defendant purchases certain pictures and gives to the claimant, the auctioneer, a cheque for the price. The claimant does not cash the cheque straight away, but nevertheless pays the price to the owner of the pictures. When the cheque is presented for payment, payment is countermanded by the defendant on the grounds that he is entitled to repudiate the contract by reason of fraud by the owner. The claimant can recover from the defendant on the cheque.[9]

5–076      4. F induces the defendant to accept five bills of exchange, each for £500, payable to the claimant's order by fraudulently representing that the claimant has advanced money to finance the acquisition of certain patents and that the bills are required to secure the claimant's advance. F is indebted to the claimant in the sum of £3,780 and delivers them to the claimant in part payment of that debt, the claimant receiving them in good faith and without notice of the fraud. At the time of such receipt the name of F, as drawer, has not been inserted in the bills. The claimant cannot recover against the defendant on the bills. The defendant can repudiate liability on the grounds of fraud even though the fraud is that of a third party. Since the bills were incomplete when received, the claimant cannot claim to be a holder in due course. In any event, as original payee, he is not a holder in due course.[10]

5. P is the executor and trustee of the estate of W.B. and opens an executor's account with the M Bank. He draws on the account eight cheques payable to the defendant, a turf accountant, signing them "G.A.P., executor of W.B. deceased". The deceased's estate can recover from the defendant the amount of the cheques. The defendant was put on

[8] *Watson v Russell* (1862) 3 B. & S. 34, (1864) 5 B. & S. 968, as interpreted in *Jones (R.E.) Ltd v Waring & Gillow Ltd* [1926] A.C. 670.
[9] *Hindle v Brown* (1908) 98 L.T. 791, CA.
[10] *Ayres v Moore* [1940] 1 K.B. 278.

inquiry and must be taken to have had notice of P's fraud and want of authority.[11]

### General Duties of the Holder

### When presentment for acceptance is necessary

39. (1) Where a bill is payable after sight, presentment for accep-   6–001
tance is necessary in order to fix the maturity of the instrument.

(2) Where a bill expressly stipulates that it shall be presented for acceptance, or where a bill is drawn payable elsewhere than at the residence or place of business of the drawee, it must be presented for acceptance before it can be presented for payment.

(3) In no other case is presentment for acceptance necessary in order to render liable any party to the bill.

(4) Where the holder of a bill, drawn payable elsewhere than at the place of business or residence of the drawee, has not time, with the exercise of reasonable diligence, to present the bill for acceptance before presenting it for payment on the day that it falls due, the delay caused by presenting the bill for acceptance before presenting it for payment is excused, and does not discharge the drawer and indorsers.

| Definitions | Comparison |
|---|---|
| "acceptance": ss.2, 17(1). | UCC: §§ 3–501. |
| "bill": s.2. | ULB: arts 21–24. |
| "holder": s.2. | UNB: arts 49, 50, 52. |

### COMMENT

**Presentment for acceptance: when required.** [1] This section, and sec-   6–002
tions 40 to 44, do not apply to cheques[2] or promissory notes.[3] Such instruments do not contemplate acceptance. But, even in the case of bills of exchange, the Act requires the bill to be presented for acceptance only

---

[11] *Nelson v Larholt* [1948] 1 K.B. 339.
[1] For the conflict of laws: see below, para.12–031. (s.72(3)).
[2] See below, para.13–003.
[3] s.89(3).

in the situations mentioned in subsections (1) and (2). In all other situations presentment for acceptance is optional. Where presentment is optional, the object of presenting is (i) to obtain the acceptance of the drawee, and thereby secure his liability as a party to the bill; (ii) to obtain an immediate right of recourse against antecedent parties in case the bill is dishonoured by non-acceptance.

An agent, *e.g.* a bank, is bound to use due diligence in presenting for acceptance, even when presentment is optional for the purposes of the Act, and (unless otherwise agreed) he is liable to his principal for damages resulting from his negligence.[4]

A bill in the form "Pay without acceptance" is valid.[5]

6–003    **Presentment by banks.** In many international trade transactions bills drawn by the seller on the buyer for the price will be presented for acceptance by utilising the services of commercial banks.[6] The seller will instruct his bank (the remitting bank) to present the bill for acceptance and the remitting bank will employ for this purpose a correspondent bank in the buyer's country. In most cases the duties and responsibilities of the banks involved will be subject to the ICC Uniform Rules for Collections.[7] By Article 22 of the Rules, the presenting bank is responsible for seeing that the form of acceptance of a bill of exchange appears to be complete and correct, but it is not responsible for the genuineness of any signature or for the authority of any signatory to sign the acceptance.

6–004    **Subsection (1): after sight bills.** A bill may be drawn payable at a fixed period after sight.[8] Since "sight" means presentment for acceptance, such a bill must be presented for acceptance since its due date for payment would not otherwise be known.[9] It may seem somewhat surprising that this subsection does not also extend to a bill which is expressed to be payable at sight,[10] but such a bill is in fact payable on demand.[11]

The consequences of a failure to present for acceptance an after sight bill which is negotiated are that the drawer and prior indorsers will be discharged if the holder neither negotiates it nor presents it for acceptance

---

[4] *cf. Bank of Van Diemen's Land v Bank of Victoria* (1871) L.R. 3 P.C. 526 (after sight bill) (s.21, Illustration 5). But see below, para.6–047 (s.45) (sub-agent).

[5] *R. v Kinnear* (1838) 2 Moo. & R. 117; *Miller v Thomson* (1841) 3 M. & G. 576.

[6] See *Benjamin's Sale of Goods* (6th ed.), §§ 22–076—22–138.

[7] 1995 Brochure No.522. See below, para.6–043 (s.45).

[8] See above, para.2–086 (s.11).

[9] For the date of payment, see ss.14(2) (3), 18(3), 65(5).

[10] The equivalent Canadian statute (at s.75(1)) includes a bill payable at sight.

[11] s.10(1). It may also be argued that the drawee who does not intend to pay the bill is unlikely to accept it, since it would be immediately presented for payment.

within a reasonable time.[12] Otherwise a failure to present entails that there is no maturity date to crystallise the obligations of the drawer and indorsers to pay the bill.[13]

**Subsection (2): other situations.**[14] Even a bill payable on demand or on a fixed date or at a fixed period after date must be presented for acceptance in the situations specified in this subsection. The consequences of a failure to present (unless excused) are that the bill cannot be presented for payment. If it is not duly presented for payment, the drawer and indorsers will be discharged.[15]   **6–005**

**Subsection (3): optional presentment.**[16] In all other cases presentment is optional and failure to present does not discharge any party liable on the bill.[17]   **6–006**

**Subsection (4): domiciled bill coming forward late.** This subsection[18] is rendered necessary by the provision of subsection (2) that a bill drawn payable elsewhere than at the residence or place of business of the drawee[19] must be presented for acceptance before it can be presented for payment. Suppose a bill, payable one month after date, is drawn in New York on a Liverpool firm, but payable at a London bank. It only reaches the English holder, or his agent, on the day that it matures. He must, by reason of subsection (2), nevertheless present it for acceptance to the drawees in Liverpool. Subsection (4) provides that he shall not be prejudiced thereby. If he acts with reasonable diligence, the delay caused by presenting the bill for acceptance before presenting it for payment is excused.   **6–007**

## Time for presenting bill payable after sight

**40.**  **(1) Subject to the provisions of this Act, when a bill payable after sight is negotiated, the holder must either present it for acceptance or negotiate it within a reasonable time.**   **6–008**

---

[12] s.40(1) (2).

[13] See below, paras 6–009, 6–017 (after sight bill which is not negotiated).

[14] This subs. settled a doubtful point.

[15] s.45.

[16] This subs. was declaratory: see *Ramchurn Mullick v Luchmeechund Radakissen* (1854) 9 Moore P.C. 46, 65, 66.

[17] Subject to s.40(2), the question of due presentment is only material when acceptance cannot be obtained. If acceptance is obtained, the informality of the acceptance is immaterial.

[18] It was added in committee. It settled a moot point, and perhaps altered the law: Chalmers (9th ed.), pp.2, 158.

[19] As to the place of payment, see s.45(4)(a).

(2) **If he do not do so, the drawer and all indorsers prior to that holder are discharged.**

(3) **In determining what is a reasonable time within the meaning of this section, regard shall be had to the nature of the bill, the usage of trade with respect to similar bills, and the facts of the particular case.**

Definitions
"acceptance": ss.2, 17(1).
"bill": s.2.
"holder": s.2.
"negotiate": s.31.

Comparison
UCC: §3–501
ULB: arts 23, 53.
UNB: arts 49, 51, 53.

COMMENT

6–009    **Time for presenting bill payable after sight.** It is in the interests of the drawer and indorsers of a bill payable after sight[20] (which must therefore be presented for acceptance)[21] that the holder present the bill for acceptance within a reasonable time,[22] lest, in the intervening period, the drawee become insolvent and the bill be dishonoured by non-acceptance. However, subsection (1) permits each holder to negotiate[23] the bill instead of presenting it for acceptance. In theory, therefore, the liability of such secondary parties could be indefinitely postponed.[24] Nevertheless, in practice, some limit is imposed by subsection (2): the drawer and prior indorsers are discharged if any holder does not, within a reasonable time, either negotiate the bill or present it for acceptance.

Subsection (3) indicates the matters to be taken into account in determining what is a reasonable time. Reasonable time is a question of mixed law and fact, and in determining it, regard must be had to the interests of the holder as well as to the interests of the drawer and indorsers.[25] There are no modern cases on this point and early nineteenth century cases[26]

---

[20] See above, para.2–086 (s.11).
[21] s.39(1).
[22] *cf.* ULB, art 23; UNB, art. 51(d) (one year to present).
[23] See s.31. The transfer of a bill payable to order without indorsement is not a negotiaton of the bill: s.31(4).
[24] *cf. Muilman v D'Eguino* (1795) 2 H.Bl. 565, 570.
[25] *Ramchurn Mullick v Luchmeechund Radakissen* (1854) 9 Moore P.C. 46, 66, 67. See also *Fry v Hill* (1817) 7 Taunt. 397, 398; *Shute v Robins* (1828) 3 C. & P. 80, 82; *Mellish v Rawdon* (1832) 9 Bing. 416, 423.
[26] *Fry v Hill* (1817) 7 Taunt. 397, 398 (Illustration 1); *Goupy v Harden* (1816) 7 Taunt. 159; *Shute v Robins* (1828) 3 C. & P. 80, 82 (Illustration 2); *Mellish v Rawdon* (1832) 9 Bing. 416, 423 (Illustration 3); *Straker v Graham* (1839) 4 M. & W. 721 (Illustration 4); *Ramchurn Mullick v Luchmeechund Radakissen* (1854) 9 Moore P.C. 46, 66, 67 (Illustration 5); *Godfray v Coulman* (1859) 13 Moore P.C. 11.

should, perhaps, be approached with caution in view of the less rapid means of communication involved.

It is to be noted that this section only applies in its terms when a bill payable after sight is negotiated. Somewhat surprisingly, therefore, it does not apply where the bill is in the hands of the original payee in whose possession it remains. It also does not apply to bills payable at sight.[27]

Subsection (1) is subject to section 41(2) (excuses for non-presentment).

**Presentment by bank.** By Article 6 of the ICC Uniform Rules for Collections,[28] in the case of documents payable at a tenor other than sight, the presenting bank must, where acceptance is called for, make presentation for acceptance without delay.    **6–010**

ILLUSTRATIONS

1. The claimant, on Friday 9th at Windsor, receives a bill for £140 drawn on a bank in London payable one month after sight. There is no post on Saturday. The bill is presented for acceptance on the 13th, and acceptance is refused. The jury find that it has been presented within a reasonable time.[29]    **6–011**

2. On November 12, 1825 a bill for £100 is drawn by E & Co., country bankers, upon B & Co., bankers in London, payable to C 20 days after sight. It is indorsed and delivered to the claimant's traveller on the 17th, and transmitted by him to the claimants after one week. On the 29th the bill is transmitted for acceptance. Acceptance is refused, the country bankers in the meantime having failed. The jury finds no unreasonable delay.[30]

3. The defendant in London draws a bill on G in Rio de Janeiro payable 60 days after sight. The claimant purchases the bill on September 10, 1830 and keeps the bill until February 1, 1831, on which day he sells the bill. G fails in the interval. The claimant pays his indorsee and seeks to recover

---

[27] See above, para.6–004. The equivalent Canadian statute (at s.77(1)) includes a bill payable at sight.

[28] (1995) Brochure No.522. See above, para.6–003 (s.39); below, para.6–043 (s.45).

[29] *Fry v Hill* (1817) 7 Taunt. 397.

[30] *Shute v Robins* (1828) 3 C. & P. 80.

from the defendant (the drawer). The jury finds the delay is not unreasonable and the court refuses to disturb the verdict.[31]

6–012     4. A bill of exchange for £176 is drawn in duplicate on August 12 in Newfoundland on S & Co. in England, payable 90 days after sight. It is not presented for acceptance to S & Co. until November 16. There are sailings three times a week from Newfoundland to England and the voyage takes 18 days. The jury finds that the bill has not been presented within a reasonable time and the court agrees, no circumstances having been proved in explanation of the delay.[32]

5. The respondents in Calcutta draw a bill on February 16, 1848 for $37,840 on D & Co. in Hong Kong payable to themselves, or order, 60 days after sight. They indorse the bill in blank and deliver it to M. Due to the depressed state of the money market in Calcutta and the unsaleability of bills on China in Calcutta at that time, M keeps the bill for five months and then negotiates it to the appellants. The appellants present the bill for acceptance on October 24. Acceptance is refused. The jury finds the delay unreasonable (even though the drawees are solvent and no damage has been sustained) and the verdict is upheld by the court.[33]

### Rules as to presentment for acceptance, and excuses for non-presentment

6–013     41. (1) A bill is duly presented for acceptance which is presented in accordance with the following rules:
  (a) The presentment must be made by or on behalf of the holder to the drawee or to some person authorised to accept or refuse acceptance on his behalf at a reasonable hour on a business day and before the bill is overdue;
  (b) Where a bill is addressed to two or more drawees, who are not partners, presentment must be made to them all, unless one has authority to accept for all, then presentment may be made to him only;
  (c) Where the drawee is dead presentment may be made to his personal representative;
  (d) Where the drawee is bankrupt, presentment may be made to him or to his trustee;

---

[31] *Mellish v Rawdon* (1832) 9 Bing. 416.
[32] *Straker v Graham* (1839) 4 M. & W. 721.
[33] *Ramchurn Mullick v Luchmeechund Radakissen* (1854) 9 Moore P.C. 46.

    (e) Where authorised by agreement or usage, a presentment through [a postal operator] is sufficient.

(2) Presentment in accordance with these rules is excused, and a bill may be treated as dishonoured by non-acceptance—

    (a) Where the drawee is dead or bankrupt, or is a fictitious person or a person not having capacity to contract by bill;

    (b) Where, after the exercise of reasonable diligence, such presentment cannot be effected;

    (c) Where although the presentment has been irregular, acceptance has been refused on some other ground.

(3) The fact that the holder has reason to believe that the bill, on presentment, will be dishonoured does not excuse presentment.

Amendment

S.41(1)(c) was amended by the Postal Services Act 2000 (Consequential Modifications No.1) Order 2001, SI 2001/1149.

Definitions
"acceptance": ss.2, 17(1).
"bankrupt": s.2.
"bill": s.2.
"business day": s.92.
"holder": s.2.
"person": s.2.
"postal operator": s.2

Comparison
UCC: §§ 3–501, 3–504.
ULB: arts 21–24, 53.
UNB: arts 51, 52.

## COMMENT

**Subsection (1): due presentment for acceptance.** This subsection sets out the rules for due presentment of a bill for acceptance.[34] It does not apply to cheques or promissory notes. Subject to section 40(2), the question of due presentment is only material when acceptance cannot be obtained. If acceptance is obtained, the informality of the presentment is immaterial.   6–014

**By whom due presentment must be made.** For a bill to be duly presented for acceptance, presentment must be made "by or on behalf of the holder". "Holder" is defined in section 2: he need not necessarily be   6–015

---

[34] For the conflict of laws, see below, para.12–031 (s.72(3)).

the lawful holder.[35] The holder need not present personally. A bill may be forwarded, unindorsed, to an agent,[36] *e.g.* to a banker, for him to procure acceptance. Presentment for acceptance does not imply a warranty that the bill and documents, if any, attached thereto are genuine.[37]

6–016      **To whom due presentment must be made.** Presentment must be made "to the drawee or to some person authorised to accept or refuse acceptance on his behalf".[38] Thus, presentment to a servant who opened the door would not be sufficient; and if a bill is domiciled for payment at a bank, presentment at the bank premises would not in itself suffice. *Byles* states[39]: "There must be proof that presentation has been made to the actual drawee (or to his accredited agent), not to a person who merely refused to accept but who did not represent himself to be the drawee." Reasonable diligence must be used to find the drawee or some person authorised to act for him. When the drawee is a trader, presentment should be made to him at his place of business if possible.

Subsection (1) also provides rules for due presentment in the following special cases:

(a) *Two or more drawees.* Paragraph (b) is mandatory where it applies. If one of two or more drawees refuses to accept, the acceptance of the other drawee or drawees is a qualified acceptance.[40]

(b) *Drawee dead.* Paragraph (c) is permissive. Presentment may be made to his personal representative. But presentment is alternatively excused where the drawee is dead.[41]

(c) *Drawee bankrupt.* Paragraph (d) is likewise permissive. Presentment may be made to the bankrupt[42] drawee or to his trustee, or may be excused.[43]

6–017      **When due presentment must be made.** To constitute due presentment, the presentment must be made "at a reasonable hour on a business

---

[35] Chalmers (9th ed.), p.160, refers to an unreported case, in December 1876, where the Court of Appeal dissolved an injunction restraining the drawee from accepting a bill where the holder was alleged to have obtained it by fraud; the proper course would have been to proceed against the holder. See also *Smith v Commercial Banking Co. of Sydney Ltd* (1910) 11 C.L.R. 667, 674.

[36] On the duty of the agent, see *Bank of Van Diemen's Land v Bank of Victoria* (1871) L.R. 3 P.C. 526, 542 (s.21, Illustration 5); ICC Uniform Rules for Collections (1995) Brochure No.522.

[37] *Guaranty Trust Co. of New York v Hannay & Co.* [1918] 2 K.B. 623. Contrast UCC, § 3–417.

[38] See also ICC Uniform Rules for Collections (1995), Brochure 522, art.5.

[39] 27th ed., 11–05, citing *Cheek v Roper* (1804) 5 Esp. 175.

[40] s.19(2)(e). As to the consequences of a qualified acceptance, see s.44.

[41] s.41(2)(a), below.

[42] Defined in s.2.

[43] s.41(2)(a), below.

day and before the bill is overdue". "Reasonable hour", in the case of a trader, means business hours, and in the case of a banker, banking hours.[44] When a bill is payable at a future date or so many days after date, it will be overdue after the expiration of its due date.[45] A bill payable at sight or on demand will presumably be overdue in the circumstances set out in section 36(3), *i.e.* when it appears on the face of it to have been in circulation for an unreasonable length of time.[46] But where a bill is payable after sight (which is one of the situations where presentment for acceptance is necessary), it is not clear when—if at all—the bill will be overdue. Section 40(1) prescribes that, when a bill payable after sight is negotiated, the holder must either present it for acceptance or negotiate it within a reasonable time.[47] But that subsection applies only where such a bill is negotiated and does not apply where the holder is the original payee of the bill in whose possession it remains. It would seem that a bill payable after sight is, while it has yet to be presented for acceptance, never overdue, since the day on which it falls due is determined by reference to the date of the acceptance.[48]

A bill may be accepted when overdue.[49] But such an acceptance preserves or revives the liability of the drawer and indorsers only in the case provided for in section 39(4), *i.e.* domiciled bill arriving late.

**Presentment by post.** Paragraph (*e*) of subsection (1) permits present-  6–018
ment through a postal operator "where authorised by agreement or usage".

**Subsection (2): excuses for non-presentment.** This subsection lists the  6–019
situations where presentment in accordance with the rules for due presentment set out in subsection (1) is excused:

(a) *Drawee dead.* In this case, presentment may at the option of the holder be made to the drawee's personal representative.[50]

(b) *Drawee bankrupt.*[51] In this case, likewise, the holder has the option to present the bill for acceptance to the bankrupt or to his trustee.[52]

(c) *Drawee fictitious person.* Section 7(3) of the Act refers to the payee being a "fictitious or non-existing person" and the case-law

---

[44] See below, para.6–053 (presentment for payment).
[45] s.14(1)(2).
[46] See above, para.5–043.
[47] See above, para.6–001.
[48] s.14(3).
[49] s.18(2). See also s.10(2) (deemed payable on demand).
[50] s.41(1)(c), above.
[51] Defined in s.2.
[52] s.41(1)(d), above.

draws a distinction between the two.[53] But section 5(2),[54] sections 46(2)(b) and 50(2)(c)(d), and paragraph (a) of the present subsection, refer merely to the case where the drawee is a "fictitious person"; it is submitted that the expression in this context includes a non-existing drawee.[55]

(d) *Drawee lacking capacity.* Incapacity to contract by bill has been dealt with in the Comment on section 22 of the Act.[56]

(e) *Inability to present.* Presentment is excused where, after the exercise of reasonable diligence,[57] it cannot be effected. This is a question of fact.[58]

(f) *Irregular presentment.*[59] The theory underlying paragraph (c) is unclear. It has been explained on the ground of waiver or estoppel[60]: that by failing to object to the irregularity the drawee acknowledges the sufficiency of the presentment, but nevertheless refuses to honour the bill on some other ground. The bill may therefore be treated as dishonoured by non-acceptance.

**6–020** **Subsection (3): reason to believe that bill will be dishonoured.**[61] Presentment for acceptance is not excused in the circumstances set out in this subsection[62] (which only applies to cases where presentment is obligatory).[63]

**6–021** **Effect of excuses.** A bill may be treated as dishonoured by non-acceptance when presentment is excused. If acceptance is nevertheless obtained, *e.g.* from a personal representative of the drawee, it will not be dishonoured. A bill is dishonoured by non-acceptance when presentment for acceptance is excused and the bill is not accepted,[64] with the result that an immediate right of recourse against the drawer and indorsers accrues to the holder, and no presentment for payment is necessary.[65]

---

[53] See above, para.2–052.

[54] Under s.5(2), where the drawee is a fictitious person or a person not having capacity to contract, the holder may treat the instrument, at his option, as a promissory note, in which case provisions relating to presentment for acceptance will not apply (s.89(3)).

[55] See *Smith v Bellamy* (1817) 2 Stark 223 (s.5, Illustration 5).

[56] See above, para.3–002. See also s.5(2) (n.54, above).

[57] *Smith v Bank of New South Wales* (1872) L.R. 4 P.C. 194, 205–208. See also ss.46(2)(a), 50(2)(a).

[58] *Smith v Bank of New South Wales*, (1872) L.R. 4 P.C. 194 at 208. See also *Bateman v Joseph* (1810) 12 East 433 (notice of dishonour).

[59] The common law on this point was very doubtful: Chalmers (9th ed.), pp.2, 162.

[60] See *Crawford and Falconbridge* (8th ed.), p. 1553.

[61] This subs. was declaratory: *Re Agra Bank* (1867) L.R. 5 Eq. 160, 165.

[62] See also ss.46(2)(a) and 50(2)(a).

[63] See s.39(1)(2).

[64] s.43(1)(b).

[65] s.43(2).

**Presentment for acceptance and payment compared.** Comparing pre-    6–022
sentment for acceptance with presentment for payment,[66] it is clear that
the two cases are governed by somewhat different considerations. Speaking generally, presentment for acceptance should be personal, while presentment for payment should be local. A bill should be presented for
payment where the money is. Anyone can then hand over the money.[67] A
bill should be presented for acceptance to the drawee himself, for he has
to write the acceptance; but the place where it is presented is compar-
atively immaterial, for all he has to do is to take the bill. Again (except in
the case of demand drafts), the day for payment is a fixed day; but the
drawee cannot tell on what day it may suit the holder to present a bill for
acceptance. These considerations are material as bearing on the question
whether the holder has exercised reasonable diligence[68] to effect
presentment.

### Non-acceptance

**42. When a bill is duly presented for acceptance and is not accepted**    6–023
**within the customary time, the person presenting it must treat it as**
**dishonoured by non-acceptance. If he do not, the holder shall lose his**
**right of recourse against the drawer and indorsers.**

| Definitions | Comparison |
|---|---|
| "acceptance": ss.2, 17(1). | UCC: § 3–502 |
| "bill": s.2. | ULB: art.44. |
| "holder": s.2. | UNB: art.54. |
| "person": s.2. | |

COMMENT

**"Duly presented."** The rules for due presentment for acceptance are    6–024
set out in section 41(1). The person who presents a bill for acceptance
must deliver it up to the drawee if required so to do.[69]

---

[66] s.45.
[67] *Royal Bank of Canada v Davidson* (1972) 25 D.L.R. (3d) 202, 209.
[68] ss.41(2)(b), 46(2)(a).
[69] But see *Brookes' Notary* (6th ed.), p.78, as to an alleged practice where it is thought unsafe
to leave the bill with the drawee. The holder, after exhibiting the bill to him, leaves a
formal notice that the bill lies for acceptance at a specified address.

**6–025** **"Not accepted."** As to what constitutes acceptance, see sections 2, 17, 18 and 19 of the Act. In a case in 1818,[70] Bayley J. said[71]:

> "Where a bill is, in the usual course of business, left for acceptance it is the duty of the party who leaves it to call again for it, and to inquire whether it has been accepted or not. It is not . . . the duty of the other person to send it to him, unless . . . there is a usual course of dealing between the particular individuals concerned so to do."

The court then proceeded to decide what the Act now makes clear,[72] namely that the prolonged retention and ultimate destruction of the bill by the drawee does not amount to an acceptance.

**6–026** **"Within the customary time."** Chalmers commented[73]: "The probable effect of [this section] as regards trade bills, is this: If a bill, left for acceptance within business hours one day, is not accepted before the close of business hours on the next day, it must be noted for non-acceptance, or otherwise treated as dishonoured." In *Bank of Van Diemen's Land v Bank of Victoria*[74] the Privy Council recognised as customary that the drawee is entitled to retain the bill for 24 hours,[75] but after the expiration of this time he must redeliver it[76] accepted or unaccepted. In reckoning the 24 hours, non-business days[77] are to be excluded.[78]

**6–027** **"Must treat it as dishonoured by non-acceptance."** Notice of dishonour must be given to the drawer and each indorser[79] and any necessary protest effected.[80]

**Dishonour by non-acceptance, and its consequences**

**6–028** **43. (1) A bill is dishonoured by non-acceptance—**
**(a) when it is duly presented for acceptance, and such an acceptance as is prescribed by this Act is refused or cannot be obtained; or**

---

[70] *Jeune v Ward* (1818) 1 B. & Ald. 653.
[71] At 659.
[72] In s.17(2).
[73] 9th ed., p.164.
[74] (1871) L.R. 3 P.C. 526.
[75] At 546, 547.
[76] See s.51(8) (protest for non-delivery).
[77] See s.92.
[78] (1871) L.R. 3 P.C. 526, 547.
[79] s.48.
[80] s.51(2).

    (b) when presentment for acceptance is excused and the bill
       is not accepted.
  (2) Subject to the provisions of this Act when a bill is dis-
     honoured by non-acceptance, an immediate right of recourse
     against the drawer and indorsers accrues to the holder, and no
     presentment for payment is necessary.

| Definitions | Comparison |
|---|---|
| "acceptance": ss.2, 17(1). | UCC: § 3–502. |
| "bill": s.2. | ULB: art.44. |
| "holder": s.2. | UNB: art.54. |

## COMMENT

**Subsection (1): dishonour by non-acceptance.** This subsection defines   6–029
those situations in which a bill is dishonoured by non-acceptance. Acceptance is dealt with in sections 2, 17, 18 and 19 of the Act, due presentment
for acceptance in section 41(1) and excuses for non-presentment for
acceptance in section 41(2). By section 44(1), the holder has an option to
take or refuse a qualified acceptance.

A bill which has been dishonoured by non-acceptance may subsequently be accepted.[81]

**Subsection (2): its consequences.** On non-acceptance the holder has   6–030
an "immediate right of recourse", that is, resort, to the drawer and
indorsers; but no right of action arises until he has performed the conditions precedent by giving notice of dishonour, and protesting, when
necessary.[82] The subsection may, therefore, be taken to be subject to the
provisions of sections 48 and 51, as to notice of dishonour and protest. It
may also be taken to be subject to section 15 (referee in case of need) and
sections 65 to 68 (acceptance for honour). The holder is under no obligation to resort to the case of need. But if he does so, or if he obtains an
acceptance for honour, his right of recourse against the drawer and
indorsers is suspended.

**Duties as to qualified acceptances**

  **44. (1) The holder of a bill may refuse to take a qualified acceptance,**   6–031
       **and if he does not obtain an unqualified acceptance may treat**
       **the bill as dishonoured by non-acceptance.**

[81] s.18(2), (3).
[82] *Castrique v Bernabo* (1844) 6 Q.B. 498. For precedents of pleadings, see Appendix B(2).

(2) Where a qualified acceptance is taken, and the drawer or an indorser has not expressly or impliedly authorised the holder to take a qualified acceptance, or does not subsequently assent thereto, such drawer or indorser is discharged from his liability on the bill.

The provisions of this sub-section do not apply to a partial acceptance, whereof due notice has been given. Where a foreign bill has been accepted as to part, it must be protested as to the balance.

(3) When the drawer or indorser of a bill receives notice of a qualified acceptance, and does not within a reasonable time express his dissent to the holder he shall be deemed to have assented thereto.

| Definitions | Comparison |
|---|---|
| "acceptance": ss.2, 17(1). | UCC: § 3–410. |
| "bill": s.2. | ULB: art.26. |
| "foreign bill": s.4. | UNB: art.43. |
| "holder": s.2. | |

COMMENT

6–032    **Subsection (1): refusal to take qualified acceptance.** The holder of a bill may refuse to take a qualified acceptance. What is a qualified acceptance is defined in section 19(2) of the Act, namely an acceptance which in express terms varies the effect of the bill as drawn.[83] If the holder refuses to take a qualified acceptance, and so elects to treat the bill as dishonoured by non-acceptance, he should promptly give notice of dishonour[84] and effect any necessary protest.[85]

6–033    **Subsections (2) and (3): qualified acceptance taken.** If the holder takes a qualified acceptance, then (except in the case of a partial acceptance, below) this will discharge the drawer and any indorser who has not expressly or impliedly authorised the holder to take a qualified acceptance. However, the drawer or such indorser may subsequently assent thereto. The holder should therefore at once give notice of the qualified

[83] For examples of qualified acceptance, see s.19(2)(a)–(e); above, para.2–127.
[84] s.48.
[85] s.51.

acceptance to the drawer and indorsers.[86] If the drawer or an indorser receives such notice, and does not within a reasonable time express his dissent to the holder, he is deemed to have assented thereto,[87] and is not discharged.

**Partial acceptance.** The holder may take a partial acceptance, that is to say, an acceptance to pay part only of the amount for which the bill is drawn.[88] A partial acceptance of which "due notice" has been given does not discharge the drawer and indorsers. The expression "due notice" is not explained or defined, but presumably is to be interpreted in the same way as notice of dishonour.[89] A foreign bill[90] accepted as to part must be protested as to the balance.

6–034

## Rules as to presentment for payment

**45.** Subject to the provisions of this Act a bill must be duly presented for payment. If it be not so presented the drawer and indorsers shall be discharged.

6–035

A bill is duly presented for payment which is presented in accordance with the following rules—

(1) Where the bill is not payable on demand, presentment must be made on the day it falls due.

(2) Where the bill is payable on demand, then, subject to the provisions of this Act, presentment must be made within a reasonable time after its issue in order to render the drawer liable, and within a reasonable time after its indorsement, in order to render the indorser liable.

In determining what is a reasonable time, regard shall be had to the nature of the bill, the usage of trade with regard to similar bills, and the facts of the particular case.

(3) Presentment must be made by the holder or by some person authorised to receive payment on his behalf at a reasonable hour on a business day, at the proper place as herein-after defined, either to the person designated by the bill as payer, or to some

---

[86] For a form of notice, see Appendix A, Notice 5.
[87] Subs.(3) settled a doubtful point in favour of the holder: see *Rowe v Young* (1820) 2 Bligh 391 HL: *Chalmers* (9th ed.), pp.2, 168.
[88] s.19(2)(b).
[89] See ss.48, 49. For a form of notice, see Appendix A, Notice 4.
[90] See s.4.

person authorised to pay or refuse payment on his behalf if with the exercise of reasonable diligence such person can there be found.

(4) A bill is presented at the proper place—

    (a) Where a place of payment is specified in the bill and the bill is there presented.

    (b) Where no place of payment is specified, but the address of the drawee or acceptor is given in the bill, and the bill is there presented.

    (c) Where no place of payment is specified and no address given, and the bill is presented at the drawee's or acceptor's place of business if known, and if not, at his ordinary residence if known.

    (d) In any other case if presented to the drawee or acceptor wherever he can be found, or if presented at his last known place of business or residence.

(5) Where a bill is presented at the proper place, and after the exercise of reasonable diligence no person authorised to pay or refuse payment can be found there, no further presentment to the drawee or acceptor is required.

(6) Where a bill is drawn upon, or accepted by two or more persons who are not partners, and no place of payment is specified, presentment must be made to them all.

(7) Where the drawee or acceptor of a bill is dead, and no place of payment is specified, presentment must be made to a personal representative, if such there be, and with the exercise of reasonable diligence he can be found.

(8) Where authorised by agreement or usage a presentment through [a postal operator] is sufficient.

Amendment

S.45(8) was amended by the Postal Services Act 2000 (Consequential Modifications No.1) Order 2001, SI 2001/1149.

| Definitions | Comparison |
|---|---|
| "bill": s.2. | UCC: §§ 3–501, 4–204. |
| "business day": s.92. | ULB: arts 38, 42, 53. |
| "holder": s.2. | ULC: arts 3, 28–31. |
| "indorsement": s.2. | UNB: arts 55, 57. |
| "issue": s.2. | |
| "person": s.2. | |
| "postal operator": s.2 | |

COMMENT

**Presentment for payment.** A bill, cheque[91] or note[92] must be duly    6–036
presented for payment.[93] The provisions of the Act to which this requirement is subject include section 46 (excuses for non-presentment and
delay), section 39(4) (domiciled bill coming forward late) and section
43(2) (no presentment for payment necessary where a bill is dishonoured
by non-acceptance).

**Consequences of failure to present.** The consequences of a failure to    6–037
make due presentment for payment vary according to the nature of the
instrument.

(i) *Bills of exchange.* If a bill is not duly presented, the drawer and    6–038
indorsers will be discharged.[94] But due presentment is not generally
required to preserve the liability of the acceptor as the party primarily
liable on the bill. By section 52(1) of the Act, when a bill is accepted
generally[95] presentment for payment is not necessary in order to render
the acceptor liable. However, by the terms of a qualified acceptance[96] the
acceptor may stipulate that presentment for payment is required, *e.g.* by
an acceptance to pay only at a particular specified place.[97] In such a case,
the bill must be presented for payment before the acceptor can be liable;
but he will nevertheless not be discharged by the omission to present the
bill for payment on the day that it matures in the absence of an express
stipulation to that effect.[98]

(ii) *Cheques.* If a cheque is not duly presented, the indorsers will be    6–039
discharged.[99] But by section 74 of the Act, where a cheque is not presented for payment within a reasonable time of its issue, the drawer is not
discharged,[1] although under certain conditions he may be discharged to
the extent that he suffers actual damage by reason of the delay.[2] It is
generally accepted that section 74 prevails over the provisions of the

---

[91] s.73.
[92] s.89(1). See also s.87(2).
[93] For the conflict of laws, see below, para.12–031 (s.72(3)).
[94] s.45. If an indorser pays in ignorance that the bill has not been duly presented, the
payment may be recoverable as having been made under a mistake of fact: *Milnes v
Duncan* (1827) 6 B. & C. 671 (s.59, Illustration 13).
[95] See s.19(1)(2), and in particular s.19(2)(c).
[96] s.19(1)(2).
[97] s.19(2)(c).
[98] s.52(2).
[99] ss.45, 73.
[1] *King & Boyd v Porter* [1925] N.I. 103. This was the position at common law: see below,
para.13–017 (s.74).
[2] s.74(1).

present section and thus establishes a different regime for cheques.[3] However, due presentment for payment to the drawee bank is in other respects necessary (unless excused)[4] before the drawer can be sued.[5]

**6–040**  (iii) *Promissory notes.* Presentment for payment is necessary in order to render the indorser of a note liable.[6] Indorsers will be discharged if the note is not duly presented for payment.[7] But the maker of a note, being the party primarily liable, will be liable even though the note is not presented for payment,[8] unless the note is in the body of the instrument payable at a particular place, in which case it must be presented for payment at that place in order to render the maker liable.[9] However, as in the case of bills, the maker will not be discharged by the omission to present the note for payment on the day that it matures in the absence of an express stipulation to that effect.[10]

**6–041**  **Guarantors.** Presentment for payment is not generally[11] a condition precedent to the liability of a person who, not being a party to the instrument, has given a separate guarantee for its payment by the acceptor or maker.[12] But, in the absence of a contrary stipulation in the contract of guarantee, the guarantor of the drawer of a bill or of an indorser of a bill, cheque or note will presumably be discharged from liability if the instrument is not duly presented for payment,[13] since his liability is prima facie co-extensive with that of the party guaranteed.[14] It may also be assumed that the guarantor of the drawer of a cheque will prima facie be liable only to the same extent and in the same circumstances as the drawer.

On the other hand, if a guarantor merely signs the instrument as anomalous indorser,[15] then, in common with any other indorser, he will

---

[3] *King & Boyd v Porter* [1925] N.I. 103. See below, para.13–017 (s.74).
[4] See s.46(2)(c); below, para.6–074.
[5] *Interlease Ltd v Georgiladakis* 1980 (1) S.A. 376; *Goodwin v Diplomat Hotel* 1982 (3) S.A. 350; *Van Vuuren v Van Vuuren* 1994 (4) S.A. 209.
[6] s.87(2). See also s.87(3).
[7] ss.45, 89(1), (2). See also s.86.
[8] s.87(1).
[9] s.87(1).
[10] ss.52(2), 89(1), (2).
[11] It might, however, be so where presentment for payment is necessary to charge the acceptor or maker.
[12] *Warrington v Furbor* (1807) 8 East 242, 245; *Holbrow v Wilkins* (1822) 1 B. & C. 10; *Hitchcock v Humfrey* (1843) 5 M. & G. 559; *Walton v Mascall* (1844) 13 M. & W. 452; *Carter v White* (1883) 25 Ch.D. 666. But in these cases it is suggested that the guarantor might be discharged if damnified.
[13] *Philips v Astling* (1809) 2 Taunt. 207; *Hitchcock v Humfrey* (1843) 5 M. & G. 559 at 564.
[14] See *Chitty on Contracts* (29th ed.), Vol.II, § 44–088.
[15] See s.56.

be discharged from liability on the instrument if it is not duly presented for payment.[16]

**Duty of creditor holding third party instrument.** There is nineteenth   6–042
century authority for the view that, where a bill,[17] upon which a debtor is not primarily liable,[18] is accepted by a creditor as conditional payment of or as security for a debt, the creditor must do all that is necessary to obtain payment of the instrument. He must, therefore, duly present it for payment. If he does not do so, and the debtor is thereby prejudiced,[19] he is guilty of "laches" and makes the instrument his own, so that he cannot hold the debtor liable on the debt or other consideration for which the instrument was given.[20] It is questionable whether this principle has survived into the modern law.[21]

**Bank collections.**[22] In international trade transactions presentment for   6–043
payment and the collection of the proceeds of bills of exchange is frequently effected by utilising the services of commercial banks. The seller's bill for the price is presented to the buyer for acceptance and payment by the seller's bank or by that bank's correspondent in the buyer's country. This procedure is convenient and relatively inexpensive, and confers certain advantages on the seller: first, where the bill is accompanied by commercial documents, those documents will not be released to the buyer except against acceptance or payment of the bill; secondly, a finance facility may be associated with the collection, enabling the seller to obtain funding from his bank in advance of the payment of the bill by the buyer; thirdly, for the most part banks operate within a well-defined set of rules, the ICC Uniform Rules for Collections, which adumbrate the duties and responsibilities of the banks involved, so that

---

[16] *Yeoman Credit Ltd v Gregory* [1963] 1 W.L.R. 343 (Illustration 2).
[17] There seems no reason in principle why this should not also apply to a cheque: see *Hopkins v Ware* (1869) L.R. 4 Ex. 268 (creditor accepts cheque drawn by agent of debtor). But see below, para.13–018 (s.74).
[18] *cf. Price v Price* (1847) 16 M. & W. 232; *Atkinson v Hawdon* (1835) 2 A. & E. 628 (s.64, Illustration 8).
[19] A number of the cases cited in n.20 (below) do not, however, stress any element of prejudice.
[20] *Anderton v Beck* (1812) 16 East 248; *Soward v Palmer* (1818) 8 Taunt. 277; *Camidge v Allenby* (1827) 6 B. & C. 373; *Robson v Oliver* (1847) 10 Q. B. 704, 715; *Peacock v Pursell* (1863) 14 C.B., N.S. 728. *cf. Robson v Oliver* (1847) 10 Q.B. 704, 715. Contrast *Goodwin v Coates* (1832) 1 M. & Rob. 221. See also *Bridges v Berry* (1810) 3 Taunt. 130 (failure to give notice of dishonour); *Alderson v Langdale* (1832) 3 B. & Ad. 660 (alteration of bill) (s.64, Illustration 7); *Hopkins v Ware* (1869) L.R. 4 Ex. 268 (where the debtor was not a party to the cheque but liable on the consideration).
[21] In particular it is disputed by Goode, *Commercial Law* (3rd ed.), 510.
[22] See *Benjamin's Sale of Goods* (6th ed.), §§ 22–076—22–138.

the seller can with confidence expect that all the necessary steps will be taken to obtain payment of the instrument.

6–044    **ICC Uniform Rules for Collections.** The Uniform Rules for Collections were first promulgated by the International Chamber of Commerce in 1956 and were revised in 1967, 1978 and 1995. The current version of the Rules is that of 1995 (URC 522).[23] They derive their force from agreement of the parties to the transaction[24] and not from any international convention, although they are adhered to by banks in many countries of the world.

The Rules apply to all collections, as defined in the Rules.[25] "Collection" means the handling by banks, in accordance with instructions received, of "documents", in order to (a) obtain payment and/or acceptance, or (b) deliver commercial documents against payment and/or acceptance, or (c) deliver documents on other terms and conditions.[26] Documents are divided into two classes: "financial documents", that is to say, bills of exchange, promissory notes, cheques, or other similar instruments used for obtaining payment of money, and "commercial documents", that is to say, invoices, transport documents, documents of title or other similar documents, or any other documents whatsoever, not being financial documents.[27] The Rules differentiate between "clean collection" and "documentary collection". The former means collection of financial documents not accompanied by commercial documents. The latter means collection of financial documents accompanied by commercial documents or commercial documents not accompanied by financial documents.[28]

The parties to a collection are defined in the Rules.[29] The customer entrusting the handling of a collection to a bank is termed the "principal". The bank to which the principal has entrusted the handling of a collection is termed the "remitting bank". Any bank, other than the remitting bank, involved in processing the collection is termed the "collecting bank". The collecting bank making presentation to the drawee is termed the "presenting bank". The person to whom presentation is to be made in accordance with the collection instruction is termed the "drawee". The drawee, as so defined, is not necessarily the drawee of the instrument. Presentation for payment may be ordered to be made to a bank of a bill drawn by

---

[23] Effective January 1, 1996.
[24] Art.1(a) (incorporation in text of the collection instruction), but *cf. Harlow and Jones Ltd v American Express Bank Ltd* [1990] 2 Lloyd's Rep. 343 (incorporation by usage). Any specific provision can be excluded by express stipulation and, in any event, is without effect if proved to be contrary to any imperative provision of the governing domestic law.
[25] Art.1(a).
[26] Art.2(a).
[27] Art.2(b).
[28] Art.2(c)(d).
[29] Art.3(a)(b).

the seller on the buyer, and in such a case the bank is the "drawee" under the rules and not the buyer upon whom the bill is drawn.

**Collection instruction.** The process of collection is initiated by the principal completing a "collection instruction" incorporating the Rules and giving complete and precise instructions.[30] Banks are only permitted to act upon the instructions given in such collection instruction, and in accordance with the Rules.[31] The collection instruction should contain details of the bank from which the collection was received, the principal, the drawee and the presenting bank, amount and currency to be collected, list of documents, terms and conditions upon which payment and/or acceptance is to be obtained, terms of delivery of documents, charges and interest to be collected, method of payment and form of payment advice and instructions in case of non-payment or non-acceptance and/or non-compliance with other instructions.[32] If any bank elects, for any reason, not to handle a collection or any related instructions received by it, it must advise the party from whom it received the collection or instructions without delay.[33] 6–045

**Process of collection.** The collection instruction is passed by the principal to the remitting bank. The remitting bank may be in a position to collect the bill through a branch in the buyer's country, but more often it will employ a correspondent for this purpose. The remitting bank must, under the Rules, utilise as the collecting bank the bank nominated by the principal, but will, in the absence of such nomination, utilise any bank, of its own or another's choice, in the country of payment or acceptance, or in the country where other terms and conditions have to be complied with.[34] The documents and the collection instruction may be sent to the collecting bank directly or through another (correspondent) bank as intermediary.[35] It is for the presenting bank to make presentation for payment or acceptance.[36] 6–046

**Liabilities and responsibilities of banks.** The liabilities and responsibilities of the banks involved are set out in the Rules, and cover such 6–047

---

[30] Art.4(a)(i).
[31] Art.4(a)(i).
[32] Art.4(b)(c).
[33] Art.1(c); *Minories Finance Ltd v Afribank Nigeria Ltd* [1995] 1 Lloyd's Rep. 134, 139.
[34] Art.5(d).
[35] Art.5(e).
[36] Where the bill is domiciled for payment with the buyer's bank, that bank may be the presenting bank, and will present for payment to itself.

matters as presentation,[37] payment,[38] acceptance,[39] protest,[40] case-of-need[41] and protection of goods,[42] advice of fate[43] and interest charges and expenses.[44] A detailed analysis of these is outside the scope of the present work.[45] The general principle is set out in Article 9 that "Banks will act in good faith and exercise reasonable care." Under Article 12, banks must determine that the documents received appear to be as listed in the collection instruction and must without delay advise the party from whom the collection instruction was received of any documents missing or found to be other than listed,[46] but they have no further obligation to examine the documents.[47] Under Article 13, "banks assume no liability for the form, sufficiency, accuracy, genuineness, falsification or legal effect of any documents, or for the general and/or particular conditions stipulated in the documents or superimposed thereon" and they are not to be responsible for the goods or for persons involved in the transaction.[48] They are specifically exempted (*inter alia*) from liability for loss or delay of items in transit or for errors in transmission, translation or the interpretation of technical terms[49] and for events of *force majeure*.[50]

At common law, in the absence of any agreement to the contrary,[51] the remitting bank would be liable to the principal for the acts of the collecting bank, its agent.[52] However, Article 11 of the Rules provides that "Banks utilizing the services of another bank or other banks for the purpose of giving effect to the instructions of the principal do so for the account of and at the risk of such principal", and further provides that banks assume no liability should the instructions they transmit not be carried out, even if they have themselves taken the initiative in the choice of such other banks. The collection instruction will also normally state

---

[37] Arts 5–8.
[38] Arts 16–19.
[39] Art.22.
[40] Art.24.
[41] *i.e.* the principal's representative in the foreign country. Art.25.
[42] Art.10.
[43] Art.26.
[44] Arts 20, 21.
[45] See *Benjamin's Sale of Goods* (6th ed.), §§ 22–076—22–138.
[46] Art.12(a).
[47] Art.12(a)(c).
[48] But in *Linklaters v HSBC Bank plc* [2003] EWHC 1113 (Comm); [2003] 2 Lloyd's Rep. 545, it was held that the disclaimer in art.13 did not prevent the implication of a warranty on the part of the remitting bank to the presenting bank that the principal was entitled to the proceeds of a cheque remitted for collection (see below, para.6–051).
[49] Art.14.
[50] Art.15.
[51] *Calico Printers' Association v Barclays Bank* (1931) 145 L.T. 51.
[52] *Mackersy v Ramsays, Bonars & Co.* (1843) 9 Cl. & Fin. 818; *Trading and General Investment Corp. v Gault Armstrong & Kemble Ltd* [1986] 1 Lloyd's Rep. 195, 201. See also *Bowstead and Reynolds on Agency* (17th ed.), § 5–011.

that the remitting bank is not to be liable for any loss, damage or delay which is not directly due to the negligence of the remitting bank.[53] The collecting bank will be liable to indemnify the remitting bank against loss (if any) sustained by the remitting bank in the event of negligence or failure by the collecting bank to act in accordance with its instructions.[54] But this would appear to leave the principal without any effective legal remedy. There is no privity of contract between the principal and his sub-agent, the collecting bank, even though the delegation was effected with the principal's authority[55]; and in the absence of such privity the rights and duties arising out of the contract between the principal and the remitting bank, and between the remitting bank and the collecting bank, respectively, are only enforceable by and against the immediate parties to those contracts.[56] The collecting bank could not therefore be sued in contract by the principal, nor would it be liable to account to the principal[57] or be susceptible to an action in restitution for money had and received.[58] In some circumstances it might be possible to bring a direct action against the collecting bank in tort[59] or for breach of fiduciary duty.[60] But otherwise the principal would have to persuade the remitting bank to bring an action against the collecting bank in its own name, which it would only do (if at all) if suitably indemnified by the principal in respect of its costs and expenses. It is however, at least arguable that, since the principal and the collecting bank both become "parties" to the collection[61] and agree to be bound by the Rules, this is sufficient to indicate an intention that the rights and liabilities created by the Rules are to be enforceable between them and so to establish privity of contract under the Rules.[62]

---

[53] This exclusion may be subject to the test of reasonableness under s.3 of the Unfair Contract Terms Act 1977.

[54] *Bank of Scotland v Dominion Bank* [1891] A.C. 592. See *Bowstead and Reynolds on Agency* (17th ed.), Ch.6.

[55] *Prince v Oriental Bank Corp.* (1878) 3 App. Cas. 325, 335; *Calico Printers' Association v Barclays Bank* (1931) 145 L.T. 51, 56; *Bowstead and Reynolds on Agency* (17th ed.), §§ 5–008—5–016.

[56] *Bowstead and Reynolds on Agency* (17th ed.), § 5–011. But see Contract (Rights of Third Parties) Act 1999, s.1(1)(2).

[57] *Lockwood v Abdy* (1845) 14 Sim. 437.

[58] *Robbins v Fennell* (1847) 11 Q.B. 248; *Cobb v Becke* (1845) 6 Q.B. 930; *New Zealand & Australian Land Co. v Watson* (1881) 7 Q.B.D. 374.

[59] *Henderson v Merrett Syndicates Ltd* [1995] 2 A.C. 145. But *cf. Balsamo v Medici* [1984] 1 W.L.R. 951.

[60] *Bowstead and Reynolds on Agency* (16th ed.), § 5–012.

[61] ICC Uniform Rules for Collections (1995), art.3.

[62] *Clarke v Earl of Dunraven* [1897] A.C. 59; *Motani Lounge (Pty) Ltd v Standard Bank of South Africa Ltd* 1995 (2) S.A. 498. See also the observations of Rix J. in *Bastone & Firminger Ltd v Nasima Enterprises (Nigeria) Ltd* [1996] C.L.C. 1902 referred to in *Benjamin's Sale of Goods* (6th ed.), § 22–092, n.43.

Article 11(c) of the Rules also provides that "A party instructing another to perform services shall be bound by and liable to indemnify the instructed party against all obligations and responsibilities imposed by foreign law and usages". It is a moot point whether this will, for example, entitle the collecting bank to an indemnity from the remitting bank against a liability arising from a pitfall in the foreign law, *e.g.* the fact that a cheque crossed "a/c payee" is not negotiable in English law,[63] or whether the indemnity is limited to taxes and similar imposts which may be imposed on a collecting bank by foreign law.[64] The latter is, it is submitted, the more reasonable interpretation.

6–048     **Subsections (1) and (2): time for due presentment for payment.** Where a bill is not payable on demand, presentment must be made on the day it falls due.[65] This also applies to notes which are not payable on demand.[66] The day on which such an instrument falls due is to be determined by reference to the terms of the instrument and section 14 of the Act.[67] Presentment on the day after[68] or the day before[69] the due date is not due presentment. If a bill is presented for payment prior to the due date and returned dishonoured by non-payment, this does not dispense with the necessity for presentment on the due date.[70]

A bill payable on demand must be presented for payment within a reasonable time after its issue[71] in order to render the drawer liable, and within a reasonable time after its indorsement[72] in order to render the indorser liable.[73] The latter rule also applies to cheques[74]; but the drawer of a cheque is in a different position in this respect from the drawer of a bill payable on demand, since the provisions of section 45 are modified by section 74 of the Act.[75] Where a note payable on demand has been

---

[63] See s.81A, below, para.14–037.
[64] *Linklaters v HSBC Bank plc* [2003] EWHC 1113 (Comm), [2003] 2 Lloyd's Rep. 545 at [61–62].
[65] s.45(1). This subsection was declaratory: *Philpot v Briant* (1828) 4 Bing. 717, 720. See also ICC Uniform Rules for Collections (1995), art.6.
[66] s.89(1).
[67] See also ss.18(3), 65(5).
[68] *Yeoman Credit Ltd v Gregory* [1963] 1 W.L.R. 343 (Illustration 2).
[69] *Hamilton Finance Co. Ltd v Coverley Westray Walbaum & Tosetti Ltd* [1969] 1 Lloyd's Rep. 53, 72 (Illustration 1).
[70] *Hamilton Finance Co. Ltd v Coverley Westray Walbaum & Tosetti Ltd* [1969] 1 Lloyd's Rep. 53, 72 (Illustration 1). See s.46(2)(a).
[71] Defined in s.2.
[72] Defined in s.2.
[73] s.45(2). See also ICC Uniform Rules for Collections (1995), Brochure 522, art.6.
[74] s.73. A particular problem arises with respect to post-dated cheques, since such a cheque may be indorsed long before the date on the face of the cheque, before which date the cheque cannot be paid. *Paget* (8th ed.), pp.223–224, suggested that post-dating extends the reasonable time for presentment for payment.
[75] *King & Boyd v Porter* [1925] N.I. 103. See below, para.13–017.

indorsed, it must be presented for payment within a reasonable time of its indorsement, otherwise the indorser is discharged.[76]

A bill or note is payable on demand which is expressed to be payable on demand, or at sight, or on presentation, or in which no time for payment is expressed.[77] A cheque is, by definition, payable on demand.[78]

**"Within a reasonable time."** Subsection (2) indicates the matters to be taken into account in determining what is a reasonable time. In a pre-Act case concerning a promissory note,[79] this was said to be a mixed question of fact and law. It is probably still so,[80] although it has been asserted that the question is now solely one of fact.[81] **6–049**

**Subsections (3) to (8): due presentment.** These subsections set out further rules for due presentment for payment. The person presenting the bill for payment must exhibit the bill to the person from whom he demands payment, and when a bill is paid must forthwith deliver it up to the person paying it.[82] If the bill be lost, a copy should be presented and an indemnity tendered.[83] As to bills in a set, see section 71. **6–050**

**By whom due presentment must be made.** For a bill to be duly presented for payment, presentment must be made "by the holder or by a person authorised to receive payment on his behalf". The obligation of the acceptor[84] is to pay the holder—that is, the person who can give a good discharge for the bill.[85] "Holder" is defined in section 2. Presentment by the holder in person is not required: "the document itself must be present, though not the holder".[86] A person presenting an instrument for payment does not, by so doing, warrant its authenticity or that of the documents attached to it.[87] But it has been held that, where a collecting **6–051**

---

[76] s.86(1).
[77] s.10.
[78] s.73.
[79] *Chartered Mercantile Bank of India, London & China v Dickson* (1871) L.R. 3 P.C. 574, 584.
[80] *Bank of British North America v Haslip* (1914) 20 D.L.R. 922.
[81] See *Byles* (29th ed.), 24–10, and the other Canadian cases there cited.
[82] s.52(4). But see (truncation of cheques), below, para.6–063.
[83] *cf.* ss.69, 70. Chalmers (9th ed.), p. 170, doubted whether this was sufficient, as s.70 hardly seems to meet the case.
[84] Or, in the case of a note, the maker: see s.88, 89(2).
[85] See s.59 and *Walker v Macdonald* (1848) 2 Exch. 527, 532.
[86] *Griffin v Weatherby* (1868) L.R. 3 Q.B. 753, 760. See also s.45(8) (presentment through the post).
[87] *East India Co. v Tritton* (1824) 3 B. & C. 280, 289, 291; *Leather v Simpson* (1871) L.R. 11 Eq. 398; *Guaranty Trust Co. of New York v Hannay & Co.* [1918] 2 K.B. 623, 631, 632; *Greenwood v Martins Bank Ltd* [1933] A.C. 51, 59–60; *Linklaters v HSBC Bank plc* [2003] EWHC (Comm) 1113, [2003] 2 Lloyd's Rep. 545 at [38].

banker employs another banker as his agent to present a cheque for payment on behalf of a customer, the collecting banker impliedly warrants to his agent that the customer is entitled to the proceeds of the cheque.[88]

A collecting agent is liable to his principal if he does not use due diligence in presenting an instrument for payment.[89] A collecting banker is liable to his customer for loss arising from such delay.[90] However, a banker is under no duty to his customer to advise him of the risks of collecting a cheque or other instrument in accordance with the customer's instructions, for example, of the tax implications of collecting a draft via London[91] or of the consequences of collecting a cheque crossed "account payee" for a person other than the named payee.[92]

**6–052**      **To whom due presentment must be made.** Presentment must be made "either to the person designated in the bill as payer, or to some person authorised to pay or refuse payment on his behalf". The person designated as the payer will be the acceptor or drawee (in the case of a bill or cheque) or the maker (in the case of a note). But, as a general rule, a personal demand on the acceptor, drawee or maker is unnecessary. It is his duty to see that the money is ready on the appointed day at the appointed place.[93] If the holder, after the exercise of reasonable diligence, cannot find there any person authorised to pay or refuse payment, he has done all that is required of him.[94] Thus the bill may be drawn or accepted payable at a bank.[95]

Special rules are set out in subsections (6) and (7):

> (a) *Two or more drawees.* Where a bill is drawn upon or accepted by two or more persons who are not partners, and no place of

---

[88] *Honourable Society of the Middle Temple v Lloyds Bank plc* [1999] 1 All E.R. (Comm) 193; *Linklaters v HSBC Bank plc* [2003] EWHC (Comm) 1113, [2003] 2 Lloyd's Rep. 545, but some doubts were expressed by Gross J. in this latter case at [40].

[89] See *Paget* (12th ed.), 22.9; *Bowstead and Reynolds on Agency* (17th ed.), § 6–013. But see above, para.6–047 (sub-agent).

[90] *Lubbock v Tribe* (1838) 3 M. & W. 607. cf. ICC Uniform Rules for Collections (1995), Brochure 522, arts 6, 9, 11; above, para.6–044.

[91] *Schioler v Westminster Bank Ltd* [1970] 2 Q.B. 719, 726.

[92] *Redmond v Allied Irish Bank plc* [1987] F.L.R. 307 (although this case was decided before the Cheques Act 1992, below, para.17–050); *Levett v Barclays Bank plc* [1995] 1 W.L.R. 1260, 1272; *Honourable Society of the Middle Temple v Lloyds Bank plc* [1999] 1 All E.R. (Comm) 193.

[93] *De Bergareche v Pillin* (1826) 3 Bing. 476, 478.

[94] s.45(5); *Hine v Allely* (1833) 4 B. & Ad. 624 (Illustration 5); *Buxton v Jones* (1840) 1 M. & G. 83 (Illustration 6).

[95] See below, para.6–055. See also ICC Uniform Rules for Collections (1995), art.3(b), definition of "drawee": above, para.6–043.

payment is specified, presentment must be made to them all.[96] Of course, if one pays, or in refusing payment acts as the agent of the others, that is enough. If a place of payment is specified, the bill may be presented there.[97]

(b) *Drawee or acceptor dead.* Where the drawee or acceptor of a bill is dead, and no place of payment is specified, presentment must be made to a personal representative, if such there be, and with the exercise of reasonable diligence he can be found.[98] It should be noted that, unlike presentment for acceptance,[99] presentment for payment in this case is not excused. But, again, if a place of payment is specified, the bill may be presented there.[1]

**Day and hour.** Presentment must be made on a business day, defined   **6–053** in section 92 of the Act.

Presentment must also be made "at a reasonable hour". The reasonableness of the hour will depend on whether the instrument is payable at a place of business or at a private house. The payer is not bound to stay at his place of business after a reasonable hour. If a bill be payable at a bank, it must be presented within banking hours[2]; if at a trader's place of business, then within business hours[3]; if at a private house, probably a presentment up to bedtime would be sufficient.[4]

These requirements do not, however, apply where a cheque is presented under section 74B (which permits the "truncation" of cheques).[5]

**Where due presentment must be made.**[6] In contrast with presentment   **6–054** for acceptance,[7] it is essential that a bill or cheque be presented for payment at the proper place. Subsection (4) sets out, in sequence, the

---

[96] Subs.(6). This was probably declaratory, but the point was not clear. See also ss.85, 89 (promissory notes).

[97] s.45(4)(a).

[98] Subs.(7). This was declaratory. See also s.89 (promissory notes).

[99] s.41(2)(a).

[1] s.45(4)(a). See *Philpot v Briant* (1827) 3 C & P. 244 (Illustration 3).

[2] *Parker v Gordon* (1806) 7 East 385; *Elford v Teed* (1813) 1 M. & S. 28; *White v Bank of England* (1835) 1 C.M. & R. 744. But *cf. Baines v National Provincial Bank* (1927) 137 L.T. 631 (cheque presented after advertised time of closing, but before the bank closed); *Eaglehill Ltd v Needham (J.) Builders Ltd* [1973] A.C. 992 (bill presented by post to bank when post opened). In *Garnett v Woodcock* (1817) 6 M. & S. 44 it was held that a bill irregularly presented outside banking hours, but refused payment on another ground, could be treated as dishonoured by non-payment (see s.41(2)(c): presentment for acceptance).

[3] *Barclay v Bailey* (1810) 2 Camp. 527; *Morgan v Davison* (1815) 1 Stark. 114. See also *Triggs v Newnham* (1825) 1 C. & P. 631 (attorney's office).

[4] *Wilkins v Jadis* (1831) 2 B. & Ad. 188, 189.

[5] s.74B(2); see below, paras 6–063, 13–023.

[6] See also ICC Uniform Rules for Collections (1995), arts 4(b)(iii), 5.

[7] See above, para.6–022 (s.41).

rules for ascertaining that place. However, under section 74A of the Act[8] a banker may specify by public notice an alternative place at which cheques drawn on him may be presented for payment and, in addition, the rules do not apply where presentment of a cheque is made under section 74B ("truncation" of cheques).[9] The rules relating to the place of payment of a promissory note are to be found in section 87 of the Act.

**6–055**    (i) *Place of payment specified.* A bill is not invalid by reason that it does not specify the place where it is payable,[10] but a place of payment may be specified in the bill either by the drawer[11] or by the acceptor.[12] If, by a qualified acceptance,[13] the acceptor undertakes to pay only at a particular specified place,[14] presentment for payment at that place is necessary to render him liable on the bill.[15] If, on the other hand, he accepts to pay at a particular place, but the acceptance does not expressly state that the bill is to be paid there only and not elsewhere, this is a general acceptance[16]: presentment for payment at that place is not necessary to render him liable,[17] but the bill must nevertheless be presented for payment at that place to preserve the liability of the drawer and indorsers.[18] Where a place of payment is specified by the drawer, presentment must be made at that place to charge the drawer and indorsers.[19]

If alternative places of payment are specified,[20] then, on the wording of paragraph (a) of the subsection, presentment at either place is sufficient.[21] If the drawer specifies one place, but the acceptor by his acceptance specifies another, this would appear to be a qualified acceptance[22] which, if taken, would probably require the bill to be duly presented at the place specified in the acceptance.[23]

---

[8] Inserted by the Deregulation (Bills of Exchange) Order 1996, SI 1996/2993.

[9] Inserted by the Deregulation (Bills of Exchange) Order 1996, SI 1996/2993. See s.74B(2) and below, paras 6–063, 13–023.

[10] s.3(4).

[11] *Banku Polski v K. J. Mulder & Co.* [1941] 2 K.B. 266; [1942] 1 K.B. 497 (s.19, Illustration 4).

[12] s.19(2)(c).

[13] s.19(2).

[14] s.19(2)(c).

[15] s.19(2). But see s.52(2) (time).

[16] s.19(1), (2)(c).

[17] s.52(1).

[18] *Gibb v Mather* (1832) 2 Cr. & J. 254 (Illustration 4). See above, para.6–038.

[19] *Beirnstein v Usher* (1895) 11 T.L.R. 356; but not the acceptor: see *Banku Polskiego v K.J. Mulder & Co.* [1941] 2 K.B. 266 (unless it is stated to be payable at that place only and not elsewhere.

[20] See above, para.2–024 (s.3).

[21] See (before the Act) *Beeching v Gower* (1816) Holt 313 (note). See also *Pollard v Herries* (1803) 3 B. & P. 335 (note).

[22] *i.e.* because it "varies the effect of the bill as drawn" (see s.19(2)). But *cf.* s.19(2)(c).

[23] *Saul v Jones* (1858) 1 E. & E. 59.

Where the specified place of payment is a bank, presentment for payment must be made at that bank,[24] and, if a branch is specified, presentment must be made at that branch.[25] This duty is not affected by the fact that the holder is informed by or on behalf of the acceptor or drawee that no funds will be available to meet the bill at the specified bank or branch and that presentment should be made at another bank or branch.[26] The substitution of a different place of payment for that specified in the bill requires the consent of the drawer and of every indorser to the change.[27] Neither the bank nor the holder is authorised to alter the place of payment specified in the bill[28]: such an alteration of the bill or of an acceptance is a material alteration of the instrument.[29]

If, when the bill matures, the bank at which the bill is domiciled for payment is the holder of the instrument, but the acceptor has no assets there, this is sufficient presentment. No personal demand on the acceptor is necessary.[30] **6–056**

Should a bill be payable at the X Bank, specifying a particular town but not a branch or address, it is uncertain whether presentment may be duly made at any branch of the X Bank in that town, or whether presentment must be made to all branches[31] or to the principal branch in that town. Probably presentment at any branch will suffice.

It has been held[32] that a crossed cheque was duly presented for payment when it was presented by the payee in person at the bank on which it was drawn, even though the payee could expect that payment would be refused since the bank would be liable[33] to the true owner and to its customer, the drawer, if it paid a crossed cheque otherwise than to a banker.

(ii) *No place of payment specified.* Where no place of payment is specified, but the address of the drawee or acceptor is given in the bill,[34] due **6–057**

---

[24] *Saunderson v Judge* (1795) 2 H.Bl. 509; *Hopley v Dufresne* (1813) 3 Camp. 463; *Gibb v Mather* (1832) 2 Cr. & J. 254 (Illustration 4); *Saul v Jones* (1858) 1 E. & E. 59; *Yeoman Credit Ltd v Gregory* [1963] 1 W.L.R. 343 (Illustration 2).

[25] *City Bank v Australian Joint Stock Bank* (1870) 9 S.C.R. (N.S.W.) 259.

[26] *Yeoman Credit Ltd v Gregory* [1963] 1 W.L.R. 343.

[27] *Thoneman v Holmes* [1945] S.A.S.R. 227, 233; *Yeoman Credit Ltd v Gregory* [1963] 1 W.L.R. 343, at 353.

[28] *Thoneman v Holmes* [1945] S.A.S.R. 227 at 233.

[29] s.64(1), (2).

[30] *Bailey v Porter* (1845) 14 M. & W. 44. See also *Royal Bank of Canada v Davidson* (1972) 25 D.L.R. (3d) 202 (note).

[31] *cf. Hardy v Woodroofe* (1818) 2 Stark. 399.

[32] *Ringham v Hackett, The Times*, February 8, 1980, referred to and criticised in *Byles* (27th ed.), 12–10.

[33] See below, para.14–020 (s.79).

[34] *cf. Saul v Jones* (1858) 1 E. & E. 59.

presentment is to be made at that address.[35] Thus if a bill is drawn on "XYZ Ltd, 156 Strand, London WC2", it should be presented for payment at that address. In the case of a note, where the address of the maker is given in the instrument, presentment to the maker elsewhere than at that address, if sufficient in other respects, will suffice to render the indorser liable.[36] But, in the case of a bill, paragraph (b) of subsection (4) requires presentment at the address given in the bill in order to render the drawer and indorsers liable.

6–058     (iii) *No address given.* If no place of payment is specified and no address given, due presentment is to be made at the drawee's or acceptor's place of business if known, and if not, at his ordinary residence if known.[37]

6–059     (iv) *In any other case.* In any other case, due presentment is made if the bill is presented to the drawee or acceptor wherever he can be found, or if it is presented at his last known place of business or residence.[38] The words "in any other case" are to be interpreted as meaning that personal presentment to the drawee or acceptor, or at his last known place of business or residence, is permitted only where none of paragraphs (a), (b) or (c) applies. It is available, therefore, only as a last resort.

6–060     **No authorised person to be found.** Subsection (5) deals with the situation where, after the exercise of reasonable diligence, no person authorised to pay or refuse payment can be found at the "proper place" for payment ascertained in accordance with subsection (4). Such a situation might arise, for example, where a place of payment is specified or an address given in the bill, but the holder or his agent finds no or no responsible person there, or that the drawee or acceptor has removed from that address,[39] or that the premises are shut up[40] or have ceased to exist.[41] In such a case, there is no necessity for the holder to proceed to the alternatives set out in paragraphs (c) and (d) of subsection (4). Since no person authorised to pay or refuse payment can be found at the proper place designated in paragraphs (a) or (b) of that subsection, no further presentment to the drawee or acceptor is required.

---

[35] *Hine v Allely* (1833) 4 B. & Ad. 624 (Illustration 5); *Buxton v Jones* (1840) 1 M. & G. 83 (Illustration 6).

[36] s.87(2).

[37] Presumably reasonable diligence must be exercised to discover the place of business or residence.

[38] These seem to be genuine alternatives.

[39] *Buxton v Jones* (1840) 1 M. & G. 83 (Illustration 6).

[40] *Hine v Allely* (1833) 4 B. & Ad. 624 (Illustration 5).

[41] Alternatively, this might be a case falling within s.46(2)(a).

Reasonable diligence must, however, be exercised at the proper place to find such a person.[42]

**Presentment by post.** Presentment through a postal operator[43] is suffi-   6–061
cient where authorised by agreement or usage.[44] The usage of bankers does not authorise presentment by post except by a bank.

**Presentment through a clearing house.** The process used for the clear-   6–062
ing of cheques through a clearing house (or "exchange centre") is described in Ellinger, Lomnicka and Hooley, *Modern Banking Law*,[45] and in the award of Bingham J. (sitting as judge–arbitrator) in *Barclays Bank plc v Bank of England*.[46] In the *Barclays Bank* case, Bingham J. held that, where Bank A ("the Presenting Bank") receives from a customer for collection a cheque drawn upon Bank B ("the Paying Bank") by a person having an account at a branch of the paying bank, and the cheque is dealt with through the inter-bank system for clearing cheques, the presenting bank's responsibility to its customer in respect of the collection of the cheque is discharged only when the cheque is physically delivered to that branch of the paying bank for decision whether it should be paid or not.[47] In arriving at this conclusion, Bingham J. rejected the view put forward in previous editions of Chalmers,[48] and adopted by the Supreme Court of Ireland in *Royal Bank of Ireland v O'Rourke*,[49] that presentment to the paying bank takes place when the cheque is delivered to the employee or agent of the paying bank at the clearing house.[50]

A general description of the clearing system can be obtained from the website of the Association for Payment Clearing Services (APACS) at *www.apacs.org.uk*. Cheque clearing is governed by Rules for the Conduct of Cheque Clearing.

---

[42] *Collins v Butler* (1738) 2 Str. 1087.
[43] Defined in s.2.
[44] See, *e.g. Prideaux v Criddle* (1869) L.R. 4 Q.B. 455; *Heywood v Pickering* (1874) L.R. 9 Q.B. 428; *Hamilton Finance Ltd v Coverley Westray Walbaum & Tosetti Ltd* [1969] 1 Lloyd's Rep. 53 (Illustration 1); *Eaglehill Ltd v Needham (J.) Builders Ltd* [1973] A.C. 992 (s.49, Illustration 16).
[45] (3rd ed., 2002), p.331. See also Goode, *Commercial Law* (3rd ed.), 535; Brindle and Cox, *Law of Bank Payments* (3rd ed.), Ch.7, Pt III.
[46] [1985] 1 All E.R. 385.
[47] At 394 (relying on *Hare v Henty* (1861) 10 C.B., N.S. 65, 69; *Prideaux v Criddle* (1869) L.R. 4 Q.B. 455; *Bank of British North America v Haslip* (1914) 19 D.L.R. 576, 581, affirmed (1914) 20 D.L.R. 922; *Riedell v Commercial Bank of Australia Ltd* [1931] V.L.R. 382; *H.H. Dimond (Rotorua 1966) Ltd v Australia & New Zealand Banking Group Ltd* [1979] 2 N.Z.L.R. 739). The same rule has been applied in Canada to presentment at a data centre: *Advance Bank v Toronto Dominion Bank* (2003) 227 D.L.R. (4th) 755.
[48] 13th ed., p.148.
[49] [1962] I.R. 159.
[50] At 392 (relying on *Bailey v Bodenham* (1864) 16 C.B., N.S. 288, 296; *Prince v Oriental Bank Corp.* (1878) 3 App. Cas. 325, 328).

**6–063**    **Truncation of cheques.** Major changes in the clearing process would, however, take place if "truncation" of cheques were generally adopted.[51] Section 74B of the Act permits, as an alternative method of presentment, the notification of the essential features of a cheque by electronic means or otherwise instead of by presenting the cheque itself.[52] Presentment can thus be made by the electronic transmission from the collecting bank to the bank on whom the cheque is drawn of the information in the magnetic ink code line at the bottom of the cheque without any movement of the cheque itself or even transmission of an electronic image of the cheque. Further, section 74A of the Act permits a bank to specify by public notice an alternative place, *e.g.* a data processing centre or its head office, where cheques drawn on it may be presented for payment.[53]

**6–064**    **Presentment and collection at same branch.** Where a cheque drawn by one customer is received by a banker from another customer for credit to his account at the same branch on which it is drawn, the cheque is not passed through the clearing system but is the subject of an "in-house" payment. It is a question of fact whether it is presented to the banker for payment in his capacity as drawee or whether it is received by him as agent for collection.[54]

ILLUSTRATIONS

**6–065**    1. Two bills of exchange are drawn by the first defendants upon and duly accepted by N Ltd payable to the first defendants at Westminster Bank Ltd, 53 Threadneedle Street, EC2, 90 days after date. They are indorsed by the first defendants to the second defendants and by them to the claimants. The due date of payment of both bills is January 1, 1966. The first bill is delivered by the claimants to their bankers for collection on December 31, but is not received by the Westminster Bank, Threadneedle Street, until January 4. It is returned dishonoured on that day. The second bill is despatched by post by the claimants' bankers for collection

---

[51] Some banks have already commenced truncation of cheques in the case of "on-us" items, that is to say, cheques drawn on the bank by one customer and payable to another customer of the same bank and deposited with the bank for collection.

[52] Inserted by art. 4 of the Deregulation (Bills of Exchange) Order 1996, SI 1996/2993, as a result of the recommendation of the Review Committee on Banking Services Law and Practice (1989) Cm. 622, reg. 7(8) (above, para.11), accepted by the Government (1990) Com. 1026, Annex 5, paras 5.11–5.13. See Vroegop [1990] L.M.C.L.Q. 244.

[53] Inserted by art.3 of the Deregulation (Bills of Exchange) Order 1996, SI 1996/2993.

[54] *Boyd v Emmerson* (1834) 2 A. & E. 184; *Sutherland v Royal Bank of Scotland plc.* 1997 S.L.T. 329. *cf. Carpenters' Co. v British Mutual Banking Co. Ltd* [1938] 1 K.B. 511 (s. 60, Illustration 1).

through general clearing on December 29. It is received by the Westminster Bank, Threadneedle Street, on December 31, and returned by them dishonoured by post on the same day. Section 45(1) of the Act has not been complied with. The first bill has been presented after the due date. The second bill has been presented before the due date, and section 46(2) of the Act cannot be relied on to excuse subsequent presentment on the due date. The first defendants as drawers and indorsers and the second defendants as indorsers are discharged.[55]

2. Two bills of exchange are drawn by the claimants upon and duly accepted by E.C. Ltd payable at the N.P. Bank, Piccadilly, to the order of the claimants. Each bill is indorsed by the defendant and two other directors of E.C. Ltd as sureties.[56] The first bill is a fixed date bill with a due date for payment December 9. The second bill is an on demand bill. The claimants send the bills to their bankers on December 8 in order that they may be presented for payment, but, before they are presented, the claimants are informed on behalf of E.C. Ltd that the bills should be presented instead to the Midland Bank, Golden Square, with whom arrangements have been made for payment. Accordingly the bills are presented on December 9, to Midland Bank, which refuses to honour them, and are subsequently represented on December 11 to National Provincial Bank, by whom they are also dishonoured. In respect of the first (fixed date) bill, failure to present at the proper place on the due date discharges the defendant as indorser. In respect of the second (on demand) bill, the question of time of presentment does not arise. Due notice of dishonour having been given by the claimants to the defendant on December 11, the defendant is liable on that bill.[57]

3. A bill is accepted "Payable at No.18 Bishopsgate Street". The acceptor dies. Presentment at 18 Bishopsgate Street is sufficient, and there is no need for presentment to the deceased's executrix. The drawer is liable.[58]

4. The acceptors of a bill accept it payable at "Messrs Jones, Lloyd & Co., bankers, London". The bill is presented for payment on the due date to the acceptors in Liverpool. The drawer is discharged, since the bill has not been presented at the proper place.[59]   **6–066**

---

[55] *Hamilton Finance Ltd v Coverley Westray Walbaum & Tosetti Ltd* [1969] 1 Lloyd's Rep. 53. See also below, para.6–095 (s.48, Illustration 2).
[56] See below, para.7–030.
[57] *Yeoman Credit Ltd v Gregory* [1963] 1 W.L.R. 343. See also below, para.6–118 (s.49, Illustration 21) and above, para.2–147 (s.20, Illustration 19).
[58] *Philpot v Briant* (1827) 3 C. & P. 244.
[59] *Gibb v Mather* (1832) 2 Cr. & J. 254.

5. A bill is drawn upon "P.P., No.6 Bridge Row, Watling Street" and is accepted generally by him. The bill is presented for payment on the due date at 6 Bridge Row, but the house is found shut up. This is sufficient and the drawer is liable.[60]

6. A bill is addressed to "F.E., No.38 Minto Street, Baal-zephon Street, Bermondsey". F.E. accepts it generally. On the due date a messenger takes the bill to 38 Minto Street and inquires for F.E. A woman lodging in the house informs him that F.E. has gone. This is sufficient. No personal demand on F.E. is necessary to charge a prior indorser.[61]

### Excuses for delay or non-presentment for payment

6–067    46. (1) Delay in making presentment for payment is excused when the delay is caused by circumstances beyond the control of the holder, and not imputable to his default, misconduct, or negligence. When the cause of delay ceases to operate presentment must be made with reasonable diligence.

     (2) Presentment for payment is dispensed with—

      (a) Where, after the exercise of reasonable diligence presentment, as required by this Act, cannot be effected.
The fact that the holder has reason to believe that the bill will, on presentment, be dishonoured, does not dispense with the necessity for presentment.

      (b) Where the drawee is a fictitious person.

      (c) As regards the drawer where the drawee or acceptor is not bound, as between himself and the drawer, to accept or pay the bill, and the drawer has no reason to believe that the bill would be paid if presented.

      (d) As regards an indorser, where the bill was accepted or made for the accommodation of that indorser, and he has no reason to expect that the bill would be paid if presented.

      (e) By waiver of presentment, express or implied.

| Definitions | Comparison |
|---|---|
| "bill": s.2. | UCC: § 3–504. |
| "holder": s.2. | ULB: art.54. |
| "person": s.2. | ULC: art.48. |
| | UNB: art.56. |

---

[60] *Hine v Allely* (1833) 4 B. & Ad. 624.
[61] *Buxton v Jones* (1840) 1 M. & G. 83.

COMMENT

**Excuses relating to presentment for payment.** This section deals with   6–068
excuses for delay in presentment for payment and with those situations
where presentment for payment is dispensed with. It applies also to
promissory notes.[62] The section is primarily of importance only where it
is sought to charge the drawer or indorser of a bill or cheque or the
indorser of a note.[63] But subsection (2) will also be of relevance where
presentment for payment is necessary to render liable the acceptor of a
bill[64] or the maker of a note.[65]

**Subsection (1): delay in presenting for payment excused.** Examples   6–069
of circumstances excusing delay might be the sudden death of the holder,
or his serious illness so that he is unable to attend to business or give
instructions, an outbreak of hostilities preventing access to the place of
payment,[66] and (where the bill can be duly presented by post)[67] a delay
in the post.[68]
  If presentment is delayed at the request of the drawer or indorser
sought to be charged, the delay is presumably excused.[69]
  See also section 39(4) (domiciled bill coming forward late).

**Subsection (2): when presentment for payment dispensed with.** The   6–070
dispensations from presentment for payment are more limited than the
excuses for non-presentment for acceptance.[70] For example, presentment
for payment is not dispensed with where the person designated by the
instrument as payer is dead[71] or bankrupt[72] or is a person not having
capacity to contract.[73] They are also more limited than the dispensations
from giving notice of dishonour.[74]

**Presentment cannot be effected.** If, after the exercise of reasonable   6–071
diligence, presentment for payment cannot be effected as required by

---

[62] s.89(1).
[63] See above, paras 6–038, 6–040 (s.45).
[64] ss.19(2)(c), 52(2).
[65] s.87(1).
[66] *Patience v Townley* (1805) 2 Smith 223.
[67] s.45(8).
[68] *cf. Hamilton Finance Co. v Coverley Westray Welbaum & Tosetti Co.* [1969] 1 Lloyd's Rep. 53, 72 (postal delay alleged not proved).
[69] *Lord Ward v Oxford Ry Co.* (1852) 2 De G.M. & G. 750. See also waiver, below, para.6–076.
[70] s.41(2).
[71] *cf.* s.41(2)(a). But see s.45(4)(a), (7).
[72] *cf.* s.41(2)(a). See s.46(2)(a).
[73] *cf.* s.41(2)(a). But such a case might fall within s.46(2)(c). See also s.5(2).
[74] s.50(2).

section 45 of the Act,[75] then it is entirely dispensed with. In practice, there will be few situations where due presentment cannot be made at the "proper place" determined in accordance with section 45(4), although in *Cornelius v Banque Franco-Serbe*[76] the holder of a cheque drawn on an Amsterdam bank was dispensed from presenting it for payment on the ground that presentment there was impossible due to the occupation of Amsterdam by hostile German forces. Cases may, however, arise where the person designated by the bill as payer, or some other person authorised to pay or refuse payment on his behalf, cannot be found.[77]

Reasonable diligence is required of the person presenting the instrument for payment.[78] This is probably a question of mixed law and fact.

6–072    **Presentment futile.** English law has never, in general,[79] favoured the view that presentment is dispensed with because it would in the circumstances be futile, *i.e.* because it is known that the bill will not in fact be paid. Thus, at common law, it was held that due presentment was not dispensed with in cases where, to the knowledge of the holder, the drawer ordered the acceptor not to pay the bill[80] or the acceptor became bankrupt[81] or absconded[82] before the due date, or where the acceptor stated that he could not or would not pay the bill at maturity.[83] Paragraph (a) of subsection (2) preserves this rule by providing that the fact that the holder has reason to believe that the bill will, on presentment, be dishonoured, does not dispense with the necessity for presentment.[84]

6–073    **Drawee a fictitious person.** Where the drawee is a fictitious person,[85] the holder may treat the instrument, at his option, either as a bill of exchange or as a promissory note.[86] If the holder elects to treat the instrument as a note, presentment for payment will not ordinarily be necessary to charge the drawer, as he will be deemed to be the maker of the note.[87] But, whether the holder elects to treat the instrument as a bill

---

[75] Or ss.86, 87 (notes).
[76] [1942] 1 K.B. 29 (Illustration 1).
[77] See s.45(3), (4)(d), (5), (7).
[78] *Collins v Butler* (1738) 2 Str. 1087; *Sands v Clarke* (1849) 8 C.B. 751 (Illustration 4) (note).
[79] But see s.46(2)(c) and (d), below.
[80] *Hill v Heap* (1823) Dowl. & Ry. N.P. 57.
[81] *Esdaile v Sowerby* (1809) 11 East 114, 117 (Illustration 3). See also *Nicholson v Gouthit* (1796) 2 H.Bl. 609 (note); *Bowes v Howe* (1813) 5 Taunt. 30 (note).
[82] *Sands v Clarke* (1849) 8 C.B. 751 (Illustration 4) (note).
[83] *Baker v Birch* (1811) 3 Camp. 107 (Illustration 5); *Bowes v Howe* (1813) 5 Taunt. 30 (note).
[84] *Hamilton Finance Co. v Coverlay Westray Walbaum & Tosetti Co.* [1969] 1 Lloyd's Rep. 53 (s.45, Illustration 1).
[85] This would appear to include a non-existing person: see above, paras 2–052 (s.5), 6–019 (s.41); below, para.6–131 (s.50). *cf.* s.7(3).
[86] s.5(2).
[87] See above, para.2–040 (s.5); *Miller v Thomson* (1841) 3 M. & G. 576 (s.5, Illustration 2); *Re British Trade Corp. Ltd* [1932] 2 Ch. 1 (s.5, Illustration 3).

or note, paragraph (b) of this subsection will dispense with the necessity for presentment, even to preserve the liability of indorsers.

**Dispensation as regards the drawer.** The prime example of the application of paragraph (c) of subsection (2) is where there are no funds in the account of the drawer of a cheque with the drawee bank and no arrangements made for an overdraft (with the result that the bank is not bound, as between itself and the drawer, to pay the cheque) and the drawer knows that the cheque will be dishonoured by non-payment.[88] It also presumably applies where the drawer of a cheque countermands payment[89] or where the cheque presented is out of date.[90]    **6–074**

In contrast with the dispensation from giving notice of dishonour provided for in section 50(2)(c) of the Act, the drawer must have no reason to believe that the bill would be paid if presented.[91] The words "no reason" mean "no tenable reason".[92] The relevant time would appear to be, in the case of a bill payable on or after a fixed date, the due date for payment,[93] and, in the case of a cheque or bill payable on demand, any time at which the holder could legitimately present the instrument for payment.[94]

It is to be noted that presentment for payment is only dispensed with under paragraph (c) in respect of the drawer. Presentment is still necessary for the liability of indorsers.[95] It is also to be noted that the fact that the *holder* has reason to believe that the instrument will, on presentment, be dishonoured does not in itself dispense with presentment for payment.[96]

**Accommodation bills.**[97] Under paragraph (d) of subsection (2), where a bill is accepted or made for the accommodation of an indorser, then, as    **6–075**

---

[88] *Wirth v Austin* (1875) L.R. 10 C.P. 689 (Illustration 6); *Re Bethell* (1887) 34 Ch.D. 561. See also *Terry v Parker* (1837) 6 A. & E. 502 (bill); *Re Boyse (No.3)* (1886) 33 Ch.D. 612 (bill).

[89] *Commercial Union Trade Finance v Republic Bottlers of South Africa (Pty) Ltd* 1992 (4) S.A. 728; *Navidos (Pty) Ltd v Essop* 1994 (4) S.A. 141. But the matter is not entirely free from doubt. In s.52(1)(c) of the Act (dispensation from notice of dishonour) countermand of payment (5) is listed separately from (4) "where the drawee or acceptor is as between himself and the drawer under no obligation to accept or pay the bill". *cf.* also *Hill v Heap* (1823) Dowl. & Ry. N.P. 57. In *Trapp & Co. v Prescott* (1912) 5 D.L.R. 183, affd 18 D.L.R. 794, countermand of payment was said to be a waiver of presentment by the drawer.

[90] *Commissioners of Inland Revenue v Thomas Cook (NZ) Ltd* [2003] 2 N.Z.L.R. 296; see below, para.13–065.

[91] *cf. Prideaux v Collier* (1817) 2 Stark. 57.

[92] *Re Boyse (No. 3)* (1886) 33 Ch.D. 612 at 624.

[93] Contrast the headnote in *Terry v Parker* (1837) 6 A. & E. 502.

[94] *Fiorentino Comm. Giuseppe Srl v Farnesi* [2005] 2 All E.R. 737 (Illustration 2). See also *Commercial Union Trade Finance v Republic Bottlers of South Africa (Pty) Ltd*, 1992 (4) S.A. 728.

[95] *Saul v Jones* (1858) 1 E. & E. 59, 70.

[96] s.46(2)(a); above.

[97] See above, para.4–041 (s.28).

regards that indorser, presentment will be dispensed with if he has no reason to expect that the bill would be paid if presented. Where, as is more usually the case, a bill is accepted for the accommodation of the drawer,[98] then, as regards the drawer, presentment may be dispensed with under paragraph (c)[99] if he has no reason to believe that the bill would be paid if presented, *e.g.* because he has failed to provide funds to the acceptor for its payment.

6–076    **Waiver.** The drawer of a bill, and any indorser, may insert therein an express stipulation waiving as regards himself the holder's duty to present the bill for payment.[1] But an express waiver outside the bill will also suffice.

Waiver may also be implied. It may be implied from the conduct of a party both before[2] and after the date for presentment. Thus if, after the date for presentment has passed, a party knows of the failure to present or of undue delay in presentment, but promises to pay the bill or makes or promises to make a part payment on account, a waiver may be implied.[3] But an admission of liability made in ignorance of the fact that the bill has not been duly presented will not constitute a waiver.[4]

A waiver will be effective only against the party making it.

ILLUSTRATIONS

6–077    1. The claimant sells and delivers coconut oil to a firm in Yugoslavia and receives in payment for the oil a cheque for 2,989 Dutch guilders drawn by the defendants, a French bank carrying on business in Belgrade, on a bank in Amsterdam. The claimant receives this cheque on May 10, 1940. On that day Germany invades Holland and on May 21 the British Government declares Holland to be enemy-occupied territory. It is

---

[98] But the drawer may also be an indorser.

[99] The acceptor is not normally bound, as between himself and the drawer, to pay the bill unless he is provided with funds to meet the bill at maturity: see above, para.4–045 (s.28).

[1] s.16(2).

[2] *Reisler v Kulcsar* (1965) 57 D.L.R. (2d) 730.

[3] *Hopley v Dufresne* (1812) 15 East 275; *Hodge v Fillis* (1813) 3 Camp. 463; *Singer v Elliott* (1887) 4 T.L.R. 34 and 524. See also *Newman v W.R. Browne & Son* [1925] 1 D.L.R. 676 (promise to renew note and pay interest). But an alternative view is that such a promise is merely prima facie evidence of due presentment for payment: see *Lundie v Robertson* (1806) 7 East 231; *Greenway v Hindley* (1814) 4 Camp. 52; *Croxon v Worthen* (1839) 5 M. & W. 5; *Sparrow v Corbett* (1913) 16 D.L.R. 184.

[4] *Keith v Burke* (1885) Cab. & El. 551. It is also submitted that the party alleged to have waived due presentment must have been aware at the time that the holder's failure duly to present the bill had the legal effect of discharging him from liability where this is the case: see *Ayer v Murray* (1909) 39 N.B.R. 170; *Peyman v Lanjani* [1985] Ch. 457.

impossible to present the cheque for payment in Amsterdam and after May 21 it is illegal to do so. Presentment for payment is dispensed with under section 46(2)(a) of the 1882 Act. Notwithstanding that presentment for payment in Amsterdam is illegal, the claimant can recover from the defendants (the drawers) on the cheque, payment by them being legal elsewhere.[5]

2. Three post-dated cheques are drawn payable to the claimants on successive dates. The first cheque is dishonoured on presentment to the drawer's bank for payament. The second and third cheques are never presented. Presentment of these cheques is excused if the drawer knew at any time at which they could be presented that the cheques would not in fact be paid.[6]

3. A bill is drawn by C upon H payable to the defendants' order and by them indorsed to the claimants. H accepts the bill. Both H (the acceptor) and C (the drawer) become insolvent. This does not dispense with due presentment for payment and notice of dishonour to charge the defendants.[7]

4. The defendant makes a promissory note payable in the body of it at    **6–078**
"No.11 Old Slip". When the note becomes due, the claimant is minded to present the note for payment at 11 Old Slip, but the defendant has absconded. There is no evidence that the note is ever presented there for payment. The claimant's action fails.[8]

5. A few days before a bill becomes due for payment, the acceptor tells the drawer that he will not be able to take it up. The bill is not presented by the holder to the acceptor for payment until some days after it has become due, and no notice of dishonour is given to the drawer. The drawer is not liable on the bill.[9]

6. The defendant draws two cheques upon the Huddersfield branch of the Midland Banking Co. payable to H or order, and these are indorsed by H to the claimant. At the time the cheques are drawn the defendant has no funds at the Huddersfield branch of the bank and has been notified by the bank that cheques drawn by him will not be paid. The claimant need not prove presentment at the Huddersfield branch or notice of dishonour

---

[5] *Cornelius v Banque Franco-Serbe* [1942] 1 K.B. 29 (a better report is to be found in [1941] 2 All E.R. 728).

[6] *Fiorentino Comm. Giuseppe Srl v Farnesi* [2005] 2 All E.R. 737.

[7] *Esdaile v Sowerby* (1809) 11 East 114.

[8] *Sands v Clarke* (1849) 8 C.B. 751. See s.87(1).

[9] *Baker v Birch* (1811) 3 Camp. 107.

in order to entitle him to sustain an action against the defendant, the drawer.[10]

### Dishonour by non-payment

6–079    47. (1) A bill is dishonoured by non-payment (a) when it is duly presented for payment and payment is refused or cannot be obtained, or (b) when presentment is excused and the bill is overdue and unpaid.

(2) Subject to the provisions of this Act, when a bill is dishonoured by nonpayment, an immediate right of recourse against the drawer and indorsers accrues to the holder.

| Definitions | Comparison |
|---|---|
| "bill": s.2. | UCC: § 3–502. |
| "holder": s.2. | ULB: arts 43, 47. |
| | ULC: arts 40, 44. |
| | UNB: art.58. |

### COMMENT

6–080    **Dishonour by non-payment.** This section deals with dishonour by non-payment and its effect. It applies to promissory notes[11] as well as to bills of exchange and cheques. Dishonour by non-payment may be an "actual dishonour" under paragraph (a) or a "deemed dishonour" under paragraph (b).

6–081    **Subsection (1)(a): actual dishonour.** Dishonour will occur if an instrument is duly presented for payment in accordance with section 45 of the Act[12] and payment is refused or cannot be obtained. Nothing less than payment will suffice, so that, for example, a cheque returned by the drawee bank with the answer "Refer to drawer" or "Present again" is dishonoured by non-payment. A holder may, but is not bound to, accept part payment: he may reject the part payment and treat the instrument as dishonoured.

A holder is entitled to demand payment in cash, unless he expressly or impliedly agrees to accept payment in some other form. Thus he cannot

---

[10] *Wirth v Austin* (1875) L.R.10 C.P. 689.
[11] s.89.
[12] Or (in the case of a note) in accordance with ss.86, 87.

be compelled, without his consent,[13] to accept a cheque or even a banker's draft for the amount. Where an instrument is drawn on or domiciled for payment with a banker and is presented for payment by a banker, payment will be made by settlement between the two bankers, and the proceeds credited to the customer's account.[14] What constitutes payment is discussed in the Comment to section 59, below.[15]

**Time of dishonour.** Since notice of dishonour can only be given after    6–082
dishonour,[16] it may be necessary to determine the time of dishonour by non-payment. In *Eaglehill Ltd v Needham Builders (J.) Ltd*,[17] on the maturity date of the bill the acceptor was in liquidation and in consequence there was no prospect of the bill being honoured on presentation. On behalf of the holder the collecting bank presented it by post for payment to the bank with whom it was domiciled for payment. Lord Cross said[18]:

> "If the acceptor is not bankrupt or in liquidation but has not a credit with the paying bank sufficient to cover the bill and that bank is not prepared to advance him the necessary money to cover it, it may well be that the bill is not dishonoured until it is returned through the post to the holder or the collecting bank. If, for instance, the paying bank were to ring up its customer saying that the bill would be dishonoured unless he put them in funds to meet it and he provided the necessary money that day I am not satisfied that the bill would have been dishonoured simply because the paying bank did not debit their customer's account with the necessary sum as soon as they saw it. But in this case where there could be no question of the acceptor meeting the bill I think that it was dishonoured as soon as the bank clerk who had authority to deal with the matter saw it and recognised that it was a bill which could not be met and would have to be returned to the holder or the collecting bank."

**Subsection (1)(b): deemed dishonour.** Dishonour will also occur    6–083
when presentment for payment is excused under section 46(2) of the Act[19] and the instrument is overdue and unpaid. A bill or note which is not payable on demand will be overdue once the due date for payment has passed, determined in accordance with section 14 of the Act.[20] Such an

---

[13] *cf. Meyer & Co. Ltd v Sze Hai Tong Banking and Insurance Co. Ltd* [1913] A.C. 847.
[14] See, in particular, cheques presented through a clearing house; above, para.6–062.
[15] para.8–005.
[16] See below, para.6–105 (s.49).
[17] [1973] A.C. 992 (s.49, Illustration).
[18] At 1011 (with whom Lords Reid, Diplock and Simon agreed at 1002, 1007).
[19] See above, para.6–070.
[20] See above, para.2–100.

instrument will therefore be dishonoured by non-payment on the day following the day on which payment falls due.

More difficulty, however, arises with respect to instruments payable on demand. By section 36(3) of the Act a bill payable on demand is deemed to be overdue, within the meaning and for the purposes of that section, when it appears on the face of it to have been in circulation for an unreasonable length of time. But that provision could not sensibly be applied to the word "overdue" in paragraph (b) of the present subsection, since it would mean that, when presentment for payment is excused, an unpaid demand instrument would not be dishonoured by non-payment until such an unreasonable length of time had elapsed. A different approach is therefore required. A demand instrument is at maturity from the date of its issue[20a] and payment is "due" as from that time. It is therefore submitted that, when presentment for payment is excused, the instrument should be deemed to be dishonoured by non-payment, for the purposes of the holder's immediate right of recourse under subsection (2),[21] immediately the event which dispenses the holder from presenting it for payment occurs.[22]

6–084     **Subsection (2): effect of dishonour.** When a bill is dishonoured by non-payment, an immediate right of recourse against the drawer and indorser accrues to the holder. The right of recourse must be distinguished from the right of action.[23] The subsection:

> "does not say that on the presentation and dishonour of the bill an immediate right of action against the drawer and the indorsers accrues to the holder, and I do not think that is the meaning. . . . In my opinion, s.47 means only that the holder of the bill may, immediately upon payment being refused by the acceptor, give notice to the drawer and the indorsers, telling them that he shall hold them liable upon it. But they, as well as the acceptor, still have the whole of the last day of grace[24] in which to pay the bill, and, if it is not paid

---

[20a] Or, in the case of a post-dated cheque, from the date on the cheque: *Fiorentino Comm. Giuseppe Srl v Farnesi* [2005] 2 All E.R. 737 (s.46, Illustration 2).

[21] And for the purposes of giving notice of dishonour under s.49(12). But delay in giving notice may be excused under s.50(1) or the circumstances may be "exceptional" (s.49(12)).

[22] *Commissioners of Inland Revenue v Thomas Cook (NZ) Ltd* [2003] 2 N.Z.L.R. 296. It must, however, be admitted that this view does not accord with *Re Boyse (No.3)* (1886) 33 Ch.D. 612 (where North J. held that the limitation period ran from the date the bill was presented and dishonoured, although he held that presentment for payment was dispensed with under s.46(2)(c)) and arguably does not accord with *Re Bethell* (1897) 34 Ch.D. 561 (where it was held that the limitation period in respect of a cheque ran from the date of its issue, or from a later promise to pay the cheque, presentment for payment being excused under s.46(2)(c)). See below, para.7–057 (s.57).

[23] *Kennedy v Thomas* [1894] 2 Q.B. 759 (Illustration).

[24] Days of grace have now been abolished: see above, para.2–100 (s.14).

before the end of that day, the holder's right of action against them becomes complete."[25]

The position is therefore that a right of recourse against the drawer and indorsers accrues to the holder immediately upon dishonour, so that he can at once give them notice of dishonour[26]; but his right of action accrues only when notice of dishonour is received,[27] and, where the instrument is not payable on demand,[28] does not in any event accrue until the day following the due date for payment.

The holder's right of action may also be subject to any necessary protest.[29]

**Collecting banker.** A collecting banker is entitled to debit his customer's account with the amount of a cheque which has been delivered to him for collection and credited to the account, if the cheque is dishonoured by non-payment.[30] This right arises out of the relationship of banker and customer and is not affected by any failure of the banker to give due notice of dishonour to the customer as indorser of the instrument.[31]   6–085

ILLUSTRATION

A bill of exchange for £75, dated October 16, 1893, is accepted by the defendant payable three months after date at the London and South Western Bank, Fleet Street Branch. The bill is presented for payment at the bank about 2.30 p.m. on January 19, 1894, *i.e.* on the third day of grace then allowed, but payment is refused. At a later hour on the same day the claimant (the holder) issues a writ against the defendant in respect of the bill. The action is dismissed as premature. The holder had no cause of action against the acceptor or the other parties to the bill until the expiration of that day.[32]   6–086

---

[25] *Kennedy v Thomas* [1894] 2 Q.B. 759 *per* Davey L.J. at 765.
[26] In *Eaglehill Ltd v Needham (J.) Builders Ltd* [1973] A.C. 992 (s.49, Illustration 16) the House of Lords held that notice of dishonour might be sent before the bill was dishonoured, provided that it was (or was deemed to be) received after dishonour.
[27] *Castrique v Bernabo* (1844) 6 Q.B. 498; see below, paras 6–105, 6–121.
[28] Where an instrument is payable on demand, the right of action accrues upon receipt of notice of dishonour.
[29] See below, para.6 143.
[30] *Capital and Counties Bank v Gordon* [1903] A.C. 240, 248. *cf. Huron & Eric Mortgage Corp. v Rumig* (1969) 10 D.L.R. (3d) 309.
[31] *Bank of Nova Scotia v Sharp* (1975) 57 D.L.R. (3d) 260.
[32] *Kennedy v Thomas* [1894] 2 Q.B. 759.

Notice of dishonour and effect of non-notice

6–087      48. Subject to the provisions of this Act, when a bill has been
dishonoured by non-acceptance or by non-payment, notice of dishonour must be given to the drawer and each indorser, and any
drawer or indorser to whom such notice is not given is discharged;
Provided that—
   (1) Where a bill is dishonoured by non-acceptance, and notice of
       dishonour is not given, the rights of a holder in due course
       subsequent to the omission, shall not be prejudiced by the
       omission.
   (2) Where a bill is dishonoured by non-acceptance and due notice
       of dishonour is given, it shall not be necessary to give notice
       of a subsequent dishonour by non-payment unless the bill
       shall in the meantime have been accepted.

| Definitions | Comparison |
|---|---|
| "acceptance": ss.2, 17(2). | UCC: § 3–503. |
| "bill": s.2. | ULB: art.45. |
| "holder": s.2. | ULC: art.42. |
| "holder in due course": s.29. | UNB: art.64. |

COMMENT

6–088      **Necessity for notice of dishonour.** This section applies to bills of
exchange, cheques and promissory notes.[33] It provides[34] that, where a bill
has been dishonoured by non-acceptance or by non-payment, notice of
dishonour is necessary to charge the drawer or indorser of a bill or
cheque[35] or the indorser of a note. The requirement of notice of dishonour
in English law has thus been explained by *Byles*[36]: "The law presumes
that, if the drawer has not had due notice, he is injured because otherwise
he might have immediately withdrawn his effects from the hands of the
drawee and that, if the indorser has not had timely notice, the remedy
against the parties liable to him is rendered more precarious." However,
the presumption, if it exists, is an absolute one: it is irrelevant that the
drawer or indorser has not in fact suffered any prejudice by reason of the

---

[33] s.89(1).
[34] Subject to s.49(15) (miscarriage by postal operator) and s.50 (excuses for non-notice and delay).
[35] But see, as regards the drawer of a cheque, the dispensations provided for in s.50(2)(c), (4), (5).
[36] 27th ed., 15–29.

absence of or delay in giving notice.[37] The giving of notice is therefore no trivial matter.[38]

**Meaning of notice of dishonour.** "Notice of dishonour" means notifi-  6–089
cation of dishonour, *i.e.* formal notice.[39] The fact that the drawer or indorser knows that the instrument has been dishonoured does not dispense with the necessity of giving him notice.[40] "That knowledge must be conveyed to him by a notification from the holder."[41] But mere knowledge of dishonour may be sufficient in certain circumstances. Where a person is an officer of two companies within the same group, knowledge of dishonour acquired by him in his capacity as an officer of the company required to give notice may be imputed to him in his capacity as an officer of the company entitled to receive it.[42] "Where a man holds a double character, it is not necessary that he should write a letter from himself in one character to himself to inform himself in another character."[43] However, the knowledge must come to him in circumstances in which it is his duty to communicate that knowledge to the company entitled to receive the notice.[44] This exception could possibly be explained also on the ground of waiver of notice.[45]

**Consequences of failure to give notice of dishonour.** Unless notice is  6–090
dispensed with or delay in giving it is excused, the drawer or indorser of a bill or cheque,[46] and the indorser of a note, to whom notice of dishonour is not duly given will be discharged from liability on the instrument.[47] No notice of dishonour need be given to the acceptor of a bill,[48] since it is his failure to pay the bill that gives rise to dishonour by non-payment. Nor is there any necessity for notice of dishonour to be given to the maker of a note.[49] This is so even though a bill is accepted or a note made payable at a bank or at an agent of the acceptor or maker.[50]

---

[37] The ULB (Art.45) and UNB (Art.68) provide only for an action for damages for loss caused by failure to give notice of dishonour.
[38] *Lombard Banking Ltd v Central Garage & Engineering Co. Ltd* [1963] 1 Q.B. 220, 231.
[39] *Burgh v Legge* (1839) 5 M. & W. 418, 422; *Carter v Flower* (1847) 16 M. & W. 743, 749.
[40] *Re Fenwick Stobart & Co.* [1902] 1 Ch. 507 (Illustration 1).
[41] *Re Leeds Banking Co.* (1865) L.R. 1 Eq. 1, 5.
[42] *Hamilton Finance Co. Ltd v Coverley Westray Walbaum & Tosetti Ltd* [1969] 1 Lloyd's Rep. 53 (Illustration 2). Contrast *Re Fenwick Stobart & Co.* [1902] 1 Ch. 507 (Illustration 1).
[43] *Re Fenwick Stobart & Co.* [1902] 1 Ch. 507 at 511.
[44] *ibid.* See also *Re Hampshire Land Co. (No.2)* [1896] 2 Ch. 743.
[45] s.50(2)(b); below, para.6–127.
[46] But see as regards the drawer of a cheque, the dispensations provided for in s.50(2)(c), (4), (5).
[47] *Berridge v Fitzgerald* (1869) L.R. 4 Q.B. 639, 642. cf. *Bank of Nova Scotia v Sharp* (1975) 57 D.L.R. (3d) 260 (collecting bank still entitled to debit its customer's account).
[48] s.52(3).
[49] ss.52(3), 89(2).
[50] *Treacher v Hinton* (1821) 4 B. & Ald. 413.

Failure to give due notice of dishonour is a complete defence to the party sought to be charged.[51]

**6–091**    **Guarantors.** Except as otherwise provided in the contract of guarantee, a guarantor of the undertaking of a party to whom notice of dishonour must be given will be discharged from liability if the failure to give due notice discharges the party guaranteed.[52]

Notice of dishonour need not be given to a person who has given his separate or collateral guarantee for its payment by the acceptor or maker.[53] However, in an old case *Philips v Astling*,[54] it was said that a person who guarantees the undertaking of the drawer is entitled to notice of dishonour unless both the drawer and drawee are bankrupt. But that case may be explained on the ground that the drawer (the principal debtor) had himself been discharged from liability by a failure of the holder duly to present the bill for payment and to give notice of dishonour to the drawer.[55] It runs contrary to the general principle that a guarantor is not, apart from special stipulation, entitled to notice of a default by the principal debtor.

On the other hand, a person who guarantees payment of an instrument by signing it as an anomalous indorser[56] will be discharged from liability on the instrument if he does not receive due notice of dishonour.[57] But this does not apply to the case of an *aval*.[58]

**6–092**    **Liability on consideration.** It has already been pointed out[59] that there is nineteenth-century authority for the view that, where a bill or note

---

[51] As to whether a party who is discharged by a failure to give notice of dishonour, but who nevertheless pays the bill, can recover the money paid from the recipient as money paid under a mistake, see *Byles* (27th ed.), 15–29; *Crawford and Falconbridge* (8th ed.), p.1576. Previously the money would be irrecoverable, having been paid under a mistake of law. But money paid under a mistake of law may now be recoverable: *Kleinwort Benson Ltd v Lincoln City Council* [1999] 2 A.C. 349. Such a party cannot recover from prior parties the amount paid: *Turner v Leech* (1821) 4 B & Ald. 451. cf. *Huntley v Sanderson* (1833) 1 Cr. & M. 467 (action by an agent against his principal for an indemnity in respect of the amount paid); *Godfrey v Hennelly* (1893) 19 V.L.R. 70 (cosureties).

[52] As his liability is normally coterminous with that of the principal debtor.

[53] *Swinyard v Bowes* (1816) 5 M. & S. 62; *Holbrow v Wilkins* (1822) 1 B. & C. 10; *Hitchcock v Humfrey* (1843) 5 M. & G. 559; *Black v Ottoman Bank* (1862) 15 Moore P.C. 472, 484; *Carter v White* (1883) 25 Ch.D. 666. See also *Murray v King* (1821) 5 B. & Ald. 165 (failure to give notice of dishonour did not discharge indorser from liability on a bond given to secure payment of the bill).

[54] (1809) 2 Taunt 207.

[55] *Hitchcock v Humfrey*, (1843) 5 M. & G. 559 at 564.

[56] s.56.

[57] *Yeoman Credit Ltd v Gregory* [1963] 1 W.L.R. 343 (s.49, Illustration 21); *Lombard Banking Ltd v Central Garage and Engineering Co. Ltd* [1963] 1 Q.B. 220 (s.49, Illustration 20). See also *Scott (S.A.) Pty Ltd v Dawson* [1962] N.S.W.R. 1166.

[58] *G. & H. Montage GmbH v Irvani* [1990] 1 W.L.R. 667 (s.72, Illustration 10).

[59] See above, para.6–042 (s.45).

upon which a debtor is not primarily liable is accepted by a creditor as conditional payment of or as security for a debt, the creditor must do all that is necessary to obtain payment of the instrument. It has also been held that, if the creditor fails to give notice of dishonour to the debtor, the debtor is discharged, not only from liability on the instrument, but also from any underlying indebtedness for which the instrument was given.[60] This harsh rule seems scarcely justifiable, unless the debtor has suffered substantial prejudice by the failure to give notice, *e.g.* where the failure renders the instrument worthless.[61] It may not in any event have survived into the modern law.

**The provisos: dishonour by non-acceptance.** It is not always neces-  6–093
sary to present a bill for acceptance.[62] But whether or not presentment for acceptance is required, if a bill is in fact presented for acceptance and acceptance is refused or cannot be obtained, notice of dishonour must be given to charge the drawer and indorsers.[63]

The first proviso protects a holder in due course from the consequences of an omission to give notice of dishonour by a previous holder.[64] "Holder in due course" is defined in section 29 of the Act. It is to be noted that only a person to whom the bill has been negotiated can be a holder in due course[65] and that a person who takes a bill with notice that it has been previously dishonoured by non-acceptance cannot be a holder in due course.[66]

By section 43(2) of the Act, when a bill is dishonoured by non-acceptance, an immediate right of recourse against the drawer and indorsers accrues to the holder,[67] and no presentment for payment is necessary. The second proviso states that, where a bill is dishonoured by non-acceptance and due notice of dishonour is given, it is not necessary to give notice of a subsequent dishonour by non-payment, unless the bill has been accepted in the meantime.[68]

---

[60] *Bridges v Berry* (1810) 3 Taunt. 130; *Camidge v Allenby* (1827) 6 B. & C. 373; *Peacock v Pursell* (1863) 14 C.B., N.S. 728; *Smith v Mercer* (1867) L.R. 3 Ex. 51. *cf. Camidge v Allenby* (1827) 6 B. & C. 373 (defendant is prior holder).
[61] *cf. Bank of Nova Scotia v Sharp* (1975) 57 D.L.R. (3d) 260.
[62] s.39(3).
[63] *Blesard v Hirst* (1770) 5 Burr. 2670, 2672; *Goodall v Dolley* (1787) 1 T.R. 712; *Roscow v Hardy* (1810) 12 East 434; *Dunn v O'Keeffe* (1816) 5 M. & S. 282.
[64] *Dunn v O'Keeffe* (1816) 5 M. & S. 282 (Illustration 3).
[65] See above, para.4–059 (s.29).
[66] s.29(1)(a). See also s.36(5)
[67] Subject to notice of dishonour to perfect the right of action: see above, para.6–030 (s.43).
[68] A bill may be accepted after it has been dishonoured by a previous refusal to accept: s.18(2).

**6–094**    **Conflict of laws.** By section 72(3) of the Act, the necessity for or sufficiency of a notice of dishonour, or otherwise, are determined by the law of the place where the bill is dishonoured.[69]

ILLUSTRATIONS

**6–095**    1. G Ltd, F Ltd and D Ltd, are companies within the same group. Their head offices are in the same room in London and one H acts as secretary for all three companies. F Ltd draw a bill on G Ltd payable to their own order. The bill is accepted by G Ltd and indorsed for value by F Ltd to D Ltd. It is dishonoured by non-payment but no formal notice of dishonour is given by D Ltd to F Ltd (the drawers). D Ltd cannot prove in the liquidation of F Ltd. The knowledge of H that the bill has been dishonoured does not constitute notice of dishonour to F Ltd, because that knowledge came to him in circumstances under which it was not his duty to communicate it to F Ltd.[70]

2. The claimants are a subsidiary company of P Ltd and the business of the two companies is carried on from the same office. One K is both a director of the claimants and the secretary of P Ltd. C Ltd draw five bills on N Ltd to their own order. These are accepted by N Ltd and indorsed by C Ltd to P Ltd and by P Ltd to the claimants. The bills are dishonoured by non-payment. No formal notice of dishonour is given by the claimants to P Ltd as indorsers. P Ltd must be taken to have had notice of dishonour. In the circumstances it would be an absurdity to require K to give himself, either in writing or by oral communication, notice of dishonour.[71]

3. On June 19 the defendants draw a bill for £1,000 on R & Co. payable one month after date to the order of S. On June 20 the bill is presented by S to R & Co. for acceptance, but acceptance is refused. No notice of dishonour is given by S to the defendants. Subsequently the bill is indorsed by S to the claimant, who takes it in good faith and for value and without notice of the dishonour. On July 13 the claimant presents the bill to R & Co. for acceptance, but acceptance is again refused. On the same

---

[69] See below, para.12–031.
[70] *Re Fenwick, Stobart & Co. Ltd* [1902] 1 Ch. 507.
[71] *Hamilton Finance Co. Ltd v Coverley Westray Walbaum & Tosetti Ltd* [1969] 1 Lloyd's Rep. 53. See also above, para.6–065 (s.45, Illustration 1).

day the claimant gives notice of dishonour to the defendants. The defendants are liable to the claimant on the bill. The claimant is not prejudiced by S's failure to give notice of dishonour to the defendants.[72]

## Rules as to notice of dishonour

**49.** Notice of dishonour in order to be valid and effectual must be given in accordance with the following rules— 6–096

(1) The notice must be given by or on behalf of the holder, or by or on behalf of an indorser who, at the time of giving it, is himself liable on the bill.

(2) Notice of dishonour may be given by an agent either in his own name, or in the name of any party entitled to give notice whether that party be his principal or not.

(3) Where the notice is given by or on behalf of the holder, enures for the benefit of all subsequent holders and all prior indorsers who have a right of recourse against the party to whom it is given.

(4) Where notice is given by or on behalf of an indorser entitled to give notice as herein-before provided, it enures for the benefit of the holder and all indorsers subsequent to the party to whom notice is given.

(5) The notice may be given in writing or by personal communication, and may be given in any terms which sufficiently identify the bill, and intimate that the bill has been dishonoured by non-acceptance or non-payment.

(6) The return of a dishonoured bill to the drawer or an indorser is, in point of form, deemed a sufficient notice of dishonour.

(7) A written notice need not be signed, and an insufficient written notice may be supplemented and validated by verbal communication. A misdescription of the bill shall not vitiate the notice unless the party to whom the notice is given is in fact misled thereby.

(8) Where notice of dishonour is required to be given to any person, it may be given either to the party himself, or to his agent in that behalf.

(9) Where the drawer or indorser is dead, and the party giving notice knows it, the notice must be given to a personal representative if such there be, and with the exercise of reasonable diligence he can be found.

[72] *Dunn v O'Keeffe* (1816) 5 M. & S. 282.

(10) Where the drawer or indorser is bankrupt, notice may be given either to the party himself or to the trustee.

(11) Where there are two or more drawers or indorsers who are not partners, notice must be given to each of them, unless one of them has authority to receive such notice for the others.

(12) The notice may be given as soon as the bill is dishonoured and must be given within a reasonable time thereafter.

In the absence of special circumstances notice is not deemed to have been given within a reasonable time, unless—

(a) where the person giving and the person to receive notice reside in the same place, the notice is given or sent off in time to reach the latter on the day after the dishonour of the bill.

(b) where the person giving and the person to receive notice reside in different places, the notice is sent off on the day after the dishonour of the bill, if there be a post at a convenient hour on that day, and if there be no such post on that day then by the next post thereafter.

(13) Where a bill when dishonoured is in the hands of an agent, he may either himself give notice to the parties liable on the bill, or he may give notice to his principal. If he give notice to his principal, he must do so within the same time as if he were the holder, and the principal upon receipt of such notice has himself the same time for giving notice as if the agent had been an independent holder.

(14) Where a party to a bill receives due notice of dishonour, he has after the receipt of such notice the same period of time for giving notice to antecedent parties that the holder has after the dishonour.

(15) Where a notice of dishonour is duly addressed and posted, the sender is deemed to have given due notice of dishonour, notwithstanding any miscarriage by the [postal operator concerned.].

Amendment

S.49(15) was amended by the Postal Services Act 2000 (Consequential Modifications No.1) Order 2001, SI 2001/1149.

| Definitions | Comparison |
|---|---|
| "bankrupt": s.2. | UCC: § 3–503. |
| "bill": s.2. | ULB: art.45. |
| "holder": s.2. | ULC: art.42. |
| "person": s.2. | UNB: art.64. |
| "postal operator": s.2. | |

"writing": s.2.
"written": s.2.

## COMMENT

**Rules as to notice of dishonour.** This section sets out 15 rules, all of    6–097
which must be complied with (where relevant) for notice of dishonour to
be duly given. The rules apply also in principle to cheques[73] and to
promissory notes.[74]

**By whom notice of dishonour must be given.** A valid notice of dis-    6–098
honour must be given by or on behalf of the holder,[75] or by or on behalf
of an indorser who, at the time of giving it, is himself liable on the
instrument.[76] Notice cannot validly be given by an indorser who has been
discharged from liability by failure to receive due notice[77] or who has
indorsed the instrument without recourse.[78] Nor can it be given by the
acceptor or drawee, or by a banker with whom the bill is domiciled for
payment, unless he is acting on behalf of a party entitled to give
notice.[79]

Notice of dishonour may be given by an agent. The notice may be given
in the agent's own name[80] and without specifying the name of his principal.[81] The notice may also be given by the agent in the name of any party
entitled to give notice,[82] and (contrary to the usual principles of agency)
whether that party be his principal or not. Thus notice given by an agent
in the name of a previous indorser liable on the bill, but without that
indorser's authority, is a valid notice.[83] An agent must, however, at the
time he gives notice, be acting under the authority of a party entitled to
give notice.[84]

---

[73] s.73. But see s.50(2)(c), (4) and (5).
[74] s.89(1).
[75] Defined in s.2.
[76] s.49, rule (1).
[77] The case usually cited (*Turner v Leech* (1821) 4 B. & Ald. 451) does not turn on notice of
dishonour, but on the inability of a discharged indorser who has paid the bill to recover
from prior parties.
[78] s.16(1).
[79] *Harrison v Ruscoe* (1846) 15 M. & W. 231, 235. *cf. Bailey v Bodenham* (1864) 16 C.B. (N.S.) 288,
296; *Heywood v Pickering* (1874) L.R. 9 Q.B. 428.
[80] *Lysaght v Bryant* (1850) 9 C.B. 46 (Illustration 2).
[81] *Woodthorpe v Lawes* (1836) 2 M. & W. 109.
[82] *Chapman v Keane* (1835) 3 A. & E. 193 (Illustration 3).
[83] *Harrison v Ruscoe* (1846) 15 M. & W. 231 (Illustration 1). See also *Rogersen v Hare* (1837) 1
Jur. 71.
[84] *Stewart v Kennett* (1809) 2 Camp. 177 (Illustration 4); *East v Smith* (1847) 16 L.J.Q.B. 292,
295.

A banker to whom an instrument is delivered for collection may, as agent or holder, give notice of dishonour to parties liable on the bill. But he is not, as a general rule, required to do so, and will satisfy his duty as agent by giving due notice to his principal.[85]

**6–099**    **For whose benefit notice enures.** Notice given by or on behalf of the holder enures for the benefit of all subsequent holders.[86] So, if the holder gives notice of dishonour to the drawer and then negotiates the bill, the new holder can avail himself of the notice so given.

Notice given by or on behalf of the holder also enures for the benefit of all prior indorsers who have a right of recourse against the party to whom it is given.[87] Thus if B draws a bill on A payable to C, which C indorses to D, notice given by the holder (D) to the drawer (B) will enure for the benefit of the indorser (C). C, if he has received due notice from D and in consequence has a right of recourse against B, can sue B.

Notice given by or on behalf of an indorser entitled to give notice[88] enures for the benefit of the holder and all indorsers subsequent to the party to whom notice is given.[89] So, in the above example, if D merely gives notice to C, but C in turn gives notice of dishonour to the drawer (B), C's notice enures for the benefit of D, and D can sue both B and C. In practice, a holder will often give notice only to his immediate indorser, relying on each indorser to give notice to the party immediately liable to himself. But if this is not done, the chain will break,[90] *e.g.* if C fails to give due notice of dishonour to B, then D can sue C, but neither D nor C can sue B. It is therefore advisable for a holder himself to give notice of dishonour to all parties (other than the acceptor, or, in the case of a note, the maker of the note)[91] against whom he might wish to recover, lest a failure to give due notice should discharge such party from liability.

**6–100**    **In what manner notice of dishonour to be given.**[92] Notice may be given in writing or by "personal communication".[93] It is submitted that notice given by telegram,[94] telex or telefax would constitute notice in

---

[85] See s.49, rule (13), below *cf.* ICC Uniform Rule for Collections (1995), Brochure 522, art. 26.
[86] s.49, rule (3).
[87] s.49, rule (3).
[88] see s.49, rule (1) above.
[89] s.49, rule (4); *Chapman v Keane* (1835) 3 A. & E. 193 (Illustration 3).
[90] See *Miers v Brown* (1843) 11 M. & W. 372; *Horne v Rouquette* (1878) 3 Q.B.D. 514, 517.
[91] See above, paras 6–088—6–090 (s.48).
[92] See also ICC Uniform Rules for Collections (1995), Brochure 522, art.26.
[93] s.49, rule (5).
[94] *Fielding & Co. v Corry* [1898] 1 Q.B. 268 (Illustration 19).

writing, and that a telephoned notice would suffice as personal communication.[95] The Government proposes to amend the Act to allow—if not already allowed—notice to be given by electronic communication or by telecommunication.[96] It is, however, submitted that notice given by email or text message is already allowed.[97]

Notice may be given by post.[98]

**Form of notice of dishonour.** Forms of notice of dishonour are set out in Appendix A. But a notice of dishonour need be in no particular form. A notice may be given "in any terms which sufficiently identify the bill,[99] and intimate that the bill has been dishonoured by non-acceptance or non-payment". The words of rule (5) are clear enough to dispense with the need to resort to pre-Act cases on this point, some of which adopted a strict,[1] but others a more liberal,[2] construction of the wording of the notice. The rule does not, however, appear to require that the notice need state in express terms that the bill has been presented for payment and dishonoured[3]: it is a sufficient intimation[4] that the bill has been dishonoured if the notice states that the bill is unpaid and in addition, for example, requests that payment be made[5] or that the recipient give his "immediate attention" to the matter.[6] It is otherwise unnecessary for any

6–101

---

[95] *Noyes Bros Ltd v Oates* [1933] S.R.Qd. 112; *Royal Bank of Ireland Ltd v O'Rourke* [1962] I.R. 159; *Ladup Ltd v Shaikh* [1983] Q.B. 225. cf. *Lombard Banking Ltd v Central Garage and Engineering Co. Ltd* [1963] 1 Q.B. 220, 232 (Illustration 20). For examples of oral communication before the Act, see *Housego v Cowne* (1837) 2 M. & W. 348 (Illustration 13); *Metcalfe v Richardson* (1852) 11 C.B. 1011 (Illustration 12).

[96] (1990) Cm. 1026, Annex 6, para.6.11 (as a result of the report of the Review Committee on Banking Services Law and Practice (1989) Cm. 622, rec. 8(10), Technical Recommendation 36); see above, para.1–008. No order has yet been made, *e.g.* under s.8 of the Electronic Communications Act 2000.

[97] Interpretation Act 1978, s.5 and Sch.1 "Writing": see above, para.1–030. See also Brindle and Cox, *Law of Bank Payments* (3rd ed.), 6–122, 7–101. Contrast *Byles* (27th ed.), 15–05.

[98] See below, para.6–110.

[99] *Shelton v Braithwaite* (1841) 7 M. & W. 436. cf. s.49, rule (7).

[1] See, *e.g. Solarte v Palmer* (1834) 1 Bing. N.C. 194, HL of which Chalmers remarked: "This inconvenient decision was frequently regretted, and was eventually got rid of by considering it merely as a finding on the particular facts. Since 1841 (*Furze v Sherwood* (1841) 2 Q.B. 288) it does not appear that any written notice of dishonour has been held bad on the ground of insufficiency in form": (9th ed.), p.184.

[2] *Bailey v Porter* (1845) 14 M. & W. 44 (Illustration 8); *Maxwell v Brain* (1864) 10 L.T. 301 (Illustration 9); *Bain v Gregory* (1866) 14 L.T. 601.

[3] cf. *Solarte v Palmer* (1834) 1 Bing. N.C. 194, HL.

[4] The word "sufficiently" appears to govern both "identify" and "intimate" in s.49, rule (5).

[5] *Armstrong v Christiani* (1848) 5 C.B. 687 (Illustration 7); *Everard v Watson* (1853) 1 E. & B. 801 (Illustration 5); *Paul v Joel* (1859) 4 H. & N. 355 (Illustration 6); *Counsell v Livingston* (1902) 4 O.L.R. 340.

[6] *Bailey v Porter* (1845) 14 M. & W. 44 (Illustration 8); *Maxwell v Brain* (1864) 10 L.T. 301 (Illustration 9); *Bain v Gregory* (1866) 14 L.T. 601 (Illustration 10).

demand for payment to be made[7] or for the notice to state that the recipient is held liable.[8] Nor is it necessary for the notice to state by whom it is given,[9] or where the bill is lying[10] or that the bill has been protested.[11]

A written notice need not be signed,[12] and an insufficient written notice may be supplemented and validated by verbal communication.[13] It may be presumed that the converse is also true. Presumably the supplementary communication must be given or sent off within the time referred to in rule (12).[14]

A misdescription of the bill will not vitiate the notice unless the party to whom the notice is given is in fact misled thereby.[15] So, for example, a notice given to the drawer which describes the bill as payable at the "J Bank" whereas in fact it is payable at the "W Bank",[16] which describes a bill of exchange as a note,[17] which transposes the names of drawer and acceptor,[18] or which describes the acceptor by the wrong name,[19] may be sufficient if the recipient is not misled.[20] The burden of showing that the notice is invalid because he was misled rests on the recipient.[21]

6–102    **Return of bill as notice.** By rule (6) the return of a dishonoured bill to the drawer or an indorser is, in point of form, deemed a sufficient notice of dishonour. Chalmers[22] commented that "This subsection approves a common practice of collecting bankers which was previously of doubtful validity." But the common practice of collecting bankers is, in fact, to return a dishonoured bill or cheque to their own customer, the payee or

---

[7] *Miers v Brown* (1843) 11 M. & W. 372; *King v Bickley* (1842) 2 Q.B. 419 (Illustration 11). *cf.* *Hartley v Case* (1825) 1 C. & P. 555; *Everard v Watson* (1853) 1 E. & B. 801.
[8] *Chard v Fox* (1849) 14 Q.B. 200. Rule (5) originally ended with the words "and that the party to whom notice is given is held liable". These words were struck out in committee. *cf. East v Smith* (1847) 16 L.J.Q.B. 292.
[9] But the notice must in fact be given by or on behalf of a person entitled to give notice: s.49, rules (1), (2), above.
[10] *Woodthorpe v Lawes* (1836) 2 M. & W. 109.
[11] *Ex p. Lowenthal* (1874) L.R. 9 Ch. App. 591. But it may be advisable to inform the recipient of the fact that the bill has been protested in order to preserve the rights of the person giving notice under a foreign law.
[12] *Bailey v Porter* (1845) 14 M. & W. 44; *Maxwell v Brain* (1864) 10 L.T. 301.
[13] s.49, rule (7); *Houlditch v Cauty* (1838) 4 Bing. N.C. 411, 419.
[14] *cf. Fielding & Co. v Corry* [1898] 1 Q.B. 268 (Illustration 19).
[15] s.49, rule (7).
[16] *Bromage v Vaughan* (1846) 9 Q.B. 608.
[17] *Stockman v Parr* (1843) 11 M. & W. 809; *Bain v Gregory* (1866) 14 L.T. 601 (Illustration 10).
[18] *Mellersh v Rippen* (1852) 7 Exch. 578.
[19] *Harpham v Child* (1859) 1 F. & F. 652.
[20] *cf. Beauchamp v Cash* (1822) Dow. & Ry. N.P. 3.
[21] *Shelton v Braithwaite* (1841) 7 M. & W. 436; *Eaglehill Ltd v Needham (J.) Builders Ltd* [1973] A.C. 992, 1011.
[22] 9th ed., p.185.

indorsee of the instrument.[23] The payee or indorsee may have indorsed the instrument to the banker for collection and so be an indorser.[24] But, in the case of cheques, section 1 of the Cheques Act 1957 has, in general, rendered indorsement unnecessary,[25] and even in the case of bills of exchange indorsement may not be required, *e.g.* because the bill is payable to bearer. It is to be noted that, in its terms, the rule does not extend to the giving of notice by a collecting banker, as agent, to his principal, as provided for in rule (13). It only applies to a return of a dishonoured bill to the drawer or an indorser.

**To whom notice of dishonour must be given.** Notice must be given to any secondary party whom it is sought to hold liable on the instrument. Rule (8) provides that notice may be given to the party himself, or to his agent in that behalf. Notice has been held to have been validly given at a non-trader's house to his wife,[26] or at a merchant's place of business to his clerk.[27] But the words "in that behalf" would appear to require that the agent have actual or ostensible authority to receive the notice on behalf of his principal,[28] or at least to be under or have assumed a duty to communicate the notice to his principal.[29] In *Re Leeds Banking Co.*[30] it was held that a referee in case of need nominated by an indorser was an agent of the indorser for payment but not for receiving notice.

6–103

Rules (9), (10) and (11) set out further provisions for giving notice in special circumstances:

    (a) *Drawer or indorser dead.* If the party giving notice knows of the death, the notice must be given to a personal representative if such there be, and with the exercise of reasonable diligence he can be found.[31] It is to be inferred from this provision, first, that if, after the exercise of reasonable diligence, the personal representative cannot be found or if there is no personal representative, then notice of dishonour is dispensed with, and, secondly, that a notice sent to a drawer or indorser in ignorance of his death is a valid notice.

[23] A collecting banker who returns a cheque to his customer may lose his rights as a holder in due course: *Westminster Bank Ltd v Zang* [1966] A.C. 182; and see above, para.4–030 (s.27).

[24] *Caisse Populaire (St Jean Baptiste) Belle Rivière Ltée v Provincial Bank of Canada* (1979) 97 D.L.R. (3d) 527 (delay in returning cheque discharged indorser).

[25] See below, para.17–005.

[26] *Housego v Cowne* (1837) 2 M. & W. 348 (Illustration 13); *Wharton v Wright* (1844) 1 C. & K. 585.

[27] *Viale v Michael* (1874) 30 L.T. 463 (Illustration 14).

[28] *Firth v Thrush* (1828) 8 B. & C. 387, 391.

[29] *Housego v Cowne* (1837) 2 M. & W. 348. See also *Re Fenwick, Stobart & Co. Ltd* [1902] 1 Ch. 507 (s.48, Illustration 1).

[30] (1865) L.R. 1 Eq. 1.

[31] s.49, rule (9).

(b) *Drawer or indorser bankrupt.*[32] Notice may be given either to the party himself or to the trustee.[33]

(c) *Two or more drawers or indorsers.* In this case, if they are not partners, notice must be given to each of them, unless one of them has authority to receive such notice for the others.[34] If they are partners, notice to one of them who habitually acts in the partnership business is normally notice to all.[35] Notice to a continuing partner after the dissolution of the partnership is sufficient to charge a partner who has retired in respect of a bill drawn before the dissolution.[36]

**6–104** **Where notice of dishonour may be given.** The Act does not state where notice of dishonour must be given. Presumably a notice, wherever given, is a valid notice if it is actually communicated to the party himself, or to his agent in that behalf. But a notice will also be valid if given at or sent to the place of business or residence of the drawer or indorser whom it is sought to charge. Where a bill has been drawn or indorsed in the way of business, it is enough that the notice is given at or sent to the party's place of business: if he has no place of business, notice may be given at or sent to his residence.[37] It is the duty of the drawer or indorser of a bill, if he be absent from his place of business or residence, to see that there is someone there to receive notice on his behalf.[38] Notice sent by post to a party at the address given by him in the bill[39] or to his only known address[40] will, it seems, also suffice. The person giving the notice is bound to exercise reasonable diligence to discover the address of the party to whom notice is to be given.[41] Notice to a company may be given by leaving it at, or sending it by post to, the company's registered office.[42]

Where the party entitled to give notice, or his agent, attends in person at the place of business or residence of the drawer or indorser sought to be charged, intending to give him oral notice of dishonour, but no person authorised to receive the notice can be found there or the premises are

---

[32] "Bankrupt" is defined in s.2.

[33] s.49, rule (10).

[34] s.49, rule (11).

[35] Partnership Act 1890, s.16.

[36] *Goldfarb v Bartlett & Kremer* [1920] 1 K.B. 639 (even if the holder knows of the dissolution).

[37] *Berridge v Fitzgerald* (1869) L.R. 4 Q.B. 639 (Illustration 15).

[38] *Crosse v Smith* (1813) 1 M. & S. 545, 554; *Housego v Cowne* (1837) 2 M. & W. 348, 349; *Allen v Edmundson* (1848) 2 Exch. 719, 723; *Eaglehill Ltd v Needham (J.) Builders Ltd* [1973] A.C. 992, 1011.

[39] *Burmester v Barron* (1852) 17 Q.B. 828 (but in this case the address "London" was held to suffice, which would not be sufficient today).

[40] *Ex p. Baker* (1877) 4 Ch.D. 795; *Lombard Banking Ltd v Central Garage and Engineering Co. Ltd* [1963] 1 Q.B. 220, 232.

[41] *Berridge v Fitzgerald* (1869) L.R. 4 Q.B. 639 at 641. See also s.50(2)(a).

[42] Companies Act 1985, s.725.

shut up, this will not support an allegation of actual notice of dishonour.[43] But it may excuse delay in giving notice,[44] or even dispense altogether with giving notice of dishonour provided reasonable diligence has been used.[45] In such a case it does not seem necessary to leave a written notice of dishonour[46] although it would no doubt be prudent to do so.

**When notice of dishonour must be given.** Notice of dishonour may     **6–105** be given at any time after the instrument has been dishonoured.[47] Where a bill is presented for payment on its due date, notice of dishonour may be given as soon as the bill is dishonoured[48]; but no cause of action accrues to the holder until that day has expired.[49]

Notice of dishonour is given when it is received, and not when it is dispatched, even if sent by post.[50] If the holder of a bill, anticipating that it will be dishonoured, posts a notice of dishonour before the bill is dishonoured, the notice will nevertheless be effective if it reaches the recipient after, or at the same time as, the dishonour, provided that it states that the bill has been (and not will be) dishonoured.[51] "There must be an assertion that it has been dishonoured, as an accomplished fact."[52] If it reaches the recipient before the dishonour, it will be ineffective. Where there is evidence to show which of the two events, *i.e.* dishonour and the receipt of notice of dishonour, first occurred, the validity of the notice will be determined according to that evidence.[53] However, if there is no or no sufficient evidence on this point, it will be presumed that each act was done in the proper order, that is to say, that the bill was first dishonoured and then notice of dishonour was given.[54]

Notice must be given within a reasonable time after dishonour. This appears to be a question of mixed law and fact.[55] Rule (12), however, sets out two provisions, that are to be applied "in the absence of special

---

[43] *Allen v Edmundson* (1818) 2 Exch. 719 (s.50, Illustration 2).

[44] s.50(1).

[45] s.50(2)(a). See *Allen v Edmundson* (1848) 2 Exch. 719; *Crosse v Smith* (1813) 1 M. & S. 545.

[46] *Crosse v Smith* (1813) 1 M. & S. 545; *Housego v Cowne* (1837) 2 M. & W. 348.

[47] For the time at which a bill is dishonoured by non-payment, see above, para.6–082 (s.47).

[48] *Burbridge v Manners* (1812) 3 Camp. 193; *Hine v Allely* (1833) 4 B. & Ad. 624; *Kennedy v Thomas* [1894] 2 Q.B. 759; *Eaglehill Ltd v Needham (J.) Builders Ltd* [1973] A.C. 992. *cf. Hartley v Case* (1825) 1 C. & P. 555, 676.

[49] *Kennedy v Thomas* [1894] 2 Q.B. 759 (s.47, Illustration).

[50] *Eaglehill Ltd v Needham (J.) Builders Ltd* [1973] A.C. 992 at 1004, 1009; see below, para.6–110. But see s.49, rule (15).

[51] *Eaglehill Ltd v Needham (J.) Builders Ltd* [1973] A.C. 992 (Illustration 16).

[52] *Jennings v Roberts* (1855) 4 E. & B. 615, 618.

[53] *Eaglehill Ltd v Needham (J.) Builders Ltd* [1973] A.C. 992.

[54] *Eaglehill Ltd v Needham (J.) Builders Ltd* [1973] A.C. 992 at 1011–1012. But *cf.* above at 1007.

[55] *Hirschfield v Smith* (1866) L.R. 1 C.P. 340, 351; *Gladwell v Turner* (1870) L.R. 5 Ex. 59, 61.

circumstances". Such circumstances have been held to exist where the person required to give notice was of the Jewish religion and forbidden to attend to any sort of business on the day of a Jewish festival[56] and where the person entitled to receive notice was the master of a ship the whereabouts of which was not known.[57] It has further been stated that, where a bill is presented by post by a collecting banker to the banker with whom it is domiciled for payment, so that neither the holder nor the collecting banker know when it is dishonoured by non-payment, these will be special circumstances which justify the holder in delaying the giving of notice until he gets the unpaid bill back in his hands.[58] Having regard to the realities of the batch processing of cheques at the present day,[59] this would appear to be a sensible rule to apply in the case of cheques as well. In this connection, it is also necessary to have regard to section 50(1) of the Act whereby delay in giving notice is excused where the delay is caused by circumstances beyond the control of the party giving notice. But "special circumstances" may exist even if they are not beyond his control.

**6–106**     The first provision of the rule prescribes that, where the person giving and the person to receive the notice reside in the same place,[60] notice is not deemed to have been given within a reasonable time unless it is given or sent off in time to reach the latter on the day after the dishonour of the bill.[61] The second provision prescribes that, where the person giving and the person to receive the notice reside in different places,[62] notice is not deemed to have been given within a reasonable time unless it is sent off on the day after the dishonour of the bill, if there be a post at a convenient hour on that day, and if there be no such post on that day then by the next post thereafter.[63] In *Hamilton Finance Co. Ltd v Coverley Westray Walbaum*

---

[56] *Lindo v Unsworth* (1811) 2 Camp. 602.

[57] *The Elmville (No.1)* [1904] P. 319 (s.50, Illustration 1). See also *Firth v Thrush* (1828) 8 B. & C. 387.

[58] *Lombard Banking Ltd v Central Garage and Engineering Co. Ltd* [1963] 1 Q.B. 220, 231 (Illustration 10). But see *Yeoman Credit Ltd v Gregory* [1963] 1 W.L.R. 343, 355 (Illustration 21).

[59] See *Caisse Populaire D'Alfred Ltd v Lapensee* (1985) 31 B.L.R. 28 (Ontario) where this aspect is examined.

[60] *Smith v Mullett* (1809) 2 Camp. 208 (both parties in London); *Hilton v Fairclough* (1811) 2 Camp. 633 (Gerard St/Panton St, in London); *Extension Investments (Pty) Ltd v Ampro Holdings (Pty) Ltd* 1961 (3) S.A. 429 (both addresses in City of Johannesburg); *Scott (S.A.) Pty Ltd v Dawson* [1962] N.S.W.R. 1166 (George St, Sydney, and Haberfield, six miles from Sydney); *Hamilton Finance Co. Ltd v Coverley Westray Walbaum & Tosetti Ltd* [1969] 1 Lloyd's Rep. 53 (below). See also *Yeoman Credit Ltd v Gregory* [1963] 1 W.L.R. 343 (point conceded).

[61] For non-business days, see s.92.

[62] *Williams v Smith* (1819) 2 B. & Ald. 496 (Wantage and Newbury); *Hawkes v Salter* (1828) 4 Bing. 715 (Norwich and address 14 miles from Norwich); *H. Rowe & Co. Pty Ltd v Pitts* [1973] 2 N.S.W.L.R. 159 (Pitt St, Sydney, and St Leonard's).

[63] *Bray v Hadwen* (1816) 5 M. & S. 68 (Illustration 17); *Hawkes v Salter* (1828) 4 Bing. 715. For non-business days, see s.92.

*& Tosetti Ltd,*[64] Mocatta J. held that Upper Brook Street, London W1, and Seething Lane, London EC3, were "in the same place" for the purposes of rule (12)(a).

His Lordship said[65]:

> "If I am to answer this question as one of fact as a Jury might, I would find that the two addresses, a modest bus or tube journey apart, both in the central area of London, are 'in the same place'. I would, however, wish to find some rationale on which the distinction between Sect. 49(12)(a) and (b) are based. A little, but not much, help is to be derived from *Smith v Mullet*[66]; and *Hilton v Fairclough*.[67] It will be noticed that sub-para. (a) makes no mention of the post, whereas sub-para. (b) does. From this it would appear that if the two addresses on other grounds would seem to be 'in the same place', the determining factor is whether it would in all the circumstances be reasonable to send the notice by hand rather than rely upon the general post. In view of the importance of giving due notice of dishonour and the relative cheapness of delivery by hand between the two addresses, this factor in the present case to my mind supports what I have called the Jury view."

It is submitted that Mocatta J. was correct in looking at the matter as a "jury" question but that it is difficult to rely on any principle[68] or rationale to determine whether the parties reside "in the same place"[69] or "in different places".

A holder has only the time referred to in rule (12) to give notice of dishonour to his immediate indorser and to any other secondary party whom he seeks to hold liable on the instrument. If he fails to give notice to such a party in due time, he will lose his rights against that party. But those rights may yet be saved if timely notice is given to that party by an indorser who has himself received due notice of dishonour.[70]

Where a party to a bill receives[71] due notice of dishonour, he has after **6–107** the receipt of such notice the same period of time for giving notice to antecedent parties that the holder has after the dishonour.[72] So, for example, if C is the payee and indorser of a dishonoured bill held by D, and D gives due notice of dishonour to C, C must give notice of dishonour to the

---

[64] [1969] 1 Lloyd's Rep. 53 (s.45, Illustration 1).
[65] At 73.
[66] (1809) 2 Camp. 208.
[67] (1811) 2 Camp. 633.
[68] The suggestion was previously made by Chalmers (11th ed.), p.158, that all places within a "postal district" were in the same place.
[69] The same expression is used in a similar sense in s.67(2).
[70] s.49, rule (4), above.
[71] See below, para.6–121 (s.50).
[72] s.49, rule (14). See *Wright v Shawcross* (1819) 2 B. & Ald. 503n.

drawer within the time referred to in rule (12) after his receipt of the notice. However, if D fails to give notice to C in due time, any notice given by C to the drawer will be ineffective, because, at the time of giving the notice, C was discharged from liability by D's delay.[73] Moreover, C cannot make up for a delay of (say) one day by D by giving notice to the drawer on the same day instead of on the following day as permitted by rule (12).

**6–108**    **Bill in the hands of an agent.** Rule (13) permits an agent who is in possession of a dishonoured bill to give notice of dishonour either to the party liable on the bill or to his principal. If he gives notice to his principal, he must do so within the same time as if he were the holder. The principal, upon receipt of the notice, then has himself the same time for giving notice as if the agent had been an independent holder.[74]

The ability of an agent to give notice to his principal is of particular importance to collecting banks.[75] For example, the holder of a bill may deliver it to his own bank (A) for collection, which passes it to a correspondent bank (B), which in turn delivers it to an agent (C) in the place where the bill is to be presented for payment. Each of these agents, A, B, and C, must give notice of dishonour to his respective principal within the time referred to in rule (12). Time runs, in the case of C, from the time of the dishonour, and, in the case of A and B, from the time at which he himself receives notice. The holder must then give notice of dishonour to secondary parties within the time referred to in rule (12) after he receives notice. Even though more than the stipulated time has elapsed from the time when the instrument was dishonoured, the liability of a secondary party will be preserved, provided that each agent and the principal has given notice in due time.[76]

For the purposes of rule (13) each branch of a bank is treated as a separate entity and has the usual time for giving notice of dishonour to the branch which acts as its principal.[77] But if the agent gives notice to his principal before the expiry of the time allowed to him, the time so saved cannot be added to the time allowed to the principal.[78]

**6–109**    In *Fielding & Co. v Corry*[79] a bill was remitted by the Cardiff branch of the G Bank to the W Bank in London for collection. It was dishonoured

---

[73] s.49, rule (1), above.

[74] *Yeoman Credit Ltd v Gregory* [1963] 1 W.L.R. 343 (Illustration 21).

[75] For early cases, see *Robson v Bennett* (1810) 2 Taunt. 388; *Langdale v Trimmer* (1812) 15 East 291. See now ICC Uniform Rules for Collections (1995), Brochure 522, art.26(c) (advice of fate).

[76] *Bray v Hadwen* (1816) 5 M. & S. 68 (Illustration 17); *Goodall v Polhill* (1845) 1 C.B. 233.

[77] *Clode v Bayley* (1843) 12 M. & W. 51 (Illustration 18); *Prince v Oriental Bank Corp.* (1878) 3 App. Cas. 325, 332. cf. *Fielding & Co. v Corry* [1898] 1 Q.B. 268 (Illustration 19).

[78] *Yeoman Credit Ltd v Gregory* [1963] 1 W.L.R. 343.

[79] [1898] 1 Q.B. 268 (Illustration 19).

on presentment and on the first business day following the date of dishonour the W Bank sent by post a notice of dishonour but by error addressed the notice to the Cirencester branch of the G Bank. The mistake was discovered the next day and the W Bank immediately gave notice of dishonour by telegram to the Cardiff branch, the telegram arriving at about the same time as the posted notice would have arrived had it been properly addressed. A majority of the Court of Appeal held that notice had been given in compliance with rules (12) and (13), since the mistake had been rectified in due time by the telegram of the next day. This decision is open to criticism. Collins L.J., who dissented, held that the postal notice was a nullity and that the telegraphed notice was out of time and ineffective. In any event it is submitted that the case is no authority for the proposition that, where no notice of dishonour is sent off by post within the proper time or at all, a notice subsequently sent off out of time will nevertheless be a good notice if it reaches the party to whom it is addressed on the same day as a notice posted within time would have reached him.[80]

Rules (12) and (13) apply also to cheques. It is clear that the holder of a cheque may deliver it to a bank as his agent for collection, whether the cheque be crossed or uncrossed. But the collecting bank must observe the time-limits specified for giving notice of dishonour to its principal,[81] otherwise (unless notice of dishonour is dispensed with)[82] the drawer and any indorser will be discharged. Where a cheque drawn by one customer is paid in by another customer at the same branch on which it is drawn, then, if the banker receives it as agent for collection,[83] he has the usual time allowed to an agent to give notice of dishonour to his principal.[84]

**Notice of dishonour by post.** Notice of dishonour may be given by    **6–110**
post.[85] But, unless miscarried by the postal operator concerned, the notice is "given" only when it is received, and not when it is posted.[86] The address to which a notice of dishonour may properly be sent has been previously considered.[87] By rule (15), where a notice of dishonour is duly addressed and posted, the sender is deemed to have given notice of

---

[80] *cf. Byles* (27th ed.), 15–11n.
[81] Or to the other parties liable; but in practice the collecting bank will elect to give notice to its principal.
[82] See, in particular, s.50(2)(c), (4) and (5).
[83] See below, para.17–031 (s.45).
[84] *Boyd v Emmerson* (1834) 2 A. & E. 184.
[85] See, *e.g.* s.49, rule 12(b). Where the address of the party to whom notice is to be given is abroad, it is submitted that the notice must be sent by air mail, if available. *cf.* ICC Uniform Rules for Collections (1995), art. 26(b).
[86] *Eaglehill Ltd v Needham (J.) Builders Ltd* [1973] A.C. 992, 1003–1004, 1009 (Illustration 16).
[87] See above, para.6–104.

dishonour, notwithstanding any miscarriage[88] by the postal operator concerned. The effect appears to be that, if the notice is delayed in the post by the fault of the postal operator, the delay will be excused,[89] and that, if it is lost in the post by such fault, notice of dishonour will be deemed to have been duly given.[90]

6–111 **Burden of proof.** The burden of proving that notice of dishonour has been duly given rests upon the claimant.[91] In particular, he bears the burden of proving that a notice sent by post was duly addressed and posted.[92]

ILLUSTRATIONS

6–112 1. A bill of exchange is drawn by the defendant on and accepted by R payable to the defendant's order. It is indorsed by the defendant to V and by V to the claimant. The bill is dishonoured by non-payment and the claimant's attorney sends to the defendant notice of dishonour, but by mistake gives it in the name of V instead of the claimant. The notice is valid, provided that V is liable to the claimant and has a right of recourse against the defendant.[93]

2. The defendant draws a bill on M payable to the defendant's order six months after date, which M accepts. The defendant indorses the bill to L & S, who indorse it to the claimant but hold the bill on behalf of the claimant. The bill is dishonoured by non-payment and L & S give notice of dishonour in their own name to the defendant. This is a valid notice.[94]

3. The claimant indorses a bill to W, who leaves it with the claimant's clerk to present it for payment to the drawee. On presentment the bill is dishonoured. The clerk gives notice of dishonour to the defendant, the drawer, but gives it in the name of the claimant and not in the name of W. The claimant takes up the bill from W. The notice given in the name of the

---

[88] It is submitted that this expression would extend to non-carriage, *e.g.* because of a postal strike.
[89] See s.50(1); *Woodcock v Houldsworth* (1846) 16 M. & W. 124.
[90] *Mackay v Judkins* (1858) 1 F. & F. 208; *Renwick v Tighe* (1860) 8 W.R. 391. See also Interpretation Act 1978, s.7.
[91] *Lawson v Sherwood* (1816) 1 Stark. 314.
[92] *Hetherington v Kemp* (1815) 4 Camp. 193; *Hawkes v Salter* (1828) 4 Bing. 715; Interpretation Act 1978, s.7. cf. *Eaglehill Ltd v Needham (J.) Builders Ltd* [1973] A.C. 992.
[93] *Harrison v Ruscoe* (1846) 15 M. & W. 231.
[94] *Lysaght v Bryant* (1850) 9 C.B. 46.

claimant is a valid notice and W (the holder) may avail himself of the notice.[95]

4. A bill indorsed to the defendant and by the defendant to the claimant **6–113** is held by A. It is dishonoured. C, who was at one time employed by the original parties to the bill to get it discounted, but is not in any way acting for A, informs the defendant that the bill has been dishonoured. This is insufficient. The defendant is discharged.[96]

5. "We beg to acquaint you with the non-payment of W.M.'s acceptance to J.W.'s draft of 29th December last, at four months, £50, amounting with expenses, to £55 5s. 1d.; which remit to us in course of post without fail, or pay to Messrs E." This is a sufficient notice of dishonour from the holder to an indorser.[97]

6. The following notice is left at the drawer's counting house by the holder's clerk: "B's acceptance to J, £500, due 12th January, is unpaid; payment to R & Co. is requested before four o'clock." This is a sufficient notice of dishonour.[98]

7. "I am the holder of a bill drawn by you on L.M. for £98 15s., which **6–114** became due yesterday, the 4th instant, and is unpaid; and I have to state that, unless the same is paid immediately, I shall take proceedings against you without delay for the amount" is, though unsigned, sufficient notice of dishonour from the holder to the drawer.[99]

8. An unsigned communication in writing from the holder's clerk to the drawer stating that "J.C.'s acceptance due that day was unpaid and requested his immediate attention to it" is a sufficient notice of dishonour.[1]

9. A letter from the holder to the drawer: "I beg to intimate that Mr S's acceptance to you for £74 15s. due 30th inst. at M & Co. is still unpaid, and have to request your immediate attention to the same" is a sufficient notice of dishonour.[2]

---

[95] *Chapman v Keane* (1835) 3 A. & E. 193.
[96] *Stewart v Kennett* (1809) 2 Camp. 177.
[97] *Everard v Watson* (1853) 1 E. & B. 801.
[98] *Paul v Joel* (1859) 4 H. & N. 355.
[99] *Armstrong v Christiani* (1848) 5 C.B. 687.
[1] *Bailey v Porter* (1845) 14 M. & W. 44.
[2] *Maxwell v Brain* (1864) 10 L.T. 301.

**6–115**   10. "Yours and P's note of hand is now due, and your attention to the same will oblige." This is a sufficient notice of dishonour by the holder to the drawer of a bill accepted by P.[3]

11. A written communication: "I hereby give notice that a bill for £50 at 3 months after date, by A upon you and accepted by B, and indorsed by you, lies at &c. dishonoured" is a sufficient notice of dishonour without any need to state that the holder looks to the indorser for payment.[4]

12. On the day after a bill becomes due, the holder's clerk calls upon the drawer and tells him that the bill has been duly presented, and that the acceptor cannot pay it. The drawer replies that he will see the holder about it. It is properly left to the jury to infer from this conversation that the drawer has received due notice of dishonour.[5]

**6–116**   13. A person sent by the holder calls at the house of the drawer, who is not a trader, on the day after a bill becomes due. The drawer being away, he sees there the drawer's wife and tells her that he has brought back the bill which has been dishonoured. The wife says that she does not know anything about it, but will tell her husband when he comes home. No written notice of dishonour is left. The oral notice to the wife is sufficient notice of dishonour.[6]

14. A foreign bill of exchange is dishonoured on June 9, and protested against the acceptor. On June 10, it is taken by the notary's clerk to the place of business of the defendant, the drawer. The notary's clerk presents the bill to the clerk there and asks for payment. Attached to the bill is the usual note with the words "No account" thereon. The defendant's clerk takes the bill in his hands, looks at it, and says the defendant is out and has left no orders. The notary's clerk then leaves the usual notice that the bill lies due at his office. Sufficient notice of dishonour has been given to the defendant.[7]

15. The claimant draws a bill on a company payable to himself. The bill is drawn at the office of the company, accepted on behalf of the company by the company's manager and, as required by the claimant, is there indorsed by the defendant and another director of the company. The bill being unpaid at maturity, the claimant immediately sends notice of dishonour to the defendant, addressed to him at the company's office. The

---

[3] *Bain v Gregory* (1866) 14 L.T. 601. *Sed quaere?*
[4] *King v Bickley* (1842) 2 Q.B. 419.
[5] *Metcalfe v Richardson* (1852) 11 C.B. 1011.
[6] *Housego v Cowne* (1837) 2 M. & W. 348.
[7] *Viale v Michael* (1874) 30 L.T. 463.

defendant does not receive the notice until long after, having ceased to attend at the company's office upon the company getting into financial difficulties. Under the circumstances, the notice of dishonour is valid.[8]

16. The respondents draw a bill on F Ltd to be paid by December 31 **6–117** (the last day of grace) and the bill is accepted payable at the High Wycombe branch of L Bank. It is discounted by the appellants. Prior to the due date for payment F Ltd go into liquidation and in consequence both the appellants and the respondents know that it will be dishonoured when presented. A notice stating that the bill has been dishonoured is prepared by the appellants, dated January 1, but by error it is sent off by post on December 30. It is delivered to the respondents at their business premises by first post on December 31. The bill is presented for payment by post and also arrives by first post on December 31. There is no evidence to show precisely when the bill was first seen by a responsible official of the L Bank or when the notice of dishonour was first seen by anyone on behalf of the respondents. The respondent drawers are not discharged. The notice is not vitiated by the fact that it was posted before dishonour, and, in the absence of evidence, it must be presumed that the required acts were done in the order in which they ought to have been done, *i.e.* that the bill was presented for payment and then notice of dishonour given.[9]

17. A bill indorsed by the defendant is accepted payable at a bank in London, and is deposited by the claimant holder with G & Co., bankers in Launceston, for collection. The bill is presented for payment by G & Co.'s London agents on July 14. It is dishonoured. The London agents return the bill with notice of dishonour on July 15, the letter reaching G & Co. on July 17 (a Sunday). The next day G & Co. send off notice of dishonour by post to the claimant at Tavistock, but do not post the letter before 12 noon when the Tavistock post departs. As a result, instead of reaching the claimant on the 19th, the notice does not arrive until the 20th. Thereafter due notice is given to the defendant. The defendant is not discharged. G & Co. had an entire day following their receipt of notice of dishonour to send off notice by post to the claimant.[10]

18. A bill drawn by the defendant is accepted payable at No.22 Essex Street, Strand, London, and is indorsed by the defendant to the claimants. The claimants deliver it to the Portmadoc branch of the N.P. Bank for collection, from where it is sent to the Pwllheli branch of the same bank,

---

[8] *Berridge v Fitzgerald* (1869) L.R. 4 Q.B. 639.
[9] *Eaglehill Ltd v Needham (J.) Builders Ltd* [1973] A.C. 992.
[10] *Bray v Hadwen* (1816) 5 M. & S. 68.

by whom it is sent to the head office of that bank in London. The bill is dishonoured. It is returned, by the same day's post, from the head office to the Pwllheli branch, and likewise from Pwllheli to Portmadoc, and from Portmadoc to the claimants, who give due notice of dishonour to the defendant. Notice of dishonour has been given in due time, each branch being considered as regards time a distinct party.[11]

**6–118**  19. A bill bearing the defendant's indorsement is delivered by the claimant holders to the Cardiff branch of the G Bank for collection, and is forwarded by that branch to the W Bank in London, who present it for payment on Saturday, November 10. The bill is dishonoured. On Monday, November 12, the W Bank sends off by post a notice of dishonour, but by error directs it to the Cirencester branch of the G Bank. On November 13 the W Bank discovers its mistake and immediately telegraphs notice of dishonour to the Cardiff branch. On November 14 the Cardiff branch gives notice of dishonour to the claimants, and subsequent notices are given in due time. Sufficient notice of dishonour has been given by the W Bank to comply with rules (12) and (13) of section 49 of the 1882 Act, the mistake having been rectified in due time by the telegram of the next day.[12]

20. Three bills of exchange indorsed by the defendants are accepted by the drawee payable at Bank B, Porthcawl. The claimants, holders of the bills, deliver them for collection to their bankers, Bank W in London, who request Bank B to present to themselves the bills for payment (it is not suggested that Bank B are the claimant's agents for this purpose). The bills are not paid. On the day of dishonour, Bank B write to Bank W notifying them of the dishonour and returning the bills, which Bank W receive on the next working day following the day of dishonour. On the same day that they receive the bills, Bank W inform the claimants by telephone of the dishonour. The claimants nevertheless wait until they receive from Bank W the bills marked unpaid, and then immediately give notice of dishonour to the defendants. The requirements of rules (12) and (13) of section 49 of the 1882 Act have been complied with. The claimants have acted reasonably in the special circumstances of the case in waiting to get the bills back in their hands before giving notice. Even if Bank B had been the agents of the claimants, the telephoned information was but a warning of what was in the post and the substantive notice of dishonour was given to the claimants only when they received from Bank W the bills marked unpaid.[13]

---

[11] *Clode v Bayley* (1845) 12 M. & W. 51.
[12] *Fielding & Co. v Corry* [1898] 1 Q.B. 268.
[13] *Lombard Banking Ltd v Central Garage and Engineering Co. Ltd* [1963] 1 Q.B. 220. See also above, para.2–146 (s.20, Illustration 17).

21. Twelve bills indorsed by the defendant are accepted by the drawee payable at the N.P. Bank, Piccadilly. They are delivered by the claimant holders to Martins Bank for collection. On January 28, Martins Bank present the bills to the N.P. Bank for payment, but they are dishonoured, a fact which is communicated on the same day to the claimants. On January 30, at the request of the claimants, Martins Bank present the bills for payment to Midland Bank, it being supposed that funds are available for their payment at that bank. The bills are again dishonoured. On the same day the claimants give notice of dishonour to the defendant. The notice is out of time. It has not been given until the second day after the claimants had knowledge of the dishonour.[14]

### Excuses for non-notice and delay

50. (1) Delay in giving notice of dishonour is excused where the 6–119
delay is caused by circumstances beyond the control of the party giving notice, and not imputable to his default, misconduct, or negligence. When the cause of delay ceases to operate the notice must be given with reasonable diligence.

(2) Notice of dishonour is dispensed with—

(a) When, after the exercise of reasonable diligence, notice as required by this Act cannot be given to or does not reach the drawer or indorser sought to be charged;

(b) By waiver express or implied. Notice of dishonour may be waived before the time of giving notice has arrived, or after the omission to give due notice;

(c) As regards the drawer in the following cases, namely, (1) where drawer and drawee are the same person, (2) where the drawee is a fictitious person or a person not having capacity to contract, (3) where the drawer is the person to whom the bill is presented for payment, (4) where the drawee or acceptor is as between himself and the drawer under no obligation to accept or pay the bill, (5) where the drawer has countermanded payment;

(d) As regards the indorser in the following cases, namely, (1) where the drawee is a fictitious person or a person not having capacity to contract and the indorser was aware of the fact at the time he indorsed the bill, (2) where the indorser is the person to whom the bill is presented for

---

[14] *Yeoman Credit Ltd v Gregory* [1963] 1 W.L.R. 343, 354 (it being conceded that the parties concerned resided in the same place). See also above, para.2–147 (s.20, Illustration 19) and para.6–065 (s.45, Illustration 2).

**payment, (3) where the bill was accepted or made for his accommodation.**

Definitions
"acceptance": ss.2, 17(1).
"bill": s.2.
"person": s.2.

Comparison
UCC: § 3–504.
ULB: art.54.
ULC: art.48.
UNB: art.67.

COMMENT

**6–120** **Excuses for delay and dispensations from notice of dishonour.** This section applies to promissory notes as well as to bills and cheques.[15] In applying its provisions the maker of a note is deemed to correspond with the acceptor of a bill, and the first indorser of a note is deemed to correspond with the drawer of an accepted bill payable to drawer's order.[16]

**6–121** **Subsection (1): excuses for delay in giving notice.** Delay in giving notice may be excused where the party entitled to notice has given the wrong address,[17] or where his address is unknown[18] or where he cannot be found at the appropriate address[19]: time taken up in making enquiries with reasonable diligence[20] to discover his whereabouts will be excused. Delay will also be excused where the person required to give notice is seriously ill, or the delay is otherwise caused by circumstances beyond his control, and not imputable to his default, misconduct, or negligence.[21]

It has already been pointed out that a notice of dishonour sent by post is "given", not when it is posted, but when it is received.[22] If a notice is sent off in due time by post to an appropriate address[23] of the party

---

[15] s.89(1).
[16] s.89(2).
[17] *Berridge v Fitzgerald* (1869) L.R. 4 Q.B. 639, 642. See also *Hewitt v Thomson* (1836) 1 M. & Rob. 543 (indistinct name inducing error).
[18] *Bateman v Joseph* (1810) 2 Camp. 461; 12 East 433; *Baldwin v Richardson* (1823) 1 B. & C. 245; *Firth v Thrush* (1828) 8 B. & C. 387; *Gladwell v Turner* (1870) L.R. 5 Ex. 59; *The Elmville (No.1)* [1904] P. 319 (Illustration 1).
[19] *Studdy v Beesty* (1889) 60 L.T. 647 (Illustration 3).
[20] *Browning v Kinnear* (1819) Gow N.P.C. 81. *cf. Beveridge v Burgis* (1812) 3 Camp. 262; *Chapcott v Curlewis* (1843) 2 M. & Rob. 484 (reasonable diligence not employed).
[21] See also s.49(12) "special circumstances".
[22] *Eaglehill Ltd v Needham (J.) Builders Ltd* [1973] A.C. 992, 1003–1004, 1009; see above, para.6–110 (s.49).
[23] See above, para.6–104 (s.49).

entitled to receive it, the person giving the notice will have satisfied his obligations under section 49 of the Act. He will not be responsible for any delay in communicating the notice to the recipient should the recipient be absent from that address when the notice arrives. The question, however, arises whether such absence will in turn excuse a delay by the recipient in giving notice of dishonour to a prior party. On one view, the recipient needs no such excuse, since he is only obliged to give notice of dishonour when he is actually aware, through receiving notice of dishonour, of the dishonour of the bill.[24] But this might mean, in the case of prolonged absence, that the prior party does not receive notice of dishonour until many months later. The better view, it is submitted, is that, since rule 14(1) of section 49 uses the words "receives due notice"[25] and since it is the duty of the drawer or of an indorser who is absent from the appropriate place to see that there is someone there to receive notice on his behalf,[26] delay in giving notice due to such absence will only be excused if it satisfies the requirements of the present subsection or constitutes "special circumstances" under rule (12) of section 49.[27] It would also seem that, where the delay in giving notice has been caused by the fault of the recipient, *e.g.* because he has given the wrong address, then, though he is liable, he himself is out of time and cannot give effective notice to prior parties.[28]

Quite apart from rule (15) of section 49, delay caused by a postal operator in delivering a properly addressed notice sent by post would be excused.[29] In the event of a postal strike, it is submitted that reasonable efforts would have to be made to give notice of dishonour by alternative means where available.

Once the cause of the delay ceases to operate, the notice must be given **6–122** "with reasonable diligence",[30] and this may be taken to mean, in most cases, within the time limits specified in rules (12), (13) and (14) of section 49. Thus if the address of the party entitled to receive notice is unknown or he cannot be found at the appropriate address, but after enquiry an effective address is obtained before action brought, notice must be given to him with reasonable diligence at that address.[31]

---

[24] In *Eaglehill Ltd v Needham (J.) Builders Ltd* [1973] A.C. 992, their Lordships appear to have assumed that notice was given when the bill was first seen by a responsible official of the bank, *i.e.* communicated.

[25] See above, para.6–107 (s.49).

[26] See above, para.6–104 (s.49).

[27] *Turner v Leech* (1818) Chitty (11th ed.), p.226, cited in *Byles* (27th ed.), 15–30.

[28] *cf. Shelton v Braithwaite* (1841) 8 M. & W. 252, 254.

[29] *Woodcock v Houldsworth* (1846) 16 M. & W. 124.

[30] *Firth v Thrush* (1828) 8 B. & C. 387; *Gladwell v Turner* (1870) L.R. 5 Ex. 59, 61.

[31] *Studdy v Beesty* (1889) 60 L.T. 647 (Illustration 3).

6–123    **Subsection (2): where notice dispensed with.** The grounds for dispensing with notice of dishonour are more extensive than those which excuse presentment for acceptance[32] or dispense with presentment for payment.[33] However, the fact that presentment for acceptance or payment is dispensed with does not in itself dispense with notice of dishonour[34] unless the respective grounds for dispensation coincide.

6–124    **Notice cannot be given.** Notice of dishonour is dispensed with when, after the exercise of reasonable diligence, notice as required by the Act cannot be given. The words in paragraph (a) "as required by this Act" must, it is submitted, be understood to exclude cases where due notice can otherwise be given but not within the time-limits prescribed by rules (12), (13) and (14) of section 49. In such cases delay in giving notice may be excused under subsection (1), but the delay will not dispense entirely with the giving of notice. It may, however, be difficult in practice to distinguish between those situations where, notwithstanding the exercise of reasonable diligence, notice cannot be given at all and those situations where, with the exercise of reasonable diligence, notice can in fact be given though out of time. For example, in one pre-Act case,[35] where the holder attended at the business premises of the drawer but found them shut up and no one there of whom to make inquiries, it was suggested that notice could thereby be dispensed with. But in a later case,[36] where the holder attended at the address given by an indorser and the indorser was not at that address, but he later discovered the indorser's address, it was held that the delay in giving notice was excused but not the omission to give it when the indorser's address was found.

6–125    **Notice does not reach the drawer or indorser.** Notice of dishonour is also dispensed with when, after the exercise of reasonable diligence, notice as required by the Act does not reach the drawer or indorser sought to be charged. A similar difficulty arises in the application of this provision. As has already been seen, it is sufficient if a notice is sent by post to the intended recipient's business address, or to his address given on the bill or to his only known address.[37] It is clear that, in view of the strict time-limits imposed by section 49, "reasonable diligence" does not require the person giving the notice first to ascertain whether or not the intended recipient is still at that address. On the other hand, if, at the time of dishonour, the person giving the notice is aware that the intended

---

[32] s.41(2); above, para.6–019.
[33] s.46(2); above, para.6–070.
[34] See also *Thackray v Blackett* (1811) 3 Camp. 164 (lost bill: notice to drawer required).
[35] *Allen v Edmondson* (1848) 2 Exch. 719 (Illustration 2).
[36] *Studdy v Beesty* (1889) 60 L.T. 647 (Illustration 3).
[37] See above, para.6–104 (s.49).

recipient is no longer at that address, but knows his actual address, it would seem reasonable for him to post the notice to that actual address.[38] The problem then arises: suppose that a notice of dishonour is duly sent to the intended recipient's supposed address, but before action brought the person giving the notice is informed that the notice did not reach him because he had moved from that address. Does "reasonable diligence" now require a fresh notice of dishonour to be sent to the intended recipient at his known actual address (the delay being excused)? Or is the position that sufficient notice has, in fact, already been given with reasonable diligence by sending the notice to an appropriate address?[39] The point is arguable,[40] but it is submitted that the last sentence of subsection (1) does not apply (the case not falling to be treated as one of delay) nor does "reasonable diligence" now require a fresh notice of dishonour to be given to satisfy the requirements of subsection (2).[41]

There appears to be an overlap between paragraph (a) of this subsection and rule (15) of section 49, where a notice, duly addressed and posted, is lost in the post. Under the latter provision, the notice is deemed to have been duly given.[42] Under the former provision, notice is dispensed with.

**Knowledge of dishonour.** The fact that the drawer or indorser knows that the acceptor or drawee is bankrupt,[43] or that for some other reason the bill will be or has been dishonoured by non-payment,[44] does not dispense with the requirement that he be given formal notice of dishonour.  **6–126**

**Waiver.** Paragraph (b) of subsection (2) recognises that a party may waive the notice to which he is entitled. Such waiver may be "express or implied" and "before the time of giving notice has arrived, or after omission to give due notice".  **6–127**

By section 16(2) the drawer of a bill, and any indorser, may insert therein an express stipulation waiving as regards himself the duty of the holder to give him notice of dishonour. No subsequent party is then required to give him notice.[45] But there may be an express waiver outside

---

[38] cf. *Crawford and Falconbridge* (8th ed.), p.1592n.
[39] As in *Berridge v Fitzgerald* (1869) L.R. 4 Q.B. 639 (s.49, Illustration 15).
[40] See Riley, *Law relating to Bills of Exchange in Australia* (3rd ed.), pp.129–130; *Crawford and Falconbridge* (8th ed.), p.1592.
[41] cf. *Studdy v Beesty* (1889) 60 L.T. 647 (Illustration 3) (but in this case no notice was given at the appropriate address).
[42] See above, para.6–110.
[43] *Esdaile v Sowerby* (1809) 11 East 114 (s.46, Illustration 3).
[44] *Staples v Okines* (1795) 1 Esp. 332; *Baker v Birch* (1811) 3 Camp. 107; *Burgh v Legge* (1839) 5 M. & W. 418, 422; *Carter v Flower* (1847) 16 M. & W. 743, 749; *Re Fenwick, Stobart & Co. Ltd* [1902] 1 Ch. 507. (s.48, Illustration 1); *Greig & Murray Ltd v Taylor* (1889) 15 V.L.R. 86.
[45] See above, para.2–111.

the instrument, as, for example, where the drawer tells the holder that he will himself call to ascertain its fate.[46]

In *Lombard Banking Ltd v Central Garage and Engineering Co. Ltd*[47] Scarman J. commented that the courts have been ready to infer waiver of notice from very slight evidence. In that case waiver was implied from the fact that the indorser of a bill, though fully aware of the fact of dishonour and the reasons for it at an early stage, nevertheless did not take the point that no notice of dishonour had been given to him until after action brought and in an application to amend his defence. Most reported cases have, however, concerned a promise to pay or an admission of liability on the bill. "A promise to pay", said Byles J.,[48] "may operate either as evidence of notice of dishonour, or as a prior dispensation, or as a subsequent waiver of notice." If a promise to pay is made before the time for giving notice has arrived, it can only have effect as a prior waiver of notice[49]; if it is made when the time for giving notice has arrived, but before it has expired, it can have effect as a prior waiver of notice or as evidence that notice of dishonour has been duly given[50]; if it is made after that time, then it may have effect as a subsequent waiver after omission to give due notice,[51] or it may be evidence either that notice of dishonour has been duly given[52] or of a prior waiver of notice.[53] Many of the nineteenth-century cases fail to distinguish between admissions of liability, which are evidence of due notice having been received, and admissions of liability when due notice has not been given, and which therefore are evidence of waiver. Since the Act, however, the above analysis[54] and distinctions no longer appear to be of importance, except

[46] *Phipson v Kneller* (1815) 4 Camp. 285 (Illustration 4).
[47] [1963] 1 Q.B. 220, 233.
[48] *Cordery v Colville* (1863) 32 L.J.C.P. 210, 211.
[49] *Wood v Brown* (1816) 1 Stark. 217; *Burgh v Legge* (1839) 5 M. & W. 418; *North Staffordshire Loan & Discount Co. v Wythies* (1861) 2 F. & F. 563; *Coulcher v Toppin* (1886) 2 T.L.R. 657, 658; *Wright Heaton & Co. v Barrett* (1892) 13 N.S.W.L.R. 206.
[50] *Cordery v Colville* (1863) 32 L.J.C.P. 210, 211 (*sub. nom. Cordery v Colvin* (1863) 14 C.B., N.S. 374).
[51] *Lundie v Robertson* (1806) 7 East 231; *Margetson v Aitken* (1828) 3 C. & P. 338; *Dixon v Elliott* (1832) 5 C. & P. 437; *Woods v Dean* (1862) 3 B. & S. 101 (Illustration 6); *Cordery v Colvin* (1863) 14 C.B., N.S. 491; *Killby v Rochussen* (1865) 18 C.B., N.S. 357.
[52] *Lundie v Robertson* (1806) 7 East 231; *Horford v Wilson* (1807) 1 Taunt. 12; *Taylor v Jones* (1809) 2 Camp. 105; *Potter v Rayworth* (1811) 13 East 417; *Gunson v Metz* (1823) 1 B. & C. 193; *Hicks v Beaufort (Duke of)* (1838) 4 Bing. N.C. 229; 4 Bing. N.C. 229, 232; *Brownell v Bonney* (1841) 1 Q.B. 39; *Curlewis v Corfield* (1841) 1 Q.B. 814; *Campbell v Webster* (1845) 15 L.J.C.P. 4; *Mills v Gibson* (1847) 16 L.J.C.P. 249; *Jackson v Collins* (1848) 17 L.J.Q.B. 142; *Bartholomew v Hill* (1862) 5 L.T. 756. Contrast (evidence not sufficient): *Borradaile v Lowe* (1811) 4 Taunt 93; *Braithwaite v Coleman* (1835) 4 N. & M. 654; *Hicks v Beaufort (Duke of)*, (1838) 4 Bing. N.C. 229; *Bell v Frankis* (1842) 4 M. & G. 446; *Holmes v Staines* (1850) 3 Car. & K. 19; *Lecaan v Kurtman* (1859) 6 Jur. N.S. 17.
[53] *Woods v Dean* (1862) 3 B. & S. 101, 106. (Illustration 6).
[54] The analysis is derived from Riley, *Law relating to Bills of Exchange in Australia* (3rd ed.), p.130.

where the promise to pay or admission of liability is made after omission to give due notice and under a misapprehension of fact,[55] for example, in ignorance that the bill has been presented for acceptance and that acceptance has been refused. In such a case the promise or admission cannot be a waiver of the omission to give due notice since the party was unaware of the fact, *i.e.* of dishonour, which entitled him to notice.[56] But it could nevertheless be evidence (in appropriate circumstances) that notice has been given or previously dispensed with.

The waiver must be unconditional[57] and if made as to part of the amount operates only as a waiver *pro tanto*.[58]    **6–128**

The waiver may be made by the party to be charged himself or by his agent.[59] But it is personal to that party: a waiver of notice by an indorser will not dispense with notice being given to parties prior to[60] or subsequent to that indorser. However, since notice is dispensed with by waiver, it seems that waiver by one party will enure for the benefit of the holder, subsequent holders and all indorsers subsequent to the party who has waived notice.[61] Waiver need not be made to the claimant, but it may be made to another party to the bill or even to a stranger.[62]

**Dispensations as regards the drawer.** Paragraph (c) of subsection (2)    **6–129**
lists five situations where notice of dishonour is dispensed with as regards the drawer. They are mainly self-explanatory: it would be otiose for notice to be required to be given to the drawer in these circumstances. With respect to cheques, it might seem anomalous that the Act should ever require (as it does) that notice of dishonour be given to the drawer, since, like the acceptor of a bill or the maker of a note, he is the party primarily liable on the instrument. But in practice notice to the drawer will ordinarily be dispensed with by virtue of the dispensations referred to in cases (4) and (5) below, since a cheque will usually be dishonoured either because there are insufficient funds to meet it or because the cheque is out of date, or because the drawer has countermanded payment.

---

[55] In *Stevens v Lynch* (1810) 12 East 38 it was held that a misapprehension of law would not suffice. But *cf. Peyman v Lanjani* [1985] Ch. 457.

[56] *Goodall v Dolley* (1787) 1 T.R. 712; *Pickin v Graham* (1833) 1 Cr. & M. 725, 729. See also *Mactavish's Judicial Factor v Michael's Trustees* 1912 S.C. 425.

[57] *Pickin v Graham* (1833) 1 Cr. & M. 725 (Illustration 7).

[58] *Fletcher v Froggatt* (1827) 2 C. & P. 569.

[59] *Standage v Creighton* (1832) 5 C. & P. 406.

[60] *Roscow v Hardy* (1810) 12 East 434; *Turner v Leech* (1821) 4 B. & Ald. 451.

[61] *Coulcher v Toppin* (1866) 2 T.L.R. 657; *Bank of Toronto v Bennett* (1925) 57 O.L.R. 326. See s.49(3)(4); above, para.6–099.

[62] *Potter v Rayworth* (1811) 13 East 417; *Woods v Dean* (1862) 3 B. & S. 101 (Illustration 6). See also *Gunson v Metz* (1823) 1 B. & C. 193 (evidence of notice); *Rabey v Gilbert* (1861) 6 H. & N. 536.

**6–130**     (1) *Drawer and drawee the same.* Section 3 of the Act defines a bill of exchange as an order addressed by one person to another. A drawer who draws a bill on himself makes, in effect, a promise to pay. By section 5(2) the holder may treat the instrument, at his option, either as a bill of exchange or as a promissory note. If it is treated as a promissory note, notice of dishonour is unnecessary to charge the drawer since he is in the same position as the maker of a note. If it is treated as a bill of exchange, notice is unnecessary because it is the drawer's own refusal to accept or pay which has given rise to the dishonour.

**6–131**     (2) *Drawee fictitious or unable to contract.* Again, by section 5(2), where the drawee is a fictitious person or a person not having the capacity to contract, the holder may treat the instrument, at his option, either as a bill of exchange or as a promissory note. In either case, the drawer now being the party primarily liable on the instrument should not require to be given notice of dishonour.[63] In this provision, as in sections 5(2), 41(2)(a) and 46(2)(b), it is submitted that the words "a fictitious person" include a non-existing person.[64] Capacity to contract is dealt with in section 22 of the Act.

**6–132**     (3) *Presentment for payment to the drawer.* Notice of dishonour is dispensed with where the drawer is the person to whom the bill is presented for payment. Such a situation may arise, for example, where the acceptor has died and the bill is presented for payment to the drawer as his personal representative.[65] Since the drawer has himself dishonoured the bill, notice need not be given to him. This provision may also be intended to cover the situation, found in the older cases,[66] where a drawer draws a bill payable at his own house, from which it may be presumed that the bill has been accepted for the accommodation of the drawer and that no notice is in consequence required. Such a situation might, however, where such accommodation was established, fall within case (4) below.

**6–133**     (4) *Drawee not bound to accept or pay.* The most obvious situation is in the case of a cheque where the banker on whom the cheque is drawn is, as between himself and his customer (the drawer), under no obligation to pay the cheque because there are insufficient funds in the drawer's account and no arrangements have been made for an overdraft. Notice to the drawer of the dishonour by non-payment is not then required to render the drawer liable on the cheque.[67] This likewise applies where the

[63] *Smith v Bellamy* (1817) 2 Stark. 223 (s.5, Illustration 5).
[64] See above, paras 2–040, 6–019, 6–073. Contrast s.7(3).
[65] *Caunt v Thompson* (1849) 7 C.B. 400 (indorser).
[66] *e.g. Sharp v Bailey* (1829) 9 B. & C. 44.
[67] *Carew v Duckworth* (1869) L.R. 4 Ex. 313 (Illustration 8); *Wirth v Austin* (1875) L.R. 10 C.P. 689 (s.46, Illustration 6); *Mohamed Amirdin v Varatharajan* [1968] 2 M.L.J. 83; *Ng Kim Lek v Wee Hok Chye* [1971] 1 M.L.J. 148.

banker is not obliged to pay the cheque because it is out of date.[68] It is to be noted that, unlike the similar provision dispensing with presentment for payment contained in section 46(2)(c) of the Act, the present provision does not contain the additional words "and the drawer has no reason to believe that the bill would be paid if presented".[69]

A similar situation may arise in respect of a bill of exchange where there are no effects of the drawer in the hands of the drawee, so that (*vis-à-vis* the drawer) the drawee is under no obligation to accept or pay the bill.[70] In particular, where a bill has been accepted for the accommodation of the drawer, the acceptor may not, as between himself and the drawer, be under any obligation to pay the bill if the drawer has failed to put him in funds to meet the bill when due.[71] Notice to the drawer is then dispensed with.[72] Notice of dishonour must, however, still be given to the drawer where the bill is drawn, not for the accommodation of the drawer, but of the acceptor,[73] or where the person accommodated is an indorser or a third party.[74]

Where a seller of goods draws a bill on the buyer payable at an earlier date than has been agreed between them for payment of the price, the buyer is under no obligation, as between himself and the seller, to accept or pay the bill. If he refuses to accept or pay, the seller is not entitled to notice of dishonour.[75]

The relevant time for determining whether the drawee is under no **6–134** obligation to accept or pay the bill would appear to be the time at which the bill is presented for acceptance or payment as the case may be.[75a] It is important to emphasise, however, that the test is one of the absence of any legal obligation. The fact that the drawer expected the instrument to be paid, though there was no obligation on the drawee to do so, does not entitle him to notice of dishonour.[76] Conversely, notice of dishonour is not dispensed with where the drawee, being obliged between himself and the drawer to accept or pay the bill, has nevertheless informed the drawer that the bill will not be accepted or paid.[77] Whether or not there are sufficient funds in the drawer's account to meet a cheque is to be decided

---

[68] See below, para.13–065.
[69] These words were struck out in committee, and so altered the previous common law.
[70] *Bickerdike v Bollman* (1786) 1 T.R. 405 (Illustration 9); *Rogers v Stephens* (1788) 2 T.R. 713; *Dennis v Morrice* (1800) 3 Esp. 158, 159; *Terry v Parker* (1837) 6 A.& E. 502, 507.
[71] See above, para.4–045 (s.28).
[72] *Sharp v Bailey* (1829) 9 B. & C. 44.
[73] *Ex. p. Heath* (1813) 2 Ves. & B. 240; *Sleigh v Sleigh* (1850) 5 Exch. 514.
[74] *Lafitte v Slatter* (1830) 6 Bing. 623 (unless the drawee is not, *vis-à-vis* the drawer, bound to pay).
[75] *Claridge v Dalton* (1815) 4 M. & S. 226.
[75a] Cf. *Fiorentino Comm. Giuseppe Srl v Farnesi* [2005] 2 All E.R. 737 (s.46, Illustration 2).
[76] Contrast the previous position at common law: *Byles* (27th ed.), 15–38.
[77] *Staples v Okines* (1795) 1 Esp. 332. See also *Baker v Birch* (1811) 3 Camp. 107 (s.46, Illustration 5).

objectively in the light of actual facts. The subjective opinion of the drawee (or any other person) is irrelevant. Nor is the reason given by the drawee for dishonour the decisive factor.[78]

**6–135**   (5) *Countermand of payment.* Where the drawer has countermanded payment, *e.g.* "stopped" payment of a cheque, he has himself authorised the dishonour and is not entitled to notice.[79]

**6–136**   **Dispensations as regards an indorser.** Three situations are listed in paragraph (d) of subsection (2) where notice of dishonour is dispensed with as regards an indorser.

**6–137**   (1) *Drawee fictitious or unable to contract.* The reader is referred to the Comment on paragraph (c)(2) above.[80] In the case of an indorser, however, for his protection it is provided that he must have been aware of the fictitious nature of the drawee or of the drawee's incapacity to contract at the time he indorsed the bill.[81]

**6–138**   (2) *Presentment for payment to the indorser.* Notice of dishonour is dispensed with where the indorser is the person to whom the bill is presented for payment, as, for example, where the acceptor has died and the bill is presented for payment to the indorser as his personal representative.[82]

**6–139**   (3) *Indorser accommodated.* Notice is also dispensed with where the bill was accepted or made for the accommodation of the indorser.[83] In contrast with the dispensation from presentment for payment contained in section 46(2)(d)[84] it is not required that the indorser has no reason to expect that the bill would be paid if presented.[85]

It is no excuse for failure to give notice of dishonour to an indorser that the drawee or acceptor is as between himself and the drawer under no obligation to accept or pay the instrument.[86] Thus, where payment of a cheque is refused due to insufficient funds or to countermand of payment by the drawer, notice must still be given to an indorser.

---

[78] *Anglo-African Factors (Pty.) Ltd v Cuppusamy* 1974 (3) S.A. 399; *Braz v Afonso* 1998 (1) S.A. 573.
[79] *Hill v Heap* (1823) Dowl. & Ry. N.P. 57.
[80] See above, para.6–131.
[81] *Leach v Hewitt* (1813) 4 Taunt. 731.
[82] *Caunt v Thompson* (1849) 7 C. B. 400.
[83] See above, para.4–041 (s.28).
[84] See above, para.6–075.
[85] Words to this effect were deleted in committee.
[86] *Wilkes v Jacks* (1794) 1 Peake 267; *Brown v Maffey* (1812) 15 East 216; *Foster v Parker* (1876) 2 C.P.D. 18; *Turner v Samson* (1876) 2 Q.B.D. 23. See also (no funds in hands of maker of promissory note) *Carter v Flower* (1847) 16 M. & W. 743. But *cf. Reid v Tustin* (1894) 13 N.Z.L.R. 745.

1. The master of the *Elmville* draws a bill on the owners of the vessel    **6–140**
payable in London to A & Co. in respect of coal supplied and disburse-
ments made by A & Co. on account of the ship. The bill is indorsed by A
& Co. to the claimants and is duly accepted by the drawees. It is handed
to the N Bank for collection, presented for payment on a Saturday, but is
dishonoured. On the following Monday the N Bank communicates the
fact of dishonour to the claimants, who seek information as to the whereabouts of the vessel and find that it is at Newcastle-upon-Tyne. They take
until Thursday in making inquiries as to the location of the vessel at
Newcastle, and then give notice of dishonour to the drawer by a letter
sent by registered post to the ship at Newcastle. The notice is in time,
since there are special circumstances to excuse the delay and the claimants acted with reasonable diligence in making inquiries and giving
notice.[87]

2. A bill drawn by the defendant is dishonoured in London by non-
payment on Saturday, October 2. It is returned to the claimant in Manchester and received by him on Tuesday, October 5. On the same day, the
claimant sends notice of dishonour by messenger during business hours
to the defendant's counting house, but, as the messenger finds the house
locked and no one answering, he comes away without leaving any notice.
On the following Monday the claimant serves the defendant with formal
notice of dishonour. The act of going to the premises and knocking on the
door is not equivalent to notice. But it would have supported an allegation that notice was dispensed with. Alternatively it might be treated as
an excuse for delay in giving the notice which was given on the following
Monday.[88]

3. A bill is drawn by the defendant and indorsed by him to the
claimant. Upon the bill being dishonoured by non-payment, the claimant's solicitor goes to the only address given by the defendant and spends
some time in searching for the defendant in order to give him notice of
dishonour, but is unable to find him there. Subsequently it comes to the
knowledge of the claimant that the defendant is living at another address,
but no notice of dishonour is given to the defendant at that address before
the issue of the writ. Since notice could have been given before the issue
of the writ, the giving of notice is not excused. Notice of dishonour is

[87] *The Elmville (No.1)* [1904] P. 319.
[88] *Allen v Edmundson* (1848) 2 Exch. 719.

dispensed with only where, after the exercise of reasonable diligence, it cannot be given at any time before action brought.[89]

**6–141**    4. The drawer of a bill of exchange, a few days before it becomes due, calls at the counting house of the claimant whom he knows to be the holder. He tells the claimant that he has no regular residence and that he will call and see whether the bill has been paid by the acceptor. This dispenses with notice of dishonour.[90]

5. A bill drawn by the defendant is made payable at the defendant's house. It is indorsed by the defendant to the claimant. On the day the bill becomes due, the claimant takes it to the house and shows it to the defendant's wife. The defendant subsequently makes repeated promises to pay the amount when he should be able. This is evidence to go to the jury either that the defendant received due notice of dishonour or of a subsequent waiver by him of such notice.[91]

6. A bill is indorsed by the defendant to J & Co. and by them to the claimant. Some time after the dishonour of the bill, the defendant, who has received no notice of dishonour, is informed by J & Co. that the claimant is about to take proceedings against him for recovery of the bill, and is asked what he is going to do about it. The defendant says he will pay the bill if the claimant gives him time to pay it. This is a waiver of the right to notice of dishonour. Alternatively it is evidence that the defendant waived that right prior to the time when notice ought to have been given.[92]

**6–142**    7. The drawer of a bill indorses it to J, who indorses it to P, who indorses it to the claimant. On the day after the bill is dishonoured in London, but before the fact of dishonour is known in Yorkshire, the drawer's clerk calls upon P in Yorkshire and informs P that he has come in consequence of an intimation that the bill will probably not be paid. He tells P, "I suppose there will be no alternative but my taking up the bill and if you will bring it next Tuesday I will pay you the money." No notice of dishonour is given by the claimant to P or the drawer. The conversation with P did not dispense with notice of dishonour being given to the drawer. It was not an express, absolute and unconditional promise to pay the bill.[93]

---

[89] *Studdy v Beesty* (1889) 60 L.T. 647.
[90] *Phipson v Kneller* (1815) 4 Camp. 285.
[91] *Cordery v Colville* (1863) 32 L.J.C.P. 210.
[92] *Woods v Dean* (1862) 3 B. & S. 101.
[93] *Pickin v Graham* (1833) 1 C. & M. 725.

8. The claimant is the holder of a cheque for £30 drawn by the defendant on the A Bank. The cheque is duly presented for payment but payment is refused because there are no funds in the defendant's account adequate for payment. No notice of dishonour is required to be given to the defendant.[94]

9. R is indebted to G & Co. in the sum of £115. He draws a bill on B for £20 payable to G & Co. two months after date and gives this to G & Co. on account of the debt. At no time are there any effects of R in the hands of B and in fact R is indebted to B in a substantial amount. The bill is presented for payment and dishonoured. No notice of dishonour need be given by G & Co. to R. R is not discharged and his debt to G & Co. is sufficient to support a petition for a commission in bankruptcy against him.[95]

## Noting or protest of bill

51. (1) Where an inland bill has been dishonoured it may, if the holder think fit, be noted for non-acceptance or non-payment, as the case may be; but it shall not be necessary to note or protest any such bill in order to preserve the recourse against the drawer or indorser.    6–143

(2) Where a foreign bill, appearing on the face of it to be such, has been dishonoured by non-acceptance it must be duly protested for non-acceptance, and where such a bill, which has not been previously dishonoured by non-acceptance, is dishonoured by non-payment it must be duly protested for non-payment. If it be not so protested the drawer and indorsers are discharged. Where a bill does not appear on the face of it to be a foreign bill, protest thereof in case of dishonour is unnecessary.

(3) A bill which has been protested for non-acceptance may be subsequently protested for non-payment.

(4) Subject to the provisions of this Act, when a bill is noted or protested [it may be noted on the day of its dishonour and must be noted not later than the next succeeding business day]. When a bill has been duly noted, the protest may be subsequently extended as of the date of the noting.

(5) Where the acceptor of a bill becomes bankrupt or insolvent or suspends payment before it matures, the holder may cause

---

[94] *Carew v Duckworth* (1869) L.R. 4 Ex. 313.
[95] *Bickerdike v Bollman* (1786) 1 T.R. 405.

the bill to be protested for better security against the drawer and indorsers.

(6) A bill must be protested at the place where it is dishonoured: Provided that—

(a) When a bill is presented through [a postal operator], and returned by post dishonoured, it may be protested at the place to which it is returned and on the day of its return if received during business hours, and if not received during business hours, then not later than the next business day;

(b) When a bill drawn payable at the place of business or residence of some person other than the drawee, has been dishonoured by non-acceptance, it must be protested for non-payment at the place where it is expressed to be payable, and no further presentment for payment to, or demand on, the drawee is necessary.

(7) A protest must contain a copy of the bill, and must be signed by the notary making it, and must specify—

(a) The person at whose request the bill is protested;

(b) The place and date of protest, the cause or reason for protesting the bill, the demand made, and the answer given, if any, or the fact that the drawee or acceptor could not be found.

(8) Where a bill is lost or destroyed, or is wrongly detained from the person entitled to hold it, protest may be made on a copy or written particulars thereof.

(9) Protest is dispensed with by any circumstance which would dispense with notice of dishonour. Delay in noting or protesting is excused when the delay is caused by circumstances beyond the control of the holder, and not imputable to his default, misconduct, or negligence. When the cause of delay ceases to operate the bill must be noted or protested with reasonable diligence.

Amendments

Subs.(4) was amended by s.1 of the Bills of Exchange (Time of Noting) Act 1917. Subs.6(a) was amended by art.4(b) of the Postal Services Act 2000 (Consequential Modifications No.1) Order 2001, SI 2001/1149.

| Definitions | Comparison |
|---|---|
| "bill": s.2. | UCC: § 3–505. |
| "business day": s.92. | ULB: arts 43, 44, 46. |
| "foreign bill": s.4. | ULC: arts 40, 41, 48. |
| "holder": s.2. | UNB: arts 59–62. |

"inland bill": s.4.
"person": s.2.
"postal operator": s.2.
"written": s.2.

## COMMENT

**Protest.** Protest is a declaration, in solemn form, that a bill has been **6–144** dishonoured. It must normally be made by a notary public. Protest derives from the ancient customs of merchants.[96] In many legal systems, it is required upon the dishonour of any bill of exchange or promissory note.[97] But in English law, as a general rule, protest is necessary only to preserve the liability of secondary parties to a foreign bill of exchange. Foreign notes need not be protested.[98] The object of requiring the protest to be made by a notary public is that his office is traditionally recognised, not only in the courts of this country, but in those of every civilised nation.[99] "A Notary Public by the Law of Nations has credit everywhere."[1]

Nevertheless, it is difficult to see why protest of a foreign bill should be mandatory in the sense that a failure to protest will discharge the drawer and indorsers. The Review Committee on Banking Services Law and Practice,[2] recommended that protesting a dishonoured foreign bill should be abolished as a mandatory requirement. Protest would be retained on a voluntary basis. But the Committee further recommended a less formal method of protest, namely, that anyone entitled to take an oath would be able to give a simple certificate of the facts, in lieu of a notarial act. The Government proposes to enact legislation amending the Act so as to give effect to these recommendations.[3]

**Noting and protest.** Noting is an act preliminary to protest. The proce- **6–145** dure is thus explained in *Brooke's Notary*[4]:

"To note a bill means to make a note or minute on the face of it. The note consists of the notary's initials, the date of noting, the noting

---

[96] *Gale v Walsh* (1793) 5 T.R. 239.
[97] ULB, arts 44, 77.
[98] ss.51(1), 52(3), 89(1)(2)(4).
[99] *Halsbury's Laws of England* (4th ed.), Vol. 34, p. 83.
[1] *Hutcheon v Mannington* (1802) 6 Ves. Jun. 823, 824.
[2] (1989) Cm. 622, Chap.8, rec. 8(8); above, para.1–008.
[3] (1990) Cm. 1026, Annex 6, paras 6.6, 6.7. It is nevertheless likely that formal protest by a notary will continue, in order to prove protest in foreign jurisdictions.
[4] 12th ed., 7–53—7–55.

charges and a reference to a mark or number in the notary's register. It is also advisable for the notary to indicate on the bill by the abbreviations 'N/A' or 'N/P' whether the noting is for non-acceptance or non-payment. A ticket is attached to the bill on which is written in abbreviated form the answer given to the clerk when he presented the bill, for instance, 'no effects', 'no orders', or other words giving the general purport of what was said or done."

"The notary should keep a register containing copies, complete in every particular, of all bills and promissory notes which he has noted, showing the minute made on the face of the instrument and the noting ticket attached. In a further register or 'protest book', entered upon a daily basis, he keeps a separate record of instruments noted, indicating the serial number he has allocated, the amount of the bill or note, the date and place of presentment, from whom it was received and to whom it was returned. The record is initialled by the clerk who actually presented the bill or note. From these records a formal instrument called the protest may afterwards be drawn up, signed by the notary, and passed under his official seal."

"Properly speaking, a protest is the formal announcement or attestation under the signature and seal of a notary that a bill has been duly presented and dishonoured by non-acceptance or non-payment. In practice, however, the word protest has a wider meaning, and includes the noting and demand, in short, all the steps that must necessarily be taken to fix liability on a dishonoured bill."

6–146      **When protest is required.** The circumstances in which, under English law, protest of an instrument is mandatory can be ascertained from the present section and from other provisions of the Act. They may be summarised as follows:

(a) *Foreign bills.* The distinction between a "foreign" bill and an "inland" bill is set out in section 4 of the Act. Where a foreign bill, appearing on the face of it to be such, has been dishonoured by non-acceptance, it must be duly protested for non-acceptance in order to preserve the liability of the drawer and indorsers[5]; and where a foreign bill has been accepted as to part, it must be protested as to the balance.[6] Where a foreign bill or cheque,[7] appearing on the face of it to be such, is dishonoured by non-payment, and (in the case of a bill) it has not been previously

[5] s.51(2).
[6] s.44(2) (the drawer and indorsers are otherwise discharged). This subs. does not contain the words "appearing on the face of it to be such": but, unless the contrary appear on the face of the bill, the holder may treat it as an inland bill (s.4(2)).
[7] However, in most cases, protest of a dishonoured cheque will be dispensed with as regards the drawer: ss.50(2)(c)(4)(5), 51(9); see below, para.6–133.

dishonoured by non-acceptance,[8] it must be duly protested for non-payment in order to preserve the liability of the drawer and indorsers.[9]

(b) *Acceptance for honour and case of need.* Protest of a bill, whether it be inland or foreign, is required where resort is made to an acceptor for honour[10] or referee in case of need.[11] Protest is always necessary to found an acceptance for honour *suprà protest*: the bill must first be protested for dishonour by non-acceptance or protested for better security.[12] Where a dishonoured bill has been accepted for honour *suprà protest*, or contains a reference in case of need, it must be protested for non-payment before it is presented for payment to the acceptor for honour, or referee in case of need.[13] If a bill is dishonoured by the acceptor for honour, it must be protested for non-payment by him.[14]

**When protest is not required.** The following provisions of the Act set  6–147
out the circumstances where protest of an instrument is not required:

(a) In order to render the acceptor of a bill liable it is not necessary to protest it.[15]

(b) It is not necessary to protest a dishonoured inland bill or cheque in order to preserve the recourse against the drawer or indorser.[16]

(c) Where an inland or foreign note is dishonoured, protest thereof is unnecessary.[17]

(d) Where a bill or cheque does not appear on the face of it to be a foreign bill or cheque, protest thereof in the case of dishonour is unnecessary.[18]

**When protest is optional.** Protest of an instrument may always be  6–148
effected even though it is not mandatory, and it may be desirable to
protest a bill or note in any event where proceedings are contemplated in
a foreign country. It may also be advantageous to protest for non-acceptance a bill payable at a fixed period after sight.[19] But there are two

---

[8] *cf.* s.51(3).
[9] s.51(2).
[10] For acceptance for honour, see below, para.9–001.
[11] For reference in case of need, see above, para.2–105.
[12] s.65(1). For protest for better security, see s.51(5).
[13] s.67(1). See also s.68 (payment for honour *suprà protest*).
[14] s.67(4).
[15] s.52(3).
[16] s.51(1).
[17] ss.51(1), 52(3), 89(1)(2)(4).
[18] s.51(2).
[19] s.14(3).

situations where the Act expressly provides for the voluntary protest of a bill:

(a) A bill which has been protested for non-acceptance may be subsequently protested for non-payment.[20]

(b) Where the acceptor of a bill becomes bankrupt or insolvent or suspends payment before it matures, the holder may cause the bill to be protested for better security against the drawer and indorsers.[21]

6–149 **Conflict of laws.** Foreign legal systems often provide strict rules governing protest of a bill or note in the event of dishonour by non-acceptance or non-payment.[22] Under section 72(3) of the Act, the necessity for or sufficiency of a protest, or otherwise, are determined by the law of the place where the instrument is dishonoured.[23] Even, therefore, where the instrument is a promissory note, or is an inland bill, or is a foreign bill not appearing on the face of it to be such, if it is payable and dishonoured in a foreign country, protest in the form and within the time-limits stipulated by the law of that country may still be required to charge the drawer or an indorser in England.

6–150 **Scotland.** Protest is required for summary diligence in Scotland.[24]

6–151 **Bank collections.** Under Article 24 of the ICC Uniform Rules for Collections,[25] the collection instruction[26] should give specific instructions regarding protest (or other legal process in lieu thereof) in the event of non-payment or non-acceptance. In the absence of such specific instructions the banks concerned with the collection have no obligation to have the documents protested (or subjected to other legal process in lieu thereof) for non-payment or non-acceptance.

6–152 **Subsection (1): noting inland bill.** An inland bill is defined in section 4. The Act attaches no legal consequences to noting an inland bill, except by making it a necessary preliminary to acceptance and payment for honour.[27] The advantages of noting appear to be purely evidentiary, since neither noting nor protest is necessary to preserve the recourse against

---

[20] s.51(3).
[21] s.51(5).
[22] See, *e.g.* ULB, arts 44, 77 (bills and notes). The requirement of protest is generally more relaxed in the case of cheques: ULC, arts 40, 41.
[23] See below, para.12–031.
[24] See the Comment on s.98; below, para.16–029.
[25] (1995) Brochure No.522; above, para.6–044 (s.45).
[26] See above, para.6–045.
[27] ss.65, 67, 93.

the drawer or indorsers of an inland bill or the indorsers of a note. By
section 57 the expenses of noting may be recovered as liquidated damages.

**Subsection (2): protest of foreign bill.**[28] A foreign bill is defined in     6–153
section 4. Unless the contrary appear on the face of the bill the holder may
treat it as an inland bill.[29] Thus the subsection requires protest only in the
case of a foreign bill "appearing on the face of it to be such".

Unless dispensed with,[30] protest is required where such a foreign bill is
dishonoured by non-acceptance.[31] Although presentment for acceptance
is only necessary in a limited number of circumstances in order to render
liable any party to the bill,[32] if in fact the bill is presented for acceptance
and dishonoured by non-acceptance, protest is required. If the drawee of
the bill is dead or bankrupt, presentment for acceptance is excused.[33] The
bill may then be treated as dishonoured by non-acceptance, and, in such
a case, protest must be effected.

Unless dispensed with,[34] protest is also required where such a foreign
bill is dishonoured by non-payment.[35] However, protest is unnecessary
where the bill has been previously dishonoured by non-acceptance,
although in such a case it may be subsequently protested for non-payment.[36] The fact that presentment for payment has been dispensed with[37]
does not eliminate the need for protest, unless the ground of dispensation
is also a ground for dispensing with notice of dishonour.[38]

Failure to effect due protest, when required, will discharge the drawer     6–154
and indorsers from liability on the bill, but will not affect the liability of
the acceptor.[39]

The requirement of protest for non-payment also extends to foreign
cheques.[40] But, in practice, as regards the drawer, it will ordinarily be
dispensed with,[41] although it remains necessary to charge an indorser of

---

[28] Chalmers stated that this subsection altered the law (9th ed.), p. 2.
[29] s.4(2).
[30] s.51(9).
[31] See also s.44(2) (partial acceptance). For forms of protest, see *Brooke's Notary* (12th ed.),
    12–01.
[32] s.39.
[33] s.40(2)(a).
[34] s.51(9).
[35] For forms of protest, see *Brooke's Notary* (12th ed.), 12–01—12–21.
[36] s.51(3).
[37] s.46(2).
[38] s.51(9).
[39] s.52(3). Nor will it discharge a person who gives an *aval* for the acceptor: see below,
    para.7–039 (s.56).
[40] s.73.
[41] ss.50(2)(c)(4)(5), 51(9).

the cheque. Where a foreign note is dishonoured, protest thereof is unnecessary.[42]

6–155    **Subsection (3): protest for non-payment after non-acceptance.** The option to protest for non-payment a bill which has been protested for non-acceptance appears to have been specifically included because, at the time of the enactment of the Act, some foreign codes did not provide for a right of recourse against the drawer and indorsers upon dishonour by non-acceptance or did not dispense with protest for non-payment after protest for non-acceptance. This is not so in the case of the Geneva Uniform Law on Bills of Exchange and Promissory Notes.[43]

6–156    **Subsection (4): time of protest.** This subsection was amended by section 1 of the Bills of Exchange (Time of Noting) Act 1917. The provisions to which it is subject are subsections (6)(a) and (9) of the present section.

Any necessary protest, or noting, must be effected not later than the next business day succeeding the day of dishonour. "Business day" is defined in section 92 of the Act. The provision that, when a bill has been duly noted, the protest may be subsequently extended as of the date of noting, is supplemented by section 93. That section enables the formal protest to be drawn up later, and ante-dated as of the date of noting.

6–157    **Subsection (5): protest for better security.**[44] The purpose of a protest for better security is (i) to enable the holder to demand security from the drawer and indorsers in a foreign country where the failure of the acceptor before maturity of the bill enables such a demand to be made, and (ii) as a precursor of acceptance for honour *suprà protest*.[45] In English law, however, a protest for better security confers no right upon the holder to demand such security; it does not accelerate the holder's right of recourse against the drawer and indorsers; and it does not dispense with the need for a further protest for non-payment if the bill is dishonoured at maturity.

6–158    **Subsection (6): place of protest.** The reference in this subsection to the "place" where the bill is dishonoured raises a problem of interpretation similar to that discussed in relation to section 49(12) of the Act,[46] although the answer is probably different having regard to the differing purposes of the two provisions. A reasonable construction is, it is submitted, that

[42] s.89(4).
[43] ULB, arts 43, 44.
[44] For the form of protest, see *Brooke's Notary* (12th ed.), 12–15.
[45] s.65.
[46] See above, para.6–105.

"place" means simply the town or city where the bill is dishonoured, and does not bear a more restricted meaning of an address, postal district, or area served by a notary, etc.

Paragraph (a) contains a sensible proviso enabling a bill presented through a postal operator,[47] and returned by post dishonoured, to be protested when and at the place to which it is returned. It is said that this proviso was inserted in committee to protect a common practice of the Liverpool notaries with regard to bills drawn on cotton spinners in Lancashire.[48] For presentment through a postal operator, see sections 41(1)(e) and 45(8). For "business day" see section 92.

The need for the second proviso, in paragraph (b), is by no means apparent. It reproduces the effect of the repealed Bills of Exchange Act 1832.[49] Suppose a bill is drawn on A in Liverpool "payable at the X Bank in London". It is dishonoured by non-acceptance. It must be protested for non-payment in London. No further presentment for payment to, or demand on, A is necessary.

**Subsection (7): requisites in form of protest.**[50] The protest must ordinarily be made by a notary public or other person authorised to act as such. However, by section 94, when the services of a notary cannot be obtained at the place where the bill is dishonoured, protest may be made by any householder or substantial resident of the place in the presence of two witnesses. The form of such a protest is set out in the First Schedule to the Act.

Dealing with the form of protest, *Brooke's Notary* states[51]:

6–159

"There is no prescribed or special form of protest. The only model provided by statute is the form of certificate that is to be used by a householder or other substantial resident, where the services of a notary cannot be obtained. The Bills of Exchange Act, however, directs that every protest must specify the person at whose request the bill is protested; the place and date of protest; the demand made; and either the answer given or the fact that the drawee or acceptor could not be found. It also provides that a protest should contain a copy of the bill and be signed by the notary who makes it. Although the Act does not require the official seal of the notary to be affixed to the instrument, this formality should never in practice be omitted."

[47] Defined in s.2.
[48] *Chalmers* (9th ed.), p.202.
[49] 2 & 3 Will IV, c.98.
[50] For various forms of protest, see *Brooke's Notary* (12th ed.).
[51] 12th ed., 7–56.

**6–160**      **Subsection (8): protest of lost bill or for non-delivery.**[52] Protest is still required in the circumstances set out in this subsection and may be made in the manner indicated. For lost bills, see sections 69 and 70.

**6–161**      **Subsection (9): excuses for non-protest or delay.** Protest is dispensed with by any circumstance which would dispense with notice of dishonour, as set out in section 50(2) of the Act. Since notice of dishonour is dispensed with as regards the drawer where a cheque is dishonoured by non-payment due to inadequate funds in the drawer's account[53] or the fact that the drawer has countermanded payment,[54] protest is not normally required to charge the drawer of a cheque. By section 16(2), the drawer of a bill, and any indorser, may insert therein an express stipulation waiving as regards himself the holder's duty to protest a bill. Since notice of dishonour is dispensed with by waiver express or implied,[55] presumably protest may likewise also be dispensed with by waiver outside the bill.

It may be assumed that a failure to protest for non-acceptance will, as in the case of a failure to give notice of dishonour,[56] not prejudice the rights of a holder in due course subsequent to the omission.

Similar language is used in this subsection to excuse delay in noting or protesting to that used in section 50(1) to excuse delay in giving notice of dishonour.[57]

**6–162**      **Notice of protest.** The Act contains no provision requiring notice of any protest effected to be given to the drawer or indorsers whom it is sought to charge.[58] Protest does not, however, do away with the necessity to give notice of dishonour. The notice of dishonour would ordinarily refer to the fact that the bill had been protested,[59] but there is no obligation to include such a reference.[60]

### Duties of holder as regards drawee or acceptor

**6–163**      **52. (1) When a bill is accepted generally presentment for payment is not necessary in order to render the acceptor liable.**

---

[52] For forms of protest, see *Brooke's Notary* (12th ed.), 12–01—12–21.
[53] s.50(2)(c)(4).
[54] s.50(2)(c)(5).
[55] s.50(2)(b).
[56] s.48(1).
[57] See above, para.6–121.
[58] See also (common law) *Cromwell v Hynson* (1796) 2 Esp. 511; *Robins v Gibson* (1813) 1 M. & S. 288.
[59] See Appendix A, Notices 1, 2, 4.
[60] *Ex p. Lowenthal* (1874) L.R. 9 Ch. 591.

(2) When by the terms of a qualified acceptance presentment for payment is required, the acceptor, in the absence of an express stipulation to that effect, is not discharged by the omission to present the bill for payment on the day that it matures.

(3) In order to render the acceptor of a bill liable it is not necessary to protest it, or that notice of dishonour should be given to him.

(4) Where the holder of a bill presents it for payment, he shall exhibit the bill to the person from whom he demands payment, and when a bill is paid the holder shall forthwith deliver it up to the party paying it.

Definitions
"acceptance": ss.2, 17(1).
"bill": s.2.
"holder": s.2.
"person": s.2.

Comparison
UCC: §§ 3–413, 3–501, 3–503.
ULB: arts 38, 39.
UNB: art.57.

COMMENT

**Subsection (1): general acceptance.** Since the acceptor is the person  6–164
primarily liable on the bill, when a bill is accepted generally, presentment for payment is not necessary in order to render him liable. The same applies to the maker of a promissory note, unless the note is in the body of it made payable at a particular place.[61] Nevertheless a holder would not be likely to bring an action without first applying to the acceptor or maker for payment and, if he did so, the court might well make him pay the costs, and deprive him of interest.[62]

A general acceptance is defined in section 19(2) of the Act. Presentment for payment is dealt with in section 45.

**Subsection (2): qualified acceptance.** The acceptor may, by the terms  6–165
of a qualified acceptance, make presentment for payment a condition precedent to his liability.[63] Thus, if a bill is accepted "Payable at the X Bank only", the holder must present it for payment at that bank before he can sue the acceptor. Nevertheless, although a bill not payable on demand must be presented for payment on the day it falls due in order

[61] s.87(1).
[62] See below, para.7–048 (s.57).
[63] s.19(2)(c).

to charge the drawer and indorsers,[64] the acceptor is not discharged by the omission to present the bill for payment on the day that it matures, unless there is an express stipulation that presentment must be made on that day. A qualified acceptance is defined in section 19(2) of the Act.

By section 87(1), where a promissory note is in the body of it made payable at a particular place, it must be presented for payment at that place in order to render the maker liable. By section 89(2), the provisions of this subsection would apply in that case.

**6–166** **Subsection (3): no notice or protest required.** Again, because the acceptor is the party primarily liable on the bill and is the author of the dishonour of the instrument, in order to render him liable it is not necessary to protest the bill,[65] or that notice of dishonour should be given to him. This is so, even though the acceptance is to pay only at a particular specified place, *e.g.* at a bank.[66] The same rule applies to the maker of a note.[67]

Notice of dishonour is dealt with in sections 48 and 49 of the Act, and protest in section 51.

**6–167** **Subsection (4): production of bill.** The party demanding payment of a bill must produce, and offer to deliver up, the instrument itself.[68] "Holder" is defined in section 2, and payment is dealt with in section 59 of the Act.

If the bill is paid, it must forthwith be delivered up to the party paying it. "The acceptor paying the bill", said Lord Tenterden,[69] "has a right to the possession of the instrument for his own security, and as his voucher and discharge *pro tanto* in his account with the drawer". This subsection applies also to cheques[70] and promissory notes.[71] However, section 74B of the Act[72] permits the "truncation" of cheques as an alternative means of presentment, that is to say the notification by a banker to the banker on whom the cheque is drawn of its essential features by electronic means or otherwise instead of presenting the cheque itself. In such a case, the subsection does not apply.[73]

---

[64] s.45(1).
[65] *Friedrich Kling GmbH v Continental Jewellery* 1993 (3) S.A. 76.
[66] *Treacher v Hinton* (1821) 4 B. & Ald. 413, 415. See also *Smith v Thatcher* (1821) 4 B. & Ald. 200.
[67] s.89(1)(2)(4).
[68] *Ramuz v Crowe* (1847) 1 Exch. 167, 174 (negotiable bill).
[69] *Hansard v Robinson* (1827) 7 B. & C. 90, 94. See also *Auchteroni & Co. v Midland Bank Ltd* [1928] 2 K.B. 294, 300.
[70] s.73.
[71] s.89(1).
[72] Inserted by the Deregulation (Bills of Exchange) Order 1996 (SI 1996/2993); above, para.6–063.
[73] s.74C.

Where a bill or note is payable at a bank, and has been duly paid, the bank will normally return the paid instrument to its customer. But it is no longer the practice of most banks to return paid cheques.[74]

For lost bills and notes, see sections 69 and 70. For bills in a set, see section 71.

## Liabilities of Parties

### Funds in hands of drawee

53. (1) A bill, of itself, does not operate as an assignment of funds in  7–001
the hands of the drawee available for the payment thereof, and the drawee of a bill who does not accept as required by this Act is not liable on the instrument. This subsection shall not extend to Scotland.

(2) [Subject to section 75A of this Act,] in Scotland, where the drawee of a bill has in his hands funds available for the payment thereof, the bill operates as an assignment of the sum for which it is drawn in favour of the holder, from the time when the bill is presented to the drawee.

Amendment
Subs.(2) was amended by s.11(a) of the Law Reform (Miscellaneous Provisions) (Scotland) Act 1985.

Definitions
"acceptance": ss.2, 17(1).
"bill": s.2.
"holder": s.2.

Comparison
UCC: §§ 3–408, 3–409.
UNB: art.37.

### COMMENT

**No liability of drawee on unaccepted bill.** A bill is an order to pay.[1]  7–002
By his acceptance the drawee signifies his assent to the order of the drawer.[2] The drawee of a bill who does not accept as required by the Act[3] is not liable on the instrument.[4]

---

[74] See also Cheques Act 1957, s.3 (evidence of receipt).
[1] s.3(1).
[2] s.17(1).
[3] ss.2, 17–19, 21.
[4] s.53(1).

Even though, as between himself and the drawer, the drawee is under an obligation to accept or pay the bill, he can incur no liability on it unless and until he accepts. The same applies to cheques. A banker may, as between himself and his customer, be under an obligation to honour cheques drawn on him by the customer. But he is under no liability on the cheque if he fails to do so.[5]

Any cause of action against the drawee of an unaccepted bill, or of a cheque, can therefore only arise otherwise than on the instrument.

7–003     **Contractual liability.** The drawee of a bill may, by an agreement external to the bill, undertake to accept or pay it.[6] Failure to accept or pay in accordance with the terms of his undertaking will then render him liable to the other party to that agreement. The relationship of banker and customer imposes upon the banker a duty to his customer to pay cheques drawn on him by the customer if there are at the time of presentment funds in current account to the credit of the customer sufficient to meet the cheque or if he has agreed to provide the customer with overdraft facilities sufficient to meet it.[7] But a banker is under no similar duty to pay bills or notes accepted or made by his customer and domiciled with him for payment,[8] or to accept or pay bills of exchange drawn on him by the customer,[9] in the absence of special agreement, express or implied. In any event, even if there is such an agreement between the drawee and drawer of the instrument, this will normally impose no contractual liability on the drawee to the payee or other holder of the instrument, as there is no privity of contract between them.[10] While it is in theory possible for the payee to acquire rights against the drawee under the Contracts (Rights of Third Parties) Act 1999 from an agreement external to the instrument, it is probable that, in most cases, the parties to the agreement will be found not to have intended to confer any rights on the payee.[11]

Privity may nevertheless be established where, for example, a banker undertakes to accept or pay bills drawn on him pursuant to a commercial letter of credit,[12] whether that undertaking is given to one person only (as

---

[5] *Hopkinson v Forster* (1874) L.R. 19 Eq. 74; *Schroeder v Central Bank of London Ltd* (1876) 34 L.T. 735 (Illustration 1); *R. v Kassim* [1992] 1 A.C. 9. The position remains unaltered as a result of the enactment of the Contracts (Rights of Third Parties) Act 1999, since s.6(1) of the Act expressly states that it does not confer any rights on a third party in the case of bills of exchange, promissory notes and other negotiable instruments.

[6] *Smith v Brown* (1815) 6 Taunt. 340, 344; *Laing v Barclay* (1823) 1 B. & C. 398.

[7] See below, para.13–032 (s.75).

[8] *Robarts v Tucker* (1851) 16 Q.B. 560, 579; *Bank of England v Vagliano Brothers* [1891] A.C. 107, 157. *cf. Kymer v Laurie* (1849) L.J.Q.B. 218 (authority to pay).

[9] *Goodwin v Robarts* (1875) L.R. 10 Ex. 337, 351 (affirmed (1876) 1 App. Cas. 476); *Re Boyse (No.3)* (1886) 33 Ch.D. 612, 624.

[10] See also *Wells v First National Commercial Bank* [1998] P.N.L.R. 552 (no liability in tort).

[11] Contracts (Rights of Third Parties) Act 1999, s.1(2).

[12] See *Benjamin's Sale of Goods* (6th ed., Sweet & Maxwell), §§ 23–131 *et seq.*

in the case of a "straight credit" directed solely to the named beneficiary of the credit) or to persons generally (as in the case of a "negotiation credit" which extends to any bona fide holder of a bill of exchange drawn by the beneficiary).

A banker may also undertake to the holder of a cheque drawn on him by his customer that the cheque will be paid when presented for payment, provided certain stipulated conditions are satisfied. Such is the case, for example, where a bank issues a cheque guarantee card, whereby it undertakes (subject to the fulfilment of certain conditions referred to on the card) to honour its customer's cheque.[13] The undertaking contained in the card is not addressed to any particular person or group of persons, but to any person who acts on it, for example, by supplying money, goods or services in return for the cheque. Similarly, in the case of travellers' letters of credit, a banker will undertake to reimburse advances made to the beneficiary against bills or cheques drawn by the beneficiary up to a specified amount. The letter of credit may be "specially advised", that is to say, addressed to a particular person or persons, such as the issuer's correspondent bank in another country, or it may be "general" (or "open") when it is addressed to all bankers or other persons in general.[14]

In one instance, a quasi-privity is established between the banker and the holder of a cheque by section 74(3) of the Act,[15] which provides that where the holder of a cheque omits to present it within a reasonable time, whereby the drawer has been damnified (*i.e.* by the bank failing), the drawer is *pro tanto* discharged, and the holder is substituted as a creditor of the bank.

7–004

A banker may be approached by a person who has accepted or is about to accept in payment a cheque drawn on the banker for an oral assurance that the cheque is "good" or "all right". If the banker chooses to give that assurance, it is submitted that he does not thereby undertake to pay the cheque on presentment. The effect of such an assurance will, of course, vary according to its precise terms, but it is likely to be construed merely as a representation that the person named as drawer maintains a current account with the banker and, possibly, that there are at the time sufficient funds in that account to meet the cheque. If that representation were untrue when made, an action might lie against the banker for negligent misstatement.[16] But otherwise no action would lie if payment were subsequently refused, for example, because there were by then insufficient funds in the account or because the drawer countermanded payment or

---

[13] See *Chitty on Contracts* (29th ed., Sweet & Maxwell), Vol.II, §§ 34–158, 38–447; and below, para.13–042.

[14] *Re Agra and Masterman's Bank* (1867) L.R. 2 Ch.App. 391 (Illustration 3).

[15] See below, para.13–020.

[16] *Hedley Byrne & Co. Ltd v Heller & Partners Ltd* [1969] A.C. 465.

because the signature of the drawer on the cheque was forged or unauthorised.

A banker may also be requested to confirm expressly that a cheque presented to him for payment has in fact been paid. Again an action might, in some circumstances, lie against him for negligent misstatement if he erroneously confirmed to the payee or other holder the payment of the cheque. Such a confirmation might also estop him from recovering from the recipient money paid by mistake[17]; but the mere fact of payment would not give rise to any estoppel.[18]

**7–005** **Assignment.** In England, a bill of itself does not operate as an assignment of funds in the hands of the drawee[19] available for the payment thereof.[20] The same principle applies to cheques. Thus the drawing and issue of a cheque, and its presentment for payment to the bank on which it is drawn, does not entitle the payee to maintain an action against the bank in respect of such part of the drawer's credit balance with the bank as is represented by the cheque, nor does it confer upon the payee any interest, whether legal or equitable, in that balance.[21]

The position is otherwise in Scotland. By subsection (2), in Scotland, where the drawee of a bill (or cheque) has in his hands funds available for the payment thereof, the bill or cheque operates as an assignment of the sum for which it is drawn in favour of the holder, from the time when it is presented to the drawee.[22] However, in view of the difficulty caused by this "funds attached" principle in relation to cheques where the drawer countermanded payment,[23] by an amendment effected by the Law Reform (Miscellaneous Provisions) (Scotland) Act 1985,[24] subsection (2) is made subject to a newly introduced section 75A. The result is that, on the

---

[17] See below, para.8–026 (s.59).
[18] *National Westminster Bank Ltd v Barclays Bank International Ltd* [1975] Q.B. 654 (s.59, Illustration 18); *Barclays Bank Ltd v W.J. Simms, Son & Cooke (Southern) Ltd* [1980] Q.B. 677 (s.59, Illustration 19).
[19] Or of funds belonging to the drawee (or acceptor) at the bank where the bill is domiciled for payment: *Yates v Bell* (1820) 3 B. & Ald. 643; *Moore v Bushell* (1857) 27 L.J. Ex. 3; *Hill v Royds* (1869) L.R. 8 Eq. 290; *Auchteroni & Co. v Midland Bank* [1928] 2 K.B. 294, 299.
[20] s.53(1). See also *Shand v Du Buisson* (1874) L.R. 18 Eq. 283, 288–289; *Citizen's Bank of Louisiana v New Orleans Bank* (1873) L.R. 6 H.L. 352; *Brown, Shipley & Co. v Kough* (1885) 29 Ch.D. 848.
[21] *Schroeder v Central Bank of London Ltd* (1876) 34 L.T. 735 (Illustration 1).
[22] *British Linen Co. v Carruthers* (1883) 10 R. 923; *British Linen Co. v Rainey* (1885) 12 R. 825; *Thompson v Jolly Carters Inn Ltd* 1972 S.C. 215; *Bank of Scotland v Richmond & Co.* 1997 S.C.L.R. 303; cf. *Kirkwood & Sons v Clydesdale Bank* 1908 S.C. 20; *Dickson v Clydesdale Bank* 1937 S.L.T. 585; *Sutherland v Royal Bank of Scotland plc* 1997 S.L.T. 329. Subs. (2) applies where a bill has been presented for acceptance, and acceptance has been refused: *Watt's Trustees v Pinkney* (1853) 16 D. 279; *Carter v McIntosh* (1862) 24 D. 925. It is irrelevant that presentment was irregular. This principle is to be the subject of re-consideration: see below, para.7–008.
[23] See Gretton (1983) 28 J.L.S.S. 333, 389, and below, para.13–072 (s.75A).
[24] s.11(a).

countermand of payment of a cheque, the bank is to be treated as having no funds available for the payment of the cheque.

It is nevertheless open to the drawer of a bill to assign to the payee or any other person the whole or part of any funds standing to his credit in the hands of the drawee by an equitable assignment[25] or a statutory assignment under section 136 of the Law of Property Act 1925,[26] and such an assignment will bind the drawee from the time when he receives notice of the assignment.[27] It is arguable that there can be no valid assignment of the credit balance on a current account until demand has been made for repayment, on the ground that there is no debt owing from the banker which is capable of being assigned until such a demand has been made.[28] But the better view is that such a credit balance can be assigned even before demand.[29]

A bill of exchange is an order to pay, but an order to pay out of a **7–006** particular fund is not unconditional within the meaning of section 3(1) of the Act and so cannot be a bill of exchange.[30] An instrument directing the drawee to pay out of a particular fund might, though invalid as a bill, nevertheless be a valid equitable assignment by the drawer to the payee of part of that fund, but only if the direction is declared to be irrevocable and is not a mere revocable mandate to pay.[31]

**Restitution.** The drawee of a bill may also be liable outside the bill in **7–007** an action for money had and received brought by the payee of the instrument where funds are remitted to the drawee by the drawer in order to meet the bill. If the drawee is directed or requested by the drawer to pay the whole or part of those funds to the payee, assents so to do and communicates such assent to the payee, *i.e.* "attorns to the payee", he thereafter holds to the use of the payee the funds (or such part thereof as has been transferred) when received from the drawer.[32] This principle was extended by Barry J. in *Shamia v Joory*[33] to a case where there was no "fund" as such in the hands of the defendant, but merely a debt owing

---

[25] See *Chitty on Contracts* (29th ed.), Vol.I, § 19–020.
[26] See *Chitty on Contracts* (29th ed.), Vol.I, § 19–006. But, in the case of a statutory assignment, part only of the debt cannot be assigned. *Forster v Baker* [1910] 2 K.B. 636; *Re Steel Wing Co.* [1921] 1 Ch. 349; *Williams v Atlantic Assurance Co.* [1933] 1 K.B. 81,100; *Walter and Sullivan Ltd v Murphy & Sons Ltd* [1955] 2 Q.B. 584.
[27] See *Chitty on Contracts* (29th ed.), Vol.I, §§ 19–016, 19–020.
[28] *Schroeder v Central Bank of London Ltd* (1876) 34 L.T. 735, 736 (approved in *Joachimson v Swiss Bank Corp.* [1921] 3 K.B. 110).
[29] *Walker v Bradford Old Bank* (1884) 12 Q.B.D. 511.
[30] See above, para.2–020 (s.3).
[31] See above, para.2–021 (s.3).
[32] *Griffin v Weatherby* (1868) L.R. 3 Q.B. 753 (Illustration 4). See also *Walker v Rostron* (1842) 9 M. & W. 411; *Greenway v Atkinson* (1881) 29 W.R. 560; *W.P. Greenhalgh & Sons v Union Bank of Manchester* [1924] 2 K.B. 153, 161.
[33] [1958] 1 Q.B. 448. *cf. Liversidge v Broadbent* (1859) 4 H. & N. 603.

from the defendant to the transferor, which at the request of the transferor the defendant promised the claimant would be paid to him. Although this extension has been criticised on the ground that it "blurs the essential distinction between assignment and attornment",[34] the transfer of the debt or fund effected by the operation of this principle is distinct from that of an equitable assignment in that the drawee must assent to the drawer's instruction and further make a promise of payment to the payee.[35]

**7–008**     **Revision of Scots Law.** The Review Committee on Banking Services Law and Practice recommended that the "funds attached" principle of Scots Law set out in subsection (2) should be abolished except in relation to instruments other than cheques.[36] The Government proposes to consult interested parties in Scotland on this recommendation and to take account of their views in reaching a conclusion whether a change in the law is necessary and desirable.[37]

**7–009**     **Marked or certified cheques.** A bank on which a cheque is drawn may be requested to mark the cheque or "certify" it as good for payment. The request may come from (i) the collecting bank, (ii) the bank's own customer, the drawer, or (iii) the payee or other holder.

Previously where a cheque was received by the collecting bank too late for presentation through the clearing house on the day of receipt, the collecting bank might request the drawee bank to mark the cheque as good for the purposes of clearance.[38] Such marking was, by the custom of bankers, recognised as constituting a promise to pay,[39] provided that the cheque was presented through clearing[40] the next day. It was not an acceptance of the cheque by the drawee bank,[41] but the marking was treated as the equivalent of paying the cheque. This practice has now ceased.

Marking or certification by the drawee bank at the request of the drawer or holder is extremely rare in the United Kingdom,[42] although it

---

[34] Goff and Jones, *The Law of Restitution* (6th ed.), 28–003.

[35] *Williams v Everett* (1811) 14 East 582, 597; *Warwick v Rogers* (1843) 5 M. & G. 340, 374; *Griffin v Weatherby* (1868) L.R. 3 Q.B. 753, 758–759.

[36] (1989) Cm. 622, rec. 7(10); above, para.1–008.

[37] (1990) Cm. 1026, Annex 5, paras 5.15–5.18.

[38] See Ellinger, Lomnicka and Hooley, *Modern Banking Law* (3rd ed.), p.349; *Paget* (10th ed.), p.209.

[39] *Robson v Bennett* (1810) 2 Taunt. 388; *Goodwin v Robarts* (1875) L.R. 10 Ex. 337, 351–352 (affirmed (1876) 1 App. Cas. 476); *Bank of Baroda Ltd v Punjab National Bank Ltd* [1944] A.C. 176, 185.

[40] See above, para.6–062 (s.45).

[41] *cf.*, *Robson v Bennett* (1810) 2 Taunt. 388 at 396.

[42] See *Paget* (10th ed.), p.209, setting out the resolution of the Committee of London Clearing Bankers (1920) but cheques are occasionally still marked for customers by merchant banks. There is now no discussion of the topic in *Paget* (12th ed.), 18.14.

is not uncommon in some North American jurisdictions[43] and in South Africa.[43a] In Canada it has been held that certification is equivalent to an acceptance.[44] The drawee bank is in consequence bound to pay the cheque[45] even if, for example, the drawer's signature on the cheque is forged.[46] Where certification is at the request of the drawer, he is precluded from countermanding payment of the cheque,[47] and it is the practice of banks in that country to transfer from the drawer's account to a special account the amount required to meet the certified cheque.[48] Moreover, since the holder has no right as between himself and the drawer to present the cheque for any purpose other than payment, if he presents the cheque to the drawee bank for certification and it is duly certified, the drawer is discharged[49]: as between the drawer and holder, certification is the equivalent of payment, the proceeds of the cheque being transferred out of the drawer's account and notionally redeposited with the bank.[50]

In English law, however, it is clear that marking or certification of a **7–010** cheque is not an acceptance of the cheque by the drawee bank, since it lacks the essential characteristics of an acceptance.[51] Such marking does not constitute an undertaking by the bank to the holder of the cheque that it will be paid on presentment.[52] At most it could be relied upon as a representation by the bank to the holder as to genuiness of the cheque and of the signature by the drawer, and possibly also as a representation that, at the time of marking, there are funds in the drawer's account

---

[43] See *Crawford and Falconbridge* (8th ed.), p.1796; UCC, § 3–409.

[43a] Bills of Exchange Act, No.34 of 1964, s.72A.

[44] *Maubach v Bank of Nova Scotia* (1987) 40 D.L.R. (4th) 134; *Citizens Trust Co. v Hong Kong Bank of Canada* (1991) 85 D.L.R. (4th) 762; *A.E. Le Page Real Estate Services Ltd v Rattray Publications* (1994) 120 D.L.R. (4th) 499; *Bank of Nova Scotia v Canada Trust Co.* (1998) 39 O.R. (3d) 84; Geva (1986) 65 Can.Bar Rev. 107. But there are significant differences between these two obligations.

[45] See the cases cited in n.14, above, and *Honeywell Ltd v Sherwood Credit Union Ltd* (1989) 58 D.L.R. (4th) 249; *Centrac Ltd v Canadian Imperial Bank of Commerce* (1994) 120 D.L.R. (4th) 250; *Crawford and Falconbridge* (8th ed.), p.1796. See also the Privy Council cases (from Canada): *Gaden v Newfoundland Savings Bank* [1899] A.C. 281, 285–286; *Imperial Bank of Canada v Bank of Hamilton* [1903] A.C. 49, 54.

[46] *Citizens Trust Co. v Hong Kong Bank of Canada* (1991) 85 D.L.R. (4th) 762. See also s.54(2) and above, para.3–056 (s.24).

[47] *Steinback Credit Union Ltd v Seitz* (1988) 50 D.L.R. (4th) 436.

[48] "funds appropriation", see *Crawford and Falconbridge* (8th ed.), pp.1797–1798.

[49] *Boyd v Nasmith* (1889) 17 O.R. 40, 42; *Broadhead v Royal Bank of Canada* (1968) 70 D.L.R. (2d) 445. See also *Marr's Marine Ltd v Rosetown Chrysler Plymouth Ltd* (1975) 61 D.L.R. (3d) 497 (cheque not cashed).

[50] *Crawford and Falconbridge* (8th ed.), pp.1791, 1796.

[51] See s.17 and *Bank of Baroda Ltd v Punjab National Bank Ltd* [1944] A.C. 176 (Illustration 5). cf. *Adaikappa Chettia v Thos Cook & Son Ltd* (1930) 31 N.L.R. (Ceylon) 385; (1932) 34 N.L.R. (Ceylon) 44; UCC, § 3–409 (d).

[52] *Bank of Baroda Ltd v Punjab National Bank Ltd* [1944] A.C. 176 at 191. The position remains unaltered as a result of the Contracts (Rights of Third Parties) Act 1999. See *ibid.*, s.6(1).

sufficient to meet the cheque.[53] Any estoppel raised against the bank by such representations would not, however, give rise to a cause of action against the bank on the part of the holder, since the bank is, *vis-à-vis* the holder, under no duty to pay the cheque.[54] An action might possibly lie against the bank for negligent misstatement on the principle enunciated in *Hedley Byrne & Co. Ltd v Heller & Partners Ltd*[55] but not on the basis of any warranty that the cheque would be honoured.[56] The marking of a cheque at the request of the drawer would not, it is submitted, justify the bank in ignoring the drawer's countermand of payment. Further, in English law, a cheque of itself does not operate as an assignment of funds in the hands of the drawee bank available for the payment thereof[57] and, since marking does not constitute an undertaking by the bank to pay the cheque, it is unlikely that it would enable the holder to claim against the bank any part of the sum standing to the drawer's credit as money had and received to his use.[58]

**7–011** **Bank giro credits.** The operation of the giro system lies outside the scope of the present work.[59] Doubts have, however, been raised as to whether or not a transfer instruction by bank giro credit constitutes a legal assignment of the funds involved.[60] The Review Committee on Banking Services Law and Practice[61] recommended that legislation should make it clear such an instruction is not an assignment,[62] and the Government proposes to introduce into legislation a clarifying provision to avoid any future uncertainty.[63]

ILLUSTRATIONS

**7–012** 1. H draws a cheque for £26 on the defendant bank, payable to bearer, and hands it to the claimants, who present it for payment. Payment is

---

[53] *Bank of Baroda Ltd v Punjab National Bank Ltd* [1944] A.C. 176 at 191; *Gaden v Newfoundland Savings Bank* [1899] A.C. 281, 285. Contrast *Thomson v Simpson* (1870) 5 Ch.App. 659 (mere business statement).

[54] In any event, it would be open to the bank to correct the representations before the holder had acted to his detriment in reliance on them.

[55] [1969] A.C. 465.

[56] See Ellinger, Lomnicka and Hooley, *Modern Banking Law* (3rd ed.), pp.349–351; *Paget* (10th ed.), p.210; *Byles* (27th ed.), 22–58; Chorley, *Law of Banking* (6th ed.), p.51.

[57] s.53(1); see above, para.7–005.

[58] See above, para.7–007.

[59] *Chitty on Contracts* (29th ed.), Vol.II, §§ 34–367—34–410; Ellinger, Lomnicka and Hooley, *Modern Banking Law* (3rd ed.), Chap.12.

[60] Chorley, *Law of Banking* (5th ed.), pp.268, 269.

[61] See above, para.1–008.

[62] (1989) Cm. 662, rec. 7(13); above, para.1–009.

[63] (1990) Cm. 1026, Annex 5, paras 5.21, 5.22.

refused. At the time of the refusal, the defendants have in their hands funds belonging to H to an amount exceeding that for which the cheque is drawn. The claimants have no remedy against the defendant bank. There is no privity of contract between them, and no assignment of any funds in the hands of the bank. A cheque is an order to pay and no more.[64]

2. The claimants agree to manufacture and sell certain machinery to buyers in Calcutta. Pursuant to the contract of sale, the defendant bank opens a confirmed irrevocable letter of credit in favour of the claimants by which the bank undertakes to pay the amounts of bills drawn on the buyers to a maximum of £70,000, provided the bills are accompanied by certain stipulated documents. The claimants duly tender to the bank bills accompanied by the required documents, but, on the instructions of the buyers, the bank refuses to pay part of the amount represented by the invoices for the goods. The refusal of the bank to take and pay the bills on presentment of the proper documents constitutes a repudiatory breach by the bank of the undertaking contained in the letter of credit for which the bank is liable to the claimants in damages.[65]

3. The A Bank gives to D & Co. a letter addressed to them in the following terms: "No.394. You are hereby authorized to draw upon this bank at six months' sight to the extent of £15,000, and such drafts I undertake duly to honour on presentation. This credit will remain in force for twelve months from its date, and parties negotiating bills under it are requested to indorse particulars on the back hereof." D & Co. draw bills under this letter to the amount of £6,000, and indorse them to the B Bank, which duly indorses particulars thereof on the letter. The bills so drawn are dishonoured and the A bank is subsequently wound up. The B bank is entitled to prove in the liquidation for the amount of the bills. The letter of credit constitutes a contract to the benefit of which all persons taking and paying for bills on the faith of it are entitled.[66]

4. J draws a bill of exchange on the defendant payable to the claimants.  **7–013** The defendant does not accept the bill but informs the claimants that he will honour it when funds of J come into his hands to meet it. Funds do so come into his hands and he repeatedly promises to pay the money to the claimants, but nothing is in fact paid owing to a dispute between the defendant and J as to the amount. The claimants can maintain an action against the defendant for money had and received to their use.[67]

[64] *Schroeder v Central Bank of London Ltd* (1876) 34 L.T. 735.
[65] *Urquhart Lindsay & Co. v Eastern Bank* [1922] 1 K.B. 318.
[66] *Re Agra and Masterman's Bank, Ex. p. Asiatic Banking Corp.* (1867) L.R. 2 Ch.App. 391.
[67] *Griffin v Weatherby* (1868) L.R. 3 Q.B. 753.

5. A cheque is drawn by G on the appellant bank in Calcutta payable to M. The cheque is post-dated June 20, 1939, and bears the notation "Marked good for payment on 20.6.39" and the signature of a branch manager of the appellant bank. M indorses the cheque generally and, on June 13, 1939, negotiates it for value to the respondent bank, which takes it in good faith as security for an overdraft. The cheque is presented for payment on the due date but is dishonoured due to absence of funds in G's account. The marking of the cheque does not constitute an acceptance. The respondent bank, as holder in due course, cannot claim against the appellant bank, either in contract on the actual words used in the certification, there being no privity of contract between themselves and the drawee bank and no consideration passing, or on an estoppel.[68]

### Liability of acceptor

7–014
54. The acceptor of a bill, by accepting it—
(1) Engages that he will pay it according to the tenor of his acceptance:
(2) Is precluded from denying to a holder in due course:
    (a) The existence of the drawer, the genuineness of his signature, and his capacity and authority to draw the bill;
    (b) In the case of a bill payable to drawer's order, the then capacity of the drawer to indorse, but not the genuineness or validity of his indorsement;
    (c) In the case of a bill payable to the order of a third person, the existence of the payee and his then capacity to indorse, but not the genuineness or validity of his indorsement.

| Definitions | Comparison |
|---|---|
| "acceptance": ss.2, 17(1). | UCC: § 3–413. |
| "bill": s.2. | ULB: art.28. |
| "holder": s.2. | UNB: art.40. |
| "holder in due course": s.29. | |
| "indorsement": s.2. | |

### COMMENT

7–015
**Subsection (1): liability of acceptor.**[69] The requirements for a valid acceptance are set out in sections 2, 17 to 19 and 21 of the Act. The drawee

---

[68] *Bank of Baroda Ltd v Punjab National Bank Ltd* [1944] A.C. 176, PC.
[69] For precedents of pleadings, see Appendix B(1)(3)(4)(5).

of a bill, by accepting it, becomes the party primarily liable thereon to the holder.[70] "His engagement", said Bayley J.,[71] "is general, that he will pay; that of the drawer and indorsers is conditional, namely, that if due diligence be used, they will pay, if the acceptor does not". When a bill is accepted generally, presentment for payment is not necessary in order to render the acceptor liable,[72] nor is it necessary to protest it or that notice of dishonour should be given to him.[73]

The words in the subsection "according to the tenor of his acceptance" take account of the fact that his acceptance may be qualified,[74] in which case his engagement to pay will be conditioned by the terms of his acceptance, including the necessity for presentment for payment where so stipulated in the acceptance.[75]

However, parol evidence[76] is admissible in certain circumstances to show that a bill has been accepted for the accommodation of the drawer,[77] and that, as between himself and the drawer, the acceptor is in substance a mere surety for the drawer.[78]

For the measure of damages recoverable against the acceptor for dishonour of a bill by non-payment, see section 57 of the Act.

**Right to securities held by acceptor.** Where a bill is on the face of it **7–016** drawn against a specific consignment of goods,[79] and the acceptor becomes insolvent, the holder does not thereby obtain any charge over the goods upon dishonour of the bill.[80] But a charge may arise if the acceptor agrees, outside the bill, that securities held by him are to be specifically appropriated to meet the bill.[81] Thus if a security has been lodged by the drawer with the acceptor in order to cover the acceptor's liability on the bill, and it has been agreed between them that the security is to be specifically appropriated to meet the bill, the drawer is entitled in equity to a charge over the security to the extent of the amount of the bill should it be dishonoured. The charge may be asserted by the party to the

---

[70] *Philpot v Briant* (1828) 4 Bing 717, 720; *Jones v Broadhurst* (1850) 9 C.B. 173, 181.
[71] *Rowe v Young* (1820) 2 Bligh H.L. 391, 467.
[72] s.52(1).
[73] s.52(3). But see ss.65(1), 67(1)(4) (acceptance for honour); above, para.6–146 (s.51).
[74] ss.19(1)(2), 44.
[75] ss.19(2)(c), 52(2).
[76] See above, para.2–155 (s.21).
[77] See above, para.2–165 (s.28).
[78] See above, para.4–043 (s.28).
[79] See above, para.2–009.
[80] *Banner v Johnston* (1871) L.R. 5 H.L. 157; *Robey & Co.'s Perseverance Ironworks v Ollier* (1872) L.R. 7 Ch. 695; *Re Entwhistle, Ex p. Arbuthnot* (1876) 3 Ch.D. 477; *Re Suse, Ex p. Dever* (1884) 13 Q.B.D. 766; *Brown Shipley & Co. v Kough* (1885) 29 Ch.D. 848.
[81] *Ex p. Flower* (1835) 4 D. & C. 449; *Ex p. Imbert* (1851) 1 De G. & J. 152; *Inman v Clare* (1858) Johns. 769, 776.

agreement in whose favour the charge is created.[82] However, "where, as between the drawer and the acceptor of a bill of exchange, a security has, by virtue of a contract between them, been specifically appropriated to meet that bill at maturity, and has been lodged for that purpose by the drawer with the acceptor; then, if both drawer and acceptor become insolvent, and their estates are brought under a forced administration, the bill-holder, though neither party nor privy to the contract, is entitled to have the specifically appropriated security applied in or towards payment of the debt".[83]

**7–017**    **Subsection (2): estoppels binding acceptor.** Certain statutory estoppels or "preclusions"[84] are raised against the acceptor of a bill by virtue of his acceptance.[85] They are available only to a holder in due course,[86] and not to any other holder, *i.e.* a holder for value,[87] a "mere" holder[88] or the original payee of the instrument.[89]

First, under paragraph (a), the acceptor is precluded from denying to a holder in due course "the existence of the drawer,[90] the genuineness of his signature,[91] and his capacity[92] and authority[93] to draw the bill". The signature of the drawer may be forged or unauthorised and so, wholly inoperative.[94] Nevertheless, the acceptor will not be permitted, as against

---

[82] *i.e.* in the example cited, the drawer. But see (holder) *Ex p. Imbert* (1851) 1 De G. & J. 152; *Ex p. Carrick* (1858) 2 De G. & J. 208; *Ranken v Alfaro* (1877) 5 Ch.D. 786.

[83] *Ex p. Waring* (1815) 19 Ves. 345, as explained in *Re Suse, Ex p. Dever (No.2)* (1885) 14 Q.B.D. 611, 620. See also *Powles v Hargreaves* (1853) 3 De G.M. & G. 430; *Re New Zealand Banking Co.* (1867) L.R. 4 Eq. 226, 229; *Re Securitibank Ltd* [1978] 1 N.Z.L.R. 97; *Byles* (27th ed.), 34–30; O'Donovan and Phillips, *The Modern Contract of Guarantee* (English ed.) 12–325. *cf. Star v Silva* (1994) 36 N.S.W.L.R 685. But see below, para.8–017, n.23.

[84] The term "precluded" was inserted in the Bill in Committee in lieu of the word "estoppel", a term unknown in Scots law. It will, however, be noted that the preclusions are absolute, and do not depend upon the holder in due course proving that he was misled or that he acted to his detriment.

[85] Other estoppels may arise on evidence, see above, paras 3–057, 3–079 (s.24).

[86] Defined in s.29(1). But see also s.29(3) (sheltered holder) who presumably is also entitled to the benefit of these estoppels.

[87] See above, para.4–024 (s.27(2)).

[88] See above, para.4–028.

[89] The original payee of the instrument is not a holder in due course *Jones (R.E.) Ltd v Waring & Gillow Ltd* [1926] A.C. 670; see above, para.4–059. But see above, para.3–079 (s.24) (possible estoppel at common law).

[90] *Cooper v Meyer* (1830) 10 B. & C. 468; *Ashpitel v Bryan* (1863) 3 B. & S. 474, affirmed 5 B. & S. 723.

[91] *Jenys v Fawler* (1733) 2 Stra. 946; *Price v Neal* (1762) 3 Burr. 1354 (s.59, Illustration 10); *Smith v Chester* (1787) 1 T.R. 654, 655; *Cooper v Meyer* (1830) 10 B. & C. 468; *Sanderson v Collman* (1842) 4 M. & G. 209; *Beeman v Duck* (1843) 11 M. & W. 251; *Phillips v Thurn* (1866) L.R. 1 C.P. 463. See also *Schultz v Astley* (1836) 2 Bing. N.C. 544 (s.20, Illustration 6); *London and South Western Bank Ltd v Wentworth* (1880) 5 Ex.D. 96 (s.20, Illustration 7) (incomplete bills).

[92] *Taylor v Croker* (1802) 4 Esp. 187.

[93] *Robinson v Yarrow* (1817) 7 Taunt. 455.

[94] s.24.

a holder in due course, to set up the forgery or want of authority, or to allege that the bill is in consequence invalid, because he will have given to the drawer's signature and to the instrument a genuineness against himself by accepting it.[95] Similarly, if the drawer is for some reason incapable of incurring liability as a party to the bill,[96] the acceptor cannot set up the want of capacity against a holder in due course.

Secondly, under paragraph (b), in the case of a bill drawn to drawer's order, the acceptor is precluded from denying to a holder in due course "the then capacity of the drawer to indorse,[97] but not the genuineness[98] or validity[99] of his indorsement."

Thirdly, under paragraph (c), in the case of a bill payable to the order **7–018** of a third person, he is, as against a holder in due course, precluded from denying "the existence of the payee and his then capacity to indorse,[1] but not the genuineness[2] or validity of his indorsement".

It will be observed that, with respect to indorsements, a distinction is drawn between the capacity of the drawer or payee to indorse and the genuineness or validity of his indorsement. Capacity is a question of status, and relates to the power of the drawer or payee to indorse so as to bind himself.[3] The acceptor cannot deny that capacity. But he can deny the genuineness of the indorsement, that is to say, allege that it is a forgery.[4] He can also contest its validity, for example, by showing that it was placed on the bill without authority.[5] It is clear that capacity to draw must be identical with capacity to indorse. But the signature of the drawer may be or be presumed to be genuine; yet his indorsement may be a forgery. And an authority to draw on behalf of another does not necessarily include an authority to indorse on his behalf.[6]

The restrictions imposed in paragraphs (b) and (c) of this subsection with respect to indorsements may, nevertheless, in certain circumstances be undermined by the operation of section 7(3) of the Act. If the drawee

---

[95] *Bank of England v Vagliano Brothers* [1891] A.C. 107, 116; *London & River Plate Bank Ltd v Bank of Liverpool Ltd* [1896] 1 Q.B. 7, 10–11. Nor, it seems, can the acceptor plead that the bill was never "issued"; *cf. Clutton & Co. v Attenborough & Son* [1897] A.C. 90.

[96] s.22.

[97] *Pitt v Chappelow* (1841) 8 M. & W. 616 (bankruptcy); *Braithwaite v Gardiner* (1846) 8 Q.B. 473 (bankruptcy); *Smith v Marsack* (1848) 6 C.B. 486 (married woman); *Hallifax v Lyle* (1849) 3 Exch. 446 (company).

[98] *Smith v Chester* (1787) 1 T.R. 654; *Beeman v Duck* (1843) 11 M. & Co. 251.

[99] *Robinson v Yarrow* (1817) 7 Taunt. 455 (bill drawn and indorsed per pro. without authority); *Garland v Jacomb* (1873) L.R. 8 Ex. 216 (bill drawn and indorsed by partner in non-trading firm without authority).

[1] *Drayton v Dale* (1823) 2 B. & C. 293, 299 (note).

[2] *Robarts v Tucker* (1851) 16 Q.B. 560 (s.24, Illustration 8).

[3] See above, para.3 002 (s.22).

[4] See *Smith v Chester* (1787) 1 T.R. 654; *Beeman v Duck* (1843) 11 M. & Co. 251; *Drayton v Dale* (1823) 2 B. & C. 293. (Even if the indorsement is on the bill at the time of acceptance.)

[5] See *Robinson v Yarrow* (1817) 7 Taunt. 455; *Garland v Jacomb* (1873) L.R. 8 Ex. 216.

[6] *Prescott v Flinn* (1832) 9 Bing. 19, 22.

accepts a bill drawn on him in a fictitious name payable to the drawer's order or payable to the order of some other fictitious or non-existing person, the bill may be treated as payable to bearer. The holder does not then have to rely on the indorsement of the drawer or payee.[7]

If the amount of the bill is altered, or if any other material alteration is made in it, the acceptor is not precluded by this subsection from setting it up.[8]

7–019 **Promissory notes.** The engagement of the maker of a promissory note and the estoppels that may be raised against him are set out in section 88 of the Act.

### Liability of drawer or indorser

7–020 55. (1) The drawer of a bill by drawing it—

    (a) Engages that on due presentment it shall be accepted and paid according to its tenor, and that if it be dishonoured he will compensate the holder or any indorser who is compelled to pay it, provided that the requisite proceedings on dishonour be duly taken;

    (b) Is precluded from denying to a holder in due course the existence of the payee and his then capacity to indorse.

(2) The indorser of a bill by indorsing it—

    (a) Engages that on due presentment it shall be accepted and paid according to its tenor, and that if it be dishonoured he will compensate the holder or a subsequent indorser who is compelled to pay it, provided that the requisite proceedings on dishonour be duly taken;

    (b) Is precluded from denying to a holder in due course the genuineness and regularity in all respects of the drawer's signature and all previous indorsements;

    (c) Is precluded from denying to his immediate or a subsequent indorsee that the bill was at the time of his indorsement a valid and subsisting bill, and that he had then a good title thereto.

| Definitions | Comparison |
|---|---|
| "acceptance": ss.2, 17(1). | UCC: §§ 3–413, 3–414, 3–415. |
| "bill": s.2. | ULB: arts 9, 15, 47. |

---

[7] See, *e.g. Bank of England v Vagliano Brothers* [1891] A.C. 107 (s.7, Illustration 4) and see above, para.2–052.
[8] For alteration of a bill, see s.64.

"holder": s.2.                     ULC: arts 12, 18, 44.
"holder in due course": s.29.      UNB: arts 38, 44, 45.
"indorsement": s.2.

## COMMENT

**Suretyship.**[9] It has been said that, in the case of a bill accepted for value, the relationship between the drawer and indorsers on the one hand and the acceptor on the other is one of suretyship.[10] But this is not an accurate expression. The relationship is not one of suretyship, though it is analogous thereto.[11] Nevertheless, the analogy is sufficiently close for the acceptor to be regarded as "the principal debtor" and the drawer and indorsers, for most purposes,[12] as his "sureties". In particular, if the acceptor is discharged, this will normally discharge all other parties liable on the bill.[13] And the same is true of the discharge of the maker of a promissory note.

A binding agreement between the holder and the acceptor,[14] at any time prior to judgment, to give time to the acceptor for payment will discharge the drawer and indorsers,[15] unless the party sought to be held liable consents to the giving of time,[16] or unless the holder, in giving time, expressly reserves his rights against them.[17] A bill must be duly presented for payment to the acceptor in order to charge the drawer and indorsers.[18]

7–021

---

[9] See *Byles* (27th ed.), Ch.33; *Rowlatt on Principal and Surety* (5th ed., Sweet & Maxwell), Ch.13; O'Donovan and Phillips, *The Modern Contract of Guarantee* (English ed.), 1–43—1–61. See also above, para.4–041 (s.28) (accommodation party).

[10] *Rowe v Young* (1820) 2 Bligh H.L. 391, 467; *Cook v Lister* (1863) 18 C.B.N.S. 543, 579; *Rouquette v Overmann* (1875) L.R. 10 Q.B. 525, 537. In this last case, Brett L.J., approving a passage in *Byles* (11th ed.), further stated that, as between the holder and the drawer, the drawer is the principal debtor and subsequent indorsers are his sureties, and that, as between the holder and the second indorser, the second indorser is the principal, and the subsequent, or third, indorser is his surety.

[11] *Duncan, Fox & Co. v North and South Wales Bank* (1880) 6 App. Cas. 1, 11, 13, 14, 19; *Re Conley* [1938] 2 All E.R. 127, 131.

[12] *cf. Duncan, Fox & Co. v North and South Wales Bank* (1880) 6 App. Cas. 1 (indorser only entitled to equities of surety when the bill has been dishonoured, but not before). See also below, para.8–017, n.23.

[13] See ss.59–63.

[14] *cf. Lyon v Holt* (1839) 5 M. & W. 250; *Frazer v Jordan* (1858) 8 E. & B. 303.

[15] *Moss v Hall* (1850) 5 Exch. 46. Contrast *Philpot v Briant* (1828) 4 Bing. 717 (unenforceable agreement) and *Badnall v Samuel* (1817) 3 Price 521; *Hewet v Goodrick* (1826) 2 C. & P. 468 (offer to extend time).

[16] *Clark v Devlin* (1803) 3 B. & P. 363; *Stevens v Lynch* (1810) 12 East 58.

[17] *Cowper v Smith* (1838) 4 M. & W. 519; *North v Wakefield* (1848) 13 Q.B. 536; *Owen v Homan* (1853) 4 H.L.C. 997; *Muir v Crawford* (1875) L.R. 2 Sc.App. 456.

[18] s.45.

But mere delay by the holder thereafter to sue the acceptor or to press him for payment will not effect a discharge.[19]

Any other conduct of the holder towards the acceptor as principal debtor which would, under the law of suretyship,[20] discharge a surety, will likewise discharge the drawer and indorsers. But such conduct towards the drawer or an indorser will discharge only the parties to whom the drawer or that indorser is liable and not the others.[21]

7–022      **Subsection (1)(a): liability of the drawer.**[22] The engagement of the drawer is that, on due presentment, the bill will be accepted and paid according to its tenor.[23] Presentment for acceptance is dealt with in sections 39 to 41 of the Act and presentment for payment in sections 45 and 46.

The drawer undertakes that the bill will be accepted generally,[24] that is to say, according to its tenor as drawn. The holder of a bill may refuse to take a qualified acceptance, and if he does not obtain an unqualified acceptance may treat the bill as dishonoured by non-acceptance.[25] As to the liability of the drawer where a qualified acceptance is taken, see section 44 of the Act.

The drawer also undertakes that the bill will be paid according to its tenor. The liability of the drawer of an accepted bill must in general be measured by that of the acceptor, since their relations resemble those of principal and surety.[26] If the bill is accepted generally, the tenor of the bill will be as drawn and accepted, since a general acceptance assents without qualification to the order of the drawer.[27] If the acceptance is qualified or partial,[28] the tenor of the bill will be that as qualified by the acceptance.

7–023      In the case of a cheque, which does not contemplate acceptance, the engagement of the drawer is that on due presentment for payment it will

---

[19] *Walwyn v St Quentin* (1797) 1 B. & P. 652 (disapproved on other grounds in *Cory v Scott* (1820) 3 B. & Ald. 619); *Goring v Edmonds* (1829) 6 Bing. 94, 99; *Carter v White* (1883) 25 Ch.D. 666; *Rowlatt on Principal and Surety* (5th ed.), pp.176, 177; O'Donovan and Phillips, *The Modern Contract of Guarantee* (English ed.), 1–43—1–61, 7–65.

[20] See *Rowlatt on Principal and Surety* (5th ed.), Ch.8; O'Donovan and Phillips, *The Modern Contract of Guarantee* (English ed.), 1–43—1–61, Ch.7.

[21] *Smith v Knox* (1800) 3 Esp. 46, 47; *Claridge v Dalton* (1815) 4 M. & S. 226; *Hall v Cole* (1836) 6 N. & M. 124.

[22] For precedents of pleadings, see Appendix B(2)(3)(4)(8).

[23] *Siggers v Lewis* (1834) 1 C.M. & R. 370, 371; *Whitehead v Walker* (1842) 9 M. & W. 506, 516; *Allen v Kemble* (1848) 6 Moore P.C. 314, 321; *Jones v Broadhurst* (1850) 9 C.B. 173, 181; *Gibbs v Fremont* (1853) 9 Exch. 25, 30; *Steele v M'Kinlay* (1880) 5 App. Cas. 754, 769; *Re Commercial Bank of South Australia* (1887) 36 Ch.D. 522, 525, 526.

[24] s.19(1).

[25] s.44(1).

[26] See above, para.7–021.

[27] s.19(2).

[28] ss.19, 44, 52(2).

be paid according to its tenor as drawn. The same is probably true of a bill of exchange drawn payable on demand.[29] In those other cases where presentment for acceptance is not necessary in order to render liable any party to the bill,[30] for example, where a bill is drawn payable at a fixed period after date, although it might be argued that the drawer engages that on due presentment it will be paid (not accepted and paid), an immediate right of recourse against the drawer accrues to the holder if the bill is in fact presented for acceptance and dishonoured.[31] It is therefore preferable to regard the drawer's engagement in such a case as an engagement both that the bill will be accepted and that it will be paid.

In contrast with the liability of the acceptor, that of the drawer is conditional.[32] It does not arise unless and until the bill is dishonoured, either by non-acceptance or by non-payment.[33] It is also conditional on the requisite proceedings on dishonour being duly taken, that is to say, the giving of notice of dishonour[34] and the effecting of any necessary protest,[35] unless these are waived or dispensed with in accordance with the Act.[36] The liability of the drawer and indorsers of an accepted bill may therefore be said to be a "secondary liability", as opposed to the "primary liability" of the acceptor.

The drawer and indorsers of a bill are nevertheless jointly and severally responsible to the holder for its due acceptance and payment.[37] If it is dishonoured the holder may enforce payment from the drawer, or an indorser, or the acceptor, or all or any of them at his option. As stated in the subsection, the drawer engages that on dishonour he will compensate, not only the holder, but any indorser who is compelled to pay the bill. Thus if B draws a bill on A payable to the order of C, which C indorses to D, D may, if he chooses, claim payment from C if the bill is dishonoured by non-acceptance or by non-payment.[38] Provided that the requisite proceedings on dishonour have been duly taken, B (the drawer) will be bound to compensate C who has been compelled to pay the bill.

However, the drawer of a bill may insert therein an express stipulation **7–024** negativing or limiting his own liability to the holder.[39] Further, parol evidence[40] is admissible, as between the drawer and an indorser, to prove

[29] See above, para.6–004 (s.39).
[30] s.39(3).
[31] s.43(2).
[32] *Rowe v Young* (1820) 2 Bligh H.L. 391, 467.
[33] *Re Boyse (No.3)* (1886) 33 Ch.D. 612, 623.
[34] ss.48, 49.
[35] s.51.
[36] ss.16(2), 50(2), 51(9).
[37] *Rouquette v Overmann* (1875) L.R. 10 Q.B. 525 at 537.
[38] s.55(2)(a).
[39] s.16(1), or waiving as regards himself some or all of the holder's duties (s.16(2)).
[40] See above, para.2–167 (s.21).

that the drawer is not liable or not fully liable to the indorser, as, for example, where it is shown that the bill was drawn for the accommodation of the indorser[41]; or that it was agreed that they should be cosureties for payment of the bill.

For the measure of damages recoverable in respect of a dishonoured bill, see section 57 of the Act.

7–025  **Subsection (1)(b): estoppels binding drawer.** The statutory estoppels or "preclusions" raised against the drawer by virtue of his drawing the bill are set out in this paragraph, although other estoppels may arise on evidence.[42] The statutory estoppels are available only to a holder in due course.[43] The drawer is precluded from denying to a holder in due course the existence of the payee and his then capacity to indorse.[44]

7–026  **Subsection (2)(a): liability of indorser.**[45] The engagement of the indorser of a bill is expressed in terms similar to that of the drawer. As in the case of the drawer, the liability of an indorser of an accepted bill is secondary to that of the party primarily liable, the acceptor. However, as between the drawer and any indorser, the drawer is primarily and the indorser secondarily liable.[46] Subject to the requisite proceedings on dishonour being duly taken[47] and to any express stipulation to the contrary,[48] the drawer and indorsers are jointly and severally liable to the holder if the bill is dishonoured by non-acceptance or non-payment. But an indorser who is compelled to pay the bill is entitled to be indemnified by the drawer[49] and, if the bill has been accepted, by the acceptor.[50]

"Indorsement" is defined in section 2 of the Act and is dealt with in sections 32 to 35. It has been said that "every indorser of a bill is in the nature of a new drawer".[51] But the question arises whether the words "according to its tenor" refer to the tenor of the bill at the time it was originally drawn or at the time of its indorsement. The latter is more

---

[41] s.28; above, para.4–41.

[42] In particular, see *London Joint Stock Bank v Macmillan* [1918] A.C. 777 (s.64, Illustration 5) and above, para.3–079.

[43] Defined in s.29(1). The original payee of a bill is not a holder in due course *Jones (R.E.) Ltd v Waring and Gillow Ltd* [1926] A.C. 670: see above, para.4–059. But see also s.29(3) (sheltered holder) who presumably is also entitled to the benefit of these estoppels.

[44] *Collis v Emett* (1790) 1 H.Bl. 313; *Drayton v Dale* (1823) 2 B. & C. 293, 300, 301; *Phillips v Thurn* (1865) 18 C.B., N.S. 694, 701.

[45] For precedents of pleadings, see Appendix B(4)(5)(7).

[46] See *Horne v Rouquette* (1878) 3 Q.B.D. 514, 518, citing *Byles* (11th ed.), p.243 (though in terms of principal and surety).

[47] See above, para.6–096.

[48] See below.

[49] s.55(1)(a).

[50] *Duncan Fox & Co. v North and South Wales Bank* (1880) 6 App. Cas. 1, 13.

[51] *Byles* (27th ed.), p.197; *Penny v Innes* (1834) 1 C.M. & R. 439, 441. cf. *Gwinnell v Herbert* (1836) 5 A. & E. 436, 439; *Steele v M'Kinlay* (1880) 5 App. Cas. 754, 769–770.

probable,[52] if its effect has been varied, *e.g.* by a qualified acceptance, or by an alteration of the sum payable.

The liability of an indorser is conditional. It does not arise until the bill has been dishonoured, either by non-acceptance or by non-payment. Moreover, unless waived or dispensed with,[53] notice of dishonour must be duly given[54] and any necessary protest effected[55] in order to render the indorser liable. His liability is to compensate, not only the holder, but any *subsequent* indorser who is compelled to pay the bill. An indorser does not, however, by indorsing the bill enter into any engagement with the drawer or *prior* indorsers.[56] Thus if a bill drawn payable to the order of C is indorsed by C to D and by D to E, E may claim payment from either C or D, or both of them, if it is dishonoured. If he claims payment from D, who is compelled to pay the bill, D may claim indemnity from C. But if C is required to and does pay the bill, he can claim no indemnity from D.

The words "subsequent indorser" mean an indorser who is subsequent in time.[57] By section 32(5) of the Act, where there are two or more indorsements on a bill, each indorsement is deemed to have been made in the order in which it appears on the bill, until the contrary is proved. Parol evidence[58] is admissible to show that the order in which indorsements were in fact made was otherwise than the order in which they appear on the bill.[59]   7–027

Any indorser may insert in the bill an express stipulation negativing or limiting his own liability to the holder.[60] But, as between an indorser and his immediate indorsee, even an unqualified indorsement may be shown by parol evidence not to have been intended to impose liability on the indorser to the indorsee.[61] Parol evidence is also admissible, for example, to show that successive indorsers were in fact cosureties[62] or otherwise to show the relationship between them and their true liability to each

---

[52] But contrast *Lebel v Tucker* (1867) L.R. 3 Q.B. 77, 81, with *Gibbs v Fremont* (1853) 9 Exch. 25, 31.

[53] ss.16(2), 50(2), 51(9).

[54] ss.48, 49.

[55] s.51.

[56] *Steele v M'Kinlay* (1880) 5 App. Cas. 754 at 769; *Ferrier v Stewart* (1912) 15 C.L.R. 32, 37.

[57] *McCall Bros Ltd v Hargreaves* [1932] 2 K.B. 423 (s.20, Illustration 18).

[58] See above, para.2–168 (s.21).

[59] *National Sales Corp. Ltd v Bernardi* [1931] 2 K.B. 188 (s.20, Illustration 16); *McCall Bros v Hargreaves* [1932] 2 K.B. 423; *Lombard Banking Ltd v Central Garage and Engineering Co. Ltd* [1963] 1 Q.B. 220 (s.20, Illustration 17); *Yeoman Credit Ltd v Gregory* [1963] 1 W.L.R. 343 (s.20, Illustration 19). See also above, para.2–135 (s.20), para.2–168 (s.21), para.5–021 (s.32).

[60] ss.16(1), See also ss.26(1), 33, 35.

[61] *Castrique v Buttigieg* (1855) 10 Moore P.C. 94 (s.21, Illustration 35). See above, para.2–167 (s.21).

[62] *Macdonald v Whitfield* (1883) 8 App. Cas. 733 (s.21, Illustration 33).

other.[63] It may therefore be said that, as between immediate parties,[64] paragraph (a) of this subsection sets out only the prima facie engagement, or contract, of the indorser, his actual contract falling to be ascertained by reference to the intention with which the indorsement was made and completed by delivery, "as evinced by the words, either spoken or written, of the parties, and the circumstances (such as the usage at the place, the course of dealing between the parties and their respective situations) under which the delivery takes place".[65]

For the measure of damages recoverable on dishonour, see section 57 of the Act.

7–028    **Subsection (2)(b) and (c): estoppels binding indorser.** The principle underlying the estoppels set out in paragraph (b) of this sub-section, that an indorser "is precluded from denying to a holder in due course the genuineness and regularity in all respects of the drawer's signature and all previous indorsements",[66] is that he is not permitted to allege any defect in the signatures which are or are normally on the bill when it leaves his hands. These estoppels, however, only arise in favour of a holder in due course.[67] Although, in principle, a person who acquires an order bill under or through a forged or unauthorised indorsement cannot be a holder, and therefore cannot be a holder in due course,[68] he can, as against one who indorsed after the forged or unauthorised indorsement, be such a holder by estoppel,[69] though not for other purposes.[70]

In contrast, the estoppels set out in paragraph (c) "that the bill was at the time of his indorsement a valid and subsisting bill, and that he had then a good title thereto"[71] are raised in favour of the indorser's immediate indorsee and any subsequent indorsee, and are not limited to a holder in due course.

Where one indorsement in a chain of indorsements is forged or unauthorised, the effect of paragraphs (b) and (c) is that the bill remains, so to speak, negotiable by estoppel,[72] even though the forged or unauthorised

---

[63] See the cases cited in n.59, above, and *Gerald McDonald & Co v Nash & Co.* [1924] A.C. 625 (s.20, Illustration 15); *Rolfe Lubell & Co. v Keith* [1979] 1 All E.R. 860. See above, para.2–164 (s.21), para.5–021 (s.32).

[64] For "immediate parties", see above, para.4–005.

[65] *Castrique v Buttigieg* (1855) 10 Moore P.C. 94 at 108–109; see above, para.2–167 (s.21).

[66] *MacGregor v Rhodes* (1856) 6 E. & B. 266.

[67] Defined in s.29(1). Or (*semble*) in favour of the "sheltered holder" (s.29(3)).

[68] See above, para.3–066 (s.24).

[69] See above, para.3–066 (s.24).

[70] See above, paras 3–066—3–076 (s.24).

[71] *Ex p. Clarke* (1792) 3 Bro.C.C. 238. *cf. Chamberlain v Young* [1893] 2 Q.B. 206, 209, 210, 211. Contrast *Ladup Ltd v Shaikh* [1983] Q.B. 225 (illegality known to indorsee: s.27, Illustration 16).

[72] See above, para.3–066 (s.24).

signature is wholly inoperative,[73] and to cause the loss ultimately to fall on the person whose indorsement immediately follows the forged or unauthorised indorsement, *i.e.* the person who took the bill from the forger.[74]

**Cheques and promissory notes.** The engagement of the indorser of a    **7–029**
bill and the estoppels that may be raised against him apply equally in the case of cheques.[75]

They also apply, with the necessary modifications, to promissory notes.[76] By section 89(2) the first indorser of a note is deemed to correspond with the drawer of an accepted bill payable to drawer's order. It is arguable that the estoppel in paragraph (a) in respect of the genuineness and regularity of the *drawer's* signature could be extended by analogy to the signature of the maker of a note.[77]

## Stranger signing bill liable as indorser

**56. Where a person signs a bill otherwise than as drawer or accep-    7–030
tor, he thereby incurs the liabilities of an indorser to a holder in due course.**

| Definitions | Comparison |
|---|---|
| "bill": s.2 | UCC: §§ 3–204, 3–205, |
| "holder": s.2 | 3–401, 3–415. |
| "holder in due course": s.29 | ULB: arts 30–32, 47. |
| "person": s.2 | ULC: arts 25–27, 44. |
| | UNB: arts 46–48. |

### COMMENT

**The anomalous indorser.** An indorsement, properly so called, must be    **7–031**
made by the holder and for the purpose of negotiating the instrument.[78] But when a person who is not the holder of a bill or note backs it with his signature, this section imposes on him the liabilities of an indorser to a

---

[73] s.24.
[74] See above, para.3–066 (s.24).
[75] s.73.
[76] s.89(1). For precedents of pleadings see Appendix B(7).
[77] *Merchants Bank v United Empire Club Co.* (1879) 44 U.C.Q.B. 468 (although by s.89(2) the maker of a note is deemed to correspond with the acceptor of a bill).
[78] ss.2, 31(3).

holder in due course.[79] Such a person is not an indorser, but has been termed a "quasi-indorser"[80] or "anomalous indorser."[81] "Holder in due course" is defined in section 29 of the Act and the liabilities of an indorser are set out in section 55(2). Although the Act does not specifically so provide, the anomalous indorser is entitled to the privileges of an indorser, for example, to be given notice of dishonour[82]; however, his right to be indemnified by the drawer and prior indorsers will usually be qualified by the circumstances in which he became a party to the instrument.[83] Ordinarily the anomalous indorser places his signature on a bill or note in order to accommodate[84] and guarantee the liabilities of another party to the instrument.

The difficulty which arises with respect to the application of section 56 is that the most frequent situation where a non-holder backs with his signature a bill or note is where he does so in order to guarantee the liability of the acceptor or maker to the payee of the instrument. Suppose that a seller of goods is only willing to supply goods or extend credit to the buyer if payment for the goods is guaranteed by a third party (X). The seller draws a bill on the buyer for the price payable to his own order, and the bill is then accepted by the buyer and indorsed by X. If the bill is dishonoured by non-payment by the buyer, the seller appears to have no claim under this section against X. As original payee of the bill, the seller is not a holder in due course,[85] and X undertakes no liability to him in his capacity as drawer.[86]

In the pre-Act case of *Steele v M'Kinlay*,[87] W drew a bill payable to his own order on a partnership firm, consisting of two partners, in respect of an advance to be made by him to the firm. He handed the bill to the father of the two partners. The father procured his sons' acceptance of the bill, wrote his own signature on the back of the bill and delivered it to W. W then discounted the bill to a bank, but, when the partners failed to pay, retired it.[88] W and the father subsequently died. An action was brought by the pursuers, the trustees of W, against the defender, the personal

---

[79] Not every signature on the back of an instrument is an indorsement. The signature of the payee on a cheque may be merely a receipt to facilitate collection: *Keene v Beard* (1860) 8 C.B. 372, 382; above, para.5–006.

[80] *Chalmers* (9th ed.), p.220.

[81] *Crawford and Falconbridge* (8th ed.), p.1620.

[82] *Yeoman Credit Ltd v Gregory* [1963] 1 W.L.R. 343 (s.49, Illustration 21), *Lombard Banking Ltd v Central Garage and Engineering Co. Ltd* [1963] 1 Q.B. 220 (s.49, Illustration 20). See also *Dotten v Bryan and McKee* (1960) 24 D.L.R. (2d) 668; *Scott (S.A.) Pty Ltd v Dawson* [1962] N.S.W.R 1166.

[83] See below, para.7–035.

[84] s.28; see above, para.4–041.

[85] *Jones (R.E.) Ltd v Waring & Gillow Ltd* [1926] A.C. 670 (s.29, Illustration 6), see above, para.4–059 (s.29).

[86] s.55(2)(a); *Steele v M'Kinlay* (1880) 5 App. Cas. 754 (Illustration).

[87] (1880) 5 App. Cas. 754 (Illustration).

[88] *i.e.* took up the bill and paid the bank.

representative of the father. There was no evidence as to the character in which and the purpose for which the father had backed the bill. The House of Lords held that the father's signature was not an acceptance of the instrument as it was not addressed to him. The view was expressed that the signature was that of an indorser,[89] and, since the Act, it would now be taken to be that of an anomalous indorser. But such an indorsement created no obligation to those who previously were parties to the bill; it was solely for the benefit of those who took subsequently.[90] Moreover, in so far as the pursuers sought to establish a collateral contract (as to which there was no evidence) of the father to be answerable to the drawer for default by the acceptors, there was no note or memorandum in writing of that contract sufficient to satisfy the Statute of Frauds.[91]

However, there is one route—though an artificial one—by which a 7–032 person who backs with his signature a bill or note may be liable to the payee of the instrument where there is evidence that he signed in order to make himself so liable in the event of dishonour by the acceptor, drawer or maker. In *McDonald (Gerald) & Co. v Nash & Co.*[92] the appellants supplied goods to A & Co. for which the latter were unable to pay. It was agreed that the respondents would provide finance in order to enable the transaction to proceed. The appellants therefore drew bills, payable to their own order, on A & Co. These were accepted by A & Co., indorsed by the respondents and handed by them to the appellants. Before the bills became due, the appellants indorsed their name as payees above the respondents' signature. The bills were dishonoured by A & Co. and the appellants claimed payment from the respondents as indorsers. The House of Lords held that the intention of the parties was that the respondents, by their signature, should become liable to the appellants in the event of default by A & Co. When handed to the appellants the bills were incomplete and, in accordance with section 20 of the Act, the appellants had implied authority to indorse their name as payees above that of the respondents, thereby completing the chain of indorsements. When so filled up, the bills became enforceable by the appellants against the respondents. In subsequent cases, it was further held that it was immaterial that the drawer-payee added his indorsement below that of the anomalous indorser, since the order of indorsements, as they appear on

[89] In particular by Lord Watson at 782.
[90] *Per* Lord Blackburn at 772.
[91] At 768. See also *MacDonald v Whitfield* (1883) 8 App. Cas. 733, 745.
[92] [1924] A.C. 625 (s.20, Illustration 15). See also *Glenie v Bruce Smith* [1908] 1 K.B. 263 (s.20, Illustration 14); *Re Gooch* [1921] 2 K.B. 593; *Ferrier v Stewart* (1912) 15 C.L.R. 32; *Durack v West Australian Trustee Executor & Agency Co. Ltd* (1944) 72 C.L.R. 189; *H. Rowe & Co. Pty Ltd v Pitts* [1973] 2 N.S.W.L.R. 159; *G. & H. Montage GmbH v Irvani* [1990] 1 W.L.R. 667, 672–673.

the bill, is not conclusive.[93] They will be read in the order that gives effect to the intention of the parties. Even a restrictive indorsement by the drawer-payee to a bank for collection has been held to suffice, the indorsement being treated, first, as an indorsement in blank which completes the chain of indorsements to the drawer-payee, and, secondly, as an indorsement by him to the bank for collection.[94]

The limitations inherent in section 56 do not therefore apply where the anomalous indorser signed a bill or note with the intention of rendering himself liable to the payee of the instrument in the event of default in payment by the acceptor, drawer or maker, and the payee, in accordance with the authority so conferred, completes the chain of indorsements by signing his own name (whether above or below that of the anomalous indorser) on the back of the instrument.[95] To this case the principle in *Steele v M'Kinlay* has no application even if the anomalous indorser signs the bill while it is still incomplete.[96] Moreover, even though the contract of the anomalous indorser to be liable for the default of the acceptor, drawer or maker is in one sense a contract of guarantee, the claim against him is a claim on the bill to which the Statute of Frauds does not apply.[97] Indeed, whenever the liability of a guarantor is not collateral, but arises directly on the instrument, it is immaterial that there is no written note or memorandum of the guarantee.[98]

7–033     It is open to the signatory to prove that his signature was placed on the instrument other than for the purpose of rendering him liable as an indorser[99] and that in consequence the payee had no authority so to complete the chain of indorsements.[1] But, in the absence of such proof, there is still the difficult case where the route made available by *McDonald (Gerald) & Co. v Nash & Co.* is not open to the payee because the payee does not in fact complete the chain of indorsements by his indorsement of the instrument. In Canada it has been held by the Supreme Court that the corresponding section of the Canadian statute does not limit the liability of the anomalous indorser only to a holder in due course[2] and that it

---

[93] *National Sales Corp. Ltd v Bernardi* [1931] 2 K.B. 188 (s.20, Illustration 16); *McCall Bros Ltd v Hargreaves* [1932] 2 K.B. 423 (s.20, Illustration 18); *Lombard Banking Ltd v Central Garage and Engineering Co. Ltd* [1963] 1 Q.B. 220 (s.20, Illustration 17). See also *Durack v West Australian Trustee Executor & Agency Co. Ltd* (1944) 72 C.L.R. 189.

[94] *Yeoman Credit Ltd v Gregory* [1963] 1 W.L.R. 343 (s.20, Illustration 19).

[95] For a precedent of a pleading, see Appendix B(5), below.

[96] *Jenkins & Sons v Coomber* [1898] 2 Q.B. 168 and *Shaw v Holland* [1913] 2 K.B. 15 to the contrary must now be taken to have been overruled by *McDonald (Gerald) & Co. v Nash & Co.* [1924] A.C. 625: see *McCall Bros Ltd v Hargreaves* [1932] 2 K.B. 423, 428.

[97] *McCall Bros Ltd v Hargreaves* [1932] 2 K.B. 423 (s.20, Illustration 18).

[98] *McCall Bros Ltd v Hargreaves* [1932] 2 K.B. 423 at 429. See also *G. & H. Montage GmbH v Irvani* [1990] 1 W.L.R. 667.

[99] See above, para.5–016 (s.32).

[1] The burden of disproving authority rests upon the person alleging authority to be absent: see above, paras 2–135, 2–136 (s.20).

[2] *Grant v Scott* (1919) 50 D.L.R. 250; *Gallagher v Murphy* [1929] 2 D.L.R. 124.

operates in a similar manner to an *aval*,[3] enabling the original payee of the instrument to sue.[4] But the Canadian Act adds to the words of section 56 "and is subject to all the provisions of this Act respecting indorsers". In Australia, the corresponding section is in the same terms as section 56 of the 1882 Act. It has nevertheless been held[5] that the drawer-payee, as holder for value of a bill, could recover against the anomalous indorser under the sections corresponding to sections 38 and 57 of the 1882 Act where the intention is that the anomalous indorser should be so liable. The same view is, in effect, expressed in Byles[6]:

"It is, perhaps, more rational to read [section 56] as enacting that the liabilities incurred are those for which any indorser would normally be liable to a holder in due course, thus placing such a person in the same category as regards liabilities as any indorser in the strict sense; it can hardly mean that the liability is to no one but a holder in due course."

However, the wording of the section appears to be unambiguous: the difficulties stem, in part at least, from the decision of the House of Lords in *Jones (R.E.) Ltd v Waring & Gillow Ltd*[7] that the original payee of a bill is not a holder in due course.

**Cheques crossed "account payee."** The interpretation to be placed on section 56 assumes greater importance now that section 81A of the 1882 Act (introduced by the Cheques Act 1992) provides that a cheque crossed "account payee" is not transferable, but is only valid between the parties thereto. Most cheques currently issued in the United Kingdom are so crossed. If such a cheque is indorsed by a third party with the intention of guaranteeing payment by the drawer, the payee cannot resort to the device of completing the chain of indorsements since the cheque is not transferable. Unless the view of Byles referred to above is adopted, the payee will have no right of action against the anomalous indorser under section 56.    **7–034**

**Evidence of co-suretyship.** Where two or more persons indorse a bill or note as anomalous indorsers to guarantee the liability of the acceptor,    **7–035**

---

[3] See below, para.7–039.
[4] *Robinson v Mann* (1901) 31 S.C.R. 484.
[5] *H. Rowe & Co. Pty Ltd v Pitts* [1973] 2 N.S.W.L.R. 159.
[6] 27th ed., 17–13. See also *Rolfe Lubell & Co. v Keith* [1979] 1 All E.R. 860 (s.26, Illustration 12; and below, n.10); *G. & H. Montage GmbH v Irvani* [1988] 1 W.L.R. 1285, 1294 (but on appeal in this case [1990] 1 W.L.R. 667, a more cautious approach was adopted by Mustill L.J. at 672–673, 679–680).
[7] [1926] A.C. 670 (s.29, Illustration 6); see above, para.4–059 (s.29).

drawer or maker, parol evidence[8] is admissible to show that their relations *inter se* are those of cosureties, and not as sureties in succession
according to the order of their indorsements on the instrument.[9]

**7–036** **Estoppels against anomalous indorser.** There is no reason to suppose
that the estoppels set out in section 55(2)(b) of the Act with respect to an
actual indorser are not equally available against an anomalous
indorser.[10]

**7–037** **Stipulations negativing or limiting liability.** The privilege of negativing or limiting his liability by a stipulation in the bill[11] extends to the
anomalous indorser.[12]

**7–038** **"Payment guaranteed."** A person may place his signature on the back
of a bill or note with the words "payment guaranteed" or other similar
words of guarantee. The signature will most probably be construed as
that of an anomalous indorser. The additional words will be disregarded
as mere surplusage, being simply a restatement of his liability under
section 56. But such words could possibly be construed as a collateral
guarantee of the liability of the acceptor, drawer or maker to the payee of
the instrument.[13] The question would then arise whether there is a sufficient note or memorandum of that guarantee to satisfy the Statute of
Frauds. It is arguable[14] that the person to whom the guarantee is given,
*i.e.* the payee, is sufficiently identified from his name on the face of the
instrument[15] and that parol evidence is admissible to determine the scope
and object of the guarantee.[16] A guarantor is, however, not entitled to the
benefit of the provisions of the Act for the protection of indorsers, for
example, to be given notice of dishonour.[17] Also, not being part of the law
of negotiable instruments, the conflict of law rules applicable to guarantees will differ.[18]

---

[8] See above, para.2–164 (s.21).
[9] *Macdonald v Whitfield* (1883) 8 App. Cas. 733 (s.21, Illustration 33).
[10] *Ferrier v Stewart* (1912) 15 C.L.R. 32; *Trimble v Thorne* [1914] V.L.R. 41; *Sydney & North Sydney Lime Burners Ltd v Phillips* (1931) 31 S.R. (N.S.W.) 505. This might be held to cover the absence of an indorsement by the payee at the time of signature by the anomalous indorser.
[11] s.16(1).
[12] *Wakefield v Alexander & Co.* (1901) 17 T.L.R. 217.
[13] *cf. Re T.C. Marines Ltd* (1973) 34 D.L.R. (3d) 489 (liability as indorser unchanged).
[14] *cf. Steele v M'Kinlay* (1880) 5 App. Cas. 754 (Illustration).
[15] *Williams v Byrnes* (1863) 1 Moo.P.C. (N.S.) 154.
[16] *Heffield v Meadows* (1869) L.R. 4 C.P. 595; *Perrylease Ltd v Imecar A.G.* [1988] 1 W.L.R. 463. Contrast *Holmes v Mitchell* (1859) 7 C.B.N.S. 361. See also *Sheers v Thimbleby & Son* (1897) 76 L.T. 709; *G. & H. Montage GmbH v Irvani* [1990] 1 W.L.R. 667.
[17] See above, para.6–091.
[18] See below, para.12–005.

**Aval.** Many legal systems, especially those of states which have 7–039
adopted the Geneva Uniform Law on Bills of Exchange and Promissory
Notes,[19] recognise the concept of an *aval*. An *aval* is essentially a guarantee
of payment of a bill.[20] It may be given by a stranger or even by a person
who has signed as a party to a bill.[21] The *aval* is given either on the bill
itself or on an "allonge".[22] It is expressed by the words *"bon pour aval"*
("good as aval") or by any other equivalent formula, and it must be
signed by the giver of the *aval*.[23] The *aval* must specify for whose account
it is given; in default of this, it is deemed to be given for the drawer.[24] The
giver of the *aval* is bound in the same manner as the person for whom he
has become guarantor. His liability is not, however, the exact equivalent
of that of a guarantor in English law: his undertaking is valid even when
the liability which he has guaranteed is inoperative for any reason other
than defect in form. He has, when he pays the bill, the rights arising out
of the instrument against the person guaranteed and against those who
are liable to the latter on the bill.[25] These provisions are also applicable to
promissory notes.[26]

It is clear that the *aval* is not the equivalent of, and is quite different
from, an anomalous indorsement under section 56 of the 1882 Act.[27] The
liability of the person giving the *aval* is not limited to those who become
parties to the instrument after the *aval* is placed on it. Where (as is usually
the case) the *aval* is for the drawee, there is no need to resort to the device
of completing the chain of indorsements by adding the indorsement of
the payee.

The obligations created by an *aval* are to be determined by the law of
the place where the contract of *aval* is made.[28] Assuming that the *aval* is
valid under that law,[29] those obligations will be recognised and enforced
in proceedings brought in the English courts against the person by whom

[19] (ULB). See above, para.1–012.
[20] The nature, requirements and effect of an *aval* may, of course, vary from country to
country. The account in this paragraph is based on the Geneva Uniform Law (ULB).
[21] ULB, art.30.
[22] See above, para.5–013 (s.32).
[23] It is deemed to be constituted by the mere signature of the giver of the *aval* placed on the
face of the bill, except in the case of the signature of drawee or of the drawer. In some
systems, a mere signature on the back of the bill operates in the same way as an
anomalous indorsement.
[24] ULB, art.31.
[25] ULB, art.32.
[26] ULB, art.77. If the *aval* does not specify on whose behalf it has been given, it is deemed to
have been given on behalf of the maker of a promissory note.
[27] cf. *Steele v M'Kinlay* (1880) 5 App. Cas. 754 at 772.
[28] s.72(2). See *G.H. Montage GmbH v Irvani* [1990] 1 W.L.R. 667 (s.72, Illustration 10); *Banco
Atlantico S.A. v British Bank of the Middle East* [1990] 2 Lloyd's Rep. 504; below,
para.12–013.
[29] s.72(1) (2).

it was given.[30] Although the *aval* is in substance a contract of guarantee, since the liability sued upon is a liability under the instrument, the Statute of Frauds cannot be set up in answer to the claim.[31]

7–040    Further, even if a bill is dishonoured in England, and in consequence the duties of the holder with respect to the necessity for or sufficiency of a protest or notice of dishonour are to be determined by English law,[32] this does not necessarily lead to the conclusion that the giver of the *aval* is discharged if protest is not duly effected or notice of dishonour is not duly given, in accordance with sections 48 and 51(2) of the Act. The nature of the cause of action arising under the foreign law from the *aval* has to be examined. In particular, if the claim is by the drawer-payee of the bill and the *aval* is for the acceptor, the facts giving rise to the cause of action are not such as to require the court to treat the *aval* as an anomalous indorsement so as to bring sections 48 and 51(2) into play.[33]

7–041    **Proposed legislation.** The Government has declared its intention to give legal recognition to the *aval*,[34] as mentioned in the report of the Review Committee on Banking Services Law and Practice.[35] It proposes to introduce legislation to amend the Act so as to recognise a guarantee given by way of *aval*.

### ILLUSTRATION

7–042    W draws a bill payable to himself or his order. It is addressed to M & Co., a partnership firm consisting of two partners to whom he has agreed to make an advance. He hands the bill to J, the father of the two partners, who procures its acceptance by his sons in the name of the firm, writes his own signature on the back of the bill and hands the bill back to W. W discounts the bill with a bank, but, the acceptors having failed to pay the bill, retires it. Both W and J die. An action is brought on the bill by the pursuers, trustees of W, against the defender, the personal representative of J. There is no evidence as to why J signed the bill. The action fails. J is

---

[30] *G.H. Montage GmbH v Irvani* [1990] 1 W.L.R. 667. *Banco Atlantico S.A. v British Bank of the Middle East* [1990] 2 Lloyd's Rep. 504.

[31] *G.H. Montage GmbH v Irvani* [1990] 1 W.L.R. 667, following *McCall Bros Ltd v Hargreaves* [1932] 2 K.B. 423 (s.20, Illustration 18). Alternatively, where, as in *Irvani*, the *aval* consisted of the signature of the person giving it accompanied by the words "*bon pour aval pour les tirés*" (good as *aval* for the drawees), the requirements of the Statute of Frauds were considered to have been sufficiently met.

[32] s.72(3).

[33] *G.H. Montage GmbH v Irvani* [1990] 1 W.L.R. 667.

[34] (1990) Cm. 1026, Annex 6, para.6.8; above, para.1–009.

[35] (1989) Cm. 622; above, para.1–008.

not an acceptor nor (in Scots law) is he liable as joint obligor with the acceptors of the bill. *Semble* the character in which J became a party to the bill was as indorser, but in such a case he has incurred no liability to W as drawer of the bill. In so far as it is sought to establish a collateral contract of guarantee that J should be answerable for the default of the acceptors, there is no sufficient note or memorandum thereof in writing to satisfy the Statute of Frauds.[36]

**Measure of damages against parties to dishonoured bill**

7–043
57. Where a bill is dishonoured, the measure of damages, which shall be deemed to be liquidated damages, shall be as follows:
(1) The holder may recover from any party liable on the bill, and the drawer who has been compelled to pay the bill may recover from the acceptor, and an indorser who has been compelled to pay the bill may recover from the acceptor or from the drawer, or from a prior indorser—
(a) The amount of the bill;
(b) Interest thereon from the time of presentment for payment if the bill is payable on demand, and from the maturity of the bill in any other case;
(c) The expenses of noting, or, when protest is necessary, and the protest has been extended, the expenses of protest.
(2) [*Repealed*]
(3) Where by this Act interest may be recovered as damages, such interest may, if justice require it, be withheld wholly or in part, and where a bill is expressed to be payable with interest at a given rate, interest as damages may or may not be given at the same rate as interest proper.

Repeal
Subs.(2) was repealed by ss.4, 32 and Sch. 5, Pt I, of the Administration of Justice Act 1977.

Definitions
"bill": s.2.
"holder": s.2.

Comparison
UCC: §§ 3–107, 3–118, 3–411.
ULB: arts 28, 48, 49.
ULC: arts 45, 46.
UNB: arts 69–71.

[36] *Steele v M'Kinlay* (1880) 5 App. Cas. 754.

## Comment

**7–044**     **Measure of damages.** This section prescribes the measure of damages, which are deemed to be liquidated damages,[37] recoverable where a bill is dishonoured.[38] Dishonour may be by non-acceptance[39] or by non-payment.[40] Its provisions apply, with the necessary modifications, to cheques[41] and promissory notes.[42]

The section, as originally enacted, contained a subsection (2), which dealt with the recovery of re-exchange in the case of a bill dishonoured abroad. That subsection ceased to have effect and was repealed by the Administration of Justice Act 1977[43] following the decision of the House of Lords in *Miliangos v George Frank (Textiles) Ltd*,[44] holding that judgments could be given in a foreign currency. However, situations may arise which are not covered by subsection (1), or which were not previously covered by subsections (1) and (2), where resort may have to be made to section 97(2) of the Act, which saves the law merchant if not inconsistent with the Act.

**7–045**     **From whom recoverable.** The several engagements of the acceptor,[45] drawer[46] and indorsers[47] of a bill, and their liability to the holder and other parties to the bill, are dealt with in sections 54 and 55 of the Act, and that of the maker of a promissory note in section 88. "Indorser" in subsection (1) will include a person who signs a bill as anomalous indorser under section 56. Precedents of pleadings are set out in Appendix B, below.

**7–046**     **Amount of the bill.** The amount of the bill is more in the nature of a debt than damages. It will include "interest proper", that is to say, interest

---

[37] By deeming the damages to be liquidated, the claim could be specially indorsed on the writ under the former RSC Ord.3, r.6, so enabling the damages to be recovered under RSC Ord 14. But the necessity for this no longer applies under CPR Part 24. See also *Commissioners of Inland Revenue v Thomas Cook (NZ) Ltd* [2003] 2 N.Z.L.R. 296 ("money").

[38] By s.35A(8) of the Supreme Court Act 1981 (inserted by s.15 and Sch.1, Pt I, of the Administration of Justice Act 1982) and by s.69(7) of the County Courts Act 1984, nothing in those sections affects the damages recoverable for dishonour of a bill exchange.

[39] s.43.

[40] s.47.

[41] s.73.

[42] s.89.

[43] ss.4, 32 and Sch.5, Part I.

[44] [1976] A.C. 443.

[45] s.54(1).

[46] s.55(1)(a).

[47] s.55(2)(a).

reserved by the instrument itself.[48] Where the amount is expressed in a foreign currency, judgment will be given for the amount in the foreign currency.[49]

**Interest.** Interest on the amount of the bill is recoverable as damages under subsection (1)(b).[50] Where the instrument is payable on demand, interest runs from the time of presentment for payment.[51] In any other case, it runs from the maturity of the bill, *i.e.* the day on which it falls due.[52] The "maturity date" rule applies even though the holder's cause of action against the drawer or an indorser does not accrue until notice of dishonour is given[53] and even though no demand for payment is made on the acceptor until some time after the bill is due.[54] It also applies even though, for example, the drawer's undertaking is to compensate an indorser who is compelled to pay the bill, and subject to the requisite proceedings on dishonour being taken.[55] Moreover, it seems that when a bill is dishonoured by non-acceptance interest can only be recovered from the date of its maturity, and not from the date of its dishonour.[56] However, it has been said[57] that subsection (1)(b) "deals only with the ordinary normal case where dishonour inevitably involves an inexcusable failure to pay at the proper time". Thus, where it was illegal to pay because the person entitled was an alien enemy, interest was held to run only from the date on which payment again became lawful,[58] and where a bank refused payment of a cheque because its authority to do so had been determined by notice of its customer's death,[59] no interest was awarded to the payee in an action against the estate of the drawer.[60]

7–047

---

[48] See s.9.
[49] *Miliangos v George Frank (Textiles) Ltd* [1976] A.C. 443; *Barclays Bank International Ltd v Levin Bros (Bradford) Ltd* [1977] Q.B. 270 (Illustration 1).
[50] See above, n.38.
[51] *cf. Pierce v Fothergill* (1835) 2 Bing N.C. 167 (from issue of writ where no prior demand); *Re East of England Banking Co.* (1868) L.R. 6 Eq. 368, 375 (bank shuts its doors rendering demand futile).
[52] See also *Blake v Lawrence* (1802) 4 Esp. 147 (note payable by instalments with acceleration clause) and s.9(1)(b). But *cf. Murray v East India Co.* (1821) 5 B. & Ald. 204 (money due to estate before appointment of administrator).
[53] The decision to the contrary in *Walker v Barnes* (1813) 5 Taunt. 240 cannot now stand.
[54] *Bank Polski v Mulder (K.J.) & Co.* [1942] 1 K. B. 497, 500. But see s.57(3).
[55] s.55(1)(a).
[56] *cf. Harrison v Dickson* (1811) 3 Camp. 52n; *Suse v Pompe* (1860) 8 C.B.N.S. 538, 566–567 (before the Act).
[57] *Ledeboter (N.V.) & Van der Held's Textiehandel v Hibbert* [1947] K.B. 964, 967.
[58] *Du Belloix v Waterpark* (1822) 1 Dow. & Ry. 16; *Biedermann & Co. v Allhausen* (1921) 37 T.L.R. 662; *Ledeboter (N.V.) & Van der Held's Textiehandel v Hibbert* [1947] K.B. 964. Contrast *The Berwickshire (No.2)* [1950] P. 204, 217. See also *Stevenson & Sons Ltd v Aktiengesellschaft für Cartonnagen Industrie* [1918] A.C. 239, 245, 256, 259.
[59] s.75(2).
[60] *Ranchers (Pvt) Ltd v McLean's Estate* 1986 (4) S.A. 271.

Interest is to be calculated down to the date of judgment.[61] The judgment carries interest in the normal way under the Judgments Act 1838 as amended (in the High Court) or under section 74 of the County Courts Act 1984 (in the County Court) as provided for in the County Courts (Interest on Judgment Debts) Order 1991.[62]

Interest on a dishonoured bill or note used to be calculated and allowed in England at the rate of 5 per cent. But there is now no "prescribed" or "correct" rate of interest. It has been said that, when a court is considering an appropriate rate of interest for a period from the date of the cause of action to the date of the judgment, the rate payable on judgment debts is a convenient starting point.[63] On the other hand, the usual practice in the Commercial Court is to award interest at one per cent above base rate, unless such rate would be unfair to one or other of the parties.[64] In the case of small claims, it is easier to claim interest at the judgment rate.[65]

By section 57(3), where a bill is expressed to be payable with interest at a given rate, interest may at the discretion of the court be given as damages at the same rate as "interest proper".[66] In the absence of any agreement to pay at that rate after dishonour,[67] it is suggested that interest at the judgment rate is more appropriate.[68]

**7–048**     **Subsection (3): discretion of court.** In addition to the discretion vested in the court with respect to the rate of interest awarded as damages,[69] such interest may, if justice requires,[70] be withheld wholly or in part.[71] For example, if a valid tender has been made, interest might be withheld from the date of tender[72]; if presentment for payment was delayed interest might be disallowed for the period before any demand was made[73]; and it might also be withheld if there was a long delay in enforcing payment

---

[61] *Robinson v Bland* (1760) 2 Burr. 1077, 1088.

[62] SI 1991/1184. But see (judgments in foreign currency) Administration of Justice Act 1970, s.44A, and County Courts Act 1984, s.74 (5A), introduced by the Private International Law (Miscellaneous Provisions) Act 1995. See CPR, Part 40.

[63] See the notes to the CPR 1998 in the White Book para. 7.0.17. Contrast *Practice Note (QBD: Indorsements for Interest on Claims for Debts on Liquidated Sums)* (1983) [1983] 1 W.L.R. 377 (short term investment rate).

[64] *Shearson Lehman Hutton Inc. v Maclaine Watson & Co. Ltd* [1990] 3 All E.R. 723.

[65] CPR, Pt 12, r.6 (default judgments).

[66] Compare *Keene v Keene* (1857) 3 C.B.N.S. 144 with *Ward v Morrison* (1842) Car. & M. 368. See also *Ackermann v Ehrensperger* (1846) 16 M. & W. 99, 103.

[67] It may be that such an agreement could only be, or be deemed to be, outside the bill: see above, para.2–071, n.30 (s.9).

[68] *Cook v Fowler* (1874) L.R. 7 H.L. 27; *Re Roberts* (1880) 14 Ch.D. 49 (not bills cases).

[69] See *Cameron v Smith* (1819) 2 B. & Ald. 305, 308; *Webster v British Empire Co.* (1880) 15 Ch.D. 169, 175, 176; *Ex p. Charman* [1887] W.N. 184; *Spaethe v Anderson* (1899) 18 N.Z.L.R. 149.

[70] *Du Belloix v Waterpark* (1822) 1 Dow. & Ry. 16, 19; *Ex p. Charman* [1887] W.N. 184; *London and Universal Bank v Clancarty* [1892] 1 Q.B. 689.

[71] See, *e.g.* the cases cited in n.58, above (payment illegal).

[72] *Dent v Dunn* (1812) 3 Camp. 296.

[73] *Phillips v Franklin* (1820) Gow 196; *Murray v East India Co.* (1821) 5 B. & Ald. 204.

after presentment.[74] The discretion of the court does not extend to "interest proper" payable by the terms of the instrument to the date of maturity or presentment

**Pleading of claim for interest.** Particulars of Claim must include, if the    7–049
claimant is seeking interest, a statement to that effect and the details set
out in paragraph (2) of CPR, rule 16.4.[75]

**Noting and protest.** Noting and protest are dealt with in section 51 of    7–050
the Act. The expenses of noting are recoverable as liquidated damages,
whether or not noting is necessary. But the expenses of protest are
recoverable only where protest is necessary, *e.g.* in the case of the dishonour of a foreign bill of exchange appearing on its face to be such.[76] The
expenses of protesting for better security are irrecoverable.[77]

**Other losses.** Subsection (1) must be regarded as establishing the    7–051
entire measure of damages in the cases to which it applies. It has been
held that, where bills drawn in a foreign country were dishonoured in
England, there could be no recovery, in one case,[78] of the commission paid
by the drawers to their bankers for accepting the bill for honour, and, in
another case,[79] of expenses incurred by the holder consisting of banker's
commission, brokerage, stamps and postage.[80] On the other hand, in *Re
Gillespie, ex p. Robarts*,[81] a bill was drawn in Tobago on London and
accepted. On the acceptor's dishonour of the bill in London, the drawers
became liable under the law of Tobago to pay to the holder the amount of
re-exchange[82] as damages. The drawers sought to prove for the re-
exchange in the bankruptcy of the acceptor, and were held entitled to do
so. The Court of Appeal considered that their entitlement did not arise
under subsection (1) as that subsection did not cover damages by way of
re-exchange, nor under (the now repealed) subsection (2) as that subsection applied only in the case of a bill dishonoured abroad, but arose by
virtue of section 97(2) of the Act which preserves the rules of the common

---

[74] *Spaethe v Anderson* (1889) 18 N.Z.L.R. 149.
[75] CPR, r.16(4)(1)(b).
[76] See above, para.6–153 (s.51). A foreign note does not need to be protested: s.89(4).
[77] *Re English Bank of the River Plate* [1893] 2 Ch. 438 (Illustration 3). For protest for better
security, see s.51(5).
[78] *Re English Bank of the River Plate* [1893] 2 Ch. 438.
[79] *Banque Populaire de Bienne v Cavé* (1895) 1 Com. Cas. 67.
[80] Both cases were decided before the repeal of s.57(2). But see *Cato v Cato* (1972) 116 S.J. 138
("attorney's fee of 15% of amount due" on default held penal).
[81] (1886) 18 Q.B.D. 286 (Illustration 2).
[82] For an explanation of re-exchange, see *Suse v Pompe* (1860) 8 C.B.N.S. 538, 563–565 (Byles
J.). But re-exchange is largely obsolete, now that judgment can be given in a foreign
currency.

law, including the law merchant, save in so far as they are inconsistent with the express provisions of the Act. Lindley L.J. said[83]:

> "The acceptor of a bill drawn abroad knows that, in the event of dishonour, there is a liability for re-exchange, and subs.-s. (1) of s.57 is not addressed to this point, and does not deal with it, but s.97 has been added to meet cases not exhaustively dealt with by other sections of the Act."

7–052    **Conflict of laws.** Prior to the repeal of subsection (2), that subsection in general[84] covered the measure of damages in the case of a bill dishonoured abroad, so that it was possible to conclude that subsection (1) only covered the case of a bill dishonoured in the United Kingdom.[85] With the repeal of subsection (2), it is to be assumed that the holder, drawer or indorser (as the case may be) of a bill dishonoured abroad is prima facie entitled to recover damages in accordance with subsection (1).[86]

Subsection (1) is, however, a rule of English law. There is no provision in the Act which deals in express terms with the measure of damages where laws conflict. It would appear that the measure of damages recoverable from a party to a bill or note is to be treated as a matter of substantive law and is therefore to be determined by the law which governs that party's contract on the instrument.[87] If the law which governs that contract is the law of part of the United Kingdom, then the measure of damages will be determined in accordance with section 57.[88]

If, on the other hand, the law which governs that contract is the law of some foreign country, section 57 will not apply, and the measure of damages will be determined by that law.[89] By section 72(2) of the Act, subject to the proviso to that subsection,[90] the interpretation of the drawing, indorsement, acceptance, or acceptance *suprà protest* of a bill, is determined by the law of the place where such contract is made.[91] The

---

[83] At 292–293.
[84] It did not, however, in its terms apply to the recovery of re-exchange by a holder from the acceptor (or the maker of a note). But re-exchange would be recoverable at common law under s.97(2).
[85] *Re Commercial Bank of South Australia* (1887) 36 Ch.D. 522, 527
[86] Or s.97(2) where applicable.
[87] *Allen v Kemble* (1848) 6 Moo. P.C. 314, 321–322; *Gibbs v Fremont* (1853) 9 Exch. 25; *Re Gillespie, Ex p. Robarts* (1886) 18 Q.B.D. 286, 292; *Re Commercial Bank of South Australia* (1887) 36 Ch.D. 522 at 526;
[88] Subject to the decision in *Re Gillespie, Ex p. Robarts* (1886) 18 Q.B.D. 286, and s.97.
[89] See the cases cited in n.87, above.
[90] See below, para.12–017 (inland bills indorsed abroad).
[91] See below, para.12–013.

weight of judicial opinion now favours the view that the word "interpretation" extends, not only to the meaning of the words used, but also to their legal effect.[92] The general rule is, therefore, that the law which governs each party's contract on the instrument is the *lex loci contractus*. Accordingly, it is that law which should determine the measure of damages recoverable against that party.[93]

However, Chalmers stated[94]:

**7–053**

> "The cases seem to regard the measure of damages on the breach of the contracts on a bill as resting on the same principles as the interpretation of those contracts; but it may be questioned whether the measure of damages comes within the meaning of the word 'interpretation' in its present context in the Act. Subject to the positive provisions of section 57, the rule with respect to damages appears to be that 'the place at which each party to a bill or note undertakes that *he himself* will pay it, determines with regard to him the *lex loci contractus* according to which his liability is governed'."[95]

But this presupposes that the law of the place where the contract of a party is made will coincide with that where he undertakes to pay. This will not always be the case. A bill may be accepted in one country payable in another. The question then arises whether it is the *lex loci contractus* or the *lex loci solutionis* which determines the measure of damages recoverable from the acceptor. The pre-Act authorities are inconclusive,[96] although *Dicey and Morris*[97] considers that "the principle which on the whole they suggest is that the law of the place of payment of each obligation governs this matter". Indeed, there is force in the contention that the measure of damages should be referred to the law of the place where the acceptor undertook to pay and the holder expected to receive payment.[98]

But it is submitted that the law of the place of contracting should apply, first, because the measure of damages, as a substantive matter, should be governed by the *lex causae* of the relevant claim, and, secondly, because it better accords with the intentions of the parties that the nature and extent of a party's liability in the event of dishonour should be determined by the law of the place of his issue, indorsement or acceptance of the bill, as the case may be.

---

[92] See below, para.12–015.
[93] See the cases cited in n.87, above.
[94] 9th ed., p.283.
[95] *Story on Conflict of Laws*, § 315. See also *Livesley v Horst Co.* [1925] 1 D.L.R. 159, 162.
[96] Since the two places coincided. See n.87, above, but *cf. Cooper v Earl Waldegrave* (1840) 2 Beav. 282 (bill accepted in Paris payable in London: rate of interest the English rate).
[97] *The Conflict of Laws* (13th ed., Sweet & Maxwell), para.33–368.
[98] See *Restatement Conflict of Laws* 2d, § 214.

**7–054**    Whichever view is adopted, since each party's contract on a bill is governed by its own law, it follows that the measure of damages recoverable from one party may differ from that recoverable from another. In particular, before the Act it was held that, where a bill was drawn in California on a drawee in Washington, and the rate of interest differed in the two places, the rate of interest recoverable in an action in England against the drawer was the Californian rate.[99] If the law which governs the measure of damages also governs the rate of interest, this would mean that a restriction of the rate, *e.g.* to 5 per cent,[1] under the applicable law would be upheld. However, it may be argued that the rate of interest—as opposed to the right to recover interest by way of damages—is a procedural matter which, in an English court, should be governed by English law as the *lex fori*.[2]

Where a party who has become liable to pay damages in accordance with a foreign law which governs his liability seeks to recover, by way of recourse, damages against a party whose liability to him is governed by English law, then the measure of damages will include any additional damages which he has become liable to pay under the foreign law.[3]

**7–055**    **Limitation of actions.**[4] By section 5 of the Limitation Act 1980, no action founded on simple contract can be brought after the expiration of six years from the date on which the cause of action accrued. This limitation period normally applies to any action against a party to a bill, cheque or note. If, however, the action is on a specialty, the limitation period is 12 years.[5] Where, as permitted by section 91(2) of the 1882 Act,[6] the contract of a corporation on the instrument is made by sealing with the corporate seal, it is submitted that this does not in itself mean that an action against the corporation is an action on a specialty.[7] But a specialty obligation will arise if a corporation or individual makes it clear on the instrument that it is intended to be executed as a deed.[8]

---

[99] *Gibbs v Fremont* (1853) 9 Exch. 25.

[1] ULB, art.47(2).

[2] See Dicey and Morris, *The Conflict of Laws* (13th ed., Sweet Maxwell), paras 33–375, 33–384.

[3] *Re Gillespie, Ex p. Robarts* (1886) 18 Q.B.D. 286 (Illustration 2).

[4] For comparison, see ULB, arts 70, 71; ULC, art.52, 53; UNB, art.84.

[5] Limitation Act 1980, s.8.

[6] See below, para.16–009. By s.36A(4) of the Companies Act 1985 (inserted by s.130(1) of the Companies Act 1989) a document signed by a director and the secretary of a company or by two directors of the company and expressed to be executed by the company has the same effect as if executed under the common seal of the company.

[7] *Re Compania de Electricidad de la Provincia de Buenos Aires Ltd* [1980] Ch. 146, 186.

[8] Companies Act 1985, s.36A(5)(6) (inserted by s.130(1) of the Companies Act 1989); Law of Property (Miscellaneous Provisions) Act 1989, s.1.

**Accrual: acceptor or maker.** As a general rule the liability to the holder   **7–056**
of the acceptor of a bill or the maker of a note payable at a fixed or
determinable future time arises on maturity of the instrument. Thus if a
bill is payable on a fixed date, or at a fixed period after date or sight, time
will begin to run in favour of the acceptor against the holder from the
date on which the bill falls due, and not from the date on which it is
drawn or from the date on which the acceptance is given.[9] But to this
general rule there are two exceptions. First, in those cases where presentment for payment is necessary to charge the acceptor of a bill or the
maker of a note,[10] time will only run from the date of such presentment.
Secondly, where a bill is accepted after its maturity,[11] time will run from
the date of acceptance.[12]

If a bill or note is payable at sight or on demand,[13] time will begin to
run in favour of the acceptor or maker from the date of acceptance or, in
the case of a note from the date of the note,[14] or from the date of issue of
the instrument if later,[15] and not from the date of the demand. Again,
however, where presentment for payment is necessary to charge the
acceptor or maker,[16] time runs from the date of presentment.[17]

It should be noted that time starts to run in favour of the acceptor or
maker when a cause of action accrues to the *then* holder of the instrument.[18] Thus, if a note is made by A payable on demand to B, and three
years after its date is transferred by B to C, C must sue A within the next
three years. The transfer of the note does not result in the accrual of a new
cause of action to the transferee, C.

**Accrual: drawer and indorsers.** The liability of the drawer of a bill and   **7–057**
of an indorser of a bill, cheque or note is a secondary liability: he engages
that on due presentment the instrument will be paid (or, in the case of a
bill, accepted and paid) according to its tenor, and that if it is dishonoured
he will compensate the holder, provided that the requisite proceedings on
dishonour be duly taken.[19] The holder's cause of action against such

---

[9] *Holmes v Kerrison* (1810) 2 Taunt. 323; *Thorpe v Booth* (1826) Ry. & M. 388; *Fryer v Roe* (1852)
12 C.B. 437; *Montague v Perkins* (1853) 22 L.J.C.P. 187; *Re Rutherford* (1880) 14 Ch.D. 687;
*Gelmini v Moriggia* [1913] 2 K.B. 549 (Illustration 4).
[10] ss.19(2)(c), 52(2), 87(1).
[11] s.18(2).
[12] s.10(2).
[13] s.10(1).
[14] *Norton v Ellam* (1837) 2 M. & W. 461. (Illustration 5); *Jackson v Ogg* (1859) Johns. 397, 400;
*Re Brown's Estate* [1893] 2 Ch. 300, 304; *Re British Trade Corp. Ltd* [1932] 2 Ch. 1 (s.5,
Illustration 3).
[15] *Savage v Aldren* (1817) 2 Stark. 232; *Watkins v Figg* (1863) 11 W.R. 258.
[16] ss.19(2)(c), 52(2), 87(1).
[17] *Oxner v Bank of Montreal* (1967) 61 D.L.R. (2d) 599, (1969) 70 D.L.R. (2d) 719n.
[18] See *Whitehead v Walker* (1842) 9 M. & W. 506 (drawer).
[19] s.55(1)(a), (2)(a).

parties therefore accrues when, following dishonour, the requisite proceedings on dishonour are duly taken, *e.g.* on the date on which the
relevant party receives notice of dishonour,[20] and the limitation period
will begin to run from that time. In cases where notice of dishonour is
dispensed with,[21] time begins to run from the date of dishonour. If the
notice of dishonour is lost or delayed in the post,[22] presumably the cause
of action is complete when the notice ought to have been received.

By section 47(1) of the Act, a bill is dishonoured by non-payment (a)
when it is duly presented for payment and payment is refused or cannot
be obtained, or (b) when presentment is excused and the bill is overdue
and unpaid. In the latter situation, a bill or note which is not payable on
demand will be overdue once the due date for payment has passed, and
it will accordingly be dishonoured by non-payment at that time.[23] More
difficulty, however, arises where a bill or note is payable on demand and
presentment is excused. It has earlier been suggested[24] that, in such a
case, the instrument will be dishonoured by non-payment under section
47(1)(b) when the event which excuses the holder from presenting it for
payment occurs.[25] The limitation period will accordingly start to run in
favour of the drawer or an indorser from the time when he receives notice
of the dishonour, or, if notice of dishonour is dispensed with, from the
time of the dishonour.

If a bill is dishonoured by non-acceptance, and afterwards by non-
payment, no fresh cause of action accrues to the holder against the
drawer by reason of the dishonour by non-payment.[26]

7–058 In the case of a cheque, the drawer is the party primarily liable on the
instrument. Nevertheless, unless presentment for payment is dispensed
with,[27] a cheque must be presented for payment in order to charge the
drawer.[28] It is therefore submitted that, in principle, time ought not to run
in favour of the drawer against the holder until the cheque is presented
to the drawee bank for payment and dishonoured by non-payment,[29] and
(unless notice of dishonour is dispensed with)[30] the drawer has received
notice of dishonour. If presentment for payment is dispensed with, then
time will start to run when the deemed dishonour occurs, *i.e.* when

---

[20] But, in the case of an instrument not payable on demand, his right of action does not in
any event accrue until the day following the due date of the instrument: see above,
para.6–084 (s.47).
[21] s.50(2)
[22] ss.49(15), 50(2).
[23] See above, para.6–083 (s.47).
[24] See above, para.6–083 (s.47).
[25] *cf. Re Bethell* (1887) 34 Ch.D. 561 (cheque). Contrast *Re Boyse (No.3)* (1886) 33 Ch.D. 612.
[26] *Whitehead v Walker* (1842) 9 M. & W. 506.
[27] See, in particular, s.46(2)(c).
[28] See, above, para.6–039 (s.45).
[29] See *Re Boyse (No.3)* (1886) 33 Ch.D. 612 (demand bill).
[30] See, in particular, s.50(2)(c)(4)(5).

presentment is excused and the cheque is overdue and unpaid.[31] Nevertheless a number of cases indicate that a cheque cannot be presented for payment once six years have elapsed.[32] This is presumably on the ground that, since a cheque is by definition payable on demand, the cause of action of the holder against the drawer accrues on the date of the cheque, or of its issue if later.[33]

**Accrual: right of recourse.** Where the drawer of a bill, or an indorser 7–059 of a bill, cheque or note, is compelled to take up and pay the instrument, he has a right of recourse against those parties liable to him on it.[34] With respect to his claim against a party primarily liable on the instrument, that is to say, against the acceptor of a bill, the drawer of a cheque or the maker of a note, since this is in effect a claim by a surety against the principal debtor, it would seem that time runs against him from the date when he pays the instrument or his liability to pay it is ascertained, *e.g.* by judgment.[35] However, it is arguable that his right to be indemnified by the party primarily liable arises immediately his own liability to the holder is established, that is, when he receives notice of dishonour, and time begins to run against him from that moment.[36]

With respect to the claim of an indorser against the drawer of a bill or prior indorsers, paragraph (a) of section 55(1) and (2) of the Act refers to the obligation of the drawer to compensate any indorser, and of an indorser to compensate a subsequent indorser, who is "compelled to pay" the bill. It might therefore be thought that any cause of action by way of recourse would accrue only when the indorser is compelled to and does in fact pay the bill. This would be on the assumption that his right to be indemnified arises when, but not before, he is damnified, *i.e.* on payment.[37] But there is pre-Act authority to the contrary,[38] and it would

---

[31] s.47(1); *Commissioners of Inland Revenue v Thomas Cook (NZ) Ltd* [2003] 2 N.Z.L.R. 296. No demand will be necessary.

[32] *Robinson v Hawksford* (1846) 9 Q.B. 52, 59; *Laws v Rand* (1857) 3 C.B.N.S. 442, 449; *Re Bethell* (1887) 34 Ch.D. 561 at 566.

[33] As in the case of the maker of a note, above. But for an alternative explanation see *Pott v Clegg* (1847) 16 M. & W. 321, which is no longer good law since *Joachimson v Swiss Bank* [1921] 3 K.B. 110.

[34] s.59(2).

[35] *County & District Properties Ltd v C. Jenner & Son Ltd* [1976] 2 Lloyd's Rep. 728; *R.H. Green & Silley Weir v British Railways Board* [1985] 1 W.L.R. 570; *Telfair Shipping Corp v Inersea Carriers S.A.* [1985] 1 W.L.R. 553; *Socony Mobil Oil Inc. v West of England Ship Owners Mutual Insurance Assoc. Ltd (No.2)* [1987] 2 Lloyd's Rep. 529, 540. *cf. Bosma v Larsen* [1966] 1 Lloyd's Rep. 22 (not bills cases).

[36] See also *Parr's Banking Co. v Yates* [1898] 2 Q.B. 460 (default of principal debtor), and *Webster v Kirk* (1852) 17 Q.B. 944.

[37] See *Wolmershausen v Gullick* [1893] 2 Ch. 514 (contribution between cosureties).

[38] *Webster v Kirk* (1852) 17 Q.B. 944 (Illustration 6). Contrast *Reynolds v Doyle* (1840) 1 M. & G. 753; *Angrove v Tippett* (1865) 11 L.T. 708 (action outside bill on implied contract to indemnify).

appear that time will begin to run against an indorser and in favour of the drawer and prior indorsers from the date on which they respectively receive notice of dishonour, this being the date on which the right of the indorser to be indemnified by them arises.

It is submitted that an action by way of recourse is not an action to recover contribution under section 1 of the Civil Liability (Contribution) Act 1978 to which the two-year period of limitation prescribed by section 10 of the Limitation Act 1980 applies.

**7–060**     **Computation of the period.** Since the acceptor of a bill or the maker of a note has the whole of the day on which it falls due to make payment, the cause of action against him is not complete until the beginning of the following day,[39] and time will begin to run from and be inclusive of that day.[40] Where the cause of action accrues by virtue of some act or event, for example, the drawing or issue of the instrument, its acceptance or dishonour, or the receipt of notice of dishonour, the day of the act or event is to be excluded from the computation of the limitation period, and time begins to run from the following day.[41]

If the limitation period ends on a Sunday or other non-juridical day when the court offices are closed, and the necessary act, that is, the issue of the claim form, is one which can only be done if the court office is open on the day when time expires, the period is extended until the next day on which the court office is open.[42]

**7–061**     **Postponement or extension of the period.** If on the date on which a right of action accrued the person to whom it accrued was under a disability, the action may be brought at any time before the expiration of six years from the date on which he ceased to be under a disability or died (whichever first occurred) notwithstanding that the limitation period has expired.[43] Also if the claimant's action is based on the fraud of the defendant or if a fact relevant to his cause of action has been deliberately concealed from him by the defendant or if his action is for relief from the consequences of a mistake, the period does not begin to run until the claimant discovers or with reasonable diligence could have discovered the fraud, concealment or mistake.[44]

---

[39] *Kennedy v Thomas* [1894] 2 Q.B. 759 (s. 47, Illustration).
[40] *Gelmini v Moriggia* [1913] 2 K.B. 549 (Illustration 4).
[41] *Radcliffe v Bartholomew* [1892] 1 Q.B. 161; *Marren v Dawson, Bentley & Co. Ltd* [1961] 2 Q.B. 135; *Pritam Kaur v S. Russell & Sons Ltd* [1973] Q.B. 336 (not bills cases).
[42] *Pritam Kaur v S. Russell & Sons Ltd* [1973] Q.B. 336, not following on this point *Gelmini v Moriggia* [1913] 2 K.B. 549. See also *Hodgson v Armstrong* [1967] 2 Q.B. 299; *The Clifford Maersk* [1982] 1 W.L.R. 1292; but see now CPR, 7PD5 (receipt of form).
[43] Limitation Act 1980, s.28.
[44] Limitation Act 1980, s.32.

By section 29 of the 1980 Act, where any right of action has accrued to recover any debt or other liquidated pecuniary claim, and the person liable therefor acknowledges the claim or makes any payment in respect of it,[45] the right is to be treated as having accrued on and not before the date of the acknowledgment or payment. A current period of limitation may be repeatedly extended under this rule by further acknowledgments or payments; but a right of action, once barred by the Act, cannot be revived by any subsequent acknowledgment or payment.[46]

There may also be an agreement not to plead the statute or the defendant may be estopped from so doing.

But these qualifications are not peculiar to bills, cheques and notes, and an account of their scope and effect should be sought elsewhere.[47]

**Collateral obligations.** When action is brought against a party to an instrument to enforce an obligation collateral to the instrument, though arising out of a transaction in connection with or underlying the instrument, the nature of the particular obligation determines the period from which time begins to run and the limitation period applicable.[48] If a bank wrongfully refuses or fails to pay its customer's cheque when presented for payment,[49] it would seem that the customer's cause of action against the bank will accrue when the cheque is first presented for payment and is dishonoured. It is unlikely that a fresh cause of action will accrue to the customer if the cheque is re-presented for payment and again dishonoured.[50]     **7–062**

**Loans.** Section 6 of the 1980 Act lays down special provisions in respect of certain loans. If (a) a contract of loan does not provide for repayment of the debt on or before a fixed or determinable date, and[51] (b) does not effectively (whether or not it purports so to do) make the obligation to repay conditional on demand for repayment made by or on behalf of the creditor or any other matter, then the right of action on the contract of loan is not barred (as it normally was at common law)[52] after six years from the date of the loan.[53] Instead, the six-year period does not start to run unless and until a demand *in writing* for repayment of the     **7–063**

---

[45] See *Marreco v Richardson* [1908] 2 K.B. 584 (part payment by cheque).
[46] s.29(7).
[47] See *Chitty on Contracts* (29th ed.), Vol.I, Ch.28.
[48] *Davies v Humphreys* (1840) 6 M. & W. 153 (contribution between co-makers); *Reynolds v Doyle* (1840) 1 M. & G. 753; *Angrove v Tippett* (1865) 11 L.T. 708 (indemnity by accommodated party); *Huntley v Sanderson* (1833) 1 Cr. & M. 467 (indemnity of agent); *Garden v Bruce* (1868) L.R. 3 C.P. 300 (loan by cheque).
[49] See below, para.13–032.
[50] But see *Mahomed v Bank of Baroda* [1999] Lloyd's Rep. Bank. 14.
[51] This may possibly mean "or".
[52] *Bradford Old Bank v Sutcliffe* [1918] 2 K.B. 833, 840, 845–846, 848, 849.
[53] s.6(2).

debt is made by or on behalf of the creditor.[54] However, the section establishes an exception

> "where in connection with taking the loan the debtor enters into any collateral obligation to pay the amount of the debt or any part of it (as, for example, by delivering a promissory note[55] as security for the debt) on terms which would exclude the application of this section to the contract of loan if they applied directly to repayment of the debt".

Thus, if in connection with the taking of the loan, the debtor delivers to the creditor a promissory note payable on a fixed date, no written demand is necessary to start time running, and (*semble*) time starts to run from the due date of the note. More difficulty, however, arises where, for example, the debtor delivers to the creditor a promissory note payable on demand. It is then arguable that, no demand being necessary to enforce payment of the note,[56] time will start to run in favour of the debtor from the date of the note, or of its issue if later.[57] But this does not appear to be the case[58] and time will start to run only from the date of the written demand.

7–064      **Foreign Limitation Periods Act 1984.** The effect of this Act is considered in the Comment on section 72 (conflict of laws).[59]

ILLUSTRATIONS

7–065      1. Sellers in New York draw four bills on the defendants, an English company, in respect of goods sold and delivered. Each of the bills is for U.S. $23,137 and they are payable at various dates between June and August 1975. The bills are accepted by the defendants payable at their bankers in Bradford. They are indorsed for value by the sellers to the claimants, but are dishonoured by non-payment. The claimants claim the value of the four bills U.S. $92,548, notarial expenses and interest. The Master, applying section 72(4) of the Act (now repealed) gives judgment for the claimants for £44,973.25, plus interest and costs. He reaches this figure by taking the rate of exchange for sight drafts on Bradford at the

---

[54] s.6(3); *Boot v Boot* [1996] 2 F.C.R. 713, CA.
[55] Defined in s.6(4).
[56] See above, para.7–056.
[57] Twenty-first Report of the Law Reform Committee, Final Report on Limitation of Actions (1977, Cmnd. 6923), para.3.25.
[58] *Boot v Boot* [1996] 2 F.C.R. 713.
[59] See below, para.12–035.

four several dates on which the bills were due: namely $2.2725, $2.1840, $2.1720 and $2.1395 to the £ sterling. The claimants appeal and their appeal is allowed. They are entitled to judgment in United States dollars for U.S. $92,548. (At the date of the appeal the rate of exchange is $1.80 to the £.)[60]

2. The executors of K in Tobago, in order to pay a legacy to H under the will, draw there bills of exchange for £3,000 on G in England, who has money of the deceased in his hands. The executors send the bills so drawn to H, who sells and indorses them to T. T presents them to G, who accepts them but dishonours them when due. The holder, T, requires H to pay him, which she does, and she in turn requires the executors (the drawers) to pay her, which they do. In addition, under the law of Tobago, the executors are liable to pay to H a further sum by way of damages for re-exchange. The executors are entitled to prove against G's estate in bankruptcy for the amount of re-exchange. Section 57(1) of the Act does not exclude the right of proof in respect of the acceptor's liability to indemnify the drawers against damages for re-exchange, which are recoverable at common law as preserved by section 97 of the Act.[61]

3. A bank in Rio de Janeiro draws bills on an English bank, the E Bank, payable to various payees and these are duly accepted by the E Bank in London where they are payable. The E Bank stops payment and goes into liquidation. The holders of some of the bills protest them for better security and all of the bills are accepted *suprà protest* for the honour of the drawers by the drawers' bankers in London. After dishonour of the bills by the E Bank, they are protested by the holders for non-payment. They are then presented to the drawers' bankers who, under their acceptance, pay the principal moneys on the bills, together with notarial expenses. The drawers can prove in the winding-up of the E Bank for the amount of the bills and the expenses of protest for non-payment (such expenses being "necessary" under sections 51(2) and 57(1) of the Act), but not in respect of the expenses of protest for better security or the commission paid by the drawers to their bankers for accepting the bills and paying them at maturity.[62]

4. The defendants make a joint and several promissory note for £313, **7–066** dated December 20, 1905, payable nine months after date to the claimant or his order. The time for payment of the note (including days of grace) expires on September 22, 1906. As the whole of that day is allowed for

---

[60] *Barclays Bank International Ltd v Levin Bros (Bradford) Ltd* [1977] Q.B. 270.
[61] *Re Gillespie, Ex p. Robarts* (1886) 18 Q.B.D. 286.
[62] *Re English Bank of the River Plate, Ex p. Bank of Brazil* [1893] 2 Ch. 438.

payment, the claimant's cause of action arises on September 23. Since action could be brought on that day, it is to be included in the computation of the limitation period.[63]

5. A promissory note is made: "I promise to pay £400 on demand, with interest." A note payable on demand is a present debt, and it is payable without any demand. The Statute of Limitations begins to run from the date of the note.[64]

6. K is indebted to the claimants, the defendant and a banking company. It is agreed that, for the purpose of securing K's debt to the company, the defendant will draw three bills of exchange payable to the claimants, and that the claimants will indorse these to the company. The bills become due in 1843, and are dishonoured. In 1847, the banking company sues the claimants on the bills and, in 1851, the claimants pay the amount. The claimants are barred by the Statute of Limitations from suing the defendant as drawer of the bills.[65]

### Transferor by delivery and transferee

7–067
58. (1) Where the holder of a bill payable to bearer negotiates it by delivery without indorsing it, he is called a "transferor by delivery".
(2) A transferor by delivery is not liable on the instrument.
(3) A transferor by delivery who negotiates a bill thereby warrants to his immediate transferee being a holder for value that the bill is what it purports to be, that he has a right to transfer it, and that at the time of transfer he is not aware of any fact which renders it valueless.

| Definitions | Comparison |
|---|---|
| "bearer": s.2. | UCC: § 3–416. |
| "bill": s.2. | UNB: art.45. |
| "holder": s.2. | |
| "holder for value": s.27(2). | |
| "negotiate": s.31. | |
| "value": s.2. | |

[63] *Gelmini v Moriggia* [1913] 2 K.B. 549.
[64] *Norton v Ellam* (1837) 2 M. & W. 461.
[65] *Webster v Kirk* (1852) 9 M. & W. 506.

COMMENT

**Subsections (1) and (2): transferor by delivery.** A bill is payable to  7–068
bearer which is expressed to be so payable, or on which the only or last
indorsement is in blank.[66] Such a bill is negotiated by the simple act of
delivery[67]: there is no need for the holder to indorse it. A holder who
negotiates the bill by delivery without indorsing it is referred to as a
"transferor by delivery".[68] He is not liable on the instrument,[69] since no
person can be so liable who has not signed it.[70] He may, however, incur
liability to his immediate transferee under the warranties set out in subsection (3). The same principles apply to the transfer without indorsement of a cheque[71] or note[72] which is payable to bearer.

A holder who indorses in blank a bill payable to his order, thereby
making the bill payable to bearer,[73] and then negotiates it, is not a
transferor by delivery; he incurs the liabilities of an indorser. Nor is the
holder of a cheque payable to order who delivers it for value to a banker
for collection without indorsing it, since, under section 2 of the Cheques
Act 1957,[74] he is deemed to have indorsed it in blank. A holder who
indorses a bill delivered to him indorsed in blank, and then negotiates it,
will also be liable as indorser.[75]

For the position of a holder of a bill payable to his order who transfers
it without indorsing it, see section 31(4) of the Act.

**Subsection (3): warranties by transferor.** By negotiating a bearer  7–069
instrument the transferor by delivery gives three warranties to his
immediate transferee,[76] being a holder for value.[77]

First, he warrants that the bill is what it purports to be. Thus if he
transfers, even in good faith, an instrument which has been previously

---

[66] s.8(3).
[67] s.31(2).
[68] s.58(1).
[69] s.58(2). See *Fenn v Harrison* (1790) 3 T.R. 757; *Ex p. Roberts* (1798) 2 Cox 171; *Van Wart v Woolley* (1824) 3 B. & C. 439, 445.
[70] s.23.
[71] s.73.
[72] s.89.
[73] s.34(1).
[74] See below, para.17–015.
[75] ss.8(3), 55(2)(a), 56. But it is otherwise if he converts the blank indorsement into a special indorsement by writing above the indorsers signature a direction to pay the bill to or to the order of some other person: s.34(4).
[76] But not to subsequent parties: *Miller Associates (Australia) Pty Ltd v Bennington Pty Ltd* (1975) 7 A.L.R. 144.
[77] See above, para.4–024 (s.27(2)). But it seems probable that the transferee must himself have given value for the instrument.

materially altered and is in consequence avoided,[78] or a bill which is ostensibly a foreign bill, but which in fact is an inland bill and so void for want of a stamp,[79] the transferee can recover. Further, if one or more of the signatures on the bill are not genuine, then, even though the other signatures are, there is a breach of this warranty.[80]

Secondly, he warrants that he has a right to transfer it. So, for example, if he transfers without indorsement a bearer instrument on which the payee's indorsement in blank is forged, he will be liable on this warranty.[81] More problematical, however, is the case where an instrument drawn payable to bearer is lost or stolen, comes into the possession of a transferor by delivery and is negotiated by him for value to a holder in due course. The transferee as such holder will acquire a good title to the instrument notwithstanding any defect in the title of the transferor. In such a case, it seems unlikely that the transferor by delivery will be liable under this warranty, since he has created in the transferee those rights which he purported to transfer.

7–070    Thirdly, he warrants that at the time of the transfer he is not aware of any fact which renders the bill valueless. The transferor is "not bound to see that he sold a bill of good quality, or to answer for the insolvency of the parties."[82] But if, for example, he *knows* that the maker of a note is in fact insolvent so that the note is valueless, then he will be liable.[83]

When the transferee discovers the defect in the bill he must repudiate the transaction with reasonable diligence.[84]

7–071    **Liability on the consideration.** Where there is no breach by the transferor by delivery of any of the warranties set out in subsection (3), but the instrument is dishonoured, the question arises whether he is under any liability on the consideration in respect of which he transferred it. Suppose, for example, the holder of a note payable to bearer transfers it without indorsement to the transferee in return for a cash payment. The maker becomes insolvent and the note is dishonoured on presentment for

---

[78] *Jones v Ryde* (1814) 5 Taunt. 488 (order bill); *Leeds and County Bank Ltd v Walker* (1883) 11 Q.B.D. 84 (Illustration 1).
[79] *Gompertz v Bartlett* (1853) 2 E. & B. 849 (stamp duty has now been abolished). *cf. Pooley v Brown* (1862) 11 C.B.N.S. 566.
[80] *Fuller v Smith* (1824) Ry. & M. 49 (Illustration 2); *Gurney v Womersley* (1854) 24 L.J.Q.B. 46 (Illustration 3) (at least if the other signatures are worthless). See also *Camidge v Allenby* (1827) 6 B. & C. 373, 385, *Burchfield v Moore* (1854) 3 E. & B. 683, 687. *cf. Emly v Nye* (1812) 15 East 7; *Ex p. Bird* (1851) 4 De G. & S. 273.
[81] *Bank of Ottawa v Harty* (1906) 12 O.L.R. 218.
[82] *Gompertz v Bartlett* (1853) 2 E. & B. 849, 854. See also *Camidge v Allenby* (1827) 6 B. & C. 373 at 385.
[83] *Fenn v Harrison* (1790) 3 T.R. 757, 759; *Camidge v Allenby* (1827) 6 B. & C. 373 at 382. *cf. Read v Hutchinson* (1813) 3 Camp. 352.
[84] *Pooley v Brown* (1862) 11 C.B.N.S. 566.

payment. May the transferee recover back the money which he has paid?

In a number of early cases[85] it was held that the transfer was to be treated as a sale and purchase of the instrument. The risk that it might be dishonoured lay upon the transferee. Since the transferor had not given his indorsement, the transferee must be taken to have received the instrument on his own credit and on the credit of those whose names appeared on the instrument. The transferor could not therefore be made liable on the consideration given for it, whether this consisted of money or money's worth, *e.g.* goods[86] or other bills or notes. But to this rule there were a number of exceptions:

(a) where the instrument was given in respect of an antecedent debt (as opposed to present value), the reason being that in such a case "it is always intended to be taken under this condition, to be payment if the money be paid thereon in convenient time"[87];

(b) where it appeared that the transfer was not intended to operate in full and complete discharge of the transferor's liability[88];

(c) where the circumstances implied an indemnity against loss, *e.g.* where A "obliges" B by cashing a cheque for B.[89]

It is suggested that, in the modern law, it is the second "exception" to which primary importance must be attached. Normally, a bill of exchange or other negotiable instrument is presumed to have been taken by a creditor as conditional payment only.[90] If the instrument is dishonoured, the creditor's right to sue on the underlying consideration revives. Only in the exceptional case where the instrument is given and received as an absolute discharge will that right be lost, and he will be relegated to his rights on the instrument itself.

There is, however, pre-Act authority that, in order for the transferor by **7–072** delivery to be held liable on the consideration, the transferee must use reasonable diligence to obtain payment[91] and must notify the transferor

---

[85] *Bank of England v Newman* (1700) 1 Ld. Raym. 442; *Fenn v Harrison* (1790) 3 T.R. 757; *Fydell v Clark* (1796) 1 Esp. 447; *Ex p. Shuttleworth* (1797) 3 Ves. Jun. 368; *Ex p. Blackburne* (1804) 10 Ves.Jun. 204, 206; *Emly v Lye* (1812) 15 East 7, 13; *Read v Hutchinson* (1813) 3 Camp. 352; *Camidge v Allenby* (1827) 6 B. & C. 373, 381–382.

[86] *cf. Owenson v Morse* (1796) 7 T.R. 64; *Evans v Whyle* (1829) 5 Bing. 485, 488.

[87] *Ward v Evans* (1703) 2 Ld. Raym. 928, 930. See also *Clerk v Mundall* (1698) 12 Mod. 203; *Moore v Warren* (1720) 1 Stra. 415; *Ex p. Blackburne* (1804) 10 Ves.Jun. 204; *Camidge v Allenby* (1827) 6 B. & C. 373 at 382. *cf. Timmins v Gibbins* (1852) 18 Q.B. 722, 726. Contrast *Guardians of Lichfield Union v Greene* (1857) 1 H. & N. 884, 889 (banknote).

[88] *Van Wart v Woolley* (1824) 3 B. & C. 439, 446. See also *Timmins v Gibbins* (1852) 18 Q.B. 722 at 726, 727.

[89] *Turner v Stones* (1843) 12 L.J.Q.B. 303. See also *Woodland v Fear* (1857) 7 E. & B. 519, 522.

[90] See *Chitty on Contracts* (29th ed.), Vol.I, § 21–074; above, para.4–021.

[91] *Clerk v Mundall* (1698) 12 Mod. 203; *Ward v Evans* (1703) 2 Ld. Raym. 928, 930; *Rogers v Langford* (1833) 1 C. & M 637; *Moule v Brown* (1838) 4 Bing. N.C. 266. See also above, para.6–042 (s.45).

within a reasonable time of the dishonour[92] and take such other steps as are necessary to preserve the liability of parties who are secondarily liable.[93] If he fails to do so, and the transferor is thereby substantially prejudiced, the transferor will not be liable.[94]

## Illustrations

7–073    1. A Bank of England note, payable to bearer, is negotiated for value without indorsement by the defendant to the claimant bank. When presented for payment, it is discovered that the note has been materially altered in number, and payment is refused. The claimant bank can recover from the defendant the money paid. Section 64 of the Act does not apply to a forged Bank of England note and, in any event, the alteration was apparent. The note was therefore worthless.[95]

2. The claimant bankers discount for the defendant bill brokers a bill of exchange indorsed in blank by the payee. The indorser absconds and the signatures of the drawer and acceptor are found to be forgeries. The claimants can recover from the defendants the money paid to them, even though the latter have paid this to their principal, the indorsee.[96]

3. The defendants, bill brokers, discount with the claimant bills which purport to have been drawn by B on and accepted by N & Co. and which purport to have been specially indorsed to A and by him indorsed in blank. All the signatures except that of A prove to be forgeries. That of A is genuine, but he was the author of the forgeries and is bankrupt. The claimants can recover the amount paid for the bills from the defendants.[97]

## Discharge of Bill

### Payment in due course

8–001    **59. (1) A bill is discharged by payment in due course by or on behalf of the drawee or acceptor.**

[92] *Camidge v Allenby* (1827) 6 B. & C. 373; *Robson v Oliver* (1847) 10 Q.B. 704.
[93] See above, para.6–092 (s.48).
[94] But it is questionable whether this has survived into the modern law.
[95] *Leeds and County Bank Ltd v Walker* (1883) 11 Q.B.D. 84.
[96] *Fuller v Smith* (1824) Ry. & M. 49.
[97] *Gurney v Womersley* (1854) 24 L.J.Q.B. 46.

"Payment in due course" means payment made at or after the maturity of the bill to the holder thereof in good faith and without notice that his title to the bill is defective.

(2) Subject to the provisions herein-after contained, when a bill is paid by the drawer or an indorser it is not discharged; but

(a) Where a bill payable to, or to the order of, a third party is paid by the drawer, the drawer may enforce payment thereof against the acceptor, but may not re-issue the bill.

(b) Where a bill is paid by an indorser, or where a bill payable to drawer's order is paid by the drawer, the party paying it is remitted to his former rights as regards the acceptor or antecedent parties, and he may, if he thinks fit strike out his own and subsequent indorsements, and again negotiate the bill.

(3) Where an accommodation bill is paid in due course by the party accommodated the bill is discharged.

Definitions
"bill": s.2.
"good faith": s.90.
"holder": s.2.

Comparison
UCC: §§ 3–207, 3–418, 3–602, 3–603, 4–407.
ULB: arts 38–42, 50.
ULC: art.35.
UNB: arts 72–77.

## COMMENT

**Subsection (1): discharge by payment in due course.** A bill (or cheque) is discharged by payment in due course, that is to say, when the instrument is paid at or after maturity by or on behalf of the drawee or acceptor to the holder in good faith and without notice that the holder's title to the bill is defective. A promissory note is likewise discharged if such a payment is made by or on behalf of the maker of a note.[1]    8–002

**Effect of discharge.** By section 36(1) of the Act, where a bill is negotiable in its origin it continues to be negotiable "until it has been . . . (b) discharged by payment or otherwise". The inference is clear: that a bill    8–003

---

[1] s.89(1)(2); *Bartrum v Caddy* (1838) 9 A. & E. 275.

which has been discharged by payment in due course ceases thereafter to be negotiable.

When a bill or note is paid, the person by whom it is paid is entitled to require that the holder forthwith deliver it up to him.[2] But he may fail to do so, and the instrument may subsequently be indorsed and delivered to a person who (but for the discharge) would be a holder in due course, and who takes it in ignorance of the fact that it has been paid. The instrument itself would not appear to be "mere waste paper",[3] since, by section 55(2)(c) of the Act, the indorser is precluded from denying to his immediate indorsee that the instrument was at the time of his indorsement valid and subsisting.[4] But the question arises whether the acceptor of the bill (or the maker of a note) incurs any liability to the person to whom the instrument has been so transferred. In the pre-Act case of *Harmer v Steele*, Wilde C.J. said[5]: "There is no doubt that, when a bill has been paid at maturity by [an] . . . acceptor to a third person, who is the holder, no action can afterwards be brought on the acceptance." Chalmers, too, was of the same view[6]: "A bill is discharged when all rights of action thereon are extinguished. It then ceases to be negotiable, and if it subsequently comes into the hands of a holder in due course, he acquires no right of action on the instrument." On the other hand, in *Glasscock v Balls*, Lord Esher M.R. said[7]: "If a negotiable instrument remains current, even though it has been paid, there is nothing to prevent a person to whom it has been indorsed for value without knowledge that it has been paid from suing." If the instrument is payable at a fixed date and the holder transfers it after maturity, the transferee could not in any event be a holder in due course, since he does not become the holder of it before it is overdue.[8] He should therefore acquire no rights on the instrument as it is his duty to inquire whether or not it has been paid.[9] But in the case of a bill which is payable on demand, then, unless it appears on the face of it to have been in circulation for an unreasonable period of time,[10] it is not overdue, and the transferee could otherwise have the status of a holder in due course. Nevertheless, under section 36(1), the bill will have ceased to be negotiable, and the bill will not have been negotiated to him. It is

---

[2] s.52(4).

[3] Contrast *Chalmers* (13th ed.), p.122.

[4] In the case of a bearer instrument, there would be a breach of warranty under s.58(3).

[5] (1849) 4 Exch. 1, 13 (Illustration 1).

[6] 9th ed., p.233, citing *Harmer v Steele* (1849) 4 Exch. 1; *Burchfield v Moore* (1854) 23 L.J.Q.B. 261; *Burbridge v Manners* (1812) 3 Camp. 193, 195; *Cundy v Marriott* (1831) 1 B. & Ad. 696. But see Kadirgamar (1959) 22 M.L.R. 146, 150–153.

[7] (1889) 24 Q.B. 13, 15.

[8] s.29(1)(a).

[9] See above, para.5–039 (s.36(2)).

[10] s.36(3). This does not apply to promissory notes: s.86(3).

therefore difficult to see how he could sue the acceptor on the instrument.[11] It has, however, been suggested[12] that, in the case of a promissory note payable on demand,[13] if the maker who has paid fails to obtain the instrument or fails to note on it that it has been paid, he might still be liable to a holder in due course, alternatively, that he might be estopped from setting up the payment as a defence to an action against him by such a holder.[14] The first proposition seems highly doubtful in view of section 36(1), which applies also to promissory notes.[15] The second proposition, which would also extend to bills payable on demand, has more substance, but would depend on whether leaving the instrument in the possession of the holder without any notation of payment is sufficient to raise an estoppel by representation or negligence against the acceptor or maker.[16]

**Rights outside the bill.** A right of action on a bill must be distin-    8–004
guished from a right of action which a party to a bill may have arising out of the bill transaction, but wholly independent of the instrument. The former is extinguished by the discharge of the instrument, the latter may or may not be so.[17] For example, if one of several joint acceptors pays the bill in due course at maturity to the holder, the contract of acceptance is performed, and no action can be maintained upon it. But the acceptor who has paid the bill may have a right of action against the other joint acceptors for contribution; that action would not be on the contract of acceptance or on the bill, but on a different contract, arising out of the state of accounts between the joint acceptors, or on the terms on which they agreed together to accept, and would not be discharged.[18] Also if an accommodation acceptor pays a bill it is discharged,[19] but he has a personal right of action for indemnity against the person accommodated.[20]

---

[11] Contrast *Paget* (12th ed.), 31.23.

[12] Kadirgamar (1959) 22 M.L.R. 146.

[13] "For such a note is a continuing security payable at any time after issue, and when it is paid it is deemed to have been paid at maturity (s.86(3))": Kadirgamar (1959) 22 M.L.R. 146 at 149.

[14] See *Mohamedally v Misso* (1957) 58 N.L.R. (Ceylon) 457, PC, on appeal from the Supreme Court of Ceylon (1954) 56 N.L.R. (Ceylon) 370.

[15] s.89(1).

[16] See Kadirgamar (1959) 22 M.L.R. 146, 153–163. Contrast *Moorgate Mercantile Co. Ltd v Twitchings* [1977] A.C. 890 (sale of goods).

[17] As a normal rule, payment of an instrument will—at least *pro tanto*—discharge the debt or other obligation for which it was given in payment.

[18] *Harmer v Steele* (1849) 4 Exch. 1, 14. cf. *Houle v Baxter* (1802) 3 East 177 (indorsement).

[19] This statement was approved by Lord Atkin in *Coats v Union Bank of Scotland Ltd* 1929 S.C.(H.L.) 114, 127.

[20] See above, para.4–045 (s.28).

**8–005**     **Meaning of "payment".** Payment must be consensual.[21] Since the order or promise to pay in a bill or note is to pay in money,[22] the holder is entitled to insist on payment in money. But when the time of payment comes he may, if he chooses, agree to accept satisfaction in any other form.[23] Any satisfaction which would operate as a discharge in the case of an ordinary contract to pay money[24] is equally effectual in the case of a bill or note.[25] Thus "payment" may be made by means of an agreement to set-off another debt,[26] or by receipt of goods,[27] bonds[28] or the cheque or draft of the person paying[29] or of a third party,[30] or by a transfer in a banker's books from one account to another.[31] The burden of proving that payment has been made by such other means rests upon the person alleging it to be so.[32]

Payment by a banker to a private individual is complete, and the property in the money passes to the payee, when the money is laid on the counter.[33] Payment by inter-bank transfer is probably complete when the recipient bank receives the paying bank's payment order and decides to credit the payee's account,[34] but it may be that a reasonable time must

---

[21] *Thompson v Big Cities Realty & Agency Co.* (1910) 21 O.L.R. 394: "It is plain that a wrongful taking of the company's money etc. cannot be pleaded as payment on the notes" (Riddell J. at p.402).

[22] ss.3(1), 17(2)(b), 83(1).

[23] *London Banking Corp. Ltd v Horsnail* (1898) 3 Com.Cas. 105, 106–107.

[24] See *Chitty on Contracts* (29th ed.), Vol.I, § 22–012.

[25] *D. Gokal & Co (HK) Ltd v Rippleworth Ltd* [1998] C.L.Y. 370 (compromise).

[26] *Re Harmony and Montague Tin and Copper Mining Co.* (1873) L.R. 8 Ch.App. 407, 414; *Lindsay v La Plante* (1912) 3 D.L.R. 449. *cf. Pease v Hirst* (1829) 10 B. & C. 122; *Callander v Howard* (1850) 19 L.J.C.P. 312 (no agreement).

[27] *Hands v Burton* (1808) 9 East 349; *Saxty v Wilkin* (1843) 11 M. & W. 622; *Smith v Battams* (1857) 26 L.J. Exch. 232; *Tyrer Co. Ltd v Eureka Lumber Co. Ltd* (1922) 55 N.S.R. 441.

[28] *Schroder's Case* (1870) L.R. 11 Eq. 131.

[29] *Meyer & Co. Ltd v Sze Hai Tong Banking and Insurance Co. Ltd* [1913] A.C. 847 (s.79, Illustration 2). See also *Sibree v Tripp* (1846) 15 M. & W. 23. But this may be only conditional payment unless accepted as absolute payment (below). *cf.* also *Pease v Hirst* (1829) 10 B. & C. 122; (note to be only security).

[30] *Belshaw v Bush* (1851) 11 C.B. 191, 207.

[31] *Bodenham v Purchas* (1818) 2 B. & Ald. 39; *Gordon v London City and Midland Bank Ltd* [1902] 1 K.B. 242, 274–275; *The Brimnes (Tenax Steamship Co. Ltd v The Brimnes)* [1975] Q.B. 929.

[32] *Beaver Lumber Co. v Gellner* [1945] 3 W.W.R. 657. Parol evidence will be admissible to ascertain the intention of the parties.

[33] *Chambers v Miller* (1862) 13 C.B.N.S. 125. But *cf. Barclays Bank Ltd v Simms, Son & Cooke (Southern) Ltd* [1980] Q.B. 677, 700.

[34] *Mardorf Peach & Co. Ltd v Attica Sea Carriers Corp. of Liberia* [1977] A.C. 850, 880, 889; *Delbrueck & Co. v Manufacturers Hanover Trust Co.* 609 F. 2d 1047 (1979). But contrast *The Chikuma (A/S Awilco of Oslo v Fulvia SpA Di Navigazione of Cagliari* [1981] 1 W.L.R. 314, HL. See also *TSB Bank of Scotland v Welwyn Hatfield D.C.* [1993] 2 Bank. L.R. 267. It cannot, however, be said that there is any uniform rule: see the Report of the Review Committee on Banking Services Law and Practice (1989) Cm. 622, Ch.12; Goode, *Payment Obligations in Commercial and Financial Transactions* (1983 Sweet & Maxwell); Goode, *Commercial Law* (3rd ed.), 469; Paget (12th ed.), 17.190; Wood, *Comparative Financial Law* (1995), 25.18; Brindle and Cox, *Law of Bank Payments* (3rd ed.), 3–102; Vroegop [1990] L.M.C.L.Q. 64, 72–76.

elapse in order to enable the recipient bank to process the order.[35] In the case of an "in-house" payment within the same branch of the same bank, payment is made when the bank decides to accept its customer's instruction to pay and sets in motion its internal process for crediting the payee's account.[36] The same is probably true of an inter-branch payment.[37] Payment of cheques through clearing is effected in accordance with Clearing House Rules, an adjustment being made if the item is subsequently dishonoured.[38] The Banking Code[39] requires information to be given to customers with respect to the cheque clearing cycle and the charging of interest.[40]

**Conditional payment.** The holder may at or after maturity take from the acceptor of a bill or the maker of a note, in satisfaction of the latter's indebtedness to him on the instrument, a new negotiable instrument,[41] whether of the acceptor, the maker or a third person.[42] The new instrument may be given and accepted as absolute payment if the parties so intend. But prima facie the delivery of the new instrument is conditional payment only, as it is in the case of any other debt.[43] The holder's right of action on the original instrument is suspended until maturity of the new instrument.[44] If the new instrument is duly paid, the payment becomes

8–006

---

[35] *Mardorf Peach & Co. Ltd v Attica Sea Carriers Corp. of Liberia* [1977] A.C. 850 at 885. See also *Afovos Shipping Co. S.A. v R. Pagnan and Filli (The Afovos)* [1980] 2 Lloyds Rep. 469, 473; on appeal [1982] 1 W.L.R. 848.

[36] *The Brimnes* [1975] Q.B. 929 at 948–951, 963–966, 969; *Momm v Barclays Bank International Ltd* [1977] Q.B. 790; Brindle and Cox, *Law of Bank Payments* (3rd ed.), 3–094; Geva [1990] 3 J.I.B.L. 108. Contrast *Sutherland v Royal Bank of Scotland plc* 1997 S.L.T. 329.

[37] *Libyan Arab Foreign Bank v Manufacturers Hanover Trust Co. (No.2)* [1989] 1 Lloyd's Rep. 608; Brindle and Cox, *Law of Bank Payments* (3rd ed.), 3–101.

[38] See Ellinger, Lomnicka and Hooley, *Modern Banking Law* (3rd ed.), pp.331–339, Brindle and Cox, *Law of Bank Payments* (3rd ed.), 7–055, 7–058; Report of the Review Committee on Banking Services Law and Practice (1989) Cm. 622, para.12.16; Goode 1990 L.M.C.L.Q. 64; Vroegop [1990] L.M.C.L.Q. 64. For older cases, see *Warwick v Rogers* (1843) 5 M. & G. 340; *London Banking Co. v Horsnail* (1898) 3 Com.Cas. 105. *cf. Riedell v Commercial Bank of Australia Ltd* [1931] V.L.R. 382; *H.H. Dimond (Rotorua 1966) Ltd v Australia and New Zealand Banking Group Ltd* [1979] 2 N.Z.L.R. 739; *National Slag v Canadian Imperial Bank of Commerce* (1982) 140 D.L.R. (3d) 473; *Barclays Bank plc v Bank of England* [1985] 1 All E.R. 385 (above, para.6–062).

[39] Para.9.4 (above, para.1–011).

[40] For the charging of interest during the clearing cycle where the customer's account is overdrawn in accordance with the bank's standard terms, see *Emerald Meats (London) Ltd v AIB Group (UK) plc* [2002] EWCA Civ 460.

[41] It is immaterial whether the new instrument is payable on demand or *in futuro*: *Currie v Misa* (1875) L.R. 10 Ex. 153, affirmed sub. nom. *Misa v Currie* (1876) 1 App. Cas. 554 (s.27, Illustration 17).

[42] *Belshaw v Bush* (1851) 11 C.B. 191; *Allen v Royal Bank of Canada* (1936) 134 L.T. 194. *cf. Oliver v Davis* [1949] 2 K.B. 727 (s.27, Illustration 18).

[43] See above, paras 4–011, 4–021.

[44] *Allen v Royal Bank of Canada* (1936) 134 L.T. 194 at 196. Where the instrument is payable on demand, *e.g.* a cheque, the remedy is suspended until the instrument is presented for payment and dishonoured.

absolute[45] and the original instrument is discharged. If the new instrument is dishonoured by non-payment, the rights of the holder against the acceptor or maker on the original instrument—and on the indebtedness for which it was given—revive.[46]

8–007    **Renewals.** When a bill is given in renewal of a former bill, and the holder retains the former bill, the renewal, in the absence of special agreement,[47] operates merely as conditional payment of the former bill. If the renewal bill is paid in due course or otherwise discharged, the original bill is likewise discharged.[48] But if the renewal bill is dishonoured, then, in principle, the liabilities of the parties to the original bill revive, and they may be sued thereon.[49] However, renewing a bill operates as an extension of the time for paying it. Hence, if the holder of a bill takes from the acceptor in lieu of payment a new bill payable at a future day, to which the drawer and indorsers are not parties, this discharges the drawer and indorsers.[50]

When there is an agreement to renew, the application for renewal must be made within a reasonable time of the maturity of the original bill, but need not be made before its maturity.[51] If the holder of a renewed bill could not have maintained an action on the original bill because there was no consideration,[52] or the consideration was illegal,[53] or because he

---

[45] *Thorne v Smith* (1851) 10 C.B. 659; *Hadley (Felix) & Co. Ltd v Hadley* [1898] 2 Ch. 680; *Allen v Royal Bank of Canada* (1936) 134 L.T. 194. The payment is deemed to have been made when the new instrument was accepted by the holder: *Thomson v Moyse* [1961] A.C. 967, 1004.

[46] *Gunn v Bolckow, Vaughan & Co.* (1875) L.R. 10 Ch.App. 491; *Cohen v Hale* (1878) 3 Q.B.D. 371; *Re Romer & Haslam* [1893] 2 Q.B. 286, 296; *DPP v Turner* [1974] A.C. 357, 367–368, 369. But this is not so if the new instrument is negotiated and is still outstanding in the hands of a third party after dishonour (*Davis v Reilly* [1898] 1 Q.B. 1; *Re a Debtor* [1908] 1 K.B. 344) unless the third party is the agent of or trustee for the holder (*Hadwen v Mendisabel* (1825) 2 C. & P. 20; *National Savings Bank Association Ltd v Tranah* (1867) L.R. 2 C.P. 556).

[47] cf. *Lewis v Lyster* (1835) 2 C.M. & R. 704 (absolute payment).

[48] *Dillon v Rimmer* (1822) 1 Bing. 100; *Kendrick v Lomax* (1832) 2 C. & J. 405. cf. *Lumley v Musgrave* (1837) 4 Bing. N.C. 9; *Lumley v Hudson* (1837) 4 Bing. N.C. 15 (interest on original bill preserved).

[49] *Ex p. Barclay* (1802) 7 Ves.Jun. 597; *Norris v Aylett* (1809) 2 Camp. 329; *Bishop v Rowe* (1815) 3 M. & S. 362. See also *Sloman v Cox* (1834) 1 C.M. & R. 471 (renewal bill void for alteration); *Bell v Buckley* (1856) 11 Exch. 631 (renewal bill forged).

[50] *Gould v Robson* (1807) 8 East 576; *Goldfarb v Bartlett* [1920] 1 K.B. 639, 648.

[51] *Maillard v Page* (1870) L.R. 5 Ex. 321. As to construction of agreements to renew, see *Innes v Munro* (1847) 1 Exch. 473; *Torrance v Bank of British North America* (1873) L.R. 5 P.C. 246.

[52] *Southall v Rigg* (1851) 11 C.B. 481; *Edwards v Chancellor* (1888) 52 J.P. 454.

[53] *Chapman v Black* (1819) 2 B. & Ald. 588; *Wynne v Callender* (1826) 1 Russ. 293; *Hay v Ayling* (1851) 16 Q.B. 423. cf. *Preston v Jackson* (1817) 2 Stark. 237; *Flight v Reed* (1863) 1 H. & C. 703.

was privy to some fraud connected therewith,[54] he cannot sue on the renewed bill.[55]

**Partial payment.** The holder is not bound to accept partial payment if tendered.[56] But, if he does so, it has been said that partial payment in due course operates as a discharge *pro tanto*.[57] While this may be correct as between payer and payee, it is submitted that the instrument remains fully negotiable.[58] If it is payable on demand,[59] a holder in due course to whom it is subsequently negotiated and who takes it without notice of the partial payment should be entitled to claim the whole amount of the bill.

8–008

On the other hand, the holder may agree to accept the partial payment in satisfaction of the amount of the bill. Normally, in the law of contract, part payment by a debtor of a greater sum which is currently due and payable is no satisfaction of that sum, since there is no consideration for the promise to forego the balance.[60] But, by section 62(1) of the Act, when the holder of a bill at or after its maturity absolutely and unconditionally renounces his rights against the acceptor the bill is discharged, provided that the renunciation is in writing or the bill delivered up to the acceptor. Partial payment coupled with an absolute and unconditional renunciation of the holder's right to the balance may, on these conditions, therefore operate as a complete discharge.

**Time of payment.** Payment, to operate as a discharge, must be made "at or after the maturity of the bill". Where an instrument is not payable on demand,[61] it is at maturity on the day on which it falls due.[62] An instrument which is payable on demand is at maturity from the date of its issue,[63] and due payment may be made at any time after that date.

8–009

---

[54] The renewal bill is in general held under the same title as the one it replaces: *Lee v Zagury* (1817) 8 Taunt. 114 (distinguished in *Mascarenhas v Mercantile Bank of India* (1931) 47 T.L.R. 611).

[55] But contrast *Mather v Maidstone* (1856) 18 C.B. 273 (Illustration 6); *Levin v Roth* [1950] 1 All E.R. 698n.

[56] *Chitty on Contracts* (29th ed.), Vol.I, § 21–085. Contrast ULB, art.39. See also ICC Uniform Rules for Collection (1995), art.19.

[57] *Chalmers* (9th ed.), p.235, citing *Graves v Key* (1832) 3 B. & Ad. 313, but that decision is to the opposite effect.

[58] s.36(1).

[59] Otherwise it will be overdue. But *cf. Graves v Key* (1832) 3 B. & Ad. 313.

[60] *Pinnel's Case* (1602) 5 Co.Rep. 117a; *Foakes v Beer* (1884) 9 App. Cas. 605; *D. & C. Builders v Rees* [1966] 2 Q.B. 617. See *Chitty on Contracts* (29th ed.), Vol.I, § 21–052. Contrast partial payment by a third party, below, para.8–010.

[61] s.10.

[62] s.14.

[63] *Re George, Francis v Bruce* (1890) 44 Ch.D. 627 (s.62, Illustration 2); *Edwards v Walters* [1896] 2 Ch. 157 (s.62, Illustration 1).

Payment by the drawee or acceptor of a bill, or by the maker of a note, before maturity operates as a mere purchase or discount of the instrument; it is not discharged.[64] In *Burbridge v Manners*, Lord Ellenborough said[65]:

> "I agree that a bill paid at maturity cannot be reissued, and that no action can afterwards be maintained upon it by a subsequent indorsee. A payment before it becomes due, however, I think does not extinguish it any more than if it were merely discounted. A contrary doctrine would add a new clog to the circulation of bills of exchange and promissory notes; for it would be impossible to know whether there had not been an anticipated payment of them. It is the duty of bankers to make some memorandum on bills and notes which have been paid; but if they do not, the holders of such securities cannot be affected by any payment made before they are due. While a bill of exchange is running, it remains in a negotiable state."

Thus, if the acceptor of a bill pays the holder before maturity, and the bill is negotiated back to him, he may reissue and further negotiate it.[66] If he negotiates it before its due date[67] to a holder in due course who is unaware that it has been paid, that holder can enforce it against the acceptor and against any prior party (*e.g.* the drawer).[68] Or if the acceptor, having paid the bill before its due date, allows it to remain in the hands of the holder who negotiates it before it is overdue to a holder in due course without notice of the payment, the bill is again enforceable by that holder against the acceptor and any party liable on the instrument.[69]

8–010    **By whom payment must be made.** Subject to subsection (3), payment in due course must be made "by or on behalf of the drawee[70] or acceptor",[71] or, in the case of a promissory note, by the maker of the note.[72] Where there are more than one joint acceptors of a bill[73] or makers of a note,[74] payment by any one of them will discharge the instrument.

---

[64] *Morley v Culverwell* (1840) 7 M. & W. 174, 182.
[65] (1812) 3 Camp. 193, 195.
[66] s.37. *cf. Bartrum v Caddy* (1838) 9 A. & E. 275 (note payable on demand).
[67] If the acceptor retains it until maturity, the bill will be discharged: s.61.
[68] *Morley v Culverwell* (1840) 7 M. & W. 174; *Attenborough v Mackenzie* (1856) 25 L.J. Exch. 244 (s.37, Illustration 2).
[69] *Dod v Edwards* (1827) 2 C. & P. 602 (premature release); *Factory Investments (Pty) Ltd v Ismails* 1960 (2) S.A. 10.
[70] *Wilkinson v Simson* (1838) 2 Moore P.C. 274, 287.
[71] *Callow v Lawrence* (1814) 3 M. & S. 95, 97; *Jones v Broadhurst* (1850) 9 C.B. 173, 181.
[72] ss.89(1), (2).
[73] *Harmer v Steele* (1849) 4 Exch. 1, 13, 14 (Illustration 1).
[74] *Beaumont v Greathead* (1846) 2 C.B. 494. See also *Bartrum v Caddy* (1838) 9 A. & E. 275.

Payment by the drawer or an indorser will not operate as a discharge.[75] Nor will payment by a stranger discharge the instrument,[76] unless the payment is made by him as agent for and on account of the drawee, acceptor or maker, and with his prior authority or subsequent ratification.[77] However, partial payment by a stranger in full satisfaction of the amount of the instrument, if accepted by the holder, may, it seems, constitute payment,[78] because it would be a fraud on the stranger to proceed.[79]

Application of moneys by the holder himself does not amount to payment in due course.[80] In *Glasscock v Balls*,[81] a promissory note payable on demand was given to secure an advance and a mortgage executed in favour of the holder as further security. The holder sold and transferred the mortgage, the amount realised being in excess of the amount advanced. The Court of Appeal held that this was not payment of the note, which was subsequently negotiated by the holder to an indorsee for value without notice. Payment was not made by the maker of the note, nor was there payment to the holder, even though the holder applied the proceeds of the transfer to the satisfaction of the advance.

**To whom payment must be made.** Payment, to operate as a discharge,    **8–011** must be made to the holder of the instrument,[82] or to some person authorised to receive payment on his behalf.[83] "Holder" is defined in section 2 of the Act to mean the payee or indorsee of a bill or note who is in possession of it, or the bearer thereof, and "bearer" is defined to mean the person in possession of a bill or note which is payable to bearer.

If an instrument is payable to bearer, payment to the person in possession of it will be payment to the holder. Such a payment can constitute

---

[75] s.59(2).
[76] *Deacon v Stodhart* (1841) 2 M. & G. 317; *Kemp v Balls* (1854) 10 Exch. 607; *Lyon v Maxwell* (1868) 18 L.T. 28. See also *Re Rowe* [1904] 2 K.B. 483; *Smith v Cox* [1940] 2 K.B. 558; *Owen v Tate* [1976] 1 Q.B. 402.
[77] *Belshaw v Bush* (1851) 11 C.B. 191; *Kemp v Balls* (1854) 10 Exch. 607 at 610; *Simpson v Eggington* (1855) 10 Exch. 845. But authority may be presumed: *Bennett v Griffin Finance Ltd* [1967] 2 Q.B. 46.
[78] *Hirachand Punamchand v Temple* [1911] 2 K.B. 330 (but some doubts were expressed by Vaughan Williams L.J. in this case).
[79] *Welby v Drake* (1825) 1 C. & P. 557. *cf. Cook v Lister* (1863) 13 C.B.N.S. 543.
[80] *Jenkins v Tongue* (1860) 26 L.J. Ex. 147.
[81] (1889) 24 Q.B.D. 13 (Illustration 3).
[82] A bill will, however, be discharged if the money, though not paid to the holder, finds its way into the holder's hands, and the holder has treated it as received in liquidation of the bill: *Field v Carr* (1828) 5 Bing. 13. See *Byles* (27th ed.), 13–07.
[83] Authority to receive payment will be determined in accordance with ordinary principles of agency. See also s.45(3) (presentment for payment).

payment in due course even though the holder stole or found the instrument[84] or obtained the payee's indorsement in blank and then fraudulently converted the proceeds,[85] provided that the payment is made in good faith and without notice that the holder's title to it is defective.[86]

If an instrument is payable to order, then, subject to the special protection afforded to a banker,[87] payment must be made to the payee or indorsee of the instrument who is in possession of it in order to constitute payment to the holder. It is immaterial that the payee or indorsee has obtained the instrument or its acceptance by fraud[88] or that his title to it is otherwise defective,[89] provided that the payment is made in good faith and without notice of the defect.[90] However, a person who takes a bill through or under a forged or unauthorised indorsement is not a holder, even though he takes it in good faith and for value and without notice that the indorsement is forged or unauthorised.[91] He is not an indorsee of the instrument, since the forged or unauthorised indorsement is wholly inoperative,[92] nor is he the payee or bearer of it. Payment to him is therefore not payment to the holder and will not discharge the payer or the instrument.[93] Also, if a thief steals an instrument payable to order and obtains payment by personating the payee or indorsee, there will be no discharge.[94] Where, however, the payee is a fictitious or non-existing person, a bill may be treated as payable to bearer, and payment to the person in possession of it may be a good discharge.[95]

If an instrument is not transferable, for example because it is drawn "Pay X only"[96] or because it is a cheque crossed "account payee"[97] no person other than the original payee can be a holder of the instrument and payment to such a person will not operate as a discharge.

8–012     **Payment by a banker.** A banker on whom a cheque is drawn must pay it in accordance with the mandate of his customer, the drawer, and cannot therefore, in principle, debit his customer's account if he pays otherwise than to a holder of the instrument.[98] But, by section 60 of the Act, a banker

---

[84] *Smith v Sheppard* (1776) cited *Chitty* (11th ed.), p.278; *Robarts v Tucker* (1851) 16 Q.B. 560, 579; *Charles v Blackwell* (1877) 2 C.P.D. 151, 158.
[85] *Auchteroni & Co. v Midland Bank Ltd* [1928] 2 K.B. 294 (Illustration 4).
[86] See below, para.8–013.
[87] See below, para.8–012.
[88] See above, para.4–063 (s.29).
[89] See s.29(2), and above, para.4–062.
[90] See below. para.8–013.
[91] See above, para.3–066 (s.24).
[92] s.24.
[93] *Robarts v Tucker* (1851) 16 Q.B. 560 (s.24, Illustration 8).
[94] See below, para.8–052 (s.60).
[95] s.7(3).
[96] s.8(1).
[97] s.81A.
[98] See above, para.3–072 (s.24).

who pays in good faith and in the ordinary course of business a cheque[99] drawn on him payable to order on which the indorsement of the payee or any subsequent indorsement is forged or unauthorised is deemed to have paid it in due course. This section applies whether the payment is made across the counter or to another banker. By section 80, where a banker upon whom a crossed cheque is drawn (or, by section 5 of the Cheques Act 1957, certain other crossed instruments) pays the cheque to another banker in good faith and without negligence and in accordance with the terms of the crossing, the banker paying the cheque, and, if the cheque has come into the hands of the payee, the drawer, are respectively entitled to the same rights and are placed in the same position as if payment had been made to the true owner thereof.[1] Further, section 1(1) of the Cheques Act 1957 provides that, where a banker in good faith and in the ordinary course of business pays a cheque drawn on him which is not indorsed or which is irregularly indorsed, he does not in doing so, incur any liability by reason only of the absence of or irregularity in, indorsement, and he is deemed to have paid in due course.[2] Section 1(2) of the 1957 Act extends to a banker a similar protection in the case of certain other instruments, and provides that the payment so made discharges the instrument.[3]

A customer of a bank may accept a bill or make a note payable at his bank. If the banker agrees to pay an instrument so domiciled with him for payment,[4] his mandate is to pay to a person who is capable of giving a good discharge for it.[5] Thus, in the case of an instrument payable to order, if the banker pays to a person who derives his title to it through or under a forged or unauthorised indorsement, he will not be entitled to debit his customer's account with the amount so paid, as he will have paid contrary to his mandate.[6] He cannot claim the protection of section 60 of the Act or of section 19 of the Stamp Act 1853 as the instrument is not drawn on him, and a bill or note does not fall within the categories of instrument protected by the Cheques Act 1957. However, the customer may, in certain circumstances, be held to be estopped from asserting that the payment was improperly made or to have ratified the unauthorised payment.[7]

---

[99] The protection extends to a bill payable to order on demand drawn on a banker (see below, para.8–043). See also s.19 of the Stamp Act 1853 (below, para.8–045).

[1] See below, paras 14–024, 17–075.

[2] See below, para.17–005.

[3] See below, para.17–013.

[4] *Robarts v Tucker* (1851) 16 Q.B. 560, 579; *Bank of England v Vagliano Bros* [1891] A.C. 107, 157. See also *Kymer v Laurie* (1849) 18 L.J.Q.B. 218.

[5] *Robarts v Tucker* (1851) 16 Q.B. 560 (s.24, Illustration 8).

[6] *Robarts v Tucker* (1851) 16 Q.B. 560.

[7] *Bank of England v Vagliano Bros* [1891] A.C. 107 at 114–115, 123–124, 134, 158. See also above, para.3–074 (s.24).

**8–013**     **Good faith and absence of notice.** Payment in due course must be made in good faith and without notice that the holder's title is defective. "Good faith" is defined in section 90 of the Act, and the concept of a defective title is illustrated (though not exhaustively) in section 29(2).[8] It would appear that "notice" in section 59(1), as in section 29(1)(b), means actual notice, and reference should be made to the Comment on section 29(1).[9]

**8–014**     **Postponement of payment.** Circumstances may arise where a banker, being under an obligation as between himself and his customer to pay an instrument, is nevertheless justified in postponing payment pending inquiries as to the identity or bona fides of the holder or pending confirmation by the customer that it should be paid. In *Robarts v Tucker*[10] Maule J. suggested that a banker might defer payment of a domiciled bill until he had satisfied himself that all the indorsements were genuine. But this suggestion was disapproved by Lord MacNaghten in *Bank of England v Vagliano Brothers*,[11] who said: "bankers who undertake the duty of paying their customer's acceptances cannot do otherwise than pay off-hand, and as a matter of course, bills presented for payment which are duly accepted and regular and complete on the face of them". A more cautious note was, however, struck by Lord Halsbury L.C.[12] in the same case, who said that, where payment in cash was required, a banker would "hesitate very much before making payment" to a person whose appearance and demeanour was calculated to raise a suspicion that he was not likely to be entrusted with a valuable document, whether the document was a cheque payable to bearer for a large amount or a bill. On the other hand, in *Auchteroni & Co. v Midland Bank Ltd*[13] Wright J. stated that a banker was required to pay cash over the counter on a bill domiciled with him for payment which was indorsed in blank "in the absence of very special circumstances of suspicion, such as presentation by a tramp, or a postman, or an office boy". But other circumstances may also exist which would justify the banker in questioning his customer's mandate, for example, where he knows or suspects that the moneys to be paid are going to be misapplied by the customer in breach of trust or of some other fiduciary relationship,[14] or where he has reasonable grounds for believing that there is a serious or reasonable possibility that the moneys are being

---

[8] See above, para.4–062. This would also, it seems, cover the case where the holder of a bearer instrument has no title to it at all: see above.
[9] See above, para.4–058.
[10] (1851) 16 Q.B. 560, 577–578.
[11] [1891] A.C. 107, 157.
[12] [1891] A.C. 107 at 117–118.
[13] [1928] 2 K.B. 294, 304.
[14] See below, para.13–056 (s.75). See also below, para.13–053 (money laundering).

misappropriated in fraud of the customer.[15] In such a case, even though the instrument itself is complete and regular, the banker will be entitled —and indeed bound—to defer immediate payment pending further investigation of the bona fides of the transaction.

**Proof of payment.** A receipt on the back of a bill imports, prima facie,   **8–015** that it has been paid by the drawee.[16] By section 3 of the Cheques Act 1957, an unindorsed cheque which appears to have been paid by the banker on whom it is drawn, or a certified copy thereof, is evidence of the receipt by the payee of the sum payable by the cheque.

**Subsection (2): payment by drawer or indorser.** The words "subject to   **8–016** the provisions hereinafter contained" refer to subsection (3). Subject to that subsection, a bill is not discharged when it is paid by the drawer or an indorser. The reason is that, since payment has been made by a party who is secondarily liable, the bill must remain valid to enable that party to exercise his rights of recourse upon it. Likewise a promissory note is not discharged by payment by an indorser. Thus it is no defence to an action by the holder against the acceptor or maker that the holder has been paid by the drawer or an indorser.[17]

When the bill is paid, the drawer or indorser should require delivery up to him of the bill, lest it be subsequently negotiated by the holder after payment to a holder in due course. He may, however, leave the bill in the hands of the holder in order that the holder may sue on it as trustee on his behalf.[18]

If a banker with whom a bill is domiciled for payment indorses the bill, it is a question of fact whether payment by him to the holder is made in his capacity as indorser or as agent for his customer, the acceptor.[19]

**Right of recourse.** A drawer or indorser who pays a bill is entitled to   **8–017** claim payment from the acceptor and antecedent parties liable to him on the bill.[20] If the bill is payable to order, he does not need to show that he is the holder of the bill by indorsement from the holder whom he has paid.[21] Where a bill payable to, or to the order of, a third party is paid by the drawer, paragraph (a) of this subsection confers upon him a right to enforce payment thereof against the acceptor. Where a bill is paid by an

---

[15] See below, para.13–062 (s.75)

[16] *Scholey v Walsby* (1791) 1 Peake 34, 35; *Graves v Key* (1832) 3 B. & Ad. 313, 318.

[17] *Jones v Broadhurst* (1850) 9 C.B. 173 (Illustration 5); *Brown, Janson & Co. v Cama & Co.* (1890) 6 T.L.R. 250.

[18] *Williams v James* (1850) 15 Q.B. 498.

[19] *Pollard v Ogden* (1853) 2 E. & B. 459.

[20] *Woodward v Pell* (1868) L.R. 4 Q.B. 55 (Illustration 7); *McKinnon v Armstrong Bros & Co.* (1877) 2 App. Cas. 531, 539 (Illustration 8).

[21] *Parminter v Symons* (1748) 2 Bro.P.C. 43; *Cossey v McManus* (1918) 40 D.L.R. 369.

indorser, or where a bill payable to drawer's order is paid by the drawer, then, by paragraph (b), the party paying it is remitted to his former rights as regards the acceptor or antecedent parties, *i.e.* he regains his former rights as holder of the instrument.[22]

The relationship between the drawer and indorsers on the one hand and the acceptor on the other is not strictly one of suretyship, but it is sufficiently analogous thereto that if the drawer or an indorser pays a dishonoured bill he is entitled to the benefit of any securities deposited by the acceptor with the holder to secure payment of the bill, and retained by the holder at the time of the dishonour of the bill.[23]

8–018    **Part payment.** The subsection does not deal with the case of part payment by the drawer or an indorser. But again it is clear that the bill or note is not discharged; nor is the liability of the acceptor or maker discharged *pro tanto* by reason of the part payment. If the holder retains possession of the bill after the payment, he can recover from the acceptor the full amount of the bill, holding it as trustee for the drawer or indorser as regards the amount received.[24] However, when the acceptor of a bill becomes bankrupt, any payment by the drawer or indorser must be deducted from the amount which the holder is entitled to prove against the bankrupt's estate.[25]

Where the drawer or indorser pays to the holder part of the amount of a bill, it would appear that he can recover the amount paid from the acceptor as money paid to the acceptor's use.[26]

8–019    **Renegotiation of bill.** Where a bill payable to, or to the order of, a third party is paid by the drawer, the drawer may not reissue the bill.[27] To

---

[22] *Callow v Lawrence* (1814) 3 M. & S. 95, 98–99.

[23] *Duncan, Fox & Co. v North and South Wales Bank* (1880) 6 App. Cas. 1 (Illustration 9); *Aga Ahmed Ispahany v Crisp* (1891) 8 T.L.R. 132. But where a bill of exchange has been dishonoured by the acceptor upon presentment and the drawer-payee of the bill is compelled to and does pay to the holder (a bank) to whom the bill has been discounted, he will normally have no claim against a third party who has guaranteed the bill by providing security to the bank in respect of the general indebtedness of the acceptor: *Scholefield Goodman & Sons Ltd v Zyngier* [1984] V.R. 445, affirmed (1985) 59 A.L.J.R. 770. Contrast *D & J Fowler (Australia) Ltd v Bank of New South Wales* [1982] 2 N.S.W.L.R. 879; *Maxal Nominees Pty. Ltd v Dalgety Ltd* [1985] 1 Qd.R.51.

[24] *Jones v Broadhurst* (1850) 9 C.B. 173, 183; *Cook v Lister* (1863) 13 C.B.N.S. 543, 579; *Agra and Mastermans Bank v Leighton* (1866) L.R. 2 Ex. 56. But he may be met by any defence available to the defendant against the payor: *Thornton v Maynard* (1875) L.R. 10 C.P. 695 (s.38, Illustration 1).

[25] *Re Oriental Commercial Bank* (1868) L.R. 6 Eq. 582. See also *Ex p. Tayler* (1857) 1 De G. & J. 302.

[26] *Pownal v Ferrand* (1827) 6 B. & C. 439.

[27] *Williams v James* (1850) 15 Q.B. 498 at 505.

allow reissue in these circumstances would be to permit the drawer to substitute himself for the payee and thereby materially to alter the effect of the instrument. But where a bill is paid by an indorser, or where a bill payable to drawer's order is paid by the drawer, the party paying it may, if he thinks fit, strike out his own and subsequent indorsements,[28] and again negotiate the bill.[29] In such a case, the bill is once more in the same state as it was when it originally came into his hands. By putting it again into circulation upon his own indorsement only, it does not prejudice any of the other parties who have subsequently indorsed the bill that the holder should be at liberty to sue the acceptor and any indorser prior to the party by whom it is paid.[30]

**Subsection (3): payment of accommodation bill.** According to Chalmers,[31] the expression "an accommodation bill" in this subsection is limited to a bill of which the *acceptor* is the accommodation party, *i.e.* is surety for another person or party ("the party accommodated"). This appears to be correct. The discharge of the bill may then be supported either on the grounds that the party accommodated pays as the acceptor's agent, or on the grounds that the bill has been paid by the person who, in substance though not in form, had the real obligation to pay.[32]   8–020

**Recovery of money paid under a mistake.** A person who has paid a bill, cheque or note may be able to recover from the recipient the sum paid as money paid under a mistake. Such a claim may be made by the drawee of a bill or the maker of a note who has paid the instrument to a person not entitled to receive the payment.[33] But a claim for money paid under a mistake may also be made, for example, by a person who has paid a bill *suprà protest* for the honour of a party liable thereon,[34] by an indorser who has paid the bill to the holder[35] and by the drawer of a cheque or payment order whose account has been debited with the   8–021

---

[28] See also s.37.
[29] *Callow v Lawrence* (1814) 3 M. & S. 95 (Illustration 6); *Hubbard v Jackson* (1827) 4 Bing. 390.
[30] *Callow v Lawrence* (1814) 3 M. & S. 95 at 97.
[31] See s.28, above, para.4–041.
[32] *Cook v Lister* (1863) 13 C.B.N.S. 543, 590. See also *Lazarus v Cowie* (1842) 3 Q.B. 459, criticised but followed in *Jewell v Parr* (1853) 13 C.B. 909, and apparently approved *Parr v Jewell* (1855) 16 C.B. 684, 709; *Jones v Broadhurst* (1850) 9 C.B. 173, 181, 189; *Ralli v Dennistoun* (1851) 6 Exch. 483, 36th plea and judgment at 493; *Strong v Foster* (1855) 17 C.B. 201, 222; *Re Oriental Commercial Bank* (1871) L.R. 7 Ch.App. 99, 102.
[33] *cf. Price v Neal* (1762) 3 Burr. 1355; *Mather v Maidstone* (1856) 18 C.B. 273; *London & River Plate Bank Ltd v Bank of Liverpool Ltd* [1896] 1 Q.B. 7.
[34] *Wilkinson v Johnson* (1824) 3 B. & C. 428 (Illustration 12).
[35] *Milnes v Duncan* (1827) 6 B. & C. 671 (Illustration 13).

amount paid.[36] In particular, a banker upon whom a cheque is drawn or with whom a bill is domiciled for payment, and who has paid the instrument, may recover money paid under a mistake from the person to whom it has been paid.[37]

A claim to recover a mistaken payment from the recipient is a personal claim in restitution for money had and received at common law.[38] It is founded upon the unjust enrichment of the recipient at the expense of the claimant.[39] Restitution will ordinarily be ordered against the recipient if he received the payment with knowledge that the claimant was acting under a mistake.[40] But restitution may be ordered even against a recipient who had no such knowledge, although certain defences may then be available in answer to the claim.[41]

"It is notoriously difficult to harmonize all the cases dealing with money paid under a mistake . . . ."[41a] Nevertheless, certain principles emerge.[42] First, the mistake may be one of fact or of law.[43] Secondly, if the payment is due under a contract between the payer and the recipient the payment cannot be recovered unless the contract itself is held void or discharged.[44] But otherwise it is sufficient that the mistake is material, in

---

[36] *Jones (R.E) Ltd v Waring & Gillow Ltd* [1926] A.C. 670 (s.29, Illustration 6); *Agip (Africa) Ltd v Jackson* [1991] Ch. 547 (Illustration 20). See also *Place v Turner* (1951) 101 L.J. 93; *Lipkin Gormon v Karpnale Ltd* [1991] 2 A.C. 548 (s. 75, Illustration 13); *Coutts & Co. v Stock* [2000] 1 W.L.R. 906, 912; *Niru Battery Manufacturing Co. v Milestone Trading Ltd* (No.1) [2002] EWHC 1425 (Comm), [2002] 2 All E.R. (Comm) 705 at [145], affirmed [2003] EWCA Civ 1446, [2004] 1 Lloyd's Rep. 344.

[37] *Imperial Bank of Canada v Bank of Hamilton* [1903] A.C. 49 (Illustration 17); *National Westminster Bank Ltd v Barclays Bank International Ltd* [1975] Q.B. 654 (Illustration 18); *Barclays Bank Ltd v W. J. Simms Ltd* [1980] Q.B. 677 (Illustration 19); *Bank of America v Arnell* [1999] Lloyd's Rep. Bank. 399. *cf. Smith v Mercer* (1815) 6 Taunt. 76; *Cocks v Masterman* (1829) 9 B. & C. 902.

[38] *Kelly v Solari* (1841) 9 M. & W. 54, 58; *Westdeutsche Landesbank Girozentrale v Islington London B.C.* [1986] A.C. 669, 683. But see below, para.8–032 (proprietary claim).

[39] *Lipkin Gorman v Karpnale Ltd* [1991] 2 A.C. 548; *Woolwich Equitable Building Society v I.R.C.* [1993] A.C. 70; *Westdeutsche Landesbank Girozentrale v Islington London BC* [1986] A.C. 669 at 710; *Kleinwort Benson Ltd v Glasgow CC* [1999] A.C. 553; *Banque Financiere de la Cite v Parc Battersea Ltd* [1999] 1 A.C. 221, 227, 234; *Kleinwort Benson Ltd v Lincoln CC (No.2)* [1999] 2 A.C. 349.

[40] *Kendal v Wood* (1853) 1 E. & B. 795; *John v Dodwell & Co.* [1918] A.C. 263; *Reckitt v Barnett, Pembroke and Slater Ltd* [1929] A.C. 176 (s.51, Illustration 3); *Barclays Bank Ltd v W.J. Simms Ltd* [1980] Q.B. 677 at 695; *Lloyds Bank plc v Independent Insurance Co. Ltd.* [2000] Q.B. 110, 130; *Niru Battery Manufacturing Co. v Milestone Trading Ltd* [2003] EWCA Civ 1446, [2004] 1 Lloyd's Rep. 344 at [152]. See also below, para.8–030.

[41] See below, paras 8–023–8–031.

[41a] *Weld-Blundell v Synott* [1940] 2 K.B. 107, 112 *per* Asquith J. See also *Morgan v Ashcroft* [1938] 1 K.B. 49, 62.

[42] See Goff and Jones, *The Law of Restitution* (6th ed., Sweet & Maxwell), Chs 4, 5.

[43] Previously, as a general rule, it had been held that money paid under a mistake of law was irrevocable. But following the decision of the House of Lords in *Kleinwort Benson Ltd v Lincoln City Council* [1999] 2 A.C. 349 this restriction was abolished.

[44] *Norwich Union v W.H. Price Ltd* [1934] A.C. 455; *Barclays Bank Ltd v W.J. Simms Ltd* [1980] Q.B. 677 at 695.

the sense that it causes the person paying to make the payment.[45] Repayment may be demanded, for example, where the signature of the drawer of a cheque[46] or of the drawee of a bill,[47] or that of an indorser of an order bill,[48] has been forged; where an instrument has been altered by raising the amount payable[49]; where an indorser pays a bill believing himself to be bound whereas in fact his liability has been discharged[50]; where a bank paying a cheque ignores or overlooks its customer's countermand of payment[51] or the fact that the customer has died[52]; where payment is made to a person other than the person directed[53]; or where a cheque is issued in the mistaken belief that it relates to an entirely different transaction.[54]

It is no longer material that the mistake is not "between" payer and recipient, that is, common to both parties.[55] Thus if A by fraud procures B to draw a cheque payable to C under a fundamental misapprehension as to the nature of transaction in respect of which the cheque is drawn,

8–022

---

[45] *Barclays Bank Ltd v W.J. Simms Ltd* [1980] Q.B. 677 at 692, 695; *Avon County Council v Howlett* [1983] 1 W.L.R. 605, 619–620; *David Securities Pty Ltd v Commonwealth Bank of Australia* (1990) 175 C.L.R. 353; *Kleinwort Benson Ltd v Lincoln City Council* [1999] 2 A.C. 349, 373, 408; *Nurdin and Peacock plc v D.B. Ramsden & Co. Ltd* [1999] 1 W.L.R. 1249, 1273; *Dextra Bank & Trust Company Ltd v Bank of Jamaica* [2002] 1 All E.R. (Comm) 193 at [28–30]; *Maersk Air Ltd v Expeditors International (UK) Ltd* [2003] 1 Lloyd's Rep. 491 at [26]; *Papamichael v National Westminster Bank plc* [2003] EWHC 164 (Comm), [2003] 1 Lloyd's Rep. 341 at [196–199].

[46] *National Westminster Bank Ltd v Barclays Bank International Ltd* [1975] Q.B. 654 (Illustration 18); *Bank of America v Arnell* [1999] Lloyd's Rep. Bank. 399. cf. *Price v Neal* (1762) 3 Burr. 1355 (Illustration 10) (bill).

[47] Cf. *Smith v Mercer* (1815) 6 Taunt. 76 (Illustration 11); *Cocks v Masterman* (1829) 9 B. & C. 902 (Illustration 14); *Mather v Maidstone* (1856) 18 C.B. 273 (Illustration 15).

[48] *Standard Bank of South Africa Ltd v ABSA Bank Ltd* 1995 (2) S.A. 740. cf. *London & River Plate Bank Ltd v Bank of Liverpool Ltd* [1896] 1 Q.B. 7 (Illustration 16).

[49] *Imperial Bank of Canada v Bank of Hamilton* [1903] A.C. 49 (Illustration 17).

[50] *Milnes v Duncan* (1827) 6 B. & C. 671 (Illustration 13).

[51] *Barclays Bank Ltd v W.J. Simms Ltd* [1980] Q.B. 677 (Illustration 19) (criticised by Goode (1981) 97 L.Q.R. 254). See also *Bank of New South Wales v Deri* (1963) 80 W.N. (N.S.W.) 1499; *Southland Savings Bank v Anderson* [1974] 1 N.Z.L.R. 118; *Commercial Bank of Australia Ltd v Younis* [1979] 1 N.S.W.L.R. 444; *Royal Bank of Canada v LVG Auctions Ltd* (1984) 2 D.L.R. (4th) 95 (affirmed (1985) 12 D.L.R. (4th) 768); *Davies (K.J.) (1976) Ltd v Bank of New South Wales* [1981] 1 N.Z.L.R. 262; *Australia and New Zealand Banking Group Ltd v Westpac Banking Corpn* (1988) 62 A.J.L.R. 292. Contrast *B & H Engineering v First National Bank of South Africa Ltd* 1995 (2) S.A. 279.

[52] *Barclays Bank Ltd v W.J. Simms Ltd* [1980] Q.B. 677 at 700.

[53] *Kleinwort, Sons & Co. v Dunlop Rubber Co.* (1907) 97 L.T. 263.

[54] *Jones (R.E.) Ltd v Waring & Gillow Ltd* [1926] A.C. 670 (s.29, Illustration 6). See also *T. Place & Sons v Turner* (1951) 101 L.J. 93. Contrast *Midland Bank plc v Brown Shipley & Co. Ltd* [1991] 1 Lloyd's Rep. 576, 584; *Dextra Bank & Trust Company Ltd v Bank of Jamaica* [2002] 1 All E.R. (Comm) 193 at [29] (Illustration 21).

[55] *Colonial Bank v Exchange Bank of Yarmouth, Nova Scotia* (1885) 11 App.Cas. 84; *Imperial Bank of Canada v Bank of Hamilton* [1903] A.C. 49 (Illustration 17); *Barclays Bank Ltd v W.J. Simms* [1980] Q.B. 677 at 694 (Illustration 19). Contrast the earlier view in *Chambers v Miller* (1862) 13 C.B., N.S. 125, 133; *Deutsche Bank v Beriro & Co. Ltd* (1895) 1 Com. Cas. 255, 259; *Barclay & Co. Ltd v Malcolm & Co.* (1925) 133 L.T. 512; *National Westminster Bank Ltd v Barclays Bank Ltd* [1975] Q.B. 654, 662.

and then delivers the cheque to C in settlement of an existing debt owed by him to C, B can recover the proceeds of the cheque from C as money paid under a mistake, even though his mistake is not shared by C.[56] It is also no longer material that, had the facts been as the payer supposed them to be, he would be under no legal liability to pay the money.[57] Thus a bank can recover money paid on a cheque even though, as between itself and the recipient, it is under no obligation to pay the cheque,[58] and (*semble*) even though, as between itself and its customer, the bank is not bound to pay the cheque because the customer's account is overdrawn.[59] However, if the payer intends that the recipient shall have the money at all events, whether the fact be true or false, or is deemed in law so to intend,[60] the money is irrecoverable.[61]

Recovery of money from the recipient is not necessarily precluded by the fact that he has given value for the instrument,[62] unless the money is paid to discharge a debt owed to the recipient[63] by the payer or by a third party by whom the payer is authorised to pay the debt.[64] The recipient cannot be said to have been unjustly enriched if he was entitled to receive

[56] *Jones (R.E.) Ltd v Waring & Gillow Ltd* [1926] A.C. 670 (s.29, Illustration 6).
[57] *Kleinwort Sons & Co. v Dunlop Rubber Co.* (1907) 97 L.T. 263, 264; *Kerrison v Glynn, Mills, Currie & Co.* (1911) 15 Com.Cas. 241; *Jones (R.E.) Ltd v Waring & Gillow Ltd* [1926] A.C. 670; *Larner v LCC* [1949] 2 K.B. 683; *Barclays Bank Ltd v W.J. Simms Ltd* [1980] Q.B. 677. *Rover International Ltd v Cannon Film Sales Ltd (No.3)* [1989] 1 W.L.R. 912, 933; *Kleinwort Benson Ltd v Lincoln City Council* [1999] 2 A.C. 349 at 407; *Nurdin and Peacock Ltd v D.B. Ramsden & Co. Ltd* [1999] 1 W.L.R. 1249, 1273; *Lloyds Bank plc v Independent Insurance Co. Ltd* [2000] Q.B. 110, 129; *Dextra Bank & Trust Co. Ltd v Bank of Jamaica* [2002] 1 All E.R. (Comm) 193 at [28]; *Customs and Excise Commissioners v National Westminster Bank plc* [2002] EWHC 2204, [2003] 1 All E.R. (Comm) 327 at [2]. Contrast the earlier view in *Kelly v Solari* (1841) 9 M. & W. 54, 58; *Aiken v Short* (1856) 1 H. & N. 210, 215; *Deutsche Bank v Beriro & Co. Ltd* (1895) 1 Com.Cas. 255, 259; *Re Bodega Co. Ltd* [1904] 1 Ch. 276, 286; *Steam Saw Mills Co. Ltd v Baring Bros & Co. Ltd* [1922] 1 Ch. 244, 250. See also *National Westminster Bank Ltd v Barclays Bank International Ltd* [1975] Q.B. 654 at 675.
[58] *Imperial Bank of Canada v Bank of Hamilton* [1903] A.C. 49; *National Westminster Bank Ltd v Barclays Bank International Ltd* [1975] Q.B. 654; *Barclays Bank Ltd v W.J. Simms Ltd* [1980] Q.B. 677.
[59] *Barclays Bank Ltd v W.J. Simms Ltd* [1980] Q.B. 677 at 700. See also *Commercial Bank of Australia Ltd v Younis* [1979] 1 N.S.W.R. 444.
[60] *Morgan v Ashcroft* [1938] 1 K.B. 49, 71, 77.
[61] *Kelly v Solari* (1841) 9 M. & W. 54 at 58, 59; *Beevor v Marler* (1898) 14 T.L.R. 289; *Barclays Bank Ltd v W.J. Simms Ltd* [1980] Q.B. 677 at 695.
[62] *Wilkinson v Johnson* (1824) 3 B. & C. 428 (Illustration 12); *Milnes v Duncan* (1827) 6 B. & C. 671 (Illustration 13); *Imperial Bank of Canada v Bank of Hamilton* [1903] A.C. 49 (Illustration 17); *Jones (R.E.) Ltd v Waring & Gillow Ltd* [1926] A.C. 670 (s.29, Illustration 6) (but see the observations on this case in *Midland Bank plc v Brown Shipley & Co. Ltd* [1991] 1 Lloyd's Rep. 576, 584, and Byles (27th ed.), 32–24); *National Westminster Bank Ltd v Barclays Bank International Ltd* [1975] Q.B. 654 (Illustration 18).
[63] Or a principal on whose behalf he is authorised to receive the payment.
[64] *Barclays Bank Ltd v W.J. Simms Ltd* [1980] Q.B. 677 at 695; *Lloyds Bank plc v Independent Insurance Co. Ltd* [2000] Q.B. 110, (Illustration 20). See *Aiken v Short* (1856) 1 H. & N. 210; *Kerrison v Glyn Mills, Currie & Co.* (1911) 15 Com.Cas. 1, at 14, 241, at 248; *Steam Saw Mills Co. Ltd v Baring Bros & Co. Ltd* [1922] 1 Ch. 244, 251, 254; *British American Continental Bank v British Bank for Foreign Trade* [1926] 1 K.B. 328, 336, 341, 344.

the money paid to him[65] and the payment discharged the debt. If a bank honours a cheque in the mistaken belief that there are sufficient funds or overdraft facilities to meet the cheque, it cannot recover the money as paid under a mistake, since it pays within its mandate from the customer and the payment discharges the debt owed by the customer to the recipient.[66] But payment made by a bank on a cheque in breach of its mandate from the customer may be recoverable: the bank is not authorised by the customer to pay the debt and, unless ratified by the customer, the payment will not discharge the customer's debt to the recipient.[67]

It would seem that, if a bank in good faith and in the ordinary course of business pays a cheque payable to order on which the indorsement of the payee or any subsequent indorsement is forged or unauthorised, the bank could recover the sum from the recipient notwithstanding that, under section 60 of the Act, the bank would be entitled to debit its customer's account.[68] The same would also apply where, due to the negligence of its customer in drawing a cheque, the amount of the cheque is fraudulently raised,[69] or the customer is estopped, as against the bank, from denying the authenticity of the drawer's signature,[70] even though in such a case the customer's account could be debited with the amount paid out by the bank in breach or in excess of its mandate.

**Denial of recovery: alleged grounds.** The older cases dealing with the 8–023 recovery of money paid under a mistake in respect of negotiable instruments exhibited a strong tendency to deny recovery,[71] and on various grounds. But the more modern cases favour recovery and reject most of the grounds put forward from time to time in the older cases to disallow recovery of money paid under a mistake.[72] Those grounds will now be examined.

The first ground was that, as between the competing equities of the payer and the recipient, the balance favoured the innocent recipient.[73]

---

[65] *Kleinwort Benson Ltd v Lincoln C.C.* [1999] 2 A.C. 349, 410 (Lord Hope).
[66] *Chambers v Miller* (1862) 13 C.B., N.S. 125; *Pollard v Bank of England* (1871) L.R. 6 Q.B. 623; *National Westminster Bank Ltd v Barclays Bank International Ltd* [1975] Q.B. 654 at 662; *Barclays Bank Ltd v W.J. Simms Ltd* [1980] Q.B. 677 at 700; *Lloyds Bank plc v Independent Insurance Co. Ltd* [2000] Q.B. 110.
[67] *Imperial Bank of Canada v Bank of Hamilton* [1903] A.C. 49; *National Westminster Bank Ltd v Barclays Bank International Ltd* [1975] Q.B. 654 at 700. *Cf. London Intercontinental Trust Ltd v Barclays Bank Ltd* [1980] 1 Lloyd's Rep. 241 (s.24, Illustration 13) (payment authorised though in breach of mandate).
[68] See below, para.8–044. But see s.80; below, para.14–024.
[69] *London Joint Stock Bank v MacMillan* [1918] A.C. 777; above, para.3–085.
[70] *Greenwood v Martins Bank Ltd* [1933] A.C. 51; above, para.3–080.
[71] See Illustrations 10, 11, 14, 15, 16.
[72] *Imperial Bank of Canada v Bank of Hamilton* [1903] A.C. 49; *National Westminster Bank Ltd v Barclays Bank International Ltd* [1975] Q.B. 654; *Barclays Bank Ltd v W.J. Simms, Son & Cooke (Southern) Ltd* [1980] Q.B. 677.
[73] *Price v Neal* (1762) 3 Burr. 1355, 1377.

This appears to be a restatement, in differing terms, of the broad principle enunciated by Ashurst J. in *Lickbarrow v Mason*[74] that "wherever one of two innocent persons must suffer by the acts of a third, he who has enabled such third person to occasion the loss must sustain it". But this dictum is much too wide: it has often been criticised[75] and seldom applied.

The second and more technical ground, where the person making the payment had been negligent in failing to discover the true facts, was that he should be precluded or estopped by his negligence from recovering the money.[76] But it has long been held, since *Kelly v Solari*[77] in 1841, that recovery is possible " . . . however careless the party paying may have been, in omitting to use due diligence to inquire into the fact".[78] And a plea of estoppel by negligence must fail in the absence of any duty of care owed by the payer to the recipient.[79]

8–024    The third ground, where the person paying the instrument paid as the result of a forged signature of another,[80] was that he impliedly represented to the recipient that the signature was genuine and might be estopped from asserting that the signature was forged.[81] However, in fact, he makes no such representation: he does not represent that the signature is genuine, but only that he believes the signature to be genuine.[82] It is

---

[74] (1787) 2 T.R. 63, 70, reversed *sub nom. Mason v Lickbarrow* (1790) 1 Hy.Bl. 357.

[75] *Farquharson Bros & Co. v King & Co.* [1902] A.C. 325, 335, 342; *London Joint Stock Bank v Macmillan* [1918] A.C. 777 at 836; *Jones (R.E.) Ltd v Waring & Gillow Ltd* [1926] A.C. 670, 693; *Mercantile Bank of India Ltd v Central Bank of India Ltd* [1938] A.C. 287, 298–299; *Wilson and Meeson v Pickering* [1946] K.B. 422, 425; *Central Newbury Car Auctions Ltd v Unity Finance Ltd* [1957] 1 Q.B. 371, 389, 396.

[76] *Smith v Mercer* (1815) 6 Taunt. 76, 81, 87; *Cocks v Masterman* (1829) 9 B. & C. 902, 908; *Mather v Maidstone* (1856) 18 C.B. 273, 294. Contrast *London & River Plate Bank Ltd v Bank of Liverpool Ltd* [1896] 1 Q.B. 7, 10–11.

[77] (1841) 9 M. & W. 54.

[78] (1841) 9 M. & W. 54 at 59. See also *Imperial Bank of Canada v Bank of Hamilton* [1903] A.C. 49; *Jones (R.E.) Ltd v Waring & Gillow Ltd* [1926] A.C. 670; *Weld-Blundell v Synott* [1940] 2 K.B. 107; *Turvey v Dentons (1923) Ltd* [1953] 1 Q.B. 218, 244; *National Westminster Bank Ltd v Barclays Bank International Ltd* [1975] Q.B. 654 at 675; *Simos v National Bank of Australasia Ltd* (1976) 10 A.C.T.L.R. 4; *Commercial Bank of Australia Ltd v Younis* [1979] 1 N.S.W.L.R. 444; *R.B.C. Dominion Securities Inc. v Dawson* (1994) 111 D.L.R. (4th) 230; *Scottish Equitable plc v Derby* [2001] 3 All E.R. 818 at [25]; *Dextra Bank & Trust Co. Ltd v Bank of Jamaica* [2002] 1 All E.R. 193 (Comm) at [207].

[79] *Jones (R.E.) Ltd v Waring & Gillow Ltd* [1926] A.C. 670 at 693; *Mercantile Credit Co. Ltd v Hamblin* [1965] 2 Q.B. 242; *National Westminster Bank Ltd v Barclays Bank International Ltd* [1975] Q.B. 654 at 662; *Moorgate Mercantile Co. Ltd v Twitchings* [1977] A.C. 890, 903.

[80] Contrast the position where the forged signature is that of the person paying: *Leach v Buchanan* (1802) 4 Esp. 226 (s.24, Illustration 10); *Mather v Maidstone* (1856) 18 C.B. 273 (Illustration 15). See also *Brook v Hook* (1871) L.R. 6 Ex. 69 (s.24, Illustration 14) (adoption).

[81] *London & River Plate Bank Ltd v Bank of Liverpool Ltd* [1986] 1 Q.B. 371 at 10–11.

[82] *Imperial Bank of India v Abeyesinghe* (1927) 29 N.L.R. (Ceylon) 257, 261; *National Westminster Bank Ltd v Barclays Bank International Ltd* [1975] Q.B. 654 at 674, 676.

also clear that the mere fact of payment is not a clear and unequivocal representation that the recipient is entitled to keep the money.[83]

The fourth ground, where the drawee or acceptor paid a bill or cheque on which the drawer's signature was forged, was that it was incumbent on him to know the signature of the drawer.[84] But although this may, in a sense, be true for example, as between banker and customer,[85] where it lies outside the mandate of the banker to pay against the forged signature of the drawer, it has no application as between payer and recipient.[86]

None of these grounds can, therefore, as a general rule now be relied on to preclude the recovery of money paid under a mistake. There is, however, one further ground to be found in the older cases which can probably still be relied on today. This is the so-called rule in *Cocks v Masterman*[87] where Bayley J., delivering the judgment of the Court of King's Bench, said[88]:

8–025

> "we are all of opinion that the holder of a bill is entitled to know, on the day when it becomes due, whether it is an honoured or dishonoured bill, and that, if he receive the money and is suffered to retain it during the whole of that day, the parties who paid it cannot recover it back. The holder, indeed, is not bound by law (if the bill be dishonoured by the acceptor) to take any steps against the other parties to the bill till the day after it is dishonoured. But he is entitled so to do, if he thinks fit and the parties who pay the bill ought not by their negligence[89] to deprive the holder of any right or privilege."

The argument is that the payment deprives the holder of the opportunity of giving notice of dishonour to prior parties liable to him on the bill,[90] so that his position will be irretrievably prejudiced by the loss of his right to claim against them. However, subsequent cases show that the rule is limited in effect. First, if the forgery is such as wholly to invalidate the instrument,[91] or the instrument is so altered as to render it void,[92] the rule

---

[83] *Jones (R.E.) Ltd v Waring & Gillow Ltd* [1926] A.C. 670.

[84] *Price v Neal* (1762) 3 Burr. 1355 at 1357; *Smith v Mercer* (1815) 6 Taunt. 76, 81. See also *Hart v Frontino and Bolivia South American Gold Mining Co. Ltd* (1870) L.R. 5 Exch. 111, 115.

[85] See above, para.3–059.

[86] *Imperial Bank of India v Abeyesinghe* (1927) 29 N.L.R. (Ceylon) 257; *National Westminster Bank Ltd v Barclays Bank International Ltd* [1975] Q.B. 654 at 666.

[87] (1829) 9 B. & C. 902 (Illustration 14). See also *Mather v Maidstone* (1856) 18 C.B. 273; *London & River Plate Bank Ltd v Bank of Liverpool Ltd* [1896] 1 Q.B. 7; *Morison v London County and Westminster Bank* [1914] 3 K.B. 356, 373, 378, 382–383.

[88] At 908–909.

[89] Contrast *London & River Plate Bank Ltd v Bank of Liverpool Ltd* [1896] 1 Q.B. 7 at 10–11, where negligence was said to be immaterial.

[90] See above, para.6–096.

[91] As where the only signature on a cheque is a forged signature of the drawer.

[92] See below, para.8–078 (s.64) and *Leeds and County Bank Ltd v Walker* (1883) 11 Q.B.D. 84.

will not apply, as it is not a negotiable instrument.[93] Secondly, the rule will have no application if there are no parties to whom notice of dishonour by non-payment must be given.[94] Thirdly, it may be argued that section 50(1) of the Act provides that delay in giving notice of dishonour is excused where the delay is caused by circumstances beyond the control of the party giving notice, and not imputable to his default, misconduct or negligence, and that this provision extends to the case where the holder of an instrument receives payment of it on presentation in ignorance of the fact that he is not entitled to the money. If this argument were accepted,[95] it is difficult to conceive of situations where the rule in *Cocks v Masterman* would in practice apply, since the payment would not deprive the holder of the opportunity of giving notice of dishonour, which could be given with reasonable diligence[96] when he is informed of the facts giving rise to the mistake and of the claim. However, the rule might be supported on the larger ground that the payment deprives the holder of his right immediately to have recourse to the drawer and any indorser on dishonour by non-payment.[97] It has also been argued[98] that, where a bank mistakenly pays a countermanded cheque,[99] the payment discharges the cheque and so deprives the payee of his right to obtain summary judgment on the cheque against the drawer. But it is questionable whether such a payment does in fact discharge the cheque[1] and in any event whether this technical detriment is sufficient to outweigh the injustice of denying the bank's claim to recover the money.[2]

8–026    **Estoppel.**[3] In certain circumstances the person making the payment may be estopped from alleging that he paid under a mistake. To establish such an estoppel, the recipient must first show a clear and unequivocal[4] representation of fact for which the person making the payment is

---

[93] *Imperial Bank of Canada v Bank of Hamilton* [1903] A.C. 49; *National Westminster Bank Ltd v Barclays Bank International Ltd* [1975] Q.B. 654.

[94] *Imperial Bank of Canada v Bank of Hamilton* [1903] A.C. 49 at 58; *Barclays Bank Ltd v W. J. Simms Ltd* [1980] Q.B. 677 at 702. Where a bank pays a cheque in disregard of the countermand of payment by the drawer, notice of dishonour to the drawer is dispensed with by s.50(2)(c) of the Act: above, para.6–135.

[95] Contrast *Barclays Bank Ltd v W. J. Simms Ltd* [1980] Q.B. 677 at 702.

[96] See s.50(1).

[97] s.47(2). See *Cocks v Masterman* (1829) 9 B. & C. 902, 908–909. But this might require that a party liable to make payment on the bill has, in the meantime, become insolvent.

[98] Goode (1981) 97 L.Q.R. 254, 259.

[99] *Barclays Bank Ltd v W.J. Simms Ltd* [1980] Q.B. 677.

[1] See s.63(3), below, para.8–073. Contrast *B. & H. Engineering v National Bank of SA Ltd* 1995 (2) SA 279, 288.

[2] See Goff and Jones, *Law of Restitution* (6th ed.), 4–038.

[3] Goff and Jones *Law of Restitution* (6th ed.), 40–010.

[4] *Weld-Blundell v Synott* [1940] 2 K.B. 107, 114.

responsible.[5] Secondly, he must show that the representation led him to believe that he was entitled to the money.[6] Thirdly, he must show that he, bona fide and without notice of the mistake,[7] has in reliance on the payment altered his position to his detriment or at least in a way which would make it inequitable to require him to repay the money.[8]

With respect to the first requirement, the mere fact of payment by itself does not amount to such a representation.[9] But in cases of overpayment due to accounting errors, as where credits are made in error by a bank to its customer's account, it will be relatively easy to spell out such a representation where, as between payer and recipient, the person making the payment is under a duty to inform the recipient of the true state of account[10] or where the recipient is entitled to assume that the account kept by the person paying is accurate.[11] A sufficient representation may also arise where the drawer of a banker's draft confirms that the draft is genuine and has been issued in the ordinary course of business,[12] or where the drawee of a bill or the purported maker of a note acknowledges to the holder that his signature is genuine, whereas it is in fact forged,[13] or where he fails on inspection to detect the forgery of his own signature and pays the instrument.[14]

With respect to the third requirement, recovery is not in general precluded by the fact that the recipient has spent the money beyond recall.[15] But it may be inequitable to compel him to refund it if he has made payments or incurred expenditure which he would not have made or

---

[5] *Jones (R.E.) Ltd v Waring & Gillow Ltd* [1926] A.C. 670; *Deutsche Bank v Beriro & Co.* (1895) 1 Com.Cas. 123, 255; *United Overseas Bank v Jiwani* [1976] 1 W.L.R. 964, 968; *Lipkin Gorman v Karpnale Ltd* [1991] 2 A.C. 548, 579.

[6] *Kendal v Wood* (1871) L.R. 6 Ex. 243; *Holt v Markham* [1923] 1 K.B. 504, 512; *Transvaal & Delagoa Bay Investment Co. v Atkinson* [1944] 1 All E.R. 579, 585; *United Overseas Bank v Jiwani* [1976] 1 W.L.R. 946 at 968; *Avon C.C. v Howlett* [1983] 1 W.L.R. 605, 620.

[7] *United Overseas Bank v Jiwani* [1976] 1 W.L.R. 964.

[8] *Skyring v Greenwood* (1825) 4 B. & C. 281, 289; *Deutsche Bank v Beriro & Co.* (1895) 1 Com. Cas. 123; *Kleinwort, Sons & Co. v Dunlop Rubber Co.* (1907) 97 L.T. 263, 264; *Holt v Markham* [1923] 1 K.B. 504; *Lloyds Bank Ltd v Brooks* (1950) 6 L.D.B. 161; *United Overseas Bank v Jiwani* [1976] 1 W.L.R. 946; *Avon C.C. v Howlett* [1983] 1 W.L.R. 605; *Davies (K.J.) (1976) Ltd v Bank of New South Wales* [1981] 1 N.Z.L.R. 262. See also *Gillett v Holt* [2001] Ch. 210.

[9] *Jones (R.E.) Ltd v Waring & Gillow Ltd* [1926] A.C. 670.

[10] *Weld-Blundell v Synott* [1940] 2 K.B. 107 at 115; *United Overseas Bank v Jiwani* [1976] 1 W.L.R. 946 at 968.

[11] *Skyring v Greenwood* (1825) 4 B. & C. 281; *Holt v Markham* [1923] 1 K.B. 504 at 512, 514; *Lloyds Bank Ltd v Brooks* (1950) 6 Legal Decisions affecting Bankers 161; *Avon C.C. v Howlett* [1983] 1 W.L.R. 605.

[12] *Midland Bank plc v Brown Shipley & Co. Ltd* [1991] 1 Lloyd's Rep. 576, 585, 586.

[13] *Leach v Buchanan* (1802) 4 Esp. 226 (s.24, Illustration 10); *Brook v Hook* (1871) L.R. 6 Ex. 89 (s.24, Illustration 14); but these are probably cases of adoption of the forged signature by the drawee. See also *Price v Neal* (1762) 3 Burr. 1355 (Illustration 10).

[14] *Mather v Maidstone* (1856) 18 C.B. 273 (Illustration 15). *Sed quaere?*

[15] *Standish v Ross* (1849) 3 Exch. 527; *Durrant v Ecclesiastical Commissioners* (1880) 6 Q.B.D. 234; *Baylis v Bishop of London* [1913] 1 Ch. 127; *Larner v LCC* [1949] 2 K.B. 683, 688–689.

incurred but for the payment, or if he has altered his mode of living in reliance on the payment.[16]

8–027   Estoppel is a rule of evidence. A successful plea of estoppel should therefore in principle prevent the person making the payment from recovering any part of the amount paid and not merely *pro tanto* to the extent that it would be inequitable to require the recipient to repay.[17] However, as an exception to the rule, it has been held that, if the detriment incurred by the recipient is significantly less in monetary terms than the amount mistakenly paid, it may be inequitable and unconscionable to allow the recipient to keep the whole of the amount. He will then be entitled to retain only the lesser sum. So, in one case,[18] the Court of Appeal upheld the trial judge's decision not to allow the recipient to retain the whole of a mistaken overpayment of £17,500 when the expense incurred by him in reliance on the payment was only £9,600, and, in another case[19] the same court held that he could not retain the whole of the sum of US $76,700 mistakenly paid when the detrimental reliance was no more than £13,180. It may be that the defence of estoppel is moving away from being an 'all or nothing' defence and is moving closer to the more flexible defence of change of position.[20] Indeed, in *Philip Collins Ltd v Davis*[21] Jonathan Parker J. even suggested (*obiter*) that "the law has now developed to the point where a defence of estoppel by representation is no longer apt in restitutionary claims where the more flexible defence of change of position is in principle available".

8–028   **Principal and agent.** An agent who has received on his principal's behalf money paid under a mistake may be liable to refund it.[22] But if an agent acting as such[23] has, before learning of the claim,[24] paid over the money to his principal or to another for his principal, then no claim in

---

[16] See the cases cited in n.11, above, and in particular *Avon C.C. v Howlett* [1983] 1 W.L.R. 605.

[17] *Avon C.C. v Howlett* [1983] 1 W.L.R. 605; *Lipkin Gorman v Karpnale Ltd* [1991] 2 A.C. 548, 579.

[18] *Scottish Equitable plc v Derby* [2000] 3 All E.R. 793, affirmed [2001] EWCA Civ 369, [2001] 3 All E.R. 818.

[19] *National Westminster Bank plc v Somer International (UK) Ltd* [2001] EWCA Civ 970, [2002] Q.B. 1286.

[20] See below, para.8–029. *Cf.* Fung and Ho (2001) 117 L.Q.R. 14.

[21] [2000] 3 All E.R. 808, 826. See also *RBC Dominion Securities Inc. v Dawson* (1994) 111 D.L.R. (4th) 236. *Cf. National Westminster Bank plc v Somer International (UK) Ltd* [2001] EWCA Civ 369 at [28] [64] [65].

[22] *Buller v Harrison* (1777) 2 Cowp. 565; *Kleinwort, Sons & Co. v Dunlop Rubber Co.* (1907) 97 L.T. 263, 264; *Pollard v Bank of England* (1871) L.R. 6 Q.B. 623, 630; *Continental Caoutchouc & Gutta Percha Co. v Kleinwort, Sons & Co.* (1904) 90 L.T. 474, 476; *National Westminster Bank Ltd v Barclays Bank Ltd* [1975] Q.B. 654 at 677.

[23] *Gurney v Womersley* (1854) 4 E. & B. 133; *Royal Exchange Assoc. v Moore* (1843) 8 L.T. 242.

[24] *Continental Caoutchouc & Gutta Percha Co. v Kleinwort, Sons & Co.* (1904) 90 L.T. 474 at 477.

restitution for money had and received will lie against the agent but only against the principal.[25] Thus no such claim can be made for money paid under a mistake against a banker who has collected a cheque for his customer and paid over the proceeds to the customer.[26] It is not enough that the banker has credited the customer with the amount received in his books, whether the customer's account is currently in credit or in over-draft.[27] But if he has, in reliance on the payment, allowed the customer new credit,[28] or (*semble*) has allowed the customer to draw against the cheque in reliance on it being honoured,[29] this will be considered as the equivalent of payment over to the customer. Where, however, no such payment or its equivalent has been made, a claim for money paid under a mistake can be made both against the banker who received the money and against his customer.[30] The banker cannot assert any lien over or set-off against the money received.[31]

**Change of position.**[32] In *Lipkin Gorman v Karpnale Ltd*[33] the House of   **8–029** Lords recognised "change of position" as a general defence to a restitutionary claim. Lord Goff stated[34] that this defence is "available to a person whose position has so changed that it would be inequitable in all the circumstances to require him to make restitution, or alternatively to make

---

[25] *Buller v Harrison* (1777) 2 Cowp. 565 at 568; *Holland v Russell* (1863) 4 B. & S. 14; *Pollard v Bank of England* (1871) L.R. 6 Q.B. 623, 631; *Kleinwort, Sons & Co. v Dunlop Rubber Co.* (1907) 97 L.T. 263 at 264; *Kerrison v Glyn, Mills, Currie & Co.* (1911) 81 L.J.K.B. 465; *Transvaal & Delagoa Bay Investment Co. Ltd v Atkinson* [1944] 1 All E.R. 579; *Thomas v Houston Corbett & Co.* [1969] N.Z.L.R. 151; *National Westminster Bank Ltd v Barclays Bank Ltd* [1975] Q.B. 654 at 671, 677; *Australia and New Zealand Banking Group Ltd v Westpac Banking Corp.* (1987–1988) 164 C.L.R. 663; *Agip (Africa) Ltd v Jackson* [1990] Ch. 265, 287 (affirmed [1991] Ch. 547) (Illustration 20); *Lipkin Gorman v Karpnale Ltd* [1991] 2 A.C. 548, 578; *Bank Tejarat v Hong Kong and Shanghai Banking Corp. (CI) Ltd* [1995] 1 Lloyd's Rep. 239, 246. See also *Gowers v Lloyds and National Provincial Foreign Bank Ltd* [1938] 1 All E.R. 766 (where the money was paid over to a fraudulent person posing as the customer-principal).

[26] But a claim may lie against him in conversion, subject to the defence available under s.4 of the Cheques Act 1957 (see below, para.17–028).

[27] *Buller v Harrison* (1777) 2 Cowp. 565; *Cox v Prentice* (1815) 3 M. & S. 344; *Kleinwort, Sons & Co. v Dunlop Rubber Co.* (1907) 97 L.T. 263; *Bavins Jr & Sims v London & South Western Bank Ltd* [1900] 1 Q.B. 270; *Scottish Metropolitan Assurance Co. Ltd v P. Samuel & Co. Ltd* [1923] 1 K.B. 348; *National Westminster Bank Ltd v Barclays Bank International Ltd* [1975] Q.B. 654.

[28] *Buller v Harrison* (1777) 2 Cowp. 565 at 568; *Kleinwort, Sons & Co. v Dunlop Rubber Co.* (1907) 97 L.T. 263 at 265, 266; *Scottish Metropolitan Assurance Co. Ltd v P. Samuel & Co. Ltd* [1923] 1 K.B. 348 at 355, 356.

[29] *National Westminster Bank Ltd v Barclays Bank International Ltd* [1975] Q.B. 654 at 677. But see *Imperial Bank of Canada v Bank of Hamilton* [1903] A.C. 49 (Illustration 17); *Admiralty Commissioners v National Provincial and Union Bank of England Ltd* (1922) 127 L.T. 452.

[30] *National Westminster Bank Ltd v Barclays Bank International Ltd* [1975] Q.B. 654; *Standard Bank of South Africa Ltd v ABSA Bank Ltd* 1995 (2) S.A. 740.

[31] *Kerrison v Glyn, Mills, Currie & Co.* (1907) 97 L.T. 263.

[32] See Goff and Jones, *Law of Restitution* (6th ed.), 40–001.

[33] [1991] 2 A.C. 548, 558, 567, 568, 577 (s.75, Illustration 13).

[34] At 580.

restitution in full". The defence is wider than that of estoppel in that it does not depend on any representation by the person making the payment,[35] but it is also narrower in that it may only provide a defence *pro tanto* to the claim.[36] It may, however, be the case that the two further defences referred to above, namely the rule in *Cocks v Masterman*[37] and the payment over by an agent to his principal of money received by the agent on behalf of his principal,[38] will be regarded in future as particular examples of this defence.[39] The justification for the defence is that "where an innocent defendant's position is so changed that he will suffer an injustice if called upon to repay or to repay in full, the injustice of requiring him so to repay outweighs the injustice of denying the plaintiff restitution".[40] Nevertheless the parameters of the defence still require to be elucidated on a "case by case basis".[41]

In the *Lipkin Gorman* case Lord Goff gave the following example of the defence[42]:

> "If the plaintiff pays money to the defendant under a mistake of fact, and the defendant then, acting in good faith, pays the money or part of it to a charity, it is unjust to require the defendant to make restitution to the extent that he has so changed his position".

On the other hand, he stressed that the mere fact that the recipient has spent the money, in whole or in part, does not render it inequitable that he should be called upon to repay "because the expenditure might in any event have been incurred by him in the ordinary course of things".[43] It would therefore appear that the recipient must, as a result of the receipt,[44] have incurred expenditure which he would not otherwise have incurred or lost a financial benefit which he would otherwise have gained and in such a way as to render it unjust that he should now be compelled to refund the payment.[45] The courts will approach the issue of the extent to

---

[35] [1991] 2 A.C. 548 at 579.

[36] [1991] 2 A.C. 548. See above, para.8–027, n.20.

[37] See above, para.8–025.

[38] See above, para.8–028.

[39] *Lipkin Gorman v Karpnale Ltd* [1991] 2 A.C. 548 at 578, 579. But payment over by an agent to his principal may now be more appropriately treated as a question of identifying the proper defendant: *Portman Building Society v Hamlyn Taylor Neck* [1998] 4 All E.R. 202, 207; *Niru Battery Manufacturing Co. v Milestone Trading Ltd* [2002] EWHC (Comm) 1425, affirmed [2003] EWCA Civ 1446, [2004] 1 Lloyd's Rep. 344.

[40] [1991] 2 A.C. 548 at 579.

[41] [1991] 2 A.C. 548 at 580.

[42] [1991] 2 A.C. 548 at 579.

[43] [1991] 2 A.C. 548 at 580.

[44] *Credit Suisse (Monaco) SA v Attar* [2004] EWHC 374 (Comm). In *Dextra Bank & Trust Co. Ltd v Bank of Jamaica* [2002] 1 All E.R. (Comm) 193 at [35–39] (Illustration 22) Lord Bingham and Lord Goff stated (obiter) that anticipatory reliance may amount to an effective change of position. See also *Commerzbank AG v Price-Jones* [2003] EWCA Civ 1663.

[45] *Midland Bank plc v Brown Shipley & Co. Ltd* [1991] 1 Lloyd's Rep. 576, 584; *Scottish Equitable plc v Derby* [2001] EWCA Civ 369, [2001] 3 All E.R. 618 at [301–31].

which the recipient has, overall, been prejudiced with a reasonably broad brush, and it is not necessary for him to prove that items of expenditure are precisely matched against particular receipts.[46] However, if the recipient has used the money to pay off an existing debt, it will not be inequitable to require him to repay as he will have been enriched by the discharge of the debt.[47] Moreover, where, for example, money has been expended by the recipient on goods or services, the benefit of which he still retains, he might still be held to have been unjustly enriched to that extent as a result of the payment.[48]

**Bad faith and negligence.** The defence of change of position is not **8–030** open to a recipient who has changed his position in bad faith, as where he has paid away the money with knowledge of the facts entitling the claimant to restitution[49] even though he was not guilty of dishonesty.[50] It is also commonly accepted that such defences would not be available to a wrongdoer.[51] It is less clear whether negligence on the part of the recipient would have any, and, if so, what, effect.[52] It has been held that recovery will not be precluded where the payment is primarily caused by the fault of, or concealment by, the recipient[53] or where, as in *National Westminster Bank Ltd v Barclays Bank International Ltd*,[54] the payee of a cheque fails to impart to the drawee bank knowledge of unusual circumstances relating to the cheque which only he has, so as to put the bank on its guard. On the other hand, since negligence on the part of the claimant is immaterial to his right of recovery,[55] it would be curious if carelessness on the part of the recipient should deprive him of the defence.[56] In *Dextra*

---

[46] *Avon C.C. v Howlett* [1981] I.R.L.R. 447, 449; [1983] 1 W.L.R. 605, 622; *Philip Collins Ltd v Davis* [2000] 3 All E.R. 808. See also *Scottish Equitable plc v Derby* [2001] EWCA Civ 369, [2001] 3 All E.R. 618 at [33]. Contrast *Rural Municipality of Storthoaks v Mobile Oil Canada Ltd* [1976] 2 S.C.R. 147.

[47] *Scottish Equitable plc v Derby* [2000] 3 All E.R. 793, affirmed [2001] EWCA Civ 369, [2001] 3 All E.R. 618 (mortgage debt reduced); *RBC Dominion Securities Inc. v Dawson* (1994) 111 D.L.R. (4th) 236 (payment of credit card debt); *National Bank of Egypt International Ltd v Oman Housing Bank SAOC* [2002] EWHC 1760 (Comm), [2003] 1 All E.R. (Comm) 246.

[48] *Reid v Rigby & Co.* [1894] Q.B. 40 (s.26, Illustration 7).

[49] *Lipkin Gorman v Karpnale Ltd* [1991] 2 A.C. 548, 580; *Niru Battery Manufacturing Co. v Milestone Trading Ltd* [2003] EWCA Civ 1446, [2004] 1 Lloyd's Rep. 344; *Papamichael v National Westminster Bank plc* [2003] EWJC 164 (Comm), [2003] 1 Lloyd's Rep. 341. See also above, para.8–026 (estoppel) and para.8–028 (principal and agent).

[50] *Niru Battery Manufacturing Co. v Milestone Trading Ltd* [2001] EWHC 1425 at [152] [191] [193].

[51] *Lipkin Gorman v Karpnale Ltd* [1991] 2 A.C. 548 at 580. See also *Barros Mattos Junior v MacDaniels Ltd* [2005] 1 W.L.R. 247 (illegality).

[52] See *Chitty on Contracts* (29th ed.), Vol.I, § 29–184.

[53] *George Whitechurch Ltd v Cavanagh* [1902] A.C. 117, 145; *Larner v LCC* [1949] 2 K.B. 683, 689; *Secretary of State for Employment v Wellworthy Ltd (No.2)* [1976] I.C.R. 13, 25.

[54] [1975] Q.B. 654 (Illustration 18). Contrast *Midland Bank plc v Brown Shipley & Co. Ltd* [1991] 1 Lloyd's Rep. 576, 585–587.

[55] See above, para.8–023.

[56] Cf. *South Tyneside Metropolitan BC v Svenska International plc* [1995] 1 All E.R. 545, 569.

*Bank & Trust Co. Ltd v Bank of Jamaica*[57] the Privy Council rejected the adoption of any criterion of the relative faults of the claimant and the recipient in considering the change of position defence. This decision should, it is submitted, also be treated as authority for the proposition that mere negligence on the part of the recipient is insufficient to deprive him of the defence.[58]

8–031      **Inter-bank transfers.** In *Agip (Africa) Ltd v Jackson*,[59] the claimants maintained a US dollar account with a bank in Tunis. One of their employees fraudulently altered a payment order addressed to the bank and thereby caused the bank to give instructions, by telex, to the L Bank in London to credit the account of a customer of the L Bank with the amount of the order. At the same time the Tunis bank gave instructions, by telex, to its correspondent bank in New York to reimburse the L Bank with a similar amount. The moneys so transferred came into the hands of the defendants. Millett J. held that no action would lie at the suit of the claimants at common law to recover the money from the defendants as money had and received, because (*inter alia*):

> "The money cannot be followed by treating it as the proceeds of a cheque presented by the collecting bank in exchange for payment by the paying bank. The money was transmitted by telegraphic transfer. There was no cheque or any equivalent. The payment order was not a cheque or its equivalent. It remained throughout in the possession of the [Tunis bank]. No copy was sent to [the L Bank or its customer] or presented to the [Tunis bank] in exchange for the money. . . . Nothing passed between Tunisia and London but a stream of electrons."[60]

Further, he held that no such action would lie because (i) the L Bank complied with the instruction by paying its customer with its own money, and (ii) the money with which the L Bank was reimbursed could not be identified, without recourse to equity,[61] as being that of the Tunis bank as it must have become mixed with other money when passed through the New York clearing system. Since money itself does not travel, and an inter-bank transfer of funds is effected by mutual credits and debits in the

---

[57] [2002] 1 All E.R. (Comm) 193 at [40–46] (Illustration 22).

[58] *Niru Battery Manufacturing Co. v Milestone Trading Ltd* [2001] EWHC 1425 (Comm) at [126], affirmed [2003] EWCA Civ 1446, [2004] 1 Lloyd's Rep. 344; *Papamichael v National Westminster Bank plc* [2003] EWHC 164 (Comm), [2003] 1 Lloyd's Rep. 341 at [209]. Contrast *Commerzbank AG v Price-Jones* [2003] EWCA Civ 1663 at [82].

[59] [1990] Ch. 265 (affirmed [1991] Ch. 547) (Illustration 21).

[60] At 286. See also *Bank Tejarat v Hong Kong and Shanghai Banking Corp. (CI) Ltd* [1995] 1 Lloyd's Rep. 239, 245; *El Ajou v Dollar Land Holdings plc* [1993] 3 All E.R. 717, 733; *Bank of America v Arnell* [1999] Lloyd's Rep. Bank. 399.

[61] See below.

books of the paying and receiving banks, this decision may in certain circumstances impose severe restrictions on the ability to obtain recovery of money paid under a mistake by the common law action for money had and received.

**Proprietary claims.** Money paid under a mistake may, in certain cir-    8–032
cumstances, be recovered from the recipient on the ground that the person making the payment has retained a proprietary interest in the money. A proprietary claim differs from a person claim for money had and received in that it is designed to vindicate the property rights of the claimant rather than to reverse the unjust enrichment of the defendant.[62] It is also, in some respects, superior to such a claim in that it may lie even against an indirect recipient of the money. A claimant may follow the money from one recipient to another and (subject to certain limitations) trace the money, or any asset required with the money, and then claim its recovery. Further, if the defendant is insolvent, it will enable the claimant to assert a proprietary interest in the money in priority to the claims of the defendant's general creditors.

At common law a claimant will be held to have retained a legal proprietary interest in money paid under a mistake where his intention to make the payment was vitiated, for example by theft[63] or by a fundamental mistake such as payment to the wrong person[64] or (*semble*) if the transaction was voidable for fraud and has been avoided.[65] The claimant will be permitted to follow his property and to trace his proprietary interest in the money, or in the product of or substitute for the money, provided that these are still identifiable and have not been mixed with other money.[66] Money can therefore be followed at common law into and out of a bank account, but this is so only if it has not been admixed with other money in the account.[67] In equity, however, whether the claim is personal or proprietary,[68] the money can be traced and identified even in

---

[62] *Foskett v McKeown* [2001] 1 A.C. 102, 108, 115, 127. Contrast Birks [1997] N.Z.L. Rev. 623; Burrows (2001) 117 L.Q.R. 412.

[63] *Lipkin Gorman v Karpnale Ltd* [1991] A.C. 548, 572; *Trustee of the Property of F.C. Jones & Sons v Jones* [1997] Ch. 159.

[64] *Citibank NA v Brown Shipley & Co. Ltd* [1991] 2 All E.R. 690, 699. *Cf. Barclays Bank Ltd v W.J. Simms, Son & Cooke (Southern) Ltd* [1980] Q.B. 677, 689.

[65] See below, n.74.

[66] *Taylor v Plumer* (1815) 3 M. & S. 562; *Banque Belge pour l'Etranger v Hambrouck* [1921] 1 K.B. 321; *Re Diplock* [1948] Ch. 465, 518; *Re J Leslie Engineers Co. Ltd* [1976] 1 W.L.R. 292, 297; *Lipkin Gorman v Karpnale Ltd* [1991] A.C. 548 at 573, 574; *Trustees of the Property of F.C. Jones & Sons v Jones* [1997] Ch. 159. But the difference between the tracing rules of common law and equity has been challenged: *Trustees of the Property of F.C. Jones & Sons v Jones* [1997] Ch. 159 at 169–170; *Foskett v McKeown* [2001] 1 A.C. 102 at 109; *Bracken Partners Ltd v Gutteridge* [2003] EWHC 1034, [2003] 2 B.C.L.C. 83 at [131] (not considered on appeal [2004] 1 B.C.L.C. 377).

[67] *Agip (Africa) Ltd v Jackson* [1990] Ch. 265, 285 (affirmed [1991] Ch. 547).

[68] *Boscawen v Bajwa* [1996] 1 W.L.R. 328, 334.

a mixed fund. Consequently the claim will not be defeated by the passage of the money through different bank accounts. In *Agip (Africa) Ltd v Jackson*,[69] notwithstanding that the claimants' claim to recover the money from the defendants as money had and received was held to have failed, the defendants were accountable for it as constructive trustees,[70] since the claimants' equitable interest in the money could be followed into their hands through the various accounts through which it had passed. However, there must be some fiduciary relationship which permits the assistance of equity to be invoked.[71] Ordinarily this will require that there be initially in existence a fiduciary relationship between the claimant and the recipient or a third party, so that the money is already the subject of fiduciary obligations when it comes into the hands of the recipient. This requirement will be satisfied, for example, where a payment made by or on behalf of an employer or principal is fraudulently misapplied in breach of his fiduciary duty by an employee or agent,[72] or where the beneficiaries of a trust seek to recover from the recipient money paid to him under a mistake by the trustees.[73] No breach of fiduciary duty need nevertheless be shown where the money paid has been obtained by fraud on the part of the recipient. In such a case equity imposes a constructive trust on the fraudulent recipient: the money is recoverable and traceable in equity.[74] In *Chase Manhattan Bank NA v Israel-British Bank (London) Ltd*,[75] however, Goulding J. held that the equitable remedy was also available where "the payment into the wrong hands itself [gives] rise to a fiduciary relationship".[76] In that case money was paid by mistake by the claimant bank to the defendant bank, which subsequently became insolvent and went into liquidation. Goulding J. granted a declaration that the defendant bank became trustee for the claimant bank of the money mistakenly

[69] See [1990] Ch. 265 (affirmed [1991] Ch. 547) (Illustration 21).
[70] For "knowing assistance", but not for "knowing receipt": see below, para.17–060 (Cheques Act, s.4).
[71] *Re Diplock* [1948] Ch. 465 (this point did not arise in the House of Lords [1951] A.C. 251); *Agip (Africa) Ltd v Jackson* [1991] Ch. 547, 566; *Boscawen v Bajwa* [1996] 1 W.L.R. 328 at 335; *Westdeutsche Landesbank Girozentrale v Islington LBC* [1996] A.C. 669. But see *Foskett v McKeown* [2001] 1 A.C. 102; Millett (1998) 114 L.Q.R. 399, 409.
[72] *Agip (Africa) Ltd v Jackson* [1990] Ch. 265.
[73] *Re Diplock* [1951] A.C. 251.
[74] *Westdeutsche Landesbank Girozentrale v Islington LBC* [1996] A.C. 669 at 716; *Bankers Trust Co. v Shapira* [1980] 1 W.L.R. 1274, 1282; *Niru Battery Manufacturing Co. v Milestone Trading Ltd* [2002] EWHC 1425 (Comm) at [54–56], affirmed [2003] EWCA Civ 1466, [2004] 1 Lloyd's Rep. 344. But see *Lonrho plc v Fayed (No.2)* [1992] 1 W.L.R. 1, 11–12; *El Ajou v Dollar Land Holdings plc (No.1)* [1993] 3 All E.R. 717, 734; *Halifax Building Society v Thomas* [1996] Ch. 217, 227; *Box v Barclays Bank plc* [1998] Lloyd's Rep. Bank. 185; *Twinsectra Ltd v Yardley* [1999] Lloyd's Rep. Bank. 438, 461 (reversed in part [2002] 2 A.C. 164); *Papamichael v National Westminster Bank plc* [2003] EWHC 164 (Comm), [2003] 1 Lloyd's Rep. 341 at [231–245 (transaction voidable for fraud must be rescinded to vest the equitable title in the claimant).
[75] [1981] Ch. 105.
[76] At 119.

paid, and directed an inquiry as to what had become of that sum and as to what assets of the defendant represented it. He said that "a person who pays money to another under a factual mistake retains an equitable property in it and the conscience of that other is subjected to a fiduciary duty to respect his proprietary right".[77] But in *Westdeutsche Landesbank Girozentrale v Islington LBC*[78] (where a claim was made to recover money paid under a contract which was subsequently held void as being *ultra vires*) Lord Browne-Wilkinson[79] stated that he could not agree with this reasoning, and the case must now be taken to have been overruled on this point.[80] Even equity cannot trace property if its identity has been lost, *e.g.* where money has been spent, and no specific asset can be identified which derives from it.[81] Further, equitable tracing does not extend to tracing through an overdrawn bank account, whether overdrawn at the time the money was paid into the account or subsequently.[82]

**Bona fide purchase defence.** Where money is the subject of a proprie-  8–033
tary claim, the defence of bona fide purchase for value is available but not the defence of change of position.[83] The bona fide purchase for value of the money by the recipient deprives the claimant of his title to the money on which his proprietary claim depends. The defence is not available where the claim is a personal one for unjust enrichment.[84]

**Interest.** Simple interest only is recoverable in an action for money had  8–034
and received under the Supreme Court Act 1981.[85] But compound interest may be recovered where the claim is equitable and a person in a fiduciary

---

[77] [1981] Ch. 105 at 119.

[78] [1996] A.C. 669.

[79] With whom all other members of the House of Lords agreed, except for Lord Goff who left the matter open.

[80] But Lord Browne-Wilkinson stated: "although I do not accept the reasoning of Goulding J., *Chase Manhatten* may well have been rightly decided. The defendant bank knew of the mistake made by the paying bank within two days of the receipt of the money... Although the mere receipt of the moneys, in ignorance of the mistake, gives rise to no trust, the retention of the moneys after the recipient bank learned of the mistake may well have given rise to a constructive trust ... " See also the explanation of this case by Millett J. in *Agip (Africa) Ltd v Jackson* [1990] Ch. 265, 290 (affirmed [1991] Ch. 547) and (1998) 114 L.Q.R. 399, 412–413; *Friends' Provident Life Office v Hillier Parker May and Rowden* [1997] Q.B. 85, 106; *Bank of America v Arnell* [1999] Lloyd's Rep. Bank 399; *Papamichael v National Westminster Bank plc* [2003] EWHC 164 (Comm), [2003] 1 Lloyd's Rep. 341 at [371–373].

[81] *Re Diplock* [1948] Ch. 465, 521, 548, *Re Goldcorp Exchange Ltd* [1995] 1 A.C. 74, 105.

[82] *Bishopsgate Investment Management Ltd v Homan* [1995] Ch. 211.

[83] *Foskett v McKeown* [2001] 1 A.C. 102, 129; *Papamichael v National Westminster Bank plc* [2003] EWHC 164 (Comm), [2003] 1 Lloyd's Rep. 341 at [253].

[84] *Papamichael v National Westminster Bank plc* [2003] EWHC 164 (Comm) at [253]. But see *Dextra Bank & Trust Co. Ltd v Bank of Jamaica* [2002] 1 All E.R. (Comm) 193 at [47] (Illustration 22) where it is said that "the defence of bona fide purchaser is only available to a third party, which includes an indirect recipient, *i.e.* a person who received the benefit from somebody other than the plaintiff or his authorised agent".

[85] *Westdeutsche Landesbank Girozentrale v Islington LBC* [1996] A.C. 669.

position has, or ought to have, received compound interest or been relieved from paying compound interest if he has used the money in his trade or business.[86]

ILLUSTRATIONS

**8–035**   1. A bill is drawn by W upon H, B and L payable to the order of W six months after date, and is accepted by them. The bill is delivered by W to H and indorsed by him to the claimant for value. In answer to a claim against them by the claimant on the bill, B and L plead that the bill was paid by H to W at maturity and subsequently indorsed by H to the claimant. The plea is a good defence. Payment by one joint acceptor to the holder at maturity discharges the bill and no action can be maintained on the acceptance.[87]

2. A bill is drawn by the defendant on R payable to himself three months after date, and accepted. It is alleged by the defendant that, before the bill became due, it was agreed between himself and R that, on R giving certain mortgage security for the amount of the bill, the defendant would deliver up the bill to R as discharged and fully satisfied. On the assumption that R nevertheless indorsed away the bill and that it came before maturity into the hands of the claimant as bona fide indorsee, there is no defence to the claimant's claim against the defendant on the bill. If an acceptor pays a bill before maturity, he purchases it, and is in the same position as if he had discounted it. The bill was not discharged.[88]

3. The defendant gives to W a promissory note for £289, payable on demand to W's order, as security for a debt. A further debt is incurred and the defendant executes in favour of W a mortgage of certain property to secure the total debt of £641, and as further security for the debt of £289. W transfers the mortgage to H, receiving therefor £700. The note remains in the hands of W after the transfer of the mortgage. W indorses and delivers the note to the claimant as security for a debt of £200 due from him to the claimant, and the claimant takes the note without knowledge of the previous transactions. After so indorsing it, W pays the claimant £60 on account of his debt. The claimant is entitled to claim from the defendant the balance of £140. Although the transactions between the defendant and W would entitle the defendant to certain rights against W,

---

[86] *Burdick v Garrick* (1870) L.R. 5 Ch.App. 233, 241; *Wallersteiner v Moir (No.2)* [1975] Q.B. 373, 397.
[87] *Harmer v Steele* (1849) 4 Exch. 1.
[88] *Morley v Culverwell* (1840) 7 M. & W. 174.

and might entitle him to an injunction to prevent W from suing on the note, the note had never been paid. The note being still current, the defendant was liable to the claimant as indorsee for value without notice of anything wrong.[89]

4. The claimants, a partnership firm, draw a bill on N Ltd payable to their own order in respect of goods supplied by them to N Ltd. N Ltd accept the bill payable at their bankers, the defendants, arrangements having been made between N Ltd and the defendants for this to be done within the limits of N Ltd's overdraft. W, the claimants' cashier, brings the bill to one of the partners in the claimant firm and induces him to indorse it in blank. He then takes the bill to the defendants, presents it for payment, obtains payment over the counter and fraudulently converts and steals the proceeds. The claimants claim against the defendants the amount of the bill. The action fails. The defendants are not liable to the claimants in negligence, as they owed the claimants no duty of care and there is no privity of contract between them. Nor are they liable in an action for money had and received, since the bill did not operate as an assignment of funds of N Ltd with the defendants. No action for conversion of the bill lies against the defendants. The bill was payable to bearer and the defendants paid it in good faith and without notice of any defect in title of W, there being no special circumstances of suspicion.[90]

8–036

5. A bill for £49 is drawn by C, payable to order, upon the defendant and accepted by the defendant. It is indorsed by C to the claimants. It is no defence to an action by the claimants against the defendant on the bill that, before action brought, C had delivered to the claimants, and the claimants had accepted, goods of the value of £50 in satisfaction and discharge of the bill.[91]

6. P draws a bill, payable to his own order, on the defendant and the defendant accepts the bill. P indorses the bill to T, who discounts it for him, and T indorses it to B, who, about two days before it becomes due, pays it short into his bankers. The bankers present the bill for payment at maturity, but it is dishonoured. The bill is returned to B. About a week afterwards P calls upon B and pays him the amount of the bill, upon which B draws his pen through his own and T's indorsement and delivers up the bill to P. P then negotiates the bill to the claimant. The claimant can recover against the defendant on the bill. Payment by P did not discharge

[89] *Glasscock v Balls* (1889) 24 Q.B.D. 13.
[90] *Auchteroni & Co. v Midland Bank Ltd* [1928] 2 K.B. 294.
[91] *Jones v Broadhurst* (1850) 9 C.B. 173.

the bill and when the bill came back to P he was remitted to his original rights.[92]

8–037      7. E & Co. draw a bill on the defendant payable to their own order, which the defendant accepts. The bill is indorsed by E & Co. to C, who indorses it in blank and delivers it to H who, in turn, delivers it to the M Bank. At maturity, the bill is dishonoured and the M Bank commences an action against the defendant, E & Co. and C. C pays H and H pays the M Bank. An order is made staying proceedings in the action on payment of taxed costs. These costs are paid by the claimants on behalf of C and the bill (indorsed in blank) is delivered by the M Bank to C. C, being indebted to the claimants in a larger amount, delivers the bill to them. The claimants can recover against the defendant on the bill. C, having paid the bill, had a right of action on it against the defendant which he could transfer to the claimants.[93]

8. H & Sons accept bills drawn upon them by A & Co. payable to drawer's order. The bills are indorsed by A & Co. to the respondents and discounted by the respondents to the C Bank. Before the bills arrive at maturity, H & Sons become bankrupt and are sequestrated. The respondents pay the bills and obtain them from the C Bank. The respondents can set off the amount of the bills against a claim made against them by the trustee of the sequestrated bankrupt estate of H & Sons in respect of another transaction.[94]

9. The claimants sell a cargo of wheat to R & Co., a partnership firm. R & Co accept bills drawn on them by the claimants, which the claimants indorse to and discount with the defendant bank. Unknown to the claimants, R, a partner in R & Co., has deposited with the defendants the deeds to two properties as security for what the defendants might advance to R & Co. in the way of discounts. The bills are dishonoured by non-payment. The claimants are entitled, on paying the bills, to the benefit *pro tanto* of the securities currently held by the defendants, since they are in a position analogous to that of sureties for R & Co. (the acceptor).[95]

*Money paid under a mistake*

8–038      10. Two bills purporting to be drawn by S on the claimant payable to R are indorsed by R to the defendant for value. Upon learning that the first

---

[92] *Callow v Lawrence* (1814) 3 M. & S. 95.
[93] *Woodward v Pell* (1868) L.R. 4 Q.B. 55.
[94] *McKinnon v Armstrong Bros & Co.* (1877) 2 App. Cas. 531.
[95] *Duncan, Fox & Co. v North and South Wales Bank* (1880) 6 App. Cas. 1.

bill has been drawn on him, the claimant sends his servant to the defendant to take up and pay the bill. The claimant then accepts the second bill and pays this to the defendant on presentation. On discovering that the signature of S, the drawer, is a forgery, the claimant seeks to recover from the defendant the money paid. His claim fails.[96]

11. The defendant bankers are holders for value of a bill which purports to have been accepted by E payable at the claimants, his bankers. The defendants indorse the bill and pass it to their correspondents for collection. The bill is paid on presentation and the money remitted to the defendants. A week later the claimants learn from E that his acceptance is a forgery. The money paid is not recoverable by the claimants from the defendants.[97]

12. The defendants are the indorsees and holders of certain bills. The claimants are requested to, and do, take up the bills for the honour of H & Co., one of the indorsers, and pay to the defendants the amount of the bills. On the same day that payment is made the claimants discover that the signatures of the drawer, the acceptor and of H & Co. are forgeries. They give immediate notice of this fact to the defendants in time to enable the defendants to give notice of dishonour to prior indorsers. The claimants are entitled to recover from the defendants the money paid.[98]

13. A bill of exchange is drawn in Ireland upon the stamp required **8–039** there by law, which is less in amount than the stamp required for such a bill in England. The bill bears several indorsements, but there is nothing to show that the bill has been drawn and indorsed in Ireland. The defendant, holder of the bill in England, neglects to present it for payment and keeps it for a month after it is due. The acceptor becomes bankrupt and the defendant applies to the claimant, his immediate indorser, for payment. The claimant pays the defendant the amount of the bill in ignorance of the fact that it has been drawn in Ireland and that he has been discharged by the defendant's omission to present it for payment. There is no laches, and the claimant can recover the money paid from the defendant.[99]

14. The defendants are the holders of a bill of exchange which bears the indorsements of the drawer and two other indorsers and which purports to have been accepted by a customer of the claimant bankers. The bill is paid by the claimants to the defendants on presentation. On the day after

[96] *Price v Neal* (1762) 3 Burr. 1355. See now s.54(2)(a)(b).
[97] *Smith v Mercer* (1815) 6 Taunt. 76.
[98] *Wilkinson v Johnson* (1824) 3 B. & C. 428.
[99] *Milnes v Duncan* (1827) 6 B. & C. 671.

payment is made the claimants discover that the signature of the acceptor has been forged by the drawer and immediately give notice of this fact to the defendants. The claimants' claim to recover the money paid from the defendants fails. The holder of a bill is entitled to know, on the day on which it becomes due, whether it is an honoured or dishonoured bill. He will otherwise be deprived of his right to take steps against the parties to the bill on the day when it becomes due.[1]

15. The claimant is the holder for value of a bill of exchange for £1,000 drawn by V payable to L and indorsed by L to C and by C to the claimant. The bill purports to bear the acceptance of the defendant. The bill is presented by the claimant to the defendant for payment and the defendant, having had an opportunity to inspect the bill, gives to the claimant a renewed bill (similarly drawn and indorsed) for £1,000 in exchange for the bill so presented. The defendant then discovers that his acceptance on the first bill is a forgery. This is no answer to a suit by the claimant on the substitute bill. The holder of a bill has a right to know whether it has been duly honoured by the acceptor at maturity, and it makes no difference that the purported acceptor, instead of paying money for the bill, takes the bill, examines it and gives another acceptance in lieu of it.[2]

8–040      16. A bill of exchange payable to order and accepted by the claimant bank is negotiated to the defendant bank, which takes it in good faith and for value. Upon presentment for payment, the bill is paid by the claimant bank. Many months after payment has been made, the indorsements on the bill are discovered to be forgeries. The claimant bank cannot recover from the defendant bank the money paid.[3]

17. B, the drawer of a cheque for $5, takes it to the claimant, his bankers, and it is certified by them. The cheque is subsequently altered by B, who raises the amount to $500. B takes the cheque as altered to the defendant bank and opens an account with it. The cheque is placed to his credit and he is allowed to draw against it. Payment of the cheque is made by the claimants on January 27. On January 28, the claimants discover the fraud and immediately demand from the defendants repayment of $495. They are entitled to recover this sum from the defendants as money paid under a mistake.[4]

18. A cheque form is stolen from B in Nigeria, his signature as drawer is forged and the amount of £8,000 inserted. The cheque comes into the

[1] *Cocks v Masterman* (1829) 9 B. & C. 902.
[2] *Mather v Maidstone* (1856) 18 C.B. 273.
[3] *London & River Plate Bank Ltd v Bank of Liverpool Ltd* [1896] 1 Q.B. 7.
[4] *Imperial Bank of Canada v Bank of Hamilton*, [1903] A.C. 49.

hands of H, who gives it to I, the second defendant. I fills in his own name as payee, but, having doubts as to the authenticity of the cheque, sends it to his London bankers, the first defendants, with a request for special collection. The cheque is presented to the claimants, the drawee bank, who fail to detect the forged signature and pay the cheque to the first defendants. Relying on the fact that the cheque has been paid, I pays to H a large sum in Nigerian currency. Two weeks later the forgery is discovered. Judgment is given for the claimants against I and against the first defendants, who have not paid over the money to I, as the money has been paid under a mistake. The claimants are not estopped.[5]

19. A housing association draws a cheque for £24,000 on its account    **8–041** with the claimant bank payable to a building company. On the following day a receiver is appointed of the building company, and the association countermands payment of the cheque. The claimant bank nevertheless overlooks this countermand and pays the cheque when presented for payment by the receiver. The error is not discovered by the claimant bank for two days and repayment is subsequently demanded from the receiver. The amount paid is recoverable from the building company as having been paid under a mistake.[6]

20. W Ltd, a customer of the claimant bank, owes £162,000 to the defendant insurance company. W Ltd pays into its account with the bank a cheque for £168,000 drawn by K Ltd payable to W Ltd with instructions to pay £162,000 of the proceeds to the defendant as soon as possible. The bank agrees to do so, but only if and when the cheque has cleared. Three days later, in the mistaken belief that the cheque has cleared, the bank transfers £162,000 by CHAPS to the defendant's bank account. When presented for payment, K. Ltd's cheque is dishonoured. The bank immediately debits W Ltd's account, putting the account into substantial overdraft. The bank claims restitution from the defendant of the money paid under the transfer. The claim fails. The bank was acting within the authority granted to it by W Ltd when it made the payment to the defendant. Although money paid under a mistake is prima facie recoverable, repayment will not be ordered where, as in this case, the payer is authorised to and does discharge a debt owed to the payee by a third party, as the payee cannot then be said to have been unjustly enriched by the payment.[7]

21. The claimants maintain a US dollar account with a bank in Tunis. An authorised signatory of the claimants signs a payment order

---

[5] *National Westminster Bank Ltd v Barclays Bank International Ltd* [1975] Q.B. 654.
[6] *Barclays Bank Ltd v W. J. Simms, Son & Cooke (Southern) Ltd* [1980] Q.B. 677.
[7] *Lloyds Bank plc v Independent Insurance Co. Ltd* [2000] Q.B. 110.

addressed to the bank authorising the payment of US $518,822 to a shipping company in respect of invoices rendered. One Z, the claimants' chief accountant, fraudulently alters the name of the payee on the order by substituting the name of B Ltd together with the address of a London branch of the L Bank and the account number of B Ltd at that branch. B Ltd is a newly formed English company. Its directors and shareholders are the defendants, who practise in partnership together as chartered accountants in the Isle of Man and who act throughout on behalf of foreign clients. On receipt of the payment order, the Tunis bank debits the claimants' account and, by telex, instructs the L Bank in London to credit B Ltd's account with the amount of the order. The Tunis bank at the same time, by telex, instructs its correspondent bank, the C bank, in New York to reimburse the L Bank with a similar amount. The L Bank accordingly credits B Ltd's account with this sum, and, on the instructions of one of the defendants, transfers this sum to the account of the defendants' firm with the L Bank. Thereafter these moneys are transferred to the client account of the defendants' firm with an Isle of Man bank and from there to various overseas recipients in accordance with the instructions of the firm's foreign clients. B Ltd is then put into liquidation. Proceedings brought by the claimants in Tunisia against the Tunis bank for the recovery of the sums debited to their account are unsuccessful. The claimants have title to maintain an action against the defendants to recover money paid by the Tunis bank as their agent but without their authority. Their claim at common law to recover that money as money had and received fails, because (i) neither the proceeds of the payment order nor any physical asset was transferred from Tunis to London or New York, but only telex messages, (ii) the money transferred could not be identified as it must have been mixed with other moneys in the New York clearing process, and (iii) the defendants, as agents, had paid over the money to or to the order of their principals. The claimants' claim in equity to trace the money through the accounts into the hands of the defendants succeeds, because (i) the money was fraudulently misapplied by Z, who was under a fiduciary duty to the claimants, (ii) the defendants were not liable as constructive trustees for knowing receipt of the money as they had never received it for their own benefit, but (iii) they were accountable for the money as constructive trustees on the grounds that, although they were not privy to and had no actual knowledge of the fraud, they had assisted in the fraud and must have realised that their clients might be involved in a fraud on the claimants yet made no proper inquiries.[8]

8–042    22. The D Bank (D) draws a cheque on its bankers for US$2,999,000 payable to the Bank of Jamaica (BOJ). Each party is deceived by the fraud

---

[8] *Agip (Africa) Ltd v Jackson* [1991] Ch. 547, affirming [1990] Ch. 265.

of one P as to the intention of the other concerning the purpose of the transaction. D draws the cheque intending to lend the amount of the cheque to BOJ against the security of a promissory note to be executed by BOJ. But BOJ intends to buy from D the US dollar amount of the cheque for an equivalent amount in Jamaican dollars, which is to be paid to certain individuals whom BOJ believes to have been nominated by D to receive the money. P is authorised by D to deliver the cheque to BOJ and P in turn uses B, an intermediary, for this purpose. On receipt of the cheque BOJ negotiates it to another bank for collection and payment is duly collected from D's bankers. The Jamaican dollar sums are paid by BOJ through its agents to a number of persons including P and B, that is to say to those who are responsible for the deception, and these persons make off with the money. D claims from BOJ damages for conversion of the cheque, alternatively repayment of US$2,999,000 as money paid under a mistake. The claim in conversion fails. Title to the cheque passed to BOJ on delivery. There was an effective delivery of the cheque because P was authorised by D to deliver the cheque to BOJ even though P chose to do this through B. The claim in restitution also fails because (i) there was no mistake of fact on the part of D but rather a misprediction as to the nature of the transaction which would come into existence when the cheque was delivered to BOJ, (ii) BOJ changed its position by relying in anticipation on the payment, and (iii) BOJ could invoke the defence of bona fide purchase of the cheque for value in answer to D's restitutionary claim. The relative fault of the party deprived and the party enriched by a mistaken payment is irrelevant to the change of position defence.[9]

### Banker paying demand draft whereon indorsement is forged

**60.  When a bill payable to order on demand is drawn on a banker, and the banker on whom it is drawn pays the bill in good faith and in the ordinary course of business, it is not incumbent on the banker to show that the indorsement of the payee or any subsequent indorsement was made by or under the authority of the person whose indorsement it purports to be, and the banker is deemed to have paid the bill in due course, although such indorsement has been forged or made without authority.**       8–043

| Definitions | Comparison |
|---|---|
| "banker": s.2. | ULC: art.35. |
| "bill": s.2. | |
| "indorsement": s.2. | |

[9] *Dextra Bank & Trust Co. Ltd v Bank of Jamaica* [2002] 1 All E.R. (Comm) 193.

"person": s.2.

### COMMENT

8–044      **Scope of section.** This section protects a paying banker who pays in good faith and in the ordinary course of business, a bill payable to order on demand, or a cheque payable to order, drawn on him, even though the indorsement of the payee or any subsequent indorsement is forged or unauthorised. But for this protection he would not be entitled to debit the account of his customer, the drawer, with the amount paid, since his mandate from the customer is to pay only to a person entitled to receive payment and who can give a good discharge.[10] It also protects him from a possible charge of conversion at the suit of the true owner.[11] The section does not apply to bearer instruments. A banker who pays a cheque drawn on him which is payable to bearer does not require protection, since payment in due course, *i.e.* in good faith and without notice that the title of the holder is defective, constitutes a good discharge.[12]

However, section 1(1) of the Cheques Act 1957[13] provides that, where a banker in good faith and in the ordinary course of business pays a cheque drawn on him which is not indorsed or is irregularly indorsed, he does not in so doing incur any liability by reason only of the absence of, or irregularity in, indorsement, and he is deemed to have paid in due course. This subsection has the effect of eliminating entirely the need for indorsements on cheques so far as the paying banker is concerned.[14] Nevertheless the Committee of London Clearing Bankers has taken the view that an indorsement should still be required in certain circumstances. Those circumstances are set out in a memorandum of the Committee dated September 23, 1957,[15] which remains the prevailing practice of bankers in the United Kingdom. To the extent that the memorandum applies to the paying banker, it provides that an indorsement is still required[16] where cheques are encashed over the counter and in respect of combined cheques and receipt forms marked "R". But in most cases where such an indorsement is required, it will not be a true indorsement effecting a negotiation of the cheque or an indorsement for collection, but merely a receipt for its payment by the payee, *e.g.* in the case of payment

---

[10] See above, para.3–066 (s.24).
[11] See above, para.3–050, n.65.
[12] See above, para.8–011 (s.59); *Charles v Blackwell* (1877) 2 C.P.D. 151, 158.
[13] See below, para.17–005.
[14] See below, para.17–002.
[15] See below, para.17–003.
[16] The memorandum also states that an indorsement is required of a bill of exchange or promissory note.

over the counter to the ostensible payee who presents it for payment, or combined cheques marked "R". To this situation section 60 of the 1882 Act probably has no application.[17] But the section still provides protection to the paying banker where an order cheque appears to have been negotiated and an indorsement is required, for example, where a cheque drawn on the banker payable to A or order, purports to have been indorsed by A to B, or to have been indorsed by A in blank, and is presented by B for payment over the counter, the signature of A as indorser being forged or unauthorised.

**Stamp Act 1853, s.19.** The precursor of section 60 of the 1882 Act is to **8–045** be found in section 19 of the Stamp Act 1853. This provides that:

> "any draft or order drawn upon a banker for a sum of money payable to order on demand which shall, when presented for payment, purport to be endorsed by the person to whom the same shall be drawn payable, shall be a sufficient authority to such banker to pay the amount of such draft or order to the bearer thereof; and it shall not be incumbent on such banker to prove that such endorsement, or any subsequent endorsement, was made by or under the direction or authority of the person to whom the said draft or order was or is made payable either by the drawer or any endorser thereof."

It will be noted, first, that this section extends to a wider class of instruments than bills of exchange and cheques, namely to "any draft or order drawn upon a banker for a sum of money payable to order on demand"; secondly, that there is no requirement (as in section 60) that the payment by the banker must be made "in good faith and in the ordinary course of business". Nevertheless, the effect of the protection afforded to the paying banker is the same in both cases: in section 19 the banker is authorised to pay the amount of the draft or order to the bearer thereof[18] and in section 60 he is deemed to have paid the bill in due course. In either case, therefore, payment to the person presenting the instrument for payment is a good discharge notwithstanding the presence of a forged or unauthorised indorsement.

The remainder of the Stamp Act 1853 has been repealed. But section 19 remains unrepealed. In *Capital and Counties Bank Ltd v Gordon*,[19] Lord Lindley considered the status of the section and said[20]:

---

[17] See below, para.8–052.
[18] See *Charles v Blackwell* (1877) 2 C.P.D. 151 (s.25, Illustration 8).
[19] [1903] A.C. 240.
[20] At 251.

"The only conclusion which I can draw... is that s.19 of the Act of 1853 was purposely left unrepealed in order that it might apply to drafts or orders which did not fall within the definitions of bills of exchange or cheques in the Codifying Act of 1882. These definitions are far more limited and scientific than the sweeping descriptions contained in the Stamp Acts; and s.19 of the Act of 1853 appears to me to be purposely preserved in order to protect bankers cashing drafts or orders on them, and which are not bills of exchange or cheques as defined in the Act of 1882, in the same way as s.60 of that Act protects them from cashing documents drawn on them, and which are bills of exchange and cheques as defined in it."

And in *Carpenters' Co. v British Mutual Banking Co. Ltd*,[21] the view was expressed that section 60 of the 1882 Act had impliedly repealed section 19 of the Act of 1853 so far as bills and cheques are concerned. Thus in the case of a bill or cheque it is not open to a paying banker who fails to establish that payment was made by him "in the ordinary course of business" to fall back on the wider protection of section 19.

**8–046**      Section 19 nevertheless continues to protect the paying banker in the case of demand drafts and orders other than bills and cheques, for example, in the case of the banker's draft payable to order on demand drawn by one branch on the head office of the bank or on another branch, or vice versa.[22] Since the drawer and drawee are the same person, such a draft is not a bill or cheque within the meaning of the 1882 Act.[23] However, section 1(2) of the Cheques Act 1957 provides that, where a banker in good faith and in the ordinary course of business pays a document issued by a customer of his which, though not a bill of exchange, is intended to enable a person to obtain payment from him of the sum mentioned in the document,[24] or similarly pays a draft payable on demand drawn by him on himself, whether payable at the head office or some other office of his bank, he does not, in doing so, incur any liability by reason only of the absence of, or irregularity in, indorsement, and the payment discharges the instrument. Again, this dispenses with the need for any indorsement, except where, under prevailing banking practice, an indorsement is required.

The Stamp Act 1853 was concerned only with stamp duty on inland bills. In *Brown, Brough & Co. v National Bank of India Ltd*[25] Bigham J. at first instance held that section 19 did not extend to foreign drafts or orders, *e.g.*

---

[21] [1938] 1 K.B. 511 (Illustration 1).

[22] *Capital and Counties Bank Ltd v Gordon* [1903] A.C. 240; *Lipkin Gorman v Karpnale Ltd* [1987] 1 W.L.R. 987, 996 ([1989] 1 W.L.R. 1340; [1991] 2 A.C. 548).

[23] Though it may be treated by the *holder* at his option, either as a bill of exchange or as a promissory note (s.5(2)).

[24] *e.g.* a cheque drawn "pay cash or order".

[25] (1902) 18 T.L.R. 669.

to a draft drawn by a branch office in India on the head office in London. But the section itself contains no such express limitation and in *Capital and Counties Bank Ltd v Gordon*[26] the point was left open by Lord Lindley in the House of Lords.

**Bills of Exchange Act 1882, s.80.** Further protection is afforded to the   8–047
paying banker who pays a crossed cheque drawn on him by section 80 of the 1882 Act.[27]

**"Bill payable to order on demand."** Section 60 clearly applies to order   8–048
cheques[28]; but it is not so confined and it will extend to a demand bill payable to order drawn on a banker, for example, under a letter of credit. Bankers' drafts do not, however, fall within this section.[29]

The instrument must be payable to order. Paget comments[30]: " . . . this seems to involve the the necessity that it must be negotiable, which is further emphasised by the reference to the indorsement of the payee and any subsequent indorsement, a reference only applicable to an instrument negotiable by indorsement". Thus a bill or cheque drawn "Pay X only" is not within the section. More significantly, since section 81A(1) prescribes that a cheque crossed "account payee" shall not be transferable[31] and most cheques are now pre-printed with this crossing, no protection is afforded by section 60 to a paying banker who pays a cheque so crossed.[32] Such a cheque is not payable to order.

A bill must be payable on demand, as defined in section 10(1) of the Act. Cheques are, by definition, payable on demand. A post-dated cheque will be payable on demand on or after the ostensible date, and it is probably so payable even before.[33]

**"Drawn on a banker."** The bill or cheque must be drawn on a banker,[34]   8–049
and on the banker by whom it is paid. This does not necessarily require that it be drawn by a customer of the banker; but it would not be in the ordinary course of business for a banker to pay a cheque drawn on him other than by his customer. Bills accepted payable at a banker's or

---

[26] [1903] A.C. 240, 251.
[27] See below, para.14–024 (s.80). See also s.5 of the Cheques Act 1957 (extension to other crossed instruments).
[28] s.73.
[29] See above, para.8–046.
[30] 12th ed., 20.15.
[31] See below, para.14–037.
[32] Where payment is made other than to the true payee, the banker must rely on the protection afforded by s.80 of the Act (and s.81A(2)): below, paras 14–024, 14–028, 14–042.
[33] See above, para.2–098.
[34] Defined in s.2. *cf. Halifax Union v Wheelwright* (1875) L.R. 10 Ex. 183.

domiciled with him for payment are not within the section, since they are not drawn on the banker.

The banker may be both paying and collecting banker, as where both the drawer of a cheque and the person presenting it for payment maintain an account at the same branch or different branches of the drawee bank or where a UK bank is instructed by a foreign bank to collect a cheque drawn on the UK bank by a customer. In such a case, as paying banker he may rely on the protection conferred by section 60, but in respect of his position as collecting banker must rely on section 4 of the Cheques Act 1957.[35]

8–050    **"Pays."** The concept of payment has been discussed in the Comment on section 59 of the Act.[36] Payment need not be in cash, and payment by mutual credits and debits within the same branch or between different branches of the same bank,[37] or between banks,[38] will suffice.

8–051    **"In good faith and in the ordinary course of business."** The expression "good faith" is defined in section 90 of the Act. Payment will be made in the ordinary course of business if it accords with the mode of transacting business which is adopted by the banking community at large,[39] not merely in accordance with the practice of a particular bank. Payment by a banker of a crossed order cheque in disregard of the crossing[40] or of an order cheque which bears an irregular indorsement[41] is not in the ordinary course of business, although, in the latter case, under section 1 of the Cheques Act 1957, irregularity in the indorsement will no longer render the paying banker liable. In *Carpenters' Co. v British Mutual Banking Co. Ltd*[42] Greer L.J. was of the opinion that payment would not be made in the ordinary course of business if the banker acted negligently, but a contrary view was taken by Slesser L.J. and Mackinnon L.J., and it is submitted that this latter view is to be preferred.[43] However, payment of a large sum in cash over the counter may not be in the ordinary course of business if circumstances occur necessarily giving rise to suspicion, for example, where the person presenting the instrument for

---

[35] *Carpenters' Co. v British Mutual Banking Co. Ltd* [1938] 1 K.B. 511 (Illustration 1); *Linklaters v HSBC Bank plc* [2003] EWHC 1113 (Comm); *Standard Bank of South Africa Ltd v Harris* 2003 (2) S.A. 23.

[36] See above, para.8–005.

[37] *Gordon v London City and Midland Bank Ltd* [1902] 1 K.B. 242, 274–275. See also *Bissell & Co. v Fox Bros & Co.* (1885) 53 L.T. 193.

[38] See above, para.8–005.

[39] *Australian Mutual Provident Soc. v Derham* (1979) 39 F.L.R. 165, 173. *cf. Lloyds Bank Ltd v Swiss Bankverein* (1913) 108 L.T. 143, 146.

[40] *Smith v Union Bank of London* (1875) L.R. 10 Q.B. 291 (affirmed (1875) 1 Q.B.D. 31).

[41] *Slingsby v District Bank Ltd* [1932] 1 K.B. 544, 565–566.

[42] [1938] 1 K.B. 511 (Illustration 1).

[43] See also *Smith v Commercial Banking Co. of Sydney Ltd* (1910) 11 C.L.R. 667, 677, 688.

payment was one "whose appearance and demeanour was calculated to raise a suspicion that he was not likely to be entrusted with a valuable document for which he was to receive payment in cash"[44] or if a cheque for a large amount was presented by "a tramp, or a postman, or an office boy".[45] Payment marginally outside a bank's official opening hours will still be in the ordinary course of business.[46]

Payment of an order cheque presented to a banker for payment by the process of cheque "truncation"[47] will be in the ordinary course of business.

**"Indorsement."** The question arises whether the banker is protected    8–052
by this section if he requests the ostensible payee to "indorse" an unindorsed order cheque presented for payment over the counter, and the ostensible payee does so, in the presence of the cashier, by forging the signature of the true payee of the instrument. Where a cheque has not been negotiated by indorsement before it is presented for payment, it would seem that the payee's signature on the back of the cheque is merely a receipt and not an indorsement.[48] The argument then is that the word "indorsement" in section 60 refers only to an indorsement for negotiation,[49] or for collection,[50] and does not extend to an "indorsement" which is no more than a receipt.[51] If, therefore, the banker pays an order cheque over the counter to a person not entitled to receive payment, but who forges the receipt of the payee, the banker is not protected since the banker is only relieved from showing that "the indorsement of the payee . . . was made by or under the authority of the person whose indorsement it purports to be". It has been so held in South Africa[52] and in Australia[53] on the wording of provisions identical with section 60.[54] However, if the purported indorsement is merely a receipt, then it is arguable that the paying banker is protected by section 1 of the Cheques Act 1957, which states that "he does not . . . incur any liability by reason only of the absence of indorsement".

---

[44] *Bank of England v Vagliano Brothers* [1891] A.C. 107, 117–118. See above, para.8–014 (s.59).
[45] *Auchteroni & Co. v Midland Bank Ltd* [1928] 2 K.B. 294, 304 (s.59, Illustration 4).
[46] *Baines v National Provincial Bank Ltd* (1927) 96 L.J.K.B. 801.
[47] ss.74B, 74C.
[48] *Keene v Beard* (1860) 8 C.B., N.S. 372, 382; *McDonald (Gerald) & Co. v Nash & Co.* [1924] A.C. 625, 634. *cf. Charles v Blackwell* (1877) 2 C.P.D. 151, 157. See above, para.5–006.
[49] s.32.
[50] s.35.
[51] *cf.* s.2.
[52] *National Bank of South Africa Ltd v Paterson* (1909) 2 L.D.B. 214; *Stapelberg N.O. v Barclays Bank D.C. & O.* 1963 (3) S.A. 120.
[53] *Smith v Commercial Banking Co. of Sydney Ltd* (1910) 11 C.L.R. 667.
[54] Contrast *Byles* (26th ed.), p.300n., which argued that the indorsement of an order cheque was more than a receipt.

The indorsement must purport to be that of the payee or of a subsequent indorser. But the fact that the signature is by procuration, *e.g.* "per pro.",[55] or that the person signing as indorser adds to his signature words indicating that he signs for or on behalf of a principal, or in a representative character, does not preclude the application of the section.

The section does not, of course, protect the paying banker where it is the signature of the drawer that is forged or unauthorised[56]; nor does it protect him if the instrument has been materially altered.[57]

**8–053**    **Effect of section.** Where the requirements of the section are fulfilled, the paying banker "is deemed to have paid the bill in due course". The instrument will be discharged.[58] In the case of a cheque, he will be entitled to debit the account of his customer, the drawer, with the amount paid and will be relieved from any liability in conversion or otherwise to the true owner of the cheque. The payee or indorsee from whose possession the cheque was taken and whose indorsement has been forged or made without authority has no claim against the drawer either on the cheque or on the underlying consideration.[59] His only remedy will be to sue in conversion[60] or for money had and received[61] the collecting banker (who will also normally be protected by section 4 of the Cheques Act 1957)[62] or the person to whom payment was made.[63]

**8–054**    **Proposed legislation.** The Review Committee on Banking Services Law and Practice[64] considered the various statutory protections available to the paying banker under this section, section 19 of the Stamp Act 1853, section 80 of the 1882 Act and section 1 of the Cheques Act 1957 and the inconsistencies which exist between them. It recommended that these sections should be combined together in a single enactment.[65] The Government has accepted this recommendation[66] and proposes to introduce legislation to repeal these sections and re-enact them in a consolidated provision which nevertheless retains the spirit of the current protection

---

[55] *Charles v Blackwell* (1877) 2 C.P.D. 151 (s.25, Illustration 8) (on s.19 of the 1853 Act).
[56] See above, para.3–059 (s.24).
[57] *Slingsby v District Bank Ltd* [1932] 1 K.B. 544 (Illustration 2); *Yorkshire Bank plc v Lloyds Bank plc* [1999] 2 All E.R. (Com) 154, 156, 158; *Smith v Lloyds TSB Bank plc* [2001] Q.B. 541.
[58] s.59(1).
[59] *Charles v Blackwell* (1877) 2 C.P.D. 151.
[60] See above, para.3–050 (s.24).
[61] See above, para.3–052 (s.24).
[62] See below, para.17–028.
[63] *Vinden v Hughes* [1905] 1 K.B. 795 (s.7, Illustration 5). Such a person cannot qualify as a holder in due course: see above, paras 3–066, 3–076 (s.24).
[64] (1989) Cm. 622; above, para.1–008.
[65] Rec. 7(5).
[66] (1990) Cm. 1026, Annex 5, para.5.9.

afforded to the paying banker. The Review Committee further recommended that the protection should be made subject to the condition that the banker had acted "in good faith and without negligence", *i.e.* the language employed by section 80 rather than that found in the present section and section 1 of the Cheques Act 1957. This recommendation has also been accepted.[67]

ILLUSTRATIONS

1. The claimants maintain an account with the defendant bank. B, an 8–055 employee of the claimants, also maintains his own account with the same office of the bank. Over a period of time cheques drawn by the claimants payable to the order of various tradesmen who have supplied goods to the claimants are misappropriated by B. He also fraudulently procures cheques to be drawn by the claimants payable to the order of tradesmen who have supplied no such goods, and misappropriates these. B forges the indorsement of the payees and pays the cheques into his account. The defendants are liable to the claimants for the amount of the cheques. (*Per* Slesser and Mackinnon L.JJ.) the defendants are protected as paying bankers by section 60 of the Act as they paid the cheques in good faith and in the ordinary course of business, but (*per* Slesser and Greer L.JJ.) they are not protected as collecting bankers by section 82 of the Act since they acted negligently.[68]

2. A cheque is drawn by the claimant on the defendant bank "Pay John Prust & Co.             or Order". One C fraudulently inserts the words "per Cumberbirch & Potts" between the payee's name and "or Order", indorses it "Cumberbirch & Potts" and pays it into the account at the W Bank of a company in which C is interested. The cheque is paid by the defendant bank. The claimant is entitled to recover from the defendant bank the amount so paid. The alteration is a material alteration which avoids the cheque under section 64 of the Act; the indorsement is invalid and irregular; and the defendant bank is not protected by sections 60, 79(2) or 80 of the Act. A cheque drawn payable "Pay X per Y or order" should be indorsed "X per Y" and not merely "Y".[69]

[67] (1990) Cm. 1026, Annex 5, para.5.9.
[68] *Carpenters' Co. v British Mutual Banking Co. Ltd* [1938] 1 K.B. 511.
[69] *Slingsby v District Bank Ltd* [1932] 1 K.B. 544.

### Acceptor the holder at maturity

8–056 **61. When the acceptor of a bill is or becomes the holder of it at or after its maturity, in his own right, the bill is discharged.**

Definitions
"bill": s.2.
"holder": s.2.

COMMENT

8–057 **Acceptor the holder at maturity.** The rule stated in this section is a deduction from the general principle that a present right and liability united in the same person cancel each other: "There is no principle", said Best C.J.,[70] "by which a man can be at the same time plaintiff and defendant." The liability is extinguished by merger.[71]

It should be noted, however, that an instrument is only discharged by virtue of this section if the acceptor, or, in the case of a promissory note, the maker of the note,[72] becomes the holder of it. So, for example, a cheque is not thereby discharged if the drawer becomes the holder, even though he is the party primarily liable.[73] Further, the acceptor or maker must be or become the holder of it at or after its maturity. An instrument which is not payable on demand is at maturity on the day on which it falls due, determined in accordance with section 14 of the Act. An instrument payable on demand is at maturity from the day of its issue.[74]

The acceptor or maker must be or become the holder "in his own right". Thus, if he comes into possession of the instrument only as agent for some other person, he does not hold it in his own right and it is not discharged. However, in *Nash v De Freville*,[75] the Court of Appeal held that these words did not mean merely "not in a representative capacity" but meant "having a right not subject to that of any one else but his own—good against all the world".[76] In that case, promissory notes indorsed in blank were delivered to their maker by a person who had acquired the notes by fraud. The maker did not take the notes as holder

---

[70] *Neale v Turton* (1827) 4 Bing. 149, 151.
[71] See *Chitty on Contracts* (29th ed.), Vol.I, Chap. 25.
[72] s.89(2).
[73] But the delivery of the cheque to the drawer could support an inferred renunciation under s.62(2).
[74] *Re George, Francis v Bruce* (1890) 44 Ch.D. 627 (s.62, Illustration 2); *Edwards v Walters* [1896] 2 Ch. 157 (s.62, Illustration 1).
[75] [1900] 2 Q.B. 72 (Illustration 1).
[76] [1900] 2 Q.B. 72 at 89, *per* Collins L.J.

in due course, since he did not take them for value and they were then overdue. Since the maker's title to the notes was defective, he did not become the holder of them in his own right, but subject to the right of another person. They were therefore not discharged.

Where the acceptor or maker dies, and the holder becomes the admin-     8–058
istrator or executor of his estate, the instrument is not discharged.[77] But the position is more doubtful where the acceptor or maker becomes the executor or administrator of the holder. On the wording of the present section, there is no discharge, since he does not become the holder of the instrument "in his own right" but in a representative capacity. On the other hand, by section 21A of the Administration Estates Act 1925,[78] as a normal rule,[79] where a debtor becomes his deceased creditor's executor by representation or administrator, his debt is thereupon extinguished but he is accountable for the amount of the debt as part of the creditor's estate. By subsection (3) of that section "debt" includes any liability, and "debtor" and "creditor" are to be construed accordingly. This provision confirms, and extends to an administrator, the common law rule that a debt is released if the debtor becomes the executor of the creditor's estate.[80]

Illustrations

1. The defendant gives to P three promissory notes payable on demand     8–059
totalling £1,800 to cover advances made by P to the defendant, and P undertakes not to negotiate them. Subsequently the defendant gives to P two further notes payable on demand totalling £3,500 in substitution for the three earlier notes and to cover further advances made to him by P, and P agrees that these notes shall also not be negotiated. P nevertheless negotiates all five notes to the claimants by indorsing them generally and delivering them to the claimants, who are ignorant of the agreement between the defendant and P. The defendant then pays to P £4,000 to meet the £3,500 and interest due on the last two notes, but does not ask for or obtain any of the notes from P, believing them still to be in P's possession. At a later date, P obtains the five notes from the claimants by fraud and hands them to the defendant, who destroys them. The defendant is liable to the claimants in an action against him on the notes and

---

[77] *Lowe v Peskett* (1855) 16 C.B. 500. But the holder may retain assets in his hands which are available for its payment, and thus pay himself.
[78] Inserted by s.10 of the Limitation Amendment Act 1980.
[79] *cf.* s.21A(2).
[80] *Jenkins v Jenkins* [1928] 2 K.B. 501 (Illustration 2). See also *Chitty on Contracts* (29th ed.), Vol.I, § 25–005.

in conversion. The notes are not discharged. The defendant did not become the holder of the notes "in his own right," since (i) P's title to the notes was defective, (ii) the defendant did not take the notes as holder in due course because, although in good faith, he did not acquire them for value or before they were overdue, and (iii) the notes were subject to the rights of the claimants.[81]

2. The claimant, the defendant and two other persons make a promissory note by which they jointly and severally promise to pay to E the sum of £100. E dies, having by his will appointed the claimant his executor. The claimant, suing as executor, brings proceedings against the defendant on the note. The action is not maintainable. Both at common law and in equity the debt is released.[82]

### Express waiver

8–060      62. (1) **When the holder of a bill at or after its maturity absolutely and unconditionally renounces his rights against the acceptor the bill is discharged.**
            **The renunciation must be in writing, unless the bill is delivered up to the acceptor.**
      (2) **The liabilities of any party to a bill may in like manner be renounced by the holder before, at, or after its maturity;**
            **but nothing in this section shall affect the rights of a holder in due course without notice of the renunciation.**

| Definitions | Comparison |
|---|---|
| "bill": s.2. | UCC: §§ 3–604, 3–605. |
| "holder": s.2. | |
| "holder in due course": s.29. | |
| "writing": s.2. | |

### COMMENT

8–061     **Discharge by renunciation.** At common law, the release by a creditor of a debt due or payable to him does not discharge the debt unless the release is made by deed or there is accord and satisfaction.[83] But, by the

---

[81] *Nash v De Freville* [1900] 2 Q.B. 72.
[82] *Jenkins v Jenkins* [1928] 2 K.B. 501.
[83] See *Chitty on Contracts* (29th ed.), Vol.I, Chap. 22.

law merchant,[84] contracts on bills of exchange form an exception to this rule: an express and unqualified renunciation by the holder of his claim on any party to the bill is effective though not made by deed, and the liability of the acceptor or other party, remote or immediate, though complete, may be discharged by an express renunciation of his claim on the part of the holder, without consideration.[85] The same principle applies to cheques[86] and promissory notes.[87]

**Subsection (1): discharge of bill.** Where the requirements of this sub-        8–062
section are satisfied, the bill is discharged. For this to occur, first, the renunciation must be made by the holder, as defined in section 2 of the Act. Secondly, the renunciation must be at or after maturity.[88] Where an instrument is not payable on demand, it will be at maturity on the day on which it falls due, as determined in accordance with section 14 of the Act.[89] An instrument payable on demand is at maturity from the day of its issue.[90] Thirdly, the renunciation must be of the holder's rights against the acceptor, or, in case of a note, against the maker of the note. It need not necessarily be made to the acceptor or maker. A renunciation to a third party may suffice, at least if made at the request of the acceptor or maker.[91] Fourthly, the renunciation must be absolute and unconditional. A promise not to enforce a bill if a certain event takes place would appear not to satisfy this requirement, even if the event occurs.[92] Further, in *Re George, Francis v Bruce*[93] a wish expressed by a dying man that a debt due to him from a relative on a promissory note should be forgiven and that the note should be destroyed when found was held not to be an absolute and unconditional renunciation, but merely the expression of an intention to cancel it.

**Writing or delivery.** The renunciation must be in writing, unless the        8–063
bill is delivered up to the acceptor.[94] These requirements are stated in the

---

[84] The law merchant was, however, modified in this case by the requirement that the renunciation must be in writing, which was introduced in Committee. See *Edwards v Walters* [1896] 2 Ch. 157, 166; *Chalmers* (9th ed.), pp.2, 250.

[85] *Foster v Dawber* (1851) 6 Exch. 839, 846, 851–852.

[86] s.73.

[87] s.89.

[88] *Dod v Edwards* (1827) 2 C. & P. 602.

[89] See above, para.2–100.

[90] *Re George, Francis v Bruce* (1890) 44 Ch.D. 627 (Illustration 2); *Edwards v Walters* [1896] 2 Ch. 157 (Illustration 1).

[91] *Re Dickinson* (1909) 101 L.T. 27.

[92] *Abrey v Crux* (1869) L.R. 5 C.P. 37 (s.21, Illustration 23).

[93] (1890) 44 Ch.D. 627 (Illustration 2).

[94] See *Rimalt v Cartwright* (1925) 132 L.T. 40, 42; *MacMillan v Macmillan* (1974) 51 D.L.R. (3d) 478, affirmed 76 D.L.R. (3d) 760.

alternative. The writing need not, it seems, be signed by the holder[95]; but:

> "What must be in writing is an absolute and unconditional renunciation of rights. It is not necessary to put these words in; but that must be the effect of the document. Then the document is not to be a note or memorandum of the renunciation or of an intention to do it, but it must be itself the record of the renunciation."[96]

With respect to delivery up of the instrument, delivery to the executor or administrator of a deceased acceptor or maker will probably suffice, but not to a devisee or legatee under his will.[97]

It is arguable that the requirement of writing or delivery up applies only to a unilateral renunciation of rights on a bill unsupported by consideration and that it would not be required in the case of an oral agreement for release supported by consideration, *i.e.* accord and satisfaction.[98] But in *Rimalt v Cartwright*[99] Scrutton L.J. said:

> "This is an action on a bill of exchange and the law affecting bills of exchange differs in many ways from the law affecting other contracts. In those cases evidence may be given of collateral agreements which will put an end to the liability of the parties in the original agreement, but if the original agreement is a bill of exchange, it can only be renounced by the holder if the renunciation is in writing, or the bill is cancelled by delivery up to the person liable as acceptor."

Since, however, a holder may agree to accept a consideration other than money as payment by or on behalf of the drawee or acceptor[1] an oral accord and satisfaction might be a sufficient discharge under section 59 of the Act even if it would be insufficient for the purposes of the present section.

8–064      **Effect of renunciation.** A renunciation which satisfies the requirements of subsection (1) discharges the instrument. Not only the acceptor or maker, but all other parties liable on the instrument are discharged.[2] It must, however, be noted that the saving provision in subsection (2) in favour of a holder in due course applies to the entire section and extends to cases falling within subsection (1). Thus, although the instrument is

---

[95] *Re George* (1890) 44 Ch.D. 627 at 632. See also *Re Dickinson* (1909) 101 L.T. 27.
[96] *Re George* (1890) 44 Ch.D. 627 at 632.
[97] *Edwards v Walters* [1896] 2 Ch. 157 (Illustration 1).
[98] *D. Gokal & Co (HK) Ltd v Rippleworth Ltd* [1998] C.L.Y. 370.
[99] (1925) 132 L.T. 40, 42.
[1] See above, para.8–005.
[2] *cf. Muir v Crawford* (1875) L.R. 2 Sc. & Div. 456; *Jones & Co. v Whitaker* (1887) 3 T.L.R. 723 (retention of bill and express reservation of rights against other parties).

stated to be discharged, it is clearly envisaged that the holder could still negotiate it to a holder in due course[3] who, if he was without notice[4] of the renunciation, could enforce the instrument.

**Partial renunciation.** It would appear that a renunciation by the holder of only part of his rights would be ineffective, since the renunciation would not be absolute.[5]    8–065

**Subsection (2): discharge of individual parties.** The liabilities of any party to a bill may in like manner be renounced by the holder. In this case the renunciation may be before, at or after maturity. The words "in like manner", however, give rise to some difficulty. It is clear that a renunciation in writing will suffice. What is not clear is whether, in the alternative, the section envisages the possibility of a discharge without writing only if the instrument is delivered up to the acceptor or maker (which could not happen in the case of a cheque) or whether delivery up to a person other than the acceptor or maker, *e.g.* to the drawer of a cheque, is sufficient. The latter interpretation is, it is submitted, to be preferred.[6] But there must be clear evidence of an intention on the part of the holder to renounce such liabilities.[7]    8–066

A further question which arises is whether a renunciation by the holder of his rights against a particular party will also operate to discharge any other party who has a right of recourse against that party. If, for example, the holder renounces his rights against the drawer, will this discharge all indorsers? Or if the holder renounces his rights against the first indorser, will this discharge all subsequent indorsers? The subsection make no express provision on this point,[8] but it is arguable that the renunciation would have no practical effect if the holder could still proceed against subsequent parties who, in turn, would have recourse against the party released. On the other hand, if the holder renounced his rights against the acceptor before maturity,[9] this would, in effect, discharge the bill, since all secondary parties would then be discharged. In any event, renunciation by the holder of his rights against a particular party will not discharge the liabilities to the holder of a prior party, *e.g.* if the holder renounces his

---

[3] Defined in s.29.

[4] See above, para.4–058 (s.29).

[5] *cf. Macmillan v Macmillan* (1975) 51 D.L.R. (3d) 478, affirmed on other grounds (1977) 76 D.L.R. (3d) 760, where a partial renunciation was held ineffective because it was oral only and without consideration.

[6] *Silk Bros Interstate Traders Pty Ltd v Security Pacific National Bank* (1989) 16 N.S.W.L.R. 446.

[7] *Silk Bros Interstate Traders Pty Ltd v Security Pacific National Bank* (1989) 16 N.S.W.L.R. 446; *Cohn & Co. v Werner & Co.* (1891) 8 T.L.R. 11.

[8] Contrast s.63(2).

[9] It may be argued that the words in subs. (2) "any party" nevertheless mean any party other than the acceptor or maker as mentioned in subs. (1).

rights against the first indorser, the drawer and acceptor will not be discharged.

The subsection expressly saves the rights of a holder in due course[10] without notice[11] of the renunciation.

8–067     **Effect on underlying transaction.** The release by holder of his rights against a party to the bill will not, it is submitted, necessarily discharge the liabilities of that party to the holder on the transaction underlying the bill.

8–068     **Collection of cheques.** A banker may endeavour, but be unable, to collect a cheque drawn payable to the order of his customer which the customer has delivered to him for collection. If he then returns the cheque to the customer, debiting the customer's account with the amount of the cheque, this will not constitute a waiver or renunciation of the liabilities of the drawer.[12]

ILLUSTRATIONS

8–069     1. E lends W £200 on the security of a promissory note made by W payable to E on demand. W dies, devising certain properties to his daughter. E delivers the note to the daughter, stating orally that it is a gift. E dies and his administrator sues the executors of W on the note. The note is not discharged. Although a note payable on demand is at maturity immediately upon its being made, there has been no renunciation in writing and the note has not been delivered up to the personal representatives of W but to a devisee.[13]

2. G lends F £2,000 and in return F executes a promissory note for that amount payable to G on demand. Being in a dying state, G orally declares that he wishes to give the £2,000 to F and forgive her the debt and that the note is to be destroyed when found. A written memorandum of this declaration is made by G's nurse. The note is not discharged. Although the note was at maturity, being payable on demand, the memorandum

---

[10] Defined in s.29.

[11] See above, para.4–058 (s.29).

[12] *Royal Bank of Canada v Wild* (1974) 51 D.L.R. (3d) 188. But the rights of the collecting banker to a lien may be lost: *Westminster Bank Ltd v Zang* [1966] A.C. 182, CA (Cheques Act 1957, s.2, Illustration 2); see *Silk Bros Interstate Traders Pty Ltd v Security Pacific National Bank* (1989) N.S.W.L.R. 446.

[13] *Edwards v Walters* [1896] 2 Ch. 157.

was not an absolute and unconditional renunciation in writing, but merely an expression by G of his intention to cancel the note.[14]

## Cancellation

63. (1) Where a bill is intentionally cancelled by the holder or his agent, and the cancellation is apparent thereon, the bill is discharged.  8–070

(2) In like manner any party liable on a bill may be discharged by the intentional cancellation of his signature by the holder or his agent. In such case any indorser who would have had a right of recourse against the party whose signature is cancelled, is also discharged.

(3) A cancellation made unintentionally, or under a mistake, or without the authority of the holder is inoperative; but where a bill or any signature thereon appears to have been cancelled the burden of proof lies on the party who alleges that the cancellation was made unintentionally, or under a mistake, or without authority.

Definitions  
"bill": s.2.  
"holder": s.2.

Comparison  
UCC: §§ 3–604, 3–605.

COMMENT

**Subsection (1): cancellation of bill.** A bill, cheque or note will be discharged if it is intentionally cancelled by the holder or his agent.[15] But, to have this effect, the cancellation must be "apparent thereon". It must therefore be obvious from the instrument itself that it has been cancelled. A cancellation expressed in a separate document could only take effect, if at all, as a renunciation by the holder of his rights under section 62 of the Act and subject to the conditions set out in that section. No particular form is prescribed; but writing the word "cancelled" prominently across the face of the bill would clearly suffice. Burning a bill would probably be  8–071

---

[14] *Re George, Francis v Bruce* (1890) 44 Ch.D. 627.
[15] *Sweeting v Halse* (1829) 9 B. & C. 365, 369; *Yglesias v Mercantile Bank of River Plate* (1877) 3 C.P.D. 60 affirmed at 330).

sufficient (at least if accompanied by words of cancellation[16] or renunciation). Tearing the instrument in half might be more doubtful.[17] Stamping by a banker of a cheque as "paid" would not, it is submitted, in itself cancel the cheque, being merely an administrative notation by the bank. A cancellation which is not apparent on the bill will not affect the rights of a holder in due course.[18]

Where a bill is effectively cancelled by or on behalf of the holder, the drawer, acceptor and indorsers are discharged from all liability on the bill. Moreover, the drawer, for example, is deprived of any remedy on the bill against the acceptor.[19] The bill cannot thereafter be negotiated.[20]

**8–072**　`**Subsection (2): cancellation of signatures.** An individual party to the instrument may in like manner be discharged by the intentional cancellation of his signature by the holder or his agent.[21] If the drawer's signature is cancelled, this will discharge all indorsers. If the signature of an indorser is cancelled, all subsequent indorsers are discharged. If the cancellation is of the signature of the acceptor (or of the maker of a note), then any indorser will be discharged and—although this is not specifically referred to—also the drawer in the case of a bill.[22] Cancellation of the signature of the party primarily liable will, therefore, in effect normally cancel the instrument itself.

Cancellation should be effected by striking through the signature, leaving it legible.

**8–073**　**Subsection (3): unintentional cancellation.** A cancellation is inoperative if made unintentionally, or under a mistake, or without the authority of the holder.[23] The burden of proof lies on the party alleging this to be so. An agent who, without the authority of the holder, allows an

---

[16] *Kaufman v Bell* [1939] 2 D.L.R. 782.

[17] See *Ingham v Primrose* (1859) 7 C.B., N.S. 82 (torn instrument pasted together: no apparent cancellation). But this case was decided at a time when it was common, for security reasons, to cut a bill into halves, and this would no longer be the case: see *Baxendale v Bennett* (1878) 3 Q.B.D. 525, 532; *Smith v Prosser* [1907] 2 K.B. 735, 746.

[18] See above, para.4–050 (s.29).

[19] *Yglesias v Mercantile Bank of River Plate* (1877) 3 C.P.D. 60.

[20] s.36(1).

[21] *Ralli v Dennistoun* (1851) 6 Ex. 483 (Illustration 1).

[22] Because cancellation of the acceptor's signature will deprive the drawer of his right of recourse against the acceptor. However, *Byles* (27th ed.), p.152, raises the question whether the drawer is discharged if the acceptance is for his accommodation, since he would not in such a case have a right of recourse against the acceptor: see above, para.4–045 (s.28).

[23] *Raper v Birkbeck* (1812) 15 East 17 (Illustration 2); *Wilkinson v Johnson* (1824) 3 B. & C. 428; *Novelli v Rossi* (1831) 2 B. & Ad. 757; *Warwick v Rogers* (1843) 5 M. & G. 340, 373 (approved in *Prince v Oriental Bank Corp.* (1878) 3 App. Cas. 325). See also *Ward v Wray* (1913) 9 D.L.R. 2 (mistake as to identity of maker of substituted note); *Davis v Nash* (1957) 7 D.L.R. (2d) 416; *Royal Securities Corp. Ltd v Montreal Trust Co.* (1966) 59 D.L.R. (2d) 666, affirmed 63 D.L.R. (2d) 15.

instrument to be cancelled may be liable for any loss sustained by the holder as a result of the unauthorised cancellation.[24]

A holder who takes a new negotiable instrument in payment of an existing instrument at or after maturity is normally presumed to have taken it as conditional satisfaction only.[25] If the new instrument is dishonoured, his rights on the original instrument revive. However, he may at the same time agree that the original instrument be cancelled. In such a case, on one view, the cancellation is effective and his sole right is to sue on the new instrument.[26] The cancellation is not unintentional or mistaken within the meaning of the subsection, as it might be, for example, where the cancellation is obtained by fraud or the new instrument is a forgery. Moreover, his assent to the cancellation would indicate that the new instrument was accepted as absolute, and not merely as conditional, payment. On the other hand, it could be argued that a cancellation in these circumstaces was made unintentionally or under a mistake, since it was made under the misapprehension that the new instrument would be honoured on presentment. It is submitted that the former view is to be preferred.

ILLUSTRATIONS

1. S draws several bills of exchange on D & Co., which they accept. S then writes to D & Co. in terms which indicate that the acceptances are to be cancelled, and D & Co. accordingly cancel their acceptances. The obligation of D & Co. as acceptors of the bills is put an end to with respect to S and all persons claiming subsequently under him.[27]  **8–074**

2. C draws a bill on S & Co., which is accepted by them payable at the L Bank and subsequently indorsed to the defendants and by them indorsed to the claimants. The bill states "In case of need apply to B & Co.". It is dishonoured when presented for payment at the L Bank and sent to B & Co. A partner in B & Co., thinking that the bill has been made payable at B & Co., by mistake cancels the acceptance. He then perceives his error and writes on the bill "Cancelled by mistake". B & Co. nevertheless pay the bill for the honour of the claimants. The claimants, on proof of cancellation by mistake, can recover against the defendants as prior indorsers.[28]

---

[24] *Bank of Scotland v Dominion Bank* [1891] A.C. 592 (Illustration 3).
[25] See above, para.8–006 (s.59).
[26] See, *e.g. Yglesias v Mercantile Bank of the River Plate* (1877) 3 C.P.D. 60.
[27] *Ralli v Dennistoun* (1851) 6 Ex. 483.
[28] *Raper v Birkbeck* (1812) 15 East 17.

3. McA Bros in Canada draw a bill on A & Co. in Scotland payable to themselves. A & Co. accept the bill payable at the London office of the defendant bank. The bill is indorsed by McA Bros to the respondent bank which transmits it for collection at maturity to the N Bank in London. Payment is refused on presentment. A & Co. then offer to pay the bill on condition that they will not be liable for interest and expenses. The agent of the appellant bank informs the N Bank of this condition, and, without waiting for authority, takes payment of the bill and delivers it up to A & Co. to be cancelled. The respondent bank refuses to ratify his act and raises an action against A & Co. for the amount of the bill, interest and expenses, relying on section 63(3); but A & Co. become bankrupt. The respondents are entitled to recover their loss from the appellants as the cancellation was made without their authority.[29]

## Alteration of bill

8–075   64. (1) Where a bill or acceptance is materially altered without the assent of all parties liable on the bill, the bill is avoided except as against a party who has himself made, authorised, or assented to the alteration, and subsequent indorsers.
Provided that,
Where a bill has been materially altered, but the alteration is not apparent, and the bill is in the hands of a holder in due course, such holder may avail himself of the bill as if it had not been altered, and may enforce payment of it according to its original tenour.

(2) In particular the following alterations are material, namely, any alteration of the date, the sum payable, the time of payment the place of payment, and where a bill has been accepted generally, the addition of a place of payment without the acceptor's assent.

| Definitions | Comparison |
|---|---|
| "acceptance": s.2. | UCC: §§ 3–407, 4–401. |
| "bill": s.2. | ULB: art.69. |
| "holder": s.2. | ULC: art.51. |
| "holder in due course": s.29. | UNB: art.35. |

---

[29] *Bank of Scotland v Dominion Bank* [1891] A.C. 592. (The respondents agreed to assign their rights against the drawers to the appellants.)

COMMENT

**Alteration of a bill.** This section deals with the effect of a material    8–076
alteration of a bill or acceptance. It applies also to cheques and promissory notes. Although the words "or acceptance" appear in subsection (1),
there is no further reference to an acceptance in the section. It has been
suggested[30] that "acceptance" is here used in the older and non-technical
sense of a bill which has been accepted by the drawee but is not yet at
maturity, rather than to denote an acceptance as defined in sections 2 and
17 of the Act. In either case, however, the alteration of an acceptance
would be an alteration of a bill.

The words "altered" and "alteration" are not confined to cases where
existing wording on an instrument is replaced by new wording, as where
the place of drawing is struck through and another place of drawing is
substituted[31] or the name of the payee is deleted and a different name is
inserted.[32] A bill may be altered by the addition of words or figures, for
example, where a stipulation as to payment of interest is inserted,[33] or by
a deletion or erasure.[34] But the accidental disfigurement of a bill, for
instance, where details are effaced by its being sent inadvertently to the
laundry in a garment to be washed,[35] is not an alteration, although if the
damage is so extensive as to obliterate the instrument it would presumably fall to be treated as a destroyed bill.[36] The alteration may be on
the face or on the back of the bill.

The section does not apply where an incomplete bill is filled up as a
complete bill or, in the case of a bill wanting in a material particular, the
omission is filled up: such insertions are dealt with in accordance with
section 20 of the Act. Nor does it apply where the instrument is altered
before it becomes a bill. So, for example, if an instrument is accepted
before it has been signed by the drawer, there is no alteration within the
meaning of the present section if the drawer inserts his signature as
drawer and at the same time alters the printed place of drawing to the
place where it is actually drawn.[37] There may also be no such alteration
where the instrument is altered before it is issued as a bill.[38]

---

[30] *Crawford and Falconbridge* (8th ed.), p.1685.
[31] *Koch v Dicks* [1933] 1 K.B. 307 (Illustration 2).
[32] *Smith v Lloyds TSB Group plc* [2001] Q.B. 541 (Illustration 6).
[33] *Payana Reena Saminathan v Pana Lana Palaniappa* [1914] A.C. 618 (Illustration 8).
[34] *Nicholson v Revill* (1836) 4 A. & E. 675.
[35] *Hong Kong and Shanghai Banking Corp. v Lo Lee Shi* [1928] A.C. 181.
[36] See below, paras 10–001, 10–005 (ss.69, 70).
[37] *Foster v Driscoll* [1929] 1 K.B. 470, 494 (s.12, Illustration).
[38] *Kennerley v Nash* (1816) 1 Stark. 452; *Downes v Richardson* (1822) 5 B. & Ald. 674. But
contrast *Walton v Hastings* (1815) 4 Camp. 223; *Outhwaite v Luntley* (1815) 4 Camp. 179;
*Engel v Stourton* (1889) 5 T.L.R. 444.

8-077     Although the fraudulent alteration of a bill and the falsification of a signature on it may both constitute forgery under the Forgery and Counterfeiting Act 1981,[39] the Act of 1882 deals distinctly with these two situations. Alteration is dealt with in the present section. The effect of a forged or unauthorised signature is dealt with in section 24 of the Act.

8-078     **Subsection (1): effect of material alteration.** The effect of any material alteration of a bill without the assent of all parties liable thereon[40] is to avoid the bill, except as against a party who has himself made, authorised or assented to the alteration,[41] and subsequent indorsers. Thus if after acceptance, a bill for £500 is altered in amount to £3,500 by the drawer and then delivered by him to a holder (other than a holder in due course), the holder cannot recover against the acceptor, even for the original amount. The acceptor is under no duty to the holder to take precautions against fraudulent alterations of the bill after acceptance.[42] The drawer who made the alteration is, however, liable to his immediate and any subsequent transferee for the full £3,500. Also, if the bill is indorsed after the alteration, the indorser is liable to the holder[43] for the raised amount.

8-079     **The proviso.**

> "Before the Act a material alteration was a complete defence, by whomsoever made, and avoided and discharged the bill, except as against a party who made or assented to the alteration. Now, under the proviso to section 64, a holder for value[44] may, when a bill has been materially altered, but the alteration is not apparent, avail himself of the bill as if it had not been altered."[45]

So, in the above example, if the bill comes into the hands of a holder in due course, that holder could (provided the alteration is not apparent) recover from the acceptor the original sum of £500.[46] However, the right to "avail himself of the bill as if it had not been altered" and to "enforce payment of it according to its original tenour" is conferred only upon a

---

[39] See above, para.3–047 (s.24).
[40] The date of payment of an accepted bill payable to the drawer, and not negotiated, may be altered by agreement between the acceptor and drawer.
[41] For conflicting views on the burden of proof, see *Kana Pana Adeyappa Chitty v Abdulrahmav* (1900) 6 S.S.L. R.76 (Straits Settlements); *Ebersohn v Claasen* 1963 (1) S.A. 467; *Bhanabai and Co. (H.K.) Ltd v Wearwell Clothing Co. Pty Ltd* 1986 (4) S.A. 350.
[42] *Scholfield v Londesborough* [1896] A.C. 514 (Illustration 1). See also *Heskell v Continental Express Ltd* [1950] 1 All E.R. 1033.
[43] Or to any subsequent indorser.
[44] By "holder for value" is meant here a holder in due course.
[45] *Scholfield v Londesborough* [1895] 1 Q.B. 536, 552, *per* Lopes L.J., CA.
[46] *Scholfield v Londesborough* [1896] A.C. 514 (Illustration 1).

holder in due course, as defined in section 29 of the Act.[47] A mere holder[48] or holder for value[49] or the original payee of the bill (who cannot be a holder in due course)[50] cannot take advantage of the proviso.

**Apparent alteration.** It is for the holder to show that an alteration is 8–080 not apparent.[51] In *Woollatt v Stanley*,[52] Salter J. stated that an alteration is apparent "if the intending holder on scrutinising the document with reasonable care would observe that it had been altered". He rejected a test earlier proposed by Denman J.[53] that the alteration should be apparent to the party sought to be bound—a test which would be inconsistent with the decision of the House of Lords in *Scholfield v Londesborough*[54] and confine the protection given to a holder in due course within very narrow limits. The formulation employed by Salter J. was adopted, with qual-ification, by the High Court of Australia in *Automobile Finance Co. of Australia Ltd v Law*.[55] In that case, a printed form of promissory note made payable to a named payee was altered after issue by the insertion of a place of payment in the space following the printed words "Payable at" adjacent to the maker's signature. The insertion was in a different hand-writing from, and was in darker ink than, the rest of the writing on the note. The majority[56] of the High Court held that, assuming the alteration was material, it was not "apparent". Four members of the Court[57] were of the opinion that it must be apparent upon inspection of the instrument that its text had undergone a change, and that its appearance must be consistent with the revision having occurred after completion or issue. The statement of Salter J. did not mean "merely that what has been substituted or added should be visible to [the holder] upon reasonable examination, but that the fact that it was put there as an addition or substitution will thus be seen".[58] Starke J.[59] in the same case said that it was not enough to say that a prudent businessman would be put upon enquiry, or that his suspicions would be aroused by the form of the document: "The alteration may be by addition, interlineation, or other-wise, but it must be visible as an alteration, upon inspection."

[47] See above, para.4–050 (or a "sheltered holder" under s.29(3)).
[48] See above, para.4–028.
[49] See above, para.4–024.
[50] See above, para.4–059; *Rapid Discount Corp. Ltd v Thomas E. Hiscott Ltd* (1977) 76 D.L.R. (3d) 450.
[51] *Woollatt v Stanley* (1928) 138 L.T. 620, 622.
[52] (1928) 138 L.T. 620.
[53] *Leeds & County Bank Ltd v Walker* (1883) 11 Q.B.D. 84, 90–91.
[54] [1896] A.C. 514 (Illustration 1).
[55] (1933) 49 C.L.R. 1.
[56] Evatt J. dissenting.
[57] Gavan Duffy C.J., Rich, Dixon and McTiernan JJ.
[58] At 10.
[59] At 12.

Whether or not an alteration is apparent seems to be a question of fact.

8–081      **Subsection (2): what alterations are material.** Five examples of material alterations are mentioned in this subsection; but, as the words "in particular" show, they are not intended to be exhaustive. In *Koch v Dicks*,[60] the Court of Appeal held to be material an alteration after issue of the place of drawing from London to Deisslingen in Germany, thus changing the bill from an inland bill to a foreign one. Scrutton L.J. said[61] that "an alteration which affects the rights as between the parties to the bill is a material alteration", and cited Lord Campbell in *Gardner v Walsh*[62]: "if the altered instrument, supposing it to be genuine, would operate differently from the original instrument, whether the alteration be or be not to his prejudice".[63] In the same case Greer L.J. referred[64] to anything which alters "the legal incidence of the bill" and Slesser L.J.[65] to "any such alteration which would produce a change in the legal nature of the instrument". But even these tests may not be wide enough. In *Suffell v Bank of England*,[66] the serial number of a Bank of England note was altered. This did not change the nature of the instrument; nor did it affect the contract which the instrument contained.[67] The alteration was nevertheless held to be material. Brett M.R. said[68]: "Any alteration of any instrument seems to be material which would alter the business effect of the instrument if used for any ordinary business purpose for which such an instrument or any part of it is used" and Cotton L.J. considered the number to be an essential part of the note, the alteration of which altered the instrument "in a material way".[69]

The following alterations have been held to be material: a particular consideration is substituted for the words "value received"[70]; the date of a bill payable at a fixed period after date is altered, and the time of payment thereby postponed[71] or accelerated[72]; a date is inserted which is

---

[60] [1933] 1 K.B. 307 (Illustration 2).

[61] At 320.

[62] (1855) 5 E. & B. 83, 89.

[63] Contrast (a non-bill case) *Raiffeisen Zentralbank Osterreich AG v Crossseas Shipping Ltd* [2000] 1 W.L.R. 1135 at [26–27] (alteration prejudicial to party making it not material).

[64] At 324.

[65] At 328.

[66] (1882) 9 Q.B.D. 555. See also *Leeds & County Bank Ltd v Walker* (1883) 11 Q.B.D. 84. *cf. Hong Kong and Shanghai Banking Corp. v Lo Lee Shi* [1928] A.C. 181.

[67] (1882) 9 Q.B.D. at 565.

[68] At 568.

[69] At 574.

[70] *Knill v Williams* (1809) 10 East 431; *cf. Wright v Inshaw* (1842) 1 Dowl.(N.S.) 802; 6 Jur. 857.

[71] *Outhwaite v Luntley* (1815) 4 Camp. 179; *Hirschman v Budd* (1873) L.R. 8 Ex. 171; *Société Générale v Metropolitan Bank* (1873) 21 W.R. 335; *Woollatt v Stanley* (1928) 138 L.T. 620.

[72] *Master v Miller* (1793) 1 Anst. 225; *Walton v Hastings* (1815) 4 Camp. 223.

not in accordance with the contract under which the bill is given[73]; a bill payable three months after date is converted into a bill payable three months after sight[74]; the date of a cheque or bill payable on demand is altered[75]; the crossing of a cheque is altered[76] or an order cheque is converted into a bearer cheque[77]; the sum payable is altered, *e.g.* from £500 to £3,500[78] or from £105 to £100[79]; a provision for interest is inserted[80]; the specified rate of interest is altered, *e.g.* from 3 per cent to $2\frac{1}{2}$ per cent[81]; a bill payable "with lawful interest" is altered by adding the words "interest at 6 per cent"[82]; a particular rate of exchange is indorsed on a bill which does not authorise this to be done[83]; a restrictive indorsement is deleted[84]; a joint note is converted into a joint and several note[85]; a new maker is added to a joint and several note[86]; the name of a maker of a joint and several note is cut off[87] or intentionally erased[88]; the place of payment is altered, *e.g.* a bill is accepted payable at X & Co.'s, and Y & Co. is substituted for X & Co.[89]; a place for payment is added without the acceptor's consent[90]; the number on a Bank of England note is altered[91]; the name of the payee on a cheque or banker's draft is deleted and a different name substituted[92]; the name of the payee on a cheque payable to order is altered by the insertion of an initial[93]; the words "per—and—" are added to payee's name on the face of a cheque[94]; the place of drawing

[73] *Foster v Driscoll* [1929] 1 K.B. 470 (s.12, Illustration).
[74] *Long v Moore* (1790) 3 Esp. 155n.
[75] *Vance v Lowther* (1876) 1 Ex.D. 176.
[76] See s.78, overriding *Simmonds v Taylor* (1858) 27 L.J.C.P. 248.
[77] *Cutfin (Pty) Ltd v Sangio Pipe CC* 2002 (5) SA 156, 172.
[78] *Scholfield v Londesborough* [1896] A.C. 514 (Illustration 1).
[79] *cf. Hamelin v Bruck* (1846) 9 Q.B. 306.
[80] *Saminathan v Palaniappa* [1914] A.C. 618 (Illustration 8).
[81] *Sutton v Toomer* (1827) 7 B. & C. 416.
[82] *Warrington v Early* (1853) 2 E. & B. 763.
[83] *Hirschfield v Smith* (1866) L.R. 1 C.P. 340.
[84] *Bhanabhai and Co. (HK) Ltd v Wearwell Clothing Co. Pty Ltd* 1986 (4) S.A. 350.
[85] *Perring v Hone* (1826) 4 Bing. 28.
[86] *Gardner v Walsh* (1855) 5 E. & B. 83; *cf. Clerk v Blackstock* (1816) Holt N.P. 474.
[87] *cf. Mason v Bradley* (1843) 11 M. & W. 590.
[88] *Nicholson v Revill* (1836) 4 A. & E. 675.
[89] *Tidmarsh v Grover* (1813) 1 M. & S. 735.
[90] *Calvert v Baker* (1838) 4 M. & W. 417; *Burchfield v Moore* (1854) 3 E. & B. 683; *cf. Hanbury v Lovett* (1868) 18 L.T. 366. *Quaere,* if the acceptor consent: *Walter v Cubley* (1833) 2 Cr. & M. 151; and *cf. Mason v Bradley* (1843) 11 M. & W. 590 at 594; but see *Gibb v Mather* (1832) 2 C. & J. 254 at 262; *Saul v Jones* (1858) 1 E. & E. 59, which show that the position of the drawer and indorsers is altered.
[91] *Suffell v Bank of England* (1882) 9 Q.B.D. 555; *Leeds Bank v Walker* (1883) 11 Q.B.D. 84.
[92] *Yorkshire Bank plc v Lloyds Bank plc* [1999] 2 All E.R. (Comm) 154; *Smith v Lloyds TSB Group plc* [2001] Q.B. 541 (Illustration 6).
[93] *Goldman v Cox* (1924) 40 T.L.R. 744.
[94] *Slingsby v Westminster Bank* [1931] 2 K.B. 583; *Slingsby v District Bank* [1932] 1 K.B. 544 (s.60, Illustration 2).

is altered from London to Germany, thus changing the bill from an inland bill to a foreign one.[95]

8–082    **Immaterial alterations.** The following have been held to be immaterial: a bill payable to C or bearer is converted into a bill payable to C or order[96]; an indorsement in blank is converted into a special indorsement[97]; the words "on demand" are added to a note in which no time of payment is expressed[98]; or a bill addressed to Brown & Co., under the style of Brown, Smith & Co., is accepted by them as Brown & Co., and the address is afterwards altered to make it correspond with the acceptance[99]; the alteration of a marginal figure on a bill[1]; the words "or order" are struck out by the acceptor in the case of a bill payable to "D or order"[2]; the number on a banknote (not issued by the Bank of England) is missing[3]; a reference to collateral security is deleted from a note[4]; the name of the addressee is inserted in a note[5]; the place of drawing is altered from Birmingham to Bristol.[6]

8–083    **Cheques crossed "account payee".** The words "account payee" or "a/c payee", either with or without the word "only", across the face of a crossed cheque render the cheque non-transferable.[7] The deletion of these words by the payee or by a third party, *e.g.* a collecting banker, without the authority or assent of the drawer will be a material alteration and avoid the cheque as against the drawer. It is, however, submitted that the addition of these words to a crossed cheque by the payee is not a material alteration. He is entitled, as holder, to prohibit the transfer of the cheque in order to reduce the risk that the cheque may be stolen, his indorsement forged and payment made to the wrong person.[8]

---

[95] *Koch v Dicks* [1933] 1 K.B. 307 (Illustration 2).

[96] *Atwood v Griffin* (1826) 2 C. & P. 368, 370; *Cutfin (Pty) Ltd v Sangio Pipe CC* 2002 (5) S.A. 156.

[97] See s.34(4).

[98] *Aldous v Cornwell* (1868) L.R. 3 Q.B. 573; see s.10.

[99] *Farquhar v Southey* (1826) M. & M. 14; but see *Bank of Montreal v Exhibit and Trading Co.* (1906) 22 T.L.R. 722; 11 Com.Cas. 250, as to adding the word "Limited" to the name of an unincorporated company; *cf. Arab Bank v Ross* [1952] 2 Q.B. 216.

[1] *Garrard v Lewis* (1882) 10 Q.B.D. 30.

[2] *Decroix, Verley & Cie v Meyer* (1890) 25 Q.B.D. 343, CA.

[3] *Hong Kong and Shanghai Banking Corp. v Lo Lee Shi* [1928] A.C. 181, PC.

[4] *Re Thompson* [1931] 4 D.L.R. 573, 579; *Ievens v Latvian (Toronto) Credit Union Ltd* (1977) 84 D.L.R. (3d) 248.

[5] *Haseldine v Winstanley* [1936] 2 K.B. 101 (Illustration 3).

[6] *Koch v Dicks* [1933] K.B. 307 at 327.

[7] s.81A(1).

[8] *cf.* the *express* provision in s.77(4) whereby the holder may add the words "not negotiable" to a crossed cheque.

**Correcting a mistake.**[9] It may be that an alteration is not material if it    8–084
is made for the purpose of correcting a mistake and bringing the instrument into accordance with the intention of the parties at the time of
issue.[10] Thus if a cheque is erroneously dated January 2, 2004, whereas the
true date on which it is drawn and that intended by the drawer was
January 2, 2005, the payee could, without the knowledge or assent of the
drawer, correct the mistake. But it is arguable that the language of
subsection (1) effectively precludes any unilateral alteration of an instrument after issue without the assent of all parties liable thereon,[11] although
in appropriate circumstances such assent could no doubt be implied.[12]

**Drawee bank.** Where a cheque is materially altered after issue by a    8–085
person other than the drawer and without the drawer's authority or
consent, the banker upon whom the cheque is drawn is not entitled to
debit the account of his customer, the drawer, with the amount paid on
the altered cheque.[13] His mandate from the customer is to pay only on
presentation of a genuine cheque and not of an instrument which has
been avoided by the alteration. The right given by the proviso to subsection (1), where the alteration is not apparent, to utilise the cheque as if it
had not been altered and to enforce payment of it according to its original
tenor is confined to a holder in due course, and does not extend to the
drawee banker.[14] Nor is any other statutory protection available to him.[15]
But if, for example, the amount of a cheque is fraudulently raised by the
payee, it is at least arguable that, as between banker and customer, the
customer's mandate is still good for the original amount and that the
customer can only require his account to be reinstated to the extent of the
increase.[16] This would not apply to a case where, for instance, the name

---

[9] See Hudson [1975] J.B.L. 108.
[10] *Brutt v Picard* (1824) Ry. & M. 37; *Hamelin v Bruck* (1846) 9 Q.B. 306, 310; *London & Provincial Bank v Roberts* (1874) 22 W.R. 402. See also *Byron v Thompson* (1839) 11 A. & E. 31; *Bradley v Bardsley* (1845) 14 M. & W. 873; *Haseldine v Winstanley* [1936] 2 K.B. 101 (Illustration 3) and (non-bill cases) *Re Howgate and Osborne's Contract* [1902] 1 Ch. 451; *Lombard Finance Ltd v Brookplain Ltd* [1991] 1 W.L.R. 271, 274.
[11] *Sutton v Blakey* (1897) 13 T.L.R. 441; *Koch v Dicks* [1933] 1 K.B. 307, 311–312; *Byles* (27th ed.), 20–22. ss.12 and 20 of the Act are not applicable in this situation.
[12] *cf. Cariss v Tattersall* (1841) 2 M. & G. 890.
[13] *Hall v Fuller* (1826) 5 B. & C. 750; *Colonial Bank of Australia Ltd v Marshall* [1906] A.C. 559 (although this case was disapproved on its facts in *London Joint Stock Bank Ltd v Macmillan* [1918] A.C. 777); *Slingsby v District Bank* [1932] 1 K.B. 544 (s.60, Illustration 2); *Yorkshire Bank plc v Lloyds Bank plc* [1999] 2 All E.R. (Comm) 154, 156; *Smith v Lloyds TSB Group plc* [2000] 1 W.L.R. 1225, 1235, (affirmed [2001] Q.B. 541). Contrast (banker's draft) *Harvey Jones Ltd v Woolwich plc* [2001] Q.B. 541 (Illustration 7).
[14] *Slingsby v District Bank Ltd* [1931] 2 K.B. 588, 600 (affirmed [1932] 1 K.B. 544).
[15] *e.g.* under ss.60, 80 of the Act or s.1 of the Cheques Act 1957.
[16] See, *e.g. Hall v Fuller* (1826) 5 B. & C. 750 at 757; *Colonial Bank of Australasia Ltd v Marshall* [1906] A.C. 559; *Imperial Bank of Canada v Bank of Hamilton* [1903] A.C. 49.

of the payee is altered or erased and another name substituted, or the words "account payee" are deleted from a crossed cheque.[17]

However, the customer of the drawee banker owes him a duty in drawing a cheque to take reasonable and ordinary precautions against forgery, and if as the natural and direct result of the neglect of these precautions the amount of the cheque is increased by forgery, the customer must bear the loss as between himself and the banker. This sufficiently appears from the speeches in the House of Lords in *London Joint Stock Bank Ltd v Macmillan*.[18] In that case a partner in a partnership firm was induced by his confidential clerk to sign as drawer a cheque payable to bearer. The cheque, prepared by the clerk with a view to fraud, bore only in figures the amount £2, but with a space before the figure "2" and nothing at all written in the space for words. The cheque so signed was then completed by the clerk by inserting "One hundred and twenty pounds" in words and the figures "1" and "0" respectively before and after the figure "2". The clerk presented the cheque to the drawee bank for payment, received £120 and absconded. It was held that the drawee bank was entitled to debit the partners' account with the larger amount. The cheque was, of course, incomplete and inchoate when signed.[19] But the earlier case of *Young v Grote*[20] was approved, and Lord Finlay L.C. said[21]:

> "It is beyond dispute that the customer is bound to exercise reasonable care in drawing the cheque to prevent the banker being misled. If he draws a cheque in a manner which facilitated fraud, he is guilty of a breach of duty as between himself and the banker, and he will be responsible to the banker for any loss sustained by the banker as a natural and direct consequence of this breach of duty... As the customer and the banker are under a contractual relation in this matter, it appears obvious that in drawing a cheque the customer is bound to take usual and reasonable precautions to prevent forgery."

And Lord Shaw said[22]:

> " ... it is the duty of the customer ... to take care to frame and fill up his cheque in such a manner that when it passes out of his, the customer's, hands it will not be so left that before presentation, alterations, interpolations, &c., can be readily made upon it without

---

[17] See above, para.8–083.
[18] [1918] A.C. 777 (Illustration 5). *cf. Société Générale v Metropolitan Bank Ltd* (1873) 27 L.T. 849; *Slingsby v District Bank Ltd* [1932] 1 K.B. 544 (s.60, Illustration 2).
[19] See above, para.2–130 (s.20).
[20] (1827) 4 Bing. 253 (Illustration 4).
[21] At 789, 793. See also Lord Haldane at 815.
[22] At 824. See also 793, 814, 826, 835.

giving reasonable ground for suspicion to the banker that they did not form part of the original body of the cheque when signed."

There is little doubt, therefore, that the principle in *Macmillan's Case* applies equally to the alteration, due to the failure of the drawer to take usual and reasonable precautions, of a completed cheque.[23]

A drawee banker who pays a cheque in ignorance of the fact that it has been materially altered is prima facie entitled to recover the amount paid from the payee or from the collecting banker (provided that the latter has not before learning of the claim paid over the money to his principal)[24] as money paid under a mistake.[25] It is arguable that a collecting banker who presents, on behalf of a customer, an altered cheque for payment impliedly warrants to the drawee banker that the cheque is a genuine document and has not been avoided by alteration.[26] However, in *Smith v Lloyds TSB Group plc*[27] Pill L.J. said: "The cheque is rendered invalid by section 64 and, by presenting it under normal banking arrangements, the collecting bank was not asserting its validity". It is submitted that this view should be followed.

The holder of a cheque from whom the cheque is stolen and subse-    8–086
quently altered by the substitution of the name of another for that of the payee owes no duty to the drawee banker to take precautions to prevent the misappropriation of the cheque or its presentation to the drawee bank for payment.[28]

A drawee banker who pays a cheque or other instrument drawn on him which has been avoided by a material alteration is not liable to the true owner in conversion for the face value of the instrument as the instrument is a nullity and worthless.[29]

**Bank where bill or note domiciled for payment.** Where a banker    8–087
agrees to pay a bill accepted by his customer or to pay a note domiciled with him for payment by his customer, his authority from the customer does not extend to paying an instrument which has been materially altered and he will not be entitled to debit his customer's account with the amount which he has paid. It is doubtful whether the customer owes

---

[23] E. A. Barbour Ltd v Ho Hong Bank Ltd [1929] S.S.L.R. 116; Will v Bank of Montreal [1931] 3 D.L.R. 526; Barclays Bank D.C.O. v Straw 1965 (2) S.A. 93. Commonwealth Trading Bank of Australia v Sydney Wide Stores Pty Ltd (1981) 148 C.L.R. 304.

[24] See above, para.8–028 (s.59).

[25] Imperial Bank of Canada v Bank of Hamilton [1903] A.C. 49 (s.59, Illustration 17).

[26] Sheffield Corporation v Barclay [1905] A.C. 392; Kai Yung v Hong Kong & Shanghai Banking Corporation [1981] A.C. 787 (forged documents); Honourable Society of the Middle Temple v Lloyds Bank plc [1993] 1 All E.R. (Comm) 193 (Cheques Act 1957, s.4. Illustration 5) (warranty that customer entitled to the proceeds).

[27] [2001] Q.B. 541, 557.

[28] Yorkshire Bank plc v Lloyds Bank plc [1999] 2 All E.R. (Comm) 154.

[29] Harvey Jones Ltd v Woolwich plc [2001] Q.B. 541 (Illustration 7).

him a duty not to accept a bill which is so drawn as to facilitate alteration; but it is submitted that, by directing the banker to pay out of a balance for which he has to account, the acceptor is under an obligation to exercise care in the framing of what is a mandate to pay, and that the banker "has a right to insist that the direction he receives to be acted upon without any delay shall be so drawn as not to require exceptional consideration and so impose delay".[30] The maker of a promissory note is, presumably, under the same duty to his banker as the drawer of a cheque to take reasonable and ordinary precautions to prevent forgery. Money paid by the banker on an altered bill or note is prima facie recoverable from the person to whom it was paid.[31]

8–088     **Collecting bank.** Where an instrument has been materially altered after issue with the result that it has been avoided under subsection (1), no claim can be made by the true owner of the instrument to recover its face value[32] from a collecting banker who has converted the instrument by dealing with it inconsistently with the true owner's rights.[33] What has been converted is no longer a negotiable instrument but a worthless piece of paper. It was so held by the Court of Appeal in *Smith v Lloyds TSB Group plc*[34] where Pill L.J. said[35]: "No party can bring an action for damages in conversion for its face value because it no longer represents a chose in action for that amount".

This is also the case where the drawer of a cheque is its true owner. It is probable that, in the case of a cheque which has been materially altered after issue, the only right of the drawer is to insist that his account be re-credited by the drawee banker[36] and that no action can be brought by him directly against the collecting banker. But the drawer might be entitled to recover from the collecting banker the sum paid as money paid under a mistake on the part of his agent, the drawee banker.[37] This

---

[30] *London Joint Stock Bank Ltd v Macmillan* [1918] A.C. 777 at 815. See also *Scholfield v Londesborough* [1896] A.C. 514, 523.

[31] See above, para.8–021 (s.59).

[32] See above, para.3–050.

[33] See above, para.3–050.

[34] [2001] Q.B. 541 (Illustration 6). This settled an issue which previously was somewhat in doubt: see *Slingsby v Westminster Bank Ltd* [1931] 2 K.B. 583; *Slingsby v District Bank Ltd* [1932] 1 K.B. 544, 559, 562; *Bank of Ceylon v Kulatilleke* (1937) 59 N.L.R. (Ceylon) 188 (disapproved on other grounds in *Daniel Silva v Johanis Appuhamy* (1965) 67 N.L.R. (Ceylon) 437, but see *De Costa v Bank of Ceylon* (1969) 72 N.L.R. (Ceylon) 457); *Lumsden & Co. v London Trustee Savings Bank* [1971] 1 Lloyd's Rep. 114 (Cheques Act 1957, s.4. Illustration 20).

[35] At p.557.

[36] See above, para.8–085.

[37] See above, para.8–021.

restitutionary remedy is, however, subject to the defence that the collecting banker has paid over the proceeds of the cheque to his principal before he became aware of the mistake.[38]

The fact that the drawer of the instrument could have been compelled,[39] or would have been prepared, to issue a duplicate instrument to the holder had the alteration been discovered before the conversion does not mean that the instrument retains its face value.[40] Nor, it is submitted, does the fact that the instrument is drawn payable to order or to bearer and might therefore (if the alteration was not apparent) be enforceable under the proviso by a holder in due course according to its original tenor mean that it has a face value as if it had not been altered. The instrument only has value in the hands of a holder in due course. If, for example, a cheque is drawn payable to order or bearer and the amount of the cheque is fraudulently raised, and he cheque is delivered to a bank for collection, the collecting banker will not be liable in conversion to the true owner of the cheque for the unaltered amount. If he is collecting for a person other than a holder in due course, the cheque is still worthless. If he is collecting for a holder in due course, then the title of the true owner of the cheque will to that extent have been extinguished.

A collecting banker may, however, be both an agent for collection and the holder of an instrument for value,[41] in which case he himself may take advantage of the proviso to subsection (1) of the present section if he is a holder in due course.

**Effect on consideration for bill.** The section deals only with the effect 8–089 of a material alteration on the bill itself and with the liability on the bill of parties to it. It does not deal with the right of a holder of a bill which has been avoided by a material alteration to sue on the consideration in respect of which it was received by him. But, under the common law before the Act, the avoidance of a bill could affect the right of the holder to resort to an action on the underlying consideration. If the bill was negotiated to him after the alteration was made, and he was not privy to the alteration, he could sue on the consideration.[42] Since the enactment of the proviso to subsection (1), this rule is of less importance, but could, for example, still benefit a holder who does not qualify as a holder in due course or (*semble*) a holder in due course who is only able to enforce a bill raised in amount according to its original tenor. However, at common law, if a bill was altered while in the holder's custody or under his

---

[38] See above, para.8–028.
[39] ss.69, 70.
[40] *Harvey Jones Ltd v Woolwich plc* [2001] Q.B. 541, 557 (Illustration 7).
[41] See below, para.17–019 (Cheques Act 1957, s.2). But see below, para.17–017.
[42] *Burchfield v Moore* (1854) 3 E. & B. 683. But *cf. McDowall v Boyd* (1848) 17 L.J.Q.B. 295 (instrument taken as absolute payment).

control, he could not recover on the consideration for which he received it unless (a) he did not intend to commit a fraud by the alteration, and (b) the alteration had not deprived the party sued of a right of recourse which he would have had if the bill had not been altered. So, for example, if a promissory note was innocently altered by the payee or at his instigation, the payee could still recover against the maker on the debt in respect of which it was given to him.[43] But if an accepted bill was indorsed by a buyer to a seller to pay for goods sold and delivered, and was materially altered by the indorsee (thereby avoiding the bill), the indorsee could not sue the indorser for the price of the goods, since, by altering the bill, he had deprived the indorser of his remedy on the bill against the acceptor.[44]

## ILLUSTRATIONS

**8–090**    1. A bill is drawn by S on the defendant and accepted by him. After acceptance, the drawer fraudulently increases the amount to £3,500 by inserting "3" before "500" and by writing "three thousand" before the words "five hundred" in the body of the bill. The bill has been drawn by S so as deliberately to facilitate this fraud. The bill is indorsed by S to another from whom the claimant acquires it in good faith and for value. The defendant is liable to the claimant for £500 only. He is not estopped.[45]

2. R Co., a company carrying on business in Deisslingen in Germany, agrees to supply goods to the defendant in England. The defendant accepts seven bills which purport to be drawn in London, but at the time of his acceptance the name of the drawer is not on them. The bills are sent in this condition to Germany, where the name of R Co. is put on them as drawers, and the R Co. then indorse them to the claimant for value. The claimant tries to discount the bills with his bankers in Germany, but they insist that the place of drawing be altered from London to Deisslingen. The claimant accordingly so alters five of the bills without the defendant's knowledge or consent. The alteration is a material alteration, changing these bills from inland to foreign bills, after they were complete. The bills are therefore avoided.[46]

---

[43] *Saminathan v Palaniappa* [1914] A.C. 618 (Illustration 8). See also *Sutton v Toomer* (1827) 7 B. & C. 416; *Atkinson v Hawdon* (1835) 2 A. & E. 628 (Illustration 10).
[44] *Alderson v Langdale* (1832) 3 B. & Ad. 660 (Illustration 9).
[45] *Scholfield v Londesborough* [1896] A.C. 514.
[46] *Koch v Dicks* [1933] 1 K.B. 307.

3. M draws two documents in the form of bills of exchange, but neither document has on it the name of any addressee or drawee. The defendant is induced by fraud to accept them. The documents are delivered by M to the claimant, who, in M's presence, writes M's name as addressee on both of them. Subsequently the claimant agrees to discount them for M, and, with the consent of M, strikes out M's name as addressee and inserts that of the defendant. The claimant acquires the bills for value and without notice of the fraud. The defendant is liable to him as acceptor. When accepted by the defendant the bills were incomplete. M had prima facie authority from the defendant to insert therein the name of the defendant as addressee, and the claimant, with M's approval, did this. Alternatively, the documents were good promissory notes. The alteration was then immaterial, as it did not affect them in any way as promissory notes.[47]

4. Y leaves home for a few days, leaving with his wife five blank cheques and requesting her in his absence to have them filled up for such sums as his business may require. His wife requires £50 2s. to pay wages. She delivers one of the cheques so signed to W, a clerk of Y, authorising him to fill it up for that amount. The clerk fills it up and shows it to Mrs Y. The cheque reads "fifty pounds 2s. 3d.," but the word "fifty" starts in the middle of the line and commences with a small letter "f". In figures there is "50,2,3," but sufficient space has been left between "£" and "50" to enable an insertion to be made. W fraudulently inserts the words "three hundred and" before "fifty" and "3" before the figure "5". The drawee bank pays W £350 2s. 3d. against the cheque, and debits Y with this amount. The bank can maintain the debit to the account.[48]

8–091

5. The claimants, a partnership firm of general merchants in the City of London, maintain an account with the defendant bank. They have in their employment a confidential clerk, K, part of whose duties is to prepare cheques for signature. A partner in the firm is approached by K who produces for his signature a bearer cheque drawn on the defendant bank. The sum (£2) is expressed in figures only, the space for words being left blank. The partner is about to go for lunch and signs the cheque in that state. K adds the words "Ourselves" before the words "or Bearer", writes "one hundred and twenty pounds" in the space left for the sum payable in words, and alters the figure "2" to "120". The bank is entitled to debit the claimants' account with the larger amount. The claimants, as customers of the bank, owe a duty to the bank to take reasonable and ordinary precautions in the mode of drawing the cheque, and the alteration of the amount of the cheque by K is the direct result of that breach of duty.[49]

---

[47] *Haseldine v Winstanley* [1936] 2 K.B. 101.
[48] *Young v Grote* (1827) 4 Bing. 253.
[49] *London Joint Stock Bank Ltd v Macmillan* [1918] A.C. 777.

6. The claimants are joint liquidators of a company in liquidation. They apply to the Central Accounting Unit of the Insolvency Service for a cheque payable to the Inland Revenue in the sum of £127,240. The Unit sends them a cheque for this amount drawn "Pay Inland Revenue only" and crossed "a/c payee only". The cheque is abstracted from the claimants' offices, the name Joseph Smitherman substituted for that of the Inland Revenue and the cheque paid into and collected for the account of Joseph Smitherman with the defendant bank. The claimants, as true owners of the cheque, claim from the defendant bank (the collecting bank) damages for conversion in the face value of the cheque. The claim fails. The instrument was rendered a nullity and worthless as a result of the alteration. No substantial damages can be awarded for converting what is a worthless piece of paper.[50]

7. The claimant company is a supplier of kitchen units. It receives a banker's draft for £7,222 drawn by the defendant bank in respect of the supply of kitchen units to a customer. The draft is stolen from the claimant's premises, its name as payee deleted from the draft and the name of "Edmund C.A. Owusu-Sekyere" substituted. The draft is collected for an account in that name at the N. Bank and is duly paid by the defendant bank. The claimant, as true owner of the draft, claims against the defendant bank (the paying bank) damages for conversion in the face value of the draft. The claim fails. The draft, having been materially altered, was a nullity and worthless. It did not follow from the fact that the defendant bank would have issued a replacement draft (had the alteration been discovered before the draft was paid) that the draft retained its face value. The payee of a banker's draft assumes the relevant risk just as much as he must assume the risk if he receives payment in banknotes which are then stolen.[51]

8–092    8. Two promissory notes for Rs.14,000 are made by the appellant payable to the respondent in respect of a debt admitted to be due under an arbitrators' award. At the instance of the respondent, the notes are materially altered by adding a stipulation for interest, the alteration being made innocently as the result of a misunderstanding. An action by the respondent on the notes is dismissed. The respondent can nevertheless recover against the appellant on the original debt, the notes having been given and accepted as conditional payment only.[52]

8–093    9. The defendant indorses to the claimant, in payment for goods sold, a bill drawn by the defendant on a third party. After the bill has been

---

[50] *Smith v Lloyds TSB Group plc* [2001] Q.B. 541.
[51] *Harvey Jones Ltd v Woolwich plc* [2001] Q.B. 541.
[52] *Saminathan v Palaniappa* [1914] A.C. 618.

accepted, the claimant alters the time of payment mentioned in the bill from four to three months. The bill thereby becomes wholly null and void. The claimant cannot recover from the defendant the price of the goods sold. By altering the bill in a material part, he has made it his own against the defendant, and caused it to operate as satisfaction of the debt for which it was originally given.[53]

10. A bill is drawn by the claimant on the defendant for £19 payable to the claimant two months after date, in respect of the balance of the amount payable by the defendant to the claimant for goods supplied. After the bill is accepted, the claimant alters the date of the bill from December 30 to December 28, 1833. The claimant can recover against the defendant for the original debt. The defendant, as acceptor, is not in any worse a situation by the alteration and avoidance of the bill.[54]

## Acceptance and Payment for Honour

### Acceptance for honour *suprà protest*

65. (1) Where a bill of exchange has been protested for dishonour by non-acceptance, or protested for better security, and is not overdue, any person, not being a party already liable thereon, may, with the consent of the holder, intervene and accept the bill *suprà protest*, for the honour of any party liable thereon, or for the honour of the person for whose account the bill is drawn.

    (2) A bill may be accepted for honour for part only of the sum for which it is drawn.

    (3) An acceptance for honour *suprà protest* in order to be valid must—

        (a) be written on the bill, and indicate that it is an acceptance for honour:

        (b) be signed by the acceptor for honour:

    (4) Where an acceptance for honour does not expressly state for whose honour it is made, it is deemed to be an acceptance for the honour of the drawer.

    (5) Where a bill payable after sight is accepted for honour, its maturity is calculated from the date of the noting for non-

9–001

---

[53] *Alderson v Langdale* (1832) 3 B. & Ad. 660.
[54] *Atkinson v Hawdon* (1835) 2 A. & E. 628.

acceptance, and not from the date of the acceptance for honour.

| Definitions | Comparison |
|---|---|
| "acceptance": s.2. | ULB: arts 55–58. |
| "bill": s.2. | |
| "holder": s.2. | |
| "person": s.2. | |
| "written": s.2. | |

## COMMENT

9–002     **Subsection (1): acceptance for honour.** Acceptance for honour is a procedure by which, notwithstanding that the drawee has refused to accept a bill or the acceptor has become insolvent, a stranger may intervene and accept the bill, thus keeping the credit of the bill alive until it falls due for payment, at which time he undertakes to pay it if the person upon whom it was originally drawn fails to pay. Acceptance for honour does not apply to cheques[1] and promissory notes[2] and is, in practice, obsolete. There is no longer any need for such intervention since numerous other devices now exist by which a substitute arrangement can be promptly effected.

The following requirements must be satisfied for an acceptance for honour to be made: first, the bill must have been protested for non-acceptance[3] or for better security.[4] Secondly, the bill must not be overdue.[5] Thirdly, the acceptor for honour must not be a party already liable on the bill. The subsection appears to permit the drawee (as well as a stranger), though he refuses to accept generally, to accept a bill *suprà protest* for the honour of the drawer or of an indorser. Fourthly, the acceptance must be for the honour of a party liable on the bill, or for the honour of the person for whose account the bill is drawn.[6] Fifthly, the acceptance must be with the consent of the holder. Such consent is necessary because the holder would otherwise, upon dishonour by non-acceptance, be entitled to an immediate right of recourse against the drawer and indorsers,[7] which right he might be unwilling to postpone.

---

[1] *Bank of Baroda v Punjab National Bank* [1944] A.C. 176, 184.
[2] s.89(3)(c).
[3] s.51; but see s.93 (noting). The bill must be protested (or noted) even if it is an inland bill. cf. *Mutford v Walcot* (1698) 1 Ld. Raym. 574, 575.
[4] s.51(5). See *Ex p. Wackerbath* (1800) 5 Ves. Jun. 574.
[5] ss.10, 14, 36(3).
[6] Sometimes referred to as the "third account".
[7] s.43(2).

The Act does not provide for more than one acceptance for honour on a bill. This leaves open the question whether, if a bill is accepted for the honour of an indorser, there may be another acceptance for the honour of a party prior to him,[8] or whether, if the acceptor for honour fails before maturity, a second acceptance for honour could be obtained.[9]

**Subsection (2): partial acceptance for honour.**  Ordinarily, if the holder   9–003
takes a partial acceptance,[10] he must give due notice to the drawer and indorsers, otherwise they will be discharged.[11] This may not apply to a partial acceptance for honour.[12]

**Subsection (3): form of acceptance for honour.**  According to the law   9–004
merchant, the acceptor had to attend personally before a notary public with witnesses and to declare in the presence of the notary that he accepted the protested bill for the honour of the drawer or indorser, as the case may be, and that he would pay the bill at the appointed time. This declaration, known as an "act of honour", would be written at the foot of the protest and attested by the notary.[13] A clause requiring this was inserted in the bill, but was struck out in committee. It may, therefore, no longer be essential,[14] but it is to be noted that section 97(2) preserves the rules of the law merchant save in so far as they are inconsistent with the express provisions of the Act. The minimum formal requirements for an acceptance for honour are, however, set out in this subsection.

**Subsection (4): for whose honour acceptance made.**  It is usual for the   9–005
acceptor to state expressly for whose honour he accepts. But, if he does not do so, he is deemed to have accepted for the honour of the drawer.

**Subsection (5): after sight bill.**  This subsection brought the law into   9–006
line with mercantile understanding, and got rid of an inconvenient rul-ing[15] that maturity was to be calculated from the date of acceptance for honour. For noting of a bill, see section 51(4).

### Liability of acceptor for honour

**66. (1) The acceptor for honour of a bill by accepting it engages that**   9–007
       **he will, on due presentment, pay the bill according to the**

---

[8] Beawes, *Lex Mercatoria* (6th ed.), No.42.
[9] *Story*, § 122.
[10] s.19(2)(b).
[11] s.44(2).
[12] But it should so apply.
[13] *Brookes' Notary* (12th ed.), pp.7–77, 12–17—12–20.
[14] *cf.* s.63(3) (payment for honour).
[15] *Williams v Germaine* (1827) 7 B. & C. 468.

tenor of his acceptance, if it is not paid by the drawee, provided it has been duly presented for payment and protested
for non-payment, and that he receives notice of these facts.

(2) The acceptor for honour is liable to the holder and to all
parties to the bill subsequent to the party for whose honour
he has accepted.

Definitions                         Comparison
"bill": s.2.                        ULB: arts 55–58.
"holder": s.2.

COMMENT

9–008    **Subsection (1): liability of acceptor for honour.** " . . . an acceptance for
honour is", said Lord Tenterden,[16] " . . . in the nature of a conditional
acceptance. It is equivalent to saying to the holder of the bill, keep this
bill, don't return it, and when the time arrives at which it ought to be
paid, if it be not paid by the party on whom it was originally drawn, come
to me, and you shall have the money." The engagement of an acceptor for
honour differs, therefore, from that of a drawee who has accepted a bill[17]
in that he does not undertake to pay in any event, but only if the bill is
presented to the drawee at maturity and is not paid.

In order to render the acceptor for honour liable on the bill, six conditions must be satisfied. First, the bill must have been duly presented for
payment to the drawee.[18] The reason for this requirement is, in the words
of Lord Ellenborough,[19] that "effects often reach the drawee, who has
refused acceptance in the first instance, out of which the bill may and
would be satisfied if presented to him again when the period of payment
had arrived". Secondly, the bill must not have been paid by the drawee.
Thirdly, the bill must have been protested for non-payment.[20] Fourthly,
the acceptor for honour must have received notice of these facts. Fifthly,
the bill must have been duly presented to him for payment in accordance
with section 67. Sixthly, the bill must be protested for non-payment by
him.[21]

[16] *Williams v Germaine* (1827) 7 B. & C. 468, 477.
[17] s.54(1).
[18] ss.45, 46.
[19] *Hoare v Cazenove* (1812) 16 East 391, 398.
[20] s.51. But see s.93 (sufficiency of noting). Protest is necessary whether the bill is an inland
or foreign bill. See also s.67(1).
[21] s.67(4).

**Subsection (2): to whom liable.** An acceptor for honour steps into the place of the party for whose honour he has accepted. He is therefore liable to the holder, and to all parties subsequent to that party. It seems that he is bound by the estoppels which bind an ordinary acceptor[22] and also by the estoppels which would bind the party for whose honour he accepted.[23]

9–009

### Presentment to acceptor for honour

67. (1) Where a dishonoured bill has been accepted for honour *suprà protest*, or contains a reference in case of need, it must be protested for non-payment before it is presented for payment to the acceptor for honour, or referee in case of need.

(2) Where the address of the acceptor for honour is in the same place where the bill is protested for non-payment, the bill must be presented to him not later than the day following its maturity; and where the address of the acceptor for honour is in some place other than the place where it was protested for non-payment, the bill must be forwarded not later than the day following its maturity for presentment to him.

(3) Delay in presentment or non-presentment is excused by any circumstance which would excuse delay in presentment for payment or non-presentment for payment.

(4) When a bill of exchange is dishonoured by the acceptor for honour it must be protested for non-payment by him.

9–010

| | |
|---|---|
| Definitions | Comparison |
| "acceptance": s.2. | ULB: arts 55–58, 60. |
| "bill": s.2. | |

COMMENT

**Presentment for payment *suprà protest*.** A bill which has been accepted for honour in accordance with section 65, or which contains a reference in case of need,[24] must be protested[25] for non-payment before it

9–011

---

[22] s.54.
[23] s.55. See *Phillips v Thurn* (1866) L.R. 1 C.P. 463, 471; on demurrer (1865) 18 C.B.N.S. 694.
[24] s.15.
[25] ss.51, 67(1). But see s.93 (sufficiency of noting). The bill must be protested whether it is an inland bill or foreign bill.

565

is presented for payment to the acceptor for honour, or referee in case of need.

In the case of an acceptance for honour, it must then be presented for payment to the acceptor for honour within the time limited by subsection (2) of this section.[26] By section 92, non-business days are to be excluded in computing the time. It seems probable that, despite the differences in purpose and wording, "place" might be construed to have the same meaning as in section 49(12) of the Act (time within which notice of dishonour must be given),[27] that is to say, two addresses are "in the same place" if it would in all the circumstances be reasonable to take the bill after protest by hand to the acceptor for presentment rather than to forward it by post for presentment to him.[28] If a bill is not presented in due time to the acceptor for honour, it is conceived that he, and any party who would have been discharged had he paid the bill, are discharged by the holder's laches; but there is no decision in point. Delay in presentment is excused in the circumstances set out in section 46(1)[29] and non-presentment is excused in the circumstances set out in section 46(2).[30]

If the bill is dishonoured by the acceptor for honour it must be protested for non-payment by him.[31]

### Payment for honour *suprà protest*

9–012　　68. (1) Where a bill has been protested for non-payment, any person may intervene and pay it *suprà protest* for the honour of any party liable thereon, or for the honour of the person for whose account the bill is drawn.

(2) Where two or more persons offer to pay a bill for the honour of different parties, the person whose payment will discharge most parties to the bill shall have the preference.

(3) Payment for honour *suprà protest*, in order to operate as such and not as a mere voluntary payment, must be attested by a notarial act of honour which may be appended to the protest or form an extension of it.

(4) The notarial act of honour must be founded on a declaration made by the payer for honour, or his agent in that behalf,

---

[26] This reproduced the effect of the Bills of Exchange Act 1836 (6 & 7 Will. 4 c. 58), s.1 (now repealed).

[27] See above, para.6–105.

[28] *Hamilton Finance Co. Ltd v Coverley Westray Walbaum & Tosetti Ltd* [1969] 1 Lloyd's Rep. 53, 73. *cf.* Bills of Exchange Act 1836, s.1 (same "City, Town or Place").

[29] See above, para.6–069.

[30] See above, para.6–070.

[31] ss.51, 67(4). But see s.93 (sufficiency of noting). The bill must be protested whether it is an inland or foreign bill.

declaring his intention to pay the bill for honour, and for whose honour he pays.

(5) Where a bill has been paid for honour, all parties subsequent to the party for whose honour it is paid are discharged, but the payer for honour is subrogated for, and succeeds to both the rights and duties of, the holder as regards the party for whose honour he pays, and all parties liable to that party.

(6) The payer for honour on paying to the holder the amount of the bill and the notarial expenses incidental to its dishonour is entitled to receive both the bill itself and the protest. If the holder do not on demand deliver them up he shall be liable to the payer for honour in damages.

(7) Where the holder of a bill refuses to receive payment *suprà protest* he shall lose his right of recourse against any party who would have been discharged by such payment.

| Definitions | Comparison |
|---|---|
| "bill": s.2. | ULB: arts 55, 59–63. |
| "holder": s.2. | |
| "person": s.2. | |

## COMMENT

**Payment for honour.** A person may, after a bill has been protested for non-payment,[32] intervene and pay it *suprà protest* for the honour of any party liable thereon,[33] or for the honour of the person for whose account the bill is drawn.[34] A cheque or promissory note could, it seems, also be paid for honour *suprà protest*. But, in practice, payment of an instrument for honour is now obsolete.     9–013

Although the bill must first have been protested for non-payment, the conditions for an effective payment are, in certain respects, less exacting than those for acceptance for honour[35]: the bill may be overdue; payment may be made by any person, including a party already liable on the bill; and the consent of the holder is not required.

**Notarial act of honour.** A notarial act of honour is in this case required, even though it may not be essential in the case of acceptance for honour.[36]     9–014

---

[32] s.51. But see s.93 (sufficiency of noting). Protest is required whether the bill is an inland or foreign bill.
[33] *Geralopulo v Wieler* (1851) 10 C.B. 690.
[34] Sometimes called "the third account".
[35] s.65(1).
[36] s.65(3); see above, para.9–004.

It is usually appended to the protest or forms an extension of it.[37] Without any prior protest for non-payment or a notarial act of honour, payment of the bill by a stranger will operate as a mere voluntary payment. It would not constitute payment in due course.[38]

**9–015**      **Effect of payment for honour.** The payer for honour "succeeds to the title of the person from whom, not for whom, he receives [the bill], and has all the title of such person to sue upon it, except that he discharges all the parties to the bill subsequent to the one for whose honour he takes it up".[39] Thus if a bill is paid for the honour of the acceptor, the payer can sue the acceptor, but the drawer and all indorsers are discharged. If he pays for the honour of the drawer, he can sue the acceptor[40] and (provided he has received due notice of dishonour)[41] the drawer, but the indorsers are discharged.

When a bill has been paid *suprà protest*, it ceases to be negotiable.[42]

**9–016**      **Right to bill and protest.** The protest referred to in subsection (6) is the protest for non-payment by the acceptor which is necessary in order to charge the acceptor for honour.[43]

**9–017**      **Refusal of payment.** In contrast with section 65(1),[44] payment for honour does not require the consent of the holder. If the holder refuses the payment, he loses his right of recourse against any party who would have been discharged by such payment.

**Lost Instruments**

**Holder's right to duplicate of lost bill**

**10–001**      **69. Where a bill has been lost before it is overdue, the person who was the holder of it may apply to the drawer to give him another bill of the same tenor, giving security to the drawer if required to indemnify him against all persons whatever in case the bill alleged to have been lost shall be found again.**

---

[37] See *Brooke's Notary* (12th ed.), p.7–77.

[38] See above, para.8–010 (s.59) (unless assented to or ratified).

[39] *Re Overend, Gurney & Co.* (1868) L.R. 6 Eq. 344, 367.

[40] Unless (possibly) the bill has been accepted for the accommodation of the drawer: *Ex p. Lambert* (1806) 13 Ves.Jun. 179. *cf. Re Overend Gurney & Co.* (1868) L.R. 6 Eq. 344.

[41] *Goodall v Polhill* (1845) 1 C.B. 233. See s.49.

[42] *Re Overend, Gurney & Co.* (1868) L.R. 6 Eq. 344 at 367.

[43] *Re English Bank of the River Plate* [1893] 2 Ch. 438, 444.

[44] See above, para.9–002.

**If the drawer on request as aforesaid refuses to give such duplicate bill, he may be compelled to do so.**

Definitions
"bill": s.2.
"holder": s.2.
"person": s.2.

## COMMENT

**Right to duplicate of lost bill.** This section[1] confers upon the former holder of a lost bill the right to obtain a duplicate of the bill from the drawer, provided that it was lost before it was overdue.[2] The section does not, however, confer any right to obtain an acceptance or indorsement over again. The holder must re-present the duplicate bill for acceptance and obtain any indorsement necessary to establish his title to the bill. As a result, the remedy given by the section has been said to be "still very inadequate".[3] But the Act does not require the former holder to obtain a duplicate and he may instead bring an action under section 70 against the acceptor and (subject to the requisite proceedings on dishonour being duly taken) against the drawer and any indorser of the lost bill.

10–002

The section applies also to cheques. But, in view of the fact that the duty to give a duplicate is placed on the drawer, it is questionable whether the maker of a promissory note is under a similar obligation to give a duplicate of a lost note. Under section 89(2) of the Act, the maker of a note is deemed to correspond with the acceptor of a bill, and not with the drawer. But section 89(1) provides that "the provisions of this Act relating to bills of exchange apply, with the necessary modifications, to promissory notes". It is therefore arguable that, for the purposes of the present section, a necessary modification requires the maker of a lost note to furnish a duplicate on request.[4]

The right to obtain a duplicate of a lost bill is not an absolute one. The former holder must give security to the drawer if required to indemnify him against all persons whatever in case the bill alleged to have been lost

---

[1] Reproducing the effect of the Bills of Exchange Act 1698 (9 Will. 3, c. 17), s.3 (now repealed).
[2] As to when a bill is overdue, see ss.10, 14, 36(3).
[3] *Chalmers* (9th ed.), p.272.
[4] *Bank of Canada v Bank of Montreal* (1971) 24 D.L.R. (3d) 13, *sub. nom. Bank of Montreal v Bay Bus Terminal (North Bay) Ltd* affirmed. (1972) 30 D.L.R. (3d) 24, (1977) 76 D.L.R. (3d) 385 (banknotes). In the United Kingdom, however, Bank of England notes are treated as cash and there would be no right to a duplicate of a lost note.

is found again. Presumably the question whether any security tendered is adequate for this purpose is a matter for decision by the court.

If the drawer on request refuses to give a duplicate bill, he may be compelled to do so. Where the former holder obtains a judgment or order to that effect, but the drawer neglects or refuses to comply, section 39 of the Supreme Court Act 1981 empowers the High Court to order that the duplicate bill be executed by such person as the court may nominate for that purpose.

10–003    **Loss by theft.** There is no reason to suppose that loss by theft is not covered by the section.[5]

10–004    **Destroyed bill.** The section does not apply in its wording to the case where a bill is destroyed, and not merely lost.[6] If a bill is intentionally destroyed by the holder or his agent, it will be taken to have been cancelled under section 63(1). But if a bill is destroyed unintentionally, or under a mistake, or without the authority of the holder, it will not be cancelled.[7] The question then arises whether the former holder has any right under the present section to require a duplicate to be given to him by the drawer. In Canada it has been held that, by virtue of the rules of common law as saved by the Act,[8] the holder of a destroyed instrument is likewise entitled to obtain a duplicate of it.[9] On the other hand, an Australian court[10] has held that the section does not apply where a bill has been destroyed: in that case the bill is gone and is no longer in existence, and therefore there is no occasion to give security.

### Action on lost bill

10–005        70. In any action or proceeding upon a bill, the court or a judge may order that the loss of the instrument shall not be set up, provided an indemnity be given to the satisfaction of the court or judge against the claims of any other person upon the instrument in question.

---

[5] cf. *Harvey Jones Ltd v Woolwich plc* [2001] Q.B. 541 (s.64, Illustration 7).
[6] Contrast s.51(8).
[7] s.63(3).
[8] s.97(2).
[9] *Bank of Canada v Bank of Montreal* (1971) 24 D.L.R. (3d) 13.
[10] *Ex p. Walker* (1892) 9 W.N. (N.S.W.) 1, 2.

Repeal

This section, as it applies to Northern Ireland, has been repealed by s.122(2) and Sched. 7 of the Judicature (Northern Ireland) Act 1978.

| Definitions | Comparison |
|---|---|
| "action": s.2. | UCC: §§ 3–309, 3–312. |
| "bill": s.2. | UNB: arts 78–83. |

## COMMENT

**Lost instruments.** The finder of a lost bill, cheque or note has no title    **10–006** to it and can maintain no action against any party to the instrument. He may be compelled to deliver up the instrument to its true owner[11] and will be liable to an action in conversion or for money had and received at the suit of the true owner if he wrongfully deals with the instrument or its proceeds.[12] However, if the instrument is payable to bearer, payment to him at or after maturity by or on behalf of the drawee, acceptor or maker in good faith and without notice that his title to the instrument is defective will constitute payment in due course and discharge the instrument.[13] But payment to the finder of an instrument payable to order will not be a good discharge,[14] except that a banker who pays a cheque or other instrument drawn on him may in certain circumstances be protected by statute[15] and be deemed to have paid the instrument in due course.

Where the finder of a lost bearer instrument transfers it by delivery to a holder in due course,[16] that holder will acquire a good title to the instrument and is entitled to compel payment by the parties liable thereon.[17] But, in the case of an instrument payable to order, if the finder forges the indorsement of the holder and purports to negotiate the instrument—even to a person who takes it in good faith and for value and without notice of the defect of title, no right to retain the instrument or to enforce payment thereof against any party thereto can be acquired through or under the forged indorsement, unless the party against whom

---

[11] See above, para.3–051 (s.24).
[12] See above, para.3–050 (s.24).
[13] See above, para.8–011 (s.59).
[14] See above, para.3–066 (s.24), 8–011 (s.59).
[15] Stamp Act 1853, s.19; Bills of Exchange Act 1882, ss.60, 80; Cheques Act 1957, s.1.
[16] Defined in s.29.
[17] See above, paras 3–078, 4–051, 5–074.

it is sought to retain or enforce payment of the instrument is precluded from setting up the forgery.[18]

**10–007**     **Action on lost instrument.** At common law, no action could be brought on a lost bill or note, if negotiable,[19] even though it was an order bill and was unindorsed by the holder[20] and even though the defendant tendered an indemnity.[21] Nor could an action be brought on the consideration.[22] The courts were concerned lest the instrument should be found and the parties exposed to the risk of a second action by a bona fide holder.[23] But the position was otherwise in equity: the former holder could obtain relief upon giving an indemnity.[24] By section 87 of the Common Law Procedure Act 1854,[25] it was provided that, in case of any action founded upon a bill of exchange[26] or other negotiable instrument, the Court or a judge might order that the loss of the instrument should not be set up, provided an indemnity was given, to the satisfaction of the Court, or judge, or a master, against the claims of any other person upon the instrument. The present section reproduces the effect of that provision and provides a remedy which is available in any court. It applies, however, only to a bill of exchange, cheque or promissory note as defined in the 1882 Act. Section 87 of the 1854 Act (which remains unrepealed)[27] applies more generally to any negotiable instrument,[28] but is limited to actions in the Supreme Court. In the present section, "action" includes counter-claim and set-off.[29]

Although the former holder cannot present the lost instrument for payment to the person designated by it as payer,[30] he should nevertheless make a demand for payment on the due date. If not paid, he must give due notice of dishonour to charge the drawer and any indorser.[31] By

---

[18] s.24. See above, para.3–066.

[19] *cf. Wain v Bailey* (1839) 10 A. & E. 616; *Charnley v Grundy* (1854) 14 C.B. 608.

[20] *Ramuz v Crowe* (1847) 1 Ex. 167. *cf. Long v Bailie* (1805) 2 Camp. 214n.; *Rolt v Watson* (1827) 4 Bing. 273.

[21] *Pierson v Hutchinson* (1809) 2 Camp. 211; *Hansard v Robinson* (1827) 7 B. & C. 90.

[22] *Crowe v Clay* (1859) 9 Ex. 604; *Champion v Terry* (1822) 3 Brod. & B. 295. *Cf. Rolt v Watson* (1827) 4 Bing. 273.

[23] *Pierson v Hutchinson* (1809) 2 Camp. 211 at 213.

[24] *Hansard v Robinson* (1827) 7 B. & C. 90 at 95; *Rolt v Watson* (1827) 4 Bing. 273 at 274; *Macartney v Graham* (1828) 2 Sim. 285; *King v Zimmerman* (1871) L.R. 6 C.P. 466, 468.

[25] 17 & 18 Vict., c.125.

[26] The words "bill of exchange or other" in s.87 of the 1854 Act were repealed by the Statute Law Revision Act 1892.

[27] Except in part: see n.26, above.

[28] *Australian Joint Stock Bank v Oriental Bank* (1866) 5 S.C.R. (N.S.W.) 129 (banknote); *Conflans Stone Quarry Ltd v Parker* (1867) L.R. 3 C.P. 1 (circular note).

[29] s.2.

[30] ss.45, 46.

[31] *Thackray v Blackett* (1811) 3 Camp. 164. See s.49.

section 51(8) of the Act, protest may be made on a copy or written particulars of a lost or destroyed instrument.

**Procedure.** The defendant should plead the non-production of the instrument in his defence.[32] He need not ask for an indemnity. The claimant[33] should then tender an indemnity and apply to strike out the defence in so far as it is based on the loss of the instrument. But a claimant who commences an action on a lost instrument without first tendering an indemnity may be penalised in costs.[34] The indemnity should be in such terms as will indemnify the defendant against any loss or expense to which he is or may be put by reason of the other party's having lost the instrument in question.[35] If the parties cannot agree on the sufficiency of the indemnity, the claimant must satisfy the Court or Judge as to its sufficiency.[36] This would seem to be a matter of discretion. Should the lost instrument be a cheque crossed "account payee", there would seem to be no good reason why any indemnity should be required since the cheque is not transferable and is only valid between the parties thereto.[37]

10–008

**Destruction of instrument.** The section does not apply in its express terms to an instrument which has been destroyed.[38] It would appear that the common law rule against actions on a lost instrument did not apply to an instrument which was proved to have been destroyed.[39] The normal principle that secondary evidence is admissible to prove the contents of a missing document applied. It is therefore arguable that, if the destruction of an instrument is proved, no indemnity need be tendered: there is no risk of a claim being made by any other person on the instrument.[40] On the other hand, the evidence may be merely that the instrument has probably been destroyed, *e.g.* in a fire. In such a case, there would seem to be no reason of policy why the section should not be extended and an indemnity required of the former holder to safeguard the defendant should the instrument reappear.[41]

10–009

---

[32] *cf. Blackie v Pidding* (1848) 6 C.B. 196; *Charnley v Grundy* (1854) 14 C.B. 608.
[33] *Aranguren v Scholfield* (1856) 1 H. & N. 494.
[34] *King v Zimmerman* (1871) L.R. 6 C.P. 466, 468.
[35] *cf. King v Zimmerman* (1871) L.R. 6 C.P. 466 at 469.
[36] See *Walmsley v Child* (1749) 1 Ves. Sen. 341.
[37] s.81A.
[38] Contrast s.51(8).
[39] *Pierson v Hutchinson* (1809) 2 Camp. 211, 212; *Woodford v Whitely* (1830) Moo. & M. 517; *Blackie v Pidding* (1848) 6 C.B. 196; *Wright v Maidstone* (1855) 1 K. & J. 701. *cf. Hansard v Robinson* (1827) 7 B. & C. 90, 95.
[40] *Ex p. Walker* (1892) 9 W.N. (N.S.W.) 1.
[41] *Pillow & Hersey Co v L'Espérance* (1902) 22 Que.S.C. 213 (Quebec).

**10–010**    **Northern Ireland.** This section, as it applies to Northern Ireland, has been repealed.[42]

Bill in a Set

Rules as to sets

**11–001**    71. (1) Where a bill is drawn in a set, each part of the set being numbered, and containing a reference to the other parts, the whole of the parts constitute one bill.

     (2) Where the holder of a set indorses two or more parts to different persons, he is liable on every such part, and every indorser subsequent to him is liable on the part he himself indorsed as if the said parts were separate bills.

     (3) Where two or more parts of a set are negotiated to different holders in due course, the holder whose title first accrues is as between such holders deemed the true owner of the bill; but nothing in this subsection shall affect the rights of a person who in due course accepts or pays the part first presented to him.

     (4) The acceptance may be written on any part, and it must be written on one part only.

       If the drawee accepts more than one part, and such accepted parts get into the hands of different holders in due course, he is liable on every such part as if it were a separate bill.

     (5) When the acceptor of a bill drawn in a set pays it without requiring the part bearing his acceptance to be delivered up to him, and that part at maturity is outstanding in the hands of a holder in due course, he is liable to the holder thereof.

     (6) Subject to the preceding rules, where any one part of a bill drawn in a set is discharged by payment or otherwise, the whole bill is discharged.

| Definitions | Comparison |
|---|---|
| "acceptance": ss.2, 17.(1). | ULB: arts 64–66. |
| "bill": s.2. | ULC: arts 49, 50. |
| "holder": s.2. | |
| "holder in due course": s.29. | |
| "indorsement": s.2. | |
| "negotiated": s.31. | |

[42] Judicature (Northern Ireland) Act 1978, s.122(2) and Sch. 7.

"person": s.2.
"written": s.2.

## COMMENT

**Bills in a set.** Bills are nowadays rarely drawn in a set. But bills so    **11–002**
drawn are still occasionally encountered in respect of international trading transactions. The bill will be drawn in a set of two or three parts. The
main purpose of issuing a bill in a set is to diminish the risk that a single
bill may be lost or delayed in the course of transmission by post. Two
parts of the bill will be forwarded by post, each under a separate cover.
Alternatively, one part may be indorsed and delivered to an indorsee, and
another part sent to the drawee for acceptance, thus giving the indorsee
security *vis-à-vis* the drawer during the interval.[1]

The Geneva Uniform Law or Bills of Exchange and Promissory Notes
likewise makes provision for bills of exchange to be drawn in a set of two
or more identical parts (*exemplaires*).[2] But it also provides that the holder
of a bill of exchange has the right to make copies of it (*copies*).[3] *Exemplaires*
and *copies* are dealt with distinctly in the Law. In contrast, the 1882 Act
makes no provision for copies, except in respect of the right of the holder
to obtain from the drawer a duplicate of a lost bill[4] and the ability to make
protest on a copy of a bill which is lost or destroyed or on written
particulars thereof.[5] It does, however, sanction an indorsement written on
a "copy" of a bill issued or negotiated in a country where "copies" are
recognised.[6]

The present section establishes the principle that the whole of the parts
of a set constitute one bill[7] but recognises that the parts may become
separated by indorsement to separate holders[8] or that the drawee may
accept more than one part, each part then getting into the hands of a
different holder in due course.[9]

The section does not apply to promissory notes.[10]

---

[1] *Byles* (27th ed.), p.43.
[2] ULB, arts 64–66.
[3] ULB, arts 67, 68.
[4] s.69.
[5] s.51(8).
[6] s.32(1).
[7] subs.(1)(6).
[8] subs.(2)(3).
[9] subs.(4).
[10] s.89(3)(d).

**11–003**     **Subsection (1): whole set but one bill.** Each part of a bill drawn in a set should be numbered ("First Bill of Exchange", "Second Bill of Exchange", etc.) and should contain a reference to the other parts ("second and third of the same tenor and date unpaid"). The whole of the parts then constitute one bill.[11] If one part of a set omits reference to the rest, it probably becomes a separate bill in the hands of a bona fide holder. In order to distinguish a separate bill from one drawn in a set, a bill may be drawn "Pay this sole Bill of Exchange" or "Pay this Sola of Exchange", and, where a printed form of bill is used with a space before "Bill of Exchange" it is advisable that the word "sole" be inserted if the bill is not drawn in a set.

**11–004**     **Subsection (2): separate indorsement of parts.** This subsection protects the holders in the event that two or more parts are indorsed to different persons. Before the Act it was held[12] that a person who negotiated a bill drawn in a set was bound to deliver up all the parts in his possession, but by negotiating one part he did not warrant that he had the rest. It was also said[13] that an indorser was not liable to pay a dishonoured set unless all the parts bearing his indorsement were delivered up to him or accounted for; but this would no longer be the case.

**11–005**     **Subsection (3): competing holders in due course.** Where two or more parts of a set are negotiated to different holders in due course, each negotiation is valid and the indorsers of each part will be liable to the respective holder.[14] But, as between competing holders in due course, the holder whose title first accrues is deemed the true holder of the bill.[15] However, this does not affect the rights of a person who in due course accepts[16] or pays the part first presented to him.

**11–006**     **Subsection (4): acceptance.** The drawee should accept only one part of a bill in a set. By accepting more than one part, he runs the risk that he will be liable on his separate acceptance to different holders in due course.[17]

**11–007**     **Subsections (5) and (6): payment and discharge.** The principle that the whole of the parts constitute one bill is maintained in subsection (6),

---

[11] *Davidson v Roberston* (1815) 3 Dow H.L. 218. *cf. Société Générale v Metropolitan Bank* (1873) 27 L.T. (N.S.) 849.

[12] *Pinard v Klockmann* (1863) 3 B. & S. s.388.

[13] *Société Générale v Metropolitan Bank* (1873) 27 L.T. (N.S.) 849 at 854.

[14] subs.(2).

[15] In *Holdsworth v Hunter* (1830) 10 B. & C. 449, 450, 454, it is suggested that the true holder is entitled to get the remaining part(s) from any holder in due course. But this is inconsistent with subs.(2).

[16] s.59(1).

[17] *Holdsworth v Hunter* (1830) 10 B. & C. 449. *cf. Ralli v Dennistoun* (1851) 6 Exch. 483, 496.

which provides that, where any one part of a bill drawn in a set is discharged by payment[18] or otherwise,[19] the whole bill is discharged. But this is subject to subsection (2) and (4), in the circumstances of which the parts separately indorsed or accepted will remain current and not be discharged. It is also subject to subsection (5). If, upon payment, the acceptor fails to require the part bearing his acceptance to be delivered up to him, and that part at maturity is outstanding in the hands of a holder in due course, he is liable to the holder thereof.[20]

## Conflict of Laws

### Rules where laws conflict

72. Where a bill drawn in one country is negotiated, accepted, or     12–001
payable in another, the rights, duties, and liabilities of the parties
thereto are determined as follows:

(1) The validity of a bill as regards requisites in form is determined by the law of the place of issue, and the validity as
regards requisites in form of the supervening contracts, such
as acceptance, or indorsement, or acceptance *suprà protest*, is
determined by the law of the place where such contract was
made.

Provided that—

(a) Where a bill is issued out of the United Kingdom it is not
invalid by reason only that it is not stamped in accordance with the law of the place of issue:

(b) Where a bill, issued out of the United Kingdom, conforms, as regard requisites in form, to the law of the
United Kingdom, it may, for the purpose of enforcing
payment thereof, be treated as valid as between all persons who negotiate, hold, or become parties to it in the
United Kingdom.

(2) Subject to the provisions of this Act, the interpretation of the
drawing, indorsement, acceptance, or acceptance *suprà protest*
of a bill, is determined by the law of the place where such
contract is made.

---

[18] Under s.59.
[19] Under ss.61–64. See *Société Général v Metropolitan Bank* (1873) 27 L.T. (N.S.) 849 (material alteration).
[20] *Kearney v West Granada Mining Co.* (1856) 1 H. & N. 412.

Provided that where an inland bill is indorsed in a foreign country the indorsement shall as regards the payer be interpreted according to the law of the United Kingdom.

(3) The duties of the holder with respect to presentment for acceptance or payment and the necessity for or sufficiency of a protest or notice of dishonour, or otherwise, are determined by the law of the place where the act is done or the bill is dishonoured.

(4) [*Repealed*].

(5) Where a bill is drawn in one country and is payable in another, the due date thereof is determined according to the law of the place where it is payable.

Repeal

Subs. (4) was repealed by ss.4, 32 and Sch.5, Pt I, of the Administration of Justice Act 1977.

Definitions

"acceptance": s.2.

"acceptance *suprà protest*": s.65.

"bill": s.2.

"holder": s.2.

"indorsement": s.2.

"inland bill": s.4.

"issue": s.2.

"person": s.2.

"United Kingdom": Interpretation Act 1978, s.5 and Sch.1.

Comparison

CCLB—see para.12–002, n.17.

CCLC—see para.12–002, n.17.

## COMMENT

**12–002**    **Conflict of laws.** This section lays down certain rules relating to the conflict of laws where a bill drawn in one country is negotiated, accepted, or payable in another.[1] It applies, with the necessary modifications, to cheques[2] and promissory notes.[3] The rights, duties and liabilities of the parties to the instrument are to be determined in accordance with the subsections which follow. Those sub-sections do not, however, resolve all the conflict of laws issues that may arise. They do not, for example, deal

---

[1] See Dicey and Morris, *Conflict of Laws* (13th ed.), 33–327; Cheshire and North, *Private International Law* (13th ed.), pp.547, 965; *Crawford and Falconbridge* (8th ed.), p.1710.

[2] s.73.

[3] s.89(1).

expressly with capacity to incur liability as a party to the instrument,[4] the need for consideration,[5] the effect of illegality,[6] the discharge of the instrument or of a party to it,[7] the transfer of the instrument,[8] the necessity for presentment for acceptance or payment,[9] the measure of damages,[10] and limitation of actions.[11] The law to be applied in such cases has to be derived by analogy from the express provisions of the section, or from the general principles of the conflict of laws applicable to contractual obligations, or from judicial decisions.

Negotiable instruments give rise to particular problems in the conflict of laws. In the first place, in every legal system by the law merchant: (1) the rights arising out of the instrument can be transferred by indorsement and delivery (and in some cases by mere delivery) of the instrument so that the parties liable thereon can be sued by the person who is for the time being in possession of the instrument, and (2) the transferee may acquire those rights free of defences available against his immediate transferor or previous holders of the instrument.[12] But legal systems differ as to the requirements for an effective transfer and as to the circumstances in which larger rights may be acquired by the transferee. These issues are dealt with only in part in section 72.[13] Otherwise, in English law, the negotiation of an instrument is to be treated as a matter involving the transfer of a chattel or tangible movable and governed by the law of the place where the instrument is at the time of the transfer.[14]

Secondly, a bill, cheque or note may involve not one but several contracts. In addition to the originating contract of the drawer of a bill or cheque or the maker of the note, there will be the "supervening"[15] contracts of the acceptor of a bill and (if the instrument has been indorsed) of the several indorsers. A bill may be drawn in one country, accepted in a second, indorsed in a third, and payable in a fourth. With certain exceptions,[16] the section adopts what is sometimes termed the "several laws" principle, that is to say, that each contract on the instrument is treated as independent of the others and is governed by its own

---

[4] See below, para.12–012.
[5] See below, para.12–011.
[6] See below, para.12–018.
[7] See below, para.12–022.
[8] See below, para.12–028.
[9] See below, para.12–031.
[10] See above, para.7–052 (s.57).
[11] See below, para.12–035.
[12] See above, para.5–002.
[13] See below, para.12–028.
[14] See below, para.12–028.
[15] s.72(1).
[16] ss.72(2) proviso, s.72(3) and s.72(5).

law.[17] It does not, as a general rule, adopt a "single law" or "interdependence" approach by which those various contracts are governed by a single law.

**12–003**      Thirdly, the object of a bill, cheque or note is to secure to the holder payment of the amount stated in the instrument. It might therefore be thought that, in determining the rights, duties and liabilities of the parties, considerable importance would be attached to the law of the place where the instrument is payable or to the law of the place where each separate obligation on the instrument is to be performed (the *lex loci solutionis*).[18] But, with respect to the several contracts on the instrument, the general rules set out in subsections (1) and (2) refer to the law of the place of contracting (the *lex loci contractus*) rather than to the *lex loci solutionis* as the law which governs requisites in form,[19] interpretation[20] and (probably) the legal effect[21] of those contracts. Those rules may be criticised as reflecting an out-dated approach to contractual obligations in the conflict of laws whereby matters both of form and of substance are governed by the *lex loci contractus*: the place of contracting may well be fortuitous.

However, it is arguable that, in the case of negotiable instruments, some simple and definite rule is required. From a practical point of view, it is preferable to avoid a more complex "proper law" approach which would require the law governing each contract on the instrument to be ascertained by reference to the system of law "with which the transaction had its closest and most real connection".[22] Suppose, for example, a seller in Germany agrees to manufacture and sell to an English buyer certain machinery to be shipped from Germany c.i.f. an English port,[23] the price being denominated in United States dollars and payment to made against tender of documents in Rotterdam, Holland. In pursuance of this contract the seller draws and issues in Germany a bill of exchange addressed to the buyer which is accepted in England by the buyer payable at a bank in Rotterdam. It is difficult to determine with which system of law the contract of the buyer as acceptor of the bill has its "closest and most real

---

[17] *Horne v Rouquette* (1878) 3 Q.B.D. 514, 520. See also the Geneva Convention for the Settlement of Certain Conflicts of Laws in Connection with Bills of Exchange and Promissory Notes ("CCLB"), arts 2, 3, 4 (but *cf*. arts 5, 8); Geneva Convention for the Settlement of Certain Conflicts of Laws in Connection with Cheques ("CCLC"), arts 4, 5 (but *cf*. arts 6, 7, 8).

[18] Story, *Conflict of Laws* (8th ed.), p.44, pl.317.

[19] s.72(1).

[20] s.72(2).

[21] See below, para.12–015.

[22] See Dicey and Morris, *Conflict of Laws* (13th ed.), 32–002. *cf. Banco Atlantico S.A. v British Bank of the Middle East* [1990] 2 Lloyd's Rep. 504, 507.

[23] In *H. Glynn (Covent Garden) Ltd v Wittleder* [1959] 2 Lloyd's Rep. 409, at 420, Pearson J. stated that there is "no general rule" as to "what you can expect the proper law of c.i.f. contracts to be". See now the Contracts (Applicable Law) Act 1990.

connection". There is also advantage in avoiding a solution which refers matters relating to the form of any contract on the bill and matters relating to the effect of the obligation to two different systems of law,[24] with resulting problems of classification.[25] While the selection of the *lex loci contractus* may not in all situations be ideal, it could be said to reflect more accurately the expectations of each of the parties to the instrument: that his contract should be governed by the law of the place where the relevant act of issue, acceptance or indorsement was done.[26]

Fourthly, in the case of bills and notes, all legal systems require certain formal steps to be taken before the holder can claim payment, at least against parties secondarily liable on the instrument, *e.g.* presentment for acceptance and payment, notice of dishonour, and protest. But the necessity for and the nature of those steps will vary in each legal system. Subsection (3) of the section deals with these issues in the conflict of laws, but the coverage of the subsection is not comprehensive.[27]

**Choice of law.** It would no doubt in theory be possible for a party to stipulate expressly on the instrument that his rights, duties and liabilities are to governed by a law other than that mentioned in section 72, and effect might then have to be given to his choice.[28] But such stipulations are never encountered. It is submitted that no implied or inferred choice of law could be set up in contradiction of the provisions of the section, nor could any express choice of law outside the instrument be regarded as valid. However, if a bill or note were to contain a heading which clearly indicated that it was subject to the United Nations Convention on International Bills of Exchange and International Promissory Notes (the UNCITRAL Convention) and were otherwise to fulfil the requirements for the application of that Convention, it could be presumed that any party to such a bill or note intended his rights, duties and obligations to be governed by that Convention to the exclusion of any national law to which, under section 72, they would be subject.[29] **12–004**

**Contracts (Applicable Law) Act 1990.** This Act provides for the Rome Convention on the Law applicable to Contractual Obligations to have **12–005**

---

[24] CCLB, arts 3, 4; CCLC, arts 4, 5.
[25] See below, para.12–015.
[26] The place of payment may also not be certain: see *Bank Polski v Mulder & Co.* [1941] 2 K.B. 266; [1942] 1 K.B. 497 (Illustration 9).
[27] See below, para.12–031.
[28] *cf. Centrax Ltd v Citibank NA* [1999] 1 All E.R. (Comm) 557 (agreement off instrument).
[29] But the UNCITRAL Convention (UNB) for the most part, deals only with the "substantive" law of bills and notes. There is still considerable scope for the application of private international law, and this raises problems in the context of an international régime. See *Crawford and Falconbridge* (8th ed.), p.1731.

effect in the United Kingdom.[30] But by Article 1(2)(c) of the Convention, its rules do not apply to "obligations arising under bills of exchange, cheques or promissory notes" or to "other negotiable instruments to the extent that the obligations under such other negotiable instruments arise out of their negotiable character".

**12–006** **Scope of section 72.** The question arises whether the provisions of section 72 are limited to bills, cheques and promissory notes as defined by the 1882 Act.[31] In *G & H Montage GmbH v Irvani*,[32] at first instance Saville J. expressed the opinion that the special conflict rules set out in the section applied only to instruments as so defined. So, for example, if the order or promise to pay contained in a bill or note drawn in a foreign country is not unconditional,[33] or if the sum to be paid is not certain,[34] these special rules would be inapplicable because the instrument would not be a bill or note recognised by the Act under English law.[35] On another view, however, it is arguable that the section should be more broadly interpreted and that subsection (1) specifically refers the issue of the validity of a bill as regards requisites in form to be determined by the law of the place of issue.[36] If, therefore, the instrument would be regarded as a valid bill under that law, then it will be so recognised in England and the rights, duties and liabilities of the parties thereto will be determined in accordance with the provisions of the section.

If it is assumed that the opinion of Saville J. is correct, the further question arises as to what conflict rules (if any) should be applied in respect of an instrument which is not a bill, cheque or note as defined by the Act. The difficulty here is that it is well established that it is for English law, as the *lex fori*, to determine whether or not an instrument is negotiable.[37] An instrument which does not comply with the statutory definitions contained in the Act will not be negotiable in English law, unless it has acquired the characteristic of negotiability by English mercantile custom. The fact that it is negotiable under a foreign law, *e.g.* the law of the place of its issue, is normally irrelevant.[38] But an instrument, for instance, a traveller's cheque,[39] might not be a bill, cheque or note as defined by the Act, yet still be negotiable by English mercantile custom.

---

[30] And also the Luxembourg Convention, and the Brussels Protocol, see s.1(b)(c).

[31] See Dicey and Morris *Conflict of Laws* (13th ed.), 33–331.

[32] [1988] 1 W.L.R. 1285, 1289. See also on appeal: [1990] 1 W.L.R. 667, 678.

[33] See above, para.2–009.

[34] See above, para.2–014.

[35] s.3(1).

[36] See below, para.12–007.

[37] *Picker v London and County Banking Co.* (1887) 18 Q.B.D. 515; Dicey and Morris *Conflict of Laws* (13th ed.), 33–315, 33–321.

[38] But see below, para.12–028 (transfers of instrument abroad).

[39] See below, para.13–011.

In such a case, it would appear that the provisions of section 72—though not directly applicable—would be applied by analogy[40] or possibly as rules of common law which are preserved by section 97(2) of the Act.

**Subsection (1): requisites in form.** The validity of a bill as regards **12–007** requisites in form is determined by the law of the place of issue. So, for example, the law of the place of issue will determine whether the term "bill of exchange" or "promissory note" must be inserted in the body of the instrument (as required by the Geneva Uniform Law on Bills of Exchange and Promissory Notes)[41] or whether this is unnecessary (as under the 1882 Act),[42] and that law may, it seems, determine whether the order or promise to pay is conditional or unconditional.[43] "Issue" is defined in section 2 of the Act to mean the first delivery of a bill or note, complete in form,[44] to a person who takes it as holder.[45]

The validity as regards requisites in form of an acceptance of a bill is determined by the law of the place where the contract of acceptance is made. "Acceptance" is defined in section 2 to mean an acceptance completed by delivery or notification. Thus the question whether the mere signature of the drawee is sufficient to constitute an acceptance[46] or whether it must be accompanied by the word "accepted" or an equivalent term is a matter to be determined by the law of the place where the acceptance is completed by delivery or notification.[47]

The validity as regards requisites in form of an indorsement is determined by the law of the place where the contract of indorsement is made.[48] So, for example, if a bill drawn in France and accepted in England is indorsed by the payee in France, the question whether the indorsement is valid as regards requisites in form is to be determined by the law of France.[49] By section 2 of the Act, "indorsement" means an indorsement completed by delivery. The contract of indorsement is therefore made where delivery is effected, not where the signature of the indorser is attached.[50]

---

[40] *G & H Montage GmbH v Irvani* [1990] 1 W.L.R. 667, 680 (Illustration 10).
[41] ULB, arts 1, 75.
[42] See above, para.2–007.
[43] *Guaranty Trust Co. of New York v Hannay & Co.* [1918] 1 K.B. 43, 55; [1918] 2 K.B. 623, 634, 670. But see above, para.12–006.
[44] See Dicey and Morris, *Conflict of Laws* (13th ed.), 33–335 on the law to be applied to determine this question.
[45] See also s.84 (notes).
[46] s.17(2)(a).
[47] s.21(1), proviso.
[48] But see s.32(1) (indorsement on a "copy").
[49] *Koechlin et Cie v Kestenbaum Bros* [1927] 1 K.B. 889 (Illustration 8).
[50] *Banco Atlantico S.A. v British Bank of the Middle East* [1990] 2 Lloyds Rep. 504, 507. *cf. G. & H. Montage GmbH v Irvani* [1990] 1 W.L.R. 667, 668, 689.

12–008     The validity of other "supervening" contracts on the instrument, *e.g.* of an acceptance *suprà protest*[51] or of an *"aval"*,[52] is likewise determined, as regards requisites in form, by the law of the place where such contract was made.

The effect of subsection (1), apart from the provisos, would therefore appear to be as follows: (i) if an instrument is in form invalid by the law of the place of its issue or if any necessary indorsement is in form invalid by the law of the place of indorsement,[53] a holder cannot enforce it in the United Kingdom; (ii) if any other supervening contract, *e.g.* an acceptance or anomalous indorsement,[54] is in form invalid by the law of the place where the contract is made, the instrument is not enforceable in the United Kingdom against the party to that contract, but may be enforceable against other parties liable thereon; (iii) if an indorsement is formally valid by the law of the place of indorsement, the fact that the indorsement is in form invalid by the law of the United Kingdom will not preclude an action upon it here; (iv) if any other supervening contract, *e.g.* an acceptance or an *"aval"*,[55] is formally valid by the law of the place where the contract is made, but not by the law of the United Kingdom, it is nevertheless enforceable here against the party who entered into such contract.

12–009     **Proviso (1)(a): foreign stamp laws.** Any objection that an instrument issued out of the United Kingdom is invalid under the law of the place of issue merely on the ground that it is not stamped or is insufficiently stamped is removed by this proviso.[56] Bills, cheques and notes issued in the United Kingdom no longer require a stamp.[57]

12–010     **Proviso (1)(b): instruments issued abroad.** The second proviso to subsection (1), which applies also to cheques and promissory notes issued out of the United Kingdom, confirms the decision (though not the reasoning) in the pre-Act case of *Re Marseilles Extension Railway and Land Co.*[58] Its scope is limited by three factors: first, the bill issued abroad must conform, as regards requisites in form, to the law of the United Kingdom; secondly, it is only to be treated as valid "for the purpose of enforcing

---

[51] s.65.
[52] See above, para.7–039.
[53] *Bradlaugh v De Rin (No.2)* (1868) L.R. 3 C.P. 538; (1870) L.R. 5 C.P. 473 (Illustration 3). But see s.55(2)(c) (estoppel of indorser) and below, para.12–028 (transfer).
[54] s.56.
[55] See above, para.7–039.
[56] Even before the Act, if a bill, through want of a stamp, was merely inadmissible in evidence according to the law of the place of its issue, it was admissible in evidence here if it conformed to the requirements of the English stamp laws relating to foreign bills. See *Boristow v Sequeville* (1850) 5 Exch. 275.
[57] Finance Act 1970, s.32 and Sch.7, para.2.
[58] (1885) 30 Ch.D. 598 (Illustration 4).

payment thereof" and not—it seems—for the purpose of obtaining a declaration that the holder of the bill who has been paid is entitled to retain the money[59]; thirdly, it is only to be treated as valid between persons who negotiate, hold or become parties to it in the United Kingdom.

For example, a bill is issued in France payable to order in a form which complies with the law of the United Kingdom. It is indorsed in France by the payee in a form which is invalid to effect a negotiation by French law. For the purpose of enforcing payment, the bill will be valid between a holder to whom it is subsequently indorsed in the United Kingdom,[60] and a drawee who accepted it in the United Kingdom,[61] between such a holder and the subsequent indorser, and between such indorser and the acceptor. But it will not be enforceable against the drawer or the payee who indorsed it in France. Nor will such a bill be enforceable, for instance, between a holder in the United Kingdom and a drawee who accepted it in France, between a holder in France and a person who accepted or indorsed the bill in the United Kingdom,[62] or between an indorser here and a drawee who accepted in France.

The purpose of the proviso may have been to facilitate the negotiation, in the United Kingdom, of bills issued (or accepted or indorsed) abroad. It is true that it does render valid, as between certain parties, the negotiation, in the United Kingdom, of a bill which, for example, is in form invalid by the law of the place of issue but which conforms, as regards requisites in form, to the law of the United Kingdom. However, in the context of section 72, it is capable of producing anomalous results.[63] In particular, the proviso only applies if the instrument is issued abroad. If a bill is drawn payable to order and issued in the United Kingdom, but is accepted and payable in France, an indorsement in France which is in form invalid under French law will pass no title to or right to sue on the bill. Subsequent indorsements in the United Kingdom will not cure the defect as to any party,[64] since the chain of indorsements to the holder is incomplete. It is curious that, under the proviso, greater validity is in certain circumstances given to a bill issued abroad which complies with

---

[59] *Guaranty Trust Co. of New York v Hannay & Co.* [1918] 1 K.B. 43; [1918] 2 K.B. 623, 648, 670.
[60] The expression "persons who ... hold ... it in the United Kingdom" is imprecise; it would seem that a person must become the holder by indorsement and delivery (or delivery) to him in the United Kingdom, *i.e.* he must receive it in the United Kingdom.
[61] *Re Marseilles Extension Railway and Land Co.* (1885) 30 Ch. D. 598.
[62] *Bradlaugh v De Rin (No.2)* (1868) L.R. 3 C.P. 538; (1870) L.R. 5.C.P. 473 (Illustration 3) (unless the claimant became a holder in the United Kingdom).
[63] See *Crawford and Falconbridge* (8th ed.), p.1714.
[64] But see s.55(2) (estoppel of indorser).

United Kingdom requirements of form than a bill which is issued in the
United Kingdom in conformity with those same requirements.

12–011    **Consideration.** The question whether consideration is required to support any contract on a bill is probably, by analogy, governed by the law of
the place where the contract was made.[65]

12–012    **Capacity.**[66] An individual's capacity to contract may be governed by
the law of his domicile and residence.[67] If he lacks capacity by the *lex
domicilii*, it would seem that he may yet have capacity by the system of
law with which the transaction is most closely connected.[68] In the case of
bills, cheques and notes, however, it is submitted that it is preferable[69] to
apply to an individual's capacity to incur liability on the instrument the
general rule embodied in subsections (1) and (2), that is to say, the
governing law is that of the place where the contract in question was
made.[70] The capacity of a corporation to incur liability on the instrument
should likewise in principle be determined by the law of the place of
contracting. But the capacity of a corporation to contract will be further
limited by its constitution, which matter must be governed by the law of
the place of its incorporation.[71]

12–013    **Subsection (2): interpretation.** Subject to the provisions of the Act,[72]
the interpretation of each several contract on the instrument is to be
determined by the law of the place where such contract was made. Thus
the law of the place of contracting will determine whether an acceptance
is to be interpreted as general or qualified,[73] whether an indorsement
with the word *für mich* ("for me") in German is to be interpreted as an
open indorsement or as a restrictive indorsement which prohibits further

[65] See Dicey and Morris, *Conflict of Laws* (13th ed.), 33–335. The point was left open in *Wragge
v Sims Cooper & Co. (Australia) Pty Ltd* (1933) 50 C.L.R. 483.
[66] See Fisher (1951) 14 M.L.R. 144.
[67] *Cooper v Cooper* (1888) 13 App. Cas. 88, 108. See also *Sottomayor v De Barros (No.1)* (1877)
3 P.D. 1, 5; *Re Cooke's Trusts* (1887) 56 L.J. Ch. 637, 639.
[68] Dicey and Morris *Conflict of Laws* (13th ed.), 32–214. See also *Charron v Montreal Trust Co.*
(1958) 15 D.L.R. (2d) 240; *Bodley Head Ltd v Flegon* [1972] 1 W.L.R. 680.
[69] But see the wording of s.22(1) which might be taken to preclude this approach.
[70] *Bondholders Securities Corp. v Manville* [1933] 4 D.L.R. 699. See also (outside bills of
exchange) *Male v Roberts* (1800) 3 Esp. 163; *McFeetridge v Stewarts and Lloyds Ltd* 1913 S.C.
773; *Baindail v Baindail* [1946] p.122, 128; *Stevensen Estate v Siewert* (2000) 191 D.L.R. (4th)
151, (2001) 20 D.L.R. (4th) 295.
[71] Dicey and Morris *Conflict of Laws* (13th ed.), 30–021.
[72] *i.e.* the remaining provisions of s.72, and (possibly) to ss.15, 53, 57.
[73] *Bank Polski v Mulder (K.J.) & Co.* [1941] 2 K.B. 266; [1942] 1 K.B. 497 (Illustration 9). See also
*Sanders v St Helens Smelting Co. Ltd* (1906) 39 N.S.R. 370.

negotiation of the bill,[74] whether an *"aval"* on a bill on which the words and figures differ is to be interpreted as a guarantee of the amount expressed in words or the amount expressed in figures,[75] and (*semble*) whether a bill or note in the terms "Pay C" without the addition of the words "or order" is or is not to be interpreted as an instrument payable to order and therefore negotiable.[76] As in the case of subsection (1), the place where the contract was made is not necessarily the place where the party signed the instrument, but the place where the contract was completed by delivery[77] or, in the case of an acceptance, by delivery or notification.[78]

Prior to the enactment of the Act the law was uncertain and incomplete. The liability of the acceptor of a bill or the maker of a note, as between himself and a person suing on the instrument, appears in principle to have been governed by the law of the place where the bill was accepted or the note was made,[79] but possibly on the assumption that it was at that place that the acceptor or maker undertook to pay.[80] If a bill payable to order was drawn and accepted in England, and then indorsed in France in a manner which was invalid to effect a negotiation by the law of France but which was valid by English law, the holder could sue the acceptor on the bill, since the contract of the acceptor was to pay to an order valid by the law of England.[81] On the other hand, if a note was made in France in favour of a payee in France, and subsequently negotiated in France, the indorsement would be subject to French law.[82]

However, in *Bradlaugh v De Rin (No.2)*,[83] an "intermediate" situation arose. A bill was drawn in France but accepted in England. It was indorsed in France in a form invalid by the law of France. In an action by an indorsee against the acceptor, a majority of the Court of Common Pleas[84] held that the indorsement was governed by the law of the place where it was made (*locus regit actum*), on the ground that it would be

---

[74] *Haarbleicher v Baerselman* (1914) 137 L.T.J. 564 (Illustration 7).
[75] *G. & H. Montage GmbH v Irvani* [1990] 1 Lloyd's Rep. 14 (Illustration 10).
[76] See ss.9(1)(4). Contrast *Robertson v Burdekin* (1843) 1 Ross, Scots L.C. 824.
[77] ss.2, 84. See also (on an *"aval"*) *G. & H. Montage GmbH v Irvani* [1990] 1 W.L.R. 667 (but see *G. & H. Montage GmbH v Irvani* at 688, 689); *Banco Atlantico S.A. v British Bank of the Middle East*, [1990] 2 Lloyd's Rep. 504, 507.
[78] *Nova (Jersey) Knit Ltd v Kammgarn Spinnerei GmbH* [1977] 1 W.L.R. 713, 718.
[79] *Trimbey v Vignier* (1834) 1 Bing. N.C. 151, 159; *Allen v Kemble* (1848) 6 Moo. P.C. 314, 321; *Lebel v Tucker* (1867) L.R. 3 Q.B. 77; *Re Marseilles and Extension Railway and Land Co.* (1885) 30 Ch.D. 598 (pre-Act cases).
[80] Story, *Conflict of Laws* (8th ed.), p.44, pl.317.
[81] *Lebel v Tucker* (1867) L.R. 3 Q.B. 77 (Illustration 2).
[82] *Trimbey v Vignier* (1834) 1 Bing. N.C. 151 (Illustration 1).
[83] (1868) L.R. 3 C.P. 538; (1870) L.R. 5 C.P. 473 (Illustration 3).
[84] Reversed (1875) L.R. 5 C.P 473, but only on the question whether the form was valid by the law of France.

anomalous if the indorsee could sue the acceptor, but not the drawer, on the bill. It seems probable that Chalmers intended, in subsection (2) and in the proviso, to codify the existing rules of the common law.[85] He appears to have been conscious of the fact that his selection of the law of the place of contracting, and not the *lex loci solutionis*, as the law governing the various contracts on a bill might attract criticism.

12–014      Commenting on subsection (2),[86] he stated:

> "Story, § 154, points out the reasons of the rule adopted in this subsection. 'It has sometimes been suggested', he says, 'that this doctrine is a departure from the rule that the law of the place of payment is to govern, But, correctly considered, it is entirely in conformity with that rule. The drawer and indorsers do not contract to pay the money in the foreign place on which the bill is drawn, but only to guarantee its acceptance and payment in that place by the drawee; and in default of such payment, they agree upon due notice to reimburse the holder in principal and damages where they respectively entered into the contract.' "

And Chalmers continued[87]:

> "The case of a bill accepted in one country but payable in another gives rise to difficulty. Suppose a bill is accepted in France, payable in England. Probably the maxim, *Contraxisse unusquisque in eo loco intelligitur in quo ut solveret se obligavit*[88] would apply. But if not, then comes the question, what is the French law, not as to bills accepted and payable in France, but as to bills accepted in France payable in England? Probably the *lex loci solutionis* would be regarded."

Whatever the intention of Chalmers may have been, the wording of subsection (2) is, in matters of interpretation, clear and unequivocal: the law to be applied is—subject to the proviso—the law of the place where the contract was made. No doubt, in practice, the place of contracting and the place where payment is to be made will often coincide. But, where they differ, as in the case where a bill is accepted in one country but payable in another, the law of the place of contracting will apply and not the law of the place of payment. There is no way, either as a matter of construction or (as suggested by Chalmers) by application of the doctrine

---

[85] *Cooper v Waldergrave* (1840) 2 Beav. 282, 284; *Allen v Kemble* (1878) 6 Moo. P.C. 314, 321.
[86] 9th ed., p.282.
[87] 9th ed., p.282.
[88] Each person is deemed to have contracted in that place which he has undertaken to perform: Dig. 44.7.21.

of *renvoi*,[89] by which reference can be made to the *lex loci solutionis* as the governing law.

**Legal effect.** The view has been expressed[90] that the word "inter- **12–015** pretation" in subsection (2) should be narrowly construed so as to exclude the legal effect or essential validity of the contract. The propo-nents of this view appear to be motivated, not only by a desire for semantic accuracy, but by a wish to apply to the contractual obligations of parties to bills and notes the more modern principle of the "proper law",[91] that is to say, in the absence of any express or inferred choice of law, a contract is governed by the system of law with which the transac-tion has its closest and most real connection. This would, in the case of bills and notes, often be the law of the place where, under the particular contract, payment was or was expected to be made.[92] The preponderance of judicial opinion is, however, that "interpretation" extends to the legal effect of the contract.[93] Chalmers, too, was of that opinion[94]: "The term 'interpretation', in this subsection, it is submitted, clearly includes the obligations of the parties as deduced from such interpretation." Indeed, it would be remarkable if section 72 dealt, in subsections (1) and (2), only with questions of form and interpretation, but did not deal with the law applicable to the legal effect of the various contracts on the instrument. Although in this respect resort to the law of the place of contracting may appear old-fashioned and (in some cases at least) inconvenient,[95] it has the merit of simplicity in that, in principle, the same law is applied to matters of formal validity, interpretation and legal effect. The court is thus

---

[89] *Renvoi* has no place in law of contract: see Dicey and Morris *Conflict of Laws* (13th ed.), 32–042.

[90] Dicey and Morris *Conflict of Laws* (13th ed.), 33–344.

[91] Dicey and Morris *Conflict of Laws* (13th ed.), 32–005. But see now the Contracts (Applicable Law) Act 1990; above, para.12–005.

[92] But (*semble*) it would also be necessary, in determining the proper law, to have regard to the place where the bill or note was itself payable and, possibly, to the transaction underlying the contract in question. See the criticism of the "proper law" solution as applied to bills and notes in *Crawford and Falconbridge* (8th ed.), p.1337 and above, para.12–003.

[93] *Alcock v Smith* [1892] 1 Ch. 238, 256, 263 (Romer J. and Lindley L.J.); *Embiricos v Anglo-Austrian Bank* [1905] 1 K.B. 677, 686, 687 (Romer J. and Stirling L.J.); *Koechlin et Cie v Kestenbaum Bros* [1927] 1 K.B. 889, 899 (Sargant L.J.); *Banku Polskiego v Mulder (K.J.) & Co.* [1942] 1 K.B. 497, 500 (Mackinnon L.J.); *Nova (Jersey) Knit v Kammgarn Spinnerei* [1977] 1 W.L.R. 713, 718 (H.L.); *G. & H. Montage GmbH v Irvani* [1990] 1 W.L.R. 667, 675; *Banco Atlantico S.A. v British Bank of the Middle East* [1990] 2 Lloyd's Rep. 504, 507. See also *Wragge v Sims Cooper & Co. (Australia) Pty Ltd* (1933) 50 C.L.R. 483, 491; *Rooney v Dawson* (1958) 15 D.L.R. (2d) 102; *Canada Life Assurance Co. v Canadian Imperial Bank of Commerce* (1979) 98 D.L.R. (3d) 670, 682. Contrast *Guaranty Trust Co. of New York v Hannay & Co.* [1918] 2 K.B. 623, 670; *Embiricos v Anglo-Austrian Bank* [1904] 2 K.B. 870, 875–876; [1905] 1 K.B. 677, 685.

[94] 9th ed., p.282.

[95] For an example, see Dicey and Morris *Conflict of Laws* (13th ed.), 33–344.

relieved, for the most part,[96] from having to decide whether a particular issue is to be characterised as one relating to the formal validity of the contract or to its essential validity—matters which, having regard to the formal nature of bills and notes, may be indistinguishable.[97]

There are, however, very few reported cases in appellate courts in England where subsection (2) has been applied to the legal effect of a contract on an instrument. In *Embiricos v Anglo-Austrian Bank*,[98] Stirling L.J.[99] considered that it determined the effect of a forged indorsement in Austria of a cheque drawn in Romania on a London Bank whereby, under Austrian law, a good title to the cheque passed by the indorsement to a bona fide indorsee. In *Nova (Jersey) Knit Ltd v Kammgarn Spinnerei GmbH*[1] a majority of the House of Lords[2] stated that, by virtue of the subsection,[3] English law applied to all questions as to the effect of acceptances of bills drawn in England on a drawee in Germany where the acceptances had been completed by delivery or notification in England. And in *G. & H. Montage GmbH v Irvani*,[4] Purchas and Woolf L.JJ.[5] in the Court of Appeal held that it operated so as to apply German law to the effect of an *"aval"* placed in Germany on bills drawn in Germany and accepted in Iran. In the same case, however, Mustill L.J.[6] was of the opinion that subsection (2) applied only by analogy, since an *"aval"* was not an indorsement as referred to in the subsection.

**12–016**     **Cheques.** Section 72 applies "where a bill drawn in one country is negotiated, accepted or payable in another". If a cheque is drawn in country A on a bank in that country and delivered to the payee in country B, it might be argued that the section does not apply because the cheque is drawn and payable in the same country. But it is clear that the reference to "the law of the place of issue" in subsection (1) and the reference to "the law of the place where such contract is made" in subsection (2) indicate that the relevant place is not the country where the drawer signed the cheque but the place where the contract of the drawer was completed by delivery to give effect thereto.[7] Subsection (2) applies

---

[96] But not entirely, since subss.(1) and (2) are subject to different provisos.
[97] A point made by Dicey and Morris *Conflict of Laws* (13th ed.), 33–344.
[98] [1904] 2 K.B. 870, 875. But see below, para.12–028.
[99] And also, with less emphasis, Romer L.J. But *cf.* Vaughan Williams L.J. See also *Koechlin et Cie v Kestenbaum Bros* [1927] 1 K.B. 889, 899.
[1] [1977] 1 W.L.R. 713, 718.
[2] [1977] 1 W.L.R. 713 at 718, 722, 729.
[3] But Lord Wilberforce stated (at 718) that the proper law would be the same.
[4] [1990] 1 W.L.R. 667. See also *Banco Atlantico S.A. v British Bank of the Middle East* [1990] 2 Lloyd's Rep. 504.
[5] [1990] 1 W.L.R. 667 at 687, 688.
[6] [1990] 1 W.L.R. 667 at 675, 679, 680. See also *Banco Atlantico S.A. v British Bank of the Middle East* [1990] 2 Lloyd's Rep. 504.
[7] s.21(1).

equally to cheques, so that the interpretation and legal effect of the contract of the drawer and indorsers on the instrument will be determined by the law of the place where each such contract was made. Thus, in the above example, the law applicable to the contract of the drawer on the cheque will be that of country B.[8] There is, it is submitted, no ground[9] on which the law may be displaced in favour of the law of the place on which the cheque is drawn and where it is payable, or the law applicable to the transaction underlying the issue or negotiation of the cheque.

**Proviso: inland bills indorsed abroad.** The proviso to subsection (2) **12–017** confirms the effect of the pre-Act case of *Lebel v Tucker*.[10] Its application is confined to the interpretation of an indorsement abroad of an inland bill (or note).[11] An inland bill is a bill which is or on the face of it purports to be (a) both drawn and payable within the British Islands, or (b) drawn within the British Islands upon some person resident there.[12] Thus if a bill is drawn, accepted and payable in England, but is indorsed in France, then in an action by the holder of the bill against the acceptor the "interpretation" of the indorsement is governed by the law of England.[13] However, the words "as regards the payer" restrict the operation of the proviso to cases where payment is claimed from or made by[14] the payer of the instrument, *i.e.* the acceptor of the bill or the maker of the note. It does not apply to a case where the issue is in reality which of two persons is entitled as against the other to claim payment from the payer as holder of the instrument.[15] Nor would it apply if an action were brought in conversion or for money had and received by the true owner against a collecting banker who had wrongfully collected the instrument. On the other hand, in contrast with proviso (b) to subsection (1), the holder need not be a holder in the United Kingdom.

**Illegality.** The general rule that the legal effect of each contract of a bill **12–018** is to be determined by the law of the place where such contract was made has to be qualified where the bill or its acceptance has been obtained for an illegal consideration.

---

[8] If a cheque is drawn in country A on a bank in country B and delivered to a payee in country B, s.72 will not in its terms apply. But it is then self-evident that the applicable law is that of country B. See *MK International Development Co. Ltd v Housing Bank* [1991] 1 Bank.L.R. 74 (concession).
[9] Except (possibly) under the proviso to the subs.
[10] (1867) L.R. 3 Q.B. 77 (but not the reasoning) (Illustration 2).
[11] s.83(4).
[12] s.4.
[13] *Lebel v Tucker* (1867) L.R. 3 Q.B. 77.
[14] *Alcock v Smith* [1892] 1 Ch. 238, 256, 257.
[15] [1892] 1 Ch. 238, 256, 257. See also at 270.

If a bill is accepted payable in England and for a consideration unlawful by the law of England, it cannot be enforced here by the original payee even though the consideration for the acceptance was lawful by the law of the place where the contract of acceptance was made.[16] Similarly, if a cheque drawn on an English bank is issued for a consideration unlawful by the law of England, the drawer cannot be sued here by the payee, even though the consideration for the cheque is lawful by the law of the place of issue.[17] The acceptance or cheque being given for a consideration illegal by the *lex loci solutionis*, the instrument cannot be enforced by a holder who received it with notice of the illegality.

The converse, however, is not necessarily true. If, for example, A draws a cheque on an English bank payable to B, and issues it to B for a consideration which is lawful by English law, B may not be able to sue A on the cheque if the consideration for it was illegal under a foreign law. In *Re Banque des Marchands de Moscou (No.2)*[18] drafts addressed to an English bank by a Russian bank in favour of a customer of the latter were held to be unenforceable because they violated Russian law. Roxburgh J. said: "The whole transaction was illegal in its inception as being a transaction carried out in Russia in breach of the Russian currency laws then in force." The drafts were not illegal by English law. But Russian law was applied as the law which governed the underlying transaction in consideration of which the drafts were issued.

12–019      The conclusion appears to be that a contract on a bill, cheque or note will not be enforced[19] in England if it is illegal by the *lex loci solutionis* of the obligation or if the consideration for the contract was a transaction which is illegal by its governing law. However, an English court will not allow a party to refuse payment merely on the ground that the payment would be illegal by the law of the foreign country where he resides or carries on business, or of which he is a national.[20] And the fact that payment is rendered illegal by the law of the foreign country where the instrument is payable will not make a party's engagement to pay unenforceable unless payment can be required of him only in that country and not elsewhere.[21]

---

[16] *Robinson v Bland* (1760) 2 Burr. 1077.

[17] *Moulis v Owen* [1907] 1 K.B. 746 (Illustration 11). See also Cohen (1911) 28 L.Q.R. 127.

[18] [1954] 1 W.L.R. 1108 (Illustration 12). See also *Rosencrantz v Union Contractors Ltd* (1960) 23 D.L.R. (2d) 473.

[19] Except by a holder in due course or (*semble*) by the original payee without notice of the illegality: see above, paras 4–050 and 5–072.

[20] *Kleinwort Sons & Co. v Ungarische Baumwolle Industrie A.G.* [1939] 2 K.B. 678.

[21] *Bank Polski v Mulder (K.J.) & Co.* [1942] 1 K.B. 497 (Illustration 9); *Cornelius v Banque Franco-Serbe* [1942] 1 K.B. 29 (s.46, Illustration 1); *Kahler v Midland Bank Ltd* [1950] A.C. 24. 48; *Zivnostenska Banka v Frankman* [1950] A.C. 57, 78; *Banco Atlantico S.A. v British Bank of the Middle East* [1990] 2 Lloyd's Rep. 504.

All of these rules are nevertheless subject to the overriding principle that a contract will not be enforced in the English courts—whatever may be the applicable law—if its enforcement would be against the public policy of this country[22] or contrary to a statute that must be applied regardless of the conflict of laws.[23]

**Bretton Woods Agreement Order 1946.** One example of such a statute 12–020 is provided by the Bretton Woods Agreement Order 1946,[24] made under the Bretton Woods Agreement Act 1945. The United Kingdom is a member of the International Monetary Fund and a party to the International Monetary Fund Agreement (the "Bretton Woods Agreement"). Article VIII (2)(b) of the Schedule to the Order states: "Exchange contracts which involve the currency of any member and which are contrary to the exchange control regulations of any member maintained or imposed consistently with this agreement shall be unenforceable in the territories of any member". This provision gives rise to a number of difficulties of interpretation, discussion of which lies outside the scope of the present work.[25] It must, however, be given effect to in the courts of the United Kingdom irrespective of the law applicable to the contract or the place of performance of the obligation.[26]

An exchange contract is a contract to exchange the currency of one country for the currency of another.[27] This "narrow" interpretation was confirmed by the House of Lords in *United City Merchants (Investments) Ltd v Royal Bank of Canada*.[28] But in the same case it was held that a monetary transaction in disguise can be an exchange contract and that the court must consider, not only the contract which is sought to be enforced, but any other contract or contracts which are part of the same overall transaction. A contract may be an exchange contract in substance even if not in form.[29] If the other requirements of the provision are satisfied, the contract will not be illegal, but it will be unenforceable.[30] Where the contract is in part a monetary transaction in disguise, and in part a

[22] Dicey and Morris *Conflict of Laws* (13th ed.), 32–235. See, *e.g. Foster v Driscoll* [1929] 1 K.B. 470; *Ispahani v Bank Melli Iran* [1998] Lloyd's Rep. Bank. 133; Dicey and Morris *Conflict of Laws* (13th ed.), 32–235.

[23] *e.g.* anti-money laundering legislation, below, para.13–053. In *Moulis v Owen* [1907] 1 K.B. 746 (Illustration 11) Collins M.R, considered that the Gaming Acts applied as part of the *lex fori*.

[24] S.R. & O. 1946, No.36.

[25] See F.A. Mann, *The Legal Aspect of Money* (5th ed.), Ch.15; Gold, *The Fund Agreement in the Courts* (1962); Dicey *Conflict of Laws* (13th ed.), 36–088.

[26] *Sharif v Azad* [1967] 1 Q.B. 605, 617.

[27] *Wilson, Smithett and Cope Ltd v Terruzzi* [1976] Q.B. 683, 703. Contrast the earlier view in *Sharif v Azad* [1967] 1 Q.B. 605, and see Gold (1984) 33 I.C.L.Q. 777.

[28] [1983] 1 A.C. 168.

[29] *Wilson, Smithett and Cope Ltd v Terruzzi* [1976] Q.B. 683 at 714.

[30] *Singh Batra v Ebrahim* [1982] 2 Lloyd's Rep. 11, 13; *United City Merchants (Investments) Ltd v Royal Bank Of Canada* [1982] Q.B. 208, 241; [1988] 1 A.C. 168, 189.

genuine transaction, *e.g.* payment for goods supplied, it will be *pro tanto* unenforceable, leaving the enforceability of the other part unimpaired.[31]

In *Sharif v Azad*[32] the Court of Appeal held that a sterling cheque drawn by a person resident in England on an English bank payable to another person resident in England, though it was an exchange contract[33] which involved the currency of a member of the Fund (Pakistan), was not contrary to Pakistan exchange control regulations. However, this case was subsequently distinguished in *Mansouri v Singh*[34] where a sterling cheque was drawn by a travel agent in England on an English bank in favour of an Iranian national resident in England as part of a wider transaction which had as its object the deposit by the Iranian national of a sum in rials in Iran and a corresponding payment to him of sterling in England, in breach of Iranian exchange control regulations. The Court of Appeal refused to enforce payment of the cheque.

12–021     One possible ground for the decision in *Sharif v Azad*,[35] that the obligation to make payment on a cheque is an autonomous obligation and quite separate from any obligations which may exist under any underlying or associated transaction, was expressly rejected by the Court of Appeal in the latter case.[36] A negotiable instrument may therefore be unenforceable by virtue of the fact that it is given and received in furtherance of a transaction which constitutes an exchange contract.

Where difficulty arises in transferring funds from a foreign country because of the existence of exchange control regulations in that country, the arrangement most usually encountered is that A, a resident in the foreign country, will make available in that country funds to or for the account of B, resident in England, and that B in return will reimburse A in England in cash or by a sterling cheque drawn on an English bank. There seems to be little doubt that, if the overall transaction is in breach of the exchange control regulations of the foreign country (being a member of the Fund), the cheque will be unenforceable here by A against B.[37] Similarly, if A in a foreign country raises false invoices with the agreement of B in this country in order to enable a transfer of funds to be made in breach of the exchange control regulations of the foreign country, a bill or note given in pursuance of this

---

[31] *United City Merchants (Investments) Ltd v Royal Bank of Canada* [1983] 1 A.C. 168.
[32] [1967] 1 Q.B. 605.
[33] *cf. Wilson, Smithett and Cope Ltd v Terruzzi* [1976] Q.B. 683, 703.
[34] [1986] 1 W.L.R. 1393 (Illustration 13).
[35] [1967] 1 Q.B. 605.
[36] [1986] 1 W.L.R. 1393 at 1403.
[37] *Mansouri v Singh* [1986] 1 W.L.R. 1393. See also *Singh Batra v Ebrahim* [1982] 2 Lloyd's Rep. 11.

agreement may be unenforceable, in whole or in part, by A against B in the English courts.[38]

Transactions which are in breach of exchange control regulations of a foreign country, but which fall outside the Bretton Woods Agreement Order, will not necessarily be valid and enforceable. They may still be unenforceable because they are illegal at common law.[39]

**Discharge.** Section 72 contains no provision to indicate which law governs the validity and effect of a discharge from liability on a bill. At common law, the discharge of a contract normally[40] depended upon the proper law of the contract.[41] If, however, it is accepted that the doctrine of the proper law cannot conveniently be applied to the contracts of the parties to a bill or note,[42] then the choice lies between the *lex loci contractus* (*i.e.*, the general rule in subsections (1) and (2)), the *lex loci solutionis*, or the law of the place where the act constituting the discharge was done (*locus regit actum*).

    12–022

(a) *Payment.* The first question which arises is as to the law which determines whether payment has been effectively made by the party primarily liable on the instrument, that is, by the acceptor of a bill or the maker of a note. It is arguable that this should in the first instance be referred to the law of the place where that party's contract was made.[43] This, in many cases, will be the same as the law of the place where the instrument is payable and of the place where it is paid.[44] But those places may diverge. Suppose that a bill payable to order is accepted in England payable in Paris. It is stolen by a thief, who forges the payee's indorsement and transfers the bill in England to C, who takes it in good faith and for value. At maturity, C presents the bill for payment in Paris and it is paid in good faith and without negligence. By English law, the acceptor is not discharged: payment has not been made to a holder, since C acquires no title to the bill through or under the forged indorsement.[45] By the law of France, there is a valid discharge: the person who pays at maturity is bound to verify the regularity of the series of indorsements, but not the signature of the indorsers.[46]

    12–023

It is submitted that the payment is a valid discharge. By the law of England, which governs the legal effect of the contract of acceptance, the

---

[38] See *United City Merchants (Investments) Ltd v Royal Bank of Canada* [1982] Q.B. 208.
[39] *Ispahani v Bank Melli Iran* [1998] Lloyd's Rep. Bank 133.
[40] But see below, para.12–027, n.66 (bankruptcy).
[41] Dicey and Morris *Conflict of Laws* (13th ed.), 32–003.
[42] See above, paras 12–003 and 12–015.
[43] Dicey and Morris *Conflict of Laws* (13th ed.), 33–347.
[44] See, *e.g. Wragge v Sims Cooper & Co. (Australia) Pty Ltd* (1933) 50 C.L.R. 483.
[45] See above, paras 3–072 and 8–011 (ss.24, 59).
[46] ULB, art.40.

acceptor engages that he will pay the bill according to the tenor of his acceptance. Having accepted the bill payable in France, it may be contended that he satisfies his obligation by making payment to any person entitled to receive payment under French law. Alternatively, it may be preferable to hold that French law, as the *lex loci solutionis* of the principal debt,[47] should prevail.

In the case of an unaccepted bill or cheque there is, or course, no contract of the drawee on the instrument. Whether payment by the drawee is an effective discharge of the instrument is, it is submitted, a matter to be determined by the law of the place where the instrument was expected to be paid.[48] In the case of a cheque this would be the office or branch on which the cheque is drawn. A banker who pays a cheque drawn on him by his customer payable in the United Kingdom will therefore be entitled to rely on the protection afforded by sections 60 and 80 of the 1882 Act and section 1 of the Cheques Act 1957 notwithstanding that the cheque was drawn abroad. The same result is reached by applying the Rome Convention to the agency contract between the banker and his customer which confers on the banker his mandate and authority to pay. For the purposes of Article 4(2) of the Convention[49] the "characteristic performance" of the contract is that of the banker. In any event, since that performance is to be effected at the office or branch on which the cheque is drawn, it is to be presumed (unless otherwise agreed) that the law of that place will apply.[50]

**12–024**     Since the relationship between the parties secondarily liable on the instrument and the party primarily liable is in the nature of suretyship,[51] it must follow that a payment by the acceptor, maker or drawee which is a valid discharge as mentioned above will also discharge the contracts of the drawer and all indorsers on the instrument. However, in the pre-Act case of *Allen v Kemble*[52] the Privy Council held that the right of the drawer and of an indorser of a bill to avail themselves of a right of set-off which the acceptor was entitled to raise against the assignees of the estate of the bankrupt holder, was governed by the law of the place where their respective contracts were entered into, and not by the law of the place where the bill was payable. This case probably turns upon a special rule of the *lex loci contractus*, which fell to be applied, that a guarantor was

---

[47] Dicey and Morris *Conflict of Laws* (13th ed.), 33–347.

[48] *Franklin v Westminster Bank*, CA; Mann, *The Legal Aspect of Money* (5th ed.), App.II, p.561.

[49] Contracts (Applicable Law) Act 1990, Sch.1, art.4(2).

[50] *Bank of Baroda v Vysya Bank Ltd* [1994] 2 Lloyd's Rep. 87; *Marconi Communications International Ltd v PT Pan Indonesia Bank Ltd TBK* [2004] EWHC 129 (Comm), [2004] 1 Lloyd's Rep. 594, affirmed *The Times*, May 17, 2005, CA. (letter of credit).

[51] *Duncan Fox & Co. v North and South Wales Bank* (1880) 6 App. Cas. 1, 11, 13, 14; see above, para.7–021 (s.55).

[52] (1848) 6 Moore P.C. 314 (Illustration 14).

entitled to rely upon any right of set-off (*compensatio*) available to a principal debtor against a creditor. But it could be taken to establish that, if according to the law of the place where the contract of the drawer or indorser was made the liability of the acceptor has been discharged by set-off or payment, the drawer or indorser will be discharged, whether or not the acceptor's liability is discharged under the applicable law.

In *Ralli v Dennistoun*[53] the question arose whether an accommodation bill was discharged by a payment made abroad by the party accommo-dated.[54] A bill was drawn in Austria on merchants in Liverpool and accepted by them payable in London for the accommodation of the drawer. The drawer negotiated the bill in Austria to a holder who, after the bill was due, received from the drawer in Austria a smaller sum in satisfaction of the bill. This, according to Austrian law, was a valid discharge. In the Court of Exchequer the acceptors pleaded the payment as a defence to an action against them by a subsequent indorsee of the bill. Parke B. said[55] that "inasmuch as it appeared that the accord and satisfaction was sufficient, according to the law of the country where the bill was negotiated and the payment was made, the bill being then due and payable and in the hands of the true holder, the defence was good"; and the rest of the Court concurred in that opinion. It may further be argued, in reliance of this case, that, where payment is made by the drawer or an indorser,[56] the validity and effect of the payment will be determined by the law of the place where that party impliedly undertook to and did pay the bill.

(b) *Renunciation and cancellation.* It also seems probable that the law of the place where the relevant party entered into his contract would be held to govern the validity and effect of a renunciation by the holder of that party's liabilities on the bill[57] and the cancellation by the holder of that party's signature,[58] subject to the qualification that a valid release of the liabilities of the acceptor[59] or a valid cancellation *vis-à-vis* the acceptor[60] will also discharge the drawer and all indorsers. **12–025**

(c) *Alteration of bill.* In *Hirschfield v Smith*,[61] a bill was drawn in Eng-land payable to drawer's order on and accepted by the drawee in France. It was indorsed by the drawer and delivered to the defendant in England, and by him indorsed and delivered to the claimant in England. The **12–026**

---

[53] (1851) 6 Exch. 483 (36th plea and judgment).
[54] See s.59(3).
[55] (1851) 6 Exch. 483 at 493.
[56] See s.59(2).
[57] s.62(2).
[58] s.63(2).
[59] s.62(1).
[60] s.63(1).
[61] (1866) L.R. 1 C.P. 340 (Illustration 16).

claimant altered the acceptance and the indorsements by writing in a rate of exchange at which the bill was payable. The Court of Common Pleas held that this was a material alteration[62] which avoided the bill in the hands of the claimant. No conflict of laws issue on this point was raised or discussed. But Erle C.J. said[63]: "The contract of the acceptor is altered by the superscription on the face of the bill; and the contract of the indorser is altered by the superscription over the indorsements on the back of the bill . . . ." This suggests that the "several laws" principle[64] and not the "single law" principle is to be applied to the alteration of a bill. On this assumption, it is submitted that the effect of an alteration on a party's contract on a bill is to be determined by the law of the place where the relevant contract was entered into.

12–027    (d) *Insolvency.* A discharge of a party from his liability on a bill under the bankruptcy law[65] of a country outside the United Kingdom[66] is a discharge therefrom in England if, and only if,[67] it is a discharge under the law applicable to his contract, *i.e.* the law of the place where such contract was made.[68] However, in the case of bankruptcies falling within Council Regulation 1346/2000 on Insolvency Proceedings,[69] where main proceedings in another Member State are closed and the closure has, under the law of that Member State, the effect of discharging the debtor, that discharge must be recognised in England even if it is not an effective discharge under the law applicable to the contract.[70] Whether a foreign corporation has been dissolved must be determined by the place of its incorporation,[71] but again recognition may have to be afforded to insolvency proceedings in another Member State where the insolvency falls within Council Regulation 1346/2000.[72]

12–028    **Transfer abroad.** The section does not deal in express terms with the law which governs the transfer of a bill, cheque or note. But it is settled

---

[62] See now s.64.

[63] (1866) L.R. 1 C.P. 340 at 353–354.

[64] See above, para.12–002.

[65] Provided that it amounts to an extinction of the liability: see Dicey and Morris *Conflict of Laws* (13th ed.), 32–083; citing *Gibbs v Société Industrielle et Commerciale des Metaux* (1890) 25 Q.B.D. 399, 405.

[66] A discharge from a liability under an English bankruptcy or under a Scottish or Northern Ireland bankruptcy is a discharge therefrom in England, irrespective of the law which governs the contract: Dicey and Morris *Conflict of Laws* (13th ed.), 31–088.

[67] *Bartley v Hodges* (1861) 1 B. & S. 375; *Gibbs v Société Industrielle et Commercialle des Metaux* (1890) 25 Q.B.D. 399.

[68] *Burrows v Jemino* (1726) 2 Stra. 733; *Potter v Brown* (1804) 5 East 124; Dicey and Morris *Conflict of Laws* (13th ed.), 31–081.

[69] art.4(2)(j).

[70] Dicey and Morris *Conflict of Laws* (4th Supp. to the 13th ed., 2004), p.387.

[71] Dicey and Morris *Conflict of Laws* (13th ed.), 30–092.

[72] Dicey and Morris *Conflict of Laws* (4th Supp. to the 13th ed., 2004), p.359.

law that, *quoad* transfer in a foreign country, negotiable instruments must be regarded as chattels, and are subject to the ordinary rules of the conflict laws which regulate the transfer of chattels.[73] The validity and effect of the transfer is governed by the law of the country where the instrument is at the time of the transfer (*lex situs*),[74] which will almost invariably coincide with the *lex loci actus*.[75] Thus "the rule that the transfer of chattels must be governed by the law of the country in which the transfer takes place applies to a bill or cheque".[76] In *Alcock v Smith*,[77] a bill drawn, accepted and payable in England, and subsequently indorsed in blank, was seized under an order of a Norwegian court and sold in Norway to a purchaser. By the law of Norway, the purchaser obtained a perfect title to the bill. By the law of England, the bill being overdue at the time of sale, he took subject to equities. The Court of Appeal held that Norwegian law applied as the law of the country where the transfer took place. In *Embiricos v Anglo-Austrian Bank*,[78] a cheque was drawn in Romania on an English bank payable to the order of the claimants, who specially indorsed the cheque to an English firm. The cheque was stolen by an employee of the claimants, the indorsement of the English firm forged and the cheque transferred in Austria to a Viennese bank, which cashed it in good faith and forwarded it to the defendant bank in London for collection. By the law of Austria, the Viennese bank acquired a good title to the cheque under the forged indorsement. By English law, no title was so acquired. The Court of Appeal held that the validity of the transfer was governed by the law of the country where the transfer took place. In both of these cases, subsection (2) of section 72 was to some extent also relied on to support the decision[79] (although it is difficult to understand why this should be so in *Alcock v Smith*,[80] since at the time of the transfer, the bill was payable to bearer, and there was in consequence no "indorsement" to which the subsection could apply). Moreover, in *Koechlin et Cie v Kestenbaum Bros*,[81] where a bill drawn in France and accepted in England was indorsed by the payee in France in a form which was valid by French law, but invalid by English law, Sargant L.J. considered[82] that the

---

[73] *Macmillan Inc. v Bishopsgate Investment Trust plc (No.3)* [1996] 1 W.L.R. 387, 400, 411.

[74] Dicey and Morris *Conflict of Laws* (13th ed.), 24–002.

[75] The same law will, it is submitted, determine whether or not the transferred instrument is negotiable. But see *Macmillan Inc. v Bishopsgate Investment Trust plc (No.3)* [1996] 1 W.L.R. 387 at 400 (*lex fori*).

[76] *Embiricos v Anglo-Austrian Bank* [1905] 1 K.B. 677, 683.

[77] [1892] 1 Ch. 238 (Illustration 5).

[78] [1905] 1 K.B. 677 (Illustration 6).

[79] *Alcock v Smith* [1892] 1 Ch. 238 at 256, 263; *Embiricos v Anglo-Austrian Bank* [1905] 1 K.B. 677 at 686, 687. See also *Canada Life Assurance Co. v Canadian Imperial Bank of Commerce* (1979) 98 D.L.R. (3d) 670, 682.

[80] See below, para.12–038.

[81] [1927] 1 K.B. 889 (Illustration 8).

[82] [1927] 1 K.B. 889 at 899.

case was covered by section 72(1),[83] but, if it was not so covered, then it was covered by subsection (2) "in view of the very wide effect of *Embiricos v Anglo-Austrian Bank*[84] . . . ".

On the assumption that subsections (1) and (2) are relevant to the issue whether or not a bill has been validly transferred abroad,[85] the position would appear to be as follows: (i) if the indorsement in fact made is, according to the law of the place where it is made, sufficient to give a title to the indorsee, then by subsections (1) and (2)[86] the indorsee is entitled to sue on the bill in this country[87]; (ii) in any event a transferee will be entitled to sue here if he obtained a good title to the bill by the law of the country where the transfer took place.[88]

**12–029**    **Transfer in England.** By the same token, the validity and effect of the transfer of an instrument in England will be governed by the law of England. In particular, if a cheque payable to order is drawn and issued abroad to the payee, and is then delivered in England by the holder to a banker for collection, English law will determine what rights the banker has by virtue of such delivery. If, therefore, a cheque payable to order is delivered to him for value unindorsed, the banker can rely on section 2 of the Cheques Act 1957[89] and maintain an action against the drawer in England, claiming as holder for value or as holder in due course.

**12–030**    **Conversion.** It has previously been pointed out[90] that an action for conversion of a bill, cheque or note lies at the suit of the "true owner" against any person who wrongfully deals with it in a manner inconsistent with the right of the true owner, the instrument being treated for this purpose as a chattel. Where the act of conversion relied on takes place in England, the courts will normally apply English law.[91] Nevertheless, the claimant may be met by the plea that he has no property in or immediate right to possession of the instrument,[92] and his title to the instrument may fall to be determined by a foreign law.[93]

---

[83] See above, para.12–007.

[84] See above, para.12–015.

[85] Cheshire and North, *Private International Law* (12th ed.), pp.965, 966. Contrast Dicey and Morris *Conflict of Laws* (13th ed), 33–353.

[86] Subject to their respective provisos.

[87] *Embiricos v Anglo-Austrian Bank* [1905] 1 K.B. 677 at 875; *Koechlin et Cie v Kestenbaum Bros* [1927] 1 K.B. 889 at 899.

[88] *Alcock v Smith* [1892] 1 Ch. 238; *Embiricos v Anglo-Austrian Bank* [1905] 1 K.B. 677.

[89] See below, para.17–015.

[90] See above, para.3–050 (s.24).

[91] Private International Law (Miscellaneous Provisions) Act 1995, ss.9(6), 11(1). See also (at common law) *Lacave v Crédit Lyonnais* [1897] 1 Q.B. 148 (Cheques Act 1957, s.4, Illustration 2). *Kleinwort Sons & Co. v Comptoir National d'Escompte de Paris* [1894] 2 Q.B. 157, 159.

[92] See above, para.3–051 (s.24).

[93] *Embiricos v Anglo-Austrian Bank* [1905] 1 K.B. 677 (Illustration 6). cf. *Lacave v Crédit Lyonnais* [1897] 1 Q.B. 148.

Where the act of conversion relied on takes place elsewhere than in England, an action brought by the true owner in England will fail if the act alleged to constitute the conversion was not actionable according to the law of the country where it was done.[94] Since, in general, civil law systems do not recognise the strict liability imposed by English law upon a person who deals with an instrument to which he has no title or a defective title,[95] a claimant in English proceedings may well encounter difficulty in establishing a liability in tort where the act complained of took place in a civil law country.[96]

The alternative claim of the true owner for money had and received,[97] which in England is based on the fictional "waiver" of the tort of conversion, would probably be held to be so closely connected with the tort as to be governed by the same rules.[98] But since the claim is in substance one that the recipient of the proceeds of the instrument has been unjustly enriched at the expense of the true owner, it is arguable that the obligation to restore the money obtained should be governed by the law of the place where the enrichment occurred.[99] If such a claim is made against a collecting banker in respect of the proceeds of a cheque delivered to him for collection, it is submitted that the governing law will normally be that of the country where he receives payment and not that of the country where the instrument is presented for payment and payment is made.[1] If a claim is made against the recipient of the proceeds of the instrument, it will probably be the law of the country where the proceeds are credited to his account rather than that of the country to which they are ultimately remitted.[2]

A banker in the United Kingdom to whom a cheque is delivered for collection should be entitled to the protection afforded by section 4 of the

---

[94] Private International Law (Miscellaneous Provisions) Act 1995, s.11. *cf.* s.12.

[95] There is no tort of conversion or its equivalent in Scots law. Liability will be in restitution, if enrichment is proved: see Cusine (1978) 23 Jur. Rev. 223.

[96] *cf. Honourable Society of Middle Temple v Lloyd's Bank plc* [1999] 1 All E.R. (Comm) 193 (Turkish law).

[97] See above, para.3–052.

[98] Dicey and Morris *Conflict of Laws* (13th ed.) 34–007, 34–015, 34–03. *cf.* Cheshire and North, *Private and International Law* (12th ed.), p.693.

[99] Dicey and Morris *Conflict of Laws* (13th ed.), 34–029. Contrast Cheshire and North, *Private International Law* (12th ed.), pp.682–692.

[1] *Hong Kong and Shanghai Banking Corp. Ltd v United Overseas Bank Ltd* [1992] 2 Sing. L.R. 495 (Singapore). But contrast *Kleinwort Sons & Co. v Comptoir National d'Escompte de Paris* [1894] 2 Q.B. 157; *Macmillan Inc. v Bishopsgate Investment Trust plc (No.3)* [1996] 1 W.L.R. 387, 397, 408.

[2] *Chase Manhattan Bank N.A. v Israel British Bank (London) Ltd* [1981] Ch. 105; *Re Jogia (A Bankrupt)* [1988] 1 W.L.R. 484, 495; *El Ajou v Dollar Land Holdings plc (No.1)* [1993] 3 All E.R. 717 (revd on other grounds [1994] 2 All E.R. 685); *Thahir v Pertamina* [1994] 3 Sing. L.R. 257 (Singapore).

Cheques Act 1957[3] if he receives payment in the United Kingdom not-withstanding that the cheque is drawn on a banker outside the United Kingdom or that his customer is resident or has his place of business outside the United Kingdom and the proceeds are remitted to him there. It is, however, questionable whether a foreign banker may rely on section 4 in proceedings brought against him in the United Kingdom in respect of his collection and conversion of a cheque in a country outside the United Kingdom, but it may be that he can do so.[4]

12–031    **Subsection (3): duties of holder.** The drafting of this subsection has been criticised[5] and indeed it is too succinct for its meaning to be readily intelligible. It is submitted that the words of the subsection must be read discretely and distributively,[6] so that it comprises two separate sub-rules: (1) "The duties of the holder with respect to presentment for acceptance and payment are determined by the law of the place where the act is done", and (2) "the necessity for or sufficiency of a protest or notice of dishonour, or otherwise,[7] are determined by the law of the place where the bill is dishonoured".

Where a bill has been presented for acceptance or payment, the first sub-rule refers to the law of the place of presentment the question whether the bill has been "duly" presented.[8] It is less clear, however, whether the same law applies to the necessity for presentment, *i.e.* whether or not presentment is required, and whether presentment is excused.[9] For this to be so, the words "where the act is done" would have to be construed as meaning "where the act is done or to be done".[10] Such a gloss on the subsection would not be unreasonable. However, in *Bank Polski v Mulder (K.J.) & Co.,*[11] a bill was accepted in London payable in Dutch florins in Amsterdam, but was not presented there for payment by the holder. In an action by the holder against the acceptors, Tucker J. held[12] that the acceptance was a general acceptance and, since the acceptors were not bound to perform the obligations under their contract by

---

[3] See below, para.17–028.

[4] *cf. Honourable Society of the Middle Temple v Lloyds Bank plc* [1999] 1 All E.R. (Comm) 193 (But this case was decided before the entry into force of the Private International Law (Miscellaneous Provisions) Act 1995, which now makes the only relevant substantive law the law of the place of conversion).

[5] Cheshire and North *Private International Law* (12th ed.), p.526.

[6] Dicey and Morris *Conflict of Laws* (13th ed.), 33–356.

[7] It is uncertain to what exactly the words "or otherwise" refer by way of duties of the holder.

[8] *Franklin v Westminster Bank* (1931) CA, Mann, *The Legal Aspect of Money* (5th ed.), App.II, p.561.

[9] See Mann (1941) 5 M.L.R. 251.

[10] Dicey and Morris *Conflict of Laws* (13th ed.), 33–357.

[11] [1941] 2 K.B. 266; [1942] 1 K.B. 497 (Illustration 9).

[12] [1941] 2 K.B. 266. The s.72 point was abandoned on appeal: [1942] 1 K.B. 497. See also *Cornelius v Banque Franco-Serbe* [1948] 2 All E.R. 728, 732 (application of the *lex fori*).

payment in Holland, section 72(3) was inapplicable. The proper law of the acceptors' contract, that is to say, English law, governed the case, and by English law presentment for payment was not necessary to charge the acceptors. This case has been taken to establish that the necessity for presentment lies outside the subsection,[13] but it would appear that Tucker J. accepted that, had the acceptance been qualified and the bill been payable in Amsterdam only and not elsewhere, Dutch law would have applied. It is suggested that it is undesirable to draw a distinction, for the purpose of the application of the subsection, between the manner of presentment and the necessity for presentment, since the question whether presentment has been duly made and the question whether it has been made at all may merge into one another.

In contrast, the second sub-rule clearly covers both the necessity for and sufficiency of a protest or notice of dishonour. These matters are referred to the law of the place where the bill is dishonoured. This reproduces the common law before the Act. In *Rothschild v Currie*,[14] where a bill was drawn in England and accepted payable in France, notice of dishonour by an indorsee in England to his indorser in England was held to be good, since it complied with the law of France, even though it was out of time in English law; and in *Hirschfield v Smith*[15] it was similarly held, in respect of an indorsement in England, that protest in accordance with the law of France was a sufficient notice of dishonour to enable the indorsee to charge his indorser, the bill being payable and dishonoured in France. In *Horne v Rouquette*[16] a bill drawn in England payable in Spain—a country where notice of dishonour for non-acceptance is not required—was dishonoured in Spain by non-acceptance. An indorsee in Spain delayed giving notice of dishonour to the claimant, his immediate indorser in England, but on receipt of the notice the claimant immediately gave notice to the defendant his indorser in England, in accordance with English law. The Court of Appeal held that the defendant was liable to the claimant on the bill.

The subsection is in no way limited in its terms to the necessity for and **12–032** sufficiency of a protest or notice of dishonour by the *last* holder of the bill. However, it has been argued[17] that, as between prior indorsers and between a prior indorser and the drawer, these matters are to be referred to the law which governs the contract of the party entitled to receive the notice. There is certainly support for this argument in *Horne v Rouquette*,[18] where emphasis was placed on the fact that the claimant had given notice

[13] Dicey and Morris *Conflict of Laws* (13th ed.), 33–257.
[14] (1841) 1 Q.B. 43 (Illustration 15).
[15] (1866) L.R. 1 C.P. 340 (Illustration 16).
[16] (1878) 3 Q.B.D. 514 (Illustration 17).
[17] Westlake, *Private International Law* (7th ed.), s.232.
[18] (1878) 3 Q.B.D. 514.

of dishonour to the defendant within the time allowed by English law; but in *Hirschfield v Smith* it was said[19]: "The indorser of a bill accepted payable in France, promises to pay in the event of dishonour in France, and notice thereof. By his contract he must be taken to know the law of France relating to the dishonour of bill; and notice of dishonour is a portion of that law." Further, if by the law of the place of dishonour no notice of dishonour need be given by the last holder to his immediate indorser, it is difficult to see why that indorser should be bound, in order to preserve his rights against prior parties in England, at once to give notice of dishonour on being informed that the bill has been dishonoured.[20] It is submitted that the intention of the subsection is to apply the "single law" principle[21] to the exclusion of the "several laws" principle with respect to the formalities attendant upon the dishonour of an instrument.[22]

In *G. & H. Montage GmbH v Irvani*[23] the defendant had given in Germany an "aval" in respect of certain bills drawn in Germany but accepted payable and dishonoured by non-payment in England. No notice of dishonour was given to him and, although the bills were protested, this was not done within the time specified in section 51(2) of the Act. The Court of Appeal held that the necessity for notice of dishonour and the sufficiency of the protest fell to be determined in accordance with English law. But since neither section 48 nor section 51 of the Act required due notice of dishonour to be given or due protest to be made in relation to a person who had given an "aval", their absence afforded the defendant no defence to his liability on the bills.

Section 89(4) of the Act provides that, where a foreign note is dishonoured, protest thereof is unnecessary. But such a note may nevertheless have to be protested if dishonoured abroad in a country where protest is required.

12–033     **Subsection (4): rate of exchange.** This subsection provided that, where a bill was drawn out of but payable in the United Kingdom and the sum payable was not expressed in the currency of the United Kingdom, the amount should, in the absence of some express stipulation, be calculated according to the rate of exchange for sight drafts at the place of payment on the day the bill was payable. It ceased to have effect and was repealed by the Administration of Justice Act 1977[24] following the decision of the

---

[19] (1866) L.R. 1 C.P. 340, 352. See also *Rothschild v Currie* (1841) 1 Q.B. 43.
[20] See Dicey and Morris *Conflict of Laws* (13th ed.), 33–358.
[21] See above, para.12–002.
[22] See also *Rouquette v Overmann* (1875) L.R. 10 Q.B. 525, 542–543 (Illustration 18).
[23] [1990] 1 W.L.R. 667 (Illustration 10).
[24] ss.4, 32 and Sch.5, Pt.I.

House of Lords in *Miliangos v George Frank (Textiles) Ltd*,[25] which enabled judgment to be given in a foreign currency. Judgment can therefore now be given in the currency in which an instrument is expressed to be payable.[26] However, the *Miliangos* case did not prescribe that a debt or liability expressed in a foreign currency can only be paid in that currency.[27] Indeed, if a sum of money expressed in a foreign currency is payable in England, the general rule is that the debtor may choose whether to pay in that currency or in sterling.[28]

In *Barclays Bank International Ltd v Levin Bros (Bradford)Ltd*,[29] Mocatta J. said[30]:

> "I think it is clear that when someone is under an obligation to pay another a sum of money expressed in a foreign currency but to pay it in this country, the person under the obligation has an option, if he is to fulfil his obligation at the date when the money is payable, either to produce the appropriate amount in the foreign currency in question or to pay the equivalent in sterling at the rate of exchange prevailing at the due date. This proposition seems to me elementary and a matter of common sense."

He further approved the rule stated in Dicey and Morris, *The Conflict of Laws*,[31] that:

> "if a sum of money expressed in a foreign currency is payable in England, it may be paid either in units of the money of account or in sterling at the rate of exchange at which units of the foreign legal tender can, on the day when the money is payable, be bought in London[32] in a recognised and accessible market, irrespective of any official rate of exchange between that currency and sterling".

It is therefore submitted that, notwithstanding its repeal, the principle set out in the subsection continues to apply by virtue of the rules of common law,[33] provided that it is understood merely to provide a formula to ascertain the amount of sterling which an acceptor should pay in

---

[25] [1976] A.C. 443.

[26] *Barclays Bank International Ltd v Levin Bros (Bradford) Ltd* [1977] Q.B. 270 (s.57, Illustration 1).

[27] *Re Lines Brothers Ltd (No.1)* [1983] Ch. 1, 25.

[28] *Marrache v Ashton* [1943] A.C. 311, 317; *Heisler v Anglo-Dal Ltd* [1954] 1 W.L.R. 1273, 1278; *Libyan Arab Foreign Bank v Bankers Trust Co.* [1989] Q.B. 728. But contrast ICC Uniform Rules for Collection (1995), Brochure 522, art. 18.

[29] [1977] Q.B. 270 (s.57, Illustration 1).

[30] [1977] Q.B. 270 at 277.

[31] 9th ed., Rule 173, p.903. See now 13th ed., Rule 210, § 36R–050.

[32] Or at the place of payment. *cf. Syndic in Bankruptcy of Salim Nasrallah Khowry v Khayat* [1943] A.C. 507, 514.

[33] s.97(2). See also *Syndic in Bankruptcy of Salim Nasrallah Khowry v Khayat* [1943] A.C. 507 at 514.

order to discharge his obligation under the bill, if he chooses to pay the bill in sterling and not in the currency in which it is drawn, and not to extend to the sum recoverable by the holder when no payment is made on the date of maturity and the holder subsequently sues the acceptor.[34] The principle would also apply where an instrument expressed in a foreign currency is both drawn and payable in the United Kingdom.[35]

Whether a liability on a bill expressed in sterling but payable in a foreign country may likewise be discharged by payment in local currency depends presumably on the law of the place where payment is or is expected to be made.[36]

12–034      **Measure of damages.** The law which governs the measure of damages recoverable in the event of dishonour of a bill has been considered in the Comment on section 57 of the Act.[37]

12–035      **Limitation.** At common law, since limitation was characterised as a matter of procedure, an English court would as a general rule apply English statutes of limitation as the *lex fori* to any action brought in England on a bill or note. So, for example, no action could be brought in England against the maker of a promissory note governed by a foreign law after the expiration of six years from the date when the cause of action accrued, even though the rights of the holder were not barred or extinguished under the foreign law.[38] Conversely, even if the foreign limitation period had expired, an action could still be brought in England on the note within six years,[39] unless in the opinion of the English court the foreign law did not merely bar the remedy but extinguished the right.[40]

However, the common law was fundamentally altered by the Foreign Limitation Periods Act 1984. The effect of section 1 of that Act is that, if by the application of section 72(2) the legal effect of a party's contract on an instrument is to be determined by the law of another country, then the law of that other country relating to limitation will apply to any action or proceedings in England on that contract, and the English law of limitation will not apply. Thus differing periods of limitation may apply to the several contracts of the parties to the instrument. Under section 2 of the

---

[34] *Barclays Bank International Ltd v Levin Bros (Bradford) Ltd* [1977] Q.B. 270 at 275, 277. *cf.* Dicey and Morris, *Conflict of Laws* (13th ed.), 36–051, 36–054.

[35] *Syndic in Bankruptcy of Salim Nasrallah Khowry v Khayat* [1943] A.C. 507 at 514.

[36] See Dicey and Morris, *Conflict of Laws* (13th ed.), 36–055, but it is there stated that the rate of exchange is determined by the law applicable to the contract. *cf. Ottoman Bank v Jebara* [1928] A.C. 269.

[37] See above, para.7–052.

[38] *British Linen Co. v Drummond* (1830) 10 B. & C. 903.

[39] *Huber v Steiner* (1835) 2 Bing. N.C. 202.

[40] (1835) 2 Bing. N.C. 202 at 211.

1984 Act an English court may nevertheless not apply section 1 to the extent that its application would conflict with public policy, that is to say, to the extent that it would cause undue hardship to a person who is, or might be made, a party to the action or proceedings. Such a situation might arise, for example, where the foreign limitation period was excessively short or where it was excessively long, or where there was no limitation period at all, or in the circumstances of the particular case.[41] The effect of such disapplication is, it seems, to impose the relevant English limitation period as part of the procedural law of the forum.[42]

See also (in Scotland) section 23A of the Prescription and Limitation (Scotland) Act 1973, inserted by section 4 of the Prescription and Limitation (Scotland) Act 1984.

**Subsection (5): due date.** Although this subsection refers only to the situation where a bill is drawn in one country and is payable in another, the same rule would apply where a bill is drawn and payable in the same country. The due date of the instrument is determined according to the law of the place where it is payable, not only in respect of the contract of the party primarily liable, *i.e.* the acceptor of the bill or the maker of a note, but also in respect of the contracts of the parties secondarily liable.[43]    **12–036**

In the pre-Act case of *Rouquette v Overmann*,[44] Cockburn C.J. said[45]:

> "it is well settled that the incidents of presentment and payment must be regulated and determined by the law of the place of performance—a rule which is strikingly illustrated by the familiar but pertinent example of the effect of days of grace being allowed by the law of the country where a bill of exchange is drawn, but not by the law of the country where it is payable, or vice versa, the payment of the bill being, as is well known, deferred until the expiration of the days of grace in the one case, but not so in the other. And this arises out of the nature of the thing, as the acceptor cannot be made liable under any law but his own."[46]

---

[41] *Hellenic Steel Co. v Svolamar Shipping Co. Ltd* [1990] 1 Lloyd's Rep. 541 (reversed on other grounds [1991] 1 Lloyd's Rep. 370); *Jones v Trollope & Colls Cementation Overseas Ltd, The Times*, January 26, 1990, CA; *Société Commerciale de Reassurance v Eras International Ltd* [1992] 1 Lloyd's Rep. 570, 604; *Arab Monetary Fund v Hashim (No.9)* [1996] 1 Lloyd's Rep. 589.

[42] *Arab Monetary Fund v Hashim* [1996] 1 Lloyd's Rep. 589 at 600.

[43] *Rouquette v Overmann* (1875) L.R. 10 Q.B. 525 (Illustration 18); *Franklin v Westminster Bank* (1931) CA; Mann, *The Legal Aspect of Money* (5th ed.), App.II, p.561.

[44] (1875) L.R. 10 Q.B. 525.

[45] (1875) L.R. 10 Q.B. 525 at 535–536.

[46] Cockburn C.J. envisaged here that the place of acceptance and place of payment will coincide.

Thus the obligations of all parties to a bill will be postponed by moratory legislation in the country where it is payable.[47]

## ILLUSTRATIONS

12–037     1. A promissory note is made by the defendant in France and is indorsed by the payee in blank in that country, each of the parties, the maker and the payee, being at the respective times of making and indorsement domiciled in France. It is proved that, by the law of France, an indorsement in blank does not operate as a transfer of the note; it is but a procuration. The claimant, a subsequent holder, cannot sue the defendant on the note in England.[48]

2. A bill drawn by C & Co. payable to their own order is accepted by the defendant. The bill is drawn, accepted and payable in England. It is indorsed in France by C & Co. to the claimant. The indorsement is in blank, and by the law of France the indorsement is invalid to enable the claimant to sue in his own name, but it is a sufficient indorsement by the law of England. The claimant can sue the defendant on the bill. The contract of the acceptor was made in England to pay in England, and it cannot be affected by the circulation and negotiation of the instrument in a foreign country.[49]

3. A bill is drawn in France upon and accepted by the defendant in England. It is indorsed in France in blank to the claimant who sues the defendant in the bill. By the law of France, a blank indorsement does not transfer any property in the bill but amounts to a procuration only. By English law, the blank indorsement would give the claimant a right of action on the bill. The formalities of acts are governed by the law of the place where the acts are done (*locus regit actum*). The claimant cannot enforce payment of the bill against the defendant.[50]

12–038     4. B, a domiciled Frenchman, in 1866 draws in France two bills in the French language, but in English form, on the M Co. in England payable to himself. These bills are accepted by the M Co. They are indorsed by B in blank and delivered by B to J in England, by J to D, and by D to the

---

[47] *Rouquette v Overmann* (1875) L.R. 10 Q.B. 525; *Re Francke and Rasche* [1918] 1 Ch. 470 (Illustration 19).

[48] *Trimbey v Vignier* (1834) 1 Bing. N.C. 151.

[49] *Lebel v Tucker* (1867) L.R. 3 Q.B. 77. See now the proviso to subs.(2).

[50] *Bradlaugh v De Rin (No.2)* (1868) L.R. 3 C.P. 538, (reversed on the effect of French law (1870) L.R. 5 C.P. 473).

applicants. The M Co. goes into liquidation and the applicants seek to prove in the winding-up. By the law of England, the indorsement by B was valid. By the law of France, that indorsement was only a procuration and did not make the bills negotiable. The applicant's proof is admitted. As regards the acceptor, the bills are to be treated as English bills, and an indorsement in accordance with English law is a good indorsement.[51]

5. A bill is drawn, accepted and payable in England, and is indorsed by the payee to M or order. M indorses it in Norway in blank and delivers it there to an agent of the claimants, an English firm. The bill is seized from the claimants' agent under an order of the Norwegian court to satisfy a judgment against a partner in the firm, and is sold by public auction to M. By the law of England, since the bill is at the time of the sale overdue, M gets only such title as his vendor has. By the law of Norway, a perfect title is conferred free from all equities. M sells the bill in Sweden (Swedish law on this point being the same as Norwegian law) to a Swedish bank, which sends the bill for collection to the N Bank in London. Injunctions having been obtained against the acceptor, the drawer, the judgment creditor and M, the case resolves itself into a dispute as to whether the claimants or the Swedish bank are entitled to the bill. The title of the Swedish bank prevails. The effect of the transactions in Norway must be determined by Norwegian law as the law of the country where the transfer took place.[52]

6. A Romanian bank draws a cheque in Romania on a London bank payable to the order of the claimants. The claimants specially indorse the cheque in Romania to E & Co., an English firm, and place it in an envelope to be posted to that firm. The cheque is stolen from the envelope by a clerk of the claimants, who forges the indorsement of E & Co. and cashes it at a Vienna bank. The Vienna bank indorses the cheque and posts it to the defendants, a London bank, for collection. The claimants sue the defendants for conversion of the cheque. By the law of England, the forged indorsement passed no title to the cheque. By the law of Austria, the Austrian bank, as a holder in good faith, obtained a good title to the cheque. The claimants' claim fails. The validity of the transfer of the cheque was governed by the law of the place where such transfer took place, *i.e.* by Austrian law. Alternatively (*per* Stirling L.J.)[53] by section

---

[51] *Re Marseilles Extension Railway Land Co.* (1885) 30 Ch.D. 598. See now proviso (b) to subs.(1). The result, but not the reasoning, would be the same.

[52] *Alcock v Smith* [1892] 1 Ch. 238.

[53] At 687.

72(2) of the Act, the legal effect of the indorsement was governed by Austrian law as the law of the place where the cheque was indorsed.[54]

**12–039**      7. A bill is drawn on and accepted by the defendants payable to the order of R, a Hamburg banker. R, in Germany, indorses the bill to the claimants, bill brokers in London, with the words "für mich" (*for me*). On presentation the bill is dishonoured. By German law, which applies, this is an open and not a restrictive indorsement. The defendants are liable to the claimants on the bill.[55]

8. A bill is drawn in France by E.V. upon the defendants payable to the order of M.V. and is accepted in England by the defendants payable at a London bank. The bill is then returned to France where it is indorsed to the claimants by E.V. in his own name only, but on behalf of and with the authority of M.V. When the bill is presented for payment the defendants refuse payment on the ground that it does not bear the indorsement of M.V. By English law, an indorsement by E.V. in his own name without any indication that he is signing on behalf of his principal is not a valid indorsement. By French law, an indorsement may be validly made by an authorised agent signing his own name. Under section 72(1) of the Act, the form of the indorsement was governed by French law. Also French law governed the legal effect of the transfer by virtue of section 72(2)[56] and it was the law of the place where the transfer was made.[57] The defendants are liable to the claimants on the bill.[58]

9. A bill is drawn in Poland for an amount in Dutch florins and is accepted in London by the defendants payable at a bank in Amsterdam. The bill is not presented for payment there. Under English law, which, by virtue of section 72(2), governs the interpretation of the acceptance, the acceptance is general and not qualified. Since the holder is therefore not bound to present the bill for payment in Amsterdam, section 72(3) of the Act has no application. The necessity to present the bill for payment is governed by English law and not by the law of Holland. Under English law, presentment for payment is not necessary to render the defendants liable.[59]

**12–040**      10. At the instance of the claimants in Germany, 30 bills are accepted in Iran payable in London. Each of the bills is "backed" by the defendant

---

[54] *Embiricos v Anglo-Austrian Bank* [1905] 1 K.B. 677.
[55] *Haarbleicher v Baerselman* (1914) 137 L.T.J. 564.
[56] At 899, 900.
[57] At 895–896, 899.
[58] *Koechlin et Cie v Kestenbaum Bros* [1927] 1 K.B. 889.
[59] *Bank Polski v Mulder (K.J.) & Co.* [1941] 2 K.B. 266; [1942] 1 K.B. 497. See also s.17, Illustration 4.

placing in Iran his signature on the reverse side. The bills are then returned to the claimants who sign them in Germany as drawers, the bills being payable to their order. Subsequently, before maturity, with the authority and consent of the defendant sent from Iran, there is added in Germany to the defendant's signature the words *bon pour aval pour les tirés* (good as an *"aval"* for the drawees). One of the bills is, in figures, for an amount of DM 464,000, but by a typing error the word "thousand" is omitted from the amount expressed in words. Upon presentment for payment in London at maturity, all the bills are dishonoured. No notice of dishonour is given in respect of any bill. The bills are protested for non-payment, but not within the time required by section 51 of the 1882 Act. The claimants sue the defendant on his *"aval"*.

(1) The legal effect of the *"aval"* was determined (*per* Purchas and Woolf L.JJ.) by section 72(2) of the Act, or (*per* Mustill L.J.) by analogy thereto, by the law of the place where the contract of *"aval"* was made, *i.e.* by the law of Germany. By German law, the effect of the *"aval"* was not that of an anomalous indorsement: the *"aval"* was a guarantee by the defendant to the claimants of payment by the drawees. (2) Whether that guarantee was required to be supported by a note or memorandum to satisfy section 4 of the Statute of Frauds 1677 was to be determined by English law as the *lex fori*. By English law, the liability of the defendant as a party to the bill did not require to be supported by such a note or memorandum, but, in any event, the bills themselves were sufficient writings to satisfy the Statute. (3) Under section 72(3) of the Act, the necessity for or sufficiency of a protest or notice of dishonour was to be determined by English law as the law of the place where the bills were dishonoured. In English law, due protest and due notice of dishonour were not necessary to charge the defendant, for there was nothing in sections 51(2) and 48 of the Act which addressed the question of protest or notice of dishonour in relation to a person who had given an *"aval"*. (4) With respect to the bill on which the amount of the words and figures differed, this was a question of interpretation which, under section 72 (2) of the Act or by analogy thereto, was to be determined by German law as the law of the place where the contract of *"aval"* was made. By German law, in this particular case, the amount in figures prevailed over the amount in words. (5) The defendant was therefore liable to the claimants on the bills.[60]

11. The defendant gives to the claimant a cheque at Algiers drawn on an English bank, partly in return for money advanced by the claimant to the defendant for the purpose of playing baccarat in a club at Algiers and partly to be applied by the claimant in payment of sums won by various persons when playing at baccarat in the club. Baccarat is not an illegal

[60] *G. & H. Montage GmbH v Irvani* [1990] 1 W.L.R. 667.

game in Algiers and, by the law of France which applies in Algiers, there is valid consideration for the cheque. By the law of England the cheque has been given for an illegal consideration under the Gaming Acts 1835 and 1892. The cheque is unenforceable against the defendant. The legality of the consideration is to be determined by English law as the *lex loci solutionis* and (*per* Collins M.R.) the *lex fori*.[61]

**12–041**  12. Drafts are drawn in Russia by a Russian bank addressed to the M. Bank in England payable to the order of a Russian citizen. The consideration for the issue of the drafts is a transaction which is illegal by the law of Russia, being in breach of Russian currency laws then in force. A proof for the amounts of the drafts will not be admitted in the English winding-up of the Russian bank.[62]

13. The claimant, an Iranian national resident in England, agrees with the defendant, a travel agent in England, that the claimant will deposit a sum in rials with a travel agent in Iran nominated by the defendant. The agent in Iran will arrange for air tickets of an equivalent amount to be sent to the defendant in England, and on their receipt the defendant will pay a commensurate sum to the claimant in England. In pursuance of these arrangements the defendant draws a post-dated cheque on an English bank payable to the claimant, but subsequently countermands payment. The cheque is dishonoured on presentment. The claimant cannot recover from the defendant on the cheque. It has been given and received by the same parties to, and in order to carry out their obligations under, an exchange contract which involves the currency of Iran and which is contrary to the exchange regulations of Iran, a member of the International Monetary Fund.[63]

14. C, resident in Demerara, draws a bill on M, resident in Scotland, payable to the order of A, resident in Demerara. The bill is accepted payable in London. A indorses it in Demerara to T Bros in Demerara, who indorse it to T in London. T becomes bankrupt, and the bill passes to the respondents, his assignees in bankruptcy. At maturity, M is the holder of two dishonoured acceptances of T, and thus has a right of set-off against T's estate in the bankruptcy. In order to avoid this right of set-off, the respondents send the bill to Demerara with instructions to sue C, the drawer, and A, the indorser. C and A are entitled to plead the set-off in an action against them in Demerara. Since they drew and indorsed the bill in Demerara, their obligations are governed by the law of Demerara, and

---

[61] *Moulis v Owen* [1907] 1 K.B. 746.
[62] *Re Banque des Marchands de Moscou (No.3)* [1954] 1 W.L.R. 1108.
[63] *Mansouri v Singh* [1986] 1 W.L.R. 1393.

not by the law of the place of payment of the bill. By the law of Demerara, a surety is entitled to avail himself of any right of set-off (*compensation*) which the principal debtor has against the creditor.[64]

15. A bill is drawn in England in favour of the defendant upon a **12–042** drawee in Paris and accepted by him payable there. It is indorsed by the defendant to the claimant, both parties being domiciled in England. The bill is dishonoured by non-payment and a protest is duly drawn up in accordance with French law, but notice of dishonour is not duly given by the claimant to the defendant within the time limited by English law. French law regulates the time of giving notice of dishonour. Since the notice was given in due time according to that law, judgment is given for the claimant.[65]

16. A bill is drawn by L in London on P in Paris payable to the order of L, and is accepted by P. The bill is indorsed by L in blank and delivered to the defendant in England and by him indorsed in blank and delivered to the claimant in England, and indorsed by the claimant and delivered to B in France. The claimant, however, alters the bill by writing on its face and above the indorsements a rate of exchange at which the bill is payable. The bill is duly presented in France, but is dishonoured. The holder takes the steps required by the law of France, *i.e.* protest, in order to enable him to recover against other parties to the bill. Since the bill is payable in France, in the event of dishonour, notice of dishonour according to the law of France is good notice. Or, if English law applies, notice valid according to the law of France is to be deemed due notice, being such notice as can reasonably be required under the circumstances. But the alteration of the bill, being a material alteration, avoided it in the hands of the claimant.[66]

17. B & Co. at Newcastle draw a bill on C in Spain payable in Spain to the order of the defendant three months after date. The bill is purchased by the claimant in London from the defendant who indorses it in London to the claimant. The claimant indorses the bill and forwards it to M in Spain, where it is further indorsed. The holder presents it in Spain to C for acceptance, but acceptance is refused and the bill is duly protested there for non-acceptance. A delay of 12 days occurs before M writes to the claimant to inform him of the dishonour and the claimant then immediately gives notice of dishonour to the defendant. By the law of Spain, no notice of dishonour for non-acceptance is required. By English law, such

---

[64] *Allen v Kemble* (1848) 6 Moo. P.C. 314.
[65] *Rothschild v Currie* (1841) 1 Q.B. 43.
[66] *Hirschfield v Smith* (1866) L.R. 1 C.P. 340.

notice is required and, the notice given being out of time, both the claimant and the defendant are discharged. The claimant is entitled to recover the amount of the bill from the defendant. The obligation of M to give notice of dishonour to the claimant was governed by the law of Spain, and the claimant gave due notice of dishonour to the defendant in accordance with English law.[67]

**12–043** 18. The defendants, merchants in England, draw a bill upon a French firm in Paris, payable to their own order. The bill is accepted in Paris and indorsed to the claimants in England. The due date of payment is October 5, 1870, but before that date the Emperor of the French, in consequence of the Franco-Prussian war, issues a decree postponing the payment of bills by one month. This moratorium is extended from time to time by the government of France, with the result that the bill does not become payable until September 5, 1871. On that day the bill is presented to the acceptor for payment and is dishonoured. It is duly protested and due notice of dishonour is given to all parties. The claimants, as indorsees, are entitled to recover against the defendants, as drawers and indorsers, on the bill. The maturity of the bill is to be determined by French law, as the law of the place where it was accepted and payable. As between an English indorsee and an English indorser, the time of payment is likewise postponed.[68]

19. Before the 1914–1918 war the M Bank purchases from the firm of F. & R. Co. certain bills drawn by the firm in England on drawees in Germany and accepted payable there. The firm is ordered to be wound-up under the Trading with the Enemy and Export of Prohibited Goods Act 1916 and the bank seeks to prove in the winding-up for the amount of the bills. The due date written on the bills has passed, but German legislation postponed the maturity of the bills until further notice. The bank's proof is not admitted. By section 72(5) of the Act, the due date of the bills is to be determined according to German law. Since, under that law, the due date has not yet arrived, the proof must be rejected.[69]

---

[67] *Horne v Rouquette* (1878) 3 Q.B.D. 514.
[68] *Rouquette v Overmann* (1875) L.R. 10 Q.B. 525.
[69] *Re Francke and Rasched* [1918] 1 Ch. 470.

# PART III

# CHEQUES ON A BANKER

## Cheque defined

73. A cheque is a bill of exchange drawn on a banker payable on   13–001
demand.

Except as otherwise provided in this Part, the provisions of this Act
applicable to a bill of exchange payable on demand apply to a
cheque.

| Definitions | Comparison |
|---|---|
| "banker": s.2. | UCC: § 3–104. |
| "bill": s.2. | ULC: arts 1–3, 28 and *passim*. |

### COMMENT

**Cheques.** A cheque has two main functions. First, it enables a cus-   13–002
tomer who maintains an account with a bank to effect withdrawals from
that account. Cheques are, however, not the only means of withdrawal. In
the case of savings or deposit accounts, withdrawals may often be made
by a withdrawal slip or voucher or on production of a pass book. Even in
the case of a current account withdrawals may be made by the customer
by use of a plastic card, encoded with the customer's account number and
PIN ("personal identification number"), to operate an automatic teller
machine (ATM). The machine may be that of the bank which issues the
card and with whom the customer's account is maintained, or it may be
that of another bank with whom reciprocal arrangements have been
made by the issuer of the card. Network systems, *e.g.* "Link", have come
into existence in order to enable such cards to be more widely employed.
As a result, the use of cheques to effect withdrawals of cash over the
counter from personal accounts has considerably declined. It is likely to
decline still further, since paper-based transactions are more expensive to
operate than those which are machine based.

The second function of a cheque is to enable a customer to utilise funds
lent by him to a bank on current account to make payments to third
parties. The customer draws a cheque on the bank payable to a third

party. A cheque may be drawn payable to order or to bearer. But nowadays most cheques issued in the United Kingdom are crossed "account payee" and are not transferable.[1] These are not negotiable instruments but are, in effect, merely payment orders directing the bank to pay the amount of the cheque to the named payee. Cheques are delivered by the payee to his bank for collection and are collected through the clearing system.[2] Again, however, they are not the only means by which such payments may be made. Payments may be effected by standing orders, direct debits and other mandates to pay.[3] In recent years there has been an enormous growth in the use of plastic cards, *e.g.* "credit cards" (where the customer is given extended credit on his account) and "charge cards" (where he is expected to discharge the entire debit balance on the account at periodic intervals, usually of one month). Such cards may be "two-party" cards, that is to say, issued by shops and stores for the purchase of their own goods or services. Or they may be "three-party" cards issued by banks, building societies, credit card and finance companies etc. for the purchase of goods and services from participating retailers. In most cases a separate card account is maintained for the customer and payments are made into the account from a current account with a bank by cheque, direct debit or (in some cases) by standing order. A still more recent phenomenon has been the appearance of the "debit card" which operates directly on the customer's current account to which debits created by the use of the card are posted within a period of a few days, or, in the case of EFTPOS transactions ("electronic funds transfer at point of sale"), immediately the retail transaction is carried out. It lies beyond the scope of the present work to consider the legal implications of the use of such cards.[4] But they may, in the course of time, displace the cheque as the most frequently used payment instrument in consumer transactions. Cards may also be used in some cases to obtain cash.

13–003      **Cheques and bills.** A cheque is essentially an instrument of payment. It is directed to a banker and instructs him to pay the instrument from funds lent to him by the drawer.[5] Being payable on demand, it is also intended as an instrument which will immediately be paid. A bill of exchange, on the other hand, is a credit instrument. It is frequently drawn payable at a future date and is indorsed and discounted or sold to a third party by the payee.

---

[1] s.81A(1); below, para.14–037.
[2] See Ellinger, Lomnicka and Hooley, *Modern Banking Law* (3rd ed.), Ch.9. But see s.74B (truncation of cheques).
[3] *e.g.* by the Giro system: see Ellinger, Lomnicka and Hooley, *Modern Banking Law*, Ch.12.
[4] See *Chitty on Contracts* (29th ed.), Vol.II, Ch.38.
[5] Or from funds made available by the banker to the customer on overdraft.

Cheques are not, and are not intended to be, accepted. A banker who has sufficient funds of his customer to enable him to pay a cheque drawn on him will be liable to the customer if he dishonours it.[6] But he incurs no liability to the payee or other holder of the cheque if he refuses or fails to pay it[7]; the remedy in such a case is to sue the drawer, who is the party ultimately liable on the instrument. In contrast, the acceptor of a bill engages that he will pay it according to the tenor of his acceptance. He is the party primarily liable. The drawer's liability on an accepted bill is a secondary liability; he engages that on due presentment it will be paid according to its tenor, and that if it be dishonoured he will compensate the holder or any indorser who is compelled to pay it, providing that the requisite proceedings on dishonour be taken.

For historical reasons, the law relating to cheques closely followed that relating to bills of exchange,[8] the cheque being viewed as an unaccepted bill. As a result, the sections on cheques are added as an appendage to those dealing with bills. But as long ago as 1854 Parke B. stated[9] that a cheque seemed to him to be:

" . . . a peculiar sort of instrument, in many respects resembling a Bill of Exchange, but in some entirely different. A cheque does not require acceptance; in the ordinary course it is never accepted; it is not intended for circulation, it is given for immediate payment; it is not entitled to days of grace; and though it is, strictly speaking, an order upon a debtor by a creditor to pay to a third person the whole or part of a debt, yet, in the ordinary understanding of persons, it is not so considered. It is more like an appropriation of what is treated as ready money in the hands of the banker, and in giving the order to appropriate to a creditor, the person giving the cheque must be considered as the person primarily liable to pay, who orders his debt to be paid at a particular place, and as being much in the same position as the maker of a promissory note, or the acceptor of a Bill of Exchange, payable at a particular place and not elsewhere, who has no right to insist on immediate presentment at that place."

It would, perhaps, be preferable to have an entirely separate regime dealing with cheques, incorporating (*inter alia*) the provisions of the Cheques Act 1957.[10] In the Geneva system, there are separate Uniform

---

[6] See below, para.13–032 (s.75).
[7] See above, para.7–002.
[8] See Holden, *History of Negotiable Instruments in English Law* (1955), Ch.7.
[9] *Ramchurn Mullick v Luchmeechund Radakissen* (1854) 9 Moo. P.C. 46, 69–70. See also *Keene v Beard* (1860) 8 C.B., N.S. 372, 380, 381, as modified by *Hopkinson v Forster* (1874) L.R. 19 Eq. 74, 76.
[10] See below, para.17–001.

Laws governing bills of exchange and promissory notes on the one hand and cheques on the other.[11] The UNCITRAL Convention on Bills of Exchange and Promissory Notes,[12] specifically excludes cheques.

**13–004** **Definition of cheque.** All cheques are bills of exchange, but all bills of exchange are not cheques. The definition of a cheque in this section prescribes that the instrument must be (i) a bill of exchange, (ii) drawn on a banker, and (iii) payable on demand. A complete definition of a cheque is therefore as follows: an unconditional order in writing, addressed by one person to another (the latter being a banker), signed by the person giving it, requiring the banker to whom it is addressed to pay on demand a sum certain in money to or to the order of a specified person, or to bearer.

It is no part of the definition that a cheque should be an inland bill, or that it should be drawn by a *customer* on his banker. But cheques will almost invariably be drawn on a banker with whom the drawer maintains an account and of whom he is therefore a customer. The exception is where a cheque is drawn by a person who forges the signature of the ostensible drawer or places it there without his authority[13]; but in that case, if no other signature is present, there is some doubt whether the instrument is in fact a cheque.[14] The indorser of such an instrument may, however, by estoppel be liable on it.[15] A banker who pays an instrument on which his customer's signature is forged or unauthorised cannot ordinarily debit the customer's account with the amount so paid.[16]

It is also no part of the definition of a cheque that it should be transferable.[17]

**13–005** **"Bill of exchange."** The requirements of a cheque *qua* bill of exchange have already been dealt with in the Comment on section 3 of the Act.[18] In particular, it was there noted that a banker's draft, drawn by a banker on himself, is not a cheque because it is not addressed by one person to another[19]; that an order addressed to a banker requiring him to pay provided that a receipt form on the instrument is duly signed is not a

---

[11] See above, para.1–012.
[12] See above, para.1–012.
[13] s.24.
[14] See above, para.3–062.
[15] s.55(2).
[16] See above, para.3–059 (s.24).
[17] cf. ss.8, 81A.
[18] See above, para.2–007.
[19] *Capital and Counties Bank v Gordon* [1903] A.C. 240, 250. See also s.5(2) and above, para.2–012.

cheque because the order is not unconditional[20]; and that an instrument drawn payable to "cash or order",[21] or to the order of something other than a person, *e.g.* to "wages",[22] is not—though addressed to a banker—a cheque, because it is not drawn payable to a specified person or to bearer. But a cheque may be drawn payable to, or to the order of, the drawer ("Pay self") or it may be drawn payable to, or to the order of, the drawee banker.[23]

**"Drawn on a banker."** By section 2 of the Act, "banker" includes a **13–006** body of persons, whether incorporated or not, who carry on the business of banking. This provision has already been considered in the Comment on that section.[24] Financial institutions other than "banks" in the popular sense, such as building societies and finance companies which are authorised to accept deposits or to provide banking services, may carry on the business of banking.

Provided that a cheque is drawn on a banker,[25] its status as such is not affected by the fact that it is not drawn on a cheque form provided by the banker[26] or that it does not specify the place where it is payable.[27] A banker is, however, entitled to insist that cheques be drawn by his customer which specify the name and address of the branch at which the customer's account is maintained and where the cheque is payable. Moreover, the banker is entitled, by agreement,[28] to require that cheque forms be used only for drawing cheques on the specified account at the specified branch. The pre-printed magnetic symbols on the cheque form, which are employed in the clearing and accounting process, set out the clearing number of the bank and of the branch, the number of the account and the number of the cheque. These numbers are read electronically and cannot be affected by pen-and-ink alterations on the face of the cheque.

---

[20] *Bavins Jnr & Sims v London and South Western Bank Ltd* [1900] 1 Q.B. 270 (s.3, Illustration 4). But see Cheques Act 1957, ss.1(2)(a), 4(2)(b), 5. Contrast *Nathan v Ogdens Ltd* (1905) 93 L.T. 553, affirmed (1905) 94 L.T. 126 (s.3, Illustration 5) and *Roberts & Co. v Marsh* [1915] 1 K.B. 42 (Illustration 1). See above, para.2–009.

[21] *North and South Insurance Corp. Ltd v National Provincial Bank Ltd* [1936] 1 K.B. 328; *Cole v Milsome* [1951] 1 All E.R. 311; *Orbit Mining and Trading Co. Ltd v Westminster Bank Ltd* [1963] 1 Q.B. 794 (s.3, Illustration 8). But see the protection afforded to the banker by ss.1, 4 of the Cheques Act 1957, and see also s.5 of the 1957 Act; above, para.2–018; below, paras 17–013, 17–064, 17–075.

[22] See above, para.2–018 (s.3).

[23] s.5(1).

[24] See above, para.1–016.

[25] *cf. Aziz v Knightsbridge Gaming and Catering Services Ltd* (1982) 79 L.S.G. 1412, where an instrument appearing to be a cheque, but drawn on a non-existent bank, was held to be a cheque for the purposes of s.16(3) of the Gaming Act 1968.

[26] *Roberts & Co. v Marsh* [1915] 1 K.B. 42 (Illustration 1).

[27] s.3(4)(c).

[28] *cf. Burnett v Westminster Bank Ltd* [1966] 1 Q.B. 742 (Illustration 2).

A banker cannot be required to pay other than at the branch indicated on the cheque.[29]

**13–007**    **"Payable on demand."** As a general rule, no time for payment is expressed on a cheque, nor is a cheque expressed to be payable on demand. But, by section 10(1) of the Act, such an instrument is payable on demand. If an instrument in the form of a cheque is drawn payable on a specified date or "not before" a specified date, then it is not a cheque but may be a bill of exchange or promissory note.

**13–008**    **Date.** A cheque is not invalid by reason that it is not dated.[30] But a banker is entitled to refuse to pay an undated cheque.[31] The date on an undated cheque may be inserted in accordance with section 20 of the Act. Where a cheque is dated, the date will, unless the contrary is proved, be deemed to be the true date.[32] An alteration of the date is a material alteration.[33]

**13–009**    **Post-dated cheques.** A cheque is not invalid by reason of the fact that it is post-dated,[34] and (if payable to order or bearer) it is fully negotiable between the time of its issue and the date written on it. These matters, and the status of the instrument during the intervening period, have been considered in the Comment on section 13(2) of the Act.[35]

A banker who inadvertently pays a post-dated cheque is not entitled at once to debit his customer's account since he has no mandate to pay until the date written on the cheque arrives. He cannot therefore refuse to honour cheques drawn on the customer's account which, but for the unauthorised payment, he would have been bound to honour. If, before the ostensible date, the customer countermands payment of the cheque[36] or for any other reason the duty and authority of the banker to pay it is revoked,[37] the loss will fall on the banker.[38] He could not, it is submitted, claim to have purchased an order cheque for value (as opposed to

---

[29] *Woodland v Fear* (1857) 7 E. &. B. 519; *Garnett v M'Kewan* (1872) L.R. 8 Exch. 10; *Joachimson v Swiss Bank Corp.* [1921] 3 K.B. 110, 127; *Arab Bank Ltd v Barclays Bank (D.C. & O.)* [1954] A.C. 495.

[30] s.3(4)(a).

[31] *Griffiths v Dalton* [1940] 2 K.B. 264.

[32] s.13(1).

[33] s.64(2).

[34] s.13(2).

[35] See above, para.2–098.

[36] s.75(1).

[37] See below, para.13–044 (s.75).

[38] *Pollock v Bank of New Zealand* (1901) 20 N.Z.L.R. 174; *Keyes v Royal Bank of Canada* [1947] 3 D.L.R. 161; *Brien v Dwyer* (1979) 141 C.L.R. 378, 394. Contrast *Magill v Bank of North Queensland* (1895) 6 Q.L.J. 262 (Aust.). But see above, para.8–021 (recovery by banker from person to whom it is paid).

effecting a payment intended as a discharge) before its due date and so be entitled to sue the drawer as a holder in due course.[39] It is not open to him to depart from his character as drawee and paying agent of the customer and claim to be the holder of an order cheque of which he is not the payee and which has not been negotiated to him.[40] Once the ostensible date arrives without countermand or revocation, it would appear that the banker may then lawfully debit his customer's account, just as if the cheque had been presented on or after the ostensible date. A banker is bound to pay a post-dated cheque presented on or within a reasonable time after its ostensible date even though he may have refused payment of the same cheque before and marked it as post-dated when presented before that date.[41]

**Application of Act.** The main exceptions referred to in Part III of the 13–010 Act are as follows:

(a) failure by a holder to present a cheque for payment within a reasonable time does not completely discharge the drawer as does failure to present a bill payable on demand under section 45 of the Act (s.74);

(b) provision is made for an alternative place of payment and alternative means of presentment for payment where a cheque is presented by a banker for payment (ss.74A to 74C);

(c) the duty and authority of the drawee banker to pay a cheque drawn on him by his customer is revoked by countermand of payment and by notice of the customer's death (s.75);

(d) the rules as to crossings apply to cheques but do not apply to bills of exchange (ss.76 to 80);

(e) special incidents attach to crossed cheques marked "not negotiable" or "account-payee" which do not apply in the case of bills of exchange (ss.81, 81A).

In addition, the provisions of the Cheques Act 1957 (which is to be construed as one with the 1882 Act) apply only to cheques and certain analogous instruments, but not to bills of exchange.

It should also be noted that (a) references in the Act to acceptance and the acceptor do not apply to cheques, since cheques are not intended to be and are not accepted; (b) protection is afforded by section 60 of the Act to a banker who pays an order cheque on which an indorsement is

---

[39] *Keyes v Royal Bank of Canada* [1947] 3 D.L.R. 161; *Paget* (12th ed.), 15.11. *cf. Canadian Bank of Commerce v Brash* (1957) 10 D.L.R. (2d) 555.

[40] See above, para.4–060 (s.29). But see *London Provincial & South Western Bank Ltd v Buszard* (1918) 35 T.L.R. 142 (s.29, Illustration 9).

[41] *Emanuel v Robarts* (1868) 17 L.T. 696 to the contrary would not now be followed: see *Paget* (12th ed.), 15.11.

forged[42]; and (c) although the drawer of a cheque is in principle entitled to receive notice of dishonour,[43] in practice notice of dishonour will normally be dispensed with as regards him since payment will be refused by the drawee banker either on the ground that, as between himself and the drawer, he is under no obligation to pay the cheque due to insufficient funds[44] or because the drawer has countermanded payment.[45]

13–011     **Traveller's cheques.**[46] The type of document known as the traveller's cheque is widely used as a means of payment by those travelling away from home. Traveller's cheques are purchased by the traveller from the issuing bank or its agents. There are a number of different forms of cheque currently in use, but they all have one feature in common. This is that they must be signed twice by the traveller, first at the time when they are issued to him ("the original signature") and secondly at the time when he cashes or negotiates them ("the countersignature"). Unlike the normal cheque, there is an undertaking on the part of the issuing bank to pay the amount stated in the instrument. The precise terms of that undertaking are not necessarily clearly spelt out. Some forms of traveller's cheque merely state, for example "Holder to countersign here in presence of paying agent". It is, however, normally stated on the cheque (or it is to be assumed) that the bank will pay only if the cheque is both signed and countersigned by the same person.

Some traveller's cheques take the form of an order addressed by the bank to itself, signed by one or more directors on behalf of the bank, requiring the bank to pay the sum stated in the cheque to the order of the traveller (who is identified by the original signature).[47] It is not envisaged that the instrument will be accepted by the bank; the bank's liability arises as drawer. In this respect, therefore, the instrument resembles a banker's draft payable on demand. It is clear, however, that a traveller's cheque in this form cannot be a bill of exchange or cheque within the meaning of the Act,[48] since it is not addressed by one person to another.[49] Other traveller's cheques are similar in form, being addressed to the bank and drawn by the chairman or a director of the bank[50]; but they are payable, when countersigned, to the order of the payee (whose name is

---

[42] See also s.1 of the Cheques Act 1957; below, para.17–005.
[43] s.48.
[44] s.50(2)(c)(4).
[45] s.50(2)(c)(5).
[46] See Ellinger (1969) 19 Univ. of Toronto L.J. 132; Stassen (1978) 95 S.A.L.J. 180; Frohlich (1980) 54 A.L.J. 388; *Chitty on Contracts* (29th ed.), Vol.II, § 34–174; Cowen, *Law of Negotiable Instruments in South Africa* (5th ed.), p.295.
[47] *e.g.* National Westminster Bank traveller's cheque.
[48] ss.3(1), 73.
[49] See above, para.2–012. But see s.5(2).
[50] It is, however, uncertain whether the signature is personal or on behalf of the bank.

left blank).[51] Another type of traveller's cheque takes the form of an order addressed to the bank by the traveller as drawer directing the bank to pay the amount of the cheque to the order of the traveller as identified by his signature.[52] The cheque bears the signature of the chairman or a director of the bank, which is presumably an acceptance.[53] It might be argued that the countersignature on a cheque in the first and third of these three forms is merely the indorsement of the original payee which is required to negotiate the instrument, since it is payable to his order. But a countersignature is demanded as a condition of payment even if the original payee presents it for payment to the drawee bank. Although it could be contended that the countersignature is then a mere receipt[54] or identification,[55] it is submitted that its requirement renders the order to pay not unconditional. For this reason, an instrument in any of these three forms cannot be a bill of exchange or a cheque.[56]

Other traveller's cheques resemble promissory notes. The issuing bank promises to pay the sum stated in the cheque to the order of the payee (whose name is left blank) when the cheque is countersigned by the person identified by the original signature.[57] But the instrument is not a promissory note within the meaning of the Act[58] because the promise to pay is again not unconditional.[59]

There is little doubt, however, that traveller's cheques are treated as **13–012** negotiable instruments throughout the world. Their negotiability can be attributed to modern mercantile custom.[60] It seems likely that the provisions of the 1882 Act would be applied, with any necessary modifications, to traveller's cheques, either by analogy or by virtue of the common law as codified by the Act. There are nevertheless certain features of the traveller's cheque which might call for special treatment.[61] The position is further complicated by the fact that most banks which issue traveller's cheques either undertake, subject to certain conditions, to refund their

---

[51] *e.g.* American Express traveller's cheque.

[52] This signature may be either the countersignature or the original signature.

[53] *S v Katsikaris* 1980 (3) S.A. 580.

[54] But see *Bavins Jnr & Sims v London and South Western Bank Ltd* [1900] 1 Q.B. 270 (s.3, Illustration 4).

[55] Stassen (1978) 95 S.A.L.J. 180, 182–183.

[56] ss.3(1), 73; *S v Katsikaris* 1980 (3) S.A. 580. Contrast UCC, § 3–106(c); Goode, *Commercial Law* (3rd ed.), p.569.

[57] *e.g.* Thomas Cook, Citibank and Bank of America traveller's cheques.

[58] s.83.

[59] Contrast UCC, § 3–106(c); Goode, *Commercial Law* (3rd ed.) p.569.

[60] For other examples, see *Goodwin v Robarts* (1875) L.R. 10 Ex. 337 (affirmed (1876) 1 App.Cas. 476); *London Joint Stock Bank v Simmons* [1892] A.C. 201; *Edelstein v Schuler & Co.* [1902] 2 K.B. 144. See also *Ashford v Thos Cook & Son (Bankers) Ltd* (1970) 471 P. 2d 531, 532; *S v Katsikaris* 1980 (3) S.A. 580 at 592.

[61] *e.g.* the inability of the traveller to countermand payment; (possibly) the fact that the cheques are transferred without completion of the name of the payee (see below); and (possibly) that travellers' cheques will not become "overdue".

face value if they are lost or stolen, or impose certain conditions upon the traveller's right to obtain reimbursement.[62] There have been a number of cases decided in the United States on transactions involving traveller's cheques,[63] but very few in this country.[64]

A holder who takes from the traveller a traveller's cheque which has been duly signed and countersigned by the traveller will be entitled to payment from the issuing bank. If the cheque is signed by the traveller, but then stolen from him and his countersignature forged, the transferee will have no right to payment.[65] Where the countersignature constitutes the indorsement of the traveller-payee, the transferee would acquire no title to the instrument through or under the forged indorsement.[66] Where the countersignature is required as a condition of the order or promise to pay, that condition would not have been satisfied. On the other hand, if the traveller both signs and countersigns the cheque, and it is then stolen from him and negotiated by the thief, the transferee will hold it free from any defect of title of prior parties[67] if he is a holder in due course[68] or derives his title to it through a holder in due course.[69] The same will be the case if the traveller neglects to sign the cheque at the outset, so that the thief is able both to sign and countersign it with the same signature.[70]

By definition, however, a holder in due course must be a holder who takes an instrument which is complete and regular on the face of it.[71] In the United States it has been held[72] that a person could be a holder in due course of a traveller's cheque where the space for the name of the payee was left blank, it being quite usual to negotiate a cheque in that state. But it is doubtful whether that decision would be followed in this country. A holder in due course must also take the instrument in good faith and for value, and before it is overdue. It may be assumed that the general

---

[62] See *Fellus v National Westminster Bank plc* (1983) 133 N.L.J. 766; *Braithwaite v Thomas Cook Travellers Cheques Ltd* [1989] Q.B. 553; *El Awadi v Bank of Credit and Commerce International S.A.* [1990] 1 Q.B. 606; Hall (1993) 143 New L.J. 360.

[63] See the books and articles cited above, para.13–011, n.46.

[64] See the cases cited above, para.13–012, n.62.

[65] *Samberg v American Express Co.* (1904) 99 N.W. 879; *Sullivan v Knauth* (1914) 146 N.Y.S. 583, (1915) 115 N.E. 460. But see now UCC, §§ 3–106(c), 3–305(a)(2).

[66] s.24.

[67] s.38(2).

[68] s.29(1). But the original payee cannot be a holder in due course (see above, para.4–059). The original payee should, however, be entitled to payment if he took the cheque in good faith and for value: see above, para.5–072 (s.38).

[69] s.29(3).

[70] *Ashford v Thos Cook & Son (Bankers) Ltd* (1970) 471 P. 2d 531. For the rights of the holder where incomplete cheques are stolen from the issuer, see *Chitty on Contracts* (29th ed.), Vol.II, § 34–187; Cowen, *Law of Negotiable Instruments in South Africa* (5th ed.), p.313.

[71] s.29(1).

[72] *Emerson v American Express Co.* (1952) 90 A. 2d. 236. *cf. Gray v American Express Co.* (1977) 239 S.E. 2d 621.

presumption[73] that every holder is prima facie deemed to be a holder in due course applies also to traveller's cheques.

More problematic is the question whether a bank which pays a travel- **13–013** ler's cheque and a bank which collects payment of such a cheque for a customer are respectively entitled to the protection of section 1 and section 4 of the Cheques Act 1957.[74] If the cheque is in the form of a promissory note, the bank could not claim to be protected, since the instrument clearly does not fall within the Act. But if it is in the form of a cheque or demand draft, then, even though it contains a conditional order to pay, it is possible that it would be an instrument referred to in sections 1(2)(a) or (b) and 4(2)(b) or (d) of the 1957 Act,[75] and the bank could be protected.

**Government payable orders and warrants.** Government payable **13–014** orders, or warrants, are documents issued mainly (but not exclusively) by one Government department to be drawn on the same or another Government department, such as a National Savings Warrant. They are treated as cheques by banks and their customers, although they are not cheques as defined by the present section. The Review Committee on Banking Services Law and Practice recommended[76] that legislation should be enacted to equate such orders and warrants (for the payment of interest or dividends, and for repayment of capital) with cheques, and the Government proposes to introduce legislation to this effect.[77]

ILLUSTRATIONS

1. The defendant, not having his cheque book with him, draws on a **13–015** blank sheet of paper a form of cheque addressed to his bankers and payable to the claimant. Not wishing this to be passed through his bank account, he writes in the face of it "to be retained" and promises the claimant to send a cheque on one of his bankers' printed forms in substitution for it. This he does not do. The instrument is presented to the

---

[73] s.30(2).
[74] Or s.19 of the Stamp Act 1853 (see above, para.8–045). The protection of s.60 of the 1882 Act would not apply, as the instrument is not a bill as defined in s.3(1), nor that of s.80, as the instrument is not a crossed cheque. It is submitted that the bank will, if not protected, be liable in conversion and for money had and received to the true owner: see *Braithwaite v Thomas Cook Travellers Cheques Ltd* [1989] Q.B. 553, 561; *El Awadi v Bank of Credit and Commerce International S.A.* [1990] Q.B. 606, 615, 627.
[75] See below, paras 17–013, 17–064. But with respect to s.1(2)(a) and 4(2)(b), the document may not be one issued by a customer of the bank.
[76] (1989) Com. 622, rec. 7(11), 7(12).
[77] (1990) Cm. 1026, Annex 5, paras 5.19, 5.20.

defendant's bankers for payment, but is dishonoured. The defendant is liable to the claimant on the instrument. It is a cheque. The words "to be retained" are only a request to the payee, and do not prevent it from being an unconditional order by the defendant to his bankers to pay.[78]

2. The claimant is a customer of the defendant bank. He maintains two current accounts, one at the Borough branch of the bank and the other at the Bromley branch. A cheque book is supplied to him to effect withdrawals from the Borough branch account. Each cheque bears the magnetic ink number of that branch. On the cover of the cheque book there is printed "The cheques and credit slips in this book will be applied to the account for which they have been prepared. Customers must therefore not permit their use on another account." Wishing to draw a cheque on the Bromley branch, the claimant uses for this purpose a "Borough" cheque, changing the address on the cheque to that of the Bromley branch. The claimant countermands payment of this cheque after issue by telephoning the Bromley branch, giving full details and the fact that it has been altered from Borough to Bromley. The cheque is dealt with by computer and is forwarded to the Borough branch, where it is paid. The defendants cannot debit his account with the amount of the cheque. There was an effective countermand of payment. The claimant knew that the cover of the cheque book had printed words on it, but did not know and could not reasonably be taken to have assumed that the cover contained conditions.[79]

### Presentment of cheque for payment

13–016       **74. Subject to provisions of this Act—**

           **(1) Where a cheque is not presented for payment within a reasonable time of its issue, and the drawer or the person on whose account it is drawn had the right at the time of presentment as between him and the banker to have the cheque paid and suffers actual damage through the delay, he is discharged to the extent of such damage, that is to say, to the extent to which such drawer or person is a creditor of such banker to a larger amount than he would have been had such cheque been paid.**

           **(2) In determining what is a reasonable time regard shall be had to the nature of the instrument, the usage of trade and of bankers, and the facts of the particular case.**

[78] *Roberts & Co. v Marsh* [1915] 1 K.B. 42.
[79] *Burnett v Westminster Bank Ltd* [1966] 1 Q.B. 742.

(3) The holder of such cheque as to which such drawer or person
is discharged shall be a creditor, in lieu of such drawer or
person, of such banker to the extent of such discharge, and
entitled to recover the amount from him.

Definitions                      Comparison
"banker": s.2.                   UCC: §§ 3–414, 3–415, 4–404.
"cheque": s.73.                  ULC: arts 29–31.
"holder": s.2.
"person": s.2.

### COMMENT

**Subsection (1): delay in presenting a cheque for payment.** This sec-   13–017
tion altered the previous law.[80] It was introduced in the Lords by Lord
Bramwell to mitigate the rigour of the common law rule. At common law
the mere omission to present a cheque for payment did not discharge the
drawer until at any rate six years had elapsed,[81] and in this respect the
common law appears unaltered.[82] But if a cheque was not presented
within a reasonable time, as defined by the cases, and the drawer suffered
actual damage by the delay, *e.g.* by failure of the bank, the drawer was
absolutely discharged, even though ultimately the bank paid a substantial proportion of its liabilities.[83] By subsection (1) the drawer is now
discharged only to the extent of the actual damage suffered by him
through the delay, that is to say, to the extent to which he is a creditor of
the bank to a larger amount than he would have been had the cheque
been paid.

The effect of the subsection may be illustrated as follows: A draws a
cheque on his banker for £1,000 payable to B, who neglects to present it
for payment within a reasonable time of its issue. At the time at which
presentment ought to have been made,[84] A had in excess of £1,000
standing to his credit on his account and would therefore have had the
right, as between himself and his banker, to have the cheque paid. Before
the cheque is presented for payment the banker fails and the cheque is
unpaid. At the time of the failure, A has £4,000 standing to his credit on

---

[80] *Chalmers* (9th ed.), pp. 2, 293.
[81] *i.e.* the limitation period. See above, para.7–058 (s.57).
[82] See below.
[83] *Alexander v Burchfield* (1842) 7 M. & G. 1061, 1067; *Robinson v Hawksford* (1846) 9 Q.B. 52,
59; *Bailey v Bodenham* (1864) 16 C.B.N.S. 288.
[84] The subs. is infelicitously drafted; the words "at the time of such presentment" must
mean "at the time at which presentment ought to have been made".

the account, and is a creditor of the banker to that amount. Had the cheque been duly presented and paid, he would have been the banker's creditor in the amount of £3,000 only. A has suffered actual damage through the delay, and is discharged to the extent of £1,000. If, at the time of the failure, he had only a credit of £500 on his account, he is discharged to the extent of £500.

It is generally accepted that subsection (1) overrides, in the case of cheques, section 45(2) of the Act, by which a bill payable on demand must be presented for payment within a reasonable time after its issue to render the drawer liable.[85] That provision, however, continues to apply in relation to the indorser of a cheque, who will be discharged if the cheque is not presented within a reasonable time after its indorsement.[86] Although it is not expressly so stated, the subsection appears to be exhaustive, that is to say, delay in presenting a cheque for payment will not affect the liability of the drawer except when and to the extent that the subsection applies. Thus, in the above example, if at the time at which presentment ought to have been made A had insufficient funds in his account to meet the cheque, and no overdraft facility, so that he would then have had no right to have the cheque paid, he will not be discharged, either in whole or in part. The subsection does not apply in such a case. A *fortiori*, however long the delay,[87] the drawer will not be discharged unless he thereby suffers loss, *e.g.* through failure of the banker, at least until the time that the limitation period expires.

13–018      It has been previously noted[88] that, at common law, where a creditor takes from a debtor the bill of a third party as conditional payment of or as security for a debt, his failure duly to present the bill for payment will—if the debtor is thereby prejudiced—release the debtor from liability for the debt or other consideration for which the instrument was given. If this principle survives in the modern law, and applies to cheques,[89] then it is submitted that it would be reasonable to extend the effect of subsection (1) so as to release the debtor only to the extent that he has been prejudiced by the discharge of the drawer due to the delay.

13–019      **Subsection (2): reasonable time.** At common law, in the absence of special circumstances, a cheque had to be presented for payment on the

---

[85] s.45 begins "Subject to the provisions of this Act", but so does s.74. *Paget* (8th ed.), p.221 commented: "Presumably this makes the effect nil either way. But s.45(2) says, 'Where a *bill* is payable on demand'; s.74 says 'Where a *cheque* is not presented'. This may be intended to turn the scale."

[86] See above, para.6–039 (s.45). *cf. King & Boyd v Porter* [1925] N.I. 103.

[87] *King & Boyd v Porter* [1925] N.I. 103 (three-year delay). See also *Shapiro v Greenstein* (1969) 10 D.L.R. (3d) 746 (post-dated cheque).

[88] See above, para.6–042 (s.45).

[89] *Hopkins v Ware* (1869) L.R. 4 Ex. 268 (creditor accepts cheque drawn by agent of debtor).

day following its receipt if the person receiving it and the banker on whom it was drawn were in the same place.[90] If they were in different places, it had to be forwarded on the day after receipt either direct to the drawee bank or to an agent for collection, who likewise had to present or forward it on the day after he received it.[91] Those rules are swept into limbo by subsection (2). So far as the payee is concerned, it may well be doubted whether the citizen in his private affairs, or even any professional man or every business man, makes a habit of paying in cheques the day after receiving them. Moreover the bank to whom the cheque is delivered for collection will pass it through the clearing system,[92] irrespective of whether the drawee bank branch is in the same or in a different place.

What is a reasonable time may differ for the purposes of section 36 (3) (when demand bill is overdue),[93] section 45(2) (liability of indorser),[94] section 74(1), and the refusal by a banker to honour a cheque which is "stale".[95]

Delay in making presentment for payment will be excused in the circumstances set out in section 46(1) of the Act.

**Subsection (3): rights of holder when drawer discharged.** By this subsection the holder is, in effect, subrogated to the rights of the drawer to the extent that the latter is discharged. Thus, in the above example, the holder could prove against the banker for the £1,000 or the £500, as the case may be.    13–020

## Presentment of cheque for payment: alternative place of presentment

**74A. Where the banker on whom a cheque is drawn—**    13–021
   **(a) has by notice published in the London, Edinburgh and Belfast Gazettes specified an address at which cheques drawn on him may be presented, and**
   **(b) has not by notice so published cancelled the specification of that address, the cheque is also presented at the proper place if it is presented there.**

---

[90] *Alexander v Burchfield* (1842) 7 M. & G. 1061.
[91] *Hare v Henty* (1861) 10 C.B.N.S. 65; *Prideaux v Criddle* (1869) L.R. 4 Q.B. 455; *Heywood v Pickering* (1874) L.R. 9 Q.B. 428.
[92] See Ellinger, Lomnicka and Hooley, *Modern Banking Law* (3rd ed.), Ch.9.
[93] See above, para.5–043.
[94] See above, para.6–048.
[95] See *Paget* (12th ed.), 18.13; below, para.13–065 (s.75).

Amendment
This section was inserted by Article 3 of the Deregulation (Bills of Exchange) Order 1996

| Definitions | Comparison. |
|---|---|
| "banker": s.2. | UCC: § 4–204. |
| "cheque": s.73. | |

COMMENT

13–022    **Presentment at proper place.** Section 45(3) of the Act requires a bill (including a cheque) to be presented "at the proper place" as defined in section 45(4).[96] It has been held that presentment of a cheque for payment through clearing is effective only when it is physically delivered to the branch of the paying bank on which it is drawn.[97] The present section permits the banker on whom a cheque is drawn to specify, by public notice, an address (*e.g.* his head office or data processing centre) on which cheques drawn on him may be presented, and the cheque is also presented at the proper place if it is presented there. It is not limited to presentment by the alternative means allowed by section 74B. But it applies only to "cheques" (as defined in section 73 of the Act) and not to the analogous instruments referred to in sections 1(2)[98] and 4(2)(b)(c)(d)[99] of the Cheques Act 1957.

**Presentment of cheque for payment: alternative means of presentment by banker.**

13–023    74B. (1) **A banker may present a cheque for payment to the banker on whom it is drawn by notifying him of its essential features by electronic means or otherwise instead of by presenting the cheque itself.**

(2) **If a cheque is presented for payment under this section, presentment need not be made at the proper place or at a reasonable hour on a business day.**

(3) **If, before the close of business on the next business day following presentment of a cheque under this section, the banker on whom the cheque is drawn requests the banker by**

---

[96] See above, para.6–050.
[97] *Barclays Bank plc v Bank of England* [1985] 1 All E.R. 385; above, para.6–062.
[98] See below, para.17–013.
[99] See below, para.17–064.

whom the cheque was presented to present the cheque itself—

(a) the presentment under this section shall be disregarded, and

(b) this section shall not apply in relation to the subsequent presentment of the cheque.

(4) A request under subsection (3) above for the presentment of a cheque shall not constitute dishonour of the cheque by non-payment.

(5) Where presentment of a cheque is made under this section, the banker who presented the cheque and the banker on whom it is drawn shall be subject to the same duties in relation to the collection and payment of the cheque as if the cheque itself had been presented for payment.

(6) For the purposes of this section, the essential features of a cheque are—

(a) the serial number of the cheque,

(b) the code which identifies the banker on whom the cheque is drawn,

(c) the account number of the drawer of the cheque, and

(d) the amount of the cheque is [as] entered by the drawer of the cheque.

Amendment

This section was inserted by Article 4 of the Deregulation (Bills of Exchange) Order 1996.

Definitions
"banker": s.2.
"business day": s.92.
"cheque": s.73.

Comparison.
UCC: §§ 4–110, 4–406.

COMMENT

**Truncation of cheques.**[1] Clearance of cheques by physical present-ment of the cheque to the paying banker on whom it is drawn requires the daily movement between banks of upwards of 10 million cheques. On the other hand, the "truncation" of cheques enables banks to reduce this flow of paper by capturing, electronically, the details contained in the magnetic ink codeline at the bottom of the cheque, and passing those

**13–024**

[1] See Vroegop [1990] L.M.C.L.Q. 244.

details to the paying bank by electronic means instead of the cheque itself. The cheques, meanwhile, remain with the collecting bank. The Review Committee on Banking Services Law and Practice recommended a change in the law to permit this to be done[2] and the Government accepted this recommendation.[3] It was implemented in the present section, which was inserted by Article 4 of the Deregulation (Bills of Exchange) Order 1996,[4] made under the Deregulation and Contracting Out Act 1994.[5]

**13–025**    **Presentment by notification of essential features.** A banker may still present the cheque itself for payment and no doubt cheques of high value will continue to be so presented. But subsection (1) affords him an alternative means of presentment by notifying the banker on whom the cheque is drawn of its essential features "by electronic means or otherwise". The words "or otherwise" are very general and could (in theory) include notification by letter, telefax or telephone, or even by word of mouth. The "essential features" referred to are listed in subsection (6) and are those which are found on collection in the magnetic codeline at the bottom of the cheque (the word "is" in subsection (6)(d) appears to be a misprint for "as").

Subsection (2) in effect amends section 45 of the Act in respect of such presentment. Under section 45(3) presentment must be made "at a reasonable hour on a business day", and "at the proper place" as defined in section 45(4).[6] These requirements are dispensed with in the case of a presentment under the present section.

**13–026**    **"Cheque."** The present section applies only to the presentment of a "cheque" as defined in section 73 of the Act, that is to say, a bill of exchange drawn on a banker payable on demand. It does not apply (by virtue of section 5 of the Cheques Act 1957)[7] to the analogous instruments referred to in section 4(2)(b)(c)(d) of the 1957 Act[8] nor to those referred to in section 1(2) of that Act.[9] This alternative method is therefore not available in the case, for example, of a banker's draft[10] drawn by the

---

[2] (1989) Cm. 622, rec. 7(8); above, para.1–008.
[3] (1990) Cm. 1026, Annex 5, paras 5–11—5–13.
[4] SI 1996/2993. It applies to all cheques drawn on or after November 28, 1996.
[5] But full cheque truncation is still "some way off", possibly due to the expense involved: see *Paget* (12th ed.), 17–21; Brindle and Cox, *Law of Bank Payments* (3rd ed.), 7–064.
[6] See above, para.6–050.
[7] s.5 refers only to "the provisions of the Bills of Exchange Act 1882 relating to *crossed* cheques . . . "; see below, para.17–075.
[8] See below, para.17–064.
[9] See below, para.17–013.
[10] This is not a cheque: see above, para.13–005.

banker on himself or of a dividend warrant.[11] It also applies only to presentment of a cheque for payment by a banker (as defined in section 2 of the 1882 Act) to the banker on whom it is drawn.

**Request for presentment of the cheque itself.** By subsection (3) the 13–027 banker on whom the cheque is drawn may request the banker by whom a cheque has been presented under this section to present the cheque itself. This request must be made before the close of business on the next business day following presentment under this section, and it is submitted must be received by the presenting banker before this time. "Business day" is defined in section 92 of the Act.[12] Where such a request is effectively made, the presentment under the present section is to be disregarded and the cheque itself must be presented for payment in accordance with the provisions of the Act.[13] Such a request is likely to be made if there is some query about the cheque. Presumably for the avoidance of doubt, subsection (4) provides that the request does not constitute dishonour of the cheque by non-payment.

**Preservation of duties of bankers.** Subsection (5) makes it clear that 13–028 the duties of the collecting and paying bankers are not altered or diminished by this alternative means of presentment.

**Cheques presented for payment under section 74B: disapplication of section 52(4).**

74C. Section 52(4) above— 13–029
    (a) **so far as relating to presenting a bill for payment, shall not apply to presenting a cheque for payment under section 74B above, and**
    (b) **so far as relating a bill which is paid, shall not apply to a cheque which is paid following presentment under that section.**

Amendment
This section was inserted by Article 4 of the Deregulation (Bills of Exchange) Order 1996.

Definitions
"bill": ss.2, 3.

---

[11] s.95 of the 1882 Act refers only to "The provisions of this Act as to crossed cheques . . .": see below, para.16–018.
[12] below, para.16–012.
[13] s.45; above, para.6–035.

"cheque": s.73.

COMMENT

**13–030**      **Disapplication of section 52(4).** This section is supplementary to section 74B.

       Section 52(4)[14] provides that, where the holder of a bill presents it for payment, he must exhibit the bill to the person from whom he demands payment. It further provides that, when a bill is paid, the holder must forthwith deliver it up to the party paying it. Neither of these provisions applies where a banker presents a cheque for payment by the alternative method permitted by section 74B, that is to say, by notification of the essential features of the cheque and not by presentment of the cheque itself. See also section 3(2) of the Cheques Act 1957 (evidence of receipt).[15]

### Revocation of banker's authority

**13–031**      **75. The duty and authority of a banker to pay a cheque drawn on him by his customer are determined by—**
     **(1) Countermand of payment:**
     **(2) Notice of the customer's death.**

| Definitions | Comparison |
|---|---|
| "banker": s.2. | UCC: §§ 4–303, 4–401–4–405. |
| "cheque": s.73. | ULC: arts 32, 33. |

COMMENT

**13–032**      **Duty of banker to pay customer's cheque.** A banker is under a duty to his customer to pay on presentation a cheque in proper form[16] drawn on him by the customer provided that he has in his hands at the time funds in current account to the credit of the customer sufficient to meet

---

[14] See above, para.6–167.
[15] See below, para.17–027.
[16] *Cunliffe Brooks & Co. v Blackburn and District Benefit Building Society* (1884) 9 App. Cas. 857, 864; *London Joint Stock Bank Ltd v Macmillan* [1918] A.C. 777, 824.

634

the cheque[17] or has agreed to provide the customer with overdraft facilities sufficient to meet it.[18] In other circumstances, he is under no obligation to honour his customer's cheques.[19] If, however, a customer draws a cheque on him when there are no funds or no overdraft facilities sufficient to meet the cheque, the cheque on presentation constitutes a request to him by the customer to provide overdraft facilities sufficient to meet it. The banker then has an option whether or not to comply with that request. If he declines to do so, he acts entirely within his rights and no legal consequences follow as between himself and his customer. If he pays the cheque, he accepts the request and the payment has the same legal consequences as if the payment had been made pursuant to previously agreed overdraft facilities.[20]

A banker who refuses or fails to honour his customer's cheque when under an obligation to do so is liable to his customer in damages,[21] unless the requisite funds were paid in so short a time before the dishonour of the cheque that the banker could not with the exercise of reasonable diligence have ascertained the state of accounts between them.[22] He may also expressly reserve the right to refuse payment of a cheque drawn against uncleared effects[23] or be held entitled to do so by established banking practice.[24] In the absence of special directions from the customer, it is his duty to pay the customer's cheques in the order in which they are presented.[25] Where several cheques are simultaneously presented, and in

---

[17] *Joachimson v Swiss Bank Corp.* [1921] 3 K.B. 110; *Bank of New South Wales v Laing* [1954] A.C. 135, 154. Contingent liabilities of the customer to the banker must be disregarded: *Bower v Foreign and Colonial Gas Co. Ltd* (1874) 22 W.R. 740; but *cf. Agra & Masterman's Bank v Hoffmann* (1865) 34 L.J. Ch. 285.

[18] *Fleming v Bank of New Zealand* [1900] A.C. 577.

[19] *Marzetti v Williams* (1830) 1 B. & Ad. 415, 424; *Bank of New South Wales v Laing* [1954] A.C. 135 at 154.

[20] *Barclays Bank Ltd v W.J. Simms Son & Cooke (Southern) Ltd* [1980] Q.B. 677, 699 *per* Robert Goff J. By implication, the customer must pay the bank's usual interest and other charges (*Lloyds Bank v Voller* [2000] 2 All E.R. (Comm) 978, 982) at standard rate for unauthorised borrowings. This case was approved in *Emerald Meats (London) Ltd v AIB Group (UK) plc* [2002] EWCA Civ. 460, with the rider that the amounts "must not be extortionate or contrary to all approved banking practice" (at [14] [16] [26])

[21] For the earlier cases, see *Marzetti v Williams* (1830) 1 B. & Ad. 415; *Whitaker v Bank of England* (1835) 1 C.M. & R. 744; *Rolin v Steward* (1854) 14 C.B. 595 (Illustration 1); *Summers v City Bank* (1874) L.R. 9 C.P. 580.

[22] *Whitaker v Bank of England* (1835) 1 C.M. & R. 744 at 749, 750. *cf. Marzetti v Williams* (1830) 1 B. & Ad. 415; *Bransby v East London Bank* (1866) 14 L.T. 403.

[23] *Westminster Bank Ltd v Zang* [1966] A.C. 182 (Cheques Act 1957, s.2, Illustration 2).

[24] The matter is of some difficulty: see *Rolin v Steward* (1854) 14 C.B. 595; *Capital and Counties Bank Ltd v Gordon* [1903] A.C. 240, 249; *Jones & Co. v Coventry* [1909] 2 K.B. 1029; *Underwood (A.L.) Ltd v Bank of Liverpool* [1924] 1 K.B. 775; Ellinger, Lomnicka and Hooley, *Modern Banking Law* (3rd ed.), p.364; *Paget* (12th ed.), 18.9; Banking Code (above, para.1–011) para.9.4.

[25] *Kilsby v Williams* (1822) 5 B. & Ald. 815; *Sednaoui Zariffa Nahas & Co. v Anglo-Austrian Bank* (1909) Journal of the Institute of Bankers, Vol.XXX, p.413; *Dublin Port and Docks Board v Bank of Ireland* [1976] I.R. 118.

total they exceed the balance available in the customer's account, it seems that he may pay them in whatever order he decides until the available balance is exhausted.[26] A banker is not, however, entitled to dishonour cheques drawn bona fide and without negligence on the faith of an incorrect entry in the customer's account.[27]

A banker is only bound to pay a cheque presented at the branch on which the cheque is drawn[28] and during ordinary business hours.[29] But where a customer has personal accounts at two or more branches the banker is normally entitled to combine such accounts against him.[30] This, however, is an option open to the banker and he cannot be required to combine accounts maintained by the customer at different branches in order to meet a cheque when there are insufficient funds in the account at the branch on which it is drawn.[31] Nor, it seems, is he obliged to combine different accounts maintained by a customer at one branch in order to refrain from dishonouring his cheque.[32]

**13–033** Where a banker dishonours his customer's cheque drawn in favour of a third party[33] without a justifiable reason, reasonable damages are recoverable by the customer for the injury done to his credit as a result of the breach by the banker of his obligation to pay.[34] Originally it was believed that, if the customer was not a trader, the damages would be merely nominal, unless the customer alleged and proved actual loss.[35] But in *Kpohraror v Woolwich Building Society*[36] the Court of Appeal held that, in modern social conditions, it was not only traders who would sustain injury to their creditworthiness if their cheques were dishonoured. Some damage could obviously be presumed whether the customer was a trader

[26] See Ellinger, Lomnicka and Hooley, *Modern Banking Law* (3rd ed.), p.366. cf. Paget (12th ed.), 18.8. In Scotland the banker must return all cheques.
[27] *Holland v Manchester and Liverpool District Banking Co. Ltd* (1909) 25 T.L.R. 386.
[28] *Woodland v Fear* (1857) 7 E. & B. 519; *Garnett v M'Kewan* (1872) L.R. 8 Exch. 10, 14; *Joachimson v Swiss Bank Corp.* [1921] 3 K.B. 110, 127; *Arab Bank Ltd v Barclays Bank (D.C. & O.)* [1954] A.C. 495. If the customer changes his branch, a cheque drawn on his previous branch will be returned.
[29] *Whitaker v Bank of England* (1835) 1 C.M. & R. 744; *Joachimson v Swiss Bank Corp.* [1921] 3 K.B. 110. cf. *Baines v National Provincial Bank Ltd* (1927) 96 L.J.K.B. 801.
[30] *Garnett v M'Kewan* (1872) L.R. 8 Exch. 10 at 14–15; *Re European Bank* (1872) L.R. 8 Ch.App. 41, 44; *Halesowen Presswork and Assemblies Ltd v National Westminster Bank Ltd* [1971] 1 Q.B. 1, 34, affirmed [1972] A.C. 785. See Ellinger, Lomnicka and Hooley, *Modern Banking Law* (3rd ed.), Ch.6.
[31] *Garnett v M'Kewan* (1872) L.R. 8 Exch. 10 at 14. cf. *Mutton v Peat* [1900] 2 Ch. 79.
[32] See Ellinger, Lomnicka and Hooley, *Modern Banking Law* (3rd ed.), p.218; *Paget* (12th ed.), 29.16.
[33] cf. *Kinlan v Ulster Bank* [1928] I.R. 171 where the cheque wrongfully dishonoured was payable to self and was presented by the drawer.
[34] *Marzetti v Williams* (1830) 1 B. & Ad. 415; *Rolin v Steward* (1854) 14 C.B. 595, 606–607 (Illustration 1); *Wilson v United Counties Bank* [1920] A.C. 102, 112; *Kpohraror v Woolwich Building Society* [1996] 4 All E.R. 119.
[35] *Gibbons v Westminster Bank* [1939] 2 K.B. 882, 888. See also *Baker v Australia and New Zealand Bank* [1958] N.Z.L.R. 907; *Rae v Yorkshire Bank, The Times*, Oct. 12, 1987 CA.
[36] [1996] 4 All E.R. 119 (Illustration 2).

or a non-trader. The customer can therefore recover general damages for the loss caused to him by the wrongful dishonour of his cheque without the need to prove actual damage.

An action for libel may also lie at the suit of the customer if a cheque is returned dishonoured due to a supposed inadequacy of funds in the customer's account.[37] A banker must exercise extreme care in the choice of words he writes on a returned cheque. The words "not sufficient" are capable of being defamatory, and where these words were written when there would in fact have been sufficient funds but for the negligence of the bank in failing to stop an earlier cheque, a bookmaker recovered £250 damages. The defence of privilege failed since, without the mistake which the bank made, there were no facts giving rise to privilege.[38] The words "Reason assigned—not stated" on a returned cheque are not actionable.[39] It had long been thought that "refer to drawer" or the letters "R/D" or "R/A" (on a bill) were equally innocuous,[40] but the phrase has now acquired a certain notoriety and in the light of more recent authority is best avoided.[41] In New Zealand "present again" has been held to be libellous.[42] The position of the banker is a delicate one for he is required by the rules of the Clearing House to make some written answer on the returned cheque. If he cannot properly[43] make use of some other phrase, e.g. "signature indistinct", it is preferable for him simply to note the fact of dishonour by the single word "unpaid".

**Nominee accounts.** A banker is not entitled without warning to refuse    13–034
to honour a customer's cheque, when there is money in his account to cover it, merely on the basis of a suspicion that the account is held by the customer as nominee for a third party who is indebted to the bank. Instead, clear and undisputable evidence is required that the customer holds his account as nominee or bare trustee for the third party before the bank can set-off the credit in one account against the debits in the other.[44] The same rule applies where the customer accepts that he is not the

---

[37] But the mere dishonour of a cheque is probably in itself insufficient to give rise to an action for libel or slander: *Kinlan v Ulster Bank* [1928] I.R. 171.

[38] *Davidson v Barclays Bank Ltd* [1940] 1 All E.R. 316 (Illustration 3).

[39] *Frost v London Joint Stock Bank Ltd* (1906) 22 T.L.R. 760.

[40] *London Joint Stock Bank Ltd v Macmillan* [1918] A.C. 777, 824, 831; *Flach v London and South Western Bank Ltd* (1915) 31 T.L.R. 334, 336; *Plunkett v Barclays Bank Ltd* [1936] 2 K.B. 107.

[41] *Pyke v Hibernian Bank Ltd* [1950] I.R. 195; *Jayson v Midland Bank Ltd* [1968] 1 Lloyd's Rep. 409; *Paget* (12th ed.), 18.21.

[42] *Baker v Australia and New Zealand Bank Ltd* [1958] N.Z.L.R. 907.

[43] cf. *Potterton (T.E.) v Northern Bank* [1993] 1 I.R. 413 (improper reason stated).

[44] *Bhogal v Punjab National Bank* [1988] 2 All E.R. 296. See also *Re Willis Percival and Co.* (1878) 12 Ch D 491; *Uttamchandani v Central Bank of India* (1989) 133 S.J. 262; *Saudi Arabian Monetary Agency v Dresdner Bank AG* [2004] EWCA Civ. 1074, [2005] 1 Lloyd's Rep. 12.

beneficial owner of the money in the account but contends that a third party, who is not the debtor of the bank, is the beneficiary.[45] The banker's entitlement may, however, be increased or decreased by express agreement with the customer.[46]

**13–035**      **Authority of banker to pay customer's cheque.** The order to pay contained in a cheque is a mandate or authority given by the customer to the banker on whom it is drawn to pay the amount of the cheque as directed by the customer from funds deposited with or made available by the banker on the account. When the drawee banker acts in accordance with the order and honours such a cheque, he acts within his mandate, with the result that he is entitled to debit the customer's account with the amount of the cheque, and further that the payment made by him is effective to discharge the obligation of the customer to the payee on the cheque, because he has paid the cheque with the authority of the customer.[47]

**13–036**      **Revocation of banker's duty and authority to pay.** Since the banker's position is similar to that of an agent acting on behalf of a principal, his duty and authority to pay may be determined by the customer giving to him notice of revocation at any time before the mandate has been carried out. That duty and authority may also be determined, or suspended, upon the happening of a number of other events.

**13–037**      **Subsection (1): countermand.** Countermanding payment, or "stopping" a cheque, is the means by which the customer revokes the banker's authority to pay a cheque drawn by him.

Unless otherwise agreed,[48] no particular form is required for an effective countermand. It may be made orally by telephone or in person,[49] or by letter, telegram, telex, fax, e-mail or other writing, provided that the banker can reasonably satisfy himself that the person communicating with him is truly the customer. The banker is not bound to accept an

---

[45] *Saudi Arabian Monetary Agency v Dresdner Bank AG* [2004] EWCA Civ. 1074, [2005] 1 Lloyd's Rep. 12.

[46] [2004] EWCA Civ. 1074, [2005] 1 Lloyd's Rep. 12 at [23].

[47] *Barclays Bank Ltd v W.J. Simms Son & Cooke (Southern) Ltd* [1980] Q.B. 677, 699, *per* Robert Goff J.

[48] The Banking Code, para.6.1 (see above, para.1–011), requires banks and building societies to provide customers with the relevant terms and conditions for the services which customers have asked to be provided: this will include information about how and when they may stop a cheque. See also paras 3.3, 9.15, 12.8.

[49] *Banque Provinciale du Canada v Beauchemin* (1959) 18 D.L.R. (2d) 584, 586.

unauthenticated message, *e.g.* a telegram, as a sufficient revocation altogether of his duty and authority to pay a cheque,[50] although he might well rely upon it to the extent of postponing payment pending confirmation.[51] He will normally provide a special form to be completed for this purpose.

The countermand must identify with sufficient certainty the cheque which is the subject-matter of the countermand. In *Westminster Bank Ltd v Hilton*[52] the House of Lords held that a bank was entitled to debit its customer's account when, having been instructed to stop payment of cheque number 117283 of a certain amount to a named payee, it paid a cheque in identical terms number 117285, which was the cheque the customer intended to be stopped. In that case, however, the cheque in question was post-dated, a fact which the customer did not mention to the bank. The bank had concluded that it was a replacement for cheque number 117283, as it bore a later serial number and was dated one day later than the customer's stop order. It is questionable whether minor discrepancies, for example, as to the precise amount of the cheque or as to its precise date, will likewise absolve the banker, or whether the banker ought, if the circumstances permit, to seek clarification from the customer if the matter is in doubt.[53] However, where the customer's instructions are ambiguous, the banker should not be penalised if he acts fairly and honestly in accordance with his interpretation of those instructions, even if that interpretation was not the one intended by the customer.[54]

**Notice of countermand.** To constitute an effective countermand it must be brought to the actual knowledge of the banker. **13–038**

"Countermand is really a matter of fact. It means much more than a change of purpose on the part of the customer. It means, in addition, the notification of that change of purpose to the bank. There is no such thing as a constructive countermand in a commercial transaction of this kind".[55]

---

[50] *Curtice v London City and Midland Bank Ltd* [1908] 1 K.B. 293, 299, 300, 302 (Illustration 5). Contrast *Reade v Royal Bank of Ireland* [1922] 2 I.R. 22.

[51] *Curtice v London City and Midland Bank Ltd* [1908] 1 K.B. 293 at 298–299.

[52] (1926) 43 T.L.R. 124, HL (Illustration 4).

[53] See *Giordano v Royal Bank of Canada* (1973) 38 D.L.R. (3d) 191; *Remfor Industries Ltd v Bank of Montreal* (1978) 90 D.L.R. (3d) 316; Crawford, *Payment Clearing and Settlement in Canada* (2002), Vol.2, 1194–1198. *cf. Westminster Bank Ltd v Hilton* (1926) 43 T.L.R. 124, 126; *Shapera v Toronto-Dominion Bank* (1970) 17 D.L.R. (3d) 122.

[54] *Curtice v London City and Midland Bank Ltd* [1908] 1 K.B. 293 at 299; *Westminster Bank Ltd v Hilton* (1926) 43 T.L.R. 124 at 126; *Bowstead and Reynolds on Agency* (17th ed.), § 3–016.

[55] *Curtice v London City and Midland Bank Ltd* [1908] 1 K.B. 293 at 298, *per* Cozens-Hardy M.R.

Thus where a telegram stopping payment of a cheque was delivered and placed in the letter-box of a bank in the evening after the bank was closed, but due to an oversight was not taken from the box and shown to the manager until two days later, by which time the cheque had been paid, it was held that payment had not been effectively countermanded.[56] But it was also said that if, due to the negligence of a bank, it did not receive notice of the customer's desire to stop the cheque, then the bank might be liable to the customer in damages.[57] Presumably a countermand will only take effect if and when it is communicated to some employee of the bank who has actual or ostensible authority to receive it, and not to a telephonist[58] or caretaker, for example.

Notice of countermand given to one branch of a bank is not an effective notice of countermand of a cheque drawn on another branch of the same bank.[59] Conversely the customer need notify only the branch of the bank on which the cheque was drawn.[60]

**13–039**   **Time of countermand.** The drawee banker must receive the countermand in time for him to refuse payment of the cheque. If a cheque has been presented for payment across the counter and has been paid,[61] then obviously any later countermand will be of no effect. Where the drawer and the payee maintain their accounts with different banks the cheque will be passed through the clearing process.[62] Notwithstanding that settlement takes place between banks at the end of each trading day, the Clearing House Rules make provision for the later dishonour of cheques by the branch on which the cheque was drawn. It might therefore at least be arguable that a notice of countermand should be effective if received before the time limited by the Rules has run out.[63] Where the drawer and the payee maintain their accounts at the same branch or at different branches of the same bank, it would appear that payment is "made"

---

[56] *Curtice v London City and Midland Bank Ltd* [1908] 1 K.B. 293 (Illustration 5).
[57] [1908] 1 K.B. 293 at 298, 300, 301.
[58] *Commonwealth Trading Bank v Reno Auto Sales Pty Ltd* [1967] V.R. 790, 794.
[59] *Burnett v Westminster Bank Ltd* [1966] 1 Q.B. 742, 760.
[60] *Burnett v Westminster Bank Ltd* [1966] 1 Q.B. 742 (s.73, Illustration 2); *Royal Bank of Canada v Boyce* (1966) 57 D.L.R. (2d) 683. But in *London Provincial and South Western Bank Ltd v Buszard* (1918) 35 T.L.R. 142 (s.29, Illustration 9), it was held that notice of countermand given to the branch on which the cheque was drawn was not notice to other branches of the same bank.
[61] *Baines v National Provincial Bank Ltd* (1927) 137 L.T. 631 (where cheque presented and paid shortly after bank's advertised time of closing, but before bank closed).
[62] See Ellinger, Lomnicka and Hooley, *Modern Law of Banking* (3rd ed.), pp.331–339.
[63] cf. *H.H. Dimond (Rotarua 1966) Ltd v Australia and New Zealand Banking Group Ltd* [1979] 2 N.Z.L.R. 739. But see Goode, *Commercial Law* (3rd ed.), 469–470; Brindle and Cox, *Law of Bank Payments* (3rd ed.), 3–092; Wood, *Comparative Financial Law* (1995), 25–18.

as soon as the bank decides to accept its customer's instruction to pay and has set in motion the bank's internal process for crediting the payee's account.[64] The advent of cheque "truncation"[65] will reduce considerably the time taken to clear cheques and will correspondingly reduce the time available for countermand.

**Authority to countermand.** Paget states: "Any one of several partners, trustees or executors has power to stop a cheque given by any or all."[66] Where a joint account is maintained in the names of two or more customers, but cheques can be signed by any one of them, it would seem that any of them could countermand payment of a cheque drawn on the account, whether drawn by himself or another. If cheques must be signed by all of them jointly, then any signatory could countermand payment of a cheque signed by him, since he thereby revokes his authority to pay the cheque.[67] Where cheques must be signed by (say) two authorised signatories in a representative capacity on behalf of a company, then presumably any person authorised by the company could countermand payment and not merely one or both of the authorised signatories alone.

13–040

**Effect of countermand.** A banker will pay without mandate if he overlooks or ignores notice of countermand of the customer who has drawn the cheque; and unless the customer is able to and does ratify the payment, the banker cannot debit the customer's account,[68] nor will his payment be effective to discharge the obligation (if any) of the customer on the cheque, because he had no authority to discharge such obligation.[69] The banker is, however, entitled to recover the money paid from the recipient as money paid under a mistake,[70] subject to any recognised defences that the recipient may raise against such recovery.[71]

13–041

If the banker obeys the countermand and stops payment of the cheque, the payee or other holder will, of course, have no claim against the banker since there is no privity of contract between them. His remedy lies against

---

[64] *Momm v Barclays Bank International Ltd* [1977] Q.B. 790. But see *Paget* (12th ed.), 17.198–17.204, 18.16; Brindle and Cox, *Law of Bank Payments*, § 3–094, 3–101. *cf. Capital Associates Ltd v Royal Bank of Canada* (1970) 15 D.L.R. (3d) 234, 36 D.L.R. (3d) 579, affirmed 65 D.L.R. (3d) 384n.

[65] See ss.74B, 74C; above, para.13–073.

[66] 12th ed., 18.16.

[67] *cf. Crawford and Falconbridge* (8th ed.), p.1769, which takes a more cautious view.

[68] *Burnett v Westminster Bank Ltd* [1966] 1 Q.B. 742 (s.73, Illustration 2).

[69] *Barclays Bank Ltd v W.J. Simms Son & Cooke (Southern) Ltd* [1980] Q.B. 677, 699, *per* Robert Goff J. The customer will therefore be obliged to pay the debt again.

[70] *Barclays Bank Ltd v W.J. Simms Son & Cooke (Southern) Ltd* [1980] Q.B. 677 (s.59, Illustration 19). See above, para.8–021 (s.59).

[71] See above, paras 8–026 and 8–029 (s.59).

the drawer on the cheque.[72] Assuming that he is a holder for value,[73] he is normally entitled to summary judgment against the drawer: a cheque (like a bill of exchange) is treated as cash.[74] The defences available to the drawer in an action against him by the holder depend upon the status of the holder[75] and whether they are immediate or remote parties.[76] But (subject to any real or absolute defences)[77] the drawer will be liable to a holder in due course.[78]

Where payment of a cheque has been countermanded by the drawer, it is unnecessary for the holder to present the cheque for payment to charge the drawer.[79] If it is presented for payment and dishonoured, the debt for which it was given revives.[80] No notice of the dishonour need be given to the drawer.[81]

A person who takes a cheque with notice of the dishonour takes it subject to any defect in title attaching thereto at the time of dishonour.[82]

**13–042**    **Cheque guarantee cards.** It is now the practice of most banks to issue to their customers plastic cards known as "cheque cards" or "cheque guarantee cards". By such a card the bank guarantees in any single transaction the payment of one cheque taken from one of its own cheque books for up to a specified amount. Payment is subject to the conditions printed on or referred to in the card. The content of these conditions may vary, but they are typically that: (i) the cheque bears the same name and code number as the card; (ii) it is dated with the actual date of issue; (iii) it is signed before the date of expiry of the card, in the United Kingdom, in the presence of the payee by the person whose signature appears on the card[83]; (iv) the card number is written on the cheque by the payee; and (v) the card has not been altered or defaced. The "guarantee" given by the bank is not a guarantee in the technical sense, but a contractual undertaking given by the bank through the agency of the customer to the payee that the bank will not dishonour the cheque on presentation for want of

---

[72] *M'Lean v Clydesdale Banking Co.* (1883) 9 App. Cas. 95 (Illustration 6); *Gaynor v McDyer* [1968] I.R. 295.
[73] See above, para.4–024 (s.27).
[74] See above, para.4–010. For precedents of pleadings, see App.B(8).
[75] See above, paras 4–024, 4–028 and 4–050.
[76] See above, para.4–005.
[77] See above, para.5–070.
[78] ss.29, 38.
[79] s.46(2)(c); but see the comment, above, para.6–075, n.89 (s.46).
[80] *Cohen v Hale* (1878) 3 Q.B.D. 371, 373.
[81] s.50(2)(c)(4).
[82] ss.29(1), 36(2); *Hornby v McLaren* (1908) 24 T.L.R. 494 (s.36, Illustration 11).
[83] In some sets of conditions, it is required that the signature corresponds with that on the card.

funds in the account, so that it is obliged if necessary to advance moneys to the customer to meet it.[84]

> "The use of the cheque card in connection with the transaction gives to the payee a direct contractual right against the bank itself to payment on presentment, provided that the use of the card by the drawer to bind the bank to pay the cheque was within the actual or ostensible authority conferred upon him by the bank."[85]

A payee who has acted reasonably and in good faith upon the bank's undertaking on the card by, for example, supplying goods or services or cash to the drawer, and complied with the conditions, is entitled to maintain an action against the bank to recover the amount of the cheque should the bank refuse to honour the cheque guaranteed.[86]

The terms and conditions on which the cheque card is supplied by the bank to its customer include an undertaking by the customer not to countermand payment of any cheque backed by the card. The question then arises whether this invalidates any countermand of payment by the customer in respect of such a cheque. It is arguable that the countermand is effective, though in breach of contract. But the better view, it is submitted, is that the customer has no longer any right of countermand.[87] He has authorised his agent, the bank, to incur a personal liability to the payee and he cannot, by purporting to revoke the bank's authority to discharge it, destroy the bank's right of reimbursement and indemnity in respect of such liability.[88]

Whether the bank is under an obligation to the payee to pay a cheque on which its customer's signature is forged depends upon the precise wording of the undertaking on the card. In *First Sport Ltd v Barclays Bank plc*[89] a majority of the Court of Appeal held that the conditions in question,[90] taken as a whole, contained no clear indication that the bank undertook liability only if the cheque was signed by its customer. The bank was therefore liable to the payee even though the cheque form had been stolen and the customer's signature forged. But it is submitted that, in such a case, the bank would not be entitled to debit its customer's account, unless the terms and conditions governing the use of the card

**13–043**

---

[84] See *Re Charge Card Services Ltd* [1987] Ch. 150, 166 (affirmed [1989] Ch. 497); *First Sport Ltd v Barclays Bank plc* [1993] 1 W.L.R. 1229, 1232, 1237, 1239.

[85] *Commissioner of Police for the Metropolis v Charles* [1977] A.C. 177, 182, *per* Lord Diplock. See also at 191, *per* Lord Edmund-Davies.

[86] *First Sport Ltd v Barclays Bank plc* [1993] 1 W.L.R. 1229. But it is submitted that the cheque is still received by the supplier as conditional payment only: *Re Charge Card Services Ltd* [1987] Ch. 150, 166 (a point left open by the Court of Appeal [1989] Ch. 497, 516).

[87] Ellinger, Lomnicka and Hooley, *Modern Banking Law* (3rd ed.), pp.539, 540 draws an analogy with irrevocable letters of credit.

[88] *Bowstead and Reynolds on Agency* (17th ed.), § 10–010.

[89] [1993] 1 W.L.R. 1229 (Kennedy L.J. dissenting).

[90] These are no longer in use.

clearly and unequivocally entitled the bank to do so and these had been sufficiently drawn to the attention of the customer.[91]

**13–044**     **Subsection (2): notice of customer's death.** The banker's duty and authority to pay cheques is determined by notice of his customer's death. This is a derogation from the normal rule[92] that the authority of an agent is determined by the death of the principal[93] and, if the agent continues to act, he may be liable for loss caused to the estate.[94] A banker is justified in paying a cheque after the customer's death but before he receives notice thereof. The rule is nevertheless inconvenient since the banker is bound to dishonour cheques drawn in respect of even essential services once he knows of the death.[95] If the banker overlooks the notice and pays, he can recover the money from the recipient as money paid under a mistake.[96]

The cheque itself remains valid notwithstanding the death, and an action on it can be brought by the holder against the drawer's estate if it is dishonoured.

**13–045**     **Joint and partnership accounts.** Upon the death of one joint account holder the legal title to the money lent to the banker usually vests in the survivor.[97] It appears that the banker would be justified in paying cheques drawn by the survivor, although the practice is to rule off the joint account and to start a new account in the name of the survivor alone.

In 1878, in *Backhouse v Charlton*,[98] Malins V.-C. stated that, where one member of a partnership firm died, the surviving partner was entitled to

---

[91] *Tai Hing Cotton Mill Ltd v Liu Chong Hing Bank Ltd* [1986] A.C. 80, 109–110. See *Chitty on Contracts* (29th ed.), Vol.I, § 12–015 (notice of unusual terms). A customer is not protected against loss caused by misuse of the card by section 84 of the Consumer Credit Act 1974 because that section deals only with limitation of liability for misuse of a "credit-token". A card which is solely a cheque guarantee card is not a credit-token within the meaning of the 1974 Act. Nor is he protected by the Consumer Protection (Distance Selling) Regulations 2000 (SI 2000/2334), reg.21(1)(2), as those provisions apply only to a "payment card" (which is defined not to include a cheque guarantee card). But a non-business customer's liability for misuse of the card is limited by the Banking Code (see above, para.1–011) to £50 unless the customer has acted without reasonable care.

[92] *Bowstead and Reynolds on Agency* (17th ed.), § 10–015.

[93] *Campanari v Woodburn* (1854) 15 C.B. 400.

[94] *Re Overweg* [1900] 1 Ch. 209.

[95] But it is probable that the personal representatives of the deceased could ratify the payment.

[96] *Barclays Bank Ltd v W.J. Simms Son & Cooke (Southern) Ltd* [1980] Q.B. 677, 699. See above, para.8–021 (s.59). For the defences which may be raised by the recipient, see above, paras 8–026 and 8–029.

[97] See Ellinger, Lomnicka and Hooley, *Modern Banking Law* (3rd ed.), p.267; *Paget* (12th ed.), 11.24.

[98] (1878) 8 Ch.D. 444, 449.

draw on the partnership account and the banker was justified in honouring cheques drawn on that account. However, section 33 of the Partnership Act 1890 now provides that, in the absence of agreement to the contrary, the death of one partner dissolves the partnership. The surviving partners nevertheless have power to continue the business of the firm so far as is necessary for winding up its affairs,[99] and the banker could honour cheques drawn for that purpose.

**Donatio mortis causa.** Because of the rule set out in subsection (2), if a customer draws a cheque and hands it to another in contemplation of death, there will be no valid *donatio mortis causa* if the cheque is not presented to and paid by the banker before he has notice of the death,[1] unless the gift has in the lifetime of the donor been completed by a dealing with the cheque.[2] Nor is there an effective gift *inter vivos* of the amount of the cheque at law or in equity, for equity will not intervene to perfect an imperfect gift.[3]    **13–046**

**Mental disorder of customer.**[4] The effect of a customer's insanity upon the duty and authority of the drawee banker to pay the customer's cheque is uncertain. Where an order has been made in relation to the customer by a judge of the Court of Protection under Part VII of the Mental Health Act 1983, it is possible that the customer would be legally incapable of giving a mandate to pay and that any mandate would automatically determine.[5] Otherwise it is submitted that the authority of a customer to pay a cheque will only be determined by his mental disorder when the banker has notice of it. However, in *Yonge v Toynbee*[6] it was held that an agent's authority is determined by the insanity of his principal, whether the agent knows of it or not. That case may nevertheless not apply to the relationship of banker and customer, which is not precisely that of principal and agent, especially if the requirement of notice in sub-section (2) is applied by analogy.[7] Even if the banker knows of the disability, but nevertheless allows another to draw cheques on the account on the customer's behalf, he may by subrogation obtain the right to reimbursement to the extent that the drawings have been used to    **13–047**

---

[99] Partnership Act 1890, s.38. See *Re Bourne* [1906] 2 Ch. 427.

[1] *Hewitt v Kaye* (1868) L.R. 6 Eq. 198; *Re Beak's Estate* (1872) L.R. 13 Eq. 489 (Illustration 7); *Re Beaumont* [1902] 1 Ch. 889 (Illustration 9). The donee, not being a holder for value, cannot sue the drawer's estate on the cheque.

[2] *Rolls v Pearce* (1877) 5 Ch.D. 730 (Illustration 8).

[3] *Re Swinburne* [1926] Ch. 38 (Illustration 10). But a gift of a cheque drawn by a third party, which the donor holds, would appear to be good: *Clement v Cheeseman* (1884) 27 Ch.D. 631; see above, para.5–068.

[4] See Ryder (1934) 55 J.I.B. 14.

[5] See *Chitty on Contracts*, (29th ed.), Vol.I, § 8–072. *cf. Paget* (12th ed.), 18.18.

[6] [1910] 1 K.B. 215. *cf. Drew v Nunn* (1874) 4 Q.B.D. 661.

[7] See also *Imperial Loan Co. Ltd v Stone* [1892] 1 Q.B. 599 (s.22, Illustration 5).

provide necessaries for the customer.[8] Where unauthorised payments have been made, it is not open to the bank to debit its customer's account on the ground that the drawings have been applied for the benefit of the customer in payment of his debts.[9] The safest course for the banker to take when he learns of the mental disorder of a customer is to place a stop on the account pending an order of the Court of Protection.

**13–048**      **Bankruptcy of customer.** The effect of the bankruptcy of the customer upon the duty and authority of a banker to pay his customer's cheques is governed by the Insolvency Act 1986. The bankruptcy of an individual commences with the day on which the bankruptcy order is made.[10] His estate vests in his trustee immediately on the trustee's appointment taking effect or, in the case of the official receiver, on his becoming trustee.[11] The banker no longer has any duty or authority to pay the bankrupt customer's cheques as from that time. If he does so, and the payment diminishes the credit balance on the account, he will be accountable to the trustee even though the payment is effected in ignorance of the making of the order.[12]

Further, under section 284(1)–(3) of the 1986 Act any payment (whether in cash or otherwise) by the bankrupt between the presentation of the petition and the vesting of the bankrupt's estate in the trustee is void except to the extent that is made with the consent of or ratified by the court. Where any void payment is made, the person paid holds the sum paid for the bankrupt as part of his estate.[13] However, these provisions do not give a remedy against any person in respect of any payment which he received before the commencement of the bankruptcy in good faith, for value and without notice that the petition had been presented.[14] It seems unlikely that the court would not ratify the payment by the banker of a cheque given by the customer to effect a payment by the customer which is void under this section if the cheque was paid in ignorance of the presentation of a petition.[15] Although the banker is therefore entitled to pay cheques drawn on him which are presented for payment during the relevant period, it is suggested that, once he becomes aware that a

---

[8] *Re Beavan (No.1)* [1912] 1 Ch. 196; (but no claim for interest or charges would lie).

[9] *Crantrave Ltd v Lloyds Bank plc* [2000] Q.B. 917; above, para.3–059 (unless ratified). Contrast *Scarth v National Provincial Bank Ltd* (1930) 4 L.D.B. 241, following *Liggett (B.) Liverpool Ltd v Barclays Bank Ltd* [1928] 1 K.B. 48.

[10] s.278(a).

[11] s.306(1).

[12] *Re Wigzell* [1921] 2 K.B. 835. The Court of Appeal further held that the banker was liable for amounts paid into the bankrupt's account without any allowance for the amounts paid out. *cf. Re Wilson* [1926] Ch. 21.

[13] s.248(2).

[14] s.248(4)(a). The previous provisions of the Bankruptcy Act 1914, ss.45, 46 have been entirely supplanted.

[15] See the cases cited in relation to winding up, below, para.13–049, n.24.

bankruptcy petition has been presented, the prudent course for him to take is to freeze the customer's account until either the petition is dismissed or the consent of the court obtained.[16]

Some measure of relief is, however, given to banks by section 284(5) of the Act.[17] The effect of this subsection is to protect a banker who, after the commencement of the bankruptcy, honours a cheque drawn and given by the bankrupt to effect a payment rendered void by section 284(1)–(3).[18] If the payment results in an overdraft on the bankrupt's account, the debt thus incurred by the bankrupt would, but for this subsection, not be provable in the bankruptcy as it was incurred after its commencement. The debt is nevertheless deemed to have been incurred before the commencement of the bankruptcy,[19] unless either (a) the banker had notice of the bankruptcy before the debt was incurred, or (b) it is not reasonably practicable for the amount of the payment to be recovered from the person to whom it was made.

**Winding up of customer company.** Neither the presentation of a winding up petition[20] nor the making of a winding up order[21] terminates the duty and authority of a banker to pay cheques drawn on the company's account. Nevertheless— 13–049

> "The normal and prudent practice of banks, upon becoming aware of a winding up petition against a corporate customer is to take prompt action. The bank freezes the company's existing bank accounts, whether in credit or in overdraft, as at the date of the presentation of the petition and insists that all subsequent dealings be on a new and separate account in respect of which a validation may be obtained".[22]

The validation order referred to is an order under section 127 of the Insolvency Act 1986 (previously section 227 of the Companies Act 1948). The section provides that, in a winding up by the court, any disposition

---

[16] See (on winding-up) *Hollicourt (Contracts) Ltd v Bank of Ireland* [2001] Ch. 555 at [7].

[17] This replaces the former provision in section 4 of the Bankruptcy (Amendment) Act 1926 (now repealed).

[18] But it is doubtful whether the subs. protects a payment out of the bankrupt customer's account when in credit. In such a case the bankrupt has not "incurred a debt to a banker" by reason of the making of the payment: see *Paget* (12th ed.), 14.37.

[19] This is the only effect of the subs. It is, however, arguable that its intent (though not its wording) is to render the debt recoverable.

[20] *Coutts & Co. v Stock* [2000] 1 W.L.R. 906, 910–911; *Hollicourt (Contracts) Ltd v Bank of Ireland* [2001] Ch. 555 at [12] (Illustration 11).

[21] *Re Loteka Property Ltd* [1990] 1 Qd. R. 322; *Hollicourt (Contracts) Ltd v Bank of Ireland* [2001] Ch. 555 at [26].

[22] *Hollicourt (Contracts) Ltd v Bank of Ireland* [2001] Ch. 555, *per* Mummery L.J. at [7], citing *Paget* (11th ed.), p.207. See also *D.B. Evans Bilston Ltd v Barclays Bank Ltd* (1961) 7 L.D.B. 283.

of the company's property made after the commencement of the winding up is, unless the court otherwise orders, void. The winding up of a company by the court is deemed to commence at the time of the presentation of the petition for winding up, unless before that time a resolution has been passed by the company for voluntary winding up, in which case the commencement of the winding up is the time of the passing of the resolution.[23] A disposition carried out in good faith in the ordinary course of business at a time when the parties are unaware that a petition has been presented, and completed before the winding up order is made, will, it seems, normally be validated by the court,[24] unless there is any ground for thinking that the transaction may involve an attempt to prefer the disponee, in which case the transaction would probably not be validated. Prospective dispositions after the setting up of the new account may be validated if they are of benefit to the company and enable the company to carry on its business.[25]

Where a payment has been made to a third party after commencement of the winding up by a cheque drawn on the company's account, but no validation order has been obtained, the disposition of the company's property constituted by payment of the cheque is rendered void by section 127. The liquidator of the company is entitled to a restitutionary remedy[26] to recover the amount of the cheque from the payee.

Previously a bank was at risk if it allowed payments to be made by a company in or out of its account after a winding up petition had been presented.[27] But in *Hollicourt (Contracts) Ltd v Bank of Ireland*[28] the Court of Appeal held that section 127 did not enable the liquidator to recover from the bank amounts paid out from the company's account, but only from the payees. This was so whether the company's account was in credit or in overdraft.[29] The bank in honouring the company's cheques obeys as agent the order of its principal and there is no disposition of the company's property to the bank. Payments into a company's bank account after the presentation of a winding up petition do not constitute a disposition of the company's property to the bank if the account is in credit as the

---

[23] s.129.
[24] *Re Wiltshire Iron Co.* (1868) L.R. 3 Ch. App. 443; *Re Neath Harbour Smelting and Rolling Works* (1887) 56 L.T. 727, 729; *Re Liverpool Civil Service Association* (1874) L.R. 9 Ch.App. 511, 512; *Re Gray's Inn Construction Co. Ltd* [1980] 1 W.L.R. 711, 718; *Denney v John Hudson & Co. Ltd* [1992] B.C.L.C. 901.
[25] *Denney v John Hudson & Co. Ltd* [1992] B.C.L.C. 901.
[26] *Hollicourt (Contracts) Ltd v Bank of Ireland* [2001] Ch. 555 at [22]; *Wily v United Telecasters Sydney Ltd* (1996) A.C.L.C. 863, 870. A defence of change of position (see above, para.8–029) may therefore be open to the payee.
[27] *Re Gray's Inn Construction Ltd* [1980] 1 W.L.R. 711.
[28] [2001] Ch. 555 (Illustration 11), distinguishing *Re Gray's Inn Construction Ltd* [1980] 1 W.L.R. 711. See also *Coutts & Co. v Stock* [2000] 1 W.L.R. 906; *Re Mal Bowers Macquarie Centre Pty Ltd* [1974] 1 N.S.W.L.R. 254; *Re Loteka Property Ltd* [1990] 1 Qd. R. 322.
[29] At [32]. See also *Coutts & Co. v Stock* [2000] 1 W.L.R. 906.

amount standing to the credit of the customer is increased[30] but payments into an overdrawn account may do so.[31]

It would appear that the duty and authority of a banker to pay the company's cheques terminates on dissolution of the company.[32]

**Third party debt order.**[33] Under Part 72 of the Civil Procedure Rules a judgment creditor may obtain an order, a "third party debt order", for a payment to him of money which a third party owes[34] to the judgment debtor.[35] This type of order was formerly known as a garnishee order. Whilst a credit balance on a current account is not due and repayable in the absence of a demand, it has long been accepted that the service of a garnishee order nisi (now replaced by an "interim third party debt order") itself operates in law as a sufficient demand for this purpose.[36] Thus a banker's obligation to honour his customer's cheques ceases if he is served with such an order[37] and this is so even though the credit balance of the customer exceeds the amount of the judgment.[38] Only if the order is stated to be for a limited amount is the banker free to pay away the surplus.

An interim third party debt order does not attach amounts paid into the account after it is served,[39] but will attach amounts of cheques paid into the account at the time of service and treated as cash even though these have not yet been cleared.[40]

The order binds a trust account as well as a private account.[41] It will operate on a customer's account even although he may have instructed his banker to close the account and transfer the balance to another person, provided the transferee has not been notified.[42] The name of the account is not necessarily conclusive: where an account was in the name of a wife but in reality the moneys were held on a resulting trust for her husband,

13–050

---

[30] *Re J. Leslie Engineers Co. Ltd* [1976] 1 W.L.R. 292; *Re Barn Crown Ltd* [1995] 1 W.L.R. 147.

[31] *Re Gray's Inn Construction Ltd* [1980] 1 W.L.R. 711; *Re Tain Construction Ltd* [2003] B.P.I.R. 1188.

[32] *Re Russian Commercial and Industrial Bank* [1955] 1 Ch 148.

[33] See *Paget* (12th ed.), Ch.25.

[34] There must be a debt "due or accruing due" to the judgment debtor from the third party: CPR, r.72.2(a).

[35] CPR, Pt 72 and 72PD.

[36] *Joachimson v Swiss Bank Corp.* [1921] 3 K.B. 110, 115, 121, 126, 131.

[37] *Choice Investments Ltd v Jeromnimon* [1981] Q.B. 149, 154–155.

[38] *Rogers v Whiteley* [1892] A.C. 118 (Illustration 12). See the reasoning of Lindley L.J. in the Court of Appeal, (1889) 23 Q.B.D. 236, 238.

[39] *Heppenstall v Jackson and Barclays Bank Ltd* [1939] 1 K.B. 585.

[40] *Jones & Co. v Coventry* [1909] 2 K.B. 1029. But contrast *Bank of New South Wales Ltd v Barlex Investments Pty Ltd* [1964–1965] N.S.W.R. 546; *Paget* (12th ed.), 25.2.

[41] *Plunkett v Barclays Bank Ltd* [1936] 2 K.B. 107. But this fact will be taken into account by the court in exercising its discretion whether to make a final order: *Deutsche Schachtbau-und Tiefbohrgesellschaft mbH v Shell International Petroleum Co. Ltd* [1990] A.C. 295.

[42] *Rekstin v Severo Sibirsko, etc., and Bank for Russian Trade Ltd* [1933] 1 K.B. 47.

it was held that the judgment creditors of the wife could not attach the moneys.[43] A joint account is attachable only in respect of a joint debt.[44]

13–051      **Freezing injunction.**[45] A freezing injunction directed to the customer of which the banker has notice may suspend the duty of the banker to pay the customer's cheques, subject to the terms of the injunction.[46] It will embrace both the existing credit balance on the account and amounts paid into the account after the date on which the order is made.[47] If a bank, having received notice of an injunction, pays its customer's cheques in contravention of the injunction, it may be held liable in negligence to the person in whose favour the injunction is granted, since it is reasonable to expect that the bank can and will take reasonable care to prevent the disposal of funds in accordance with the injunction.[48]

13–052      **Writ of sequestration.** Moneys standing to the credit of a customer in a bank account are liable to sequestration, the banker being normally ordered to pay them into court.[49]

13–053      **Investigation and proceeds of crime and money laundering.** The duty of a banker to pay his customer's cheques may be affected by a restraint order or a confiscation order made under the Proceeds of the Crime Act 2002.[50] Also in Part 7 of the Act, which deals with money laundering, section 327 makes it an offence to conceal, disguise, convert or transfer criminal property or remove it from the United Kingdom, and section 328 makes it an offence for a person to enter into or become concerned in an arrangement which he knows or suspects facilitates (by whatever means) the acquisition, retention, use or control of criminal

---

[43] *Harrods Ltd v Tester* [1937] 2 All E.R. 236.

[44] *Macdonald v Tacquah Gold Mines Co.* (1884) 13 Q.B.D. 535; *Beasley v Roney* [1891] 1. Q.B. 509, 512; *Hirschorn v Evans* [1938] 2 K.B. 801; *Westcoast Commodities Inc. v Chen* (1986) 28 D.L.R. (4th) 635.

[45] CPR, r. 25.1(f). See *Paget* (12th ed.), Ch.26.

[46] *Z Ltd v A-Z and AA-LL* [1982] Q.B. 558, 572, 574, 592. The terms of the order may allow payment of trade creditors in the ordinary course of business: *Iraqi Ministry of Defence v Arcepey Shipping Co.* [1981] Q.B.65, 73; *Avant Petroleum Inc. v Gatoil Overseas Inc.* [1986] 2 Lloyd's Rep. 236, 242. See also on the obligation of the bank to honour a cheque guaranteed by a cheque card: *Z Ltd v A-Z and AA-LL* [1982] Q.B. 558 at 592, and documentary collections: *Lewis & Peat (Produce) Ltd v Almatu Properties Ltd* [1993] 2 Bank.L.R. 45.

[47] *TDK Tape Distributor (U.K.) Ltd v Videochoice Ltd* [1985] 3 All E.R. 345, 349.

[48] *Customs and Excise Commissioners v Barclays Bank plc* [2004] EWCA Civ 1555, [2005] 1 Lloyd's Rep. 164.

[49] R.S.C. Ord.46, r.5.8, *Miller v Huddlestone* (1883) 22 Ch.D. 233; *Guerrine v Guerrine* [1959] 1 W.L.R. 760.

[50] ss.6–13, 40–47, 92–98, 119–127, 156–163, 189–195, and ss.67, 215 (seizure of money). See also the Terrorism Act 2000 ss.18, 25, the Anti-Terrorism, Crime and Security Act 2001, ss.1, 4–16, and the Crime (International Co-operation) Act 2003, ss.32–46. See *Paget* (12th ed.), Ch.4.

property. Property is "criminal property" if (broadly) it constitutes a person's benefit from criminal conduct or if it represents such a benefit.[51] Banks are obviously at risk from these provisions and they may justify a bank in refusing to pay out moneys held in an account or to transfer or otherwise deal with them in accordance with instructions given by a customer.[51a]

**"Tipping off".** The Proceeds of Crime Act 2002 further requires a  **13–054** bank, of its own initiative, to inform the relevant authorities if it knows or suspects, or has reasonable grounds for knowing or suspecting, that another person is engaged in money laundering.[52] The bank should not, however, disclose that it has done so, since section 333 of the Act[53] establishes the offence of "tipping off" if the disclosure is likely to prejudice any investigation which might be conducted following the disclosure. Moreover, if the bank knows or suspects that an "appropriate officer" (for example, the Police or Customs and Excise) is conducting or is about to conduct a money laundering investigation, it will commit an offence under section 342 of the Act if it makes a disclosure which is likely to prejudice that investigation. A bank which suspects the provenance of moneys in its customer's account is therefore faced with a dilemma. If it pays out those moneys, it could be liable to third parties as an accessory to a breach of trust.[54] If it refuses to pay out, it may not be able to reveal the reason to its customer or, if sued by the customer, be able effectively to defend itself, lest it commit the offence of "tipping off".[55] In *Bank of Scotland v A. Ltd*[56] the Court of Appeal held that, in such a situation, the bank can apply to the court for interim declaratory relief in proceedings to which the relevant enforcement authority (but not the customer) would be made a party. The court will then determine what, if any, disclosure should be made by the bank to the customer. This will not, so Lord Woolf C.J. pointed out,[57] automatically provide protection against any action by the customer or by third parties. If proceedings are brought by the customer against the bank, the bank will have to make a commercial decision whether to contest the proceedings or not. But the view was

---

[51] s.340(3).
[51a] *Squirrel Ltd v National Westminster Bank plc*, The Times, May 25, 2005.
[52] s.330. This section implements Arts 6, 7 of the Directive on Prevention of the use of the financial system for the purpose of money laundering (Council Directive 91/308 [1991] O.J. L166/77, as amended by Council Directive 2001/97 [2001] O.J. L344/76).
[53] See Art.8 of the Directive.
[54] See below, paras 13–055—13–060. A criminal offence may also be committed under s.327.
[55] cf. *Linklaters v HSBC Bank plc* [2003] EWHC 1113 (Comm) at [115]; *Squirrel Ltd v National Westminster Bank plc*, The Times, May 25, 2005.
[56] [2001] EWCA Civ 52, [2001] 1 W.L.R. 751.
[57] [2001] EWCA Civ 52, [2001] 1 W.L.R. 751 at [43] [47].

expressed that it was almost inconceivable that, having sought the guidance of the court, the bank would incur accessory liability to third parties for "dishonest assistance".[58]

13–055      **Assistance in a breach of trust.** In the nineteenth century, the duty of a banker to pay his customer's cheque when he had in his hands funds of the customer sufficient to meet it was sometimes stated in almost absolute terms: the banker could not refuse the payment of the cheque on the ground that he was aware that the customer, being in a fiduciary or representative capacity, intended a breach of trust, and had drawn the cheque for that purpose.[59] But in 1868, in *Gray v Johnston*,[60] Lord Cairns L.C. said:

> " . . . it would be a most serious matter if bankers were to be allowed, on light and trifling grounds—on grounds of mere suspicion or curiosity—to refuse to honour a cheque drawn by their customer, even although the customer might happen to be an administrator or an executor. On the other hand, it would be equally of serious moment if bankers were to be allowed to shelter themselves under that title, and to say that they were at liberty to become parties or privies to a breach of trust committed with regard to trust property, and, looking to their position as bankers merely, to insist that they were entitled to pay away money which constituted a part of trust property at a time when they knew it was going to be misapplied, and for the purpose of its being so misapplied."

It has subsequently become clear that a banker will be entitled, and indeed bound, to refuse to pay a cheque drawn on his customer's account if, in all the circumstances actually known to the banker, a reasonable banker would conclude that the payment would render him liable as accessory to a breach of trust.[61] Such liability may arise, for example, where loss is occasioned by withdrawals improperly made by trustees, partners, employees or agents or by the directors of a company.

13–056      **Dishonest assistance.** Previously it was held that liability would be incurred if, in making the payment, the paying banker knowingly assisted in a dishonest and fraudulent design on the part of a trustee.[62] But the law relating to accessory liability was reformulated by the Judicial

---

[58] See below, para.13–056.
[59] *Gray v Johnston* (1868) L.R. 3 H.L. 1, 14. See also *Bodenham v Hoskyns* (1852) 21 L.J. Eq. 864, 869.
[60] (1868) L.R. 3 H.L. 1, 11.
[61] *U.S. International Marketing Ltd v National Bank of New Zealand Ltd* [2004] 1 N.Z.L.R. 589.
[62] *Barnes v Addy* (1874) 9 Ch.App. 244, 251–252.

Committee of the Privy Council in *Royal Brunei Airlines Sdn Bhd v Tan*.[63]
That case established, first, that it is unnecessary to show a dishonest and
fraudulent design on the part of the trustee. An innocent breach of trust
will suffice.[64] Secondly, assuming that the paying banker has not received
on his own account and become chargeable with any part of the trust
property, it established that the touchstone of his liability is dishonesty.[65]
As a result, the principle has come to be known as that of "dishonest
assistance". Liability will attach to the paying banker if the following are
proved: (1) a trust or other fiduciary relationship; (2) breach of trust or
fiduciary duty, even if innocent, by the trustee or person under the duty;
(3) assistance by the banker in that breach of trust or fiduciary duty; (4)
dishonesty on the part of the banker.

**(1) Trust or other fiduciary relationship.** Although the principal of    13–057
accessory liability was originally developed in relation to the misapplication of trust funds by trustees, it is clear that it can now apply where there
is no trust but only a fiduciary relationship, for example, between a
company and its directors or other officers.[66]

**(2) Breach of trust or fiduciary duty.** There must be a breach of trust or    13–058
fiduciary duty by the trustee or person under the duty. In the *Royal Brunei
Airlines* case[67] the Privy Council dispensed with the need to show a
dishonest or fraudulent breach of trust or fiduciary duty. The breach may
therefore be innocent. It is, however, still not yet settled whether accessory liability requires that the defendant must have assisted in a breach of
trust or fiduciary duty in relation to property, or whether assistance in
any breach of fiduciary duty will suffice.[68] Since, in relation to the liability
of banks, the act relied on to establish the claim will almost inevitably
consist in the disposal of property, *i.e.* money from a bank account, it is
unnecessary to come to a conclusion on this issue, although it is submitted that the better view is that the principle is not limited to property.[69]

---

[63] [1995] 2 A.C. 378.
[64] [1955] 2 A.C. 378 at 384.
[65] [1955] 2 A.C. 378 at 392.
[66] *Agip (Africa) Ltd v Jackson* [1991] Ch. 547 (s.69, Illustration 20).
[67] See above, para.13–056.
[68] *Brown v Bennett* [1991] 1 B.C.L.C. 649; *Satnam Investments Ltd v Dunlop Heywood & Co. Ltd*
[1999] 3 All E.R. 652, 671; *Petrotrade Inc. v Smith* [2000] 1 Lloyd's Rep. 496 at [27] [28]; *Fyffes
Group Ltd v Templeman* [2000] 2 Lloyd's Rep. 643; *Goose v Wilson Sandford & Co. (No.2)*
[2000] EWCA Civ 73, [2001] Lloyd's Rep. P.N. 189 at [88]; *Gencor ACP Ltd v Dalby* [2000]
2 B.C.L.C. 734, 758.
[69] The limitation did not form part of the original formulation by Lord Nicholls in *Royal
Brunei Airlines Sdn Bhd v Tan* [1995] 2 A.C. 378, 392.

**13–059**    **(3) Assistance in the breach of trust or fiduciary duty.** The banker must have assisted in the breach of trust or fiduciary duty. This is a question of fact. Typical examples will be the payment out of money deposited with the bank or the movement of funds from one bank to another or the collection of a cheque and the payment of the proceeds to a fraudster. A causal connection between the assistance and the claimant's loss must be shown.

**13–060**    **(4) Dishonesty on the part of the banker.** In *Twinsectra Ltd v Yardley*[70] a majority of the House of Lords held that the standard to be applied to determine whether a person had acted dishonestly was a standard which combined both an objective and a subjective test: "it must be established that the defendant's conduct was dishonest by the ordinary standards of reasonable and honest people and that he himself realised that by those standards his conduct was dishonest".[71] It was, however, emphasised that "he should not escape a finding of dishonesty because he sets his own standards of honesty and does not regard as dishonest what he knows would offend the normally accepted standards of dishonest conduct".[72] Nevertheless, the rejection by a majority of their Lordships[73] of a purely objective test and their insistence upon a subjective element in determining whether or not conduct is dishonest means that even a deliberate and flagrant departure by a banker from standard banking practice might not necessarily involve the banker in accessory liability.

**13–061**    **Constructive trust.** The justification for the accessory liability of the paying banker is sometimes said to derive from a constructive trust: that the banker, by assisting in the breach of trust, has become a constructive trustee. This, however, may be a misnomer, as he has received no part of the trust property on his own account. It is a personal liability—a liability in equity to make good resulting loss, and not proprietary.[74]

**13–062**    **Duty of care to customer.** A banker is under a contractual[75] duty of care to his customer in carrying out the mandate given to him by the

---

[70] [2002] UKHL 12, [2002] 2 A.C. 164, applied in *Papamichael v National Westminster Bank plc* [2003] EWHC 164 (Comm), [2003] 1 Lloyd's Rep. 341 at [375].

[71] [2002] UKHL 12, [2002] 2 A.C. 164 at [27], [35], [38].

[72] [2002] UKHL 12, [2002] 2 A.C. 164 at [36].

[73] Lord Millett dissenting.

[74] *Royal Brunei Airlines Sdn Bhd v Tan* [1995] 2 A.C. 378, 387; *Agip (Africa) Ltd v Jackson* [1990] Ch. 265, 292 (affirmed [1991] Ch. 547); *Paragon Finance plc v D.B. Thakerar & Co.* [1999] 1 All E.R. 400, 409; *Bank of Scotland v A. Ltd* [2001] EWCA Civ 52, [2001] 1 W.L.R. 751 at [27]; *Grupo Torras SA v Al-Sabah (No.5)* [2001] Lloyd's Bank Rep. 36 at [123]; *Dubai Aluminium Co. Ltd v Salaam* [2002] UKHL 48, [2003] 2 A.C. 366 at [141].

[75] There is no wider duty of care in tort: *Tai Hing Cotton Mill Ltd v Liu Chong Hing Bank Ltd (No.1)* [1986] A.C. 80; *National Bank of Greece S.A. v Pinios Shipping Co. (No. 1)* [1990] A.C. 637, CA (revd *ibid.*, on other grounds).

customer to pay cheques drawn on the customer's account.[76] He is therefore entitled (and bound in his own interests) to refuse to pay a cheque drawn on him if to do so would involve a breach of that duty. The duty appears to be that of exercising reasonable care and skill, the standard of care being that of a reasonably prudent banker.[77] It is clear, however, that the duty does not require the banker to consider the commercial wisdom of the transaction.[78] The circumstances in which a banker may be negligent must necessarily vary from case to case. But he will be considered to have acted in breach of that duty where he pays, without inquiry, a cheque drawn on him when he has reasonable grounds for believing that there is a serious or reasonable possibility that the funds withdrawn are being misappropriated in fraud of the customer.[79]

In *Lipkin Gorman v Karpnale Ltd*,[80] a partner in a solicitors' firm, with authority to draw cheques on the firm's client account with the defendant bank, over a period of time withdrew large sums from the account, which he misappropriated and used for the purpose of gambling. Alliott J. at first instance found that the branch manager of the defendant bank had reasonable grounds for believing that the probability was that the solicitor was operating the clients' account in fraud. But this finding was reversed by the Court of Appeal[81] which stressed the necessity of having regard to the realities of how banking business is conducted at a branch of a bank. Parker L.J. also pointed out[82] that it would place on banks a wholly unrealistic burden if the manager of a branch which held a solicitors' client account and a personal account of one or more of the partners, with powers of signature on the client account, had continually to monitor the personal and client accounts for signs that one of the partners might be abusing his signing powers. Regard must therefore be had to current banking practice to determine what facts ought to be known to the banker, what facts should cause him to suspect that a fraud is being attempted, and what inquiries he should make. In *Barclays Bank plc v Quincecare*[83] Steyn J. said:

---

[76] *Selangor United Rubber Estates Ltd v Cradock (No. 3)* [1968] 1 W.L.R. 1555, 1634; *Varker v Commercial Banking Co. of Sydney* [1972] 2 N.S.W.L.R. 967; *Karak Rubber Co. Ltd v Burden (No.2)* [1972] 1 W.L.R. 602, 629; *Ryan v Bank of New South Wales* [1978] V.R. 555, 579; *Lipkin Gorman v Karpnale Ltd* [1989] 1 W.L.R. 1340, 1376 ([1991] 2 A.C. 548); *Barclays Bank plc v Quincecare Ltd* [1992] 4 All E.R. 363, 376; *Venty & Spindler v Lloyds Bank plc* [1995] C.L.C. 1557; Supply of Goods and Services Act 1982, s.13.

[77] *Lipkin Gorman v Karpnale Ltd* [1989] 1 W.L.R. 1340 at 1377. *cf.* at 1356; *Barclays Bank plc v Quincecare Ltd* [1992] 4 All E.R. 363, 376. See also below, para.17–039 (Cheques Act 1957, s.4) and *Marfani & Co. Ltd v Midland Bank Ltd* [1968] 1 W.L.R. 956, 972; *Linklaters v HSBC Bank plc* [2003] EWHC 1113 (Comm) at [106]. (Cheques Act 1957, s.4).

[78] *Lipkin Gorman v Karpnale Ltd* [1989] 1 W.L.R. 1340 at 1356.

[79] [1989] 1 W.L.R. 1340 at 1376, 1377.

[80] [1987] 1 W.L.R. 987 (Illustration 13).

[81] [1989] 1 W.L.R. 1340. This point did not arise in the House of Lords: [1991] 2 A.C. 548.

[82] At 1381.

[83] [1992] 4 All E.R. 363, 376.

"The law should not impose too burdensome an obligation on bankers, which hampers the effective transacting of banking business unnecessarily. On the other hand, the law should guard against the facilitation of fraud, and exact a reasonable standard of care in order to combat fraud and to protect bank customers and innocent third parties. To hold that a bank is only liable when it has displayed a lack of probity would be too restrictive an approach. On the other hand, to impose liability whenever speculation might suggest dishonesty would impose wholly impractical standards on bankers. In my judgment the sensible compromise, which strikes a fair balance between competing considerations, is simply to say that a banker must refrain from executing an order if and for so long as the banker is 'put on inquiry' in the sense that he has reasonable grounds (although not necessarily proof) for believing that the order is an attempt to misappropriate funds . . . And the external standard of the likely perception of an ordinary prudent banker is the governing one".

The duty of care owed by the banker is owed to his customer[84] and not to third parties[85] although a similar duty may be owed by a banker to the true owner of a cheque collected by him.[86] Where the customer is a trustee, any rights against the banker in respect of breach of that duty form part of the trust property and can be enforced in appropriate cases by the beneficiaries if the trustee is unable or unwilling to do so. But a dishonest trustee will have no claim against the banker. In such a situation, it is unlikely that (save in exceptional circumstances) any duty of care would be held to be owed directly to the beneficiaries.[87]

13–063    **Solicitors' accounts.** Section 85 of the Solicitors Act 1974 provides:

"Where a solicitor keeps an account with a bank in pursuance of rules under section 32 [of the 1974 Act]—(a) the bank shall not incur any liability, or be under any obligation to make any inquiry, or be deemed to have any knowledge of any right of any person to any money paid or credited to the account, which it would not incur or be under or be deemed to have in the case of an account kept by a person entitled absolutely to all the money paid or credited to it . . . "

---

[84] cf. *Weir v National Westminster Bank* 1994 S.L.T. 125 (customer is agent).
[85] *Chapman v Barclays Bank plc* [1995] 6 Bank L.R. 315; *Wells v First National Commercial Bank* [1998] P.N.L.R. 552.
[86] See below, para.17–030.
[87] *Royal Brunei Airlines Sdn Bhd v Tan* [1995] 2 A.C. 318, 391–392.

In *Lipkin Gorman v Karpnale Ltd.*[88] Alliott J. took the view that the intention of the legislature in this provision was not to give the bank a special advantage in maintaining and operating a clients' account but to ensure that there was no disadvantage.

**Postponement of payment.** A banker may be justified in postponing **13–064** payment of a cheque drawn on him by his customer pending inquiries as to the identity or bona fides of the holder or pending confirmation by the customer that it should be paid.[89]

**Out of date cheques.** It is the practice of bankers,[90] in the absence of **13–065** specific instructions to the contrary from their customer, to refuse payment of out of date, or "stale", cheques drawn by the customer. The time after which payment will be refused varies from bank to bank, but it is submitted that there is sufficient *consensus* to establish an implied term in the banker-customer relationship that a banker may refuse to pay a cheque which is presented to him for payment six months or more after the date written on the cheque.[91]

**Closure of account.** The duty and authority to pay a customer's **13–066** cheque is brought to an end by the closure of the account, either by the banker or by the customer.[92]

**Conflict of laws.** As a general rule the contract between a banker and **13–067** his customer is governed by the law of the place where the account is kept, in the absence of agreement to the contrary.[93]

ILLUSTRATIONS

1. The claimants, carrying on business as merchants and shipowners in **13–068** Norfolk, are customers of the defendants, the East of England Bank. The

---

[88] [1987] 1 W.L.R. 987, 997 (Illustration 13). This point did not arise in the Court of Appeal or the House of Lords; [1989] 1 W.L.R. 1340, [1991] 2 A.C. 508.

[89] See above, para.8–014 (s.59).

[90] See *Paget* (12th ed.), 18.13.

[91] *Commissioners of Inland Revenue v Thomas Cook (NZ) Ltd* [2003] 2 N.Z.L.R. 296 at [31–39]. The Review Committee on Banking Services Law and Practice (1989) Cm. 622 (above, para.1–008) recommended that the Code of Practice should provide that a banker should not return, within six months from the date of issue, a cheque on the grounds that it was out of date: rec. 7(15). See the Banking Code (above, para.1–011), para.9.9.

[92] The banker is required to give reasonable notice: *Prosperity Ltd v Lloyds Bank Ltd* (1923) 39 T.L.R. 372; *Paget* (12th ed.), 7.13.

[93] *X A.G. v A Bank* [1983] 2 All E.R. 464; *Mackinnon v Donaldson, Lufkin & Jenrette Securities Corp.* [1986] Ch. 482, 494; *Libyan Arab Foreign Bank v Bankers Trust Co.* [1989] Q.B. 728. *cf.* Contracts (Applicable Law) Act 1990; *Bank of Baroda v Vysya Bank Ltd* [1994] 2 Lloyd's Rep. 87. See Dicey and Morris, *Conflict of Laws* (13th ed.), 33–296.

defendants wrongfully dishonour three cheques drawn on them by the claimants payable to third parties when there are funds in the claimants' account sufficient to meet the cheques. There is no evidence of any special damage, but the jury return a verdict for the claimants in the sum of £500. The jury's verdict is upheld subject to an agreed reduction of damages to £200. For wrongful dishonour of a customer's cheque, where it is alleged and proved that the customer is a trader, an action lies for substantial damages without proof of special damage.[94]

2. The claimant, a Nigerian, maintains a current account with the defendant building society. He draws a cheque on this account for £4,550 payable to P Ltd in respect of goods to be supplied for shipment to Nigeria. There are funds in the account sufficient to meet the cheque but, when it is presented to the defendants for payment by special clearance, payment is wrongfully refused on the ground that the cheque has been reported lost. Later the same day the error is discovered and on the following day the defendants persuade P Ltd to accept their own corporate cheque for the amount. P Ltd thereupon releases to the claimant the goods destined for Nigeria. An award to the claimant of £5,500 general damages for injury to his credit is upheld. A bank's customer can recover substantial damages for injury to his credit by the wrongful dishonour of a cheque without proof of special damage. This is so whether or not the customer is a trader, since, in modern conditions, the credit rating of individuals is as important for their personal transactions as it is for those engaged in trade. A further claim by the claimant for special damages in respect of trading losses incurred by the delay in the shipment in question and the cancellation of further shipments is dismissed. Such losses are too remote to be recoverable.[95]

3. The claimant, a bookmaker, draws a cheque for £2 15s. 8d. on the Kennington branch of the defendant bank. The cheque is dishonoured due to an error on the part of the bank in paying a previous cheque, the payment of which had been countermanded by the claimant. The dishonoured cheque is returned marked "Not sufficient". These words are libellous of the claimant. Although they have been published only to the payee, they are not subject to qualified privilege. It was the bank's mistake which created the alleged privileged occasion. Damages of £250 are awarded.[96]

**13–069**    4. On July 31, 1924, the claimant, a customer of the defendant bank, draws a cheque numbered 117285 for £8 1s. 6d. payable to P. The cheque

[94] *Rolin v Steward* (1854) 14 C.B. 595.
[95] *Kpohraror v Woolwich Building Society* [1996] 4 All E.R. 119.
[96] *Davidson v Barclays Bank Ltd* [1940] 1 All E.R. 316.

is post-dated August 2. On August 1, he telegraphs the bank to stop payment of the cheque, stating the amount and the payee, but giving as its number 117283. He does not notify the bank that the cheque is post-dated. In fact, cheque number 117283 has been previously paid by the bank. On August 6, cheque number 117285 is presented for payment. The bank concludes that this cheque is a replacement for number 117283 and pays it. The claimant's action against the bank for negligence fails.[97]

5. The claimant, C, draws a cheque for £63 on the Willesden Green branch of the defendant bank payable to J. The same day, after business hours, he telegraphs the branch "please stop cheque to J for £63. C." The telegram messenger, finding the branch closed, places the telegram in the bank's letter box at 6.15 p.m. By an oversight, the telegram is not taken out of the box until two days later and shown to the manager. The cheque in the meantime has been paid. The countermand is ineffective, and the defendants can debit the claimant's account with the amount of the cheque. Actual notice of countermand brought to the attention of the bank is required: constructive notice is insufficient. Further the bank is not bound to accept an unauthenticated telegram as sufficient authority for refusing to pay the cheque.[98]

6. The defendant draws a crossed order cheque for £265 payable to C, who indorses it and pays it into his account with the claimant bank. The account is overdrawn, and the cheque is applied by the claimants in reduction of the overdraft. The defendant countermands payment and, on presentment, payment is refused. The claimants, as holders for value, can recover from the defendant the amount of the cheque.[99]

7. B, in contemplation of death, draws a cheque in favour of his nephew **13–070** for £4,000, and conveys it to him accompanied by his bank pass-book. On the day after B's death the nephew presents the cheque for payment, but payment is refused as the bank has been informed of B's death. There is no valid *donatio mortis causa*.[1]

8. P, in contemplation of death, draws in Italy two cheques on a London bank payable to the order of his wife. During P's lifetime, his wife negotiates the cheques for value to an Italian bank, and they are subsequently further negotiated until they come into the possession of the U Bank in London. The U Bank presents them for payment to the drawee bank, but payment is refused by reason of P's death. P's wife is obliged

[97] *Westminster Bank Ltd v Hilton* (1926) 43 T.L.R. 124, HL.
[98] *Curtice v London City and Midland Bank Ltd* [1908] 1 K.B. 293.
[99] *Mclean v Clydesdale Banking Co.* (1883) 9 App. Cas. 95.
[1] *Re Beak's Estate* (1872) L.R. 13 Eq. 489.

to refund what she received on the cheques. The dealing with the cheques completes the gift as a valid *donatio mortis causa*.[2]

9. B, in contemplation of death, draws a cheque for £300 payable to E, who indorses it and hands it to her bankers for collection. The cheque is presented for payment to the drawee bank before B's death, but B's account is overdrawn and payment is refused because of doubts about the drawer's signature. Before confirmation of the signature is obtained, B dies and the cheque is never cashed. There is no valid *donatio mortis causa*.[3]

10. Shortly before her death, S gives to the defendant a cheque for £700 drawn by her on the N Bank. The cheque is not honoured on presentment because the bank has doubts about S's signature on it. It is returned marked "Signature differs". S dies before anything further is done. There has been no effective gift of £700 to the defendant. There was an incomplete gift *inter vivos* of the amount of the cheque, which would not be perfected with the assistance of equity.[4]

**13–071**     11. A company maintains an account with the defendant bank. On February 5, 1996, a petition is presented for the compulsory winding up of the company and on June 7, 1996, a winding up order is made. Unaware of the presentation of the petition, between these two dates the bank pays out of the account a number of cheques drawn by the company in favour of third parties and presented to the bank for payment. At all material times the company's account is in credit. The liquidator of the company claims a declaration that the payments are void under section 127 of the Insolvency Act 1986 and an order that the bank reconstitute the account. This relief is refused. Section 127 only invalidates dispositions by a company of its property to the payees of the cheques and enables the company to recover from them the amount of the cheques. It does not enable the payments to be recovered from the bank, whether the company's account is in credit or overdraft at the time the payments are made.[5]

12. There is standing to the credit of the appellants on current and deposit account at the respondents' bank a balance of over £6,800. A

---

[2] *Rolls v Pearce* (1877) 5 Ch.D. 730.
[3] *Re Beaumont* [1902] 1 Ch. 889.
[4] *Re Swinburne* [1926] Ch. 38.
[5] *Hollicourt (Contracts) Ltd v Bank of Ireland* [2001] Ch. 555.

judgment creditor of the appellants for £6,000 obtains a garnishee order nisi which orders that "all debts owing and accruing due" from the bank to the appellants be attached to answer for the sum of £6,000. In consequence the bank refuses to honour cheques drawn by the appellants on the credit balance over £6,000. An action is brought by the appellants against the bank claiming damages for injury to their credit and reputation. The action fails. An order made in these terms attaches the whole of the moneys, and the bank was right in dishonouring the cheques.[6]

13. C is a partner in the claimant firm of solicitors and has authority to draw on the firm's client account with the second defendant bank by his signature alone. He is a compulsive gambler and, in order to finance his gambling activities, fraudulently withdraws over a period some £300,000 by means of cheques drawn on the account. He uses most of the stolen money to gamble at the first defendants' gaming club, there exchanging cash for the chips employed in gambling at the club. The claimants are unaware of these defalcations or of his gambling propensities. Upon discovering the theft the claimants claim against the bank as constructive trustee and for breach of its contractual duty of care, and against the club in an action for money had and received to recover the money derived from the account which has been received by the club. Their claim against the bank fails. The bank would have been liable as accessory to C's breach of trust had it known of C's dishonest and fraudulent design, or if it had wilfully or recklessly turned a blind eye to it.[7] The bank would also have been in breach of its contractual duty to the claimants had it continued to pay without inquiry cheques drawn on it in the knowledge that there was a serious or real possibility that C was appropriating moneys drawn from the account for his own purposes. But, on the evidence, the bank was not aware of facts which would have led a reasonable and honest banker to conclude that there was such a possibility. The claimants' claim against the club succeeds to the extent of the net amount of the stolen moneys received by the club, taking account of C's winnings at the club. No valuable consideration was given by the club for the cash it received in exchange for chips. But the defence of change of position is open to the club and it would be unjust to require the club to repay the totality of the sums received without deducting the sums paid out by the club to C with respect to winning bets.[8]

[6] *Rogers v Whiteley* [1892] A.C. 118.
[7] See now *Royal Brunei Airlines Sdn Bhd v Tan* [1995] 2 A.C. 378; above, para.13–056.
[8] *Lipkin Gorman v Karpnale Ltd* [1987] 1 W.L.R. 987; [1989] 1 W.L.R. 1340; [1991] 2 A.C. 548. See also above, paras 3–089 (s.24) and 4–077 (s.29, Illustration 7).

### Countermanded cheques in Scotland

13–072    75A. **(1) On the countermand of payment of a cheque, the banker shall be treated as having no funds available for the payment of the cheque.**

**(2) This section applies to Scotland only.**

Amendment
This section was inserted by section 11(b) of the Law Reform (Miscellaneous Provisions) (Scotland) Act 1985.

Definitions
"banker": s.2.
"cheque": s.73.

COMMENT

13–073    **Amendment of law.** Section 53(2) provides that, in Scotland, where the drawee of a bill has in his hands funds available for the payment thereof, the bill operates as an assignment of the sum for which it is drawn in favour of the holder, from the time when the bill is presented to the drawee. The present section, introduced by section 11(b) of the Law Reform (Miscellaneous Provisions) (Scotland) Act 1985 removes one of the difficulties arising out of such an assignment in relation to cheques. This was that, if the drawer countermanded payment of a cheque, the amount for which the cheque was drawn was transferred by the drawee banker to a non-interest bearing suspense account until the dispute giving rise to the countermand was settled or a court order obtained to release the funds or the period of prescription expired. The difficulty is overcome by the simple expedient of treating the banker as having no funds available to meet the cheque. Section 53(2) accordingly does not apply in the case of a countermanded cheque.

### Crossed Cheques

### General and special crossings defined

14–001    **76. (1) Where a cheque bears across its face an addition of—**

**(a) The words "and company" or any abbreviation thereof between two parallel transverse lines, either with or without the words "not negotiable"; or**

(b) **Two parallel transverse lines simply, either with or without the words "not negotiable";
that addition constitutes a crossing, and the cheque is crossed
generally.**

(2) **Where a cheque bears across its face an addition of the name
of a banker, either with or without the words "not negotiable", that addition constitutes a crossing, and the cheque is
crossed specially and to that banker.**

| | |
|---|---|
| Definitions | Comparison |
| "banker": s.2. | ULC: arts 37–39. |
| "cheque": s.73. | |

COMMENT

**Crossed cheques.** The practice of crossing cheques originated in the 14–002
bankers' clearing house in the late eighteenth or early nineteenth century.
Clerks of the various bankers to whom cheques had been delivered for
collection were accustomed to write across such cheques the names of
their employers in order to facilitate the making up of accounts by the
clerks of the clearing house.[1] The crossing of cheques by the drawer is a
later development.[2] Crossing of cheques is unknown in the United States,
and the Uniform Commercial Code contains no provisions on this subject.
Crossing is very unusual in Canada,[3] but the practice is well known in
Australia, New Zealand, South Africa and many Commonwealth countries. Crossed cheques are referred to in the Geneva Convention providing a Uniform Law for Cheques,[4] but the effects of a crossing are
somewhat different from those in English law.

The first statute to recognise crossings was the Drafts on Bankers Act
1856.[5] This enactment was supplemented by the Drafts on Bankers Act
1858,[6] which made the fraudulent alteration or obliteration of a crossing
a forgery. Then came the case of *Smith v Union Bank of London*.[7] A cheque
crossed to the London and County Bank was stolen from the payee after
he had indorsed it in blank. It came into the hands of a holder in due

---

[1] *Bellamy v Marjoribanks* (1852) 7 Exch. 389, 402.
[2] Holden, *History of Negotiable Instruments in English Law*, p.230.
[3] *Crawford and Falconbridge* (8th ed.), p.1805.
[4] ULC, arts 37–39.
[5] 19 & 20 Vict. c.25.
[6] 21 & 22 Vict., c.79, passed in consequence of the decision in *Simmons v Taylor* (1858) 4
C.B.N.S. 463 that the crossing was not an integral part of the cheque, and that its
obliteration was not a forgery.
[7] (1875) 1 Q.B.D. 31 (s.79, Illustration 1).

course, who obtained payment through the London and Westminster Bank, notwithstanding the crossing. The court held that the payee had no remedy against the drawee bank because the negotiability of the cheque was not affected by the crossing. As a result, the Crossed Cheques Act 1876[8] was passed, which repealed and replaced the earlier statutes. The 1876 Act introduced the "not negotiable" crossing.[9] It also gave a remedy to the true owner of a crossed cheque if it was paid contrary to the crossing[10] and provided protection to a banker who paid a crossed cheque,[11] and to a banker who collected such a cheque,[12] in accordance with the crossing. The 1882 Act repealed the Act of 1876, but in part reproduced its provisions in sections 76 to 82. Section 82 was in turn repealed by the Cheques Act 1957, which, by section 4, extended the protection of the collecting banker to uncrossed, as well as to crossed, cheques.[13]

**14–003**      **Crossed instruments other than cheques.** By section 95 of the 1882 Act, the provisions of the Act as to crossed cheques apply to dividend warrants. By section 5 of the Cheques Act 1957, the provisions of the 1882 Act relating to crossed cheques, so far as applicable, have effect in relation to the following instruments other than cheques: (i) any document issued by a customer of a banker which, though not a bill of exchange, is intended to enable a person to obtain payment from that banker of the sum mentioned in the document,[14] *e.g.* an instrument drawn payable to "cash or order"[15]; (ii) any document issued by a public officer which is intended to enable a person to obtain payment from the Paymaster General or the Queen's and Lord Treasurer's Remembrancer of the sum mentioned in the document but is not a bill of exchange[16]; and (iii) any draft payable on demand drawn by a banker upon himself, whether payable at the head office or some other office of his bank,[17] *i.e.* a banker's demand draft.[18]

---

[8] 39 & 40 Vict., c. 81.

[9] s.12. See now s.81 of the 1882 Act.

[10] s.10. See now s.79(2) of the 1882 Act.

[11] ss. 9, 11. See now ss.79(2), 80.

[12] s.12. See s.82 of the 1882 Act (repealed).

[13] See below, para.17–064.

[14] ss.4(2)(b), 5. See, previously, Revenue Act 1883, s.17 (repealed by s.6(3) and the Sch. to the Cheques Act 1957).

[15] *Orbit Mining and Trading Co. v Westminster Bank Ltd* [1963] 1 Q.B. 794 (s.3, Illustration 8).

[16] ss.4(2)(c), 5. See, previously, Revenue Act 1883, s.17 (repealed by s.6(3) and the Sch. to the Cheques Act 1957).

[17] ss.4(2)(d), 5. See previously Bills of Exchange Act (1882), Amendment Act 1932 (repealed by s.6(3) and the Sch. to the Cheques Act 1957).

[18] *Capital and Counties Bank v Gordon* [1903] A.C. 240, 250.

**Purpose of crossing.** The purpose of crossing a cheque is to diminish the risk that the item may be misappropriated and payment made to a person not entitled to it. Payment of a crossed cheque will not be made by the drawee bank across the counter. If it does so, it disregards the mandate of its customer, the drawer, and may not be entitled to debit his account with the payment made.[19] The cheque must be presented for payment through a bank, to which the payment will be made. Crossing does not, however, in itself affect the negotiability of the instrument. If payable to order it can be negotiated, *i.e.,* transferred, by one holder to another by indorsement and delivery or (if payable to bearer) by mere delivery, just as if it were not crossed. And a crossed order or bearer cheque is a negotiable instrument in the sense that the crossing does not prevent a holder from becoming a holder in due course and thus acquiring a better title to it than the person from whom he took it had.[20] But further restrictions may be imposed by crossing the cheque "not negotiable"[21] and/or "account payee".[22]

14–004

**Methods of crossing.** Both order and bearer cheques may be crossed. A cheque may be crossed either generally or specially. In practice, special crossings by drawers are now obsolete.

14–005

**Subsection (1): general crossing.** A cheque may be crossed generally in any of the ways set out in the subsection. The minimum requirement is that of two parallel transverse lines on the face of the cheque. Cheques are normally now pre-printed in this form, which is in itself sufficient to constitute a general crossing. The two lines need not be at right angles to the cheque; nor need they extend across the entire cheque[23]; nor need they be any particular distance apart. Whether a cheque is crossed or not is essentially a question of fact.[24]

14–006

**Subsection (2): special crossing.** An addition across the face of the cheque of the name of a banker constitutes a special crossing and to that banker. Two parallel transverse lines are in this case unnecessary, but may be added.

14–007

**Addition of words "not negotiable".** Strictly the words "not negotiable", if placed on a crossed cheque, need not be added to the crossing.[25]

14–008

---

[19] See below, para.14–020 (s.79). See also s.79(2) (liability to true owner).
[20] *Smith v Union Bank of London Ltd* (1875) 1 Q.B.D. 31 (s.79, Illustration 1); *Midland Bank Ltd v Charles Simpson Motors Ltd* [1960] C.L.Y. 217. But see the legislation proposed on this matter, below, para.14–010.
[21] s.81.
[22] s.81A.
[23] *Hunter BNZ Finance Ltd v C.G. Maloney Pty Ltd* (1988) 18 N.S.W.L.R. 420.
[24] *Mather v Bank of New Zealand* (1918) 18 S.R. (N.S.W.) 49, 52.
[25] See below, para.14–034.

But where these words are used, they are normally written or printed within the crossing. Their effect is provided for in section 81 of the Act.

**14–009**    **Addition of words "account payee".** Normally in the United Kingdom the words "account payee" or "a/c payee" or "account payee only" accompany the crossing. The effect of such words is, under section 81A,[26] to render the cheque non-transferable, and it is only valid as between the parties thereto.

**14–010**    **Proposed legislation.** The Government intends to introduce legislation that will fundamentally alter the effect of a general crossing on a cheque.[27] As at present, payment of a cheque crossed generally will have to be made to a bank. But a cheque so crossed will be "non-negotiable", that is to say, it will remain transferable, but the holder will not acquire a better title than the person from whom he received it had. The special crossing will be abolished, as being no longer necessary.

### Crossing by drawer or after issue

**14–011**    77. (1) A cheque may be crossed generally or specially by the drawer.
      (2) Where a cheque is uncrossed, the holder may cross it generally or specially.
      (3) Where a cheque is crossed generally the holder may cross it specially.
      (4) Where a cheque is crossed generally or specially, the holder may add the words "not negotiable".
      (5) Where a cheque is crossed specially, the banker to whom it is crossed may again cross it specially to another banker for collection.
      (6) Where an uncrossed cheque, or a cheque crossed generally, is sent to a banker for collection, he may cross it specially to himself.

| Definitions | Comparison |
|---|---|
| "banker": s.2. | ULC: arts 37–39. |
| "cheque": s.73. | |
| "holder": s.2. | |

---

[26] See below, para.14–037.

[27] (1990) Cm. 1026, Annex 5, para.5.5. This proposal is the result of the investigation conducted by the Review Committee on Banking Services Law and Practice ((1989) Cm. 622).

COMMENT[28]

**Subsection (1): crossing by drawer.** A general crossing on a cheque is 14–012
normally made by the drawer or is pre-printed on the cheque when he
draws it.

**Subsections (2), (3), (4): crossing by holder.** A holder, or successive 14–013
holders, may cross a cheque generally or specially, or turn a general
crossing into a special crossing, or add the words "not negotiable" to the
crossing. "Holder" is defined by section 2 and has been held to include an
agent for collection.[29] Accordingly a collecting banker is not restricted to
the right under subsection (6) of crossing a cheque specially to himself,
but may exercise the rights conferred by these subsections.

**Subsection (5): second special crossing by banker.** This subsection, 14–014
for example, enables a banker who is not a member of a clearing house,
but to whom a cheque has been crossed specially, to cross it specially to
a clearing house banker for collection. It is this second crossing that is
referred to in the exception to section 79(1).

**Subsection (6): special crossing by banker to himself.** This subsection 14–015
appears now to be of little significance.[30] Chalmers suggested[31] that it
might serve to protect the banker from possible frauds by his clerks, but
it is difficult to see what protection the subsection confers that is not
already available. In the opinion of Lord Birkenhead[32] it was possibly
inserted *ex abundanti cautela* lest it might be argued that the practice of
crossing specially by the banker to himself was unlawful as constituting
a breach of the relation of principal and agent, inasmuch as it recognised
only payment made to the agent.

### Crossing a material part of cheque

78. A crossing authorised by this Act is a material part of the 14–016
cheque; it shall not be lawful for any person to obliterate or, except
as authorised by this Act, to add to or alter the crossing.

[28] This section is derived from s.5 of the Crossed Cheques Act 1876.
[29] *Akrokerri (Atlantic) Mines Ltd v Economic Bank* [1904] 2 K.B. 465, 472; *Sutters v Briggs* [1922]
1 A.C. 1, 16. See also *Baker v Barclays Bank Ltd* [1955] 1 W.L.R. 822.
[30] A banker crossing an open cheque deposited with him for collection was not thereby
enabled to claim the protection of what was then s.82: *Gordon v London City and Midland
Bank Ltd* [1902] 1 K.B. 242, affirmed [1903] A.C. 240. s.4 of the Cheques Act 1957 is not
confined to crossed cheques.
[31] 9th ed., p.305.
[32] *Sutters v Briggs* [1922] 1 A.C. 1 at 16–18.

Definitions
"cheque": s.73.
"person": s.2.

COMMENT

**14–017**     **Crossing obliterated, added to or altered.**[33] For the effect of material alterations generally, see section 64.

    The drawer of a cheque sometimes strikes out a crossing and writes "Pay cash" on it, adding his signature or initials. This practice of "opening the crossing" is sanctioned by bankers. If this is done before the cheque is issued because the drawer wishes himself to obtain cash across the counter or to enable the payee to do so, then the cheque may be regarded as having been issued uncrossed.[34] If the crossing is opened by the drawer after issue at the request of the payee, there is a technical breach of this section, but it is difficult to see who in such a case could have an effective cause for complaint. Neither the drawer nor the payee would be in a position to assert, as against the drawee banker, that the banker had wrongfully paid in disregard of the crossing since both have assented to such payment being made.[35] The banker is, however, at risk if the crossing is opened by a fraudulent person who forges the drawer's signature or initials and obtains payment in cash,[36] since he is not protected in such a case by the proviso to section 79(2).

    Where a cheque was paid into the E Bank for collection, and the bank (not being a clearing bank) crossed it specially to a clearing bank with the words "account E Bank", it was held that this was not an unlawful addition to the crossing, but a mere direction to the clearing bank as to how the money was to be dealt with after receipt.[37] For the same reason the words "account payee",[38] when added to a general crossing on a cheque, did not previously contravene the provisions of this section. But now, by section 81A(1) of the Act, the effect of such words is to render the cheque non-transferable[39] Nevertheless, it is submitted that the addition of these words by the payee to the crossing is not an unlawful addition under the present section. However, the deletion of these words from the crossing after issue of the cheque, whether made by the payee or any

---

[33] This section reproduced s.6 of the Crossed Cheques Act 1876, which in turn embodied in part the provisions of the Drafts on Bankers Act 1858.
[34] *cf. Smith and Baldwin v Barclays Bank Ltd* (1944) 5 L.B.D. 370, 375.
[35] *Smith v Union Bank of London* (1875) 1 Q.B.D. 31, 34–35.
[36] Contrast *Mercantile Bank of India Ltd v Ratnam* (1955) 57 N.L.R. (Ceylon) 193.
[37] *Akrokerri (Atlantic) Mines Ltd v Economic Bank* [1904] 2 K.B. 465, 472.
[38] See above, para.14–009.
[39] See above, para.14–009; below, para.14–037.

person other than the drawer, will be a material alteration of the cheque.[40]

## Duties of banker as to crossed cheques

79. (1) Where a cheque is crossed specially to more than one banker except when crossed to an agent for collection being a banker, the banker on whom it is drawn shall refuse payment thereof.

(2) Where the banker on whom a cheque is drawn which is so crossed nevertheless pays the same, or pays a cheque crossed generally otherwise than to a banker, or if crossed specially otherwise than to the banker to whom it is crossed, or his agent for collection being a banker, he is liable to the true owner of the cheque for any loss he may sustain owing to the cheque having been so paid.

Provided that where a cheque is presented for payment which does not at the time of presentment appear to be crossed, or to have had a crossing which has been obliterated, or to have been added to or altered otherwise than as authorised by this Act, the banker paying the cheque in good faith and without negligence shall not be responsible or incur any liability, nor shall the payment be questioned by reason of the cheque having been crossed, or of the crossing having been obliterated or having been added to or altered otherwise than as authorised by this Act, and of payment having been made otherwise than to a banker or to the banker to whom the cheque is or was crossed, or to his agent for collection being a banker, as the case may be.

14–018

Definitions
"banker": s.2.
"cheque": s.73.
"good faith": s.90.

## COMMENT

**Subsection (1): Cheque crossed specially to more than one bank-er.**[41] The exception in this subsection is that referred to in section 77(5).

14–019

---

[40] See above, para.8–081 (s.64).
[41] This subs. was previously s.8 of the Crossed Cheques Act 1876.

**14–020**    **Subsection (2): Payment contrary to the crossing.**[42] A banker pays a
cheque contrary to the crossing if he pays it in any of the ways mentioned
in this subsection. In particular, if the cheque is crossed generally, he must
not pay it otherwise than to a banker. Payment is not defined, but it has
been held that a banker pays a crossed cheque within the meaning of this
section if he gives in exchange his own cheque drawn on another bank.[43]
When a banker receives a crossed cheque on behalf of one customer
which is drawn on that same banker by another customer, the banker is
to be treated as paying the crossed cheque to a banker even though he
merely credits the account of the one customer and debits the account of
the other. And this is so whether the two accounts are maintained at the
same branch or at different branches of the bank.[44] The banker acts in two
capacities: as paying banker and as receiving banker.[45]

The main sanction imposed upon a banker who pays a cheque in
disregard or in contravention of a crossing on it is that he is not entitled
to debit his customer's account if payment is made otherwise than to a
lawful holder.[46] By paying the cheque in a manner prohibited by the
crossing, he acts contrary to the mandate of his customer, which is to pay
only in accordance with the crossing. It would appear that the mandate is
none the less that of the customer if the crossing is put on or added to by
a subsequent holder, provided it is done under the authority of and in
accordance with the Act.[47]

The subsection, however, also renders the banker liable to the true
owner of the cheque for any loss that the latter may sustain owing to the
cheque having been paid contrary to the crossing. The concept of the
"true owner" of an instrument is a difficult one and has been discussed
in the Comment on section 24 of the Act.[48] But suppose that A draws a
crossed cheque payable to B or order. It is stolen, unindorsed, from B by
a thief who personates B and presents it for payment at the counter of the
drawee bank. If the bank pays the thief, it will be liable to B, the true
owner of the cheque, for the loss he has sustained owing to the cheque
having been paid contrary to the crossing. It would seem that the same
conclusion should be reached if the cheque were drawn by A payable to
bearer and delivered to B from whom it was stolen. However, if the

---

[42] This subs. was previously s.10 of the Crossed Cheques Act 1876.
[43] *Meyer & Co. Ltd v Sze Hai Tong Banking & Insurance Co. Ltd* [1913] A.C. 847 (Illustration 2).
[44] *Gordon v London City and Midland Bank Ltd* [1902] 1 K.B. 242, 274–275, 281 (not dealt with on appeal [1903] A.C. 20); *Carpenters' Co. v British Mutual Banking Co. Ltd* [1938] 1 K.B. 511, 537–539.
[45] *Carpenters' Co. v British Mutual Banking Co. Ltd* [1938] 1 K.B. 511 (s.60, Illustration 1).
[46] *Bellamy v Majoribanks* (1852) 7 Exch. 389. 404; *Smith v Union Bank of London* (1875) 1 Q.B.D. 31, 35, 36; *Bobbett v Pinkett* (1876) 1 Ex. D. 368, 372. Contrast *Mercantile Bank of India Ltd v Ratnam* (1955) 57 N.L.R. (Ceylon) 193.
[47] *Paget* (11th ed.), p.246.
[48] See above, para.3–051 (s.24).

cheque was drawn payable to bearer, or was indorsed by B in blank before it was stolen, and came into the hands of a holder in due course, payment to that holder by the drawee bank across the counter contrary to the crossing will not give B any remedy against the bank.[49] At the time the cheque was presented for payment, B would no longer be the true owner of the instrument since title to it would have passed to the holder in due course.

In order to maintain an action under this subsection the true owner must prove that he has sustained loss owing to the cheque having been paid contrary to the crossing. If the true owner of the cheque is the drawer, he will have no claim, since, as a customer of the banker, he can require the banker to reinstate his account.[50]

**Proviso.** The proviso to the subsection is clumsily expressed.[51] The subject-matter of the words "or to have been added to or altered otherwise than as authorised by this Act" is the crossing on the cheque and not the cheque itself.[52] The purpose of the proviso is to protect a banker who pays in good faith and without negligence a cheque presented to him which does not at the time of presentment appear (i) to be crossed, or (ii) to have had a crossing which has been obliterated, or (iii) to have a crossing which has been added to or altered in an unauthorised manner.    **14–021**

Where the proviso applies, the drawee banker is protected, not only against any liability to the true owner under subsection (2), but also, by virtue of the words "nor shall the payment be questioned", against any claim by the drawer that the banker is not entitled to debit his account with the payment made. On a somewhat forced construction,[53] however, those words could be taken to mean that the drawer's liability on the cheque and the consideration are discharged and that the true owner cannot as against the drawer question the payment.

Good faith is defined in section 90 of the Act.[54] The burden of proving that payment was made without negligence appears to rest on the banker.[55]

**Other protection.** A banker who pays a cheque contrary to the crossing could not rely on the protection afforded to a paying banker by    **14–022**

---

[49] *Smith v Union Bank of London* (1875) 1 Q.B.D. 31 (Illustration 1).
[50] *Channon v English, Scottish & Australian Bank* (1918) 18 S.R. (N.S.W.) 30, 38.
[51] It was previously s.11 of the Crossed Cheques Act 1876.
[52] *Slingsby v District Bank Ltd* [1932] 1 K.B. 544, 559, 562, 567.
[53] *Paget* (8th ed.), p.248. But see s.80.
[54] See below, para.16–001.
[55] *Mather v Bank of New Zealand* (1918) 18 S.R. (N.S.W.) 49.

section 60 of the Act[56] or section 1 of the Cheques Act 1957[57] as it would not be in the ordinary course of business so to do.

ILLUSTRATIONS

**14–023**  1. M draws a cheque upon the defendants, a banking company, payable to the claimant's order and delivers it to the claimant in conditional payment of a debt owed by him to the claimant. The claimant indorses the cheque and crosses it specially to his bankers, the L Bank. While the claimant's servant is taking the cheque to the bank it is stolen from him and sold by the thief to T who passes it for full value to C who receives it in good faith. C is a customer of the W Bank and pays it into his account with that bank, which presents it to the defendants for payment. In contravention of the crossing, the defendants pay the cheque to the W Bank. The claimant's action against the defendants for conversion of the cheque fails. The Drafts on Bankers Act 1858 did not affect the negotiability of the cheque. The claimant had indorsed the cheque before it was stolen from him and C had become the bona fide holder of it before it was presented to the defendants. The claimant had ceased to be the owner of the cheque.[58]

2. The appellants are dealers in opium and other goods in Singapore and employ one Abed as their clerk. The respondents are bankers. Abed presents at the respondents' bank certain cheques drawn by third parties on the respondents payable to the appellants. The cheques are crossed generally. The respondents hand to Abed a cheque for an equivalent amount drawn by the respondents on the N Bank payable to the appellants. This cheque is paid by Abed into his own account with the N Bank and he misappropriates the proceeds. The appellants claim the amount of the cheques from the respondents under section 79(2) of the Act as loss sustained by them owing to payment having been made in contravention of the crossing. The action fails. The handing to Abed of the respondents' cheque was payment by them of the cheques presented. But, having held out Abed to have authority to collect cheques in this manner, the appellants are estopped from denying Abed's authority to receive payment of the cheques from the respondents.[59]

---

[56] See above, para.8–043.
[57] See below, para.17–013.
[58] *Smith v Union Bank of London* (1875) 1 Q.B.D. 31.
[59] *Meyer & Co. Ltd v Sze Hai Tong Banking & Insurance Co. Ltd* [1913] A.C. 847.

## Protection to banker and drawer where cheque is crossed

80. Where the banker, on whom a crossed cheque (including a    14–024
cheque which under section 81A below or otherwise is not transferable) is drawn, in good faith and without negligence pays it, if
crossed generally, to a banker, and if crossed specially, to the banker
to whom it is crossed, or his agent for collection being a banker, the
banker paying the cheque, and, if the cheque has come into the
hands of the payee, the drawer, shall respectively be entitled to the
same rights and be placed in the same position as if payment of the
cheque had been made to the true owner thereof.

Amendment
The words in brackets in this section were inserted by s.2 of the Cheques
Act 1992.

Definitions
"banker": s.2.
"cheque": s.73.
"good faith": s.90.

### COMMENT

**Protection of banker and drawer where cheque is crossed.** The cross-    14–025
ing of a cheque[60] has the effect of protecting (i) the drawee banker who
pays it in accordance with the crossing, provided he does so in good faith
and without negligence, and (ii) in consequence the drawer, if the cheque
has come into the hands of the payee. For example, A draws a crossed
cheque payable to B or order and delivers it to B as conditional payment
of the price of goods sold and delivered by B to A. It is stolen from B by
a thief who forges B's indorsement and pays it into his own bank account
for collection. The collecting bank presents the cheque for payment to the
drawee bank which pays it in good faith and without negligence.
Although the thief is not a holder of, and has no title to, the instrument,
both the drawee bank and A, the drawer, are entitled to the same rights
and are placed in the same position as if payment had been made to the
true owner of the cheque. The drawee bank is protected against any
action against it by B, the true owner, and can debit the account of its
customer, A. Moreover, A will be deemed to have paid B. B's only remedy
will be to recover from the thief, if he can be found.[61]

---

[60] Or certain other crossed instruments: see above, para.14–003.
[61] *Ogden v Benas* (1874) L.R. 9 C.P. 513.

The section is nevertheless limited in scope and does not protect the drawee banker in every case where he pays what purports to be a crossed cheque in good faith and without negligence in accordance with the crossing. First, it does not permit him to debit his customer's account if his customer's signature as drawer on the cheque is forged or unauthorised.[62] Secondly, the protection given by the section is excluded where a material alteration has made the paper a null and void document, no longer a cheque.[63] Thirdly, it has been said that the section only applies to a case where the true owner is somebody other than the drawer.[64]

14–026    **"Pays it to a banker."** A banker pays to a banker a crossed cheque drawn on him if the payee is also his customer and the cheque is paid in at a different branch from, or at the same branch as, that where the drawer maintains his account.[65] In such a case "payment" as required by this section is made by debiting the account of the drawer and crediting the account of the payee, and the banker acts both as paying and collecting banker. In his capacity as paying banker he will be entitled to the protection of this section but as collecting banker must rely on section 4 of the Cheques Act 1957.[66] However, in *Universal Guarantee Pty Ltd v National Bank of Australasia Ltd*,[67] an employee of the appellant company procured crossed cheques to be drawn on the company's account with the respondent bank payable to fictitious payees, indorsed these in the name of the payees and paid them into the company's account. By so doing he was able to steal equivalent sums received in cash from the company's customers. The Privy Council held that, when the bank received such a cheque, it did not "pay" it to anyone and it did not "collect" it on behalf of anyone. It made two contra entries in the same account of its customer. Nothing was paid out and nothing was collected or paid in. In the result the debtor/creditor relationship between the bank and the company remained entirely unaffected.

14–027    **Other provisions.** This section is one of three statutory provisions designed to protect the drawee banker who pays a cheque.[68] Section 60 of

---

[62] See above, para.3–059 (s.24).

[63] *Slingsby v District Bank Ltd* [1932] 1 K.B. 544, 559, 562.

[64] [1932] 1 K.B. 544 at 562. *Sed quaere?*

[65] See above, para.14–020 (s.79).

[66] *Carpenters' Co. v British Mutual Banking Co. Ltd* [1938] 1 K.B. 511 (s.60, Illustration 1); *Standard Bank of South Africa Ltd v Nair* 2001 (1) S.A. 998; *Standard Bank of South Africa Ltd v Harris* 2003 (2) S.A. 23.

[67] [1965] 1 W.L.R. 691; Megrah (1966) 29 M.L.R. 72.

[68] The need for the protection given by this section has been questioned: Holden, *History of Negotiable Instruments in English Law*, p.229.

the Act protects the drawee banker against forged or unauthorised indorsements if he pays a cheque payable to order in good faith and in the ordinary course of business.[69] That section is not limited, as is the present section, to crossed cheques paid to a banker. On the other hand, it is limited to cheques payable to order. The present section is not so limited. It applies to cheques which are not transferable and so are not payable to order. It also applies to bearer cheques, but in that respect the banker is in no need of this statutory protection, since payment to the holder of a stolen bearer cheque, if made in good faith and without notice that his title to the cheque is defective, is payment in due course and discharges the instrument.[70] Section 1 of the Cheques Act 1957 further relieves the drawee banker from liability if he pays a cheque, whether crossed or uncrossed, which is not indorsed or which is irregularly indorsed, provided that he does so in good faith and in the ordinary course of business.[71]

The cumulative protection afforded by the three sections is due to historical reasons. Section 60 is derived from section 19 of the Stamp Act 1853.[72] The present section reproduced section 9 of the Crossed Cheques Act 1876, which was repealed by the 1882 Act. Section 1 of the Cheques Act 1957 was intended to relieve the paying banker from liability if he paid a cheque which was irregularly indorsed and to dispense with the necessity for the indorsement of cheques as a pre-condition for payment.[73] It would clearly be preferable if their effect were now combined in a single legislative provision, and the Government proposes to effect such a consolidation by legislation.[74]

**"In good faith and without negligence."** Both the two sections mentioned above and the present section require that the banker should act "in good faith". But there is a further difference between them in that the former sections protect the banker who acts "in the ordinary course of business" whereas the present section protects him if he acts "without negligence". It would seem that a paying banker may be acting in the

**14–028**

---

[69] See above, para.8–043 (s.60).
[70] See above, para.8–011 (s.59).
[71] See below, para.17–005.
[72] s.19 of the 1853 Act remains unrepealed, but, by interpretation, it does not now apply to cheques: see above, para.8–045 (s.60).
[73] But "indorsement" is still required where a cheque is paid across the counter: see below, para.17–003.
[74] (1990) Cm. 1026, Annex 5, para.5.9 (as a result of Recommendation 7(5) of the Review Committee on Banking Services Law and Practice: (1989) Cm. 622); above, para.1–008. The consolidation will follow the wording of the present section, *i.e.* "good faith and without negligence", and not that of s.60 and the Cheques Act 1957, s.1.

ordinary course of business despite his negligence.[75] Whether a paying banker can deviate from the ordinary course of business and still act without negligence is more doubtful.[76]

Where a cheque is crossed and bears across its face the words "account payee" or "a/c payee", it is not transferable.[77] It might be thought negligent for a banker to pay such a non-transferable cheque if it bore a purported indorsement by the payee: the inference from such an indorsement would be that it was being collected for a person other than the named payee, who would be the only person entitled to claim payment of the cheque.[78] However, in such a case and in the case of any other non-transferable cheque (*e.g.* one drawn "Pay X only"), by section 81A(2): "A banker is not to be treated for the purposes of section 80 . . . as having been negligent by reason only of his failure to concern himself with any purported indorsement" of the cheque. The effect of this provision —though somewhat obliquely expressed—is to relieve the paying banker from scrutinising non-transferable cheques for indorsements.[79] It also seems that the banker can normally ignore any purported indorsement on such a cheque and safely pay the banker presenting the cheque for payment. It is the responsibility of the collecting, and not of the paying, banker to ensure that a non-transferable cheque is collected only for the account of the original payee.[80] There may nevertheless be additional circumstances, for example where the paying banker is reliably informed that the cheque has been stolen from the payee,[81] in which it might be negligent for the banker to pay a non-transferable cheque bearing a purported indorsement without first satisfying himself that it was in fact being paid to the person entitled to receive payment.

**14–029**    **Banker both collects and pays.** Where a banker acts both as paying banker and collecting banker, as where he collects a cheque drawn on the same or a different branch of the same bank, he can be negligent in the performance of his collecting functions without being negligent in performance of his functions as paying banker.[82]

---

[75] *Carpenters' Co. v British Mutual Banking Co. Ltd* [1938] 1 K.B. 511; above, para.8–051.
[76] But see *Australian Mutual Provident Soc. v Derham* (1979) 39 F.L.R. 165, where the Australian equivalent of s.80 was read together with the equivalent of s.1 of the Cheques Act 1957. See also above, para.13–062 (s.75).
[77] s.81A(1).
[78] Contrast *Gishen v Nedbank Ltd* 1984(2) S.A. 378.
[79] As under s.1 of the Cheques Act 1957; below, para.17–005.
[80] See below, para.17–049 (Cheques Act 1957, s.4).
[81] Assuming that the drawer has not, or has not yet, countermanded payment.
[82] *Carpenters' Co. v British Mutual Banking Co. Ltd* [1938] 1 K.B. 511 (s.60, Illustration 1); *Linklaters v HSBC Bank plc* EWHC 1113 (Comm); *Standard Bank of South Africa v Harris* 2003 (2) S.A. 23; see also above, para.8–049; below, para.17–052.

**Effect of crossing on holder**

**81. Where a person takes a crossed cheque which bears on it the   14–030
words "not negotiable," he shall not have and shall not be capable of
giving a better title to the cheque than that which the person from
whom he took it had.**

Definitions
"cheque": s.73.
"person": s.2.

COMMENT

**"Not negotiable" crossing.** The "not negotiable" crossing was intro-   14–031
duced by section 12 of the Crossed Cheques Act 1876.[83] An order or
bearer cheque crossed "not negotiable" is still transferable, but its negotiable quality is limited. It is put on much the same footing as an overdue
bill.[84] A holder who has a good title can still transfer it,[85] and the
transferee is entitled to receive payment; but where the transferor has no
title or a defective title to the cheque, a subsequent holder who takes it in
good faith and for value will not acquire the rights or gain the protection
ordinarily afforded to a holder in due course. In *Great Western Railway Co.
v London and County Banking Co. Ltd*[86] Lord Lindley said: "Every one who
takes a cheque marked 'not negotiable' takes it at his own risk, and his
title to the money got by its means is as defective as his title to the cheque
itself."

Suppose that a cheque payable to bearer and crossed "not negotiable"
is stolen from the drawer before it reaches the payee. The thief gets a
tradesman to cash it for him, and the tradesman gets the cheque paid on
presentment through a banker. The drawee banker who pays will ordinarily be protected by section 80 of the Act[87] and the collecting banker by
section 4 of the Cheques Act 1957.[88] But the tradesman will be liable to an
action for conversion or in restitution for money had and received at the

[83] See above, para.14–002.
[84] See s.36(2).
[85] See *Sutters v Briggs* [1922] 1 A.C. 1.
[86] [1901] A.C. 414, 424. See also *Commissioners of the State Savings Bank of Victoria v Permewan
Wright & Co. Ltd* (1914) 19 C.L.R. 457, 467; *Universal Guarantee Pty Ltd v National Bank of
Australasia Ltd* [1965] 1 W.L.R. 691, 697; *Universal Stores Ltd v O.K. Bazaars (1929) Ltd* 1973
(4) S.A. 747, 760.
[87] Or by s.1 of the Cheques Act 1957.
[88] See below, para.17–028.

677

suit of the drawer.[89] And if payment of the cheque was countermanded by the drawer before it was paid, the tradesman could not sue the drawer.

The effect of a "not negotiable" crossing is not, however, confined to the situation where a cheque is taken from a person who had no title to it at all. It also extends to cases where that person's title is defective within the meaning of section 29(2) of the Act, *e.g.* where the cheque was obtained by fraud.[90] Moreover, the word "person" in the phrase "[W]here a person takes a crossed cheque" includes the original payee. In *Wilson and Meeson v Pickering*[91] a blank cheque form crossed "not negotiable" was signed by one of the partners in the claimant firm and handed by him to a secretary for completion as a cheque payable to the Inland Revenue. The secretary fraudulently filled it in as a cheque for a larger amount payable to the defendant, who received it in good faith and without notice of the fraud in payment of a debt owed to her by the secretary. It was held that the defendant was a "person" and "took" the cheque within the meaning of the section, and had no better title to it than the secretary had.

14–032      The fact that a cheque is crossed "not negotiable" appears to have no adverse effect on the protection given to the collecting banker by section 4 of the Cheques Act 1957.[92] But if such a banker failed to establish that he had acted without negligence in collecting the cheque, he would be unable to fall back on the alternative ground of defence, which may in certain circumstances be open to him,[93] that he was a holder in due course.

The "not negotiable" crossing is now rarely seen. The majority of cheques issued in the United Kingdom are now crossed instead with the pre-printed words "account payee". These words render the cheque non-transferable[94] and for the most part provide a greater measure of protection to the payee.

14–033      **Bills and notes.** The words "not negotiable" have only the specialised and restricted meaning attached in this section where they are found on a crossed cheque. Where a bill of exchange payable three months after date was crossed "not negotiable" and drawn payable to the payee *only*,

---

[89] *Great Western Ry Co. v London and County Banking Co. Ltd* [1901] A.C. 414, 418, 424; (Cheques Act 1957, s.4, Illustration 3).

[90] *Fisher v Roberts* (1896) 116 T.L.R. 354; *Great Western Ry Co. v London and County Banking Co. Ltd* [1901] A.C. 414; *Union Bank of Australia Ltd v Schulte* [1914] V.L.R. 183; *Wilson & Meeson v Pickering* [1946] K.B. 422 (s.20, Illustration 22). *cf. Cheney v Holschier* [1958] V.L.R. 64; *Bank of New South Wales v Ross, Stuckey and Morawa* [1974] 2 Lloyd's Rep. 110.

[91] [1946] K.B. 422 (s.20, Illustration 22).

[92] See below, para.17–057.

[93] See below, para.17–058.

[94] s.81A(1).

the Court of Appeal refused[95] to hold that the negotiability of the instrument alone was affected, leaving its transferability unimpaired. The bill contained words prohibiting transfer within the terms of section 8(1) and an indorsee could not sue on it. It is, perhaps, less certain what would be the effect where a bill or note merely bore the words "not negotiable"[96]: this would probably be construed as "indicating an intention that [the instrument] should not be transferable", as mentioned in section 8(1),[97] but might possibly be regarded as an error and to have no legal effect.

**Relationship to crossing.** The section does not in its terms require that the words "not negotiable" be added to the crossing itself,[98] although it is usual to place them within the two transverse lines of the crossing. The section refers to "a crossed cheque which bears on it the words 'not negotiable'" and it is submitted that this requirement will be satisfied wherever the words are placed, provided that they are on the face of the crossed cheque.  **14–034**

**Uncrossed cheques.** The appearance of the words "not negotiable" on a cheque which is not crossed gives rise to difficulty. It does not seem reasonable to ascribe to these words the same effect as that set out in section 81 when the section is a statutory provision specifically limited to crossed cheques.[99] On the other hand, the drawer presumably intended them to mean something. On that supposition, they would have to be construed as indicating an intention that the cheque should not be transferable within section 8(1),[1] unless they were simply regarded as an error and deemed not to have been written on the cheque.[2]  **14–035**

**By whom written.** The words "not negotiable" may be written on a crossed cheque by the drawer or added by any holder.[3]  **14–036**

### Non-transferable cheques

81A. (1) **Where a cheque is crossed and bears across its face the words "account payee" or "a/c payee", either with or without the word "only", the cheque shall not be transferable, but shall only be valid as between the parties thereto.**  **14–037**

---

[95] *Hibernian Bank v Gysin and Hanson* [1939] 1 K.B. 483 (s.8, Illustration 1).
[96] These could only be placed on a bill by the drawer.
[97] See *Hibernian Bank v Gysin and Hanson* [1938] 2 K.B. 384, 390–392 (Lewis J.)
[98] But see s.76(1)(b), 77(4).
[99] *Paget* (12th ed.), 15.32. *Byles* (27th ed.), 8–02.
[1] See above, para.2–061.
[2] *cf. National Bank v Silke* [1891] 1 Q.B. 435, 438.
[3] s.77(4).

(2) **A banker is not to be treated for the purposes of section 80 above as having been negligent by reason only of his failure to concern himself with any purported indorsement of a cheque which under subsection (1) above or otherwise is not transferable.**

Amendment

This section was inserted by section 1 of the Cheques Act 1992.

Definitions

"banker": s.2

"cheque": s.73

"indorsement": s.2

COMMENT

14–038     **Background to the section.** It has long been the practice of commercial enterprises to place on crossed cheques drawn by them the words "account payee" or "a/c payee" or "account payee only".[4] There was previously no statutory authority for this practice. The purpose of adding these words was, however, to reduce the risk that the cheque and its proceeds might be fraudulently appropriated by some person other than the named payee.[5] But the effect of the words was often misunderstood. They did not affect the transferability of a cheque. They were not, when added to a cheque payable to order or bearer, "words prohibiting transfer or indicating that the cheque should not be transferable" within section 8(1) of the Act.[6] Nor did they in themselves have the effect, unless accompanied by the words "not negotiable",[7] of preventing a transferee from acquiring a good title to a cheque to which his transferor had no title

---

[4] *Bellamy v Marjoribanks* (1852) 7 Exch. 389; Holden, *History of Negotiable Instruments in English Law*, pp.241, 282–285.

[5] The "payee" is the person named as such in the cheque and not the person who, by negotiation, has become the owner of the cheque: *House Property Co. of London Ltd v London County & Westminster Bank* (1915) 84 L.J.K.B. 1846.

[6] *National Bank v Silke* [1891] 1 Q.B. 435; *Universal Guarantee Pty Ltd v National Bank of Australia Ltd* [1965] 1 W.L.R. 691, 697; *Standard Bank of South Africa Ltd v Sham Magazine Centre* 1977 (1) S.A. 484; *Algemene Bank Nederland NV v Happy Valley Restaurant Pte Ltd* [1991] 2 M.L.J. 289.

[7] s.81; see above, para.14–030.

or a defective title.[8] Being normally added to the crossing on the cheque, which is a direction to the drawee banker not to pay the cheque otherwise than to a banker, it might have been supposed that they were likewise a direction to the drawee banker to pay the cheque only when presented for the account of the named payee. But it would be impossible for the drawee banker to know, when a cheque was passed through clearing, for whose account it was collected and he could not be expected to assume responsibility for ensuring that the proceeds were credited to the payee's account. It was therefore held that the words were not to be treated as a direction to the drawee banker: they were in fact to be regarded as a direction, or rather as a warning, to the receiving banker that the proceeds when collected were to be applied to the credit of the payee's account.[9] If the collecting banker collected a cheque for a person other than the person named as the original payee, then he ran the risk that he might be liable to the true owner in conversion should that person have no title or a defective title to the cheque. In the absence of special circumstances, the banker would not be able to rely on the protection afforded to him by section 4 of the Cheques Act 1957 as he would not have acted "without negligence" in so collecting the cheque.[10]

In 1989 the Review Committee on Banking Services Law and Practice recommended the introduction of a new non-transferable instrument (the "bank payment order"), the proceeds of which could be collected only by a bank and solely for the account of the named payee.[11] The Government did not accept this recommendation, but proposed instead to achieve the same result by giving statutory recognition to the words "account payee" written on a crossed cheque.[12] This proposal was implemented in the Cheques Act 1992. Section 1 of the 1992 Act introduced into the 1882 Act the current section 81A, subsection (1) of which renders non-transferable a crossed cheque bearing these words across its face.[12a] Since most cheque forms supplied by United Kingdom banks to their customers, whether commercial or private, are now crossed and pre-printed with the words "account payee only" within the crossing, it follows that the vast majority of cheques issued in the United Kingdom are no longer negotiable instruments but merely payment orders by which the customer instructs his

---

[8] *Underwood (A.L.) Ltd v Bank of Liverpool* [1924] 1 K.B. 775, 793–794. See also *Sutters v Briggs* [1922] 1 A.C. 1.

[9] *Akrokerri (Atlantic) Mines Ltd v Economic Bank* [1904] 2 K.B. 465, 472; *Importers Ltd v Westminster Bank Ltd* [1927] 2 K.B. 297; *Morison v London County and Westminster Bank Ltd* [1914] 3 K.B. 356, 373–374; *Universal Guarantee Pty Ltd v National Bank of Australia Ltd* [1965] 1 W.L.R. 691, at 697.

[10] See below, para.17–049.

[11] (1989) Cm. 622, rec. 7(7); see above, para.1–008.

[12] (1990) Cm. 1026, Annex 5, para.5.6.

[12a] Similar amendments have been made in New Zealand in 1995 and in South Africa in 2000.

banker to pay the sum of money specified in the cheque to the person named therein as the payee.

**14–039**    **Form of cheque.** Subsection (1) applies not only to crossed cheques as defined in section 73 of the Act ("a bill of exchange drawn on a banker payable on demand") but also, by virtue of section 5 of the Cheques Act 1957,[13] to the three further categories of instruments analogous to cheques mentioned in subsection (2) of section 4 of the 1957 Act.[14] So, for example, the same words across the face of a crossed banker's draft payable on demand, or of a crossed dividend warrant, render the instrument not transferable. The same applies to crossed post-dated cheques.[15] But such words on a bill of exchange or promissory note would not have this effect: nor would they have this effect if placed on an uncrossed cheque. In such a case they would, as previously, be a direction to the collecting banker not to collect the instrument for the account of any person other than the named payee. The instrument itself would nevertheless remain transferable.

A cheque or other instrument falling within section 81A(1), not being transferable, is not payable to order. Pre-printed cheque forms accordingly now omit the words "or Order" previously printed after the space for the insertion of the name of the payee. It is submitted that a crossed cheque drawn (in handwriting) "Pay John Smith or Order" or "Pay to the order of John Smith" but bearing the printed words "account payee" across its face would still be non-transferable. Although it might be argued that the handwritten words should prevail over the printed and show the intention of the drawer that the cheque should nevertheless be transferable,[16] it would appear that subsection (1) would still apply. The printed words would have to be deleted by the drawer for his intention to be carried into effect. More difficulty, however, arises if such a pre-printed cheque is drawn payable to "Bearer". The draftsman of the 1992 Act seems to have overlooked this possibility. The inference that a cheque so drawn was intended by the drawer to be transferable is, it is submitted, very strong indeed. But if the subsection is mandatory, the cheque would not be transferable by the person to whom it was originally delivered, even though a collecting banker who was asked to collect such a cheque for a customer would have no means of knowing from the cheque itself whether his customer was that person. A cheque drawn payable to "John Smith or bearer", though normally payable to bearer,[17]

---

[13] See below, para.17–075.
[14] See below, para.17–063.
[15] See above, para.2–089 (s.13).
[16] Contrast *Aboobaker v Gableiter Distributors Pty Ltd* 1978 (4) S.A. 615 ("not transferable" stamped on cheque prevails over handwritten "or order").
[17] See above, para.2–065 (s.8).

would, it seems, be non-transferable and payable only to the named payee, John Smith.[18]

**Exact words required.** It is submitted that subsection (1) only renders   **14–040**
a cheque non-transferable if the precise words referred to in the subsection are used. Thus if a cheque is drawn "Pay M £450" and crossed "Account of M, National Bank, Croydon", the subsection does not apply. The cheque remains transferable.[19] It is, however, arguable that, having regard to the enactment of section 81A(1), a similar or cognate expression such as "Account of M" would now be words "indicating an intention that [the cheque] should not be transferable" within section 8(1) of the Act. But it is doubtful whether it would be so held.

The cheque must bear the words referred to in subsection (1) "across its face". They are usually printed within the two transverse lines of the crossing, although the subsection does not require this. On the other hand, in contrast to section 81 which refers to a crossed cheque "which bears *on it* the words 'not negotiable' ",[20] the expression "across" suggests that the words must be printed or written transversely across the cheque. If, for example, a cheque were drawn "Pay John Smith a/c payee" this would not be sufficient. Again, however, it could be argued that these are now words "indicating an intention that [the cheque] should not be transferable" within section 8(1).

**Cancelling or adding the words "account payee".** It is open to the   **14–041**
drawer, before or at the time of issuing a cheque, to delete, and so cancel, the words "account payee" printed on the cheque. He will normally do this by striking through the words and signing his name or placing his initials next to the deletion. The cheque then becomes transferable and payable to order or bearer as the case may be. It is not open to the payee or any other person (*e.g.* a collecting banker) without the authority of the drawer so to delete the words. Such an unauthorised deletion would be a material alteration which would avoid the cheque under section 64 of the Act.[21]

The drawer could add the words "account payee" to a crossed cheque on which these words were not pre-printed. It is submitted that this could also be done after issue by the payee (with or without the authority of the

---

[18] See, by analogy, *House Property Co. of London Ltd v London County and Westminster Bank* (1915) 31 T.L.R. 479; *Impala Plastics (Pty) Ltd v Coetzee* 1984 (2) S.A. 392; *Gishen v Nedbank Ltd* 1984 (2) S.A. 378.
[19] *National Bank v Silke* [1891] 1 Q.B. 435.
[20] See above, para.14–034.
[21] See above, para.8–083.

drawer) and that this would not be a material alteration of the cheque or contravene section 78 of the Act.[22]

**14–042**     **Subsection (2).** This subsection has been considered in the Comment on section 80 of the Act.[23]

**14–043**     **General effect of the section.** The section appears to have achieved its purpose of reducing fraud. If a thief steals a crossed cheque marked "account payee", he will experience considerable difficulty in obtaining cash for the cheque. If he delivers it to his bank for collection, the bank should refuse to collect it for him unless (without the knowledge of the bank) he has previously managed to open a bank account in the name of the payee or unless his name is identical with that of the payee. No third party, *e.g.* a shopkeeper, to whom the thief purports to transfer the cheque in exchange for cash will acquire a good title to the cheque even though he takes it in good faith and for value, and the third party will likewise be unable to have the cheque collected.

Should the thief nevertheless succeed in obtaining payment of a stolen cheque marked "account payee", the question arises as to the rights (if any) of the drawer or true owner of the cheque against the paying banker and the collecting banker. In this respect, the insertion of section 81A by the Cheques Act 1992 appears to have made no substantial difference.

     (i) *Paying banker.* Since the cheque is not transferable, the paying banker will have paid the cheque to a person who is not entitled to receive the payment and in consequence will *prima facie* not be able to debit the drawer's account with the amount paid out. The paying banker can no longer rely on the protection conferred by section 60 of the Act since that section applies only to cheques payable to order.[24] However, he can still rely on the protection conferred by section 80 of the Act and ordinarily this will—as previously—provide a defence to any claim against him in respect of the wrongful payment.[25]

     (ii) *Collecting banker.* By collecting a cheque for a person other then the named payee the collecting banker will *prima facie* be liable to the true owner of the cheque in conversion. Whether or not the collecting banker can rely upon the statutory defence available to him under section 4 of the Cheques Act 1957 depends on whether he can prove that he acted "without negligence" and in this respect his position has not been materially altered by the

---

[22] See (before the 1992 Act) *Akrokerri (Atlantic) Mines Ltd v Economic Bank* [1904] 2 K.B. 465, 472, and above, para.14–017.
[23] See above, para.14–028.
[24] See above, para.8–048.
[25] See above, para.14–028.

enactment of section 81A. Normally, in the absence of special circumstances, it will be negligent for him to collect such a cheque for a person other than the named payee.[26]

There is, nevertheless, one situation where the collecting banker is now in a less favourable position than he was before. Since the cheque is not transferable, a collecting banker who has in good faith given value to his customer for the cheque cannot claim to be a holder, still less a holder in due course, of the cheque should it be dishonoured on presentation. He will have no claim against the drawer of the cheque and, in particular, cannot rely on section 2 of the Cheques Act 1957.[27]

**Assignment.** The question has earlier been discussed[28] whether the indorsement and delivery of a non-transferable instrument by the original payee to a third party could constitute an assignment by the payee to the third party of the payee's contractual rights on the instrument. It is submitted that, by drawing a cheque crossed "account payee", the drawer sufficiently indicates his intention to incur liability only to the payee and that, so far as he is concerned, any purported assignment by the payee would be ineffective.[29] The purported assignment might, however, still be effective as a contract between the payee and the third party[30] or as a declaration of trust of the benefit of the payee's contractual rights in favour of the third party.[31] Moreover, by such indorsement and delivery, the third party might become the true owner of the paper and so the payee would be precluded from bringing any action in conversion against a collecting banker who had collected the cheque on behalf of a person other than the payee.[32]

14–044

**The "unbanked" payee.**[33] Although section 81A performs a useful function in reducing fraud, it gives rise to particular problems for the "unbanked" payee, that is to say, a payee who does not have a bank account into which the cheque may be paid. It is no longer open to the payee to indorse the cheque and deliver it to a friend who does have such an account so that the cheque may be collected through that account. A bank is unlikely to accept for collection a cheque drawn payable to a

14–045

---

[26] See below, para.17–049.
[27] See below, para.17–017.
[28] See above, paras 2–062 and 5–067.
[29] *Linden Gardens Trust Ltd v Lenesta Sludge Disposals Ltd* [1994] 1 A.C. 85.
[30] [1994] 1 A.C. 85 at 108. See *Chitty on Contracts* (29th ed.), Vol.I, para.19–045.
[31] *Re Turcan* (1888) 40 Ch.D.5; *Spellman v Spellman* [1961] 1 W.L.R. 921, 925; *Don King Productions Ltd v Warren* [2000] Ch. 291.
[32] *Absa Bank Ltd v Greyvenstein* 2003 (4) SA 537; above, para.2–062; below, paras 17–030 and 17–049. Alternatively the payee might be estopped if he had, by his signature, misled the bank into collecting the cheque.
[33] See Macleod (1997) 113 L.Q.R. 133.

person other than its customer without a full investigation of the circumstances of the case, if indeed it is prepared to do so at all.

### Protection to collecting banker

14–046      82. [*Repealed.*]

Repeal

This section, together with the amendment effected by the Bills of Exchange (Crossed Cheques) Act 1906, was repealed by section 6(3) of and the Schedule to the Cheques Act 1957. It is replaced by section 4 of the 1957 Act; see below, para.17–064.

# PART IV

# PROMISSORY NOTES

## Promissory note defined

83. (1) A promissory note is an unconditional promise in writing    15–001
made by one person to another signed by the maker, engag-
ing to pay, on demand or at a fixed or determinable future
time, a sum certain in money, to, or to the order of, a specified
person or to bearer.

(2) An instrument in the form of a note payable to maker's order
is not a note within the meaning of this section unless and
until it is indorsed by the maker.

(3) A note is not invalid by reason only that it contains also a
pledge of collateral security with authority to sell or dispose
thereof.

(4) A note which is, or on the face of it purports to be, both made
and payable within the British Islands is an inland note. Any
other note is a foreign note.

Definitions                      Comparison
"bearer": s.2.                   UCC: §§ 3–104—3–113.
"British Islands": s.4(1).       ULB: arts 75, 76.
"determinable future time": s.11.    UNB: arts 2, 3.
"note": s.2.
"person": s.2.
"writing": s.2.

## COMMENT

**Promissory notes.** Part IV of the Act (sections 83 to 89) deals with    15–002
promissory notes. By section 89(1) of the Act, subject to certain qualifications, the provisions of the Act relating to bills of exchange apply, with the
necessary modifications, to promissory notes. As a result, much of the law
relating to promissory notes is to be found in Part II of the Act and has
been discussed in the Comment on the various sections which make up
that part. In the Comment on sections 83 to 89 which follows, the discussion is for the most part limited to matters which are peculiar to notes as
opposed to bills of exchange.

Promissory notes were originally not negotiable at common law.[1] They were made so by the statute of Anne in 1704,[2] which statute was repealed by section 96 of and the Second Schedule to the 1882 Act.

15–003 **Subsection (1): definition of note.**[3] As in the case of bills of exchange, no particular form of words is essential to the validity of a note[4] provided the requirements of this subsection are fulfilled. There is no necessity, as there is under the Geneva Convention providing a Uniform Law for Bills of Exchange and Promissory Notes, for the term "promissory note" to be inserted in the instrument.[5] Nor need it be expressly payable "to order" or to bearer.[6] On the other hand, the form of words will not suffice to make a document a note which the parties did not intend to be a negotiable instrument. In *Sibree v Tripp*,[7] a document in the form: "Memorandum. Mr Sibree has this day deposited with me £500, on the sale of £10,300 £3 p.c. Spanish, to be returned on demand" was held not to be a note. Pollock C.B. said[8]:

> "We cannot suppose that the legislature intended to prevent parties making written contracts relating to the payment of money, other than bills and notes; and this appears to me to be merely an instrument recording the agreement of the parties . . . and to be rather an agreement than a promissory note."

The difference between an agreement and a promissory note was also emphasised by Bowen L.J. in 1888[9] when he said that promissory notes "are meant to include documents the contents of which consist substantially of a promise to pay a definite sum of money, and of nothing else". And more recently, in *Claydon v Bradley*, it has been stated by Dillon L.J.[10]:

> "If the statutory definition of a promissory note in section 83 of the Act of 1882 is applied literally, it would seemingly cover a range of

---

[1] *Clerke v Martin* (1701) 2 Ld. Raym. 757; *Buller v Crips* (1703) 6 Mod. 29.

[2] Promissory Notes Act 1704. (3 & 4 Anne c. 9).

[3] A wider definition of promissory note was contained in s.33 of the Stamp Act 1891, but that section was repealed by s.32(a) of the Finance Act 1970 following the abolition of stamp duty on notes. In particular the section did not require the note to be unconditional.

[4] *Brooks v Elkins* (1836) 2 M. & W. 74; *Lovell v Hill* (1836) 6 C. & P. 238; *Hooper v Williams* (1848) 2 Exch. 13, 20.

[5] ULB, art.75.

[6] Contrast UCC, § 3–104(a)(e).

[7] (1846) 15 M. & W. 23.

[8] (1846) 15 M. & W. 23 at 29.

[9] *Mortgage Insurance Corp. v IRC* (1888) 21 Q.B.D. 352, 358 (a Stamp Act case). See also *Thomson v Bill* 1894, 22 R. (Ct Sess.) 16.

[10] *Claydon v Bradley* [1987] 1 W.L.R. 521, 526. See also at 528 and *Wirth v Weigal Leygonie & Co. Ltd* [1939] 3 All E.R. 712 (Illustration 4).

documents which no one would ordinarily dream of regarding as promissory notes or bills of exchange or in any other way negotiable: such as four-year covenants in favour of charities, or legal charges on land containing the usual covenant by the mortgagor for payment on a fixed date or on demand."

**"Promise."** The subsection requires a note to contain a promise to pay. The actual word "promise" need not, however, be used, and any other words which clearly constitute a promise to pay are sufficient.[11] But a mere acknowledgment of indebtedness, though it imports a promise to repay, is not a note.[12] In *Akbar Khan v Attar Singh*,[13] a receipt for Rs. 43,900 with the addition "this amount to be payable after two years. Interest at the rate of Rs. 5.4.0 per cent per year to be charged" was held by the Privy Council not to be a promissory note. Lord Atkin, delivering the advice of the Board, stated[14]:

15–004

> "It is . . . doubtful whether a document can properly be styled a promissory note which does not contain an undertaking to pay, not merely an undertaking which has to be inferred from the words used. It is plain that the implied promise to pay arising from an acknowledgement of a debt will not suffice".

But he also emphasised the point, referred to above, that the document must be such as to show the intention to make a note, for he continued[15]:

> "Their Lordships prefer to decide this point on the broad ground that such a document as this is not and could not be intended to be brought within the definition[16] relating to documents which are to be negotiable instruments. Such documents must come into existence for the purpose only of recording an agreement to pay money and nothing more, though of course they may state the consideration. Receipts and agreements generally are not intended to be negotiable, and serious embarrassment would be caused in commerce if the negotiable net were cast too wide. This document plainly is a receipt for money containing the terms on which it is to be repaid . . . Being

---

[11] *Wheatley v Williams* (1836) 1 M. & W. 533; *Brooks v Elkins* (1836) 2 M. & W. 74 (but these cases would probably be decided otherwise today).

[12] *Horne v Redfearn* (1838) 4 Bing. N.C. 433; *Gould v Coombs* (1845) 1 C.B. 543 (Illustration 2); *Sibree v Tripp* (1846) 15 M. & W. 23; *White v North* (1849) 3 Exch. 689 (Illustration 2); *Hyne v Dewdney* (1852) 21 L.J.Q.B. 278 (Illustraton 2); *Hopkins v Abbott* (1875) L.R. 19 Eq. 222 (Illustration 3); *Claydon v Bradley* [1987] 1 W.L.R. 521 (Illustration 5). *cf. Ellis v Mason* (1839) 7 Dowl. P.C. 598.

[13] [1936] 2 All E.R. 545.

[14] [1936] 2 All E.R. 545 at 549.

[15] [1936] 2 All E.R. 545 at 550.

[16] In the Indian Negotiable Instruments Act 1881.

primarily a receipt even if coupled with a promise to pay it is not a promissory note."

**15–005**    **"Unconditional."** The promise to pay contained in a promissory note must be unconditional.[17] This requirement has been discussed in the Comment on section 3 of the Act.[18] As in the case of bills of exchange, an instrument expressed to be payable on a contingency is not a note and the happening of the event does not cure the defect.[19] The provisions of section 3(3) of the Act also apply to a promise to pay out of a particular fund.[20] The fact that a note is in the body of it made payable at a particular place does not make it conditional.[21]

**15–006**    **"Writing."** By section 2 of the Act, writing includes print. See also section 5 of and Schedule 1 to the Interpretation Act 1978 and the Comment on section 3 of the Act.[22]

**15–007**    **"Made by one person to another."** The maker and the payee of a note must be different persons[23]; but see subsection (2), below, para.15–027. See also section 85 of the Act for a note made by two or more makers and sections 7(2) and 32(3) for a note payable to two or more payees.

**15–008**    **"Signed by the maker."** For the meaning of "signature," see the Comment on sections 23[24] and 91[25] of the Act. See also section 23(1) (2) (signature in assumed or firm name), section 24 (forged or unauthorised signature), section 25 (procuration signature), sections 26 and 91(1) (signature by agent or representative) and section 91(2) (seal of corporation as signature).

**15–009**    **"Engaging to pay."** The engagement of the maker to pay is a contract on the note.[26] In English law[27] it can be enforced only by a payee who has given valuable consideration for the promise or by a holder for value of the instrument. "Valuable consideration" is defined in section 27(1) and "holder for value" in section 27(2).

---

[17] *Colehan v Cooke* (1742) Willes 393, 397–398.
[18] See above, para.2–009.
[19] s.11. But see s.11(2). Contrast Stamp Act 1891, s.33(2) (now repealed).
[20] See above, para.2–020. Contrast Stamp Act 1891, s.33(2) (now repealed).
[21] s.87(1).
[22] See above, para.2–011.
[23] *Brown v De Winton* (1848) 6 C.B. 336, 356. *cf. Beecham v Smith* (1858) E.B. & E. 442.
[24] See above, para.3–023.
[25] See below, para.16–004.
[26] See above, para.4–002 (s.27) and s.88.
[27] See above, para.4–004 (s.27).

**"On demand or at a fixed or determinable future time."** Section 10  **15–010**
defines when a bill is payable on demand and section 89 applies that
provision to notes. For specific provisions dealing with notes payable on
demand, see section 86.

A note may be made payable at a fixed time, *i.e.* on a specified date, or
at a determinable future time, as defined in section 11.

The concept of "sight"[28] does not apply to notes.[29]

**"A sum certain in money."** For the requirement of certainty, see the  **15–011**
Comment on section 3 of the Act.[30] This requirement is also dealt with in
section 9. Notes frequently stipulate that the sum payable is to be paid by
stated instalments, with a provision that upon default in payment of any
instalment the whole shall become due[31]: as to which, see section
9(1)(c).

"Money" is not defined in the Act, but see the Comment on its meaning
in section 3.[32] Section 3(2) of the Act (instrument which orders any act to
be done in addition to the payment of money is not a bill) also applies to
the promise contained in a note; but see subsection (3), *infra*.

**"To or to the order of a specified person."** As to when a note is  **15–012**
payable to order, see section 8, subsections (4) and (5). A note payable "to
C or order", "to the order of C" or simply "to C" is an order instrument.
For the certainty required as to the payee, see section 7 of the Act. The
omission of the name of the payee is dealt with in the Comment on
sections 7[33] and 20[34] of the Act.

**"Or to bearer."** As to when a note is payable to bearer, see section 8(3)  **15–013**
of the Act. "Bearer" is defined in section 2.

**Form of a note.** The following is an illustration of a promissory  **15–014**
note:

£10,000—                                          London, 10th March 2005.

On demand I promise to pay to Mr John Charles or order ten thousand
pounds, with interest at six per cent per annum until payment, for value
received.

(Signed) Henrietta Black

---

[28] See above, para.2–086 (s.11).
[29] s.89(3)(a).
[30] See above, para.2–014.
[31] *Kirkwood v Carroll* [1903] 1 K.B. 531 (Illustration 1).
[32] See above, para.2–014.
[33] See above, para.2–049.
[34] See above, para.2–130.

**15–015**     **Instruments treated as notes.** By section 5(2) of the Act, where in a bill drawer and drawee are the same person, the holder may treat the instrument, at his option, either as a bill of exchange or as a promissory note.[35] Such an instrument is not in fact a bill of exchange, since it is not an order addressed by one person to another.[36] The advantage of treating it as a promissory note is that it need not normally be presented for payment to render the maker (the drawer) liable.[37] A holder may also so treat the instrument where the drawee is a fictitious person or a person not having the capacity to contract.[38]

Where a bill is not addressed to anyone, but a person writes his "acceptance" on it, that person may be liable on the instrument as the maker of a promissory note.[39]

**15–016**     **Agreement.** An instrument which fails as a promissory note may yet be valid as an agreement or be evidence of an agreement.[40]

**15–017**     **IOUs.** An IOU is not a promissory note,[41] and is merely evidence of an indebtedness. If it contains an express promise to pay, it might qualify as a note,[42] but this is unlikely having regard to the observations of Lord Atkin in *Akbar Khan v Attar Singh*.[43]

**15–018**     **Certificates of deposit.** A bankers' deposit note or receipt is not a negotiable instrument.[44] But, in recent years, banks and building societies have issued "negotiable certificates of deposit" (NCDs) payable to bearer. These are negotiable by custom.[45] But they are not promissory notes, since they appear to be primarily an acknowledgment that a sum of money has been deposited with the banker and setting out the terms on which it is to be repaid; and they may not be unconditional.

---

[35] See above, para.2–040 (s.5).

[36] s.3(1).

[37] s.87(1). See *Re British Trade Corp. Ltd* [1932] 2 Ch. 1 (s.5, Illustration 3).

[38] For the consequences, see above, para.2–041 (s.5).

[39] *Peto v Reynolds* (1854) 9 Exch. 410; *Mason v Lack* (1929) 45 T.L.R. 363 (s.6, Illustration 2); *Haseldine v Winstanley* [1936] 2 K.B. 101 (s.64, Illustration 3); *Novaknit Hellas S.A. v Kumar Brothers International Ltd* [1998] Lloyd's Bank Rep. 287. *cf. Britannia Electric Lampworks Ltd v D. Mandler & Co. Ltd* [1939] 2 K.B. 129 (s.87, Illustration 3). Contrast *Credit Agricole Indosuez v Ecumet (UK) Ltd*, unreported, March 29, 2001 (Tomlinson, J.).

[40] *Black v Pilcher* (1909) 25 T.L.R. 497; see also above, para.2–019 (s.3); *Abacus Cities Ltd v Cornwall* (1982) 43 C.B.R. (N.S.) 56 (Alberta).

[41] *Gould v Coombs* (1845) 1 C.B. 543 (Illustration 2).

[42] *Brooks v Elkins* (1836) 2 M. & W. 74 ("IOU £20 to be paid on 22nd inst.").

[43] See above, para.15–004. But see *Zebrarise Ltd v de Nieffe* [2004] All E.R.(D) 364.

[44] *Clegg v Burnett* (1887) 56 L.T. 775. See also *Hopkins v Abbott* (1875) L.R. 19 Eq. 222 Illustration 3).

[45] *Customs and Excise Commissioners v Guy Butler (International) Ltd* [1977] Q.B. 377, 382. *cf.* Ellinger, Lomnicka and Hooley *Modern Banking Law* (3rd ed.), 319; Goode, *Commercial Law* (3rd ed.), 572.

**Bearer bonds.** Bonds issued by transnational institutions, foreign gov-  15–019
ernments and corporations payable to bearer have been recognised as
negotiable instruments, and bearer bonds issued by English companies
may likewise be negotiable by custom.[46] But they are unlikely to be
promissory notes, as the promise to pay is subject to the conditions
referred to in the bond.[47]

**Debentures to bearer.** Debentures framed payable to bearer are sel-  15–020
dom encountered nowadays but may be negotiable by custom or estoppel,[48] and so transferable by delivery free from equities. Whether a
debenture so framed is a promissory note may depend, *inter alia*, on
whether the promise to pay is unconditional.

**Bearer scrip, shares, share warrants and letters of allotment.** Bearer  15–021
scrip is a negotiable instrument.[49] Bearer shares, share warrants and
letters of allotment might in certain circumstances be negotiable.[50] But
such instruments will not be promissory notes.

**Notes issued pursuant to a trust deed.** Notes may be made with an  15–022
express notation that the note is issued pursuant to and secured by a trust
deed or trust indenture, and it is a question in each case whether the
terms of the notation qualify the maker's promise to pay.[51] But such
instruments might also fail as promissory notes on the ground that they
do not satisfy one or more of the other requirements of section 83(1), or

---

[46] See *Glyn v Baker* (1811) 13 East 509; *Gorgier v Mieville* (1824) 3 B. & C. 45; *Lang v Smyth*
(1831) 7 Bing. 284; *Att.-Gen. v Bouwens* (1838) 4 M. & W. 171, 190; *Picker v London and
County Bank* (1887) 18 Q.B.D. 515, 518 (approved *Williams v Colonial Bank* (1888) 38 Ch.D.
388, 404); *London and County Bank v River Plate Bank* (1888) 21 Q.B.D. 535; *Sheffield v London
Joint Stock Bank Ltd* (1888) 13 App. Cas. 333; *London Joint Stock Bank v Simmons* [1892] A.C.
201; *Venables v Baring Bros* [1892] 3 Ch. 527; *Bentinck v London Joint Stock Bank* [1893] 2 Ch.
120; *Edelstein v Schuler & Co.* [1902] 2 K.B. 144. See also *Easton v London Joint Stock Bank*
(1887) 34 Ch.D. 95; *Lloyds Bank Ltd v Swiss Bankverein* (1913) 108 L.T. 143 (negotiability by
estoppel); Ewart (1900) 16 L.Q.R. 135; Goode, *Commercial Law* (3rd ed.), 572; Tennekoon,
*The Law and Regulation of International Finance* (1991), 161.
[47] *Weidman Bros Ltd v Guaranty Trust Co.* [1955] 5 D.L.R. 107 (government bond).
[48] *Re Blakely Ordinance Co.* (1867) L.R. 3 Ch.App. 154; *Re Natal Investment Co.* (1868) L.R. 3
Ch.App. 355; *Re Imperial Land Co. of Marseilles* (1871) 11 Eq. 478; *Goodwin v Robarts* (1875)
L.R. 10 Ex. 337, 356; (1876) 1 App. Cas. 476; *Re Romford Canal Co.* (1883) 24 Ch.D. 85;
*Bechuanaland Exploration Co. v London Trading Bank Ltd* [1898] 2 Q.B. 658; Palmer (1889) 15
L.Q.R. 245; Ewart (1900) 16 L.Q.R. 135.
[49] *Goodwin v Robarts* (1875) L.R. 10 Ex. 337; (1876) 1 App. Cas. 476; *Rumball v Metropolitan
Bank* (1877) 2 Q.B.D. 194.
[50] *Colonial Bank v Cady and Williams* (1890) 15 App. Cas. 267; *Fry v Smellie* [1912] 3 K.B. 282;
*Fuller v Glyn Mills, Currie & Co.* [1914] 2 K.B. 168.
[51] *cf. Royal Securities Corp. Ltd v Montreal Trust Co.* (1966) 59 D.L.R. (2d) 666, affirmed 63
D.L.R. (2d) 15; *Crawford and Falconbridge* (8th ed.), p.1232.

fail to state those requirements, which have to be ascertained from some other document referred to in the instrument.[52]

**15–023**    **Floating rate notes.** These may be negotiable by mercantile custom, but they are not promissory notes as the sum payable is not certain.[53]

**15–024**    **Sterling commercial paper.** Sterling commercial paper, issued by financial institutions other than banks, usually takes the form of a promissory note payable to bearer[54] and is negotiable if unconditional.

**15–025**    **Bank of England notes.** Notes of the Bank of England expressed to be payable to bearer on demand are legal tender for the payment of any amount.[55]

**15–026**    **Postal and money orders.** These are *sui generis* and are not negotiable.[56] The Postal Services Act 2000 empowers the Post Office company to issue postal and money orders, but only in accordance with a scheme under section 112 of the Act and published in the London Gazette. The Act protects the Post Office company against liability for loss and damage caused by a reasonable refusal to pay or a reasonable delay in paying a postal or money order[57] and further protects the Post Office company and a collecting banker against liability for paying or collecting a postal or money order to or on behalf of a person other than the true owner of the order.[58]

**15–027**    **Subsection (2): note payable to maker's order.** By subsection (1) a note must be made "by one person to another." But this is qualified by the present subsection. The indorsement referred to must be completed by delivery.[59] Thus if B makes a form of note payable to his own order, and indorses and delivers it to C, it will be a valid note payable to C or order.[60]

---

[52] *cf.* 83(3), below, para.15–028.
[53] See above, para.2–014.
[54] MacVicar (1986) Butterworth J.I.B.F.L. 40.
[55] Currency and Bank Notes Act 1954, ss.1(2), (6). For the prohibition (in England and Wales) against any other banker issuing notes payable to bearer on demand, see s.3 of the Bank Notes Act 1826 and s.11 of the Bank Charter Act 1844 (as amended); *Halsbury's Statutes* (4th ed.), Vol.4, pp.377 *et seq.* Contrast (Scotland) Bank Notes (Scotland) Act 1845, ss.16, 20.
[56] *Fine Art Society Ltd v Union Bank of London Ltd* (1886) 17 Q.B.D. 705.
[57] s.111(1).
[58] s.111(2)–(7).
[59] s.2 "Indorsement."
[60] *Gay v Lander* (1848) 6 C.B. 336; *Davis v Clarke* (1844) 6 Q.B. 16 (s.5, Illustration 1).

If B indorses it in blank and delivers it to C, it will be a valid note payable to bearer.[61] Until so indorsed, it is not a note.[62]

Where A, B and C make a joint and several note payable to C and D or order, this is a valid note without indorsement, and C and D may sue B on his several liability.[63]

**Subsection (3): note containing pledge of collateral security.** A state- 15–028 ment in a note that the maker has deposited collateral security with the payee, or a pledge contained in a note with a power of sale, does not invalidate it.[64] But the promise to pay must not be qualified.[65]

A promissory note given together with some other security, *e.g.* a bill of sale, is not necessarily invalid because the security is void.[66]

**Subsection (4): inland and foreign notes.** The corresponding provi- 15–029 sion in relation to bills of exchange is section 4, where "British Islands" is defined for the purposes of this subsection as well. Unlike a foreign bill, which must be protested upon dishonour to charge the drawer and indorsers,[67] protest of a foreign note is unnecessary.[68] The definition therefore appears now to serve no useful purpose, except in relation to the proviso to section 72(2) of the Act.[69]

ILLUSTRATIONS

1. The defendants make and give to the claimant an instrument pur- 15–030 porting to be a promissory note by which they jointly and severally promise to pay to the claimant £125 by instalments, the whole sum to become due on default in payment of any instalment. The instrument contains a clause as follows: "No time given, or security taken from, or

---

[61] *Brown v De Winton* (1848) 6 C.B. 336; *Hooper v Williams* (1848) 2 Exch. 13; *Masters v Baretto* (1849) 8 C.B. 433 (s.87, Illustration 2) *Stevenson v Brown* (1902) 18 T.L.R. 268.

[62] *Britannia Electric Lamp Works Ltd v D. Mandler & Co.* [1939] 2 K.B. 129 (s.87, Illustration 3).

[63] *Beecham v Smith* (1858) E.B. & E. 442.

[64] *Wise v Charlton* (1836) 4 A. & E. 786; *Fancourt v Thorne* (1846) 9 Q.B. 312; *Chesney v St John* (1879) 4 O.A.R. 150, 156; *O'Grady v Lecomte* (1918) 40 D.L.R. 378. But care should be taken to ensure that the document does not constitute a bill of sale within the Bills of Sale Act 1878 and the Bills of Sale Act 1878 (Amendment) Act 1882: *Fook Lee Tin Mining Kongsi v Gurdev Singh* [1952] M.L.J. 55.

[65] See above, para.2–009 (s.3).

[66] *Monetary Advance Co. v Cater* (1888) 20 Q.B.D. 785. *Aliter* if the security is illegal.

[67] s.51(2).

[68] s.89(4).

[69] See above, para.12–017. But in that proviso the words "indorsed in a foreign country" appear to relate to a foreign country outside the United Kingdom (as defined in s.5 and Sch.1 of the Interpretation Act 1978).

composition or arrangements entered into with either party hereto shall prejudice the rights of the holder to proceed against any other party." The instrument complies with section 83(1) and is a valid promissory note.[70]

2. The following are invalid as notes:

(a) "I O Mr John Gould two hundred pounds, for value received."[71]

(b) "Borrowed of Mr Joseph White the sum of £200, to account for, on behalf of the Alliance Club, at — months' notice, if required."[72]

(c) "Borrowed, this day, of Mr John Hyne, Stonehouse, the sum of £100 for one or two months; cheque, £100, on the Naval Bank".[73]

3. B, by her will, bequeaths "all bonds promissory notes and other securities in my hands at the time of my decease, and all moneys due thereon" on certain trusts. At the time of her death, she has placed money with her bankers on deposit, and received in return deposit notes in the form "Received of B one hundred and fifty pounds, to account for on demand. Signed X". These deposit notes are merely acknowledgments and are not included in the bequest.[74]

**15–031**   4. The claimant agrees to finance certain transactions of one Kischner. A letter is addressed by the defendants to the claimant in respect of each transaction in the following form: "Reference A.C.3 T.R./W.L.1 S. Kischner, London, WC1. We confirm herewith that we undertake to pay irrevocably the sum of £200 to you or into your banking account on May 25, 1935, in respect of the above reference." This document is not and was not intended to be a promissory note.[75]

5. The claimants make certain advances to a company. The defendant, who is the principal shareholder in and a director and secretary of the company, signs and gives to the claimants a letter as follows: "Received from Mr & Mrs C the sum of £10,000 (ten thousand pounds) as a loan to be paid back in full by July 1, 1983 with an interest rate of 20% (twenty per cent) per annum." This is a receipt for money containing the terms on which the money was to be repaid and is not a promissory note. Further,

---

[70] *Kirkwood v Carroll* [1903] 1 K.B. 531.
[71] *Gould v Coombs* (1845) 1 C.B. 543.
[72] *White v North* (1849) 3 Exch. 689.
[73] *Hyne v Dewdney* (1852) 21 L.J.Q.B 278.
[74] *Hopkins v Abbott* (1875) L.R. 19 Eq. 222.
[75] *Wirth v Weigel Leygonie & Co. Ltd* [1939] 3 All E.R. 712.

since the document contained an option to pay at an earlier date than 1 July, it was not a promise to pay on demand or at a fixed or determinable future time within section 83(1) of the Act.[76]

### Delivery necessary

**84. A promissory note is inchoate and incomplete until delivery thereof to the payee or bearer.** 15–032

| Definitions | Comparison |
|---|---|
| "bearer": s.2. | UCC: § 3–115. |
| "delivery": s.2. | ULB: arts 10, 77. |
| "promissory note": s.83(1). | UNB: art.12. |

### COMMENT

**Inchoate note.** Delivery to the payee or bearer is necessary to complete the contract contained in a promissory note.[77] This corresponds with the provision in section 21(1) of the Act relating to bills of exchange.[78] By section 2, "delivery" means transfer of possession, actual or constructive, from one person to another. For the requirements for an effectual delivery, see section 21(2)(a)[79]; for conditional delivery, see section 21(2)(b)[80]; and for the presumptions as to delivery, see section 21, subsections (2) and (3).[81] 15–033

On the admissibility of extrinsic evidence to qualify the promise of the maker on the note, see the Comment on section 21 of the Act.[82]

### Joint and several notes

**85. (1) A promissory note may be made by two or more makers, and they may be liable thereon jointly, or jointly and severally according to its tenour.** 15–034

[76] *Claydon v Bradley* [1987] 1 W.L.R. 521; see also above, para.2–085 (s.11).
[77] *Latter v White* (1872) L.R. 5 H.L. 578 (s.21, Illustration 6). *cf. Re Richards* (1887) 36 Ch.D. 541 (s.21, Illustration 3).
[78] See above, para.2–150.
[79] See above, para.2–152.
[80] See above, para.2–152.
. See *Jefferies v Austin* (1725) 1 Stra. 674 (s.21, Illustration 8).
[81] See above, para.2–154.
[82] See above, para.2–155.

**(2) Where a note runs "I promise to pay" and is signed by two or more persons it is deemed to be their joint and several note.**

| Definitions | Comparison |
|---|---|
| "note": s.2. | UCC: §§ 3–412, 3–502. |
| "person": s.2. | UNB: art.10. |
| "promissory note": s.83(1). | |

## Comment

**15–035**    **Joint, and joint and several liability.** Joint liability arises when two or more persons jointly promise to do the same thing.[83] There is but one obligation,[84] which is that of all of the promisors. Thus if A and B make a joint note to pay £100, this is a single obligation of both A and B. Payment or satisfaction by one joint maker discharges the others.[85] Joint liability is subject to a number of technical rules of law, although most of these have been alleviated by statute or by rules of court. The common law rule was that all surviving joint promisors had to be joined as defendants to the action[86]; if this was not done, those who were sued could plead the non-joinder in abatement. This rule does not now apply in the case of actions in the County Court,[87] the Civil Procedure Rules enable the court to order a person to be added as a new party[88] so that an action cannot be defeated by the non-joinder of a joint maker of a note.[89] Again at common law, since there was only one obligation and one cause of action, the general rule was that judgment against one joint promisor barred any further action against the others, even though the judgment was unsatisfied.[90] This rule was abrogated by section 3 of the Civil Liability (Contribution) Act 1978, which provides that judgment recovered against any person liable in respect of any debt or damage shall not be a bar to an action, or to the continuance of an action, against any other person who is (apart from any such bar) jointly liable with him in respect

---

[83] *Chitty on Contracts*, (29th ed.), Vol.I, § 17–001.

[84] *King v Hoare* (1844) 13 M. & W. 494, 504; *Kendall v Hamilton* (1879) 4 App. Cas. 504; *Re Hodgson* (1885) 31 Ch.D. 177, 188.

[85] *Re W.E.A.* [1901] 2 K.B. 642; *Morris v Wentworth-Stanley* [1999] Q.B. 1004; *Banco Santander SA v Bayfern Ltd* [2000] 1 All E.R. (Comm) 776, 780.

[86] *Cabell v Vaughan* (1669) 1 Wms. Saund. 291; *Richards v Heather* (1817) 1 B. & Ald. 29; *Kendall v Hamilton* (1879) 4 App. Cas. 504 at 542–544. But a number of exceptions existed: *Chitty on Contracts* (29th ed.), Vol.I, § 17–010.

[87] County Courts Act 1984, s.48(1).

[88] CPR, s.19.20 See also Insolvency Act 1986, s.345(4).

[89] But see CPR, r.19.3.

[90] *King v Hoare* (1844) 13 M. & W. 494; *Kendall v Hamilton* (1879) 4 App. Cas. 504.

of the same debt or damage.[91] But if one joint promisor dies, his liability passes to the other joint promisors, and not to his estate,[92] although in respect of the joint liability of partners in a firm the estate of a deceased partner is also severally liable, subject however to the prior payment of his separate debts.[93]

Joint and several liability arises when two or more persons in the same instrument jointly promise to do the same thing and also severally make separate promises to do the same thing. Joint and several liability gives rise to one joint obligation and to as many several obligations as there are joint and several promisors.[94] Thus if A and B make a joint and several note to pay £100, their total obligation is £100, but either or both may be made liable to pay it. The note, "though it is one instrument, contains both a joint contract and distinct and separate contracts by the several makers".[95] Payment or satisfaction by one joint and several maker again discharges the others,[96] but joint and several liability was never subject to the technical rules of law which applied to joint liability. On the death of a joint and several promisor his several liability remains enforceable against his estate.[97]

The discharge in bankruptcy of one joint or joint and several debtor does not discharge the others.[98]

**Subsection (1): interpretation of promise.** It is a question of construc- **15–036** tion whether the liability of two or more makers of a promissory note is joint, or joint and several. Their liability may be one or other "according to its tenour". The acceptors of a bill can only be liable jointly, and not jointly and severally.[99] But this subsection allows for either possibility in the case of the makers of a note. However, there cannot be a series of makers liable severally, and not jointly and severally. Nor can two makers be liable in the alternative.[1] Where a minor and a person of full age and

---

[91] *cf. Morris v Wentworth-Stanley* [1999] Q.B. 1004 (consent judgment).
[92] *Godson v Good* (1816) 6 Taunt, 587; *White v Tyndall* (1888) 13 App. Cas. 263 (on the death of the last surviving joint promisor, his liability passes to his estate: *Calder v Rutherford* (1822) 3 Brod. & B. 302). But see Treitel, *Law of Contract* (11th ed.), p.570, who argues that this rule has been abolished by s.1(1) of the Law Reform (Miscellaneous Provisions) Act 1934.
[93] Partnership Act 1890, s.9.
[94] *Chitty on Contracts* (29th ed.), Vol.I, § 17–001.
[95] *Ex p. Honey* (1871) L.R. 7 Ch.App. 178, 183, *per* Mellish L.J. See also *Re Davison* (1884) 13 Q.B.D. 50, 53.
[96] *Nicholson v Revill* (1836) 4 A. & E. 675; *Beaumont v Greathead* (1846) 2 C.B. 494; *Thorne v Smith* (1851) 10 C.B. 659; *Re W.E.A.* [1901] 2 K.B. 642: but not if there is an express or implied reservation of the creditors rights against them: *Re E.W.A.* [1901] 2 K.B. 642 at 648; *Johnson v Davies* [1999] Ch. 217.
[97] *Read v Price* [1909] 1 K.B. 577 (affd [1909] 2 K.B. 724).
[98] Insolvency Act 1986, s.281(7).
[99] See above, para.2–046 (s.6).
[1] *Ferris v Bond* (1821) 4 B. & Ald. 679.

capacity make a joint or a joint and several note, the minor is not liable,[2] but the other person is liable as principal debtor.[3]

15–037   **Subsection (2): deemed joint and several note.** This subsection to some extent constitutes a departure from the general rule of law by which a promise by two persons together is considered to be joint, unless it is qualified in some way.[4] A note which runs "I promise to pay", and is signed by two or more persons, is deemed to be their joint and several note. Conversely a note which runs "We promise to pay", and is signed by two or more persons, is deemed to be a joint note only.[5] Perhaps if a note runs, "I, John Brown, promise to pay", and is signed by Smith as well as Brown, Smith would only be liable as an anomalous indorser under section 56, and not as comaker.

15–038   **Liability of partners.** By section 9 of the Partnership Act 1890 "Every partner in a firm is liable jointly with the other partners . . . for all debts and obligations of the firm incurred while he is a partner . . .". One partner has no authority, as such, to bind his co-partners severally, but by a *joint and several* note he may bind the firm jointly[6] and himself severally.[7] If a partner makes a note which runs "I promise to pay" and signs it for himself and the other partners in the firm, this is a joint note of the firm.[8] But where several partners make a note in the form "I promise to pay", and simply sign it themselves, all who sign the note are liable on it jointly and severally.[9]

15–039   **Alteration of note.** If after issue a joint note is converted into a joint and several note,[10] or a maker is added to[11] or erased from[12] a joint and several note, it has been held that this is a material alteration which may avoid the instrument.[13]

---

[2] See above, para.3–014.

[3] *Gibbs v Merrill* (1810) 3 Taunt. 307; *Burgess v Merrill* (1812) 4 Taunt. 468; *Lovell and Christmas v Beauchamp* [1894] A.C. 607; *Wauthier v Wilson* (1912) 28 T.L.R. 239 (s.22, Illustration 6). See also Minors' Contracts Act 1987, s.2 (guarantee).

[4] *Levy v Sale* (1877) 37 L.T. 709; *White v Tyndall* (1888) 13 App. cas. 263; *The Argo Hellas* [1984] 1 Lloyd's Rep. 296, 300.

[5] This was the view of Chalmers, citing *Parsons on Bills*, Vol.1, p.247. See also *Crawford and Falconbridge* (8th ed.), p.1835. *cf. Gordon v Matthews* (1909) 19 O.L.R. 564.

[6] *Maclae v Sutherland* (1854) 3 E. & B. 1.

[7] *Penkivil v Connell* (1850) 5 Exch. 381. See also *Healey v Story* (1848) 3 Exch. 3; *Bottomley v Fisher* (1862) 1 H. & C. 211.

[8] *Ex p. Buckley* (1845) 14 M. & W. 469.

[9] s.85(2). See also *Clerk v Blackstock* (1816) Holt N.P. 474.

[10] *Perring v Hone* (1826) 4 Bing. 28.

[11] *Gardner v Walsh* (1855) 5 E. & B. 83 (unless the note is incomplete).

[12] *Nicholson v Revill* (1836) 4 A. & E. 675.

[13] s.64.

Note payable on demand

86. (1) Where a note payable on demand has been indorsed, it must   15–040
        be presented for payment within a reasonable time of the
        indorsement. If it be not so presented the indorser is dis-
        charged.

    (2) In determining what is a reasonable time, regard shall be had
        to the nature of the instrument, the usage of trade, and the
        facts of the particular case.

    (3) Where a note payable on demand is negotiated, it is not
        deemed to be overdue, for the purpose of affecting the holder
        with defects of title of which he had no notice, by reason that
        it appears that a reasonable time for presenting it for payment
        has elapsed since its issue.

| Definitions | Comparison |
|---|---|
| "holder": s.2. | UCC: § 3–502. |
| "note": ss.2, 83. | ULB: arts 38–42, 77, 78. |
| | UNB: arts 55–57. |

COMMENT

**Note payable on demand.** Promissory notes payable on demand differ   15–041
from cheques and bills payable on demand in that a cheque is an instrument intended for immediate payment[14] and a bill payable on demand is
usually intended to be presented and paid within a short space of time.
But a note is often made and given as a continuing security, or as a
collateral security for the performance of some other obligation which
involves the payment of money, and is intended to remain such for an
extended period.[15] Notes payable on demand are frequently expressed to
carry interest to the date of payment and are not intended to be presented
for payment speedily. The provisions of this section make certain concessions in the light of this function of a promissory note.

As to when a note is payable on demand, see section 10 of the Act,[16]
which applies by virtue of section 89.

**Subsections (1) and (2): liability of indorser.** Since the maker of a   15–042
promissory note is the person primarily liable on the instrument, it need
not be presented for payment within a reasonable time, or even (except as

---

[14] See above, para.13–003 (s.73).
[15] *Brooks v Mitchell* (1841) 9 M. & W. 15, 18; *Chartered Bank of India, London and China v Dixon*
    (1871) L.R. 3 P.C. 574, 579.
[16] See above, para.2–079.

provided in section 87(1)) at all, in order to render him liable.[17] But presentment for payment is necessary in order to render the indorser of a note liable[18]; and this must be done, in the case of a note payable on demand, within a reasonable time of the indorsement. If such a note be not so presented, the indorser is discharged. The reason for this rule appears to be that the indorser has a right to expect that he will not be prejudiced by undue delay, as he has an interest in knowing at an early date whether the maker will pay the note.[19] It corresponds with that set out in relation to bills in section 45(2) of the Act.

Subsection (2) is similar in wording to sections 45(2) and 74(2) of the Act. In the pre-Act case of *Chartered Bank of India, London and China v Dixon*,[20] where the note in question was meant to be a continuing security, it was held that a delay of 10 months in presenting it for payment after indorsement[21] did not discharge the indorser. Presumably the reference to "the nature of the instrument" would take account of the fact that it was expressed to be payable with interest[22] and the reference to "the facts of the particular case" would render admissible evidence that it was intended as a continuing security[23] and (possibly) whether or not the indorser has been prejudiced by the delay. What is a reasonable time appears to be a question of mixed law and fact.[24]

Delay in making presentment for payment will be excused in the circumstances set out in section 46(1) of the Act.

**15–043**    **Subsection (3): negotiation of demand note.** By section 36(2) of the Act, when an overdue bill is negotiated, it can only be negotiated subject to any defect of title affecting it at its maturity,[25] and by section 36(3), a bill payable on demand is deemed to be overdue when it appears on the face of it to have been in circulation for an unreasonable length of time.[26] The present subsection negatives[27] the application of section 36(3) to promissory notes payable on demand.[28] Since such notes are or may be a

---

[17] See below, para.15–045 (s.87).
[18] s.87(2).
[19] *Cliff v Devlin* [1953] 1 D.L.R. 627, 635.
[20] (1871) L.R. 3 P.C. 574 (Illustration 1).
[21] The actual date of indorsement is not stated, but appears to have been about the time of the date of the note.
[22] *Barough v White* (1825) 4 B. & C. 325, 327.
[23] *Chartered Bank of India, London and China v Dixon* (1871) L.R. 3 P.C. 574.
[24] (1871) L.R. 3 P.C. 574 at 584. But contrast *Byles* (27th ed.), 24–10 (question of fact).
[25] See above, para.5–039.
[26] See above, para.5–043.
[27] But it is arguable that a note which appears on the face of it to have been in *circulation* for an unreasonable length of time is deemed to be overdue (s.36(3)) even though it is not deemed to be overdue by reason that it appears that a reasonable time for presenting it for payment has elapsed since its *issue* (s.86(3)).
[28] *Brooks v Mitchell* (1841) 9 M. & W. 15 (Illustration 2); *Glasscock v Balls* (1889) 24 Q.B.D. 13 (s.59, Illustration 3). See also *Cohen v Quigley* (1899) 20 N.S.W.R. 136, 139.

continuing security, they ought to remain fully negotiable while they are still current.[29] Where, however, a demand note has been presented for payment and dishonoured, nothing in this subsection prevents the application of the principle that a holder who takes it with notice that it has been dishonoured is not a holder in due course[30] and takes it subject to any defect of title attaching to it at the time of dishonour.[31]

ILLUSTRATIONS

1. S Bros make a note promising to pay the defendants or order on **15–044** demand the sum of £5,000. The note is dated February 16, 1864. It is indorsed by the defendants to T who indorses it for value to the claimants. The note is not presented for payment until December 14, in that year, when it is dishonoured. Having regard to the fact that the note was meant to be—to a greater or lesser extent—a continuing security, there was no undue delay in presentment of the note and the defendants are not discharged.[32]

2. On December 24, 1824, L makes a note for £2,000 payable to E or order on demand with interest. E, on March 12, 1836, indorses and delivers it to R. In August 1836 E becomes bankrupt. On January 16, 1838, R indorses it to the defendant, who takes it bona fide and for value and without notice of any claim by the assignees of E's estate. The claimants, as such assignees, bring an action in trover against the defendant to recover the note. The action fails. At the time of the indorsement to the defendant the note was still a negotiable instrument. A promissory note payable on demand is intended to be a continuing security.[33]

**Presentment of note for payment**

87. (1) **Where a promissory note is in the body of it made payable at**    **15–045**
   **a particular place, it must be presented for payment at that**
   **place in order to render the maker liable. In any other case,**

---

[29] *Brooks v Mitchell* (1841) 9 M. & W. 15 at 18. For the problem which arises where a demand note is paid, but is then negotiated to a holder who is ignorant of the payment, see above, para.8–003 (s.59).

[30] s.29(1)(a).

[31] s.36(5).

[32] *Chartered Mercantile Bank of India, London & China v Dixon* (1871) L.R. 3 P.C. 574.

[33] *Brooks v Mitchell*, (1841) 9 M. & W. 15.

presentment for payment is not necessary in order to render the maker liable.

(2) Presentment for payment is necessary in order to render the indorser of a note liable.

(3) Where a note is in the body of it made payable at a particular place, presentment at that place is necessary in order to render an indorser liable; but when a place of payment is indicated by way of memorandum only, presentment at that place is sufficient to render the indorser liable, but a presentment to the maker elsewhere, if sufficient in other respects, shall also suffice.

| Definitions | Comparison |
|---|---|
| "note": s.2. | UCC: §§ 3–412, 3–415, 3–501, |
| "promissory note": s.83(1). | 3–502. |
| | ULB: arts 4, 27, 77. |
| | UNB: art.55. |

## COMMENT

15–046     **Subsection (1): note payable at a particular place.** A promissory note is not invalid by reason that it does not specify the place where it is payable.[34] But where a note is in the body of it made payable at a particular place, it must be presented for payment at that place in order to render the maker liable.[35] There is no further requirement, as there is in the case of a local acceptance of a bill,[36] that the note expressly states that it is to be paid "there only, and not elsewhere".

However, the place of payment must be specified in the *body* of the note. This has been interpreted to mean "in the terms of the actual contract to pay which is contained in the note".[37] A statement of a place of payment in the margin or at the foot of the note beneath the signature[38]

---

[34] s.3(4)(c).

[35] *Saunderson v Bowes* (1811) 14 East 500; *Spindler v Grellet* (1847) 1 Exch. 384 (Illustration 1); *Sands v Clark* (1849) 8 C.B. 751 (s.46, Illustration 4); *Van der Donckt v Thellusson* (1849) 8 C.B. 812; *Randall v Thorn & Co.* [1878] W.N. 150. The fact that it has so been made payable to give a court jurisdiction is immaterial: *Josolyne v Roberts* [1908] 2 K.B. 349.

[36] s.19(2)(c).

[37] *Re British Trade Corp. Ltd* [1932] 2 Ch. 1, 9.

[38] *Price v Mitchell* (1815) 4 Camp. 200; *Exon v Russell* (1816) 4 M. & S. 505; *Williams v Waring* (1829) 10 B. & C. 2; *Masters v Baretto* (1849) 8 C.B. 433 (Illustration 2). *cf. Van der Donckt v Thellusson* (1849) 8 C.B. 812.

or written across the face of the note[39] is to be treated by way of memorandum only,[40] and not as part of the contract to pay. If an instrument purporting to be a bill of exchange is drawn by one branch of the drawer upon another branch, then by section 5(2) of the Act the holder may at his option treat it as a promissory note. Should he do so, the address of the drawee in the instrument is not to to be regarded for the purposes of the present subsection as contained in the body of the note.[41] It would seem that a note is only made payable at a "particular" place if it specifies a precise address or office, and not merely a country or town, *e.g.* England or Salt Lake City.[42]

Even though a note is in the body of it made payable at a particular place, the maker is not discharged by the omission to present the note for payment there on the date that it matures.[43] Presentment for payment at the particular place may also be dispensed with under section 46(2) of the Act,[44] as necessarily modified with respect to its application to promissory notes.[45]

**Presentment of note to charge maker.** Except as provided in this 15–047 subsection, presentment for payment is not necessary in order to render the maker liable. The maker of a note, like the acceptor of a bill,[46] is the party primarily liable on the instrument and presentment for payment is normally unnecessary to charge such a party in either case.[47]

**Subsection (2): presentment for payment to charge indorser.** As in the 15–048 case of a bill,[48] a note must be duly presented for payment in order to render an indorser liable. If it be not so presented, the indorser is discharged. For the rules as to due presentment, see section 45 of the Act[49]; for excuses for delay or non-presentment for payment, see section 46.

**Subsection (3): place of presentment.** Where a note is in the body of it 15–049 made payable at a particular place, presentment at that place is necessary

---

[39] *Stevenson v Brown* (1902) 18 T.L.R. 268. *cf. Britannia Electric Lampworks Ltd v D. Mandler & Co. Ltd* [1939] 2 K.B. 129 (Illustration 3).

[40] See s.87(3) below, para.15–049.

[41] *Re British Trade Corp. Ltd* [1932] 2 Ch. 1 (s.5, Illustration 3).

[42] *Eimco Corp. v Tutt Bryant Ltd* [1970] 2 N.S.W.R. 249. *cf. Day v Bate* (1979) 41 F.L.R. 222 ("at Toorak, Victoria").

[43] s.52(2) (in the absence of an express stipulation to that effect). See *Isaac v Kerr* (1897) 25 S.C. 570; *Day v Bate* (1979) 41 F.L.R. 222.

[44] See above, para.6–070.

[45] s.89(1).

[46] s.89(2).

[47] s.52(1).

[48] s.45.

[49] Subject to s.87(3).

in order to render an indorser liable.[50] In *Britannia Electric Lampworks Ltd
v D. Mandler & Co. Ltd*,[51] where a document in the form of a bill which
was not addressed to anyone and on which no name of the drawer
appeared was "accepted" payable at a particular place and indorsed by
an anomalous indorser,[52] it was held that, if it was a note, no action could
be maintained against the indorser in the absence of any proof that it had
been presented for payment at that place.

When a place of payment is indicated "by way of memorandum only",
presentment at that place is permissive, but not mandatory, in order to
render an indorser liable; but due presentment to the maker elsewhere
will suffice.[53] This is to be contrasted with section 45(4) of the Act in
relation to bills.

ILLUSTRATIONS

**15–050**    1. The defendant makes a promissory note for £200 payable to the
claimant "by the name and addition of Miss Jessie Hop at 10 Duncan-
street Edinburgh". This note is payable at a particular place, and the
claimant's declaration is bad for want of averment of presentment at that
place.[54]

2. A promissory note for £65 is made by the defendant payable to his
own order and indorsed in blank by him. Beneath his signature is written
"Payable at Messrs W & B". This is a mere memorandum, and the
introduction of the word "payable" makes no difference. It is unnecessary
for the claimant to plead in his declaration that the note was payable at
Messrs W & B.[55]

3. A document is made in this form: "Two months after date pay to our
order the sum of £100 for value received". It is not addressed to anyone
and no signature of the drawer or maker appears, but across the document is written "Accepted and payable at 2 Manville Road, Balham,
London SW17". This is followed by a rubber stamp with the words "D.
Mandler & Co. Ltd—[gap]—Managing Director". The gap is filled by the
signature of "D. Mandler", and on the back of the document there is the
signature of "D. Mandler" only. The claimants sue as holders for value of

---

[50] *Roche v Campbell* (1812) 3 Camp. 247.
[51] [1939] 2 K.B. 129 (Illustration 3).
[52] s.56.
[53] *Saunderson v Judge* (1795) 2 H.Bl. 509.
[54] *Spindler v Grellet* (1847) 1 Exch. 384.
[55] *Masters v Baretto* (1849) 8 C.B. 433.

the document. D. Mandler alone defends. The signature on the face of the document is the signature of the company and not of D. Mandler, but the signature on the back is that of D. Mandler and not of the company. D. Mandler is nevertheless not liable on it. If it is a promissory note, then it has not been proved that presentment has been made at the address stated, and D. Mandler is therefore not liable as indorser. Moreover, the note is inchoate, as it has not been indorsed by the maker.[56]

## Liability of maker

**88. The maker of a promissory note by making it—**      15–051
    **(1) Engages that he will pay it according to its tenour;**
    **(2) Is precluded from denying to a holder in due course the existence of the payee and his then capacity to indorse.**

| Definitions | Comparison |
|---|---|
| "holder": s.2. | UCC: § 3–412. |
| "holder in due course": s.29. | ULB: art.78. |
| "promissory note": s.83(1). | UNB: art.39 |

### COMMENT

**Maker of note.** The maker of a promissory note is the party who, by      15–052
his signature of the note, promises to pay it.[57] He is the principal obligor on the instrument.

The maker is sometimes called the drawer, but the primary and absolute liability of the maker of a note must be distinguished from the secondary and conditional liability of the drawer of a bill of exchange.[58] The maker of a note corresponds with the acceptor of a bill,[59] and in general the same rules apply to both. A note indorsed by the payee resembles an accepted bill payable to drawer's order and indorsed by the drawer, the payee corresponding with the drawer.[60] The distinctions that exist between maker and acceptor arise from this: the acceptor is not the creator of a bill; his contract is supervening, while the maker of a note originates the instrument. Hence (a) a note can be made by any person or,

---

[56] *Britannia Electric Lampworks Ltd v D. Mandler & Co. Ltd* [1939] 2 K.B. 129.
[57] *Crawford and Falconbridge* (8th ed.), p.1853.
[58] s.55(1).
[59] s.89(2).
[60] s.89(2).

persons, whereas only the drawee can accept a bill,[61] unless the acceptance is for honour[62]; (b) a note cannot be made conditionally,[63] whereas a bill may be accepted conditionally[64]; (c) maker and payee are normally immediate parties in direct relation with each other, whereas acceptor and payee, except in the case of a bill payable to drawer's order, are normally remote parties.[65] A further distinction should also be noted. The maker of a note is entitled to require, as a pre-condition of his liability on it, that the note be presented for payment at a particular place by making it payable in the body of it at that place,[66] whereas the acceptor of a bill can only so qualify his acceptance by expressly stating that the bill is to be paid there only, and not elsewhere.[67]

15–053  **Subsection (1): liability of maker.** The maker of a promissory note engages that he will pay it "according to its tenour," that is to say, in accordance with the terms of his promise written on the instrument.[68] By making the note, he becomes the party primarily and absolutely liable thereon to the holder.[69] As a general rule, presentment for payment is not necessary to render him liable.[70] In the case of a note which is not payable on demand, his liability will arise on the date of payment stipulated in the instrument.[71] In the case of a note payable on demand, the note will be at maturity from the date of its issue and his liability will arise at that time. Even though a note is made expressly payable "on demand", no demand is in fact necessary to crystallise that liability. Accordingly the limitation period runs in favour of the maker from the date of issue.[72]

The "engagement" of the maker is a contract. In English law, like any other contract it requires to be supported by consideration.[73] As between immediate parties,[74] there must be valuable consideration moving from

---

[61] s.17(1).
[62] s.65.
[63] s.83.
[64] s.19(2)(a).
[65] See *Bishop v Young* (1800) 2 B. & P. 78, 83. For the distinction between immediate and remote parties, see above, para.4–005 (s.27).
[66] s.87(1).
[67] s.19(2)(c).
[68] For precedents of pleadings, see App.B.
[69] For the measure of damages when a note is dishonoured, see s.57(1)(3).
[70] s.87(1).
[71] s.14. But the holder cannot commence an action against the maker until the following day: *Kennedy v Thomas* [1894] 2 Q.B. 759 (s.47, Illustration).
[72] *Norton v Ellam* (1837) 2 M. & W. 461 (s.57, Illustration 5). See above, para.7–056.
[73] See the Comment on s.27, above, para.4–002.
[74] For the distinction between immediate and remote parties, see above, para.4–005 (s.27).

the promisee. As between remote parties,[75] however, the maker will be liable to a holder for value as defined in section 27(2) of the Act.

**Subsection (2): estoppels binding maker.** The estoppels (or "preclusions") which bind the maker are set out in this subsection. They are raised only in favour of a holder in due course.[76] They have been said to reflect the fact that the first indorser of a note is deemed to correspond with the drawer of an accepted bill payable to drawer's order,[77] and an analogy has been drawn with the estoppels raised against the acceptor by section 54(2)(b) of the Act in such a case. But they are in fact precisely those raised against the drawer of a bill by section 55(1)(b). This is understandable, since both the drawer of a bill and the maker of a note initiate the instrument.

  **15–054**

It should be noted that the maker is not precluded from denying the genuineness or validity of the payee's indorsement.[78] But other estoppels may arise on evidence.

### Application of Part II to notes

89. (1) Subject to the provisions in this part and, except as by this section provided, the provisions of this Act relating to bills of exchange apply, with the necessary modifications, to promissory notes.

  **15–055**

  (2) In applying those provisions the maker of a note shall be deemed to correspond with the acceptor of a bill, and the first indorser of a note shall be deemed to correspond with the drawer of an accepted bill payable to drawer's order.

  (3) The following provisions as to bills do not apply to notes; namely, provisions relating to—

   (a) Presentment for acceptance;

   (b) Acceptance;

   (c) Acceptance suprà protest;

   (d) Bills in a set.

  (4) Where a foreign note is dishonoured, protest thereof is unnecessary.

---

[75] See above, para.4–005.
[76] Defined in s.29(1).
[77] s.89(2).
[78] But see s.7(3) (payee fictitious or non-existing person).

| Definitions | Comparison |
|---|---|
| "bill": s.2. | UCC: §§ 3–104, 3–412, 3–501, |
| "foreign note": s.83(4). | 3–502. |
| "note": s.2. | ULB: arts 44, 77, 78. |
| "promissory note": s.83(1). | UNB: art.63. |

## COMMENT

15–056   **Subsections (1) and (2): application of Act to notes.** No substantial problems arise in applying to notes "with the necessary modifications" the provisions of the Act relating to bills of exchange.[79] Part III of the Act (Cheques on a Banker) does not, of course, apply to notes.

The maker of a note is bound in the same manner as the acceptor of a bill of exchange. This has already been considered in the Comment on section 88 of the Act.[80]

The analogy[81] referred to in subsection (2) is as follows: (i) A makes a note payable to B's order which B indorses to C; (ii) B draws a bill on A payable to B's order, which A accepts, and B indorses the bill to C. A, as maker or acceptor, is the party primarily liable on each instrument to C. B is jointly and severally liable with A if the instrument is not paid, as indorser in the case of a note and as drawer and indorser in the case of a bill.

15–057   **Subsection (3): disapplication to notes.** The following provisions do not apply to notes: sections 39 to 43 (presentment for acceptance), sections 17 to 19, 44 (acceptance), sections 65 to 67 (acceptance *suprà protest*) and section 71 (bills in a set).

15–058   **Subsection (4): protest of foreign note not required.** Although foreign bills must normally be protested,[82] this is not so in the case of foreign notes. However, by virtue of the operation of section 72(3), which provides that the necessity for or sufficiency of a protest are determined by the law of the place where the note is dishonoured, protest may still be required by that law.[83] In any event, it is advisable to protest a foreign note for the purposes of charging a foreign party in his own country.

A foreign note is defined in section 83(4) of the Act.

---

[79] Subject to the provisions of Pt IV (*e.g.* ss.86(3), 87(3)) and subject to subss.(3) and (4) of the present section). For an example, see *Central Bank of Yemen v Cardinal Financial Investments Corpn.* [2001] Lloyd's Rep. Bank 1.

[80] See above, para.15–052.

[81] See *Heylyn v Adamson* (1758) 2 Burr. 669, 676.

[82] s.51(2).

[83] See above, para.12–031.

# PART V

# SUPPLEMENTARY

## Good faith

**90. A thing is deemed to be done in good faith, within the meaning**  16–001
**of this Act, where it is in fact done honestly, whether it is done**
**negligently or not.**

Comparison
UCC: § 1–201(19).
ULB: arts 10, 16, 40.
ULC: arts 13, 21.
UNB: art.6.

COMMENT

**Good faith.** "Good faith" is required by section 12 (holder inserts a   16–002
wrong date), 29(1) (definition of holder in due course), 30(2) (re-establishing status of holder in due course), 59(1) (payment in due course), 60
(banker paying demand draft whereon indorsement is forged), 79(2)
(banker paying a crossed cheque) and 80 (protection to banker and
drawer where cheque is crossed) of the 1882 Act. It is also required by
sections 1 (protection of bankers paying unindorsed or irregularly
indorsed cheques) and 4 (protection of bankers collecting payment of
cheques) of the Cheques Act 1957, which is to be construed as one with
the 1882 Act.

The section adopts the principle, to be found in the cases decided
before the Act,[1] that a thing done honestly is done in good faith, whether
it is done negligently or not. In *Swan v North British Australasian Land Co.
Ltd*,[2] Byles J., in a judgment where he distinguished deeds from negotiable instruments, said in respect of the latter: "However gross the

---

[1] *Crook v Jadis* (1834) 5 B. & Ad. 910; *Bank of Bengal v Fagan* (1849) 7 Moore P.C. 61, 72; *Raphael
v Bank of England* (1855) 17 C.B. 161; *Jones v Gordon* (1877) 2 App. Cas. 616, 628.
[2] (1863) 2 H. & C. 175, 185.

711

holder's negligence, if it stops short of fraud, he has a title." Negligence cannot therefore be equated with bad faith.

However, in the later case of *Re Gomersall*[3] Baggallay L.J. stated:

> "I fully recognise the importance of maintaining the well-established principle that negligence or carelessness on the part of the holder of a bill is not of itself sufficient to deprive him of his remedies for procuring payment of its amount. But negligence or carelessness when considered in connection with the surrounding circumstances may be evidence of *mala fides*; and the question in this case is, whether the surrounding circumstances accompanying the negligence or carelessness of [the holder] were such as to affect him with notice of the fraudulent character of the transaction out of which these bills originated."

**16–003**    On appeal to the House of Lords *sub. nom. Jones v Gordon*,[4] Lord Blackburn drew a distinction between "carelessness, negligence, or foolishness in not suspecting the bill was wrong" and suspicion, coupled with wilfully refraining from further inquiry. He said[5]:

> "If he was ... honestly blundering and careless, and so took a bill of exchange or a banknote when he ought not to have taken it, still he would be entitled to recover. But if the facts and circumstances are such that the jury, or whoever has to try the question, came to the conclusion that he was not honestly blundering and careless, but that he must have had a suspicion that there was something wrong, and that he refrained from asking questions, not because he was an honest blunderer or a stupid man, but because he thought in his own secret mind—I suspect there is something wrong, and, if I ask questions and make further inquiry, it will no longer be my suspecting it, but my knowing it, and then I shall not be able to recover—I think that is dishonesty."

The distinction between mere negligence and "wilfully shutting one's eyes" has also been recognised in other cases.[6]

---

[3] (1875) 1 Ch.D. 137, 146.

[4] (1877) 2 App. Cas. 616 (s.29, Illustration 5).

[5] At 629.

[6] *May v Chapman* (1847) 16 M. & W. 355, 361; *Raphael v Bank of England* (1855) 17 C.B. 161, 174; *London Joint Stock Bank v Simmons* [1892] A.C. 201, 221; *White v Dominion Bank* [1935] 1 D.L.R. 42, 46, 57; *Hasan v Willson* [1977] 1 Lloyd's Rep. 431, 444; *Bank of Montreal v Tourangeau* (1980) 118 D.L.R. (3d) 293, 301; *Lipkin Gorman v Karpnale Ltd.* [1987] 1 W.L.R. 987, 994–995; [1989] 1 W.L.R. 1340, 1360 (C.A.) (claim against club). *cf. Manifest Shipping Co Ltd v Uni-Polaris Shipping Co Ltd* [2003] 1 A.C. 469. See above, para.4–055 (s.29).

## Signature

91.  (1)  **Where, by this Act, any instrument or writing is required to**   **16–004**
**be signed by any person, it is not necessary that he should**
**sign it with his own hand, but it is sufficient if his signature**
**is written thereon by some other person by or under his**
**authority.**

     (2)  **In the case of a corporation, where, by this Act, any instru-**
**ment or writing is required to be signed, it is sufficient if the**
**instrument or writing be sealed with the corporate seal.**
**But nothing in this section shall be construed as requiring the**
**bill or note of a corporation to be under seal.**

| | |
|---|---|
| Definitions | Comparison |
| "bill": s.2. | UCC: §§ 1–201(39), 3–402. |
| "note": ss.2, 83. | ULB: art.8. |
| "person": s.2. | ULC: art.11. |
| "writing": s.2. | UNB: arts 33, 36. |
| "written": s.2 | |

## COMMENT

**Subsection (1): authority to sign.** Section 23 of the Act provides that   **16–005**
no person is liable as drawer, indorser, or acceptor of a bill[7] who has not
signed it as such, and the same applies to the maker of a promissory
note.[8] What constitutes a "signature" for the purposes of the Act has been
discussed in the Comment on that section.[9]

The present subsection makes it clear that a party to a bill, cheque or
note need not sign it personally. It is sufficient if his signature is written
on the instrument by some other person by or under his authority.
Usually that person will himself sign the instrument, and add words to
his signature indicating that he signs for or on behalf of a principal.[10] But
the simple signature of the principal alone in the hand of the agent will
suffice.[11]

The question whether a person's signature on an instrument has been
written there by another "by or under his authority" depends upon the

---

[7] Or cheque: see s.73.
[8] s.89(1).
[9] See above, para.3–023.
[10] See above, para.3–104 s.26 (signature as agent or in representative capacity).
[11] *London County Council v Agricultural Food Products Ltd* [1955] 2 Q.B. 218, 223; *Van Tondere en Andere v Vorster* 1996 (3) S.A. 383.

law of agency. The principles of agency lie outside the scope of the present work.[12] Reference can only be made to one or two points which are particularly relevant to bills and notes. It is, of course, trite law that actual authority given by a principal to his agent may be express or implied. But even if there is no actual authority, a principal may nevertheless be bound by acts done by another where there is apparent (or ostensible) authority.[13]

**16–006** A power of attorney in general terms to recover, receive and discharge debts owing to the principal or to transact the affairs of the principal confers no authority to accept or indorse bills of exchange in the name of the principal.[14] Moreover, powers of attorney are strictly construed, and are interpreted as giving only such authority as they confer expressly or by necessary implication.[15] Thus, even where a power of attorney to manage the principal's affairs or business includes a power to draw, accept and indorse bills of exchange or to draw cheques on the principal's account, this does not authorise the agent to borrow money and give bills in respect of a loan[16] or to draw cheques in payment of his own private debts.[17] And a clause in the power of attorney whereby the principal agrees to ratify and confirm whatsoever the agent shall do by virtue of the power does not enlarge the scope of the power.[18]

An agent has implied authority to do whatever is necessary for, or ordinarily incidental to, the effective execution of his express authority in the usual way.[19] But an express authority to draw does not confer authority to draw a bill payable to the agent's own order[20] or to indorse bills[21]; an express authority to discount a bill does not necessarily confer authority to indorse it in the name of the principal[22]; and an authority to a partner in a non-trading firm to draw cheques does not authorise the drawing of post-dated cheques.[23]

[12] See *Bowstead and Reynolds on Agency* (17th ed.).
[13] *Bowstead and Reynolds on Agency* (17th ed.), § 3–005.
[14] *Gardner v Baillie* (1795) 6 T.R. 591; *Hay v Goldsmid* (1804) 1 Taunt. 349; *Hogg v Snaith* (1808) 1 Taunt. 347 (Illustration 1); *Murray v East India Co.* (1821) 5 B. & Ald. 204; *Esdaile v La Nauze* (1835) 1 Y. & C. Ex. 394; *Brown v Byers* (1847) 16 M. & W. 252, *Jonmenjoy Condo v Watson* (1884) 9 App. Cas. 561 (s.25, Illustration 2); see also (general authority on dissolution of partnership) *Kilgour v Finlyson* (1789) 1 H.Bl. 155; *Abel v Sutton* (1800) 3 Esp. 108; *Odell v Cormack Bros* (1887) 19 Q.B.D. 223.
[15] *Bowstead and Reynolds on Agency* (17th ed.), § 3–010.
[16] *Jacobs v Morris* [1902] 1 Ch. 816 (Illustration 2).
[17] *Reckitt v Barnett, Pembroke and Slater Ltd* [1929] A.C. 176 (Illustration 3). See also *Morison v Kemp* (1912) 29 T.L.R. 70 (s.25, Illustration 4); *Midland Bank Ltd v Reckitt* [1933] A.C. 1 (s.25, Illustration 9). *cf. Bryant, Powis and Bryant Ltd v Quebec Bank* [1893] A.C. 170 (s.25, Illustration 6).
[18] *Midland Bank Ltd v Reckitt* [1933] A.C. 1.
[19] *Bowstead and Reynolds on Agency* (17th ed.), § 3–018.
[20] *Hogarth v Wherley* (1875) L.R. 10 C.P. 630.
[21] *cf. Prescott v Flinn* (1832) 9 Bing. 19.
[22] *Fenn v Harrison* (1790) 3 T.R. 757; (1791) 4 T.R. 177.
[23] *Foster v Mackreth* (1867) L.R. 2 Ex. 163.

A managerial agent who is employed to conduct a trade or business or to act generally in certain matters has implied authority to do whatever is incidental to the ordinary conduct of such trade or business, or of matters of that nature, and whatever is necessary for the proper and effective performance of his duties, but not to do anything that is outside the ordinary scope of his employment or duties.[24] So, for example, the managing director of a company has (subject to the company's memorandum and articles of association) authority to sign bills and cheques[25]; but a farm bailiff has not, as such, authority to draw or indorse bills in the name of his principal.[26]

For the signature of the name of a partnership firm, and the authority **16–007** of a partner to bind the firm, see the Comment on section 23(2) of the Act.[27]

A principal may, as between himself and his agent, limit the authority of the agent to sign bills, cheques and notes in the principal's name. But he may yet be bound by the signature if the agent was acting within the limits of his apparent (or ostensible) authority.[28] However, a signature by procuration operates as notice that the agent has but a limited authority to sign, and the principal is only bound by such signature if the agent so signing was acting within the actual limits of his authority.[29]

A person whose signature is placed on an instrument without his authority may be estopped from setting up the want of authority.[30] He may also be held to have ratified the unauthorised signature.[31]

**Delegation of authority.** Where an agent has actual authority to sign **16–008** bills in the name of his principal, it may be inferred from the circumstances of the case that he also has authority to appoint another, *e.g.* his clerk, to do so in his place.[32] Authority to sign a particular bill in the principal's name may be delegated by the agent to another, because the act of signing is purely ministerial and does not involve the exercise of discretion.[33]

---

[24] *Bowstead and Reynolds on Agency* (17th ed.), § 3–024.
[25] *Dey v Pullinger Engineering Co.* [1921] 1 K.B. 77. (ostensible authority). Contrast *Re Cunningham & Co. Ltd* (1887) 36 Ch.D. 532 (s.25, Illustration 3). See also s.35A of the Companies Act 1985; above, para.3–006 (s.22).
[26] *Davidson v Stanley* (1841) 2 M. & G. 721.
[27] See above, para.3–029.
[28] *Bowstead and Reynolds on Agency* (17th ed.), § 8–013; *Edmunds v Bushell & Jones* (1865) L.R. 1 Q.B. 97 (Illustration 4), but see *Bowstead and Reynolds on Agency* (17th ed.) § 8–079.
[29] s.25.
[30] s.24; above, para.3–079.
[31] s.24; above, para.3–087.
[32] *Re Marshall* (1788) 2 Cox 84; *Lord v Hall* (1849) 8 C.B. 627; *Brown v Tombs* [1891] 1 Q.B. 253.
[33] *Re London and Mediterranean Bank* (1868) L.R. 3 Ch.App. 651, 653–654.

16–009    **Subsection (2): seal of corporation.** The seal of a corporation, duly affixed[34] to an instrument or writing, is by this subsection declared to be the equivalent of any signature required by the Act.[35] A document is executed by a company by the affixing of its common seal.[36] However, a company need not have a common seal.[37] Whether it does or not, a document signed by a director and the secretary of a company, or by two directors of a company, and expressed (in whatever form of words) to be executed by the company has the same effect as if executed under the common seal of the company.[38]

But a bill or note of a corporation does not necessarily have to be under seal.[39]

16–010    **Cross references.** As to the capacity of a corporation to incur liability on a bill and the effect of an instrument which purports to be made by or on behalf of a company at a time when the company has not been formed, see the Comment on section 22[40]; as to the personal liability of officers, etc., of a company under section 349 of the Companies Act 1985, see the Comment on section 23[41]; as to the power of directors to bind a company and the effect of forged or unauthorised signatures, see the Comment on section 24[42]; as to procuration signatures, see section 25[43]; and as to persons signing as agent or in a representative capacity, see section 26.[44]

ILLUSTRATIONS

16–011    1. The claimant, by a power of attorney, constitutes A his attorney to claim, demand, recover and receive from the Commissioners of His Majesty's Navy all salary, wages, etc., and all other moneys whatsoever

---

[34] See Law of Property Act 1925, s.74.
[35] This resolved doubts as to whether a bill or note issued by a corporation under its seal constituted a negotiable instrument: *Crouch v Crédit Foncier* (1873) L.R. 8 Q.B. 374, 382–384. See *Chalmers* (9th ed.), pp.2, 331.
[36] Companies Act 1985, s.36A(2) (s.36A was inserted by s.130(2) of the Companies Act 1989).
[37] Companies Act 1985, s.36A(3).
[38] Companies Act 1985, s.36A(4). For execution of documents in Scotland, see Companies Act 1985, s.36B (inserted by s.130(3) of the Companies Act 1989).
[39] In particular, see s.37 of the Companies Act 1985; above, para.3–025 (s.23).
[40] See above, para.3–007.
[41] See above, para.3–026.
[42] See above, paras 3–048 and 3–049.
[43] See above, para.3–095.
[44] See above, para.3–104.

due to the claimant. By virtue of this power, E receives from the Commissioners two bills of exchange payable to the claimant or his order. E indorses these bills "E, attorney" and discounts them with the defendants, his bankers. A power of attorney in these terms, or a power "to transact all business" on behalf of a principal, does not authorise the attorney to negotiate bills. The bills are recoverable by the claimant from the defendants.[45]

2. The claimant, who carries on business as a tobacco merchant in Australia, appoints J as his agent in England with a power of attorney to purchase goods in connection with the business, either for cash or on credit, and "where necessary in connection with any purchase on the claimant's behalf, or in connection with the business, to make, draw, sign, accept or indorse any bill of exchange or promissory note which shall be requisite or proper". J, purporting to exercise this power, borrows money from the defendants, handing to the defendants as security bills of exchange accepted in his own name per pro. the claimant, and misappropriates the money borrowed. The power of attorney gives no power to J to borrow on the security of the bills.[46]

3. The appellant gives a power of attorney to T to manage his affairs while he is abroad, and amplifies this by a letter addressed to his bankers extending the power "to cover the drawing of cheques upon you without restriction". T draws a cheque payable to the order of the respondents and signs it as the appellant's attorney. The respondents know that the cheque is given in payment of a private debt of T. The power of attorney, as amplified, confers no authority on T to use the appellant's money for paying his private debts. The authority to draw cheques is limited to the management of the appellant's affairs. The respondents are not entitled to retain the proceeds of the cheque.[47]

4. Jones carries on business in London under the name of "Bushell & Co." and appoints Bushell to manage the business. Authority to draw and accept bills of exchange is incidental to that business, but Jones expressly forbids Bushell to accept bills. Bushell nevertheless accepts bills in the name of Bushell & Co. Jones is liable on the bill to an indorsee who takes it for value without any knowledge of Jones or Bushell or the business.[48]

---

[45] *Hogg v Snaith* (1808) 1 Taunt. 347.
[46] *Jacobs v Morris* [1902] 1 Ch. 816.
[47] *Reckitt v Barnett, Pembroke and Slater Ltd* [1929] A.C. 176.
[48] *Edmunds v Bushell and Jones* (1865) L.R. 1 Q.B. 97.

### Computation of time

16–012      92. Where, by this Act, the time limited for doing any act or thing is less than three days, in reckoning time, non-business days are excluded.

"Non-business days" for the purposes of this Act mean—

(a) [Saturday,] Sunday, Good Friday, Christmas Day:

(b) A bank holiday under the [Banking and Financial Dealings Act 1971:]

(c) A day appointed by Royal proclamation as a public fast or thanksgiving day:

[(d) A day declared by an order under section 2 of the Banking and Financial Dealings Act 1971 to be a non-business day.]

Any other day is a business day.

Amendments
Banking and Financial Dealings Act 1971, ss.3(1), 4(4).

Comparison
UCC: § 4–104.

### COMMENT

16–013     **Business and non-business days.** This section was amended by sections 3(1) and 4(4) of the Banking and Financial Dealings Act 1971. It defines "non-business days" and also what is a business day, and is relevant to section 14(1) (computation of time of payment), 41(1)(a) (presentment for acceptance), 44(3) (presentment for payment), 49(12) (notice of dishonour), section 51(4)(6) (protest) and section 67(2) (presentment to acceptor for honour).

### When noting equivalent to protest

16–014      93. For the purposes of this Act, where a bill or note is required to be protested within a specified time or before some further proceeding is taken, it is sufficient that the bill has been noted for protest before the expiration of the specified time or the taking of the proceeding; and the formal protest may be extended at any time thereafter as of the date of the noting.

Definitions
"bill": s.2.
"note": ss.2, 83.


COMMENT


**Noting and protest.** This section affirmed the rule in *Geralopulo v*    **16–015**
*Wieler*.[49] The noting is in fact an incipient protest.[50] As to the application
of this section, see sections 51(4), 65, 67 and 68.


### Protest when notary not accessible

**94. Where a dishonoured bill or note is authorised or required to be**    **16–016**
**protested, and the services of a notary cannot be obtained at the place**
**where the bill is dishonoured, any householder or substantial resi-**
**dent of the place may, in the presence of two witnesses, give a**
**certificate, signed by them, attesting the dishonour of the bill, and**
**the certificate shall in all respects operate as if it were a formal protest**
**of the bill.**

**The form given in Schedule 1 to this Act may be used with neces-**
**sary modifications, and if used shall be sufficient.**

Definitions                        Comparison
"bill": s.2.                        ULB: art.44.
"note": ss.2, 83.                  UNB: art.60.


COMMENT


**Householder's protest.** As to protest being "authorised or required",    **16–017**
see sections 51, 65, 66, 67 and 68 of the Act. The word "place" in this
section possibly suggests an area ordinarily served by a notary.[51]

For the form referred to, see Schedule 1 to the Act.[52]

---

[49] (1851) 20 L.J.C.P. 105. But *Chalmers* (9th ed.), at p.2, stated that s.93 changed the law.
[50] See above, para.6–145 (s.51).
[51] *cf.* ss.49(12), 51(6)(7), 67(2).
[52] See below, para.16–033.

**Dividend warrants may be crossed**

16–018      95. The provisions of this Act as to crossed cheques shall apply to a warrant for payment of dividend.

Definition
"cheque": s.73.

COMMENT

16–019      **Dividend warrants.** For the provisions as to crossed cheques, see sections 76 to 81A. See also section 97(3)(d). It is probable that dividend warrants come within sections 1(2)(a), 4(2)(b) and 5 of the Cheques Act 1957.[53]

The word "dividend" includes sums payable as interest on Government Stock.[54]

16–020      **Government payable orders and warrants.** Following the recommendations of the Review Committee on Banking Services Law and Practice,[55] it is proposed to introduce legislation to equate Government payable orders and warrants (for the payment of interest or dividends, or for repayment of capital) with cheques.[56]

**Repeal**

16–021      96. [*Repealed*]

COMMENT

16–022      **Spent repeals.** This section, which repealed the enactments set out in the second schedule to the Act, was repealed as spent by the Statute Law Revision Act 1898.

---

[53] See below, paras 17–013, 17–064 and 17–075.
[54] *Slingsby v Westminster Bank Ltd* [1931] 1 K.B. 173 (disapproved on other grounds in *Slingsby v District Bank Ltd* [1932] 1 K.B. 544).
[55] (1989) Com. 622, rec. 7(11), 7(12)
[56] (1990) Com. 1026, Annex 5, paras 5.19, 5.20.

**Savings**

97. (1) The rules in bankruptcy relating to bills of exchange, promissory notes, and cheques, shall continue to apply thereto notwithstanding anything in this Act contained.   **16–023**

  (2) The rules of common law including the law merchant, save in so far as they are inconsistent with the express provisions of this Act, shall continue to apply to bills of exchange, promissory notes, and cheques.

  (3) Nothing in this Act or in any repeal effected thereby shall affect—

    (a) [. . . . ] any law or enactment for the time being in force relating to the revenue:

    (b) The provisions of the Companies Act, 1862, or Acts amending it, or any Act relating to joint stock banks or companies:

    (c) The provisions of any Act relating to or confirming the privileges of the Bank of England or the Bank of Ireland respectively:

    (d) The validity of any usage relating to dividend warrants, or the indorsements thereof.

**Repeal**
Subs. 3(a) was repealed in part by s.1 of the Statute Law Revision Act 1898.

| **Definitions** | **Comparison** |
|---|---|
| "bill of exchange": s.3. | UCC: § 1–103. |
| "cheque": s.73. | |
| "indorsement": s.2. | |
| "promissory note": s.83. | |

## COMMENT

**Subsection (1): bankruptcy law.** Chalmers' comment[57] on this subsection was as follows:   **16–024**

"This provision was intended to preserve such rules as the rule against double proof,[58] the rule as to proof in respect of bills not yet

---

[57] *Chalmers* (9th ed.), p.335.
[58] *Banco de Portugal v Waddell* (1880) 5 App. Cas. 161.

due,[59] or the rule that when a bill is pledged for less than its amount, the holder may prove for the full amount, though he cannot receive dividend for more than the sum advanced."[60]

Bankruptcy, or the insolvency of individuals, in England and Wales is dealt with in the Insolvency Act 1986[61] and in Scotland in the Bankruptcy (Scotland) Act 1985. Company insolvency in England, Wales and Scotland is dealt with in the Insolvency Act 1986.

**16–025**    **Subsection (2): common law.** When considering the scope of this subsection it is necessary to bear in mind the statement of Lord Herschell in *Bank of England v Vagliano Brothers*[62] that, in construing the Act "the proper course is in the first instance to examine the language of the statute and to ask what is its natural meaning, uninfluenced by any considerations derived from the previous state of the law". For that purpose only a limited resort may be made to the common law before the Act, for example, where a provision is of doubtful import, or where words are found in the Act which have previously acquired a technical meaning or have been used in a sense other than their ordinary one. The subsection itself also makes it clear that common law rules do not apply "in so far as they are inconsistent with the express provisions of this Act".

Nevertheless, certain sections of the Act expressly import the rules of the common law relating to contracts. For example, section 22(1) states that capacity to incur liability as a party to a bill is coextensive with capacity to contract,[63] and section 27(1)(a) declares that valuable consideration for a bill may be constituted by any consideration sufficient to support a simple contract.[64] Moreover, the Act was never intended to be a complete and exclusive regulatory code, containing the entire law relating to bills of exchange, promissory notes and cheques: it is "more in the nature of a digest of the law on the subject".[65] There is therefore considerable room for the application of the common law, as preserved by the present subsection, in areas not dealt with, or not comprehensively dealt with, in the Act. Examples are: where the damages claimed for dishonour of a bill include a claim in respect of liability for re-exchange which falls outside of section 57(1),[66] where there is an incomplete bill

---

[59] *Wood v De Mattos* (1865) L.R. 1 Ex. 91. See now ss.322, 382(1)(b) of the Insolvency Act 1986.

[60] *Re Bunyard* (1880) 16 Ch.D. 330 (s.27, Illustration 30).

[61] And in the Insolvency Rules 1986 (as amended).

[62] [1891] A.C. 107, 144–145; above, para.1–005.

[63] See above, para.3–003.

[64] See above, para.4–011.

[65] *Embiricos v Anglo-Austrian Bank* [1904] 2 K.B. 870, 876 (Walton J.).

[66] *Re Gillespie, Ex p. Robarts* (1886) 18 Q.B.D. 286; above, para.7–051.

and the holder relies on an estoppel at common law in a case where he would otherwise not be protected by the proviso to section 20(2),[67] and where a bill is transferred abroad.[68] Of a somewhat different nature are those situations where the rules of the common law are applied to or superimposed on the provisions of the Act. Examples of such situations are: the defence of *non est factum*,[69] limitation[70]; the common law relating to fraud, duress and illegality[71]; and the operation of accord and satisfaction as equivalent to payment.[72] Many other examples could no doubt be given.

Rules of evidence and procedure are also of considerable importance, particularly in respect of the admissibility of extrinsic evidence[73] and the right to summary judgment without set-off of a counterclaim.[74]

The Act has therefore to be read against the background of the common law. Commenting on this aspect, Dixon J. has said[75]:  **16–026**

" . . . [I]t was inevitable that what was stated should, not only for its proper understanding but for its practical application, continue to depend upon the whole content of the law of which it formed a coherent part. The subject could not be isolated. Bills of exchange and promissory notes have very special characteristics, but they are not and could not be removed from the general law of status, of obligation, and of remedies. Further, heads of law which deal with particular relations, with transactions of a special nature and with general conceptions of property must continue to include bills and notes within their operation."

**Subsection (3): savings.** As to paragraph (a), stamp duty on bills and  **16–027** notes was abolished by section 32(a), and paragraph 2(2)(a) of Schedule 7 to, the Finance Act 1970.

As to paragraph (b), see now the Companies Act 1985[76] and the Financial Services and Markets Act 2000.

As to paragraph (c), see *Halsbury's Statutes of England and Wales* (4th ed.), Volume 4, Title "Banking", and in particular the Bank Charter Act 1844, section 11 (prohibition on the issue by a banker in England and Wales of bills of exchange and promissory notes payable to bearer on

---

[67] *Lloyds Bank Ltd v Cooke* [1907] 1 K.B. 794; above, para.2–139.
[68] *Embiricos v Anglo-Austrian Bank* [1905] 1 K.B. 677.
[69] See above, para.3–022.
[70] See above, para.7–055.
[71] See above, paras 4–015, 4–063, 4–065.
[72] See above, para.8–005.
[73] See above, para.2–155.
[74] See above, para.4–010.
[75] *Stock Motor Ploughs Ltd v Forsyth* (1932) 48 C.L.R. 125, 137.
[76] As amended by the Companies Act 1989.

demand). See also the Currency and Bank Notes Act 1954, the Coinage Act 1971 and the Currency Act 1983 (legal tender).

Paragraph (d) was introduced in committee. It was probably intended to protect the usage of paying dividend warrants on the indorsement of one of several payees.[77] See also section 95.

### Saving of summary diligence in Scotland

16–028      **98. Nothing in this Act or in any repeal effected thereby shall extend or restrict, or in any way alter or affect the law and practice in Scotland in regard to summary diligence.**

### COMMENT

16–029      **Summary diligence on bill or note.** This section preserves the law and practice in Scotland[78] whereby the procedure for obtaining warrant for diligence, known as summary diligence, may be done on a bill of exchange or promissory note, but not on a cheque,[79] without first resorting to court action. Protest is required.[80]

See the Bills of Exchange Act 1681, the Inland Bills Act 1696, the Bank Notes (Scotland) Act 1765, the Bills of Exchange (Scotland) Act 1772, the Debtors (Scotland) Act 1987 and the Debt Arrangement and Attachment (Scotland) Act 2002.

### Construction with other Acts, &c.

16–030      **99. Where any Act or document refers to any enactment repealed by this Act, the Act or document shall be construed, and shall operate, as if it referred to the corresponding provisions of this Act.**

### Parole evidence allowed in certain judicial proceedings in Scotland

16–031      **100. In any judicial proceeding in Scotland, any fact relating to a bill of exchange, bank cheque, or promissory note, which is relevant**

---

[77] See above, para.5–019 (s.32).
[78] See Walker, *Principles of Scottish Private Law* (4th ed.), Vol.II, p.470; Wilson, *The Law of Scotland relating to Debt* (1982), p.240.
[79] *Glickman v Linda* 1950 S.C. 18.
[80] See s.51; above, para.6–150.

to any question of liability thereon, may be proved by parole evidence: Provided that this enactment shall not in any way affect the existing law and practice whereby the party who is, according to the tenour of any bill of exchange, bank cheque, or promissory note, debtor to the holder in the amount thereof, may be required, as a condition of obtaining a list of diligence, or suspension of a charge, or threatened charge, to make such consignation, or to find such caution as the court or judge before whom the cause is depending may require. [ ... ]

Repeal
The final words of this section were repealed by the Prescription and Limitation (Scotland) Act 1973, Sch.5, Pt I.

Definitions
"bill of exchange": s.3.
"cheque": s.73.
"holder": s.2.
"promissory note": s.83.

## COMMENT

**Parole evidence in Scotland.** This section was added in committee. Its object was to remove certain technicalities from the Scots law of evidence which had frequently been adversely commented upon by the courts. In general, in Scots law, facts relevant to liability could be proved only by writ or oath. The section permits any fact relating to a bill, cheque or note, which is relevant to any question of liability thereon, to be proved by parole evidence.[81] As originally enacted, the section did not apply to any case where the instrument had undergone the sesennial prescription, but this exception was repealed by the Prescription and Limitation (Scotland)

**16–032**

---

[81] It has, however, been held incompetent by parole to contradict liability appearing on the face of the instrument: see *National Bank of Australasia v Turnbull & Co.* (1891) 18 R. 629; *Gibson's Trustees v Galloway* (1896) 23 R. 414; *Robertson v Thomson* (1900) 3 F. (Ct. of Sess.) 5; *Semple v Kyle* (1902) 4 F. 421; *Manchester and Liverpool District Banking Co. v Ferguson & Co.* (1905) 7 F. 865; *Adam's Trustees v Young* (1905) 13 S.L.T. 113; *Stagg & Robson v Stirling* 1908 S.C. 675; *Jackson v Ogilvie* 1935 S.C. 154; *Nicol's Trustees v Sutherland* 1951 S.C. (H.L.) 21. *cf. Ferguson, Davidson & Co. v Jolly's Trustees* (1880) 7 R. 500, 504; *Thompson v Jolly Carters Inn Ltd* 1972 S.C. 215. It does not appear that this rule has been changed by the Contract (Scotland) Act 1997.

Act 1973.[82] The quinquennial prescription now applies to any obligation under a bill of exchange or promissory note.[83]

# SCHEDULES

## FIRST SCHEDULE

16–033    **Section 94.**

**Form of protest which may be used when the services of a notary cannot be obtained**

Know all men that I, *A.B.* [householder], of                          in the county of                          , in the United Kingdom, at the request of *C.D.*, there being no notary public available, did on the                          day          of                          188          at demand payment [*or* acceptance] of the bill of exchange hereunder written, from *E.F.*, to which demand he made answer [state answer, if any] wherefore I now, in the presence of *G.H.* and *J.K.* do protest the said bill of exchange.

(Signed) *A.B.*

*G.H.*
*J.K.* } Witnesses.

N.B.—The bill itself should be annexed, or a copy of the bill and all that is written thereon should be underwritten.

## SECOND SCHEDULE

16–034    **Section 96.**          **Enactments Repealed**

[*This Schedule was repealed as spent by s.1 of the Statute Law Revision Act 1898.*]

---

[82] Sch.5, Pt I.
[83] Prescription and Limitation (Scotland) Act 1973, s.6 and Sch.1(1)(e). The vicennial prescription also applies: s.7(2). By s.7 and Sch.1(2)(b) a bank note prescribes only after 20 years.

# CHEQUES ACT 1957

## (5 & 6 Eliz. 2, c. 36)

*An Act to amend the law relating to cheques and certain other instruments.*  **17–001**
[July 17, 1957]

**Be it enacted by the Queen's most Excellent Majesty, by and with the advice and consent of the Lords Spiritual and Temporal, and Commons, in this present Parliament assembled, and by the authority of the same, as follows:—**

### COMMENT

**General note.** This Act, which is to be construed as one with the Bills  **17–002**
of Exchange Act 1882, came into force on October 17, 1957. Until that date it had been the practice of bankers to require as a matter of course the indorsement of all order cheques prior to payment, whether or not there had been previous negotiation by the payee. This practice, which was equally applicable whether payment was made over the counter or through a collecting banker, had arisen prior to the Stamp Act 1853, and had become the more firmly established by reason of the emphasis placed in the Bills of Exchange Act upon the need for a banker to act in the ordinary course of business.

The amount of work involved for both business firms in indorsing cheques and for collecting and paying bankers in scrutinising them led to the suggestion[1] that the indorsement of an order cheque should be dispensed with when presented for payment by the payee. In 1955 the Mocatta Committee on Cheque Endorsement was appointed to inquire whether and to what extent it was desirable to reduce the need for indorsement of order cheques and of similar instruments received for collection by a banker and what amendments of the Bills of Exchange Act,

---

[1] *Bankers' Magazine* (1934), Vol.CXXXVII, p.595, See also *Bankers' Magazine* (1934), Vol.CXXXVIII, p.39, and *Journal of the Institute of Bankers* (1934), Vol.LV, p.388; *The Banker* (1949), Vol.XCL, p.24; *Bankers' Magazine* (1949), Vol.CLXVII, p.469; *The Accountant* (1949), Vol.CXX, p.277; (1951) 14 M.L.R. 44 and 314.

1882, or other statutory provision should be made for that purpose. The Committee recommended[2] legislation which would state that indorsement would no longer be required on cheques being collected for the payee by his banker.

The draftsman of the 1957 Act adopted the objective of the Mocatta Committee's recommendation but chose a slightly different course from that envisaged. The Act does not specifically do away with such indorsements: instead it seeks to make them pointless. It enables the banker in normal circumstances to ignore the absence of, or irregularity in, the indorsement whilst still retaining the statutory protection hitherto available. The Act has nevertheless achieved its desired effect and cheques are no longer indorsed when delivered by the payee to his banker for collection. But in one significant respect the Act goes further than either the Mocatta Committee or the bankers themselves desired, for section 1 in effect dispenses with the need for the paying banker to concern himself with indorsements, not only where a cheque drawn on him is paid to a banker, but also where it is paid across the counter. Bankers may yet avail themselves of the wider protection there afforded, but for the present time, at any rate, they have by agreement limited the effect of that section.

**17–003**     **CLCB Memorandum.** This was done by a memorandum of the Committee of London Clearing Bankers dated September 23, 1957. The memorandum sets out detailed instructions for the guidance of all branches of the Clearing Banks in the United Kingdom. It is to be noted in particular that indorsement remains necessary as a matter of banking practice for cheques cashed across the counter. The procedure adopted (which establishes a course of business from which it may be difficult to depart) as set out in the memorandum is as follows:

> "1. *Paying banks*
>     (a) *Cheques and other instruments presented in the clearings, or specially presented, and 'house debits.'*
>         It will not be necessary to examine instruments for endorsement unless the instruments are:
>         Combined cheque and receipt forms marked 'R';
>         Travellers' cheques;
>         Bills of exchange (other than cheques);
>         Promissory notes.
>         In these cases endorsement or discharge will be required as heretofore.

---

[2] See the Report presented to Parliament, November 1956 (Cmnd. 3).

(b) *Cheques and other instruments cashed at the counter (including those cashed under open credits).*

 The Banks have agreed to continue to require endorsement or receipt in all cases where at present it is the practice to look for this. It is felt that the public interest would best be served by a continuance of the present practice. The Mocatta Committee attached importance to the endorsement of cheques encashed over the counter as possibly affording some evidence of the identity of the recipient and some measure or protection for the public.

2. *Collecting banks*

(a) With the exception of the instruments referred to in the Schedule to this Circular cheques and other instruments collected for the account of the ostensible payee will not require examination for endorsement, or in the case of dividend and interest warrants for discharge.

(b) Cheques and other instruments payable to a bank to be applied after collection for the credit of a customer's account, *e.g.* when dividends are mandated to a bank, will not require endorsement or discharge by the payee bank.

(c) Endorsement or discharge will be required as heretofore if the instrument is tendered for the credit of an account other than that of the ostensible payee. If a cheque is specially endorsed to the customer for whose account it is tendered for collection no further endorsement will be necessary.

(d) The banks will not be concerned with the completion of the discharge at the foot of a dividend or interest or redemption warrant unless the instrument is being collected for the account of a third party. If, as a result of the Act, such warrants cease to be printed with a space for the payee's signature, they will nevertheless require endorsement if negotiated. (It is understood that the Bank of England intend to omit the space from warrants in respect of Government, etc., Stocks issued by them.)

(e) If the payee's name is mis-spelt or he is incorrectly designated, the instrument may be accepted for collection without endorsement or discharge unless there are circumstances to suggest that the customer is not the person to whom payment is intended to be made.

(f) The instruments referred to in the Schedule to this Circular will require endorsement or discharge as heretofore.

(g) Instruments payable to one or more of a number of joint account holders may be collected for the credit of the joint account without endorsement or discharge. For this purpose joint accounts include accounts of partners, trustees, etc.

(h) Instruments payable to joint payees will require endorsement or discharge if tendered for the credit of an account to which all are not parties.

(i) The foregoing sub-paragraphs of this paragraph also apply when the account is domiciled with another branch of the collecting bank or with another bank.

3. *Clearing Banks acting as collecting agents for Non-Clearing Banks, the Post Office, or Trustee Savings Banks*

Instruments received from a Non-Clearing Bank, the Post Office or a Trustee Savings Bank need not be examined for endorsement or discharge. It may be assumed that any requisite of indorsement will have been seen to by the Non-Clearing Bank, the Post Office or the Trustee Savings Bank as the case may be, to whom the collecting bank will be entitled to have recourse.

4. *Exchanging cheques and other instruments*

Cheques and other instruments exchanged at the counter will require endorsement or discharge as heretofore.

5. *Exchange Control markings*

All markings in connection with the Exchange Control must in future be placed upon the face of the instrument.

6. *Combined cheque and receipt forms*

Cheques and other instruments bearing receipts which paying banks have agreed to continue to examine have been dealt with fully in the Committee of London Clearing Bankers' Circular dated September 2, 1957. All such instruments without exception will bear a denoting 'R' on the face of them, and they will require examination by both the collecting and paying banks as heretofore.

[7. *Banks in Isle of Man: Channel Islands: Republic of Ireland . . .* ][3]

## SCHEDULE

Combined Cheque and Receipt Forms marked 'R.'
Bills of Exchange (other than cheques).
Promissory Notes.
Drafts and other instruments drawn on the General Post Office or payable at a Post Office.

---

[3] The circular originally required indorsement of all instruments drawn on bankers in such areas, but similar legislation has been adopted in the Isle of Man, The Bills of Exchange Act 1958; in the Channel Isles, The Cheques (Jersey) Law 1957, and The Bills of Exchange (Guernsey) Law 1958; in the Republic of Ireland, The Cheques Act 1959. References in the circular to those areas are now inapplicable.

Inland Revenue warrants.

Drafts drawn on H.M. Paymaster-General or the Queen's and Lord Treasurer's Remembrancer.

Drafts drawn on the Crown Agents, High Commissioners for the Union of South Africa, Pakistan and India, the Commonwealth Relations Office and other paying agents.

Travellers' Cheques.

Instruments payable by banks abroad."[4]

**Cheques Act 1992.** This Act amended the 1882 Act by introducing a new section 81A, subsection (1) of which provides that where a cheque is crossed and bears across its face the words "account payee" or "a/c payee", either with or without the word "only", the cheque shall not be transferable, but shall only be valid as between the parties thereto. Most cheques issued in the United Kingdom are now crossed with these words pre-printed on them. They are therefore non-transferable and are, in effect, merely payment orders. This development has no significant effect upon the provisions of the 1957 Act, except that (as will be later noted) it has deprived the collecting banker of certain benefits conferred upon him by section 2 of the 1957 Act.

    **17–004**

**Protection of bankers paying unindorsed or irregularly indorsed cheques, etc.**

1. (1) Where a banker in good faith and in the ordinary course of business pays a cheque drawn on him which is not indorsed or is irregularly indorsed, he does not, in doing so, incur any liability by reason only of the absence of, or irregularity in, indorsement, and he is deemed to have paid it in due course.

    **17–005**

  (2) Where a banker in good faith and in the ordinary course of business pays any such instrument as the following, namely—

    (a) a document issued by a customer of his which, though not a bill of exchange, is intended to enable a person to obtain payment from him of the sum mentioned in the document;

    (b) a draft payable on demand drawn by him upon himself, whether payable at the head office or some other office of his bank;

---

[4] As to the Isle of Man, Channel Islands and the Republic of Ireland, see above.

**he does not, in doing so, incur any liability by reason only of the absence of, or irregularity in, indorsement, and the payment discharges the instrument.**

Definitions
"banker": 1882 Act, s.2.
"bill of exchange": 1882 Act, s.3.
"cheque": 1882 Act, s.73.
"good faith": 1882 Act, s.90.
"person": 1882 Act, s.2.

COMMENT

**17–006** **Liability of paying banker.** The relationship between a banker and his customer when he pays a cheque drawn on him by the customer is in essence that of an agent acting for a principal. The banker is obliged to adhere strictly to the terms of the mandate given to him by the customer. If he pays a cheque in a manner not authorised by the customer, he does so at his peril and he is not entitled to debit the customer's account with the amount paid. So, for example, at common law, if a cheque drawn payable to order is stolen from the payee, the payee's indorsement is forged and the instrument is presented to and paid by the drawee banker, the banker cannot debit the account of his customer (the drawer) and must bear the loss himself.[5] His mandate is to pay only to a holder of the instrument and it is immaterial that the payment has been made in good faith and without negligence on his part. Moreover the banker will probably be liable to the payee, as true owner of the cheque, in an action for conversion.[6]

**17–007** **Subsection (1): protection of paying banker.** Under section 59 of the 1882 Act, payment by a banker of a cheque to the holder thereof in good faith and without notice that the holder's title is defective is "payment in

---

[5] See above, para.3–072 (s.24).
[6] *Smith v Union Bank of London* (1875) L.R. 10 Q.B. 291 (affirmed (1875) 1 Q.B.D. 31) (s.79, Illustration 1); *El Awadi v Bank of Credit and Commerce International S.A.* [1990] Q.B. 606, 615, 627; *Smith v Lloyds TSB Bank plc* [2000] 2 All E.R. (Comm) 693, 697; above, para.3–050. Contrast *Charles v Blackwell* (1877) 2 C.P.D. 151, 162–163. See also *Lacave & Co. v Crédit Lyonnais* [1897] 1 Q.B. 148, and s.79(2) of the 1882 Act.

due course" and discharges the instrument. The banker will be entitled to debit his customer's account with the amount paid. However, a person who derives his title to a cheque payable to order through or under a forged or unauthorised indorsement is not a holder.[7] Payment to him is not payment in due course and does not discharge the instrument.[8]

The present subsection is only one of several statutory provisions designed to protect the paying banker. It is unfortunate that the opportunity was not taken in the 1957 Act to rationalise these provisions and to combine them in a single enactment.[9]

First, since the paying banker has no means of verifying the genuineness of an indorsement, section 60 of the 1882 Act protects him if he pays in good faith and in the ordinary course of business a cheque payable to order drawn on him, in the event that the indorsement of the payee or any subsequent indorsement is forged or unauthorised.[10] This section is limited to order cheques.[11]

Secondly, section 80 of the 1882 Act protects him if he pays to a banker **17–008** a crossed cheque drawn on him provided he does so in accordance with the crossing and in good faith and without negligence.[12] This protection is somewhat narrower than that afforded by section 60, being confined to crossed cheques paid to a banker, although it is not limited to order cheques.[13] Further, by section 5 of the present Act, the protection is extended to certain crossed instruments analogous to cheques referred to in section 4(2)(b)(c) and (d). Payment of such instruments is not protected by section 60.[14]

As the law stood before the enactment of the present Act, it would have been outside the ordinary course of business (and would probably have been negligent) for a banker to pay an order cheque drawn on him which

[7] See above, paras 1–022 (s.2), and 3–066 (s.24).
[8] See above, para.8–011 (s.59).
[9] But the Government now proposes to introduce such consolidating legislation: (1990) Cm. 1026, Annex 5, para.5.9 (following the recommendations of the Review Committee on Banking Services Law and Practice (1989) Cm. 622, rec. 7(5)). See above, paras 8–054 and 14–027 (ss.60, 80).
[10] See above, para.8–043.
[11] The banker has no need of the protection if the cheque is payable to bearer, and is paid in good faith and without notice that the holder's title is defective (s.59). But the protection would not apply to a cheque crossed "account payee" or to a cheque drawn "Pay X only". These are not transferable and so not payable to order. See above, para.8–048.
[12] See above, para.14–025.
[13] By an amendment made by the Cheques Act 1992, s.2, the protection of s.80 is expressly extended to crossed cheques which under s.81A(1) of the 1882 Act (cheques marked "account payee") or otherwise (*e.g.* cheques drawn "Pay X only") are not transferable.
[14] But the banker may be protected by the (unrepealed) s.19 of the Stamp Act 1853; see above, para.8–045 (s.60) and *Lipkin Gorman v Karpnale Ltd* [1987] 1 W.L.R. 987, 996 ([1989] 1 W.L.R. 1340; [1991] 2 A.C. 548).

was not indorsed or which was irregularly indorsed,[15] even if the cheque had not been negotiated by the payee. The paying banker was therefore at risk if he paid such a cheque, since he would be unable to rely on the protection afforded by section 60 and section 80 of the 1882 Act. The present subsection in effect removes that risk by providing that the banker does not, in paying such a cheque, incur any liability by reason only of the absence of, or irregularity in, indorsement, provided that he otherwise pays the cheque in good faith and in the ordinary course of business. The paying banker has, therefore, no longer any duty or incentive to scrutinise cheques presented to him for payment through clearing in order to ascertain whether an indorsement is missing or is irregular. In consequence, as the Mocatta Committee recommended, the need for indorsements on cheques so presented has been virtually eliminated.

Nevertheless, the Committee of London Clearing Bankers, in its memorandum of September 23, 1957,[16] stated that paying banks should still require indorsement (i) of cheques encashed over the counter, and (ii) of combined cheque and receipt forms marked "R".

17–009    **"Good faith."** Section 90 of the 1882 Act provides that a thing is deemed to be done in good faith, whether it is done negligently or not.

17–010    **"In the ordinary course of business."** This phrase is also used in section 60 of the 1882 Act and may be interpreted in the same manner.[17] It would appear to be outside the ordinary course of business for a banker to pay a cheque without an indorsement, or bearing an irregular indorsement, in the situations referred to in the Committee of London Clearing Bankers' memorandum.

17–011    **"Cheque."** A cheque is defined in section 73 of the 1882 Act as a bill of exchange drawn on a banker payable on demand. Although subsection (2), below, para.17–013, applies the same rule to certain instruments analogous to cheques, the protection does not extend to bills of exchange (other than cheques) or to promissory notes.

In *Slingsby v District Bank Ltd*[18] the Court of Appeal held that a cheque which had been materially altered, and so rendered void by section 64 of the 1882 Act, was no longer a cheque, so that the paying banker could not rely on sections 60 and 80 of that Act. Presumably the same rule applies to the present subsection. Whether or not an instrument is a cheque if the

---

[15] As to when an indorsement is irregular, see above, para.4–053 (s.29)
[16] See above, para.17–003.
[17] See above, para.8–051 (s.60).
[18] [1932] 1 K.B. 544, 559 (s.60, Illustration 2).

signature of the drawer thereon is forged or unauthorised,[19] the subsection does not protect the banker in that event, and he is not entitled to debit his customer's account.

**Scope of protection.** The words "by reason only" show that the sole   **17–012**
effect of the subsection is to relieve the paying banker of liability if an indorsement is absent or irregular. It does not do away with the necessity for an indorsement to negotiate a cheque payable to order. Nor does it relieve the banker of liability if any necessary indorsement is forged or unauthorised, in which case he must rely on section 60 or section 80 of the 1882 Act. On the other hand, the subsection is not limited in its terms to crossed cheques, or to cheques payable to order, or to cheques paid to another banker.[20]

If a cheque is crossed "account payee"[21] or is otherwise not transferable (for example, because it is drawn "Pay X only")[22] any indorsement can only be a receipt. It cannot operate to negotiate the cheque as the cheque is incapable of transfer. The present subsection protects the paying banker if such an indorsement by the payee is absent or irregular.[23] But it does not protect him if payment is made to a person other than the payee, for which purpose he must rely on section 80 of the 1882 Act.[24]

**Subsection (2): analogous instruments.** This subsection extends the   **17–013**
same protection to certain instruments analogous to cheques. Paragraph (a) covers conditional orders for payment, "cheques" requiring a receipt,[25] interest and dividend warrants,[26] and those payable to "cash or order".[27] Paragraph (b) covers bankers' drafts.[28] It is not required that these instruments be payable on demand. There appears to be no significance in the change of wording from "and he is deemed to have paid

---

[19] See above, para.3–062 (s.24); below, para.17–063 (s.4).

[20] But see the Committee of London Clearing Bankers' Memorandum, above, para.17–003.

[21] s.81A of the 1882 Act.

[22] s.8(1) of the 1882 Act.

[23] But see the Committee of London Clearing Bankers' Memorandum, above, para.17–003.

[24] See above, para.14–024.

[25] *Bavins Junr & Sims v London and South Western Bank Ltd* [1900] 1 Q.B. 270 (s.3, Illustration 4).

[26] s.95. Legislation will be introduced to equate Government payable orders and warrants (for the payment of interest or dividends, or for the repayment of capital) with cheques: (1990) Cm. 1026, Annex 5, paras 5.20, 5.21. This was recommended by the Review Committee on Banking Services Law and Practice (1989) Cm. 622, rec. 7(11), 7(12).

[27] *Orbit Mining and Trading Co. Ltd v Westminster Bank Ltd* [1963] 1 Q.B. 794 (Cheques Act 1957, s.4, Illustration 17).

[28] These are not cheques: see above, paras 2–012 and 13–005. See also Stamp Act 1853, s.19 (above, para.8–045) and *Lipkin Gorman v Karpnale Ltd* [1987] 1 W.L.R. 987, 996 ([1989] 1 W.L.R. 1340; [1991] 2 A.C. 548).

it in due course" in subsection (1) to "and the payment discharges the instrument" in subsection (2).

**17–014**　**Other defences.** Section 1 does not affect the other defences which may be available to the paying banker, *e.g.* estoppel,[29] ratification,[30] adoption of a forged signature[31] and (possibly) contributory negligence.[32]

### Rights of bankers collecting cheques not indorsed by holders

**17–015**　**2. A banker who gives value for, or has a lien on, a cheque payable to order which the holder delivers to him for collection without indorsing it, has such (if any) rights as he would have had if, upon delivery, the holder had indorsed it in blank.**

Definitions
"banker": 1882 Act, s.2.
"cheque": 1882 Act, s.73.
"delivers": 1882 Act, s.2.
"holder": 1882 Act, s.2.
"value": 1882 Act, s.2.

Comparison
UCC: § 4–205.

### COMMENT

**17–016**　**Purpose of section.** Before the enactment of the 1957 Act, in practically all cases a banker to whom a cheque was delivered for collection received the instrument as holder. If the cheque was payable to bearer, the mere delivery of it to the collecting banker would suffice to make him a holder of it.[33] If the cheque was payable to order, an indorsement would be required and he would become a holder of it by negotiation.[34] As holder, by section 38(1) of the 1882 Act, he could sue on it in his own name. The exception was where, in the case of an order cheque, the indorsement of the payee or any other necessary indorsement was forged or unauthorised. In that case the banker would not be a holder of the cheque[35] and would acquire no title to it through or under that indorsement.[36]

---

[29] See above, para.3–079 (s.24).
[30] See above, para.3–087 (s.24).
[31] See above, para.3–088 (s.24).
[32] See above, para.3–089 (s.24).
[33] s.31(2). See *Sutters v Briggs* [1922] 1 A.C. 1.
[34] s.31(3).
[35] See above, para.3–066 (s.24).
[36] s.24.

It has previously been noted[37] that the main object of the 1957 Act was to dispense with the need for an indorsement where a cheque was deposited by a payee with a banker for collection. The present section seeks to ensure that a banker who collects a cheque payable to order will not be prejudiced by the absence of an indorsement. It provides that a banker who gives value for, or who has a lien on, a cheque payable to order which the holder delivers to him for collection without indorsing it, has such (if any) rights as he would have had if, upon delivery, the holder had indorsed it in blank. The unindorsed cheque is therefore treated as payable to bearer in the hands of the collecting banker.

As to when a cheque is payable to order, see section 8(4) of the 1882 Act; as to the nature and effect of an indorsement in blank, see section 34(1) of that Act (cheque so indorsed becomes payable to bearer).

**Cheques crossed "account payee".** The benefits conferred upon the    **17–017** collecting banker by this section have, however, largely been abrogated by the Cheques Act 1992. Section 81A(1) of the 1882 Act (inserted by section 1 of the Act of 1992) now provides that, where a cheque is crossed and bears across its face the words "account payee" or "a/c payee", either with or without the word "only", the cheque shall not be transferable, but shall only be valid as between the parties thereto.[38] If a cheque so crossed is delivered by the holder (the payee) to a banker for collection without indorsing it,[39] the banker acquires no rights against the drawer of the cheque under this section or otherwise. Since the cheque is not transferable, it is not payable "to order". Moreover, the banker would not have acquired any such rights had the payee indorsed it in blank. The indorsement would have been nugatory. The banker cannot therefore become a holder of the cheque and in consequence cannot be a holder for value or a holder in due course. Most cheque forms pre-printed by bankers in the United Kingdom are crossed and now bear the words "account payee" or "a/c payee" across their face. A banker who gives value for such a cheque, for example, by allowing the customer to borrow further against it, has no rights against the drawer of the cheque if it is dishonoured and he suffers loss.[40]

The paragraphs which follow must therefore be read in the light of these observations. They will now apply only in the rare cases where a cheque is uncrossed, or where the words "account payee" are absent or have been deleted by the drawer of the cheque.

---

[37] See above, para.17–002.
[38] See above, para.14–037.
[39] It is immaterial for the purposes of s.81A(1) of the 1882 Act whether or not the cheque is indorsed.
[40] Illustration 3.

**17–018**     **Scope of the section.** The section only applies where a cheque payable to order is delivered by the holder to a banker for collection. In *Westminster Bank Ltd v Zang*[41] the defendant drew a cheque for £1,000 on Lloyds Bank payable to "J. Tilley or order". The cheque was not indorsed by Tilley but was handed by him to the claimant bank to be credited to the account of Tilley's Autos Ltd, a company of which Tilley was the managing director and the controlling shareholder. In an action by the bank against the defendant on the cheque, it was argued (i) that the cheque had not been delivered to the bank by the holder (Tilley), but by the company through Tilley as its agent, and (ii) that the words "which the holder delivers to him for collection" meant that the cheque had to be delivered to the bank for collection for the credit of the account of Tilley, and of no one else. The first argument was rejected by the Court of Appeal.[42] The second argument was rejected by the House of Lords: the section was not limited to collection only for the holder's account.[43] However, the section does not apply where an order cheque is stolen from the payee or other holder and delivered to a banker for collection, as the cheque will then not have been so delivered by the holder. "Holder" is defined by section 2 of the 1882 Act (with which the 1957 Act is to be construed as one) to mean the payee or indorsee of a bill or note who is in possession of it, or the bearer thereof. The thief is not the payee or indorsee of the cheque; nor is he the bearer of it, since it is not payable to bearer.

The section refers only to cheques. It does not relate to those instruments which are not cheques but come within sections 1(2) and 4(2)(b)(c) and (d) of the 1957 Act. It also refers only to cheques payable to order which the holder delivers to the banker without indorsing them. If an order cheque is in fact indorsed, the section does not relieve the banker from concerning himself with the regularity of the indorsement.[44] Indeed, even where it applies, the only effect of the section is to confer upon the banker "such (if any) rights as he would have had if, upon delivery, the holder had indorsed it in blank".

The section further requires that the banker must either give value for the cheque or have a lien on it.

**17–019**     **The collecting banker as holder for value.** Where a cheque is delivered to a banker for the purposes of collection the banker is prima facie a mere collecting agent. His role is to receive payment on behalf of, and to credit the proceeds to the account designated by, the person who

---

[41] [1966] A.C. 182 (Illustration 2).
[42] [1966] A.C. 182 at 200, 206, 208. It was also rejected by the House of Lords at 217.
[43] [1966] A.C. 182 at 218–219, 222.
[44] With respect to becoming a holder in due course, below, para.17–022.

deposited the cheque. That person will normally be a customer of the banker. But in some circumstances the collecting banker may give value for the cheque and become a holder of it in his own right.[45] For example, where he gives immediate cash for an order cheque, he in effect purchases it and becomes a holder for value of the instrument.[46] A banker may therefore collect a cheque either as the agent of his customer or as holder for value on his own account. But the two roles are not mutually exclusive. This point was made by Milmo J. in *Barclays v Astley Industrial Trust Ltd*,[47] where he said:

"I am unable to accept the contention that a banker cannot at one and the same time be an agent for collection of a cheque and a holder of that cheque for value. It seems to me that the language of section 2 of the Cheques Act, 1957, negatives this proposition since it presupposes that a banker who has been given a cheque for collection may nevertheless have given value for it. . . . A banker who permits his customer to draw £5 against an uncleared cheque for £100 has given value for it but is it to be said that in consequence he is no longer the customer's agent for collection of that cheque? I readily accept that if a banker holds a cheque merely—and I emphasise the word "merely"—as his customer's agent for collection he cannot be a holder for value and still less a holder in due course; but that is an entirely different proposition."

Whether or not the collecting banker gave value for a cheque has been in issue in a number of cases.[48] The following principles emerge.

First, the mere fact that the banker credits his customer's account with the amount of the cheque before clearance does not mean that he gives value for it.[49] In *A.L. Underwood Ltd v Bank of Liverpool*,[50] Atkin L.J. said: "I think it is sufficient to say that the mere fact that the bank in their books enter the value of the cheques on the credit side of the account on the day on which they receive the cheques for collection does not without more

---

[45] *Capital and Counties Bank Ltd v Gordon* [1903] A.C. 240 (Cheques Act 1957, s.4, Illustration 1).

[46] *London Provincial & South Western Bank Ltd v Buszard* (1918) 35 T.L.R. 142 (s.29, Illustration 9) where one branch of the bank was held to have given value for a cheque drawn on another branch of the same bank.

[47] [1970] 2 Q.B. 527, 538. See also *Sutters v Briggs* [1922] 1 A.C. 1.

[48] See *National Australia Bank Ltd v KDS Construction Services Pty Ltd* (1988) 76 A.L.R. 27 (Aust.) for a discussion of the cases.

[49] *Akrokerri (Altantic Mines) Ltd v Economic Bank* [1904] 2 K.B. 465; *Re Farrow's Bank* [1923] 1 Ch. 41 (s.27, Illustration 26); *Underwood (A.L.) Ltd v Bank of Liverpool Ltd* [1924] 1 K.B. 775 (Cheques Act 1957, s.4, Illustration 9); *Westminster Bank Ltd v Zang* [1966] A.C. 182 (Illustration 2); *National Australia Bank Ltd v KDS Construction Services Pty Ltd* (1988) 76 A.L.R. 27 (Aust.). But see s.27(3) of the 1882 Act, and below, para.17–021.

[50] [1924] 1 K.B. 775, 805.

constitute the bank a holder for value." This statement is now generally accepted as representing the present law.[51]

**17–020**     Secondly, the banker will give value if he expressly or impliedly agrees that he will, before receipt of the proceeds, honour cheques of the customer drawn against the cheque paid in for collection, or if he does in fact allow the customer so to draw against that cheque.[52] However, in *Westminster Bank Ltd v Zang*,[53] where there was no finding that the bank had in fact allowed its customer to draw against an uncleared cheque, the House of Lords held that there was no agreement to allow this to be done. Although the bank had, in practice, constantly allowed the customer to draw against uncleared cheques, it was not obliged to do so, and on the paying-in slip the bank expressly reserved the right to postpone payment of cheques drawn against uncleared effects.[54]

Thirdly, the banker will give value if he allows the customer to borrow further on the strength of the cheque paid in for collection or if he honours cheques drawn on him by the customer which he would not have honoured had the cheque not been paid in.[55]

Fourthly, the banker will give value if the cheque is paid in for the express purpose of reducing the customer's overdraft or if the bank expressly or impliedly agrees to accept the cheque in conditional reduction of the customer's overdraft, the condition being that the cheque will not be dishonoured on presentation.[56] But where the banker credits a cheque to the overdrawn account of a customer, with the result that the customer's overdraft is reduced by the amount of the cheque, but nevertheless continues to charge interest on that amount pending clearance, it

---

[51] *Importers Co. Ltd v Westminster Bank Ltd* [1927] 2 K.B. 297, 309–310; *Baker v Barclays Bank Ltd* [1955] 1 W.L.R. 822, 835; *Westminster Bank Ltd v Zang* [1966] A.C. 182 at 192, 203, 209. cf. *Capital and Counties Bank Ltd v Gordon* [1903] A.C. 240 at 245.

[52] *Royal Bank of Scotland v Tottenham* [1894] 2 Q.B. 715 (s.13, Illustration); *Capital and Counties Bank Ltd v Gordon* [1903] A.C. 240 (Cheques Act 1957, s.4, Illustration 1); *Underwood (A.L.) Ltd v Bank of Liverpool Ltd* [1924] 1 K.B. 775, 804, 805–806; *Midland Bank Ltd v Charles Simpson Motors Ltd* [1960] C.L.Y. 217; *Westminster Bank Ltd v Zang* [1966] A.C. 182, 191, 202–203, 207, 209–210, 219–221; *Barclays Bank Ltd v Astley Industrial Trust Ltd* [1970] 2 Q.B. 527, 539–540. Contrast *First National Bank of South Africa Ltd v Richards Bay Taxi Centre (Pty) Ltd* 1999 (3) S.A. 883.

[53] [1966] A.C. 182 (Illustration 2).

[54] *Re Farrow's Bank Ltd* [1923] 1 Ch. 41 (s.27, Illustration 26); *Bank of New South Wales v Barlex Investments Pty Ltd* [1964–1965] N.S.W.R. 546, 549–550. The Banking Code, para.9.4 (above, para.1–011) requires banks and building societies to tell customers about the clearing cycle, including when the customer can withdraw money after paying into his account, and when the customer will start to earn interest.

[55] *Barclays v Astley Industrial Trust Ltd* [1970] 2 Q.B. 527 at 539–540.

[56] *Currie v Misa* (1875) L.R. 10 Ex. 153; *M'Lean v Clydesdale Banking Co.* (1883) 9 App. Cas. 95 (s.75, Illustration 6); *Midland Bank Ltd v Reckitt* [1933] A.C. 1, 18; *Re Keever* [1967] Ch. 182; *Barclays v Astley Industrial Trust Ltd* [1970] 2 Q.B. 527 at 539, see also *Sidney Raper Pty Ltd v Commonwealth Trading Bank of Australia* [1975] 2 N.S.W.L.R. 227, 244, 250.

is hard to see that by crediting the account and reducing the overdraft the banker gives value for the cheque.[57]

For the purposes of the section, the collecting banker may give value in any of the ways mentioned above. He must, however, himself give value. It is not sufficient that, under section 27(2) of the 1882 Act,[58] value has at some time previously been given for the cheque.

**Lien of the collecting banker.** Where a cheque is delivered by a    **17–021** customer to a banker for collection (whether the banker receives it as agent for collection or on his own account)[59] then, in the absence of an express agreement or circumstances evincing an indication to the contrary, the banker has by implication of law a lien over the cheque to the extent of the customer's indebtedness to him at the time.[60] By section 27(3) of the 1882 Act, where the holder of a bill has a lien on it arising either from contract or by implication of law, he is deemed to be a holder for value to the extent of the sum for which he has a lien. Under the present section a banker who has a lien on a cheque payable to order which the holder delivers to him for collection without indorsing it becomes a holder of the cheque notwithstanding the absence of an indorsement. In consequence, by virtue of section 27(3) of the 1882 Act, he becomes a holder for value of the instrument. Thus, in *Barclays Bank Ltd v Astley Industrial Trust Ltd*,[61] a company which was a customer of the claimant bank paid into its account for collection five unindorsed order cheques drawn by the defendants totalling £2,850. The company's overdraft was then in excess of £4,600. Milmo J. held that, quite apart from whether the bank had given value for the cheques, it was a deemed holder for value of them to the extent of the amount of the overdraft.

In *Westminster Bank Ltd v Zang*,[62] however, an unindorsed cheque payable to order which was deposited with the claimant bank for collection and dishonoured when presented for payment was delivered back to the payee's solicitors in order that the payee might sue the drawer. The payee's action was dismissed for non-compliance with a court order. The bank then recovered the cheque and itself sued the drawer. The Court of Appeal held that the bank had lost its lien when it redelivered the cheque

---

[57] *Westminster Bank Ltd v Zang* [1966] A.C. 182 at 219. See n.54, above.
[58] See above, para.4–024.
[59] *Sutters v Briggs* [1922] 1 A.C. 1, 18.
[60] *Johnson v Robarts* (1875) 10 Ch.App. 505; *Misa v Currie* (1876) 1 App. Cas. 554, 565, 569, 573; *Sutters v Briggs* [1922] 1 A.C. 1 at 18; *Midland Bank Ltd v Reckitt* [1933] A.C. 1 at 19; *Re Keever* [1967] Ch. 182 (s.27, Illustration 27); *Barclays v Astley Industrial Trust Ltd* [1970] 2 Q.B. 527 at 539; *Bank of New South Wales v Ross, Stuckley and Morawa* [1974] 2 Lloyd's Rep. 110; *National Australia Bank Ltd v KDS Construction Services Pty Ltd* (1988) 76 A.L.R. 27; see above, para.4–029 (s.27)
[61] [1970] 2 Q.B. 527 (s.27, Illustration 27).
[62] [1966] A.C. 182 (Illustration 2).

to the payee's solicitors.[63] Lord Denning M.R. and Salmon L.J. further held that, although the bank could in the beginning have relied on section 2 of the 1957 Act, when the cheque was redelivered to the bank it was not for collection, nor did the bank then give value for it.[64] The bank could not therefore rely on section 2. Before starting the action against the payee the bank should have asked the payee to indorse the cheque in blank. This point was not considered by the House of Lords.

17–022      **The collecting banker as holder in due course.** If a collecting banker is a holder of another cheque and gives value for it, he may qualify as a holder in due course. By section 29(1) of the 1882 Act, in order to be a holder in due course, he must take a cheque, complete and regular on the face of it, in good faith and without notice of any defect in the title of the person who negotiated it to him. He must also become the holder of it before it was overdue, and without notice that it had been previously dishonoured, if such was the fact. Where an order cheque is delivered to him for collection unindorsed, it is neither incomplete nor irregular by reason of the absence of an indorsement. The lack of an indorsement is cured by section 2 of the 1957 Act.[65]

In *Midland Bank Ltd v R.V. Harris Ltd*,[66] the claimant bank received for collection from its customer two cheques drawn by the defendants payable to the customer or order. The cheques were not indorsed by the customer. The bank gave value for the cheques, but payment of them was countermanded by the defendants. The bank sued the defendants on the cheques, claiming as holder for value and holder in due course. It was argued that section 2 did not make the bank a holder, but merely gave it the rights of a holder, and that the bank could not therefore be a holder in due course. This argument was rejected by Megaw J.. The two cheques were in the hands of the bank payable to bearer; the bank was an indorsee of the cheques and a bearer of them, as defined in section 2 of the 1882 Act, and it was the holder of them as defined in the same section.

Where a banker has a lien on a cheque delivered to him by a holder for collection and is in consequence deemed to be a holder for value of the instrument to the extent of the sum for which he has a lien, he may likewise qualify as a holder in due course. In *Barclays v Astley Industrial Trust Ltd*,[67] Milmo J. held that the claimant bank, having a lien on the cheques delivered to it for collection, was deemed to have taken them for

---

[63] [1966] A.C. 182 at 202, 207, 211. Contrast *Midland Bank Ltd v R.V. Harris Ltd* [1963] 1 W.L.R. 1021.

[64] [1966] A.C. 182 at 203, 211.

[65] *Westminster Bank Ltd v Zang* [1966] A.C. 182, 190.

[66] [1963] 1 W.L.R. 1021 (Illustration 1).

[67] [1970] 2 Q.B. 527 (s.27, Illustration 28). Contrast *Bank of Credit and Commerce International S.A. v Dawson and Wright* [1987] Fin.L.R. 342 (absence of a good faith).

value and that the other conditions in section 29(1) of the 1882 Act to make it a holder in due course were satisfied.

**"Not negotiable" crossing.** If a crossed order cheque delivered to the    **17–023**
banker for collection bears on it the words "not negotiable", then, notwithstanding that he is a holder for value of the cheque, he cannot acquire a better title than the person from whom he took it had.[68] Section 2 affords him no assistance in this respect.

ILLUSTRATIONS

1. S maintains a current account with the claimant bank and, by agree-    **17–024**
ment, is permitted to draw against uncleared cheques credited to the account. He pays into the account for collection two cheques, for £1,640 and £1,740 respectively, drawn by the defendants payable to himself or order. S does not indorse the cheques when paid in. Payment of the cheques is countermanded by the defendants and they are returned unpaid. Notice of dishonour is duly given. The claimant bank, as holder in due course, can recover from the defendants on the cheques. The bank is both an indorsee and a bearer of the cheques by virtue of section 2 of the 1957 Act and as such is a "holder" of them within the meaning of section 2 of the 1882 Act.[69]

2. The defendant draws a cheque for £1,000 payable to "J. Tilley or Order" which he hands to Tilley in exchange for £1,000 in cash. The money so given is the property of Tilley's Autos Ltd, a company controlled by Tilley and of which he is the managing director. Tilley pays in the cheque, without indorsing it, for credit to the account which the company maintains with the claimant bank. He does so by means of a paying-in slip which reserves the right of the bank, at its discretion, to postpone payment of cheques drawn against uncleared effects. When presented the cheque is dishonoured by non-payment. He decides to sue the defendant and his solicitors write to the bank asking it to let them have the dishonoured cheque on their undertaking to return it on demand. Tilley's action against the defendant is dismissed for failure to comply with an order for disclosure. The cheque is returned to the bank, which itself commences an action against the defendant on the cheque, claiming as holder in due course and for value. The bank relies on section 2 of the 1957 Act. The holder of the cheque (Tilley) delivered it to the bank

---

[68] s.81.
[69] *Midland Bank Ltd v R.V. Harris Ltd* [1963] 1 W.L.R. 1021.

and delivered it for collection. For the purposes of the section, it was not necessary for the bank to show that the cheque was after collection to be credited to the payee's account. But the bank did not give value for the cheque. Although it credited the cheque in reduction of the company's overdraft, it charged interest on the £1,000 pending its clearance. There was no evidence that the bank in fact allowed the company to draw against the uncleared cheque, and there was no agreement by the bank to allow the company to do so. The bank's action fails.[70]

3. The defendant draws a cheque "Pay M £450". It is drawn on a pre-printed cheque form which is crossed and bears across its face the words "account payee". M delivers the cheque to the claimants, his bankers, for collection without indorsing it, and they credit him with the amount. M's account is overdrawn and he is permitted to draw further against the credited amount. The cheque is dishonoured. By section 81A(1) of the 1882 Act (introduced by section 1 of the Cheques Act 1992) the cheque is not transferable. The claimants do not acquire the rights of a holder under section 2 of the 1957 Act or otherwise. They have no claim against the defendant on the cheque.

## Unindorsed cheques as evidence of payment

17–025      3. (1) An unindorsed cheque which appears to have been paid by the banker on whom it is drawn is evidence of the receipt by the payee of the sum payable by the cheque.

         (2) For the purposes of subsection (1) above, a copy of a cheque to which that subsection applies is evidence of the cheque if—

             (a) the copy is made by the banker in whose possession the cheque is after presentment and,

             (b) it is certified by him to be a true copy of the original.

Amendment
Subsection (2) was inserted by art.5 of Deregulation (Bills of Exchange) Order 1996.

Definitions
"banker": 1882 Act, s.2.
"cheque": 1882 Act, s.73.

---

[70] *Westminster Bank Ltd v Zang* [1966] A.C. 182.

COMMENT

**Payment as evidence of receipt.** An indorsement, properly so called, **17–026** is only necessary where it is sought to negotiate an instrument payable to order. The original payee of a cheque is not bound to indorse it when presenting it to the drawee banker for payment. Before the Act, the payee or other holder of a cheque would usually sign his name on the back when presenting it for payment or delivering it for collection. A cheque so indorsed which appeared to have been paid by the drawee banker had long been held to be prima facie evidence of the receipt by the payee of the amount of the cheque[71] and was effective as if a simple receipt form on the back of the cheque had been completed. This section, in the words of Lord Reid,[72] "makes it clear—if there were any doubt—that an unindorsed cheque which appears to have been paid by the payer's banker is, without evidence as to who actually received the money, in itself prima facie evidence of receipt of the money by the payee".

Contrary to the recommendations of the Mocatta Committee, however, the section strangely does not extend to the analogous instruments referred to in sections 1(2) and 4(2)(b) (c) and (d). In the absence of any indorsement, the drawer of such an instrument payable to order cannot rely on the section in seeking to prove payment.

In view of the fact that it is the practice now of many banks not to return paid cheques to their customers unless special arrangements are made for this to be done, and it is increasingly the practice even of public utilities and government departments, *e.g.* the Inland Revenue and the Commissioners of Customs and Excise, not to make provision for the person paying to request a receipt should he wish to do so, the drawer of a cheque may in any event be in difficulty in proving payment. It is therefore always advisable for a formal receipt to be demanded where proof of payment is important, *e.g.* for rent under a lease, in connection with the sale of land, or upon a settlement or compromise. Such a receipt will, moreover, connect the payment with the discharge of a particular debt.

**Truncation of cheques.** The Review Committee on Banking Services **17–027** Law and Practice recommended that the 1882 Act be amended to permit the "truncation" of cheques.[73] The Committee also recommended the amendment of the present section so as to accord to a photocopy, or some equivalent reproduction in legible form, of a cheque, suitably marked and

---

[71] *Egg v Barnett* (1800) 3 Esp. 196; *Keene v Beard* (1860) 8 C.B.N.S. 372.
[72] *Westminster Bank Ltd v Zang* [1966] A.C. 182 at 221.
[73] See above, para.13–024.

authenticated by the collecting bank, the status of "evidence of the receipt by the payee of the sum payable by the cheque".[74] The Government accepted these recommendations.[75] They were implemented by the Deregulation (Bills of Exchange) Order 1996,[76] which introduced into the 1882 Act new sections 74B and 74C, so as to permit the truncation of cheques,[77] and introduced into the present section a new subsection (2). The drafting of subsection (2) is somewhat economical, but it appears to achieve the purpose recommended by the Committee. The subsection does not lay down any particular form for the certification referred to.

### Protection of bankers collecting payment of cheques, etc.

17–028     4. (1) Where a banker, in good faith and without negligence—

(a) receives payment for a customer of an instrument to which this section applies; or

(b) having credited a customer's account with the amount of such an instrument, receives payment thereof for himself;

and the customer has no title, or a defective title, to the instrument, the banker does not incur any liability to the true owner of the instrument by reason only of having received payment thereof.

(2) This section applies to the following instruments, namely—

(a) cheques (including cheques which under section 81A(1) of the Bills of Exchange Act 1882 or otherwise are not transferable);

(b) any document issued by a customer of a banker which, though not a bill of exchange, is intended to enable a person to obtain payment from that banker of the sum mentioned in the document;

(c) any document issued by a public officer which is intended to enable a person to obtain payment from the Paymaster General or the Queen's and Lord Treasurer's Remembrancer of the sum mentioned in the document but is not a bill of exchange;

---

[74] (1989) Com. 622, rec. 7(8).

[75] (1990) Com. 1026, Annex 5, para.15. The Banking Code (above, para.1–011) requires banks and building societies to keep original cheques paid from a customer's account, or copies, for at least six years, unless these have already been returned to the customer (para.9.7). Presumably a "copy" made from a microfilmed image of the cheque will suffice, but not merely information stored in electronic form.

[76] SI 1996/2993

[77] See above, paras 13–023 and 13–029.

    **(d) any draft payable on demand drawn by a banker upon himself, whether payable at the head office or some other office of his bank.**

  **(3) A banker is not to be treated for the purposes of this section as having been negligent by reason only of his failure to concern himself with absence of, or irregularity in, indorsement of an instrument.**

Amendment

The words in brackets in subs. 2(a) were inserted by s.3 of the Cheques Act 1992.

Definitions

"banker": 1882 Act, s.2.

"bill of exchange": 1882 Act, s.3.

"cheque": 1882 Act, s.73.

"good faith": 1882 Act, s.90.

COMMENT

**The collecting banker.** It has previously been pointed out[78] that a   **17–029** banker to whom a cheque is delivered by a customer for collection is prima facie merely the customer's agent to present the cheque to the bank on which it is drawn and to receive payment from that bank for the customer. However, a collecting banker may go further and himself give value for the cheque. In such a case, if the cheque is payable to order, when he receives payment of the instrument, he does so not simply as agent for collection but as holder for value on his own account. The character in which a banker receives payment of a cheque is a question of fact.[79] If, having given value, he becomes a holder in due course, then he will hold the cheque free from any defect of title of prior parties.[80] But otherwise, whether he receives payment for his customer or for himself, he will be exposed to the risk of liability if the person who delivers the cheque to him for collection has no title, or a defective title, to the

---

[78] See above, para.17–019.

[79] *M'Lean v Clydesdale Banking Co.* (1883) 9 App. Cas. 95, 115; *Capital and Counties Bank Ltd v Gordon* [1903] A.C. 240, 244; *Re Farrow's Bank Ltd* [1923] 1 Ch. 41, 47.

[80] s.38(2) of the 1882 Act.

instrument.[81] He may, therefore, be justified in refusing to collect a cheque which would expose him to such liability.[82]

**17–030**      **Liability of collecting banker.** The liability of the collecting banker is a liability at common law to the "true owner" of the cheque.[83] He is liable for conversion of the cheque at the suit of its true owner, the cheque being regarded for this purpose as a chattel.[84] In an action for conversion, the cheque is deemed to have a value equal to the amount for which it is drawn.[85] Alternatively the amount received for the cheque may be recovered from him by the true owner in an action in restitution for money had and received.[86] In either case the liability of the collecting banker is strict. Conversion is a tort of strict liability, and, at common law, it is no defence that the banker had no knowledge that his customer's title to the cheque was defective or that he acted throughout in good faith and with proper care. In *Marfani & Co. Ltd v Midland Bank Ltd*,[87] Diplock L.J. said:

> "A banker's business, of its very nature, exposes him daily to this peril. His contract with his customer requires him to accept possession of cheques delivered to him by his customer, to present them for payment to the banks upon which the cheques are drawn, to receive payment of them, and to credit the amount thereof to his own customer's account, either upon receipt of the cheques themselves from the customer or upon receipt of actual payment of the cheques from the banks on which they are drawn. If the customer is not entitled to the cheque which he delivers to his banker for collection, the banker, however innocent and careful he might have been, would at common law be liable to the true owner of the cheque for the amount of which he receives payment, either as damages for conversion or under the cognate cause of action, based historically upon assumpsit, for money had and received."

---

[81] He may, however, if innocent, be entitled to debit his customer's account with the amount which he is required to pay in settlement of the liability: *Redmond v Allied Irish Bank plc* [1987] F.L.R. 307 (concessions made). But in this case Saville J. doubted whether the concessions had been properly made. See also *Sheffield Corpn. v Barclay* [1905] A.C. 392; *Kai Yung v Hong Kong Banking Corp.* [1981] A.C. 787; *National Commercial Banking Corp. of Australia Ltd v Batty* (1985–1986) 160 C.L.R. 251, 273; *Honourable Society of the Middle Temple v Lloyd's Bank plc* [1999] 1 All E.R. (Comm) 193, (Illustration 5).

[82] *Tan ah Sam v Chartered Bank* (1971) 45 A.L.R. 770.

[83] See above, para.3–051 (s.24).

[84] See above, para.3–050 (s.24). Even mere receipt from a customer for the purposes of collection may be said to be conversion: *Fine Art Society v Union Bank* (1886) 17 Q.B.D. 705, 709. There is no equivalent of conversion in Scots Law. Liability will be in restitution, but only if the collecting banker is enriched. See Cusine (1978) 23 Jur. Rev. 233.

[85] But see above, paras 3–050, 3–062 (s.24) for possible exceptions.

[86] See above, paras 3–052, 8–021 (ss.24, 59).

[87] [1968] 1 W.L.R. 956, 971.

**Protection of collecting banker.** The present section incorporates, 17–031
extends and replaces the provisions of section 82 of the 1882 Act, which
gave protection to a banker collecting upon a crossed cheque. Section 82
provided that, where a banker in good faith and without negligence
received payment for a customer of a cheque crossed generally or specially to himself, and the customer had no title or a defective title thereto,
the banker should not incur any liability to the true owner of the cheque
by reason only of having received such payment. In 1903 the House of
Lords held in *Capital and Counties Bank Ltd v Gordon*[88] that bankers were
only protected by section 82 when they received payment of a crossed
cheque as mere agents for collection for a customer. They were not so
protected when they credited a customer with the amount of a cheque as
soon as it was handed in to his account and allowed him to draw against
the amount so credited before the cheque was cleared. In such a case they
received payment as holders of the cheque on their own account. As a
result the Bills of Exchange (Crossed Cheques) Act 1906 was passed. This
provided that a banker would receive payment of a crossed cheque for a
customer within the meaning of section 82 of the 1882 Act notwithstanding that he credited his customer's account with the amount of the cheque
before receiving payment thereof. The 1957 Act repealed both section 82
and the 1906 Act, and it embodied in section 4 the protection afforded to
the collecting banker by their provisions.

Section 4, however, also enlarged those provisions. First, the protection
is no longer confined to cheques that are crossed. Secondly, the protection
is extended to three other types of instrument which, although they are
not cheques, are analogous to cheques and were brought within the
protection by previous legislation.[89] Thirdly, the collecting banker is not
to be treated as having been negligent by reason only of his failure to
concern himself with absence of, or irregularity in, indorsement of an
instrument. Subject to these changes and to certain differences in wording
between section 4 and the repealed provisions, cases decided under
section 82 of the 1882 Act may still be of relevance, *e.g.* as to the scope of
the protection, as to who is a "customer", and (with due regard to
changes in banking practice) as to when a collecting banker has acted
"without negligence".

**Subsection (1): scope of protection.** Notwithstanding certain doubts 17–032
which were previously raised as to the wording of paragraph (b),[90] it is

---

[88] [1903] A.C. 240 (Illustration 1).
[89] Revenue Act 1883, s.17; Bills of Exchange Act (1882) Amendment Act 1932. The protection
was further extended by the Cheques Act 1992, s.3, to non-transferable cheques.
[90] *Byles* (26th ed.), p.319. These doubts were, however, withdrawn in the 27th ed., 23–23,
n.39.

clear that the banker may claim protection both when he receives payment for a customer as a mere agent for collection and when, having credited the customer's account with the amount of an order or bearer cheque before clearance, he receives payment of it for himself, *i.e.* as holder in his own right. However, he would not be protected if (exceptionally) he paid cash for the instrument instead of crediting the customer's account, although he could still, in an appropriate case, rely upon his status as a holder in due course.

It is also clear that, despite the words "by reason only of having received payment thereof", the protection afforded by the section extends, not only to the actual receipt of the money by the banker, but also to any prior dealing with the cheque by him in the ordinary course of collecting it. Commenting on section 82 of the 1882 Act, Lord Macnaghten said in *Capital and Counties Bank Ltd v Gordon*[91]:

> "The only question, therefore, is, Did the banks receive payment of these cheques for their customer? If they did, it is obvious that they are relieved from any liability which, perhaps, might otherwise attach to some preliminary action on their part taken in view and anticipation of receiving payment. The section would be nugatory—it would be worse than nugatory —it would be a mere trap if the immunity conferred in respect of receipt of payment, and in terms confined to such receipt, did not extend to cover every step taken in the ordinary course of business and intended to lead up to that result."

And in *Gordon v London, City and Midland Bank Ltd*[92] Stirling L.J. said that section 82 " . . . must be construed so as to cover every act which is necessarily incidental to the transaction of receiving payment, from the receipt of the cheque in the first instance down to the conclusion of the transaction by receipt of payment of the cheque". The protection continues to apply when the banker pays out the proceeds to the customer.[93]

A customer may pay in a cheque at a different branch of the same bank on which the cheque is drawn, or pay it in at the same branch of the bank on which it is drawn. In both situations, when the banker pays the cheque drawn on himself, he acts as paying banker, and—at least in the second situation—could be said merely to be paying a cheque presented to him for payment and not acting in the role of collecting agent at all.[94] In

---

[91] [1903] A.C. 240, 244.
[92] [1902] 1 K.B. 242, 277.
[93] *Marfani & Co. Ltd v Midland Bank Ltd* [1968] 1 W.L.R. 956, 973–975.
[94] *Sutherland v Royal Bank of Scotland plc* 1997 S.L.T. 329. But see *Boyd v Emmerson* (1834) 2 A. & E. 184 and above, para.6–064 (s.45).

certain earlier cases[95] the Court of Appeal accepted that a banker who, in either situation, paid a cheque drawn on himself was entitled to rely on the protection afforded to a paying banker by section 19 of the Stamp Act 1853 or section 60 of the 1882 Act. But in *Carpenters' Co. v British Mutual Banking Co. Ltd*[96] the Court of Appeal held that the banker in fact acts in a dual capacity, both as a collecting and as a paying banker. In that case, crossed order cheques drawn by the claimant corporation payable to tradesmen were stolen by a clerk, the necessary indorsements were forged and the cheques paid in to the credit of his private account at the same branch of the defendant bank on which they were drawn. In an action for conversion brought by the corporation against the bank, a majority of the Court of Appeal[97] held that section 60 of the 1882 Act only protected a banker when that banker was merely a paying banker, and not when he received a cheque for collection. The only defence available to the defendant bank as collecting bank was under section 82 of the 1882 Act—or, now, under the present section. A banker who, therefore, collects a customer's cheque drawn on himself to which the customer has no title, or a defective title, is prima facie liable in conversion to the true owner of the cheque. But, if he can otherwise bring himself within its provisions, he is equally entitled to the protection of the present section as when collecting a customer's cheque drawn on another banker.

**"Banker."** This expression is defined by section 2 of the 1882 Act. The **17–033** protection extends only to a banker. A customer who delivers a cheque to a banker for collection is not protected and will be liable to the true owner in an action for conversion or in restitution for money had and received.[98]

**"Customer."** The word "customer" is not defined in the 1957 or in the **17–034** 1882 Act.[99] The mere performance for a person of some casual service by a banker, even on a regular basis and over an extended period of time, does not suffice to make that person a customer. Thus, where a person had been allowed to cash cheques for many years at a certain bank, he was not a customer of the bank for "nothing was put to his debit or credit

---

[95] *Bissell & Co. v Fox Bros & Co.* (1885) 53 L.T. 193; *Gordon v London City and Midland Bank Ltd* [1902] 1 K.B. 242, 274–275

[96] [1938] 1 K.B. 511 (s.60, Illustration 1). See also *Standard Bank of South Africa Ltd v Nair* 2001 (1) S.A. 998; *Standard Bank of South Africa Ltd v Harris* 2003 (2) S.A. 23.

[97] Greer and Slesser L.JJ., Mackinnon L.J dissenting.

[98] *Ogden v Benas* (1874) L.R. 9 C.P. 513; *Bobbett v Pinkett* (1876) 1 Ex.D. 368 (s.24, Illustration 9); *Vinden v Hughes* [1905] 1 K.B. 795 (s.7, Illustration 5); *Lipkin Gorman v Karpnale Ltd* [1987] 1 W.L.R. 987; [1989] 1 W.L.R. 1340; [1991] 2 A.C. 548 (s.29, Illustration 7). See above, paras 3–050, 3–052 (s.24).

[99] It is, however, defined in s.138(7) of the Financial Services and Markets Act 2000.

in any book or paper kept by the bank".[1] On the other hand a person who has an account with the banker,[2] or for whom the banker has agreed to open an account, is a customer, and the duration of the relationship is of no significance.

In *Commissioners of Taxation v English, Scottish and Australian Bank Ltd*,[3] Lord Dunedin said[4]:

> "Their Lordships are of opinion that the word 'customer' signifies a relationship in which duration is not of the essence. A person whose money has been accepted by a bank on the footing that they undertake to honour cheques up to the amount standing to his credit is . . . a customer of the bank in the sense of the statute, irrespective of whether his connection is of short or long standing. The contrast is not between an habitué and a newcomer, but between a person for whom the bank performs a casual service, such as, for instance, cashing a cheque for a person introduced by one of their customers, and a person who has an account of his own at the bank."

In that case the Privy Council held that the bank was protected by the New South Wales equivalent of section 82 of the 1882 Act when the cheque in question had been paid in by a person who only the day before had opened an account with the bank. Indeed a person may open an account with the very cheque for the collection of which the banker may later successfully claim the statutory protection.[5]

The relationship of banker and customer comes into existence when the banker agrees to accept the instruction of a person to open an account in that person's name.[6] However, if a person steals a cheque drawn payable to a named payee and opens an account in the name of the payee, the payee does not thereby become a customer of the banker, but the thief is such a customer despite the misrepresentation of his identity.[7] One person may nevertheless open an account in the name of another, as where a grandparent opens an account in the name of his or her grandchild. In such a case, it would seem that the "customer" is the person in whose

---

[1] *Great Western Railway Co. v London and County Banking Co. Ltd* [1901] A.C. 414 (Illustration 3). See also *Lacave & Co. v Crédit Lyonnais* [1897] 1 Q.B. 148 (Illustration 2).

[2] Even if overdrawn: *Clarke v London and County Banking Co.* [1897] 1 Q.B. 552. A deposit account will suffice: *Great Western Railway Co. v London and County Banking Co. Ltd* [1901] A.C. 414 at 421.

[3] [1920] A.C. 683 (Illustration 4).

[4] [1920] A.C. 683 at 687.

[5] *Ladbroke & Co. v Todd* (1914) 30 T.L.R. 433 (Illustration 7); *Honourable Society of the Middle Temple v Lloyds Bank plc* [1999] 1 All E.R. (Comm) 193. (Illustration 5).

[6] *Ladbroke & Co. v Todd* (1914) 30 T.L.R. 433; *Woods v Martins Bank Ltd* [1959] 1 Q.B. 55, 63; *Barclays Bank Ltd v Okenhare* [1966] 2 Lloyd's Rep. 87.

[7] *Stoney Stanton Supplies (Coventry) Ltd v Midland Bank Ltd* [1966] 2 Lloyd's Rep. 373.

name the account is opened,[8] unless the named account holder is a mere nominee for the person who opens the account.[9]

One banker may be a customer of another, as when one who is not a **17–035** clearing house member regularly employs a clearing banker to collect cheques deposited with him for collection by his customers.[10]

Arrangements now exist between banks whereby a customer of one bank ("Bank A") may deliver a cheque to another bank ("Bank B") with a request that the proceeds be remitted to his account with Bank A. The cheque is then passed by Bank B through the clearing system to the drawee bank, and Bank B advises Bank A and accounts to it for the proceeds. Whether Bank B acts as principal or merely as agent for Bank A, it seems probable that it would be liable to the true owner in conversion if the person delivering the cheque had no title, or a defective title, to the instrument. It would also appear that Bank B would not be entitled to the protection of the section, since that person is not its customer, but a customer of Bank A.[11] The word "customer" in subsection (1) must surely mean a customer of the banker who receives payment or who credits the account, and not of some other banker. It could, however, possibly be argued (depending on the precise nature of the arrangements between the two banks) that Bank B is acting as agent of Bank A and, in that capacity, would be entitled to the protection afforded to its principal. It would not be too unreasonable a construction of the subsection to assume that the statutory protection was intended to extend, not only to the banker referred to, but to persons acting on his behalf, *i.e.* his employees and agents.

**"The customer has no title, or a defective title."** The words "a defec- **17–036** tive title" must be construed by reference to section 29(2) of the 1882 Act. The examples given in that subsection are not, however, exhaustive, and there may be other defects in the title of the customer not there mentioned.[12] The protection extends also to cases where the customer has no title to the instrument, that is to say, where he has obtained it through or under a forged or unauthorised indorsement,[13] or where the instrument has been stolen, or where the instrument is not transferable and the customer is not the payee.

**Burden of proof.** In order to claim the protection of the section the **17–037** collecting banker must show that he received payment "in good faith and

---

[8] *Rowlandson v National Westminster Bank Ltd* [1978] 1 W.L.R. 798.
[9] *Thavorn v Bank of Credit and Commerce International S.A.* [1985] 1 Lloyd's Rep. 259, 263.
[10] *Importers Co. Ltd v Westminster Bank Ltd* [1927] 2 K.B. 297; see below, para.17–049.
[11] See Ellinger and Lomnicka, and Hooley, *Modern Banking Law* (3rd ed.), pp.590–591; Brindle and Cox, *Law of Bank Payments* (3rd ed.), 7–088.
[12] See above, para.4–062 (s.29).
[13] s.24; above, para.3–066.

without negligence". The burden of proof is on him. Lord Wright said in *Lloyds Bank Ltd v E.B. Savory & Co.*[14]:

> "In an ordinary action in conversion, once the true owner proves his title and the act of taking by the defendants, absence of negligence or of intention or knowledge are alike immaterial as defences. Sect. 82 is therefore not the imposition of a new burden or duty on the collecting banker, but is a concession affording him the means of avoiding a liability in conversion to which otherwise there would be no defence. As it is for the banker to show that he is entitled to this defence, the onus is on him to disprove negligence."

The burden is the same under the present section.[15] The banker may therefore be required to give particulars of all facts and matters on which he relies to establish that he acted without negligence.[16]

Unless he discharges the burden of proof, the banker remains liable to the true owner in conversion or in restitution for money had and received.

17–038    **"Good faith."** Section 90 of the 1882 Act provides that a thing is deemed to be done in good faith, whether it is done negligently or not. It is unlikely that the good faith of the collecting banker will be called into question.[17]

17–039    **"Without negligence."** According to the words of subsection (1), the time for determining whether the collecting banker has acted without negligence is the time at which he receives payment. But Diplock L.J. has said[18]:

> "The relevant time for determining whether the banker has complied with his duty of care towards the true owner of the cheque is, in my opinion, the time at which he pays out the proceeds of the cheque to his own customer, so depriving the true owner of his right to follow the money into the banker's hands."

The concept of "negligence" as used in the subsection is the subject-matter of some controversy. On one view, it consists of a breach of a duty

---

[14] [1933] A.C. 201, 228–229. See also *Lloyds Bank Ltd v Chartered Bank of India Australia and China* [1929] 1 K.B. 40, 59, 77; *Midland Bank Ltd v Reckitt* [1933] A.C. 1, 14; *Baker v Barclays Bank Ltd* [1955] 1 W.L.R. 822, 835.

[15] *Orbit Mining and Trading Co. Ltd v Westminster Bank Ltd* [1963] 1 Q.B. 794, 829; *Thackwell v Barclays Bank plc* [1986] 1 All E.R. 676; *Hunter BNZ Finance Ltd v C.G. Maloney Pty Ltd* (1988) 18 N.S.W.L.R. 420.

[16] *Griggs Bartlett Ltd v Coutts & Co.* (1968) (Donaldson J.) unreported.

[17] But see *Lawrie v The Commonwealth Trading Bank of Australia* [1970] Q.R. 373; *Bank of Montreal v Tourangeau* (1981) 118 D.L.R. (3d) 293.

[18] *Marfani & Co. Ltd v Midland Bank Ltd* [1968] 1 W.L.R. 956, 975.

of care,[19] although the negligence referred to is not the breach of a duty owed by the banker to his customer, but the breach of a duty owed to the true owner, and "must mean the neglect of such reasonable precautions as ought to be taken with reference to [his] interests . . . ".[20] On another view, however, it does not involve the breach of any duty of care to the true owner but consists of a failure by the banker to achieve a certain standard of conduct in his business.[21] The adoption of one or other view may of relevance to the question whether negligence on the part of the banker is to be disregarded if it is shown not to have had any causative effect upon the loss suffered by the true owner.[22] But it appears to make no difference to the standard of care expected of him. It has been emphasised that the question whether the banker has been negligent is a question of fact which must be decided on the circumstances of each case[23] and must be determined separately with regard to each instrument paid in.[24] Nevertheless, there have been a number of general statements concerning the standard of care required of the banker.

In *Commissioners of Taxation v English, Scottish and Australian Bank Ltd*,[25] Lord Dunedin stated that "the test of negligence is whether the transaction of paying in any given cheque coupled with the circumstances antecedent and present was so out of the ordinary course that it ought to have aroused doubts in the bankers' mind, and caused them to make inquiry". The Privy Council in that case rejected the view that the care to be taken was not less than a man invited to purchase or cash such a

---

[19] *Marfani & Co. Ltd v Midland Bank Ltd* [1968] 1 W.L.R. 956, 972.

[20] *Bissell & Co. v Fox Bros & Co.* (1884) 51 L.T. 663, 666, per Denman J., approved on appeal (1885) 53 L.T. 193. See also *Hannan's Lake View Central Ltd v Armstrong & Co.* (1900) 16 T.L.R. 236, 237; *London Bank of Australia Ltd v Kendall* (1920) 28 C.L.R. 401, 410; *London & Montrose Shipbuilding & Repairing Co. Ltd v Barclays Bank Ltd* (1925) 31 Com.Cas. 67, 72; *Lloyds Bank Ltd v Chartered Bank of India, Australia and China* [1929] 1 K.B. 40, 73; *Honourable Society of the Middle Temple v Lloyds Bank plc* [1999] 1 All E.R. (Comm) 193.

[21] *Ladbroke & Co. v Todd* (1914) 30 T.L.R. 433, 434; *Lloyds Bank Ltd v E.B. Savory & Co.* [1933] A.C. 201, 221; *Orbit Mining and Trading Co. Ltd v Westminster Bank Ltd* [1963] 1 Q.B. 794, 822; *Hunter BNZ Finance Ltd v C.G. Maloney Pty Ltd* (1988) 18 N.S.W.L.R. 420, 447–451; *Dairy Containers Ltd v NZI Bank Ltd* [1995] 2 N.Z.L.R. 30, 114.

[22] See below, para.17–055.

[23] *Commissioners of Taxation v English, Scottish and Australian Bank Ltd* [1920] A.C. 683, 688; *Lloyds Bank Ltd v Chartered Bank of India, Australia and China* [1929] 1 K.B. 40 at 59, 73; *Orbit Mining and Trading Co. Ltd v Westminster Bank Ltd* [1963] 1 Q.B. 794 at 822.

[24] *Morison v London County and Westminster Bank Ltd* [1914] 3 K.B. 365, 368; *Commissioners of the State Savings Bank of Victoria v Permewan Wright & Co. Ltd* (1914) 19 C.L.R. 457; *Commissioners of Taxation v English, Scottish and Australian Bank Ltd* [1920] A.C. 683 at 688; *Lloyds Bank Ltd v Chartered Bank of India, Australia and China* [1929] 1 K.B. 40 at 59, 72.

[25] [1920] A.C. 683, 688. See also *Underwood (A.L.) Ltd v Bank of Liverpool Ltd* [1924] 1 K.B. 775, 793; *Hampstead Guardians v Barclays Bank Ltd* (1923) 39 T.L.R. 229, 231; *Francis and Taylor Ltd v Commercial Bank of Australia Ltd* [1932] N.Z.L.R. 1028, 1033; *Orbit Mining and Trading Co. Ltd v Westminster Bank Ltd* [1963] 1 Q.B. 794 at 823. *New Zealand Law Socy v ANZ Banking Group Ltd* [1985] 1 N.Z.L.R. 280, 286.

cheque for himself might reasonably be expected to take, for the simple reason that:

"it is no part of the business or ordinary practice of individuals to cash cheques which are offered to them, whereas it is part of the ordinary business or practice of a bank to collect cheques for their customers. If, therefore, a standard is sought, it must be the standard derived from the ordinary practice of bankers, not individuals."[26]

**17–040**    However, in *Lloyds Bank Ltd v Chartered Bank of India, Australia and China*,[27] Sankey L.J. said:

"I think the duty of the defendants to the true owner of the cheque was (1.) to exercise the same care and forethought with regard to the cheque paid in by the customer as a reasonable man would bring to bear on similar business of his own... , and (2.) to provide a reasonable and competent staff to carry out this duty."

In *Lloyds Bank Ltd v E.B. Savory & Co.*[28] Lord Warrington expressed the following view:

"The standard by which the absence, or otherwise, of negligence is to be determined must in my opinion be ascertained by reference to the practice of reasonable men carrying on the business of bankers, and endeavouring to do so in such a manner as may be calculated to protect themselves and others against fraud."

In *Marfani & Co. Ltd v Midland Bank Ltd*,[29] Diplock L.J. described the duty of the banker as "a qualified duty to take reasonable care to refrain from taking any such step which he foresees is, or ought reasonably to have foreseen was, likely to cause loss or damage to the true owner".[30] The banker was entitled to assume that the customer was the owner of the cheque unless there were facts which were, or ought to have been, known to him which would cause a reasonable banker to suspect that the customer was not the true owner. His Lordship pointed out[31] that what facts ought to be known to the banker, *i.e.* what inquiries he should make, and what facts should cause him reasonably to suspect that the customer was not the true owner, would depend on current banking practice, and

---

[26] [1920] A.C. 683 at 689.
[27] [1929] 1 K.B. 40, 69.
[28] [1933] A.C. 201, 221.
[29] [1968] 1 W.L.R. 956.
[30] [1968] 1 W.L.R. 956 at 972.
[31] [1968] 1 W.L.R. 956 at 972.

change as that practice changed. Cases decided 30 years ago might not be a reliable guide to what the duty of the careful banker was today.[32] Diplock L.J. then formulated the following principle[33]:

> "What the court has to do is to look at all the circumstances at the time of the acts complained of and to ask itself: were those circumstances such as would cause a reasonable banker possessed of such information about his customer as a reasonable banker would possess, to suspect that his customer was not the true owner of the cheque?"

More recently, in *Linklaters v HSBC Bank plc*.[34] Gross J. Stated that, as a    **17–041** matter of English law, a bank which collected a cheque and paid over the proceeds to its customer—

> "had to balance: (1) its duty to exercise reasonable care in and about executing its customer's order to transfer funds, such duty extending to the true owner of the cheque; (2) its duty, when a customer is in credit, to execute, promptly, valid and proper orders as to the transfer of funds".

and he applied the test[35] whether an "ordinary prudent banker" in the position of the collecting banker should have been put on inquiry.

In any event, the banker cannot be held liable merely because he has not subjected the customer's account to microscopic examination,[36] or—unless there is something markedly irregular in the transaction —because he has not made a thorough inquiry into the history of each cheque, which would render banking business impracticable.[37] To cashiers and clerks there must be attributed the degree of intelligence and care ordinarily required of persons in their position to fit them for the discharge of their duties[38]; but "it is not expected that the officials of banks

---

[32] However, the wheel may have come full circle. In the South African case of *ABSA Bank Ltd v Mutual and Federal Insurance Co. Ltd* 2003 (1) S.A. 635, 642, it was pointed out that "these are fraudulent times. What would have been acceptable in an instrument 20 years ago without any cause for suspicion is no longer so."

[33] [1968] 1 W.L.R. 956 at 973.

[34] [2003] EWHC 1113 (Comm); [2003] 2 Lloyd's Rep. 545 at [106].

[35] Derived from the statement (in a different context) of Steyn J. in *Barclays Bank plc v Quincecare* [1992] 4 All E.R. 363, 376, 377; above, para.13–062.

[36] *Lloyds Bank Ltd v Chartered Bank of India, Australia and China* [1929] 1 K.B. 40, 73.

[37] *Commissioners of Taxation v English, Scottish and Australian Bank Ltd* [1920] A.C. 683, 689–690; *Lloyds Bank Ltd v Chartered Bank of India, Australia and China* [1929] 1 K.B. 40 at 59.

[38] *Ross v London County Westminster and Parr's Bank* [1919] 1 K.B. 678, 685; *Lloyds Bank Ltd v Chartered Bank of India, Australia and China* [1929] 1 K.B. 40 at 72.

should also be amateur detectives".[39] Evidence of the practice of bankers is admissible.[40]

**17–042**     **Misappropriation by employees, agents and other fiduciaries.** In *Lloyds Bank Ltd v E.B. Savory & Co.*, Lord Wright said[41]:

> "The most obvious circumstances which should put the banker on his guard (apart from manifest irregularities in the indorsement and such like) are where a cheque is presented for collection which bears on its face a warning that the customer may have misappropriated it, as for instance where a customer known to be a servant or agent pays in for collection a cheque drawn by third parties in favour of his employer or principal. Such a case carries even a clearer warning if the cheque is indorsed per pro. the employer or principal by the servant or agent. . . . Similarly, if a cheque payable to a one-man company is paid in by the 'one-man', who is also managing director, to his private account. . . . A second type of case is where a servant steals cheques drawn by his employers and pays them or procures their payment into his own account. . . . In all these cases the cheque in itself, apart from knowledge possessed of the customer's position, indicates a possibility or even probability that the servant or agent may have misappropriated it and hence the bank may be converting it."

As examples he cited *Bissell & Co. v Fox Bros & Co.*,[42] where a salesman of the claimant firm indorsed by per pro. indorsements a number of cheques payable to the firm and arranged for them to be credited to his private account with the defendant bank; *Lloyds Bank Ltd v Chartered Bank of India, Australia and China*,[43] where the claimants' chief accountant drew cheques on the claimants' account payable to the defendant bank, which he sent to the defendants with instructions to place them to the credit of his private account; *Underwood (A.L.) Ltd v Bank of Liverpool*,[44] where the sole director of a one-man company indorsed on behalf of the company a number of cheques drawn by third parties payable to the company and paid them into his private account with the defendant bank; and *Morison*

---

[39] *Lloyds Bank Ltd v Chartered Bank of India, Australia and China* [1929] 1 K.B. 40 at 73, *per* Sankey L.J.; *Penmount Estates Ltd v National Provincial Bank Ltd* (1945) 173 L.T. 344, 346.

[40] *Importers Co. Ltd v Westminster Bank Ltd* [1927] 2 K.B. 297, 303; *Orbit Mining and Trading Co. Ltd v Westminster Bank Ltd* [1963] 1 Q.B. 794, 816; *Honourable Society of the Middle Temple v Lloyds Bank plc* [1999] 1 All E.R. (Comm) 193; *Linklaters v HSBC Bank plc* [2003] EWHC 1113 (Comm), [2003] 2 Lloyd's Rep. 545.

[41] [1933] A.C. 201, 229–230.

[42] (1884) 53 L.T. 193.

[43] [1929] 1 K.B. 40 (Illustration 10).

[44] [1924] 1 K.B. 775 (Illustration 9). See also *Hannan's Lake View Central Ltd v Armstrong & Co.* (1900) 16 T.L.R. 236 (secretary of company).

*v London County and Westminster Bank*,[45] where an employee of the claimants, with authority to draw cheques, drew and where necessary indorsed per pro. the claimants a large number of cheques which were then delivered by him to the defendant bank for the credit of his private account. Similar cases have arisen where cheques drawn payable to a corporation[46] or partnership[47] or to a public official[48] or to a principal per the agent[49] or to an agent per the principal,[50] or cheques drawn by the customer on a trustee account[51] or on a client's account under a power of attorney,[52] were paid into the private account of a customer of the bank. Some alleviation is, however, afforded in the case of solicitors' accounts by section 85 of the Solicitors Act 1974.[53]

**Per pro. signatures.**[54] The mere fact that a cheque is drawn per pro. or    **17–043** in a representative capacity is not a matter to excite suspicion. But if a cheque is drawn or indorsed by a customer per pro. another and then paid into the customer's private account, this should put the banker on inquiry, for it indicates to him that the customer is in a fiduciary position and that there is a possibility of an abuse of authority.[55] In *Orbit Mining & Trading Co. Ltd v Westminster Bank Ltd*,[56] however, cheques drawn on behalf of the claimant company required the signature of two directors. A director of the company procured the signature by a codirector of crossed cheque forms in blank. He then added his own (but illegible) signature as drawer beneath that of his codirector, made the cheques payable to "cash or order", indorsed them and paid them into his private account with the defendant bank. The Court of Appeal held that the bank was not put on inquiry, and was not negligent. It had no knowledge of the director's connection with the company, and the cashier did not look on the back of the cheque since there was no named payee and the cheque did not

---

[45] [1914] 3 K.B. 356 (s.24, Illustration 1). See also *Bennett and Fisher Ltd v Commercial Bank of Australia Ltd* [1930] S.A.S.R. 26.

[46] *Carpenters' Co. v British Mutual Banking Co. Ltd* [1938] 1 K.B. 511 (s.60, Illustration 1).

[47] *Baker v Barclays Bank Ltd* [1955] 1 W.L.R. 822 (Illustraton 15); *Tan Ah Sam v Chartered Bank* [1971] 1 M.L.J. 28. *cf. Smith and Baldwin v Barclays Bank Ltd* (1944) 5 L.D.B. 370.

[48] *Ross v London County, Westminster and Parr's Bank Ltd* [1919] 1 K.B. 678 (Illustration 8). See also *Commercial Bank of Australia v Flannagan* (1932) 47 C.L.R. 461; *Commissioners of the State Savings Bank of Victoria v Permewan, Wright & Co.* (1914) 19 C.L.R. 457.

[49] *Slingsby v District Bank Ltd* [1931] 2 K.B. 588 (action agaist paying bankers) (s.60, Illustration 2).

[50] *Bute (Marquess of) v Barclays Bank Ltd* [1955] 1 Q.B. 202 (Illustration 14).

[51] *House Property Co. of London Ltd v London County and Westminster Bank Ltd* (1915) 31 T.L.R. 479.

[52] *Midland Bank Ltd v Reckitt* [1933] A.C. 1 (s.25, Illustration 9).

[53] See above, para.13–063. But see *Lipkin Gorman v Karpnale Ltd* [1987] 1 W.L.R. 987, 997.

[54] See above, para.3–095 (s.25).

[55] *Midland Bank Ltd v Reckitt* [1933] A.C. 1. See also *Morison v London County and Westminster Bank Ltd* [1914] 3 K.B. 356, 368; *Day v Bank of New South Wales* (1978) 19 A.L.R. 32 (Aust.). Contrast *Crumplin v London Joint Stock Bank Ltd* (1913) 30 T.L.R. 99 (Illustration 6).

[56] [1963] 1 Q.B. 794 (Illustration 17).

require indorsement. There was nothing therefore to connect the one signature with the other to require scrutiny by the cashier. Also in *Australia and New Zealand Bank Ltd v Ateliers de Constructions Electriques de Charleroi*[56a] a bank was sued by the claimant company in conversion for wrongfully receiving and crediting to the personal account of an agent cheques drawn payable to the claimants and indorsed on their behalf by the agent, the proceeds of which were subsequently misappropriated by the agent. On the facts of the case it was found that this was the only practical way by which the proceeds of cheques payable to order could be remitted to the claimants abroad and that they had never objected to the clearance of cheques in this manner. They had therefore, by implication, conferred on the agent authority to indorse cheques on their behalf and pay them into his own account.

On the other hand, in 1941 Lord Atkin said[57]: "In these days every bank clerk sees the red light when a company's cheque is endorsed by a company's official into an account which is not the company's." Banks generally forbid acceptance for the credit of private accounts cheques drawn in favour of limited companies, even where there is no connection between the payee and the persons for whom they are asked to collect.[58]

**17–044**     **Opening the account.** Whilst negligence must relate to collection if the banker is to lose the protection of the section, a failure to make proper inquiries concerning a new customer on opening an account may mean that he is negligent in collecting a cheque for that customer.[59] It must, however, be emphasised that, on the wording of the section, "it is not a question of negligence in opening an account, though the circumstances

---

[56a] [1967] 1 A.C. 86 (Illustration 18). See also *Souhrada v Bank of New South Wales* [1976] 2 Lloyd's Rep. 444.

[57] *United Australia Ltd v Barclays Bank Ltd* [1941] A.C. 1, 23–24. See also *Motor Traders Guarantee Corp. Ltd v Midland Bank Ltd* [1937] 4 All E.R. 90. *cf. London and Montrose Shipbuilding and Repairing Co. Ltd v Barclays Bank Ltd* (1926) 31 Com.Cas. 67, 76 (revd (1926) 31 Com.Cas. 182).

[58] *Paget* (12th ed.), 24.20.

[59] *Turner v London and Provincial Bank Ltd* (1903) 2 L.D.B. 33; *Ladbroke & Co. v Todd* (1914) 30 T.L.R. 433; *London Bank of Australia Ltd v Kendall* (1920) 28 C.L.R. 401; *Hampstead Guardians v Barclays Bank* (1923) 39 T.L.R. 229; *Lloyds Bank Ltd v E.B. Savory & Co.* [1933] A.C. 201; *Saving Bank of South Australia v Wallman* (1935) 52 C.L.R. 688, 695; *Rubber Industry (Replanting) Board v Hong Kong and Shanghai Banking Corp.* [1957] M.L.J. 103; *Lumsden & Co. v London Trustee Savings Bank* [1971] 1 Lloyd's Rep. 114 (Illustration 20); *Honourable Society of the Middle Temple v Lloyds Bank plc* [1999] 1 All E.R. (Comm) 193 (Illustration 5); *Linklaters v HSBC Bank plc* [2003] EWHC 1113 (Comm), [2003] 2 Lloyd's Rep. 545 at [175]. *cf. Commissioners of Taxation v English, Scottish and Australian Bank Ltd* [1920] A.C. 683 (Illustration 4); *Savings Bank of South Australia v Wallman* (1935) 52 C.L.R. 688; *Nu-Stilo Footwear Ltd v Lloyds Bank Ltd* (1956) 7 L.D.B. 33 (Illustration 16); *Marfani & Co. Ltd v Midland Bank Ltd* [1968] 1 W.L.R. 956.

connected with the opening of an account may shed light on the question of whether there was negligence in collecting a cheque".[60] A cheque may, for example, be paid into a new account which has been deliberately opened by a customer with a view to facilitating a fraud. In *Ladbroke & Co. v Todd*[61] a crossed order cheque was stolen while in the post by a thief who forged the payee's indorsement and opened an account with it in the payee's name. The bank did not verify the identity of its new customer or inquire as to how the account would be funded, nor did it take up references, but merely accepted the thief's story that the cheque had been received in respect of a gambling transaction which he did not wish to come to the attention of his college authorities at Oxford. It was held that the bank had failed to discharge the burden of proving that it had acted without negligence under section 82 of the 1882 Act. On the other hand, in *Marfani & Co. Ltd v Midland Bank Ltd*,[62] a cheque drawn by his employers payable to a third party was stolen by a clerk. The clerk then opened an account in the payee's name with a small deposit, indicating that he intended to start a restaurant business and that further funds would be paid in later. The bank did not inquire as to his occupation or verify his identity, but obtained from him the names of two referees. It then collected the cheque and, having received a satisfactory oral report from one of the referees, allowed him to draw out the proceeds. The bank successfully relied on section 4 of the 1957 Act.

The high-water mark in this respect is the case, in 1933, of *Lloyds Bank Ltd v E.B. Savory & Co.*,[63] where two employees of a stockbrokers' firm stole a large number of crossed bearer cheques drawn by their employers, one of them paying the cheques into his own private account and the other into that of his wife. One of the reasons why the bank failed in its defence under section 82 of the 1882 Act was, in the view of Lord Wright, that on the opening of the account the bank had failed to make inquiry as to its prospective customer's employers, or, in the case of the wife, as to the position of her husband. He said[64]:

> "at least where the new customer is employed in some position which involves his handling, and having the opportunity of stealing, his employers' cheques, the bankers fail in taking adequate precautions if they do not ask the name of his employers . . . because they fail to ascertain a most relevant fact as to the intending customer's circumstances. This is specially true of a stockbroker's clerk . . . or other similar employment."

[60] *Commissioners of Taxation v English, Scottish and Australian Bank Ltd* [1920] A.C. 683, *per* Lord Dunedin at 688.
[61] (1914) 30 T.L.R. 433 (Illustration 7).
[62] [1968] 1 W.L.R. 956 (Illustration 19).
[63] [1933] A.C. 201 (Illustration 11).
[64] [1933] A.C. 201 at 231.

But banking practices change. In modern times, to inquire of a customer the occupation of his or her spouse might be regarded as offensive. Moreover, it has been pointed out[65] that the answer given to an inquiry regarding the prospective customer's employers may cease to be accurate immediately it is given, and, as Harman L.J. stated in a later case[66]: "It cannot at any rate be the duty of the bank continually to keep itself up to date as to the identity of the customer's employers."

Although reasonable precautions should no doubt be taken by a banker when opening a new account to establish the bona fides of the customer, it is more than probable that a rogue who intends to operate the account for a dishonest purpose will weave a tissue of lies in answer to any inquiries made. A banker cannot reasonably be expected to subject all prospective customers to a cross examination, and so give the impression that the bank doubts their honesty. "If" said Diplock L.J.,[67] "there is some other independent and apparently trustworthy source from which the honesty of the potential customer may be verified, then to rely upon that source of information is not only less likely than the interrogation of the customer himself to damage the bank's own business by driving away honest customers but is also more likely to result in the successful detection of the occasional dishonest one." To obtain and take up references might appear to be an obvious precaution,[68] especially where a reference can be obtained from the prospective customer's own bankers. References can also be obtained from individuals, but these, if honest, may be erroneous,[69] or may even be written by the prospective customer himself under another name.[70] To attempt to obtain references from the prospective customer's employers would probably nowadays be regarded as an unwarranted intrusion into the customer's private affairs.[71]

**17–045**  The Banking Code[72] requires banks and building societies to tell potential customers, what identification is needed to prove identity. Proof of identity is now a legal requirement imposed by the Money Laundering

---

[65] Borrie (1960) 23 M.L.R. 16, 19.

[66] *Orbit Mining & Trading Co. Ltd v Westminster Bank Ltd* [1963] 1 Q.B. 956, 825.

[67] *Marfani & Co. Ltd v Midland Bank Ltd* [1968] 1 W.L.R. 968, 976.

[68] *Turner v London and Provincial Bank Ltd* (1903) 2 L.D.B. 33; *Ladbroke & Co. v Todd* (1914) 30 T.L.R. 433; *Harding v London Joint Stock Bank Ltd* (1914) 3 L.D.B. 81. But see Ellinger, Lomnicka and Hooley, *Modern Banking Law* (3rd ed.), p.578.

[69] *Marfani & Co. Ltd v Midland Bank Ltd* [1968] 1 W.L.R. 956.

[70] *Nu-Stilo Footwear Ltd v Lloyds Bank Ltd* (1956) 7 L.D.B. 121 (Illustration 16); *Lumsden & Co. v London Trustee Savings Bank* [1971] 1 Lloyd's Rep. 114 (Illustration 20).

[71] Contrast (South Africa) *Kwa Mashu Bakery Ltd v Standard Bank of South Africa* 1995 (1) S.A. 377; *Columbus Joint Venture v ABSA Bank Ltd* 2002 (1) S.A. 90 at [22–23].

[72] Para.3.1; above, para.1–011.

Regulations 2003[73] and by rules made by the Financial Services Authority under section 146 of the Financial Services and Markets Act 2000. The current rules are contained in the Authority's "Money Laundering Sourcebook".[74] A bank or building society is required to obtain sufficient information to establish the ownership of the customer (if a corporate entity)[75] or the customer's true name and residential address (if a natural person). The current practice in relation to individuals is to require identification (*e.g.* a passport or driving licence) together with the customer's date of birth and proof of residence at the given address (*e.g.* by production of a public utility or local authority bill). Information as to the source of funds deposited may also be required. Although there is no necessary correlation between the standard of care required of a banker in opening an account in respect of his duty of care to the true owner of a cheque[76] and the stringent requirements of the Money Laundering Regulations and the Money Laundering Sourcebook, it is likely that a breach by the banker of the statutory requirements would make it difficult for him to prove that he has acted without negligence for the purposes of the Cheques Act 1957. In any event, under section 150 of the Financial Services and Markets Act 2000, a contravention by a banker of a rule in the Money Laundering Sourcebook is actionable as a breach of statutory duty at the suit of a private person who has suffered loss as a result of the contravention.

Lesser precautions may, however, be justified where a banker opens a new account for an existing customer.[77]

**Conduct of the account.** Certain movements in the customer's account 17–046 may not be easily explicable and invite inquiry, for example, the opening of an account with a nominal sum followed by payment in of a cheque for a large amount.[78] The payment in of a number of "third party" cheques, that is to say, cheques originally made payable to a third party and purporting to be indorsed, especially if followed by withdrawal of the proceeds in cash, may also excite suspicion. "Of course cheques are

---

[73] SI 2003/3075, regs 3, 4. These regulations implement Council Directive 91/308 OJ/L166/77, as amended by Council Directive 2001/97 OJ/L344/76. They replace SI 1993/1933 and SI 2001/3641. See also the Money Laundering Guidance Notes 2003 provided by the Joint Money Laundering Steering Group (JMLSG), 10 Lombard Street, London EC3 9EL (*www.jmlsg.org.uk*). The Financial Services Authority will have regard to these Guidance Notes in assessing compliance.

[74] *www.fsa.gov.uk/vhb/html/ml/Mltoc.html.*

[75] *cf., Linklaters v HSBC Bank plc* [2003] EWHC 1113 (Comm), [2003] 2 Lloyd's Rep. 545 at [88].

[76] *cf. Linklaters v HSBC Bank plc* [2005] EWHC 1113 (Comm), [2003] 2 Lloyd's Rep. 545 at [110].

[77] *Columbus Joint Venture v ABSA Bank Ltd* 2001 (1) S.A. 90.

[78] *Crumplin v London Joint Stock Bank Ltd* (1913) 30 T.L.R. 99, 101. *cf. Commissioners of Taxation v English, Scottish and Australian Bank Ltd* [1920] A.C. 683.

indorsed over to third parties, but usually for small sums and only occasionally. When the bank manager sees it happening for large sums and quite regularly, I think that he is put on inquiry."[79] Even the payment in of a single third party cheque for a large amount may prompt the need for further enquiry in the particular circumstances of the case.[80] And grounds for suspicion arising from other circumstances may be enhanced if cheques are paid in for amounts disproportionate to the position known to be held by the customer.[81] The timing, nature, amount and purpose of withdrawals of the proceeds may also sound a warning.[82] But sudden fluctuations in the account are not necessarily of any significance.

The past banking history of the customer may be relevant. Where cheques drawn by the customer have had to be dishonoured on several occasions for lack of funds, and a third party cheque for a substantial amount is paid into the account, the extent of the inquiries to be made and the reasonableness of accepting the customer's own uncorroborated explanation may be affected by the unsatisfactory banking record of the customer,[83] although clearly such a record should not in itself deprive the banker of protection. Indeed, it is submitted that no single feature in the past conduct of the account, taken in isolation, could sensibly be regarded as indicating subsequent negligence on the part of the collecting banker. Rather it is a combination with other suspicious circumstances that may render the banker liable.

Special collection of a cheque at the request of the customer would ordinarily not be a matter inviting inquiry.[84]

**17–047**      **Failure to comply with the banker's own rules.** The rules of the individual banker are not necessarily to be accepted as conclusive of the standard of care, since the banker is not under any duty to observe his own rules and they may be laid down as "counsels of perfection".[85] But

---

[79] *Baker v Barclays Bank Ltd* [1955] 1 W.L.R. 822, 825.
[80] *Motor Traders' Guarantee Corp. Ltd v Midland Bank Ltd* [1937] 4 All E.R. 90 (Illustration 12); *Honourable Society of the Middle Temple v Lloyds Bank plc* [1999] 1 All E.R. (Comm) 193 (Illustration 5); *Linklaters v HSBC Bank plc* [2003] EWHC 1113 (Comm), [2003] 2 Lloyd's Rep. 545 at [99].
[81] *Nu-stilo Footwear Ltd v Lloyds Bank Ltd* (1956) 7 L.D.B. 121. (Illustration 16).
[82] *Linklaters v HSBC Bank plc* [2003] EWHC 1113 (Comm), [2003] 2 Lloyd's Rep 545 at [100] [107].
[83] *Motor Traders' Guarantee Corp. Ltd v Midland Bank Ltd* [1937] 4 All E.R. 90.
[84] *Turner v London and Provincial Bank Ltd* (1903) 2 L.D.B. 33. See also *Marfani & Co. Ltd v Midland Bank Ltd* [1968] 1 W.L.R. 956.
[85] *Motor Traders' Guarantee Corp. Ltd v Midland Bank Ltd* [1937] 4 All E.R. 90 at 96; *Orbit Mining & Trading Co. Ltd v Westminster Bank Ltd* [1963] 1 Q.B. 794, 826. See also *Savings Bank of South Australia v Wallman* (1935) 52 C.L.R. 688, 695; *New Zealand Law Soc. v ANZ Banking Group Ltd* [1985] 1 N.Z.L.R. 280, 287, 290; *Commercial Securities & Finance Ltd v ANZ Banking Group Ltd* [1985] 1 N.Z.L.R. 728, 732.

it has been said that they are clearly a useful guide[86] and offer some evidence of what may reasonably be expected,[87] and that where such rules are not kept the matter needs "close attention".[88]

**Form of cheque.** Features of the cheque delivered to the banker for collection may sometimes be such as to sound a "note of alarm"[89] and render the banker liable if he overlooks or disregards them. Manifest forgeries, erasures or alterations on the cheque may be of this nature.[90]   **17–048**

**Cheques crossed "account payee".** It will ordinarily be negligent for a banker to collect, without inquiry, a cheque crossed "account payee" for the account of a person other than the original payee.[91] It has been pointed out[92] that the words "account payee" were previously no more than a direction to the collecting banker as to how the proceeds were to be dealt with after receipt. They did not in themselves affect the negotiability or transferability of the cheque.[93] But in *Importers Co. Ltd v Westminster Bank Ltd* Atkin L.J. said[94] " . . . there is a duty upon the bank which takes a cheque in these circumstances to see that, in fact, they are collecting money for the account of the payee, and that the proceeds, when received, will go to the payee". However, section 81A(1) of the 1882 Act (introduced by section 1 of the Cheques Act 1992) now provides that, where a cheque is crossed and bears across its face the words "account   **17–049**

---

[86] *Orbit Mining & Trading Co. Ltd v Westminster Bank Ltd* [1963] 1 Q.B. 794 at 818; *Dairy Containers Ltd v NZI Bank Ltd* [1995] 2 N.Z.L.R. 30, 103.

[87] *Lumsden & Co. v London Trustee Savings Bank* [1971] 1 Lloyd's Rep. 114, 121.

[88] *Orbit Mining & Trading Co. Ltd v Westminster Bank Ltd* [1963] 1 Q.B. 794 at 826.

[89] *Commissioners of Taxation v English, Scottish and Australian Bank Ltd* [1920] A.C. 683, 690.

[90] *Commissioners of the State Savings Bank of Victoria v Permewan Wright & Co. Ltd* (1914) 19 C.L.R. 457, 485; *Souchette Ltd v London County, Westminster & Parr's Bank Ltd* (1920) 36 T.L.R. 195; *London and Montrose Shipbuilding and Repairing Co. Ltd v Barclays Bank Ltd* (1926) 31 Com.Cas. 67, 73; *Thackwell v Barclays Bank* [1986] 1 All E.R. 676; *IPF Nominees (Pty.) Ltd v Nedcor Bank Ltd* 2002 (5) S.A. 101; *ABSA Bank Ltd v Mutual & Federal Insurance Co. Ltd* 2003 (1) S.A. 635.

[91] *Bevan v National Bank Ltd* (1906) 23 T.L.R. 65; *Morison v London County and Westminster Bank Ltd* [1914] 3 K.B. 356, 373–374; *House Property Co. of London Ltd v London County and Westminster Bank Ltd* (1915) 31 T.L.R. 479; *Ross v London County, Westminster and Parr's Bank Ltd* [1919] 1 K.B. 678, 687; *Underwood (A.L.) Ltd v Bank of Liverpool Ltd* [1924] 1 K.B. 775, 793–794. *Redmond v Allied Irish Bank plc* [1987] F.L.R. 307. See also *Ladbroke & Co. v Todd* (1914) 30 T.L.R. 433; *Asiatic European Corp. Ltd v Overseas Trust Bank Ltd* [1967] H.K.L.R. 1; *Rhostar (Pvt) Ltd v Netherlands Bank of Rhodesia Ltd* 1972 (2) S.A. 703, 717; *National Commercial Banking Corp. of Australia Ltd v Robert Bushby Ltd* [1984] 1 N.S.W.L.R. 559 (affirmed sub. nom. *National Commercial Banking Corp. of Australia Ltd v Batty* (1985–1986) 160 C.L.R. 251); *Commercial Securities & Finance Ltd v ANZ Bank Group Ltd* [1985] 1 N.Z.L.R. 728; *Woodland Development Sdn Bhd v Chartered Bank* [1986] 1 M.L.J. 84.

[92] See above, para.14–038.

[93] *National Bank v Silke* [1891] 1 Q.B. 435.

[94] [1927] 2 K.B. 297, 309.

payee" or "a/c payee", either with or without the word "only", the cheque shall not be transferable, but shall only be valid as between the parties thereto.[95] There is little doubt that the duty referred to by Atkin L.J. remains unchanged—and indeed is reinforced—by this enactment.

Nevertheless, the duty does not appear to be absolute. The protection afforded to the collecting banker by section 4 expressly extends to cheques which, under section 81A(1) of the 1882 Act or otherwise,[96] are not transferable.[97] There could be circumstances where it would not be negligent for a banker to collect a non-transferable cheque for a person other than the original payee. The name of the account holder (real or assumed) might be indistinguishable from that of the named payee.[98] There may also, for example, be situations where the named payee has no bank account and requests a friend to pay the cheque into his account and obtain the proceeds for him. It is arguable that the banker could accept a credible explanation of this nature.[99] But, in the absence of special circumstances,[1] it would certainly be negligent not to require any explanation at all. Where a clearing bank is asked to collect a cheque as agent for a non-clearing bank or building society in the United Kingdom, it will be justified in assuming that its principal is aware of the principal's responsibilities in collecting an "account payee" cheque. The clearing bank will succeed in discharging the burden of proof under section 4 that it acted without negligence if it collects "without scrutiny for the identity of the person receiving payment and the named payee and in accordance with the practicalities of general banking practice, provided . . . that there is nothing exceptional in the circumstances which bring a particular cheque to its notice or ought to do so and which should then put it on enquiry".[2]

**17–050**      Where, however, a United Kingdom bank is acting on behalf of a foreign correspondent bank, the same degree of awareness of its responsi-

---

[95] See above, para.14–037.

[96] *e.g.* cheques drawn "Pay X only".

[97] s.4(2)(a), as amended by s.3 of the Cheques Act 1992.

[98] *Powell v ABSA Bank Ltd* 1998 (2) S.A. 807. But see *Energy Measurements (Pty) Ltd v First National Bank of South Africa Ltd* 2001 (3) S.A. 132; *IPF Nominees (Pty) Ltd v Nedcor Bank Ltd* 2002 (5) S.A. 101; *ABSA Bank Ltd v Mutual Federal Insurance Co. Ltd* 2003 (1) S.A. 635.

[99] *Importers Co. Ltd v Westminster Bank Ltd* [1927] 2 K.B. 297, 309. But see *Far Eastern Bank Ltd v Bee Hong Finance Co. Ltd* [1971] 2 M.L.J. 6; *Standard Bank of South Africa Ltd v Sham Magazine Centre* 1977 (1) S.A. 484; *Souhrada v Bank of New South Wales* [1976] 2 Lloyd's Rep. 444, 452. It is also arguable that the payee would no longer be the true owner of the cheque or would be estopped as against the collecting bank from making any claim in conversion or in restitution against the bank: *ABSA Bank Ltd v Greyvenstein* 2003 (4) S.A. 537.

[1] See *New Zealand Law Soc. v ANZ Banking Group Ltd* [1985] 1 N.Z.L.R. 280 (payment into solicitor's trust account).

[2] *Honourable Society of the Middle Temple v Lloyds Bank plc* [1999] 1 All E.R. (Comm) 193.

bilities on the part of the foreign bank cannot be presumed. The UK bank may be under a duty to inform the foreign bank of the effect of section 81A(1) of the 1882 Act, *i.e.* that cheques crossed "account payee" are not transferable and should be collected only for the named payee. Moreover there may be circumstances surrounding the transaction, such as the high value of the cheque or the name of the drawer or of the payee, which should sound a note of alarm as to why the cheque is being sent for collection by a foreign bank. The status of the foreign bank and its relationship with the UK bank may also be relevant. In *Honourable Society of the Middle Temple v Lloyds Bank plc*[3] these points were emphasised by Rix J. In that case, an "account payee" cheque for a substantial sum drawn by the Middle Temple payable to its insurers was stolen and deposited for collection with a Turkish Bank in Istanbul. The Turkish bank employed a UK bank as its agent to present the cheque for payment in London. The proceeds of the cheque were credited to the Turkish bank and then withdrawn by the fraudster and dissipated. Rix J. held that both the UK bank and the Turkish bank had been negligent and that neither was protected by section 4.

Nevertheless, the UK bank was to be indemnified against liability by its principal, the Turkish bank.[4] Alternatively, the Turkish bank was liable to the UK bank for breach of an implied warranty that its customer was entitled to receive the proceeds of the cheque paid to him.[5] The loss therefore ultimately fell in this case upon the foreign bank.

**Cheques crossed "not negotiable".** The fact that a crossed order **17–051** cheque bears on it the words "not negotiable" will be a relevant matter if the collecting banker claims to be a holder for value and a holder in due course, since section 81 of the 1882 Act provides that, where a person takes a crossed cheque so marked, he shall not have a better title to the cheque than that which the person from whom he took it had. But the protection of section 4 applies to cheques marked "not negotiable" as well as to cheques not so marked[6] and these words appear to have little

[3] [1999] 1 All E.R. (Comm) 193 (Illustration 5) distinguishing *Importers Co. Ltd v Westminster Bank Ltd* [p.1927] 2 K.B. 297. See also *Linklaters v HSBC Bank plc* [2003] EWHC 1113 (Comm), [2003] 2 Lloyd's Rep. 545.
[4] [1999] 1 All E.R. (Comm) 193. See also *Linklaters v HSBC Bank plc* [2003] EWHC 1113 (Comm), [2003] 2 Lloyd's Rep. 545.
[5] [1999] 1 All E.R. (Comm) 193. See also *Linklaters v HSBC Bank plc* [2003] EWHC 1113 (Comm), [2003] 2 Lloyd's Rep. 545.
[6] *Morison v London County and Westminster Bank Ltd* [1914] 3 K.B. 356, 373 (on s.82 of the 1882 Act); *Commissioners of the State Savings Bank of Victoria v Permewan Wright & Co. Ltd* (1914) 19 C.L.R. 457, 478, 485, 488 (*cf.* at 467); *Francis and Taylor Ltd v Commercial Bank of Australia Ltd* [1932] N.Z.L.R. 1028; *Day v Bank of New South Wales* (1978) 19 A.L.R. 32.

bearing upon the question whether the collecting banker is negligent.[7] These words alone do not make the cheque non-transferable and it can be collected for the account of a person other than the original payee.[8]

**17–052**    **Banker both collects and pays.** It has been previously noted[9] that, where a banker receives from a customer a cheque drawn on him to be credited to the customer's account at the same or another branch, he performs the dual role of collecting and paying banker. Even though he may have acted in good faith and in the ordinary course of business and so be entitled to the statutory protection afforded to him as paying banker, yet he may still fail to discharge the burden of proving that he acted without negligence as collecting banker.[10] It is, however, submitted that a failure to act in the ordinary course of business as paying banker does not necessarily mean that he is, as collecting banker, deprived of the protection of section 4.

**17–053**    **Exigencies of business.** "A banker", says Paget,[11] "is not normally permitted to plead the exigencies of business as a defence to a charge of negligence." The standard of care is that of a reasonable banker. In *Crumplin v London Joint Stock Bank Ltd* Pickford J. said[12]: "It is no defence for a bank to say that they were so busy and had such a small staff that they could not make inquiries. If they could not make inquiries when necessary they must take the consequences." Nowadays the plea is likely to be that a clearing bank receives each day many thousands of cheques for clearance and that the need for rapid (and automated) processing of cheques makes it impractical to scrutinise the circumstances connected with each individual cheque.[13] Nevertheless when a bank collects a cheque for its own branch customer, there are at least two points where

---

[7] *Paget* (12th ed.), 24, 28. But elsewhere it is suggested that the presence of such a crossing is a circumstance to be taken into account: *Great Western Railway Co. v London and County Banking Co. Ltd* [1901] A.C. 414, 422; *Crumplin v London Joint Stock Bank Ltd* (1913) 30 T.L.R. 99; *Morison v London County and Westminster Bank Ltd* [1914] 3 K.B. 356 at 373; *London Bank of Australia Ltd v Kendall* (1920) 28 C.L.R. 401, 413; *Mason v Savings Bank of South Australia* [1925] S.A.S.R. 198, 206; *Savings Bank of South Australia v Wallman* (1935) 52 C.L.R. 688, 695. See also *Day v Bank of New South Wales* (1978) 19 A.L.R. 31.

[8] *Crumplin v London Joint Stock Bank Ltd* (1913) 30 T.L.R. 99; *Smith and Baldwin v Barclays Bank Ltd* (1944) 5 L.D.B. 370, 375.

[9] See above, para.8–049.

[10] *Carpenters' Co. v British Mutual Banking Co. Ltd* [1938] 1 K.B. 511 (s.60, Illustration 1); *Linklaters v HSBC Bank plc* [2003] EWHC 1113. (Comm), [2003] 2 Lloyd's Rep. 545; *Standard Bank of South Africa Ltd v Harris* 2003 (2) S.A. 23. But see *London Provincial & South Western Bank Ltd v Buszard* (1918) 35 T.L.R. 142 (s.29, Illustration 9), and above, para.4–060 (s.29).

[11] 12th ed., 24.19.

[12] (1913) 30 T.L.R. 99, 101.

[13] *Honourable Society of the Middle Temple v Lloyds Bank plc* [1999] 1 All E.R. (Comm) 193, (Illustration 5).

it is feasible for the bank to carry out a check. The first is when the customer first applies to open an account (though not exclusively then).[14] The second is when the name of the customer on the paying in slip is compared with the payee's name on the cheque.[15] But other circumstances may exist which excite suspicion and give rise to a need to examine the individual cheque or its provenance despite the exigencies of modern banking business.[16]

**Inquiry as to fate.** It is no defence to the collecting banker that, before crediting a cheque, he inquired whether it would be paid when presented.[17]     **17–054**

**Causation.** Differing views have from time to time been expressed as to whether a banker should be held to have acted without negligence if he proves that his failure to make the inquiries which a prudent banker would have made would not have protected the true owner's interest in the cheque, or, to put it in another way, that his failure to make proper inquiry had no causative effect upon the loss sustained by the true owner. In *Baker v Barclays Bank Ltd*[18] Devlin J. reviewed a number of previous dicta on this issue,[19] the tenor of which was that this consideration was irrelevant. The most important of these is the statement of Lord Wright in the House of Lords[20]:     **17–055**

> "Nor is it any answer to a charge under section 82 of neglecting a proper precaution, that if it had been taken it might have been fruitless. Nor does a precaution cease to be proper for purposes of section 82 merely because, though generally effective, it may in special circumstances be ineffectual."

In *Marfani & Co. Ltd v Midland Bank Ltd*,[21] however, Diplock L.J. thought that these dicta were wrong. But he continued[22]:

> " . . . it is, however, obviously difficult to prove something so speculative as what would have happened if inquiries had been made

[14] [1999] 1 All E.R. (Comm) 193; above, para.17–044.
[15] [1999] 1 All E.R. (Comm) 193; above, para.17–049.
[16] See *Honourable Society of the Middle Temple v Lloyds Bank plc* [1999] 1 All E.R. (Comm) 193; *Linklaters v HSBC Bank plc* [2003] EWHC 1113 (Comm), [2003] 2 Lloyd's Rep. 545.
[17] *London Bank of Australia Ltd v Kendall* (1920) 28 C.L.R. 401, 413–414. See also *Bissell & Co. v Fox Bros & Co.* (1884) 53 L.T. 193; *Ogden v Benas* (1874) L.R. 9 C.P. 513, 516.
[18] [1955] 1 W.L.R. 822, 836–837.
[19] *Jones v Williams* (1857) 24 Beav. 47, 62; *Underwood (A.L.) Ltd v Bank of Liverpool Ltd* [1924] 1 K.B. 775, 789; *Lloyds Bank Ltd v E.B. Savory & Co.* [1932] 2 K.B. 112, 148; [1933] A.C. 201, 233.
[20] *Lloyds Bank Ltd v E. B. Savory & Co.* [1933] A.C. 201, 233.
[21] [1968] 1 W.L.R. 956.
[22] [1968] 1 W.L.R. 956 at 977.

which were not made, and I do not think the defendant bank has sustained the onus of proving it here. I prefer to put it in the alternative way I have already indicated. It does not constitute any lack of reasonable care to refrain from making inquiries which it is improbable will lead to detection of the potential customer's dishonest purpose, if he is dishonest, and which are calculated to offend him and maybe drive away his custom if he is honest."

A not dissimilar approach was adopted by Devlin J. in the *Baker* case[23]:

"I do not think that in this case I need go so far as to hold that every failure to make proper inquiries, whether or not they appear to be material, is fatal to a defence under section 82. I do not think it is necessary that I should hold that such carelessness is fatal even if the bank can affirmatively show that the failure was immaterial; but, in my judgment, if a bank manager fails to make inquiries which he should have made, there is at the very least a heavy burden on him to show that such inquiries could not have led to any action which could have protected the interests of the true owner; and that burden the bank has, in my judgment, failed to discharge in this case."

The controversy is still far from settled.[24] The arguments are finely balanced. Paget[25] argues that "it is illogical that a bank should be liable for damages where it proves that the claimant would have suffered loss even if the bank had discharged its duty to make inquiries". This is possibly the more rational view. But it must be conceded that a banker who fails to establish to defence under section 4, that he acted "without negligence", is exposed to a claim for conversion of the cheque, which is a tort of strict liability. Nothing in the section requires that the negligence should have had a causative effect.

**17–056**     **"Lulling to sleep."** In *Morison v London County and Westminster Bank Ltd*,[26] Buckley L.J. suggested that a collecting banker would not be negligent where he had been "lulled to sleep" by the failure of the true owner over a period of time to discover the misappropriations taking place and

---

[23] [1955] 1 W.L.R. 822, 838.
[24] In favour of the view that causation is irrelevant, see *Thompson v J. Barke & Co. (Caterers) Ltd* 1975 S.L.T. 67, 73; *Thackwell v Barclays Bank plc* [1986] 1 All E.R. 676, 684; *Hunter BNZ Finance Ltd v C.G. Maloney Pty Ltd* (1988) 18 N.S.W.L.R. 420, 447–451; *Dairy Containers Ltd v NZI Bank Ltd* [1995] 2 N.Z.L.R. 30, 104–106; *Kuwait Airways Corpn. v Iraq Airways Co.* [2001] 1 Lloyd's Rep. 161 at [437]. In favour of the *Marfani* view, see *Gippsland and Northern Co-operative Co. Ltd v English Scottish and Australian Bank Ltd* [1922] V.L.R. 670; *Savings Bank of South Australia v Wallman* (1935) 25 C.L.R. 688, 695; *New Zealand Law Soc. v ANZ Banking Group Ltd* [1985] N.Z.L.R. 280, 292; *Honourable Society of the Middle Temple v Lloyds Bank plc* [1999] 1 All E.R. (Comm) 193, 226.
[25] 12th ed., 24.41. Contrast Brindle and Cox, *Law of Bank Payments* (3rd ed.) 7–167.
[26] [1914] 3 K.B. 356, 377.

to raise any question as to the validity of the cheques: the collecting banker was entitled to assume that there was no cause for suspicion or inquiry. But the concept of "lulling to sleep" met with disapproval in subsequent cases.[27] The true owner may nevertheless be held to have ratified an unauthorised transaction[28] or to be estopped[29] from alleging the conversion.[30]

**Contributory negligence.** The defence of contributory negligence was not thought to be available to a collecting banker charged with conversion prior to the decision of Donaldson J. in *Lumsden & Co. v London Trustee Savings Bank.*[31] In that case it was held that a want of due care on the part of the claimants in drawing certain cheques had facilitated the misappropriation of the cheques by their employee. The claimants' damages against the collecting bank (which was found to have been negligent) were reduced by 10 per cent on the ground of contributory negligence. Although this decision has been questioned or not followed in a number of Australian cases,[32] it has received statutory recognition in section 47 of the Banking Act 1979, which provides: "In any circumstances in which proof of absence of negligence on the part of a banker would be a defence in proceedings by reason of section 4 of the Cheques Act 1957, a defence of contributory negligence shall also be available to a banker . . . ".[33]

**17–057**

**Holder in due course.** Even though a collecting banker fails to discharge the burden of proving that he acted without negligence, and in consequence is not protected by section 4, he will nevertheless be entitled (if such is the case) to raise the defence that he acquired the cheque from his customer as holder in due course and obtained an indefeasible title to

**17–058**

---

[27] *Ross v London County, Westminster & Parr's Bank Ltd* [1919] 1 K.B. 678, 687; *Lloyds Bank Ltd v Chartered Bank of India, Australia and China* [1929] 1 K.B. 40, 60, 79; *Lloyds Bank Ltd v E.B. Savory & Co.* [1933] A.C. 201, 236; *Carpenters' Co. v British Mutual Banking Co. Ltd* [1938] 1 K.B. 511, 530, 535.

[28] See above, para.3–087.

[29] See above, para.3–079. *cf. Orbit Mining & Trading Co. Ltd v Westminster Bank Ltd* [1963] 1 Q.B. 794, 828.

[30] *Bank of Montreal v Dominion Gresham Guarantee & Casualty Co. Ltd* [1930] A.C. 659, 666.

[31] [1971] 1 Lloyd's Rep. 114 (Illustration 20).

[32] *Wilton v Commonwealth Trading Bank of Australia* [1973] 2 N.S.W.L.R. 644; *Day v Bank of New South Wales* (1978) 19 A.L.R. 32, 42; *Grantham Holmes Pty Ltd v Interstate Permanent Building Soc. Ltd* (1979) 37 F.L.R. 191. *Australian Guarantee Corp. v Commissioners of the State Bank of Victoria* [1989] V.R. 617. Contrast *Dairy Container Ltd v NZI Bank Ltd* [1995] 2 N.Z.L.R. 30, 109–114. In *Boma Manufacturing Ltd v Canadian Imperial Bank of Commerce* (1997) 140 D.L.R. (4th) 463, 477 the Supreme Court of Canada rejected the defence.

[33] It will, however, be noted that the defence is only available where proof of absence of negligence would be a defence in proceedings *by reason of section 4 of the Cheques Act 1957*, and not otherwise.

the instrument.[34] But this defence is not open to him if the cheque is not transferable, *e.g.* if it is crossed "account payee".[35]

**17–059**    **Constructive trust.** No protection is afforded to a collecting banker by section 4 or otherwise where, by collecting a cheque or other instrument on behalf of a customer, he has become a constructive trustee of the proceeds of the instrument. But the mere fact that the customer is a trustee or fiduciary and that the banker has, by collecting the instrument, as stranger to the trust and as agent of the customer, assisted in a breach of trust by the customer is not sufficient in itself to constitute the banker a constructive trustee. This point was clearly made by Lord Selborne L.C. in the leading case of *Barnes v Addy*[36]:

> "... strangers are not to be made constructive trustees merely because they act as the agents of trustees in transactions within their legal powers, transactions, perhaps of which a Court of Equity may disapprove, unless those agents receive and become chargeable with some part of the trust property, or unless they assist with knowledge in a dishonest and fraudulent design on the part of the trustees."

The two situations envisaged by Lord Selborne where a stranger to a trust may incur liability as a constructive trustee have been given the convenient labels of "knowing receipt" and "dishonest assistance".

**17–060**    (i) *Knowing receipt.* A banker who collects a cheque for a customer cannot normally be charged with knowing receipt of trust property, since he will not have received the proceeds of the instrument for his own use and benefit but as agent of the customer.[37] But if he applies the proceeds to reduce or discharge the customer's overdraft, then in doing so he receives the money for his own benefit.[38] A potential liability may therefore arise. In order to render the banker liable in this situation, it will be necessary for the claimant to show "first, a disposal of his assets in breach of fiduciary duty; secondly, the beneficial receipt by the defendant of assets which are traceable as representing the assets of the [claimant]; and thirdly, knowledge on the part of the defendant that the assets he received are traceable to a breach of fiduciary duty".[39] Dishonesty on the part of

---

[34] See above, paras 17–019, 17–021 and 17–022.

[35] See above, para.17–017.

[36] (1874) 9 Ch.App. 244, 251.

[37] *Agip (Africa) Ltd Jackson* [1990] Ch.265, 292 (affirmed [1991] Ch. 547). See also *Adams v Bank of New South Wales* [1984] 1 N.S.W.L.R. 285; *Westpac Banking Corp v Savin* [1985] 2 N.Z.L.R. 41; *Cigma Life Insurance NZ v Westpac Securities* [1996] 1 N.Z.L.R. 80, 86.

[38] *Agip (Africa) Ltd v Jackson* [1990] Ch. 265, 292; *Citadel General Assurance Co. v Lloyds Bank Canada* (1997) 152 D.L.R. (4th) 411, 422; Millett (1991) 107 L.Q.R. 71, 83.

[39] *El Ajou v Dollar Land Holdings plc* [1994] 2 All E.R. 685, 700, *per* Hoffman L.J.; *Bank of Credit and Commerce International (Overseas) Ltd v Akindele* [2001] Ch. 437, 448.

the banker is not a necessary ingredient of liability in knowing receipt.[40] But, for a considerable period of time, there was much debate as to the degree of knowledge required to establish liability. In particular, the question was posed whether, short of actual knowledge, the recipient banker must have wilfully shut his eyes to the obvious or wilfully and recklessly failed to make such inquiries as an honest and reasonable man would make,[41] or whether "constructive knowledge" was sufficient, that is to say, knowledge of circumstances which would indicate the facts to an honest and reasonable man or knowledge of facts which would put an honest and reasonable man on inquiry.[42] The authorities were divided. More recently, however, in *Bank of Credit and Commerce International (Overseas) Ltd v Akindele*[43] the Court of Appeal stated that, just as there was now a single test of dishonesty for accessory liability,[44] so ought there to be a single test of knowledge for knowing receipt, *viz.* "The recipient's state of knowledge must be such as to make it unconscionable for him to retain the benefit of the receipt".[45] Nourse L.J. considered that the adoption of this test would avoid the "over refined categorisations of knowledge previously formulated"[46] and "should better enable the courts to give commonsense decisions in the commercial context in which claims in knowing receipt are now frequently made".[47] Despite what has been called the "elegant generalisation"[48] of the grounds for relief set out in

---

[40] *Belmont Finance Corp. Ltd v Williams Furniture Ltd* [1979] Ch. 250; *Polly Peck International plc v Nadir (No. 2)* [1992] 4 All E.R. 769, 777; *Eagle Trust plc v SBC Securities Ltd* [1993] 1 W.L.R. 484, 487; *Bank of Credit and Commerce International (Overseas) Ltd v Akindele* [2001] Ch. 437 at 448.

[41] *i.e.* categories (ii) and (iii) in *Baden Delvaux and Lecuit v Société Generale pour Favoriser le Developpement du Commerce et de L'Industrie en France S.A.* [1993] 1 W.L.R. 509, at 575, 576. See *Thomson v Clydesdale Bank Ltd* [1893] A.C. 282, 291; *Carl-Zeiss-Stiftung v Herbert Smith & Co. (No.2)* [1969] 2 Ch. 276, 290, 296–299, 301; *Competitive Insurance Co. Ltd v Davies Investments Ltd* [1975] 1 W.L.R. 1240; *Re Montagu's Settlement Trusts* [1987] Ch. 264, 285; *Eagle Trust place v SBC Securities Ltd* [1993] 1 W.L.R. 484, 504–506; *Cowan de Groot Properties v Eagle Trust plc* [1992] 4 All E.R. 700, 760; *Polly Peck International plc v Nadir (No.2)* [1992] 4 All E.R. 769, 776–777.

[42] *i.e.* categories (iv) and (v) in the *Baden Delvaux* case [1993] 1 W.L.R. 509 at 575, 576. See *Imperial Bank of Canada v Begley* [1936] 2 All E.R. 367; *Belmont Finance Corp. Ltd v Williams Furniture Ltd (No.2)* [1979] Ch. 250, 272; *International Sales and Agencies Ltd v Marcus* [1982] 3 All E.R. 551; *Baden Delvaux* case, [1993] 1 W.L.R. 509 at 572; *Westpac Banking Corp. v Savin* [1985] 2 N.Z.L.R. 41; *Agip (Africa) Ltd v Jackson* [1990] Ch. 265, 292 (this point did not arise in the Court of Appeal [1991] Ch. 547); *Powell v Thompson* [1991] 1 N.Z.L.R. 597, 607; *Equiticorp Industries Group Ltd v Hawkins* [1991] 3 N.Z.L.R. 700; *El Ajou v Dollar Land Holdings plc* [1993] 3 All E.R. 717, 739 (revd [1994] 2 All E.R. 685); *Citadel General Assurance Co. v Lloyds Bank Canada* (1997) 152 D.L.R. (4th) 411, 422; Harpum (1987) 50 M.L.R. 217.

[43] [2001] Ch. 437.

[44] See above, para.13–056; below, para.17–061.

[45] [2001] Ch. 437 at 455.

[46] Notably in the *Baden Delvaux* case, [1993] 1 W.L.R. 509 at 575–576.

[47] [2001] Ch. 437 at 455.

[48] *Papamichael v National Westminster Bank plc* [2003] EWHC 164 (Comm), [2003] 1 Lloyd's Rep. 341 at [247].

this test, there are signs that the old controversies are not entirely dead and buried. In one case[49] Hart J. held that it was unconscionable to retain the benefit of the receipt where the recipient had actual knowledge of circumstances which made the payment a misapplication of assets but then went on to express the opinion that the purpose of the new test was "not to destroy the old authorities which say in general terms that 'constructive' knowledge is enough". On the other hand, in another case,[50] Judge Chambers Q.C. said that actual and not merely constructive notice was required. He did, however, add that, even if the claimant could not show actual knowledge that the assets received were traceable to a breach of fiduciary duty, nevertheless the dishonest receipt of assets in circumstances where they were in fact traceable to such a breach of duty would make it unconscionable for the recipient to retain the benefit of the receipt. It therefore seems possible that the "over refined categorisations of knowledge previously formulated" may yet be resurrected, though perhaps not in such an extreme form.

**17–061**    (ii) *Dishonest assistance.* Even if a collecting banker receives the proceeds of an instrument solely as agent for his customer, he may yet be liable as accessory to a breach of trust by the trustee. According to Lord Selborne L.C.,[51] such liability would arise if the banker assisted with knowledge in a dishonest and fraudulent design on the part of the trustee. However, the difficulties inherent in this formulation, especially with respect to the degree of knowledge required, led to a restatement of the principle by the Judicial Committee of the Privy Council in *Royal Brunei Airlines Sdn Bhd v Tan.*[52] In that case it was held that an innocent breach of trust by the trustee would suffice, but that the touchstone for the liability of the accessory was dishonesty.[53] As a result, in order to render the banker liable in this situation, it is necessary to establish (1) a trust or other fiduciary relationship, (2) breach of trust or fiduciary duty, albeit innocent, by the trustee or person under the duty, (3) assistance by the banker in that breach of trust or fiduciary duty, and (4) dishonesty on the part of the banker.[54] This accessory liability of the banker is a personal one in equity and not proprietary.[55]

---

[49] *Criterion Properties plc v Stafford Properties plc* [2002] EWHC 496 (Ch), [2002] B.C.L.C. 151 at [36].
[50] *Papamichael v National Westminster Bank plc.* [2003] EWHC 164 (Comm), [2003] 1 Lloyd's Rep. 341 at [247–248].
[51] *Barnes v Addy* (1874) 9 Ch.App. 244 at 251.
[52] [1995] 2 A.C. 378; see above, para.13–056.
[53] For the meaning of "dishonesty" in this context, see *ante*, para.13–060.
[54] See above, paras 13–056—13–060.
[55] *Royal Brunei Airlines Sdn Bhd v Tan* [1995] 2 A.C. 378, 387.

**Further advantages of the equitable remedies.** There may be other    **17–062**
reasons why a claimant would wish to pursue a claim against the collecting banker as constructive trustee rather than by a common law action in
conversion or for money had and received. If, for example, a trustee with
authority to draw cheques on the trust account, fraudulently and in
breach of trust draws a cheque payable to himself and delivers it to his
banker for collection, a beneficiary of the trust would probably have no
claim against the collecting banker in conversion or for money had and
received since he is not the owner of the cheque nor does he have a right
to immediate possession of it.[56] But he could claim against the banker in
equity in respect of the loss suffered by the trust fund if the banker was
guilty of knowing receipt of trust money or of dishonest assistance in the
breach of trust by the trustee. Also, compound interest may be recoverable in equity but not in an action for money had and received.[57]

**Subsection (2): instruments to which section 4 applies.**[58] The first    **17–063**
category of instruments to which the section applies is "Cheques". A
cheque is defined in section 73 of the 1882 Act as: "a bill of exchange
drawn on a banker payable on demand". By an amendment made by the
Cheques Act 1992,[59] this category was extended to include cheques which
under section 81A(1) of the 1882 Act[60] or otherwise[61] are not transferable.[62]

It is difficult to escape the conclusion[63] that, since an instrument in the
form of a cheque to which the drawer's signature is a forgery is not a
cheque, it is not within section 4. By section 24 of the 1882 Act, where a
signature on a bill is forged, the forged signature is wholly inoperative,
and in consequence the instrument is a nullity if there is no other signature on it.[64] Although it might be argued that the instrument is, in fact,
"drawn on a banker", *i.e.* by the forger,[65] the word "inoperative" would
appear to mean that there is no drawer's signature on the instrument. In
Canada, it has been held that there can be no substantial damages for
conversion of a "cheque" on which the drawer's signature is forged, since

---

[56] *MCC Proceeds Inc. v Lehman Brothers International (Europe)* [1998] 4 All E.R. 675; *Hounslow London BC v Jenkins* [2004] All E.R. (D) 160.
[57] *Westdeutsche Landesbank Girozentrale v Islington LBC* [1996] A.C. 669.
[58] See also (warrants issued by the Director of Savings), SI 1972/641, SI 1972/765, SI 1976/1543, SI 1976/2012, SI 1980/767; SI 1984/789, SI 1991/1031, SI 1991/1407.
[59] s.3.
[60] See above, para.14–037 (crossed cheques marked "account payee").
[61] *e.g.* cheques drawn "Pay X only".
[62] But see above, para.3–050 (s.24).
[63] See *Paget* (12th ed.), 23.57.
[64] See above, paras 3–056 and 3–062 (s.24). But see *First Sport Ltd v Barclays Bank Ltd* [1993] 1 W.L.R. 1229, 1235, 1241.
[65] But it is not a document issued by a customer of a banker under para.(b).

what is converted is a mere piece of paper.[66] But even if the true owner of such an instrument could not obtain substantial damages for conversion, he may have a claim to recover the amount paid on it by the paying bank as his agent in an action in restitution for money had and received, *e.g.* where a cheque form is stolen from its owner, his signature as drawer forged and the "cheque" is passed to a banker for collection.[67] If a forged "cheque" is not a cheque, the collecting banker cannot claim the protection of section 4 in this situation.

On the other hand, it could be argued that the unauthorised raising of the amount or other material alteration of a cheque gives rise to different considerations, and that the instrument still remains a cheque, or at least a document falling within paragraph (b). But alteration avoids the cheque under section 64 of the 1882 Act[68] although it is true to say that that section does not always deprive the instrument entirely of any effect.[69] In the absence of any relevant limitation in section 64, it is submitted that the instrument is a nullity and is no longer a cheque or payment instrument within section 4(2).[70] The protection of section 4 is therefore not available. This should, however, be of no serious concern to the collecting banker as the true owner cannot recover substantial damages for conversion of what is a worthless piece of paper.[71]

**17–064**     The second category, referred to in paragraph (b), covers conditional orders for payment, "cheques" requiring a receipt,[72] interest and dividend warrants,[73] and instruments such as those in *Orbit Mining & Trading Co. Ltd v Westminster Bank Ltd*[74] drawn payable to "cash or order". The paragraph derives from section 17 of the Revenue Act 1883, which was repealed by section 6(3) and the Schedule to the 1957 Act.

The third category, referred to in paragraph (c), also derives from section 17 of the 1883 Act.

The fourth category, referred to in paragraph (d), covers bankers' drafts which, because they are not "addressed by one person to another", are

---

[66] *Arrow Transfer Co. Ltd v Royal Bank of Canada* (1972) 27 D.L.R. (3d) 81, 87, 104; *Number 10 Management Ltd v Royal Bank of Canada* (1977) 69 D.L.R. (3d) 99. Contrast *Boma Manufacturing Ltd v Canadian Imperial Bank of Commerce* (1997) 140 D.L.R. (4th) 463 (unauthorised signature). See also *Koster's Premier Pottery Pty Ltd v Bank of Adelaide* (1981) 28 S.A.S.R. 355 (Australia).

[67] See above, paras 3–056 and 3–062 (s.24).

[68] See above, para.8–078.

[69] See above, para.8–079.

[70] *Smith v Lloyds TSB Bank plc* [2000] 1 W.L.R. 1225 (s.64, Illustration 6); *Slingsby v District Bank Ltd* [1932] 1 K.B. 544, 549 (section 60, Illustration 2); above, para.8–088.

[71] *Smith v Lloyds TSB Bank plc* [2000] 1 W.L.R. 1225 (s.64, Illustration 6); *Slingsby v District Bank Ltd* [1932] 1 K.B. 544, 549 (section 60, Illustration 2); above, para.8–088.

[72] *Bavins Jnr & Sims v London and South Western Bank Ltd* [1900] 1 Q.B. 270 (s.3, Illustration 4).

[73] See s.95.

[74] [1963] 1 Q.B. 794 (Illustration 17).

not bills of exchange and therefore not cheques.[75] This paragraph derives from the Bills of Exchange Act (1882) Amendment Act 1932 (now repealed) which extended the crossed cheque provisions of the 1882 Act, including section 82, to such drafts.

Bills of exchange other than cheques are not covered by the sub-section, and are specifically excluded from paragraph (b). A banker has no statutory protection with respect to the collection of such instruments.

**Post-dated cheques.** It is submitted that a post-dated cheque is still a cheque,[76] and an instrument to which this subsection applies. 17–065

**Subsection (3): indorsements.** This subsection does not do away with the necessity for indorsement where an instrument payable to order is negotiated. But consistently with the policy of the Act, which was to relieve bankers of the burden of verifying indorsements on cheques paid in to the credit of the payee's account, it enables the collecting banker in some instances to ignore the absence of, or irregularity in, an indorsement whilst still retaining the statutory protection hitherto available. Prior to the enactment of the Act, if a banker collected a crossed cheque on which the payee's indorsement was absent or irregular, he forfeited by his negligence the protection of section 82 of the 1882 Act. Now, a banker is not to be treated for the purposes of the present section as having been negligent by reason only of his failure to concern himself with absence of, or irregularity in, indorsement of a cheque or other instrument to which the section applies. Thus, where a customer delivers to a banker for collection a cheque ostensibly drawn payable to himself, but which is not indorsed or is irregularly indorsed, the banker will not ordinarily require an indorsement and will not, by reason only of dispensing with this requirement, lose the protection otherwise afforded to him. 17–066

However, even though the subsection is in broad terms, the Committee of London Clearing Bankers has, in its memorandum of September 23, 1957, decided that indorsement (or discharge) will still be required in certain instances. The full terms of this memorandum have been previously set out.[77] Those instances are: first, where an instrument is tendered for the credit of an account other than that of the ostensible payee. In this case, the banker must verify the existence and regularity of any necessary indorsements, except that, if an order cheque is specially indorsed to the customer for whose account it is tendered for collection, no further indorsement is necessary. The second instance is where the payee's name is misspelt or he is incorrectly designated, and there are

[75] See above, paras 2–012 and 13–005.
[76] See above, paras 2–098 and 13–009 (s.13).
[77] See above, para.17–003.

circumstances to suggest that the customer is not the person to whom payment is intended to be made. The third is where an instrument payable to joint payees is tendered for the credit of an account to which all are not parties.

The effect of a failure by a collecting banker to comply with the Committee's memorandum (assuming the failure to be material) would appear to be that he will normally be unable to discharge the burden of proving that he acted without negligence. He will have failed to comply with the standard of care expected of a reasonable banker according to current banking practice. If he complies with the memorandum and in fact requires an indorsement, *i.e.* does "concern himself" with the indorsement, then he must ensure that it is regular.

ILLUSTRATIONS

**17–067**      1. G employs in his business a ledger clerk, J, who maintains an account in the name of W & Co. with the defendant bank. J steals crossed cheques payable to G or order, forges the necessary indorsement and pays them into that account for collection. The defendants allow him to draw against the amounts credited before the cheques are cleared. G sues the defendants in conversion and for money had and received. The jury finds that the defendants were not negligent in collecting the cheques. Nevertheless the defendants are not protected by section 82 of the 1882 Act. That section protects only a banker who receives payment for a customer as a mere agent for collection. In this case, the defendants, having credited their customer's account, thereafter received payment for themselves.[78]

2. A crossed order cheque for £600 is drawn on the London branch of the defendant bank in favour of the claimants in Cadiz. It is indorsed by the claimants payable to the order of their bankers in London and posted to those bankers. After the cheque has been posted some person obtains possession of it, obliterates the indorsement and places a forged indorsement on the cheque. The cheque is presented to the defendants' Paris branch by a person who purports to be the last indorsee but who has no account with the bank. The Paris branch pays the cheque and sends it to the London branch, which credits the Paris branch with its value. The London branch refuses to deliver up the cheque to the claimants. The defendants have converted the cheque in England, and therefore the case is governed by English law. The person who obtained payment was not a customer of the defendant bank within the meaning of section 82 of the

---

[78] *Capital and Counties Bank Ltd v Gordon* [1903] A.C. 240. See now s.4(1)(b).

1882 Act. Having paid the cheque on a forged indorsement the defendants were not protected, but were liable under section 24 of the Act for the value of the cheque.[79]

3. H, a rate collector, by falsely representing to the appellants that a rate has been made on them, obtains from them a cheque drawn on the J Bank payable to H or order and crossed "not negotiable". The appellants deliver the cheque to him as the collector and agent of the overseers and in the belief that this will discharge the rate alleged to be due. H takes the cheque to a branch of the respondent bank, indorses it and hands it to the bank clerk to be cashed. H has no account with the bank, but the bank has for several years been in the habit of cashing cheques for H in this manner. The respondent bank is liable to the appellants in conversion. H is not a customer of the bank within the meaning of section 82 of the 1882 Act. Further, as H obtained no property in the cheque and it was crossed "not negotiable" the respondents could obtain no better title than he had.[80]

4. F puts into an envelope a crossed cheque for £786 drawn by himself **17–068** on the A Bank. He hands the envelope, addressed to the Commissioners for Taxation, to be delivered by a clerk to the letter box at the Taxation Department. The cheque is drawn payable to "053 or bearer" (the figure 053 corresponding with final figures on the number of the cheque). The cheque is stolen by an unknown person. Shortly afterwards a man, giving a false name and address, opens an account with the respondent bank in Sydney with a deposit of £20. No steps are taken by the bank to verify his name and address. On the following day the man pays in the cheque for £786 and immediately draws out that amount by cheques payable to third persons. The respondent bank is protected by section 88 of the Bills of Exchange Act 1909 (Australia), corresponding to section 82 of the 1882 Act. The man is a customer of the bank, though of short standing. The negligence referred to in the section is negligence in collecting the cheque, not in opening the account. The cheque was not paid in in circumstances of an unusual character calculated to arouse suspicion and provoke inquiry.[81]

5. Middle Temple draws a cheque for £183,189 payable to its insurers. The cheque is crossed "Not Negotiable. A/c payee only".[82] The cheque is stolen and turns up (purportedly indorsed) in Istanbul. It is deposited

---

[79] *Lacave & Co. v Crédit Lyonnais* [1897] 1 Q.B. 148.
[80] *Great Western Railway Co. v London and County Banking Co. Ltd* [1901] A.C. 414.
[81] *Commissioners of Taxation v English, Scottish and Australian Bank Ltd* [1920] A.C. 683.
[82] By s.81A(1) of the 1882 Act (inserted by s.1 of the Cheques Act 1992) the cheque is not transferable.

there by one S for collection with Sekerbank, a Turkish bank. Despite the fact that S is not an existing customer of Sekerbank, the bank agrees to collect the cheque for him and instructs Lloyds Bank to present the cheque on its behalf to Middle Temple's bankers for payment. Lloyds Bank does so and credits the proceeds to Sekerbank. Before the fraud is discovered S withdraws the proceeds in cash from Sekerbank and the money disappears. Both Lloyds Bank and Sekerbank are liable to Middle Temple in conversion. Neither bank succeeds in proving that it acted without negligence for the purposes of section 4 of the 1957 Act. Lloyds did not do what it could, and should, have done to inform Sekerbank of the effect of the Cheques Act 1992 and it was also put on enquiry in the particular circumstances of the transaction. Sekerbank was clearly negligent in agreeing to collect the cheque for S. But Lloyds is entitled to be indemnified against liability by its principal, Sekerbank. Alternatively, Sekerbank is liable to Lloyds for breach of an implied warranty that S was entitled to have the proceeds of the cheque paid to him.[83]

6. The claimant, a stockbroker, employs one R as manager, bookkeeper and cashier. From time to time R introduces business to the claimant, receiving commission. R introduces in this way one Davies, for whom a genuine transaction is carried out. Subsequently over four years R engages in a number of speculative transactions under cover of the name of Davies. When small amounts become due to "Davies", he draws cheques payable to Davies or order which are signed by the claimant and crossed "not negotiable". Some of the cheques are drawn "per pro.". R indorses these and pays them into his own account with the defendant bank. The bank can rely on section 82 of the 1882 Act. The "not negotiable" crossing is only one matter to be taken into account among others, and does not go higher than that. The cheques being for small amounts and paid in at such long intervals, the circumstances are not such as to have put the bank on inquiry.[84]

**17–069**     7. The claimants, who are bookmakers, draw a cheque payable to R.H. Jobson, an undergraduate at Oxford University, and cross it "Account payee".[85] They put the cheque into the post, but it is stolen by a thief who forges Jobson's indorsement and takes it to the defendant banker in London, requesting the defendant to open an account for him in the name of Jobson. The thief explains that he needs to open this new account as the cheque has been given to him in respect of a gambling debt which he does not wish to become known to his college authorities. The defendant

---

[83] *Honourable Society of the Middle Temple v Lloyds Bank plc* [1999] 1 All E.R. (Comm) 193.
[84] *Crumplin v London Joint Stock Bank Ltd* (1913) 30 T.L.R. 99.
[85] By s.81A(1) of the 1882 Act (inserted by s.1 of the Cheques Act 1992) such a cheque would not now be transferable.

accepts this story and makes no inquiries as to the position or character of his new customer. The account is opened by paying in the stolen cheque, the cheque is specially cleared and the thief withdraws the proceeds and absconds. The defendant is not protected by section 82 of the 1882 Act. The thief became a customer of the defendant when he handed the cheque to the defendant and it was agreed that an account was to be opened in Jobson's name. But the defendant had failed to discharge the burden of proving that he had collected the cheque for his customer without negligence.[86]

8. A sergeant employed at the office of the Overseas Military Forces of Canada misappropriates during a period of 10 months 32 crossed cheques to the value of £3,900. The cheques are drawn payable to "the Officer in Charge, Estates Office, Canadian Overseas Military Forces" or order, and are indorsed generally by that officer under the same description with a view to being sent to the Paymaster General of those forces for payment to the beneficiaries. The sergeant pays the first two cheques into a branch of the defendant bank where he has an account and the remainder into another branch which passes them to the first branch. No inquiry is made at either branch whether he is entitled to the cheques. The defendant bank is liable in conversion and is not protected by section 82 of the 1882 Act. The defendants never took steps to inquire why cheques drawn payable to and indorsed by a public official were being paid into the sergeant's personal account.[87]

9. One U converts himself into a limited company in which he holds all the shares save one, which is held by his wife. He is the sole director of the company. After the formation of the company, U keeps his private account at the defendant bank. The company has a separate account at another bank. U, as director, comes into possession of a number of order cheques drawn payable to the company, some of which are crossed and others uncrossed. He indorses them in the name of the company, adding his own name as director, and pays them into his private account. The defendants do not inquire whether the company has a separate account, but collect the cheques and credit U with the proceeds, which he misappropriates. The defendants are liable to the company in conversion. The payment into U's private account of cheques payable to the company was so unusual as to put the defendants on inquiry, and they are not protected by section 82 of the 1882 Act. The mere fact that the defendants credited U's account with the amount of the cheques before clearance did not make them holders for value; for this to be the case, there must have

---

[86] *Ladbroke & Co. v Todd* (1914) 30 T.L.R. 433.
[87] *Ross v London County, Westminster and Parrs Bank Ltd* [1919] 1 K.B. 678.

been an agreement, express or implied, that U should be entitled to draw against the cheques before clearance, and that agreement must have been acted upon.[88]

**17–070**      10. L is the chief accountant at the Bombay branch of the claimant bank, having express authority to draw cheques on other bankers with whom the claimants maintain accounts. Over a period of two years he draws 19 crossed cheques totalling £17,000 on the claimants' bankers payable to the defendant bank, to which he sends instructions to place the proceeds to the credit of his private account. He conceals his fraud by false entries in the books of the branch. When cheques require a countersignature, he obtains this by misrepresenting the purpose for which the cheques are drawn. The defendants are liable in conversion and cannot rely on the protection of section 131 of the Indian Negotiable Instruments Act 1881. They have failed to discharge the onus of disproving negligence, since (i) large sums were being transferred to the defendants without any apparent cause, (ii) the defendants knew L to be an officer of the claimant bank, (iii) the cheques were not drawn upon any account of L, but upon an account which the claimants had with another bank, (iv) L both drew the cheques and gave directions as to how they were to be applied, and (v) as soon as the cheques were credited, sums were drawn out payable to persons whom the defendants knew to be stockbrokers. The claimants are not estopped.[89]

11. The respondents are stockbrokers on the London Stock Exchange. Cheques drawn in favour of jobbers are by a rule of the stock exchange made payable to bearer and crossed. The respondents have in their employment two clerks, P and S. P has an account at the Wallington branch of the appellant bank. S's wife has an account, first at the Redhill branch, and subsequently at the Weybridge branch, of the same bank. The bank officials at Wallington know that P is a stockbrokers' clerk, but have never made any enquiries as to the name of his employers. Neither at the Redhill branch nor at the Weybridge branch has S's wife been asked as to her husband's occupation. Upon opening their accounts both P and Mrs S gave satisfactory references. Over a period of two and a half years P steals from the respondents 43 cheques of a total value of £2,295, most of which he hands in at a London branch of the appellant bank, merely making out a paying-in slip in the name of the payee and directing payment to be made through the Wallington branch. Over a period of three and a half years S steals 46 cheques of a total value of £3,717, most of which are paid in at the head office of the appellant bank in the same

---

[88] *Underwood (A.L.) Ltd v Bank of Liverpool Ltd* [1924] 1 K.B. 775.
[89] *Lloyds Bank Ltd v Chartered Bank of India, Australia and China* [1929] 1 K.B. 40.

way, payment being directed to be made to the account of Mrs S at the Redhill or Weybridge branches. In both cases, the paying-in slips are sent to the country branches, no mention being made of the names of the drawers. The appellants are liable to the respondents in conversion, and are not protected by section 82 of the 1882 Act as they have failed to prove they acted without negligence. The procedures at the bank were defective, since the branch receiving a cheque never informed the country branches of the name of the drawer of the cheque. Also the managers of the country branches had failed to make sufficient inquiries when accepting P and Mrs S as customers.[90]

12. T, a motor dealer, maintains an account with the defendant bank. He induces the claimants, a finance company, to draw an order cheque for £189 15s., crossed "not negotiable", payable to a firm of car dealers, W & Co. He forges the indorsement of W & Co. and pays the cheque into his account, informing the defendants' cashier that it has been negotiated to him by W & Co. T explains to the cashier that he has obtained the cheque under a hire-purchase transaction entered into with the claimants in respect of a car bought from W & Co. and let to one of T's customers. The cashier inspects T's account in the ledger and sees a number of transactions between T and W & Co. He accepts the cheque for credit to T's account and does not, as required by the bank's regulations, refer the matter to the branch manager. In the six months that T's account has been open, some 35 cheques have been dishonoured, or only honoured after repeated presentation. The bank is liable to the claimants in conversion. Neglect to comply with the bank's internal rules did not establish negligence on the part of the bank, but the past history of the conduct of T's account should have prompted further inquiry.[91]

13. A fraudulent solicitor pays into his clients' account at the defendant bank a cheque crossed "not negotiable" payable to the order of the claimants, whose indorsement has been forged. On previous occasions when third party cheques paid into the account have been queried by the bank the solicitor has explained that the payees had no bank accounts. On this occasion he explains that the claimants have indorsed the cheque so that it may be paid into his account and he may issue his own cheque for the amount less his costs. The bank has not been negligent. The officials of a bank, doing their duty under section 82 of the 1882 Act, need not be abnormally suspicious.[92]

**17–071**

[90] *Lloyds Bank Ltd v E.B. Savory & Co.* [1933] A.C. 201.
[91] *Motor Traders Guarantee Corp. Ltd v Midland Bank Ltd* [1937] 4 All E.R. 90.
[92] *Penmount Estates Ltd v National Provincial Bank Ltd* (1945) 173 L.T. 344.

14. McG is employed by the claimant, the Marquess of Bute, as a farm manager. Part of his duties consists of making applications to the Department of Agriculture in Scotland for subsidies in respect of the farms. After he leaves his employment, three warrants in respect of such applications are sent to him by the Department. They are payable to "McG (for the Marquis of Bute)" and are crossed "not negotiable". McG applies to the defendant bank to open an account with the warrants. Although McG is unknown to the defendants, they open the account, credit the warrants to it and forward them for collection. Having taken up references, they then allow McG to draw on the account. The defendants are liable to the claimant for conversion. The claimant was entitled to immediate possession of the warrants. The warrants bore a clear indication that McG was receiving them as agent in a fiduciary capacity, and they should not have been credited to the personal account of McG without further inquiry. The defendants, having failed to discharge the onus of proving that they acted without negligence, cannot claim the protection of section 82 of the 1882 Act.[93]

15. The claimant and B are partners in a confectionery business. B misappropriates nine crossed order cheques, totalling £1,160, payable to the partnership. He indorses them himself and hands them to J, who pays them into an account of J with the defendant bank. When questioned by the defendants' branch manager as to why cheques payable to the partnership are being paid into J's account, J explains that B is the sole proprietor of the business, that J is helping him with the financial side of the business and that B owes J £450. The claimant's action against the bank for conversion of the cheques succeeds. The bank is not a holder in due course. As B was guilty of fraud, the burden lies on the bank under section 30(2) of the 1882 Act to prove that value has in good faith been given for the cheques. The bank has not discharged that burden, since J's explanation was inconsistent with his having given value for the cheques and the bank did not itself give value. The cheques could not be applied to reduce J's overdraft and the bank did not agree to honour cheques drawn by J before clearance. Further, the bank is not entitled to rely on the protection afforded by section 82 of the 1882 Act in respect of the collection of the cheques, as it was negligent in failing to make sufficient inquiries as to why third party cheques were being paid into J's account.[94]

**17–072**      16. One Montague is employed by the claimant company as its secretary and works accountant. He opens an account with the defendant bank

[93] *Bute (Marquess of) v Barclays Bank Ltd* [1955] 1 Q.B. 202.
[94] *Baker v Barclays Bank Ltd* [1955] 1 W.L.R. 822.

in the false name of Edward Bauer, describing himself as a freelance agent. He gives his own name as a reference. The bank takes up the reference, and is informed that "Bauer" has recently come down from Oxford and intends starting up business on his own account. The bank also receives a satisfactory report from the referee's bankers. The claimants sue the bank for conversion of nine crossed cheques collected for the account of "Bauer". The first cheque, for £172, is drawn payable to Bauer by Montague and another officer of the claimant company and is not so large as to raise suspicion. The second cheque is a third party cheque for £550, and subsequent cheques, some payable to Bauer and others to third parties, are likewise for sums so large as to be quite out of harmony with the description of his trade and prospects as revealed to the bank. The bank is not in a position, save as regards the first cheque, to plead the protection of section 82 of the 1882 Act.[95]

17. The claimant company maintains an account with the M Bank, authorising the bank to honour cheques signed by any two directors. Specimen signatures of E and W, directors of the company, are supplied to the bank. W is often abroad, so E asks him to sign several crossed cheque forms in blank, and W does so. E adds his signature as drawer to three such cheques made out for £147, £1,269 and £415 respectively, inserts the word "cash" between "Pay" and "order", indorses them and delivers them to the W Bank for the credit of his personal account with that bank. The only person to examine the cheques is the bank's cashier, who compares the name of the payee with that on the credit slip. If there is no variance, or the cheque is payable to "cash", he looks no further. The W Bank collects payment of the cheques and E misappropriates the proceeds. E's account has been properly conducted and the bank is unaware of his connection with the claimants. The W Bank is protected by section 4 of the 1957 Act. The three instruments, being payable to "cash or order", are not bills of exchange within the meaning of section 3 of the 1882 Act and are accordingly not cheques. But they are "documents issued by a customer" within section 4(2)(b) of the 1957 Act. As the drawer's signature was illegible and no indorsement needed, there was nothing to connect the one signature with the other so as to require further scrutiny by the cashier. "Pay cash or order" is regularly, if not frequently, found on crossed cheques and the W Bank has discharged the burden of proving that it acted without negligence.[96]

18. The claimants, a Belgian company, appoint H to be the sole representative for the sale of their products in Australia. The arrangements by

---

[95] *Nu-Stilo Footwear Ltd v Lloyds Bank Ltd* (1956) 7 L.D.B. 121.
[96] *Orbit Mining & Trading Co. Ltd v Westminster Bank Ltd* [1963] 1 Q.B. 794.

which the price of the products is to be received in Australian currency, converted into Belgian currency and credited to the claimants are left to H. The claimants have no bank account in Australia. 15 cheques for large sums are drawn over a period of time by an Australian purchaser payable to the order of the claimants care of H. These are indorsed by H in his own name and paid into H's account with the defendant bank. Initially the proceeds of the cheques are duly remitted by H to the claimants in Belgium; then delays begin to occur; and subsequently no remittances are made. H goes into liquidation. The defendant bank is not liable to the claimants for conversion of the cheques. The inference in law is that there was implied actual authority from the claimants to H to indorse cheques payable to the claimants and to pay them into his own account.[97]

**17–073**     19. K, a Pakistani, is employed by the claimant company as a clerk. He is given a crossed cheque for £3,000 drawn by the company on the I Bank payable to "Eliaszade", a firm with whom the company does business, and is instructed to post the cheque to that firm. Instead he goes to the defendant bank and requests the bank to open an account for him, giving his name as "Eliaszade". Appearing to be a person of substance, he makes a deposit of £80 and states that he intends to open a restaurant business and that the rest of the funds will arrive later. He supplies the names of two referees who are customers of the bank. No identification is requested of him, nor is he asked about his occupation or whether he has any other bank account. On the following day he indorses and pays in the cheque for £3,000, which is specially cleared by the defendants. Having received a satisfactory (though erroneous) oral reference from one of the referees, the defendants provide him with a cheque book and allow him to draw on the account. K draws out the £3,000 and leaves the country. The defendants are protected by section 4 of the 1957 Act. The standard of care required of them was to be judged by the current practice of reasonable bankers. It was not incumbent on them to make inquiries of a customer which it was improbable would lead to the detection of a fraudulent purpose on the part of a dishonest customer and which would offend him if he were honest. They were entitled to rely on the reference and were not negligent at the time they paid out the proceeds of the cheque to K.[98]

20. The claimants, a firm of stockbrokers, employ an Australian, one Blake, as a temporary accountant. Part of his duties consists of making out cheques payable to other stockbrokers, which cheques are then signed

---

[97] *Australia and New Zealand Bank Ltd v Ateliers de Constructions Electriques de Charleroi* [1967] 1 A.C. 86.
[98] *Marfani & Co. Ltd v Midland Bank Ltd* [1968] 1 W.L.R. 956.

by a partner in the firm. The payees of the cheques are designated in an abbreviated form, *e.g.* "Brown" instead of "Brown, Mills & Co.". Blake, posing as a self-employed chemist, opens an account with the defendant bank in the name of "J.A.G. Brown" with a cash deposit of £1. He is asked by the branch manager to provide a reference, and gives as the name of a referee "a family friend, Dr Blake". He provides an address for Dr Blake which is an accommodation address. Blake signs the reference himself, but fails to provide the name of his bankers as requested by the manager. The manager makes no further inquiries. Blake abstracts a number of cheques drawn by the claimants payable to "Brown", inserts the initials "J.A.G." in the gap before the name and pays the cheques into his account. The defendants are liable to the claimants in conversion. They are guilty of negligence and cannot rely on section 4 of the 1957 Act. But the claimants' damages are reduced by 10 per cent on account of their contributory negligence.[99]

### Application of certain provisions of Bills of Exchange Act 1882 to instruments not being bills of exchange

**5. The provisions of the Bills of Exchange Act, 1882, relating to** **17–074** **crossed cheques shall, so far as applicable, have effect in relation to instruments (other than cheques) to which the last foregoing section applies as they have effect in relation to cheques.**

Definition
"cheque": 1882 Act, s.73.

### COMMENT

**Crossed instruments.** This section added nothing to the previous law. **17–075** It was necessary because section 6(3) repealed both section 17 of the Revenue Act 1883 and section 1 of the Bills of Exchange Act (1882) Amendment Act 1932, which extended the provisions of sections 76 to 82 of the 1882 Act relating to crossed cheques to the analogous instruments referred to in section 4(2)(b), (c) and (d) of the present Act.

"The provisions of the Bills of Exchange Act, 1882, relating to crossed cheques" are now sections 76 to 81A. In particular, section 80 of the 1882 Act protects the banker paying such an instrument to a banker (and, if the

---

[99] *Lumsden & Co. v London Trustee Savings Bank* [1971] 1 Lloyd's Rep. 114.

instrument has come into the hands of the payee, the drawer) where the instrument is paid in good faith and without negligence.

The present section does not, however, afford to a banker who pays such an instrument the protection of section 60 of the 1882 Act. If in need of that protection, the banker must rely so far as he can upon section 19 of the Stamp Act 1853.[1]

### Construction, saving and repeal

17–076      6. (1) **This Act shall be construed as one with the Bills of Exchange Act 1882.**

            (2) **The foregoing provisions of this Act do not make negotiable any instrument which, apart from them, is not negotiable.**

            (3) **[*Repealed.*]**

Repeal
Subs. (3) was repealed by the Statute Law (Repeals) Act 1974, s.1 and Sch., Pt XI.

### COMMENT

17–077      **Subsection (1): construction as one with 1882 Act.** Where statutes are to be construed as one, then every part of each of them is to be construed as if it had been contained in one Act, unless there is some manifest discrepancy.[2] It is not permissible to make what is clear in the earlier statute obscure by reference to part of the later statute, but where the earlier is ambiguous then recourse may be had to the later statute to resolve the ambiguity.[3]

17–078      **Subsection (2): no new negotiability.** This subsection reiterates the proviso formerly contained in section 17 of the Revenue Act 1883.[4] There can be little doubt that a banker's draft is a negotiable instrument.

---

[1] See above, para.8–045.

[2] *Canada Southern Ry v International Bridge Co.* (1883) 8 App. Cas. 723, 727; *Phillips v Parnaby* [1934] 2 K.B. 299, 302. Definitions in the earlier Act may be relevant to construction of provisions in the later Act: *Solomons v R Gerzenstein Ltd* [1954] 2 Q.B. 243; *Crowe (Valuation Officer) v Lloyds British Testing Co. Ltd* [1960] 1 Q.B. 592.

[3] *Kirkness v John Hudson & Co.* [1955] A.C. 696, and see the cases there cited.

[4] Repealed by subs.(3).

**Subsection (3): repeals.** This subsection and the Schedule to the Act 17–079
were repealed as spent by the Statute Law (Repeals) Act 1974.[5]

**Provisions as to Northern Ireland**

7. This Act extends to Northern Ireland [. . . . ]. 17–080

Repeal
The words omitted were repealed by the Northern Ireland Constitution
Act 1973, s.41 and Sch.6.

**Short title and commencement**

8. (1) **This Act may be cited as the Cheques Act 1957.** 17–081
   (2) **This Act shall come into operation at the expiration of a
   period of three months beginning with the day on which it is
   passed.**

## SCHEDULE

### Enactments Repealed

[*This was repealed as spent by the Statute Law (Repeals) Act 1974, s.1 and* 17–082
*Sched., Part XI.*]

[5] s.1 and Sch., Pt XI.

# APPENDIX A: NOTICES

## 1.

### Notice to the Drawer of Dishonour of a Bill

*[Address and date]*

I hereby give you notice that the bill of exchange for £    , drawn by you on (*name of drawee*) and dated the    day of    20  , has been dishonoured by non-payment [*or* non-acceptance]\*, and is unpaid.

(*Signed*)

\**In the case of a foreign bill, add "and protested", if it has been noted or protested.*

## 2.

### Notice to an Indorser of Dishonour of a Bill or Note

*[Address and date]*

I hereby give you notice that the bill of exchange [*or* promissory note] for £    , drawn [*or* made] by (*name of drawer or maker*) [*in the case of a bill* on (*name of drawee*)] and dated the    day of    20  , which bears your indorsement, has been dishonoured by non-payment [*or, in the case of a bill,* non-acceptance]\*, and is unpaid.

(*Signed*)

\**In the case of a foreign bill, add "and protested", if it has been noted or protested.*

## 3.

### Notice to the Drawer or Indorser of Dishonour of a Cheque

*[Address and date]*

I hereby give you notice that the cheque for £    , drawn by you [*or* by    (*name of drawer*)] on (*name and address of drawee bank*) and dated the    day of    20  , [*where the notice is given to an indorser* which bears your indorsement,] has been dishonoured by non-payment, and is unpaid.

(*Signed*)

## 4.

### Notice to the Drawer of Partial Acceptance of a Bill

*[Address and date]*

I hereby give you notice that the bill of exchange for £    , drawn by you on (*name of drawee*) and dated the    day of    20  , has been accepted by the drawee for £    only.* You are held responsible for the balance.*

*(Signed)*

*In the case of a foreign bill, add "and has been protested as to the balance" and at the end add "and expenses", if it has been noted or protested.*

## 5.

### Notice to the Drawer or Indorser of Qualified Acceptance of a Bill

*[Address and date]*

I hereby give you notice that, as holder of the bill of exchange for £    , drawn by you [*or* by    (*name of drawer*)] on (*name of drawee*) and dated the    day of    20  , [*where the notice is given to an indorser* which bears your indorsement,] I have taken from the drawee a qualified acceptance which in express terms varies the effect of the said bill as drawn, namely (*set out the terms of the qualified acceptance, for example* "Accepted payable only at the    branch of the    Bank").

*(Signed)*

# APPENDIX B: PRECEDENTS OF PLEADINGS

*1.*

Claim by the Drawer-Payee Against the Acceptor in Respect of the
Dishonour of an After-Sight Bill by Non-Payment

[*Either*           CLAIM FORM    [IN THE HIGH COURT OF JUSTICE
                                    [QUEEN'S BENCH DIVISION
                                    COMMERCIAL COURT *or*
                                    DISTRICT REGISTRY
                                    MERCANTILE COURT]

*Or*            CLAIM FORM   [IN THE          COUNTY COURT *or*
                         IN THE CENTRAL LONDON COUNTY COURT
                                        MERCANTILE LIST]

                                      Claim No.
                                      Issue date

CLAIMANT     A.B.

and

DEFENDANT     C.D.

**BRIEF DETAILS OF CLAIM**

The Claimant's claim against the Defendant is for damages for dishonour by non-payment of a bill of exchange for £        drawn by and payable to the Claimant and accepted by the Defendant and for interest under section 57(1) of the Bills of Exchange Act 1882.

VALUE
£
Defendant's name
and address:

| | |
|---|---|
| Amount claimed | £ |
| Court fee | £ |
| Solicitor's costs | £ |
| Total amount | £ |

The claim does not include any issues under the Human Rights Act 1998

## PARTICULARS OF CLAIM

[Attached [*or if served separately* To follow]]

1. The Claimant drew a bill of exchange for £     dated     20   upon the Defendant, payable to the Claimant 90 days after sight, which bill the Defendant accepted on     20  .

2. On     20   the Claimant duly presented the bill for payment at but it was dishonoured by non-payment.

3. The Claimant claims as liquidated damages the amount of the bill £       .

4. Further the Claimant claims and is entitled to recover interest under section 57(1) of the Bills of Exchange Act 1882 on the said sum of £     from (*date of maturity*) to (*date of issue of the claim form*) at the rate of     per centum per annum and continuing at the said rate (£     per day) until judgment or sooner payment.

And the Claimant claims:
(i) £     ; and
(ii) under paragraph 4 above, interest of £     to the date of issue of the claim form and £     per day thereafter.

Dated     20  .             (*Signature of legal representative*)

## STATEMENT OF TRUTH

I believe [*or* The Claimant believes] that the facts stated in these Particulars of Claim are true.

I am duly authorised by the Claimant to sign this statement (*indicate in which capacity, e.g.* as solicitor).

Full name                          (*Signature*)
                              (*indicate office or position held if signing on behalf of a firm or company*)

Claimant's [*or* Claimant's solicitor's] address to which documents or payments should be sent if different from above including (if appropriate) details of CX, fax or e-mail.

The Court at            is open between 10 a.m. and 4 p.m. Monday to Friday. When corresponding with the Court, please address forms or letters to the Court Manager and quote the claim number.

## 2.

## CLAIM BY INDORSEE AGAINST THE DRAWER IN RESPECT OF THE DISHONOUR OF AN AFTER-SIGHT BILL BY NON-ACCEPTANCE

### BRIEF DETAILS OF CLAIM

The Claimant's claim against the Defendant is for damages for dishonour by non-acceptance of a bill of exchange for £            drawn by the Defendant payable to himself and indorsed by the Defendant to the Claimant, and for interest under section 57(1) of the Bills of Exchange Act 1882.

### PARTICULARS OF CLAIM

1. The Defendant drew a bill of exchange for £            dated            20    upon X.Y. payable 3 months after sight to the Defendant or to his order.

2. On or about            20    the Defendant indorsed and delivered the bill to the Claimant. The Claimant thereby became and is the holder of the bill.

3. On            20    the Claimant presented the bill to X.Y. for acceptance but the bill was dishonoured by non-acceptance. [*If the bill is a foreign bill, add* On            20    the bill was duly protested.]

4. The Claimant by a notice in writing dated            20    , a copy of which is annexed, duly gave notice of the dishonour to the Defendant.

5. The Claimant claims as liquidated damages the amount of the bill £            .

6. Further the Claimant claims and is entitled to recover interest under section 57(1) of the Bills of Exchange Act 1882 on the said sum of £            from (*date of maturity*) to (*date of issue of the claim form*) at the rate of            per centum per annum and continuing at the same rate (£            per day) until judgment or sooner payment.

And the Claimant claims:
(i) £            ; and
(ii) Under paragraph 6 above, interest of £            to the date of issue of the claim form and £            per day thereafter. [and
(iii) £            the expenses of noting [and protest]]

795

*3.*

## CLAIM BY THE PAYEE AGAINST THE ACCEPTOR AND DRAWER IN RESPECT OF THE DISHONOUR OF A FIXED-DATE BILL BY NON-PAYMENT

CLAIMANT      A.B.

and

DEFENDANTS      C.D.
                           E.F.

### BRIEF DETAILS OF CLAIM

The Claimant's claim against the Defendants is for damages for dishonour by non-payment of a bill of exchange for £      drawn by the Defendant C.D. payable to the Claimant and accepted by the Defendant E.F. and for interest under section 57(1) of the Bills of Exchange Act 1882.

### PARTICULARS OF CLAIM

1. The Defendant C.D. drew a bill of exchange for £     dated      20 upon the Defendant E.F. payable to the Claimant on      20 , which bill was accepted by the Defendant E.F.

2. On      20    the Claimant duly presented the bill for payment at        , but it was dishonoured by non-payment. [*If the bill is a foreign bill, add* On      20    the bill was duly protested.]

3. The Claimant by a notice in writing dated      20 , a copy of which is annexed, duly gave notice of the dishonour to the Defendant C.D.

4. The Claimant claims as liquidated damages the amount of the bill £      .

5. Further the Claimant claims and is entitled to recover interest under section 57(1) of the Bills of Exchange Act 1882 on the said sum of £     from (*date of maturity*) to (*date of issue of claim form*) at the rate of     per centum per annum and continuing at the same rate (£     per day) until judgment or sooner payment.

And the Claimant claims against the Defendants C.D. and E.F. and each of them:
(i) £     ; and
(ii) Under paragraph 5 above, interest of £     to the issue of the claim form and £     per day thereafter. [and

(iii) £      the expenses of noting [and protest]]

### 4.

## CLAIM BY AN INDORSEE AGAINST THE ACCEPTOR, THE DRAWER AND A PRIOR INDORSER IN RESPECT OF THE DISHONOUR OF A FIXED DATE BILL BY NON-PAYMENT

CLAIMANT      A.B.

and

DEFENDANTS      C.D.
E.F.
G.H.

## BRIEF DETAILS OF CLAIM

The Claimant's claim against the Defendants is for damages for dishonour by non-payment of a bill of exchange for £     drawn by the Defendant C.D. on and accepted by the Defendant E.F. payable to Defendant G.H. and by him indorsed to the Claimant, and for interest under section 57(1) of the Bills of Exchange Act 1882.

## PARTICULARS OF CLAIM

1. The Defendant C.D. drew a bill of exchange for £    dated    20 upon the Defendant E.F. payable to the Defendant G.H. on    20  , which bill the Defendant E.F. accepted on    20  .

2. On or about    20  the Defendant G.H. indorsed and delivered the bill to the Claimant. The Claimant thereby became and is the holder of the bill.

3. On    20  the Claimant duly presented the bill for payment at    , but it was dishonoured by non-payment. [*If the bill is a foreign bill, add* On    20  the bill was duly protested.]

4. The Claimant by a notice in writing dated    20  , a copy of which is annexed, duly gave notice of the dishonour to the Defendant C.D. and to the Defendant G.H.

5. The Claimant claims as liquidated damages the amount of the bill £    .

6. Further the Claimant claims and is entitled to recover interest under section 57(1) of the Bills of Exchange Act 1882 on the said sum of £    from (*date of*

*maturity*) to (*date of issue of claim form*) at the rate of          per centum per annum and continuing at the same rate (£          per day) until judgment or sooner payment.

And the Claimant claims against the Defendants C.D., E.F. and G.H. and each of them:
(i) £          ; and
(ii) Under paragraph 6 above, interest of £          to the issue of the claim form and £          per day thereafter. [and
(iii) £          the expenses of noting [and protest]]

<br>

## 5.

### CLAIM BY THE PAYEE AGAINST THE ACCEPTOR AND AN ANOMALOUS INDORSER IN RESPECT OF THE DISHONOUR OF A FIXED DATE BILL BY NON-PAYMENT

CLAIMANT          A.B.

and

DEFENDANTS          C.D.
                              E.F.

## BRIEF DETAILS OF CLAIM

The Claimant's claim against the Defendants is for damages for dishonour by non-payment of a bill of exchange for £          drawn by the Claimant on the Defendant C.D. payable to the Claimant and accepted by the Defendant C.D. and indorsed by the Defendant E.F. and for interest under section 57(1) of the Bills of Exchange Act 1882.

## PARTICULARS OF CLAIM

1. The Claimant drew a bill of exchange for £          dated          20   upon the Defendant C.D., payable to the Claimant on          20  , which bill the Defendant C.D. accepted on          20  .

2. On or about          20   the Defendant E.F. indorsed the bill in blank.

3. On          20  , before the bill became due, the Claimant indorsed the bill in blank placing his signature on the back of the bill above that of the Defendant E.F. The Claimant thereby became and is the holder of the bill in due course.

4. On          20   , the Claimant duly presented the bill for payment at             ,
but it was dishonoured by non-payment. [*If the bill is a foreign bill, add*
On          20    the bill was duly protested.]

5. The Claimant by a notice in writing dated          20   , a copy of which is
annexed, duly gave notice of the dishonour to the Defendant E.F.

6. The Claimant claims as liquidated damages the amount of the bill £          .

7. Further the Claimant claims and is entitled to recover interest under section
57(1) of the Bills of Exchange Act 1882 on the said sum of £          from (*date of*
*maturity*) to (*date of issue of the claim form*) at the rate of          per centum per
annum and continuing at the said rate (£          per day) until judgment or sooner
payment.

And the Claimant claims against the Defendants C.D. and E.F. and each of
them:
(i) £          ; and
(ii) under paragraph 7 above, interest of £          to the date of issue of the claim
form and £          per day thereafter. [and
(iii) £          the expenses of noting [and protest]]

*6.*

CLAIM BY THE PAYEE AGAINST THE MAKER IN RESPECT OF THE NON-
PAYMENT OF A FIXED DATE NOTE

## BRIEF DETAILS OF CLAIM
The Claimant's claim against the Defendant is for damages for non-payment of a
promissory note for £          made by the Defendant payable to the Claimant and
for interest under section 57(1) of the Bills of Exchange Act 1882.

## PARTICULARS OF CLAIM
1. The Defendant made a promissory note for £          dated          20    payable to the Claimant on          20    [at (*place*) ].

2. The defendant failed to pay the note on the said          20    or at all. [*or if the*
*note is in the body of it made payable at a particular place* On          20    the
Claimant duly presented the note for payment at (*place of presentment*) but the note
was dishonoured by non-payment].

3. The Claimant claims as liquidated damages the amount of the note £          .

4. Further the Claimant claims and is entitled to recover interest under section
57(1) of the Bills of Exchange Act 1882 on the said sum of £          from (*date of*

*maturity*) to (*date of issue of claim form*) at the rate of       per centum per annum and continuing at the same rate (£       per day) until judgment or sooner payment.

And the Claimant claims
(i) £       ; and
(ii) Under paragraph 4 above, interest of £       to the issue of the claim form and £       per day thereafter.

## 7.

### CLAIM BY AN INDORSEE AGAINST THE MAKER AND A PRIOR INDORSER IN RESPECT OF THE DISHONOUR OF A DEMAND NOTE BY NON-PAYMENT

CLAIMANT       A.B.

and

DEFENDANTS       C.D.
       E.F.

## BRIEF DETAILS OF CLAIM

The Claimant's claim against the Defendants is for damages for dishonour by non-payment of a promissory note for £       made by the Defendant C.D. payable to the Defendant E.F. and by him indorsed to the Claimant and for interest under section 57(1) of the Bills of Exchange Act 1882.

## PARTICULARS OF CLAIM

1. The Defendant C.D. made a promissory note for £       dated       20 payable to the Defendant E.F. on demand.

2. On or about       20     the Defendant E.F. indorsed and delivered the note to the Claimant. The Claimant thereby became and is the holder of the note.

3. On       20     the Claimant duly presented the note for payment [*if the note is in the body of it made payable at a particular place at* (*place of presentment*)] but the note was dishonoured by non-payment.

4. The Claimant by a notice in writing dated       20     a copy of which is annexed duly gave notice of the dishonour to the Defendant E.F.

5. The Claimant claims as liquidated damages the amount of the note £       .

6. Further the Claimant claims and is entitled to recover interest under section 57(1) of the Bills of Exchange Act 1882 on the said sum of £      from (*date of presentment*) to (*date of issue of claim form*) at the rate of      per centum per annum and continuing at the same rate (£      per day) until judgment or sooner payment.

And the Claimant claims against the Defendants C.D. and E.F. and each of them:
(i) £      ; and
(ii) Under paragraph 6 above, interest of £      to the issue of the claim form and £      per day thereafter.

## 8.

### CLAIM BY THE PAYEE AGAINST THE DRAWER IN RESPECT OF THE DISHONOUR OF A CHEQUE BY NON-PAYMENT

### BRIEF DETAILS OF CLAIM

The Claimant's claim against the Defendant is for damages for dishonour by non-payment of a cheque for £      drawn by the Defendant on      Bank plc payable to the Claimant and for interest under section 57(1) of the Bills of Exchange Act 1882.

### PARTICULARS OF CLAIM

1. The Defendant drew a cheque for £      dated      20   on      Bank plc payable to the Claimant.

2. On the      20   the Claimant's bank on his behalf duly presented the cheque for payment but the cheque was dishonoured by non-payment.

3. *Either* The Claimant by a notice in writing dated      20   , a copy of which is annexed, duly gave notice of the dishonour to the Defendant.
   *or* Payment of the cheque was countermanded by the Defendant.
   *or* At the time the cheque was presented for payment there were insufficient funds standing to the credit of the Defendant in his account with      Bank plc and the bank was, as between itself and the Defendant, under no obligation to pay the cheque.

4. The Claimant claims as liquidated damages the amount of the cheque £      .

5. Further the Claimant claims and is entitled to recover interest under section 57(1) of the Bills of Exchange Act 1882 on the said sum of £      from (*date of presentment*) to (*date of issue of the claim form*) at the rate of      per centum per

801

annum and continuing at the same rate (£      per day) until judgment or sooner payment.

And the Claimant claims:
(i) £      ; and
(ii) Under paragraph 5 above, interest of £      to the issue of the claim form and £      per day thereafter.

# INDEX